LO

G000025413

Mini Street Atlas

CONTENTS

Key to Map Pages	2-3
Large Scale Map Pages	4-27
Map Pages	28-125
Congestion Charging Overview	126-127
Congestion Charging Information	128
Index to Streets, etc.	129-358
Index to Hospitals	359-364
Index to Stations	365-368
Underground Map	back cover

SCALE

Map Pages 28-125	Map Pages 4-11
1:21477 Approx. 3 inches to 1 mile	1:10560 6 inches to 1 mile
0 ⅛ ¼ Mile	0 1/16 ⅛ Mile
0 100 200 300 Metres	0 100 200 Metres
4.66 cm to 1 km 7.49 cm to 1 mile	9.47 cm to 1km 15.24 cm to 1 mile

Geographers' A-Z Map Company Ltd.

Fairfield Road, Borough Green, Sevenoaks, Kent TN15 8PP
Enquiries & Trade Sales 01732 781000   Retail Sales 01732 783422
www.a-zmaps.co.uk

Edition 6   2007   Copyright © Geographers' A-Z Map Co. Ltd.

Ordnance Survey® This product includes mapping data licensed from Ordnance Survey ® with the permission of the Controller of Her Majesty's Stationery Office.
© Crown Copyright 2006. All rights reserved. Licence number 100017302

KEY TO MAP PAGES

2

Kingsbury

HENDON

HORNSEY

Golders Green

Highgate

| 28 | 29 | 30 | 31 | 32 | 33 | 34 |

Cricklewood

Neasden

HAMPSTEAD

| 42 | 43 | 44 | 45 | 46 | 47 | 48 |

WILLESDEN

CAMDEN TOWN

ISLIN

Kensal Green

Kilburn

MARYLEBONE

FINS

| 56 | 57 | 58 | 59 | 60 | 61 | 62 |

LARGE S

Holborn

ACTON

Shepherd's Bush

PADDINGTON

WEST END

SECTIO

| 70 | 71 | 72 | 73 | 74 | 75 | 76 |

KENSINGTON

Westminster

LAM

CHISWICK

HAMMERSMITH

CHELSEA

| 84 | 85 | 86 | 87 | 88 | 89 | 90 |

BARNES

FULHAM

BATTERSEA

PUTNEY

CLAPHAM

BRIX

| 98 | 99 | 100 | 101 | 102 | 103 | 104 |

WANDSWORTH

Roehampton

Richmond Park

Balham

| 112 | 113 | 114 | 115 | 116 | 117 | 118 |

Tooting

WIMBLEDON

STREATHAM

SCALE

0   1   2 Miles

0   1   2   3 Kilometres

MITCHAM

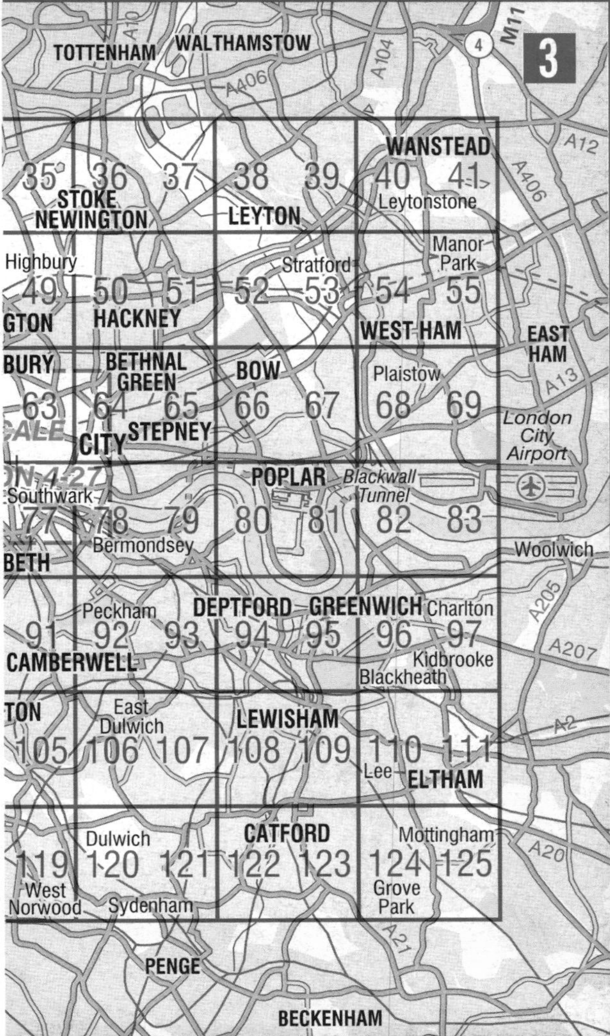
3
A10
TOTTENHAM
WALTHAMSTOW
A104
4
M11
A406
A12
WANSTEAD
35
36
37
38
39
40
41
STOKE NEWINGTON
LEYTON
Leytonstone
A406
Highbury
Stratford
Manor Park
49
50
51
52
53
54
55
GTON
HACKNEY
WEST HAM
EAST HAM
BURY
BETHNAL GREEN
BOW
Plaistow
A13
63
64
65
66
67
68
69
CITY
STEPNEY
London City Airport
POPLAR
Blackwall Tunnel
Southwark
77
78
79
80
81
82
83
Bermondsey
BETH
Woolwich
A205
Peckham
DEPTFORD
GREENWICH
Charlton
91
92
93
94
95
96
97
A207
CAMBERWELL
Kidbrooke
Blackheath
TON
East Dulwich
LEWISHAM
A2
105
106
107
108
109
110
111
Lee
ELTHAM
Dulwich
CATFORD
Mottingham
A20
119
120
121
122
123
124
125
West Norwood
Sydenham
Grove Park
A21
PENGE
BECKENHAM

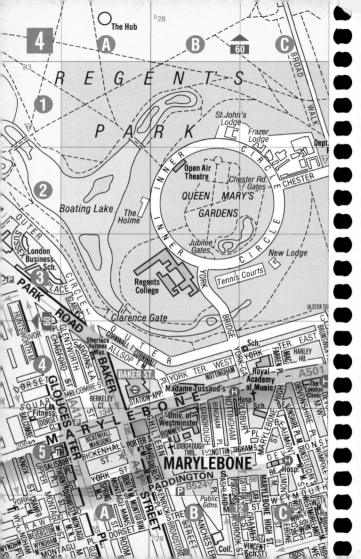

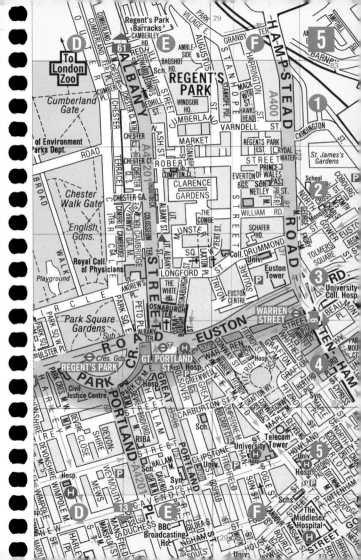

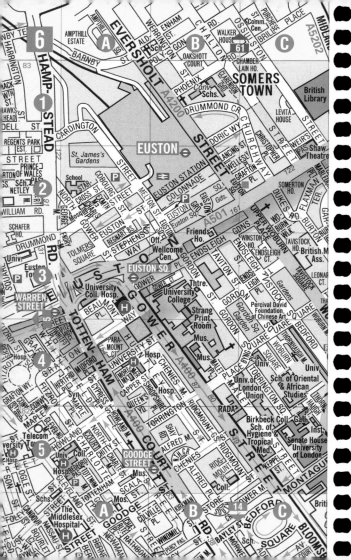

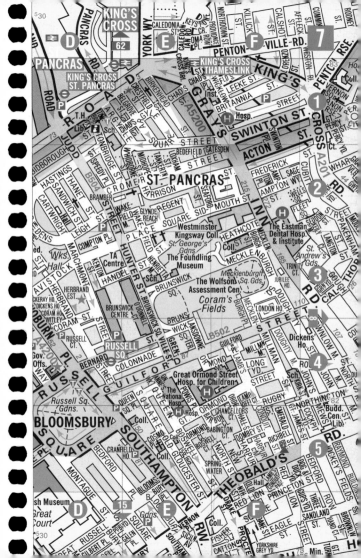

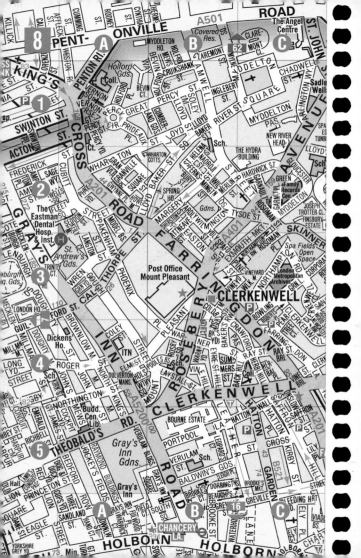

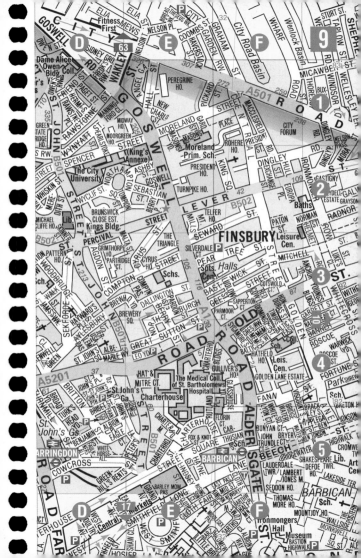

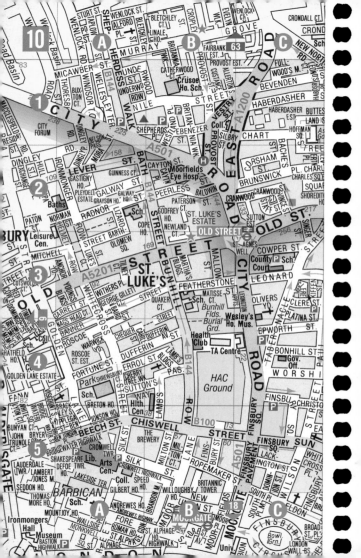

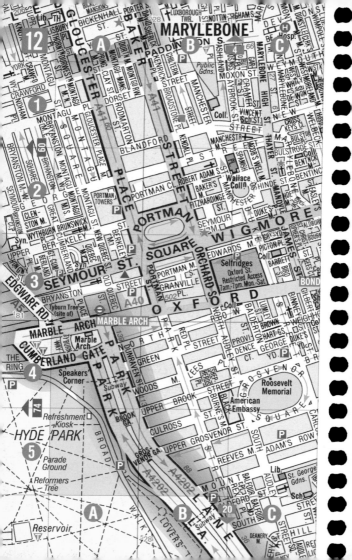

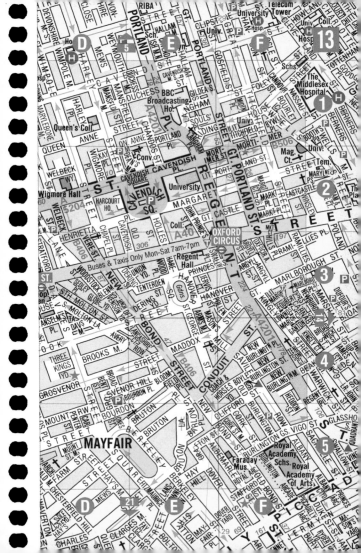

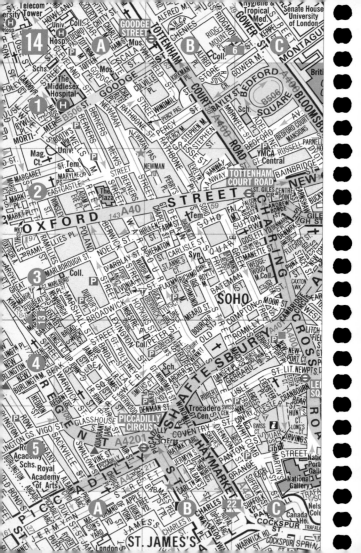

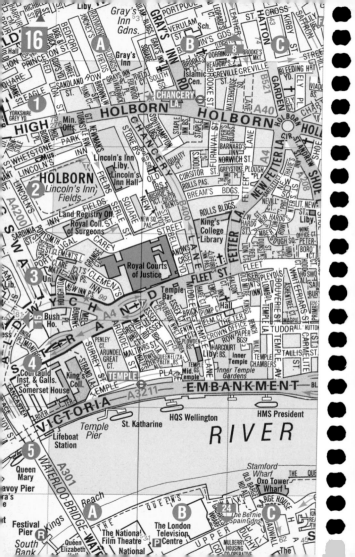

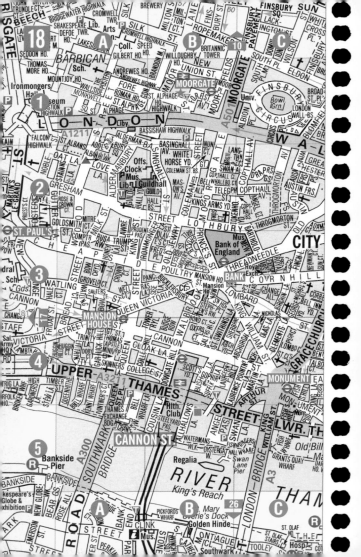

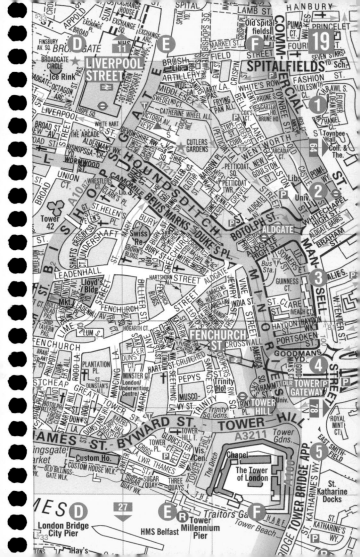

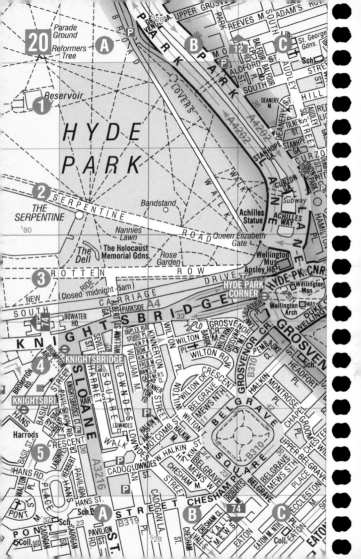

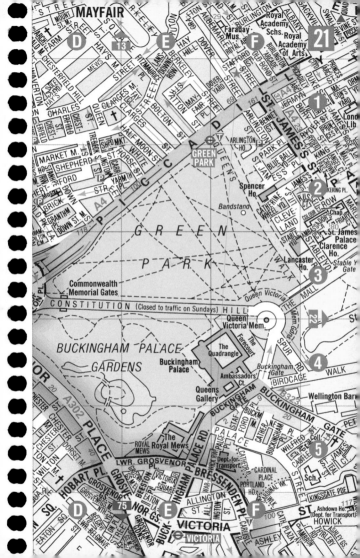

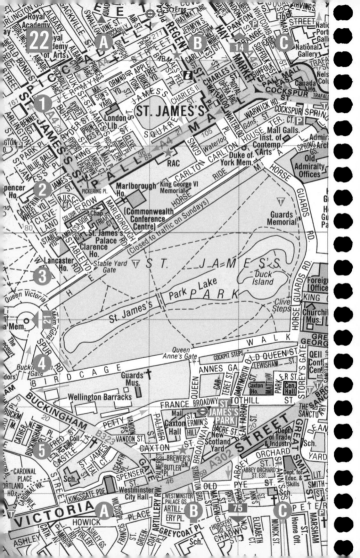

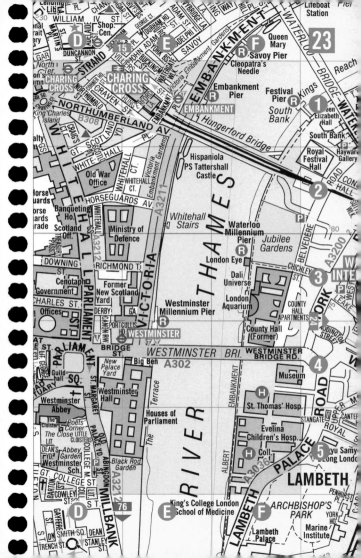

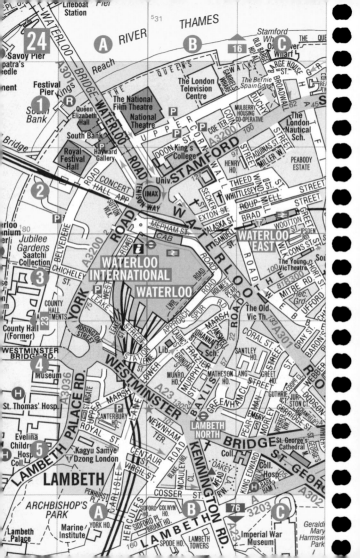

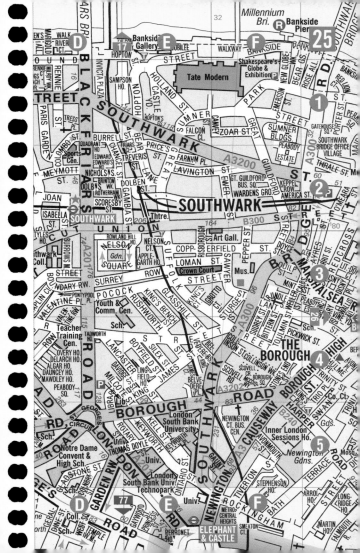

Millennium
Bri.
R Bankside
Pier

Bankside
Gallery

D WALK
RIVER CT.

17 HOPTON ST.

E JUBILEE

HOPTON ST.

STREET

F WALKWAY

BANKSIDE

Shakespeare's
Globe &
Exhibition

Tate Modern

1

SOUTHWARK

SUMNER
BLDGS

SOUTHWARK
BOROUGH OFFICE
VILLAGE

FALCON
CL.

ZOAR ST.

GT. GUILDFORD
BUS. EST.

KEPPEL
CROWN

AMERICA ST.

2

SOUTHWARK

UNION

Art Gall.

COPP-

ERFIELD
ST.

LOMAN
ST.

PEPPER ST.

BIRDCAGE

MARSHALSEA

3

SURREY

POCOCK

GLASSHILL

KING'S BENCH

STURGEON

LANT ST.

SUDREY ST.

PICKWICK ST.

BOROUGH

HIGH

4

Teacher
Training
Cen.

BOTFIELD ST.

KING
FIELD

BELVE-
DERE

St.Col.LINSON WK.

BOROUGH

Co.Ct.

TRINITY

BOROUGH

ROAD

SOUTHWARK

BOROUGH

HARPER

Inner London
Sessions Ho.

5

Newington
Gdns.

London
South Bank
University

NEWINGTON

London
South Bank Univ.
Technopark

STEPHENSON
BATH

Notre Dame
Convent &
High Sch.

GLADSTONE ST.

Univ

D Coll. Sch.

TEMPLE

77

E Univ

ROAD

F METRO-
CENTRAL
HEIGHTS

ROCKINGHAM

**ELEPHANT
& CASTLE**

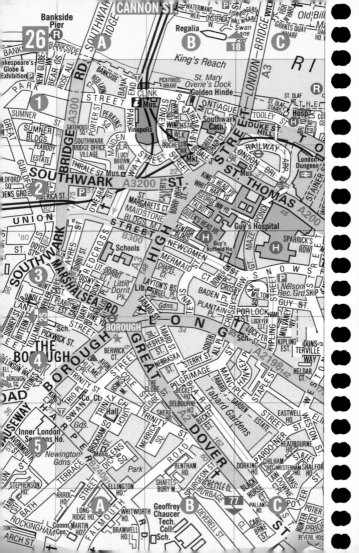

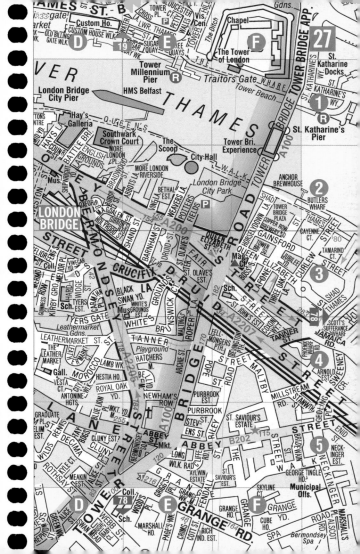

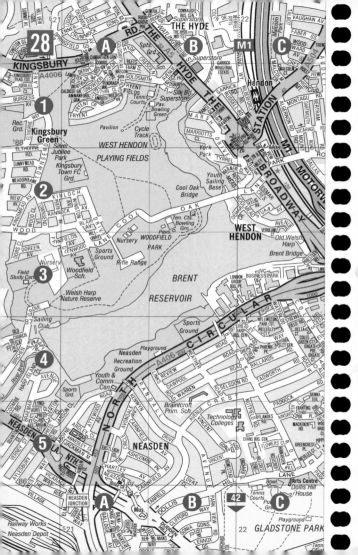

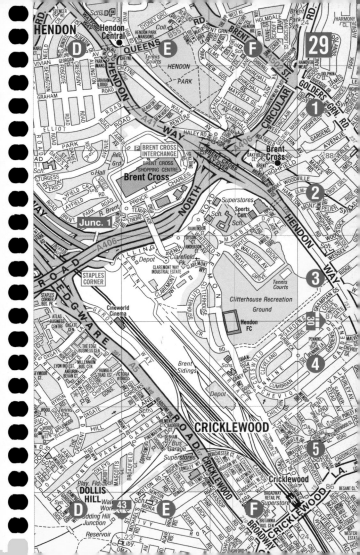

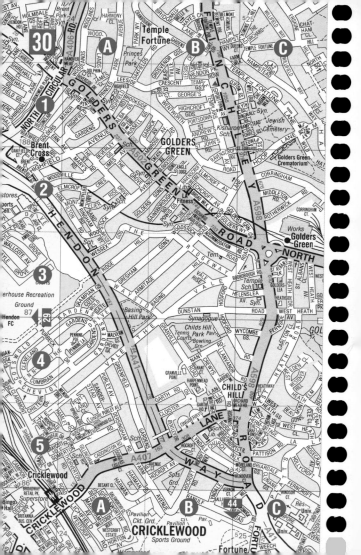

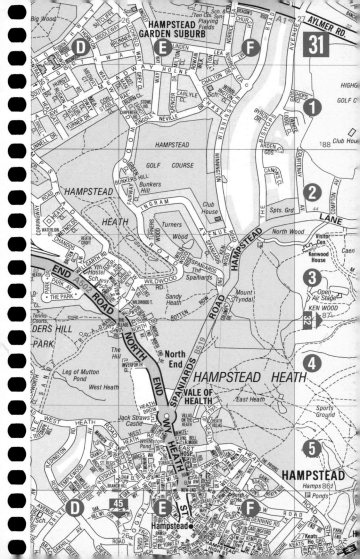

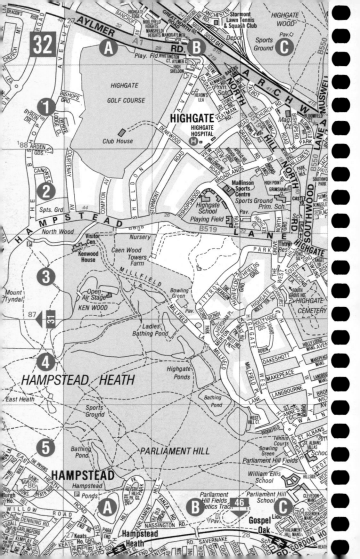

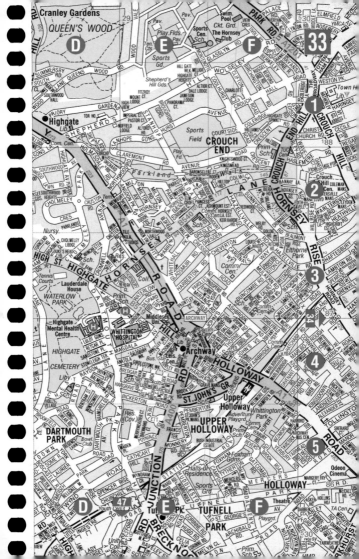

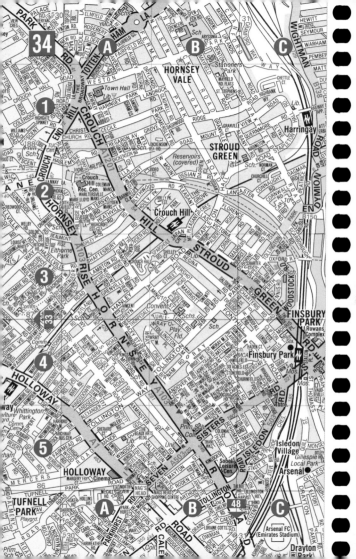

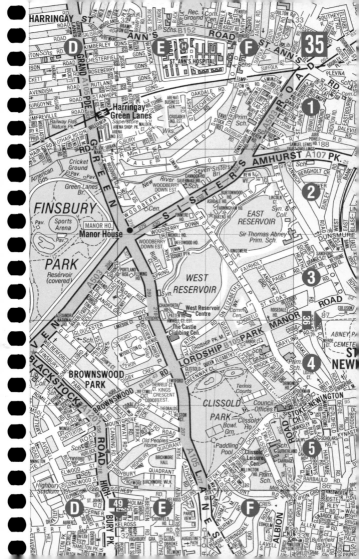

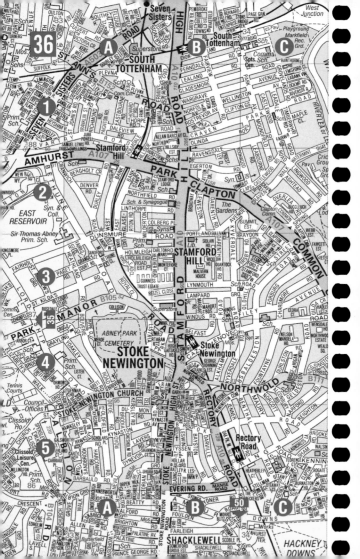

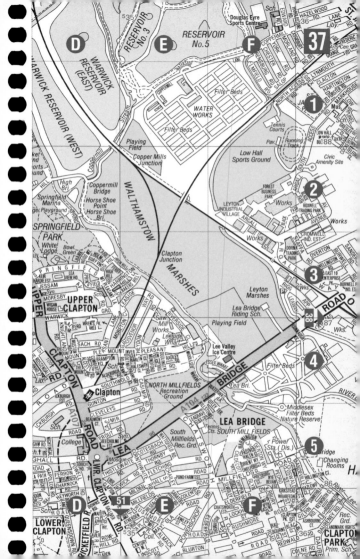

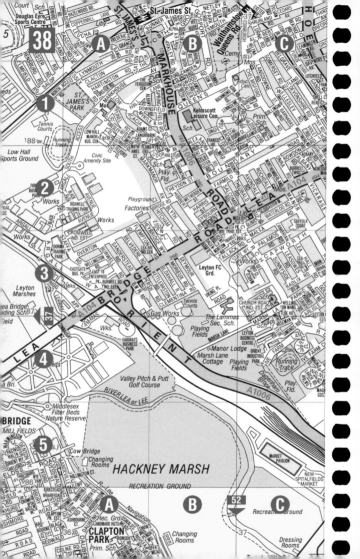

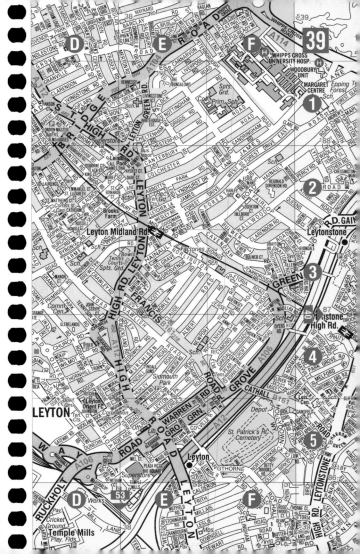

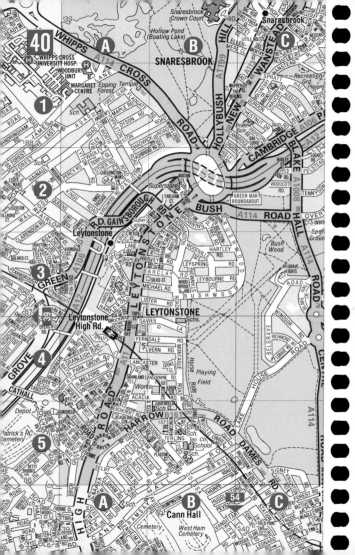

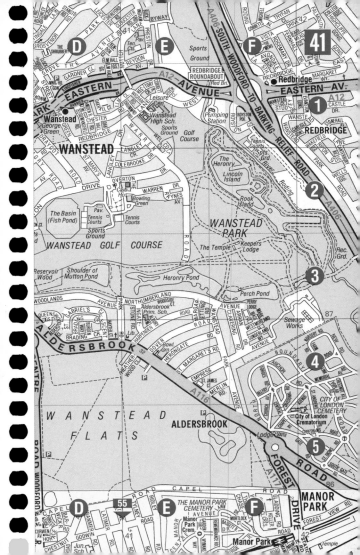

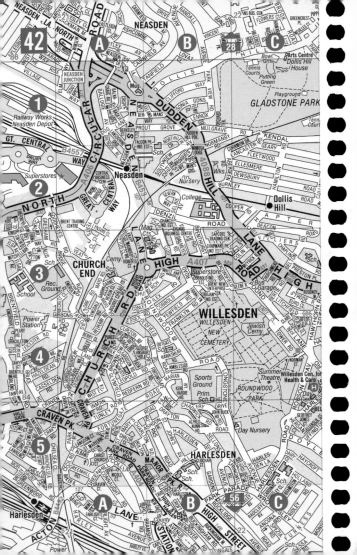

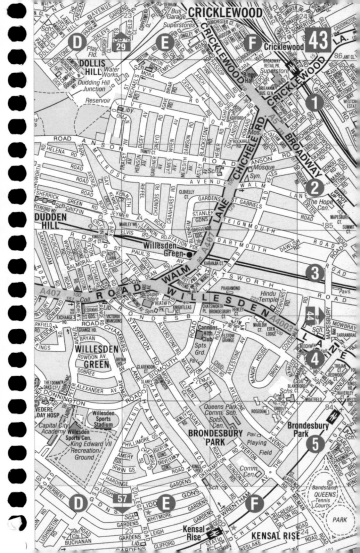

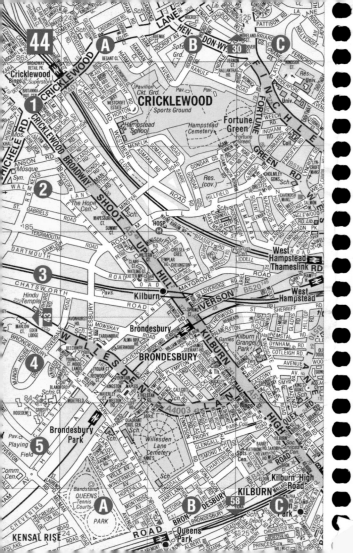

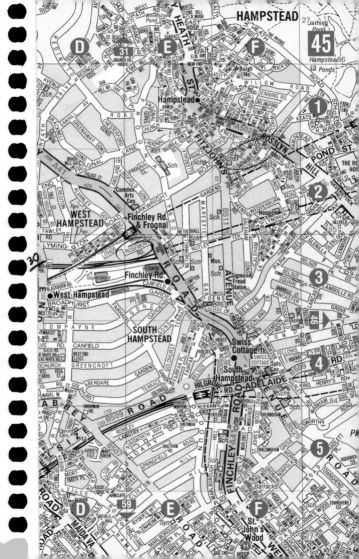

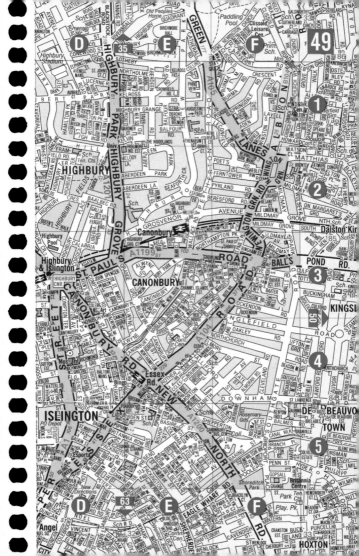

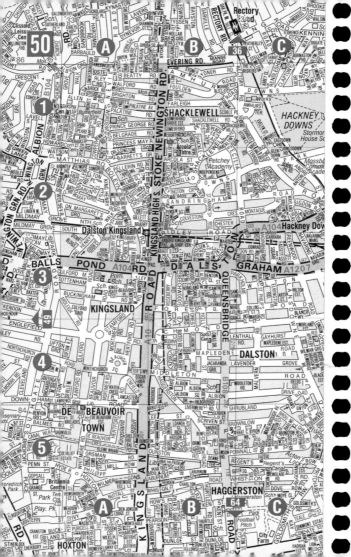

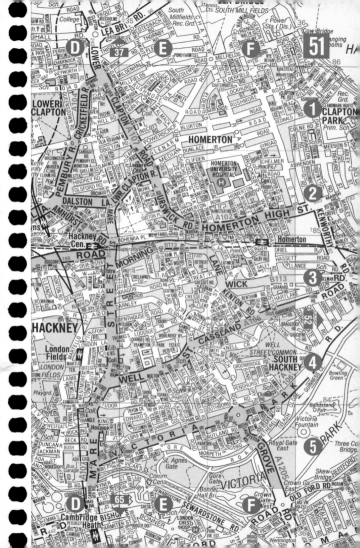

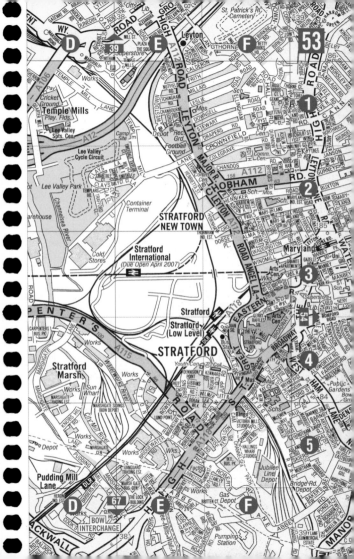

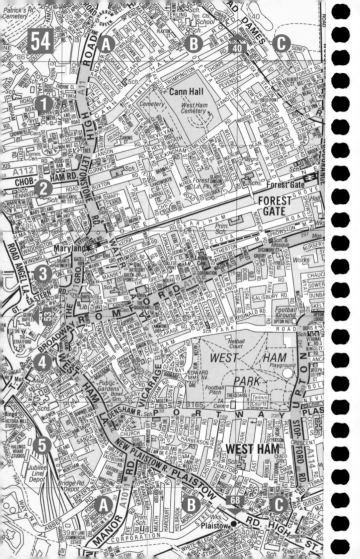

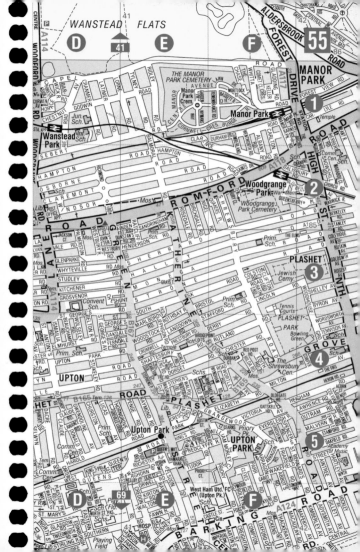

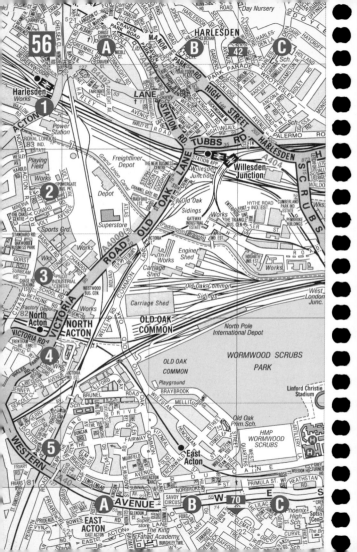

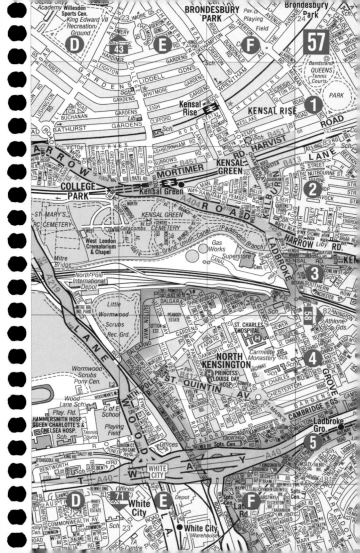

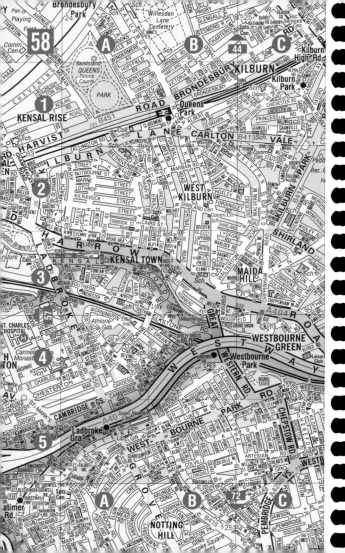

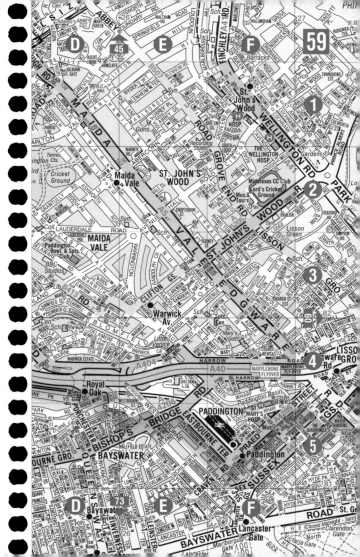

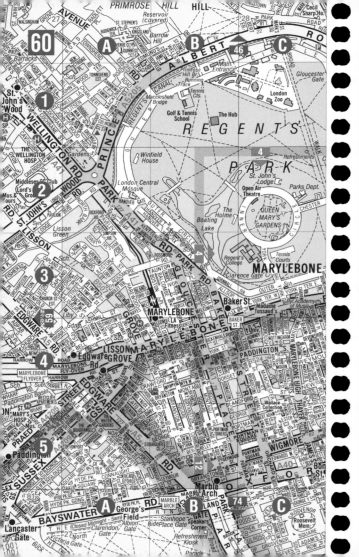

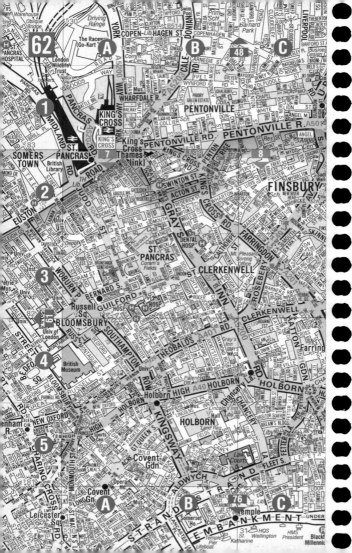

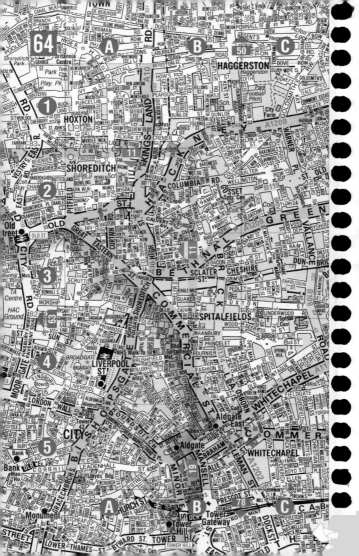

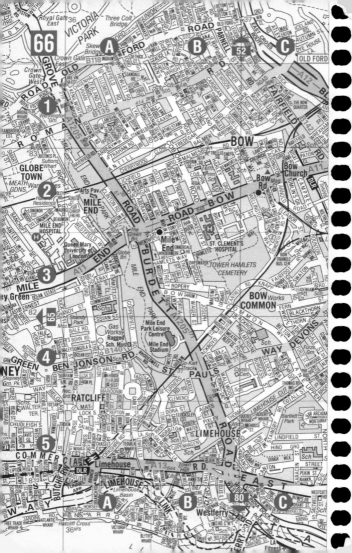

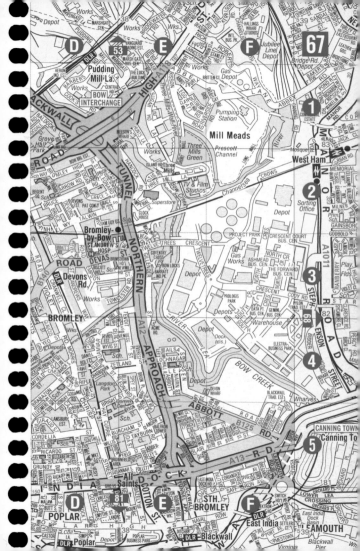

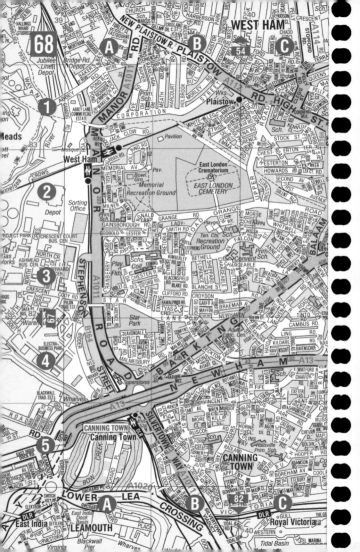

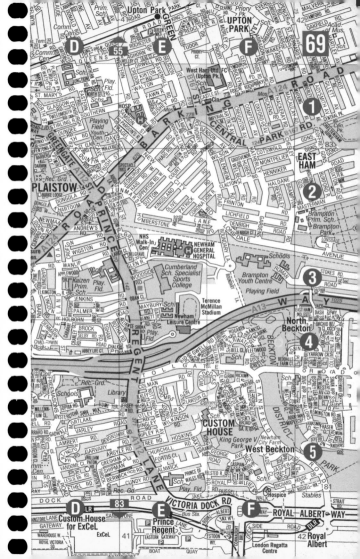

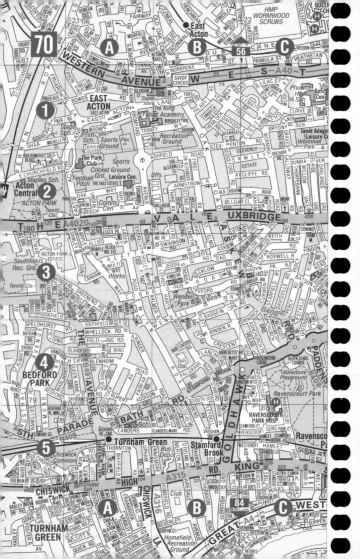

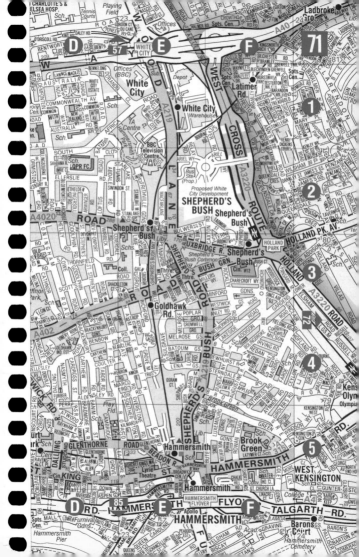

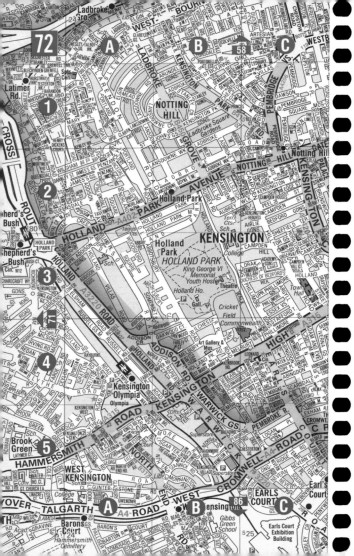

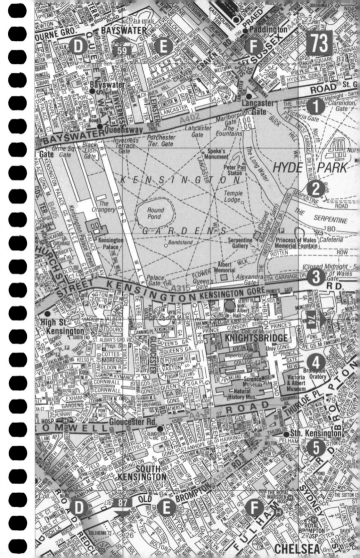

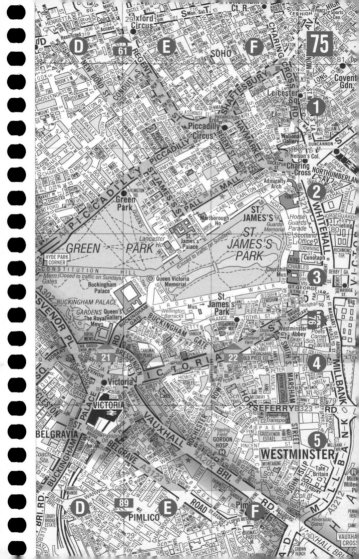

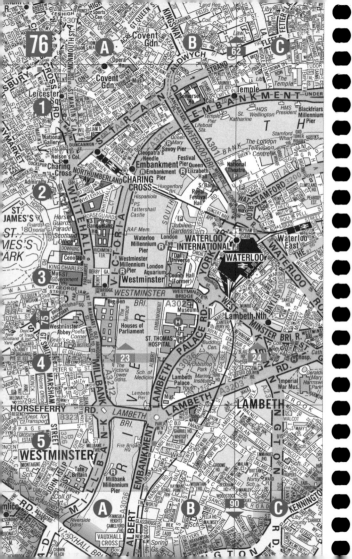

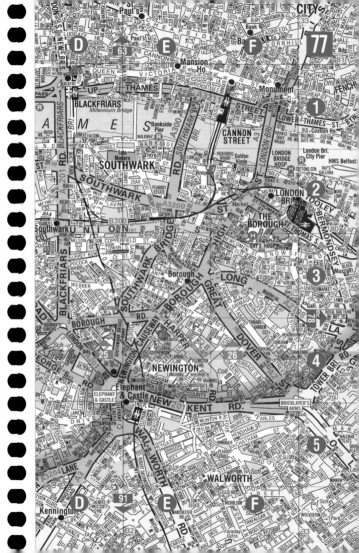

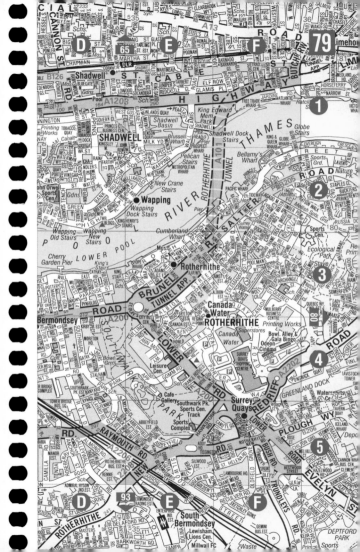

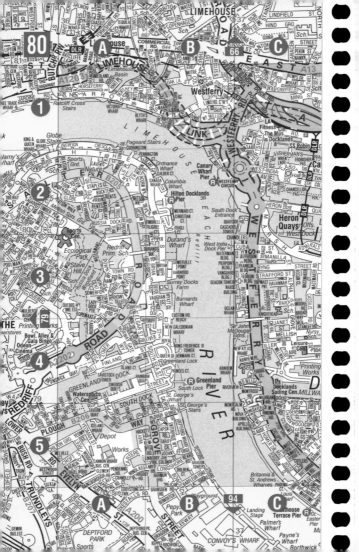

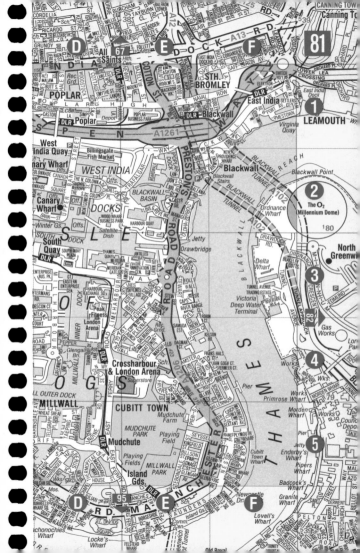

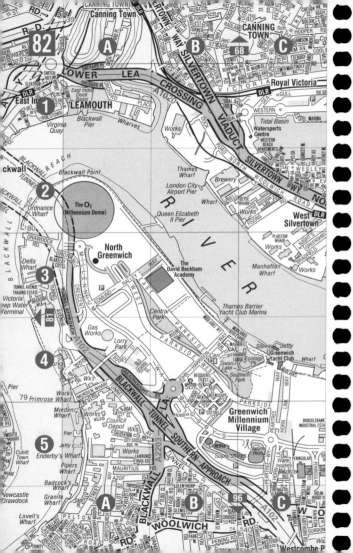

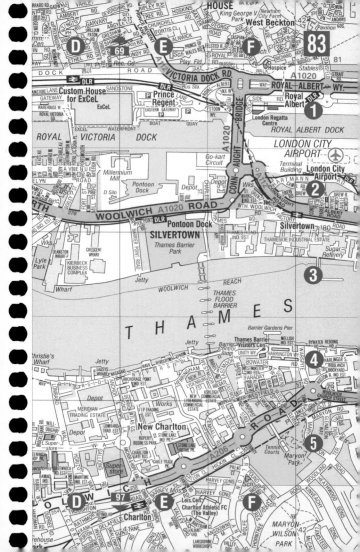

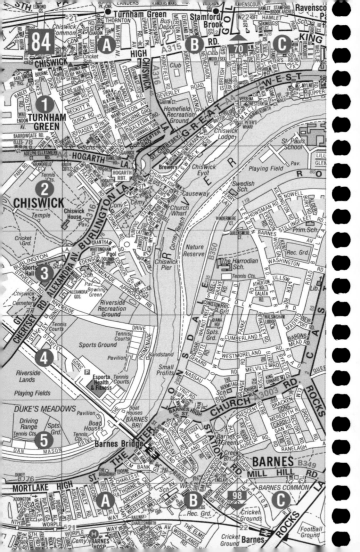

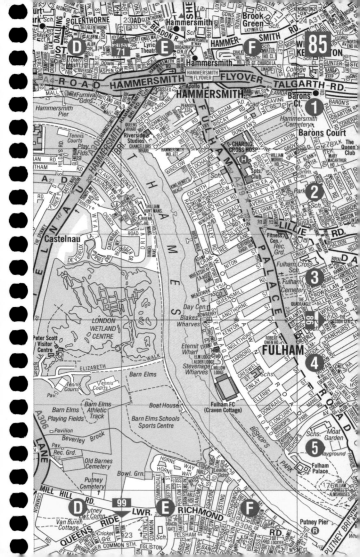

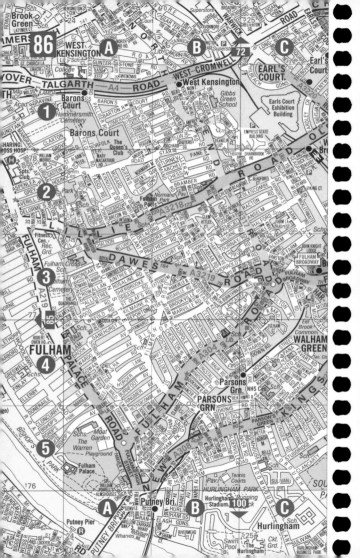

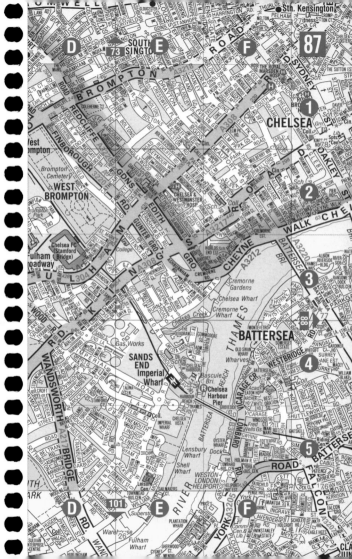

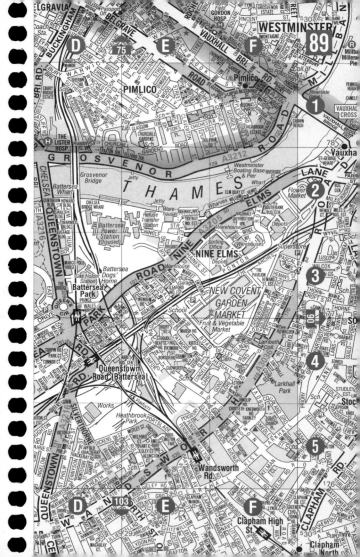

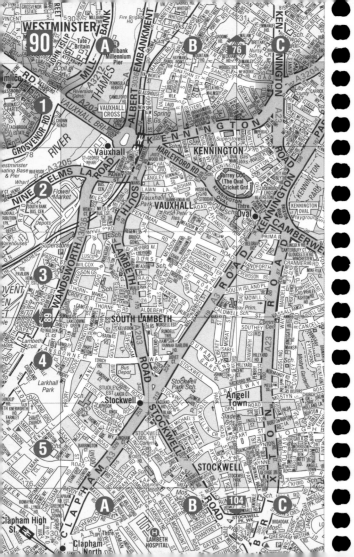

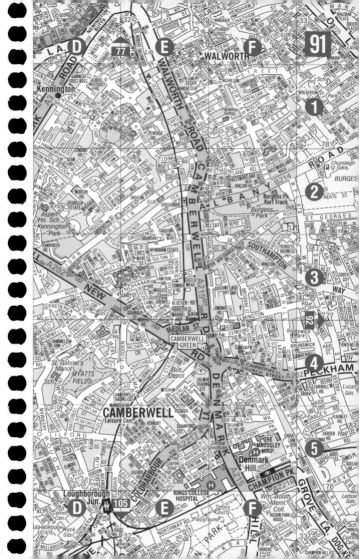

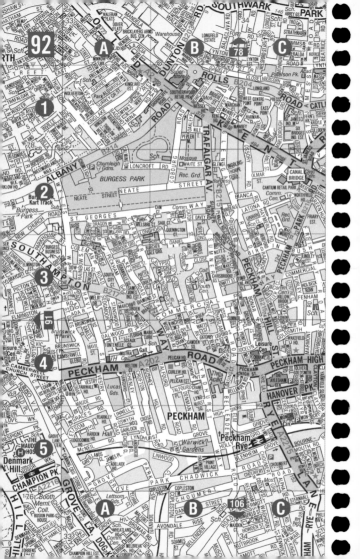

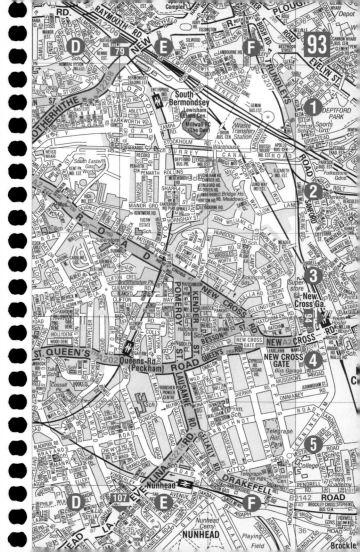

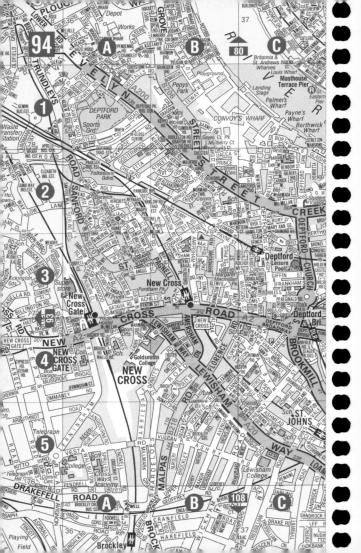

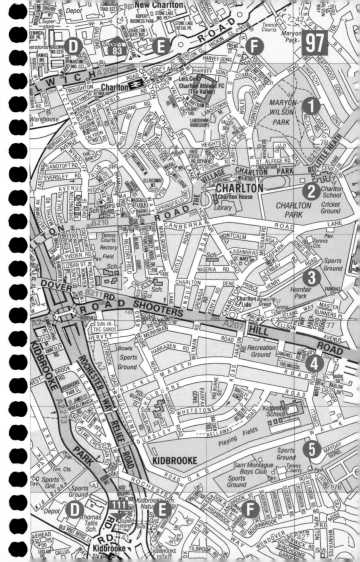

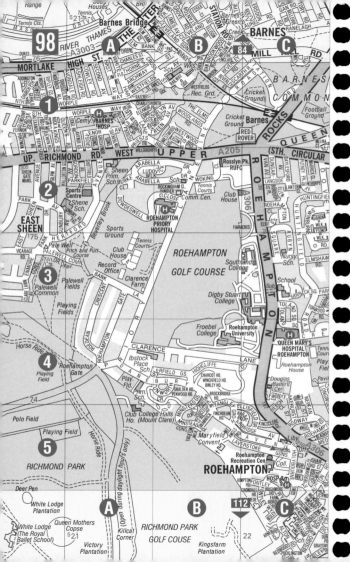

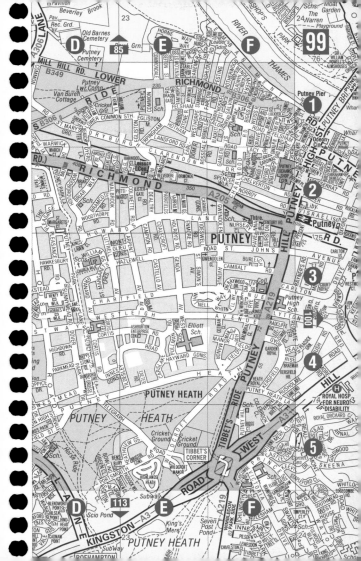

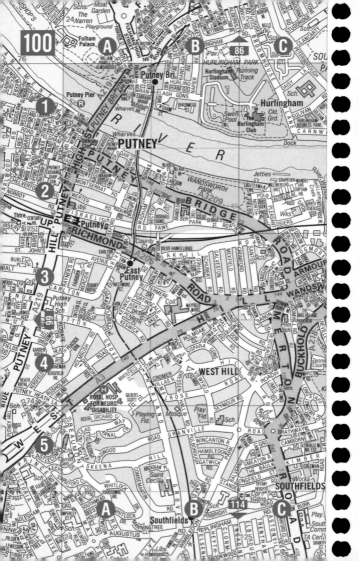

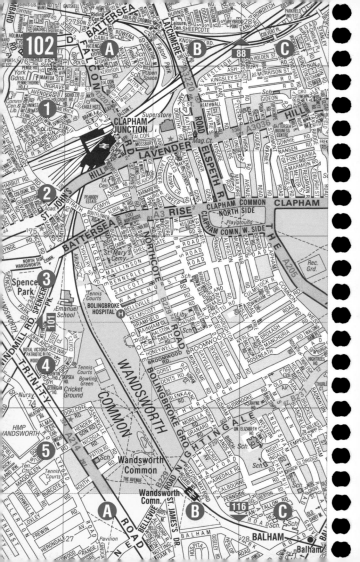

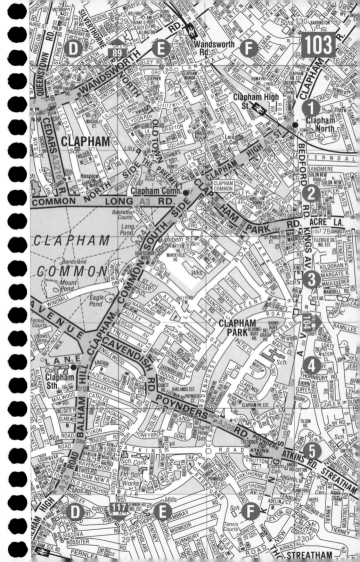

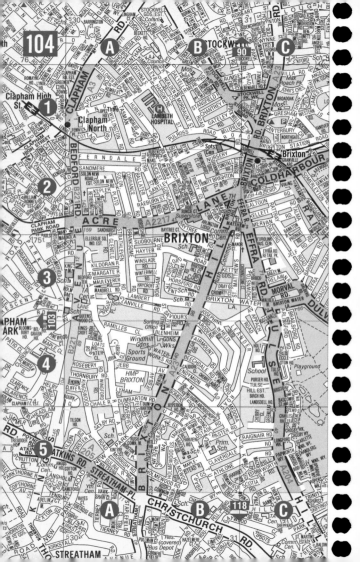

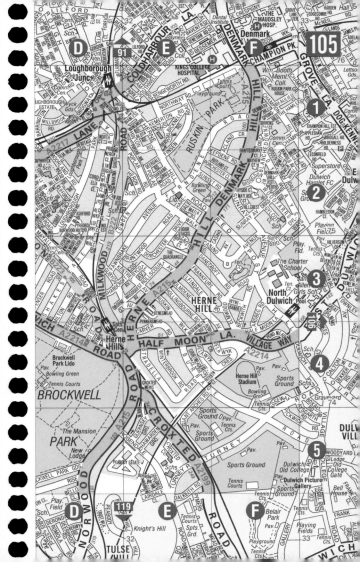

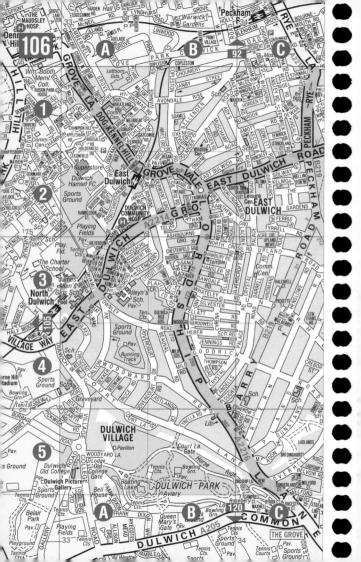

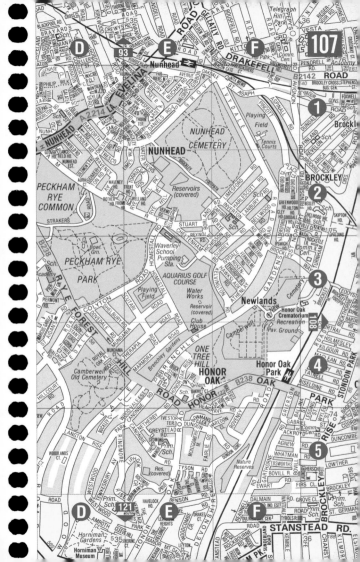

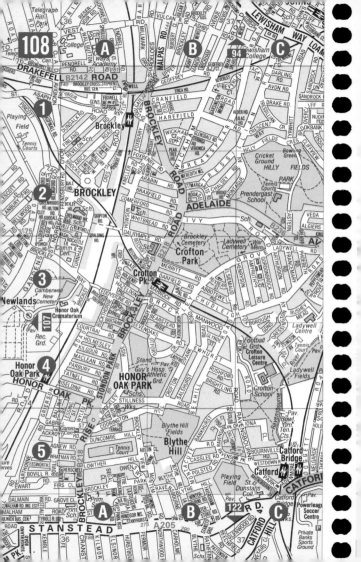

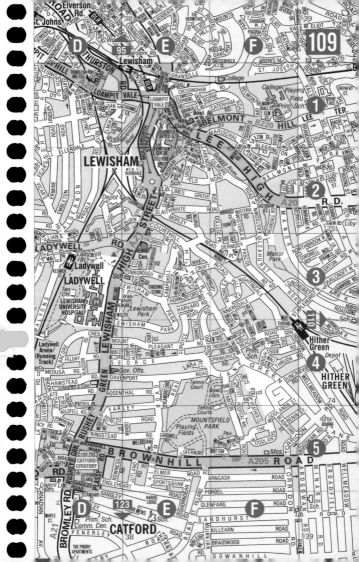

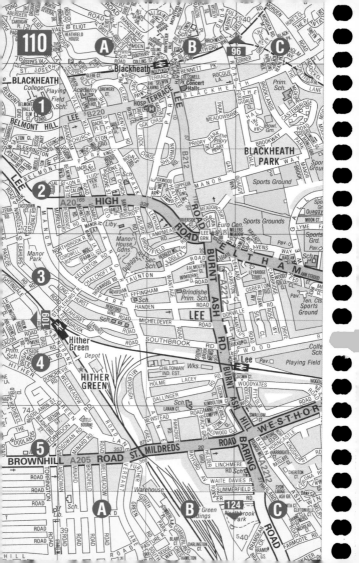

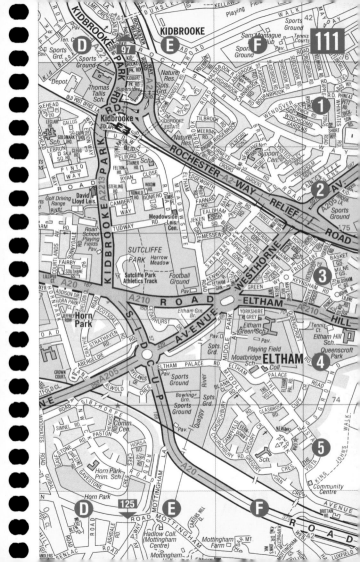

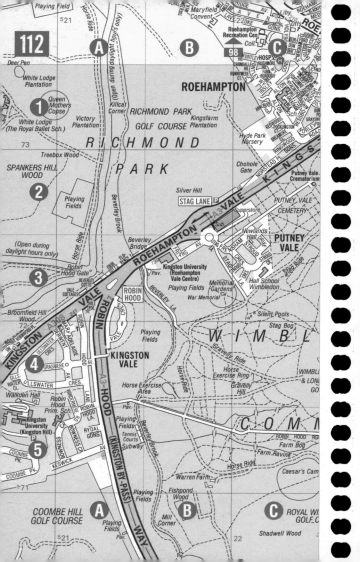

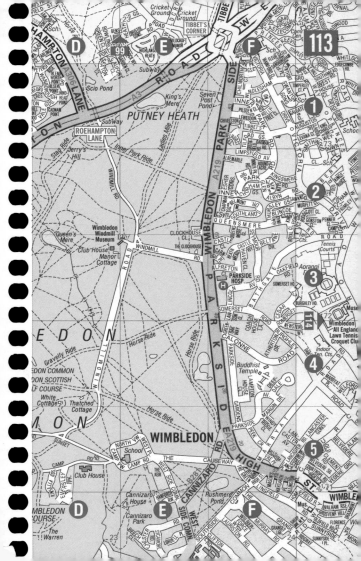

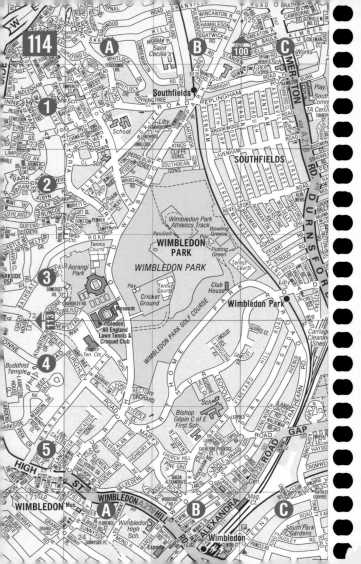

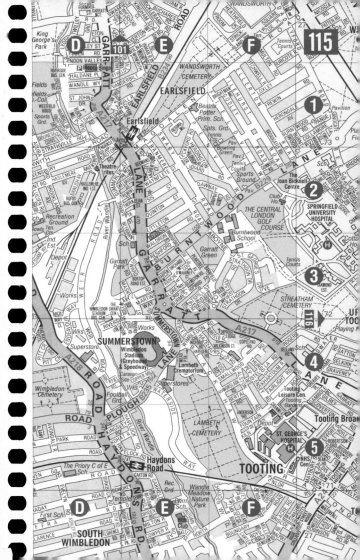

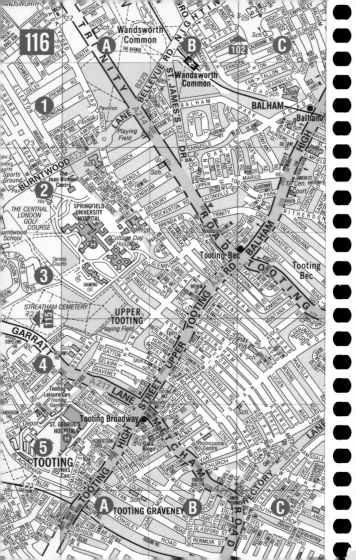

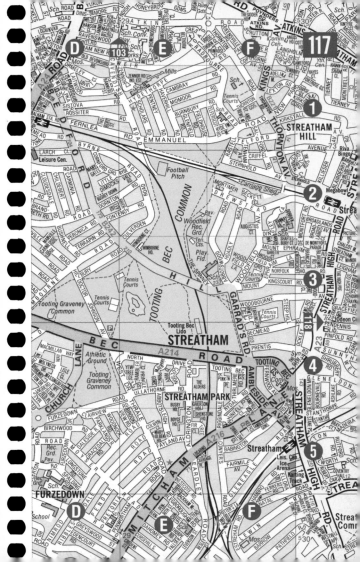

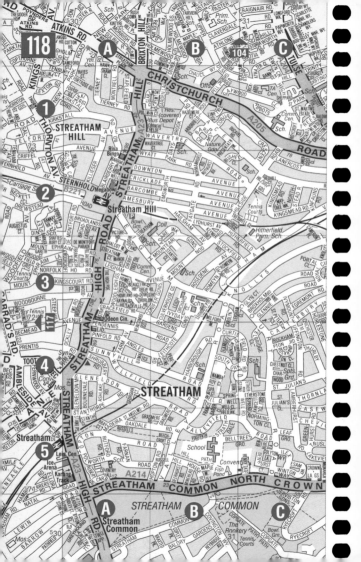

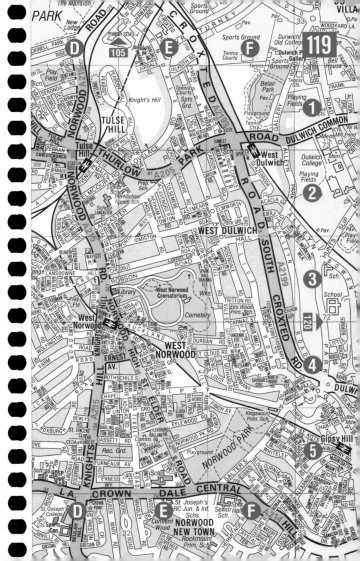

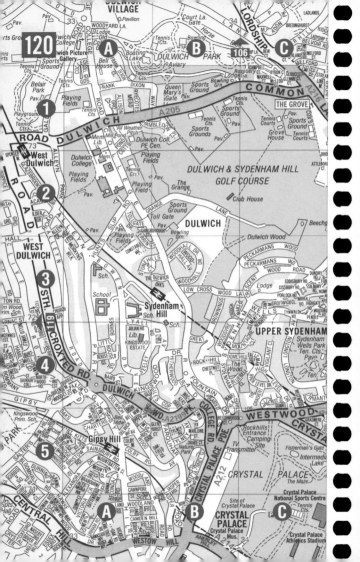

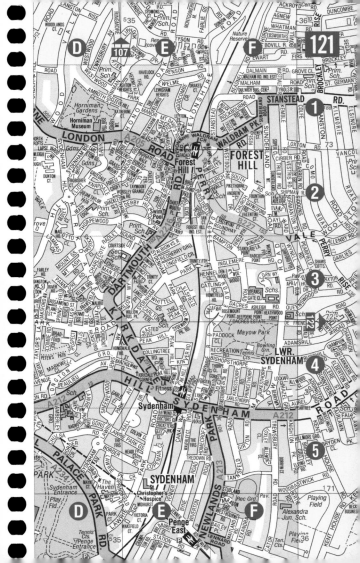

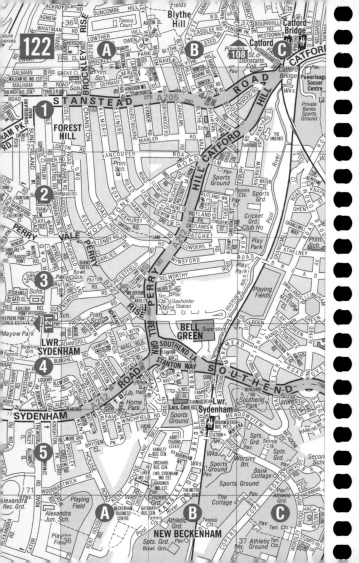

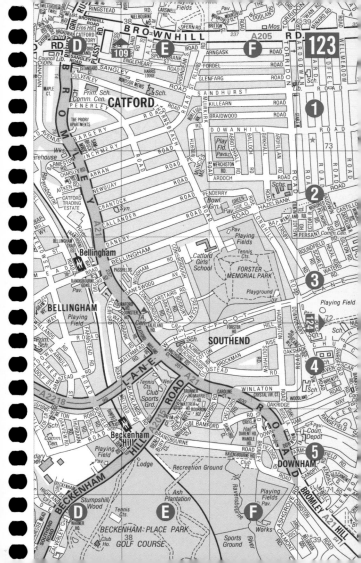

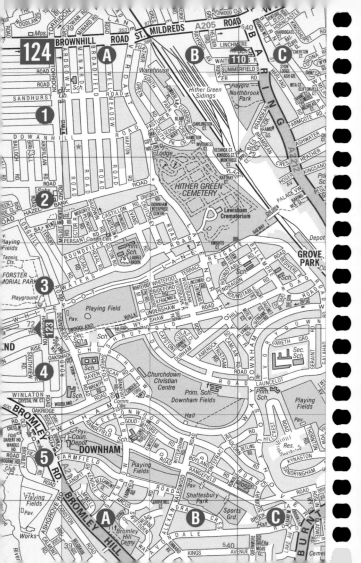

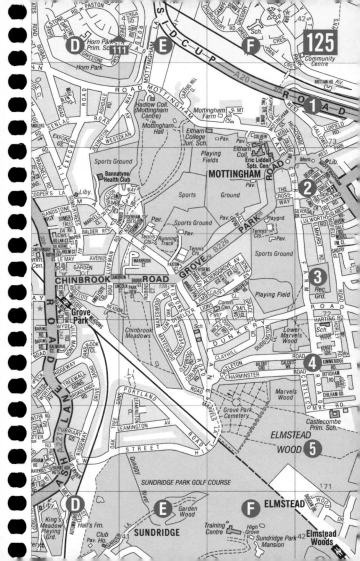

125

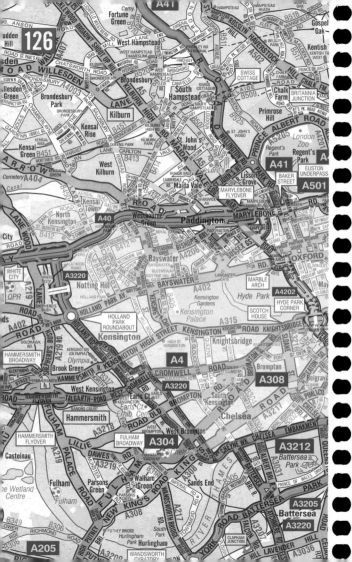

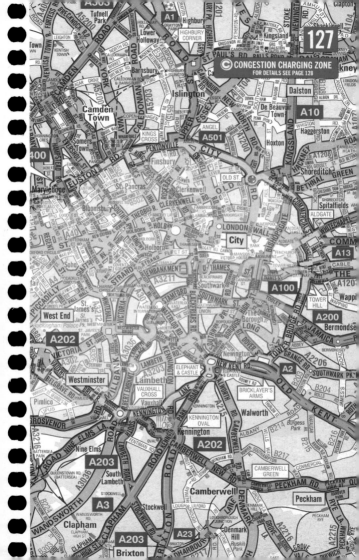

CONGESTION CHARGING ZONE
FOR DETAILS SEE PAGE 128

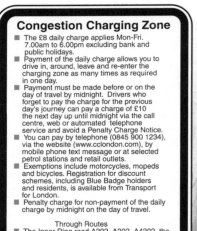

Congestion Charging Zone

- The £8 daily charge applies Mon-Fri. 7.00am to 6.00pm excluding bank and public holidays.
- Payment of the daily charge allows you to drive in, around, leave and re-enter the charging zone as many times as required in one day.
- Payment must be made before or on the day of travel by midnight. Drivers who forget to pay the charge for the previous day's journey can pay a charge of £10 the next day up until midnight via the call centre, web or automated telephone service and avoid a Penalty Charge Notice.
- You can pay by telephone (0845 900 1234), via the website (www.cclondon.com), by mobile phone text message or at selected petrol stations and retail outlets.
- Exemptions include motorcycles, mopeds and bicycles. Registration for discount schemes, including Blue Badge holders and residents, is available from Transport for London.
- Penalty charge for non-payment of the daily charge by midnight on the day of travel.

Through Routes

- The Inner Ring road A202, A302, A4202, the A5 linking Vauxhall with the Marylebone flyover and the A40 Westway remain outside the charge zone.
- Through Routes not subject to Charging Zone regulations.

For further information www.cclondon.com

Date and charges correct at time of going to press.

INDEX

Including Streets, Places & Areas, Industrial Estates,
Selected Flats & Walkways, Junction Names and
Selected Places of Interest.

HOW TO USE THIS INDEX

1. Each street name is followed by its Postcode District (or, if outside the London Postcodes, by its Locality Abbreviation(s)) and then by its map reference;
e.g. **Abbeville Rd.** SW4 . . . .4E **103** is in the SW4 Postcode District and is to be found in square 4E on page **103**. The page number is shown in bold type.

2. A strict alphabetical order is followed in which Av., Rd., St., etc. (though abbreviated) are read in full and as part of the street name; e.g. **Abbotsleigh Rd.** appears after **Abbots La.** but before **Abbots Mnr.**

3. Streets and a selection of flats and walkways too small to be shown on the maps, appear in the index with the thoroughfare to which it is connected shown in brackets;
e.g. **Abady Ho.** SW1 . . . .5F **75** (off Page St.)

4. Addresses that are in more than one part are referred to as not continuous.

5. Places and areas are shown in the index in **BLUE TYPE** and the map reference is to the actual map square in which the town centre or area is located and not to the place name shown on the map; e.g. **ALDERSBROOK** 4D **41**

6. An example of a selected place of interest is Admiralty Arch 1C **22** (2F **75**)

7. Junction names are shown in the index in **BOLD TYPE**; e.g. **ANGEL** 1C **62**

8. Map references for entries that appear on large scale pages **4-27** are shown first, with small scale map references shown in brackets; e.g. **Abbey Orchard St.** SW1 . . . .5B **22** (4F **75**)

GENERAL ABBREVIATIONS

All. : Alley	**Ent.** : Enterprise	**Pal.** : Palace
App. : Approach	**Est.** : Estate	**Pde.** : Parade
Arc. : Arcade	**Fld.** : Field	**Pk.** : Park
Av. : Avenue	**Flds.** : Fields	**Pas.** : Passage
Bk. : Back	**Gdn.** : Garden	**Pav.** : Pavilion
Blvd. : Boulevard	**Gdns.** : Gardens	**Pl.** : Place
Bri. : Bridge	**Gth.** : Garth	**Pct.** : Precinct
B'way. : Broadway	**Ga.** : Gate	**Prom.** : Promenade
Bldg. : Building	**Gt.** : Great	**Quad.** : Quadrant
Bldgs. : Buildings	**Grn.** : Green	**Ri.** : Rise
Bus. : Business	**Gro.** : Grove	**Rd.** : Road
C'way. : Causeway	**Hgts.** : Heights	**Rdbt.** : Roundabout
Cen. : Centre	**Ho.** : House	**Shop.** : Shopping
Chu. : Church	**Ho's.** : Houses	**Sth.** : South
Chyd. : Churchyard	**Ind.** : Industrial	**Sq.** : Square
Circ. : Circle	**Info.** : Information	**Sta.** : Station
Cir. : Circus	**Junc.** : Junction	**St.** : Street
Cl. : Close	**La.** : Lane	**Ter.** : Terrace
Coll. : College	**Lit.** : Little	**Twr.** : Tower
Comn. : Common	**Lwr.** : Lower	**Trad.** : Trading
Cnr. : Corner	**Mnr.** : Manor	**Up.** : Upper
Cott. : Cottage	**Mans.** : Mansions	**Va.** : Vale
Cotts. : Cottages	**Mkt.** : Market	**Vw.** : View
Ct. : Court	**Mdw.** : Meadow	**Vs.** : Villas
Cres. : Crescent	**Mdws.** : Meadows	**Vis.** : Visitors
Cft. : Croft	**M.** : Mews	**Wlk.** : Walk
Dr. : Drive	**Mt.** : Mount	**W.** : West
E. : East	**Mus.** : Museum	**Yd.** : Yard
Emb. : Embankment	**Nth.** : North	

Beck : **Beckenham**
Brom : **Bromley**

Chst : **Chislehurst**
Ilf : **Ilford**

King T :
Kingston Upon Thames

198 Gallery 4D **105**
  (off Railton Rd.)

A

Abady Ho. SW1. . . . . . . 5F **75**
  (off Page St.)
Abberley M. SW4. . . . . 1D **103**
Abbess Cl. SW2. . . . . . 1D **119**
Abbeville M. SW4. . . . . 2F **103**
Abbeville Rd. SW4. . . . . 4E **103**
Abbey Bus. Cen.
  SW8 . . . . 4E **89**
Abbey Cl. E5. . . . . 1C **50**
  SW8 . . . . 4F **89**
Abbey Ct. NW8 . . . . 1E **59**
  (off Abbey Rd.)
SE17 . . . . 1E **91**
  (off Macleod St.)
Abbey Dr. SW17 . . . . . . 5C **116**
Abbey Est. NW8 . . . . . . 5D **45**
Abbeyfield Est. SE16 . . . 5E **79**
Abbeyfield Rd. SE16 . . . 5E **79**
  (not continuous)
Abbey Gdns. NW8 . . . . . 1E **59**
SE16 . . . . 5C **78**
W6 . . . . 2A **86**
Abbey Ho. E15 . . . . 1A **68**
  (off Baker's Row)
NW8 . . . . 2E **59**
  (off Garden Rd.)
Abbey La. E15. . . . . 1E **67**
Abbey La. Commercial Est.
  E15. . . . . 1A **68**
Abbey Life Ct. E16 . . . . . 4D **69**
Abbey Lodge NW8 . . . . . 2A **60**
  (off Park Rd.)
Abbey M. E17. . . . . 1C **38**
Abbey Orchard St.
  SW1 . . . . 5B **22** (4F **75**)
Abbey Orchard St.
  SW1 . . . . 5C **22** (4F **75**)
  (not continuous)
Abbey Rd. E15. . . . . 1F **67**
NW6 . . . . 4D **45**
NW8 . . . . 4D **45**
Abbey St. E13. . . . . 3C **68**
SE1 . . . . 5E **27** (4B **78**)
Abbey Trad. Est.
  SE26 . . . . 5B **122**
Abbot Ct. SW8 . . . . 3A **90**
  (off Hartington Rd.)
Abbot Ho. E14 . . . . 1D **81**
  (off Smythe St.)
Abbotsbury NW1. . . . . . 4F **47**
  (off Camley St.)
Abbotsbury Cl. E15. . . . . 1E **67**
W14 . . . . 3A **72**
Abbotsbury Ho. W14 . . . 3A **72**
Abbotsbury M. SE15. . . 1E **107**

Abbotsbury Rd. W14 . . . 3A **72**
Abbots Ct. W8 . . . . 3D **73**
  (off Thackeray St.)
Abbotshade Rd. SE16. . . 2F **79**
Abbotshall Rd. SE6 . . . . 1F **123**
Abbot's Ho. W14 . . . . . . 4B **72**
  (off St Mary Abbots Ter.)
Abbots La.
  SE1 . . . . 2E **27** (2A **78**)
Abbotsleigh Rd.
  SW16 . . . . 4E **117**
Abbots Mnr. SW1. . . . . . 5D **75**
Abbots Pk. SW2. . . . . . 1C **118**
Abbot's Pl. NW6. . . . . . . 5D **45**
Abbot's Rd. E6 . . . . 5F **55**
Abbots Ter. N8 . . . . 1A **34**
Abbotstone Rd.
  SW15 . . . . 1E **99**
Abbot St. E8. . . . . 3B **50**
Abbots Wlk. W8. . . . . . . 4D **73**
Abbotswell Rd. SE4. . . . 3B **108**
Abbotswood Rd.
  SE22 . . . . 2A **106**
SW16 . . . . 3F **117**
Abbott Rd. E14. . . . . 4E **67**
  (not continuous)
Abbotts Cl. N1 . . . . 3E **49**
Abbotts Ho. SW1 . . . . . 1F **89**
  (off Aylesford St.)
Abbotts Pk. Rd. E10. . . . 2E **39**
Abbott's Wharf E14 . . . . 5C **66**
  (off Stainsby Pl.)
Abchor Ho. SW1 . . . . . . 1D **89**
  (off Warwick Way)
Abchurch La.
  EC4. . . . . 4C **18** (1F **77**)
  (not continuous)
Abchurch Yd.
  EC4. . . . . 4B **18** (1F **77**)
Abdale Rd. W12. . . . . . . 2D **71**
Abel Ho. SE11 . . . . 2C **90**
  (off Kennington Rd.)
Aberavon Rd. E3 . . . . . . 2A **66**
Abercorn Cl. NW8 . . . . . 2E **59**
Abercorn Cotts. NW8 . . . 2E **59**
  (off Abercorn Wlk.)
Abercorn Ho. SE10 . . . . 3D **95**
  (off Tarves Way)
Abercorn Mans.
  NW8 . . . . 1E **59**
  (off Abercorn Pl.)
Abercorn Pl. NW8 . . . . . 2E **59**
Abercorn Wlk. NW8 . . . . 2E **59**
Abercorn Way SE1. . . . . 1C **92**
Abercrombie St.
  SW11 . . . . 5A **88**
Aberdale Ct. SE16 . . . . . 3F **79**
  (off Garter Way)
Aberdare Gdns. NW6. . . 4D **45**
Aberdeen Ct. W9 . . . . . 3E **59**
  (off Maida Va.)
Aberdeen La. N5 . . . . . . 2E **49**
Aberdeen Mans. WC1 . . 3D **7**
  (off Kenton St.)

Aberdeen Pk. N5 . . . . . . 2E **49**
Aberdeen Pl. NW8 . . . . . 3F **59**
Aberdeen Rd. N5 . . . . . . 1E **49**
NW10 . . . . 2B **42**
Aberdeen Sq. E14 . . . . . 2B **80**
Aberdeen Ter. SE3 . . . . 5F **95**
Aberdeen Wharf E1 . . . . 2D **79**
  (off Wapping High St.)
Aberdour St. SE1 . . . . . . 5A **78**
Aberfeldy Ho. SE5 . . . . . 3D **91**
  (not continuous)
Aberfeldy St. E14. . . . . . 4E **67**
  (not continuous)
Aberford Gdns. SE18 . . . 4F **97**
Abergeldie Rd.
  SE12 . . . . 4D **111**
Abernethy Rd. SE13. . . . 2A **110**
Abersham Rd. E8 . . . . . . 2B **50**
Ability Towers EC1. . . . . 1F **9**
  (off Macclesfield Rd.)
Abingdon W14 . . . . 5B **72**
  (off Kensington Village)
Abingdon Cl. NW1 . . . . . 3F **47**
SE1 . . . . 5B **78**
  (off Bushwood Dr.)
Abingdon Ct. W8 . . . . . . 4C **72**
  (off Abingdon Vs.)
Abingdon Gdns. W8. . . . 4C **72**
Abingdon Ho. E2. . . . . . 3F **11**
  (off Boundary St.)
Abingdon Lodge W8. . . . 4C **72**
Abingdon Mans. W8 . . . 4C **72**
  (off Pater St.)
Abingdon Rd. W8. . . . . . 4C **72**
Abingdon St.
  SW1. . . . . 5D **23** (4A **76**)
Abingdon Vs. W8 . . . . . . 4C **72**
Abinger Gro. SE8. . . . . . 2B **94**
Abinger Ho. SE1. . . . . . . 4B **26**
  (off Gt. Dover St.)
Abinger M. W9. . . . . 3C **58**
Abinger Rd. W4 . . . . 4A **70**
Ablett St. SE16. . . . . 1E **93**
Abney Gdns. N16. . . . . . 4B **36**
Abney Pk. Ter. N16 . . . . 4B **36**
  (off Cazenov Rd.)
Aborfield NW5 . . . . 2E **47**
Aboyne Rd. NW10 . . . . . 5A **28**
SW17 . . . . 3F **115**
Abyssinia Cl. SW11 . . . . 2A **102**
Abyssinia Ct. N8 . . . . . . 1B **34**
Abyssinia Rd.
  SW11 . . . . 2A **102**
Acacia Bus. Cen.
  E11 . . . . 5A **40**
Acacia Cl. SE8 . . . . 5A **80**
Acacia Gdns. NW8 . . . . . 1F **59**
Acacia Gro. SE21 . . . . . 2F **119**
Acacia Pl. NW8 . . . . 1F **59**
Acacia Rd. E11. . . . . 4A **40**
E17. . . . . 1A **38**
NW8 . . . . 1F **59**
Acacia Wlk. SW10 . . . . . 3E **87**
  (off Tadema Rd.)

Academy Apartments
E8 . . . . 2D **51**
E8 . . . . 2D **51**
(off Dalston La.)
Academy Bldgs. *N1* . . . 1D **11**
(off Fanshaw St.)
Academy Ct. *E2* 2E **65**
(off Kirkwall Pl.)
Academy Gdns. W8 . . . 3C **72**
Academy Ho. *E3* 4D **67**
(off Violet Rd.)
Acanthus Dr. SE1 . . . . 1C **92**
Acanthus St. SW11 . . . 1C **102**
Accommodation Rd.
NW11 . . . . 3B **30**
Acfold Rd. SW6 . . . . . 4D **87**
Achilles Cl. SE1 . . . . . 1C **92**
Achilles Ho. *E2* 1D **65**
(off Old Bethnal Grn. Rd.)
Achilles Rd. NW6 . . . . 2C **44**
Achilles Statue
. . . . 2C **20**
Achilles St. SE14 . . . . 3A **94**
Achilles Way
W1 . . . . 2C **20** (2C **74**)
Acklam Rd. W10 . . . . 4A **58**
(not continuous)
Ackmar Rd. SW6 . . . . 4C **86**
Ackroyd Dr. E3 . . . . . . 4B **66**
Ackroyd Rd. SE23 . . . 5F **107**
Acland Cres. SE5 . . . 1F **105**
Acland Ho. SW9 . . . . . 4B **90**
Acland Rd. NW2 . . . . . 3D **43**
Acme Ho. E14 . . . . . . 4E **67**
Acol Ct. NW6 . . . . 4C **44**
Acol Rd. NW6 . . . . . . 4C **44**
Acorn Ct. E6 . . . . 4F **55**
Acorn Gdns. W3 . . . . . 4A **56**
Acorn Pde. SE15 . . . . 3D **93**
Acorn Production Cen.
N7 . . . . 4A **48**
Acorn Wlk. SE16 . . . . 2A **80**
Acorn Wlk. SE23 . . . . 3F **121**
Acre Dr. SE22 . . . . . . 2C **106**
Acre La. SW2 . . . . . . 2A **104**
Acre Rd. SW19 . . . . . 5F **115**
Acris St. SW18 . . . . . 3E **101**
Acton Ho. *E8* 5B **50**
(off Lee St.)
Acton La. NW10 . . . . . 1A **56**
Acton M. E8 . . . . 5B **50**
Acton Pk. Est. W3 . . . . 3A **70**
Acton St. WC1 . . 2F **7** (2B **62**)
Acton Va. Ind. Pk.
W3 . . . . 3B **70**
Acuba Rd. SW18 . . . . 2D **115**
Ada Ct. *N1* 5E **49**
(off Packington St.)
W9 . . . . 2E **59**
Ada Gdns. E14 . . . . . . 5F **67**
E15 . . . . 5B **54**
Ada Ho. *E2* 5C **50**
(off Ada Pl.)
Adair Ho. *SW3* 2A **88**
(off Oakley St.)
Adair Rd. W10 . . . . . . 3A **58**
Adair Twr. *W10* 3A **58**
(off Appleford Rd.)

Ada Kennedy Ct.
SE10 . . . . 3E **95**
(off Greenwich Sth. St.)
Adam & Eve Cl. W1 . . 2A **14**
Adam & Eve M. W8 . . . 4C **72**
Adam Cl. SE6 . . . . . . 4B **122**
Adam Ct. *SE11* 5D **77**
(off Opal St.)
SW7 . . . . 5E **73**
(off Gloucester Rd.)
Adams Ct. E17 . . . . . 1A **38**
EC2 . . . . . . 2C **18** (5A **64**)
Adams Gdns. Est.
SE16 . . . . 3E **79**
Adams Ho. *E14* 5F **67**
(off Aberfeldy St.)
Adams M. SW17 . . . . 2B **116**
Adamson Rd. E16 . . . . 5C **68**
NW3 . . . . 4F **45**
Adams Pl. *E14* 2D **81**
(off The Nth. Colonnade)
N7 . . . . 2B **48**
Adamsrill Rd.
SE26 . . . . 4F **121**
Adam's Row
W1 . . . . . . 5C **12** (1C **74**)
Adam St.
WC2 . . . . . . 5E **15** (1A **76**)
Adam Wlk. SW6 . . . . . 3E **85**
Ada Pl. *E2* 5C **50**
Adare Wlk. SW16 . . . . 3B **118**
Ada Rd. SE5 . . . . 3A **92**
Adastral Ho. *WC1* 5F **7**
(off New Nth. St.)
Ada St. E8 . . . . 5D **51**
Ada Workshops E8 . . . 5D **51**
Adderley Gro.
SW11 . . . . 3C **102**
Adderley St. E14 . . . . . 5E **67**
Addey Ho. SE8 . . . . . . 3B **94**
Addington Ct. SW14 . . 1A **98**
Addington Gro.
SE26 . . . . 4A **122**
Addington Ho. *SW9* . . 5B **90**
(off Stockwell Rd.)
Addington Rd. *E3* 2C **66**
E16 . . . . 3A **68**
N4 . . . . 1C **34**
Addington Sq. SE5 . . . 2F **91**
(not continuous)
Addington St.
SE1 . . . . . . 4A **24** (3B **76**)
Addis Ho. *E1* 4E **65**
(off Lindley St.)
Addisland Ct. *W14* . . . 3A **72**
(off Holland Vs. Rd.)
Addison Av. W11 . . . . 2A **72**
Addison Bri. Pl.
W14 . . . . 5B **72**
Addison Ct. NW6 . . . . 5C **44**
(off Brondesbury Rd.)
Addison Cres. W14 . . . 4A **72**
(not continuous)
Addison Dr. SE12 . . . 3D **111**
Addison Gdns.
W14 . . . . 4F **71**
Addison Gro. W4 . . . . 4A **70**
Addison Ho. *NW8* 2F **59**
(off Grove End Rd.)

Addison Pk. Mans.
W14 . . . . 4F **71**
(off Richmond Way)
Addison Pl. W11 . . . . . 2A **72**
Addison Rd. E11 . . . . . 1C **40**
W14 . . . . 3A **72**
Addle Hill
EC4 . . . . 3E **17** (5D **63**)
Addlestone Ho. *W10* . . 4E **57**
(off Sutton Way)
Addle St. EC2 . . 2A **18** (5E **63**)
Addy Ho. SE16 . . . . . . 5E **79**
Adela Ho. *W6* 1E **85**
(off Queen Caroline St.)
Adelaide Av. SE4 . . . . 2B **108**
Adelaide Cl. SW9 . . . . 2C **104**
Adelaide Ct. *NW8* 1E **59**
(off Abbey Rd.)
Adelaide Gro. W12 . . . 2C **70**
Adelaide Ho. E15 . . . . 1B **68**
SE5 . . . . 5A **92**
W11 . . . . 5B **58**
(off Portobello Rd.)
Adelaide Rd. E10 . . . . 5D **39**
NW3 . . . . 4F **45**
SW18 . . . . 3C **100**
Adelaide St.
WC2 . . . . . . 5D **15** (1A **76**)
Adela St. W10 . . . . . . 3A **58**
Adelina Gro. E1 . . . . . 4E **65**
Adelina M. SW12 . . . . 1F **117**
Adelina Yd. *E1* 4E **65**
(off Adelina Gro.)
Adeline Pl.
WC1 . . . . . . 1C **14** (4F **61**)
Adelphi Ct. *E8* 4B **50**
(off Celandine Dr.)
SE16 . . . . 3F **79**
(off Garter Way)
W4 . . . . 2A **84**
Adelphi Ter.
WC2 . . . . . . 5E **15** (1A **76**)
Adelphi Theatre 5E **15**
(off Strand)
Adeney Cl. W6 . . . . . . 2F **85**
Aden Gro. N16 . . . . . . 1F **49**
Aden Ho. *E1* 4F **65**
(off Duckett St.)
Adenmore Rd. SE6 . . . 5C **108**
Aden Ter. N16 . . . . . . 1F **49**
Adeyfield Ho. *EC1* 2C **10**
(off Cranwood St.)
Adie Rd. W6 . . . . 4E **71**
Adine Rd. E13 . . . . . . 3D **69**
Adler St. E1 . . . . 5C **64**
Adley St. E5 . . . . 2A **52**
Admiral Ct. *SW10* 4E **87**
(off Admiral Sq.)
W1 . . . . 1B **12**
(off Blandford St.)
Admiral Ho. *SW1* 5E **75**
(off Willow Pl.)
Admiral Hyson Ind. Est.
SE16 . . . . 1D **93**
Admiral M. W10 . . . . . 3F **57**
Admiral Pl. SE16 . . . . 2A **80**
Admirals Ct. SE1 . . . . 2F **27**
(off Horselydown La.)
Admiral's Ga. SE10 . . . 4D **95**

Admiral Sq. NW10.....4E 87
Admiral St. SE8.....5C 94
Admirals Wlk. NW3.....5E 31
Admirals Way E14.....3C 80
Admiralty Arch
.....1C 22 (2F 75)
Admiralty Cl. SE8.....3C 94
Admiral Wlk. W9.....4C 58
Adolf St. SE6.....4D 123
Adolphus Rd. N4.....4D 35
Adolphus St. SE8.....3B 94
Adpar St. W2.....4F 59
Adrian Av. NW2.....3D 29
Adrian Boult Ho. E2.....2D 65
(off Mansford St.)
Adrian Ho. N1.....5B 48
(off Barnsbury Est.)
SW8.....3A 90
(off Wyvil Rd.)
Adrian M. SW10.....2D 87
(off Horseferry Rd.)
Adriatic Bldg. E14.....1A 80
Adriatic Ho. E1.....3F 65
(off Ernest St.)
Adron Ho. SE16.....5E 79
(off Millender Wlk.)
Adstock Ho. N1.....4D 49
(off The Sutton Est.)
Advance Rd. SE27.....4E 119
Adventurers Ct. E14.....1F 81
(off Newport Av.)
Adys Lawn NW2.....3D 43
Ady's Rd. SE15.....1B 106
Aegean Apartments
E16.....1C 82
(off Western Gateway)
Aegon Ho. E14.....4D 81
(off Lanark Sq.)
Affleck St. N1.....1F 7 (1B 62)
Afghan Rd. SW11.....5A 88
Afsil Ho. EC1.....1C 16
(off Viaduct Bldgs.)
Aftab Ter. E1.....3D 65
(off Tent St.)
Agamemnon Rd.
NW6.....1B 44
Agar Gro. NW1.....4E 47
Agar Gro. Est. NW1.....4E 47
Agar Pl. NW1.....4E 47
Agar St.
WC2.....5D 15 (1A 76)
Agate Cl. E16.....5F 69
Agate Rd. W6.....4E 71
Agatha Cl. E1.....2D 79
Agave Rd. NW2.....1E 43
Agdon St. EC1.....3D 9 (3D 63)
Agincourt Rd. NW3.....1B 46
Agnes Ho. W11.....1F 71
(off St Ann's Rd.)
Agnes Rd. W3.....2B 70
Agnes St. E14.....5B 66
Agnew Rd. SE23.....5F 107
Aigburth Mans.
SW9.....3C 90
(off Mowll St.)
Aileen Wlk. E15.....4B 54
Ailsa St. E14.....4E 67
Ailsa Wlk. E14.....3C 80
(off Cassilis Rd.)

Ainger M. NW3.....4B 46
(off Ainger Rd.,
not continuous)
Ainger Rd. NW3.....4B 46
Ainsdale NW1.....1F 5
Ainsdale Dr. SE1.....1C 92
Ainsley St. E2.....2D 65
Ainslie Wlk. SW12.....5D 103
Ainsty Est. SE16.....3F 79
Ainsty St. SE16.....3E 79
Ainsworth Cl. NW2.....5C 28
SE15.....5A 92
Ainsworth Ho. NW8.....5D 45
(off Ainsworth Way)
W10.....2A 58
(off Kilburn La.)
Ainsworth Rd. E9.....4E 51
Ainsworth Way NW8.....5E 45
Aintree Av. E6.....5F 55
Aintree Est. SW6.....3A 86
(off Aintree St.)
Aintree St. SW6.....3A 86
Aird Ho. SE1.....5F 25
(off Rockingham St.)
Airdrie Cl. N1.....4B 48
Airedale Av. W4.....5B 70
Airedale Av. Sth.
W4.....1B 84
Airedale Rd. SW12.....5B 102
Airlie Gdns. W8.....2C 72
Air St. W1.....5A 14 (1E 75)
Aisgill Av. W14.....1B 86
(not continuous)
Aislibie Rd. SE12.....2A 110
Aiten Pl. W6.....5C 70
Aithan Ho. E14.....5B 66
(off Copenhagen St.)
Aitken Cl. E8.....5C 50
Aitken Rd. SE6.....2C 123
Ajax Ho. E2.....1D 65
(off Old Bethnal Grn. Rd.)
Ajax Rd. NW6.....1B 44
Akbar Ho. E14.....5D 81
(off Cahir St.)
Akehurst St. SW15.....4C 98
Akenside Rd. NW3.....2F 45
Akerman Rd. SW9.....5D 91
Akintaro Ho. SE8.....2B 94
(off Alverton St.)
Alamaro Lodge SE10.....4B 82
Aland Ct. SE16.....4A 80
Alan Hocken Way
E15.....1A 68
Alan Preece Ct.
NW6.....4F 43
Alan Rd. SW19.....5A 114
Alanthus Cl. SE12.....4C 110
Alaska Bldg. SE8.....4D 95
(off Deal's Gateway)
Alaska Bldgs. SE1.....5A 78
Alaska St.
SE1.....2B 24 (2C 76)
Alastor Ho. E14.....4E 81
(off Strattondale Ho.)
Albacore Cres.
SE13.....4D 109
Alba Gdns. NW11.....1A 30
Alba M. SW18.....2C 114

Alban Highwalk EC2.....2A 18
(not continuous)
Albany W1.....5F 13 (1E 75)
Albany Cl. E10.....2C 38
NW8.....1F 59
(off Abbey Rd.)
NW10.....2D 57
(off Trenmar Gdns.)
Albany Courtyard
W1.....5A 14 (1E 75)
Albany Mans. SW11.....3A 88
Albany M.
BR1: Brom.....5C 124
N1.....4C 48
SE5.....2E 91
Albany Pl. N7.....1C 48
Albany Rd. E10.....2C 38
E12.....1F 55
E17.....1A 38
N4.....1C 34
SE5.....2F 91
SW19.....5D 115
Albany St.
NW1.....1E 5 (1D 61)
Albany Ter. NW1.....4E 5
Alba Ti. W1.....5B 58
Albatross Way SE16.....3F 79
Albemarle SW19.....2F 113
Albemarle Ho. SE8.....5B 80
(off Foreshore)
SW9.....1C 104
Albemarle St.
W1.....5E 13 (1D 75)
Albemarle Way
EC1.....4D 9 (3D 63)
Alberta Est. SE17.....1D 91
(off Alberta St.)
Alberta Ho. E14.....2E 81
(off Gaselee St.)
Alberta St. SE17.....1D 91
Albert Av. SW8.....3B 90
Albert Barnes Ho.
SE1.....4E 77
(off New Kent Rd.)
Albert Bigg Point E15.....1F 67
(off Godfrey St.)
Albert Bri. SW3.....3A 88
Albert Bri. Rd. SW11.....3A 88
Albert Carr Gdns.
SW16.....5A 118
Albert Cl. E9.....5D 51
Albert Cotts. E1.....4C 64
(off Deal St.)
Albert Ct. E7.....1C 54
SW7.....4F 73
Albert Ct. Ga. SW1.....3B 74
(off Knightsbridge)
Albert Dr. SW19.....2A 114
Albert Emb.
SE1.....5F 23 (4B 76)
(Lambeth Pal. Rd.)
SE1.....1A 90
(Vauxhall Bri.)
Albert Gdns. E1.....5F 65
Albert Ga.
SW1.....3A 20 (3B 74)
Albert Gray Ho.
SW10.....3F 87
(off Worlds End Est.)

Albert Hall Mans.
SW7 . . . . 3F **73**
(not continuous)
Albert Memorial 3F **73**
Albert M. E14 . . . . 1A **80**
(off Northey St.)
N4 . . . . 3B **34**
SE4 . . . . 2A **108**
W8 . . . . 4E **73**
Albert Pal. Mans.
SW11 . . . . 4D **89**
(off Lurline Gdns.)
Albert Pl. W8 . . . . 4D **73**
Albert Rd. E10 . . . . . . 4E **39**
E16 . . . . 2F **83**
E17 . . . . 1C **38**
N4 . . . . 3B **34**
N15 . . . . 1A **36**
NW6 . . . . 1B **58**
Alberts Ct. NW1 . . . . . . 3A **60**
(off Palgrave Gdns.)
Albert Sq. E15 . . . . . . 2A **54**
SW8 . . . . 3B **90**
Albert Starr Ho. SE8 . . . 5F **79**
(off Bush Rd.)
Albert St. NW1 . . . . . . 5D **47**
Albert Studios SW11 . . 4B **88**
Albert Ter. NW1 . . . . . 5C **46**
W6 . . . . 1C **84**
(off Beavor La.)
Albert Ter. M. NW1 . . . 5C **46**
Albert Way SE15 . . . . 3D **93**
Albert Westcott Ho.
SE17 . . . . 1D **91**
Albery Ct. E8 . . . . 4B **50**
(off Middleton Rd.)
Albery Theatre 4D **15**
(off St Martin's La.)
Albion Av. SW8 . . . . . . 5F **89**
Albion Bldgs. N1 . . . . 1A **62**
(off Albion Yd.)
Albion Cl. W2 . . . . 1A **74**
Albion Cl. W6 . . . . 5D **71**
(off Albion Pl.)
Albion Dr. E8 . . . . 4B **50**
Albion Est. SE16 . . . . . 3F **79**
Albion Gdns. W6 . . . . . 5D **71**
Albion Ga. W2 . . . . . . 1A **74**
(off Albion St., not continuous)
Albion Gro. N16 . . . . . 1A **50**
Albion Ho. SE8 . . . . . . 3C **94**
(off Watsons St.)
Albion M. N1 . . . . 5C **48**
NW6 . . . . 4B **44**
W2 . . . . 1A **74**
W6 . . . . 5D **71**
Albion Pde. N16 . . . . . 1F **49**
Albion Pl. EC1 . . 5D **9** (4D **63**)
EC2 . . . . 1C **18** (4F **63**)
W6 . . . . 5D **71**
Albion Riverside Bldg.
SW11 . . . . 3A **88**
Albion Rd. N16 . . . . . . 1F **49**
Albion Sq. E8 . . . . 4B **50**
(not continuous)
Albion St. SE16 . . . . . 3E **79**
W2 . . . . 5A **60**
Albion Ter. E8 . . . . . . 4B **50**
Albion Vs. Rd. SE26 . . 3E **121**

Albion Wlk. N1 . . . . 1E **7**
(off York Way)
Albion Way
EC1 . . . . . . 1F **17** (4E **63**)
SE13 . . . . 2E **109**
Albion Yd. E1 . . . . 4D **65**
N1 . . . . 1A **62**
Albon Ho. SW18 . . . . 4D **101**
(off Neville Gill Cl.)
Albrighton Rd. SE22 . . 1A **106**
Albury Ho. SE1 . . . . . . 4E **25**
(off Boyfield St.)
Albury M. E12 . . . . 4E **41**
Albury St. SE8 . . . . . . 2C **94**
Albyn Rd. SE8 . . . . . . 4C **94**
Alcester Cres. E5 . . . . 4D **37**
Alconbury Rd. E5 . . . . . 4C **36**
Aldam Pl. N16 . . . . 4B **36**
Aldbourne Rd. W12 . . . 2B **70**
(not continuous)
Aldbridge St. SE17 . . . 1A **92**
Aldburgh M.
W1 . . . . . . 2C **12** (5C **60**)
(not continuous)
Aldbury Ho. SW3 . . . . . 5A **74**
(off Marlborough St.)
Aldebert Ter. SW8 . . . . 3A **90**
Aldeburgh Cl. E5 . . . . . 4D **37**
Aldeburgh Pl. SE10 . . . 5C **82**
(off Aldeburgh St.)
Aldeburgh St. SE10 . . . 1C **96**
Alden Av. E15 . . . . 2B **68**
Aldenham Ho. NW1 . . . . 1A **6**
(off Aldenham St.)
Aldenham St.
NW1 . . . . . . 1A **6** (1E **61**)
Alden Ho. E8 . . . . 5D **51**
(off Duncan Rd.)
Aldensley Rd. W6 . . . . 4D **71**
Alderbrook Rd.
SW12 . . . . 4D **103**
Alderbury Rd. SW13 . . 2C **84**
Alder Cl. SE15 . . . . . . 2B **92**
Alder Gro. NW2 . . . . . 4C **28**
Alder Ho. NW3 . . . . . . 3B **46**
SE4 . . . . 1C **108**
SE15 . . . . 2B **92**
(off Cator St.)
Alder Lodge SW6 . . . . 4E **85**
Aldermanbury
EC2 . . . . . . 2A **18** (5E **63**)
Aldermanbury Sq.
EC2 . . . . . . 1A **18** (4E **63**)
Aldermans Wlk.
EC2 . . . . . . 1D **19** (4A **64**)
Alder M. N19 . . . . 4E **33**
Aldermoor Rd. SE6 . . . 3B **122**
Alderney Ho. N1 . . . . . . 3E **49**
(off Arran Wlk.)
Alderney Rd. E1 . . . . . 3F **65**
Alderney St. SW1 . . . . 5D **75**
Alders, The SW16 . . . 4E **117**
ALDERSBROOK 4D **41**
Aldersbrook Rd. E11 . . 4D **41**
E12 . . . . 4D **41**
Alders Cl. E11 . . . . 4D **41**
Aldersford Cl. SE4 . . . 3F **107**
Aldersgate St.
EC1 . . . . 5F **9** (4E **63**)

Aldersgrove Av. SE9 . . . 3F **125**
Aldershot Rd. NW6 . . . . 5B **44**
Alderson St. W10 . . . . 3A **58**
Alderton Cl. NW10 . . . . 5A **28**
Alderton Cres. NW4 . . . 1D **29**
Alderton Rd. SE24 . . . 1E **105**
Alderton Way NW4 . . . 1D **29**
Alderville Rd. SW6 . . . 5B **86**
Alderwick Ct. N7 . . . . . 3B **48**
(off Cornelia St.)
Aldford Ho. W1 . . . . . . 1B **20**
(off Park St.)
Aldford St.
W1 . . . . . . 1C **20** (2C **74**)
ALDGATE 5B **64**
Aldgate E1 . . . . 2F **19**
(off Whitechapel High St.)
EC3 . . . . . . 3E **19** (5A **64**)
Aldgate Av.
E1 . . . . 2F **19** (5B **64**)
Aldgate Barrs E1 . . . . 2F **19**
Aldgate High St.
EC3 . . . . . . 3F **19** (5B **64**)
Aldgate Triangle E1 . . 5C **64**
(off Coke St.)
Aldham Ho. SE14 . . . . 5B **94**
(off Malpas Rd.)
Aldine Ct. W12 . . . . . . 3E **71**
(off Aldine St.)
Aldine Pl. W12 . . . . . . 3E **71**
Aldine St. W12 . . . . . . 3E **71**
Aldington Ct. E8 . . . . . 4C **50**
(off London Flds. W. Side)
Aldington Rd. SE18 . . . 4F **83**
Aldis M. SW17 . . . . . 5A **116**
Aldis St. SW17 . . . . . 5A **116**
Aldred Rd. NW6 . . . . . . 2C **44**
Aldren Rd. SW17 . . . . 3E **115**
Aldrich Ter. SW18 . . . 2E **115**
Aldrick Ho. N1 . . . . . . 5B **48**
(off Barnsbury Est.)
Aldridge Ct. W11 . . . . 4B **58**
(off Aldridge Rd. Vs.)
Aldridge Rd. Vs.
W11 . . . . 4B **58**
Aldrington Rd.
SW16 . . . . 5E **117**
Aldsworth Cl. W9 . . . . 3D **59**
Aldworth Gro. SE13 . . 4E **109**
Aldworth Rd. E15 . . . . 4A **54**
Aldwych
WC2 . . . . . . 4F **15** (5B **62**)
Aldwych Cl. E8 . . . . . . 4B **50**
(off Middleton Rd.)
Aldwych Theatre 3F **15**
(off Aldwych)
Aldwyn Ho. SW8 . . . . . 3A **90**
(off Davidson Gdns.)
Alestan Beck Rd. E16 . . 5F **69**
Alexa Ct. W8 . . . . 5C **72**
Alexander Av. NW10 . . 4D **43**
Alexander Evans M.
SE23 . . . . 2F **121**
Alexander Fleming
Laboratory Mus. 5F **59**
(off Praed St.)
Alexander Ho. E14 . . . . 4C **80**
(off Tiller Rd.)
Alexander M. W2 . . . . 5D **59**

Alexander Pl. SW7 . . . . . 5A 74
Alexander Rd. N19 . . . . . 5A 34
Alexander Sq. SW3 . . . . . 5A 74
Alexander St. W2 . . . . . 5C 58
Alexander Studios
   SW11 . . . . *2F 101*
   (off Haydon Way)
Alexandra Av. SW11 . . . . 4C 88
   W4 . . . . 3A 84
Alexandra Cl. SE8 . . . . . 2B 94
Alexandra Cotts.
   SE14 . . . . 4B 94
Alexandra Ct. *SW7* *4E 73*
   (off Queen's Ga.)
   W2 . . . . *1D 73*
   (off Moscow Rd.)
   W9 . . . . *3E 59*
   (off Maida Va.)
Alexandra Cres.
   BR1: Brom 5B 124
Alexandra Dr. SE19 . . . . 5A 120
Alexandra Gdns.
   W4 . . . . 3A 84
Alexandra Gro. N4 . . . . . 3D 35
Alexandra Pl. *E16* *2D 83*
   (off Wesley Av.)
   W6 . . . . *1E 85*
   (off Queen Caroline St.)
Alexandra Mans.
   SW3 . . . . *2F 87*
   (off King's Rd.)
Alexandra M. SW19 . . . . 5B 114
Alexandra National Ho.
   N4 . . . . 3D 35
Alexandra Pl. NW8 . . . . . 5E 45
Alexandra Rd. E10 . . . . . 5E 39
   E17 . . . . 1B 38
   NW8 . . . . 5E 45
   SE26 . . . . 5F 121
   SW14 . . . . 1A 98
   SW19 . . . . 5B 114
   W4 . . . . 3A 94
Alexandra St. E16 . . . . . 4C 68
   SE14 . . . . 3A 94
Alexandra Ter. *E14* *1D 95*
   (off Westferry Rd.)
Alexandra Wlk.
   SE19 . . . . 5A 120
Alexandra Yd. E9 . . . . . . 5F 51
Alexandria Apartments
   SE17 . . . . *5A 78*
   (off Townsend St.)
Alexis St. SE16 . . . . . . 5C 78
Alfearn Rd. E5 . . . . 1E 51
Alford Ct. *N1* *1A 10*
   (off Shepherdess Wlk.,
   not continuous)
Alford Ho. N6 . . . . 1E 33
Alford Pl.
   N1 . . . . 1A 10 (1E 63)
Alfreda St. SW11 . . . . . 4D 89
Alfred Dickens Ho.
   E16 . . . . *5B 68*
   (off Hallsville Rd.)
Alfred Ho. *E9* *2A 52*
   (off Homerton Rd.)
   E12 . . . . *4F 55*
   (off Tennyson Av.)
Alfred M. W1 . . . . 5B 6 (4F 61)

Alfred Nunn Ho.
   NW10 . . . . 5B 42
Alfred Pl. WC1 . . . 5B 6 (4F 61)
Alfred Rd. E15 . . . . 2B 54
   W2 . . . . 4C 58
Alfred St. E3 . . . . 2B 66
Alfreton Cl. SW19 . . . . . 3F 113
Alfriston Rd. SW11 . . . . 3B 102
Algar Ho. SE1 . . . . 4D 25
Algarve Rd. SW18 . . . . 1D 115
Algernon Rd. NW4 . . . . 1C 28
   NW6 . . . . 5C 44
   SE13 . . . . 2D 109
Algiers Rd. SE13 . . . . . 2C 108
Alice Gilliatt Ct.
   W14 . . . . *2B 86*
   (off Star Rd.)
Alice La. E3 . . . . 5B 52
Alice Owen Technology Cen.
   EC1 . . . . *1D 9*
   (off Goswell Rd.)
Alice Shepherd Ho.
   E14 . . . . *3E 81*
   (off Manchester Rd.)
Alice St. SE1 . . . 5D 27 (4A 78)
   (not continuous)
Alice Thompson Cl.
   SE12 . . . . 2E 125
Alice Walker Cl.
   SE24 . . . . 2D 105
Alie St. E1 . . . . 3F 19 (5B 64)
Alison Ct. SE1 . . . . 1C 92
Aliwal M. SW11 . . . . . . 2A 102
Aliwal Rd. SW11 . . . . . 2A 102
Alkerden Rd. W4 . . . . . 1A 84
Alkham Rd. N16 . . . . . . 4B 36
Allan Barclay Cl.
   N15 . . . . 1A 36
Allanson Ct. *E10* *4C 38*
   (off Leyton Grange Est.)
Allard Gdns. SW4 . . . . . 3F 103
Allardyce St. SW4 . . . . 2B 104
Allcott Ho. *W12* *5D 57*
   (off Du Cane Rd.)
Allcroft Rd. NW5 . . . . . 2C 46
Allenby Rd. SE23 . . . . . 3A 122
Allen Ct. *E17* *1C 38*
   (off Yunus Khan Cl.)
Allendale Cl. SE5 . . . . . 5F 91
   SE26 . . . . 5F 121
Allen Edwards Dr.
   SW8 . . . . 4A 90
Allenford Ho. *SW15* *4B 98*
   (off Tunworth Cres.)
Allen Ho. *W8* *4C 72*
   (off Allen St.)
Allen Mans. *W8* *4C 72*
   (off Allen St.)
Allen Rd. E3 . . . . 1B 66
   N16 . . . . 1A 50
Allensbury Pl. NW1 . . . . 4F 47
Allen St. W8 . . . . 4C 72
Allenswood SW19 . . . 1A 114
Allerford Rd. SE6 . . . . . 3D 123
Allerton Ho. *N1* *1B 10*
   (off Fairbank Est.)
Allerton Rd. N16 . . . . . 4E 35
Allerton St.
   N1 . . . . 1B 10 (2F 63)

Allerton Wlk. N7 . . . . . . 4B 34
Allestree Rd. SW6 . . . . . 3A 86
Alleyn Cres. SE21 . . . . . 2F 119
Alleyn Ho. *SE1* *5C 26*
   (off Burbage Cl.)
Alleyn Pk. SE21 . . . . . . 2F 119
Alleyn Rd. SE21 . . . . . . 3F 119
Allfarthing La.
   SW18 . . . . 4D 101
Allgood St. E2 . . . . 1B 64
Allhallows La.
   EC4 . . . . 5B 18 (1F 77)
Allhallows Rd. E6 . . . . . 4F 69
Alliance Rd. E13 . . . . . . 4E 69
Allied Ind. Est. W3 . . . . 3A 70
Allied Way W3 . . . . 3A 70
Allingham M. *N1* *1E 63*
   (off Allingham St.)
Allingham St. N1 . . . . . 1E 63
Allington Cl. SW19 . . . . 5F 113
Allington Ct. *SW1* *5E 21*
   (off Allington St.)
   SW8 . . . . 5E 89
Allington Rd. NW4 . . . . . 1D 29
   W10 . . . . 2A 58
Allington St.
   SW1 . . . . 5E 21 (4D 75)
Allison Cl. SE10 . . . . . . 4E 95
Allison Gro. SE21 . . . . . 1A 120
Alliston Ho. *E2* *2B 64*
   (off Gibraltar Wlk.)
Allitsen Rd. NW8 . . . . . . 1A 60
   (not continuous)
All Nations Ho. *E8* *4D 51*
   (off Martello St.)
Allnutt Way SW4 . . . . . 3F 103
Alloa Rd. SE8 . . . . 1F 93
Allom Ho. *W11* *1A 72*
   (off Clarendon Rd.)
Allonby Ho. *E14* *4A 66*
   (off Aston St.)
Alloway Rd. E3 . . . . 2A 66
Allport Ho. *SE5* *1F 105*
   (off Denmark Hill)
Allport M. *E1* *3E 65*
   (off Hayfield Pas.)
All Saints Cl. SW8 . . . . . 4A 90
All Saints Ct. *E1* *1E 79*
   (off Johnson St.)
   SW11 . . . . *3D 89*
   (off Prince of Wales Dr.)
All Saints Dr. SE3 . . . . . 5A 96
   (not continuous)
All Saints Ho. *W11* *4B 58*
   (off All Saints Rd.)
All Saints Pas.
   SW18 . . . . 3C 100
All Saints Rd. W11 . . . . 4B 58
   SW11 . . . . 1B 62
All Saints St. N1 . . . . . . 1B 62
All Saints Twr. E10 . . . . 2D 39
Allsop Pl.
   NW1 . . . . 4A 4 (3B 60)
All Souls Av. NW10 . . . . 1D 57
All Souls' Pl.
   W1 . . . . 1E 13 (4D 61)
Alluvium Ct. *SE1* *5D 27*
   (off Long La.)
Allwood Cl. SE26 . . . . . 4F 121
Alma Birk Ho. NW6 . . . . 4A 44

Almack Rd. E5 . . . . 1E 51
Alma Gro. SE1 . . . . 5B 78
Alma Pl. NW10 . . . . 2D 57
Alma Rd. SW18 . . . . 2E 101
Alma Sq. NW8 . . . . 1E 59
Alma St. E15 . . . . 3F 53
  NW5 . . . . 3D 47
Alma Ter. E3 . . . . 5B 52
  (off Beale Rd.)
  SW18 . . . . 5F 101
  W8 . . . . 4C 72
Almeida St. N1 . . . . 5D 49
Almeida Theatre 5D 49
  (off Almeida St.)
Almeric Rd. SW11 . . . . . . 2B 102
Almington St. N4 . . . . 3B 34
Almond Cl. SE15 . . . . 5C 92
Almond Rd. SE16 . . . . . . 5D 79
Almorah Rd. N1 . . . . 4F 49
Alnwick Rd. E16 . . . . 5E 69
  SE12 . . . . 4D 111
Alperton St. W10 . . . . 3B 58
Alphabet Sq. E3 . . . . 4C 66
Alpha Bus. Cen.
  E17 . . . . 1B 38
Alpha Cl. NW1 . . . . 3A 60
Alpha Gro. E14 . . . . 3C 80
Alpha Ho. NW6 . . . . 1C 58
  NW8 . . . . 3A 60
  (off Ashbridge St.)
  SW4 . . . . 2B 104
Alpha Pl. NW6 . . . . 1C 58
  SW3 . . . . 2A 88
Alpha Rd. SE14 . . . . 4B 94
  SE15 . . . . 5C 92
Alpine Gro. E9 . . . . 4E 51
Alpine Rd. E10 . . . . 4D 39
  SE16 . . . . 5E 79
Alric Av. NW10 . . . . 4A 42
Alroy Rd. N4 . . . . 2C 34
Alsace Rd. SE17 . . . . 1A 92
Alscot Rd.
  SE1 . . . . 5F 27 (5B 78)
  (not continuous)
Alscot Rd. Ind. Est.
  SE1 . . . . 4B 78
Alscot Way SE1 . . . . 5B 78
Alston Rd. SW17 . . . . 4F 115
Altenburg Gdns.
  SW11 . . . . 2B 102
Althea St. SW6 . . . . 5D 87
Althorpe M. SW11 . . . . . . 4F 87
Althorp Rd. SW17 . . . . . . 1B 116
Altima Ct. SE22 . . . . 2C 106
Altior Ct. N6 . . . . 1E 33
Alton Rd. SW15 . . . . 1C 112
Alton St. E14 . . . . 4D 67
Aluna Ct. SE15 . . . . 1E 107
Alvanley Gdns. NW6 . . . . 2D 45
Alverstone Av.
  SW19 . . . . 2C 114
Alverstone Ho.
  SE11 . . . . 2C 90
Alverstone Rd. NW2 . . . . . 4E 43
Alverton St. SE8 . . . . 1B 94
  (not continuous)
Alvey St. SE17 . . . . 1A 92
Alvington Cres. E8 . . . . . . 2B 50
Alwold Cres. SE12 . . . . . . 4D 111

Alwyne La. N1 . . . . 4D 49
Alwyne Pl. N1 . . . . 3E 49
Alwyne Rd. N1 . . . . 4E 49
  SW19 . . . . 5B 114
Alwyne Sq. N1 . . . . 3E 49
Alwyne Vs. N1 . . . . 4D 49
Alyth Gdns. NW11 . . . . . . 1C 30
Alzette Ho. E2 . . . . 1F 65
  (off Mace St.)
Amazon St. E1 . . . . 5C 64
Ambassadors Ct. E8 . . . . 4B 50
  (off Holly St.)
  SW1 . . . . 2A 22
Ambassador Sq. E14 . . . . 5D 81
Ambassadors Theatre
  . . . . 4C 14
  (off West St.)
Ambergate St. SE17 . . . . 1D 91
Amber Gro. NW2 . . . . . . 3F 29
Amberley Gro.
  SE26 . . . . 5D 121
Amberley Rd. E10 . . . . . . 2C 38
  W9 . . . . 4C 58
Amber Wharf E2 . . . . 5B 50
  (off Nursery La.)
Amblecote Cl. SE12 . . . . 3D 125
Amblecote Mdws.
  SE12 . . . . 3D 125
Amblecote Rd.
  SE12 . . . . 3D 125
Ambleside
  BR1: Brom 5F 123
  NW1 . . . . 1E 5
  SW19 . . . . 1A 114
Ambleside Av.
  SW16 . . . . 4F 117
Ambleside Cl. E9 . . . . . . 2E 51
  E10 . . . . 2D 39
Ambleside Gdns.
  SW16 . . . . 5F 117
Ambleside Point
  SE15 . . . . 3E 93
  (off Tustin Est.)
Ambleside Rd.
  NW10 . . . . 4B 42
Ambrosden Av.
  SW1 . . . . 5A 22 (4E 75)
Ambrose Av. NW11 . . . . . 2A 30
Ambrose Ho. E14 . . . . . . 4C 66
  (off Selsey St.)
Ambrose M. SW11 . . . . . . 5B 88
Ambrose St. SE16 . . . . . . 5D 79
Ambrose Wlk. E3 . . . . . . 1C 66
Amelia Ho. W6 . . . . 1E 85
  (off Queen Caroline St.)
Amelia St. SE17 . . . . 1E 91
Amen Cnr.
  EC4 . . . . 3E 17 (5D 63)
  SW17 . . . . 5B 116
Amen Ct. EC4 . . . 3E 17 (5D 63)
America Sq.
  EC3 . . . . 4F 19 (1B 78)
America St.
  SE1 . . . . 2F 25 (2E 77)
Amerland Rd.
  SW18 . . . . 3B 100
Amersham Gro.
  SE14 . . . . 3B 94

Amersham Rd. SE14 . . . . 4B 94
Amersham Va. SE14 . . . . 3B 94
Amery Gdns. NW10 . . . . . 5E 43
Amery Ho. SE17 . . . . 1A 92
  (off Kinglake St.)
Amesbury Av. SW2 . . . . . 2A 118
Amesbury Twr. SW8 . . . . 5E 89
Ames Cotts. E14 . . . . 4A 66
  (off Maroon St.)
Ames Ho. E2 . . . . 1F 65
  (off Mace St.)
Amethyst Rd. E15 . . . . . . 1F 53
AMF Bowling
  Lewisham 1E 109
Amherst Ho. SE16 . . . . . . 3F 79
  (off Wolfe Cres.)
Amherst Pde. N16 . . . . . . 2B 36
  (off Amhurst Pk.)
Amhurst Pk. N16 . . . . . . 2F 35
Amhurst Pas. E8 . . . . 1C 50
Amhurst Rd. E8 . . . . 2D 51
  N16 . . . . 1B 50
Amhurst Ter. E8 . . . . 1C 50
Amias Ho. EC1 . . . . 3F 9
  (off Central St.)
Amiel St. E1 . . . . 3E 65
Amies St. SW11 . . . . 1B 102
Amigo Ho. SE1 . . . . 5C 24
  (off Morley St.)
Amina Way SE16 . . . . . . 4C 78
Amity Rd. E15 . . . . 4B 54
Ammanford Grn.
  NW9 . . . . 1A 28
Ammonite Ho. E15 . . . . . . 4B 54
Amner Rd. SW11 . . . . . . 4C 102
Amor Rd. W6 . . . . 4E 71
Amory Ho. N1 . . . . 5B 48
  (off Barnsbury Est.)
Amott Rd. SE15 . . . . 1C 106
Amoy Pl. E14 . . . . 1C 80
  (not continuous)
Ampthill Est. NW1 . . . . . . 1E 61
Ampthill Sq.
  NW1 . . . . 1A 6 (1E 61)
Ampton Pl.
  WC1 . . . . 2F 7 (2B 62)
Ampton St.
  WC1 . . . . 2F 7 (2B 62)
Amroth Cl. SE23 . . . . 1D 121
Amroth Grn. NW9 . . . . . . 1A 28
Amstel Ct. SE15 . . . . 3B 92
Amsterdam Rd. E14 . . . . . 4E 81
Amundsen Ct. E14 . . . . . 1C 94
  (off Napier Av.)
Amwell Ct. Est. N4 . . . . . 4E 35
Amwell St.
  EC1 . . . . 1B 8 (2C 62)
Amyruth Rd. SE4 . . . . . . 3C 108
Anatola Rd. N19 . . . . 4E 33
Anchor St. SW18 . . . . . . 2D 101
Anchorage Cl.
  SW19 . . . . 5C 114
Anchorage Ho. E14 . . . . . 1F 81
  (off Clove Cres.)
Anchorage Point
  E14 . . . . 3B 80
  (off Cuba St.)
Anchorage Point Ind. Est.
  SE7 . . . . 4E 83

Anchor & Hope La.
　SE7 . . . . 4D 83
Anchor Brewhouse
　SE1 . . . . 2F 27 (2B 78)
Anchor Ct. SW1 . . . . 5F 75
　(off Vauxhall Bri. Rd.)
Anchor Ho. E16 . . . . 4B 68
　(off Barking Rd.)
　E16 . . . . 5E 69
　(off Prince Regent La.)
　EC1 . . . . 3F 9
　(off Old St.)
　SW10 . . . . 2F 87
　(off Moravian St.)
Anchor M. SW12 . . . . . 4D 103
Anchor Retail Pk. E1 . . . 3E 65
Anchor Rd. E12 . . . . 4F 41
Anchor St. SE16 . . . . . . 5D 79
Anchor Ter. E1 . . . . 3E 65
Anchor Wharf E3 . . . . 4F 67
　(off Yeo St.)
Anchor Yd.
　EC1 . . . . 3A 10 (3E 63)
Ancill Cl. W6 . . . . 2A 86
Ancona Rd. NW10 . . . . . 1C 56
Andalus Rd. SW9 . . . . . 1A 104
Andaman Ho. E1 . . . . . . 4A 66
　(off Duckett St.)
Anderson Cl. W3 . . . . . . 5A 56
Anderson Cl. NW2 . . . . . 3E 29
Anderson Ho. E14 . . . . . 1E 81
　(off Woolmore St.)
　SW17 . . . . 5F 115
　W12 . . . . 5D 57
　(off Du Cane Rd.)
Anderson Rd. E9 . . . . . . 3F 51
Anderson Sq. N1 . . . . . . 5D 49
　(off Gaskin St.)
Anderson St. SW3 . . . . . 1B 88
Anderton Cl. SE5 . . . . . 1F 105
Andover Av. E16 . . . . . . 5F 69
Andover Pl. NW6 . . . . . . 1D 59
Andover Rd. N7 . . . . 4B 34
Andoversford Ct.
　SE15 . . . . 2A 92
　(off Bibury Cl.)
Andre St. E8 . . . . 2C 50
Andrew Borde St.
　WC2 . . . . 2C 14 (5F 61)
Andrew Ct. SE23 . . . . . . 2F 121
Andrewes Gdns. E6 . . . . 5F 69
Andrewes Highwalk
　EC2 . . . . 1A 18
Andrewes Ho. EC2 . . . . . 1A 18
Andrew Pl. SW8 . . . . 3F 89
Andrew Reed Ho.
　SW18 . . . . 5A 100
　(off Linstead Way)
Andrews Crosse
　WC2 . . . . 3B 16
Andrews Ho. NW3 . . . . . 4B 46
　(off Fellows Rd.)
Andrew's Rd. E8 . . . . . . 5D 51
Andrew St. E14 . . . . 5E 67
Andrews Wlk. SE17 . . . . 2D 91
Anerley Hill SE19 . . . . . 5B 120
Aneurin Bevan Ct.
　NW2 . . . . 4D 29
Anfield Cl. SW12 . . . . . . 5E 103

ANGEL 1C 62
Angela Davies Ind. Est.
　SE24 . . . . 2D 105
Angel All. E1 . . . . 5B 64
　(off Whitechapel High St.)
Angel Cen., The N1 . . . . 1C 8
Angel Ct. EC2 . . 2C 18 (5F 63)
　SW1 . . . . 2A 22 (2E 75)
Angel Ga. EC1 . . . . 1E 9
　(not continuous)
Angelina Ho. SE15 . . . . . 4C 92
　(off Goldsmith Rd.)
Angelis Apartments
　N1 . . . . 1E 9
　(off Graham St.)
Angel La. E15 . . . . 3F 53
Angell Pk. Gdns.
　SW9 . . . . 1C 104
Angell Rd. SW9 . . . . . . 1C 104
ANGELL TOWN 4C 90
Angell Town Est.
　SW9 . . . . 5C 90
Angel M. E1 . . . . 1D 79
　N1 . . . . 1C 62
　SW15 . . . . 5C 98
Angel Pas.
　EC4 . . . . 5B 18 (1F 77)
Angel Pl. SE1 . . 3B 26 (3F 77)
Angel Sq. EC1 . . . . 1D 63
Angel St. EC1 . . 2F 17 (5E 63)
Angel Wlk. W6 . . . . 5E 71
Angel Yd. N6 . . . . 3C 32
Angerstein Bus. Pk.
　SE10 . . . . 5C 82
Angerstein La. SE3 . . . . . 4B 96
Anglebury W2 . . . . 5C 58
　(off Talbot Rd.)
Angler's La. NW5 . . . . . . 3D 47
Anglesea Ter. W6 . . . . . . 4D 71
Anglesey Ho. E14 . . . . . . 5C 66
　(off Lindfield St.)
Angles Rd. SW16 . . . . . 4A 118
Anglia Ho. E14 . . . . 4A 66
　(off Salmon La.)
Anglian Rd. E11 . . . . . . 5F 39
Anglo Rd. E3 . . . . 1B 66
Angrave Ct. E8 . . . . 5B 50
　(off Scriven St.)
Angrave Pas. E8 . . . . . . 5B 50
Angus Ho. SW2 . . . . 5F 103
Angus Rd. E13 . . . . 2E 69
Angus St. SE14 . . . . 3A 94
Anhalt Rd. SW11 . . . . . . 3A 88
Anley Rd. W14 . . . . 3F 71
Annabel Cl. E14 . . . . 5D 67
Anna Cl. E8 . . . . 5B 50
Annandale Rd. SE10 . . . 2B 96
　W4 . . . . 1A 84
Anna Neagle Cl. E7 . . . . 1C 54
Anne Compton M.
　SE12 . . . . 5B 110
Anne Goodman Ho.
　E1 . . . . 5E 65
　(off Jubilee St.)
Annes Ct. NW1 . . . . 3A 60
　(off Palgrave Gdns.)
Annesley Cl. NW10 . . . . 5A 28
Annesley Ho. SW9 . . . . . 4C 90
Annesley Rd. SE3 . . . . . 4D 97

Annesley Wlk. N19 . . . . . 4E 33
Anne St. E13 . . . . 3C 68
Annette Cres. N1 . . . . . . 4E 49
Annette Rd. N7 . . . . 5B 34
　(not continuous)
Annie Besant Cl. E3 . . . . 5B 52
Anning St.
　EC2 . . . . 3E 11 (3A 64)
Annis Rd. E9 . . . . 3A 52
Ann La. SW10 . . . . 2F 87
Ann Moss Way SE16 . . . 4E 79
Ann's Cl. SW1 . . . . 4A 20
Ann's Pl. E1 . . . . 1F 19
Ann Stroud Ct.
　SE12 . . . . 3C 110
Ansar Rd. E17 . . . . 1B 38
Ansdell Rd. SE15 . . . . . . 5E 93
Ansdell St. W8 . . . . 4D 73
Ansdell Ter. W8 . . . . 4D 73
Ansell Ho. E1 . . . . 4E 65
　(off Mile End Rd.)
Ansell Rd. SW17 . . . . . 3A 116
Anselm Rd. SW6 . . . . . . 2C 86
Ansford Rd.
　BR1: Brom 5E 123
Ansleigh Pl. W11 . . . . . . 1F 71
Anson Ho. E1 . . . . 3A 66
　(off Shandy St.)
　SW1 . . . . 2E 89
　(off Churchill Gdns.)
Anson Rd. N7 . . . . 1E 47
　NW2 . . . . 1D 43
Anstey Ho. E9 . . . . 5E 51
　(off Templecombe Rd.)
Anstey Rd. SE15 . . . . . . 1C 106
Anstice Cl. W4 . . . . 3A 84
Antenor Ho. E2 . . . . 1D 65
　(off Old Bethnal Grn. Rd.)
Anthony Cope Ct. N1 . . . 1C 10
　(off Chart St.)
Anthony Ho. NW8 . . . . . 3A 60
　(off Ashbridge St.)
Anthony St. E1 . . . . 5D 65
Antigua Wlk. SE19 . . . . . 5F 119
Antill Rd. E3 . . . . 2A 66
Antill Ter. E1 . . . . 5F 65
Antoine Hgts. SE1 . . . . . 4D 27
Anton St. E8 . . . . 2C 50
Antony Ho. SE14 . . . . . . 3F 93
　(off Barlborough St.)
　SE16 . . . . 5E 79
　(off Raymouth Rd.)
Antrim Gro. NW3 . . . . . . 3B 46
Antrim Ho. E3 . . . . 5B 52
　(off Birdsfield La.)
Antrim Mans. NW3 . . . . . 3B 46
Antrim Rd. NW3 . . . . . . 3B 46
Apex Ind. Est. NW10 . . . 3B 56
Aphrodite Ct. E14 . . . . . 5C 80
　(off Homer Dr.)
Apollo Bldg. E14 . . . . . . 5C 80
Apollo Bus. Cen.
　SE8 . . . . 1F 93
Apollo Ct. E1 . . . . 1C 78
　(off Thomas More St.)
　SW9 . . . . 4C 90
　(off Southey Rd.)
Apollo Ho. E2 . . . . 1D 65
　(off St Jude's Rd.)

Apollo Ho. N6 . . . . 2B **32**
  SW10 . . . . *3F 87*
    (off Milman's St.)
Apollo Pl. E11 . . . . 5A **40**
  SW10 . . . . *3F 87*
Apollo Theatre
  Soho *4B 14*
    (off Shaftesbury Av.)
  Victoria *4E 75*
    (off Wilton Rd.)
Apollo West End Cinema
  . . . . *5B 14*
    (off Regent St.)
Apothecary St.
  EC4 . . . . 3D **17** (5D **63**)
Appach Rd. SW2 . . . . . 3C **104**
Apple Blossom Ct.
  SW8 . . . . *3F 89*
    (off Pascal St.)
Appleby Cl. N15 . . . . . . 1F **35**
Appleby Rd. E8 . . . . . . 4C **50**
  E16 . . . . 5B **68**
Appleby St. E2 . . . . . . 1B **64**
Appledore Cl.
  SW17 . . . . 2B **116**
Appleford Ho. *W10* . . . *3A 58*
    (off Bosworth Rd.)
Appleford Rd. W10 . . . 3A **58**
Applegarth Ho. SE1 . . . 3E **25**
  SE15 . . . . *3C 92*
    (off Bird in Bush Rd.)
Applegarth Rd. W14 . . 4F **71**
Appleshaw Ho. SE5 . . 1A **106**
Appleton Rd. SE9 . . . . 1F **111**
Apple Tree Yd.
  SW1 . . . . 1A **22** (2E **75**)
Applewood Rd. NW2 . . 5D **29**
Applewood Dr. E13 . . . 3D **69**
Appold St.
  EC2 . . . . 5D **11** (4A **64**)
Apprentice Way E5 . . . 1D **51**
Approach, The NW4 . . . 1F **29**
  W3 . . . . 5A **56**
Approach Cl. N16 . . . . 1A **50**
Approach Rd. E2 . . . . . 1E **65**
April Ct. *E2* *1C 64*
    (off Teale St.)
April Glen SE23 . . . . . 3F **121**
April St. E8 . . . . 1B **50**
Apsley Cen., The
  NW2 . . . . 4C **28**
Apsley House 3C **20**
Apsley Ho. *E1* *4E 65*
    (off Stepney Way)
  NW8 . . . . *1F 59*
    (off Finchley Rd.)
Apsley Way NW2 . . . . . 4C **28**
  W1 . . . . 3C **20** (3C **74**)
    (not continuous)
Aquarius Bus. Pk.
  NW2 . . . . *3C 28*
    (off Priestley Way)
Aquila St. NW8 . . . . . . 1F **59**
Aquinas St.
  SE1 . . . . 2C **24** (2C **76**)
Arabella Dr. SW15 . . . . 2A **98**
Arabian Ho. *E1* *3A 66*
    (off Ernest St.)

Arabin Rd. SE4 . . . . . . 2A **108**
Aragon Ho. *E16* *2C 82*
    (off Capulet M.)
Aragon Twr. SE8 . . . . . 5B **80**
Aral Ho. *E1* *3F 65*
    (off Ernest St.)
Arapiles Ho. E14 . . . . . 5F **67**
    (off Blair St.)
Arbery Rd. E3 . . . . 2A **66**
Arbon Ct. *N1* *5E 49*
    (off Linton St.)
Arbor Ct. N16 . . . . 4F **35**
Arboretum Ct. *N1* *3F 49*
    (off Dove Rd.)
Arborfield Cl. SW2 . . . 1B **118**
Arborfield Ho. *E14* . . . *1C 80*
    (off E. India Dock Rd.)
Arbour Ho. *E1* *5F 65*
    (off Arbour Sq.)
Arbour Sq. E1 . . . . 5F **65**
Arbury Ter. SE26 . . . . . 3C **120**
Arbuthnot Rd.
  SE14 . . . . 5F **93**
Arbutus St. E8 . . . . . . 5B **50**
Arcade, The EC2 . . . . . 1D **19**
  N7 . . . . *1A 48*
    (off Macready Pl.)
Arcadia Ct. E1 . . . . 2F **19**
Arcadia Ct. E14 . . . . . . 5C **66**
Archangel St. SE16 . . . 3F **79**
Archbishop's Pl.
  SW2 . . . . 5B **104**
Archdale Ct. W12 . . . . . 2D **71**
Archdale Ho. *SE1* *5D 27*
    (off Long La.)
Archdale Rd. SE22 . . . 3B **106**
Archel Rd. W14 . . . . . . 2B **86**
Archer Apartments
  N1 . . . . *1A 64*
    (off Fern Cl.)
Archer Ho. *N1* *5A 50*
    (off Whitmore Est.)
  SE14 . . . . 4A **94**
  SW11 . . . . 4F **87**
  W11 . . . . *1B 72*
    (off Westbourne Gro.)
Archers Lodge SE16 . . . *1C 92*
    (off Culloden St.)
Archer Sq. SE14 . . . . . 2A **94**
Archer St.
  W1 . . . . 4B **14** (1F **75**)
Archery Cl. W2 . . . . . . 5A **60**
Archery Steps W2 . . . . 1A **74**
    (off St George's Flds.)
Arches, The NW1 . . . . . 4D **47**
  SW8 . . . . 3F **89**
  WC2 . . . . 1E **23**
    (off Villiers St.)
Arches Leisure Cen. . . . 2A **96**
Archibald M.
  W1 . . . . 5D **13** (1C **74**)
Archibald Rd. N7 . . . . . 1F **47**
Archibald St. E3 . . . . . . 2C **66**
Archie St.
  SE1 . . . . 4E **27** (3A **78**)
Arch St. SE1 . . . . 4E **77**
ARCHWAY 4E **33**
Archway Bus. Cen.
  N19 . . . . 5F **33**

Archway Cl. N19 . . . . . 4E **33**
  SW19 . . . . 3D **115**
  W10 . . . . 4F **57**
Archway Leisure Cen.
  . . . . 4E **33**
Archway Mall N19 . . . . 4E **33**
Archway M. *SW15* . . . *2A 100*
    (off Putney Bri. Rd.)
Archway Rd. N6 . . . . . . 1C **32**
  N19 . . . . 1C **32**
Archway St. SW13 . . . . 1A **98**
Arcola St. E8 . . . . 2B **50**
Arcola Theatre 1B **50**
Arctic St. NW5 . . . . . . 2D **47**
Arcus Rd.
  BR1: Brom 5A **124**
Ardbeg Rd. SE24 . . . . . 3F **105**
Arden Cl. Gdns. N2 . . . 1F **31**
Arden Cres. E14 . . . . . 5C **80**
Arden Est. N1 . . . . 1A **64**
Arden Ho. N1 . . . . 1D **11**
  SE11 . . . . *5B 76*
    (off Black Prince Rd.)
  SW9 . . . . *5A 90*
    (off Grantham Rd.)
Ardent Ho. E3 . . . . *1A 66*
    (off Roman Rd.)
Ardfillan Rd. SE6 . . . . . 1F **123**
Ardgowan Rd. SE6 . . . 5A **110**
Ardilaun Rd. N5 . . . . . 1E **49**
Ardleigh Rd. N1 . . . . . . 3A **50**
Ardley Cl. NW10 . . . . . 5A **28**
  SE6 . . . . 3A **122**
Ardlui Rd. SE27 . . . . . 2E **119**
Ardmere Rd. SE13 . . . . 4F **109**
Ardoch Rd. SE6 . . . . . . 2F **123**
Ardshiel Cl. SW15 . . . . 1F **99**
Ardwell Rd. SW2 . . . . 2A **118**
Ardwick Rd. NW2 . . . . 1C **44**
Arena Bus. Cen. N4 . . . 1E **35**
Arena Ind. Est. N4 . . . 1D **35**
Arena Shopping Pk.
  N4 . . . . 1E **35**
Ares Ct. *E14* *5C 80*
    (off Homer Dr.)
Arethusa Ho. *E14* *5C 80*
    (off Cahir St.)
Argall Av. E10 . . . . 2F **37**
Argall Way E10 . . . . . . 3F **37**
Argo Bus. Cen. *NW6* . . *2C 58*
    (off Kilburn Pk. Rd.)
Argon M. SW6 . . . . 3C **86**
Argos Ct. SW9 . . . . . . *4C 90*
    (off Caldwell St.)
Argos Ho. *E2* *1D 65*
    (off Old Bethnal Grn. Rd.)
Argosy Ho. SE8 . . . . . . 5A **80**
Argyle Ho. E14 . . . . . . 4E **81**
Argyle Pl. W6 . . . . 5D **71**
Argyle Rd. E1 . . . . 3F **65**
  E15 . . . . 1A **54**
  E16 . . . . 5D **69**
Argyle Sq.
  WC1 . . . . 1E **7** (2A **62**)
Argyle St.
  WC1 . . . . 1D **7** (2A **62**)
Argyle Wlk.
  WC1 . . . . 2E **7** (2A **62**)
Argyle Way SE16 . . . . . 1C **92**

Argyll Cl. SW9 . . . . 1B 104
Argyll Mans. SW3. . . . . 2F 87
    W14 . . . . 5A 72
        (off Hammersmith Rd.)
Argyll Rd. W8. . . . . 3C 72
Argyll St. W1 . . 3F 13 (5E 61)
Arica Ho. SE16. . . . . . . 4D 79
        (off Slippers Pl.)
Arica Rd. SE4. . . . . 2A 108
Ariel Cl. SE11. . . . . 5D 77
Ariel Rd. NW6. . . . . 3C 44
Ariel Way W12 . . . . 2E 71
Aristotle Rd. SW4. . . . . 1F 103
Arizona Bldg. SE8 . . . . 4D 95
        (off Deal's Gateway)
Ark, The W6 . . . . 1F 85
        (off Talgarth Rd.)
Arkindale Rd. SE6 . . . . 3E 123
Arkley Cres. E17. . . . . . 1B 38
Arkley Rd. E17 . . . . 1B 38
Arklow Ho. SE17. . . . . . 2F 91
Arklow Rd. SE14 . . . . . 2B 94
Arklow Rd. Trad. Est.
    SE14 . . . . 2A 94
Arkwright Ho. SW2. . . . 5A 104
        (off Streatham Pl.)
Arkwright Rd. NW3. . . . 2E 45
Arlesey Cl. SW15. . . . . 3A 100
Arlesford Rd. SW9 . . . . 1A 104
Arlidge Ho. EC1 . . . . . . 5C 8
        (off Kirby St.)
Arlingford Rd. SW2 . . . 3C 104
Arlington Av. N1. . . . . . 5E 49
        (not continuous)
Arlington Cl. SE13 . . . . 3F 109
Arlington Ho. EC1. . . . . 1C 8
        (off Arlington Way)
    SE8 . . . . 2B 94
        (off Evelyn St.)
    SW1 . . . . 1F 21 (2E 75)
    W12 . . . . 2D 71
        (off Tunis Rd.)
Arlington Lodge
    SW2 . . . . 2B 104
Arlington Pl. SE10 . . . . 3E 95
Arlington Rd. NW1. . . . 5D 47
Arlington Sq. N1. . . . . . 5E 49
Arlington St.
    SW1 . . . . 1F 21 (2E 75)
Arlington Way
    EC1 . . . . 1C 8 (2C 62)
Armada Ct. SE8 . . . . . . 2C 94
Armadale Rd. SW6 . . . . 3C 86
Armada St. SE8 . . . . . . 2C 94
        (off McMillan St.)
Armagh Rd. E3. . . . . . . 5B 52
Arminger Rd. W12. . . . . 2D 71
Armitage Ho. NW1. . . . 4A 60
        (off Cosway St.)
Armitage Rd. NW11. . . 3A 30
    SE10 . . . . 1B 96
Armour Cl. N7. . . . . 3B 48
Armoury Rd. SE8 . . . . . 5D 95
Armoury Way SW18. . . 3C 100
Armsby Ho. E1. . . . . . . 4E 65
        (off Stepney Way)
Armstrong Rd. SW7 . . . 4F 73
    W3 . . . . 2B 70
Arnal Cres. SW18. . . . . 5A 100

Arncliffe NW6. . . . . 1D 59
Arndale Wlk. SW18. . . . 3D 101
Arne Ho. SE11. . . . . . . 1B 90
        (off Worgan St.)
Arne St. WC2. . . 3E 15 (5A 62)
Arne Wlk. SE3 . . . . 2B 110
Arnewood Cl. SW15. . . 1C 112
Arngask Rd. SE6. . . . . . 5F 109
Arnhem Pl. E14 . . . . . . 4C 80
Arnhem Way SE22 . . . . 3A 106
Arnhem Wharf E14. . . . 4B 80
Arnold Cir.
    E2. . . . . 2F 11 (2B 64)
Arnold Est.
    SE1 . . . . 4F 27 (3B 78)
        (not continuous)
Arnold Ho. SE3 . . . . . . 2F 111
        (off Shooters Hill Rd.)
    SE17 . . . . 1D 91
        (off Doddington Gro.)
Arnold Mans. W14. . . . 2B 86
        (off Queen's Club Gdns.)
Arnold Rd. E3. . . . . 2C 66
Arnot Ho. SE5. . . . . 3E 91
        (off Comber Gro.)
Arnott Cl. W4. . . . . 5A 70
Arnould Av. SE5. . . . . . 2F 105
Arnside Ho. SE17. . . . . 2F 91
        (off Merrow St.)
Arnside St. SE17 . . . . . 2F 91
Arnulf St. SE6 . . . . 4D 123
Arnulls Rd. SW16 . . . . . 5D 119
Arodene Rd. SW2 . . . . . 4B 104
Arragon Rd. E6. . . . . . . 5F 55
    SW18 . . . . 1C 114
Arran Cl. NW10 . . . . . . 5A 28
Arran Dr. E12 . . . . 3F 41
Arran Ho. E14. . . . . 2E 81
        (off Raleana Rd.)
Arran Rd. SE6 . . . . 2D 123
Arran Wlk. N1. . . . . 4E 49
Arrol Ho.
    SE1 . . . . 5A 26 (4E 77)
Arrow Cl. SW5 . . . . 5C 72
        (off W. Cromwell Rd.)
Arrow Ho. N1 . . . . 5A 50
        (off Wilmer Gdns.)
Arrow Rd. E3 . . . . 2D 67
Arrows Ho. SE15 . . . . . 3E 93
        (off Clifton Way)
Arrowsmith Ho. SE11. . 1B 90
        (off Wickham St.)
Arsenal FC 1C 48
Arta Ho. E1. . . . . 5E 65
        (off Devonport St.)
Artemis Ct. E14 . . . . . . 5C 80
        (off Homer Dr.)
Artesian Cl. NW10. . . . 4A 42
Artesian Rd. W2. . . . . . 5C 58
Artesian Wlk. E11 . . . . 5A 40
Arthingworth St. E15. . 5A 54
Arthur Ct. SW11. . . . . . 4C 88
    W2 . . . . 5D 59
        (off Queensway)
    W10. . . . . 5F 57
Arthur Deakin Ho. E1. . 4C 64
        (off Hunton St.)

Arthurdon Rd. SE4. . . . 3C 108
Arthur Henderson Ho.
    SW6 . . . . 5B 86
        (off Fulham Rd.)
Arthur Horsley Wlk.
    E7 . . . . 2B 54
        (off Twr. Hamlets Rd.)
Arthur Ho. N1. . . . . 5A 50
        (off New Era Est.)
Arthur Rd. N7. . . . . 1B 48
    SW19 . . . . 5B 114
Arthur St.
    EC4. . . . . 4C 18 (1F 77)
Artichoke Hill E1 . . . . . 1D 79
Artichoke M. SE5. . . . . 4F 91
        (off Artichoke Pl.)
Artichoke Pl. SE5. . . . . 4F 91
Artillery Ho. E15. . . . . . 3A 54
Artillery La.
    E1. . . . . 1E 19 (4A 64)
    W12 . . . . 5C 56
Artillery Pas. E1. . . . . . 1F 19
Artillery Pl.
    SW1 . . . . 5B 22 (4F 75)
Artillery Row
    SW1 . . . . 5B 22 (4E 75)
Artisan Ct. E8. . . . . 3C 50
Artisan M. NW10 . . . . . 2F 57
        (off Warfield Rd.)
Artisan Quarter
    NW10 . . . . 2F 57
        (off Wellington Rd.)
Artizan St. E1. . . . . 2F 19
Arts Theatre 4D 15
        (off St Martin's St.)
Arundel Bldgs. SE1 . . . 4A 78
        (off Swan Mead)
Arundel Cl. E15. . . . . . . 1A 54
    SW11 . . . . 3A 102
Arundel Ct. SE16 . . . . . 1D 93
        (off Varcoe Rd.)
    SW3 . . . . 1A 88
        (off Jubilee Pl.)
    SW13 . . . . 2D 85
        (off Arundel Ter.)
Arundel Gdns. W11 . . . 1B 72
Arundel Gt. Ct.
    WC2 . . . . 4A 16 (1B 76)
Arundel Gro. N16. . . . . 2A 50
Arundel Mans. SW6. . . 4B 86
        (off Kelvedon Rd.)
Arundel Pl. N1. . . . . 3C 48
Arundel Sq. N7. . . . . . . 3C 48
Arundel St.
    WC2 . . . . 4A 16 (1B 76)
Arundel Ter. SW13. . . . 2D 85
Arvon Rd. N5 . . . . 2C 48
        (not continuous)
Asbridge Ct. W6. . . . . . 4D 71
        (off Dalling Rd.)
Ascalon Ho. SW8. . . . . 3E 89
        (off Thessaly Rd.)
Ascalon St. SW8 . . . . . 3E 89
Ascham St. NW5 . . . . . 2E 47
Ascot Ct. NW8 . . . . 2F 59
        (off Grove End Rd.)
Ascot Ho. NW1. . . . . . . 1E 5
    W9 . . . . 3C 58
        (off Harrow Rd.)

Ascot Lodge NW6 . . . . . . 5D **45**
Ascot Rd. N15 . . . . 1F **35**
   SW17 . . . . 5C **116**
Ashanti M. E8 . . . . 2E **51**
Ashbee Ho. E2 . . . . 2E **65**
   (off Portman Pl.)
Ashbourne Ct. E5 . . . . 1A **52**
Ashbourne Gro.
   SE22 . . . . 2B **106**
   W4 . . . . 1A **84**
Ashbridge Rd. E11 . . . . . . 2A **40**
Ashbridge St. NW8 . . . . . . 3A **60**
Ashbrook Rd. N19 . . . . 3F **33**
Ashburn Gdns. SW7 . . . . . 5E **73**
Ashburnham Gro.
   SE10 . . . . 3D **95**
Ashburnham Mans.
   SW10 . . . . *3E 87*
   (off Ashburnham Rd.)
Ashburnham Pl.
   SE10 . . . . 3D **95**
Ashburnham Retreat
   SE10 . . . . 3D **95**
Ashburnham Rd.
   NW10 . . . . 2E **57**
   SW10 . . . . 3E **87**
Ashburnham Twr.
   SW10 . . . . *3F 87*
   (off Worlds End Est.)
Ashburn Pl. SW7 . . . . 5E **73**
Ashburton Ent. Cen.
   SW15 . . . . 4E **99**
Ashburton Gro. N7 . . . . . . 1C **48**
Ashburton Ho. W9 . . . . . . *3B 58*
   (off Fernhead Rd.)
Ashburton Rd. E16 . . . . . . 5C **68**
Ashburton Ter. E13 . . . . . 1C **68**
Ashburton Triangle
   N7 . . . . 1C **48**
Ashbury Pl. SW19 . . . . . . 5E **115**
Ashbury Rd. SW11 . . . . . . 1B **102**
Ashby Ct. NW8 . . . . *3F 59*
   (off Pollitt Dr.)
Ashby Gro. N1 . . . . 4E **49**
   (not continuous)
Ashby Ho. N1 . . . . *4E 49*
   (off Essex Rd.)
   SW9 . . . . 5D **91**
Ashby M. SE4 . . . . 5B **94**
   SW2 . . . . *3A 104*
   (off Prague Pl.)
Ashby Rd. SE4 . . . . 5B **94**
Ashby St. EC1 . . 2E **9** (2D **63**)
Ashchurch Gro. W12 . . . 4C **70**
Ashchurch Pk. Vs.
   W12 . . . . 4C **70**
Ashchurch Ter. W12 . . . . 4C **70**
Ashcombe Pk. NW2 . . . . . 5A **28**
Ashcombe Rd.
   SW19 . . . . 5C **114**
Ashcombe St. SW6 . . . . . 5D **87**
Ashcroft Ho. SW8 . . . . . . *4E 89*
   (off Wadhurst Rd.)
Ashcroft Sq. W6 . . . . 5E **71**
Ashdale Ho. N4 . . . . 2F **35**
Ashdale Rd. SE12 . . . . . . 1D **125**
Ashdene SE15 . . . . 3D **93**
Ashdon Rd. NW10 . . . . . 5B **42**
Ashdown Cres. NW5 . . . . 2C **46**

Ashdown Ho. SW1 . . . . . . 5A **22**
Ashdown Wlk. E14 . . . . . . *5C 80*
   (off Copeland Dr.)
Ashdown Way
   SW17 . . . . 2C **116**
Ashenden SE17 . . . . *5E 77*
   (off Deacon Way)
Ashenden Rd. E5 . . . . 2A **52**
Ashen Gro. SW19 . . . . . . 3C **114**
Ashentree Ct. EC4 . . . . . 3C **16**
Asher Way E1 . . . . 1C **78**
Ashfield Cl. SW9 . . . . *5A 90*
   (off Clapham Rd.)
Ashfield Ho. W14 . . . . . . *1B 86*
   (off W. Cromwell Rd.)
Ashfield Rd. N4 . . . . 1E **35**
   W3 . . . . 2B **70**
Ashfield St. E1 . . . . 4D **65**
Ashfield Yd. E1 . . . . 4E **65**
Ashford Cl. E17 . . . . 1B **38**
Ashford Ho. SE8 . . . . 2B **94**
   SW9 . . . . 2D **105**
Ashford Pas. NW2 . . . . . . 1F **43**
Ashford Rd. NW2 . . . . 1F **43**
Ashford St.
   N1 . . . . 1D **11** (2A **64**)
Ash Gro. E8 . . . . 5D **51**
   (not continuous)
   NW2 . . . . 1F **43**
   SE12 . . . . 1C **124**
Ashgrove Ct. W9 . . . . *4C 58*
   (off Elmfield Way)
Ashgrove Ho. SW1 . . . . . . *1F 89*
   (off Lindsay Sq.)
Ashgrove Rd.
   BR1: Brom 5F **123**
Ash Ho. E14 . . . . *3E 81*
   (off E. Ferry Rd.)
   SE1 . . . . *5B 78*
   (off Longfield Est.)
   W10 . . . . *3A 58*
   (off Heather Wlk.)
Ashington Ho. E1 . . . . *3D 65*
   (off Barnsley St.)
Ashington Rd. SW6 . . . . . 5B **86**
Ashlake Rd. SW16 . . . . . . 4A **118**
Ashland Pl.
   W1 . . . . 5B **4** (4C **60**)
Ashleigh Commercial Est.
   SE7 . . . . 4E **83**
Ashleigh Point SE23 . . 3F **121**
Ashleigh Rd. SW14 . . . . 1A **98**
Ashley Ct. SW1 . . . . *4E 75*
   (off Morpeth Ter.)
Ashley Cres. SW11 . . 1C **102**
Ashley Gdns.
   SW1 . . . . 5A **22** (4E **75**)
   (not continuous)
Ashley Pl.
   SW1 . . . . 5F **21** (4E **75**)
   (not continuous)
Ashley Rd. E7 . . . . 4E **55**
   N19 . . . . 3A **34**
   SW19 . . . . 5D **115**
Ashlin Rd. E15 . . . . 1F **53**
Ashlone Rd. SW15 . . . . . 1E **99**
Ashmead Bus. Cen.
   E16 . . . . 3F **67**

Ashmead Ho. E9 . . . . 2A **52**
   (off Homerton Rd.)
Ashmead M. SE8 . . . . 5C **94**
Ashmead Rd. SE8 . . . . . . 5C **94**
Ashmere Gro. SW2 . . 2A **104**
Ash M. NW5 . . . . 2E **47**
Ashmill St. NW1 . . . . 4A **60**
Ashmole Pl. SW8 . . . . . . 2B **90**
   (not continuous)
Ashmole St. SW8 . . . . . . 2B **90**
Ashmore NW1 . . . . *4F 47*
   (off Agar Gro.)
Ashmore Cl. SE15 . . . . . 3B **92**
Ashmore Ho. W14 . . . . . *4A 72*
   (off Russell Rd.)
Ashmore Rd. W9 . . . . 1B **58**
Ashmount Est. N19 . . . . . 2F **33**
Ashmount Rd. N19 . . . . . 2E **33**
Ashness Rd. SW11 . . . . 3B **102**
Ashpark Ho. E14 . . . . *5B 66*
   (off Norbiton Rd.)
Ash Rd. E15 . . . . 2A **54**
Ashtead Rd. E5 . . . . 2C **36**
Ashton Hgts. SE23 . . . . 1E **121**
Ashton Ho. SW9 . . . . 3C **90**
Ashton Rd. E15 . . . . 2F **53**
Ashton St. E14 . . . . 1E **81**
Ash Tree Ho. SE5 . . . . . . *3E 91*
   (off Pitman St.)
Ashurst Gdns. SW2 . . 1C **118**
Ashvale Rd. SW17 . . . . 5B **116**
Ashville Rd. E11 . . . . 4F **39**
Ashwater Rd. SE12 . . . 1C **124**
Ashwin St. E8 . . . . 3B **50**
Ashworth Cl. SE5 . . . . . . 5F **91**
Ashworth Mans.
   W9 . . . . *2D 59*
   (off Elgin Av.)
Ashworth Rd. W9 . . . . . . 2D **59**
Aske Ho. N1 . . . . 1D **11**
   (not continuous)
Asker Ho. N7 . . . . 1A **48**
Askew Cres. W12 . . . . . . 3B **70**
Askew Est. W12 . . . . *2B 70*
   (off Uxbridge Rd.)
Askew Rd. W12 . . . . 3B **70**
Askham Ct. W12 . . . . 2C **70**
Askham Rd. W12 . . . . 2C **70**
Askill Dr. SW15 . . . . 3A **100**
Asland Rd. E15 . . . . 5A **54**
Aslett St. SW18 . . . . 5D **101**
Asmara Rd. NW2 . . . . . 2A **44**
Asmuns Hill NW11 . . . . . 1C **30**
Asmuns Pl. NW11 . . . . . . 1B **30**
Asolando Dr. SE17 . . . . . 5E **77**
Aspect Ct. E14 . . . . *3E 81*
   (off Manchester Rd.)
Aspen Cl. N19 . . . . 4E **33**
Aspen Gdns. W6 . . . . 1D **85**
Aspen Ho. SE15 . . . . *2E 93*
   (off Sharratt St.)
Aspenlea Rd. W6 . . . . . . 2F **85**
Aspen Lodge W8 . . . . . . *4D 73*
   (off Abbots Wlk.)
Aspen Way E14 . . . . 1D **81**
Aspern Gro. NW3 . . . . . 2A **46**
Aspinall Rd. SE4 . . . . 1F **107**
   (not continuous)

Aspinden Rd. SE16 . . . . . 5D 79
Aspley Rd. SW18 . . . . . . 3D 101
Assam St. E1 . . . . 5C 64
   (off White Church La.)
Assata M. N1 . . . . 3D 49
Assembly Pas. E1 . . . . . . 4E 65
Association Gallery, The
   . . . . 3D 11
   (off Leonard St.)
Astbury Bus. Pk.
   SE15 . . . . 4E 93
Astbury Ho. SE11 . . . . . 4C 76
   (off Lambeth Wlk.)
Astbury Rd. SE15 . . . . . 4E 93
Astell Ho. SW3 . . . . 1A 88
   (off Astell St.)
Astell St. SW3 . . . . 1A 88
Aste St. E14 . . . . 3E 81
Astey's Row N1 . . . . 4E 49
Astle St. SW11 . . . . 5C 88
Astley Av. NW2 . . . . 2E 43
Astley Ho. SE1 . . . . 1B 92
   (off Rowcross St.)
   SW13 . . . . 2D 85
   (off Wyatt Dr.)
   W2 . . . . 4C 58
   (off Alfred Rd.)
Aston Ho. SW8 . . . . 4F 89
   (off Westbourne Gro.)
   W11 . . . . 1B 72
Aston St. E14 . . . . 4A 66
Aston Ter. SW12 . . . . . . 4D 103
Astonville St. SW18 . . . 1C 114
Aston Webb Ho. SE1 . . . 2D 27
   (off Braidwood St.)
Astor Ct. E16 . . . . 5E 69
   (off Ripley St.)
   SW6 . . . . 3E 87
   (off Maynard Cl.)
Astoria, The 2C 14
   (off Falconberg M.)
Astoria Ct. E8 . . . . 4B 50
   (off Queensbridge Rd.)
Astoria Mans.
   SW16 . . . . 3A 118
Astoria Wlk. SW9 . . . . . 1C 104
Astra Ho. SE14 . . . . 2B 94
   (off Arklow Rd.)
Astrop M. W6 . . . . 4E 71
Astrop Ter. W6 . . . . 3E 71
Astwood M. SW7 . . . . . . 5E 73
Asylum Rd. SE15 . . . . . . 3D 93
Atalanta St. SW6 . . . . . . 3F 85
Atheldene Rd.
   SW18 . . . . 1D 115
Athelney St. SE6 . . . . . . 3C 122
Athelstan Gro. E3 . . . . . 1B 66
Athelstane M. N4 . . . . . . 3C 34
Athelstan Gdns.
   NW6 . . . . 4A 44
Athenaeum Ct. N5 . . . . . 1E 49
Athene Pl. EC4 . . . . 2C 16
   (off St Andrew St.)
Athenia Ho. E14 . . . . 5F 67
   (off Blair St.)
Athenlay Rd. SE15 . . . . . 3F 107
Athens Gdns. W9 . . . . . . 3C 58
   (off Harrow Rd.)
Atherden Rd. E5 . . . . 1E 51

Atherfold Rd. SW9 . . . . . 1A 104
Atherstone Ct. W2 . . . . . 4D 59
   (off Delamere Ter.)
Atherstone M. SW7 . . . . 5E 73
Atherton Dr. SW19 . . . . 4F 113
Atherton Leisure Cen.
   . . . . 3B 54
Atherton M. E7 . . . . 3B 54
Atherton Rd. E7 . . . . 3B 54
   SW13 . . . . 3C 84
Atherton St. SW11 . . . . . 5A 88
Athlone Cl. E5 . . . . 2D 51
Athlone Ho. E1 . . . . 5E 65
   (off Sidney St.)
Athlone Rd. SW2 . . . . . . 5B 104
Athlone St. NW5 . . . . . . 3C 46
Atholl Ho. W9 . . . . 2E 59
   (off Maida Va.)
Athol Sq. E14 . . . . 5E 67
Atkin Bldg. WC1 . . . . 5A 8
   (off Raymond Bldgs.)
Atkinson Ct. E10 . . . . . . 2D 39
   (off Kings Cl.)
Atkinson Ho. E2 . . . . 1C 64
   (off Pritchards Rd.)
   E13 . . . . 3B 68
   (off Sutton Rd.)
   SE17 . . . . 5F 77
   (off Catesby St.)
Atkinson Rd. E16 . . . . . . 4E 69
Atkins Rd. E10 . . . . 1D 39
   SW12 . . . . 5E 103
Atlanta Bldg. SE10 . . . . . 4D 95
   (off Deal's Gateway)
Atlanta Ho. SE16 . . . . . . 4A 80
   (off Brunswick Quay)
Atlantic Ct. E14 . . . . 1F 81
   (off Jamestown Way)
Atlantic Ho. E1 . . . . 4A 66
   (off Harford St.)
Atlantic Rd. SW9 . . . . . . 2C 104
Atlantic Wharf E1 . . . . . . 1F 79
Atlas Bus. Cen.
   NW2 . . . . 3D 29
Atlas Gdns. SE7 . . . . 5E 83
Atlas M. E8 . . . . 3B 50
   N7 . . . . 3B 48
Atlas Rd. E13 . . . . 1C 68
   NW10 . . . . 2A 56
Atlas Wharf E9 . . . . 3C 52
Atley Rd. E3 . . . . 5C 52
Atney Rd. SW15 . . . . 2A 100
Atrium Apartments
   N1 . . . . 5F 49
   (off Felton St.)
Atterbury Rd. N4 . . . . . . 1C 34
Atterbury St. SW1 . . . . . 5A 76
Attewood Av. NW10 . . . . 5A 28
Attilburgh Ho. SE1 . . . . . 5F 27
   (off Abbey St.)
Attleborough Ct.
   SE23 . . . . 2C 120
Attneave St.
   WC1 . . . . 2B 8 (2C 62)
Atunbi Ct. NW1 . . . . 4E 47
   (off Farrier St.)
Atwater Cl. SW2 . . . . . . 1C 118
Atwell Cl. E10 . . . . 1D 39
Atwell Rd. SE15 . . . . 5C 92

Atwood Ho. W14 . . . . . . 5B 72
   (off Beckford Cl.)
Atwood Rd. W6 . . . . 5D 71
Aubert Ct. N5 . . . . 1D 49
Aubert Pk. N5 . . . . 1D 49
Aubert Rd. N5 . . . . 1D 49
Aubrey Beardsley Ho.
   SW1 . . . . 5E 75
   (off Vauxhall Bri. Rd.)
Aubrey Mans. NW1 . . . . 4A 60
   (off Lisson St.)
Aubrey Moore Point
   E15 . . . . 1E 67
   (off Abbey La.)
Aubrey Pl. NW8 . . . . 1E 59
Aubrey Rd. N8 . . . . 1A 34
   W8 . . . . 2B 72
Aubrey Wlk. W8 . . . . 2B 72
Auburn Cl. SE14 . . . . . . 3A 94
Aubyn Hill SE27 . . . . 4E 119
Aubyn Sq. SW15 . . . . . . 3C 98
Auckland Hill
   SE27 . . . . 4E 119
Auckland Ho. W12 . . . . . 1D 71
   (off White City Est.)
Auckland Rd. E10 . . . . . . 5D 39
   SW11 . . . . 2A 102
Auckland St. SE11 . . . . . 1B 90
Auden Pl. NW1 . . . . 5C 46
   (not continuous)
Audley Cl. SW11 . . . . . . 1C 102
Audley Dr. E16 . . . . 2D 83
Audley Rd. NW4 . . . . . . 1C 28
Audley Sq.
   W1 . . . . 1C 20 (2C 74)
Audrey St. E2 . . . . 1C 64
Augurs La. E13 . . . . 2D 69
Augusta St. E14 . . . . 5D 67
Augustine Rd. W14 . . . . 4F 71
Augustus Cl. W12 . . . . . 3D 71
Augustus Ct. SE1 . . . . . . 5A 78
   (off Old Kent Rd.)
   SW16 . . . . 2F 117
Augustus Ho. NW1 . . . . . 1F 5
   (off Augustus St.)
Augustus Rd. SW19 . . . 1F 113
Augustus St.
   NW1 . . . . 1E 5 (1D 61)
Aulton Pl. SE11 . . . . 1C 90
Aura Ct. SE15 . . . . 2D 107
Auriga M. N1 . . . . 2F 49
Auriol Ho. W12 . . . . 2D 71
   (off Ellerslie Rd.)
Auriol Mans. W14 . . . . . 5A 72
   (off Edith Rd.)
Auriol Rd. W14 . . . . 5A 72
Aurora Bldg. E14 . . . . . . 2E 81
   (off Blackwall Way)
Aurora Ho. E14 . . . . 5D 67
   (off Kerbey St.)
Austen Ho. NW6 . . . . . . 2C 58
   (off Cambridge Rd.)
Austin Cl. SE23 . . . . 5A 108
Austin Ct. E6 . . . . 5E 55
   SE15 . . . . 1C 106
   (off Philip Wlk.)
Austin Friars
   EC2 . . . . 2C 18 (5F 63)
   (not continuous)

Austin Friars Pas.
EC2 . . . . 2C 18
Austin Friars Sq.
EC2 . . . . 2C 18
Austin Ho. SE14 . . . . 3B 94
(off Achilles St.)
Austin Rd. SW11 . . . . . 4C 88
Austin St. E2 . . 2F 11 (2B 64)
Austin Ter. SE1 . . . . 5C 24
(off Morley St.)
Australian War Memorial
. . . . 3C 20
(off Duke of Wellington Pl.)
Australia Rd. W12 . . . . 1D 71
Austral St. SE11 . . . . . . 5D 77
Autumn Cl. SW19 . . . . 5E 115
Autumn Gro.
BR1: Brom 5D 125
Autumn St. E3 . . . . 5C 52
Avalon Rd. SW6 . . . . . 4D 87
Avarn Rd. SW17 . . . . . 5B 116
Avebury Ct. N1 . . . . 5F 49
(off Imber St.)
Avebury Rd. E11 . . . . . . 3F 39
Avebury St. N1 . . . . 5F 49
Aveline St. SE11 . . . . . . 1C 90
Ave Maria La.
EC4 . . . . . . 3E 17 (5D 63)
Avenell Mans. N5. . . . . . 1D 49
Avenell Rd. N5 . . . . 5D 35
Avenfield Ho. W1 . . . . . . 4A 12
(off Park La.)
Avening Rd. SW18 . . . . 5C 100
Avening Ter. SW18 . . . . 5C 100
Avenons Rd. E13 . . . . . . 3C 68
Avenue, The E11 . . . . . 1D 41
NW6 . . . . 5F 43
SE10 . . . . 3F 95
SW4 . . . . 3C 102
SW18 . . . . 5A 102
W4 . . . . 4A 70
Avenue Cl. NW8 . . . . . . 5A 46
Avenue Cl. NW2 . . . . . . 5B 30
SW3 . . . . 5B 74
(off Draycott Av.)
Avenue Gdns.
SW14 . . . . 1A 98
Avenue Ho. NW8 . . . . . 1A 60
(off Allitsen Rd.)
NW10 . . . . 1D 57
(off All Souls Av.)
Avenue Lodge NW8 . . . 4F 45
(off Avenue Rd.)
Avenue Mans. NW3 . . . 2D 45
(off Finchley Rd.)
Avenue Pk. Rd.
SE27 . . . . 2D 119
Avenue Rd. E7 . . . . 1D 55
N6 . . . . 2E 33
N15 . . . . 1F 35
NW3 . . . . 4F 45
NW8 . . . . 4F 45
NW10 . . . . 1B 56
Averill St. W6 . . . . 2F 85
Avery Farm Row
SW1 . . . . 5C 74
Avery Row
W1 . . . . 4D 13 (1D 75)
Aviary Cl. E16 . . . . 4B 68

Avignon Rd. SE4 . . . . . 1F 107
Avington Ct. SE1 . . . . . . 5A 78
(off Old Kent Rd.)
Avis Sq. E1 . . . . 5F 65
Avoca Rd. SW17 . . . . . 4C 116
Avocet Cl. SE1 . . . . 1C 92
Avon Ct. SW15 . . . . . . 3A 100
W9 . . . . 4C 58
(off Elmfield Way)
Avondale Av. NW2 . . . . 5A 28
Avondale Ct. E11 . . . . . . 3A 40
E16 . . . . 4A 68
Avondale Cres.
IG4: Ilf 1F 41
Avondale Ho. SE1 . . . . . 1C 92
(off Avondale Sq.)
Avondale Pk. Gdns.
W11 . . . . 1A 72
Avondale Pk. Rd.
W11 . . . . 1A 72
Avondale Pavement
SE1 . . . . 1C 92
Avondale Ri. SE15 . . . . 1B 106
Avondale Rd. E16 . . . . . 4A 68
E17 . . . . 2C 38
N15 . . . . 1D 35
SE9 . . . . 2F 125
SW14 . . . . 1A 98
SW19 . . . . 5D 115
Avondale Sq. SE1 . . . . . 1C 92
Avon Ho. W8 . . . . 4C 72
(off Allen St.)
W14 . . . . 5B 72
(off Kensington Village)
Avonhurst Ho. NW2 . . . 4A 44
Avonley Rd. SE14 . . . . . 3E 93
Avonmore Gdns.
W14 . . . . 5B 72
Avonmore Pl. W14 . . . . 5A 72
Avonmore Rd. W14 . . . 5A 72
Avonmouth St.
SE1 . . . . . . 5F 25 (4E 77)
Avon Pl. SE1 . . 4A 26 (3E 77)
Avon Rd. SE4 . . . . 1C 108
Avro Ho. SW8 . . . . 3D 89
(off Havelock Ter.)
Axis Ct. SE10 . . . . 2A 96
(off Woodland Cres.)
SE16 . . . . 3C 78
(off Nth. Flock St.)
Axminster Rd. N7 . . . . . 5A 34
Aybrook St.
W1 . . . . . 1B 12 (4C 60)
Aycliffe Ho. SE17 . . . . . 2F 91
(off Portland St.)
Aycliffe Rd. W12 . . . . . . 2C 70
Ayerst Ct. E10 . . . . 2E 39
Aylesbury Cl. E7 . . . . . . 3B 54
Aylesbury Ho. SE15 . . . 2C 92
(off Friary Est.)
Aylesbury Rd. SE17 . . . 1F 91
Aylesbury St.
EC1 . . . . . . 4D 9 (3D 63)
NW10 . . . . 5A 28
Aylesford Ho. SE1 . . . . . 4C 26
(off Long La.)
Aylesford St. SW1 . . . . . 1F 89
Aylesham Cen., The
SE15 . . . . 4C 92

Aylestone Av. NW6 . . . . 4F 43
Aylmer Ct. N2 . . . . 1B 32
Aylmer Ho. SE10 . . . . . . 1F 95
Aylmer Pde. N2 . . . . 1B 32
Aylmer Rd. E11 . . . . 3B 40
N2 . . . . 1A 32
W12 . . . . 3B 70
Aylton Est. SE16 . . . . . . 3E 79
Aylward Rd. SE23 . . . . 2F 121
Aylward St. E1 . . . . 5E 65
(Jamaica St.)
E1 . . . . 5E 65
(Jubilee St.)
Aylwin Est.
SE1 . . . . . . 5E 27 (4A 78)
Aynhoe Mans. W14 . . . . 5F 71
(off Aynhoe Rd.)
Aynhoe Rd. W14. . . . . . 5F 71
Ayres Cl. E13 . . . . 2C 68
Ayres St. SE1 . . 3A 26 (3E 77)
Ayrsome Rd. N16. . . . . . 5A 36
Ayrton Gould Ho.
E2 . . . . 2F 65
(off Roman Rd.)
Ayrton Rd. SW7 . . . . . . 4F 73
Aysgarth Rd. SE21 . . . 5A 106
Ayshford Ho. E2. . . . . . . 2D 65
(off Viaduct St.)
Ayston Ho. SE16 . . . . . . 5F 79
(off Plough Way)
Ayton Ho. SE5 . . . . 3F 91
(off Edmund St.)
Aytoun Pl. SW9 . . . . 5B 90
Aytoun Rd. SW9 . . . . . . 5B 90
Azalea Ho. SE14 . . . . . . 3B 94
(off Achilles St.)
Azania M. NW5 . . . . 3D 47
Azenby Rd. SE15 . . . . . . 5B 92
Azof St. SE10 . . . . 5A 82
Azov Ho. E1 . . . . 3A 66
(off Commodore St.)
Azure Ho. E2 . . . . 2C 64
(off Buckfast St.)

B

Baalbec Rd. N5 . . . . 2D 49
Babington Ct. WC1 . . . . . 5F 7
Babington Ho. SE1 . . . . 3A 26
(off Disney St.)
Babington Rd.
SW16 . . . . 5F 117
Babmaes St.
SW1 . . . . . . 5B 14 (1F 75)
Bacchus Wlk. N1 . . . . . . 1A 64
(off Regan Way)
Bache's St.
N1 . . . . 1C 10 (2F 63)
Back All. EC3 . . . . 3E 19
Bk. Church La. E1 . . . . . 5C 64
Back Hill
EC1 . . . . . . 4C 8 (3C 62)
Backhouse Pl. SE17 . . . 5A 78
Back La. N8 . . . . 1A 34
NW3 . . . . 1E 45
Bk. Passage EC1 . . . . . . 5E 9
(off Long La.)
Bacon Gro. SE1 . . . . 4B 78

Bacon's College Sports Cen.
. . . . 2A 80
Bacons La. N6 . . . . 3C 32
Bacon St. E1 . . 3F 11 (3B 64)
 E2 . . . . 3B 64
Bacton NW5 . . . . 2C 46
Bacton St. E2 . . . . 2E 65
Baddesley Ho. SE11 . . . . 1B 90
 (off Jonathan St.)
Baddow Wlk. N1 . . . . . . 5E 49
 (off New Nth. Rd.)
Baden Pl.
 SE1 . . . . 3B 26 (3F 77)
Baden Powell Ho.
 SW7 . . . . 5E 73
 (off Queen's Ga.)
Badger Ct. NW2 . . . . . . 5E 29
Badminton M. E16 . . . . 2C 82
Badminton Ho.
 SW12 . . . . 4C 102
Badric Ct. SW11 . . . . . . 5F 87
Badsworth Rd. SE5 . . . . 4E 91
Baffin Way E14 . . . . 2E 81
Bagley's La. SW6 . . . . . . 4D 87
Bagnigge Ho. WC1 . . . . . 2B 8
 (off Margery St.)
Bagshot Ho. NW1 . . . . . . 1E 5
Bagshot St. SE17 . . . . . 1A 92
Baildon E2 . . . . 1E 65
 (off Cyprus St.)
Baildon St. SE8 . . . . . . 3B 94
Bailey Cotts. E14 . . . . . 4A 66
 (off Maroon St.)
Bailey Ho. SW10 . . . . . . 3D 87
 (off Coleridge Gdns.)
Bailey M. SW2 . . . . . . 3C 104
Bailey Pl. SE26 . . . . . 5F 121
Bainbridge St.
 WC1 . . . . 2C 14 (5F 61)
Baird Ho. E10 . . . . 3C 38
Baird Gdns. SE19 . . . . 4A 120
Baird Ho. W12 . . . . 1D 71
 (off White City Est.)
Baird St. EC1 . . . 3A 10 (3E 63)
Baizdon Rd. SE3 . . . . . . 5A 96
Baker Ho. WC1 . . . . 4E 7
 (off Colonnade)
Baker Pas. NW10 . . . . . 5A 42
Baker Rd. NW10 . . . . . . 5A 42
Bakers Av. E17 . . . . 1D 39
Baker's Fld. N7 . . . . 1A 48
Bakers Hall Ct. EC3 . . . . 5D 19
Bakers Hill E5 . . . . 3E 37
Bakers La. N6 . . . . 1B 32
Baker's M.
 W1 . . . . 2B 12 (5C 60)
Bakers Pas. NW3 . . . . . . 1E 45
 (off Heath St.)
Baker's Rents
 E2 . . . . 2F 11 (2B 64)
Baker's Row E15 . . . . . . 1A 68
 EC1 . . . . 4B 8 (3C 62)
BAKER STREET. 4B 60
Baker St.
 NW1 . . . . 4A 4 (3B 60)
 W1 . . . . 4A 4 (3B 60)
Baker's Yd. EC1 . . . . 4B 8
Bakery Cl. SW9 . . . . 3B 90
Bakery Pl. SW11 . . . . . 2B 102

Balaam Leisure Cen.
 . . . . 3C 68
Balaam St. E13 . . . . 3C 68
Balaclava Rd. SE1 . . . . . 5B 78
Bala Grn. NW9 . . . . 1A 28
 (off Ruthin Cl.)
Balchen Rd. SE3 . . . . . . 5F 97
Balchier Rd. E22 . . . . . 4D 107
Balcombe Ho. NW1 . . . . 3A 60
 (off Taunton Pl.)
Balcombe St.
 NW1 . . . . 5A 4 (3B 60)
Balcorne St. E9 . . . . 4E 51
Balder Ri. SE12 . . . . . . 2D 125
Balderton Flats W1 . . . . 3C 12
 (off Balderton St.)
Balderton St.
 W1 . . . . 3C 12 (5C 60)
Baldock St. E3 . . . . 1D 67
Baldrey Ho. SE10 . . . . . 1B 96
 (off Blackwall La.)
Baldry Gdns. SW16 . . . 5B 118
Baldwin Cres. SE5 . . . . 4E 91
Baldwin Ho. SW2 . . . . . 1C 118
Baldwins Gdns.
 EC1 . . . . 5B 8 (4C 62)
Baldwin St.
 EC1 . . . . 2B 10 (2F 63)
Baldwin Ter. N1 . . . . . . 1E 63
Balearic Apartments
 E16 . . . . 1C 82
 (off Western Gateway)
Bale Rd. E1 . . . . 4A 66
Balfern Gro. W4 . . . . . . 1A 84
Balfern St. SW11 . . . . . 5A 88
Balfe St. N1 . . . . 1A 62
Balfour Ho. W10 . . . . . . 4F 57
 (off St Charles Sq.)
Balfour M.
 W1 . . . . 1C 20 (2C 74)
Balfour Pl. SW15 . . . . . 2D 99
 W1 . . . . 5C 12 (1C 74)
Balfour Rd. N5 . . . . 1E 49
Balfour St. SE17 . . . . . . 5F 77
Balfron Twr. E14 . . . . . . 5E 67
BALHAM 1C 116
Balham Continental Mkt.
 SW12 . . . . 1D 117
 (off Shipka Rd.)
Balham Gro. SW12 . . . . 5C 102
Balham High Rd.
 SW12 . . . . 3C 116
 SW17 . . . . 3C 116
Balham Hill SW12 . . . . 5D 103
Balham Leisure Cen.
 . . . . 2D 117
Balham New Rd.
 SW12 . . . . 5D 103
Balham Pk. Rd.
 SW12 . . . . 1B 116
Balham Sta. Rd.
 SW12 . . . . 1D 117
Balin Ho. SE1 . . . . 3B 26
 (off Long La.)
Balkan Wlk. E1 . . . . 1D 79
Balladier Wlk. E14 . . . . 4D 67
Ballamore Rd.
 BR1: Brom 3C 124
Ballance Rd. E9 . . . . . . 3F 51

Ballantine St. SW18 . . . 2E 101
Ballantrae Ho. NW2 . . . 1B 44
Ballard Ho. SE10 . . . . . 2D 95
 (off Thames St.)
Ballards Rd. NW2 . . . . . 4C 28
Ballast Quay SE10 . . . . 1F 95
Ballater Rd. SW2 . . . . . 2A 104
Ball Ct. EC3 . . . . 3C 18
 (off Cornhill)
Ballina St. SE23 . . . . . . 5F 107
Ballin Ct. E14 . . . . 3E 81
 (off Stewart St.)
Ballingdon Rd.
 SW11 . . . . 4C 102
Balliol Rd. W10 . . . . . . 5E 57
Balloch Rd. SE6 . . . . . . 1F 123
Ballogie Av. NW10 . . . . 1A 42
Ballow Cl. SE5 . . . . 3A 92
Balls Pond Pl. N1 . . . . . 3F 49
Balls Pond Rd. N1 . . . . . 3F 49
Balman Ho. SE16 . . . . . 5F 79
 (off Rotherhithe New Rd.)
Balmer Rd. E3 . . . . 1B 66
Balmes Rd. N1 . . . . 5F 49
Balmoral Apartments
 W2 . . . . 4A 60
 (off Praed St.)
Balmoral Cl. SW15 . . . . 4F 99
Balmoral Ct. SE12 . . . . 4D 125
 SE16 . . . . 2F 79
 (off King & Queen Wharf)
 SE17 . . . . 1F 91
 (off Lytham St.)
 SE27 . . . . 4E 119
Balmoral Gro. N7 . . . . . 3B 48
Balmoral Ho. E14 . . . . . 4D 81
 (off Lanark Sq.)
 E16 . . . . 2D 83
 (off Keats Av.)
 W14 . . . . 5A 72
 (off Windsor Way)
Balmoral M. W12 . . . . . 4B 70
Balmoral Rd. E7 . . . . . . 1E 55
 E10 . . . . 4D 39
 NW2 . . . . 3D 43
Balmore Cl. E14 . . . . . . 5E 67
Balmore St. N19 . . . . . . 4D 33
Balmuir Gdns. SW15 . . 2E 99
Balnacraig Av. NW10 . . 1A 42
Balniel Ga. SW1 . . . . . . 1F 89
Balsam Ho. E14 . . . . . . 1D 81
 (off E. India Dock Rd.)
Baltic Apartments
 E16 . . . . 1C 82
 (off Western Gateway)
Baltic Ct. SE16 . . . . 3F 79
Baltic Ho. SE5 . . . . 5E 91
Baltic Pl. N1 . . . . 5A 50
Baltic St. E.
 EC1 . . . . 4F 9 (3E 63)
Baltic St. W.
 EC1 . . . . 4F 9 (3E 63)
Baltimore Ct. SW1 . . . . 5F 75
 (off Chapter St.)
Baltimore Ho. SE11 . . . 5C 76
 (off Hotspur St.)
Balvaird Pl. SW1 . . . . . 1F 89
Balvernie Gro.
 SW18 . . . . 5B 100

Balvernie M. SW18 . . . 5C **100**
Bamber Rd. SE15 . . . . . 4B **92**
Bamborough Gdns.
   W12 . . . . 3E **71**
Bamford Ct. *E15* 2D **53**
   (off Clays La.)
Bamford Rd.
   BR1: Brom 5E **123**
Bampton Rd. SE23 . . . 3F **121**
Banbury Ct. WC2 . . . . . 4D **15**
Banbury Ho. E9 . . . . . . 4F **51**
Banbury Rd. E9 . . . . . . 4F **51**
Banbury St. SW11 . . . . 5A **88**
Banchory Rd. SE3 . . . . 3D **97**
Bancroft Av. N2 . . . . . . 1A **32**
Bancroft Ct. *SW8* *3A* **90**
   (off Allen Edwards Dr.)
Bancroft Ho. *E1* *3E* **65**
   (off Cephas St.)
Bancroft Rd. E1 . . . . . . 2E **65**
Banfield Rd. SE15 . . . 1D **107**
Bangalore St.
   SW15 . . . . 1E **99**
Banim St. W6 . . . . 5D **71**
Banister Ho. E9 . . . . . . 2F **51**
   SW8 . . . . *4E* **89**
   (off Wadhurst Rd.)
   W10 . . . . *2A* **58**
   (off Bruckner St.)
Banister M. NW6 . . . . . 4D **45**
Banister Rd. W10 . . . . . 2F **57**
Bank, The N6 . . . . 3D **33**
Bank End
   SE1 . . . . 1A **26** (2E **77**)
Bankfoot Rd.
   BR1: Brom 4A **124**
Bankhurst Rd. SE6 . . . 5B **108**
Bank La. SW15 . . . . . . 3A **98**
Bank of England
   . . . . 3B **18** (5F **63**)
Bank of England Mus.
   . . . . 3C **18**
Banks Ho. *SE1* *5F* **25**
   (off Rockingham St.)
Bankside SE1 . . 5F **17** (1E **77**)
   (not continuous)
Bankside Art Gallery
   . . . . 5F **17** (1D **77**)
Bankside Way SE19 . . . 5A **120**
Bank St. E14 . . . . 2D **81**
Bankton Rd. SW2 . . . . 2C **104**
Bankwell Rd. SE13 . . . 2A **110**
Bannatyne's Health Club
   Grove Park 2D **125**
Banner Ct. *SE16* *5E* **79**
   (off Rotherhithe New Rd.)
Bannerman Ho. SW8 . . 2B **90**
Banner St.
   EC1 . . . . . . 4A **10** (3E **63**)
Banning St. SE10 . . . . 1A **96**
Bannister Cl. SW2 . . . . 1C **118**
Bannister Ho. *SE14* . . . *2F* **93**
   (off John Williams Cl.)
Banqueting House
   . . . . 2D **23** (2A **76**)
Banstead St. SE15 . . . 1E **107**
Banting Ho. NW2 . . . . . 5C **28**
Bantock Ho. *W10* *2A* **58**
   (off Third Av.)

Bantry Ho. *E1* *3F* **65**
   (off Ernest St.)
Bantry St. SE5 . . . . 3F **91**
Banyard Rd. SE16 . . . . 4D **79**
Baptist Gdns. NW5 . . . 3C **46**
Barandon M. *W11* *1F* **71**
   (off Grenfell Rd.)
Barandon Wlk. W11 . . . 1F **71**
Barbanel Ho. *E1* *3E* **65**
   (off Cephas St.)
Barbara Brosnan Ct.
   NW8 . . . . 1F **59**
Barbara Castle Cl.
   SW6 . . . . *2B* **86**
   (off Coomer Pl.)
Barbauld Rd. N16 . . . . 5A **36**
Barber Beaumont Ho.
   E1 . . . . *2F* **65**
   (off Bancroft Rd.)
Barbers All. E13 . . . . . 2D **69**
Barbers Rd. E15 . . . . . 1D **67**
Barbican Arts Cen.
   . . . . 5A **10** (4E **63**)
Barbican Cinema *5A* **10**
   (in Arts Cen.)
Barbican Theatre *5A* **10**
   (off Silk St.)
Barbican Trade Cen.
   EC1 . . . . *5A* **10**
   (off Beech St.)
Barb M. W6 . . . . 4E **71**
Barbon All. *EC2* *2E* **19**
   (off Houndsditch)
Barbon Cl.
   WC1 . . . . 5E **7** (4B **62**)
Barchard St. SW18 . . . 3D **101**
Barchester St. E14 . . . 4D **67**
Barclay Cl. SW6 . . . . . 3C **86**
Barclay Ho. *E9* *4E* **51**
   (off Well St.)
Barclay Path E17 . . . . 1E **39**
Barclay Rd. E11 . . . . . 3B **40**
   (not continuous)
   E13 . . . . 3E **69**
   E17 . . . . 1E **39**
   SW6 . . . . 3C **86**
Barcombe Av. SW2 . . . 2A **118**
Bardell Ho. *SE1* *3C* **78**
   (off Parkers Row)
Bardolph Rd. N7 . . . . . 1A **48**
Bard Rd. W10 . . . . 1F **71**
Bardsey Pl. *E1* *3E* **65**
   (off Mile End Rd.)
Bardsey Wlk. N1 . . . . . *3E* **49**
   (off Douglas Rd. Nth.)
Bardsley Ho. *SE10* . . . *2E* **95**
   (off Bardsley La.)
Bardsley La. SE10 . . . 2E **95**
Barents Ho. *E1* *3F* **65**
   (off White Horse La.)
Barfett St. W10 . . . . . . 3B **58**
Barfield Rd. E11 . . . . . 3B **40**
Barfleur La. SE8 . . . . . 5B **80**
Barford St. N1 . . . . 5C **48**
Barforth Rd. SE15 . . . 1D **107**
Barge Ho. St.
   SE1 . . . . . . 1C **24** (2C **76**)
Barge La. E3 . . . . 5A **52**
Bargery Rd. SE6 . . . . . 1D **123**

Bargrove Cres. SE6 . . . 2B **122**
Barham Ho. *SE17* *1A* **92**
   (off Kinglake St.)
Baring Cl. SE12 . . . . . 2C **124**
Baring Ct. *N1* *5A* **50**
   (off Baring St.)
Baring Ho. *E14* *5C* **66**
   (off Canton St.)
Baring Rd. SE12 . . . . . 5C **110**
Baring St. N1 . . . . 5F **49**
Barker Dr. NW1 . . . . . . 4E **47**
Barker M. SW4 . . . . . . 2D **103**
Barkers Arc. W8 . . . . . 3D **73**
Barker St. SW10 . . . . . 2E **87**
Barker Wlk. SW16 . . . 3F **117**
Barkham Ter. SE1 . . . . 5C **24**
Barking Rd. E6 . . . . . . 1E **69**
   E13 . . . . 1E **69**
   E16 . . . . 4B **68**
Bark Pl. W2 . . . . 1D **73**
Barkston Gdns. SW5 . . 5D **73**
Barkway Ct. *N4* *4E* **35**
   (off Queen's Dr.)
Barkwith Ho. *SE14* . . . *2F* **93**
   (off Cold Blow La.)
Barkworth Rd. SE16 . . 1D **93**
Barlborough St. SE14 . . 3F **93**
Barlby Gdns. W10 . . . . 3F **57**
Barlby Rd. W10 . . . . . . 4E **57**
Barleycorn Way E14 . . . 1B **80**
Barley Mow Pas. EC1 . . 5E **9**
   W4 . . . . 1A **84**
Barley Shotts Bus. Pk.
   W10 . . . . 4B **58**
Barling NW1 . . . . *3D* **47**
   (off Castlehaven Rd.)
Barlings Ho. *SE4* *2F* **107**
   (off Frendsbury Rd.)
Barlow Dr. SE18 . . . . . 4F **97**
Barlow Ho. *N1* *1B* **10**
   (off Fairbank Est.)
   SE16 . . . . *5D* **79**
   (off Rennie Est.)
   W11 . . . . *1A* **72**
   (off Walmer Rd.)
Barlow Pl.
   W1 . . . . 5E **13** (1D **75**)
Barlow Rd. NW6 . . . . . 3B **44**
Barlow St. SE17 . . . . . 5F **77**
Barmeston Rd. SE6 . . . 2D **123**
Barmouth Rd.
   SW18 . . . . 4E **101**
Barnabas Rd. E9 . . . . . 2F **51**
Barnaby Ct. *SE16* *3C* **78**
   (off Scott Lidgett Cres.)
Barnaby Pl. *SW7* *5F* **73**
   (off Old Brompton Rd.)
Barnard Gro. E15 . . . . 4B **54**
Barnard Ho. *E2* *2D* **65**
   (off Ellsworth St.)
Barnard Lodge *W9* . . . *4C* **58**
   (off Admiral Wlk.)
Barnard M. SW11 . . . . 2A **102**
Barnardo Gdns. E1 . . . 1F **79**
Barnardo St. E1 . . . . . 5F **65**
Barnard Rd. SW11 . . . 2A **102**
Barnards Ho. *SE16* . . . *3B* **80**
   (off Wyatt Cl.)
Barnard's Inn EC1 . . . . 1B **16**

Barnbrough NW1 . . . . . . 5E **47**
  (off Camden St.)
Barnby Sq. E15. . . . . 5A **54**
Barnby St. E15 . . . . 5A **54**
  NW1. . . . . 1A **6** (1E **61**)
Barn Cl. NW5 . . . . 2F **47**
  (off Torriano Av.)
Barn Elms Athletic Track
. . . . 4D **85**
Barn Elms Pk. SW15 . . 1F **99**
BARNES 5B **84**
Barnes Av. SW13 . . . . . 3C **84**
Barnes Cl. E12 . . . . 1F **55**
Barnes Ct. E16 . . . . 4E **69**
  N1. . . . . 4C **48**
Barnes High St.
  SW13 . . . . 5B **84**
Barnes Ho. E2. . . . . 1E **65**
  (off Wadeson St.)
  SE14 . . . . 2F **93**
  (off John Williams Cl.)
Barnes St. E14 . . . . 5A **66**
Barnes Ter. SE8 . . . . . . 1B **94**
Barnet Gro. E2 . . . . 2C **64**
Barnett St. E1. . . . . 5D **65**
Barney Cl. SE7 . . . . 1E **97**
Barn Fld. NW3 . . . . 2B **46**
Barnfield Cl. N4 . . . . 2A **34**
  SW17 . . . . 3F **115**
Barnfield Pl. E14 . . . . . . 5C **80**
Barnham St.
  SE1 . . . . 3E **27** (3A **78**)
BARNSBURY 4B **48**
Barnsbury Est. N1 . . . . 5B **48**
  (not continuous)
Barnsbury Gro. N7 . . . . 4B **48**
Barnsbury Ho. SW4 . . . 4F **103**
Barnsbury Pk. N1 . . . . . 4C **48**
Barnsbury Rd. N1. . . . . 1C **62**
Barnsbury Sq. N1 . . . . . 4C **48**
Barnsbury St. N1. . . . . . 4C **48**
Barnsbury Ter. N1. . . . . 4B **48**
Barnsdale Av. E14. . . . . 5D **81**
Barnsdale Rd. W9 . . . . 3B **58**
Barnsley St. E1 . . . . 3D **65**
Barnstable La.
  SE13. . . . . 2E **109**
Barnstaple Ho. SE10 . . 3D **95**
  (off Devonshire Dr.)
  SE12 . . . . 3B **110**
  (off Taunton Rd.)
Barnston Wlk. N1 . . . . . . 5E **49**
  (off Popham St.)
Barn St. N16 . . . . 4A **36**
Barnwell Ho. SE5. . . . . . 4A **92**
  (off St Giles Rd.)
Barnwell Rd. SW2 . . . . 3C **104**
Barnwood Cl. W9 . . . . . 3D **59**
Baroness Rd.
  E2. . . . . 1F **11** (2B **64**)
Baronsclere Ct. N6 . . . . 2E **33**
BARONS COURT 1A **86**
Baron's Ct. Rd. W14 . . 1A **86**
Barons Court Theatre
. . . . 1A **86**
  (off Comeragh Rd.)
Barons Keep W14 . . . . 1A **86**
Baronsmead Rd.
  SW13 . . . . 4C **84**

Baron's Pl.
  SE1. . . . . 4C **24** (3C **76**)
Baron St. N1 . . . . 1C **62**
Baron Wlk. E16 . . . . 4B **68**
Barque M. SE8 . . . . 2C **94**
Barratt Ho. N1 . . . . 4D **49**
  (off Sable St.)
Barratt Ind. Pk. E3 . . . . 3E **67**
Barrett Ho. NW6 . . . . . . 5C **44**
  SW9 . . . . 1B **104**
  (off Benedict Rd.)
Barrett Ho. SE17 . . . . . . 1E **91**
  (off Browning St.)
Barrett's Gro. N16 . . . . 2A **50**
Barrett St.
  W1. . . . . 3C **12** (5C **60**)
Barrhill Rd. SW2 . . . . . 2A **118**
Barriedale SE14 . . . . . . 5A **94**
Barrie Est. W2 . . . . 1F **73**
Barrie Ho. W2 . . . . 1F **73**
  (off Lancaster Ga.)
Barrier App. SE7 . . . . . . 4F **83**
Barrier Point Rd. E16. . . 2E **83**
Barringer Sq.
  SW17 . . . . 4C **116**
Barrington Cl. NW5 . . . 2C **46**
Barrington Ct. SW4 . . . 5A **90**
Barrington Rd. SW9. . . 1D **105**
Barrow Ct. SE6. . . . . . . 1B **124**
  (off Cumberland Pl.)
Barrowgate Rd. W4 . . . 1A **84**
Barrow Hill Est. NW8 . . 1A **60**
  (off Barrow Hill Rd.)
Barrow Hill Rd. NW8 . . 1A **60**
Barrow Rd. SW16. . . . . 5F **117**
Barrow Store Ct. SE1. . 5D **27**
  (off Decima St.)
Barry Av. N15. . . . . 1B **36**
Barry Ho. SE16 . . . . 5D **79**
  (off Rennie Est.)
Barry Rd. SE22. . . . . . . 4C **106**
Barset Rd. SE15. . . . . . 1E **93**
  (not continuous)
Barston Rd. SE27. . . . . 3E **119**
Barstow Cres. SW2 . . . 1B **118**
Barter St.
  WC1 . . . . 1E **15** (4A **62**)
Bartholomew Cl.
  EC1. . . . . 1E **17** (4E **63**)
  (not continuous)
  SW18 . . . . 2E **101**
Bartholomew Ct. E14. . . 1F **81**
  (off Newport Av.)
  EC1 . . . . 3A **10**
  (off Old St.)
Bartholomew La.
  EC2 . . . . 3C **18** (5F **63**)
Bartholomew Pl. EC1 . . 1F **17**
Bartholomew Rd.
  NW5 . . . . 3E **47**
Bartholomew Sq. E1 . . 3D **65**
  EC1 . . . . 3A **10** (3E **63**)
Bartholomew Vs.
  NW5 . . . . 3E **47**
Bartle Rd. W11 . . . . 5A **58**
Bartlett Cl. E14. . . . . . . 5C **66**
Bartlett Ct.
  EC4 . . . . 2C **16** (5C **62**)

Bartletts Pas. EC4 . . . . . 2C **16**
  (off Fetter La.)
Bartok Ho. W11 . . . . 2B **72**
  (off Lansdowne Wlk.)
Barton Cl. E9 . . . . 2E **51**
  SE15. . . . . 1D **107**
Barton Ct. W14. . . . . 1A **86**
  (off Baron's Ct. Rd.)
Barton Ho. N1 . . . . 4D **49**
  (off Sable St.)
  SW6 . . . . 1D **101**
  (off Wandsworth Bri. Rd.)
Barton Rd. W14 . . . . . . 1A **86**
Barton St.
  SW1. . . . . . . 5D **23** (4A **76**)
Bartonway NW8 . . . . 5F **45**
  (off Queen's Ter.)
Bartram Rd. SE4 . . . . . 3A **108**
Bartrip St. E9 . . . . 3B **52**
Barville Cl. SE4 . . . . . . 2A **108**
Barwell Ho. E2. . . . . 3C **64**
  (off Menotti St.)
Barwick Rd. E7 . . . . 1D **55**
Bascombe St.
  SW2 . . . . 4C **104**
Baseline Bus. Studios
  W11. . . . . 1F **71**
  (off Barandon Wlk.)
Basevi Way SE8. . . . . . . 2D **95**
Bashley Rd. NW10. . . . 3A **56**
Basildon Ct. W1. . . . . 5C **4**
  (off Devonshire Rd.)
Basil Gdns. SE27 . . . . 5E **119**
Basil Ho. SW8 . . . . 3A **90**
  (off Wyvil Rd.)
Basil Mans. SW3 . . . . . 4A **20**
  (off Basil St.)
Basil St.
  SW3. . . . . 5A **20** (4B **74**)
Basin App. E14. . . . . . . 5A **66**
Basing Ct. SE15. . . . . . 4B **92**
Basingdon Way SE5 . . 2F **105**
Basinghall Av.
  EC2. . . . . 2B **18** (5F **63**)
Basinghall St.
  EC2. . . . . 2B **18** (5F **63**)
Basing Hill NW11. . . . . 3B **30**
Basing Ho. Yd.
  E2. . . . . 1E **11** (2A **64**)
Basing Pl. E2 . . . 1E **11** (2A **64**)
Basing St. W11 . . . . 5B **58**
Basire St. N1 . . . . 5E **49**
Baskerville Gdns.
  NW10 . . . . 1A **42**
Baskerville Rd.
  SW18 . . . . 5A **102**
Basket Gdns. SE9 . . . . 3F **111**
Baslow Wlk. E5 . . . . 1E **51**
Basnett Rd. SW11 . . . . 1C **102**
Basque Ct. SE16. . . . . . . 3F **79**
  (off Garter Way)
Bassano St. SE22. . . . . 3B **106**
Bassein Pk. Rd.
  W12 . . . . 3B **70**
Bassett Rd. E7 . . . . 1F **55**
  W10. . . . . 5F **57**
Bassett St. NW5 . . . . . 3C **46**
Bassingbourn Ho. N1. . 4C **48**
  (off The Sutton Est.)

Bassingham Rd.
SW18 . . . . 5E **101**
Bassishaw Highwalk
EC2 . . . . 1A **18**
Basswood Cl. SE15 . . 1D **107**
Basterfield Ho. *EC1* *4F 9*
(off Golden La. Est.)
Bastion Highwalk
EC2 . . . . 1F **17**
Bastion Ho. *EC2* *1A 18*
(off London Wall)
Bastwick St.
EC1 . . . . 3F **9** (3E **63**)
Basuto Rd. SW6 . . . . . 4C **86**
Batavia Cl. *SE14* *3A 94*
(off Batavia Rd.)
Batavia M. SE14 . . . . . 3A **94**
Batavia Rd. SE14 . . . . . 3A **94**
Batchelor St. N1 . . . . . 5C **48**
Bateman Ho. *SE17* *2D 91*
(off Otto St.)
Bateman's Bldgs.
W1 . . . . 3B **14**
Bateman's Row
EC2 . . . . 3E **11** (3A **64**)
Bateman St.
W1 . . . . 3B **14** (5F **61**)
Bates Point *E13* *5C 54*
(off Pelly Rd.)
Bate St. E14 . . . . 1B **80**
Bath Cl. SE15 . . . . 3D **93**
Bath Ct. EC1 . . . . 4B **8**
SE26 . . . . *3C 120*
(off Droitwich Cl.)
Bathgate Rd. SW19 . . . 3F **113**
Bath Gro. *E2* *1C 64*
(off Horatio St.)
Bath Ho. *E2* *3C 64*
(off Ramsey St.)
SE1 . . . . *5A 26*
(off Bath Ter.)
Bath Pl. EC2 . . . 2D **11** (2A **64**)
W6 . . . . *1E 85*
(off Peabody Est.)
Bath Rd. E7 . . . . 3F **55**
W4 . . . . 5A **70**
Baths App. SW6 . . . . . 3B **86**
Bath St. EC1 . . 2A **10** (2E **63**)
Bath Ter. SE1 . . 5F **25** (4E **77**)
Bathurst Gdns.
NW10 . . . . 1D **57**
Bathurst Ho. *W12* *1D 71*
(off White City Est.)
Bathurst M. W2 . . . . . . 5F **59**
Bathurst St. W2 . . . . . . 1F **73**
Batley Pl. N16 . . . . 5B **36**
Batley Rd. N16 . . . . 5B **36**
Batman Cl. W12 . . . . . . 2D **71**
Batoum Gdns. W6 . . . . . 4E **71**
Batson Ho. *E1* *5C 64*
(off Fairclough St.)
Batson St. W12 . . . . . . 3C **70**
Battenberg Wlk.
SE19 . . . . 5A **120**
Batten Cotts. *E14* *4A 66*
(off Maroon St.)
Batten Ho. SW4 . . . . . 3E **103**
W10 . . . . *2A 58*
(off Third Av.)

Batten St. SW11 . . . . . 1A **102**
Battersby Rd. SE6 . . . . 2F **123**
BATTERSEA 4C **88**
Battersea Bri. SW11 . . . 3B **87**
Battersea Bri. Rd.
SW11 . . . . 3A **88**
Battersea Bus. Cen.
SW11 . . . . 1C **102**
Battersea Church Rd.
SW11 . . . . 4F **87**
Battersea High St.
SW11 . . . . 4F **87**
(not continuous)
Battersea Pk. 3B **88**
Battersea Pk. Children's Zoo
. . . . 3C **88**
Battersea Pk. Equestrian Cen.
. . . . 5A **88**
Battersea Pk. Rd.
SW8 . . . . 5A **88**
SW11 . . . . 5A **88**
Battersea Ri. SW11 . . . . 3A **102**
Battersea Sports Cen.
. . . . 1F **101**
Battersea Sq.
SW11 . . . . 4F **87**
Battishill St. N1 . . . . . . 4D **49**
Battlebridge Ct. *N1* . . . *1A 62*
(off Wharfdale Rd.)
Battle Bri. La.
SE1 . . . . 2D **27** (2A **78**)
Battle Bri. Rd. NW1 . . . 1A **62**
Battle Cl. SW19 . . . . . . 5E **115**
Battledean Rd. N5 . . . . 2D **49**
Battle Ho. *SE15* *2C 92*
(off Haymerle Rd.)
Batty St. E1 . . . . 5C **64**
Baudwin Rd. SE6 . . . . . 2A **124**
Baulk, The SW18 . . . . . 5C **100**
Bavaria Rd. N19 . . . . . . 4A **34**
(not continuous)
Bavent Rd. SE5 . . . . . . 5E **91**
Bawdale Rd. SE22 . . . . 3B **106**
Bawtree Rd. SE14 . . . . . 3A **94**
Baxendale St. E2 . . . . . 2C **64**
Baxter Rd. E16 . . . . 5E **69**
N1 . . . . 3F **49**
Bay Cl. *E1* *3F 65*
(off Frimley Way)
Bayer Ho. *EC1* *4F 9*
(off Golden La. Est.)
Bayes Cl. SE26 . . . . . . 5E **121**
Bayes Ct. *NW3* *4B 46*
(off Primrose Hill Rd.)
Bayfield Ho. *SE4* *2F 107*
(off Coston Wlk.)
Bayfield Rd. SE9 . . . . . 2F **111**
Bayford M. *E8* *4D 51*
(off Bayford St.)
Bayford Rd. NW10 . . . . 2F **57**
Bayford St. E8 . . . . 4D **51**
Bayford St. Bus. Cen.
E8 . . . . *4D 51*
(off Sidworth St.)
Bayham Pl. NW1 . . . . . 5E **47**
Bayham Rd. W4 . . . . . . 4A **70**
Bayham St. NW1 . . . . . 5E **47**
Bayley St.
WC1 . . . . 1B **14** (4F **61**)

Baylis Rd.
SE1 . . . . . . 4B **24** (3C **76**)
Baynes M. NW3 . . . . . . 3F **45**
Baynes St. NW1 . . . . . . 4E **47**
Bayonne Rd. W6 . . . . . . 2A **86**
Bayston Rd. N16 . . . . . . 5B **36**
BAYSWATER 1E **73**
Bayswater Rd. W2 . . . . . 1D **73**
Baythorne St. E3 . . . . . 4B **66**
Bayton Ct. *E8* *4C 50*
(off Lansdowne Dr.)
Baytree Ct. SW2 . . . . . 2B **104**
Baytree Rd. SW2 . . . . . 2B **104**
Bazalgette Ho. *NW8* . . . *3F 59*
(off Orchardson St.)
Bazeley Ho. SE1 . . . . . . *4D 25*
(off Library St.)
Bazely St. E14 . . . . 1E **81**
BBC Broadcasting House
. . . . 1E **13** (4D **61**)
BBC Television Cen. . . . 1E **71**
BBC Worldwide 5E **57**
(off Wood La.)
Beacham Cl. SE7 . . . . . 1F **97**
Beachborough Rd.
BR1: Brom 4E **123**
Beachcroft Rd. E11 . . . . 5A **40**
Beachcroft Way N19 . . . 3F **33**
Beach Ho. *SW5* *1C 86*
(off Philbeach Gdns.)
Beachy Rd. E3 . . . . 4C **52**
Bacon Bingo Hall 1F **43**
Beacon Ga. SE14 . . . . . 1F **107**
Beacon Hill N7 . . . . 2A **48**
Beacon Ho. *E14* *1D 95*
(off Burrells Wharf Sq.)
SE5 . . . . *3A 92*
(off Southampton Way)
Beacon Rd. SE13 . . . . . 4F **109**
Beaconsfield Cl. SE3 . . . 2C **96**
Beaconsfield Rd.
E10 . . . . 4E **39**
E16 . . . . 3B **68**
E17 . . . . 1B **38**
NW10 . . . . 3B **42**
SE3 . . . . 3B **96**
SE9 . . . . 2F **125**
SE17 . . . . 1F **91**
Beaconsfield Ter. Rd.
W14 . . . . 4A **72**
Beaconsfield Wlk.
SW6 . . . . 4B **86**
Beacontree Rd. E11 . . . 3B **40**
Beadman Pl. SE27 . . . . 4D **119**
Beadman St. SE27 . . . . 4D **119**
Beadnell Rd. SE23 . . . . 1F **121**
Beadon Rd. W6 . . . . . . 5E **71**
Beak St. W1 . . . 4A **14** (1E **75**)
Beale Pl. E3 . . . . 1B **66**
Beale Rd. E3 . . . . 5B **52**
Beames Rd. NW10 . . . . 5A **42**
Beaminster Ho.
SW8 . . . . *3B 90*
(off Dorset Rd.)
Beamish Ho. *SE16* *5D 79*
(off Rennie Est.)
Beanacre Cl. SE9 . . . . . 3B **52**
Bear All.
EC4 . . . . . . 2D **17** (5D **63**)

Beardell St. SE19. . . . . . 5B 120
Beardsfield E13 . . . . 1C 68
Bear Gdns.
  SE1. . . . . 1F 25 (2E 77)
Bear La. SE1 . . 1E 25 (2D 77)
Bearstead Ri.
  SE4 . . . . 3B 108
Bear St. WC2 . . . 4C 14 (1F 75)
Beaton Cl. SE15 . . . . . . 4B 92
Beatrice Cl. E13 . . . . . . 3C 68
Beatrice Ho. W6 . . . . . . 1E 85
  (off Queen Caroline St.)
Beatrice Pl. W8 . . . . 4D 73
Beatrice Rd. E17 . . . . . . 1C 38
  N4. . . . . 2C 34
  SE1 . . . . 5C 78
Beatrix Ho. SW5 . . . . . . 1D 87
  (off Old Brompton Rd.)
Beatson Wlk. SE16. . . . . 2A 80
  (not continuous)
Beattie Ho. SW8. . . . . . . 4E 89
Beatty Ho. E14 . . . . 3C 80
  (off Admirals Way)
  NW1 . . . . .3F 5
  (off Drummond St.)
  SW1 . . . . 2D 89
  (off Dolphin Sq.)
Beatty Rd. N16. . . . . 1A 50
Beatty St. NW1. . . . . 1E 61
Beauchamp Pl.
  SW3 . . . . 4A 74
Beauchamp Rd. E7 . . . . 4D 55
  SW11. . . . . 2A 102
Beauchamp St.
  EC1 . . . . 1B 16 (4C 62)
Beauchamp Ter.
  SW15 . . . . 1D 99
Beauclerc Rd. W6 . . . . . 4D 71
Beauclerk Ho.
  SW16 . . . . 3A 118
Beaufort Cl. SW15 . . . . . 5D 99
Beaufort Ct. E14 . . . . . . 3C 80
  (off Admirals Way)
  SW6 . . . . 2C 86
Beaufort Gdns. NW4 . . . 1E 29
  SW3 . . . . 4A 74
Beaufort Ho. E16 . . . . . . 2D 83
  (off Fairfax M.)
  SW1 . . . . .1F 89
  (off Aylesford St.)
  SW1 . . . . 1D 89
  (off Sutherland Row)
  SW3 . . . . 2F 87
  (off Beaufort St.)
Beaufort Mans.
  SW10 . . . . 2F 87
Beaufort M. SW6 . . . . . . 2B 86
Beaufort St. SW3 . . . . . . 2F 87
Beaufort Ter. E14 . . . . . . 1E 95
  (off Ferry St.)
Beaufoy Ho. SE27 . . . . . 3D 119
  SW8 . . . . 3B 90
  (off Rita Rd.)
Beaufoy Wlk. SE11. . . . . 5B 76
Beaulieu Av. E16 . . . . . . 2D 83
  SE26. . . . . 4D 121
Beaulieu Cl. SE5. . . . . . 1F 105
Beaulieu Lodge E14 . . . . 4F 81
  (off Schooner Cl.)

Beaumanor Mans.
  W2. . . . . 1D 73
  (off Queensway)
Beaumaris Grn. NW9. . . 1A 28
Beaumont W14. . . . . 5B 72
  (off Kensington Village)
Beaumont Av. W14 . . . . 1B 86
Beaumont Bldgs.
  WC2 . . . . 3E 15
  (off Martlett Ct.)
Beaumont Ct. E1 . . . . . . 2A 66
  E5. . . . . 5D 37
  NW1 . . . . 5F 47
  W1 . . . . .5C 4
  (off Beaumont St.)
Beaumont Cres. W14. . . 1B 86
Beaumont Gdns.
  NW3 . . . . 5C 30
Beaumont Gro. E1 . . . . . 3F 65
Beaumont Ho. E10. . . . . 2D 39
  (off Skelton's La.)
  E15. . . . . 5B 54
  (off John St.)
  W9 . . . . 2B 58
  (off Denholme Rd.)
Beaumont Lodge E8. . . . 3C 50
  (off Greenwood Rd.)
Beaumont M.
  W1. . . . . 5C 4 (4C 60)
Beaumont Pl.
  W1. . . . . 3A 6 (3E 61)
Beaumont Ri. N19 . . . . . 3F 33
Beaumont Rd. E10. . . . . 2D 39
  (not continuous)
  E13. . . . . 2D 69
  SW19 . . . . 5A 100
Beaumont Sq. E1 . . . . . 4F 65
Beaumont St.
  W1. . . . . 5C 4 (4C 60)
Beaumont Ter. SE13. . . . 5A 110
  (off Wellmeadow Rd.)
Beaumont Wlk. NW3 . . . 4B 46
Beauvale NW1 . . . . 4C 46
  (off Ferdinand St.)
Beauval Rd. SE22 . . . . . 4B 106
Beaux Arts Bldg., The
  N7. . . . . 5A 34
Beavor Gro. W6 . . . . 1C 84
  (off Beavor La.)
Beavor La. W6 . . . . 1C 84
Beccles St. E14 . . . . 5B 66
Bechervaise Ct. E10 . . . 3D 39
  (off Leyton Grange Est.)
Bechtel Ho. W6 . . . . 5F 71
  (off Hammersmith Rd.)
Beck Cl. SE13 . . . . 4D 95
Beckenham Bus. Cen.
  BR3: Beck. 5A 122
Beckenham Hill Est.
  BR3: Beck. 5D 123
Beckenham Hill Rd.
  BR3: Beck. 5D 123
  SE6. . . . . 5D 123
Beckers, The N16. . . . . . 1C 50
Becket Ho. E16 . . . . 2D 83
  (off Constable Av.)
Becket St.
  SE1. . . . . 5B 26 (4F 77)

Beckett Cl. NW10. . . . . . 3A 42
  SW16 . . . . 2F 117
Beckett Ho. E1 . . . . 4E 65
  (off Jubilee St.)
  SW9 . . . . 5A 90
Beckfoot NW1. . . . . 1A 6
  (off Ampthill Est.)
Beckford Cl. W14 . . . . . . 5B 72
Beckford Ho. N16. . . . . . 2A 50
Beckford Pl. SE17 . . . . . 1E 91
Beckham Ho. SE11 . . . . 5B 76
Becklow Gdns. W12. . . . 3C 70
  (off Becklow Rd.)
Becklow M. W12 . . . . . . 3C 70
  (off Becklow Rd.)
Becklow Rd. W12. . . . . . 3B 70
  (not continuous)
Beck Rd. E8 . . . . 5D 51
Beckton Rd. E16. . . . . . . 4B 68
Beckway St. SE17 . . . . . 5A 78
  (not continuous)
Beckwith Ho. E2. . . . . . . 1D 65
  (off Wadeson St.)
Beckwith Rd. SE24. . . . . 3F 105
Beclands Rd. SW17. . . . 5C 116
Becmead Av. SW16 . . . . 4F 117
Becondale Rd.
  SE19. . . . . 5A 120
Becquerel Ct. SE10 . . . . 4B 82
Bective Pl. SW15. . . . . . 2B 100
Bective Rd. E7. . . . . 1C 54
  SW15 . . . . 2B 100
Bedale St.
  SE1. . . . . 2B 26 (2F 77)
Beddalls Farm Ct. E6. . . 4F 69
Bedefield
  WC1. . . . . 2E 7 (2A 62)
Bede Ho. SE4. . . . . 4B 94
  (off Clare Rd.)
Bedford Av.
  WC1. . . . . 1C 14 (4F 61)
Bedfordbury
  WC2. . . . . 4D 15 (1A 76)
Bedford Cl. W4 . . . . 2A 84
Bedford Cnr. W4. . . . . . . 5A 70
  (off South Pde.)
Bedford Ct.
  WC2. . . . . 5D 15 (1A 76)
  (not continuous)
Bedford Ct. Mans.
  WC1. . . . . 1C 14
Bedford Gdns. W8 . . . . . 2C 72
Bedford Gdns. Ho.
  W8 . . . . 2C 72
  (off Bedford Gdns.)
Bedford Hill SW12. . . . . 1D 117
  SW16 . . . . 1D 117
Bedford Ho. SW4. . . . . . 2A 104
  (off Solon New Rd. Est.)
Bedford M. SE6. . . . . . . 2D 123
BEDFORD PARK 4A 70
Bedford Pk. Cnr. W4 . . . 5A 70
Bedford Pk. Mans.
  W4 . . . . 5A 70
Bedford Pas. SW6 . . . . . 3A 86
  (off Dawes Rd.)
  W1 . . . . 5A 6 (4E 61)
Bedford Pl.
  WC1. . . . . 5D 7 (4A 62)

Bedford Rd. N8 . . . . 1F 33
SW4 . . . . 2A 104
W4 . . . . 4A 70
Bedford Row
WC1 . . . . 5A 8 (4B 62)
Bedford Sq.
WC1 . . . . 1C 14 (4F 61)
Bedford St.
WC2 . . . . 4D 15 (1A 76)
Bedford Ter. SW2 . . . . . 3A 104
Bedford Way
WC1 . . . . 4C 6 (3F 61)
Bedgebury Gdns.
SW19 . . . . 2A 114
Bedgebury Rd. SE9 . . . . 2F 111
Bedivere Rd.
BR1: Brom 3C 124
Bedlam M. SE11 . . . . 5C 76
(off Walnut Tree Wlk.)
Bedmond Ho. SW3 . . . . 1A 88
(off Ixworth Pl.)
Bedser Cl. SE11 . . . . . . 2B 90
Bedwell Ho. SW9 . . . . . 5C 90
Beeby Rd. E16 . . . . 4D 69
Beech Av. W3 . . . . 2A 70
Beech Cl. SE8 . . . . 2C 94
SW15 . . . . 5C 98
SW19 . . . . 5E 113
Beech Ct. W9 . . . . 4C 58
(off Elmfield Way)
Beech Cres. Ct. N5 . . . . 1D 49
Beechcroft Av. NW11 . . . 2B 30
Beechcroft Cl.
SW16 . . . . 5B 118
Beechcroft Ct. NW11 . . . 2B 30
(off Beechcroft Av.)
Beechcroft Rd.
SW17 . . . . 2A 116
Beechdale Rd. SW2 . . . . 4B 104
Beechdene SE15 . . . . 4D 93
(off Carlton Gro.)
Beechen Pl. SE23 . . . . 2F 121
Beeches Rd. SW17 . . . . 3A 116
Beechey Ho. E1 . . . . . . 2D 79
(off Watts St.)
Beechfield Rd. N4 . . . . . 1E 35
SE6 . . . . 1B 122
Beech Gdns. EC2 . . . . . 5F 9
(off Beech St.)
Beech Ho. SE16 . . . . . . 3E 79
(off Ainsty Est.)
Beechmont Cl.
BR1: Brom 5A 124
Beechmore Rd.
SW11 . . . . 4B 88
Beecholme Est. E5 . . . . 5D 37
Beech St. EC2 . . . 5F 9 (4E 63)
Beech Tree Cl. N1 . . . . . 4C 48
Beechwood Cl. W4 . . . . 2A 84
Beechwood Gro. W3 . . . 1A 70
Beechwood Ho. E2 . . . . 1C 64
(off Teale St.)
Beechwood Rd. E8 . . . . 3B 50
Beechwoods Ct.
SE19 . . . . 5B 120
Beechworth NW6 . . . . . 4A 44
Beechworth Cl. NW3 . . . 4C 30
Beecroft La. SE4 . . . . . 3A 108
Beecroft M. SE4 . . . . . 3A 108

Beecroft Rd. SE4 . . . . 3A 108
Beehive Cl. E8 . . . . 4B 50
Beehive Pl. SW9 . . . . . 1C 104
Beemans Row
SW18 . . . . 2E 115
Bee Pas. EC3 . . . . 3D 19
(off Lime St.)
Beeston Cl. E8 . . . . 2C 50
Beeston Ho. SE1 . . . . 5B 26
(off Burbage Cl.)
Beeston Pl.
SW1 . . . . 5E 21 (4D 75)
Beethoven St. W10 . . . . 2A 58
Begbie Rd. SE3 . . . . 4E 97
Begonia Wlk. W12 . . . . 5B 56
Beira St. SW12 . . . . . . 5D 103
Bekesbourne St. E14 . . 5A 66
Beldanes Lodge
NW10 . . . . 4C 42
Belfast Rd. N16 . . . . 4B 36
Belfont Wlk. N7 . . . . 1A 48
(not continuous)
Belford Ho. E8 . . . . 5B 50
Belfort Rd. SE15 . . . . . . 5E 93
Belfry Cl. SE16 . . . . 1D 93
Belfry Rd. E12 . . . . 4F 41
Belgrade Rd. N16 . . . . . 1A 50
Belgrave Ct. E2 . . . . . . 1D 65
(off Temple St.)
E13 . . . . 3E 69
E14 . . . . 1B 80
(off Westferry Cir.)
SW8 . . . . 3E 89
(off Ascalon St.)
Belgrave Gdns. NW8 . . . 5D 45
Belgrave Hgts. E11 . . . . 3C 40
Belgrave Ho. SW9 . . . . . 3C 90
Belgrave Mans. NW8 . . 5D 45
(off Belgrave Gdns.)
Belgrave M. Nth.
SW1 . . . . 4B 20 (3C 74)
Belgrave M. Sth.
SW1 . . . . 5C 20 (4C 74)
Belgrave M. W. SW1 . . 5B 20
Belgrave Pl.
SW1 . . . . 5C 20 (4C 74)
Belgrave Rd. E10 . . . . . . 3E 39
E11 . . . . 4C 40
E13 . . . . 3E 69
E17 . . . . 1C 38
SW1 . . . . 5D 75
SW13 . . . . 3B 84
Belgrave Sq.
SW1 . . . . 5B 20 (4C 74)
Belgrave St. E1 . . . . 1F 65
Belgrave Yd. SW1 . . . . . 5D 21
BELGRAVIA 4C 74
Belgravia Ct. SW1 . . . . 4D 75
(off Ebury St.)
Belgravia Gdns.
BR1: Brom 5A 124
Belgravia Ho. SW1 . . . 5B 20
(off Halkin Pl.)
Belgravia Workshops
N19 . . . . 4A 34
(off Marlborough Rd.)
Belgrove St.
WC1 . . . . 1E 7 (2A 62)

Belham Wlk. SE5 . . . . . 4F 91
Belinda Rd. SW9 . . . . . 1D 105
Belitha Vs. N1 . . . . 4B 48
Bella Best Ho. SW1 . . . 1D 89
(off Westmoreland Ter.)
Bellamy Cl. E14 . . . . . . 3C 80
W14 . . . . 1B 86
Bellamy Ho. SW17 . . . . 4F 115
Bellamy's Ct. SE16 . . . 2F 79
(off Abbotsbade Rd.)
Bellamy St. SW12 . . . . 5D 103
Bellasis Av. SW2 . . . . . 2A 118
Bell Dr. SW18 . . . . 5A 100
Bellefields Rd.
SW9 . . . . 1B 104
Bellenden Rd. SE15 . . . 4B 92
Belleville Rd.
SW11 . . . . 3A 102
Bellevue Pde.
SW17 . . . . 1B 116
Bellevue Pl. E1 . . . . 3E 65
Bellevue Rd. SW13 . . . . 5C 84
SW17 . . . . 1A 116
Bellew St. SW17 . . . . . 3E 115
Bellfield Cl. SE3 . . . . . . 3C 96
Bellflower Cl. E6 . . . . . . 4F 69
Bell Gdns. E10 . . . . . . 3C 38
(off Church Rd.)
Bellgate M. NW5 . . . . . 1D 47
BELL GREEN 4A 122
Bell Grn. SE26 . . . . 4B 122
Bell Grn. La.
SE26 . . . . 5B 122
Bell Ho. SE10 . . . . 2E 95
(off Haddo St.)
Bellina M. NW5 . . . . . . 1D 47
BELLINGHAM 3C 122
Bellingham Grn.
SE6 . . . . 3C 122
Bellingham Rd.
SE6 . . . . 3D 123
Bellingham Trad. Est.
SE6 . . . . 3D 123
Bell Inn Yd.
EC3 . . . . 3C 18 (5F 63)
Bell La. E1 . . . . 1F 19 (4B 64)
E16 . . . . 2B 82
Bellmaker Ct. E3 . . . . . 4C 66
Bell Mdw. SE19 . . . . . . 5A 120
Bell Moor NW3 . . . . . . 5E 31
(off E. Heath Rd.)
Bello Cl. SE24 . . . . 5D 105
Bellot Gdns. SE10 . . . . 1A 96
(off Bellot St.)
Bellot St. SE10 . . . . 1A 96
Bells All. SW6 . . . . 5C 86
Bellsize Ct. NW3 . . . . . . 2F 45
Bell St. NW1 . . . . 4A 60
SE18 . . . . 4F 97
Belltrees Gro.
SW16 . . . . 5B 118
Bell Wharf La.
EC4 . . . . 5A 18 (1E 77)
Bellwood Rd.
SE15 . . . . 2F 107
Bell Yd. WC2 . . 3B 16 (5C 62)
Bell Yd. M.
SE1 . . . . 4E 27 (3A 78)
Belmont Cl. SW4 . . . . . 1E 103

Belmont Ct. N5 . . . . 1E **49**
NW11 . . . . 1B **30**
Belmont Gro. SE13 . . 1F **109**
W4 . . . . 5A **70**
Belmont Hall Ct.
SE13 . . . . 1F **109**
Belmont Hill SE13 . . . 1E **109**
Belmont M. SW19 . . . . 2F **113**
Belmont Pde. NW11 . . 1B **30**
Belmont Pk. SE13 . . . 2F **109**
Belmont Pk. Cl.
SE13 . . . . 2A **110**
Belmont Pk. Rd. E10 . . 1D **39**
Belmont Rd. SW4 . . . . 1E **103**
Belmont St. NW1 . . . . . 4C **46**
Belmore Ho. N7 . . . . . . 2F **47**
Belmore La. N7 . . . . . . 2F **47**
Belmore St. SW8 . . . . . 4F **89**
Beloe Cl. SW15 . . . . . . 2C **98**
Belsham St. E9 . . . . 3E **51**
Belsize Av. NW3 . . . . . 3F **45**
Belsize Ct. Garages
NW3 . . . . 2F **45**
(off Belsize La.)
Belsize Cres. NW3 . . . 3F **45**
Belsize Gro. NW3 . . . . 3A **46**
Belsize La. NW3 . . . . . 3F **45**
Belsize M. NW3 . . . . . . 3F **45**
Belsize Pk. NW3 . . . . . 3F **45**
Belsize Pk. Gdns.
NW3 . . . . 3F **45**
Belsize Pk. M. NW3 . . 3F **45**
Belsize Pl. NW3 . . . . . 3F **45**
Belsize Rd. NW6 . . . . . 5D **45**
Belsize Sq. NW3 . . . . . 3F **45**
Belsize Ter. NW3 . . . . . 3F **45**
Beltane Dr. SW19 . . . . 3F **113**
Belthorn Cres.
SW12 . . . . 5E **103**
Belton Rd. E7 . . . . 4D **55**
E11 . . . . 1A **54**
NW2 . . . . 3C **42**
Belton Way E3 . . . . . . 4C **66**
Beltran Rd. SW6 . . . . . 5D **87**
Belvedere, The
SW10 . . . . 4E **87**
(off Chelsea Harbour)
Belvedere Av.
SW19 . . . . 5A **114**
Belvedere Bldgs.
SE1 . . . . . . 4E **25** (3D **77**)
Belvedere Ct. N1 . . . . . 5A **50**
(off De Beauvoir Cres.)
NW2 . . . . 3F **43**
(off Willesden La.)
SW15 . . . . 2E **99**
Belvedere Dr.
SW19 . . . . 5A **114**
Belvedere Gro.
SW19 . . . . 5A **114**
Belvedere M. SE3 . . . 3D **97**
SE15 . . . . 1E **107**
Belvedere Pl.
SE1 . . . . . . 4E **25** (3D **77**)
SW2 . . . . 2B **104**
Belvedere Rd. E10 . . . 3A **38**
SE1 . . . . . . 3A **24** (2B **76**)
Belvedere Sq.
SW19 . . . . 5A **114**

Belvoir Rd. SE22 . . . . 5C **106**
Bembridge Cl. NW6 . . 4A **44**
Bembridge Ho. SE8 . . 5B **80**
(off Longshore)
SW18 . . . . 4D **101**
(off Iron Mill Rd.)
Bemersyde Point E13 . 2D **69**
(off Dongola Rd. W.)
Bemerton Est. N1 . . . . 4A **48**
Bemerton St. N1 . . . . . 5B **48**
Bemish Rd. SW15 . . . . 1F **99**
Benbow Ct. W6 . . . . . . 4E **71**
(off Benbow Rd.)
Benbow Ho. SE8 . . . . . 2C **94**
(off Benbow St.)
Benbow Rd. W6 . . . . . 4D **71**
Benbow St. SE8 . . . . . 2C **94**
Benbury Cl.
BR1: Brom 5E **123**
Bence Ho. SE8 . . . . . . 5A **80**
(off Rainsborough Av.)
Bendall Ho. NW1 . . . . . 4A **60**
(off Bell St.)
Bendall M. NW1 . . . . . 4A **60**
(off Bell St.)
Bendemeer Rd.
SW15 . . . . 1F **99**
Benden Ho. SE13 . . . . 3E **109**
(off Monument Gdns.)
Bendish Rd. E6 . . . . . . 4F **55**
Bendon Valley
SW18 . . . . 5D **101**
Benedict Rd. SW9 . . . 1B **104**
Benenden Ho. SE17 . . 1A **92**
(off Mina Rd.)
Ben Ezra Ct. SE17 . . . 5E **77**
(off Asolando St.)
Benfleet Ct. E8 . . . . . . 5B **50**
Bengal Ct. EC3 . . . . . . 3C **18**
(off Birchin La.)
Bengal Ho. E1 . . . . 4F **65**
(off Duckett St.)
Bengeworth Rd.
SE5 . . . . 1E **105**
Benham Cl. SW11 . . . 1F **101**
Benham Ho. SW10 . . . 3D **87**
(off Coleridge Gdns.)
Benham's Pl. NW3 . . . 1E **45**
Benhill Rd. SE5 . . . . . . 3F **91**
Benhurst Ct. SW16 . . 5C **118**
Benhurst La.
SW16 . . . . 5C **118**
Benin St. SE13 . . . . . . 5F **109**
Benjamin Cl. E8 . . . . . 5C **50**

Benjamin Franklin House
. . . . 1D **23**
(off Craven St.)

Benjamin St.
EC1 . . . . . . 5D **9** (4D **63**)
Ben Jonson Ct. N1 . . . 1A **64**
Ben Jonson Ho. EC2 . . 5A **10**
Ben Jonson Pl. EC2 . . 5A **10**
Ben Jonson Rd. E1 . . . 4F **65**
Benledi St. E14 . . . . . . 5F **67**
Bennelong Cl. W12 . . . 1D **71**
Bennerley Rd.
SW11 . . . . 3A **102**
Bennet's Hill
EC4 . . . . . . 4E **17** (1E **77**)

Bennet St.
SW1 . . . . . . 1F **21** (2E **75**)
Bennett Ct. N7 . . . . . . 5B **34**
Bennett Gro. SE13 . . . 4D **95**
Bennett Ho. SW1 . . . . 5F **75**
(off Page St.)
Bennett Pk. SE3 . . . . . 1B **110**
Bennett Rd. E13 . . . . . 3E **69**
N16 . . . . 1A **50**
SW9 . . . . 5C **90**
Bennett St. W4 . . . . . . 2A **84**
Bennett's Yd. SW1 . . . 4F **75**
Benn St. E9 . . . . 3A **52**
Bensbury Cl. SW15 . . 5D **99**
Ben Smith Way
SE16 . . . . 4C **78**
Benson Av. E6 . . . . 1E **69**
Benson Ho. E2 . . . . 3F **11**
(off Ligonier St.)
SE1 . . . . 2C **24**
(off Hatfields)
Benson Quay E1 . . . . . 1E **79**
Benson Rd. SE23 . . . . 1E **121**
Bentfield Gdns. SE9 . . 3F **125**
Benthal Rd. N16 . . . . . 4C **36**
Bentham Ct. N1 . . . . . . 4E **49**
(off Ecclesbourne Rd.)
Bentham Ho. SE1 . . . . 5B **26**
Bentham Rd. E9 . . . . . 3F **51**
Bentinck Cl. NW8 . . . . 1A **60**
Bentinck Ho. W12 . . . . 1D **71**
(off White City Est.)
Bentinck Mans. W1 . . 2C **12**
(off Bentinck St.)
Bentinck M.
W1 . . . . 2C **12** (5C **60**)
Bentinck St.
W1 . . . . 2C **12** (5C **60**)
Bentley Cl. SW19 . . . . 3C **114**
Bentley Ct. SE13 . . . . 2E **109**
(off Whitburn Rd.)
Bentley Dr. NW2 . . . . . 5B **30**
Bentley Ho. SE5 . . . . . 4A **92**
(off Peckham Rd.)
Bentley Rd. N1 . . . . . . 3A **50**
Bentons La. SE27 . . . . 4E **119**
Benton's Ri. SE27 . . . . 5F **119**
Bentworth Ct. E2 . . . . 3C **64**
(off Granby St.)
Bentworth Rd. W12 . . 5D **57**
Benville Ho. SW8 . . . . 3B **90**
(off Oval Pl.)
Benwell Rd. N7 . . . . . . 1C **48**
Benwick Cl. SE16 . . . . 5D **79**
Benworth St. E3 . . . . . 2B **66**
Benyon Ct. N1 . . . . 5A **50**
(off De Beauvoir Est.)
Benyon Ho. EC1 . . . . . 1C **8**
(off Myddelton Pas.)
Benyon Rd. N1 . . . . . . 5F **49**
Benyon Wharf N1 . . . . 5A **50**
(off Kingsland Rd.)
Berberis Ho. E3 . . . . . 4C **66**
(off Gale St.)
Berber Pl. E14 . . . . . . 1C **80**
Berber Rd. SW11 . . . . 3B **102**
Berenger Twr.
SW10 . . . . 3F **87**
(off Worlds End Est.)

Berenger Wlk. SW10 . . . 3F **87**
  (off Worlds End Est.)
Berens Rd. NW10 . . . . . . 2F **57**
Beresford Rd. N5 . . . . . . 2F **49**
Beresford Ter. N5 . . . . . . 2E **49**
Berestede Rd. W6 . . . . . . 1B **84**
Bere St. E1 . . . . 1F **79**
Bergen Ho. SE5 . . . . 5E **91**
  (off Carew St.)
Bergen Sq. SE16 . . . . . . 4A **80**
Berger Rd. E9 . . . . 3F **51**
Berghem M. W14 . . . . . . 4F **71**
Bergholt Cres. N16. . . . . 2A **36**
Bergholt M. NW1 . . . . . . 4F **47**
Berglen Ct. E14 . . . . 5A **66**
Bering Sq. E14 . . . . 1C **94**
Bering Wlk. E16 . . . . 5F **69**
Berisford M. SW18. . . 4E **101**
Berkeley Ct. NW1. . . . . . . 4A **4**
  NW10 . . . . 1A **42**
  NW11 . . . . 2B **30**
  (off Ravenscroft Av.)
Berkeley Gdns. W8 . . . . 2C **72**
Berkeley Ho. SE8 . . . . . . 1B **94**
  (off Grove St.)
Berkeley M.
  W1 . . . . 3A **12** (5B **60**)
Berkeley Rd. E12 . . . . . . 2F **55**
  N8 . . . . 1F **33**
  N15 . . . . 1F **35**
  SW13 . . . . 4C **84**
Berkeley Sq.
  W1 . . . . 5E **13** (1D **75**)
Berkeley St.
  W1 . . . . 5E **13** (1D **75**)
Berkeley Twr. E14. . . . . . 2B **80**
  (off Westferry Cir.)
Berkeley Wlk. N7. . . . . . . 4B **34**
  (off Durham Rd.)
Berkley Gro. NW1 . . . . . 4C **46**
Berkley Rd. NW1 . . . . . . 4B **46**
Berkshire Ho. SE6 . . . 4C **122**
Berkshire Rd. E9 . . . . . . 3B **52**
Bermans Way NW10 . . . 1A **42**
BERMONDSEY 3C **78**
Bermondsey Sq.
  SE1 . . . . 5E **27** (4A **78**)
Bermondsey St.
  SE1 . . . . 2D **27** (2A **78**)
Bermondsey Trad. Est.
  SE16 . . . . 1E **93**
Bermondsey Wall E.
  SE16 . . . . 3C **78**
Bermondsey Wall W.
  SE16 . . . . 3C **78**
Bernard Angell Ho.
  SE10 . . . . 2F **95**
  (off Trafalgar Rd.)
Bernard Ashley Dr.
  SE7 . . . . 1D **97**
Bernard Cassidy St.
  E16 . . . . 4B **68**
Bernard Gdns.
  SW19 . . . . 5B **114**
Bernard Hegarty Lodge
  E8 . . . . 4C **50**
  (off Lansdowne Dr.)
Bernard Mans. WC1. . . . 4D **7**
  (off Bernard St.)

Bernard Rd. N15 . . . . . . 1B **36**
Bernard Shaw Ct.
  NW1 . . . . 4E **47**
  (off St Pancras Way)
Bernard Shaw Ho.
  NW10 . . . . 5A **42**
  (off Knatchbull Rd.)
Bernard St.
  WC1 . . . . 4D **7** (3A **62**)
Bernard Sunley Ho.
  SW9 . . . . 3C **90**
  (off Sth. Island Pl.)
Bernays Gro. SW9 . . . . 2B **104**
Berners Ho. N1 . . . . 1C **62**
  (off Barnsbury Est.)
Berners M.
  W1 . . . . 1A **14** (4E **61**)
Berners Pl.
  W1 . . . . 2A **14** (5E **61**)
Berners Rd. N1 . . . . 5D **49**
Berners St.
  W1 . . . . 1A **14** (4E **61**)
Berner Ter. E1 . . . . 5C **64**
  (off Fairclough St.)
Bernhardt Cres. NW8. . . 3A **60**
Berridge M. NW6 . . . . . 2C **44**
Berridge Rd. SE19 . . . . 5F **119**
Berriman Rd. N7 . . . . . . 5B **34**
Berrington Ho. W2 . . . . . 1C **72**
  (off Hereford Rd.)
Berry Cl. NW10 . . . . 4A **42**
Berry Cotts. E14 . . . . 5A **66**
  (off Maroon St.)
Berryfield Rd. SE17 . . . . 1D **91**
Berry Ho. E1 . . . . 3D **65**
  (off Headlam St.)
Berry La. SE21 . . . . 4F **119**
Berryman's La.
  SE26 . . . . 4F **121**
Berry Pl. EC1. . . . 2E **9** (2D **63**)
Berry St. EC1. . . . 3E **9** (3D **63**)
Bertal Rd. SW17. . . . . . 4F **115**
Berthon St. SE8 . . . . 3C **94**
Bertie Rd. NW10 . . . . . . 3C **42**
  SE26 . . . . 5F **121**
Bertram Rd. NW4 . . . . . 1C **28**
Bertram St. N19. . . . . . . 4D **33**
Bertrand Ho. SW16 . . . 3A **118**
  (off Leigham Av.)
Bertrand St. SE13 . . . . 1D **109**
Berwick Ct. SE1 . . . . . . 4A **26**
Berwick Rd. E16 . . . . . . 5D **69**
Berwick St.
  W1 . . . . 2A **14** (5E **61**)
Berwyn Rd. SE24 . . . . 1D **119**
Beryl Rd. W6 . . . . 1F **85**
Besant Cl. NW2 . . . . . . 5A **30**
Besant Ct. N1 . . . . 2F **49**
Besant Ho. NW8. . . . . . . 5E **45**
  (off Boundary Rd.)
Besant Pl. SE22 . . . . . . 2B **106**
Besant Rd. NW2 . . . . . . 1A **44**
Besant Wlk. N7 . . . . 4B **34**
Besford Ho. E2 . . . . 1C **64**
  (off Pritchard's Rd.)
Besley St. SW16 . . . . . . 5E **117**
Bessborough Gdns.
  SW1 . . . . 1F **89**
Bessborough Pl. SW1. . . 1F **89**

Bessborough Rd.
  SW15 . . . . 1C **112**
Bessborough St. SW1. . . 1F **89**
Bessemer Ct. NW1. . . . . 4E **47**
  (off Rochester Sq.)
Bessemer Pk. Ind. Est.
  SE24 . . . . 2D **105**
Bessemer Rd. SE5 . . . . . 5E **91**
Bessingham Wlk.
  SE4 . . . . 2F **107**
  (off Aldersford Cl.)
Besson St. SE14 . . . . . . 4E **93**
Bessy St. E2 . . . . 2E **65**
Bestwood St. SE8 . . . . . 5F **79**
Beswick M. NW6 . . . . . . 3D **45**
Beta Pl. SW4 . . . . 2B **104**
Bethal Est. SE1 . . . . 2E **27**
Bethel Cl. NW4 . . . . 1F **29**
Bethell Av. E16. . . . . 3B **68**
Bethersden Ho.
  SE17 . . . . 1A **92**
  (off Kinglake St.)
Bethlehem Ho. E14 . . . . 1B **80**
  (off Limehouse C'way.)
BETHNAL GREEN 2D **65**
Bethnal Green Cen. for Sports
  & Performing Arts. . . . 2B **64**
Bethnal Green Mus. of
  Childhood 2E **65**
Bethnal Grn. Rd.
  E1. . . . . 3F **11** (3B **64**)
  E2. . . . . 3F **11** (3B **64**)
Bethune Cl. N16. . . . . . . 3A **36**
Bethune Rd. N16 . . . . . . 2F **35**
  NW10 . . . . 3A **56**
Bethwin Rd. SE5 . . . . . . 3D **91**
Betsham Ho. SE1. . . . . . 3B **26**
  (off Newcomen St.)
Betterton Ho. WC2. . . . . 3E **15**
  (off Betterton St.)
Betterton St.
  WC2 . . . . 3D **15** (5A **62**)
Bettons Pk. E15 . . . . 5A **54**
Bettridge Rd. SW6. . . . . 5B **86**
Betts Ho. E1 . . . . 1D **79**
  (off Betts St.)
Betts M. E17 . . . . 1B **38**
Betts Rd. E16 . . . . 1D **83**
Betts St. E1 . . . . 1D **79**
Betty Brooks Ho. E11. . . 5F **39**
Betty May Gray Ho.
  E14 . . . . 5E **81**
  (off Pier St.)
Beulah Hill SE19 . . . . . 5D **119**
Beulah Rd. E17 . . . . 1D **39**
Bevan Ct. E3 . . . . 1C **66**
  (off Tredegar Rd.)
Bevan Ho. N1. . . . . 5A **50**
  (off New Era Est.)
  WC1 . . . . 5E **7**
  (off Boswell St.)
Bevan St. N1 . . . . 5E **49**
Bev Callender Cl.
  SW8 . . . . 1D **103**
Bevenden St.
  N1 . . . . 1C **10** (2F **63**)
Beveridge Rd. NW10. . . 4A **42**
Beverley Cl. SW11. . . . 2F **101**
  SW13 . . . . 5C **84**

Beverley Cotts.
SW15 . . . . .3A 112
Beverley Ct. SE4 . . . . .1B 108
(not continuous)
Beverley Gdns.
NW11 . . . . .2A 30
SW13 . . . . .1B 98
Beverley Ho. BR1: Brom5F 123
(off Brangbourne Rd.)
Beverley La. SW15 . . .3B 112
Beverley Path SW13 . . .5B 84
Beverley Rd. E6 . . . . . .2F 69
SW13 . . . . .1B 98
W4 . . . . .1B 84
Beversbrook Rd. N19 . .5F 33
Beverstone Rd.
SW2 . . . . .3B 104
Beverston M. W1 . . . . .1A 12
Bevill Allen Cl.
SW17 . . . . .5B 116
Bevin Cl. SE16 . . . . . . .2A 80
Bevin Ct. WC1 . . . .1A 8 (2B 62)
Bevington Path SE1 . . .4F 27
Bevington Rd. W10 . . . .4A 58
Bevington St. SE16 . . . .3C 78
Bevin Ho. E2 . . . . .2E 65
(off Butler St.)
Bevin Sq. SW17 . . . . . .3B 116
Bevin Way
WC1 . . . . . . .1B 8 (1C 62)
Bevis Marks
EC3 . . . . . . .2E 19 (5A 64)
Bew Ct. SE22 . . . . . . .5C 106
Bewdley St. N1 . . . . . . .4C 48
Bewick M. SE15 . . . . . .3D 93
Bewick St. SW8 . . . . . .5D 89
Bewley Ho. E1 . . . . . . .1D 79
(off Bewley St.)
Bewley St. E1 . . . . . . .1E 79
Bewlys Rd. SE27 . . . . .5D 119
Bexhill Rd. SE4 . . . . . .4B 108
Bexhill Wlk. E15 . . . . . .5A 54
Bexley Ho. SE4 . . . . . .2A 108
Bianca Ho. N1 . . . . . . .1D 11
(off Crondall St.)
Bianca Rd. SE15 . . . . . .2C 92
Bibury Cl. SE15 . . . . . .2A 92
(not continuous)
Bickenhall Mans. W1 . . .5A 4
(not continuous)
Bickenhall St.
W1 . . . . .5A 4 (4B 60)
Bickersteth Rd.
SW17 . . . . .5B 116
Bickerton Rd. N19 . . . . .4E 33
Bickley Rd. E10 . . . . . .2D 39
Bickley St. SW17 . . . . .5A 116
Bicknell Ho. E1 . . . . . . .5C 64
(off Ellen St.)
Bicknell Rd. SE5 . . . . . .1E 105
Bidborough St.
WC1 . . . . .2D 7 (2A 62)
Biddenham Ho. SE16 . . .5F 79
(off Plough Way)
Bidder St. E16 . . . . .3A 68
(not continuous)
Biddesden Ho. SW3 . . .5B 74
(off Cadogan St.)
Biddestone Rd. N7 . . . .1B 48

Biddulph Mans. W9 . . .2D 59
(off Elgin Av.)
Biddulph Rd. W9 . . . . .2D 59
Bideford Rd.
BR1: Brom 3B 124
Bidwell St. SE15 . . . . . .4D 93
Biggerstaff Rd. E15 . . . .5E 53
Biggerstaff St. N4 . . . . .4C 34
Biggs Row SW15 . . . . .1F 99
Big Hill E5 . . . . .3D 37
Bigland St. E1 . . . . . . .5D 65
Bignold Rd. E7 . . . . . . .1C 54
Bigwood Ct. NW11 . . . .1D 31
Bigwood Rd. NW11 . . . .1D 31
Bilberry Ho. E3 . . . . . . .4C 66
(off Watts Gro.)
Billingford Cl. SE4 . . . . .2F 107
Billing Ho. E1 . . . . .5F 65
(off Bower St.)
Billingley NW1 . . . . . . .5E 47
(off Pratt St.)
Billing Pl. SW10 . . . . . .3D 87
Billing Rd. SW10 . . . . . .3D 87
Billingsgate Fish Market
. . . . .2D 81
Billing St. SW10 . . . . . .3D 87
Billington Rd. SE14 . . . .3F 93
Billiter Sq. EC3 . . . . . . .3E 19
Billiter St.
EC3 . . . . .3E 19 (5A 64)
Billson St. E14 . . . . . . .5E 81
Bilsby Gro. SE9 . . . . . .4F 125
Bilton Towers W1 . . . . .3A 12
(off Gt. Cumberland Pl.)
Bina Gdns. SW5 . . . . . .5E 73
Binbrook Ho. W10 . . . . .4E 57
(off Sutton Way)
Binden Rd. W12 . . . . . .4B 70
Binfield Rd. SW4 . . . . . .4A 90
Bingfield St. N1 . . . . . . .5A 48
(not continuous)
Bingham Ct. N1 . . . . . . .4D 49
(off Halton Rd.)
Bingham Pl.
W1 . . . . .5B 4 (4C 60)
Bingham St. N1 . . . . . . .3F 49
Bingley Rd. E16 . . . . . . .5E 69
Binley Ho. SW15 . . . . . .4B 98
Binney St.
W1 . . . . .3C 12 (5C 60)
Binnie Ct. SE10 . . . . . . .3D 95
(off Greenwich High Rd.)
Binnie Ho. SE1 . . . . . . .5F 25
(off Bath Ter.)
Binns Rd. W4 . . . . .1A 84
Binns Ter. W4 . . . . .1A 84
Bircham Path SE4 . . . . .2F 107
(off Aldersford Cl.)
Birch Cl. E16 . . . . .4A 68
N19 . . . . .4E 33
SE15 . . . . .5C 92
Birchdale Rd. E7 . . . . . .2E 55
Birchen Cl. NW9 . . . . . .4A 28
Birchen Gro. NW9 . . . . .4A 28
Birches, The E12 . . . . . .1F 55
SE7 . . . . .2D 97
Birchfield Ho. E14 . . . . .1C 80
(off Birchfield St.)

Birchfield St. E14 . . . . . .1C 80
Birch Gro. E11 . . . . .1A 54
SE12 . . . . .5B 110
Birch Ho. SE14 . . . . . . .4B 94
SW2 . . . . .4C 104
(off Tulse Hill)
W10 . . . . .3A 58
(off Droop St.)
Birchington Ct. NW6 . . .5D 45
(off West End La.)
Birchington Ho. E5 . . . . .2D 51
Birchington Rd. N8 . . . . .1F 33
NW6 . . . . .5C 44
Birchin La.
EC3 . . . . .3C 18 (5F 63)
Birchlands Av.
SW12 . . . . .5B 102
Birchmere Lodge
SE16 . . . . .1D 93
(off Sherwood Gdns.)
Birchmere Row SE3 . . . .5B 96
Birchmore Hall N5 . . . . .5E 35
Birchmore Wlk. N5 . . . . .5E 35
Birch Va. Ct. NW8 . . . . .3F 59
(off Pollitt Dr.)
Birchwood Dr. NW3 . . . .5D 31
Birchwood Rd.
SW17 . . . . .5D 117
Birdbrook Ho. N1 . . . . . .4E 49
(off Popham Rd.)
Birdbrook Rd. SE3 . . . . .2E 111
Birdcage Wlk.
SW1 . . . . .4F 21 (3E 75)
Birdhurst Rd. SW18 . . . .3E 101
Bird in Bush BMX Track
. . . . .3D 93
(off Bird in Bush Rd.)
Bird in Bush Rd.
SE15 . . . . .3C 92
Bird-in-Hand Pas.
SE23 . . . . .2E 121
Bird in Hand Yd.
NW3 . . . . .1E 45
(off Holly Bush Va.)
NW3 . . . . .1E 45
(Perrin's Ct.)
Birdsall Ho. SE5 . . . . . .1A 106
Birdsfield La. E3 . . . . . . .5B 52
Bird St. W1 . . . .3C 12 (5C 60)
Birkbeck College 5C 6
Birkbeck Hill SE21 . . . . .1D 119
Birkbeck M. E8 . . . . . . .2B 50
Birkbeck Pl. SE21 . . . . .2E 119
Birkbeck Rd. E8 . . . . . . .2B 50
SW19 . . . . .5D 115
Birkbeck St. E2 . . . . . . .2D 65
Birkbeck Cl. SE16 . . . . .1D 93
Birkenhead St.
WC1 . . . . .1E 7 (2A 62)
Birkhall Rd. SE6 . . . . . . .1F 123
Birkwood Cl. SW12 . . . .5F 103
Birley Lodge NW8 . . . . .1F 59
(off Acacia Rd.)
Birley St. SW11 . . . . . . .5C 88
Birnam Rd. N4 . . . . .4B 34
Birrell Ho. SW9 . . . . . . .5B 90
(off Stockwell Rd.)
Birse Cres. NW10 . . . . .5A 28
Birstall Rd. N15 . . . . . . .1A 36

Biscay Ho. *E1* *3F 65*
(off Mile End Rd.)
Biscayne Av. E14 . . . . 2F 81
Biscay Rd. W6 . . . . 1F 85
Biscoe Way SE13 . . . . . . 1F 109
Biscott Ho. E3 . . . . 3D 67
Bisham Gdns. N6 . . . . 3C 32
Bishopsgate Chu. Yd.
EC2 . . . . 2D 19 (4A 64)
Bishop King's Rd.
W14 . . . . 5A 72
Bishop's Av. E13. . . . . . . 5D 55
SW6 . . . . 5F 85
Bishops Av., The N2 . . . . 2F 31
Bishop's Bri. Rd. W2 . . . 5D 59
Bishop's Cl. N19. . . . . . . 5E 33
Bishops Ct. EC4 . . . . 2D 17
W2 . . . . *5D 59*
(off Bishop's Bri. Rd.)
WC2 . . . . 2B 16
Bishopsdale Ho.
NW6 . . . . *5C 44*
(off Kilburn Va.)
Bishopsgate
EC2 . . . . 3D 19 (5A 64)
Bishopsgate Arc.
EC2 . . . . 1E 19
Bishopsgate Institute &
Libraries *1E 19*
(off Bishopsgate)
Bishops Gro. N2. . . . . . . 1A 32
Bishops Ho. *SW8* *3A 90*
(off Sth. Lambeth Rd.)
Bishop's Mans. SW6 . . . 5F 85
(not continuous)
Bishops Mead *SE5* *3E 91*
(off Camberwell Rd.)
Bishop's Pk. Rd.
SW6 . . . . 5F 85
Bishops Rd. N6 . . . . 1C 32
SW6 . . . . 4A 86
SW11 . . . . 3A 88
Bishops Sq. E1 . . . . . 4A 64
Bishop's Ter. SE11 . . . . . 5C 76
Bishopsthorpe Rd.
SE26 . . . . 4F 121
Bishop St. N1 . . . . 5E 49
Bishop's Way E2 . . . . . . 1D 65
Bishops Wood Almshouses
E5. . . . . *1D 51*
(off Lwr. Clapton Rd.)
Bishopswood Rd. N6 . . 2B 32
Bishop Way NW10 . . . . . 4A 42
Bishop Wilfred Wood Cl.
SE15 . . . . 5C 92
Bishop Wilfred Wood Ct.
E13 . . . . *1E 69*
(off Pragel St.)
Bissextile Ho. SE13 . . . 5D 95
Bisson Rd. E15. . . . . 1E 67
Bittern Ct. SE8 . . . . 2C 94
Bittern Ho. *SE1* *4F 25*
(off Gt. Suffolk St.)
Bittern St.
SE1. . . . . 4F 25 (3E 77)
Blackall St.
EC2 . . . . 3D 11 (3A 64)
Blackbird Yd. E2. . . . . . . 2B 64
Black Boy La. N15 . . . . . 1E 35

Black Bull Yd. EC1 . . . . . 5C 8
(off Hatton Wall)
Blackburne's M.
W1 . . . . 4B 12 (1C 74)
Blackburn Rd. NW6 . . . . 3D 45
Blackett St. SW15 . . . . . 1F 99
Blackford's Path
SW15 . . . . 5C 98
Blackfriars Bri. EC4 . . . . 4D 17
SE1 . . . . 5D 17 (1D 77)
Blackfriars Ct. EC4 . . . . . 4D 17
Black Friars La.
EC4 . . . . 4D 17 (5D 63)
(not continuous)
Blackfriars Pas.
EC4 . . . . 4D 17 (1D 77)
Blackfriars Rd.
SE1 . . . . 1D 25 (3D 77)
Blackfriars Underpass
EC4 . . . . 4D 17 (1C 76)
BLACKHEATH 5B 96
Blackheath Av. SE10. . . . 3F 95
Blackheath Bus. Est.
SE10 . . . . *4E 95*
(off Blackheath Hill)
Blackheath Concert Halls
. . . . 1B 110
Blackheath Gro. SE3 . . . 5B 96
Blackheath Hill SE10 . . . 4E 95
BLACKHEATH PARK. . 2C 110
Blackheath Pk. SE3. . . . 1B 110
Blackheath Ri. SE13 . . . 5E 95
(not continuous)
Blackheath Rd. SE10 . . . 4D 95
BLACKHEATH VALE. . . . 5B 96
Blackheath Va. SE3 . . . . 5A 96
Blackheath Village
SE3 . . . . 5B 96
Black Horse Ct. SE1 . . . . 5C 26
Blackhorse Rd. SE8 . . . . 2A 94
Blacklands Rd. SE6 . . . . 4E 123
Blacklands Ter. SW3 . . . 5B 74
Black Lion La. W6 . . . . . 5C 70
Black Lion M. W6. . . . . . 5C 70
Blackmans Yd. *E2* *2C 64*
(off Grimsby St.)
Blackmore Ho. *N1* *5B 48*
(off Barnsbury Est.)
Black Path E10 . . . . 2A 38
Blackpool Rd. SE15 . . . . 5D 93
Black Prince Rd. SE1. . . . 5B 76
SE11. . . . . 5B 76
Blackshaw Rd.
SW17 . . . . 4E 115
Blacks Rd. W6 . . . . 1E 85
Blackstock M. N4. . . . . . 4D 35
Blackstock Rd. N4 . . . . . 4D 35
N5. . . . . 4D 35
Blackstone Est. E8 . . . . . 4C 50
Blackstone Rd. *SW1* . . . *1E 89*
(off Churchill Gdns.)
Blackstone Rd. NW2 . . . 2E 43
Black Swan Yd.
SE1 . . . . 3E 27 (3A 78)
Blackthorn Ct. *E11* *1F 53*
(off Hall Rd.)
Blackthorne Ct. *SE15*. . . *3B 92*
(off Cator St.)
Blackthorn St. E3 . . . . . 3C 66

Blacktree M. SW9 . . . . 1C 104
BLACKWALL 2E 81
Blackwall La. SE10 . . . . 1A 96
Blackwall Trad. Est.
E14 . . . . 4F 67
Blackwall Tunnel E14. . . 2F 81
(not continuous)
SE10 . . . . 2F 81
Blackwall Tunnel App.
E14 . . . . 5E 67
Blackwall Tunnel
Northern App. E3 . . . 1D 67
E14 . . . . 1C 66
Blackwall Tunnel Southern
App. SE10. . . . . 4A 82
Blackwall Way E14. . . . . 2E 81
Blackwater Cl. E7 . . . . . . 1B 54
Blackwater Ho. *NW8* . . . *4F 59*
(off Church St.)
Blackwater St. SE22. . . 3B 106
Blackwell Cl. E5. . . . . . . 1F 51
Blackwell Ho. SW4 . . . 4F 103
Blackwood St. SE17. . . . 1F 91
Blade M. SW15 . . . . . . 2B 100
Blades Ct. SW15 . . . . . 2B 100
W6 . . . . *1D 85*
(off Lower Mall)
Blades Ho. *SE11* *2C 90*
(off Kennington Oval)
Bladon Ct. SW16 . . . . . 5A 118
Blagdon Rd. SE13 . . . . 4D 109
Blagrove Rd. W10 . . . . . 4A 58
Blair Av. NW9. . . . . 2A 28
Blair Cl. N1 . . . . 3E 49
Blair Ct. NW8 . . . . 5F 45
SE6. . . . . 1B 124
Blairderry Rd. SW2 . . . 2A 118
Blairgowrie Ct. *E14* *5F 67*
(off Blair St.)
Blair Ho. SW9 . . . . 5B 90
Blair St. E14. . . . . 5E 67
Blake Ct. *NW6* *2C 58*
(off Malvern Rd.)
SE16. . . . . *1D 93*
(off Stubbs Dr.)
Blake Gdns. SW6. . . . . . 4D 87
Blake Hall Cres. E11 . . . 3C 40
Blake Hall Rd. E11 . . . . . 2C 40
Blake Ho. *E14* *3C 80*
(off Admirals Way)
SE1 . . . . 5B 24 (4C 76)
SE8 . . . . *2C 94*
(off New King St.)
Blakeley Cotts. SE10 . . . 3F 81
Blakemore Rd.
SW16 . . . . 3A 118
Blakeney Cl. E8 . . . . 2C 50
NW1 . . . . 4F 47
Blakenham Rd.
SW17 . . . . 4B 116
Blaker Ct. SE7 . . . . 3E 97
(not continuous)
Blake Rd. E16 . . . . 3B 68
Blaker Rd. E15. . . . . 1E 67
Blakes Cl. W10 . . . . 4E 57

Blake's Rd. SE15 . . . . . . 3A 92
Blanchard Way E8 . . . . . 3C 50
Blanch Cl. SE15 . . . . 3E 93
Blanchedowne SE5. . . . 2F 105
Blanche St. E16 . . . . 3B 68
Blandfield Rd.
 SW12 . . . . 5C 102
Blandford Ct. N1 . . . . . . 4A 50
 (off St Peter's Way)
 NW6 . . . . 4F 43
Blandford Ho. SW8 . . . . 3B 90
 (off Richborne Ter.)
Blandford Rd. W4 . . . . . . 4A 70
Blandford Sq. NW1 . . . . 3A 60
Blandford St.
 W1 . . . . 2A 12 (5B 60)
Bland Ho. SE11 . . . . 1B 90
 (off Vauxhall St.)
Bland St. SE9 . . . . 2F 111
Blann Cl. SE9 . . . . 4F 111
Blantyre St. SW10 . . . . . 3F 87
Blantyre Twr. SW10 . . . . 3F 87
 (off Blantyre St.)
Blantyre Wlk. SW10 . . . . 3F 87
 (off Worlds End Est.)
Blashford NW3 . . . . 4B 46
 (off Adelaide Rd.)
Blashford St. SE13 . . . . 5F 109
Blasker Wlk. E14 . . . . . . 1D 95
Blaxland Ho. W12 . . . . . 1D 71
 (off White City Est.)
Blazer Ct. NW8 . . . . 2F 59
 (off St John's Wood Rd.)
Blechynden Ho. W10 . . . 5F 57
 (off Kingsdown Cl.)
Blechynden St. W10 . . . 1F 71
Bledlow Cl. NW8 . . . . . . 3F 59
Bleeding Heart Yd.
 EC1 . . . . 1C 16
Blegborough Rd.
 SW16 . . . . 5E 117
Blemundsbury WC1 . . . . 5F 7
 (off Dombey St.)
Blendon Row SE17 . . . . 5F 77
 (off Townley St.)
Blendworth Point
 SW15 . . . . 1D 113
Blenheim Cl. SE12 . . . . 1D 125
Blenheim Cl. N19 . . . . . . 4A 34
 SE16 . . . . 2F 79
 (off King & Queen Wharf)
Blenheim Cres. W11 . . . . 1A 72
Blenheim Gdns. NW2 . . . 3E 43
 SW2 . . . . 4B 104
Blenheim Gro. SE15. . . . 5C 92
Blenheim Ho. E16 . . . . . 2D 83
 (off Constable Av.)
 SW3 . . . . 1A 88
 (off Kings Rd.)
Blenheim Pas. NW8 . . . . 1E 59
 (not continuous)
Blenheim Rd. E6. . . . . . . 2F 69
 E15 . . . . 1A 54
 NW8 . . . . 1E 59
 W4 . . . . 4A 70
Blenheim St.
 W1 . . . . 3D 13 (5D 61)
Blenheim Ter. NW8 . . . . 1E 59
Blenkarne Rd. SW11 . . . 4B 102

Blessington Cl.
 SE13 . . . . 1F 109
Blessington Rd.
 SE13 . . . . 1F 109
Bletchley Ct. N1 . . . . 1B 10
 (not continuous)
Bletchley St.
 N1 . . . . 1A 10 (1F 63)
Bletsoe Wlk. N1 . . . . 1E 63
Blick Ho. SE16 . . . . 4E 79
 (off Neptune St.)
Blincoe Cl. SW19 . . . . . 2F 113
Bliss Cres. SE13 . . . . . . 5D 95
Blissett St. SE10 . . . . . . 4E 95
Bliss M. W10 . . . . 2A 58
Blisworth Ho. E2 . . . . . . 5C 50
 (off Whiston Rd.)
Blithfield St. W8 . . . . 4D 73
Block Wharf E14. . . . . . . 3C 80
 (off Cuba St.)
Bloemfontein Av.
 W12 . . . . 2D 71
Bloemfontein Rd.
 W12 . . . . 1D 71
Bloemfontein Way
 W12 . . . . 2D 71
Blomfield Ct. W9 . . . . . . 3E 59
 (off Maida Va.)
Blomfield Mans.
 W12 . . . . 2E 71
 (off Stanlake Rd.)
Blomfield Rd. W9 . . . . . . 4D 59
Blomfield St.
 EC2 . . . . 1C 18 (4F 63)
Blomfield Vs. W9 . . . . . . 4D 59
Blondel St. SW11 . . . . . . 5C 88
Blondin St. E3 . . . . 1C 66
Bloomburg St. SW1 . . . . 5F 75
Bloomfield Ct. E10 . . . . . 5D 39
 (off Brisbane Rd.)
 N6 . . . . 1C 32
Bloomfield Ho. E1 . . . . . 4C 64
 (off Old Montague St.)
Bloomfield Pl. W1 . . . . . 4E 13
Bloomfield Rd. N6 . . . . . 1C 32
Bloomfield Ter. SW1 . . . 1C 88
Bloom Gro. SE27 . . . . . 3D 119
Bloomhall Rd.
 SE19 . . . . 5F 119
Bloom Pk. Rd. SW6 . . . . 3B 86
BLOOMSBURY
 . . . . 5D 7 (4A 62)
Bloomsbury Ct. WC1 . . . 1E 15
Bloomsbury Ho.
 SW4 . . . . 4F 103
Bloomsbury Pl.
 SW18 . . . . 3E 101
 WC1 . . . . 5E 7 (4A 62)
Bloomsbury Sq.
 WC1 . . . . 1E 15 (4A 62)
Bloomsbury St.
 WC1 . . . . 1C 14 (4F 61)
Bloomsbury Theatre 3B 6
Bloomsbury Way
 WC1 . . . . 1D 15 (4A 62)
Blore Cl. SW8 . . . . 4F 89
Blore Ct. W1 . . . . 3B 14
Blore Ho. SW10 . . . . 3D 87
 (off Coleridge Gdns.)

Blossom St.
 E1 . . . . 4E 11 (3A 64)
Blount St. E14 . . . . 5A 66
Bloxam Gdns. SE9 . . . . 3F 111
Bloxhall Rd. E10 . . . . . . 3B 38
Blucher Rd. SE5 . . . . . . 3E 91
Blue Anchor La.
 SE16 . . . . 5C 78
Blue Anchor Yd. E1 . . . . 1C 78
Blue Ball Yd.
 SW1 . . . . 2F 21 (2E 75)
Bluebell Av. E12 . . . . . . 2F 55
Bluebell Cl. E9 . . . . 5E 51
Blueberry Cl. NW8 . . . . 4B 120
Blue Elephant Theatre
 . . . . 3E 91
 (off Bethwin Rd.)
Bluegate M. E1 . . . . 1D 79
Blue Lion Pl.
 SE1 . . . . 5D 27 (4A 78)
Blueprint Apartments
 SW12 . . . . 5D 103
 (off Balham Gro.)
Blue Water St. SE18 . . . 2D 101
Blundell Cl. E8 . . . . 2C 50
Blundell St. N7 . . . . 4A 48
Blurton Rd. E5 . . . . 1E 51
Blyth Cl. E14 . . . . 5F 81
BLYTHE HILL 5B 108
Blythe Cl. SE6 . . . . 5B 108
Blythe Hill SE6. . . . . 5B 108
Blythe Hill La. SE6. . . . . 5B 108
Blythe Hill Pl. SE23. . . . 5A 108
Blythe Ho. SE11 . . . . . . 2C 90
Blythe M. W14 . . . . 4F 71
Blythendale Ho. E2 . . . . 1C 64
 (off Mansford St.)
Blythe Rd. W14 . . . . 4F 71
 (not continuous)
Blythe St. E2 . . . . 2D 65
Blythe Va. SE6 . . . . 1B 122
Blyth Hill Pl. SE23 . . . . 5A 108
 (off Brockley Pk.)
Blyth Rd. E17 . . . . 2B 38
Blyth's Wharf E14. . . . . . 1A 80
Blythwood Rd. N4 . . . . . 2A 34
Boades M. NW3 . . . . 1F 45
Boadicea St. N1. . . . . . . 5B 48
Boardwalk Pl. E14 . . . . . 2E 81
Boarley Ho. SE17 . . . . . 5A 78
 (off Massinger St.)
Boathouse Cen., The
 W10 . . . . 3F 57
 (off Canal Cl.)
Boathouse Wlk.
 SE15 . . . . 3B 92
 (not continuous)
Boat Lifter Way SE16. . . 5A 80
Boat Quay E16 . . . . 1E 83
Bobbin Cl. SW4 . . . . 1E 103
Bob Anker Cl. E13 . . . . . 2C 68
Bob Marley Way
 SE24 . . . . 2C 104
Bocking St. E8 . . . . 5D 51
Boddicott Cl. SW19 . . . . 2A 114
Boddington Ho. SE14 . . 4E 93
 (off Pomeroy St.)
 SW13 . . . . 2D 85
 (off Wyatt Dr.)

Bodeney Ho. SE5 . . . . 4A 92
  (off Peckham Rd.)
Boden Ho. E1 . . . . 4C 64
  (off Woodseer St.)
Bodington Ct. W12 . . . . . 3F 71
Bodley Mnr. Way
  SW2 . . . . 5C 104
Bodmin St. SW18 . . . . . 1C 114
Bodney Rd. E8 . . . . 2D 51
Bogart Ct. E14 . . . . 1C 80
  (off Premiere Pl.)
Bohemia Pl. E8 . . . . 3E 51
Bohn Rd. E1 . . . . 4A 66
Boileau Rd. SW13 . . . . . 3C 84
Boisseau Ho. E1 . . . . . . 4E 65
  (off Stepney Way)
Bolden St. SE8 . . . . 5D 95
Boldero Pl. NW8 . . . . . . 3A 60
  (off Gateforth St.)
Boleyn Ho. E16 . . . . 2C 82
  (off Southey M.)
Boleyn Rd. E6 . . . . 1F 69
  E7 . . . . 4C 54
  N16 . . . . 2A 50
Bolina Rd. SE16 . . . . 1E 93
Bolingbroke Gro.
  SW11 . . . . 2A 102
Bolingbroke Rd. W14 . . 4F 71
Bolingbroke Wlk.
  SW11 . . . . 4F 87
Bolney Ga. SW7 . . . . 3A 74
Bolney St. SW8 . . . . 3B 90
Bolsover St.
  W1 . . . . 4E 5 (3D 61)
Bolt Ct. EC4 . . . . 3C 16
Bolton Cres. SE5 . . . . . . 3D 91
Bolton Gdns. NW10 . . . . 1F 57
  SW5 . . . . 1D 87
Bolton Gdns. M.
  SW10 . . . . 1E 87
Bolton Ho. SE10 . . . . 1A 96
  (off Trafalgar Rd.)
Bolton Pl. NW8 . . . . 5D 45
  (off Bolton Rd.)
Bolton Rd. E15 . . . . 3B 54
  NW8 . . . . 5D 45
  NW10 . . . . 5A 42
Boltons, The SW10 . . . . 1E 87
Boltons Ct. SW5 . . . . . . 1D 87
  (off Old Brompton Rd.)
Boltons Pl. SW5 . . . . . . 1E 87
Bolton St.
  W1 . . . . 1E 21 (2D 75)
Bolton Studios SW10 . . 1E 87
Bolton Wlk. N7 . . . . 4B 34
  (off Durham Rd.)
Bombay Ct. SE16 . . . . . . 3E 79
  (off St Marychurch St.)
Bombay St. SE16 . . . . . . 5D 79
Bomore Rd. W11 . . . . . . 1A 72
Bonar Rd. SE15 . . . . 3C 92
Bonchurch Rd. W10 . . . 4A 58
Bond Ct. EC4 . . . . 4B 18 (1F 77)
Bond Ho. NW6 . . . . 1B 58
  (off Rupert Rd.)
  SE14 . . . . 3A 94
  (off Goodwood Rd.)
Bonding Yd. Wlk.
  SE16 . . . . 4A 80

Bond St. E15 . . . . 2A 54
  W4 . . . . 5A 70
Bondway SW8 . . . . 2A 90
Bonfield Rd. SE13 . . . . . 2E 109
Bonham Ho. W11 . . . . . . 2B 72
  (off Boyne Ter. M.)
Bonham Rd. SW2 . . . . . 3B 104
Bonheur Rd. W4 . . . . 3A 70
Bonhill St.
  EC2 . . . . 4C 10 (3F 63)
Bonita M. SE4 . . . . 1F 107
Bon Marche Ter. M.
  SE27 . . . . 4A 120
  (off Gypsy Rd.)
Bonner Rd. E2 . . . . 1E 65
Bonner St. E2 . . . . 1E 65
Bonneville Gdns.
  SW4 . . . . 4E 103
Bonnington Ho. N1 . . . . 1B 62
Bonnington Sq.
  SW8 . . . . 2B 90
Bonny St. NW1 . . . . 4E 47
Bonsor Ho. SW8 . . . . . . 4E 89
Bonsor St. SE5 . . . . 3A 92
Bonville Rd.
  BR1: Brom 5B 124
Booker Cl. E14 . . . . 4B 66
Boones Rd. SE13 . . . . . . 2A 110
Boone St. SE13 . . . . 2A 110
Boord St. SE10 . . . . 4A 82
Boothby Rd. N19 . . . . . . 4F 33
Booth Cl. E9 . . . . 5D 51
Booth La. EC4 . . . . 4F 17
Booth's Pl.
  W1 . . . . 1A 14 (4E 61)
Boot St. N1 . . . . 2D 11 (2A 64)
Border Cres. SE26 . . . . . 5D 121
Border Rd. SE26 . . . . . . 5D 121
Bordon Wlk. SW15. . . . . 5C 98
Boreas Wlk. N1 . . . . 1E 9
Boreham Av. E16 . . . . . . 5C 68
Boreham Cl. E11 . . . . . . 3E 39
Boreman Ho. SE10 . . . . . 2E 95
  (off Thames St.)
Borland Rd. SE15 . . . . . . 2E 107
Borneo St. SW15 . . . . . . 1E 99
BOROUGH, THE
  . . . . 4A 26 (3F 77)
Borough High St.
  SE1 . . . . 4A 26 (3F 77)
Borough Mkt. SE1 . . . . . 2B 26
Borough Rd.
  SE1 . . . . 5E 25 (4D 77)
Borough Sq. SE1 . . . . . . 4F 25
Borrett Cl. SE17 . . . . 1E 91
Borrodaile Rd.
  SW18 . . . . 4D 101
Borrowdale NW1 . . . . . . 2F 5
  (off Robert St.)
Borthwick M. E15. . . . . . 1A 54
Borthwick Rd. E15 . . . . . 1A 54
  NW9 . . . . 1B 28
Borthwick St. SE8 . . . . . 1C 94
Bosbury Rd. SE6 . . . . . . 3E 123
Boscastle Rd. NW5 . . . . 5D 33
Boscobel Ho. E8 . . . . . . 3D 51
Boscobel Pl. SW1 . . . . . 5C 74
Boscobel St. NW8 . . . . . 3F 59
Boscombe Av. E10 . . . . . 2F 39

Boscombe Cl. E5 . . . . . . 2A 52
Boscombe Rd.
  SW17 . . . . 5C 116
  W12 . . . . 2C 70
Boss Ho. SE1 . . . . 3F 27
  (off Boss St.)
Boss St. SE1 . . . . 3F 27 (3B 78)
Boston Gdns. W4 . . . . . . 2A 84
Boston Ho. SW5 . . . . 5D 73
  (off Collingham Rd.)
Boston Pl. NW1 . . . . 3B 60
Boston Rd. E6 . . . . 2F 69
  E17 . . . . 1C 38
Bosun Cl. E14 . . . . 3C 80
Boswell Ct. W14 . . . . . . 4F 71
  (off Blythe Rd.)
  WC1 . . . . 5E 7 (4A 62)
Boswell Ho. WC1 . . . . . . 5E 7
  (off Boswell St.)
Boswell St.
  WC1 . . . . 5E 7 (4A 62)
Bosworth Ho. W10 . . . . 3A 58
  (off Bosworth Rd.)
Bosworth Rd. W10 . . . . 3A 58
Botha Rd. E13 . . . . 4D 69
Bothwell Cl. E16 . . . . . . 4B 68
Bothwell St. W6 . . . . 2F 85
Botolph All. EC3 . . . . 4D 19
Botolph La.
  EC3 . . . . 5D 19 (1A 78)
Botts M. W2 . . . . 5C 58
Boughton Ho. SE1 . . . . . 3B 26
  (off Tennis St.)
Boulcott St. E1 . . . . 5F 65
Boulevard, The SW6 . . . 4E 87
  SW17 . . . . 2C 116
  SW18 . . . . 2D 101
Boulogne Ho. SE1 . . . . . 5F 27
  (off Abbey St.)
Boulter Ho. SE14 . . . . . . 4E 93
  (off Kender St.)
Boundaries Rd.
  SW12 . . . . 2B 116
Boundary Av. E17 . . . . . . 2B 38
Boundary Ho. SE5 . . . . . 3E 91
  W11 . . . . 2F 71
  (off Queensdale Cres.)
Boundary La. E13 . . . . . . 2F 69
  SE17 . . . . 2E 91
Boundary Pas.
  E2 . . . . 3F 11 (3B 64)
Boundary Rd. E13 . . . . . 1E 69
  E17 . . . . 2B 38
  NW8 . . . . 5D 45
  SW19 . . . . 5F 115
Boundary Row
  SE1 . . . . 3D 25 (3D 77)
Boundary St.
  E2 . . . . 2F 11 (2B 64)
Boundfield Rd. SE6 . . . . 3A 124
Bourbon Ho. SE6 . . . . . . 5E 123
Bourchier St.
  W1 . . . . 4B 14 (1F 75)
  (not continuous)
Bourdon Pl. W1 . . . . 4E 13
Bourdon St.
  W1 . . . . 5D 13 (1D 75)
Bourke Cl. NW10 . . . . . . 3A 42
  SW4 . . . . 4A 104

Bourlet Cl.
  W1 . . . . 1F **13** (4E **61**)
Bournbrook Rd. SE3 . . 1F **111**
Bourne Est.
  EC1 . . . . 5B **8** (4C **62**)
Bourne M.
  W1 . . . . 3C **12** (5C **60**)
Bournemouth Cl.
  SE15 . . . . 5C **92**
Bournemouth Rd.
  SE15 . . . . 5C **92**
Bourne Pl. W4 . . . . . . 1A **84**
Bourne Rd. E7 . . . . . . 5B **40**
  N8 . . . . 1A **34**
Bournes Ho. N15 . . . . . 1A **36**
  (off Chisley Rd.)
Bourneside Gdns.
  SE6 . . . . 5E **123**
Bourne St. SW1 . . . . . 5C **74**
Bourne Ter. W2 . . . . . 4D **59**
Bournevale Rd.
  SW16 . . . . 4A **118**
Bournville Rd. SE6 . . . 5C **108**
Bousfield Rd. SE14 . . . 5F **93**
Boutflower Rd.
  SW11 . . . . 2A **102**
Boutique Hall SE13 . . . 2E **109**
Bouverie M. N16 . . . . . 4A **36**
Bouverie Pl. W2 . . . . . 5F **59**
Bouverie Rd. N16 . . . . 3A **36**
Bouverie St.
  EC4 . . . . . . 3C **16** (5C **62**)
Boveney Ho. SE23 . . . . 5F **107**
Bovill Rd. SE23 . . . . . . 5F **107**
Bovingdon Cl. N19 . . . . 4E **33**
Bovingdon Rd. SW6 . . . 4D **87**
BOW 2B **66**
Bowater Cl. SW2 . . . . . 4A **104**
Bowater Ho. EC1 . . . . . 4F **9**
  (off Golden La. Est.)
  SW1 . . . . 3A **20**
Bowater Pl. SE3 . . . . . 3D **97**
Bowater Rd. SE18 . . . . 4F **83**
Bow Bri. Est. E3 . . . . . 2D **67**
Bow Brook, The E2 . . . 1F **65**
  (off Mace St.)
Bow Chyd. EC4 . . . . . . 3A **18**
BOW COMMON 4C **66**
Bow Comn. La. E3 . . . . 3B **66**
Bowden St. SE11 . . . . . 1C **90**
Bowditch SE8 . . . . 5B **80**
  (not continuous)
Bowdon Rd. E17 . . . . . 2C **38**
Bowen Dr. SE21 . . . . . 3A **120**
Bowen St. E14 . . . . . . 5D **67**
Bower Av. SE10 . . . . . . 4A **96**
Bowerdean St. SW6 . . . 4D **87**
Bower Ho. SE14 . . . . . 4F **93**
  (off Besson St.)
Bowerman Av. SE14 . . . 2A **94**
Bowerman Ct. N19 . . . . 4F **33**
  (off St John's Way)
Bower St. E1 . . . . 5F **65**
Bowes-Lyon Hall
  E16 . . . . 2C **82**
  (off Wesley Av.,
  not continuous)
Bowes Rd. W3 . . . . . . 1A **70**
Bowfell Rd. W6 . . . . . . 2E **85**

Bowhill Cl. SW9 . . . . . . 3C **90**
Bowie Cl. SW4 . . . . . . 5F **103**
BOW INTERCHANGE . . . 1D **67**
Bow Ind. Pk. E15 . . . . . 4C **52**
Bowland Rd. SW4 . . . . 2F **103**
Bowland Yd. SW1 . . . . 4A **20**
Bow La. EC4 . . . 3A **18** (5E **63**)
Bowl Ct. EC2 . . . 4E **11** (3A **64**)
Bowles Rd. SE1 . . . . . . 2C **92**
Bowley Cl. SE19 . . . . . 5B **120**
Bowley Ho. SE16 . . . . . 4C **78**
Bowley La. SE19 . . . . . 5B **120**
Bowling Grn. Cl.
  SW15 . . . . 5D **99**
Bowling Grn. Ho.
  SW10 . . . . 3F **87**
  (off Riley St.)
Bowling Grn. La.
  EC1 . . . . 3C **8** (3C **62**)
Bowling Grn. Pl.
  SE1 . . . . 3B **26** (3F **77**)
Bowling Grn. St.
  SE11 . . . . 2C **90**
Bowling Grn. Wlk.
  N1 . . . . 1D **11** (2A **64**)
Bow Locks E3 . . . . 3E **67**
Bowman Av. E16 . . . . . 1B **82**
Bowman M. SW18 . . . . 1B **114**
Bowman's Bldgs.
  NW1 . . . . 4A **60**
  (off Penfold Pl.)
Bowmans Lea SE3 . . . . 5E **107**
Bowman's M. E1 . . . . . 1C **78**
  N7 . . . . 5A **34**
Bowman's Pl. N7 . . . . . 5A **34**
Bowmore Wlk. NW1 . . . 4F **47**
Bowness Cl. E8 . . . . . . 3B **50**
  (off Beechwood Rd.)
Bowness Cres.
  SW15 . . . . 5A **112**
Bowness Ho. SE15 . . . . 3E **93**
  (off Hillbeck Cl.)
Bowness Rd. SE6 . . . . . 5D **109**
Bowood Rd. SW11 . . . . 3C **102**
Bow Quarter, The E3 . . 1C **66**
Bow Rd. E3 . . . . 2B **66**
Bowry Ho. E14 . . . . . . 4B **66**
  (off Wallwood St.)
Bow St. E15 . . . . 2A **54**
  WC2 . . . . 3E **15** (5A **62**)
Bow Triangle Bus. Cen.
  E3 . . . . 3C **66**
Bowyer Ho. N1 . . . . . . 5A **50**
  (off Mill Row)
Bowyer Pl. SE5 . . . . . . 3E **91**
Bowyer St. SE5 . . . . . . 3E **91**
Boxall Rd. SE21 . . . . . 4A **106**
Boxley St. E16 . . . . . . 2D **83**
Boxmoor Ho. E2 . . . . . 5C **50**
  (off Whiston Rd.)
  W11 . . . . 2F **71**
  (off Queensdale Cres.)
Box Tree Ho. SE8 . . . . 2A **94**
Boxworth Gro. N1 . . . . 5B **48**
Boyce Ho. SW16 . . . . . 5E **117**
  W10 . . . . 2B **58**
  (off Bruckner St.)

Boyce Way E13 . . . . . . 3C **68**
Boydell Ct. NW8 . . . . . 4F **45**
  (not continuous)
Boyd Av. SW19 . . . . . . 5F **115**
Boyd St. E1 . . . . 5C **64**
Boyfield St.
  SE1 . . . . 4E **25** (3D **77**)
Boyland Rd.
  BR1: Brom 5B **124**
Boyle St. W1 . . . 4F **13** (1E **75**)
Boyne Rd. SE13 . . . . . 1E **109**
Boyne Ter. M. W11 . . . 2B **72**
Boyson Rd. SE17 . . . . . 2E **91**
  (not continuous)
Boyson Wlk. SE17 . . . . 2F **91**
Boyton Cl. E1 . . . . 3E **65**
Boyton Ho. NW8 . . . . . 1F **59**
  (off Wellington Rd.)
Brabant Ct. EC3 . . . . . 4D **19**
Brabazon St. E14 . . . . 5D **67**
Brabner Ho. E2 . . . . . . 2C **64**
  (off Wellington Row)
Brabourne Cl. SE19 . . . 5A **120**
Braburn Gro. SE15 . . . 5E **93**
Bracer Ho. N1 . . . . 1A **64**
  (off Whitmore Est.)
Bracewell Rd. W10 . . . . 4E **57**
Bracey M. N4 . . . . 4A **34**
Bracey St. N4 . . . . 4A **34**
Bracken Av. SW12 . . . . 4C **102**
Brackenbury N4 . . . . . 3C **34**
  (off Osborne Rd.)
Brackenbury Gdns.
  W6 . . . . 4D **71**
Brackenbury Rd. W6 . . 4D **71**
Brackenfield Cl. E5 . . . 5D **37**
Bracken Gdns. SW13 . . 5C **84**
Bracken Ho. E3 . . . . . . 4C **66**
  (off Devons Rd.)
Brackley Av. SE15 . . . . 1E **107**
Brackley Cl. NW8 . . . . 3F **59**
  (off Pollitt Dr.)
Brackley Rd. W4 . . . . . 1A **84**
Brackley St.
  EC1 . . . . 5A **10** (3E **63**)
Brackley Ter. W4 . . . . . 1A **84**
Bracklyn Ct. N1 . . . . . 1F **63**
  (not continuous)
Bracklyn St. N1 . . . . . 1F **63**
Bracknell Gdns.
  NW3 . . . . 1D **45**
Bracknell Ga. NW3 . . . 2D **45**
Bracknell Way NW3 . . . 1D **45**
Bradbeer Ho. E2 . . . . . 2E **65**
  (off Cornwall Av.)
Bradbourne St. SW6 . . 5C **86**
Bradbury M. N16 . . . . . 2A **50**
  (off Bradbury St.)
Bradbury St. N16 . . . . 2A **50**
Bradby Ho. NW8 . . . . . 1D **59**
  (off Hamilton Ter.)
Braddyll St. SE10 . . . . 1A **96**
Bradenham SE17 . . . . . 2F **91**
  (off Bradenham Cl.)
Bradenham Cl. SE17 . . 2F **91**
Braden St. W9 . . . . . . 3D **59**
Bradfield Ct. NW1 . . . . 4D **47**
  (off Hawley Rd.)
Bradfield Rd. E16 . . . . 3C **82**

Bradford Cl. SE26 . . . . . 4D **121**
Bradford Ho. *W14* *4F 71*
    (off Spring Va. Ter.)
Bradford Rd. W3 . . . . 3A **70**
Bradgate Rd. SE6 . . . . . 4D **109**
Brading Cres. E11 . . . . . . 4D **41**
Brading Rd. SW2 . . . . . . 5B **104**
Brading Ter. W12 . . . . . . 4C **70**
Bradiston Rd. W9 . . . . . . 2B **58**
Bradley Cl. N7 . . . . 3A **48**
Bradley Ho. *SE16* *5E 79*
    (off Raymouth Rd.)
Bradley M. SW7 . . . . . 1B **116**
Bradley Rd. SE19 . . . . . 5E **119**
Bradley's Cl. N1 . . . . 1C **62**
Bradmead SW8 . . . . 3D **89**
Bradmore Pk. Rd.
   W6 . . . . 5D **71**
Bradshaw Cl. SW19 . . . . 5C **114**
Bradshaw Cotts. *E14* . . . *5A 66*
    (off Repton St.)
Bradstock Ho. E9 . . . . . . 4F **51**
Bradstock Rd. E9 . . . . . . 3F **51**
Brad St. SE1 . . . 2C **24** (2C **76**)
Bradwell Ho. *NW6* *5D 45*
    (off Mortimer Cres.)
Brady Ho. *SW8* *4E 89*
    (off Corunna Rd.)
Brady St. E1 . . . . 3D **65**
Braemar SW15 . . . . 4F **99**
Braemar Av. NW10 . . . . . 5A **28**
   SW19 . . . . 2C **114**
Braemar Cl. *SE16* *1D 93*
    (off Masters Dr.)
Braemar Ct. SE6 . . . . . . 1B **124**
Braemar Ho. *W9* *2E 59*
    (off Maida Va.)
Braemar Mans. *SW7* . . *4D 73*
    (off Cornwall Gdns.)
Braemar Rd. E13 . . . . . . 3B **68**
Braeside BR3: Beck . . 5C **122**
Braes St. N1 . . . . 4D **49**
Braganza St. SE17 . . . . . 1D **91**
Braham Ho. SE11 . . . . . 1B **90**
Braham St.
   E1 . . . . 3F **19** (5B **64**)
Braid Av. W3 . . . . 5A **56**
Braid Ho. *SE10* *4E 95*
    (off Blackheath Hill)
Braidwood Pas. *EC1* . . . *5F 9*
    (off Aldersgate St.)
Braidwood Rd. SE6 . . . . 1F **123**
Braidwood St.
   SE1 . . . . . . 2D **27** (2A **78**)
Brailsford Rd. SW2 . . . . 3C **104**
Braintree Ho. *E1* *3E 65*
    (off Malcolm Rd.)
Braintree St. E2 . . . . 2E **65**
Braithwaite Ho. *EC1* . . . *3B 10*
    (off Bunhill Row)
Braithwaite Twr. *W2* . . . *4F 59*
    (off Hall Pl.)
Bramah Grn. SW9 . . . . . 4C **90**
Bramah Tea & Coffee Mus.
   . . . . 2A **26** (2E **77**)
Bramalea Cl. N6 . . . . . . 1C **32**
Bramall Cl. E15 . . . . 2B **54**
Bramall Ct. *N7* *2B 48*
    (off George's Rd.)

Bramber WC1 . . . . 2D **7**
Bramber Ct. *W14* *2B 86*
    (off North End Rd.)
Bramber Rd. W14 . . . . . . 2B **86**
Bramble Gdns. W12 . . . 1B **70**
Bramble Ho. *E3* *4C 66*
    (off Devons Rd.)
Brambles, The
   SW19 . . . . *5B 114*
    (off Woodside)
Brambling Ct. *SE8* *2B 94*
    (off Abinger Gro.)
Bramcote Gro. SE16 . . . 1E **93**
Bramcote Rd. SW15 . . . 2D **99**
Bramdean Cres.
   SE12 . . . . 1C **124**
Bramdean Gdns.
   SE12 . . . . 1C **124**
Bramerton *NW6* *4F 43*
    (off Willesden La.)
Bramerton St. SW3 . . . . 2A **88**
Bramfield Ct. *N4* *4E 35*
    (off Queens Dr.)
Bramfield Rd.
   SW11 . . . . 4A **102**
Bramford Rd. SW18 . . . 2E **101**
Bramham Gdns.
   SW5 . . . . 1D **87**
Bramhope La. SE7 . . . . . 2D **97**
Bramlands Cl.
   SW11 . . . . 1A **102**
Bramley Cres. SW8 . . . 3F **89**
Bramley Ho. SW15 . . . . *4B 98*
    (off Tunworth Cres.)
   W10 . . . . 5F **57**
Bramley Rd. W10 . . . . . . 5F **57**
    (not continuous)
Brampton *WC1* *1F 15*
    (off Red Lion Sq.)
Brampton Cl. E5 . . . . 4D **37**
Brampton Gdns. N15 . . 1E **35**
Brampton Rd. E6 . . . . . . 2F **69**
   N15 . . . . 1E **35**
Bramshaw Rd. E9 . . . . . 3F **51**
Bramshill Gdns.
   NW5 . . . . 5D **33**
Bramshill Rd. NW10 . . 1B **56**
Bramshot Av. SE7 . . . . . 2C **96**
Bramshurst *NW8* *5D 45*
    (off Abbey Rd.)
Bramston Rd. NW10 . . 1C **56**
   SW17 . . . . 3E **115**
Bramwell Ho.
   SE1 . . . . . . 5A **26** (4E **77**)
   SW1 . . . . *1E 89*
    (off Churchill Gdns.)
Bramwell M. N1 . . . . 5B **48**
Brancaster Ho. *E1* *2F 65*
    (off Moody St.)
Brancaster Rd.
   SW16 . . . . 3A **118**
Branch Hill NW3 . . . . 5E **31**
Branch Hill Ho. NW3 . . . 5D **31**
Branch Pl. N1 . . . . 5F **49**
Branch Rd. E14 . . . . 1A **80**
Branch St. SE15 . . . . . . 3A **92**
Brand Cl. N4 . . . . 3D **35**
Brandlehow Rd.
   SW15 . . . . 2B **100**

Brandon Est. SE17 . . . . . 2D **91**
Brandon Ho.
   BR3: Beck *5D 123*
    (off Beckenham Hill Rd.)
Brandon Mans. *W14* . . . *2A 86*
    (off Queen's Club Gdns.)
Brandon M. EC2 . . . . 1B **18**
Brandon Rd. N7 . . . . 4A **48**
Brandon St. SE17 . . . . . . 5E **77**
    (not continuous)
Brandram M. *SE13* . . . *2A 110*
    (off Brandram Rd.)
Brandram Rd. SE13 . . . 1A **110**
Brandreth Rd.
   SW17 . . . . 2D **117**
Brand St. SE10 . . . . 3E **95**
Brangbourne Rd.
   BR1: Brom 5E **123**
Brangton Rd. SE11 . . . . 1B **90**
Brangwyn Ct. *W14* *4A 72*
    (off Blythe Rd.)
Branksea St. SW6 . . . . . 3A **86**
Branksome Ho. *SW8* . . *3B 90*
    (off Meadow Rd.)
Branksome Rd.
   SW2 . . . . 3A **104**
Branscombe *NW1* *5E 47*
    (off Plender St.)
Branscombe St.
   SE13 . . . . 1D **109**
Bransdale Cl. NW6 . . . . 5C **44**
Brantwood Ho. *SE5* . . . *3E 91*
    (off Wyndam Est.)
Brantwood Rd.
   SE24 . . . . 3E **105**
Brasenose Dr. SW13 . . . 2E **85**
Brassett Point *E15* *5A 54*
    (off Abbey Rd.)
Brassey Ho. *E14* *5D 81*
    (off Cahir St.)
Brassey Rd. NW6 . . . . . 3B **44**
Brassey Sq. SW11 . . . 1C **102**
Brassie Av. W3 . . . . 5A **56**
Brass Talley All.
   SE16 . . . . 3F **79**
Brasted Cl. SE26 . . . . . 4E **121**
Brathay *NW1* *1A 6*
    (off Ampthill Est.)
Brathway Rd. SW18 . . . 5C **100**
Bratley St. E1 . . . . 3C **64**
Bravington Pl. W9 . . . . . 3B **58**
Bravington Rd. W9 . . . . 1B **58**
Bravingtons Wlk. *N1* . . . *1E 7*
    (off York Way)
Brawne Ho. *SE17* *2D 91*
    (off Brandon Est.)
Braxfield Rd. SE4 . . . . . 2A **108**
Braxted Pk. SW16 . . . . 5B **118**
Bray NW3 . . . . 4A **46**
Brayards Rd. SE15 . . . . 5D **93**
Brayards Rd. Est.
   SE15 . . . . *5E 93*
    (off Brayards Rd.)
Braybrook St. W12 . . . . 4B **56**
Brayburne Av. SW4 . . . . 5E **89**
Bray Ct. SW16 . . . . 5A **118**
Bray Cres. SE16 . . . . 3F **79**
Braydon Rd. N16 . . . . . . 3C **36**
Bray Dr. E16 . . . . 1B **82**

Brayfield Ter. N1 . . . . 4C 48
Brayford Sq. E1 . . . . 5E 65
Bray Pas. E16 . . . . 1C 82
Bray Pl. SW3 . . . . 5B 74
Bread St.
  EC4 . . . . . . 3A 18 (5E 63)
    (not continuous)
Breakspears M. SE4 . . . . 5B 94
Breakspears Rd.
  SE4 . . . . 2B 108
Breakwell Ct. W10 . . . . 3A 58
    (off Wornington Rd.)
Breamore Cl. SW15 . . 1C 112
Breamore Ho. SE15 . . . 3C 92
    (off Friary Est.)
Bream's Bldgs.
  EC4 . . . . . . 2B 16 (5C 62)
Bream St. E3 . . . . 4C 52
Breasley Cl. SW15 . . . . 2D 99
Brechin Pl. SW7 . . . . 5E 73
Brecknock Rd. N7 . . . . . . 2F 47
  N19 . . . . 1E 47
Brecknock Rd. Est.
  N19 . . . . 1E 47
Brecon Grn. NW9 . . . . . 1A 28
Brecon Ho. W2 . . . . 5E 59
    (off Hallfield Est.)
Brecon M. N7 . . . . 2F 47
Brecon Rd. W6 . . . . 2A 86
Bredel Ho. E14 . . . . 4C 66
    (off St Paul's Way)
Bredgar SE13 . . . . 3D 109
Bredgar Rd. N19 . . . . . . 4E 33
Bredhurst Cl. SE20 . . . 5E 121
Bredinghurst SE22 . . . 5C 106
Bredin Ho. SW10 . . . . . 3D 87
    (off Coleridge Gdns.)
Breer St. SW6 . . . . 1D 101
Breezers Ct. E1 . . . . 1C 78
    (off The Highway)
Breezer's Hill E1 . . . . . . 1C 78
Bremner Rd. SW7 . . . . . 4E 73
Brenchley Gdns.
  SE23 . . . . 4E 107
Brenda Rd. SW17 . . . . 2B 116
Brendon Av. NW10 . . . 1A 42
Brendon St. W1 . . . . . . 5A 60
Brenley Gdns. SE9 . . . . 2F 111
Brenley Ho. SE1 . . . . . . 3B 26
    (off Tennis St.)
Brennand Ct. N19 . . . . 5E 33
Brent Cl. NW11 . . . . 2E 29
BRENT CROSS 2E 29
Brent Cross Fly-Over
  NW2 . . . . 2F 29
  NW4 . . . . 2F 29
Brent Cross Gdns.
  NW4 . . . . 1F 29
BRENT CROSS INTERCHANGE
  . . . . 1E 29
Brent Cross Shop. Cen.
  NW4 . . . . 2E 29
Brentfield Gdns.
  NW2 . . . . 2F 29
Brentfield Ho. NW10 . . 4A 42
Brentfield Rd. NW10 . . 3A 42
Brent Grn. NW4 . . . . . . 1E 29
Brent Ho. E9 . . . . 3E 51
    (off Frampton Pk. Rd.)

Brenthouse Rd. E9 . . . . . 4E 51
Brenthurst Rd. NW10 . . 3B 42
Brentmead Pl. NW11 . . 1F 29
Brent New Ent. Cen.
  NW10 . . . . 3B 42
Brenton St. E14 . . . . 5A 66
Brent Pk. Rd. NW4 . . . . 2D 29
  NW9 . . . . 2D 29
Brent Rd. E16 . . . . 5C 68
Brent St. NW4 . . . . 1F 29
Brent Ter. NW2 . . . . 3E 29
    (not continuous)
Brent Trad. Cen.
  NW10 . . . . 2A 42
Brent Vw. Rd. NW9 . . . . 1C 28
Brentwood Ho. SE18 . . 3F 97
    (off Portway Gdns.)
Brentwood Lodge
  NW4 . . . . 1F 29
    (off Holmdale Gdns.)
Bressenden Pl.
  SW1 . . . . 5E 21 (4D 75)
Breton Highwalk EC2 . . 5A 10
    (off Golden La.)
Breton Ho. EC2 . . . . 4A 10
  SE1 . . . . 5E 27
    (off Abbey St.)
Brett Cl. N16 . . . . 4A 36
Brettell St. SE17 . . . . . . 1F 91
Brett Ho. Cl. SW15 . . . . 5F 99
Brettinghurst SE1 . . . . . 1C 92
    (off Avondale Sq.)
Brett Pas. E8 . . . . 2D 51
Brett Rd. E8 . . . . 2D 51
Brewer's Grn. SW1 . . . . 5B 22
Brewer's Hall Gdn.
  EC2 . . . . 1A 18
    (off London Wall)
Brewer St.
  W1 . . . . 4A 14 (1E 75)
Brewery, The
  EC2 . . . . 5D 10 (4E 63)
Brewery Ind. Est., The
  N1 . . . . 1A 10
    (off Wenlock Rd.)
Brewery Rd. N7 . . . . 4A 48
Brewery Sq.
  EC1 . . . . . . 3D 9 (3D 63)
  SE1 . . . . 2F 27
Brewhouse La. E1 . . . . . 2D 79
  SW15 . . . . 1A 100
Brewhouse Wlk.
  SE16 . . . . 2A 80
Brewhouse Yd.
  EC1 . . . . 3D 9 (3D 63)
Brewster Gdns. W10 . . 4E 57
Brewster Ho. E14 . . . . . 1B 80
    (off Three Colt St.)
  SE1 . . . . 5B 78
    (off Dunton Rd.)
Brewster Ho. E10 . . . . 3D 39
Briant Ho. SE1 . . . . 5B 24
Briant St. SE14 . . . . 4F 93
Briar Cl. SW15 . . . . 2D 99
Briardale Gdns. NW3 . . 5C 30
Briar Rd. NW2 . . . . 1E 43
Briar Wlk. SW15 . . . . . . 2D 99
  W10 . . . . 3A 58
Briarwood Rd. SW4 . . . 3F 103

Briary Cl. NW3 . . . . 4A 46
Briary Ct. E16 . . . . 5B 68
Briary Gdns.
  BR1: Brom 5D 125
Brickbarn Cl. SW10 . . . 3E 87
    (off King's Barn)
Brick Ct. EC4 . . . . 3B 16 (5C 62)
Brickfield Rd.
  SW19 . . . . 4D 115
Brick La. E1 . . . . 4B 64
  E2 . . . . 2F 11 (2B 64)
Brick Lane Music Hall
  . . . . 2F 83

BRICKLAYER'S
  . . . . 5F 77
Bricklayers Arms Bus. Cen.
  SE1 . . . . 5A 78
Brick St. W1 . . . 2D 21 (2D 75)
Brickwood Cl. SE26 . . . 3D 121
Brideale Cl. SE15 . . . . . 2B 92
Bride Ct. EC4 . . . . 3D 17
Bride La.
  EC4 . . . . 3D 17 (5D 63)
Bridel M. N1 . . . . 5D 49
    (off Colebrook Row)
Brides Pl. N1 . . . . 4A 50
    (off De Beauvoir Rd.)
Bride St. N7 . . . . 3B 48
Bridewain St.
  SE1 . . . . 5F 27 (4B 78)
    (not continuous)
Bridewell Pl. E1 . . . . 2D 79
  EC4 . . . . 3D 17 (5D 63)
Bridford M.
  W1 . . . . 5E 5 (4D 61)
Bridge, The SW8 . . . . . . 3D 89
Bridge App. NW1 . . . . . 4C 46
Bridge Av. W6 . . . . 5E 71
Bridge Av. Mans. W6 . . 1E 85
    (off Bridge Av.)
Bridge Cl. W10 . . . . 5F 57
Bridge Ct. E10 . . . . 3B 38
  E14 . . . . 1F 81
    (off Newport Av.)
Bridgefoot SE1 . . . . 1A 90
Bridge Gdns. N16 . . . . . 1F 49
Bridge Ho. E9 . . . . 3F 51
    (off Shepherds La.)
  NW3 . . . . 4C 46
    (off Adelaide Rd.)
  NW10 . . . . 1F 57
    (off Chamberlayne Rd.)
  SE4 . . . . 2B 108
  SW1 . . . . 1D 89
    (off Ebury Bri.)
  W2 . . . . 4F 59
    (off Nth. Wharf Rd.)
Bridgehouse Ct. SE1 . . 4D 25
    (off Blackfriars Rd.)
Bridge Ho. Quay E14 . . 2E 81
Bridgeland Rd. E16 . . . 1C 82
Bridge La. NW11 . . . . . 1B 30
  SW11 . . . . 4A 88
Bridge Leisure Cen., The
  . . . . 4B 122
Bridgeman Ho. E9 . . . . 4E 51
    (off Frampton Pk. Rd.)
Bridgeman Rd. N1 . . . . 4B 48
Bridgeman St. NW8 . . . 1A 60

Bridge Mdws. SE14 . . . . 2F **93**
Bridgend Rd. SW18 . . . . 2E **101**
Bridgen Ho. E1. . . . . 5D **65**
(off Nelson St.)
Bridgepark SW18 . . . . 3C **100**
Bridge Pl. SW1 . . . . 5D **75**
Bridgepoint Lofts E7. . . . 4E **55**
Bridgepoint Pl. N6 . . . . . 3E **33**
(off Hornsey La.)
Bridgeport Pl. E1 . . . . . 2C **78**
Bridge Rd. E15 . . . . 4F **53**
E17. . . . . 2B **38**
NW10 . . . . 3A **42**
Bridges Ct. SW11 . . . . . 1F **101**
(not continuous)
Bridges Ho. SE5 . . . . 3F **91**
(off Elmington Est.)
Bridgeside Ho. N1 . . . . . 1E **63**
(off Wharf Rd.)
Bridges Pl. SW6 . . . . . . 4B **86**
Bridge St.
SW1 . . . . . . 4D **23** (3A **76**)
Bridge Ter. E15 . . . . 4F **53**
Bridgetown Cl.
SE19 . . . . 5A **120**
Bridge Vw. W6 . . . . 1E **85**
Bridge Vw. Ct. SE1 . . . . 5E **27**
(off Grange Rd.)
Bridgewalk Hgts.
SE1 . . . . 3C **26**
(off Weston St.)
Bridgewater Highwalk
EC2 . . . . 5F **9**
Bridgewater Rd. E15 . . . 5E **53**
Bridgewater Sq.
EC2 . . . . 5F **9** (4E **63**)
Bridgewater St.
EC2 . . . . 5F **9** (4E **63**)
Bridge Way NW11 . . . . . 1B **30**
Bridgeway St. NW1 . . . . 1E **61**
Bridge Wharf E2 . . . . . . 1F **65**
Bridge Yd.
SE1. . . . . 1C **26** (2F **77**)
Bridgford St. SW18 . . . 3E **115**
Bridgnorth Ho. SE15 . . . 2C **92**
(off Friary Est.)
Bridgwater Ho. W2 . . . . 5E **59**
(off Hallfield Est.)
Bridle La. W1 . . 4A **14** (1E **75**)
Bridport SE17 . . . . 1F **91**
(off Date St.)
Bridport Ho. N1 . . . . 5F **49**
(off Bridport Pl.)
Bridport Pl. N1 . . . . 5F **49**
(not continuous)
Bridstow Pl. W2 . . . . . . 5C **58**
Brief St. SE5 . . . . 4D **91**
Brierfield NW1 . . . . 5E **47**
(off Arlington Rd.)
Brierley Rd. E11 . . . . . . 1F **53**
SW12 . . . . 2E **117**
Brierly Gdns. E2 . . . . . . 1E **65**
Brigade St. SE3 . . . . 5B **96**
(off Tranquil Va.)
Briggeford Cl. E5 . . . . . 4C **36**
Briggs Ho. E2 . . . . 1F **11**
(off Chambord St.)
Brightfield Rd.
SE12 . . . . 3A **110**

Brightling Rd. SE4 . . . . 4B **108**
Brightlingsea Pl. E14 . . 1B **80**
Brightman Rd.
SW18 . . . . 1F **115**
Brighton Av. E17 . . . . . 1B **38**
Brighton Bldgs. SE1 . . . 5D **27**
(off Tower Bri. Rd.)
Brighton Gro. SE14 . . . . 4A **94**
Brighton Rd. N16 . . . . . 1A **50**
Brighton Ter. SW9 . . . . 2B **104**
Brightside Rd. SE13 . . . 4F **109**
Bright St. E14 . . . . 5D **67**
Brightwell Cres.
SW17 . . . . 5B **116**
Brig M. SE8 . . . . 2C **94**
Brigstock Rd. SE5 . . . . . 5E **91**
Brill Pl. NW1 . . . 1C **6** (1F **61**)
Brimsdown Ho. E3 . . . . 3D **67**
Brimstone Ho. E15 . . . . 4A **54**
(off Victoria St.)
Brindley Ho. W2 . . . . . . 4C **58**
(off Alfred Rd.)
Brindley St. SE14 . . . . . 4B **94**
Brindley Way
BR1: Brom 5C **124**
Brinklow Ho. W2 . . . . . 4D **59**
(off Torquay St.)
Brinkworth Way E9 . . . . 3B **52**
Brinsley Ho. E1 . . . . 5E **65**
(off Tarling St.)
Brinsley St. E1 . . . . 5D **65**
Brinton Wlk. SE1 . . . . . 2D **25**
Brion Pl. E14 . . . . 4E **67**
Brisbane Ho. W12 . . . . . 1D **71**
(off White City Est.)
Brisbane Rd. E10 . . . . . 4D **39**
E19 . . . . 5D **39**
Brisbane St. SE5 . . . . . . 3F **91**
Briscoe Cl. E11 . . . . 4B **40**
Briscoe Rd. SW19 . . . . 5F **115**
Briset Rd. SE9 . . . . 1F **111**
Briset St. EC1 . . 5D **9** (4D **63**)
Briset Way N7 . . . . 4B **34**
Bristol Gdns. SW15 . . . 5E **99**
W9 . . . . 3D **59**
Bristol Ho. SE11 . . . . . . 4C **76**
(off Lambeth Wlk.)
SW1 . . . . 1C **88**
(off Holbein M.)
WC1 . . . . 5E **7**
(off Southampton Row)
Bristol M. W9 . . . . 3D **59**
Bristol Rd. E7 . . . . 3E **55**
Briston Gro. N8 . . . . . . 1A **34**
Bristowe Cl. SW2 . . . . 4C **104**
Bristow Rd. SE19 . . . . 5A **120**
Britain & London Vis. Cen.
. . . . 1B **22**
(off Regent St.)
Britain at War Experience
. . . . 2D **27**
Britannia Bri. E14 . . . . 5B **66**
(off Commercial Rd.)
Britannia Bldg. N1 . . . . 1B **10**
(off Ebenezer St.)
Britannia Bus. Cen.
NW2 . . . . 1F **43**
Britannia Cl. SW4 . . . . 2F **103**

Britannia Ga. E16 . . . . . 2C **82**
BRITANNIA JUNC. 5D **47**
Britannia Leisure Cen.
. . . . 5F **49**
Britannia Rd. E14 . . . . . 5C **80**
SW6 . . . . 3D **87**
(not continuous)
Britannia Row N1 . . . . . 5D **49**
Britannia St.
WC1 . . . . 1F **7** (2B **62**)
Britannia Wlk.
N1 . . . . 1B **10** (1F **63**)
(not continuous)
Britannia Way SW6 . . . 3D **87**
(off Britannia Rd.)
Britannic Highwalk
EC2 . . . . 1B **18**
(off Moor La.)
Britannic Twr. EC2 . . . . 5B **10**
British Genius Site 3C **88**
British Gro. W4 . . . . . . 1B **84**
British Gro. Pas. W4 . . . 1B **84**
British Gro. Sth. W4 . . . 1B **84**
(off British Gro. Pas.)
British Library . 1C **6** (2F **61**)
British Mus. . . 1D **15** (4A **62**)
British St. E3 . . . . 2B **66**
British Telecom Cen.
EC1 . . . . 2F **17**
SE14 . . . . 1F **93**
Britley Ho. E14 . . . . 5B **66**
(off Copenhagen Pl.)
Brittain Ho. SE9 . . . . . 1F **125**
Brittany Point SE11 . . . 5C **76**
Britten Ct. NW11 . . . . . 3D **31**
Britten St. E15 . . . . 1F **67**
Britten Ho. SW3 . . . . . . 1A **88**
(off Britten St.)
Britten St. SW3 . . . . . . 1A **88**
Britton Cl. SE6 . . . . . . 5F **109**
Britton St.
EC1 . . . . 4D **9** (3D **63**)
BRIXTON 2B **104**
Brixton Academy 1C **104**
(off Stockwell Rd.)
Brixton Hill SW2 . . . . . 5A **104**
Brixton Hill Ct. SW2 . . 3B **104**
Brixton Hill Pl. SW2 . . 5A **104**
Brixton Oval SW2 . . . . 2C **104**
Brixton Recreation Cen.
. . . . 1C **104**
(off Brixton Sta. Rd.)
Brixton Rd. SE11 . . . . . 2C **90**
SW9 . . . . 2C **104**
Brixton Sta. Rd.
SW9 . . . . 1C **104**
Brixton Water La.
SW2 . . . . 3B **104**
Broadbent Cl. N6 . . . . . 3D **33**
Broadbent St.
W1 . . . . 4D **13** (1D **75**)
Broadbridge Cl. SE3 . . 3C **96**
Broad Comn. Est.
N16 . . . . 3C **36**
(off Osbaldeston Rd.)
Broad Ct.
WC2 . . . . 3E **15** (5A **62**)
Broadfield NW6 . . . . . . 3D **45**

Broadfield Cl. NW2 . . . . 5E **29**
Broadfield La. NW1 . . . . 4A **48**
Broadfield Rd. SE6. . . . 5A **110**
Broadfields Way
  NW10 . . . . 2B **42**
Broadford Ho. E1 . . . . . . 3A **66**
  (off Commodore St.)
Broadgate EC2 . . . . 1C **18**
Broadgate Circ.
  EC2 . . . . 5D **11** (4A **64**)
Broadgate Ice Rink 1D **19**
Broadgate Rd. E16 . . . . 5F **69**
Broadgates Ct. SE11 . . . 1C **90**
  (off Cleaver St.)
Broadgates Rd.
  SW18 . . . . 1F **115**
Broadhinton Rd.
  SW4 . . . . 1D **103**
Broadhurst Cl. NW6 . . . . 3E **45**
Broadhurst Gdns.
  NW6 . . . . 3D **45**
Broadlands Av.
  SW16 . . . . 2A **118**
Broadlands Cl. N6 . . . . . 2C **32**
  SW16 . . . . 2A **118**
Broadlands Lodge
  N6 . . . . 2B **32**
Broadlands Rd.
  BR1: Brom 4D **125**
  N6 . . . . 2B **32**
Broad La.
  EC2 . . . . 5D **11** (4A **64**)
  N8 . . . . 1B **34**
Broadley St. NW8 . . . . . 4F **59**
Broadley Ter. NW1 . . . . . 3A **60**
Broadmayne SE17 . . . . . 1F **91**
  (off Portland St.)
Broadmead SE6 . . . . . . 3C **122**
  W14 . . . . 5A **72**
Broadoak Ct. SW9 . . . . . 1C **104**
Broadoak Ho. NW6 . . . . . 5D **45**
  (off Mortimer Cres.)
Broad Sanctuary
  SW1 . . . . 4C **22** (3F **75**)
Broadstone NW1 . . . . 4F **47**
  (off Agar Gro.)
Broadstone Ho. SW8 . . . 3B **90**
  (off Dorset Rd.)
Broadstone Pl.
  W1 . . . . 1D **12** (4C **60**)
Broad St. Av.
  EC2 . . . . 1D **19** (4A **64**)
Broad St. Pl. EC2 . . . . . 1C **18**
Broad Wlk.
  NW1 . . . . 1C **4** (5C **46**)
  SE3 . . . . 5E **97**
  W1 . . . . 5A **12** (1B **74**)
Broad Wlk., The
  W8 . . . . 2D **73**
Broadwalk Ct. W8 . . . . . 2C **72**
  (off Palace Gdns. Ter.)
Broadwalk Ho.
  EC2 . . . . 5D **11** (3A **64**)
  SW7 . . . . 3E **73**
  (off Hyde Pk. Ga.)
Broad Wlk. La.
  NW11 . . . . 2B **30**
Broadwall
  SE1 . . . . 1C **24** (2C **76**)

Broadwater Rd.
  SW17 . . . . 4A **116**
Broadway E13 . . . . 1D **69**
  E15 . . . . 4F **53**
  SW1 . . . . . . 4B **22** (4F **75**)
Broadway, The N8 . . . . 1A **34**
  NW9 . . . . 1B **28**
  SW13 . . . . 5A **84**
Broadway Arc. W6 . . . . . 5E **71**
  (off Hammersmith B'way.)
Broadway Cen., The
  W6 . . . . 5E **71**
Broadway Chambers
  W6 . . . . 5E **71**
  (off Hammersmith B'way.)
Broadway Ho.
  BR1: Brom 5F **123**
  (off Bromley Rd.)
  E8 . . . . 5D **51**
  (off Ada St.)
Broadway Mans.
  SW6 . . . . 3C **86**
  (off Fulham Rd.)
Broadway Mkt. E8 . . . . . 5D **51**
  SW17 . . . . 4B **116**
Broadway Mkt. M.
  E8 . . . . 5C **50**
Broadway M. E5 . . . . . . 2B **36**
Broadway Pde. N8 . . . . 1A **34**
Broadway Retail Pk.
  NW2 . . . . 1F **43**
Broadway Shop. Mall
  SW1 . . . . . . 5B **22** (4F **75**)
Broadway Squash &
  Fitness Cen. 5F **71**
Broadway Theatre, The
  Catford 5D **109**
Broadway Wlk. E14 . . . . 3C **80**
Broadwell Pde. NW6 . . . 3D **45**
  (off Broadhurst Gdns.)
Broadwick St.
  W1 . . . . 4A **14** (1E **75**)
Broadwood Ter. W8 . . . . 5B **72**
Broad Yd.
  EC1 . . . . 4D **9** (3D **63**)
Brocas Cl. NW3 . . . . . . 4A **46**
Brockbridge Ho.
  SW15 . . . . 4B **98**
Brocket Ho. SW8 . . . . . 5F **89**
Brockham Cl. SW19 . . . 5B **114**
Brockham Dr. SW2 . . . . 5B **104**
Brockham Ho. NW1 . . . . 5E **47**
  (off Bayham Pl.)
  SW2 . . . . 5B **104**
  (off Brockham Dr.)
Brockham St.
  SE1 . . . . 5A **26** (4E **77**)
Brockill Cres. SE4 . . . . 2A **108**
Brocklebank Ind. Est.
  SE7 . . . . 5C **82**
Brocklebank Rd. SE7 . . . 5D **83**
  SW18 . . . . 5E **101**
Brocklehurst St.
  SE14 . . . . 3F **93**
BROCKLEY 2F **107**
Brockley Cross SE4 . . . 1A **108**
Brockley Cross Bus. Cen.
  SE4 . . . . 1A **108**

Brockley Footpath
  SE4 . . . . 3A **108**
  (not continuous)
  SE15 . . . . 2E **107**
Brockley Gdns. SE4 . . . 5B **94**
Brockley Gro. SE4 . . . . 3B **108**
Brockley Hall Rd.
  SE4 . . . . 3A **108**
Brockley Jack Theatre
  . . . . 3A **108**
Brockley M. SE4 . . . . . . 3A **108**
Brockley Pk. SE23 . . . . 5A **108**
Brockley Ri. SE23 . . . . . 1A **122**
Brockley Rd. SE4 . . . . . 1B **108**
Brockley Vw. SE23 . . . . 5A **108**
Brockley Way SE4 . . . . 3F **107**
Brockman Ri.
  BR1: Brom 4F **123**
Brockmer Ho. E1 . . . . . . 1D **79**
  (off Crowder St.)
Brock Pl. E3 . . . . 3D **67**
Brock Rd. E13 . . . . 4D **69**
Brock St. SE15 . . . . 1E **107**
Brockway Cl. E11 . . . . . 4A **40**
Brockweir E2 . . . . 1E **65**
  (off Cyprus St.)
Brockwell Ct. SW2 . . . . 3C **104**
Brockwell Ho. SE11 . . . 2B **90**
  (off Vauxhall St.)
Brockwell Pk. 4D **105**
Brockwell Pk. Gdns.
  SE24 . . . . 5C **104**
Brockwell Pk. Lido 4D **105**
Brockwell Pk. Row
  SW2 . . . . 5C **104**
Brodia Rd. N16 . . . . . . 5A **36**
Brodie Ho. SE1 . . . . 1B **92**
  (off Cooper's Rd.)
Brodie St. SE1 . . . . 1B **92**
Brodlove La. E1 . . . . . . 1F **79**
Brodrick Rd. SW17 . . . 2A **116**
Broken Wharf
  EC4 . . . . 4F **17** (1E **77**)
Brokesley St. E3 . . . . . . 2B **66**
Broke Wlk. E8 . . . . 5B **50**
Bromar Rd. SE5 . . . . . . 1A **106**
Bromell's Rd. SW4 . . . . 2E **103**
Bromfelde Rd. SW4 . . . 1F **103**
Bromfelde Wlk. SW4 . . . 5F **89**
Bromfield St. N1 . . . . . . 5C **48**
Bromhead Rd. E1 . . . . . 5E **65**
  (off Jubilee St.)
Bromhead St. E1 . . . . . . 5E **65**
Bromleigh Ct. SE23 . . . 2C **120**
Bromleigh Ho. SE1 . . . . 5F **27**
  (off Abbey St.)
BROMLEY 2D **67**
Bromley Hall Rd.
  E14 . . . . 4E **67**
Bromley High St. E3 . . . 2D **67**
Bromley Hill
  BR1: Brom 5A **124**
Bromley Pl.
  W1 . . . . 5F **5** (4E **61**)
Bromley Rd.
  BR1: Brom 1D **123**
  E10 . . . . 1D **39**
  SE6 . . . . 1D **123**
Bromley St. E1 . . . . 4F **65**

BROMPTON 4A 74
Brompton Arc. SW3 . . . 4A 20
Brompton Cotts.
  SW10 . . . . 2E 87
  (off Hollywood Rd.)
Brompton Oratory 4A 74
Brompton Pk. Cres.
  SW6 . . . . 2D 87
Brompton Pl. SW3 . . . . . 4A 74
Brompton Rd.
  SW1 . . . . . 4A 20 (5A 74)
  SW3 . . . . . 4A 20 (5A 74)
Brompton Sq. SW3 . . . . 4A 74
Brompton Vs. SW6 . . . . 2C 86
  (off Ongar Rd.)
Bromwich Av. N6 . . . . . 4C 32
Bromyard Av. W3 . . . . . 1A 70
Bromyard Ho. SE15 . . . 3D 93
  (off Commercial Way)
Bromyard Leisure Cen.
  . . . . 2A 70
Bron Ct. NW6 . . . . 5C 44
BRONDESBURY 4B 44
Brondesbury Ct. NW2 . . 3F 43
Brondesbury M. NW6 . . 4C 44
BRONDESBURY PARK
  . . . . 5A 44
Brondesbury Pk.
  NW2 . . . . 3E 43
  NW6 . . . . 4E 43
Brondesbury Rd.
  NW6 . . . . 1B 58
Brondesbury Vs.
  NW6 . . . . 1B 58
Bronsart Rd. SW6 . . . . 3A 86
Bronte Cl. E7 . . . . 1C 54
Bronte Ct. W14 . . . . . . 4F 71
  (off Girdler's Rd.)
Bronte Ho. N16 . . . . . . 2A 50
  NW6 . . . . 2C 58
  SW4 . . . . 5E 103
Bronti Cl. SE17 . . . . . . 1E 91
Bronwen Ct. NW8 . . . . 2F 59
  (off Grove End Rd.)
Bronze St. SE8 . . . . . . 3C 94
Brookbank Rd.
  SE13 . . . . 1C 108
Brook Cl. SW17 . . . . . 2C 116
Brook Ct. E11 . . . . 5A 40
  E15 . . . . 2D 53
  (off Clays La.)
  SE12 . . . . 3E 125
Brookdale Rd. SE6 . . . 4D 109
  (not continuous)
Brook Dr. SE11 . . . . . . 4C 76
Brooke Ho. SE14 . . . . . 4A 94
Brookehowse Rd.
  SE6 . . . . 2C 122
Brooke Rd. E5 . . . . 5C 36
  N16 . . . . 5B 36
Brooke's Ct.
  EC1 . . . . . . 5B 8 (4C 62)
Brooke's Mkt. EC1 . . . . 5C 8
Brooke St.
  EC1 . . . . . . 1B 16 (4C 62)
Brookfield N6 . . . . 5C 32
Brookfield Pk. NW5 . . . 5D 33
Brookfield Rd. E9 . . . . 3A 52
  W4 . . . . 3A 70

Brook Gdns. SW13 . . . . 1B 98
Brook Ga.
  W1 . . . . . . 5A 12 (1B 74)
BROOK GREEN 5F 71
Brook Grn. W6 . . . . 4F 71
Brook Grn. Flats W14 . . 4F 71
  (off Dunsany Rd.)
Brook Ho. W6 . . . . 5E 71
  (off Shepherd's Bush Rd.)
Brook Ho's. NW1 . . . . . 1E 61
  (off Cranleigh St.)
Brooking Rd. E7 . . . . . 2C 54
Brooklands Av.
  SW19 . . . . 2D 115
Brooklands Cl. NW6 . . . 4B 44
Brooklands Pk. SE3 . . . 1C 110
Brooklands Pas. SW8 . . 4F 89
Brook La.
  BR1: Brom 5C 124
  SE3 . . . . 5D 97
Brook Lodge NW11 . . . 1F 29
  (off Nth. Circular Rd.)
Brooklyn Pas. W12 . . . . 3E 71
  (off Lime Gro.)
Brookmarsh Ind. Est.
  SE10 . . . . 3D 95
Brook M. WC2 . . . . 3C 14
Brook M. Nth. W2 . . . . 1E 73
Brookmill Rd. SE8 . . . . 4C 94
Brook Rd. NW2 . . . . . . 4B 28
Brooksbank Ho. E9 . . . . 3E 51
  (off Brooksbank St.)
Brooksbank St. E9 . . . . 3E 51
Brooksby Ho. N1 . . . . . 4C 48
  (off Liverpool Rd.)
Brooksby M. N1 . . . . . . 4C 48
Brooksby St. N1 . . . . . 4C 48
Brooksby's Wlk. E9 . . . 2F 51
Brooks Ct. SW8 . . . . . 3E 89
Brooks Farm 2D 39
Brookside Rd. N19 . . . . 4E 33
  NW11 . . . . 1A 30
Brooks Lodge N1 . . . . . 1A 64
  (off Hoxton St.)
Brooks M.
  W1 . . . . . . 4D 13 (1D 75)
Brook Sq. SE18 . . . . . . 4F 97
Brooks Rd. E13 . . . . . . 5C 54
Brook St.
  W1 . . . . . . 4D 13 (1D 75)
  W2 . . . . 1F 73
Brooksville Av. NW6 . . . 5A 44
Brookview Rd.
  SW16 . . . . 5E 117
Brookville Rd. SW6 . . . 3B 86
Brookway SE3 . . . . 1C 110
Brookwood Av. SW13 . . 5B 84
Brookwood Ho. SE1 . . . 4E 25
  (off Webber St.)
Brookwood Rd.
  SW18 . . . . 1B 114
Broome Way SE5 . . . . . 3F 91
Broomfield E17 . . . . . . 2B 38
  NW1 . . . . 4C 46
  (off Ferdinand St.)
Broomfield Cl. SE16 . . . 4C 78
  (off Ben Smith Way)
Broomfield Ho. SE17 . . 5A 78
  (off Massinger St.)

Broomfield St. E14 . . . . 4C 66
Broomgrove Rd.
  SW9 . . . . 5B 90
Broomhill Rd.
  SW18 . . . . 3C 100
Broomhouse La.
  SW6 . . . . 5C 86
  (not continuous)
Broomhouse Rd.
  SW6 . . . . 5C 86
Broomsleigh Bus. Pk.
  SE26 . . . . 5B 122
Broomsleigh St.
  NW6 . . . . 2B 44
Broomwood Rd.
  SW11 . . . . 4B 102
Broseley Gro. SE26 . . . 5A 122
Brougham Rd. E8 . . . . . 5C 50
Brougham St. SW11 . . . 5B 88
Brough Cl. SW8 . . . . . . 3A 90
Broughton Dr. SW9 . . . 2C 104
Broughton Gdns. N6 . . . 1E 33
Broughton Rd. SW6 . . . 5D 87
Broughton St. SW8 . . . 5C 88
Broughton St. Ind. Est.
  SW11 . . . . 5C 88
Browne No. 88 . . . . 3C 94
  (off Deptford Church St.)
Brownfield Area E14 . . . 5D 67
Brownfield St. E14 . . . . 5D 67
Brown Hart Gdns.
  W1 . . . . . . 4C 12 (1C 74)
Brownhill Rd. SE6 . . . . 5D 109
Browning Cl. W9 . . . . . 3E 59
Browning Ct. W14 . . . . 2B 86
  (off Turneville Rd.)
Browning Ho. N16 . . . . 1A 50
  (off Shakspeare Wlk.)
  SE14 . . . . 4A 94
  (off Loring Rd.)
  W12 . . . . 5E 57
  (off Wood La.)
Browning M.
  W1 . . . . . . 1C 12 (4D 61)
Browning Rd. E11 . . . . 2B 40
Browning St. SE17 . . . . 1E 91
Brownlow Ho. SE16 . . . 3C 78
  (off George Row)
Brownlow M.
  WC1 . . . . 4A 8 (3B 62)
Brownlow Rd. E7 . . . . . 1C 54
  E8 . . . . 5B 50
  NW10 . . . . 4A 42
Brownlow St.
  WC1 . . . . . . 1A 16 (4B 62)
Browns Arc. W1 . . . . . . 5A 14
  (off Regent St.)
Brown's Bldgs.
  EC3 . . . . . . 3E 19 (5A 64)
Browns La. NW5 . . . . . 2D 47
Brown St. W1 . . . . 5B 60
BROWNSWOOD PARK
  . . . . 4D 35
Brownswood Rd. N4 . . . 5D 35
Broxash Rd. SW11 . . . . 4C 102
Broxbourne Rd. E7 . . . . 5C 40
Broxholme Ho. SW6 . . . 4D 87
  (off Harwood Rd.)
Broxholm Rd. SE27 . . . 3C 118

Broxted Rd. SE6.....2B 122
Broxwood Way NW8....5A 46
Bruce Cl. W10......4F 57
Bruce Hall M.
   SW17.........4C 116
Bruce Ho. W10......4F 57
Bruce Rd. E3.......2D 67
   NW10............4A 42
Bruckner St. W10....2A 58
Brudenell Rd.
   SW17.........3B 116
Bruford Ct. SE8.....2C 94
Bruges Pl. NW1......4E 47
      (off Randolph St.)
Brune Ho. E1........1F 19
Brunei Gallery
   ....5C 6 (4F 61)
Brunel Engine House Mus.
   ....3E 79
Brunel Est. W2......4C 58
Brunel Ho. E14......1D 95
      (off Ship Yd.)
Brunel Rd. E17......1A 38
   SE16............3E 79
   W3..............4A 56
Brunel St. E16......5B 68
Brunel Wlk. SW10....3F 87
      (off Cheyne Rd.)
Brune St. E1...1F 19 (4B 64)
Brunlees Ho. SE16....5F 25
      (off Bath Ter.)
Brunner Cl. NW11....1D 31
Brunner Ho. SE6.....4E 123
Brunner Rd. E17.....1A 38
Brunswick Cen.
   WC1.......3D 7 (3A 62)
Brunswick Cl. Est.
   EC1.......2D 9 (2D 63)
Brunswick Ct. EC1....2D 9
      (off Tompion St.)
   SE1.......4E 27 (3A 78)
   SW1.............5F 75
      (off Regency St.)
Brunswick Flats W11..5C 58
      (off Westbourne Gro.)
Brunswick Gdns. W8..2C 72
Brunswick Ho. E2....1B 64
      (off Thurtle Rd.)
   SE16............4A 80
      (off Brunswick Quay)
Brunswick Mans. WC1..3E 7
      (off Handel St.)
Brunswick M. SW16..5F 117
   W1.......2A 12 (5B 60)
Brunswick Pk. SE5...4A 92
Brunswick Pl.
   N1.......2C 10 (2F 63)
   NW1.......4C 4 (3C 60)
      (not continuous)
Brunswick Quay SE16..4F 79
Brunswick Rd. E10...3E 39
   E14.............5E 67
Brunswick Sq.
   WC1.......3E 7 (3A 62)
Brunswick Vs. SE5...4A 92
Brunton Pl. E14.....5A 66
Brushfield St.
   E1........5E 11 (4A 64)
Brushwood Cl. E14...4D 67

Brussels Rd. SW11...2F 101
Bruton La.
   W1........5E 13 (1D 75)
Bruton Pl.
   W1........5E 13 (1D 75)
Bruton St.
   W1........5E 13 (1D 75)
Brutus Ct. SE11......5D 77
      (off Kennington La.)
Bryan Av. NW10.....4D 43
Bryan Ho. NW10.....4D 43
   SE16............3B 80
Bryan Rd. SE16.....3B 80
Bryan's All. SW6....5D 87
Bryanston Ct. W1....2A 12
      (not continuous)
Bryanston Ho. N8....1F 33
      (off York St.)
Bryanston M. E.
   W1........1A 12 (4B 60)
Bryanston M. W.
   W1........2A 12 (4B 60)
Bryanston Pl. W1....4B 60
Bryanston Sq.
   W1........2A 12 (5B 60)
Bryanston St.
   W1........3A 12 (5B 60)
Bryant Ct. E2........1B 64
      (off Whiston Rd.)
      not continuous)
Bryant St. E15......4F 53
Bryantwood Rd. N7...2C 48
Bryce Ho. SE14......2F 93
      (off John Williams Cl.)
Brydale Ho. SE16....5F 79
      (off Rotherhithe New Rd.)
Bryden Cl. SE26....5A 122
Brydges Pl.
   WC2.......5D 15 (1A 76)
Brydges Rd. E15.....2F 53
Brydon Wlk. N1.....5A 48
Bryer Ct. EC2.......5F 9
Bryett Rd. N7.......5A 34
Bryher Ct. SE11.....1C 90
      (off Sancroft St.)
Brymay Cl. E3.......1C 66
Brynmaer Rd.
   SW11............4B 88
Bryony Rd. W12.....1C 70
Buccleugh Ho. E5....2C 36
Buchanan Ct. SE16...5F 79
      (off Worgan St.)
Buchanan Gdns.
   NW10............1D 57
Buchan Rd. SE15....1E 107
Bucharest Rd.
   SW18...........5E 101
Buckden Cl. SE12...4C 110
Buckfast St. E2......2C 64
Buckhold Rd. SW18...4C 100
Buckhurst Ho. N7....2F 47
Buckhurst St. E1....3D 65
Buckingham Arc.
   WC2............5D 15
Buckingham Chambers
   SW1.............5E 75
      (off Greencoat Pl.)

Buckingham Ct. W11..1C 72
      (off Kensington Pk.)
Buckingham Ga.
   SW1.......5F 21 (4E 75)
Buckingham La.
   SE23...........5A 108
Buckingham Mans.
   NW6.............2D 45
      (off West End La.)
Buckingham M. N1...3A 50
   NW10............1B 56
   SW1.............5F 21
Buckingham Palace
   ....4E 21 (3D 75)
Buckingham Pal. Rd.
   SW1.......5E 21 (5D 75)
Buckingham Pl.
   SW1.......5F 21 (4E 75)
Buckingham Rd. E10..5D 39
   E11.............1E 41
   E15.............2B 54
   N1..............3A 50
   NW10............1B 56
Buckingham St.
   WC2.......1E 23 (1A 76)
Buckland Ct. N1......1A 64
      (off St John's Est.)
Buckland Cres. NW3...4F 45
Buckland Ho. SW1....1D 89
      (off Abbots Mnr.)
Buckland Rd. E10....4E 39
Buckland St. N1.....1F 63
Bucklebury NW1......3F 5
      (off Stanhope St.)
Bucklers All. SW6....2B 86
      (not continuous)
Bucklersbury
   EC4........3B 18 (5F 63)
Bucklersbury Pas.
   EC2.............5F 63
Buckle St. E1.......5B 64
Buckley Cl. SE23....5D 107
Buckley Ct. NW6.....4B 44
Buckley Ho. W14.....3A 72
      (off Holland Pk. Av.)
Buckley Rd. NW6.....4B 44
Buckmaster Cl.
   SW9............1C 104
      (off Stockwell Pk. Rd.)
Buckmaster Ho. N7...1B 48
Buckmaster Rd.
   SW11...........2A 102
Bucknall St.
   WC2.......2C 14 (5A 62)
Bucknell Cl. SW2....2B 104
Buckner Rd. SW2....2B 104
Bucknill Ho. SW1....1D 89
      (off Ebury Bri. Rd.)
Buckridge Ho. EC1....5B 8
      (off Portpool La.)
Buckshead Ho. W2...4C 58
      (off Brunel Est.)
Buckstone Cl. SE23..4E 107
Buck St. NW1........4D 47
Buckstone Cl. SE23..4E 107
Buckthorne Rd. SE4..3A 108
Bude Cl. E17........1B 38
Budge Row
   EC4........4B 18 (1F 77)

Budge's Wlk. *W2* 2E **73**
(off The Broad Wlk.)
Budleigh Ho. *SE15* 3C **92**
(off Bird in Bush Rd.)
Buer Rd. SW6 . . . . 5A **86**
Bugsby's Way SE7 . . . . . . 5B **82**
SE10 . . . . 5B **82**
Bulbarrow *NW8* 5D **45**
(off Abbey Rd.)
Bulinga St. *SW1* 5A **76**
(off John Islip St.)
Bullace Row SE5 . . . . 4F **91**
Bullard's Pl. E2 . . . . 2F **65**
Bulleid Way SW1 . . . . . . 5D **75**
Bullen Ho. *E1* 3D **65**
(off Collingwood St.)
Bullen St. SW11 . . . . 5A **88**
Buller Cl. SE15 . . . . 3C **92**
Buller Rd. NW10 . . . . 2F **57**
Bullingham Mans.
W8 . . . . 3C **72**
(off Pitt St.)
Bull Inn Ct. WC2 . . . . 5E **15**
Bullivant St. E14 . . . . 1E **81**
Bull Rd. E15 . . . . 1B **68**
Bulls Gdns. SW3 . . . . 5A **74**
Bulls Head Pas. EC3 . . . 3D **19**
(not continuous)
Bull Wharf La.
EC4 . . . . . . 4A **18** (1E **77**)
Bull Wharf Wlk.
EC4 . . . . 5A **18**
(off Bull Wharf La.)
Bull Yd. SE15 . . . . 4C **92**
Bulmer M. W11 . . . . 1C **72**
Bulmer Pl. W11 . . . . 2C **72**
Bulow Est. *SW6* 4D **87**
(off Pearscroft Rd.)
Bulrington Cnr. *NW1* . . . 4E **47**
(off Camden Rd.)
Bulstrode Pl.
W1 . . . . 1C **12** (4C **60**)
Bulstrode St.
W1 . . . . 2C **12** (5C **60**)
Bulwer Ct. E11 . . . . 3F **39**
Bulwer Ct. Rd. E11 . . . . . 3F **39**
Bulwer Rd. E11 . . . . 2F **39**
Bulwer St. W12 . . . . 2E **71**
Bunbury Ho. SE15 . . . . . . 3C **92**
(off Fenham Rd.)
Bungalows, The E10 . . . . 1E **39**
Bunhill Row
EC1 . . . . . . 3B **10** (3F **63**)
Bunhouse Pl. SW1 . . . . . 1C **88**
Bunkers Hill NW11 . . . . . 2E **31**
Bunning Way N7 . . . . 4A **48**
Bunsen Ho. *E3* 1A **66**
(off Grove Rd.)
Bunsen St. E3 . . . . 1A **66**
Bunyan Ct. EC2 . . . . 5F **9**
Buonaparte M. SW1 . . . . 1F **89**
Burbage Cl.
SE1 . . . . . . 5B **26** (4F **77**)
Burbage Ho. *N1* 5F **49**
(off Poole St.)
SE14 . . . . 2F **93**
(off Samuel Cl.)
Burbage Rd. SE21 . . . . . 4E **105**
SE24 . . . . 4E **105**

Burcham St. E14 . . . . 5D **67**
Burchell Ho. *SE11* 1B **90**
(off Jonathan St.)
Burchell Rd. E10 . . . . 3D **39**
SE15 . . . . 4D **93**
Burcher Gale Gro.
SE15 . . . . 3B **92**
Burcote Rd. SW18 . . . . . 5F **101**
Burden Ho. *SW8* 3A **90**
(off Thorncroft St.)
Burden Way E11 . . . . 4D **41**
Burder Cl. N1 . . . . 3A **50**
Burder Rd. N1 . . . . 3A **50**
Burdett M. NW3 . . . . 3F **45**
W2 . . . . 5D **59**
Burdett Rd. E3 . . . . 3A **66**
E14 . . . . 3A **66**
Burfield Cl. SW17 . . . . . . 4F **115**
Burford Rd. E6 . . . . 2F **69**
E15 . . . . 5F **53**
SE6 . . . . 2B **122**
Burford Wlk. SW6 . . . . . . 3E **87**
Burford Wharf Apartments
E15 . . . . 5F **53**
(off Cam Rd.)
Burge Rd. E7 . . . . 1F **55**
Burges Gro. SW13 . . . . . 3D **85**
Burgess Av. NW9 . . . . . . 1A **28**
Burgess Bus. Pk. SE5 . . 3F **91**
Burgess Hill NW2 . . . . . . 1C **44**
Burgess Ho. *SE5* 3E **91**
(off Bethwin Rd.)
Burgess Pk. Kart Track
. . . . 2F **91**
Burgess Rd. E15 . . . . 1A **54**
Burgess St. E14 . . . . 4C **66**
Burge St.
SE1 . . . . . . 5C **26** (4F **77**)
Burgh House 1F **45**
Burghill Rd. SE26 . . . . . 4A **122**
Burghley Hall Cl.
SW19 . . . . 1A **114**
Burghley Ho. SW19 . . . . 3A **114**
Burghley Rd. E11 . . . . . . 3A **40**
NW5 . . . . 1D **47**
SW19 . . . . 4F **113**
Burghley Twr. W3 . . . . . . 1B **70**
Burgh St. N1 . . . . 1D **63**
Burgon St.
EC4 . . . . . . 3E **17** (5D **63**)
Burgos Gro. SE10 . . . . . . 4D **95**
Burgoyne Rd. N4 . . . . . . 1D **35**
SW9 . . . . 1B **104**
Burke Cl. SW15 . . . . 2A **98**
Burke Lodge E13 . . . . . . 2D **69**
Burke St. E16 . . . . 4B **68**
(not continuous)
Burland Rd. SW11 . . . . . 3B **102**
Burleigh Ho. *SW3* 2F **87**
(off Beaufort St.)
W10 . . . . 4A **58**
(off St Charles Sq.)
Burleigh Pl. SW15 . . . . . 3F **99**
Burleigh St.
WC2 . . . . . . 4F **15** (1B **76**)
Burleigh Wlk. SE6 . . . . . 1E **123**
Burley Ho. *E1* 5F **65**
(off Chudleigh St.)
Burley Rd. E16 . . . . 5E **69**

Burlington Arc.
W1 . . . . 5F **13** (1E **75**)
Burlington Cl. W9 . . . . . . 3C **58**
Burlington Gdns.
SW6 . . . . 5A **86**
W1 . . . . 5F **13** (1E **75**)
Burlington La. W4 . . . . . . 3A **84**
Burlington M. SW15 . . . . 3B **100**
Burlington Pl. SW6 . . . . . 5A **86**
Burlington Rd. SW6 . . . . 5A **86**
Burma M. N16 . . . . 1F **49**
Burma Rd. N16 . . . . 1F **49**
Burmarsh NW5 . . . . 3C **46**
Burma Ter. SE19 . . . . . . 5A **120**
Burmester Rd.
SW17 . . . . 3E **115**
Burnaby St. SW10 . . . . . 3E **87**
Burnand Ho. *W14* 4F **71**
(off Redan St.)
Burnard Pl. N7 . . . . 2B **48**
Burnaston Ho. E5 . . . . . . 5C **36**
Burnbury Rd. SW12 . . . . 1E **117**
Burne Jones Ho.
W14 . . . . 5A **72**
Burnell Wlk. *SE1* 1B **92**
(off Abingdon Cl.)
Burness Cl. N7 . . . . 3B **48**
Burne St. NW1 . . . . 4A **60**
Burnett Cl. E9 . . . . 2E **51**
Burnett Ho. *SE13* 5E **95**
(off Lewisham Hill)
Burney St. SE10 . . . . 3E **95**
Burnfoot Av. SW6 . . . . . . 4A **86**
Burnham NW3 . . . . 4A **46**
Burnham Cl. SE1 . . . . . . 5B **78**
Burnham Ct. *W2* 1D **73**
(off Moscow Rd.)
Burnham Est. *E2* 2E **65**
(off Burnham St.)
Burnham St. E2 . . . . 2E **65**
Burnham Way SE26 . . . . 5B **122**
Burnhill Cl. SE15 . . . . . . 3D **93**
Burnley Rd. NW10 . . . . . 2B **42**
SW9 . . . . 5B **90**
Burnsall St. SW3 . . . . . . 1A **88**
Burns Cl. SW19 . . . . 5F **115**
Burns Ho. *E2* 2E **65**
(off Cornwall Av.)
SE17 . . . . 1D **91**
(off Doddington Gro.)
Burnside Cl. SE16 . . . . . 2F **79**
Burns Rd. NW10 . . . . . . 5B **42**
SW11 . . . . 5B **88**
Burnt Ash Hgts.
BR1: Brom 5D **125**
Burnt Ash Hill SE12 . . . . 4B **110**
Burnt Ash La.
BR1: Brom 5C **124**
Burnt Ash Rd. SE12 . . . . 3B **110**
Burnthwaite Rd. SW6 . . . 3B **86**
Burntwood Cl.
SW18 . . . . 1A **116**
Burntwood Grange Rd.
SW18 . . . . 1F **115**
Burntwood La.
SW17 . . . . 3E **115**
Burntwood Vw.
SE19 . . . . 5B **120**
Buross St. E1 . . . . 5D **65**

Burrage Ct. SE16 . . . . 5F 79
(off Worgan St.)
Burrard Ho. E2 . . . . 1E 65
(off Bishop's Way)
Burrard Rd. E16 . . . . 5D 69
NW6 . . . . 2C 44
Burr Cl. E1 . . . . 2C 78
Burrell Ho.
SE1 . . . . . . 1D 25 (2D 77)
Burrells Wharf Sq.
E14 . . . . 1D 95
Burrell Towers E10 . . . . . 2C 38
Burrhill Ct. SE16 . . . . 4F 79
(off Worgan St.)
Burroughs Cotts. E14 . . . 4A 66
(off Halley St.)
Burrow Ho. SW9 . . . . 5C 90
(off Stockwell Pk. Rd.)
Burrow Rd. SE22 . . . . . . 2A 106
Burrows M.
SE1 . . . . . . 3D 25 (3D 77)
Burrows Rd. NW10 . . . . . 2E 57
Burrow Wlk. SE21 . . . . . 5E 105
Burr Rd. SW18 . . . . 1C 114
Bursar St.
SE1 . . . . . . 2D 27 (2A 78)
Burslem St. E1 . . . . 5C 64
Burstock Rd. SW15 . . . . . 2A 100
Burston Rd. SW15 . . . . . . 3F 99
Burston Vs. SW15 . . . . . . 3F 99
(off St John's Av.)
Burtley Cl. N4 . . . . 3E 35
(off Yeate St.)
Burton Bank N1 . . . . 4F 49
(off Yeate St.)
Burton Ct. SW3 . . . . 1B 88
(off Franklin's Row,
not continuous)
Burton Gro. SE17 . . . . 1F 91
Burton Ho. SE16 . . . . 3D 79
(off Cherry Gdn. St.)
Burton La. SW9 . . . . 5C 90
(not continuous)
Burton M. SW1 . . . . 5C 74
Burton Pl.
WC1 . . . . 2C 6 (2F 61)
Burton Rd. NW6 . . . . 4B 44
SW9 . . . . 5D 91
(Akerman Rd.)
SW9 . . . . 5C 90
(Evesham Wlk.)
Burton St.
WC1 . . . . 2C 6 (2F 61)
Burtonwood Ho. N4 . . . . . 2F 35
Burtop Rd. Est.
SW17 . . . . 3E 115
Burt Rd. E16 . . . . 2E 83
Burtt Ho. N1 . . . . 1D 11
(off Aske St.)
Burtwell La. SE27 . . . . . . 4F 119
Burwash Ho. SE1 . . . . . . 4C 26
(off Kipling St.)
Burwell Cl. E1 . . . . 5D 65
Burwell Rd. E10 . . . . 3A 38
Burwell Rd. Ind. Est.
E10 . . . . 3A 38
Burwell Wlk. E3 . . . . 3C 66
Burwood Ho. SW9 . . . . . 2D 105
Burwood Pl. W2 . . . . 5A 60
Bury Cl. SE16 . . . . 2F 79

Bury Pl.
WC1 . . . . . . 1D 15 (4A 62)
Bury St. EC3 . . 3E 19 (5A 64)
SW1 . . . . 1A 22 (2E 75)
Bury Wlk. SW3 . . . . 5A 74
Busbridge Ho. E14 . . . . . . 4C 66
(off Brabazon St.)
Busby Ho. SW16 . . . . 4E 117
Busby M. NW5 . . . . 3F 47
Busby Pl. NW5 . . . . 3F 47
Bushbaby Cl.
SE1 . . . . 5D 27 (4A 78)
Bushberry Rd. E9 . . . . 3A 52
Bush Cotts. SW18 . . . . . . 3C 100
Bush Ct. W12 . . . . 3F 71
Bushell Cl. SW2 . . . . 2B 118
Bushell St. E1 . . . . 2C 78
Bushey Down SW12 . . . . 2D 117
Bushey Hill Rd. SE5 . . . . . 4A 92
Bushey Rd. E13 . . . . 1E 69
N15 . . . . 1A 36
Bush Ind. Est. N19 . . . . . . 5E 33
Bush La. EC4 . . 4B 18 (1F 77)
Bushnell Rd. SW17 . . . . . 2D 117
Bush Rd. E8 . . . . 5D 51
E11 . . . . 2B 40
SE8 . . . . 5F 79
(off Rotherhithe New Rd.)
Bush Theatre 3E 71
Bushwood E11 . . . . 3B 40
Bushwood Dr. SE1 . . . . . . 5B 78
Business Design Cen.
. . . . 5C 48
(off Upper St.)
Buspace Studios
W10 . . . . 3A 58
(off Conlan St.)
Butcher Row E1 . . . . 1F 79
E14 . . . . 1F 79
Butchers Rd. E16 . . . . 5C 68
Bute Gdns. W6 . . . . 5F 71
Bute St. SW7 . . . . 5F 73
Bute Wlk. N1 . . . . 3F 49
Butfield Ho. E9 . . . . 3E 51
(off Stevens Av.)
Butler Ho. E2 . . . . 2E 65
(off Bacton St.)
E14 . . . . 5B 66
(off Burdett St.)
SW9 . . . . 4D 91
(off Lothian Rd.)
Butler Pl.
SW1 . . . . . . 5B 22 (4F 75)
Butler Rd. NW10 . . . . 4B 42
Butlers & Colonial Wharf
SE1 . . . . 3F 27
(off Shad Thames)
Butler St. E2 . . . . 2E 65
Butlers Wharf Est. 2B 78
Butlers Wharf W.
SE1 . . . . 2F 27
(off Shad Thames)
Butley Ct. E3 . . . . 1A 66
(off Ford St.)
Butterfield Cl. SE16 . . . . . 3D 79
Butterfields E17 . . . . 1E 39
Butterfly Wlk. SE5 . . . . . . 4F 91
(off Denmark Hill)

Buttermere NW1 . . . . 1E 5
(off Augustus St.)
Buttermere Cl. E15 . . . . . . 1F 53
SE1 . . . . 5B 78
Buttermere Ct. NW8 . . . . . 5F 45
(off Boundary Rd.)
Buttermere Dr.
SW15 . . . . 3A 100
Buttermere Wlk. E8 . . . . . 3B 50
Butterwick W6 . . . . 5F 71
Butterworth Ter.
SE17 . . . . 1E 91
(off Sutherland Wlk.)
Buttesland St.
N1 . . . . 1C 10 (2F 63)
Butts Rd.
BR1: Brom 5A 124
Buxhall Cres. E9 . . . . 3B 52
Buxted Rd. E8 . . . . 4B 50
SE22 . . . . 2A 106
Buxton Ct. E11 . . . . 2B 40
N1 . . . . 1A 10
Buxton M. SW4 . . . . 5F 89
Buxton Rd. E6 . . . . 2F 69
E15 . . . . 2A 54
N19 . . . . 3F 33
NW2 . . . . 3D 43
SW14 . . . . 1A 98
Buxton St. E1 . . . . 3B 64
Byam St. SW6 . . . . 5E 87
Byards Ct. SE16 . . . . 5F 79
(off Worgan St.)
Bye, The W3 . . . . 5A 56
Byelands Cl. SE16 . . . . . . 2F 79
Byfeld Gdns. SW13 . . . . . 4C 84
Byfield Cl. SE16 . . . . 3B 80
Byford Cl. E15 . . . . 4A 54
Bygrove St. E14 . . . . 5D 67
(not continuous)
Byne Rd. SE26 . . . . 5E 121
Byng Pl. WC1 . . 4C 6 (3F 61)
Byng St. E14 . . . . 3C 80
Byrne Rd. SW12 . . . . 1D 117
Byron Av. E12 . . . . 3F 55
Byron Cl. E8 . . . . 5C 50
SE26 . . . . 4A 122
SW16 . . . . 5A 118
Byron Ct. NW6 . . . . 4E 45
(off Fairfax Rd.)
SE22 . . . . 1C 120
SW3 . . . . 5A 74
(off Whiteheads Gro.)
W9 . . . . 3C 58
(off Lanhill Rd.)
WC1 . . . . 3F 7
(off Mecklenburgh Sq.)
Byron Dr. N2 . . . . 1F 31
Byron M. NW3 . . . . 1A 46
W9 . . . . 3C 58
Byron Rd. E10 . . . . 3D 39
NW2 . . . . 4D 29
Byron St. E14 . . . . 5E 67
Bythorn St. SW9 . . . . 1B 104
Byton Rd. SW17 . . . . 5B 116
Byward St.
EC3 . . . . . . 5E 19 (1A 78)
Bywater Ho. SE18 . . . . . . 4F 83
Bywater Pl. SE16 . . . . 2A 80
Bywater St. SW3 . . . . 1B 88

Byway E11 . . . . 1E **41**
Bywell Pl. W1 . . . . . . 1F **13**
Byworth Wlk. N19 . . . 3A **34**

C

Cabbell St. NW1 . . . . . . 4A **60**
Cable Ho. WC1 . . . . 1B **8**
   (off Gt. Percy St.)
Cable Pl. SE10 . . . . . . 4E **95**
Cable St. E1 . . . . 1C **78**
Cable Trade Pk. SE7 . . 5E **83**
Cabot Ct. SE16 . . . . . 5F **79**
   (off Worgan St.)
Cabot Sq. E14 . . . . . . 2C **80**
Cabot Way E6 . . . . . . 5F **55**
Cabul Rd. SW11 . . . . . 5A **88**
Caci Ho. W14 . . . . 5B **72**
   (off Kensington Village)
Cactus Cl. SE15 . . . . . 5A **92**
Cactus Wlk. W12 . . . . 5B **56**
Cadbury Way SE16 . . . 4B **78**
Caddington Rd. NW2 . 5A **30**
Cadell Cl. E2 . . . . 1B **64**
Cade Rd. SE10 . . . . . . 4F **95**
Cader Rd. SW18 . . . . . 4E **101**
Cadet Dr. SE1 . . . . . . 5B **78**
Cadet Pl. SE10 . . . . . . 1A **96**
Cadiz St. SE17 . . . . . . 1E **91**
Cadley Ter. SE23 . . . . 2E **121**
Cadman Cl. SW9 . . . . . 3D **91**
Cadmore Ho. N1 . . . . . 4D **49**
   (off The Sutton Est.)
Cadmus Cl. SW4 . . . . 1F **103**
Cadmus Cl. SW9 . . . . . 4C **90**
   (off Southey Rd.)
Cadnam Lodge E14 . . 4E **81**
   (off Schooner Cl.)
Cadnam Point
  SW15 . . . . 1D **113**
Cadogan Cl. E9 . . . . . . 4B **52**
Cadogan Ct. SW3 . . . . 5B **74**
   (off Draycott Av.)
Cadogan Ct. Gdns.
  SW1 . . . . 5C **74**
   (off D'Oyley St.)
Cadogan Gdns. SW3 . 5B **74**
Cadogan Ga. SW1 . . . . 5B **74**
Cadogan Hall 5C **74**
   (off Wilbraham Pl.)
Cadogan Ho. SW3 . . . 2F **87**
   (off Beaufort St.)
Cadogan La.
  SW1 . . . . . 5B **20** (4C **74**)
Cadogan Mans. SW3 . 5B **74**
   (off Cadogan Gdns.)
Cadogan Pl.
  SW1 . . . . . 5A **20** (4B **74**)
Cadogan Sq.
  SW1 . . . . . 5A **20** (4B **74**)
Cadogan St. SW3 . . . . 5B **74**
Cadogan Ter. E9 . . . . . 3B **52**
Cadoxton Av. N15 . . . . 1B **36**
Caedmon Rd. N7 . . . . . 1B **48**
Caernarvon Ho. E16 . . 2D **83**
   (off Audley Dr.)
  W2 . . . . 5E **59**
   (off Hallfield Est.)

Caesar Ct. E2 . . . . 1F **65**
   (off Palmer's Rd.)
Cafe Gallery 4E **79**
Cahill St.
  EC1 . . . . . . 4A **10** (3E **63**)
Cahir St. E14 . . . . 5D **81**
Caird St. W10 . . . . 2A **58**
Cairncross M. N8 . . . . 1A **34**
   (off Felix Av.)
Cairnfield Av. NW2 . . 5A **28**
Cairns Rd. SW11 . . . . 3A **102**
Caister Ho. N7 . . . . . . 3B **48**
Caistor Rd. E15 . . . . . 5B **54**
   (off Caistor Pk. Rd.)
Caistor M. SW12 . . . . 5D **103**
Caistor Pk. Rd.
  E15 . . . . 5B **54**
Caistor Rd. SW12 . . . 5D **103**
Caithness Ho. N1 . . . . 5B **48**
   (off Twyford St.)
Caithness Rd. W14 . . . 4F **71**
Calabria Rd. N5 . . . . . 3D **49**
Calais Ga. SE5 . . . . . . 4D **91**
Calais St. SE5 . . . . . . 4D **91**
Calbourne Rd.
  SW12 . . . . 5B **102**
Calcott Ct. W14 . . . . . 4A **72**
   (off Blythe Rd.)
Calcott Wlk. SE9 . . . . 4F **125**
Calcraft Ho. E2 . . . . . 1E **65**
   (off Bonner Rd.)
Caldecot Rd. SE5 . . . . 5E **91**
Caldecott Way E5 . . . . 5F **37**
Calder Ct. SE16 . . . . . 2B **80**
Calderon Ho. NW8 . . . 1A **60**
   (off Townshend Est.)
Calderon Pl. W10 . . . . 4E **57**
Calderon Rd. E11 . . . . 1E **53**
Caldervale Rd.
  SW4 . . . . 3F **103**
Caldew St. SE5 . . . . . . 3F **91**
Caldicot Grn. NW9 . . . 1A **28**
Caldwell Ho. SW13 . . . 3E **85**
   (off Trinity Church Rd.)
Caldwell St. SW9 . . . . 3B **90**
Caldy Wlk. N1 . . . . . . 4E **49**
Caleb St. SE1 . . 3F **25** (3E **77**)
Caledonia Ho. E14 . . . 5A **66**
   (off Salmon La.)
Caledonian Rd.
  N1 . . . . 1E **7** (1A **62**)
  N7 . . . . 1B **48**
Caledonian Sq. NW1 . 3F **47**
Caledonian Wharf
  E14 . . . . 5F **81**
Caledonia St.
  N1 . . . . 1E **7** (1A **62**)
Cale St. SW3 . . . . 1A **88**
Caletock Way SE10 . . 1A **96**
Calgarth NW1 . . . . . . 1A **6**
   (off Ampthill Est.)
Calgary Ct. SE16 . . . . 3E **79**
   (off Canada Est.)
Caliban Twr. N1 . . . . . 1A **64**
   (off Arden Est.)
Calico Ho. EC4 . . . . . . 3A **18**
   (off Well Ct.)
Calico Row SW11 . . . 1E **101**
Calidore Cl. SW2 . . . . 4B **104**

California Bldg.
  SE10 . . . . 4D **95**
   (off Deal's Gateway)
Callaby Ter. N1 . . . . . . 3F **49**
Callaghan Cl. SE13 . . 2A **110**
Callahan Cotts. E1 . . . 4E **65**
   (off Lindley St.)
Callander Rd. SE6 . . . 2D **123**
Callcott Ct. NW6 . . . . 4B **44**
Callcott Rd. NW6 . . . . 4B **44**
Callcott St. W8 . . . . . . 2C **73**
Callender Rd. SW7 . . . 4F **73**
Callingham Cl. E14 . . . 4B **66**
Callisons Pl. SE10 . . . 1A **96**
Callis Rd. E17 . . . . . . 1B **38**
Callow St. SW3 . . . . . 2F **87**
Cally Swimming Pool
  . . . . 5B **48**
Calmington Rd. SE5 . . 2A **92**
Calmont Rd.
  BR1: Brom 5F **123**
Calonne Rd. SW19 . . . 4F **113**
Calshot Ho. N1 . . . . . . 1B **62**
   (off Calshot St.)
Calshot St. N1 . . 1F **7** (1B **62**)
Calstock NW1 . . . . 5E **47**
   (off Royal Coll. St.)
Calstock Ho. SE11 . . . 1C **90**
   (off Kennings Way)
Calthorpe St.
  WC1 . . . . . . 3A **8** (3B **62**)
Calton Av. SE21 . . . . 4A **106**
Calverley Cl.
  BR3: Beck 5D **123**
Calverley Gro. N19 . . . 3F **33**
Calvert Av.
  E2 . . . . 2E **11** (2A **64**)
Calvert Ho. W12 . . . . . 1D **71**
   (off White City Est.)
Calverton SE5 . . . . . . 2A **92**
   (off Albany Rd.)
Calvert Rd. SE10 . . . . 1B **96**
Calvert's Bldgs.
  SE1 . . . . . . 2B **26** (2F **77**)
Calvert St. NW1 . . . . . 5C **46**
Calvin St. E1 . . 4F **11** (3B **64**)
Calydon Rd. SE7 . . . . 1D **97**
Calypso Cres. SE15 . . 3B **92**
Calypso Way SE16 . . . 4B **80**
Camarthen Grn. NW9 . 1A **28**
Cambalt Rd. SW15 . . . 3F **99**
Cambay Ho. E1 . . . . . . 3A **66**
   (off Harford St.)
Camber Ho. SE15 . . . . 2E **93**
Camberley Ho. NW1 . . 1E **5**
Cambert Way SE3 . . . 2D **111**
CAMBERWELL 4F **91**
Camberwell Chu. St.
  SE5 . . . . 4F **91**
Camberwell Glebe
  SE5 . . . . 4A **92**
CAMBERWELL GREEN
  . . . . 4F **91**
Camberwell Grn. SE5 . 4F **91**
Camberwell Gro. SE5 . 4F **91**
Camberwell Leisure Cen.
  . . . . 4F **91**
Camberwell New Rd.
  SE5 . . . . 2C **90**

Camberwell Pl. SE5 . . . . . 4E 91
Camberwell Rd. SE5 . . . . . 2E 91
Camberwell Sta. Rd.
SE5 . . . . 4E 91
Camberwell Trad. Est.
SE5 . . . . 4D 91
Camborne Rd.
SW18 . . . . 5C 100
Cambray Rd. SW12 . . . . 1E 117
Cambria Ho. E14 . . . . 5A 66
(off Salmon La.)
SE26 . . . . 4C 120
(off High Level Dr.)
Cambrian Cl. SE27 . . . . . 3D 119
Cambrian Grn. NW9 . . . . 1A 28
(off Snowden Dr.)
Cambrian Rd. E10 . . . . . . 2C 38
Cambria Rd. SE5 . . . . . . 1E 105
Cambria St. SW6 . . . . 3D 87
Cambridge Arc. E9 . . . . . 4E 51
(off Elsdale St.)
Cambridge Av. NW6 . . . . 1C 58
NW10 . . . . 5F 57
Cambridge Cir.
W1 . . . . 3C 14 (5F 61)
Cambridge Cl. E17 . . . . . . 1B 38
Cambridge Ct. E2 . . . . . . 1D 65
(off Cambridge Heath Rd.)
N16 . . . . 2A 36
(off Amhurst Pk.)
NW6 . . . . 1C 58
W2 . . . . 4A 60
(off Edgware Rd.)
W6 . . . . 5E 71
(off Shepherd's Bush Rd.)
Cambridge Cres. E2 . . . . 1D 65
Cambridge Dr.
SE12 . . . . 3C 110
Cambridge Gdns.
NW6 . . . . 1C 58
W10 . . . . 5F 57
Cambridge Ga.
NW1 . . . . 3D 5 (3D 61)
Cambridge Ga. M.
NW1 . . . . 3D 5 (3D 61)
Cambridge Gro. W6 . . . . . 5D 71
Cambridge Heath Rd.
E1 . . . . 4D 65
E2 . . . . 3E 65
Cambridge Ho. W6 . . . . . 5D 71
(off Cambridge Gro.)
Cambridge Pk. E11 . . . . . 2C 40
Cambridge Pk. Rd.
E11 . . . . 2C 40
(off Lonsdale Rd.)
Cambridge Pl. W8 . . . . . . 3D 73
Cambridge Rd. E11 . . . . . 1B 40
NW6 . . . . 1C 58
SW11 . . . . 4B 88
SW13 . . . . 5B 84
Cambridge Sq. W2 . . . . . 5A 60
Cambridge St. SW1 . . . . . 5D 75
Cambridge Ter.
NW1 . . . . 2D 5 (2D 61)
Cambridge Ter. M.
NW1 . . . . 2E 5 (2D 61)
Cambridge Theatre 3D 15
(off Earlham St.)

Cambus Rd. E16 . . . . 4C 68
Cam Ct. SE15 . . . . 2B 92
Camden Arts Cen. 2D 45
Camden Cl. NW1 . . . . 4E 47
(off Rousden St.)
Camden Gdns. NW1 . . . . 4D 47
Camden High St.
NW1 . . . . 4D 47
Camden Hill Rd.
SE19 . . . . 5A 120
Camden Ho. SE8 . . . . 1B 94
Camdenhurst St. E14 . . . 5A 66
Camden La. N7 . . . . 2F 47
Camden Lock Market
 . . . . 4D 47
(off Camden Lock Pl.)
Camden Lock Pl.
NW1 . . . . 4D 47
Camden Market 5D 47
(off Dewsbury Ter.)
Camden M. NW1 . . . . 4E 47
Camden Pk. Rd.
NW1 . . . . 3F 47
Camden Pas. N1 . . . . 5D 49
(not continuous)
Camden Peoples Theatre
 . . . . 3F 5
(off Hampstead Rd.)
Camden Rd. E11 . . . . 1D 41
E17 . . . . 1B 38
N7 . . . . 1A 48
NW1 . . . . 4E 47
Camden Row SE3 . . . . . . 5A 96
Camden Sq. NW1 . . . . . . 4F 47
(not continuous)
SE15 . . . . 4B 92
Camden St. NW1 . . . . 4E 47
Camden Studios
NW1 . . . . 5E 47
(off Camden St.)
Camden Ter. NW1 . . . . . . 3F 47
CAMDEN TOWN 5D 47
Camden Wlk. N1 . . . . 5D 49
(not continuous)
Cameford Ct. SW2 . . . . . 5A 104
Camelford NW1 . . . . 4E 47
(off Royal Coll. St.)
Camelford Ct. W11 . . . . . 5A 58
Camelford Ho. SE1 . . . . . 1A 90
Camelford Wlk.
W11 . . . . 5A 58
Camellia Ho. SE8 . . . . . . 3B 94
(off Idonia St.)
Camellia St. SW8 . . . . . . 3A 90
Camelot Cl. SW19 . . . . . . 4B 114
Camelot Ho. NW1 . . . . . . 3F 47
Camel Rd. E16 . . . . 2F 83
Camera Pl. SW10 . . . . . . 2F 87
Cameret Ct. W11 . . . . 3F 71
(off Holland Rd.)
Cameron Ho. NW8 . . . . . 1A 60
(off St John's Wood St.)
SE5 . . . . 3E 91
Cameron Pl. E1 . . . . 5D 65
SW16 . . . . 2C 118
Cameron Rd. SE6 . . . . . . 2B 122
Cameron Ter. SE12 . . . . . 3D 125
Camerton Cl. E8 . . . . 3B 50

Camgate Mans. SE5 . . . . 2E 91
(off Red Lion Row)
Camilla Rd. SE16 . . . . . . 5D 79
Camlan Rd.
BR1: Brom 4B 124
Camlet St.
E2 . . . . 3F 11 (3B 64)
Camley St. NW1 . . . . 4F 47
Camomile St.
EC3 . . . . 2E 19 (5A 64)
Campana Rd. SW6 . . . . . 4C 86
Campania Bldg. E1 . . . . . 1F 79
(off Jardine Rd.)
Campbell Cl. SW16 . . . . . 4F 117
Campbell Ct. SE21 . . . . . 1C 120
SW7 . . . . 4E 73
(off Gloucester Rd.)
Campbell Gordon Way
NW2 . . . . 1D 43
Campbell Ho. SW1 . . . . . 1E 89
(off Churchill Gdns.)
W2 . . . . 4F 59
(off Hall Pl.)
W12 . . . . 1D 71
(off White City Est.)
Campbell Rd. E3 . . . . 2C 66
E15 . . . . 1B 54
Campbell Wlk. N1 . . . . . . 5A 48
(off Outram Pl.)
Campdale Rd. N7 . . . . . . 5F 33
Campden Gro. W8 . . . . . . 3C 72
Campden Hill W8 . . . . 3C 72
Campden Hill Ct. W8 . . . . 3C 72
Campden Hill Gdns.
W8 . . . . 2C 72
Campden Hill Ga.
W8 . . . . 3C 72
Campden Hill Mans.
W8 . . . . 2C 72
(off Edge St.)
Campden Hill Pl.
W11 . . . . 2B 72
Campden Hill Rd.
W8 . . . . 2C 72
Campden Hill Sq.
W8 . . . . 2B 72
Campden Hill Towers
W11 . . . . 2C 72
Campden Ho. NW6 . . . . . 4F 45
(off Harben Rd.)
W8 . . . . 2C 72
(off Sheffield Ter.)
Campden Ho. Cl. W8 . . . . 3C 72
Campden Ho's. W8 . . . . . 2C 72
Campden Ho. Ter.
W8 . . . . 2C 72
(off Kensington Chu. St.)
Campden Mans. W8 . . . . 2C 72
(off Kensington Chu. St.)
Campden St. W8 . . . . 2C 72
Campen Cl. SW19 . . . . . . 2A 114
Camperdown St. E1 . . . . 5B 64
Campfield Rd. SE9 . . . . . 5F 111
Campion Ho. SW15 . . . . . 2E 99
Campion Ter. NW2 . . . . . 5F 29
Camplin St. SE14 . . . . . . 3F 93
Camp Rd. SW19 . . . . 5D 113
(not continuous)
Campshill Pl. SE13 . . . . . 3E 109

Campshill Rd. SE13 . . . 3E 109
Campus Rd. E17 . . . . 1B 38
Camp Vw. SW19 . . . . . . 5D 113
Cam Rd. E15 . . . . 5F 53
Canada Est. SE16 . . . . . . 4E 79
Canada Gdns. SE13 . . 3E 109
Canada Ho. SE16 . . . . . . 4A 80
    (off Brunswick Quay)
Canada Memorial 3F 21
    (off Green Pk.)
Canada Pl. E14 . . . . 2D 81
    (off Up. Bank St.)
Canada Sq. E14 . . . . 2D 81
Canada St. SE16 . . . . . . 3F 79
Canada Way W12 . . . . . 1D 71
Canada Wharf
    SE16 . . . . 2B 80
Canadian Av. SE6 . . . 1D 123
Canal App. SE8 . . . . 1A 94
Canal Blvd. N1 . . . . 3F 47
CANAL BRIDGE. 2C 92
Canal Bldg. N1 . . . . 1E 63
    (off Shepherdess Wlk.)
Canal Cl. E1 . . . . 3A 66
    W10. . . . . 3F 57
Canal Gro. SE15. . . . . . . 2D 93
Canal Mkt. NW1 . . . . 4D 47
    (off Castlehaven Rd.)
Canal Path E2 . . . . 5B 50
Canalside Activity Cen.
    . . . . 3F 57
Canal Side Studios
    NW1 . . . . 5F 47
    (off St Pancras Way)
Canal St. SE5 . . . . 2F 91
Canal Wlk. N1. . . . . 5F 49
    SE26 . . . . 5E 121
Canal Way W10 . . . . 3F 57
Canberra Rd. SE7. . . . . . 2E 97
Canbury M. SE26 . . . . . 3C 120
Cancell Rd. SW9 . . . . . . 4C 90
Candahar Rd. SW11. . . . 5A 88
Candida Ct. NW1 . . . . . . 4D 47
Candid Ho. NW10 . . . . . . 2D 57
    (off Trenmar Gdns.)
Candle Gro. SE15 . . . . . 1D 107
Candlelight Ct. E15 . . . . 3B 54
    (off Romford Rd.)
Candler St. N15 . . . . 1F 35
Candover St.
    W1 . . . . 1F 13 (4E 61)
Candy St. E3 . . . . 5B 52
Caney M. NW2 . . . . 4F 29
Canfield Gdns.
    NW6 . . . . 4D 45
Canfield Ho. N15 . . . . . . 1A 36
    (off Albert Rd.)
Canfield Pl. NW6 . . . . . . 3E 45
Canford Rd. SW11 . . . . 3C 102
Canham Rd. W3 . . . . 3A 70
CANN HALL 1A 54
Cann Hall Rd. E11 . . . . . 1A 54
Cann Ho. W14 . . . . 4A 72
    (off Russell Rd.)
Canning Cross SE5. . . . . 5A 92
Canning Ho. W12. . . . . . 1D 71
    (off Australia Rd.)
Canning Pas. W8 . . . . . . 4E 73
    (not continuous)

Canning Pl. W8 . . . . 4E 73
Canning Pl. M. W8. . . . . 4E 73
    (off Canning Pl.)
Canning Rd. E15 . . . . . . 1A 68
    N5. . . . . 5D 35
CANNING TOWN 5B 68
CANNING TOWN 5A 68
Cannizaro Rd.
    SW19 . . . . 5E 113
Cannock Ho. N4 . . . . 2E 35
Cannon Ct. EC1 . . . . 3E 9
    (off Brewhouse Yd.)
Cannon Dr. E14 . . . . 1C 80
Cannon Hill NW6 . . . . . . 2C 44
Cannon Ho. SE11 . . . . . . 5B 76
    (off Beaufoy Wlk.)
Cannon La. NW3 . . . . . . 5F 31
Cannon Pl. NW3 . . . . 5F 31
Cannons Health Club
    Cannon Street 4B 18
    Fulham 4F 85
    Willesden Green . . 4E 43
Cannon St. EC2. . . . . 5F 63
    EC4. . . . . . . 3F 17 (5E 63)
Cannon St. Rd. E1. . . . . 5D 65
Cannon Wharf Bus. Cen.
    SE8 . . . . 5A 80
Cannon Workshops
    E14 . . . . 1C 80
    (off Cannon Dr.)
Canon All. EC4 . . . . 3F 17
    (off Queen's Head Pas.)
Canon Beck Rd.
    SE16 . . . . 3E 79
Canonbie Rd. SE23 . . . 1E 107
CANONBURY 3E 49
Canonbury Bus. Cen.
    N1 . . . . 5E 49
Canonbury Ct. N1. . . . . . 4D 49
    (off Hawes St.)
Canonbury Cres. N1 . . . . 4E 49
Canonbury Gro. N1. . . . . 4E 49
Canonbury Hgts. N1 . . . 3F 49
    (off Dove Rd.)
Canonbury La. N1 . . . . . 4D 49
Canonbury Pk. Nth.
    N1 . . . . 3E 49
Canonbury Pk. Sth.
    N1 . . . . 3E 49
Canonbury Pl. N1 . . . . . . 3D 49
    (not continuous)
Canonbury Rd. N1 . . . . . 3D 49
Canonbury Sq. N1. . . . . . 4D 49
Canonbury St. N1 . . . . . . 4E 49
Canonbury Vs. N1 . . . . . 4D 49
Canon Row
    SW1. . . . . . . 4D 23 (3A 76)
    (not continuous)
Canon's Cl. N2 . . . . 2F 31
Canons Ct. E15. . . . . . . 1A-54
Canon St. N1 . . . . 5E 49
Canrobert St. E2 . . . . . . 1D 65
Cantelowes Rd.
    NW1 . . . . 3F 47
Canterbury Av.
    IG1: Ilf. 2F 41
Canterbury Cl. SE5. . . . . 5E 91
    (off Lilford Rd.)

Canterbury Ct. NW6. . . . 1C 58
    (off Canterbury Rd.)
    SE12. . . . . 3D 125
    SW9 . . . . 3C 90
Canterbury Cres.
    SW9 . . . . 1C 104
Canterbury Gro.
    SE27 . . . . 4C 118
Canterbury Ho.
    SE1 . . . . 5A 24 (4B 76)
Canterbury Ind. Pk.
    SE15 . . . . 2E 93
Canterbury Pl. SE17 . . . 1D 91
Canterbury Rd. E10 . . . . 2E 39
    NW6 . . . . 1B 58
Canterbury Ter. NW6 . . . 1C 58
Cantium Retail Pk.
    SE1 . . . . 2C 92
Canton St. E14. . . . . 5C 66
Cantrell Rd. E3 . . . . 3B 66
Canute Gdns. SE16 . . . . 5F 79
Canvey St.
    SE1 . . . . 1F 25 (2E 77)
Cape Henry Ct. E14 . . . 1F 81
    (off Jamestown Way)
Cape Ho. E8 . . . . 3B 50
    (off Dalston La.)
Capel Ct. EC2. . . . . 3C 18
    (off Bartholomew La.)
Capel Ho. E9 . . . . 4E 51
    (off Loddiges Rd.)
Capel Rd. E7 . . . . 1D 55
    E12. . . . . 1D 55
Capener's Cl. SW1 . . . . 4A 20
Capern Rd. SW18 . . . . 1E 115
Cape Yd. E1 . . . . 1C 78
Capital E. Apartments
    E16 . . . . 1C 82
    (off Western Gateway)
Capital Wharf E1 . . . . . . 2C 78
Capland Ho. NW8. . . . . . 3F 59
    (off Capland St.)
Capland St. NW8 . . . . . . 3F 59
Caple Ho. SW10 . . . . . . 3E 87
    (off King's Rd.)
Caple Rd. NW10 . . . . . . 1B 56
Capper St.
    WC1 . . . . 4A 6 (3E 61)
Capstan Ct. E1 . . . . 1E 79
    (off Wapping Wall)
Capstan Ho. E14. . . . . . . 1F 81
    (off Clove Cres.)
    E14 . . . . 5E 81
    (off Stebondale St.)
Capstan Rd. SE8 . . . . . . 5B 80
Capstan Sq. E14 . . . . . . 3E 81
Capstan Way SE16 . . . . 2A 80
Capstone Rd.
    BR1: Brom 4B 124
Capulet M. E16 . . . . 2C 82
Capworth St. E10 . . . . . . 3C 38
Caradoc Cl. W2 . . . . 5C 58
Caradoc St. SE10. . . . . . 1A 96
Caradon Cl. E11. . . . . . . 3A 40
Cara Ho. N1 . . . . 4C 48
    (off Liverpool Rd.)
Caranday Vs. W11 . . . . . 2F 71
    (off Norland Rd.)
Caravel Cl. E14 . . . . 4C 80

Caravel M. SE8 . . . . 2C 94
Caraway Apartments
　SE1 . . . . 3F 27
　　　　　(off Cayenne Ct.)
Caraway Cl. E13. . . . . . . 4D 69
Caraway Hgts. E14 . . . . . 1E 81
　　　　(off Poplar High St.)
Carbis Rd. E14 . . . . 5B 66
Carbrooke Ho. E9 . . . . . . 5E 51
　　　　(off Templecombe Rd.)
Carburton St.
　W1 . . . . 5E 5 (4D 61)
Cardale St. E14 . . . . 3E 81
Cardamon Bldg. SE1 . . . 2F 27
　　　　　(off Shad Thames)
Carden Rd. SE15 . . . . . . 1D 107
Cardiff Ho. SE15. . . . . . . 2C 92
　　　　　　(off Friary Est.)
Cardigan Pl. SE3 . . . . . . 5F 95
Cardigan Rd. E3 . . . . 1B 66
　SW13 . . . . 5C 84
Cardigan St. SE11 . . . . . 1D 90
Cardigan Wlk. N1 . . . . . . 4E 49
　　　　　　(off Ashby Gro.)
Cardinal Bourne St.
　SE1 . . . . 5C 26 (4F 77)
Cardinal Cap All.
　SE1 . . . . 2E 77
Cardinal Ct. E1 . . . . 1C 78
　　　　(off Thomas More St.)
Cardinal Hinsley Cl.
　NW10 . . . . 1C 56
Cardinal Mans. SW1 . . . 5E 75
　　　　　　(off Carlisle Pl.)
Cardinal Pl. SW1 . . . . . . 5F 21
　SW15 . . . . 2F 99
Cardinals Way N19 . . . . . 3F 33
Cardinal Wlk. SW1 . . . . . 5F 21
Cardine M. SE15 . . . . . . 3D 93
Cardington St.
　NW1 . . . . 1A 6 (2E 61)
Cardozo Rd. N7 . . . . 2A 48
Cardross Ho. W6 . . . . . . 4D 71
　　　　　　(off Cardross St.)
Cardross St. W6. . . . . . . 4D 71
Cardwell Rd. N7 . . . . 1A 48
Cardwell Ter. N7. . . . . . . 1A 48
　　　　　　(off Cardwell Rd.)
Career Ct. SE16 . . . . 3F 79
　　　　(off Christopher Cl.)
Carew Cl. N7 . . . . 4B 34
Carew Ct. SE14. . . . . 2F 93
　　　　　　(off Samuel Cl.)
Carew St. SE5. . . . . 5E 91
Carey Ct. SE5 . . . . 3E 91
Carey Gdns. SW8 . . . . . . 4E 89
Carey La.
　EC2 . . . . 2F 17 (5E 63)
Carey Mans. SW1 . . . . . . 5F 75
　　　　　(off Rutherford St.)
Carey Pl. SW1 . . . . 5F 75
Carey St.
　WC2 . . . . 3A 16 (5B 62)
Carfax Pl. SW4 . . . . 2F 103
Carfree Cl. N1 . . . . 4C 48
Cargill Rd. SW18 . . . . . . 1D 115
Carholme Rd. SE23 . . . . 1B 122
Carinthia Ct. SE16 . . . . . 5A 80
　　　　　　(off Plough Way)

Carisbrooke Ct. W1 . . . . 1C 12
　　　　(off Weymouth St.)
Carisbrooke Gdns.
　SE15 . . . . 3B 92
Carker's La. NW5 . . . . . . 2D 47
Carleton Gdns. N19 . . . . 2E 47
Carleton Rd. N7 . . . . 2F 47
Carleton Vs. NW5 . . . . . . 2E 47
Carlile Cl. E3 . . . . 1B 66
Carlile Ho. SE1 . . . . 4F 77
　　　　　　(off Tabard St.)
Carlingford Rd. NW3 . . . 1F 45
Carlisle Av.
　EC3 . . . . 3F 19 (5B 64)
　W3 . . . . 5A 56
Carlisle La. SE1: llf. : llf. 1F 41
　SE1 . . . . 5A 24 (4B 76)
Carlisle Mans. SW1 . . . . 5E 75
　　　　　　(off Carlisle Pl.)
Carlisle Pl.
　SW1 . . . . 5F 21 (4E 75)
Carlisle Rd. E10. . . . . 3C 38
　N4 . . . . 2C 34
　NW6 . . . . 5A 44
Carlisle St.
　W1 . . . . 3B 14 (5F 61)
Carlisle Wlk. E8 . . . . 3B 50
Carlisle Way SW17 . . . . 5C 116
Carlos Pl.
　W1 . . . . 5C 12 (1C 74)
Carlow St. NW1 . . . . 1E 61
Carlson Ct. SW15 . . . . . 2B 100
Carlton Cl. NW3 . . . . 4C 30
Carlton Ct. SW9 . . . . 4D 91
　W9 . . . . 1D 59
　　　　　　(off Maida Va.)
Carlton Dr. SW15 . . . . . . 3F 99
Carlton Gdns.
　SW1 . . . . 2B 22 (2F 75)
Carlton Gro. SE15 . . . . . 4D 93
Carlton Hill NW8 . . . . . . 1D 59
Carlton Ho. NW6 . . . . . . 1C 58
　　　　　(off Canterbury Ter.,
　　　　　　　not continuous)
　SE16 . . . . 3F 79
　　　　　(off Wolfe Cres.)
Carlton Ho. Ter.
　SW1 . . . . 2B 22 (2F 75)
Carlton Lodge N4 . . . . . . 2C 34
　　　　　　(off Carlton Rd.)
Carlton Mans. N16 . . . . . 3B 36
　NW6 . . . . 4C 44
　　　　　(off West End La.)
　W9 . . . . 2D 59
　W14 . . . . 3A 72
　　　　　(off Holland Pk. Gdns.)
Carlton M. NW6 . . . . 2C 44
　　　　　　(off West Cotts.)
　NW6 . . . . 2C 44
　　　　　　　(Carlton Va.)
Carlton Rd. E11 . . . . 3B 40
　E12 . . . . 1F 55
　N4 . . . . 2C 34
Carlton Sq. E1 . . . . 3F 65
　　　　　　(not continuous)
Carlton St.
　SW1 . . . . 5B 14 (1F 75)
Carlton Ter. SE26 . . . . . 3E 121

Carlton Ter. St. E7 . . . . . 4E 55
Carlton Twr. Pl. SW1 . . . 4B 74
Carlton Va. NW6 . . . . . . 1B 58
Carlton Vs. SW15. . . . . . 3A 100
Carlwell St. SW17 . . . . . 5A 116
Carlyle Cl. N2. . . . . 1E 31
　NW10 . . . . 5A 42
Carlyle Ct. SW6 . . . . 4D 87
　　　　　　(off Imperial Rd.)
　SW10 . . . . 4E 87
　　　　(off Chelsea Harbour Dr.)
Carlyle Ho. N16 . . . . 5A 36
　SE5 . . . . 3E 91
　　　　　　(off Bethwin Rd.)
　SW3 . . . . 2F 87
　　　　　(off Old Church St.)
Carlyle Mans. SW3 . . . . 2A 88
　　　　　　(off Cheyne Wlk.)
　W8 . . . . 2C 72
　　　　　(off Kensington Mall.)
Carlyle M. E1 . . . . 3F 65
Carlyle Pl. SW15 . . . . . . 2F 99
Carlyle Rd. E12 . . . . 1F 55
Carlyle's House 2A 88
　　　　　　(off Cheyne Row)
Carlyle Sq. SW3 . . . . 1F 87
Carmalt Gdns. SW15 . . . 2E 99
Carmarthen Pl.
　SE1 . . . . 3D 27 (3A 78)
Carmel Ct. W8 . . . . 3D 73
　　　　　　(off Holland St.)
Carmelite St.
　EC4 . . . . 4C 16 (1C 76)
Carmel Lodge SW6 . . . . 2C 86
　　　　　　(off Lillie Rd.)
Carmen St. E14 . . . . 5D 67
Carmichael Cl.
　SW11 . . . . 1F 101
Carmichael Ct.
　SW13 . . . . 5B 84
　　　　　　(off Grove Rd.)
Carmichael Ho. E14 . . . . 1E 81
　　　　　(off Poplar High St.)
Carmichael M.
　SW18 . . . . 5F 101
Carminia Rd. SW17. . . . 2D 117
Carnaby St.
　W1 . . . . 3F 13 (5E 61)
Carnac St. SE27 . . . . . . 4F 119
Carnarvon Rd. E10. . . . . 1E 39
　E15 . . . . 3B 54
Carnbrook Rd. SE3 . . . . 1F 111
Carnegie Pl. SW19. . . . . 3F 113
Carnegie St. N1 . . . . 5B 48
Carnie Lodge SW17 . . . . 3D 117
Carnival Ho. SE1 . . . . . . 3F 27
　　　　　　(off Gainsford St.)
Carnoustie Dr. N1 . . . . . 4B 48
　　　　　　(not continuous)
Carnwath Rd. SW6. . . . . 1C 100
Carole Ho. NW1 . . . . 5B 46
　　　　　(off Regent's Pk. Rd.)
Carolina Cl. E15. . . . . . . 2A 54
Caroline Cl. SW16 . . . . . 3B 118
　W2 . . . . 1D 73
Caroline Ct. SE6 . . . . . . 4F 123
Caroline Gdns.
　E2 . . . . 1E 11 (2A 64)
　SE15 . . . . 3D 93

Caroline Ho. W2 . . . . . . 1D 73
(off Caroline Cl.)
W6 . . . . 1E 85
(off Queen Caroline St.)
Caroline Pl. SW11 . . . . . 5C 88
W2 . . . . 1D 73
Caroline Pl. M. W2 . . . . 1D 73
Caroline St. E1 . . . . 5F 65
Caroline Ter. SW1 . . . . . 5C 74
Caroline Wlk. W6 . . . . . 2A 86
(off Lillie Rd.)
Carol St. NW1 . . . . 5E 47
Coronia Ct. SE16 . . . . . 5A 80
(off Plough Way)
Carpenter Ho. E14 . . . . 4C 66
(off Burgess St.)
NW11 . . . . 1E 31
Carpenters Bus. Pk.
E15 . . . . 4D 53
Carpenters Ct. NW1 . . . 5E 47
(off Pratt St.)
Carpenters M. N7 . . . . . 2A 48
Carpenters Pl. SW4 . . . 2F 103
Carpenter's Rd. E15 . . . 3C 52
Carpenter St.
W1 . . . . 5D 13 (1D 75)
Carradale Ho. E14 . . . . 5E 67
(off St Leonard's Rd.)
Carrara Cl. SE24 . . . . . 2C 104
SW9 . . . . 2D 105
Carrara M. E8 . . . . 3C 50
Carrara Wharf SW6 . . . 1A 100
Carre M. SE5 . . . . 4D 91
(off Calais St.)
Carriage Dr. E.
SW11 . . . . 3C 88
Carriage Dr. Nth.
SW11 . . . . 2C 88
(Carriage Dr. E.)
SW11 . . . . 3B 88
(Parade, The)
Carriage Dr. Sth.
SW11 . . . . 4B 88
(not continuous)
Carriage Dr. W.
SW11 . . . . 3B 88
Carriage Pl. N16 . . . . . . 5F 35
SW16 . . . . 5E 117
Carrick Ho. N7 . . . . 3B 48
(off Caledonian Rd.)
SE11 . . . . 1C 90
Carrick M. SE8 . . . . 2C 94
Carrington Ct.
SW11 . . . . 2A 102
(off Barnard St.)
Carrington Gdns. E7 . . . 1C 54
Carrington Ho. W1 . . . . 2D 21
(off Carrington St.)
Carrington St.
W1 . . . . 2D 21 (2D 75)
Carrol Cl. NW5 . . . . 1D 47
Carroll Cl. E15 . . . . 2B 54
Carroll Ho. W2 . . . . 1F 73
(off Craven Ter.)
Carronade Ct. N7 . . . . . 2B 48
Carron Cl. E14 . . . . 5D 67
Carroun Rd. SW8 . . . . . 3B 90
Carr St. E14 . . . . 4A 66
Carslake Rd. SW15 . . . . 4E 99

Carson Rd. E16 . . . . 3C 68
SE21 . . . . 2F 119
Carstairs Rd. SE6 . . . . . 3E 123
Carston Cl. SE12 . . . . . . 3B 110
Carswell Rd. SE6 . . . . . . 5E 109
Carter Ct. EC4 . . . . 3D 17
Carteret Ho. W12 . . . . . . 1D 71
(off White City Est.)
Carteret St.
SW1 . . . . 4B 22 (3F 75)
Carteret Way SE8 . . . . . . 5A 80
Carter Ho. E1 . . . . 1F 19
Carter La.
EC4 . . . . 3E 17 (5D 63)
Carter Pl. SE17 . . . . 1E 91
Carter Rd. E13 . . . . 5D 55
SW19 . . . . 5F 115
Carters Cl. SW5 . . . . 2F 47
(off Torriano Av.)
Carters Hill Cl. SE9 . . . . 1E 125
Carters La. SE23 . . . . . . 2A 122
Carter St. SE17 . . . . 2E 91
Carthew Rd. W6 . . . . 4D 71
Carthew Vs. W6 . . . . 4D 71
Carthusian St.
EC1 . . . . 5F 9 (4E 63)
Cartier Circ. E14 . . . . . . 2D 81
Carting La.
WC2 . . . . 5E 15 (1A 76)
Cartmel NW1 . . . . 1F 5
(off Hampstead Rd.)
Carton Ho. SE16 . . . . . . 4C 78
(off Marine St.)
W11 . . . . 1F 71
(off St Ann's Rd.)
Cartoon Mus. 1D 15
(off Museum St.)
Cartwright Gdns.
WC1 . . . . 2D 7 (2A 62)
Cartwright Ho. SE1 . . . . 4E 77
(off County St.)
Cartwright St. E1 . . . . . . 1B 78
Cartwright Way
SW13 . . . . 3D 85
Carvel Ho. E14 . . . . 1E 95
(off Manchester Rd.)
Carver Rd. SE24 . . . . . . 4E 105
Cary Rd. E11 . . . . 1A 54
Carysfort Rd. N16 . . . . . 5F 35
Casby Ho. SE16 . . . . 4C 78
(off Marine St.)
Cascades Twr. E14 . . . . 2B 80
Casella Rd. SE14 . . . . . 3F 93
Casewick Rd. SE27 . . . . 5C 118
Casey Cl. NW8 . . . . 2A 60
Casimir Rd. E5 . . . . 4E 37
Casino Av. SE24 . . . . . . 3E 105
Caspian Ho. E1 . . . . 4F 65
(off Shandy St.)
Caspian St. SE5 . . . . . . 3F 91
Caspian Wlk. E16 . . . . . 5F 69
Casselden Rd. NW10 . . 4A 42
Cassell Ho. SW9 . . . . . . 5A 90
(off Stockwell Gdns. Est.)
Cassidy Rd. SW6 . . . . . 3C 86
(not continuous)
Cassilis Rd. E14 . . . . . . 3C 80
Cassiobury Rd. E17 . . . 1A 38

Cassland Rd. E9 . . . . . . 4F 51
Casslee Rd. SE6 . . . . . . 5B 108
Casson Ho. E1 . . . . 4C 64
(off Spelman St.)
Castalia Sq. E14 . . . . . . 3E 81
Castellain Mans. W9 . . . 3D 59
(off Castellain Rd.,
not continuous)
Castellain Rd. W9 . . . . . 3D 59
Castell Ho. SE8 . . . . 3C 94
Castello Av. SW15 . . . . . 3E 99
CASTELNAU 2D 85
Castelnau SW13 . . . . . . 4C 84
Castelnau Gdns.
SW13 . . . . 2D 85
Castelnau Mans.
SW13 . . . . 2D 85
(off Castelnau,
not continuous)
Castelnau Row SW13 . . 2D 85
Casterbridge NW6 . . . . 5D 45
(off Abbey Rd.)
W11 . . . . 5B 58
(off Dartmouth Cl.)
Casterbridge Rd.
SE3 . . . . 1C 110
Casterton St. E8 . . . . . . 3D 51
Castillon Rd. SE6 . . . . . 2A 124
Castlands Rd. SE6 . . . . 2B 122
Castleacre W2 . . . . 5A 60
(off Hyde Pk. Cres.)
Castle Baynard St.
EC4 . . . . 4E 17 (1D 77)
Castlebrook Cl. SE11 . . 5D 77
Castle Climbing Cen., The
. . . . 4E 35
Castle Cl. E9 . . . . 2A 52
SW19 . . . . 3F 113
Castlecombe Dr.
SW19 . . . . 5F 99
Castlecombe Rd.
SE9 . . . . 4F 125
Castle Ct. EC3 . . . . 3C 18
(off Birchin La.)
SE26 . . . . 4A 122
Castleden Ho. NW6 . . . 4F 45
(off Hilgrove Rd.)
Castle Dr. IG4: Ilf 1F 41
Castleford St. NW8 . . . . 3F 59
(off Henderson Dr.)
Castlehaven Rd.
NW1 . . . . 4D 47
Castle Ho. SE1 . . . . 5E 77
(off Walworth Rd.)
SW8 . . . . 3A 90
(off Sth. Lambeth Rd.)
Castle Ind. Est. SE17 . . 5E 77
Castle La.
SW1 . . . . 5A 22 (4E 75)
Castlemaine SW11 . . . . 5B 88
Castlemain St. E1 . . . . . 4D 65
Castle Mead SE5 . . . . . 3E 91
Castle M. NW1 . . . . 3D 47
SW17 . . . . 4A 116
Castle Pl. NW1 . . . . 3D 47
W4 . . . . 5A 70
Castle Point E13 . . . . . . 1E 69
(off Boundary Rd.)
Castlereagh St. W1 . . . . 5B 60

Castle Rd. NW1 . . . . 3D **47**
Castle St. E6 . . . . 1E **69**
Castleton Ho. *E14* *5E 81*
(off Pier St.)
Castleton Rd. SE9 . . . . . . 4F **125**
Castletown Rd. W14 . . 1A **86**
Castleview Cl. N4 . . . . . . 4E **35**
Castle Way SW19 . . . . . 3F **113**
Castle Wharf *E14* *1A 82*
(off Orchard Pl.)
Castlewood Rd. N15 . . 1C **36**
N16 . . . . 1C **36**
Castle Yd. N6 . . . . 2C **32**
SE1 . . . . 1E **25** (2D **77**)
Castor La. E14 . . . . 1D **81**
Caterham Rd. SE13 . . 1F **109**
Catesby Ho. *E9* *4E 51*
(off Frampton Pk. Rd.)
Catesby St. SE17 . . . . . . 5F **77**
CATFORD 5D **109**
Catford Art Gallery . . 5D **109**
Catford B'way. SE6 . . 5D **109**
CATFORD GYRATORY
. . . . 5D **109**
Catford Hill SE6 . . . . . . 1B **122**
Catford Island SE6 . . 5D **109**
Catford M. SE6 . . . . . . 5D **109**
Catford Rd. SE6 . . . . . . 5C **108**
Catford Trad. Est.
SE6 . . . . 2D **123**
Cathall Leisure Cen. . . 4A **40**
Cathall Rd. E11 . . . . 4F **39**
Cathay Ho. SE16 . . . . . . 3D **79**
Cathay St. SE16 . . . . . . 3D **79**
Cathcart Hill N19 . . . . . 5E **33**
Cathcart Rd. SW10 . . 2D **87**
Cathcart St. NW5 . . . . . 3D **47**
Cathedral Lodge *EC1* . . *5F 9*
(off Aldersgate St.)
Cathedral Mans.
SW1 . . . . *5E 75*
(off Vauxhall Bri. Rd.)
Cathedral Piazza
SW1 . . . . 5F **21** (4E **75**)
Cathedral St.
SE1 . . . . 1B **26** (2F **77**)
Catherall Rd. N5 . . . . . . 5E **35**
Catherine Ct. *SW3* *2E 87*
(off Park Wlk.)
SW19 . . . . 5B **114**
Catherine Griffiths Ct.
EC1 . . . . *3C 8*
(off Northampton Rd.)
Catherine Gro. SE10 . . 4D **95**
Catherine Ho. *N1* *5A 50*
(off Whitmore Est.)
Catherine Pl.
SW1 . . . . 5F **21** (4E **75**)
Catherine St.
WC2 . . . . 4F **15** (1B **76**)
Catherine Wheel All.
E1 . . . . 1E **19** (4A **64**)
(not continuous)
Catherine Wheel Yd.
SW1 . . . . 2F **21**
Catherwood Ct. *N1* *1B 10*
(off Murray Gro.,
not continuous)

Cathles Rd. SW12 . . . 4D **103**
Cathnor Rd. W12 . . . . . 3D **71**
Catling Cl. SE23 . . . . . 3E **121**
Catlin St. SE16 . . . . 1C **92**
Cato Rd. SW4 . . . . 1F **103**
Cator Rd. SE26 . . . . . . 5F **121**
Cator St. SE15 . . . . 3B **92**
(Commercial Way)
SE15 . . . . 2B **92**
(Ebley Cl.)
Cato St. W1 . . . . 4A **60**
Catton St.
WC1 . . . . 1F **15** (4B **62**)
Caudwell Ter. SW18 . . 4F **101**
(off Lambeth Wlk.)
Caughley Ho. *SE11* . . . *4C 76*
(off Lambeth Wlk.)
Caulfield Rd. SE15 . . . 5D **93**
Causeway, The
SW18 . . . . 3D **101**
(not continuous)
SW19 . . . . 5E **113**
Causton Cotts. *E14* . . . *5A 66*
(off Galsworthy Av.)
Causton Ho. SE5 . . . . . 3E **91**
Causton Rd. N6 . . . . . . 2D **33**
Cautley Av. SW4 . . . . . 3E **103**
Cavalry Gdns.
SW15 . . . . 3B **100**
Cavaye Ho. *SW10* *2E 87*
(off Cavaye Pl.)
Cavaye Pl. SW10 . . . . . 1E **87**
Cavell Ho. *N1* *5A 50*
(off Colville St.)
Cavell St. E1 . . . . 4D **65**
Cavendish Av. NW8 . . . 1F **59**
Cavendish Cl. NW6 . . 3B **44**
NW8 . . . . 2F **59**
Cavendish Ct. EC3 . . . 2E **19**
SE6 . . . . *1D 123*
(off Bromley Rd.)
Cavendish Dr. E11 . . . 3F **39**
Cavendish Gdns.
SW4 . . . . 4E **103**
Cavendish Ho. *NW8* . . *1F 59*
(off Wellington Rd.)
Cavendish Mans. *EC1* . . *4B 8*
(off Rosebery Av.)
NW6 . . . . 2C **44**
Cavendish M. Nth.
W1 . . . . 5E **5** (4D **61**)
Cavendish M. Sth.
W1 . . . . 1E **13** (4D **61**)
Cavendish Pde.
SW4 . . . . *4D 103*
(off Clapham Comn. Sth. Side)
Cavendish Pl. SW4 . . 3F **103**
W1 . . . . 2E **13** (5D **61**)
Cavendish Rd. N4 . . . 1D **35**
NW6 . . . . 4A **44**
SW12 . . . . 4D **103**
Cavendish Sq.
W1 . . . . 2E **13** (5D **61**)
Cavendish St. N1 . . . . . 1F **63**
Cavendish Ter. E3 . . . . 2B **66**
Cave Rd. E13 . . . . 2D **69**
Caversham Ho. *SE15* . . *2C 92*
(off Haymerle Rd.)
Caversham Rd. NW5 . . . 3E **47**

Caversham St. SW3 . . . 2B **88**
Caverswall St. W12 . . 5E **57**
Cavour Ho. *SE17* *1D 91*
(off Alberta Est.)
Cawnpore St. SE19 . . 5A **120**
Caxton Ct. SW11 . . . . . 5A **88**
Caxton Gro. E3 . . . . . . 2C **66**
Caxton Rd. SW19 . . . . 5E **115**
W12 . . . . 3F **71**
Caxton St.
SW1 . . . . 5B **22** (4E **75**)
Caxton St. Nth. E16 . . 5B **68**
Caxton Wlk.
WC2 . . . . 3C **14** (5F **61**)
Cayenne Ct.
SE1 . . . . 2F **27** (3B **78**)
Cayton Pl. EC1 . . . . 2B **10**
Cayton St.
EC1 . . . . 2B **10** (2F **63**)
Cazenove Rd. N16 . . . 4B **36**
Cearns Ho. E6 . . . . 5F **55**
Cecil Cl. NW6 . . . . 4D **45**
SW10 . . . . *2E 87*
(off Fawcett St.)
Cecile Pk. N8 . . . . 1A **34**
Cecilia Rd. E8 . . . . 2B **50**
Cecil Rhodes Ho.
NW1 . . . . *1F 61*
(off Goldington St.)
Cecil Rd. E11 . . . . 5B **40**
E13 . . . . 5C **54**
NW10 . . . . 5A **42**
Cecil Sharp House . . . 5C **46**
Cedar Cl. E3 . . . . 5B **52**
SE21 . . . . 1E **119**
Cedar Ct. N1 . . . . 4E **49**
SE1 . . . . *4D 27*
(off Royal Oak Yd.)
SE7 . . . . 2E **97**
SW19 . . . . 3F **113**
Cedar Hgts. NW2 . . . . 3B **44**
Cedar Ho. *E2* *1D 65*
(off Mowlem St.)
E14 . . . . *3E 81*
(off Manchester Rd.)
SE14 . . . . 4F **93**
SE16 . . . . *3F 79*
(off Woodland Cres.)
W8 . . . . *4D 73*
(off Marloes Rd.)
Cedarhurst Dr. SE9 . . 3E **111**
Cedar Mt. SE9 . . . . . . 1F **125**
Cedarne Rd. SW6 . . . . 3D **87**
Cedar Pl. SE7 . . . . 1E **97**
Cedar Rd. NW2 . . . . . . 1E **43**
Cedars, The E15 . . . . . 4B **54**
Cedars Av. E17 . . . . . . 1C **38**
Cedars Cl. SE13 . . . . . 1F **109**
Cedars M. SW4 . . . . . 2D **103**
(not continuous)
Cedars Rd. E15 . . . . . . 3A **54**
SW4 . . . . 1D **103**
SW13 . . . . 5C **84**
Cedar Tree Gro.
SE27 . . . . 5D **119**
Cedar Way NW1 . . . . 4F **47**
Cedar Way Ind. Est.
NW1 . . . . 4F **47**

Cedra Ct. N16. . . . . 3C 36
Celandine Cl. E14. . . . . 4C 66
Celandine Dr. E8. . . . . . 4B 50
Celandine Way E15 . . . 2A 68
Celbridge M. W2 . . . . . . 4D 59
Celestial Gdns.
SE13 . . . . 2F 109
Celia Ho. N1. . . . . 1A 64
(off Arden Est.)
Celia Rd. N19. . . . . 1E 47
Celtic St. E14. . . . . 4D 67
Cemetery La. SE7. . . . . 2F 97
Cemetery Rd. E7. . . . . . 2B 54
Cenacle Cl. NW3 . . . . . 5C 30
Cenotaph 3D 23 (3A 76)
Centaur St.
SE1 . . . . 5A 24 (4B 76)
Central Av. E11. . . . . . . 4F 39
E12 . . . . 5F 41
SW11 . . . . 3B 88
Central Bus. Cen.
NW10 . . . . 2A 42
Central Church Sports Club
. . . . 2F 121
Central Cir. NW4 . . . . . 1D 29
Central Hill SE19 . . . . . 5E 119
Central Ho. E15 . . . . . . 1D 67
Central Mall SW18 . . . 4D 101
(off South Mall)
Central Mans. 1D 29
(off Watford Way)
Central Markets (Smithfield)
. . . . 1D 17
Central Pk. Rd. E6 . . . . 1F 69
Central St Martins College of
Art & Design 1F 15
Central Sq. NW11 . . . . 1D 31
Central St.
EC1. . . . . 1F 9 (2E 63)
Central Wharf E14 . . . . 5C 66
(off Thomas Rd.)
Centre Av. NW10 . . . . . 2E 57
W3 . . . . 2A 70
Centre Ct. Shop. Cen.
SW19 . . . . 5B 114
Centre Dr. E7 . . . . 1E 55
Cen. for the Magic Arts, The
. . . . 3A 6
(off Stephenson Way)
Centre Hgts. NW3. . . . . 4F 45
(off Finchley Rd.)
Centre Point SE1 . . . . . 1C 92
Centrepoint WC2 . . . . . 2C 14
Centre Point Ho.
WC2 . . . . 2C 14
(off St Giles High St.)
Centre Rd. E7. . . . . 4C 40
E11 . . . . 4C 40
Centre Sq. SW18 . . . . . 3C 100
(off Buckhold Rd.)
Centre St. E2 . . . . 1D 65
Centric Cl. NW1 . . . . . . 5C 46
Centurion Bldg.
SW8 . . . . 2D 89
Centurion Cl. N7. . . . . . 4B 48
Centurion La. E3 . . . . . 5B 52
Century Cl. NW4 . . . . . 1F 29
Century Ho. SW15 . . . . 2F 99
Century M. E5. . . . . 1E 51

Century Yd. SE23 . . . . . 2E 121
(not continuous)
Cephas Av. E1. . . . . 3E 65
Cephas Ho. E1 . . . . 3E 65
(off Doveton St.)
Cephas St. E1. . . . . 3E 65
Cerise Rd. SE15. . . . . . 4C 92
Cerney M. W2. . . . . 1F 73
Cervantes Ct. W2. . . . . 5D 59
Cester St. E2 . . . . 5C 50
Ceylon Rd. W14 . . . . . . 4F 71
Chabot Dr. SE15. . . . . . 1D 107
Chadacre Ct. E15. . . . . . 5C 54
(off Vicars Cl.)
Chadacre Ho. SW9 . . . . 2D 105
(off Loughborough Pk.)
Chadbourn St. E14. . . . . 4D 67
Chadd Grn. E13 . . . . . . 5C 54
(not continuous)
Chadston Ho. N1 . . . . . 4D 49
(off Halton Rd.)
Chadswell WC1 . . . . . . 2E 7
(off Cromer St.)
Chadwell Ho. SE17. . . . 1F 91
(off Merrow St.)
Chadwell St.
EC1. . . . . 1C 8 (2C 62)
Chadwick Av. SW19 . . . 5C 114
Chadwick Cl. SW15 . . . 5B 98
Chadwick Rd. E11 . . . . 1A 40
NW10. . . . . 5B 42
SE15 . . . . 5B 92
Chadwick St.
SW1 . . . . 5B 22 (4F 75)
Chadwin Rd. E13. . . . . . 4D 69
Chadworth Ho. EC1 . . . 2F 9
(off Lever St.)
N4 . . . . 3E 35
Chagford St.
NW1 . . . . 4A 4 (3B 60)
Chailey St. E5. . . . . 5E 37
Chalbury Wlk. N1 . . . . . 1B 62
Chalcot Cres. NW1 . . . . 5B 46
Chalcot Gdns. NW3 . . . 3B 46
Chalcot M. SW16 . . . . . 3A 118
Chalcot Rd. NW1 . . . . . 4C 46
Chalcot Sq. NW1 . . . . . 4C 46
(not continuous)
Chalcroft Rd. SE13. . . . 3A 110
Chaldon Rd. SW6. . . . . 3A 86
Chale Rd. SW2. . . . . . . 4A 104
Chalfont Ct. NW1 . . . . . 4A 4
(off Baker St.)
Chalfont Ho. SE16 . . . . 4D 79
(off Keetons Rd.)
Chalford NW3 . . . . 3E 45
(off Finchley Rd.)
Chalford Rd. SE21 . . . . 4F 119
CHALK FARM 4C 46
Chalk Farm Rd.
NW1 . . . . 4C 46
Chalk Hill Rd. W6. . . . . 5F 71
Chalk Rd. E13 . . . . 4D 69
Chalkwell Ho. E1 . . . . . 5F 65
(off Pitsea St.)
Challenge Cl. NW10 . . . 5A 42
Challenger Ho. E14 . . . 1A 80
(off Victory Pl.)
Challice Way SW2 . . . . 1B 118

Challoner Ct. W14 . . . . 1B 86
(off Challoner St.)
Challoner Cres. W14 . . . 1B 86
Challoner Mans.
W14 . . . . 1B 86
(off Challoner St.)
Challoner St. W14 . . . . 1B 86
Chalmers Wlk. SE17 . . . 2D 91
(off Hillingdon St.)
Chalsey Rd. SE4 . . . . . 2B 108
Chalton Dr. N2 . . . . 1F 31
Chalton Ho. NW1 . . . . . 1B 6
(off Chalton St.)
Chalton St.
NW1 . . . . 1B 6 (1E 61)
(not continuous)
Chamberlain Cotts.
SE5 . . . . 4F 91
Chamberlain Ho. E1. . . . 1E 79
(off Cable St.)
NW1 . . . . 1C 6
SE1 . . . . 4B 24
(off Westminster Bri. Rd.)
Chamberlain St.
NW1 . . . . 4B 46
Chamberlayne Mans.
NW10 . . . . 2F 57
(off Chamberlayne Rd.)
Chamberlayne Rd.
NW10 . . . . 5E 43
Chamberlens Garages
W6 . . . . 5D 71
(off Dalling Rd.)
Chambers, The
SW10 . . . . 4E 87
(off Chelsea Harbour Dr.)
Chambers La. NW10 . . . 4D 43
Chambers Rd. N7 . . . . . 1A 48
Chambers St. SE16 . . . . 3C 78
Chamber St. E1 . . . . . . 1B 78
Chambers Wharf
SE16. . . . . 3C 78
Chambon Pl. W6 . . . . . 5C 70
Chambord St.
E2. . . . . 2F 11 (2B 64)
Chamomile Ct. E17 . . . 1C 38
(off Yunus Khan Cl.)
Champion Cres.
SE26 . . . . 4A 122
Champion Gro. SE5 . . . 1F 105
Champion Hill SE5 . . . . 1F 105
Champion Hill Est.
SE5 . . . . 1A 106
Champion Pk. SE5 . . . . 5F 91
Champion Rd. SE26. . . 4A 122
Champlain Ho. W12 . . . 1D 71
(off White City Est.)
Champness Cl.
SE27 . . . . 4F 119
Chancel Ind. Est.
NW10 . . . . 2B 42
Chancellor Gro.
SE21 . . . . 2E 119
Chancellor Ho. E1 . . . . 2D 79
(off Green Bank)
SW7 . . . . 4E 73
(off Hyde Pk. Ga.)
Chancellor Pas. E14 . . . 2C 80
Chancellors Ct. WC1 . . . 5F 7

Chancellor's Rd. W6 . . . 1E **85**
Chancellor's St. W6 . . . 1E **85**
Chancellors Wharf
W6 . . . . 1E **85**
Chancel St.
SE1 . . . . . 2D **25** (2D **77**)
Chancery Bldgs. E1 . . . . 1D **79**
(off Lowood St.)
Chancery La.
WC2 . . . . 1A **16** (5C **62**)
Chancery M. SW17 . . . 2A **116**
Chance St.
E1 . . . . . . 3F **11** (3B **64**)
E2 . . . . . . 3F **11** (3B **64**)
Chandler Av. E16 . . . . . 4C **68**
Chandler Ho. NW6 . . . . 5B **44**
(off Willesden La.)
WC1 . . . . 4E **7**
(off Colonnade)
Chandlers Ct. SE12 . . . 1D **125**
Chandlers M. E14 . . . . . 3C **80**
Chandler St. E1 . . . . . . 2D **79**
Chandlers Way SW2 . . 5C **104**
Chandler Way SE15 . . . 2A **92**
Chandlery, The SE1 . . . 5C **24**
(off Gerridge St.)
Chandlery Ho. E1 . . . . . 5C **64**
(off Bk. Church La.)
Chandos Pl.
WC2 . . . . . 5D **15** (1A **76**)
Chandos Rd. E15 . . . . . 2F **53**
NW2 . . . . 2E **43**
NW10 . . . . 3A **56**
Chandos St.
W1 . . . . 1E **13** (4D **61**)
Chandos Way NW11 . . . 3D **31**
Change All.
EC3 . . . . . . 3C **18** (5F **63**)
Channel Ga. Rd.
NW10 . . . . 2A **56**
Channel Ho. E14 . . . . . 4A **66**
(off Aston St.)
Channel Islands Est.
N1 . . . . 3E **49**
(off Guernsey Rd.)
Channelsea Path E15 . . 5F **53**
Channelsea Rd. E15 . . . 5F **53**
Chanticleer St. SE1 . . . 1B **92**
(off Rolls Rd.)
Chantrey Rd. SW9 . . . 1B **104**
Chantry Cl. W9 . . . . . . 3C **58**
Chantry Cres. NW10 . . . 3B **42**
Chantry Sq. W8 . . . . . . 4D **73**
Chantry St. N1 . . . . . . 5D **49**
Chant Sq. E15 . . . . 4F **53**
Chant St. E15 . . . . 4F **53**
Chapel Av. E12 . . . . . . 5F **41**
Chapel Cl. NW10 . . . . . 2B **42**
Chapel Ct.
SE1 . . . . 3B **26** (3F **77**)
Chapel Ho. St. E14 . . . 1D **95**
Chapelier Ho. SW18 . . 2C **100**
Chapel Mkt. N1 . . . . . . 1C **62**
Chapel of St John the
Evangelist 5F **19**
(in The Tower of London)
Chapel of St Peter & St Paul
. . . . 2F **95**
(in Old Royal Naval College)

Chapel Path E11 . . . . . 1D **41**
(off Woodbine St.)
Chapel Pl.
EC2 . . . . . . 2D **11** (2A **64**)
N1 . . . . 1C **62**
W1 . . . . 3D **13** (5D **61**)
Chapel Rd. SE27 . . . . . 4D **119**
Chapel Side W2 . . . . . . 1D **73**
Chapel St. NW1 . . . . . . 4A **60**
SW1 . . . . . 5C **20** (4C **74**)
Chapel Way N7 . . . . . . 5B **34**
Chapel Yd. SW18 . . . . 3D **101**
(off Wandsworth High St.)
Chaplin Cl.
SE1 . . . . . 3C **24** (3C **76**)
Chaplin Rd. E15 . . . . . 1B **68**
NW2 . . . . 3C **42**
Chapman Ho. E1 . . . . . 5D **65**
(off Bigland St.)
Chapman Pl. N4 . . . . . . 4D **35**
Chapman Rd. E9 . . . . . . 3B **52**
Chapmans Pk. Ind. Est.
NW10 . . . . 3B **42**
Chapman Sq.
SW19 . . . . 2F **113**
Chapman St. E1 . . . . . . 1D **79**
Chapone Pl.
W1 . . . . 3B **14** (5F **61**)
Chapter Chambers
SW1 . . . . 5F **75**
(off Chapter St.)
Chapter House
. . . . 3F **17** (5D **63**)
Chapter Rd. NW2 . . . . . 2C **42**
SE17 . . . . 1D **91**
Chapter St. SW1 . . . . . 5F **75**
Charcot Ho. SW15 . . . . 4B **98**
Charcroft Ct. W14 . . . . 3F **71**
(off Minford Gdns.)
Chardin Ho. SW9 . . . . . 4C **90**
(off Gosling Way)
Chardin Rd. W4 . . . . . . 5A **70**
Chardmore Rd. N16 . . . 3C **36**
Charecroft Way
W12 . . . . 3F **71**
Charfield Ct. W9 . . . . . 3D **59**
(off Shirland Rd.)
Charford Rd. E16 . . . . . 4C **68**
Chargeable La.
E13 . . . . 3B **68**
Chargeable St. E16 . . . 3B **68**
Chargrove Cl. SE16 . . . 3F **79**
Charing Cross SW1 . . . 1D **23**
Charing Cross Rd.
WC2 . . . . . . 2C **14** (5F **61**)
Charing Cross Sports Club
. . . . 2F **85**
Charing Cross Underground
Shop. Cen. WC2 . . . 5D **15**
Charing Ho. SE1 . . . . . 3C **24**
(off Windmill Wlk.)
Chariot Cl. E3 . . . . 5C **52**
Charlbert Ct. NW8 . . . . 1A **60**
(off Charlbert St.)
Charlbert St. NW8 . . . . 1A **60**
Charlecote Gro.
SE26 . . . . 3D **121**
Charles II Pl.
SW3 . . . . 1B **88**

Charles II St.
SW1 . . . . . 1B **22** (2F **75**)
Charles Auffray Ho.
E1 . . . . 4E **65**
(off Smithy St.)
Charles Barry Cl.
SW4 . . . . 1E **103**
Charles Coveney Rd.
SE15 . . . . 4B **92**
Charles Darwin Ho.
E2 . . . . 2D **65**
(off Canrobert St.)
Charles Dickens Ho.
E2 . . . . 2C **64**
(off Mansford St.)
Charlesfield SE9 . . . . . 3E **125**
Charles Flemwell M.
E16 . . . . 2C **82**
Charles Gardner Ct.
N1 . . . . 1C **10**
(off Haberdasher Est.)
Charles Haller St.
SW2 . . . . 5C **104**
Charles Harrod Ct.
SW13 . . . . 2E **85**
(off Somerville Av.)
Charles House 5B **72**
(off Kensington High St.)
Charles La. NW8 . . . . . 1A **60**
Charles Mackenzie Ho.
SE16 . . . . 5C **78**
(off Linsey St.)
Charles Nex M.
SE21 . . . . 2E **119**
Charles Pl.
NW1 . . . . . . 2A **6** (2E **61**)
Charles Rd. E7 . . . . . . 4E **55**
Charles Rowan Ho.
WC1 . . . . 2B **8**
(off Margery St.)
Charles Simmons Ho.
WC1 . . . . 2B **8**
(off Margery St.)
Charles Sq.
N1 . . . . 2C **10** (2F **63**)
Charles Sq. Est. N1 . . . 2C **10**
Charles St. E16 . . . . . . 2E **83**
SW13 . . . . 5A **84**
W1 . . . . 1D **21** (2D **75**)
Charleston St. SE17 . . . 5E **77**
Charles Townsend Ho.
EC1 . . . . 3D **9**
(off Skinner St.)
Charles Uton Ct. E8 . . . 1C **50**
Charles Whincup Rd.
E16 . . . . 2D **83**
Charlesworth Ho.
E14 . . . . 5B **66**
(off Dod St.)
Charlesworth Pl.
SW13 . . . . 1A **98**
Charleville Cir.
SE26 . . . . 5C **120**
Charleville Ct. W14 . . . 1B **86**
(off Charleville Rd.)
Charleville Mans.
W14 . . . . 1A **86**
(off Charleville Rd.)
Charleville Rd. W14 . . . 1A **86**

Charlie Chaplin Wlk.
SE1 . . . . 2A **24**
(off Waterloo Rd.)
Charlmont Rd.
SW17 . . . . 5A **116**
Charlotte Ct. N8 . . . . . . 1F **33**
SE1 . . . . 5A **78**
(off Old Kent Rd.)
W6 . . . . 5C **70**
(off Invermead Cl.)
Charlotte Despard Av.
SW11 . . . . 4C **88**
Charlotte Ho. E16 . . . . . 2D **83**
(off Fairfax M.)
W6 . . . . 1E **85**
(off Queen Caroline St.)
Charlotte M.
W1 . . . . 5A **6** (4E **61**)
W10 . . . . 5F **57**
W14 . . . . 5A **72**
Charlotte Pl. SW1 . . . . . 5E **75**
W1 . . . . 1A **14** (4E **61**)
Charlotte Rd.
EC2 . . . . . . 2D **11** (2A **64**)
SW13 . . . . 4B **84**
Charlotte Row SW4 . . . 1E **103**
Charlotte St.
W1 . . . . 5A **6** (4E **61**)
Charlotte Ter. N1 . . . . . 5B **48**
Charlow Cl. SW6 . . . . . . 5E **87**
CHARLTON 3F **97**
Charlton Athletic FC . . . 1E **97**
Charlton Chu. La.
SE7 . . . . 1E **97**
Charlton Ct. E2 . . . . 5B **50**
NW5 . . . . 2F **47**
Charlton Dene SE7 . . . . 3E **97**
Charlton Ga. Bus. Pk.
SE7 . . . . 3E **83**
Charlton House 2F **97**
Charlton King's Rd.
NW5 . . . . 2F **47**
Charlton La. SE7 . . . . . . 5F **83**
Charlton Lido 3F **97**
Charlton Pk. La. SE7 . . . 3F **97**
Charlton Pk. Rd. SE7 . . . 2F **97**
Charlton Pl. N1 . . . . 1D **63**
Charlton Rd. NW10 . . . . 5A **42**
SE3 . . . . 3C **96**
SE7 . . . . 3C **96**
Charlton Way SE3 . . . . . 4A **96**
Charlwood Ho. SW1 . . . 5F **75**
(off Vauxhall Bri. Rd.)
Charlwood Ho's. WC1 . . . 2E **7**
(off Midhope St.)
Charlwood Pl. SW1 . . . . 5E **75**
Charlwood Rd. SW15 . . . 2F **99**
Charlwood St. SW1 . . . . 1E **89**
(not continuous)
Charlwood Ter. SW15 . . . 2F **99**
Charmans Ho. SW8 . . . . 3A **90**
(off Wandsworth Rd.)
Charmian Ho. N1 . . . . . . 1D **11**
(off Crondall St.)
Charminster Rd.
SE9 . . . . 4F **125**
Charmouth Ho. SW8 . . . 3B **90**
Charnock Rd. SW12 . . . 1D **71**
(off White City Est.)

Charnock Rd. E5 . . . . . . 5D **37**
Charnwood Gdns.
E14 . . . . 5C **80**
Charnwood St. E5 . . . . . 4D **37**
Charrington St.
NW1 . . . . 1F **61**
Charsley Rd. SE6 . . . . . 2D **123**
Charter Ct. N4 . . . . 3C **34**
Charterhouse 4E **9**
Charter Ho. WC2 . . . . . . 3E **15**
(off Crown Ct.)
Charterhouse Bldgs.
EC1 . . . . 4E **9** (3E **63**)
Charterhouse M.
EC1 . . . . 5E **9** (4D **63**)
Charterhouse Rd. E8 . . 1C **50**
Charterhouse Sq.
EC1 . . . . 5E **9** (4D **63**)
Charterhouse St.
EC1 . . . . . . 1C **16** (4C **62**)
Charteris Rd. N4 . . . . . . 3C **34**
NW6 . . . . 5B **44**
Charters Cl. SE19 . . . . . 5A **120**
Chartes Ho. SE1 . . . . . . 5E **27**
(off Stevens St.)
Chartfield Av. SW15 . . . 3D **99**
Chartfield Sq. SW15 . . . 3F **99**
Chartham Ct. SW9 . . . . 1C **104**
(off Canterbury Cres.)
Chartham Gro.
SE27 . . . . 3D **119**
Chartham Ho. SE1 . . . . . 5C **26**
(off Weston St.)
Chart Ho. E14 . . . . 1D **95**
(off Burrells Wharf Sq.)
Chartley Av. NW2 . . . . . 5A **28**
Chartridge SE17 . . . . . . 2F **91**
(off Westmoreland Rd.)
Chart St. N1 . . . . 1C **10** (2F **63**)
Chartwell Ho. W11 . . . . 2B **72**
(off Ladbroke Rd.)
Charwood SW16 . . . . . . 4C **118**
Chase, The E12 . . . . 1F **55**
SW4 . . . . 1D **103**
Chase Cen., The
NW10 . . . . 2A **56**
Chase Ct. SW3 . . . . 4B **74**
(off Beaufort Gdns.)
Chasefield Rd.
SW17 . . . . 4B **116**
Chaseley St. E14 . . . . . . 5A **66**
Chasemore Ho. SW6 . . . 3A **86**
(off Williams Cl.)
Chase Rd. NW10 . . . . . . 3A **56**
Chase Rd. Trad. Est.
NW10 . . . . 3A **56**
Chaston Pl. NW5 . . . . . . 2C **46**
(off Grafton Ter.)
Chater Ho. E2 . . . . 2F **65**
(off Roman Rd.)
Chateris Community
Sports Cen. 5C **44**
Chatfield Rd. SW11 . . . 1E **101**
Chatham Cl. NW11 . . . . 1C **30**
Chatham Pl. E9 . . . . 3E **51**
Chatham Rd. SW11 . . . 4B **102**
Chatham St. SE17 . . . . . 5F **77**
Chats Palace Arts Cen.
. . . . 2F **51**

Chatsworth Av.
BR1: Brom 4D **125**
Chatsworth Ct. W8 . . . . 5C **72**
(off Pembroke Rd.)
Chatsworth Est. E5 . . . . 1F **51**
Chatsworth Ho. E16 . . . 2D **83**
(off Wesley Av.)
W4 . . . . 1A **84**
(off Bourne Pl.)
Chatsworth Pl. NW2 . . . 3E **43**
E15 . . . . 2B **54**
NW2 . . . . 3E **43**
Chatsworth Rd. E5 . . . . 5E **37**
E15 . . . . 2B **54**
NW2 . . . . 3E **43**
Chatsworth Way
SE27 . . . . 3D **119**
Chatterton M. N4 . . . . . 5D **35**
(off Chatterton Rd.)
Chatterton Rd. N4 . . . . 5D **35**
Chatto Rd. SW11 . . . . . 3B **102**
Chaucer Av. N16 . . . . . . 1A **50**
Chaucer Dr. SE1 . . . . . . 5B **78**
Chaucer Ho. SW1 . . . . . 1E **89**
(off Churchill Gdns.)
Chaucer Mans. W14 . . . 2A **86**
(off Queen's Club Gdns.)
Chaucer Rd. E7 . . . . 3C **54**
E11 . . . . 1C **40**
SE24 . . . . 3C **104**
Chaucer Theatre 2F **19**
(off Braham St.)
Chaucer Way SW19 . . . 5F **115**
Chaulden Ho. EC1 . . . . . 2C **10**
(off Cranwood St.)
Chauntler Cl. E16 . . . . . 5D **69**
Cheadle Ct. NW8 . . . . . . 3F **59**
(off Henderson Dr.)
Cheadle Ho. E14 . . . . . . 5B **66**
(off Copenhagen Pl.)
Cheam St. SE15 . . . . . . 1E **107**
Cheapside
EC2 . . . . 3A **18** (5E **63**)
Chearsley SE17 . . . . 5E **77**
(off Deacon Way)
Cheddington Ho. E2 . . . 5C **50**
(off Whiston Rd.)
Chedworth Cl. E16 . . . . 5B **68**
Cheesemans Ter.
W14 . . . . 1B **86**
(not continuous)
Cheethams Rd. E12 . . . . 5F **41**
Chelford Rd.
BR1: Brom 5F **123**
Chelmer Rd. E9 . . . . 2F **51**
Chelmsford Cl. W6 . . . . 2F **85**
Chelmsford Ho. N7 . . . . 1B **48**
(off Holloway Rd.)
Chelmsford Rd. E11 . . . 3F **39**
E17 . . . . 1C **38**
Chelmsford Sq.
NW10 . . . . 5E **43**
CHELSEA 1A **88**
Chelsea Barracks 1C **88**
Chelsea Bri. SW1 . . . . . . 2D **89**
Chelsea Bri. Rd.
SW1 . . . . 1C **88**
Chelsea Bri. Wharf
SW8 . . . . 2D **89**
Chelsea Cinema 1A **88**

Chelsea Cloisters
SW3 . . . . 5A **74**
Chelsea Cl. NW10 . . . 5A **42**
Chelsea College of Art &
Design 1A **88**
Chelsea Ct. SW3 . . . . 2B **88**
(off Embankment Gdns.)
Chelsea Cres. NW2 . . 3B **44**
SW10 . . . . 4E **87**
Chelsea Emb. SW3 . . 2A **88**
Chelsea Farm Ho. Studios
SW10 . . . . 2F **87**
(off Moravian Pl.)
Chelsea FC 3D **87**
Chelsea Gdns. SW1 . . 1C **88**
Chelsea Ga. SW1 . . . 1C **88**
(off Ebury Bri. Rd.)
Chelsea Harbour
SW10 . . . . 4E **87**
Chelsea Harbour Design Cen.
SW10 . . . . 4E **87**
(off Chelsea Harbour Dr.)
Chelsea Harbour Dr.
SW10 . . . . 4E **87**
Chelsea Lodge SW3 . . 2B **88**
(off Tite St.)
Chelsea Mnr. Ct.
SW3 . . . . 2A **88**
Chelsea Mnr. Gdns.
SW3 . . . . 1A **88**
Chelsea Mnr. St.
SW3 . . . . 1A **88**
Chelsea Mnr. Studios
SW3 . . . . 1A **88**
(off Flood St.)
Chelsea Pk. Gdns.
SW3 . . . . 2F **87**
Chelsea Physic Garden
. . . . 2B **88**
Chelsea Reach Twr.
SW10 . . . . 3F **87**
(off Worlds End Est.)
Chelsea Sports Cen. . . 1A **88**
Chelsea Sq. SW3 . . . 1F **87**
Chelsea Studios
SW6 . . . . 3D **87**
(off Fulham Rd.)
Chelsea Towers SW3 . . 2A **88**
(off Chelsea Mnr. Gdns.)
Chelsea Village SW6 . . 3D **87**
(off Fulham Rd.)
Chelsea Vista SW6 . . 5E **87**
Chelsea Wharf SW10 . . 3F **87**
(off Lots Rd.)
Chelsfield Gdns.
SE26 . . . . 3E **121**
Chelsfield Ho. SE17 . . . 5A **78**
(off Massinger St.)
Chelsham Rd. SW4 . . 1F **103**
Cheltenham Gdns. E6 . . 1F **69**
Cheltenham Rd. E10 . . 1E **39**
SE15 . . . . 2E **107**
Cheltenham Ter.
SW3 . . . . 1B **88**
Chelverton Rd. SW15 . . 2F **99**
Chelwood Ho. W2 . . . . 5F **59**
(off Gloucester Sq.)
Chelwood Wlk. SE4 . . 2A **108**
Chenappa Cl. E13 . . . . 2C **68**

Cheney Ct. SE23. . . . . 1F **121**
Cheneys Rd. E11 . . . . 5A **40**
Chenies, The NW1 . . . 1F **61**
(off Pancras Rd.)
Chenies Ho. W2. . . . . . 1D **73**
(off Moscow Rd.)
W4 . . . . 3B **84**
(off Corney Reach Way)
Chenies M.
WC1 . . . . 4B **6** (3F **61**)
Chenies Pl. NW1 . . . . 1F **61**
Chenies St.
WC1 . . . . 5B **6** (4F **61**)
Cheniston Gdns.
W8 . . . . 4D **73**
Chepstow Cl. SW15 . . 3A **100**
Chepstow Cnr. W2. . . . 5C **58**
(off Chepstow Pl.)
Chepstow Ct. W11. . . . 1C **72**
(off Chepstow Vs.)
Chepstow Cres. W11 . . 1C **72**
Chepstow Pl. W2 . . . . 5C **58**
Chepstow Rd. W2 . . . . 5C **58**
Chepstow Vs. W11. . . . 1B **72**
Chequers Ct. EC1. . . . . 4A **10**
(off Chequer St.)
Chequers Ho. NW8 . . . 3A **60**
(off Jerome Cres.)
Chequer St.
EC1 . . . . 4A **10** (3E **63**)
(not continuous)
Cherbury Ct. N1 . . . . . 1F **63**
(off St John's Est.)
Cherbury St. N1 . . . . . 1F **63**
Cheriton Ct. SE12. . . . 5C **110**
Cheriton Sq. SW17 . . 2C **116**
Cherry Cl. SW2 . . . . . 5C **104**
Cherry Ct. W3. . . . . . . 2A **70**
Cherry Gdn. Ho.
SE16. . . . . 3D **79**
(off Cherry Gdn. St.)
Cherry Gdn. St. SE16. . 3D **79**
Cherry Laurel Wlk.
SW2 . . . . 4B **104**
Cherry Orchard SE7 . . 2E **97**
Cherry Tree Cl. E9 . . . 5E **51**
(off Camden St.)
SE7 . . . . 2E **97**
Cherry Tree Dr.
SW16 . . . . 3A **118**
Cherry Tree Rd. E15. . . 2A **54**
Cherry Tree Ter. SE1 . . 4E **27**
(off Whites Grounds)
Cherry Tree Wlk.
EC1 . . . . 4A **10** (3E **63**)
Cherrywood Cl. E3 . . . 2A **66**
Cherrywood Dr.
SW15 . . . . 3F **99**
Chertsey Rd. E11 . . . . 4F **39**
Chertsey St. SW17 . . 5C **116**
Cherwell Ho. NW8 . . . 3F **59**
(off Church St. Est.)
Cheryls Cl. SW6. . . . . 4D **87**
Cheseman St. SE26 . . 3D **121**
Chesham Cl. SW1 . . . 5B **20**
Chesham Flats W1 . . 4C **12**
(off Brown Hart Gdns.)
Chesham M. SW1 . . . . 5B **20**

Chesham Pl.
SW1 . . . . 5B **20** (4C **74**)
(not continuous)
Chesham Rd. SW19 . . 5F **115**
Chesham St.
SW1 . . . . 5B **20** (4C **74**)
Cheshire Cl. SE4 . . . . 5B **94**
Cheshire Ct. EC4 . . . . 3C **16**
(off Fleet St.)
Cheshire St. E2 . . . . . 3B **64**
Chesholm Rd. N16. . . . 5A **36**
Cheshunt Ho. NW6 . . . 5D **45**
(off Mortimer Cres.)
Cheshunt Rd. E7 . . . . 3D **55**
Chesil Ct. E2. . . . . 1E **65**
SW3 . . . . 2A **88**
Chesilton Rd. SW6. . . . 4B **86**
Chesley Gdns. E6 . . . . 1F **69**
Chesney Ct. W9 . . . . . 3C **58**
(off Shirland Rd.)
Chesney Ho. SE13 . . . 2F **109**
(off Mercator St.)
Chesney St. SW11. . . . 4C **88**
Chessington Ho.
SW8 . . . . 5F **89**
Chessington Mans.
E10. . . . . 2C **38**
E11. . . . . 2A **40**
Chesson Rd. W14 . . . 2B **86**
Chester Cl.
SW1 . . . . 4D **21** (3D **75**)
SW13 . . . . 1D **99**
Chester Cl. Nth.
NW1. . . . . 1E **5** (2D **61**)
Chester Cl. Sth.
NW1. . . . . 2E **5** (2D **61**)
Chester Cotts. SW1 . . . 5C **74**
(off Bourne St.)
Chester Ct.
NW1 . . . . 1E **5** (2D **61**)
SE5 . . . . 3F **91**
(off Lomond Gro.)
SE8 . . . . 1F **93**
W6. . . . . 5F **71**
(off Wolverton Gdns.)
Chester Cres. E8 . . . . 2B **50**
Chesterfield Cl. SE13. . 5F **95**
Chesterfield Gdns.
N4. . . . . 1D **35**
SE10 . . . . 4F **95**
W1. . . . . 1D **21** (2D **75**)
Chesterfield Gro.
SE22 . . . . 3B **106**
Chesterfield Hill
W1. . . . . 1D **21** (2D **75**)
Chesterfield Ho. W1 . . 1C **20**
(off Chesterfield Gdns.)
Chesterfield M. N4 . . . 1D **35**
Chesterfield Rd. E10 . . 1E **39**
Chesterfield St.
W1. . . . . 1D **21** (2D **75**)
Chesterfield Wlk.
SE10 . . . . 4F **95**
Chesterfield Way
SE15 . . . . 3E **93**
Chesterford Gdns.
NW3 . . . . 1D **45**
Chesterford Ho. SE18. . 4F **97**
(off Tellson Av.)

Chester Ga.
  NW1 . . . . 2D **5** (2D **61**)
Chester Ho. SE8 . . . . 2B **94**
  SW1 . . . . *5D **75***
                (off Eccleston Pl.)
  SW9 . . . . *3C **90***
                (off Brixton Rd.)
Chesterman Ct. *W4* *3A **84***
                (off Corney Reach Way)
Chester M.
  SW1 . . . . 5D **21** (4D **75**)
Chester Pl.
  NW1 . . . . 1D **5** (2D **61**)
Chester Rd. E7 . . . . 4F **55**
  E11 . . . . 1D **41**
  E16 . . . . 3A **68**
  E17 . . . . 1F **37**
  N19 . . . . 4D **33**
  NW1 . . . . 2C **4** (2C **60**)
  SW19 . . . . 5E **113**
Chester Row SW1 . . . . . . 5C **74**
Chester Sq. SW1 . . . . 5C **74**
Chester Sq. M. SW1 . . . . . 5D **21**
Chester St. E2 . . . . 3C **64**
  SW1 . . . . 5C **20** (4C **74**)
Chester Ter.
  NW1 . . . . 1D **5** (2D **61**)
                (not continuous)
Chesterton Cl.
  SW18 . . . . 3C **100**
Chesterton Ho. *W10* *4A **58***
                (off Portobello Rd.)
Chesterton Rd. E13 . . . . . 2C **68**
  W10 . . . . 4F **57**
Chesterton Sq. W8 . . . . . . 5C **72**
Chesterton Ter. E13 . . . . . 2C **68**
Chester Way SE11 . . . . . . 5C **76**
Chestnut All. SW6 . . . . . . 2B **86**
Chestnut Av. E7 . . . . 1D **55**
  E12 . . . . 4F **41**
Chestnut Cl. N16 . . . . 4F **35**
  SE6 . . . . 5E **123**
  SE14 . . . . 4B **94**
  SW16 . . . . 4C **118**
Chestnut Ct. SW6 . . . . 2B **86**
  W8 . . . . 4D **73**
                (off Abbots Wlk.)
Chestnut Dr. E11 . . . . 1C **40**
Chestnut Gro.
  SW12 . . . . 5C **102**
Chestnut Ho. *W4* *5A **70***
                (off The Orchard)
Chestnut Pl. SE26 . . . . . . 4B **120**
Chestnut Rd. SE27 . . . . . 3D **119**
Chestnuts, The *N5* *1E **49***
                (off Highbury Grange)
Chettle Cl. SE1 . . . . 5B **26**
Chettle Ct. N8 . . . . 1C **34**
Chetwode Ho. *NW8* *3A **60***
                (off Grendon St.)
Chetwode Rd.
  SW17 . . . . 3B **116**
Chetwood Wlk. E6 . . . . . . 4F **69**
                (off Greenwich Cres.)
Chetwynd Rd. NW5 . . . . . 1D **47**
Chetwynd Vs. NW5 . . . . . 1D **47**
                (off Chetwynd Rd.)
Cheval Pl. SW7 . . . . 4A **74**
Cheval St. E14 . . . . 4C **80**

Chevening Rd. NW6 . . . . . 1F **57**
  SE10 . . . . 1B **96**
Cheverell Ho. *E2* *1C **64***
                (off Pritchard's Rd.)
Cheverton Rd. N19 . . . . . . 3F **33**
Chevet St. E9 . . . . 2A **52**
Cheviot Ct. *SE14* *2E **93***
                (off Avonley Rd.)
Cheviot Gdns. NW2 . . . . . 4F **29**
  SE27 . . . . 4D **119**
Cheviot Ga. NW2 . . . . 4A **30**
Cheviot Ho. *E1* *5D **65***
                (off Commercial Rd.)
Cheviot Rd. SE27 . . . . . . 5C **118**
Chevron Cl. E16 . . . . 5C **68**
Cheylesmore Ho.
  SW1 . . . . *1D **89***
                (off Ebury Bri. Rd.)
Cheyne Cl. NW4 . . . . 1E **29**
Cheyne Ct. SW3 . . . . 2B **88**
Cheyne Gdns. SW3 . . . . . 2A **88**
Cheyne M. SW3 . . . . 2A **88**
Cheyne Pl. SW3 . . . . 2B **88**
Cheyne Row SW3 . . . . . . 2A **88**
Cheyne Wlk. NW4 . . . . . . 1E **29**
  SW3 . . . . 3F **87**
                (not continuous)
Chichele Rd. NW2 . . . . . . 2F **43**
Chicheley St.
  SE1 . . . . 3A **24** (3B **76**)
Chichester Cl. SE3 . . . . . . 3E **97**
Chichester Ct. *NW1* *4E **47***
                (off Royal Coll. St.)
Chichester Ho. NW6 . . . . . 1C **58**
  SW9 . . . . *3C **90***
                (off Brixton Rd.)
Chichester M. SE27 . . . 4C **118**
Chichester Rents
  WC2 . . . . 2B **16**
Chichester Rd. E11 . . . . . 5A **40**
  NW6 . . . . 1C **58**
  W2 . . . . 4D **59**
Chichester St. SW1 . . . . . 1E **89**
Chichester Way E14 . . . . . 5F **81**
Chicksand Ho. *E1* *4C **64***
                (off Chicksand St.)
Chicksand St. E1 . . . . 4B **64**
                (not continuous)
Chiddingstone SE13 . . . 3E **109**
Chiddingstone St.
  SW6 . . . . 5C **86**
Chigwell Hill E1 . . . . 1D **79**
Chilcombe Ho.
  SW15 . . . . *5C **98***
                (off Fontley Way)
Chilcot Cl. E14 . . . . 5D **67**
Childebert Rd.
  SW17 . . . . 2D **117**
Childeric Rd. SE14 . . . . . . 3A **94**
Childerley St. SW6 . . . . . . 4A **86**
Childers St. SE8 . . . . 2A **94**
Child La. *SE10* *4B **82***
                (off School Bank Rd.)
Children's Discovery Cen.
                . . . . 4F **53**
CHILD'S HILL. 5C **30**
Childs Hill Wlk. NW2 . . . . *5B **30***
                (off Cricklewood La.)

Child's M. *SW5* *5C **72***
                (off Child's Pl.)
Child's Pl. SW5 . . . . 5C **72**
Child's St. SW5 . . . . 5C **72**
Child's Wlk. *SW5* *5C **72***
                (off Child's St.)
Chilham Ho.
  SE1 . . . . 5C **26** (4F **77**)
  SE15 . . . . 2E **93**
Chilham Rd. SE9 . . . . 4F **125**
Chilianwallan Memorial
                . . . . 2C **88**
Chillerton Rd.
  SW17 . . . . 5C **116**
Chillingford Ho.
  SW17 . . . . 4E **115**
Chillington Dr.
  SW11 . . . . 2F **101**
Chillingworth Rd. N7 . . . . 2C **48**
Chiltern Ct. *NW1* *4A **4***
                (off Baker St.)
  SE14 . . . . *3E **93***
                (off Avonley Rd.)
Chiltern Gdns. NW2 . . . . . 5F **29**
Chiltern Ho. *SE17* *2F **91***
                (off Portland Wlk.)
  W10 . . . . *4A **58***
                (off Telford Rd.)
Chiltern Rd. E3 . . . . 3C **66**
Chiltern St.
  W1 . . . . 5B **4** (4C **60**)
Chilthorne Cl. SE6 . . . . . 5B **108**
Chilton Gro. SE8 . . . . 5F **79**
Chiltonian Ind. Est.
  SE12 . . . . 4B **110**
Chilton St. E2 . . . . 3B **64**
Chilver St. SE10 . . . . 1B **96**
Chilworth Ct. SW19 . . . . 1F **113**
Chilworth M. W2 . . . . 5F **59**
Chilworth St. W2 . . . . 5E **59**
Chimney Ct. *E1* *2D **79***
                (off Brewhouse La.)
China Ct. *E1* *1C **79***
                (off Asher Way)
China Hall M. SE16 . . . . . 4E **79**
China M. SW2 . . . . 5B **104**
China Wlk. SE11 . . . . 4B **76**
China Wharf SE1 . . . . 3C **78**
Chinbrook Cres.
  SE12 . . . . 3D **125**
Chinbrook Rd. SE12 . . . . 3D **125**
Ching Ct. *WC2* *3D **15***
                (off Monmouth St.)
Chingley Cl.
  BR1: Brom 5A **124**
Chinnock's Wharf
  E14 . . . . *1A **80***
                (off Narrow St.)
Chipka St. E14 . . . . 3E **81**
                (not continuous)
Chipley St. SE14 . . . . 2A **94**
Chippendale Ho.
  SW1 . . . . *1D **89***
                (off Churchill Gdns.)
Chippendale St. E5 . . . . . 5F **37**
Chippenham Gdns.
  NW6 . . . . 2C **58**
Chippenham M. W9 . . . . . 3C **58**
Chippenham Rd. W9 . . . . 3C **58**

Chipperfield Ho.
SW3 . . . . 1A 88
(off Ixworth Pl.)
Chipstead Gdns.
NW2 . . . . 4D 29
Chipstead St. SW6 . . . . 4C 86
Chip St. SW4 . . . . 1F 103
Chisenhale Rd. E3 . . . . 1A 66
Chisholm Ct. W6 . . . . . 1C 84
Chisledon Wlk. E9 . . . . 3B 52
(off Osborne Rd.)
Chisley Rd. N15 . . . . . . 1A 36
Chiswell Sq. SE3 . . . . . 5D 97
Chiswell St.
EC1 . . . . 5B 10 (4E 63)
SE5 . . . . 3F 91
(off Edmund St.)
CHISWICK 1A 84
Chiswick Comn. Rd.
W4 . . . . 5A 70
Chiswick Community
Sports Hall. 3A 84
Chiswick High Rd.
W4 . . . . 1A 84
Chiswick House 2A 84
Chiswick La. W4 . . . . . 1A 84
Chiswick La. Sth. W4 . . 2B 84
Chiswick Mall W4 . . . . 2B 84
W6 . . . . 2B 84
Chiswick Sq. W4 . . . . . 2A 84
Chiswick Wharf W4 . . . 2B 84
Chitty St. W1 . . . . 5A 6 (4E 61)
Chivalry Rd. SW11 . . . . 3A 102
Chivelston SW19 . . . . . 1F 113
Chobham Gdns.
SW19 . . . . 2F 113
Chobham Rd. E15 . . . . 2F 53
Chocolate Studios N1 . . 1B 10
(off Shepherdess Pl.)
Cholmeley Cres. N6 . . . 2D 33
Cholmeley Lodge N6 . . 3D 33
Cholmeley Pk. N6 . . . . 3D 33
Cholmley Gdns. NW6 . . 2C 44
Cholmondeley Av.
NW10 . . . . 1C 56
Choppin's Ct. E1 . . . . . 2D 79
Chopwell Cl. E15 . . . . . 4F 53
Choumert Gro. SE15 . . . 5C 92
Choumert M. SE15 . . . . 5C 92
Choumert Rd. SE15 . . 1B 106
Choumert Sq. SE15 . . . 5C 92
Chow Sq. E8 . . . . 2B 50
Chrisp Ho. SE10 . . . . . 2A 96
(off Maze Hill)
Chrisp St. E14 . . . . 4D 67
(not continuous)
Christchurch Av.
NW6 . . . . 5F 43
Christ Chu. Ct. NW10 . . 5A 42
Christchurch Ct. EC4 . . 2E 17
(off Warwick La.)
Christchurch Hill
NW3 . . . . 5F 31
Christchurch Ho.
SW2 . . . . 1B 118
(off Christchurch Rd.)
Christchurch Pas.
NW3 . . . . 5E 31
Christchurch Pl. SW8 . . 5F 89

Christchurch Rd. N8 . . 1A 34
SW2 . . . . 1B 118
Christchurch Sq. E9 . . . 5E 51
Christchurch St. SW3 . . 2B 88
Christchurch Ter.
SW3 . . . . 2B 88
(off Christchurch St.)
Christchurch Way
SE10 . . . . 1A 96
Christian Ct. SE16 . . . . 2B 80
Christian Pl. E1 . . . . . . 5C 64
(off Burslem St.)
Christian St. E1 . . . . . . 5C 64
Christie Ct. N19 . . . . . . 4A 34
Christie Ho. SE10 . . . . . 1B 96
(off Blackwall La.)
Christie Rd. E9 . . . . . . 3A 52
Christina Sq. N4 . . . . . 3D 35
Christina St.
EC2 . . . . 3D 11 (3A 64)
Christopher Cl. SE16 . . 3F 79
Christopher Pl.
NW1 . . . . 1C 6 (2F 61)
Christophers M. W11. . . 2A 72
Christopher St.
EC2 . . . . 4C 10 (3F 63)
Chryssell Rd. SW9 . . . . 3C 90
Chubworthy St. SE14 . . 2A 94
Chudleigh Rd. NW6 . . . 4F 43
SE4 . . . . 3B 108
Chudleigh St. E1 . . . . . 5F 65
Chulsa Rd. SE26 . . . . . 5D 121
Chumleigh Gdns.
SE5 . . . . 2A 92
(off Chumleigh St.)
Chumleigh St. SE5 . . . . 2A 92
Church App. SE21. . . . . 3F 119
Church Av. E12 . . . . . . 5F 41
NW1 . . . . 3D 47
Churchbury Rd. SE9 . . . 5F 111
Church Cloisters EC3 . . 5D 19
Church Cl. W8 . . . . 3D 73
Church Ct. SE16 . . . . . . 3B 80
(off Rotherhithe St.)
Church Cres. E9 . . . . . . 4F 51
Churchcroft Cl.
SW12 . . . . 5C 102
Churchdown
BR1: Brom 4A 124
CHURCH END. 4A 42
Church Entry EC4 . . . . 3E 17
Churchfield Mans.
SW6 . . . . 5B 86
(off New Kings Rd.)
Churchfields SE10 . . . . 2E 95
Church Gth. N19 . . . . . 4F 33
(off St John's Gro.)
Church Ga. SW6. . . . . . 1A 100
Church Grn. SW9 . . . . . 4C 90
Church Gro. SE13 . . . . 3D 109
Church Hill SW19 . . . . 5B 114
Church Ho. EC1 . . . . . . 3E 9
(off Compton St.)
SW1 . . . . 5C 22
(off Gt. Smith St.)
Churchill Ct. N4 . . . . . . 2C 34
Churchill Gdns. SW1 . . 1E 89
Churchill Gdns. Rd.
SW1 . . . . 1D 89

Churchill Mus.
(Cabinet War Rooms)
. . . . 3C 22 (3F 75)
Churchill Pl. E14 . . . . . 2D 81
Churchill Rd. E16. . . . . 5E 69
NW2 . . . . 3D 43
NW5 . . . . 1D 47
Churchill Wlk. E9 . . . . . 2E 51
Church La. E11. . . . . . . 3A 40
SW17 . . . . 5B 116
Churchley Rd.
SE26. . . . . 4D 121
Church Mead SE5. . . . . 3E 91
(off Camberwell Rd.)
Churchmead Rd.
NW10 . . . . 3C 42
Church Mt. N2 . . . . 1F 31
Church Pas. EC2 . . . . . 2A 18
(off Guildhall Yd.)
Church Path E11. . . . . . 1C 40
N5. . . . . 2D 49
NW10 . . . . 4A 42
SW14 . . . . 1A 98
(not continuous)
Church Pl.
SW1 . . . . 5A 14 (1E 75)
Church Ri. SE23 . . . . . . 2F 121
Church Rd. E10 . . . . . . 3C 38
E12 . . . . 2F 55
N1 . . . . 3E 49
N6 . . . . 1C 32
NW10 . . . . 4A 42
SW13 . . . . 5B 84
SW19 . . . . 5A 114
Church Rd. Almshouses
E10 . . . . 4D 39
(off Church Rd.)
Church Rd. Ind. Est.
E10 . . . . 3C 38
Church Row NW3 . . . . 1E 45
SW6 . . . . 3D 87
(off Park Rd.)
Church St. E15 . . . . . . 5A 54
NW8 . . . . 4F 59
W2. . . . . 4F 59
W4 . . . . 2B 84
Church St. Est. NW8. . . 3F 59
(not continuous)
Church St. Nth. E15. . . 5A 54
Church St. Pas. E15. . . 5A 54
(off Church St.)
Church Ter. SE13 . . . . 1A 110
Church Va. SE23. . . . . 2F 121
Church Wlk. N6 . . . . . . 5C 32
N16 . . . . 5F 35
(not continuous)
NW2 . . . . 5B 30
SW13 . . . . 4C 84
SW15 . . . . 3D 99
Churchward Ho.
SE17. . . . . 2D 91
(off Lorrimore Sq.)
W14 . . . . 1B 86
(off Ivatt Pl.)
Churchway
NW1 . . . . 1C 6 (2F 61)
Churchwell Path E9 . . . 2E 51
Churchyard Pas. SE5 . . 5F 91

Churchyard Row
SE11 . . . . 5D **77**
Church Yd. Wlk. W2 . . . . 4F **59**
(off St Mary's Sq.)
Churnfield N4 . . . . 4C **34**
Churston Av. E13 . . . . . . 5D **55**
Churston Cl. SW2 . . . . . . 1C **118**
Churston Mans. WC1 . . . . 4A **8**
Churton Pl. SW1 . . . . 5E **75**
Churton St. SW1 . . . . 5E **75**
Chusan Pl. E14 . . . . 5B **66**
Chute Ho. SW9 . . . . 5C **90**
(off Stockwell Pk. Rd.)
Chuter Ede Ho. SW6 . . . 2B **86**
(off North End Rd.)
Cibber Rd. SE23 . . . . . . 2F **121**
Cicada Rd. SW18 . . . . . 4E **101**
Cicely Ho. NW8 . . . . 1F **59**
(off Cochrane St.)
Cicely Rd. SE15 . . . . . . 4C **92**
Cinderella Path
NW11 . . . . 3D **31**
Cinderford Way
BR1: Brom 4A **124**
Cine Lumiere 5F **73**
(off Queensberry Pl.)
Cineworld Cinema
Chelsea 2F **87**
Fulham Road 1E **87**
Hammersmith 5D **71**
Shaftesbury Avenue
. . . . 1F **75**
Staples Corner 3D **29**
Wandsworth 3D **101**
West India Quay . . . 1C **80**
Cinnabar Wharf Central
E1 . . . . 2C **78**
(off Wapping High St.)
Cinnabar Wharf E.
E1 . . . . 2C **78**
(off Wapping High St.)
Cinnabar Wharf W.
E1 . . . . 2C **78**
(off Wapping High St.)
Cinnamon Cl. SE15 . . . . 3B **92**
Cinnamon Row
SW11 . . . . 1E **101**
Cinnamon St. E1 . . . . . . 2D **79**
Cinnamon Wharf SE1 . . . 3B **78**
(off Shad Thames)
Circa Apartments
NW1 . . . . 4C **46**
Circle, The NW2 . . . . . . 5A **28**
SE1 . . . . 3F **27**
(off Queen Elizabeth St.)
Circus Lodge NW8 . . . . 2F **59**
(off Circus Rd.)
Circus M. W1 . . . . 4B **60**
(off Enford St.)
Circus Pl.
EC2 . . . . 1C **18** (4F **63**)
Circus Rd. NW8 . . . . . . 2F **59**
Circus St. SE10 . . . . . . 3E **95**
Cirencester St. W2 . . . . 4D **59**
Cissbury Ho. SE26 . . . . 3C **120**
Cissbury Rd. N15 . . . . . 1F **35**
Citadel Pl. SE11 . . . . . . 1B **90**
Citizen Ho. N7 . . . . 1C **48**
Citizen Rd. N7 . . . . 1C **48**

Citrus Ho. SE8 . . . . 1B **94**
(off Alverton St.)
City Apartments E1 . . . . 5C **64**
(off White Chu. La.)
City Bus. Cen. SE16 . . . . 4E **79**
City Central Est.
EC1 . . . . 2F **9**
(off Seward St.)
City Cross Bus. Cen.
SE10 . . . . 5A **82**
City Forum
EC1 . . . . 1F **9** (2E **63**)
City Gdn. Row
N1 . . . . 1E **9** (1D **63**)
City Harbour E14 . . . . . . 4D **81**
(off Selsdon Way)
City Hgts. SE1 . . . . 2E **27**
(off Weavers La.)
CITY OF LONDON
. . . . 3B **18** (5F **63**)
City of London Almshouses
SW9 . . . . 2B **104**
City of London Crematorium
E12 . . . . 5F **41**
City of London Point
N7 . . . . 3F **47**
(off York Way)
City of Westminster College
. . . . 4B **14** (1E **75**)
City Pav. EC1 . . . . 5D **9**
(off Britton St.)
City Rd. EC1 . . 1D **9** (1D **63**)
City Twr. EC2 . . . . 1B **18**
(off Basinghall St.)
City University
. . . . 2D **9** (2D **63**)
City University
Saddlers Sports Cen.
. . . . 3E **9** (3D **63**)
Cityview SE7 . . . . 2E **97**
City Vw. Ct. SE22 . . . . . 5C **106**
City Wlk. SE1 . . . . 3A **78**
City Wlk. Apartments
EC1 . . . . 2F **9**
(off Seward St.)
Clabon M. SW1 . . . . 4B **74**
Clack St. SE16 . . . . 3E **79**
Clacton Rd. E6 . . . . 2F **69**
E17 . . . . 1A **38**
Claire Ct. NW2 . . . . 3A **44**
Claire Pl. E14 . . . . 4C **80**
Clairview Rd.
SW16 . . . . 5D **117**
Clairville Point
SE23 . . . . 3F **121**
(off Dacres Rd.)
Clancarty Rd. SW6 . . . . 5C **86**
Clandeboye Ho. E15 . . . 5B **54**
(off John St.)
Clandon Ho. SE1 . . . . . . 4E **25**
(off Webber St.)
Clandon St. SE8 . . . . . . 5C **94**
Clanricarde Gdns.
W2 . . . . 1C **72**
CLAPHAM 2E **103**
CLAPHAM COMMON
. . . . 2F **103**
Clapham Comn. Nth. Side
SW4 . . . . 2B **102**

Clapham Comn. Sth. Side
SW4 . . . . 4D **103**
Clapham Comn. W. Side
SW4 . . . . 2B **102**
(not continuous)
Clapham Cres. SW4 . . . 2F **103**
Clapham High St.
SW4 . . . . 2F **103**
CLAPHAM JUNCTION
. . . . 1A **102**
Clapham Junc. App.
SW11 . . . . 1A **102**
Clapham Leisure Cen.
. . . . 1F **103**
Clapham Mnr. Ct.
SW4 . . . . 1E **103**
Clapham Mnr. St.
SW4 . . . . 1E **103**
CLAPHAM PARK 5F **103**
Clapham Pk. Est.
SW4 . . . . 4F **103**
Clapham Pk. Rd.
SW4 . . . . 2E **103**
Clapham Pk. Ter.
SW2 . . . . 3A **104**
(off Kings Av.)
Clapham Picturehouse
. . . . 2E **103**
Clapham Rd. SW9 . . . . . 1A **104**
Clapham Rd. Est.
SW4 . . . . 1A **104**
Clapton Comn. E5 . . . . . 2B **36**
(not continuous)
CLAPTON PARK 1F **51**
Clapton Pk. Est. E5 . . . . 1F **51**
Clapton Pas. E5 . . . . . . 2E **51**
Clapton Sq. E5 . . . . 2E **51**
Clapton Ter. N16 . . . . . . 3C **36**
Clapton Way E5 . . . . . . 1C **50**
Clara Grant Ho. E14 . . . . 4C **80**
(off Mellish St.)
Clara Nehab Ho.
NW11 . . . . 1B **30**
(off Leeside Cres.)
Clare Ct. W11 . . . . 1A **72**
(off Clarendon Rd.)
WC1 . . . . 2E **7**
(off Judd St.)
Claredale Ho. E2 . . . . . . 1D **65**
(off Claredale St.)
Claredale St. E2 . . . . . . 1C **64**
Clare Gdns. E7 . . . . 1C **54**
W11 . . . . 5A **58**
Clare Ho. E3 . . . . 5B **52**
SE1 . . . . 1B **92**
(off Brodie St.)
Clare La. N1 . . . . 4E **49**
Clare Lawn Av. SW14 . . 3A **98**
Clare Mkt.
WC2 . . . . 3A **16** (5B **62**)
Clare M. SW6 . . . . 3D **87**
Claremont Cl.
N1 . . . . 1C **8** (1C **62**)
SW2 . . . . 1A **118**
Claremont Ct. W2 . . . . . 5D **59**
(off Queensway)
W9 . . . . 1B **58**
(off Claremont Rd.)
Claremont Gro. W4 . . . 3A **84**

Claremont Rd. E7. . . . . . .2D 55
E11 . . . . .5F 39
N6 . . . . 2E 33
NW2 . . . . .2F 29
W9 . . . . .1A 58
Claremont Sq.
N1 . . . . .1B 8 (1C 62)
Claremont St. SE10 . . . . .2D 95
Claremont Vs. SE5 . . . . .3F 91
(off Southampton Way)
Claremont Way NW2 . . .3E 29
(not continuous)
Claremont Way Ind. Est.
NW2 . . . . .3E 29
Clarence Av. SW4. . . . .5F 103
Clarence Ct. W6 . . . . . . .5D 71
(off Cambridge Gro.)
Clarence Cres. SW4 . . . .4F 103
Clarence Gdns.
NW1 . . . . . . .2E 5 (2D 61)
Clarence Ga. Gdns.
NW1 . . . . 4A 4
(off Glentworth St.)
Clarence House 3A 22
Clarence Ho. SE17 . . . . . .2E 91
(off Merrow St.)
Clarence La. SW15 . . . . . 4A 98
Clarence M. E5 . . . . 2D 51
SE16 . . . . .2F 79
SW12 . . . . .5D 103
Clarence PI. E5 . . . . 2D 51
Clarence Rd. E5 . . . . 1D 51
E12 . . . . .1E 55
E16 . . . . .3A 68
NW6 . . . . .4B 44
SE8 . . . . .2D 95
SE9 . . . . .2F 125
SW19 . . . . .5D 115
Clarence Ter.
NW1 . . . . 3A 4 (3B 60)
Clarence Wlk. SW4 . . . . .5A 90
Clarence Way NW1 . . . . .4D 47
Clarendon Cl. E9 . . . . . . .4E 51
W2 . . . . 1A 74
Clarendon Ct. NW2. . . . .4E 43
Clarendon Cross
W11 . . . . 1A 72
Clarendon Dr. SW15. . . .2E 99
Clarendon Flats W1 . . . .3C 12
(off Balderton St.)
Clarendon Gdns. W9 . . .3E 59
Clarendon Gro.
NW1 . . . . . . .1B 6 (2F 61)
Clarendon Ho. NW1 . . . .1A 6
(off Werrington St.)
W2 . . . . 1A 74
(off Strathearn Pl.)
Clarendon M. W2. . . . . .1A 74
Clarendon Pl. W2. . . . . .1A 74
Clarendon Ri. SE13 . . . .2E 109
Clarendon Rd. E11 . . . . .3F 39
E17 . . . . .1D 39
W11 . . . . 1A 72
Clarendon St. SW1 . . . . .1D 89
Clarendon Ter. W9 . . . . .3E 59
Clarendon Wlk.
W11 . . . . 5A 58
Clarens St. SE6 . . . . 2B 122
Clare PI. SW15. . . . . 5B 98

Clare Point NW2. . . . . . . .3F 29
(off Whitefield Av.)
Clare Rd. E11 . . . . 1F 39
NW10 . . . . .4C 42
SE14 . . . . .4B 94
Clare St. E2 . . . . 1D 65
Clareville Ct. SW7 . . . . . .5E 73
(off Clareville St.)
Clareville Gro. SW7 . . . . .5E 73
Clareville Gro. M.
SW7 . . . . .5E 73
Clareville St. SW7 . . . . . .5E 73
Clarewood Ct. W1 . . . . . .4B 60
(off Seymour Pl.)
Clarewood Wlk.
SW9 . . . . .2C 104
Clarges M.
W1. . . . . .1D 21 (2D 75)
Clarges St.
W1. . . . . .1E 21 (2D 75)
Claribel Rd. SW9. . . . . . .5D 91
Claridge Ct. SW6. . . . . . .5B 86
Clarion Ho. E3 . . . . 1A 66
(off Roman Rd.)
SW1 . . . . 1E 89
(off Moreton Pl.)
W1 . . . . 3B 14
(off St Anne's Ct.)
Clarissa Ho. E14 . . . . . . .5C 67
(off Cordelia St.)
Clarissa St. E8 . . . . 5B 50
Clarke Path N16. . . . . . . 3C 36
Clarke's M.
W1. . . . . .5C 4 (4C 60)
Clark Ho. SW10 . . . . .3E 87
(off Coleridge Gdns.)
Clarkson Rd. E16. . . . . . .5B 68
Clarkson Row NW1 . . . . .1F 61
(off Mornington Ter.)
Clarkson St. E2 . . . . 2D 65
Clark's Pl.
EC2 . . . . .2D 19 (5A 64)
Clark St. E1 . . . . 4D 65
Classic Mans. E9 . . . . . . .4D 51
(off Wells St.)
Claude Rd. E10 . . . . 4E 39
E13 . . . . .5D 55
SE15 . . . . .5D 93
Claude St. E14 . . . . 5C 80
Claudia Jones Way
SW2 . . . . .4A 104
Claudia PI. SW19. . . . . . .1A 114
Claughton Rd. E13 . . . . .1E 69
Clavell St. SE10 . . . . . . .2E 95
Claverdale Rd.
SW2 . . . . 5B 104
Clavering Av. SW13. . . . .2D 85
Clavering Ho. SE13 . . .2F 109
(off Blessington Rd.)
Clavering Rd. E12 . . . . . .3F 41
Claverton St. SW1 . . . . . .1E 89
Clave St. E1 . . . . 2E 79
Claxton Gro. W6. . . . . . . .1F 85
Claxton Path SE4 . . . . . .2F 107
(off Coston Wlk.)
Claybank Gro. SE13. . . . .1D 109
Claybridge Rd.
SE12 . . . . .4E 125
Claybrook Rd. W6 . . . . . .2F 85

Clay Ct. SE1. . . . . 5D 27
(off Long La.)
Claydon SE17 . . . . .5E 77
(off Deacon Way)
Clayhill Cres. SE9 . . . . . .4F 125
Claylands Pl. SW8. . . . . . 3C 90
Claylands Rd. SW8 . . . . . 2B 90
Claypole Ct. E17 . . . . 1C 38
(off Yunus Khan Cl.)
Claypole Rd. E15. . . . . . . 1E 67
Clays La. E15. . . . . 2D 53
Clays La. Cl. E15. . . . . . . 2D 53
Clay St. W1. . . . . 1A 12 (4B 60)
Clayton Cres. N1. . . . . . . 5A 48
Clayton Dr. SE8 . . . . 1A 94
Clayton Ho. E9. . . . . .4E 51
(off Frampton Pk. Rd.)
SW13 . . . . 3E 85
(off Trinity Church Rd.)
Clayton M. SE10. . . . . . . 4F 95
Clayton Rd. SE15. . . . . . .4C 92
Clayton St. SE11 . . . . 2C 90
Clearbrook Way E1. . . . . .5E 65
Clearwater Ter.
W11. . . . . 3F 71
Clearwell Dr. W9. . . . . . . 3D 59
Cleaver Ho. NW3 . . . . 4B 46
(off Adelaide Rd.)
Cleaver Sq. SE11. . . . . . . 1C 90
Cleaver St. SE11. . . . . . . 1C 90
Cleeve Hill SE23 . . . . 1D 121
Cleeve Ho. E2. . . . . 2E 11
Cleeve Way SW15 . . . . . .5B 98
Cleeve Workshops
E2 . . . . .2E 11
(off Boundary Rd.)
Clegg Ho. SE3 . . . . 2D 111
SE16 . . . . .4E 79
(off Moodkee St.)
Clegg St. E1. . . . . 2D 79
E13 . . . . .1C 68
Cleland Ho. E2 . . . . .1E 65
(off Sewardstone Rd.)
Clematis St. W12. . . . . . . 1C 70
Clem Attlee Ct. SW6 . . . .2B 86
Clem Attlee Pde.
SW6 . . . . 2B 86
(off North End Rd.)
Clemence St. E14 . . . . . . 4B 66
Clement Av. SW4 . . . . . . 2F 103
Clement Cl. NW6 . . . . . . .4E 43
Clement Ho. SE8 . . . . . . 5A 80
W10 . . . . .4E 57
(off Dalgarno Gdns.)
Clementina Rd. E10. . . . . 3B 38
Clement Rd. SW19 . . . . . 5A 114
Clement's Av. E16. . . . . . 1C 82
Clement's Inn
WC2. . . . . .3A 16 (5B 62)
Clement's Inn Pas.
WC2. . . . . 3A 16
Clements La.
EC4. . . . . .4C 18 (1F 77)
Clement's Rd. SE16. . . . .4C 78
Clemson Ho. E8. . . . . 5B 50
Clennam St.
SE1 . . . . .3A 26 (3E 77)
Clenston M.
W1. . . . . .2A 12 (5B 60)

Cleopatra's Needle
. . . . 5F **15** (2A *76*)
Clephane Rd. N1 . . . . . 3E **49**
Clephane Rd. Nth.
N1 . . . . 3E **49**
Clephane Rd. Sth. N1 . . . 3F **49**
Clere Pl. EC2 . . . 3C **10** (3F *63*)
Clere St. EC2 . . . 3C **10** (3F *63*)
CLERKENWELL
. . . . 3B **8** (3C *62*)
Clerkenwell Cl.
EC1 . . . . 3C **8** (3C *62*)
(not continuous)
Clerkenwell Grn.
EC1 . . . . 4C **8** (3C *62*)
Clerkenwell Rd.
EC1 . . . . 4B **8** (3C *62*)
Clermont Rd. E9 . . . . . . 5E **51**
Clevedon Cl. N16 . . . . . 5B **36**
Clevedon Mans.
NW5 . . . . 1C **46**
Clevedon Pas. N16. . . . 4B **36**
Cleve Ho. NW6. . . . . . . 4D **45**
Cleveland Av. W4 . . . . . 5B **70**
Cleveland Gdns. N4 . . 1E **35**
NW2 . . . . 4F **29**
SW13 . . . . 5B **84**
W2 . . . . 5E **59**
Cleveland Gro. E1 . . . . 3E **65**
Cleveland Mans.
SW9 . . . . *3C 90*
(off Mowll St.)
W9 . . . . 3C **58**
Cleveland M.
W1 . . . . 5F **5** (4E *61*)
Cleveland Pl.
SW1 . . . . 1A **22** (2E *75*)
Cleveland Rd. N1 . . . . 4F **49**
SW13 . . . . 5B **84**
Cleveland Row
SW1 . . . . 2F **21** (2E *75*)
Cleveland Sq. W2. . . . . 5E **59**
Cleveland St.
W1 . . . . 4E **5** (3D *61*)
Cleveland Ter. W2 . . . . 5E **59**
Cleveland Way E1. . . . . 3E **65**
Cleveley Cl. SE7 . . . . . 5F **83**
Cleveleys Rd. E5 . . . . . 5D **37**
Cleverly Est. W12. . . . . 2C **70**
Cleve Rd. NW6. . . . . . . 4C **44**
Cleves Ho. *E16*. *2C 82*
(off Southey St.)
Cleves Rd. E6 . . . . 5F **55**
Clewer Ct. *E10* *3C 38*
(off Leyton Grange Est.)
Cley Ho. SE4 . . . . 2F **107**
Clichy Est. E1 . . . . 4E **65**
Clichy Ho. *E1* *4E 65*
(off Stepney Way)
Clifden M. E9 . . . . 2F **51**
Clifden Rd. E5 . . . . 2E **51**
Cliffe Ho. *SE10*. *1B 96*
(off Blackwall La.)
Clifford Ct. *W2*. *4D 59*
(off Westbourne Pk. Vs.)
Clifford Dr. SW9. . . . . 2D **105**
Clifford Gdns. NW10 . . 1E **57**
Clifford Haigh Ho.
SW6 . . . . 3F **85**

Clifford Ho.
BR3: Beck. *5D 123*
(off Calverley Cl.)
W14 . . . . *5B 72*
(off Edith Vs.)
Clifford Rd. E16 . . . . . 3B **68**
N1 . . . . 5A **50**
Clifford's Inn Pas.
EC4 . . . . 3B **16** (5C *62*)
Clifford St.
W1 . . . . 5F **13** (1E *75*)
Clifford Way NW10. . . . 1B **42**
Cliff Rd. NW1 . . . . 3F **47**
Cliffsend Ho. *SW9* . . . *4C 90*
(off Cowley Rd.)
Cliff Ter. SE8 . . . . 5C **94**
Cliffview Rd. SE13. . . . 1C **108**
Cliff Vs. NW1 . . . . 3F **47**
Cliff Wlk. E16. . . . . 4B **68**
Clifton Av. W12 . . . . . . 2B **70**
Clifton Ct. N4 . . . . 4C **34**
NW8 . . . . *3F 59*
(off Maida Va.)
SE15. . . . . 3D **93**
Clifton Cres. SE15 . . . . 3D **93**
Clifton Est. SE15 . . . . . 4D **93**
Clifton Gdns. N15. . . . . 1B **36**
NW11 . . . . 1B **30**
W4 . . . . 5A **70**
(not continuous)
W9 . . . . 3E **59**
Clifton Ga. SW10 . . . . . 2E **87**
Clifton Gro. E8 . . . . . . 3C **50**
Clifton Hill NW8 . . . . . 1D **59**
Clifton Ho. *E2*. *3F 11*
(off Club Row)
E11 . . . . 4A **40**
Clifton Pl. SE16 . . . . . . 3E **79**
SW10 . . . . *2E 87*
(off Hollywood Rd.)
W2. . . . . 5F **59**
Clifton Ri. SE14 . . . . . . 3A **94**
(not continuous)
Clifton Rd. E7 . . . . 3F **55**
E16 . . . . 4A **68**
N1 . . . . 3E **49**
N8 . . . . 1F **33**
NW10 . . . . 1C **56**
SW19 . . . . 5F **113**
W9 . . . . 3E **59**
EC2 . . . . 4D **11** (3A *64*)
Clifton Ter. N4 . . . . 4C **34**
Clifton Vs. W9 . . . . 4E **59**
Cliftonville Ct. SE12 . . 1C **124**
Clifton Wlk. *W6* *5D 71*
(off King St.)
Clifton Way SE15 . . . . 3D **93**
Climsland Ho.
SE1 . . . . 1C **24** (2C *76*)
Clinch Ct. *E16* *4C 68*
(off Plymouth Rd.)
Clinger Ct. *N1* *5A 50*
(off Hobbs Pl. Est.)
Clink Exhibition, The
. . . . 1B **26**
Clink St. SE1 . . 1B **26** (2F *77*)
Clink Wharf *SE1* *1B 26*
(off Clink St.)

Clifford Rd. E3 . . . . 2A **66**
E7 . . . . 1C **54**
Clipper Cl. SE16. . . . . . 3F **79**
Clipper Ho. *E14* *1E 95*
(off Manchester Rd.)
Clipper Way SE13 . . . 2E **109**
Clipstone M.
W1 . . . . 5F **5** (4E *61*)
Clipstone St.
W1 . . . . 5E **5** (4D *61*)
Clissold Ct. N4 . . . . . . 4E **35**
Clissold Cres. N16 . . . 5F **35**
Clissold Leisure Cen.
. . . . 5F **35**
Clissold Rd. N16 . . . . . 5F **35**
Clitheroe Rd. SW9 . . . . 5A **90**
Clitterhouse Cres.
NW2 . . . . 3E **29**
Clitterhouse Rd.
NW2 . . . . 3E **29**
Clive Ct. W9 . . . . 3E **59**
Cliveden Ho. *E16*. *2C 82*
(off Fitzwilliam M.)
SW1 . . . . *5C 74*
(off Cliveden Pl.)
Cliveden Pl. SW1. . . . . 5C **74**
Clive Ho. *SE10*. *2E 95*
(off Haddo St.)
Clive Lloyd Ho. *N15*. . . *1E 35*
(off Woodlands Pk. Rd.)
Clive Lodge NW4 . . . . . 1F **29**
Clive Pas. SE21 . . . . . 3F **119**
Clive Rd. SE21 . . . . . . 3F **119**
SW19 . . . . 5A **116**
Cloak La.
EC4 . . . . 4A **18** (1E *77*)
Clochar Ct. NW10. . . . . 5B **42**
Clock Ho. E3. . . . . 2E **67**
Clockhouse, The
SW19 . . . . 3E **113**
Clockhouse Cl.
SW19 . . . . 2E **113**
Clock Ho. Pde. E11. . . . 1D **41**
Clockhouse Pl.
SW15 . . . . 4A **100**
Clock Mus., The 2A **18**
Clock Pl. *SE1*. *5D 77*
(off Newington Butts)
Clock Twr. M. N1 . . . . . 5E **49**
Clock Twr. Pl. N7 . . . . . 3A **48**
Cloister Rd. NW2. . . . . 5B **30**
Cloisters, The 5D **23**
Cloisters, The E1 . . . . . 4F **11**
SW9 . . . . 4C **90**
Cloisters Bus. Cen.
SW8 . . . . *3D 89*
(off Battersea Pk. Rd.)
Clonbrock Rd. N16. . . . 1A **50**
Cloncurry St. SW6 . . . . 5F **85**
Clonmel Rd. SW6 . . . . 3B **86**
Clonmore St. SW18 . . 1B **114**
Clorane Gdns. NW3. . . . 5C **30**
Close, The SE3 . . . . . . 5F **95**
Cloth Ct. EC1 . . . . 1E **17**
Cloth Fair
EC1 . . . . 1E **17** (4D *63*)
Clothier St.
E1 . . . . 2E **19** (5A *64*)
Cloth St. EC1 . . . . 5F **9** (4E *63*)

Cloudesdale Rd.
SW17 . . . . 2D 117
Cloudesley Mans. N1 . . 5C 48
(off Cloudesley Pl.)
Cloudesley Pl. N1 . . . . 5C 48
Cloudesley Rd. N1 . . . . 5C 48
(not continuous)
Cloudesley Sq. N1 . . . . 5C 48
Cloudesley St. N1 . . . . 5C 48
Clova Rd. E7 . . . . . . 3B 54
Clove Cres. E14 . . . . . 1E 81
Clove Hitch Quay
SW11 . . . . 1E 101
Clovelly Ct. NW2 . . . . 2E 43
Clovelly Ho. W2 . . . . . 5E 59
(off Hallfield Est.)
Clovelly Way E1 . . . . . 5E 65
Clover Cl. E11 . . . . . . 4F 39
Clover M. SW3 . . . . . 2B 88
Clove St. E13 . . . . . . 3C 68
Clowders Rd. SE6 . . . . 3B 122
Cloysters Grn. E1 . . . . 2C 78
Club Row E1 . . 3F 11 (3B 64)
E2 . . . . 3F 11 (3B 64)
Clunbury St. N1 . . . . . 1F 63
Clunie Ho. SW1 . . . . . 5A 20
(off Pavillion Rd.)
Cluny Est.
SE1 . . . . 5D 27 (4A 78)
Cluny M. SW5 . . . . . . 5C 72
Cluny Pl.
SE1 . . . . 5D 27 (4A 78)
Cluse Ct. N1 . . . . 1E 63
(off St Peters St.,
not continuous)
Clutton St. E14 . . . . . 4D 67
Clyde Ct. NW1 . . . . . . 1F 61
(off Hampden Cl.)
Clyde Flats SW6 . . . . . 3B 86
(off Rhylston Rd.)
Clyde Pl. E10 . . . . . . 2D 39
Clydesdale Ho. W11 . . 5B 58
(off Clydesdale Rd.)
Clydesdale Rd. W11 . . 5B 58
Clyde St. SE8 . . . . . . 2B 94
Clyde Ter. SE23 . . . . . 2E 121
Clyde Va. SE23 . . . . . 2E 121
Clyde Wharf E16 . . . . 2C 82
Clynes Ho. E2 . . . . . . 2F 65
(off Knottisford St.)
Clyston St. SW8 . . . . . 5E 89
Coach & Horses Yd.
W1 . . . . 4E 13 (1E 75)
Coach Ho. La. N5 . . . . 1D 49
SW19 . . . . 4F 113
Coach Ho. M. SE1 . . . . 4D 27
(off Blue Lion Pl.)
SE23 . . . . 4F 107
Coach Ho. Yd. NW3 . . 1E 45
(off Heath St.)
SW18 . . . . 2D 101
Coachmaker M.
SW4 . . . . 1A 104
(off Fenwick Pl.)
Coach Yd. M. N19 . . . . 3A 34
Coaldale Wlk. SE21 . . 5E 105
Coalecroft Rd. SW15 . . 2E 99
Coalport Ho. SE11 . . . . 5C 76
(off Walnut Tree Wlk.)

Coates Av. SW18 . . . . 4A 102
Coate St. E2 . . . . 1C 64
Cobalt Sq. SW8 . . . . . 2B 90
(off Sth. Lambeth Rd.)
Cobbetts Av. IG4: Ilf . . 1F 41
Cobbett St. SW8 . . . . 3B 90
Cobble La. N1 . . . . . . 4D 49
Cobble M. N5 . . . . . . 5E 35
Cobbold Ct. SW1 . . . . 5F 75
(off Elverton St.)
Cobbold Ind. Est.
NW10 . . . . 3B 42
Cobbold M. W12 . . . . 3B 70
Cobbold Rd. E11 . . . . 5B 40
NW10 . . . . 3B 42
W12 . . . . 3A 70
Cobb's Ct. EC4 . . . . . 3E 17
Cobb's Hall SW6 . . . . 2F 85
(off Fulham Pal. Rd.)
Cobbsthorpe Vs.
SE26 . . . . 4F 121
Cobb St. E1 . . . . 1F 19 (4B 64)
Cobden Bldgs. WC1 . . 1F 7
(off Weston Rd.)
Cobden Ho. E2 . . . . . 2C 64
(off Nelson Gdns.)
NW1 . . . . 1E 61
(off Arlington Rd.)
Cobden M. SE26 . . . . 5D 121
Cobden Rd. E11 . . . . . 5A 40
Cobham Cl. SW11 . . . . 4A 102
Cobham M. NW1 . . . . 4F 47
Cobland Rd. SE12 . . . 4E 125
Coborn Rd. E3 . . . . . 1B 66
Coborn St. E3 . . . . . . 2B 66
Cobourg Rd. SE5 . . . . 2B 92
Cobourg St.
NW1 . . . . 2A 6 (2E 61)
Coburg Cl. SW1 . . . . . 5E 75
Coburg Cres. SW2 . . . 1B 118
Coburg Dwellings E1 . . 5E 65
(off Hardinge St.)
Cochrane Cl. NW8 . . . 1F 59
(off Cochrane St.)
Cochrane Ct. E10 . . . . 3C 38
(off Leyton Grange Est.)
Cochrane Ho. E14 . . . . 3C 80
(off Admirals Way)
Cochrane M. NW8 . . . 1F 59
Cochrane St. NW8 . . . 1F 59
Cochrane Theatre 1E 15
(off Southampton Row)
Cockburn Ho. SW1 . . . 1F 89
(off Aylesford St.)
Cockerell Rd. E17 . . . . 2A 38
Cock Hill E1 . . 1E 19 (4A 64)
Cock La.
EC1 . . . . 1D 17 (4D 63)
Cockpit Steps SW1 . . . 4B 22
Cockpit Theatre 3A 60
(off Gateforth St.)
Cockpit Yd.
WC1 . . . . 5A 8 (4B 62)
Cockspur Ct.
SW1 . . . . 1C 22 (2F 75)
Cockspur St.
SW1 . . . . 1C 22 (2F 75)
Coda Cen., The SW6 . . 3A 86
Code St. E1 . . . . 3B 64

Codicote Ho. SE8 . . . . 5F 79
(off Chilton Gro.)
Codicote Ter. N4 . . . . . 4E 35
Codling Cl. E1 . . . . . . 2C 78
Codrington Ct. E1 . . . . 3D 65
SE16 . . . . 1A 80
Codrington Hill
SE23 . . . . 5A 108
Codrington M. W11 . . . 5A 58
Cody Rd. E16 . . . . . . 3F 67
Coffey St. SE8 . . . . . . 3C 94
Coin St. SE1 . . 1B 24 (2C 76)
(not continuous)
Coity Rd. NW5 . . . . . . 3C 46
Cokers La. SE21 . . . . . 1F 119
Coke St. E1 . . . . 5C 64
Colas M. NW6 . . . . . . 5C 44
Colbeck M. SW7 . . . . 5D 73
Colberg Pl. N16 . . . . . 2B 36
Colborne Ho. E14 . . . . 1C 80
(off E. India Dock Rd.)
Colby M. SE19 . . . . . . 5A 120
Colby Rd. SE19 . . . . . 5A 120
Colchester Rd. E10 . . . 2E 39
E17 . . . . 1C 38
Colchester St. E1 . . . . 5B 64
Coldbath Sq.
EC1 . . . . 3B 8 (3C 62)
Coldbath St. SE13 . . . 4D 95
Cold Blow La. SE14 . . 3F 93
(not continuous)
Coldharbour E14 . . . . 3E 81
Coldharbour La.
SE5 . . . . 1E 105
SW9 . . . . 2C 104
Coldharbour Pl. SE5 . . 5E 91
Coldstream Gdns.
SW18 . . . . 4B 100
Colebeck M. N1 . . . . . 3D 49
Colebert Av. E1 . . . . . 3E 65
Colebert Ho. E1 . . . . . 3E 65
(off Colebert Av.)
Colebrook Cl. SW15 . . 5F 99
Colebrook Ct. SW3 . . . 5A 74
(off Makins St.)
Colebrooke Dr. E11 . . . 2E 41
Colebrooke Pl. N1 . . . 5D 49
Colebrooke Row N1 . . 1D 63
Colebrook Ho. E14 . . . 5D 67
(off Ellesmere St.)
Coleby Path SE5 . . . . 3F 91
Colechurch Ho. SE1 . . 1C 92
(off Avondale Sq.)
Coleford Rd. SW18 . . . 3E 101
Colegrave Rd. E15 . . . 2F 53
Colegrove Rd. SE15 . . 2B 92
Coleherne Ct. SW5 . . . 1D 87
Coleherne Mans.
SW5 . . . . 1D 87
(off Old Brompton Rd.)
Coleherne M. SW10 . . 1D 87
Coleherne Rd.
SW10 . . . . 1D 87
Colehill Gdns. SW6 . . . 5A 86
Colehill La. SW6 . . . . . 4A 86
Cole Ho. SE1 . . . . 4B 24
(off Baylis Rd.)
Coleman Ct. SW18 . . . 5C 100
Coleman Flds. N1 . . . . 5E 49

Coleman Mans. N8 . . . . . 2A **34**
Coleman Rd. SE5 . . . . . 3A **92**
Coleman St.
  EC2. . . . . 2B **18** (5F **63**)
Coleman St. Bldgs.
  EC2 . . . . 2B **18**
Colenso Rd. E5. . . . . . . 1E **51**
Coleraine Rd. SE3 . . . . . 2B **96**
Coleridge Av. E12 . . . . . 3F **55**
Coleridge Cl. SW8 . . . . . 5D **89**
Coleridge Ct. SW1 . . . . . 5F **75**
  (off Fynes St.)
  W14. . . . . 4F **71**
  (off Blythe Rd.)
Coleridge Gdns.
  NW6 . . . . 4E **45**
  SW10 . . . . 3D **87**
Coleridge Ho. SE17 . . . . 1E **91**
  (off Browning St.)
  SW1 . . . . 1E **89**
  (off Churchill Gdns.)
Coleridge La. N8 . . . . . . 1A **34**
Coleridge Rd. N4 . . . . . . 4C **34**
  N8 . . . . 1F **33**
Coleridge Sq. SW10. . . . 3E **87**
  (off Coleridge Gdns.)
Coles Grn. Ct. NW2 . . . . 4C **28**
Coles Grn. Rd. NW2 . . . 3C **28**
Coleshill Flats SW1 . . . 5C **74**
  (off Pimlico Rd.)
Colestown St. SW11 . . . 5A **88**
Cole St. SE1 . . . 4A **26** (3E **77**)
Colet Ct. W6 . . . . 5F **71**
  (off Hammersmith Rd.)
Colet Flats E1 . . . . 5A **66**
  (off Troon St.)
Colet Gdns. W14. . . . . . 5F **71**
Colet Ho. SE17 . . . . 1D **91**
  (off Doddington Gro.)
Colette Cl. SE16 . . . . . . 3F **79**
  (off Eleanor Cl.)
Coley St. WC1 . . 4A **8** (3B **62**)
Colfe & Hatcliffe Glebe
  SE13 . . . . 3D **109**
  (off Lewisham High St.)
Colfe Rd. SE23 . . . . . . 1A **122**
Colin Ct. SE6 . . . . 5B **108**
Colin Dr. NW9 . . . . 1B **28**
Colinette Rd. SW15 . . . . 2E **99**
Colin Rd. NW10 . . . . . . 3C **42**
Colin Winter Ho. E1 . . . . 3E **65**
  (off Nicholas Rd.)
Coliseum Theatre 5D **15**
  (off St Martin's La.)
Coliston Pas. SW18. . . . 5C **100**
  (off Coliston Rd.)
Coliston Rd. SW18. . . . 5C **100**
Collamore Av.
  SW18 . . . . 1A **116**
Collard Pl. NW1 . . . . . . 4D **47**
Collards Almshouses
  E17 . . . . 1E **39**
  (off Maynard Rd.)
College App. SE10 . . . . 2E **95**
College Cl. E9. . . . . 2E **51**
College Ct. NW3 . . . . . . 3F **45**
  (off College Cres.)
  SW3 . . . . 1B **88**
  (off West Rd.)

College Ct. W6 . . . . 1E **85**
  (off Queen Caroline St.)
College Cres. NW3. . . . . 3E **45**
College Cross 4C **48**
College E. E1 . . . . 4B **64**
College Gdns.
  IG4: Ilf 1F **41**
  SE21 . . . . 1A **120**
  SW17 . . . . 2A **116**
  (not continuous)
College Gro. NW1 . . . . . 5E **47**
College Hill
  EC4 . . . . 4A **18** (1E **77**)
College La. NW5 . . . . . . 1D **47**
College Mans. NW6 . . . . 5A **44**
  (off Winchester Av.)
College M. N1 . . . . 4C **48**
  (off College Cross,
    not continuous)
  SW1 . . . . 5D **23**
  SW18 . . . . 3D **101**
College of Arms 4F **17**
College Pde. NW6 . . . . . 5A **44**
COLLEGE PARK 2D **57**
College Pk. Cl.
  SE13 . . . . 2F **109**
College Pl. NW1 . . . . . . 5E **47**
  SW10 . . . . 3E **87**
College Point E15 . . . . . 3B **54**
College Rd. E17 . . . . . . 1E **39**
  NW10 . . . . 1E **57**
  SE19 . . . . 5A **106**
  SE21 . . . . 5A **106**
College Row E9 . . . . . . 2F **51**
College St.
  EC4 . . . . 4A **18** (1E **77**)
College Ter. E3. . . . . . . 2B **66**
College Vw. SE9 . . . . . . 1F **125**
College Yd. NW5 . . . . . . 1D **47**
Collent St. E9 . . . . 3E **51**
Collerston Ho. SE10 . . . . 1B **96**
  (off Armitage Rd.)
Colless Rd. N15 . . . . . . 1B **36**
Collett Rd. SE16. . . . . . 4C **78**
Collett Ho. N1 . . . . 1B **62**
Collingbourne Rd.
  W12 . . . . 2D **71**
Collingham Gdns.
  SW5 . . . . 5D **73**
Collingham Pl. SW5 . . . . 5D **73**
Collingham Rd. SW5 . . . 5D **73**
Collington St. SE10 . . . . 1F **95**
Collingtree Rd.
  SE26 . . . . 4E **121**
Collingwood Ho. E1 . . . . 3D **65**
  (off Darling Row)
  SE16. . . . . 3D **79**
  (off Cherry Gdn. St.)
  SW1 . . . . 1F **89**
  (off Dolphin Sq.)
  W1. . . . . 5F **5**
  (off Clipstone St.)
Collingwood Rd. E17 . . . 1C **38**
Collingwood St. E1 . . . . 3D **65**
Collins Ct. E8 . . . . 3C **50**
Collins Ho. E14 . . . . . . 1E **81**
  (off Newby Pl.)
  E15. . . . . 5B **54**
  (off John St.)

Collins Ho. SE10 . . . . . 1B **96**
  (off Armitage Rd.)
Collinson Ct. SE1 . . . . . 4F **25**
  (off Gt. Suffolk St.)
Collinson Ho. SE15 . . . . 3C **92**
  (off Peckham Pk. Rd.)
Collinson St.
  SE1 . . . . 4F **25** (3E **77**)
Collinson Wlk.
  SE1 . . . . 4F **25** (3E **77**)
Collins Rd. N5 . . . . 1E **49**
Collins Sq. SE3 . . . . . . 5B **96**
Collins St. SE3 . . . . 5A **96**
  (not continuous)
Collin's Yd. N1. . . . . . . 5D **49**
Collison Pl. N16. . . . . . . 3A **36**
Coll's Rd. SE15 . . . . . . 4E **93**
Collyer Pl. SE15 . . . . . . 4C **92**
Colman Rd. E16 . . . . . . 4E **69**
Colmans Wharf E14 . . . . 4D **67**
  (off Morris Rd.)
Colmar Cl. E1 . . . . 3F **65**
Colmore M. SE15 . . . . . 4D **93**
Colnbrook St.
  SE1 . . . . 5D **25** (4D **77**)
Colne Ho. NW8 . . . . 3F **59**
  (off Penfold St.)
Colne Rd. E5 . . . . 1A **52**
Colne St. E13. . . . . 2C **68**
Cologne Rd. SW11 . . . . 2F **101**
Colombo St.
  SE1 . . . . 2D **25** (2D **77**)
Colombo Street Sports Cen. &
  Community Cen. 2D **25**
Colomb St. SE10 . . . . . 1A **96**
Colonial Ct. N7 . . . . 5B **34**
Colonnade
  WC1 . . . . 4E **7** (3A **62**)
Colonnade, The SE8 . . . 5B **80**
Colonnades, The W2 . . . 5D **59**
Colonnade Wlk. SW1 . . . 5D **75**
Colorado Bldg. SE8 . . . . 4D **95**
  (off Deal's Gateway)
Colosseum Ter. NW1 . . . 2E **5**
Colour Ct. SW1 . . . . . . 2A **22**
Colson Way SW16 . . . . 4E **117**
Colstead Ho. E1 . . . . . . 5D **65**
  (off Watney Mkt.)
Colston Rd. E7 . . . . 3F **55**
Colthurst Cres. N4 . . . . 4D **35**
Coltman Ho. SE10 . . . . 2E **95**
  (off Welland St.)
Coltman St. E14 . . . . . . 4A **66**
Columbas Dr. NW3 . . . . 3F **31**
Columbia Point SE16 . . . 4E **79**
  (off Surrey Quays Rd.)
Columbia Rd.
  E2 . . . . 1F **11** (2B **64**)
  E13 . . . . 3B **68**
Columbia Road Flower Market
  . . . . 1F **11**
  (off Columbia Rd.)
Columbine Av. E6 . . . . . 4F **69**
Columbine Way SE13. . . 5E **95**
Columbus Ct. SE16 . . . . 2E **79**
  (off Rotherhithe St.)
Columbus Ct. Yd.
  E14 . . . . 2C **80**
Colva Wlk. N19 . . . . . . 4D **33**

Colverson Ho. E1 . . . . . . 4E 65
(off Lindley St.)
Colvestone Cres. E8. . . 2B 50
Colview Ct. SE9 . . . . 1F 125
Colville Est. N1 . . . . 5A 50
Colville Est. W. E2 . . . . . 2B 64
(off Turin St.)
Colville Gdns. W11 . . . . . 5B 58
(not continuous)
Colville Ho. E2 . . . . 1E 65
(off Waterloo Gdns.)
Colville Ho's. W11 . . . . . 5B 58
Colville M. W11 . . . . 5B 58
Colville Pl.
W1 . . . . 1A 14 (4E 61)
Colville Rd. E11 . . . . 5E 39
W11 . . . . 5B 58
Colville Sq. W11 . . . . . . 5B 58
Colville Ter. W11 . . . . . . 5B 58
Colvin Cl. SE26. . . . . . . 5E 121
Colvin Rd. E6 . . . . 4F 55
Colwell Rd. SE22 . . . . . 3B 106
Colwick Cl. N6 . . . . 2F 33
Colwith Rd. W6 . . . . 2E 85
Colworth Gro. SE17 . . . . 5E 77
Colworth Rd. E11 . . . . . . 1A 40
Colwyn Cl. SW16 . . . . . 5E 117
Colwyn Grn. NW9 . . . . . 1A 28
(off Snowdon Dr.)
Colwyn Ho.
SE1 . . . . . . 5B 24 (4C 76)
Colwyn Rd. NW2 . . . . . . 5D 29
Colyer Cl. N1 . . . . 1B 62
Colyton La. SW16 . . . . . 5C 118
Colyton Rd. SE22 . . . . . 3D 107
Combe,
NW1. . . . . . . 2E 5 (2D 61)
Combe Av. SE3. . . . . . . 3B 96
Combedale Rd.
SE10 . . . . 1C 96
Combe Ho. W2. . . . . . . 4C 58
(off Brunel Est.)
Combemartin Rd.
SW18 . . . . 5A 100
Combe M. SE3 . . . . 3B 96
Comber Cl. NW2 . . . . . . 5D 29
Comber Gro. SE5 . . . . . 3E 91
Comber Ho. SE5. . . . . . 3E 91
Combermere Rd.
SW9 . . . . 1B 104
Comberton Rd. E5 . . . . . 4D 37
Comedy Store 5B 14
(off Oxendon St.)
Comedy Theatre 5B 14
(off Panton St.)
Comeragh M. W14 . . . . 1A 86
Comeragh Rd. W14 . . . . 1A 86
Comerell Pl. SE10 . . . . . 1B 96
Comerford Rd. SE4 . . . . 2A 108
Comet Cl. E12. . . . . 1F 55
Comet Pl. SE8 . . . . 3C 94
(not continuous)
Comet St. SE8 . . . . 3C 94
Comfort St. SE15 . . . . . 2A 92
Commercial Dock Path
SE16. . . . . 4B 80
(off Gulliver St.)
Commercial Rd. E1 . . . . 5C 64
E14 . . . . 5A 66

Commercial St.
E1. . . . . 4F 11 (3B 64)
Commercial Way
SE15. . . . . 3B 92
Commerell St. SE10 . . . 1A 96
Commodity Quay E1. . . 1B 78
Commodore Ct. SE8. . . . 4C 94
(off Albyn Rd.)
Commodore Ho. E14 . . . 1E 81
(off Poplar High St.)
SW18 . . . . 1E 101
Commodore Sq.
SW10 . . . . 4E 87
Common, The E15 . . . . . 3A 54
Commondale SW15 . . . . 1E 99
Commonfield La.
SW17 . . . . 5A 116
Common Mile Cl.
SW4 . . . . 3F 103
Common Rd. SW13. . . . 1D 99
W4 . . . . 5A 70
Commonwealth Av.
W12 . . . . 1D 71
(not continuous)
Commonwealth Conference
Cen. 2A 22 (2E 75)
Commonwealth Institute
. . . . 4B 72
Community La. N17 . . . . 2F 47
Community Rd. E15 . . . . 2F 53
Como Rd. SE23 . . . . . . 2A 122
Compass Ct. SE1 . . . . . 2F 27
(off Shad Thames)
Compass Ho. SW18. . . . 2D 101
Compass Point E14 . . . . 1B 80
(off Grenade St.)
Companye Gdns.
NW6 . . . . 4D 45
Compter Pas. EC2 . . . . . 3A 18
Compton Av. E6 . . . . . . 1F 69
N1. . . . . 3D 49
N6. . . . . 2A 32
Compton Cl. E3 . . . . 4C 66
NW1 . . . . 2E 5
NW11 . . . . 5F 29
SE15 . . . . 3C 92
Compton Ct. SE19 . . . . 5A 120
Compton Pas.
EC1 . . . . 3E 9 (3D 63)
Compton Pl.
WC1 . . . . 3D 7 (3A 62)
Compton Rd. N1 . . . . . . 3D 49
NW10 . . . . 2F 57
SW19 . . . . 5B 114
Compton St.
EC1 . . . . 3D 9 (3D 63)
Compton Ter. N1 . . . . . . 3D 49
Comus Ho. SE17 . . . . . . 5A 78
(off Comus Pl.)
Comus Pl. SE17 . . . . . . 5A 78
Comyn Rd. SW11 . . . . . 2A 102
Comyns Cl. E16 . . . . 4B 68
Conant Ho. SE11 . . . . . 2D 91
(off St Agnes Pl.)
Conant Rd. E1 . . . . 1C 78
Concanon Rd. SW2 . . . 2B 104
Concert Hall App.
SE1 . . . . 2A 24 (2B 76)

Concordia Wharf E14. . . 2E 81
(off Coldharbour)
Condell Rd. SW8 . . . . . . 4E 89
Conder St. E14. . . . . 5A 66
Condray Pl. SW11 . . . . . 3A 88
Conduit Av. SE10 . . . . . . 4F 95
Conduit Ct. WC2 . . . . . . 4D 15
Conduit M. W2 . . . . 5F 59
Conduit Pas. W2. . . . . . . 5F 59
(off Conduit Pl.)
Conduit Pl. W2. . . . . 5F 59
Conduit St.
W1. . . . . . . 4E 13 (1D 75)
Conewood St. N5. . . . . . 5D 35
Coney Acre SE21 . . . . . 1E 119
Coney Way SW8. . . . . . . 2B 90
Congers Ho. SE8 . . . . . . 3C 94
Congreve Ho. N16 . . . . 2A 50
Congreve St. SE17 . . . . . 5A 78
Congreve Wlk. E16. . . . . 4F 69
(off Fulmer Rd.)
Conifer Gdns.
SW16 . . . . 3A 118
Conifer Ho. SE4 . . . . . . 2B 108
(off Brockley Rd.)
Coniger Rd. SW6 . . . . . . 5C 86
Coningham Ct. SW10. . . 3E 87
(off King's Rd.)
Coningham M. W12. . . . 2C 70
Coningham Rd.
W12 . . . . 3D 71
Coningsby Rd. N4 . . . . . 2D 35
Conington Rd. SE13. . . . 5D 95
Conisborough Cres.
SE6 . . . . 3E 123
Conisbrough NW1 . . . . 5E 47
(off Bayham St.)
Coniston NW1. . . . . 1F 5
(off Harrington St.)
Coniston Cl. SW13 . . . . 3B 84
Coniston Ct. SE16. . . . . 3F 79
(off Eleanor Cl.)
W2 . . . . 5A 60
(off Kendal St.)
Coniston Ho. E3 . . . . . . 3B 66
(off Southern Gro.)
SE5 . . . . 3E 91
(off Wyndham Rd.)
Coniston Rd.
BR1: Brom 5A 124
Coniston Wlk. E9 . . . . . 2E 51
Conlan St. W10 . . . . 3A 58
Conley Rd. NW10. . . . . . 3A 42
Conley St. SE10 . . . . . . 1A 96
Connaught Bri. E16 . . . . 2F 83
Connaught Bus. Cen.
NW9 . . . . 1B 28
Connaught Cl. E10 . . . . 4F 37
W2 . . . . 5A 60
(off Connaught St.)
Connaught Ct. W2 . . . . 5B 60
(off Connaught Ct.)
Connaught Ho.
NW10 . . . . 2D 57
(off Trenmar Gdns.)
W1 . . . . 5D 13
(off Davies St.)

Connaught Lodge. N4 . . . 2C **34**
(off Connaught Rd.)
Connaught M. NW3 . . . . . . 1A **46**
SE11 . . . . 5C **76**
(off Walcot Sq.)
SW6 . . . . 4A **86**
Connaught Pl. W2 . . . . . . 1B **74**
Connaught Rd. E11 . . . . . 3F **39**
E16 . . . . 2F **83**
E17 . . . . 1C **38**
N4 . . . . 2C **34**
NW10 . . . . 5A **42**
Connaught Rdbt. E16 . . . 1F **83**
(off Victoria Dock Rd.)
Connaught Sq. W2 . . . . . 5B **60**
Connaught St. W2 . . . . . . 5A **60**
Connell Ct. SE14 . . . . . . 2F **93**
(off Myers La.)
Connor Cl. E11 . . . . 2A **40**
Connor Ct. SW11 . . . . . . 4D **89**
Connor St. E9 . . . . 5F **51**
Conrad Ho. E8 . . . . 3C **50**
E14 . . . . 1A **80**
(off Victory Pl.)
E16 . . . . 2D **83**
(off Wesley Av.)
N16 . . . . 2A **50**
(off Matthias St.)
SW8 . . . . 3A **90**
(off Wyvil Rd.)
Consort Ct. W8 . . . . 4D **73**
(off Wright's La.)
Consort Ho. E14 . . . . . . 1D **95**
(off St Davids Sq.)
W2 . . . . 1D **73**
(off Queensway)
Consort Lodge NW8 . . . 5B **46**
(off Prince Albert Rd.)
Consort Rd. SE15 . . . . . 4D **93**
Cons St. SE1 . . . 3C **24** (3C **76**)
Constable Av. E16 . . . . . 2D **83**
Constable Cl. NW11 . . . . 1D **31**
Constable Ct. SE16 . . . . 1D **93**
(off Stubbs Dr.)
Constable Ho. NW3 . . . . 4B **46**
Constable Ho's. E14 . . . 3C **80**
(off Cassilis Rd.)
Constable Wlk.
SE21 . . . . 3A **120**
Constance Allen Ho.
W10 . . . . 5F **57**
(off Bridge Cl.)
Constance St. E16 . . . . . 2F **83**
Constant Ho. E14 . . . . . . 1D **81**
(off Harrow La.)
Constantine Ct. E1 . . . . . 5C **64**
(off Fairclough St.)
Constantine Rd. NW3 . . . 1A **46**
Constitution Hill
SW1 . . . . 3D **21** (3D **75**)
Content St. SE17 . . . . . . 5F **77**
Convent Gdns. W11 . . . . 5A **58**
Convent Hill SE19 . . . . . 5E **119**
Conway Gro. W3 . . . . . . 4A **56**
Conway Ho. E14 . . . . . . 5C **80**
(off Cahir St.)
SW3 . . . . 1B **88**
(off Ormonde Ga.)
Conway M. W1 . . . . 4F **5**

Conway Rd. NW2 . . . . . . 4E **29**
Conway St.
W1 . . . . 4F **5** (3E **61**)
(not continuous)
Conybeare NW3 . . . . 4A **46**
Conyer's Rd. SW16 . . . . 5F **117**
Conyer St. E3 . . . . 1A **66**
Cook Ct. SE16 . . . . 2E **79**
(off Rotherhithe St.)
Cookes Cl. E11 . . . . 4B **40**
Cookham Cres. SE16 . . . 3F **79**
Cookham Ho. E2 . . . . 3F **11**
(off Montclare St.)
Cook's Rd. E15 . . . . 1D **67**
SE17 . . . . 2D **91**
Coolfin Rd. E16 . . . . 5C **68**
Coolhurst Rd. N8 . . . . . . 1F **33**
Cool Oak La. NW9 . . . . . 2A **28**
Coomassie Rd. W9 . . . . . 3B **58**
Coombe Ho. N7 . . . . 2F **47**
Coombe Lodge SE7 . . . . 2E **97**
Coombe Pk.
KT2: King T. 5A **112**
Coomber Ho. SW6 . . . . . 1D **101**
(off Wandsworth Bri. Rd.)
Coombe Rd. NW10 . . . . . 5A **28**
SE26 . . . . 4D **121**
W4 . . . . 1A **84**
Coombs St. N1 . . . 1E **9** (1D **63**)
Coomer M. SW6 . . . . 2B **86**
Coomer Pl. SW6 . . . . 2B **86**
Coomer Rd. SW6 . . . . . . 2B **86**
Cooperage, The SE1 . . . 2F **27**
(off Gainsford St.)
Cooper Cl.
SE1 . . . . 4C **24** (3C **76**)
Cooper Ct. E15 . . . . 2D **53**
Cooper Ho. NW8 . . . . . . 3F **59**
(off Lyons Pl.)
Cooper Rd. NW4 . . . . . . 1F **29**
NW10 . . . . 2C **42**
Coopersale Rd. E9 . . . . . 2F **51**
Coopers Cl. E1 . . . . 3E **65**
Coopers Ct. E3 . . . . 3B **66**
(off Eric St.)
Coopers La. E10 . . . . 3D **39**
NW1 . . . . 1F **61**
(not continuous)
SE12 . . . . 2D **125**
Coopers Lodge SE1 . . . . 3F **27**
(off Tooley St.)
Cooper's Rd. SE1 . . . . . . 1B **92**
Coopers Row
EC3 . . . . 4F **19** (1B **78**)
Coopers St. E16 . . . . 4B **68**
Coopers Wlk. E15 . . . . . . 2A **54**
Cooper's Yd. SE19 . . . . . 5A **120**
Cope Ho. EC1 . . . . 2A **10**
Copeland Dr. E14 . . . . . . 5C **80**
Copeland Ho. SE11 . . . . 4C **76**
(off Lambeth Wlk.)
SW17 . . . . 4F **115**
Copeland Rd. E17 . . . . . . 1D **39**
SE15 . . . . 5C **92**
Copeman Cl. SE26 . . . . . 5E **121**
Copenhagen Ho. N1 . . . . 5B **48**
(off Barnsbury Est.)
Copenhagen Pl. E14 . . . . 5B **66**
(not continuous)

Copenhagen St. N1 . . . . 5A **48**
Cope Pl. W8 . . . . 4C **72**
Copers Cope Rd.
BR3: Beck. 5B **122**
Cope St. SE16 . . . . 5F **79**
Copford Wlk. N1 . . . . 5E **49**
(off Popham St.)
Copgate Path
SW16 . . . . 5B **118**
Copleston M. SE15 . . . . . 5B **92**
Copleston Pas. SE5 . . . . 5B **92**
Copleston Rd.
SE15 . . . . 1B **106**
Copley Cl. SE17 . . . . 2E **91**
Copley Pk. SW16 . . . . . . 5B **118**
Copley Rd. St. 1 . . . . 4F **65**
Coppelia Rd. SE3 . . . . . . 2B **110**
Copperas St. SE8 . . . . . . 2D **95**
Copperbeech Cl.
NW3 . . . . 2F **45**
Copperfield Ho. SE1 . . . . 3C **78**
(off Wolseley St.)
W1 . . . . 5C **4**
(off Marylebone High St.)
W11 . . . . 2F **71**
(off St Ann's Rd.)
Copperfield Rd. E3 . . . . . 3A **66**
Copperfield St.
SE1 . . . . 3E **25** (3D **77**)
Coppermead Cl.
NW2 . . . . 5E **29**
Copper Mill La.
SW17 . . . . 4E **115**
Coppermill La. E17 . . . . . 1E **37**
(not continuous)
Copper Row SE1 . . . . . . 2F **27**
Copperworks, The
N1 . . . . 1A **62**
(off Railway St.)
Coppice Dr. SW15 . . . . . 4D **99**
Coppock Cl. SW11 . . . . . 5A **88**
Copse Cl. SE7 . . . . 2D **97**
Coptain Ho. SW18 . . . . . 2C **100**
Copthall Av.
EC2 . . . . 2C **18** (5F **63**)
(not continuous)
Copthall Bldgs. EC2 . . . . 2C **18**
Copthall Cl.
EC2 . . . . 2B **18** (5F **63**)
Copthorne Av.
SW12 . . . . 5F **103**
Coptic St.
WC1 . . . . 1D **15** (4A **62**)
Coral Apartments
E16 . . . . 1C **82**
(off Western Gateway)
Coral Ho. E1 . . . . 3A **66**
(off Harford St.)
Coral Row SW11 . . . . . . 1E **101**
Coral St.
SE1 . . . . 4C **24** (3C **76**)
Coram Ho. W4 . . . . 1A **84**
(off Wood St.)
WC1 . . . . 3D **7**
Coram St.
WC1 . . . . 4D **7** (3A **62**)
Corbden Cl. SE15 . . . . . . 4B **92**
Corbet Ct.
EC3 . . . . 3C **18** (5F **63**)

Corbet Ho. *N1* *1C 62*
   (off Barnsbury Est.)
SE5 . . . . *3E 91*
   (off Wyndham Rd.)
Corbet Pl. E1 . . . 5F 11 (4B 64)
Corbett Ct. SE26 . . . . . 4B 122
Corbett Ho. *SW10* *2E 87*
   (off Cathcart Rd.)
Corbett Rd. E11 . . . . 1E 41
Corbetts La. SE16 . . . . . . 5E 79
   (not continuous)
Corbetts Pas. *SE16* *5E 79*
   (off Corbetts La.)
Corbetts Wharf
SE16 . . . . *3D 79*
   (off Bermondsey Wall E.)
Corbicum E11 . . . . 2A 40
Corbidge Ct. *SE8* *2D 95*
   (off Glaisher St.)
Corbiere Ho. *N1* *5F 49*
   (off De Beauvoir Est.)
Corbridge Cres. E2 . . . 1D 65
Corbyn St. N4 . . . . 3A 34
Corby Way E3 . . . . 3C 66
Cordelia Cl. SE24 . . . 2D 105
Cordelia Ho. *N1* *1A 64*
   (off Arden Est.)
Cordelia St. E14 . . . . . . 5D 67
Cording St. E14 . . . . . . 4D 67
Cordwainers Ct. *E9* *4E 51*
   (off St Thomas's Sq.)
Cordwainers Wlk.
E13 . . . . 1C 68
Cord Way E14 . . . . 4C 80
Cordwell Rd. SE13 . . . 3A 110
Corelli Ct. *SW5* *5C 72*
   (off W. Cromwell Rd.)
Corelli Rd. SE3 . . . . 5F 97
Corfe Ho. *SW8* *3B 90*
   (off Dorset Rd.)
Corfield St. E2 . . . . 2D 65
Coriander Av. E14 . . . . . 5F 67
Coriander Ct. *SE1* *3B 78*
   (off Gainsford St.)
Corinne Rd. N19 . . . . . . 1E 47
Corker Wlk. N7 . . . . 4B 34
Cork Sq. E1 . . . . 2D 79
Cork St. W1 . . . 5F 13 (1E 75)
Cork St. M. W1 . . . . 5F 13
Cork Tree Ho. *SE27* . . . *5D 119*
   (off Lakeview Rd.)
Corlett St. NW1 . . . . 4A 60
Cormont Rd. SE5 . . . . . . 4D 91
Cormorant Ct. *SE8* *2B 94*
   (off Pilot Cl.)
Cormorant Lodge *E1* . . . *2C 78*
   (off Thomas More St.)
Cormorant Rd. E7 . . . . . . 2B 54
Cornbury Ho. *SE8* *2B 94*
   (off Evelyn St.)
Cornelia St. N7 . . . . 3B 48
Cornell Bldg. *E1* *5C 64*
   (off Coke St.)
Corner Fielde SW2 . . . 1B 118
Corner Grn. SE3 . . . . . . 5C 96
Corner Ho. St. WC2 . . . 1D 23
Corney Reach Way
W4 . . . . 3A 84
Corney Rd. W4 . . . . 2A 84

Cornflower Ter.
SE22 . . . . 4D 107
Conford Gro. SW12 . . . 2D 117
Cornhill EC3 . . . 3C 18 (5F 63)
Cornick Ho. *SE16* *4D 79*
   (off Slippers Pl.)
Cornish Ho. *SE17* *2D 91*
   (off Brandon Est.)
Cornmill La. SE13 . . . . . 1E 109
Cornmow Dr. NW10 . . . . 2B 42
Cornthwaite Rd. E5 . . . . 5E 37
Cornwall Av. E2 . . . . . . 2E 65
Cornwall Cres. W11 . . . 5A 58
Cornwall Gdns.
NW10 . . . . 3D 43
SW7 . . . . 4D 73
Cornwall Gdns. Wlk.
SW7 . . . . 4D 73
Cornwall Gro. W4 . . . . . 1A 84
Cornwall Ho. *SW7* *4D 73*
   (off Cornwall Gdns.)
Cornwallis Ct. *SW8* *4A 90*
   (off Lansdowne Grn.)
Cornwallis Ho. *SE16* . . . *3D 79*
   (off Cherry Gdn. St.)
W12 . . . . *1D 71*
   (off India Way)
Cornwallis Rd. N19 . . . 4A 34
Cornwallis Sq. N19 . . . 4A 34
Cornwall Mans.
SW10 . . . . *3E 87*
   (off Cremorne Rd.)
W8 . . . . *3D 73*
   (off Kensington Ct.)
W14 . . . . *4F 71*
   (off Blythe Rd.)
Cornwall M. Sth.
SW7 . . . . 4E 73
Cornwall M. W. SW7 . . 4D 73
Cornwall Rd. N4 . . . . . 2C 34
N15 . . . . 1F 35
SE1 . . . 1B 24 (2C 76)
Cornwall Sq. *SE11* *1D 91*
   (off Seaton Cl.)
Cornwall St. E1 . . . . . . 1D 79
Cornwall Ter.
NW1 . . . . . . 4A 4 (3B 60)
Cornwall Ter. M. NW1 . . 4A 4
Corn Way E11 . . . . 5F 39
Cornwell Cres. E7 . . . . 1E 55
Cornwood Dr. E1 . . . . . 5E 65
Corona Bldg. *E14* *2E 81*
   (off Blackwall Way)
Corona Rd. SE12 . . . . 5C 110
Coronation Av. N16 . . . 1B 50
Coronation Ct. E15 . . . 3B 54
W10 . . . . *4E 57*
   (off Brewster Gdns.)
Coronation Rd. E13 . . . 2E 69
Coroners Ct. *NW1* *5F 47*
   (off Camley St.)
Coronet Cinema 2C 72
   (off Notting Hill Ga.)
Coronet St.
N1 . . . . 2D 11 (2A 64)
Corporation Row
EC1 . . . . 3C 8 (3C 62)
Corporation St. E15 . . . 1A 68
N7 . . . . 2A 48

Corrance Rd. SW2 . . . . 2A 104
Corringham Ct.
NW11 . . . . 2C 30
Corringham Ho. *E1* *5F 65*
   (off Pitsea St.)
Corringham Rd.
NW11 . . . . 2C 30
Corringway NW11 . . . . 2D 31
Corris Grn. NW9 . . . . . 1A 28
Corry Dr. SW9 . . . . . . 2D 105
Corry Ho. *E14* *1D 81*
   (off Wade's Pl.)
Corsehill St. SW16 . . . 5E 117
Corsham St.
N1 . . . . 2C 10 (2F 63)
Corsica St. N5 . . . . . . 3D 49
Corsley Way *E9* *3B 52*
   (off Osborne Rd.)
Cortayne Rd. SW6 . . . . 5B 86
Cortis Rd. SW15 . . . . . 4D 99
Cortis Ter. SW15 . . . . . 4D 99
Corunna Rd. SW8 . . . . 4E 89
Corunna Ter. SW8 . . . . 4E 89
Corvette Sq. SE10 . . . . 2F 95
Coryton Path *W9* *3B 58*
   (off Ashmore Rd.)
Cosbycote Av. SE24 . . . 3E 105
Cosgrove Ho. *E2* *5C 50*
   (off Whiston Rd.)
Cosmo Pl.
WC1 . . . . 5E 7 (4A 62)
Cosmur Cl. W12 . . . . . 4B 70
Cossall Wlk. SE15 . . . . 5D 93
Cossar M. SW2 . . . . . 3C 104
Cosser St.
SE1 . . . . 5B 24 (4C 76)
Costa St. SE15 . . . . . . 5C 92
Coston Wlk. SE4 . . . . . 2F 107
Cosway Mans. *NW1* . . . *4A 60*
   (off Shroton St.)
Cosway St. NW1 . . . . . 4A 60
Cotall St. E14 . . . . 4C 66
Coteford St. SW17 . . . 4B 116
Cotesbach Rd. E5 . . . . 5E 37
Cotes Ho. *NW8* *3A 60*
   (off Broadley St.)
Cotham St. SE17 . . . . . 5E 77
Cotherstone Rd.
SW2 . . . . 1B 118
Cotleigh Rd. NW6 . . . . 4C 44
Cotman Cl. NW11 . . . . 1E 31
SW15 . . . . 4F 99
Cotman Ho. *NW8* *1A 60*
   (off Townshend Est.)
Cotswold Ct. EC1 . . . . . 3F 9
Cotswold Gdns. E6 . . . 2F 69
NW2 . . . . 4F 29
Cotswold Ga. NW2 . . . 3A 30
Cotswold M. SW11 . . . 4F 87
Cotswold St. SE27 . . . 4D 119
Cottage Cl. *E1* *3E 65*
   (off Hayfield Pas.)
Cottage Grn. SE5 . . . . 3F 91
Cottage Gro. SW9 . . . 1A 104
Cottage Pl. SW3 . . . . . 4A 74
Cottage Rd. N7 . . . . . . 2B 48
Cottage St. E14 . . . . . 1D 81
Cottage Wlk. N16 . . . . 5B 36
Cottesbrook St. SE14 . . 3A 94

Cottesloe Ho. NW8 . . . . 3A 60
(off Jerome Cres.)
Cottesloe M. SE1 . . . . . 5C 24
(off Emery St.)
Cottesloe Theatre 1B 24
(in National Theatre)
Cottesmore Ct. W8 . . . . . 4D 73
(off Stanford Rd.)
Cottesmore Gdns.
W8 . . . . 4D 73
Cottingham Rd. SW8 . . 3B 90
Cottington St. SE11 . . . 1C 90
Cottle Way SE16 . . . . . . 3D 79
(off Paradise St.)
Cotton Av. W3 . . . . 5A 56
Cotton Cl. E11 . . . . 4A 40
Cotton Hill
BR1: Brom 4E 123
Cotton Ho. SW2 . . . . . . 5A 104
Cotton Row SW11 . . . . . 1E 101
Cottons Cen.
SE1 . . . . . 1D 27 (2A 78)
Cotton's Gdns.
E2 . . . . 1E 11 (2A 64)
Cottons La.
SE1 . . . . 1C 26 (2F 77)
Cotton St. E14 . . . . 1E 81
Cottrell Ct. SE10 . . . . . . 5B 82
Cottrill Gdns. E8 . . . . . . 3D 51
Coulgate St. SE4 . . . . . 1A 108
Coulson St. SW3 . . . . . 1B 88
Coulter Rd. W6 . . . . 4D 71
Councillor St. SE5 . . . . . 3E 91
Counter Ct. SE1 . . . . . . 2B 26
(off Borough High St.)
Counters Ct. E14 . . . . . 4A 72
(off Holland Rd.)
Counter St.
SE1 . . . . 2D 27 (2A 78)
Countess Rd. NW5 . . . . . 2E 47
County Gro. SE5 . . . . . . 4E 91
County Hall Apartments
SE1 . . . . 3F 23
County Hall (Former)
. . . . 4F 23 (3B 76)
County St. SE1 . . . . 4E 77
Courland Gro. SW8 . . . . 4F 89
Courland St. SW8 . . . . . 4F 89
Courtauld Ho. E2 . . . . . . 5C 50
(off Goldsmith's Row)
Courtauld Institute Galleries
. . . . 4F 15
Courtauld Rd. N19 . . . . . 3A 34
Court Cl. NW8 . . . . 4F 45
(off Boydell Ct.,
not continuous)
Courtenay Av. N6 . . . . . 2A 32
Courtenay M. E17 . . . . . 1A 38
Courtenay Pl. E17 . . . . . 1A 38
Courtenay Rd. E11 . . . . 5B 40
Courtenay Sq. SE11 . . . 1C 90
Courtenay St. SE11 . . . . 1C 90
Court Farm Rd. SE9 . . . 2F 125
Courtfield Gdns.
SW5 . . . . 5D 73
Courtfield Ho. EC1 . . . . . 5B 8
(off Baldwins Gdns.)
Courtfield M. SW5 . . . . . 5E 73
Courtfield Rd. SW7 . . . . 5E 73

Court Gdns. N7 . . . . . . 3C 48
(not continuous)
Courthill Rd. SE13 . . . 2E 109
Courthope Ho. SE16 . . . 4E 79
(off Lower Rd.)
SW8 . . . . 3A 90
(off Hartington Rd.)
Courthope Rd. NW3 . . 1B 46
SW19 . . . . 5A 114
Courthouse La. E8 . . . . 1B 50
Courtland Rd. E6 . . . . . 5F 55
Courtlands Av.
SE12 . . . . 3D 111
Court La. SE21 . . . . . . 4A 106
Court La. Gdns.
SE21 . . . . 5A 106
Courtleigh NW11 . . . . . 1B 30
Court Lodge SW1 . . . . . 5C 74
(off Sloane Sq.)
Courtmead Cl. SE24 . . . 4E 105
Courtnell St. W2 . . . . . . 5C 58
Courtney Ct. N7 . . . . . . 2C 48
Courtney Ho. W14 . . . . . 4A 72
(off Russell Rd.)
Courtney Rd. N7 . . . . . . 2C 48
Courtrai Rd. SE23 . . . . 4A 108
Court Royal SW15 . . . . 3A 100
Courtside N8 . . . . 1F 33
SE26 . . . . 3D 121
Court St. E1 . . . . 4D 65
Courtville Ho. W10 . . . . 2A 58
(off Third Av.)
Courtyard, The E3 . . . . . 1C 66
EC3 . . . . 3C 18
(in Royal Exchange)
N1 . . . . 4B 48
NW1 . . . . 4C 46
SW3 . . . . 2F 87
(off Waldron M.)
Courtyard Theatre, The
King's Cross 1A 62
(off York Way)
Cousin La.
EC4 . . . . . 5B 18 (1F 77)
Couthurst Rd. SE3 . . . . 2D 97
Coutt's Cres. NW5 . . . . 5C 32
Couzens Ho. E3 . . . . . . 4B 66
(off Weatherley Cl.)
Covell Ct. SE8 . . . . 3C 94
COVENT GARDEN
. . . . 4E 15 (1A 76)
Covent Garden
. . . . 4E 15 (1A 76)
Covent Gdn.
WC2 . . . . . 4E 15 (1A 76)
Coventry Cl. NW6 . . . . . 1C 58
Coventry Cross E3 . . . . 3E 67
Coventry Hall
SW16 . . . . 5A 118
Coventry Rd. E1 . . . . . . 3D 65
E2 . . . . 3D 65
Coventry St.
W1 . . . . 5B 14 (1F 75)
Coverdale Rd. NW2 . . . . 4F 43
W12 . . . . 3D 71
Coverley Cl. E1 . . . . . . 4C 64
Coverley Point SE11 . . . 5B 76
(off Tyers St.)
Coverton Rd. SW17 . . . 5A 116

Covington Way
SW16 . . . . 5B 118
(not continuous)
Cowcross St.
EC1 . . . . 5D 9 (4D 63)
Cowdenbeath Path
N1 . . . . 5B 48
Cowden St. SE6 . . . . . . 4C 122
Cowdrey Rd. SW19 . . . 5D 115
Cowick Rd. SW17 . . . . 4B 116
Cowley La. E11 . . . . . . 5A 40
Cowley Rd. E11 . . . . . . 1D 41
SW9 . . . . 4C 90
(not continuous)
SW14 . . . . 1A 98
W3 . . . . 2B 70
Cowley St.
SW1 . . . . . . 5D 23 (4A 76)
Cowling Cl. W11 . . . . . . 2A 72
Cowper Av. E6 . . . . 4F 55
Cowper Ho. SE17 . . . . . 1E 91
(off Browning St.)
SW1 . . . . 1F 89
(off Aylesford St.)
Cowper Rd. N16 . . . . . . 2A 50
SW19 . . . . 5E 115
Cowper's Ct. EC3 . . . . . 3C 18
(off Birchin La.)
Cowper St.
EC2 . . . . . . 3C 10 (3F 63)
Cowper Ter. W10 . . . . . 4F 57
Cowthorpe Rd. SW8 . . . 4F 89
Cox Ho. W6 . . . . 2A 86
(off Field Rd.)
Coxmount Rd. SE7 . . . . 1F 97
Cox's Ct. E1 . . . . 1F 19
Coxson Way
SE1 . . . . 4F 27 (3B 78)
Cox's Wlk. SE21 . . . . . 1C 120
Crabtree Cl. E2 . . . . . . 1B 64
Crabtree Ct. E15 . . . . . 2D 53
Crabtree La. SW6 . . . . . 3E 85
(not continuous)
Crabtree Wlk. SE15 . . . 4B 92
(off Peckham Rd.)
Crace St. NW1 . . . 1B 6 (2F 61)
Craddock St. NW5 . . . . 3C 46
Crafts Council & Gallery
. . . . 1C 62
Cragie Ho. SE1 . . . . . . 5B 78
(off Balaclava Rd.)
Craigerne Rd. SE3 . . . . 3D 97
Craignair Rd. SW2 . . . . 5C 104
Craig's Ct.
SW1 . . . . . . 1D 23 (2A 76)
Craik Ct. NW6 . . . . 1B 58
(off Carlton Va.)
Crail Row SE17 . . . . . . 5F 77
Cramer St.
W1 . . . . 1C 12 (4C 60)
Crammond Cl. W6 . . . . 2A 86
Crampton Ho. SW8 . . . . 4E 89
Crampton Rd. SE20 . . . 5E 121
Crampton St. SE17 . . . . 5E 77
Cranberry La. E16 . . . . 3A 68
Cranbourn All. WC2 . . . 4C 14
(off Cranbourn St.)
Cranbourne NW1 . . . . . 4F 47
(off Agar Gro.)

Cranbourne Gdns.
NW11 . . . . 1A **30**
Cranbourne Pas.
SE16 . . . . 3D **79**
Cranbourne Rd. E12 . . 2F **55**
E15 . . . . 1E **53**
Cranbourn Ho. SE16 . . . 3D **79**
(off Marigold St.)
Cranbourn St.
WC2 . . . . 4C **14** (1F **75**)
(off Camden St.)
Cranbrook NW1 . . . . 5E **47**
Cranbrook Est. E2 . . . . 1F **65**
Cranbrook Rd. SE8 . . . . 4C **94**
W4 . . . . 1A **84**
Cranbrook St. E2 . . . . . 1F **65**
Cranbury Rd. SW6 . . . . 5D **87**
Crandley Cl. SE8 . . . . . 5A **80**
Crane Ct. EC4 . . . . 5C **62**
Crane Gro. N7 . . . . 3C **48**
Crane Ho. E3 . . . . 1A **66**
(off Roman Rd.)
SE15 . . . . 4B **92**
Crane Mead SE16 . . . . . 5F **79**
(not continuous)
Crane St. SE10 . . . . . . 1F **95**
SE15 . . . . 4B **92**
Cranfield Cl. SE27 . . . 3E **119**
Cranfield Ct. W1 . . . . . . 4A **60**
(off Homer St.)
Cranfield Ho. WC1 . . . . . 5D **7**
Cranfield Rd. SE4 . . . 1B **108**
Cranfield Row SE1 . . . . 5C **24**
Cranford Cotts. E1 . . . . 1F **79**
(off Cranford St.)
Cranford St. E1 . . . . . . 1F **79**
Cranford Way N8 . . . . . 1B **34**
Cranhurst Rd. NW2 . . . . 2E **43**
Cranleigh W11 . . . . 2B **72**
(off Ladbroke Rd.)
Cranleigh Ho's. NW1 . . . 1E **61**
(off Cranleigh St.)
Cranleigh M. SW11 . . . 5A **88**
Cranleigh St. NW1 . . . . 1E **61**
CRANLEY GARDENS . . . 1D **33**
Cranley Gdns. SW7 . . . 1E **87**
Cranley M. SW7 . . . . . . 1E **87**
Cranley Pl. SW7 . . . . . . 5F **73**
Cranley Rd. E13 . . . . . . 4D **69**
Cranmer Ct. SW3 . . . . . 5A **74**
SW4 . . . . 1F **103**
Cranmere Ct. SE5 . . . . 4E **91**
Cranmer Ho. SW9 . . . . . 3C **90**
(off Brixton Rd.)
SW11 . . . . 4A **88**
(off Surrey La. Est.)
Cranmer Rd. E7 . . . . . . 1D **55**
SW9 . . . . 3C **90**
Cranmer Ter. SW17 . . . 5F **115**
Cranmore Rd.
BR1: Brom 3B **124**
Cranston Est. N1 . . . . . 1F **63**
Cranston Rd. SE23 . . 1A **122**
Cranswick Rd.
SE16 . . . . 1D **93**
Crantock Rd. SE6 . . . 2D **123**
Cranwell Cl. E3 . . . . . . 3D **67**
Cranwich Rd. N16 . . . . 2F **35**
Cranwood Ct. EC1 . . . . 2C **10**

Cranwood St.
EC1 . . . . 2C **10** (2F **63**)
Cranworth Gdns.
SW9 . . . . 4C **90**
Craster Rd. SW2 . . . . . 5B **104**
Crathie Rd. SE12 . . . . 4D **111**
Craven Cl. N16 . . . . . . 2C **36**
Craven Cottage 5F **85**
Craven Ct. NW10 . . . . . 5A **42**
Craven Gdns. SW19 . . 5C **114**
Craven Hill W2 . . . . 1E **73**
Craven Hill Gdns.
W2 . . . . 1E **73**
(not continuous)
Craven Hill M. W2 . . . . 1E **73**
Craven Lodge W2 . . . . 1E **73**
(off Craven Hill)
Craven M. SW11 . . . . 1C **102**
Craven Pk. NW10 . . . . . 5A **42**
Craven Pk. M.
NW10 . . . . 4A **42**
Craven Pk. Rd. N15 . . . 1B **36**
NW10 . . . . 5A **42**
Craven Pas. WC2 . . . . . 1D **23**
(off Craven St.)
Craven Rd. NW10 . . . . . 5A **42**
W2 . . . . 1E **73**
Craven St.
WC2 . . . . 1D **23** (2A **76**)
Craven Ter. W2 . . . . . . 1E **73**
Craven Wlk. N16 . . . . . 2C **36**
Crawford Bldgs. W1 . . . 4A **60**
(off Homer St.)
Crawford Est. SE5 . . . . 5E **91**
Crawford Mans. W1 . . . 4A **60**
(off Crawford St.)
Crawford M.
W1 . . . . 1A **12** (4B **60**)
Crawford Pas.
EC1 . . . . 4C **8** (3C **62**)
Crawford Pl. W1 . . . . . 5A **60**
Crawford Point E16 . . . 5B **68**
(off Wouldham Rd.)
Crawford Rd. SE5 . . . . 4E **91**
Crawford St.
W1 . . . . 1A **12** (4A **60**)
Crawley Rd. E10 . . . . . 3D **39**
Crawshay Ct. SW9 . . . . 4C **90**
Crawthew Gro.
SE22 . . . . 2B **106**
Crayford Cl. E6 . . . . . . 5F **69**
Crayford Ho. SE1 . . . . . 4C **26**
(off Long La.)
Crayford Rd. N7 . . . . . 1F **47**
Cray Ho. NW8 . . . . 4F **59**
(off Penfold St.)
Crayle Ho. EC1 . . . . 3E **9**
(off Malta St.)
Crealock St. SW18 . . . 4D **101**
Creasy Est. SE1 . . . . . 4A **78**
Crebor St. SE22 . . . . . 4C **106**
Credenhill Ho. SE15 . . . 3D **93**
Credenhill St.
SW16 . . . . 5E **117**
Crediton Hill NW6 . . . . 2D **45**
Crediton Rd. E16 . . . . . 5C **68**
NW10 . . . . 5F **43**
Credon Rd. E13 . . . . . . 1E **69**
SE16 . . . . 1D **93**

Creechurch La.
EC3 . . . . 3E **19** (5A **64**)
(not continuous)
Creechurch Pl. EC3 . . . 3E **19**
Creed Ct. E1 . . . . 2A **66**
EC4 . . . . 3E **17**
Creed La.
EC4 . . . . 3E **17** (5D **63**)
Creek Ho. W14 . . . . 4A **72**
(off Russell Rd.)
Creek Rd. SE8 . . . . 2C **94**
SE10 . . . . 2C **94**
Creekside SE8 . . . . 3D **95**
Creekside Dev't SE8 . . 2D **95**
(off Stowage)
Creeland Gro. SE6 . . . 1B **122**
Crefeld Cl. W6 . . . . 2A **86**
Creighton Av. E6 . . . . . 1F **69**
Creighton Cl. W12 . . . . 1C **70**
Creighton Rd. NW6 . . . 1F **57**
Cremer Bus. Cen. E2 . . . 1F **11**
(off Cremer St.)
Cremer Ho. SE8 . . . . . . 3C **94**
(off Deptford Chu. St.)
Cremer St.
E2 . . . . 1F **11** (1B **64**)
Cremorne Est.
SW10 . . . . 2F **87**
(not continuous)
Cremorne Rd. SW10 . . 3E **87**
Creon Ct. SW9 . . . . 3C **90**
Crescent EC3 . . 4F **19** (1B **78**)
Crescent, The E17 . . . . 1A **38**
NW2 . . . . 5D **29**
SW13 . . . . 5B **84**
SW19 . . . . 3C **114**
W3 . . . . 5A **56**
Crescent Arc. SE10 . . . . 2E **95**
(off Creek Rd.)
Crescent Ct. SW4 . . . . 3F **103**
(off Park Hill)
Crescent Ct. Bus. Cen.
E16 . . . . 3F **67**
Crescent Gdns.
SW19 . . . . 3C **114**
Crescent Gro. SW4 . . . 2E **103**
Crescent Ho. EC1 . . . . . . 4F **9**
(off Golden La. Est.)
SE13 . . . . 5D **95**
Crescent La. SW4 . . . . 2E **103**
Crescent Mans. W11 . . . 1A **72**
(off Elgin Cres.)
Crescent Pl. SW3 . . . . . 5A **74**
Crescent Rd. E6 . . . . . . 5E **55**
E10 . . . . 4D **39**
E13 . . . . 5C **54**
N8 . . . . 1F **33**
Crescent Row
EC1 . . . . 4F **9** (3E **63**)
Crescent Stables
SW15 . . . . 3A **100**
Crescent St. N1 . . . . . . 4B **48**
Crescent Way SE4 . . . 1C **108**
Crescent Wharf E16 . . . 3D **83**
Crescent Wood Rd.
SE26 . . . . 3C **120**
Cresford Rd. SW6 . . . . 4D **87**
Crespigny Rd. NW4 . . . 1D **29**

Cressal Ho. *E14* 4C **80**
   (off Tiller Rd.)
Cresset Ho. E9 . . . . 3E **51**
Cresset Rd. E9 . . . . 3E **51**
Cresset St. SW4 . . . . . . 1F **103**
Cressfield Cl. NW5 . . . . . 2C **46**
Cressida Rd. N19 . . . . . . 3E **33**
Cressingham Rd.
  SE13 . . . . 1E **109**
Cressington Cl. N16 . . . . 2A **50**
Cress M. BR1: Brom . . 5F **123**
Cresswell Gdns.
  SW5 . . . . 1E **87**
Cresswell Pk. SE3 . . . . 1B **110**
Cresswell Pl. SW10 . . . . 1E **87**
Cressy Ct. E1 . . . . 4E **65**
  W6 . . . . 4D **71**
Cressy Ho's. *E1* 4E **65**
   (off Hannibal Rd.)
Cressy Pl. E1 . . . . 4E **65**
Cressy Rd. NW3 . . . . . . 2B **46**
Cresta Ho. *NW3* 4F **45**
   (off Finchley Rd.)
Crestfield St.
  WC1 . . . . 1E **7** (2A **62**)
Crest Rd. NW2 . . . . 4B **28**
Crestway SW15 . . . . 4C **98**
Creswick Wlk. E3 . . . . . . 2C **66**
Crewdson Rd. SW9 . . . . 3C **90**
Crewe Pl. NW10 . . . . . . 2B **56**
Crewkerne Ct. *SW11* . . . 4F **87**
   (off Bolingbroke Wlk.)
Crews St. E14 . . . . 5C **80**
Crewys Rd. NW2 . . . . . . 4B **30**
  SE15 . . . . 5D **93**
Crichton St. SW8 . . . . . . 5E **89**
Cricketers Ct. *SE11* 5D **77**
   (off Kennington La.)
Cricketers M. SW18 . . . 3D **101**
Cricketers Wlk.
  SE26 . . . . 5E **121**
Cricketfield Rd. E5 . . . . 1D **51**
Cricket La.
  BR3: Beck 5A **122**
Cricklade Av. SW2 . . . . 2A **118**
CRICKLEWOOD **5A 30**
Cricklewood B'way.
  NW2 . . . . 5E **29**
Cricklewood La. NW2 . . 1F **43**
Cridland St. E15 . . . . . . 5B **54**
Crieff Rd. SW18 . . . . . . 4E **101**
Criffel Av. SW2 . . . . . . 2F **117**
Crimscott St.
  SE1 . . . . . . 5E **27** (4A **78**)
Crimsworth Rd. SW8 . . . 4F **89**
Crinan St. N1 . . . . 1A **62**
Cringle St. SW8 . . . . 3E **89**
Cripplegate St.
  EC2 . . . . 5A **10** (4E **63**)
Crispe Ho. *N1* 5B **48**
   (off Barnsbury Est.)
Crispian Cl. NW10 . . . . . 1A **42**
Crispin Pl. E1 . . . . 4B **64**
Crispin St. E1 . . 1F **19** (4B **64**)
Crisp Rd. W6 . . . . 1E **85**
Cristowe Rd. SW6 . . . . . 5B **86**
Criterion Ct. *E8* 4B **50**
   (off Middleton Rd.)
Criterion M. N19 . . . . . . 4F **33**

Criterion Theatre 5B **14**
   (off Piccadilly)
Crockerton Rd.
  SW17 . . . . 2B **116**
Croft, The NW10 . . . . . . 1B **56**
Croft Ct. SE13 . . . . 4E **109**
Croftdown Rd. NW5 . . . . 5C **32**
Crofters Ct. *SE8* 5A **80**
   (off Croft St.)
Crofters Way NW1 . . . . . 5F **47**
Croft Ho. *W10* 2A **58**
   (off Third Av.)
Croftongate Way
  SE4 . . . . 3A **108**
Crofton Ho. *SW1* 1D **89**
   (off Sutherland St.)
  SW3 . . . . 2A **88**
   (off Up. Cheyne Row)
Crofton Leisure Cen.
   . . . . 4C **108**
CROFTON PARK 3B **108**
Crofton Pk. Rd. SE4 . . . 4B **108**
Crofton Rd. E13 . . . . 3D **69**
  SE5 . . . . 4A **92**
Crofton Ter. E5 . . . . 2A **52**
Crofts Ho. *E2* 1C **64**
   (off Teale St.)
Crofts St. E1 . . . . 1C **78**
Croft St. SE8 . . . . 5A **80**
Croftway NW3 . . . . 1C **44**
Crogsland Rd. NW1 . . . . 4C **46**
Cromartie Rd. N19 . . . . . 2F **33**
Cromarty Ct. SW2 . . . . 3B **104**
Cromarty Ho. *E1* 4A **66**
   (off Ben Jonson Rd.)
Crombie M. SW1 . . . . . . 5A **88**
Crome Ho. NW10 . . . . . . 3A **42**
Cromer Rd. E10 . . . . 2F **39**
  SW17 . . . . 5C **116**
Cromer St.
  WC1 . . . . 2D **7** (2A **62**)
Cromer Ter. E8 . . . . 2C **50**
Cromer Vs. Rd.
  SW18 . . . . 4B **100**
Cromford Path E5 . . . . . 1F **51**
Cromford Rd. SW18 . . . 3C **100**
Crompton Ct. SW3 . . . . . 5A **74**
Crompton Ho. *SE1* 4E **77**
   (off County St.)
  W2 . . . . 3F **59**
   (off Hall Pl.)
Crompton St. W2 . . . . . . 3F **59**
Cromwell Av. N6 . . . . . . 3D **33**
  W6 . . . . 1D **85**
Cromwell Cl. E1 . . . . 2C **78**
Cromwell Cres. SW5 . . . 5C **72**
Cromwell Gdns. SW7 . . . 4F **73**
Cromwell Gro. W6 . . . . . 4E **71**
Cromwell Highwalk
  EC2 . . . . 5A **10**
Cromwell Ho. *SW11* . . . 4C **88**
   (off Charlotte Despard Av.)
Cromwell Ind. Est.
  E10 . . . . 3A **38**
Cromwell Lodge *E1* . . . 3E **65**
   (off Cleveland Gro.)
Cromwell Mans.
  SW5 . . . . 5C **72**
   (off Cromwell Rd.)

Cromwell M. SW7 . . . . . 5F **73**
Cromwell Pl. *EC2* 5A **10**
   (off Beech St.)
  N6 . . . . 3D **33**
  SW7 . . . . 5F **73**
Cromwell Rd. E7 . . . . . . 4E **55**
  E17 . . . . 1E **39**
  SW5 . . . . 5C **72**
  SW7 . . . . 5C **72**
  SW9 . . . . 4D **91**
  SW19 . . . . 5C **114**
Cromwell Twr. EC2. . . . . 5A **10**
Crondace Rd. SW6 . . . . 4C **86**
Crondall Ct. N1 . . . . 1C **10**
Crondall Ho. SW15 . . . . 5C **98**
Crondall St.
  N1 . . . . 1C **10** (1F **63**)
Crone Ct. NW6 . . . . 1B **58**
   (off Denmark Rd.)
Cronin St. SE15 . . . . 3B **92**
Crooked Billet Yd.
  N1 . . . . 2E **11** (2A **64**)
Crooke Rd. SE8 . . . . 1A **94**
Crookham Rd. SW6 . . . . 4B **86**
Croombs Rd. E16 . . . . . . 4E **69**
Croom's Hill SE10 . . . . . 3E **95**
Croom's Hill Gro.
  SE10 . . . . 3E **95**
Cropley Ct. *N1* 1F **63**
   (off Cropley St.),
   not continuous
Cropley St.
  N1 . . . . 1B **10** (1F **63**)
Cropthorne Ct. W9 . . . . 2E **59**
Crosby Ct.
  SE1 . . . . 3B **26** (3F **77**)
Crosby Ho. E7 . . . . 3C **54**
  E14 . . . . 4E **81**
   (off Manchester Rd.)
Crosby Rd. E7 . . . . 3C **54**
Crosby Row
  SE1 . . . . 4B **26** (3F **77**)
Crosby Sq.
  EC3 . . . . 3D **19** (5A **64**)
Crosby Wlk. E8 . . . . 3B **50**
  SW2 . . . . 5C **104**
Crosby Way SW2 . . . . . 5C **104**
Crosier Cl. SE3 . . . . 4F **97**
Crosland Pl. SW11 . . . . 1C **102**
Cross Av. SE10 . . . . 2F **95**
Crossbow Ho. *N1* 5A **50**
   (off Whitmore Est.)
Crossbrook Rd. SE3 . . . 5F **97**
Cross Cl. SE15 . . . . 5D **93**
Crossfield Rd. NW3 . . . . 3F **45**
Crossfield St. SE8 . . . . . 3C **94**
   (not continuous)
Crossford St. SW9 . . . . . 5B **90**
Cross Keys Cl.
  W1 . . . . 1C **12** (4C **60**)
Cross Keys Sq. *EC1* . . . 1F **17**
   (off Little Britain)
Cross La.
  EC3 . . . . 5D **19** (1A **78**)

Crossleigh Ct. *SE14* 3B **94**
  (off New Cross Rd.)
Crosslet St. *SE17* 5F **77**
Crosslet Va. *SE10* 4D **95**
Crossley St. *N7* 3C **48**
Crossmount Ho. *SE5* *3E **91***
  (off Bowyer Rd.)
Cross Rd. *SE5* 5A **92**
Cross St. *N1* 5D **49**
  SE5 . . . . 1F **105**
  SW13 . . . . 5A **84**
Crossthwaite Av.
  SE5 . . . . 2F **105**
Crosstrees Ho. *E14* *4C **80***
  (off Cassilis Rd.)
Crosswall
  EC3 . . . . 4F **19** (1B **78**)
Crossway *N16* 2A **50**
Crossway, The *SE9* . . . 2F **125**
Crossway Ct. *SE4* 5A **94**
Crossways Ter. *E5* 1E **51**
Croston St. *E8* 5C **50**
CROUCH END 2F **33**
Crouch Hall Ct. *N19* 3A **34**
Crouch Hall Rd. *N8* 1F **33**
Crouch Hill *N4* 1A **34**
  N8 . . . . 1A **34**
Crouch Hill Recreation Cen.
  . . . . 2A **34**
Crouchman's Cl.
  SE26 . . . . 3B **120**
Crowborough Rd.
  SW17 . . . . 5C **116**
Crowder St. *E1* 1D **79**
Crowfield Ho. *N5* 1E **49**
Crowfoot Cl. *E9* 2B **52**
Crowhurst Cl. *SW9* 5C **90**
Crowhurst Ho. *SW9* . . . *5B **90***
  (off Aytoun Rd.)
Crowland Ho. *NW8* . . . *5E **45***
  (off Springfield Rd.)
Crowland Rd. *N15* 1B **36**
Crowland Ter. *N1* 4F **49**
Crowline Wlk. *N1* 3E **49**
Crowmarsh Gdns.
  SE23 . . . . 5E **107**
Crown Cl. *E3* 5C **52**
  NW6 . . . . 3D **45**
Crown Cl. Bus. Cen.
  E3 . . . . *5C **52***
  (off Crown Cl.)
Crown Ct. *EC2* 3A **18**
  NW8 . . . . 2A **60**
  (off Park Rd.)
  SE12 . . . . 4D **111**
  WC2 . . . . . . 3E **15** (5A **62**)
Crown Dale *SE19* 5D **119**
Crowndale Ct. *NW1* *1F **61***
  (off Crowndale Rd.)
Crowndale Rd. *NW1* . . . 1E **61**
Crownfield Rd. *E15* 1F **53**
Crowngate Ho. *E3* *1B **66***
  (off Hereford Rd.)
Crown Hill Rd.
  NW10 . . . . 5B **42**
Crown La. *SW16* 5C **118**
Crown La. Gdns.
  SW16 . . . . 5C **118**

Crown Lodge *SW3* . . . *5A **74***
  (off Elystan St.)
Crown M. *E1* *4F **65***
  (off White Horse La.)
  E13 . . . . 5E **55**
  W6 . . . . 5C **70**
Crown Office Row
  EC4 . . . . 4B **16** (1C **76**)
Crown Pas.
  SW1 . . . . . . 2A **22** (2E **75**)
Crown Pl.
  EC2 . . . . 5D **11** (4A **64**)
  (not continuous)
  NW5 . . . . 3D **47**
  SE16 . . . . 1D **93**
Crown Point *SE19* 5D **119**
Crown Reach *SW1* 1F **89**
Crownstone Ct.
  SW2 . . . . 3C **104**
Crownstone Rd.
  SW2 . . . . 3C **104**
Crown St. *SE5* 3E **91**
Crown Wharf *E14* *2E **81***
  (off Coldharbour)
  SE8 . . . . *1B **94***
  (off Grove St.)
Crows Rd. *E15* 2F **67**
Crowther Cl. *SW6* *2B **86***
  (off Bucklers All.)
Crowthorne Cl.
  SW18 . . . . 5B **100**
Crowthorne Rd. *W10* . . . 5F **57**
Croxley Rd. *W9* 2B **58**
Croxted Cl. *SE21* 5E **105**
Croxted M. *SE24* 4E **105**
Croxted Rd. *SE21* 5E **105**
  SE24 . . . . 5E **105**
Croxteth Ho. *SW8* 5F **89**
Croydon Ho. *SE1* *3C **24***
  (off Wootton St.)
Croydon Rd. *E13* 3B **68**
Crozier Dri. *SE3* 1D **111**
  SW8 . . . . *3B **90***
  (off Wilkinson St.)
Crozier Ter. *E9* 2F **51**
Crucifix La.
  SE1 . . . . 3E **27** (3A **78**)
Cruden Ho. *SE17* *2D **91***
  (off Brandon Est.)
Cruden St. *N1* 5D **49**
Cruikshank Ho.
  NW8 . . . . *1A **60***
  (off Townshend Rd.)
Cruikshank Rd. *E15* . . . 1A **54**
Cruikshank St.
  WC1 . . . . 1B **8** (2C **62**)
Crummock Gdns.
  NW9 . . . . 1A **28**
Crusader Ind. Est. *N4* . . 1E **35**
Crusoe M. *N16* 4F **35**
Crutched Friars
  EC3 . . . . 4E **19** (1A **78**)
Crutchley Rd. *SE6* 2A **124**
Crystal Ct. *SE19* *5B **120***
  (off College Rd.)
CRYSTAL PALACE 5B **120**
Crystal Palace
Athletics Stadium
  . . . . 5C **120**

Crystal Palace Mus.
  . . . . 5B **120**
Crystal Palace National
  Sports Cen. 5C **120**
Crystal Pal. Pde.
  SE19 . . . . 5B **120**
Crystal Pal. Pk. Rd.
  SE26 . . . . 5C **120**
Crystal Pal. Rd.
  SE22 . . . . 4B **106**
Crystal Ter. *SE19* 5F **119**
Crystal Vw. Ct.
  BR1: Brom 4F **123**
Crystal Wharf *N1* 1D **63**
Cuba St. *E14* 3C **80**
Cube Ho.
  SE16 . . . . 5F **27** (4B **78**)
Cubitt Ho. *SW4* 4E **103**
Cubitt Steps *E14* 2C **80**
Cubitt St.
  WC1 . . . . 2A **8** (2B **62**)
Cubitt's Yd. *WC2* 4E **15**
Cubitt Ter. *SW4* 1E **103**
CUBITT TOWN 5E **81**
Cuddington *SE17* *5E **77***
  (off Deacon Way)
Cudham St. *SE6* 5E **109**
Cudworth Ho. *SW8* 4E **89**
Cudworth St. *E1* 3D **65**
Cuff Cres. *SE9* 4F **111**
Cuff Point *E2* *1F **11***
  (off Columbia Rd.)
Cuff Point *E2* *4E **57***
  (off Sutton Way)
Cuff Point *E2* *1F **11***
  (off Columbia Rd.)
Culford Gdns. *SW3* 5B **74**
Culford Gro. *N1* 3A **50**
Culford Mans. *SW3* . . . *5B **74***
  (off Culford Gdns.)
Culford M. *N1* 3A **50**
Culford Rd. *N1* 4A **50**
Culford Ter. *N1* *3A **50***
  (off Balls Pond Rd.)
Culham Ho. *E2* *2F **11***
  (off Palissy St.)
  W2 . . . . *4C **58***
  (off Brunel Est.)
Culling Rd. *SE16* 4E **79**
Cullingworth Rd.
  NW10 . . . . 2C **42**
Culloden Cl. *SE16* 1C **92**
Cullum St.
  EC3 . . . . 4D **19** (1A **78**)
Cullum Welch Ct. *N1* . . *1C **10***
  (off Haberdasher St.)
Cullum Welch Ho. *EC1* . . *4F **9***
  (off Goswell Rd.)
Culmore Rd. *SE15* 3D **93**
Culmstock Rd.
  SW11 . . . . 3C **102**
Culpepper Ct. *SE11* . . . *5C **76***
  (off Kennington Rd.)
Culross Bldgs. *NW1* . . . *1A **62***
  (off Battle Bri. Rd.)
Culross Ho. *W10* *5F **57***
  (off Bridge Cl.)
Culross St.
  W1 . . . . 5B **12** (1C **74**)
Culverden Rd.
  SW12 . . . . 2E **117**

Culverhouse WC1 . . . . . . 1F **15**
(off Red Lion Sq.)
Culverhouse Gdns.
SW16 . . . . 3B **118**
Culverley Rd. SE6 . . . . 1D **123**
Culvert Pl. SW11 . . . . . . 5C **88**
Culvert Rd. N15 . . . . 1A **36**
(off Lydford Rd.)
N15 . . . . 1A **36**
(Oulton Rd.)
SW11 . . . . 5B **88**
Culworth Ho. NW8 . . . . . 1A **60**
(off Allitsen Rd.)
Culworth St. NW8 . . . . . 1A **60**
Culzean Cl. SE27 . . . . . 3D **119**
Cumberland Cl. E8 . . . . 3B **50**
Cumberland Ct.
SW1 . . . . 1D **89**
(off Cumberland St.)
W1 . . . . 3A **12**
(off Gt. Cumberland Pl.)
Cumberland Cres.
W14 . . . . 5A **72**
(not continuous)
Cumberland Gdns.
WC1 . . . . . . 1B **8** (2C **62**)
Cumberland Ga.
W1 . . . . 4A **12** (1B **74**)
Cumberland Ho.
E16 . . . . 2C **82**
(off Wesley Av.)
W8 . . . . 3D **73**
(off Kensington Ct.)
Cumberland Mans.
W1 . . . . 5B **60**
(off George St.)
Cumberland Mkt.
NW1 . . . . 1E **5** (2D **61**)
Cumberland M. SE11 . . 1C **90**
Cumberland Mills Sq.
E14 . . . . 1F **95**
Cumberland Pk. Ind. Est.
NW10 . . . . 2C **56**
Cumberland Pl.
NW1 . . . . 1D **5** (2D **61**)
SE6 . . . . 1B **124**
Cumberland Rd. E12 . . 1F **55**
E13 . . . . 4D **69**
SW13 . . . . 4B **84**
Cumberland St. SW1 . . 1D **89**
Cumberland Ter.
NW1 . . . . 1D **5** (1D **61**)
Cumberland Ter. M.
NW1 . . . . 1D **5**
(not continuous)
Cumbrian Gdns. NW2 . . 4F **29**
Cuming Mus. 5E **77**
(off Walworth Rd.)
Cumming St.
N1 . . . . 1A **8** (1B **62**)
Cumnor Cl. SW9 . . . . . . 5B **90**
(off Robsart St.)
Cunard Pl.
EC3 . . . . 3E **19** (5A **64**)
Cunard Rd. NW10 . . . . 2A **56**
Cunard Wlk. SE16 . . . . . 5F **79**
Cundy Rd. E16 . . . . 5C **69**
Cundy St. SW1 . . . . 5C **74**
Cunliffe St. SW16 . . . . 5E **117**

Cunningham Ct. E10 . . . 5D **39**
(off Oliver Rd.)
W9 . . . . 3E **59**
Cunningham Ho. SE5 . . . 3F **91**
(off Elmington Est.)
Cunningham Pl. NW8 . . . 3F **59**
Cupar Rd. SW11 . . . . . . 4C **88**
Cupola Cl.
BR1: Brom 5D **125**
Cureton St. SW1 . . . . . . 5F **75**
Curlew Ho. SE4 . . . . . . 2A **108**
(off St Norbert Rd.)
SE15 . . . . 4B **92**
Curlew St.
SE1 . . . . 3F **27** (3B **78**)
Curness St. SE13 . . . . . 2E **109**
Curnick's La. SE27 . . . . 4E **119**
Curran Ho. SW3 . . . . . . 5A **74**
(off Lucan Pl.)
Curricle St. W3 . . . . 2A **70**
Currie Hill Cl.
SW19 . . . . 4B **114**
Currie Ho. E14 . . . . 5F **67**
(off Abbott Rd.)
Cursitor St.
EC4 . . . . 2B **16** (5C **62**)
Curtain Pl.
EC2 . . . . 3E **11** (2A **64**)
Curtain Rd.
EC2 . . . . 2E **11** (3A **64**)
Curtis Dr. W3 . . . . 5A **56**
Curtis Fld. Rd.
SW16 . . . . 4B **118**
Curtis Ho. SE17 . . . . . . 1F **91**
(off Morecambe St.)
Curtis St. SE1 . . . . 5B **78**
Curtis Way SE1 . . . . 5B **78**
Curve, The W12 . . . . 1C **70**
Curwen Av. E7 . . . . 1D **55**
Curwen Rd. W12 . . . . . . 3C **70**
Curzon Cinema
Mayfair 2D **21**
(off Curzon St.)
Soho 4C **14**
(off Shaftesbury Av.)
Curzon Ct. SW6 . . . . . . 4E **87**
(off Imperial Rd.)
Curzon Cres. NW10 . . . 4A **42**
Curzon Ga.
W1 . . . . 2C **20** (2C **74**)
Curzon Sq.
W1 . . . . 2C **20** (2C **74**)
Curzon St.
W1 . . . . 2C **20** (2C **74**)
Custance Ho. N1 . . . . . 1B **10**
(off Fairbank Est.)
Custance St.
N1 . . . . 1B **10** (2F **63**)
CUSTOM HOUSE 5E **69**
Custom Ho.
EC3 . . . . 5D **19** (1A **78**)
Custom Ho. Reach
SE16 . . . . 3B **80**
Custom Ho. Wlk.
EC3 . . . . 5D **19** (1A **78**)
Cut, The SE1 . . . 3C **24** (3C **76**)
Cutbush Ho. N7 . . . . . . 2F **47**
Cutcombe Rd. SE5 . . . . 5E **91**

Cuthbert Harrowing Ho.
EC1 . . . . 4F **9**
(off Golden La. Est.)
Cuthbert Ho. W2 . . . . . . 4F **59**
(off Hall Pl.)
Cuthbert St. W2 . . . . . . 4F **59**
Cuthill Wlk. SE5 . . . . . . 4F **91**
Cutlers Gdns. EC2 . . . . 1E **19**
Cutlers Sq. E14 . . . . . . 5C **80**
Cutler St. E1 . . 2E **19** (5A **64**)
Cutty Sark 2E **95**
Cutty Sark Gdns.
SE10 . . . . 2E **95**
(off King William Wlk.)
Cuxton Ho. SE17 . . . . . . 1A **92**
(off Mina Rd.)
Cyclops M. E14 . . . . 5C **80**
Cygnet Cl. NW10 . . . . . 2A **42**
Cygnet Ho. SW3 . . . . . . 1A **88**
(off King's Rd.)
SW18 . . . . 1E **101**
Cygnet Ho. Nth. E14 . . 5D **67**
(off Chrisp St.)
Cygnet Ho. Sth. E14 . . 5D **67**
(off Chrisp St.)
Cygnet St. E1 . . 3B **11** (3B **64**)
Cygnus Bus. Cen.
NW10 . . . . 3B **42**
Cynthia St. N1 . . 1A **8** (1B **62**)
Cyntra Pl. E8 . . . . 4D **51**
Cypress Cl. E5 . . . . 4C **36**
Cypress Gdns. SE4 . . . 3A **108**
Cypress Ho. SE14 . . . . . 4F **93**
SE16 . . . . 3F **79**
(off Woodland Cres.)
Cypress Pl.
W1 . . . . 4A **6** (3E **61**)
Cyprus Cl. N4 . . . . 1D **35**
Cyprus Pl. E2 . . . . 1E **65**
Cyprus St. E2 . . . . 1E **65**
(not continuous)
Cyrena Rd. SE22 . . . . . 4B **106**
Cyril Mans. SW11 . . . . . 4B **88**
Cyrus Ho. EC1 . . . . 3E **9**
Cyrus St. EC1 . . . . 3E **9**
Czar St. SE8 . . . . 2C **94**

D

Dabbs La. EC1 . . . . 4C **8**
(off Farringdon Rd.)
Dabin Cres. SE10 . . . . . 4E **95**
Dacca St. SE8 . . . . 2B **94**
Dace Rd. E3 . . . . 5C **52**
Dacre Gdns. SE13 . . . 2A **110**
Dacre Ho. SW3 . . . . 2F **87**
(off Beaufort St.)
Dacre Pk. SE13 . . . . . . 1A **110**
Dacre Pl. SE13 . . . . . . 1A **110**
Dacre Rd. E11 . . . . 3B **40**
E13 . . . . 5D **55**
Dacres Est. SE23 . . . . . 3F **121**
Dacres Ho. SW4 . . . . . 1D **103**
Dacres Rd. SE23 . . . . . 2F **121**
Dacre St.
SW1 . . . . 5B **22** (4F **75**)
Daffodil St. W12 . . . . . . 1B **70**
Dafforne Rd. SW17 . . . 3C **116**

Da Gama Pl. E14 . . . . 1C 94
Dagenham Rd. E10 . . . . 3B 38
Dagmar Ct. E14 . . . . 4E 81
Dagmar Gdns. NW10 . . . . . 1F 57
Dagmar Pas. N1 . . . . 5D 49
    (off Cross St.)
Dagmar Rd. N4 . . . . 2C 34
SE5 . . . . 4A 92
Dagmar Ter. N1 . . . . 5D 49
Dagnall St. SW11 . . . . 4A 102
Dagnan Rd. SW12 . . . . 5D 103
Dagobert Ho. E1 . . . . 4E 65
    (off Smithy St.)
Dagonet Gdns.
  BR1: Brom 3C 124
Dagonet Rd.
  BR1: Brom 3C 124
Dahomey Rd. SW16 . . . 5E 117
Dain Ct. W8 . . . . 5C 72
    (off Lexham Gdns.)
Dainford Cl.
  BR1: Brom 5F 123
Dainton Ho. W2 . . . . 4C 58
    (off Brunel Est.)
Daintry Way E9 . . . . 3B 52
Dairy Cl. NW10 . . . . 5C 42
Dairyman Cl. NW2 . . . . 5F 29
Dairy M. SW9 . . . . 1A 104
Dairy Wlk. SW19 . . . . 4A 114
Daisy Dobbings Wlk.
  N19 . . . . 2A 34
    (off Jessie Blythe La.)
Daisy La. SW6 . . . . 1C 100
Daisy Rd. E16 . . . . 3A 68
Dakin Pl. E1 . . . . 4A 66
Dakota Bldg. SE8 . . . . 4D 95
    (off Deal's Gateway)
Dakota Gdns. E6 . . . . 3F 69
Dalberg Rd. SW2 . . . . 2C 104
    (not continuous)
Dalby Rd. SW18 . . . . 2E 101
Dalby St. NW5 . . . . 3D 47
Dalebury Rd. SW17 . . . . . . 2B 116
Dale Cl. SE3 . . . . 1C 110
Daleham Gdns.
  NW3 . . . . 2F 45
Daleham M. NW3 . . . . 3F 45
Dalehead NW1 . . . . 1F 5
    (off Hampstead Rd.)
Dale Ho. N1 . . . . 5A 50
    (off New Era Est.)
NW8 . . . . 5E 45
    (off Boundary Rd.)
SE4 . . . . 2A 108
Dale Lodge N6 . . . . 1E 33
Dalemain M. E16 . . . . 2C 82
Dale Rd. NW5 . . . . 2C 46
SE17 . . . . 2D 91
Dale Row W11 . . . . 5A 58
Daleside Rd. SW16 . . . . . . 5D 117
Dale St. W4 . . . . 1A 84
Daleview Rd. N15 . . . . 1A 36
Daley Ho. W12 . . . . 5D 57
Daley St. E9 . . . . 3F 51
Daley Thompson Way
  SW8 . . . . 5D 89
Dalgarno Gdns. W10 . . . . . 4E 57
Dalgarno Way W10 . . . . . . 3E 57
Dalgleish St. E14 . . . . 5A 66

Daling Way E3 . . . . 5A 52
Dali Universe 3F 23 (3B 76)
Dalkeith Ct. SW1 . . . . 5F 75
    (off Vincent St.)
Dalkeith Ho. SW9 . . . . 4D 91
    (off Lothian Rd.)
Dalkeith Rd. SE21 . . . . 1E 119
Dallas Rd. NW4 . . . . 2C 28
SE26 . . . . 3D 121
Dallinger Rd. SE12 . . . . . . 4B 110
Dalling Rd. W6 . . . . 5D 71
Dallington Sq. EC1 . . . . 3E 9
    (off Berry St.)
Dallington St.
  EC1 . . . . 3E 9 (3D 63)
Dalmain Rd. SE23 . . . . 1F 121
Dalmeny Av. N7 . . . . 1F 47
Dalmeny Rd. N7 . . . . 5F 33
    (not continuous)
Dalmeyer Rd. NW10 . . . . . 3B 42
Dalmore Rd. SE21 . . . . 2E 119
Dalo Lodge E3 . . . . 4C 66
    (off Gale St.)
Dalrymple Rd. SE4 . . . . . . 2A 108
DALSTON 3B 50
Dalston La. E8 . . . . 3B 50
Dalton Ho. SE14 . . . . 2F 93
    (off John Williams Cl.)
SW1 . . . . 1D 89
    (off Ebury Bri. Rd.)
Dalton St. SE27 . . . . 2D 119
Dalwood St. SE5 . . . . 4A 92
Daly Ct. E15 . . . . 2D 53
Dalyell Rd. SW9 . . . . 1B 104
Damascene Wlk.
  SE21 . . . . 1E 119
Damask Cres. E16 . . . . 3A 68
Damer Ter. SW10 . . . . 3E 87
Dames Rd. E7 . . . . 5C 40
Dame St. N1 . . . . 1E 63
Damien Ct. E1 . . . . 5D 65
    (off Damien St.)
Damien St. E1 . . . . 5D 65
Damory Ho. SE16 . . . . 5D 79
    (off Abbeyfield Est.)
Danbury St. N1 . . . . 1D 63
Danby Ho. E9 . . . . 4E 51
    (off Frampton Pk. Rd.)
W10 . . . . 2A 58
    (off Bruckner St.)
Danby St. SE15 . . . . 1B 106
Dancer Rd. SW6 . . . . 4B 86
Dando Cres. SE3 . . . . 1D 111
Dandridge Cl. SE10 . . . . . . 1B 96
Dandridge Ho. E1 . . . . 5F 11
    (off Lamb St.)
Danebury Av. SW15 . . . . . . 4A 98
    (not continuous)
Daneby Rd. SE6 . . . . 3D 123
Danecroft Rd. SE24 . . . . . . 3E 105
Danehurst St. SW6 . . . . . . 4A 86
Danemere St. SW15 . . . . . 1E 99
Dane Pl. E3 . . . . 1A 66
Danescombe SE12 . . . . 1C 124
Danes Ct. NW8 . . . . 5B 46
    (off St Edmund's Ter.)
Danescroft Av. NW4 . . . . . . 1F 29

Danescroft Gdns.
  NW4 . . . . 1F 29
Danesdale Rd. E9 . . . . 3A 52
Danesfield SE5 . . . . 2A 92
    (off Albany Rd.)
Danes Ho. W10 . . . . 4E 57
    (off Sutton Way)
Dane St.
  WC1 . . . . 1F 15 (4B 62)
Daneswood Av. SE6 . . . . . 3E 123
Daneville Rd. SE5 . . . . 4F 91
Dangan Rd. E11 . . . . 1C 40
Daniel Bolt Cl. E14 . . . . . . 4D 67
Daniel Ct. SW17 . . . . 5A 116
Daniel Gdns. SE15 . . . . . . 3B 92
Daniell Ho. N1 . . . . 1F 63
    (off Cranston Est.)
Daniel Pl. NW4 . . . . 2D 29
Daniels Rd. SE15 . . . . 1E 107
Dan Leno Wlk. SW6 . . . . . 3D 87
Dansey Pl. W1 . . . . 4B 14
Danson Rd. SE17 . . . . 1D 91
Dante Pl. SE11 . . . . 5D 77
Dante Rd. SE11 . . . . 5D 77
Danube Ct. SE15 . . . . 3B 92
    (off Daniel Gdns.)
Danube St. SW3 . . . . 1A 88
Danvers Ho. E1 . . . . 5C 64
    (off Christian St.)
Danvers St. SW3 . . . . 2F 87
Da Palma Ct. SW6 . . . . 2C 86
    (off Anselm Rd.)
Daphne St. SW18 . . . . 4E 101
D'Arblay St.
  W1 . . . . 3A 14 (5E 61)
Darcy Ho. E8 . . . . 5D 51
    (off London Flds. E. Side)
Dare Ct. E10 . . . . 2E 39
Darent Ho.
  BR1: Brom 5F 123
NW8 . . . . 4F 59
    (off Church St. Est.)
Darenth Rd. N16 . . . . 2B 36
Darfield NW1 . . . . 5E 47
    (off Bayham St.)
Darfield Rd. SE4 . . . . 3B 108
Darfield Way W10 . . . . 5F 57
Darfur St. SW15 . . . . 1F 99
Darien Ho. E1 . . . . 4F 65
    (off Shandy St.)
Darien Rd. SW11 . . . . 1F 101
Daring Ho. E3 . . . . 1A 66
    (off Roman Rd.)
Dark Ho. Wlk.
  EC3 . . . . 5D 19 (1F 77)
Darlan Rd. SW6 . . . . 3B 86
Darley Ho. SE11 . . . . 1B 90
    (off Laud St.)
Darley Rd. SW11 . . . . 4B 102
Darling Rd. SE4 . . . . 1C 108
Darling Row E1 . . . . 3D 65
Darlington Ct. SE6 . . . . 1B 124
Darlington Ho.
  SW8 . . . . 3F 89
    (off Hemans St.)
Darlington Rd.
  SE27 . . . . 5D 119

Darnall Ho. *SE10* 4E **95**
  (off Royal Hill)
Darnaway Pl. *E14* 4E **67**
  (off Aberfeldy St.)
Darnay Ho. *SE16* 4C **78**
Darnley Ho. *E14* 5A **66**
  (off Camdenhurst St.)
Darnley Rd. *E9* 3E **51**
Darnley Ter. *W11* 2F **71**
Darrell Rd. *SE22* 3C **106**
Darren Cl. *N4* 2B **34**
Darren Ct. *N7* 1A **48**
Darsley Dr. *SW8* 4F **89**
Dartford Ho. *SE1* 5B **78**
  (off Longfield Est.)
Dartford St. *SE17* 2E **91**
Dartington *NW1* 5E **47**
  (off Plender St.)
Dartington Ho. *SW8* 5F **89**
  (off Union Gro.)
  W2 . . . . 4D **59**
  (off Senior St.)
Dartle Ct. *SE16* 3C **78**
  (off Scott Lidgett Cres.)
Dartmoor Wlk. *E14* 5C **80**
  (off Charnwood Gdns.)
Dartmouth Cl. *W11* 5B **58**
Dartmouth Ct. *SE10* 4E **95**
Dartmouth Gro. *SE10* . . . 4E **95**
Dartmouth Hill *SE10* 4E **95**
Dartmouth Ho. *SE10* 4D **95**
  (off Catherine Gro.)
DARTMOUTH PARK. 5D **33**
Dartmouth Pk. Av.
  NW5 . . . . 5D **33**
Dartmouth Pk. Hill
  N19 . . . . 3D **33**
  NW5 . . . . 3D **33**
Dartmouth Pk. Rd.
  NW5 . . . . 1D **47**
Dartmouth Pl. *SE23* 2E **121**
  W4 . . . . 2A **84**
Dartmouth Rd. *NW2* 3F **43**
  NW4 . . . . 1C **28**
  SE23 . . . . 3D **121**
  SE26 . . . . 3D **121**
Dartmouth Row
  SE10 . . . . 5E **95**
Dartmouth St.
  SW1 . . . . . . 4C **22** (3F **75**)
Dartmouth Ter. *SE10* 4F **95**
Dartrey Twr. *SW10* 3E **87**
  (off Worlds End Est.)
Dartrey Wlk. *SW10* 3E **87**
Dart St. *W10* 2A **58**
Darvell Ho. *SE17* 1F **91**
  (off Merrow St.)
Darville Ho. *N16* 5B **36**
Darwen Pl. *E2* 1D **65**
Darwin Ct. *E13* 2D **69**
  NW1 . . . . 5D **47**
  SE17 . . . . 5F **77**
  (off Barlow St.)
Darwin Ho. *SW1* 2E **89**
  (off Grosvenor Rd.)
Darwin St. *SE17* 5F **77**
  (not continuous)
Daryngton Ho. *SE1* 4C **26**
  (off Manciple St.)

Daryngton Ho. *SW8* 3A **90**
  (off Hartington Rd.)
Dashwood Rd. *N8* 1B **34**
Dassett Rd. *SE27* 5D **119**
Data Point Bus. Cen.
  E16 . . . . 3F **67**
Datchelor Pl. *SE5* 4F **91**
Datchet Ho. *NW1* 1E **5**
  (off Augustus St.)
Datchet Rd. *SE6* 2B **122**
Datchworth Ho. *N1* 4D **49**
  (off The Sutton Est.)
Date St. *SE17* 1F **91**
Daubeney Rd. *E5* 1A **52**
Daubeney Twr. *SE8* 1B **94**
  (off Bowditch)
Dault Rd. *SW18* 4E **101**
Dauncey Ho. *SE1* 4D **25**
Davenant Rd. *N19* 4F **33**
Davenant St. *E1* 4C **64**
Davenport Ho. *SE11* 5C **76**
  (off Walnut Tree Wlk.)
Davenport Rd. *SE6* 4D **109**
Daventry Av. *E17* 1C **38**
Daventry St. *NW1* 4A **60**
Daver Ct. *SW3* 1A **88**
Davern Cl. *SE10* 5B **82**
Davey Cl. *N7* 3B **48**
Davey Rd. *E9* 4C **52**
Davey's Ct. *WC2* 4D **15**
Davey St. *SE15* 2B **92**
David Beckham Academy, The
  . . . . 3B **82**
Davidge Ho. *SE1* 4C **24**
  (off Coral St.)
Davidge St.
  SE1 . . . . . . 4D **25** (3D **77**)
David Hewitt Ho. *E3* 4D **67**
  (off Watts Gro.)
David Ho. *SW8* 3A **90**
  (off Wyvil Rd.)
David Lee Point *E15* 5A **54**
  (off Leather Gdns.)
David Lloyd Leisure
  Kidbrooke 2D **111**
  South Kensington 5D **73**
  (in Point West)
David M. *W1* 5A **4** (4B **60**)
Davidson Gdns. *SW8* . . . 3A **90**
Davidson Terraces
  E7 . . . . 2D **55**
  (off Claremont Rd.,
  not continuous)
David's Rd. *SE23* 1E **121**
David St. *E15* 3F **53**
Davies La. *E11* 4A **40**
Davies M.
  W1 . . . . 4D **13** (1D **75**)
Davies St.
  W1 . . . . 3D **13** (5D **61**)
Da Vinci Ct. *SE16* 1D **93**
  (off Rossetti Rd.)
Davis Ho. *W12* 1D **71**
  (off White City Est.)
Davis Rd. *W3* 2B **70**
Davis St. *E13* 1D **69**
Davisville Rd. *W12* 3C **70**
Dawes Ho. *SE17* 5F **77**
  (off Orb St.)

Dawes Rd. *SW6* 3A **86**
Dawes St. *SE17* 1F **91**
Dawlish Av. *SW18* 2D **115**
Dawlish Rd. *E10* 3E **39**
  NW2 . . . . 3F **43**
Dawnay Gdns.
  SW18 . . . . 2F **115**
Dawnay Rd. *SW18* 2E **115**
Dawn Cres. *E15* 5F **53**
Dawpool Rd. *NW2* 4B **28**
Dawson Ho. *E2* 2E **65**
  (off Sceptre Rd.)
Dawson Pl. *W2* 1C **72**
Dawson Rd. *NW2* 2E **43**
Dawson St.
  E2 . . . . 1F **11** (1B **64**)
Day Ho. *SE5* 3E **91**
  (off Bethwin Rd.)
Daylesford Av. *SW15* . . . 2C **98**
Daynor Ho. *NW6* 5C **44**
  (off Quex Rd.)
Daysbrook Rd. *SW2* . . . 1B **118**
Dayton Gro. *SE15* 4E **93**
Deacon Ho. *SE11* 5B **76**
  (off Black Prince Rd.)
Deacon M. *N1* 4F **49**
Deacon Rd. *NW2* 2C **42**
Deacon's Ri. *N2* 1F **31**
Deacons Ter. *N1* 3E **49**
  (off Harecourt Rd.)
Deacon Way *SE17* 5E **77**
Deal Ho. *SE15* 2F **93**
  (off Lovelinch La.)
  SE17 . . . . 1A **92**
  (off Mina Rd.)
Deal Porters Wlk.
  SE16 . . . . 3F **79**
Deal Porters Way
  SE16 . . . . 4E **79**
Deal Rd. *SW17* 5C **116**
Deal's Gateway *SE10* . . . 4C **94**
Deal St. *E1* 4C **64**
Dealtry Rd. *SW15* 2E **99**
Deal Wlk. *SW9* 3C **90**
Dean Abbott Ho.
  SW1 . . . . 5F **75**
  (off Vincent St.)
Dean Bradley St.
  SW1 . . . . 4A **76**
Dean Cl. *E9* 2E **51**
  SE16 . . . . 2F **79**
Dean Ct. *SW8* 3A **90**
  (off Thorncroft St.)
Deancross St. *E1* 5E **65**
Deanery M. *W1* 1C **20**
Deanery Rd. *E15* 3A **54**
Deanery St.
  W1 . . . . 1C **20** (2C **74**)
Dean Farrar St.
  SW1 . . . . . . 5C **22** (4F **75**)
Dean Ho. *E1* 5E **65**
  (off Tarling St.)
  SE14 . . . . 3A **94**
  (off New Cross Rd.)
Dean Rd. *NW2* 3E **43**
Dean Ryle St. *SW1* 5A **76**
Dean's Bldgs. *SE17* 5F **77**
Dean's Ct.
  EC4 . . . . 3E **17** (5D **63**)

Deans Ga. Cl. SE23 . . . . . 3F **121**
Deanshanger Ho.
   SE8 . . . . 5F **79**
   (off Chilton Gro.)
Dean's M.
   W1 . . . . 2E **13** (5D **61**)
Dean Stanley St.
   SW1 . . . . . . 5D **23** (4A **76**)
Deanston Wharf E16 . . . 3D **83**
Dean St. E7 . . . . 2C **54**
   W1 . . . . 2B **14** (5F **61**)
Dean's Yd. SW1 . . . . . . 5C **22**
Dean Trench St.
   SW1 . . . . . . 5D **23** (4A **76**)
Deason St. E15 . . . . 5E **53**
Deauville Ct. *SE16* 3F **79**
   (off Eleanor Cl.)
   SW4 . . . . 4E **103**
De Barowe M. N5 . . . . . . 1D **49**
Debdale Ho. *E2* 5C **50**
   (off Whiston Rd.)
De Beauvoir Ct. N1 . . . . 4F **49**
   (off Northchurch Rd.)
De Beauvoir Cres.
   N1 . . . . 5A **50**
De Beauvoir Est. N1 . . . 1A **50**
De Beauvoir Pl. N1 . . . . 3A **50**
De Beauvoir Rd. N1 . . . . 5A **50**
De Beauvoir Sq. N1 . . . . 4A **50**
DE BEAUVOIR TOWN
   . . . . 5A **50**
Debenham Ct. *E8* 5C **50**
   (off Pownall Rd.)
Debham Ct. NW2 . . . . . . 5E **29**
Debnams Rd. SE16 . . . . 5E **79**
De Bruin Ct. *E14* 1E **95**
   (off Ferry St.)
Decima St.
   SE1 . . . . . . 5D **27** (4A **78**)
Deck Cl. SE16 . . . . 2F **79**
De Crespigny Pk.
   SE5 . . . . 5F **91**
Deeley Rd. SW8 . . . . . . 4F **89**
Deepdale SW19 . . . . . . 4F **113**
Deepdene Gdns.
   SW2 . . . . 5B **104**
Deepdene Point
   SE23 . . . . 3F **121**
Deepdene Rd. SE5 . . . . 2F **105**
Deerbrook Rd.
   SE24 . . . . 1D **119**
Deerdale Rd. SE24 . . . . 2E **105**
Deerfield Cotts.
   NW9 . . . . 1B **28**
Deerhurst Ho. *SE15* . . 2C **92**
   (off Haymerle Rd.)
Deerhurst Rd. NW2 . . . . 3F **43**
   SW16 . . . . 5B **118**
Deeside Rd. SW17 . . . . 3F **115**
Dee St. E14 . . . . 5E **67**
Defoe Cl. SE16 . . . . 3B **80**
   SW17 . . . . 5A **116**
Defoe Ho. EC2 . . . . 5A **10**
Defoe Pl. *EC2* 5F **9**
   (off Beech St.)
   SW17 . . . . 4B **116**
Defoe Rd. N16 . . . . 5A **36**
De Frene Rd. SE26 . . . . 4F **121**
Dehar Cres. NW9 . . . . . 2B **28**

Dekker Ho. *SE5* 3F **91**
   (off Elmington Est.)
Dekker Rd. SE21 . . . . . 4A **106**
Delacourt Rd. SE3 . . . . 3D **97**
Delafield Ho. *E1* 5C **64**
   (off Christian St.)
Delafield Rd. SE7 . . . . . 1D **97**
Delaford Ho. SE16 . . . . 1D **93**
Delaford St. SW6 . . . . . 3A **86**
Delamere St. W2 . . . . . 4D **59**
Delamere Ter. W2 . . . . . 4D **59**
Delancey Pas. *NW1* . . . 5D **47**
   (off Delancey St.)
Delancey St. NW1 . . . . 5D **47**
Delancey Studios
   NW1 . . . . 5D **47**
Delany Ho. SE10 . . . . . 2E **95**
   (off Thames St.)
Delarch Ho. SE1 . . . . . 4D **25**
De Laune St. SE17 . . . . 1D **91**
Delaware Mans. *W9* . . 3D **59**
   (off Delaware Rd.)
Delaware Rd. W9 . . . . . 3D **59**
Delawyk Cres.
   SE24 . . . . 4E **105**
Delfina Studio Trust . . 3D **27**
   (off Bermondsey St.)
Delft Way SE22 . . . . . . 3A **106**
Delhi St. N1 . . . . 5A **48**
   (not continuous)
Delia St. SW18 . . . . 5D **101**
Delius Gro. E15 . . . . . . 1F **67**
Della Path E15 . . . . 5C **36**
Dell Cl. E15 . . . . 5F **53**
Dellow Ho. *E1* 1D **79**
   (off Dellow St.)
Dellow St. E1 . . . . 1D **79**
Dell's M. *SW1* 5E **75**
   (off Churton Pl.)
Delmare Cl. SW9 . . . . . 2B **104**
Delme Cres. SE3 . . . . . 5D **97**
Delmerend Ho.
   SW3 . . . . 1A **88**
   (off Ixworth Pl.)
Deloraine Ho. SE8 . . . . 4C **94**
Delorme St. W6 . . . . . . 2F **85**
Delta Bldg. *E14* 5E **67**
   (off Ashton St.)
Delta Ct. NW2 . . . . 4C **28**
Delta Pk. SW18 . . . . . . 2D **101**
Delta Point *E2* 2C **64**
   (off Delta St.)
Delta St. E2 . . . . 2C **64**
Delverton Ho. *SE17* . . . 1D **91**
   (off Delverton Rd.)
Delverton Rd. SE17 . . . 1D **91**
Delvino Rd. SW6 . . . . . 4C **86**
De Montfort Pde.
   SW16 . . . . 3A **118**
De Montfort Rd.
   SW16 . . . . 3A **118**
De Morgan Rd.
   SW6 . . . . 1D **101**
Dempster Rd.
   SW18 . . . . 3E **101**
Den, The 1E **93**
Denbigh Cl. NW10 . . . . 4A **42**
   W11 . . . . 1B **72**
Denbigh Ct. E6 . . . . 2F **69**

Denbigh Ho. *SW1* 5A **20**
   (off Hans Pl.)
   W11 . . . . 1B **72**
   (off Westbourne Gro.)
Denbigh M. *SW1* 5E **75**
   (off Denbigh St.)
Denbigh Pl. SW1 . . . . . 1E **89**
Denbigh Rd. E6 . . . . . . 2F **69**
   W11 . . . . 1B **72**
Denbigh St. SW1 . . . . . 5E **75**
   (not continuous)
Denbigh Ter. W11 . . . . . 1B **72**
Denby Ct. *SE11* 5B **76**
   (off Lambeth Wlk.)
Dence Ho. *E2* 2C **64**
   (off Turin St.)
Denchworth Ho.
   SW9 . . . . 5C **90**
Dene Cl. SE4 . . . . 1A **108**
Denehurst Gdns.
   NW4 . . . . 1E **29**
Denesmead SE24 . . . . 3E **105**
Denewood Rd. N6 . . . . 1B **32**
Denford St. *SE10* 1B **96**
   (off Glenforth St.)
Dengie Wlk. *N1* 5E **49**
   (off Basire St.)
Denham Ct. *SE26* 3D **121**
   (off Kirkdale)
Denham Ho. *W12* 1D **71**
   (off White City Est.)
Denham St. SE10 . . . . . 1C **96**
Denholme Rd. W9 . . . . 2B **58**
Denison Ho. *E14* 5C **66**
   (off Farrance St.)
Denison Rd. SW19 . . . . 5F **115**
Denis Way SW4 . . . . . . 1F **103**
Denland Ho. *SW8* 3B **90**
   (off Dorset Rd.)
Denman Ho. N16 . . . . . 4A **36**
Denman Pl. W1 . . . . 4B **14**
Denman Rd. SE15 . . . . 4B **92**
Denman St.
   W1 . . . . 5B **14** (1F **75**)
Denmark Gro. N1 . . . . . 1C **62**
DENMARK HILL 1E **105**
Denmark Hill SE5 . . . . . 4F **91**
Denmark Hill Est.
   SE5 . . . . 2F **105**
Denmark Mans. *SE5* . . 5E **91**
   (off Coldharbour La.)
Denmark Pl. E3 . . . . . . 2C **66**
   WC2 . . . . 2C **14** (5F **61**)
Denmark Rd. NW6 . . . . 1B **58**
   (not continuous)
   SE5 . . . . 4E **91**
Denmark St. E11 . . . . . 5A **40**
   E13 . . . . 4D **69**
   WC2 . . . . 2C **14** (5F **61**)
Denmark Wlk. SE27 . . . 4E **119**
Denmead Ho. *SW15* . . 4B **98**
   (off Highcliffe Dr.)
Denne Ter. E8 . . . . 5B **50**
Dennett's Rd. SE14 . . . 4E **93**
Denning Cl. NW8 . . . . . 2E **59**
Denning Point *E1* 2F **19**
   (off Commercial St.)
Denning Rd. NW3 . . . . 1F **45**
Dennington Cl. E5 . . . . 4E **37**

Dennington Pk. Rd.
  NW6 . . . . 3C 44
Dennison Point E15 . . . 4E 53
Denny Cl. E6. . . . . 4F 69
Denny Cres. SE11 . . . 1C 90
Denny St. SE11 . . . . . . 1C 90
Densham Ho. NW8 . . . 1F 59
  (off Cochrane St.)
Densham Rd. E15 . . . . 5A 54
Denstone Ho. SE15 . . . 2C 92
  (off Haymerle Rd.)
Dent Ho. SE17 . . . . 5A 78
  (off Tatum St.)
Denton NW1 . . . . 3C 46
Denton Ho. N1 . . . . 4D 49
  (off Halton Rd.)
Denton Rd. N8 . . . . 1B 34
Denton St. SW18 . . . . 4D 101
Denton Way E5 . . . . . . 5F 37
Dents Rd. SW11 . . . . . 4B 102
Denver Rd. N16 . . . . . . 2A 36
Denwood SE23 . . . . . 3F 121
Denyer St. SW3 . . . . . . 5A 74
Denys Ho. EC1 . . . . 5B 8
  (off Bourne Est.)
Denzil Rd. NW10 . . . . . 2B 42
Deodar Rd. SW15 . . . 2A 100
Depot App. NW2 . . . . . 1F 43
Depot Rd. W12 . . . . 1E 71
Depot St. SE5 . . . . 2F 91
DEPTFORD 3C 94
Deptford Bri. SE8 . . . . 4C 94
Deptford B'way. SE8 . . 4C 94
Deptford Bus. Pk.
  SE15 . . . . 2E 93
Deptford Chu. St.
  SE8 . . . . 2C 94
Deptford Creek Bri.
  SE8 . . . . 2D 95
  (off Creek Rd.)
Deptford Ferry Rd.
  E14 . . . . 5C 80
Deptford Grn. SE8 . . . . . .
Deptford High St.
  SE8 . . . . 2C 94
Deptford Pk. Bus. Cen.
  SE8 . . . . 1A 94
Deptford Strand SE8 . . 5B 80
Deptford Trad. Est.
  SE8 . . . . 1A 94
Deptford Wharf SE8 . . 5B 80
De Quincey Ho. SW1 . . 1E 89
  (off Lupus St.)
De Quincey M. E16 . . . 2C 82
Derby Ga.
  SW1 . . . . 3D 23 (3A 76)
  (not continuous)
Derby Hill SE23 . . . . . 2E 121
Derby Hill Cres.
  SE23 . . . . 2E 121
Derby Ho. SE11 . . . . . . 5C 76
  (off Walnut Tree Wlk.)
Derby Lodge WC1 . . . . . 1F 7
  (off Britannia St.)
Derby Rd. E7 . . . . 4F 55
  E9 . . . . 5F 51
Derbyshire St. E2 . . . . 2C 64
  (not continuous)
Derby St. W1 . . . 2C 20 (2C 74)

Dereham Ho. SE4 . . . . 2F 107
  (off Frendsbury Rd.)
Dereham Pl.
  EC2 . . . . 2E 11 (2A 64)
Derek Walcott Cl.
  SE24 . . . . 3D 105
Dericote St. E8 . . . . . . 5D 51
Dering St.
  W1 . . . . 3D 13 (5D 61)
Dering Yd.
  W1 . . . . 3E 13 (5D 61)
Derinton Rd. SW17 . . . 4B 116
Dermody Gdns.
  SE13 . . . . 3F 109
Dermody Rd. SE13 . . . 3F 109
Deronda Rd. SE24 . . . 1D 119
Derrick Gdns. SE7 . . . . 4E 83
Derrycombe Ho. W2 . . 4C 58
  (off Brunel Est.)
Derry Ho. NW8 . . . . 3F 59
  (off Penfold St.)
Derry St. W8 . . . . 3D 73
Dersingham Rd.
  NW2 . . . . 5A 30
Derwent NW1 . . . . 2F 5
  (off Robert St.)
Derwent Av. NW9 . . . . 1A 28
  SW15 . . . . 4A 112
Derwent Ct. SE16 . . . . 3F 79
  (off Eleanor Cl.)
Derwent Gro. SE22 . . . 2B 106
Derwent Ho. E3 . . . . . . 3B 66
  (off Southern Gro.)
  SW7 . . . . 5E 73
  (off Cromwell Rd.)
Derwent Ri. NW9 . . . . 1A 28
Derwent St. SE10 . . . . 1A 96
Desborough Cl. W2 . . . 4D 59
Desborough Ho.
  W14 . . . . 2B 86
  (off North End Rd.)
Desborough St. W2 . . . 4D 59
  (off Cirencester St.)
Desenfans Rd.
  SE21 . . . . 4A 106
Desford Rd. E16 . . . . . 3A 68
Design Mus. 3B 78
Desmond St. SE14 . . . 2A 94
Desmond Tutu Dr.
  SE23 . . . . 1B 122
Despard Rd. N19 . . . . . 3E 33
Dethick Ct. E3 . . . . . . 5A 52
Detling Ho. SE17 . . . . . 5A 78
  (off Congreve St.)
Detling Rd.
  BR1: Brom 5C 124
Detmold Rd. E5 . . . . . . 4E 37
Devas St. E3 . . . . 3D 67
Devenay Rd. E15 . . . . . 4B 54
Deventer Cres.
  SE22 . . . . 3A 106
De Vere Cotts. W8 . . . . 4E 73
  (off De Vere Gdns.)
De Vere Gdns. W8 . . . . 3E 73
Deverell St.
  SE1 . . . . 5B 26 (4F 77)
De Vere M. W8 . . . . 4E 73
  (off De Vere Gdns.)
Devereux Ct. WC2 . . . . 3B 16
Devereux La. SW13 . . . 3D 85

Devereux Rd. SW11 . . 4B 102
Devitt Ho. E14 . . . . 1D 81
  (off Wade's Pl.)
Devizes St. N1 . . . . 5F 49
Devon Gdns. N4 . . . . . 1D 35
Devonia Rd. N1 . . . . . . 1D 63
Devon Mans. SE1 . . . . 3F 27
  (off Tooley St.)
Devonport W2 . . . . 5A 60
Devonport Ho. W2 . . . . 4C 58
  (off Brunel Est.)
Devonport M. W12 . . . 3D 71
Devonport Rd. W12 . . . 2D 71
  (not continuous)
Devonport St. E1 . . . . . 5F 65
Devonshire Cl. E15 . . . 1A 54
  W1 . . . . 5D 5 (4D 61)
Devonshire Ct. E1 . . . . 2E 65
  (off Bancroft Rd.)
  WC1 . . . . 5E 7
  (off Boswell St.)
Devonshire Dr. SE10 . . 3D 95
Devonshire Gro.
  SE15 . . . . 2D 93
Devonshire Hall E9 . . . 3E 51
  (off Frampton Pk. Rd.)
Devonshire Ho. E14 . . . 5C 80
  (off Westferry Rd.)
  NW6 . . . . 3B 44
  (off Kilburn High Road)
  SE1 . . . . 5F 25
  (off Bath Ter.)
  SW1 . . . . 1F 89
  (off Lindsay Sq.)
Devonshire M. SW10 . . 2F 87
  (off Park Wlk.)
  W4 . . . . 1A 84
Devonshire M. Nth.
  W1 . . . . 5D 5 (4D 61)
Devonshire M. Sth.
  W1 . . . . 5D 5 (4D 61)
Devonshire M. W.
  W1 . . . . 4C 4 (3C 60)
Devonshire Pas. W4 . . 1A 84
Devonshire Pl. NW2 . . 5C 30
  W1 . . . . 4C 4 (3C 60)
  W8 . . . . 4D 73
Devonshire Pl. M.
  W1 . . . . 4C 4 (4D 60)
Devonshire Rd. E16 . . . 5D 69
  E17 . . . . 1C 38
  SE9 . . . . 2F 125
  SE23 . . . . 1E 121
  W4 . . . . 1A 84
Devonshire Road
  Nature Reserve 5F 107
Devonshire Row
  EC2 . . . . 1E 19 (4A 64)
Devonshire Row M.
  W1 . . . . 4E 5
Devonshire Sq.
  EC2 . . . . 1E 19 (5A 64)
Devonshire St.
  W1 . . . . 5C 4 (4C 60)
  W4 . . . . 1A 84
Devonshire Ter. W2 . . . 5E 59
Devons Rd. E3 . . . . 2D 67
Devon St. SE15 . . . . . . 2D 93

Devon Wharf E14 . . . . . . 4E 67
De Walden Ho. NW8 . . . . 1A 60
    (off Allitsen Rd.)
De Walden St.
  W1 . . . . 1C 12 (4C 60)
Dewar St. SE15 . . . . . . 1C 106
Dewberry Gdns. E6 . . . . . 4F 69
Dewberry St. E14 . . . . . . 4E 67
Dewey La. SW2 . . . . 4C 104
    (off Tulse Hill)
Dewey Rd. N1 . . . . 1C 62
Dewey St. SW17 . . . . 5B 116
Dewhurst Rd. W14 . . . . . . 4F 71
Dewsbury Rd. NW10 . . . . 2C 42
Dewsbury Ter. NW1 . . . . . 5D 47
D'Eynsford Rd. SE5 . . . . . 4F 91
Dhonau Ho. SE1 . . . . 5B 78
    (off Longfield St.)
Diadem Ct. W1 . . . . 2B 14
Dial Wlk., The W8 . . . . . . 3D 73
    (off The Broad Wlk.)
Diamond Est. SW17 . . . . . 3A 116
Diamond Ho. E3 . . . . 1A 66
    (off Roman Rd.)
Diamond St. SE15 . . . . . . 3A 92
Diamond Ter. SE10 . . . . . 4E 95
Diamond Way SE8 . . . . . . 2C 94
Diana Cl. SE8 . . . . 2B 94
Diana Ho. SW13 . . . . 4B 84
Diana, Princess of Wales
  Memorial Walk. 2D 73
    (in Kensington Gdns.)
Dianne Ct. SE12 . . . . . . 1C 124
Dibden Ho. SE5 . . . . 3A 92
Dibden St. N1 . . . . 5E 49
Dibdin Ho. W9 . . . . 1D 59
Dicey Av. NW2 . . . . 1E 43
Dickens Est. SE1 . . . . . . 3C 78
  SE16 . . . . 4C 78
Dickens House 4F 7
Dickens Ho. NW6 . . . . . . 2C 58
    (off Malvern Rd.)
  NW8 . . . . 3F 59
    (off Fisherton St.)
  SE17 . . . . 1D 91
    (off Doddington Gro.)
  WC1 . . . . 3D 7
Dickens M. EC1 . . . . 5D 9
    (off Turnmill St.)
Dickenson Ho. N8 . . . . . . 1B 34
Dickenson Rd. N8 . . . . . . 2A 34
Dickens Rd. E6 . . . . 1F 69
Dickens Sq.
  SE1 . . . . 5A 26 (4E 77)
Dickens St. SW8 . . . . 5D 89
Dickinson Ct. EC1 . . . . . . 3E 9
    (off Brewhouse Yd.)
Dicksee Ho. NW8 . . . . . . 3F 59
    (off Lyons Pl.)
Dickson Ho. E1 . . . . 5D 65
    (off Philpot St.)
Dickson Rd. SE9 . . . . . . 1F 111
Dieppe Cl. W14 . . . . 1B 86
Digby Bus. Cen. E9 . . . . . 3F 51
    (off Digby Rd.)
Digby Cres. N4 . . . . 4E 35
Digby Mans. W6 . . . . 1D 85
    (off Hammersmith Bri. Rd.)
Digby Rd. E9 . . . . 3F 51

Digby St. E2 . . . . 2E 65
Diggon St. E1 . . . . 4F 65
Dighton Ct. SE5 . . . . 2E 91
Dighton Rd. SW18 . . . . . 3E 101
Dignum St. N1 . . . . 1C 62
Digswell St. N7 . . . . 3C 48
Dilhorne Cl. SE12 . . . . . . 3D 125
Dilke St. SW3 . . . . 2B 88
Dillwyn Cl. SE26 . . . . 4A 122
Dilston Gro. SE16 . . . . . . 5E 79
Dilton Gdns. SW15 . . . . . 1C 112
Dimes Pl. W6 . . . . 5D 71
Dimond Cl. E7 . . . . 1C 54
Dimsdale Wlk. E13 . . . . . 1C 68
Dimson Cres. E3 . . . . 2C 66
Dinerman St. NW8 . . . . . . 5E 45
Dingle Gdns. E14 . . . . . . 1C 80
Dingley La. SW16 . . . . . 2F 117
Dingley Pl.
  EC1 . . . . 1A 10 (2E 63)
Dingley Rd.
  EC1 . . . . 2F 9 (2E 63)
Dingwall Gdns.
  NW11 . . . . 1C 30
Dingwall Rd. SW18 . . . . . 5E 101
Dinmont Est. E2 . . . . 1C 64
Dinmont St. E2 . . . . 1C 64
    (off Pritchard's Rd.)
Dinmont St. E2 . . . . 1D 65
Dinmore Ho. E9 . . . . 5E 51
    (off Templecombe Rd.)
Dinnington Ho. E1 . . . . . . 3D 65
    (off Coventry Rd.)
Dinsdale Rd. SE3 . . . . . . 2B 96
Dinsmore Rd.
  SW12 . . . . 5D 103
Dinton Ho. NW8 . . . . 3A 60
    (off Lilestone St.)
Dinton Rd. SW19 . . . . . . 5F 115
Diprose Lodge
  SW17 . . . . 4F 115
Dirleton Rd. E15 . . . . 5B 54
Disbrowe Rd. W6 . . . . . . 2A 86
Discovery Bus. Pk.
  SE16 . . . . 4C 78
    (off St James's Rd.)
Discovery Ho. E14 . . . . . . 1E 81
    (off Newby St.)
Discovery Wlk. E1 . . . . . . 2D 79
Disney Pl.
  SE1 . . . . 3A 26 (3E 77)
Disney St.
  SE1 . . . . 3A 26 (3E 77)
Disraeli Gdns.
  SW15 . . . . 2B 100
Disraeli Rd. E7 . . . . 3C 54
  SW15 . . . . 2A 100
Diss St. E2 . . . . . . 1F 11 (2B 64)
Distaff La.
  EC4 . . . . 4F 17 (1E 77)
Distillery La. W6 . . . . 1E 85
Distillery Rd. W6 . . . . 1E 85
Distin St. SE11 . . . . 5C 76
Ditch All. SE13 . . . . 4D 95
Ditchburn St. E14 . . . . . . 1E 81
Dittisham Rd. SE9 . . . . . . 4F 125
Divisional Rd. E12 . . . . . . 4F 41
Divis Way SW15 . . . . 4D 99
    (off Dover Pk. Dr.)

Dixon Clark Ct. N1 . . . . . 3D 49
Dixon Ho. W10 . . . . 5F 57
    (off Darfield Way)
Dixon Rd. SE14 . . . . 4A 94
Dobree Av. NW10 . . . . . . 4D 43
Dobson Cl. NW6 . . . . 4F 45
Dobson Ho. SE5 . . . . 3F 91
    (off Edmund St.)
  SE14 . . . . 2F 93
    (off John Williams Cl.)
Doby Cl. EC4 . . . . 4A 18
Dock Cotts. E1 . . . . 1E 79
    (off The Highway)
Dockers Tanner Rd.
  . . . . 4C 80
Dockhead SE1 . . . . 3B 78
Dockhead Wharf SE1 . . . 4F 27
    (off Shad Thames)
Dock Hill Av. SE16 . . . . . 2F 79
Docklands Sailing Cen.
  . . . . 4C 80
Dockley Rd. SE16 . . . . . . 4C 78
Dockley Rd. Ind. Est.
  SE16 . . . . 4C 78
    (off Dockley Rd.)
Dock Offices SE16 . . . . . 4E 79
    (off Surrey Quays Rd.)
Dock Rd. E16 . . . . 1B 82
Dockside Rd. E16 . . . . . . 1F 83
Dock St. E1 . . . . 1C 78
Doctor Johnson Av.
  SW17 . . . . 3D 117
Doctors Cl. SE26 . . . . . . 5E 121
Docwra's Bldgs. N1 . . . . 3A 50
Dodbrooke Rd.
  SE27 . . . . 3C 118
Dodd Ho. SE16 . . . . 5D 79
    (off Rennie Est.)
Doddington Gro.
  SE17 . . . . 2D 91
Doddington Pl. SE17 . . . . 2D 91
Dodson St.
  SE1 . . . . 4C 24 (3C 76)
Dod St. E14 . . . . 5B 66
Dog & Duck Yd. WC1 . . . 5F 7
Doggett Rd. SE6 . . . . 5C 108
Dog Kennel Hill
  SE22 . . . . 1A 106
Dog Kennel Hill Est.
  SE22 . . . . 1A 106
    (off Albrighton Rd.)
Dog La. NW10 . . . . 1A 42
Doherty Rd. E13 . . . . 3C 68
Dolben Ct. SE8 . . . . 5B 80
  SW1 . . . . 5F 75
    (off Montaigne Cl.)
Dolben St.
  SE1 . . . . 2D 25 (2D 77)
    (not continuous)
Dolby Rd. SW6 . . . . 5B 86
Dolland Ho. SE11 . . . . . . 1B 90
    (off Newburn St.)
Dolland St. SE11 . . . . . . 1B 90
Dollar Bay Ct. E14 . . . . . 3E 81
    (off Lawn Ho. Cl.)
DOLLIS HILL 4D 29
Dollis Hill Av. NW2 . . . . . 5D 29
Dollis Hill La. NW2 . . . . . 1B 42

Dolman Rd. W4 . . . . 5A **70**
Dolman St. SW4 . . . . . . 2B **104**
Dolphin Cl. SE16 . . . . . . 3F **79**
Dolphin Ct. NW11 . . . . . 1A **30**
   SE8 . . . . 2B **94**
   (off Wotton Rd.)
Dolphin Ho. SW18 . . . . 2D **101**
Dolphin La. E14 . . . . 1D **81**
Dolphin Sq. SW1 . . . . . . 1E **89**
   W4 . . . . 3A **84**
Dolphin Twr. SE8 . . . . . 2B **94**
   (off Abinger Gro.)
Dombey Ho. SE1 . . . . . . 3C **78**
   (off Wolseley St.)
   W11 . . . . 2F **71**
   (off St Ann's Rd.)
Dombey St.
   WC1 . . . . . . 5F **7** (4B **62**)
   (not continuous)
Domecq Ho. EC1 . . . . 3E **9**
   (off Dallington St.)
Dome Hill Pk.
   SE26 . . . . 4B **120**
Domelton Ho.
   SW18 . . . . 4D **101**
   (off Iron Mill Rd.)
Domett Cl. SE5 . . . . 2F **105**
Domfe Pl. E5 . . . . 1E **51**
Domingo St.
   EC1 . . . . 3F **9** (3E **63**)
Dominica Cl. E13 . . . . . . 1F **69**
Dominion Ct. E8 . . . . 4B **50**
   (off Middleton Rd.)
Dominion Ho. E14 . . . . . 1D **95**
   (off St Davids Sq.)
Dominion St.
   EC2 . . . . 5C **10** (4F **63**)
Dominion Theatre 2C **14**
   (off Tottenham Ct. Rd.)
Donald Hunter Ho.
   E7 . . . . 2D **55**
   (off Woodgrange Rd.)
Donald Rd. E13 . . . . 5D **55**
Donaldson Rd. NW6 . . . . 5B **44**
Donato Dr. SE15 . . . . 2A **92**
Doncaster Gdns. N4 . . . . 1E **35**
Donegal Ho. E1 . . . . 3D **65**
   (off Cambridge Heath Rd.)
Donegal St. N1 . . . . 1B **62**
Doneraile Ho. SW1 . . . . . 1D **89**
   (off Ebury Bri. Rd.)
Doneraile St. SW6 . . . . . 5F **85**
Dongola Rd. E1 . . . . 4A **66**
   E13 . . . . 2D **69**
Dongola Rd. W. E13 . . . . 2D **69**
Don Gratton Ho. E1 . . . . 4C **64**
   (off Old Montague St.)
Donkey All. SE22 . . . . . 5C **106**
Donkin Ho. SE16 . . . . . . 5D **79**
   (off Rennie Est.)
Donmar Warehouse Theatre
   . . . . 3D **15**
   (off Earlham St.)
Donnatt's Rd. SE14 . . . . 4B **94**
Donne Ct. SE24 . . . . 4E **105**
Donne Ho. E14 . . . . 5C **66**
   (off Dod St.)
   SE14 . . . . 2F **93**
   (off Samuel Cl.)

Donnelly Ct. SW6 . . . . . 3A **86**
   (off Dawes Rd.)
Donne Pl. SW3 . . . . 5A **74**
Donnington Ct. NW1 . . . 4D **47**
   (off Castlehaven Rd.)
   NW10 . . . . 4D **43**
Donnington Mans.
   NW10 . . . . 5E **43**
   (off Donnington Rd.)
Donnington Rd.
   NW10 . . . . 4D **43**
Donoghue Cotts. E14 . . . 4A **66**
   (off Galsworthy Av.)
Donovan Ct. SW10 . . . . . 1F **87**
   (off Drayton Gdns.)
Donovan Ho. E1 . . . . 1E **79**
   (off Cable St.)
Don Phelan Cl. SE5 . . . . 4F **91**
Doon St. SE1 . . . 2B **24** (2C **76**)
Dora Ho. E14 . . . . 5B **66**
   (off Rhodeswell Rd.)
   W11 . . . . 1F **71**
   (off St Ann's Rd.)
Dorando Cl. W12 . . . . . . 1D **71**
Doran Mnr. N2 . . . . 1B **32**
   (off Great Nth. Rd.)
Doran Wlk. E15 . . . . 4E **53**
Dora Rd. SW19 . . . . 5C **114**
Dora St. E14 . . . . 5B **66**
Dora Way SW9 . . . . 5C **90**
Dorchester Ct. N1 . . . . . 4A **50**
   (off Englefield Rd.)
   NW2 . . . . 5F **29**
   SE24 . . . . 3E **105**
   SW1 . . . . 5A **20**
   (off Pavillion Rd.)
Dorchester Dr. SE24 . . . 3E **105**
Dorchester Gro. W4 . . . . 1A **84**
Dorchester Ter. NW2 . . . 5F **29**
   (off Needham Ter.)
Dordrecht Rd. W3 . . . . . 2A **70**
Doreen Av. NW9 . . . . 3A **28**
Doreen Capstan Ho.
   E11 . . . . 5A **40**
   (off Apollo Pl.)
Doria Rd. SW6 . . . . 5B **86**
Doric Ho. E2 . . . . 1F **65**
   (off Mace St.)
Doric Way
   NW1 . . . . . . 1B **6** (2F **61**)
Doris Emmerton Ct.
   SW11 . . . . 2E **101**
Doris Rd. E7 . . . . 4C **54**
Dorking Cl. SE8 . . . . 2B **94**
Dorking Ho.
   SE1 . . . . 5C **26** (4F **77**)
Dorlcote Rd. SW18 . . . . . 5A **102**
Dorman Way NW8 . . . . . 5F **45**
Dorma Trad. Pk. E10 . . . 3F **37**
Dormay St. SW18 . . . . . . 3D **101**
Dormer Cl. E15 . . . . 3B **54**
Dormstone Ho. SE17 . . . 5A **78**
   (off Beckway St.)
Dornberg Cl. SE3 . . . . . . 3C **96**
Dornberg Rd. SE3 . . . . . 3D **97**
Dorncliffe Rd. SW6 . . . . 5A **86**
Dorney NW3 . . . . 4A **46**
Dornfell St. NW6 . . . . . . 2B **44**
Dornton Rd. SW12 . . . . . 2D **117**

Dorothy Rd. SW11 . . . . . 1B **102**
Dorrell Pl. SW9 . . . . 1C **104**
Dorrien Wlk.
   SW16 . . . . 2F **117**
Dorrington St.
   EC1 . . . . 5B **8** (4C **62**)
Dorrit Ho. W11 . . . . 2F **71**
   (off St Ann's Rd.)
Dorrit St.
   SE1 . . . . 3A **26** (3E **77**)
Dorryn Ct. SE26 . . . . . . 5F **121**
Dors Cl. NW9 . . . . 3A **28**
Dorset Bldgs.
   EC4 . . . . 3D **17** (5D **63**)
Dorset Cl.
   NW1 . . . . 5A **4** (4B **60**)
Dorset Ct. N1 . . . . 4A **50**
   (off Hertford Rd.)
Dorset Ho. NW1 . . . . 5A **4**
   (off Gloucester Pl.)
Dorset M.
   SW1 . . . . 5D **21** (4D **75**)
Dorset Pl. E15 . . . . 3F **53**
Dorset Ri.
   EC4 . . . . 3D **17** (5D **63**)
Dorset Rd. E7 . . . . 4E **55**
   SE9 . . . . 2F **125**
   SW8 . . . . 3A **90**
Dorset Sq.
   NW1 . . . . 4A **4** (3B **60**)
Dorset St.
   W1 . . . . 1A **12** (4B **60**)
Dorset Wharf W6 . . . . . . 3E **85**
   (off Rainville Rd.)
Dorton Cl. SE15 . . . . 3A **92**
Dorville Cres. W6 . . . . . . 4D **71**
Dorville Rd. SE12 . . . . . . 3B **110**
Doughty Ct. E1 . . . . 2D **79**
   (off Prusom St.)
Doughty Ho. SW10 . . . . . 2E **87**
   (off Netherton Gro.)
Doughty M.
   WC1 . . . . 4F **7** (3B **62**)
Doughty St.
   WC1 . . . . 3F **7** (3B **62**)
Douglas Ct. NW6 . . . . . . 4C **44**
   (off Quex Rd.)
Douglas Est. N1 . . . . 3E **49**
   (off Oransay Rd.)
Douglas Eyre Sports Cen.
   . . . . 1F **37**
Douglas Johnstone Ho.
   SW6 . . . . 2B **86**
   (off Clem Attlee Ct.)
Douglas M. NW2 . . . . . . 5A **30**
Douglas Path E14 . . . . . 1E **95**
   (off Manchester Rd.)
Douglas Pl. SW1 . . . . . . 5F **75**
   (off Douglas St.)
Douglas Rd. E16 . . . . . . 4C **68**
   N1 . . . . 4E **49**
   NW6 . . . . 5B **44**
Douglas Rd. Nth. N1 . . . 3E **49**
Douglas Rd. Sth. N1 . . . 3E **49**
Douglas St. SW1 . . . . . . 5F **75**
Douglas Waite Ho.
   NW6 . . . . 4C **44**
Douglas Way SE8 . . . . . 3B **94**
   (Stanley St.)

Douglas Way SE8 . . . . 3C **94**
 (Watsons St.)
Doulton Ho. SE11 . . . . . . 4B **76**
 (off Lambeth Wlk.)
Doulton M. NW6 . . . . 3D **45**
Dounesforth Gdns.
 SW18 . . . . 1D **115**
Douro Pl. W8 . . . . 4D **73**
Douro St. E3 . . . . 1C **66**
Douthwaite Sq. E1 . . . . 2C **78**
Dove App. E6 . . . . 4F **69**
Dove Commercial Cen.
 NW5 . . . . 2E **47**
Dovecote Gdns.
 SW14 . . . . 1A **98**
Dove Ct. EC2 . . . . 3B **18**
Dovedale Bus. Est.
 SE15 . . . . 5C **92**
 (off Blenheim Gro.)
Dovedale Rd. SE22 . . . . 3D **107**
Dovehouse St. SW3 . . . 1F **87**
Dove M. SW5 . . . . 5E **73**
Dover Cl. NW2 . . . . 4F **29**
Dover Ct. EC1 . . . . 3D **9**
 (off St John St.)
Dovercourt Est. N1 . . . 3F **49**
Dovercourt Rd.
 SE22 . . . . 4A **106**
Doverfield Rd. SW2 . . . 5A **104**
Dover Flats SE1 . . . . 5A **78**
Dover Ho. SE15 . . . . . . 2E **93**
Dover Ho. Rd.
 SW15 . . . . 2C **98**
Dove Rd. N1 . . . . 3F **49**
Dove Row E2 . . . . 5C **50**
Dover Pk. Dr. SW15 . . . 4D **99**
Dover Patrol SE3 . . . . . 5D **97**
Dover Rd. E12 . . . . 4E **41**
 SE19 . . . . 5F **119**
Dover St. W1 . . 5E **13** (1D **75**)
Doves Yd. N1 . . . . 5C **48**
Dovet Ct. SW9 . . . . 4B **90**
Doveton Ho. E1 . . . . 3E **65**
 (off Doveton St.)
Doveton St. E1 . . . . 3E **65**
Dove Wlk. SW1 . . . . 1C **88**
Dovey Lodge N1 . . . . . . 4C **48**
 (off Bewdley St.)
Dowanhill Rd. SE6 . . 1F **123**
Dowdeswell Cl.
 SW15 . . . . 2A **98**
Dowding Ho. N6 . . . . . . 2C **32**
 (off Hillcrest)
Dowdney Cl. NW5 . . . . 2E **47**
Dowe Ho. SE3 . . . . . . 1A **110**
Dowes Ho. SW16 . . . . 3A **118**
Dowgate Hill
 EC4 . . . . 4B **18** (1F **77**)
Dowland St. W10 . . . . 2A **58**
Dowlas St. SE5 . . . . 3A **92**
Dowler Ho. E1 . . . . 5C **64**
 (off Burslem St.)
Downbury M. SW18 . . 3C **100**
Downderry Rd.
 BR1: Brom 3F **123**
Downend Ct. SE15 . . . 2A **92**
 (off Longhope Cl.)
Downer's Cott. SW4 . . 2E **103**

Downesbury NW3 . . . . . 3B **46**
 (off Steele's Rd.)
Downey Ho. E1 . . . . 3F **65**
 (off Globe Rd.)
Downfield Cl. W9 . . . . . . 3D **59**
DOWNHAM 5F **123**
Downham Ct. N1 . . . . . . 4F **49**
 (off Downham Rd.)
Downham Ent. Cen.
 SE6 . . . . 2B **124**
Downham La.
 BR1: Brom 5F **123**
Downham Rd. N1 . . . . . . 4F **49**
Downham Way
 BR1: Brom 5F **123**
Downing Ho. W10 . . . . . 5F **57**
 (off Cambridge Gdns.)
Downing St.
 SW1 . . . . 3D **23** (3A **76**)
Downland Ct. E11 . . . . . . 4A **40**
Down Pl. W6 . . . . 5D **71**
Downs Ct. Pde. E8 . . . . . 2D **51**
 (off Amhurst Rd.)
Downsell Rd. E15 . . . . . . 1E **53**
Downsfield Rd. E17 . . . 1A **38**
Downshire Hill NW3 . . 1F **45**
Downside Cres. NW3 . . 2A **46**
Downs La. E5 . . . . 1D **51**
Downs Pk. Rd. E5 . . . . . 2B **50**
 E8 . . . . 2B **50**
Downs Rd. E5 . . . . 1C **50**
Down St. W1 . . 2D **21** (2D **75**)
Down St. M.
 W1 . . . . 2D **21** (2D **75**)
Downton Av. SW2 . . . 2A **118**
Downtown Rd.
 SE16 . . . . 3A **80**
Dowrey St. N1 . . . . 5C **48**
Dowson Cl. SE5 . . . . . . 2F **105**
Dowson Ho. E1 . . . . 5F **65**
 (off Bower St.)
Doyce St.
 SE1 . . . . 3F **25** (3E **77**)
Doyle Gdns. NW10 . . . . 5C **42**
Doyle Ho. SW13 . . . . . . 3E **85**
 (off Trinity Chu. Rd.)
D'Oyley St. SW1 . . . . . . 5C **74**
Doynton St. N19 . . . . . . 4D **33**
Draco Ga. SW15 . . . . . . 1E **99**
Draco St. SE17 . . . . 2E **91**
Dragonfly Cl. E13 . . . . . . 2D **69**
Dragon Rd. SE15 . . . . . . 2A **92**
Dragon Yd.
 WC1 . . . . 2E **15** (5A **62**)
Dragoon Rd. SE8 . . . . . . 1B **94**
Drake Cl. SE16 . . . . 3F **79**
Drake Ct. SE1 . . . . 4A **26**
 (off Swan St.)
 SE19 . . . . 5B **120**
 W12 . . . . 3E **71**
 (off Scott's Rd.)
Drakefell Rd. SE4 . . . . 1A **108**
 SE14 . . . . 5F **93**
Drakefield Rd.
 SW17 . . . . 3C **116**
Drake Hall E16 . . . . 2D **83**
 (off Wesley Av.)
Drake Ho. E1 . . . . 4E **65**
 (off Stepney Way)

Drake Ho. E14 . . . . 1A **80**
 (off Victory Pl.)
 SW1 . . . . 2F **89**
 (off Dolphin Sq.)
Drakeland Ho. W9 . . . . . 3B **58**
 (off Fernhead Rd.)
Drakeley Ct. N5 . . . . 1D **49**
Drake Rd. SE4 . . . . 1C **108**
Drakes Ct. SE23 . . . . . . 1E **121**
Drakes Courtyard
 NW6 . . . . 4B **44**
Drake St.
 WC1 . . . . . . 1F **15** (4B **62**)
Draper Ho. SE1 . . . . 5D **77**
 (off Elephant & Castle)
Draper Pl. N1 . . . . 5D **49**
 (off Dagmar Ter.)
Drapers Gdns.
 EC2 . . . . 2C **18** (5F **63**)
Drapers Rd. E15 . . . . . . 1F **53**
Drappers Way SE16 . . . 5C **78**
Drawdock Rd. SE10 . . 3F **81**
Draxmont SW19 . . . . . 5A **114**
Draycot Rd. E11 . . . . . . 1D **41**
Draycott Av. SW3 . . . . . 5A **74**
Draycott Cl. NW2 . . . . . 5F **29**
 SE5 . . . . 3F **91**
 (not continuous)
Draycott M. SW6 . . . . . 5B **86**
 (off Laurel Bank Gdns.)
Draycott Pl. SW3 . . . . . 5B **74**
Draycott Ter. SW3 . . . . 5B **74**
Drayford Cl. W9 . . . . . . 3B **58**
Dray Gdns. SW2 . . . . 3B **104**
Draymans M. SE15 . . . . 5B **92**
Drayson M. W8 . . . . 3C **72**
Drayton Gdns.
 SW10 . . . . 1E **87**
Drayton Ho. E11 . . . . . . 3F **39**
 SE5 . . . . 3F **91**
 (off Elmington Rd.)
Drayton Pk. N5 . . . . 1C **48**
Drayton Pk. M. N5 . . . . 2C **48**
Drayton Rd. E11 . . . . . . 3F **39**
 NW10 . . . . 5B **42**
Dreadnought St.
 SE10 . . . . 4A **82**
Dreadnought Wharf
 SE10 . . . . 2D **95**
 (off Thames St.)
Dresden Cl. NW6 . . . . . 3D **45**
Dresden Ho. SE11 . . . 5B **76**
 (off Lambeth Wlk.)
 SW11 . . . . 5C **88**
 (off Dagnall St.)
Dresden Rd. N19 . . . . . 3E **33**
Dressington Av.
 SE4 . . . . 4C **108**
Drewery Ct. SE3 . . . . . 1A **110**
Drewett Ho. E1 . . . . 5C **64**
 (off Christian St.)
Drew Ho. SW16 . . . . . 3A **118**
Drew Rd. E16 . . . . 2F **83**
 (not continuous)
Drewstead Rd.
 SW16 . . . . 2F **117**
Driffield Rd. E3 . . . . . . 1A **66**
Drill Hall Arts Cen. . . . 5B **6**
 (off Chenies St.)

Drinkwater Ho. *SE5* *3F 91*
  (off Picton St.)
Drive, The N7 . . . . 3B 48
  (not continuous)
NW10 . . . . 5B 42
NW11 . . . . 2A 30
SW6 . . . . 5A 86
Drive Mans. *SW6* *5A 86*
  (off Fulham Rd.)
Driveway, The *E17* . . . *1D 39*
  (off Hoe St.)
Dr Johnson's House . . *3C 16*
  (off Pemberton Row)
Droitwich Cl. SE26 . . 3C 120
Dromore Rd. SW15 . . 4A 100
Dron Ho. *E1* *4E 65*
  (off Adelina Gro.)
Droop St. W10 . . . . . . 2F 57
Drovers Pl. SE15 . . . . . 3E 93
Druce Rd. SE21 . . . . . 4A 106
Druid St. SE1 . . 3E 27 (3A 78)
Drummond Cres.
  NW1 . . . . 1B 6 (2F 61)
Drummond Ga. SW1 . . . 1F 89
Drummond Ho. *E2* . . . *1C 64*
  (off Goldsmiths Row)
Drummond Rd. E11 . . . 1E 41
  SE16 . . . . 4D 79
Drummond St.
  NW1 . . . . . . 3F 5 (3E 61)
Drum St. E1 . . . . 5B 64
Drury Ho. SW8 . . . . . . 4E 89
Drury La.
  WC2 . . . . . . 2E 15 (5A 62)
Drury Lane Theatre . . *3F 15*
  (off Catherine St.)
Drury Way NW10 . . . . 2A 42
Dryad St. SW15 . . . . . 1F 99
Dryburgh Ho. *SW1* . . . *1D 89*
  (off Abbots Mnr.)
Dryburgh Rd. SW15 . . 1D 99
Dryden Cl. SE11 . . . . . 5D 77
Dryden Mans. *W14* . . *2A 86*
  (off Queen's Club Gdns.)
Dryden Rd. SW19 . . . 5E 115
Dryden St.
  WC2 . . . . . . 3E 15 (5A 62)
Dryfield Wlk. SE8 . . . . 2C 94
Drylands Rd. N8 . . . . . 1A 34
Drysdale Dwellings
  E8 . . . . *2B 50*
  (off Dunn St.)
Drysdale Ho. *N1* *1E 11*
  (off Drysdale St.)
Drysdale Pl.
  N1 . . . . 1E 11 (2A 64)
Drysdale St.
  N1 . . . . 1E 11 (2A 64)
Dublin Av. E8 . . . . 5C 50
Ducal St. E2 . . . . 2B 64
Du Cane Cl. W12 . . . . 5E 57
Du Cane Ct. SW17 . . . 1C 116
Du Cane Rd. W12 . . . . 5B 56
Ducavel Ho. SW2 . . . . 1B 118
Duchess M.
  W1 . . . . 1E 13 (4D 61)
Duchess of Bedford Ho.
  W8 . . . . *3C 72*
  (off Duchess of Bedford's Wlk.)

Duchess of Bedford's Wlk.
  W8 . . . . 3C 72
Duchess St.
  W1 . . . . 1E 13 (4D 61)
Duchess Theatre *4F 15*
  (off Catherine St.)
Duchy St.
  SE1 . . . . . . 1C 24 (2C 76)
  (not continuous)
Ducie St. SW4 . . . . . . 2B 104
Duckett M. N4 . . . . . . 1D 35
Duckett Rd. N4 . . . . . 1C 34
Duckett St. E1 . . . . . . 3F 65
Duck La. W1 . . . . 3B 14
DUDDEN HILL 2D 43
Dudden Hill La.
  NW10 . . . . 1B 42
Dudden Hill Pde.
  NW10 . . . . 1B 42
Duddington Cl. SE9 . . 4F 125
Dudley Cl. *W1* *5B 60*
  (off Up. Berkeley St.)
WC2 . . . . . . 2D 15 (5A 62)
Dudley Ho. *W2* *4F 59*
  (off Nth. Wharf Rd.)
Dudley M. SW4 . . . . . 4C 104
Dudley Rd. NW6 . . . . 1A 58
  SW19 . . . . 5C 114
Dudley St. W2 . . . . . . 4F 59
Dudlington Rd. E5 . . . 4E 37
Dudmaston M. *SW3* . . *1F 87*
  (off Fulham Rd.)
Dudrich M. SE22 . . . . 3B 106
Duffell Ho. *SE11* *1B 90*
  (off Loughborough St.)
Dufferin Av. EC1 . . . . 4B 10
Dufferin Ct. *EC1* *4B 10*
  (off Dufferin St.)
Dufferin St.
  EC1 . . . . . . 4A 10 (3E 63)
Duff St. E14 . . . . 5D 67
Dufour's Pl.
  W1 . . . . 3A 14 (5B 61)
Dugard Way SE11 . . . 5D 77
Duggan Dr.
  BR7: Chst 5F 125
Duke Humphrey Rd.
  SE3 . . . . 4A 96
Duke of Wellington Pl.
  SW1 . . . . . . 3C 20 (3C 74)
Duke of York Column
  (Memorial) 2C 22
Duke of Yorks Sq.
  SW3 . . . . 5B 74
Duke of York's Theatre
  . . . . *5D 15*
  (off St Martin's La.)
Duke of York St.
  SW1 . . . . . . 1A 22 (2E 75)
Duke Rd. W4 . . . . 1A 84
Duke's Av. W4 . . . . . . 1A 84
Dukes Ct. SE13 . . . . . 5E 95
  SW14 . . . . 5A 84
  W2 . . . . *1D 73*
  (off Queensway)
Duke's Head Yd. N6 . . . 3D 33
Duke Shore Wharf
  E14 . . . . 1B 80

Duke's Ho. *SW1* *5F 75*
  (off Vincent St.)
Dukes La. W8 . . . . . . 3D 73
Duke's La. Chambers
  W8 . . . . *3D 73*
  (off Dukes La.)
Duke's La. Mans.
  W8 . . . . *3D 73*
  (off Dukes La.)
Duke's M. W1 . . . . . . 2C 12
Duke's Pl.
  EC3 . . . . . . 3E 19 (5A 64)
Dukes Point *N6* *3D 33*
  (off Dukes Head Yd.)
Duke's Rd.
  WC1 . . . . . . 2C 6 (2F 61)
Dukesthorpe Rd.
  SE26 . . . . 4F 121
Duke St.
  SW1 . . . . . . 1A 22 (2E 75)
  W1 . . . . 2C 12 (5C 60)
Duke St. Hill
  SE1 . . . . . . 1C 26 (2F 77)
Duke St. Mans. *W1* . . *3C 12*
  (off Duke St.)
Duke's Yd.
  W1 . . . . 4C 12 (1C 74)
Dulas St. N4 . . . . 3B 34
Dulford St. W11 . . . . . 1A 72
Dulka Rd. SW11 . . . . 3B 102
Dulverton *NW1* *5E 47*
  (off Royal College St.)
Dulverton Mans.
  WC1 . . . . 4A 8
DULWICH 2A 120
Dulwich Bus. Cen.
  SE23 . . . . 1F 121
Dulwich Comn.
  SE21 . . . . 1A 120
  SE22 . . . . 1A 120
Dulwich Lawn Cl.
  SE22 . . . . 3B 106
Dulwich Leisure Cen.
  . . . . 2C 106
Dulwich Oaks, The
  SE21 . . . . 3B 120
Dulwich Picture Gallery
  . . . . 5F 105
Dulwich Ri. Gdns.
  SE22 . . . . 3B 106
Dulwich Rd. SE24 . . . 3C 104
Dulwich Upper Wood
  Nature Pk. 5B 120
DULWICH VILLAGE . . 5A 106
Dulwich Village
  SE21 . . . . 4F 105
Dulwich Wood Av.
  SE19 . . . . 4A 120
Dulwich Wood Pk.
  SE19 . . . . 4A 120
Dumain Ct. *SE11* *5D 77*
  (off Opal St.)
Dumbarton Ct. SW2 . . 4A 104
Dumbarton Rd.
  SW2 . . . . 4A 104
Dumont Rd. N16 . . . . 5A 36
Dumpton Pl. NW1 . . . . 4C 46
Dunbar Rd. E7 . . . . . . 3C 54
Dunbar St. SE27 . . . . 3E 119

Dunbar Wharf E14 . . . . . 1B 80
(off Narrow St.)
Dunboyne Ho. NW3 . . . 2B 46
Dunbridge Ho. SW15 . . . 4B 98
(off Highcliffe Dr.)
Dunbridge St. E2 . . . . . 3C 64
Duncan Ct. E14. . . . . . . 4E 67
(off Teviot St.)
Duncan Gro. W3 . . . . . . 5A 56
Duncan Ho. NW3 . . . . . 4B 46
(off Fellows Rd.)
SW1 . . . . 1E 89
(off Dolphin Sq.)
Duncannon Ho. SW1 . . . 1F 89
(off Lindsay Sq.)
Duncannon St.
WC2. . . . . 5D 15 (1A 76)
Duncan Rd. E8 . . . . 5D 51
Duncan St. N1 . . . . 1D 63
Duncan Ter. N1. . . . . . . 1D 63
(not continuous)
Dunch St. E1 . . . . 5D 65
Duncombe Hill
SE23 . . . . 5A 108
Duncombe Rd. N19 . . . 3F 33
Duncrievie Rd.
SE13 . . . . 4F 109
Dundalk Ho. E1. . . . . . . 5E 65
(off Clark St.)
Dundalk Rd. SE4 . . . . 1A 108
Dundas Ho. E2 . . . . 1E 65
(off Bishop's Way)
Dundas Rd. SE15 . . . . . 5E 93
Dundee Ct. E1 . . . . 2D 79
(off Wapping High St.)
SE1. . . . . 5D 27
(off Long La.)
Dundee Ho. W9 . . . . . . 2E 59
(off Maida Va.)
Dundee Rd. E13. . . . . . 1D 69
Dundee St. E1 . . . . 2D 79
Dundee Wharf E14 . . . 1B 80
Dundonald Ho. E14 . . . 3D 81
(off Admirals Way)
Dundonald Rd.
NW10 . . . . 5F 43
Dundry Ho. SE26 . . . . 3C 120
Dunedin Rd. E10 . . . . . 5D 39
Dunelm Gro. SE27 . . . 3E 119
Dunelm St. E1 . . . . 5F 65
Dunfield Gdns. SE6 . . . 5D 123
Dunfield Rd. SE6 . . . . 5D 123
(not continuous)
Dunford Rd. N7 . . . . . . 1B 48
Dungarvan Av. SW15 . . 2C 98
Dunhill Point SW15 . . . 1C 112
Dunkeld Ho. E14. . . . . . 5E 67
(off Abbott Rd.)
Dunkery Rd. SE9. . . . . . 4F 125
Dunkirk St. SE27 . . . . . 4E 119
Dunlace Rd. E5. . . . . . . 1E 51
Dunlin Ho. SE16 . . . . . . 5F 79
(off Tawny Way)
Dunloe Ct. E2. . . . . 1B 64
Dunloe St. E2. . . . . 1B 64
Dunlop Pl. SE16. . . . . . 4B 78
Dunmore Point E2. . . . . 2F 11
(off Gascoigne Pl.)
Dunmore Rd. NW6 . . . . 5A 44

Dunmow Ho. SE11 . . . . 1B 90
(off Newburn St.)
Dunmow Rd. E15. . . . . . 1F 53
Dunmow Wlk. N1 . . . . . 5E 49
(off Popham St.)
Dunnage Cres. SE16 . . 5A 80
(not continuous)
Dunnico Ho. SE17 . . . . 1A 92
(off East St.)
Dunn's Pas. WC1 . . . . . 2E 15
Dunn St. E8 . . . . 2B 50
Dunollie Pl. NW5 . . . . . 2E 47
Dunollie Rd. NW5 . . . . . 2E 47
Dunoon Gdns. SE23 . . 5F 107
Dunoon Ho. N1. . . . . . . 5B 48
(off Bemerton Est.)
Dunoon Rd. SE23 . . . . . 5E 107
Dunraven Rd. W12. . . . . 2C 70
Dunraven St.
W1 . . . . 4A 12 (1B 74)
Dunsany Rd. W14. . . . . 4F 71
Dunsford Way SW15 . . . 4D 99
Dunsmure Rd. N16 . . . . 3A 36
Dunstable M.
W1 . . . . 5C 4 (4C 60)
Dunstan Ho's. E1 . . . . . 4E 65
(off Stepney Grn.)
Dunstan Rd. NW11 . . . . 3B 30
Dunstan's Gro.
SE22 . . . . 4D 107
Dunstan's Rd. SE22 . . . 5C 106
Dunster Ct.
EC3 . . . . 4E 19 (1A 78)
Dunster Gdns. NW6 . . . 4B 44
Dunster Ho. SE6. . . . . . 3E 123
Dunsterville Way
SE1. . . . . 4C 26 (3F 77)
Dunston Rd. E8 . . . . . . 5B 50
SW11 . . . . 5C 88
Dunston St. E8 . . . . 5A 50
Dunton Ct. SE23. . . . . . 2D 121
Dunton Rd. E10 . . . . . . 2D 39
SE1. . . . . 1B 92
Duntshill Rd. SW18. . . . 1D 115
Dunworth M. W11 . . . . . 5B 58
Duplex Ride
SW1 . . . . 4A 20 (3B 74)
Dupree Rd. SE7 . . . . . . 1D 97
Durand Gdns. SW9 . . . . 4B 90
Durands Wlk. SE16 . . . . 3B 80
Durant St. E2 . . . . 1C 64
Durban Ct. E7. . . . . 4F 55
Durban Ho. W12 . . . . . . 1D 71
(off White City Est.)
Durban Rd. E15. . . . . . . 2A 68
SE27 . . . . 4E 119
Durdans Ho. NW1 . . . . . 4D 47
(off Farrier St.)
Durell Ho. SE16 . . . . . . 3F 79
(off Wolfe Cres.)
Durfey Pl. SE5 . . . . 3F 91
Durford Cres. SW15. . . 1D 113
Durham Ct. NW6 . . . . . 1C 58
(off Kilburn Pk. Rd.)
Durham Hill
BR1: Brom 4B 124
Durham Ho. NW8 . . . . . 2A 60
(off Grove Gdns.)
Durham Ho. St. WC2 . . . 5E 15

Durham Pl. SW3 . . . . . . 1B 88
Durham Rd. E12. . . . . . 1F 55
E16 . . . . 3A 68
N7 . . . . 4B 34
Durham Row E1 . . . . . . 4F 65
Durham St. SE11 . . . . . 1B 90
Durham Ter. W2. . . . . . 5D 59
Durham Yd. E2 . . . . . . 2D 65
Durley Rd. N16 . . . . . . 2A 36
Durlston Rd. E5 . . . . . . 4C 36
Durnford Ho. SE6. . . . . 3E 123
Durnford St. N15 . . . . . 1A 36
SE10 . . . . 2E 95
Durning Rd. SE19 . . . . 5F 119
Durnsford Av. SW19. . . 2C 114
Durnsford Rd.
SW19 . . . . 2C 114
Durrell Rd. SW6. . . . . . 4B 86
Durrels Ho. W14 . . . . . . 5B 72
(off Warwick Gdns.)
Durrington Rd. E5 . . . . . 1A 52
Durrington Twr. SW8 . . . 5E 89
Durrisdeer Ho. NW2 . . . 1B 44
(off Lyndale)
Dursley Cl. SE3 . . . . . . 5E 97
Dursley Gdns. SE3 . . . . 4F 97
Dursley Rd. SE3 . . . . . . 5E 97
Durward St. E1 . . . . . . 4D 65
Durweston M. W1 . . . . . 5A 4
Durweston St.
W1 . . . . 1A 12 (4B 60)
Dutch Yd. SW18 . . . . . 3C 100
Dutton St. SE10 . . . . . . 4E 95
Duval Ho. N19 . . . . 4F 33
(off Ashbrook Rd.)
Dye Ho. La. E3. . . . . . . 5C 52
Dyer's Bldgs.
EC1 . . . . 1B 16 (4C 62)
Dyers Hall Rd. E11 . . . . 3A 40
Dyers Hill Rd. E11 . . . . 4F 39
Dyers La. SW15. . . . . . 2D 99
Dylan Rd. SE24 . . . . . 2D 105
Dylways SE5. . . . . 2F 105
Dymes Path SW19 . . . 2F 113
Dymock St. SW6 . . . . . 1D 101
Dyneley Rd. SE12 . . . . 3E 125
Dyne Rd. NW6. . . . . . . 4A 44
Dynevor Rd. N16 . . . . . 5A 36
Dynham Rd. NW6 . . . . . 4C 44
Dyott St.
WC1 . . . . 2C 14 (5F 61)
Dysart St.
EC2 . . . . 4D 11 (3F 63)
Dyson Ct. NW2 . . . . . . 3E 29
Dyson Ho. SE10. . . . . . 1B 96
(off Blackwall La.)
Dyson Rd. E11 . . . . . . 1A 40
E15 . . . . 3B 54

E

Eade Rd. N4. . . . . 2E 35
Eagle Cl. SE16 . . . . 1E 93
Eagle Ct. EC1 . . . 5D 9 (4D 63)
Eagle Hgts. SW11 . . . . 1A 102
Eagle Hill SE19. . . . . . 5F 119

Eagle Ho. E1 . . . . 3D **65**
(off Headlam St.)
N1 . . . . 1F **63**
(off Eagle Wharf Rd.)
Eagle Ho. M. SW4 . . . 3E **103**
Eagle Lodge NW11 . . . 2B **30**
Eagle M. N1 . . . . 3A **50**
Eagle Pl. SW1 . . . . 5A **14**
SW7 . . . . 1E **87**
Eagle St.
WC1 . . . . 1F **15** (4B **62**)
Eagle Wharf SE1 . . . . 2F **27**
(off Lafone St.)
Eagle Wharf E. E14 . . . 1A **80**
(off Narrow St.)
Eagle Wharf Rd. N1 . . . 1E **63**
Eagle Wharf W. E14 . . . 1A **80**
(off Narrow St.)
Eagle Works E. E1 . . . . 4F **11**
Eagle Works W.
E1 . . . . 4F **11** (3B **64**)
Eagling Cl. E3 . . . . 2C **66**
Ealdham Sq. SE9 . . . . 2E **111**
Eamont Ct. NW8 . . . . . 1A **60**
(off Eamont St.)
Eamont St. NW8 . . . . . 1A **60**
Eardley Cres. SW5 . . . 1C **86**
Eardley Rd. SW16 . . . 5E **117**
Earldom Rd. SW18 . . . 2E **99**
Earle Ho. SW1 . . . . 5F **75**
(off Montaigne Cl.)
Earlham Ct. E11 . . . . . 2B **40**
Earlham Gro. E7 . . . . . . 2B **54**
Earlham St.
WC2 . . . . 3C **14** (5A **62**)
Earl Ho. NW1 . . . . 3A **60**
(off Lisson Gro.)
Earlom Ho. WC1 . . . . 2B **8**
(off Margery St.)
EARL'S COURT 1C **86**
Earls Court Exhibition Building
. . . . 1C **86**
Earl's Ct. Gdns. SW5 . . 5D **73**
Earls Ct. Rd. SW5 . . . . 4C **72**
W8 . . . . 4C **72**
Earl's Ct. Sq. SW5 . . . 1D **87**
Earlsferry Way N1 . . . . 4A **48**
(not continuous)
EARLSFIELD 1E **115**
Earlsfield Rd. SW18 . . 1E **115**
Earlsmead Rd. NW10 . . 2E **57**
Earls Ter. W8 . . . . 4B **72**
Earlsthorpe M.
SW12 . . . . 4C **102**
Earlsthorpe Rd.
SE26 . . . . 4F **121**
Earlstoke St.
EC1 . . . . 1D **9** (2D **63**)
Earlston Gro. E9 . . . . . 5D **51**
Earl St. EC2 . . . 5D **11** (4F **63**)
(not continuous)
Earls Wlk. W8 . . . . 4C **72**
Earlswood Cl. SE10 . . 2A **96**
Earlswood Cl. SE10 . . 1A **96**
Early M. NW1 . . . . 5D **47**
Earnshaw St.
WC2 . . . . 2C **14** (5F **61**)
Earsby St. W14 . . . . . . 5A **72**
(not continuous)

Eashing Point
SW15 . . . . 1D **113**
(off Wanborough Dr.)
Easleys M.
W1 . . . . 2C **12** (5C **60**)
East 10 Ent. Pk. E10 . . 3A **38**
EAST ACTON 1B **70**
E. Acton Arc. W3 . . . . . 5A **56**
E. Acton Ct. W3 . . . . . . 1A **70**
E. Acton La. W3 . . . . . . 2A **70**
East Bank N16 . . . . 2A **36**
East Block SE1 . . . . . . 3A **24**
(off York Rd.)
Eastbourne M. W2 . . . . 5E **59**
Eastbourne Rd. E15 . . 5A **54**
N15 . . . . 1A **36**
SW17 . . . . 5C **116**
Eastbourne Ter. W2 . . 5E **59**
Eastbrook Rd. SE3 . . . 4D **97**
Eastbury Gro. W4 . . . . 1A **84**
Eastbury Ter. E1 . . . . . 3F **65**
Eastcastle St.
W1 . . . . 2F **13** (5E **61**)
Eastcheap
EC3 . . . . 4D **19** (1A **78**)
E. Churchfield Rd.
W3 . . . . 2A **70**
Eastcombe Av. SE7 . . . 2D **97**
Eastcote St. SW9 . . . . 5B **90**
E. Cross Cen. E15 . . . . 3C **52**
E. Cross Route E3 . . . . 4B **52**
E9 . . . . 2B **52**
(Crowfoot Cl.)
E9 . . . . 4B **52**
(Wansbeck Rd.)
E15 . . . . 2B **52**
Eastdown Ct. SE13 . . . 2F **109**
Eastdown Ho. E8 . . . . . 1C **50**
Eastdown Pk. SE13 . . . 2F **109**
EAST DULWICH 2B **106**
E. Dulwich Gro.
SE22 . . . . 3A **106**
E. Dulwich Rd.
SE22 . . . . 2B **106**
(not continuous)
Eastern Av. E11 . . . . . . 1D **41**
IG4: Ilf. 1F **41**
Eastern Gateway E16 . . 1E **83**
Eastern Ho. E2 . . . . . . 2D **65**
(off Bethnal Grn. Rd.)
Eastern Quay Apartments
E16 . . . . 2D **83**
(off Portsmouth St.)
Eastern Rd. E13 . . . . . 1D **69**
E17 . . . . 1E **39**
SE4 . . . . 2C **108**
E. Ferry Rd. E14 . . . . . 5D **81**
Eastfields Av. SW18 . . 2C **100**
Eastfield St. E14 . . . . . 4A **66**
East Gdns. SW17 . . . 5A **116**
Eastgate Bus. Pk.
E10 . . . . 3A **38**
EAST HAM 2F **69**
E. Ham Ind. Est. E6 . . . 3F **69**
E. Harding St.
EC4 . . . . 2C **16** (5C **62**)
E. Heath Rd. NW3 . . . . 5E **31**
East Hill SW18 . . . . . . 3D **101**

E. India Bldgs. E14 . . . 1C **80**
(off Saltwell St.)
E. India Ct. SE16 . . . . . 3E **79**
(off St Marychurch St.)
East India Dock Ho.
E14 . . . . 5E **67**
E. India Dock Rd.
E14 . . . . 5C **66**
Eastlake Ho. NW8 . . . . 3F **59**
(off Frampton St.)
Eastlake Rd. SE5 . . . . 5E **91**
Eastlands Cres.
SE21 . . . . 4B **106**
East La. SE16 . . . . 3C **78**
(not continuous)
Eastlea M. E16 . . . . . . 3A **68**
Eastleigh Cl. NW2 . . . . 5A **28**
Eastleigh Wlk.
SW15 . . . . 5C **98**
East Lodge E16 . . . . . . 2C **82**
(off Wesley Av.)
E. London Crematorium
E13 . . . . 2B **68**
Eastman Ho. SW4 . . . 4E **103**
Eastman Rd. W3 . . . . . 3A **70**
East Mascalls SE7 . . . 2E **97**
Eastmearn Rd.
SE21 . . . . 2E **119**
Eastmoor Pl. SE7 . . . . 4F **83**
Eastmoor St. SE7 . . . . 4F **83**
East Mt. St. E1 . . . . 4D **65**
(not continuous)
Eastney St. SE10 . . . . . 1F **95**
Easton St.
WC1 . . . . 3B **8** (3C **62**)
East Parkside SE10 . . . 3A **82**
East Pas. EC1 . . . . 5F **9**
East Pl. SE27 . . . . 4E **119**
East Point SE1 . . . . 1C **92**
E. Poultry Av.
EC1 . . . . 1D **17** (4D **63**)
East Rd. E15 . . . . 5C **54**
N1 . . . . 2B **10** (2F **63**)
SW3 . . . . 1C **88**
East Row E11 . . . . 1C **40**
W10 . . . . 3A **58**
East Row Ho. SW8 . . . 3A **90**
(off Hartington Rd.)
EAST SHEEN 2A **98**
E. Sheen Av. SW14 . . . 3A **98**
East Smithfield
E1 . . . . 5F **19** (1B **78**)
East St. SE17 . . . . 1E **91**
E. Surrey Gro. SE15 . . 3B **92**
E. Tenter St. E1 . . . . . . 5B **64**
East Va. W3 . . . . 2B **70**
Eastville Av. NW11 . . . 1B **30**
Eastway E9 . . . . 3B **52**
Eastwell Ho. SE1 . . . . 5C **26**
Eastwood Cl. N7 . . . . . 2C **48**
Eatington Rd. E10 . . . . 1F **39**
Eaton Cl. SW1 . . . . 5C **74**
Eaton Dr. SW9 . . . . . 2D **105**
Eaton Ga. SW1 . . . . . . 5C **74**
Eaton Ho. E14 . . . . 1B **80**
(off Westferry Cir.)
Eaton Mans.
SW11 . . . . 4F **87**
Eaton La.
SW1 . . . . 5E **21** (4D **75**)

Eaton Mans. *SW1* 5C **74**
        (off Bourne St.)
Eaton M. Nth.
    SW1 . . . . . . 5C **20** (5C **74**)
Eaton M. Sth. SW1 . . . . 5C **74**
Eaton M. W. SW1 . . . . . . 5C **74**
Eaton Pl.
    SW1 . . . . . . 5C **20** (5C **74**)
Eaton Row SW1 . . . . . . 4D **75**
Eaton Sq.
    SW1 . . . . . . 5C **20** (5C **74**)
Eaton Ter. E3 . . . . 2A **66**
    SW1 . . . . 5C **74**
Eaton Ter. M. *SW1* 5C **74**
        (off Eaton Ter.)
Eatonville Rd.
    SW17 . . . . 2B **116**
Eatonville Vs.
    SW17 . . . . 2B **116**
Ebbett Ct. W3 . . . . 4A **56**
Ebbisham Dr. SW8 . . . . . 2B **90**
Ebbsfleet Rd. NW2 . . . . 2A **44**
Ebdon Way SE3 . . . . . . 1D **111**
Ebenezer Ho. SE11 . . . . 5D **77**
Ebenezer Mussel Ho.
    E2 . . . . 1E **65**
        (off Patriot Sq.)
Ebenezer St.
    N1 . . . . . . 1B **10** (2F **63**)
Ebley Cl. SE15 . . . . 2B **92**
Ebner St. SW18 . . . . . . 3D **101**
Ebony Ho. *E2* 2C **64**
        (off Buckfast St.)
Ebor Cotts. SW15 . . . . . 3A **112**
Ebor St. E1 . . . . . 3F **11** (3B **64**)
Ebsworth St. SE23 . . . . 5F **107**
Eburne Rd. N7 . . . . 5A **34**
Ebury Bri. SW1 . . . . 1D **89**
Ebury Bri. Est. SW1 . . . . 1D **89**
Ebury Bri. Rd. SW1 . . . . 1C **88**
Ebury M. SE27 . . . . 3D **119**
    SW1 . . . . 5D **75**
Ebury M. E. SW1 . . . . . . 4D **75**
Ebury Sq. SW1 . . . . 5C **74**
Ebury St. SW1 . . . . 5C **74**
Ecclesbourne Rd. N1 . . . 4E **49**
Eccles Rd. SW11 . . . . . . 2B **102**
Eccleston Bri. SW1 . . . . 5D **75**
Eccleston Ho. SW2 . . . . 4C **104**
Eccleston M.
    SW1 . . . . . . 5C **20** (4C **74**)
Eccleston Pl. SW1 . . . . . 5D **75**
Eccleston Sq. SW1 . . . . 5D **75**
Eccleston Sq. M.
    SW1 . . . . 5D **75**
Eccleston St. SW1 . . . . . 4D **75**
Eckford St. N1 . . . . 1C **62**
Eckington Ho. *N15* 1F **35**
        (off Fladbury Rd.)
Eckstein Rd. SW11 . . . . 2A **102**
Eclipse Rd. E13 . . . . . . 4D **69**
Ecology Cen. and Arts Pavilion
    . . . . 2A **66**
Ector Rd. SE6 . . . . 2A **124**
Edans Ct. W12 . . . . 3B **70**
Edbrooke Rd. W9 . . . . . . 3C **58**
Eddisbury Ho. SE26 . . . 3C **120**
Eddiscombe Rd.
    SW6 . . . . 5B **86**

Eddystone Rd. SE4 . . . . 3A **108**
Eddystone Twr. SE8 . . . . 1A **94**
Edenbridge Cl. *SE16* . . . 1D **93**
        (off Masters Dr.)
Edenbridge Rd. E9 . . . . . 4F **51**
Eden Cl. NW3 . . . . 4C **30**
    W8 . . . . 4C **72**
Edencourt Rd.
    SW16 . . . . 5D **117**
Eden Gro. E17 . . . . 1D **39**
    N7 . . . . 2B **48**
Edenham Way W10 . . . . 3B **58**
Eden Ho. *NW8* 3A **60**
        (off Church St.)
Edenhurst Av. SW6 . . . . 1B **100**
Eden Lodge NW6 . . . . . . 4F **43**
Eden M. SW17 . . . . 3E **115**
Eden Rd. E17 . . . . 1D **39**
    SE27 . . . . 4D **119**
Edensor Gdns. W4 . . . . . 3A **84**
Edensor Rd. W4 . . . . 3A **84**
Edenvale St. SW6 . . . . . 5E **87**
Eden Way E3 . . . . 5B **52**
Edgar Ho. *E9* 2A **52**
        (off Homerton Rd.)
    E11 . . . . 2C **40**
    SW8 . . . . 3A **90**
        (off Wyvil Rd.)
Edgar Kail Way
    SE22 . . . . 2A **106**
Edgarley Ter. SW6 . . . . . 4A **86**
Edgar Rd. E3 . . . . 2D **67**
Edgar Wallace Cl.
    SE15 . . . . 3B **92**
Edgcott Ho. *W10* 4E **57**
        (off Sutton Way)
Edge Bus. Cen., The
    NW2 . . . . 4D **29**
Edgecombe Ho. SE5 . . . 5A **92**
    SW19 . . . . 1A **114**
Edgecot Gro. N15 . . . . . 1A **36**
Edgehill Ho. SW9 . . . . . 5D **91**
Edgeley La. SW4 . . . . . . 1F **103**
Edgeley Rd. SW4 . . . . . 1F **103**
Edgel St. SW18 . . . . . . 2D **101**
Edgepoint Cl. SE27 . . . . 5D **119**
Edge St. W8 . . . . 2C **72**
Edgeworth Ho. *NW8* . . . 5E **45**
        (off Boundary Rd.)
Edgeworth Rd. SE9 . . . . 2E **111**
Edgson Ho. *SW1* 1D **89**
        (off Ebury Bri. Rd.)
Edgware Rd. NW2 . . . . . 3D **29**
    W2 . . . . 3A **12** (3F **59**)
Edinburgh Cl. E2 . . . . . . 1E **65**
Edinburgh Ct. *SE16* 2F **79**
        (off Rotherhithe St.)
Edinburgh Ga. SW1 . . . . 3B **74**
Edinburgh Ho. *W9* 2D **59**
        (off Maida Va.)
Edinburgh Rd. E13 . . . . 1D **69**
    E17 . . . . 1C **38**
        (not continuous)
Edington NW5 . . . . 3C **46**
Edison Bldg. E14 . . . . . . 3C **80**
Edison Ct. SE10 . . . . . . 4B **82**
Edison Ho. *SE1* 5F **77**
        (off Balfour St.)
Edison Rd. N8 . . . . 1F **33**

Edis St. NW1 . . . . 5C **46**
Editha Mans. *SW10* 2E **87**
        (off Edith Gro.)
Edith Brinson Ho.
    E14 . . . . 5F **67**
        (off Oban St.)
Edith Cavell Cl. N19. . . . 2A **34**
Edith Gro. SW10 . . . . . . 2E **87**
Edith Ho. *W6* 1E **85**
        (off Queen Caroline St.)
Edithna St. SW9 . . . . . . 1A **104**
Edith Neville Cotts.
    NW1 . . . . 1B **6**
        (off Drummond Cres.)
Edith Ramsay Ho. *E1* . . . 4A **66**
        (off Duckett St.)
Edith Rd. E6 . . . . 4F **55**
    E15 . . . . 2F **53**
    SW19 . . . . 5D **115**
    W14 . . . . 5A **72**
Edith Row SW6 . . . . 4D **87**
Edith St. E2 . . . . 1C **64**
Edith Summerskill Ho.
    SW6 . . . . 3B **86**
        (off Clem Attlee Est.)
Edith Ter. SW10 . . . . . . 3E **87**
Edith Vs. W14 . . . . 5B **72**
Edith Yd. SW10 . . . . . . 3E **87**
Edmeston Cl. E9 . . . . . . 3A **52**
Edmond Ct. SE14 . . . . . 4E **93**
Edmonton Ct. *SE16* 4E **79**
        (off Canada Est.)
Edmund Halley Way
    SE10 . . . . 3A **82**
Edmund Ho. SE17 . . . . . 2D **91**
Edmundsbury Ct. Est.
    SW9 . . . . 2B **104**
Edmund St. SE5 . . . . . . 3F **91**
Ednam Ho. *SE15* 2C **92**
        (off Haymerle Rd.)
Edna St. SW11 . . . . 4A **88**
Edred Ho. *E9* 1A **52**
        (off Lindisfarne Way)
Edrich Ho. SW4 . . . . 4A **90**
Edric Ho. *SW1* 5F **75**
        (off Page St.)
Edric Rd. SE14 . . . . 3F **93**
Edward VII Mans.
    NW10 . . . . 2F **57**
        (off Chamberlayne Rd.)
Edward Bond Ho. *WC1*. . . 2E **7**
        (off Cromer St.)
Edward Cl. NW2 . . . . . . 1F **43**
Edward Cl. E16 . . . . 4C **68**
Edward Dodd Ct. *N1*. . . 1C **10**
        (off Haberdasher St.)
Edward Edward's Ho.
    SE1 . . . . 2D **25**
Edwardes Pl. W8 . . . . . . 4B **72**
Edwardes Sq. W8 . . . . . 4B **72**
Edward Ho. *SE11* 1B **90**
        (off Newburn St.)
    W2. . . . . 3F **59**
        (off Hall Pl.)
Edward Kennedy Ho.
    W10 . . . . 3A **58**
        (off Wornington Rd.)
Edward Mann Cl. *E1*. . . . 5F **65**
        (off Caroline St.)

Edward M.
NW1. . . . . 1E **5** (2D **61**)
Edward Pl. SE8. . . . . 2B **94**
Edward Rd. E17. . . . . . . 1F **37**
Edward Robinson Ho.
SE14 . . . . 3F **93**
(off Reaston St.)
Edward's Cotts. N1. . . . 3D **49**
Edward's La. N16. . . . . . 4A **36**
Edwards M. N1. . . . . 4C **48**
W1. . . . . 3B **12** (5C **60**)
Edward Sq. N1 . . . . 5B **48**
SE16. . . . . 2A **80**
Edward St. E16. . . . . . . 3C **68**
(not continuous)
SE8. . . . . 2B **94**
SE14. . . . . 3A **94**
Edward Temme Av.
E15. . . . . 4B **54**
Edward Tyler Rd.
SE12 . . . . 2E **125**
Edwina Gdns. IG4: Ilf . . 1F **41**
Edwin Ho. SE15. . . . . . . 3C **92**
Edwin's Mead E9 . . . . . 1A **52**
Edwin St. E1. . . . . 3E **65**
E16. . . . . 4C **68**
Edwyn Ho. *SW18*. 4D **101**
(off Neville Gill Cl.)
Eel Brook Cl. SW6. . . . . 4D **87**
Effie Pl. SW6. . . . . 3C **86**
Effie Rd. SW6. . . . . 3C **86**
Effingham Rd. SE12. . . 3A **110**
Effort St. SW17. . . . . . . 5A **116**
Effra Ct. *SW2* 3B **104**
(off Brixton Hill)
Effra Pde. SW2. . . . . . . 3C **104**
Effra Rd. SW2. . . . . 2C **104**
SW19. . . . . 5D **115**
Effra Rd. Retail Pk.
SW2. . . . . 3C **104**
Egbert St. NW1. . . . . . . 5C **46**
Egbury Ho. *SW15*. 4B **98**
(off Tangley Gro.)
Egeremont Rd. SE13 . . 5D **95**
Egerton Ct. E11. . . . . . . 2F **39**
Egerton Cres. SW3. . . . 5A **74**
Egerton Dr. SE10. . . . . . 4D **95**
Egerton Gdns. NW10 . . 5E **43**
SW3. . . . . 5A **74**
Egerton Gdns. M.
SW3. . . . . 4A **74**
Egerton Pl. SW3. . . . . . 4A **74**
Egerton Rd. N16. . . . . . 2B **36**
Egerton Ter. SW3 . . . . . 4A **74**
Egham Cl. SW19. . . . . . 2A **114**
Egham Rd. E13. . . . . . . 4D **69**
Eglantine Rd.
SW18. . . . . 3E **101**
Eglington Ct. SE17 . . . . 2E **91**
Egliston M. SW15. . . . . . 1E **99**
Egliston Rd. SW15. . . . . 1E **99**
Eglon M. NW1. . . . . 4B **46**
Egmont St. SE14. . . . . . 3F **93**
Egremont Ho. *SE13*. . . 5D **95**
(off Russett Way)
Egremont Rd. SE27. . . . 3C **118**
Egret Ho. *SE16* 5F **79**
(off Tawny Way)
Eider Cl. E7. . . . . 2B **54**

Eider Ct. *SE8* 2B **94**
(off Pilot Cl.)
Eisenhower Dr. E6 . . . . 4F **69**
Elaine Gro. NW5 . . . . . . 2C **46**
Elam Cl. SE5. . . . . 5D **91**
Elam St. SE5. . . . . 5D **91**
Elan Ct. E1. . . . . 4D **65**
Eland Ho. *SW1*. 5F **21**
(off Bressenden Pl.)
Eland Rd. SW11. . . . . . 1B **102**
Elba Pl. SE17. . . . . 5E **77**
Elbe St. SW6 . . . . 5E **87**
Elborough St. SW18. . . 1C **114**
Elbourne Ct. *SE16* 4F **79**
(off Worgan St.)
Elbourn Ho. *SW3* 5C **68**
(off Cale St.)
Elbury Dr. E16 . . . . 5C **68**
Elcho St. SW11. . . . . . . 3A **88**
Elcot Av. SE15 . . . . 3D **93**
Elden Ho. *SW3* 5A **74**
(off Sloane Av.)
Elder Av. N8. . . . . 1A **34**
Elderberry Gro.
SE27. . . . . 4E **119**
Elderfield Ho. E14 . . . . 1C **80**
Elderfield Pl.
SW17 . . . . 4D **117**
Elderfield Rd. E5 . . . . . 1F **51**
Elderflower Way
E15. . . . . 4A **54**
Elder Gdns. SE27 . . . . 5E **119**
Elder Rd. SE27. . . . . . . 4E **119**
Elder St. E1 . . . . 5F **11** (3B **64**)
(not continuous)
Elderton Rd. SE26 . . . . 4A **122**
Elder Wlk. *N1*. 5D **49**
(off Popham St.)
Elderwood Pl. SE27 . . . 5E **119**
Eldon Ct. NW6 . . . . 5C **44**
Eldon Gro. NW3 . . . . . . 2F **45**
Eldon Rd. W8. . . . . 4D **73**
Eldon St. EC2. . . . 1C **18** (4F **63**)
Eldridge Ct. SE16 . . . . . 4C **78**
Eleanor Cl. SE16 . . . . . 3F **79**
Eleanor Ct. *E2* 5C **50**
(off Whiston Rd.)
Eleanor Gro. SW13 . . . 1A **98**
Eleanor Ho. *W6* 1E **85**
(off Queen Caroline St.)
Eleanor Rathbone Ho.
N6 . . . . 2F **33**
(off Avenue Rd.)
Eleanor Rd. E8. . . . . . . 3D **51**
E15. . . . . 3B **54**
Eleanor St. E3 . . . . 2C **66**
Electra Bus. Pk. E16. . . 4F **67**
Electric Av. SW9. . . . . . 2C **104**
Electric La. SW9 . . . . . . 2C **104**
(not continuous)
Elektron Ho. E14. . . . . . 1F **81**
ELEPHANT & CASTLE
. . . . 4D **77**
Elephant & Castle
SE1. . . . . 5D **77**
Elephant & Castle Superbowl
. . . . 5E **77**
(off Elephant & Castle)
Elephant La. SE16 . . . . 3E **79**

Elephant Rd. SE17. . . . . 5E **77**
Elfindale Rd. SE24. . . . 3E **105**
Elford Cl. SE3 . . . . 2D **111**
Elford M. SW4. . . . . . . 3E **103**
Elfort Rd. N5 . . . . 1C **48**
Elfrida Cres. SE6. . . . . 4C **122**
Elf Row E1 . . . . 1E **79**
Elgar Av. NW10 . . . . . . 3A **42**
(not continuous)
Elgar Cl. E13. . . . . 1E **69**
SE8. . . . . 3C **94**
Elgar Ct. *W14*. 4A **72**
(off Blythe Rd.)
Elgar Ho. *NW6*. 4E **45**
(off Fairfax Rd.)
SW1 . . . . 1D **89**
(off Churchill Gdns.)
Elgar St. SE16 . . . . 4A **80**
Elgin Av. W9. . . . . 3B **58**
W12 . . . . 4D **71**
Elgin Cl. W12. . . . . 3D **71**
Elgin Ct. W9. . . . . 3D **59**
Elgin Cres. W11. . . . . . 1A **72**
Elgin Est. *W9* 3C **58**
(off Elgin Av.)
Elgin Ho. *E14*. 5D **67**
(off Ricardo St.)
Elgin Mans. W9. . . . . . . 2D **59**
Elgin M. W11 . . . . 5A **58**
Elgin M. Nth. W9 . . . . . . 2D **59**
Elgin M. Sth. W9. . . . . . 2D **59**
Elgood Cl. W11 . . . . 1A **72**
Elgood Ho. *NW8*. 1F **59**
(off Wellington Rd.)
Elham Ho. E5. . . . . 2D **51**
Elia M. N1. . . . . 1D **9** (1D **63**)
Elias Pl. SW8. . . . . 2C **90**
Elia St. N1. . . . . 1D **9** (1D **63**)
Elim Est.
SE1 . . . . 5D **27** (4A **78**)
Elim St. SE1 . . . 5C **26** (4F **77**)
(not continuous)
Elim Way E13. . . . . 2B **68**
Eliot Bank SE23 . . . . . 2D **121**
Eliot Cotts. SE3 . . . . . . 5A **96**
Eliot Ct. SW18 . . . . . . 4D **101**
Eliot Gdns. SW15. . . . . 2C **98**
Eliot Hill SE13 . . . . 5E **95**
Eliot M. NW8. . . . . 1E **59**
Eliot Pk. SE13 . . . . 5E **95**
Eliot Pl. SE3. . . . . 5A **96**
Eliot Va. SE3. . . . . 5F **95**
Elizabeth Av. N1. . . . . . 5E **49**
Elizabeth Barnes Ct.
SW6 . . . . 5D **87**
(off Marinefield Rd.)
Elizabeth Blount Ct.
E14 . . . . 5A **66**
(off Carr St.)
Elizabeth Bri. SW1 . . . . 5D **75**
Elizabeth Cl. E14. . . . . . 5D **67**
W9 . . . . 3E **59**
Elizabeth Ct. *NW1* 3A **60**
(off Palgrave Gdns.)
SW1. . . . . 5C **22**
SW10 . . . . 2F **87**
(off Milman's St.)
Elizabeth Fry M. E8 . . . 4D **51**
Elizabeth Gdns. W3 . . . 2B **70**

Elizabeth Ho. *SE11* 5C **76**
   (off Reedworth St.)
W6 . . . . 1E **85**
   (off Queen Caroline St.)
Elizabeth Ind. Est.
  SE14 . . . . 2F **93**
Elizabeth M. NW3 . . . . 3A **46**
Elizabeth Newcomen Ho.
  SE1 . . . . 3B **26**
   (off Newcomen St.)
Elizabeth Rd. E6 . . . . 5F **55**
N15 . . . . 1A **36**
Elizabeth Sq. *SE16* 1A **80**
   (off Sovereign Cres.)
Elizabeth St. SW1 . . . . 5C **74**
Elkington Point
  SE11 . . . . 5C **76**
   (off Lollard St.)
Elkington Rd. E13 . . . . 3D **69**
Elkstone Rd. W10. . . . . 4B **58**
Ellaline Rd. W6 . . . . 2F **85**
Ella M. NW3 . . . . 1B **46**
Elland Rd. *E14* 5B **66**
   (off Copenhagen Pl.)
Elland St. SE15 . . . . 2E **107**
Ella Rd. N8 . . . . 2A **34**
Ellenborough Ho.
  W12 . . . . 1D **71**
   (off White City Est.)
Ellenborough Pl.
  SW15 . . . . 2C **98**
Ellen St. E1 . . . . 5C **64**
Ellen Terry Ct. *NW1* 4D **47**
   (off Farrier St.)
Ellen Wilkinson Ho.
  E2 . . . . 2F **65**
   (off Usk St.)
  SW6 . . . . 3B **86**
   (off Clem Attlee Ct.)
Ellerby St. SW6 . . . . 4F **85**
Ellerdale Cl. NW3 . . . . 1E **45**
Ellerdale Rd. NW3 . . . . . . 2E **45**
Ellerdale St. SE13 . . . . . . 2D **109**
Ellerslie Gdns.
  NW10 . . . . 5C **42**
Ellerslie Rd. W12. . . . . . . 2D **71**
Ellerslie Sq. Ind. Est.
  SW2 . . . . 3A **104**
Ellerton Rd. SW13 . . . . . . 4C **84**
SW18 . . . . 1F **115**
Ellery Ho. SE17 . . . . 5F **77**
Ellery St. SE15 . . . . 5D **93**
Ellesmere Cl. E11 . . . . 1B **40**
Ellesmere Ct. SE12 . . . . . 1C **124**
  W4 . . . . 1A **84**
Ellesmere Rd. E3 . . . . 1A **66**
  NW10 . . . . 2C **42**
  W4 . . . . 2A **84**
Ellesmere St. E14 . . . . 5D **67**
Ellingfort Rd. E8 . . . . 4D **51**
Ellingham Rd. E15 . . . . . . 1F **53**
  W12 . . . . 3C **70**
Ellington Ho.
  SE1 . . . . 5A **26** (4E **77**)
Ellington St. N7 . . . . 3C **48**
Elliot Cl. E15 . . . . 4A **54**
Elliot Ho. *W1* 4A **60**
   (off Cato St.)
Elliot Rd. NW4 . . . . 1D **29**

Elliott Rd. SW9 . . . . 4D **91**
  W4 . . . . 5A **70**
Elliott's Pl. N1 . . . . 5D **49**
Elliott Sq. NW3 . . . . 4A **46**
Elliotts Row SE11 . . . . 5D **77**
Ellis Cl. NW10 . . . . 3D **43**
Elliscombe Mt. SE7 . . . . . 2E **97**
Elliscombe Rd. SE7 . . . . . 2E **97**
Ellisfield Dr. SW15 . . . . . . 5C **98**
Ellis Franklin Ct.
  NW8 . . . . 1E **59**
   (off Abbey Rd.)
Ellis Ho. *SE17*. 1F **91**
   (off Brandon St.)
Ellison Ho. SE13 . . . . 5D **95**
   (off Lewisham Rd.)
Ellison Rd. SW13. . . . . . . 5B **84**
Ellis St. SW1 . . . . 5C **74**
Ellora Rd. SW16. . . . . 5F **117**
Ellsworth St. E2 . . . . 2D **65**
Ellwood Ct. *W9* 3D **59**
   (off Clearwell Dr.)
Elm Bank Gdns.
  SW13 . . . . 5A **84**
Elmbourne Rd.
  SW17 . . . . 3D **117**
Elmbridge Wlk. E8. . . . . . . 4C **50**
Elm Cl. E11 . . . . 1D **41**
  N19 . . . . 4E **33**
  NW4 . . . . 1F **29**
Elm Ct. EC4 . . . . 3B **16**
  SE13 . . . . 1F **109**
  W9 . . . . 4C **58**
   (off Admiral Wlk.)
Elmcourt Rd. SE27 . . . . . . 2D **119**
Elmcroft N6 . . . . 2E **33**
Elmcroft Av. NW11 . . . . . . 2B **30**
Elmcroft Cres. NW11 . . . . 2A **30**
Elmcroft St. E5 . . . . 1E **51**
Elmer Ho. *NW8* 4A **60**
   (off Penfold St.)
Elmer Rd. SE6 . . . . 5E **109**
Elmfield Av. N8 . . . . 1A **34**
Elmfield Ho. *NW8* 1D **59**
   (off Carlton Hill)
  W9 . . . . 3C **58**
   (off Goldney Rd.)
Elmfield Rd. E17 . . . . 1F **37**
  SW17 . . . . 2C **116**
Elmfield Way W9. . . . . 4C **58**
Elm Friars Wlk. NW1 . . . . 4F **47**
Elm Grn. W3 . . . . 5A **56**
Elmgreen Cl. E15 . . . . 5A **54**
Elm Gro. N8 . . . . 1A **34**
  NW2 . . . . 1F **43**
  SE15 . . . . 5B **92**
Elm Gro. Rd. SW13 . . . . . 4C **84**
Elm Hall Gdns. E11 . . . . . 1D **41**
  (not continuous)
Elm Ho. *E14* 3E **81**
   (off E. Ferry Rd.)
  W10 . . . . 3A **58**
   (off Briar Wlk.)
Elmhurst Mans.
  SW4 . . . . 1F **103**
Elmhurst Rd. E7. . . . . 4D **55**
  SE9 . . . . 2F **125**
Elmhurst St. SW4 . . . . . . 1F **103**
Elmington Est. SE5. . . . . . 3F **91**

Elmington Rd. SE5 . . . . . . 3F **91**
Elmira St. SE13 . . . . 1D **109**
Elm La. SE6 . . . . 2B **122**
Elm Lodge SW6 . . . . 4E **85**
Elmore Ho. SW9 . . . . 5D **91**
Elmore Rd. E11 . . . . 5E **39**
Elmore St. N1. . . . . 4E **49**
Elm Pk. SW2 . . . . 4B **104**
Elm Pk. Av. N15. . . . . 1B **36**
Elm Pk. Chambers
  SW10 . . . . 1F **87**
   (off Fulham Rd.)
Elm Pk. Gdns. NW4 . . . . . 1F **29**
  SW10 . . . . 1F **87**
Elm Pk. Ho. SW10 . . . . . . 1F **87**
Elm Pk. La. SW3 . . . . 1F **87**
Elm Pk. Mans. *SW10*. 2E **87**
   (off Park Wlk.)
Elm Pk. Rd. E10. . . . . 3A **38**
  SW3 . . . . 2F **87**
Elm Pl. SW7 . . . . 1F **87**
Elm Quay Ct. SW8 . . . . . . 2F **89**
Elm Rd. E7 . . . . 3B **54**
  E11 . . . . 4F **39**
  E17 . . . . 1E **39**
Elm Row NW3 . . . . 5E **31**
Elms, The E12 . . . . 3F **55**
  SW13 . . . . 1B **98**
Elms Av. NW4 . . . . 1F **29**
Elmscott Rd.
  BR1: Brom 5A **124**
Elms Cres. SW4 . . . . 4E **103**
Elmshaw Rd. SW15 . . . . . 3C **98**
Elmslie Point *E3*. 4B **66**
   (off Leopold St.)
Elms M. W2 . . . . 1F **73**
Elms Rd. SW4 . . . . 3E **103**
ELMSTEAD. 5F **125**
Elmstone Rd. SW6. . . . . . 4C **86**
Elm St. WC1 . . . . . . 4A **8** (3B **62**)
Elm Ter. NW2 . . . . 5C **30**
  NW3 . . . . 1A **46**
Elmton Ct. *NW8* 3F **59**
   (off Cunningham Pl.)
Elmton Way E5. . . . . 5C **36**
Elm Tree Cl. NW8. . . . . . . 2F **59**
Elm Tree Ct. NW8 . . . . . . 2F **59**
   (off Elm Tree Rd.)
  SE7 . . . . 2E **97**
Elm Tree Rd. NW8 . . . . . . 2F **59**
Elm Wlk. NW3 . . . . 4C **30**
Elm Way NW10 . . . . 1A **42**
Elmwood Ct. *E10*. 3C **38**
   (off Goldsmith Rd.)
  SW11 . . . . 4D **89**
Elmwood Ho. *NW10*. 1D **57**
   (off All Souls Av.)
Elmwood Rd. SE24. . . . . . 3F **105**
Elmworth Gro. SE21 . . . . 2F **119**
Elnathan M. W9. . . . . 3D **59**
Elphinstone Ct.
  SW16 . . . . 5A **118**
Elphinstone St. N5. . . . . . 1D **49**
Elrington Rd. E8. . . . . 3C **50**
Elsa Cotts. *E14*. 4A **66**
   (off Halley St.)
Elsa St. E1 . . . . 4A **66**
Elsdale St. E9. . . . . 3E **51**
Elsden M. E2 . . . . 1E **65**

Elsenham St. SW18 . . . 1B 114
Elsham Rd. E11 . . . . 5A 40
  W14 . . . . 3A 72
Elsham Ter. W14 . . . . . 4A 72
  (off Elsham Rd.)
Elsie La. Ct. W2 . . . . . . 4C 58
  (off Westbourne Pk. Vs.)
Elsiemaud Rd. SE4 . . 3B 108
Elsie Rd. SE22 . . . . . . 2B 106
Elsinore Gdns. NW2 . . 5A 30
Elsinore Ho. N1 . . . . . . 5C 48
  (off Denmark Gro.)
  SE5 . . . . 5E 91
  (off Denmark Rd.)
  W6 . . . . 1F 85
  (off Fulham Pal. Rd.)
Elsinore Rd. SE23 . . . 1A 122
Elsley Rd. SW11 . . . . . 1B 102
Elspeth Rd. SW11 . . . . 2B 102
Elstead Ho. SW2 . . . . . 5B 104
  (off Redlands Way)
Elsted St. SE17 . . . . 5F 77
Elstow Grange NW6 . . . 4F 43
Elswick Rd. SE13 . . . . . 5D 95
Elswick St. SW6 . . . . . . 5E 87
Elsworthy Rd. NW3 . . . 4B 46
  (off Primrose Hill Rd.)
Elsworthy Ri. NW3 . . . . 4A 46
Elsworthy Rd. NW3 . . . 5A 46
Elsworthy Ter. NW3 . . . 4A 46
Elsynge Rd. SW18 . . . . 3F 101
ELTHAM 5F 111
Eltham Grn. SE9 . . . . . 3F 111
Eltham Grn. Rd.
  SE9 . . . . 2E 111
Eltham Hill SE9 . . . . . . 3F 111
Eltham Pal. Rd.
  SE9 . . . . 4E 111
Eltham Rd. SE9 . . . . . . 3B 110
  SE12 . . . . 3B 110
Elthiron Rd. SW6 . . . . . 4C 86
Elthorne Rd. N19 . . . . . 4F 33
  NW9 . . . . 2A 28
Elthorne Way NW9 . . . . 1A 28
Elthruda Rd. SE13 . . . . 4F 109
Elton Ho. E3 . . . . 5B 52
  (off Candy St.)
Elton Pl. N16 . . . . 2A 50
Eltringham St.
  SW18 . . . . 2E 101
Eluna Apartments E1 . . 1D 79
  (off Wapping La.)
Elvaston M. SW7 . . . . . 4E 73
Elvaston Pl. SW7 . . . . . 4E 73
Elveden Ho. SE24 . . . 3D 105
Elver Gdns. E2 . . . . . . 2C 64
Elverson Rd. SE8 . . . . 5D 95
Elverton St. SW1 . . . . . 5F 75
Elvino Rd. SE26 . . . . . 5A 122
Elvis Rd. NW2 . . . . 3E 43
Elwin St. E2 . . . . 2C 64
Elwood St. N5 . . . . 5D 35
Elworth Ho. SW8 . . . . . 3B 90
  (off Oval Pl.)
Elwyn Gdns. SE12 . . . 5C 110
Ely Cotts. SW8 . . . . 3B 90
Ely Ct. EC1 . . . . 1C 16
  NW6 . . . . 1C 58
  (off Chichester Rd.)

Ely Ho. SE15 . . . . 3C 92
  (off Friary Est.)
Elyne Rd. N4 . . . . 1C 34
Ely Pl. EC1 . . . . . 1C 16 (4C 62)
Ely Rd. E10 . . . . 1E 39
Elysium Pl. SW6 . . . . . . 5B 86
  (off Elysium St.)
Elysium St. SW6 . . . . . . 5B 86
Elystan Pl. SW3 . . . . . . 1A 88
Elystan St. SW3 . . . . . . 5A 74
Elystan Wlk. N1 . . . . . . 5C 48
Emanuel Ho. SW1 . . . . 4F 75
Embankment SW15 . . . . 5F 85
  (not continuous)
Embankment Gdns.
  SW3 . . . . 2B 88
Embankment Pl.
  WC2 . . . . 1E 23 (2A 76)
  (off Wellington St.)
Embassy Ct. NW8 . . . . . 1F 59
  (off Wellington Rd.)
Embassy Ho. NW6 . . . . 4D 45
Embassy Theatre 4F 45
  (off College Cres.)
Emba St. SE16 . . . . 3C 78
Emberton SE5 . . . . 2A 92
  (off Albany Rd.)
Emberton Ct. EC1 . . . . . 2D 9
  (off Tompion St.)
Embleton Rd. SE13 . . . 2D 109
Emden St. SW6 . . . . . . 4D 87
Emerald Cl. E16 . . . . . . 5F 69
Emerald Rd. NW10 . . . . 5A 42
  (not continuous)
Emerald St.
  WC1 . . . . 5F 7 (4B 62)
Emerson St.
  SE1 . . . . 1F 25 (2E 77)
Emery Hill St. SW1 . . . . 4E 75
Emery St.
  SE1 . . . . 5C 24 (4C 76)
Emery Theatre 5D 67
  (off Annabel Cl.)
Emily Ho. W10 . . . . 3A 58
  (off Kensal Rd.)
Emily Pl. N7 . . . . 1C 48
Emily St. E16 . . . . 5B 68
  (off Jude St.)
Emirates Stadium 1C 48
Emlyn Gdns. W12 . . . . . 3A 70
Emlyn Rd. W12 . . . . 3A 70
Emmanuel Ct. E10 . . . . 2D 39
Emmanuel Ho. SE11 . . . 5C 76
Emmanuel Rd.
  SW12 . . . . 1E 117
Emma Rd. E13 . . . . 1B 68
Emma St. E2 . . . . 1D 65
Emminster NW6 . . . . . . 5D 45
  (off Abbey Rd.)
Emmott Cl. E1 . . . . 3A 66
  NW11 . . . . 1E 31
Emperor's Ga. SW7 . . . 4E 73
Empingham Ho. SE8 . . . 5F 79
  (off Chilton Ro.)
Empire Cinema
  Leicester Sq. 4C 14
  (off Leicester Sq.)
Empire Ho. SW7 . . . . . . 4A 74
  (off Thurloe Pl.)
Empire Sq. N7 . . . . 5A 34

Empire Wharf E3 . . . . . . 5A 52
  (off Old Ford Rd.)
Empire Wharf Rd.
  E14 . . . . 5F 81
Empress App. SW6 . . . 1C 86
Empress Av. E12 . . . . . 4E 41
Empress M. SE5 . . . . . . 5E 91
Empress Pl. SW6 . . . . . 1C 86
Empress State Bldg.
  SW6 . . . . 1C 86
Empress St. SE17 . . . . . 2E 91
Empson St. E3 . . . . 3D 67
Emsworth St. SW16 . . 3A 118
Emsworth St. SW2 . . . 2B 118
Emu Rd. SW8 . . . . 5D 89
Enbrook St. W10 . . . . . 2A 58
Enclave, The SW13 . . . 5B 84
Endeavour Way
  SW19 . . . . 4D 115
Endell St.
  WC2 . . . . 2D 15 (5A 62)
Enderby St. SE10 . . . . . 1F 95
Endlesham Rd.
  SW12 . . . . 5C 102
Endsleigh Ct. WC1 . . . . 3C 6
Endsleigh Gdns.
  WC1 . . . . 3B 6 (3F 61)
Endsleigh Pl.
  WC1 . . . . 3C 6 (3F 61)
Endsleigh St.
  WC1 . . . . 3C 6 (3F 61)
Endwell Rd. SE4 . . . . . 5A 94
Endymion Rd. N4 . . . . . 2C 34
  SW2 . . . . 4B 104
Energen St. NW10 . . . . 3A 42
Energize Fitness Club
  . . . . 1A 86
  (in Hammersmith &
    West London College)
Enfield Cloisters N1 . . . 1D 11
  (off Fanshaw St.)
Enfield Ho. SW9 . . . . . . 5A 90
  (off Stockwell Rd.)
Enfield Rd. N1 . . . . 4A 50
Engadine St. SW18 . . . 1B 114
Engate St. SE13 . . . . . . 2E 109
Engine Ct. SW1 . . . . . . 2A 22
  (off Ambassador's Ct.)
England's La. NW3 . . . . 3B 46
Englefield NW1 . . . . 2F 5
  (off Clarence Gdns.)
Englefield Rd. N1 . . . . . 4F 49
Engleheart Rd. SE6 . . . 5D 109
Englewood Rd.
  SW12 . . . . 4D 103
English Grounds
  SE1 . . . . 2D 27 (2A 78)
English St. E3 . . . . 3B 66
Enid St. SE16 . . . . 5F 27 (4B 78)
Enmore Gdns.
  SW14 . . . . 3A 98
Enmore Rd. SW15 . . . . 2E 99
Ennerdale NW1 . . . . . . 1F 5
  (off Varndell St.)
Ennerdale Rd. E11 . . . . 2C 40
  (off Cambridge Rd.)
Ennerdale Dr. NW9 . . . 1A 28
Ennerdale Ho. E3 . . . . . 3B 66

Ennersdale Rd.
SE13 . . . . 3F **109**
Ennis Ho. E14. . . . . . . 5D **67**
(off Vesey Path)
Ennismore Av. W4 . . . . 5B **70**
Ennismore Gdns.
SW7 . . . . 3A **74**
Ennismore Gdns. M.
SW7 . . . . 4A **74**
Ennismore M. SW7 . . . 4A **74**
Ennismore St. SW7 . . . 4A **74**
Ennis Rd. N4 . . . . 3C **34**
Ensbury Ho. SW8 . . . . 3B **90**
(off Carroun Rd.)
Ensign Ho. E14 . . . . . . 2C **80**
(off Admirals Way)
Ensign Ind. Cen. E1 . . 1C **78**
(off Ensign St.)
Ensign St. E1 . . . . 1C **78**
Ensor M. SW7 . . . . . . 1F **87**
Enterprise Bus. Pk.
E14 . . . . 3D **81**
Enterprise Cen., The
BR3: Beck 5A **122**
(off Cricket La.)
Enterprise Ho. E9 . . . . 4E **51**
(off Tudor Gro.)
E14 . . . . 1D **95**
(off St Davids Sq.)
Enterprise Ind. Est.
SE16 . . . . 1E **93**
Enterprise Row N15 . . 1B **36**
Enterprise Way
NW10 . . . . 2B **56**
SW18 . . . . 2C **100**
Enterprize Way SE8 . . 5B **80**
Epcot M. NW10 . . . . . . 2F **57**
Epirus M. SW6 . . . . . . 3C **86**
Epirus Rd. SW6 . . . . . 3B **86**
Epping Cl. E14 . . . . . . 5C **80**
Epping Pl. N1 . . . . 3C **48**
Epple Rd. SW6 . . . . . . 4B **86**
Epsom Rd. E10 . . . . . . 1E **39**
Epworth St.
EC2 . . . . . . 4C **10** (3F **63**)
Equity Sq. E2 . . . . 2B **64**
(off Shacklewell St.)
Erasmus St. SW1 . . . . 5F **75**
Erconwald St. W12 . . . 5B **56**
Eresby Ho. SW7 . . . . . 3A **74**
(off Rutland Ga.)
Eresby Ho. NW6 . . . . . 4C **44**
Erica Ho. SE4 . . . . 1B **108**
Erica St. W12 . . . . 1C **70**
Eric Cl. E7 . . . . 1C **54**
Ericson Cl. SW18 . . . . 3C **100**
Eric Fletcher Ct. N1 . . 4E **49**
(off Essex Rd.)
Eric Liddell Sports Cen.
. . . . 2F **125**
Eric Rd. E7 . . . . 1C **54**
NW10 . . . . 3B **42**
Eric Shipman Ter.
E13 . . . . 3C **68**
(off Balaam St.)
Ericson Ho. SE13 . . . . 2F **109**
(off Blessington Rd.)
Eric St. E3 . . . . 3B **66**
(not continuous)

Eric Wilkins Ho. SE1 . . 1C **92**
(off Old Kent Rd.)
Eridge Rd. W4 . . . . . . 4A **70**
Erlanger Rd. SE14 . . . 4F **93**
Erlich Cotts. E1 . . . . . . 4E **65**
(off Sidney St.)
Ermine Rd. N15 . . . . . 1B **36**
SE13 . . . . 2D **109**
Ernest Av. SE27 . . . . . 4D **119**
Ernest Harriss Ho.
W9 . . . . 3C **58**
(off Elgin Av.)
Ernest St. E1 . . . . 3F **65**
Ernshaw Pl. SW15 . . . 3A **100**
Eros 5B **14** (1F **75**)
Eros Ho. Shops SE6 . . 5D **109**
(off Brownhill Rd.)
Erpingham Rd. SW15 . . 1E **99**
Errington Rd. W9 . . . . 3B **58**
Errol St. EC1 . . 4A **10** (3E **63**)
Erskine Hill NW11 . . . 1C **30**
Erskine Ho. SW1 . . . . 1E **89**
(off Churchill Gdns.)
Erskine M. NW3 . . . . . 4B **46**
(off Erskine Rd.)
Erskine Rd. NW3 . . . . 4B **46**
Esam Way SW16 . . . . 5C **118**
Escott Gdns. SE9 . . . . 4F **125**
Esher Gdns. SW19 . . . 2F **113**
Eskdale NW1 . . . . 1F **5**
(off Stanhope St.)
Esk Rd. E13 . . . . 3C **68**
Esmar Cres. NW9 . . . . 2C **28**
Esmeralda Rd. SE1 . . . 5C **78**
Esmond Ct. W8 . . . . . . 4D **73**
(off Thackeray St.)
Esmond Gdns. W4 . . . 5A **70**
Esmond Rd. NW6 . . . . 5B **44**
W4 . . . . 5A **70**
Esmond St. SW15 . . . 2A **100**
Esparto St. SW18 . . . . 5D **101**
Esporta Health & Fitness
Finchley Rd. 3E **45**
(in O2 Cen.)
Grove Park 4A **84**
Islington 5D **49**
Wandsworth 2D **101**
Wimbledon 5B **114**
Esprit Ct. E1 . . . . 1F **19**
(off Brune St.)
Essendine Mans. W9 . . 2C **58**
Essendine Rd. W9 . . . . 2C **58**
Essex Cl. EC4 . . . . 3B **16**
SW13 . . . . 5B **84**
Essex Gdns. N4 . . . . . 1D **35**
Essex Gro. SE19 . . . . 5F **119**
Essex Ho. E14 . . . . . . 5D **67**
(off Giraud St.)
Essex Mans. E11 . . . . 2F **39**
Essex Pk. M. W3 . . . . . 2A **70**
Essex Rd. E10 . . . . . . 1E **39**
E17 . . . . 1A **38**
N1 . . . . 5D **49**
NW10 . . . . 4A **42**
Essex Rd. Sth. E11 . . . 2F **39**
Essex St. E7 . . . . 2C **54**
WC2 . . . . 3B **16** (5C **62**)
Essex Vs. W8 . . . . 3C **72**
Essex Wharf E5 . . . . . 4F **37**

Essian St. E1 . . . . 4A **66**
Estate Way E10 . . . . . 3B **38**
Estcourt Rd. SW6 . . . . 3B **86**
Estella Ho. W11 . . . . . 1F **71**
(off St Ann's Rd.)
Estelle Rd. NW3 . . . . . 1B **46**
Esterbrooke St.
SW1 . . . . 5F **75**
Este Rd. SW11 . . . . . . 1A **102**
Esther Rd. E11 . . . . . . 2A **40**
Estoria Cl. SW2 . . . . . 5C **104**
Estorick Collection of
Modern Italian Art
. . . . 3D **49**
Estreham Rd. SW16 . . 5F **117**
Eswyn Rd. SW17 . . . . 4B **116**
Etal Ho. N1 . . . . 4D **49**
(off The Sutton Est.)
Etcetera Theatre 4D **47**
(off Camden High St.)
Etchingham Rd. E15 . . 1E **53**
Eternit Wlk. SW6 . . . . 4E **85**
Ethelbert St. SW12 . . . 1D **117**
Ethelburga St. SW11 . . 4A **88**
Ethelburga Twr.
SW11 . . . . 4A **88**
(off Maskelyne Cl.)
Ethelden Rd. W12 . . . . 2D **71**
Ethel Rd. E16 . . . . 5D **69**
Ethel St. SE17 . . . . . . 5E **77**
Etheridge Rd. NW4 . . . 2E **29**
(not continuous)
Etherow St. SE22 . . . . 5C **106**
Etherstone Grn.
SW16 . . . . 4C **118**
Etherstone Rd.
SW16 . . . . 4C **118**
Ethnard Rd. SE15 . . . . 2D **93**
Etloe Ho. E10 . . . . 3C **38**
Etloe Rd. E10 . . . . 4C **38**
Eton Av. NW3 . . . . 4F **45**
SW18 . . . . 5D **101**
Eton Coll. Rd. NW3 . . . 3B **46**
Eton Ct. NW3 . . . . 4F **45**
Eton Garages NW3 . . . 3A **46**
Eton Gro. SE13 . . . . . 1A **110**
Eton Hall NW3 . . . . . . 3B **46**
Eton Ho. N5 . . . . 1D **49**
(off Leigh Rd.)
Eton Mnr. Ct. E10 . . . . 4C **38**
(off Leyton Grange Est.)
Eton Pl. NW3 . . . . 4C **46**
Eton Ri. NW3 . . . . 3B **46**
Eton Rd. NW3 . . . . . . 4B **46**
Eton Vs. NW3 . . . . 3B **46**
Etta St. SE8 . . . . 2A **94**
Ettrick St. E14 . . . . . . 5E **67**
(not continuous)
Eugene Cotter Ho.
SE17 . . . . 5F **77**
(off Tatum St.)
Eugenia Rd. SE16 . . . 5E **79**
Euro Cl. NW10 . . . . . . 3C **42**
Eurolink Bus. Cen.
SW2 . . . . 3C **104**
Europa Pl. EC1 . . 2F **9** (2E **63**)
Eustace Bldg. SW8 . . . 2D **89**
Eustace Ho. SE11 . . . . 5B **76**
(off Old Paradise St.)

Eustace Rd. E6 . . . . 2F 69
  SW6 . . . . 3C 86
Euston Cen.
  NW1 . . . . 3F 5 (3E 61)
  (not continuous)
Euston Gro. NW1 . . . . . . 2B 6
  (off Euston Sq.)
Euston Rd.
  NW1 . . . . 4F 5 (3D 61)
Euston Sq.
  NW1 . . . . 2B 6 (2F 61)
  (not continuous)
Euston Sta. Colonnade
  NW1 . . . . 2B 6 (2F 61)
Euston St.
  NW1 . . . . 2A 6 (2E 61)
Euston Twr.
  NW1 . . . . 3F 5 (3E 61)
EUSTON UNDERPASS
  . . . . 3E 61
Evandale Rd. SW9 . . . . 5C 90
Evangalist Ho. EC4 . . . . 3D 17
  (off Black Friars La.)
Evangelist Rd. NW5 . . . 1D 47
Evans Bus. Cen. NW2 . . 5C 28
Evans Cl. E8 . . . . 3B 50
Evans Ho. SW8 . . . . 3F 89
  (off Wandsworth Rd.)
  W12 . . . . 1D 71
  (off White City Est.)
Evans Rd. SE6 . . . . . . 2A 124
Evanston Gdns.
  IG4: Ilf. 1F 41
Evedon Ho. N1 . . . . 5A 50
  (off New Era Est.)
Evelina Mans. SE5 . . . . 3F 91
Evelina Rd. SE15 . . . . . 1E 107
Evelyn Ct. E8 . . . . 1C 50
  N1 . . . . 1B 10
  (off Evelyn Wlk.,
  not continuous)
Evelyn Denington Ct.
  N1 . . . . 4D 49
  (off The Sutton Est.)
Evelyn Fox Ct. W10 . . . 4E 57
Evelyn Gdns. SW7 . . . . 1E 87
Evelyn Ho. SE14 . . . . . . 4A 94
  (off Loring Rd.)
  W8 . . . . 3D 73
  (off Hornton Pl.)
  W12 . . . . 3B 70
  (off Cobbold Rd.)
Evelyn Lowe Est.
  SE16 . . . . 4C 78
Evelyn Mans. SW1 . . . . 5F 21
  (off Carlisle Pl.)
  W14 . . . . 2A 86
  (off Queen's Club Gdns.)
Evelyn Rd. E16 . . . . . . 2C 82
  SW19 . . . . 5D 115
Evelyn St. SE8 . . . . 5A 80
Evelyn Wlk.
  N1 . . . . 1B 10 (1F 63)
Evelyn Yd.
  W1 . . . . 2B 14 (5F 61)
Evenwood Cl. SW15 . . . 3A 100
Everard Ho. E1 . . . . . . 5C 64
  (off Boyd St.)
Everatt Cl. SW18 . . . . . 4B 100

Everdon Rd. SW13 . . . . 2C 84
Everest Pl. E14 . . . . . . 4E 67
  (off East St.)
Evergreen Sq. E8 . . . . . 4B 50
Everilda St. N1 . . . . . . 5B 48
Evering Rd. E5 . . . . . . 5B 36
  N16 . . . . 5B 36
Everington St. W6 . . . . 2F 85
  (not continuous)
Everitt Rd. NW10 . . . . . 2A 56
Everleigh St. N4 . . . . . 3B 34
Eve Rd. E11 . . . . 1A 54
  N17 . . . . 1A 68
Evershot St.
  NW1 . . . . 1A 6 (1E 61)
Evershot Rd. N4 . . . . . 3B 34
Eversleigh Rd. E6 . . . . 5F 55
  SW11 . . . . 1B 102
Eversley Ho. E2 . . . . . . 2C 64
  (off Gossett St.)
Eversley Pk. SW19. . . . 5D 113
Eversley Rd. SE7 . . . . . 2D 97
Everthorpe Rd.
  SE15 . . . . 1B 106
Everton Bldgs.
  NW1 . . . . 2F 5 (2E 61)
Evesham Ho. E2 . . . . . . 1E 65
  (off Old Ford Rd.)
  NW8 . . . . 5E 45
  (off Abbey Rd.)
  SW1 . . . . 1D 89
  (off Sutherland Row)
Evesham Rd. E15 . . . . . 4B 54
Evesham St. W11 . . . . . 1F 71
Evesham Wlk. SE5 . . . . 5F 91
  SW9 . . . . 5C 90
Evesham Way
  SW11 . . . . 1C 102
Ewald Rd. SW6 . . . . . . 5B 86
Ewart Pl. E3 . . . . 1B 66
Ewart Rd. SE23 . . . . . . 5F 107
Ewe Cl. N7 . . . . 3A 48
Ewelme Rd. SE23 . . . . 1E 121
Ewen Cres. SW2 . . . . . 5C 104
Ewen Henderson Ct.
  SE14 . . . . 3A 94
  (off Goodwood Rd.)
Ewen Ho. N1 . . . . 5B 48
  (off Barnsbury Est.)
Ewer St. SE1 . . . 2F 25 (2E 77)
Ewhurst Cl. E1 . . . . . . 4E 65
Ewhurst Rd. SE4 . . . . 4B 108
Exbury Ho. E9 . . . . 4E 51
  SW1 . . . . 1F 89
  (off Rampayne St.)
Exbury Rd. SE6 . . . . . 2C 122
ExCeL 1D 83
Excel Cl. WC2 . . . . 5C 14
Excel Marina E16 . . . . . 1C 82
Excelsior Gdns. SE13 . . 5E 95
Excelsior Ind. Est.
  SE15 . . . . 2E 93
Excel Waterfront
  E16 . . . . 1D 83
Exchange Arc.
  EC2 . . . . 5E 11 (4A 64)
Exchange Bldg. E1 . . . . 4F 11
  (off Commercial St.)

Exchange Ct.
  WC2 . . . . 5E 15 (1A 76)
Exchange Ho. EC2 . . . . 5E 11
  NW10 . . . . 4D 43
  SW1 . . . . 5F 75
  (off Vauxhall Bri. Rd.)
Exchange Mans.
  NW11 . . . . 2B 30
Exchange Pl.
  EC2 . . . . 5D 11 (4A 64)
Exchange Sq.
  EC2 . . . . 5D 11 (4A 64)
Exchange St.
  EC1 . . . . 2F 9 (2E 63)
Exeter Ct. NW6 . . . . . . 1C 58
  (off Cambridge Rd.)
Exeter Ho. N1 . . . . 5A 50
  (off New Era Est.)
  SE15 . . . . 2C 92
  (off Friary Est.)
  SW15 . . . . 4E 99
  SE15 . . . . 5E 59
  (off Hallfield Est.)
Exeter Mans. NW2 . . . . 3A 44
Exeter M. NW6 . . . . . . 3D 45
  SW6 . . . . 3C 86
Exeter Rd. E16 . . . . . . 4C 68
  E17 . . . . 1C 38
  NW2 . . . . 2A 44
Exeter St.
  WC2 . . . . 4E 15 (1A 76)
Exeter Way SE14 . . . . . 3B 94
  SW15 . . . . 4E 99
Exford Gdns. SE12 . . . . 1D 125
Exford Rd. SE12 . . . . . 2D 125
Exhibition Cl. W12 . . . . 1E 71
Exhibition Rd.
  SW7 . . . . 3F 73
Exmoor Ho. E3 . . . . . . 1A 66
  (off Gernon Rd.)
Exmoor St. W10 . . . . . 3F 57
Exmouth Ho. E14 . . . . . 5D 81
  (off Cahir St.)
  EC1 . . . . 3B 8
  (off Pine St.)
Exmouth Mkt.
  EC1 . . . . 3B 8 (3C 62)
Exmouth M.
  NW1 . . . . 2A 6 (2E 61)
Exmouth Pl. E8 . . . . . . 4D 51
Exmouth Rd. E17 . . . . . 1B 38
Exmouth St. E1. . . . . . 5E 65
Exning Rd. E16 . . . . . . 3B 68
Exonbury NW8 . . . . . . 5D 45
  (off Abbey Rd.)
Exon St. SE17 . . . . 1A 92
Export Ho. SE1 . . . . . . 4E 27
  (off Tower Bri. Rd.)
Express Newspapers
  SE1 . . . . 1D 25
  (off Blackfriars Rd.)
Exton St.
  SE1 . . . . 2B 24 (2C 76)
Eyhurst Cl. NW2 . . . . . 4C 28
Eylewood Rd. SE27 . . . 5E 119
Eynella Rd. SE22 . . . . . 5B 106
Eynham Rd. W12 . . . . . 5E 57
Eynsford Ho. SE1 . . . . 4B 26
  (off Crosby Row)
  SE15 . . . . 2E 93

Eynsford Ho. *SE17* 5A *78*
(off Beckway St.)
Eyot Gdns. W6 . . . . 1B *84*
Eyot Grn. W4 . . . . 1B *84*
Eyre Ct. NW8 . . . . 1F *59*
Eyre St. Hill
EC1 . . . . 4B **8** (3C *62*)
Eythorne Ho. SW9 . . . . 4C *90*
Ezra St. E2 . . . . 2B *64*

F

F1 City Go-Kart Circuit
. . . . 2E *83*
(off Connaught Bri.)
Faber Gdns. NW4 . . . . 1C *28*
Fabian Rd. SW6 . . . . 3B *86*
Facade, The SE23 . . . . 2E *121*
Factory Rd. E16 . . . . 2F *83*
Fairacres SW15 . . . . 2B *98*
Fairbairn Grn. SW9 . . . . 4D *91*
Fairbank Est.
N1 . . . . 1B **10** (1F *63*)
Fairbriar Residence
SW7 . . . . 5E *73*
(off Cromwell Rd.)
Fairbridge Rd. N19 . . . . 4F *33*
Fairburn Ct. SW15 . . . . 3A *100*
Fairburn Ho. W14 . . . . 1B *86*
(off Ivatt Pl.)
Fairby Ho. SE1 . . . . 5B *78*
(off Longfield Est.)
Fairby Rd. SE12 . . . . 3D *111*
Faircharm Trad. Est.
SE8 . . . . 3D *95*
Fairchild Cl. SW11 . . . . 5F *87*
Fairchild Ho. E9 . . . . 4E *51*
(off Frampton Pk. Rd.)
N1 . . . . 1D *11*
(off Fanshaw St.)
Fairchild Pl. EC2 . . . . 4E *11*
Fairchild St.
EC2 . . . . 3E **11** (3A *64*)
Fairclough St. E1 . . . . 5C *64*
Fairdale Gdns.
SW15 . . . . 2D *99*
Fairfax Gdns. SE3 . . . . 4E *97*
Fairfax Mans. NW3 . . . . 3E *45*
(off Finchley Rd.)
Fairfax M. E16 . . . . 2D *83*
SW15 . . . . 2E *99*
Fairfax Pl. NW6 . . . . 4E *45*
W14 . . . . 4A *72*
Fairfax Rd. NW6 . . . . 4E *45*
W4 . . . . 4A *70*
Fairfield E1 . . . . 4E *65*
(off Redman's Rd.)
NW1 . . . . 5E *47*
(off Arlington Rd.)
Fairfield Av. NW4 . . . . 1D *29*
Fairfield Ct. NW10 . . . . 5C *42*
Fairfield Dr. SW18 . . . . 3D *101*
Fairfield Gdns. N8 . . . . 1A *34*
Fairfield Gro. SE7 . . . . 2F *97*
Fairfield Rd. E3 . . . . 1C *66*
N8 . . . . 1A *34*
Fairfield St. SW18 . . . . 3D *101*
Fairfoot Rd. E3 . . . . 3C *66*

Fairford SE6 . . . . 1C *122*
Fairford Ho. SE11 . . . . 5C *76*
Fairhazel Gdns. NW6 . . . 3D *45*
Fairhazel Mans.
NW6 . . . . 4E *45*
(off Fairhazel Gdns.)
Fairholme Rd. W14 . . . 1A *86*
Fairholt Cl. N16 . . . . 3A *36*
Fairholt Rd. N16 . . . . 7F *35*
Fairholt St. SW7 . . . . 4A *74*
Fairland Rd. E15 . . . . 3B *54*
Fairlawn SE7 . . . . 3E *97*
Fairlawn Ct. SE7 . . . . 3E *97*
(not continuous)
Fairlawn Mans.
SE14 . . . . 4F *93*
Fairlawn Pk. SE26 . . . . . . 5A *122*
Fairlead Ho. E14 . . . . 4C *80*
(off Alpha Gro.)
Fairlie Gdns. SE23 . . . . . . 5E *107*
Fairlight Av. NW10 . . . . . . 1A *56*
Fairlight Ct. NW10 . . . . . . 1A *56*
Fairlight Rd. SW17 . . . . . . 4F *115*
Fairlop Ct. E11 . . . . 3F *39*
Fairlop Rd. E11 . . . . 2F *39*
Fairmead Gdns.
IG4: IIf 1F *41*
Fairmead Ho. E9 . . . . 1A *52*
Fairmead Rd. N19 . . . . . . 5F *33*
Fairmile Av. SW16 . . . . . . 5F *117*
Fairmont Av. E14 . . . . 2F *81*
Fairmount Rd. SW2 . . . . . 4B *104*
Fairstead Wlk. N1 . . . . . . 5E *49*
(off Popham St.)
Fair St. SE1 . . . . . 3E **27** (3A *78*)
Fairthorn Rd. SE7 . . . . . . 1C *96*
Fairview Cl. SE26 . . . . 5A *122*
Fairview Ho. SW2 . . . . . . 5B *104*
Fairview Pl. SW2 . . . . 5B *104*
Fairview Rd. N15 . . . . 1B *36*
Fairwall Ho. SE5 . . . . 4A *92*
Fairway, The W3 . . . . 5A *56*
Fairway Cl. NW11 . . . . . . 2E *31*
Fairway Ct. SE16 . . . . 3F *79*
(off Christopher Cl.)
Fairways Bus. Pk.
E10 . . . . 4A *38*
Fairweather Ho. N7 . . . . . 1A *48*
Fairweather Rd. N16 . . . . 1C *36*
Fairwyn Rd. SE26 . . . . . . 4A *122*
Fakruddin St. E1 . . . . 3C *64*
Falcon WC1 . . . . 5E **7**
(off Old Gloucester St.)
Falconberg Ct.
W1 . . . . 2C **14** (5F *61*)
Falconberg M.
W1 . . . . 2C **14** (5F *61*)
Falcon Cl.
SE1 . . . . 1E **25** (2D *77*)
Falcon Ct.
EC4 . . . . 3C **16** (5C *62*)
N1 . . . . 1E **9**
(off City Gdn. Row)
Falconer Wlk. N7 . . . . 4B *34*
Falconet Ct. E1 . . . . 2D *79*
(off Wapping High St.)
Falcon Gro. SW11 . . . . . . 1A *102*
Falcon Highwalk
EC2 . . . . 1F *17*

Falcon Ho. E14 . . . . 1D *95*
(off St Davids Sq.)
SW5 . . . . 1D *87*
(off Old Brompton Rd.)
Falcon La. SW11 . . . . 1A *102*
Falcon Lodge W9 . . . . . . 4C *58*
(off Admiral Wlk.)
Falcon Pk. Ind. Est.
NW10 . . . . 1A *42*
Falcon Point
SE1 . . . . 5E **17** (1D *77*)
Falcon Rd. SW11 . . . . 5A *88*
Falcon St. E13 . . . . 3B *68*
Falcon Ter. SW11 . . . . 1A *102*
Falcon Way E14 . . . . 5D *81*
Falconwood Ct. SE3 . . . . 5B *96*
(off Montpelier Row)
Falkirk Ct. SE16 . . . . 2F *79*
(off Rotherhithe St.)
Falkirk Ho. W9 . . . . 1D *59*
(off Maida Va.)
Falkirk St.
N1 . . . . 1E **11** (1A *64*)
Falkland Ho. SE6 . . . . 4E *123*
W8 . . . . 4D *73*
W14 . . . . 1B *86*
(off Edith Vs.)
Falkland Pl. NW5 . . . . 2E *47*
Falkland Rd. NW5 . . . . . . 2E *47*
Fallodon Ho. W11 . . . . . . 4B *58*
(off Tavistock Cres.)
Fallow Ct. SE16 . . . . 1C *92*
(off Argyle Way)
Fallsbrook Rd.
SW16 . . . . 5E *117*
Falmouth Cl. SE12 . . . . . . 3B *110*
Falmouth Gdns.
IG4: IIf 1F *41*
Falmouth Ho. SE11 . . . . . 1C *90*
(off Seaton Cl.)
W2 . . . . 1A *74*
(off Clarendon Pl.)
Falmouth Rd.
SE1 . . . . 5A **26** (4F *77*)
Falmouth St. E15 . . . . 2F *53*
Falmouth Way E17 . . . . . . 1B *38*
Falstaff Bldg. E1 . . . . 1D *79*
(off Cannon St. Rd.)
Falstaff Ct. SE11 . . . . 5D *77*
(off Opal St.)
Falstaff Ho. N1 . . . . 1D *11*
(off Crondall St.)
Fambridge Cl. SE26 . . 4B *122*
Fane Ho. E2 . . . . 5E *51*
Fane St. W14 . . . . 2B *86*
Fan Mus., The 3E *95*
Fann St. EC1 . . . . 4F **9** (3E *63*)
(not continuous)
EC2 . . . . 4F **9** (3E *63*)
Fanshaw St.
N1 . . . . 1D **11** (2A *64*)
Fanthorpe St. SW15 . . . . . 1E *99*
Faraday Cl. N7 . . . . 3B *48*
Faraday Ho. E14 . . . . 1B *80*
(off Brightlingsea Pl.)
SE1 . . . . 4B *26*
(off Cole St.)
W10 . . . . 4A *58*
(off Wornington Rd.)

Faraday Lodge SE10 . . . . 4B 82
Faraday Mans. W14 . . . . . 2A 86
  (off Queen's Club Gdns.)
Faraday Mus.
  . . . . 5F 13 (1E 75)
Faraday Rd. E15 . . . . 3B 54
  SW19 . . . . 5C 114
  W10 . . . . 4A 58
Faraday Way SE18 . . . . . 4F 83
Fareham St.
  W1 . . . . 2B 14 (5F 61)
Faringford Rd. E15 . . . . . 4A 54
Farjeon Ho. NW6 . . . . . . 4F 45
  (off Hilgrove Rd.)
Farjeon Rd. SE3 . . . . 4F 97
Farleigh Pl. N16 . . . . 1B 50
Farleigh Rd. N16 . . . . . . 1B 50
Farley Ct. NW1 . . . . 4B 4
  (off Allsop Pl.)
  W14 . . . . 4B 72
Farley Ho. SE26 . . . . . . 3D 121
Farley Rd. SE6 . . . . 5D 109
Farlington Pl. SW15 . . . . 5D 99
Farlow Rd. SW15 . . . . . . 1F 99
Farlton Rd. SW18 . . . . . 1D 115
Farm Av. NW2 . . . . 5A 30
  SW16 . . . . 4A 118
Farm Cl. SW6 . . . . 3C 86
Farmcote Rd. SE12 . . . . 1C 124
Farmdale Rd. SE10 . . . . 1C 96
Farmer Rd. E10 . . . . 3D 39
Farmer's Rd. SE5 . . . . . . 3D 91
Farmer St. W8 . . . . 2C 72
Farmfield Rd.
  BR1: Brom 5A 124
Farmilo Rd. E17 . . . . 2B 38
Farm La. SW6 . . . . 2C 86
  (not continuous)
  SW6 . . . . 2C 86
Farm La. Trad. Est.
  SW6 . . . . 2C 86
Farmleigh Ho. SW9 . . . . 3D 105
Farm Pl. W8 . . . . 2C 72
Farm Rd. E12 . . . . 4F 41
  NW10 . . . . 5A 42
Farmstead Rd. SE6 . . . . 4D 123
Farm St. W1 . . . 5D 13 (1D 75)
Farm Wlk. NW11 . . . . . . 1B 30
Farnaby Ho. W10 . . . . . . 2B 58
  (off Bruckner St.)
Farnaby Rd. SW9 . . . . . 2E 111
Farnan Rd. SW16 . . . . . 5A 118
Farnborough Ho.
  SW15 . . . . 1C 112
Farncombe St. SE16 . . . 3C 78
Farndale Ct. SE18 . . . . . 3F 97
Farndale Ho. NW6 . . . . . 5D 45
  (off Kilburn Va.)
Farnell M. SW5 . . . . 1D 87
Farnham Ho. NW1 . . . . . 3A 60
  (off Harewood Av.)
  SE1 . . . . 2F 25
  (off Pepper St.)
Farnham Pl.
  SE1 . . . . 2E 25 (2D 77)
Farnham Royal SE11 . . . 1B 90
Farningham Ho. N4 . . . . 2F 35
Farnley Ho. SW8 . . . . . . 5F 89
Farnsworth Ct. SE10 . . . 4B 82
  (off Greenroof Way)

Farnworth Ho. E14 . . . . . 5F 81
  (off Manchester Rd.)
Faroe Rd. W14 . . . . 4F 71
Farquhar Rd. SE19 . . . . 5B 120
  SW19 . . . . 3C 114
Farrance St. E14 . . . . . . 5C 66
Farrell Ho. E1 . . . . 5E 65
  (off Ronald St.)
Farren Rd. SE23 . . . . . . 2A 122
Farrer Ho. SE8 . . . . 3C 94
Farriers Ho. EC1 . . . . 4A 10
  (off Errol St.)
Farriers M. SE15 . . . . . . 1E 107
Farrier St. NW1 . . . . 4D 47
Farrier Wlk. SW10 . . . . . 2E 87
Farringdon La.
  EC1 . . . . 4C 8 (3C 62)
Farringdon Rd.
  EC1 . . . . 3B 8 (3C 62)
Farringdon St.
  EC4 . . . . 1D 17 (4D 63)
Farrins Rents SE16 . . . . 2A 80
Farrow La. SE14 . . . . . . 3E 93
Farrow Pl. SE16 . . . . 4A 80
Farthingale Wlk. E15 . . . 4F 53
Farthing All. SE1 . . . . . . 3C 78
Farthing Flds. E1 . . . . . . 2D 79
Fashion & Textile Mus.
  . . . . 3E 27
Fashion St.
  E1 . . . . 1F 19 (4B 64)
Fassett Rd. E8 . . . . 3C 50
Fassett Sq. E8 . . . . 3C 50
Faulkners All.
  EC1 . . . . 5D 9 (4D 63)
Faulkner St. SE14 . . . . . 4E 93
Faunce Ho. SE17 . . . . . . 2D 91
  (off Doddington Gro.)
Faunce St. SE17 . . . . . . 1D 91
Favart Rd. SW6 . . . . 4C 86
Faversham Ho. NW1 . . . . 5E 47
  (off Bayham Pl.)
  SE17 . . . . 1A 92
  (off Kinglake St.)
Faversham Rd. SE6 . . . . 5B 108
Fawcett Cl. SW11 . . . . . 5F 87
  SW16 . . . . 5C 118
Fawcett Ct. SW10 . . . . . 2E 87
  (off Fawcett St.)
Fawcett Est. E5 . . . . 3C 36
Fawcett Rd. NW10 . . . . . 4B 42
Fawcett St. SW10 . . . . . 2E 87
Fawe Pk. M. SW15 . . . . 2B 100
Fawe Pk. Rd.
  SW15 . . . . 2B 100
Fawe St. E14 . . . . 4D 67
Fawkham Ho. SE1 . . . . . 5B 78
  (off Longfield Est.)
Fawley Lodge E14 . . . . . 5F 81
  (off Millennium Dr.)
Fawley Rd. NW6 . . . . . . 2D 45
Fawnbrake Av.
  SE24 . . . . 3D 105
Fawn Rd. E13 . . . . 1E 69
Fawood Av. NW10 . . . . . 4A 42
Faygate Rd. SW2 . . . . . 2B 118
Fayland Av. SW16 . . . . . 5E 117
Fazeley Ct. W9 . . . . 4C 58
  (off Elmfield Way)

Fearnley Ho. SE5 . . . . . . 5A 92
Fearon St. SE10 . . . . . . 1C 96
Feathers Pl. SE10 . . . . . 2F 95
Featherstone Av.
  SE23 . . . . 2D 121
Featherstone St.
  EC1 . . . . 3B 10 (3F 63)
Featley Rd. SW9 . . . . . 1D 105
Feeny Cl. NW10 . . . . . . 1B 42
Felbridge Cl. SW16 . . . . 4C 118
Felbridge Ho. SE22 . . . . 1A 106
Felday Rd. SE13 . . . . . . 4D 109
Felden St. SW6 . . . . 4B 86
Feldman Cl. N16 . . . . . . 3C 36
Felgate M. W6 . . . . 5D 71
Felix Av. N8 . . . . 1A 34
Felixstowe Rd.
  NW10 . . . . 2D 57
Felix St. E2 . . . . 1D 65
Fellbrigg Rd. SE22 . . . . 3B 106
Fellbrigg St. E1 . . . . 3D 65
Fellmongers Path
  SE1 . . . . 4F 27
Fellows Ct.
  E2 . . . . 1F 11 (1B 64)
  (not continuous)
Fellows Rd. NW3 . . . . . . 4F 45
Felltram M. SE7 . . . . 1C 96
  (off Felltram Way)
Felltram Way SE7 . . . . . 1C 96
Felmersham Cl.
  SW4 . . . . 2A 104
Felsberg Rd. SW2 . . . . . 4A 104
Felsham M. SW15 . . . . . 1F 99
  (off Felsham Rd.)
Felsham Rd. SW15 . . . . 1E 99
Felstead Gdns. E14 . . . . 1E 95
Felstead Rd. E9 . . . . 3B 52
  E11 . . . . 2C 40
Felstead St. E9 . . . . 3B 52
Felstead Wharf E14 . . . . 1E 95
Felsted Rd. E16 . . . . 5F 69
Felton Ho. N1 . . . . 5F 49
  (off Branch Pl.)
  SE3 . . . . 2D 111
Felton St. N1 . . . . 5F 49
Fenchurch Av.
  EC3 . . . . 3D 19 (5A 64)
Fenchurch Bldgs.
  EC3 . . . . 3E 19 (5A 64)
Fenchurch Ho. EC3 . . . . 3F 19
  (off Minories)
Fenchurch Pl.
  EC3 . . . . 4E 19 (5A 64)
Fenchurch St.
  EC3 . . . . 4D 19 (1A 78)
Fen Ct. EC3 . . . 4D 19 (5A 64)
Fendall St.
  SE1 . . . . 5E 27 (4A 78)
  (not continuous)
Fendt Cl. E16 . . . . 5B 68
Fenelon Pl. W14 . . . . . . 5B 72
Fenham Rd. SE15 . . . . . 3C 92
Fen La. SW13 . . . . 4D 85
Fennel Apartments
  SE1 . . . . 2F 27
  (off Cayenne St.)
Fennel Cl. E16 . . . . 3A 68
Fenner Cl. SE16 . . . . . . 5D 79

Fenner Ho. *E1* 2D *79*
    (off Watts St.)
Fenner Sq. SW11 . . . . . . 1F **101**
Fenning St.
  SE1 . . . . 3D **27** (3A **78**)
Fenn St. E9 . . . . 2F **51**
Fenstanton *N4* 3B *34*
    (off Marquis Rd.)
Fen St. E16. . . . . 1B **82**
Fentiman Rd. SW8. . . . . 2A **90**
Fenton Cl. E8 . . . . 3B **50**
  SW9 . . . . 5B **90**
Fenton House. *1E 45*
    (off Windmill Hill)
Fenton Ho. SE14 . . . . . . 3A **94**
Fentons Av. E13 . . . . . . 2D **69**
Fenton St. E1 . . . . 5D **65**
Fenwick Gro. SE15. . . . 1C **106**
Fenwick Pl. SW9 . . . . . 1A **104**
Fenwick Rd. SE15 . . . . 1C **106**
Ferdinand Ho. *NW1* 4C *46*
    (off Ferdinand Pl.)
Ferdinand Pl. NW1. . . . . 4C **46**
Ferdinand St. NW1. . . . . 4C **46**
Ferguson Cen., The
  E17 . . . . 1A **38**
Ferguson Cl. E14. . . . . . 5C **80**
Ferguson Dr. W3 . . . . . . 5A **56**
Ferguson Ho. SE10. . . . . 4E **95**
Fergus Rd. N5 . . . . 2D **49**
Fermain Ct. E. *N1* *5A 50*
    (off De Beauvoir Est.)
Fermain Ct. Nth. *N1*. . . . *5A 50*
    (off De Beauvoir Est.)
Fermain Ct. W. *N1* *5A 50*
    (off De Beauvoir Est.)
Ferme Pk. Rd. N4 . . . . . 1B **34**
  N8. . . . . 1A **34**
Fermor Rd. SE23 . . . . . 1A **122**
Fermoy Ho. *W9* 3B *58*
    (off Fermoy Rd.)
Fermoy Rd. W9 . . . . 3B **58**
Fernbank M. SW12. . . . 4E **103**
Fernbrook Cres.
  SE13. . . . . *4A 110*
    (off Leahurst Rd.)
Fernbrook Rd. SE13. . . 3A **110**
Ferncliff Rd. E8 . . . . . . 2C **50**
Fern Cl. N1. . . . . 1A **64**
Fern Ct. SE14 . . . . 5F **93**
Ferncroft Av. NW3 . . . . . 5C **30**
Ferndale Community
  Sports Cen. 1B **104**
Ferndale Rd. E7 . . . . . . 4D **55**
  E11. . . . . 4A **40**
  N15. . . . . 1B **36**
  SW4 . . . . 2A **104**
  SW9 . . . . 2A **104**
Ferndene Rd. SE24 . . . 2E **105**
Ferndown *NW1* *4F 47*
    (off Camley St.)
Ferndown Lodge *E14* . . . *4E 81*
    (off Manchester Rd.)
Ferndown Rd. SE9 . . . . 5F **111**
Fernhall Dr. IG4: Ilf. . . . 1F **41**
Fernhead Rd. W9. . . . . . 1B **58**
Fernholme Rd.
  SE15 . . . . 3F **107**
Fernhurst Rd. SW6. . . . . 4A **86**

Fernlea Rd. SW12 . . . . 1D **117**
Fernleigh Cl. W9 . . . . . . 2B **58**
Fernsbury St.
  WC1. . . . . . . 2B **8** (2C **62**)
Fernshaw Cl. SW10 . . . . 2E **87**
Fernshaw Mans.
  SW10 . . . . *2E 87*
    (off Fernshaw Rd.)
Fernshaw Rd. SW10 . . . . 2E **87**
Fernside NW11. . . . . 4C **30**
Fernside Rd. SW12 . . . 1B **116**
Ferns Rd. E15 . . . . 3B **54**
Fern St. E3 . . . . 3C **66**
Fernthorpe Rd.
  SW16. . . . . 5E **117**
Ferntower Rd. N5. . . . . . 2F **49**
Fern Wlk. SE16 . . . . 1C **92**
Fernwood SW19. . . . . . 1B **114**
Fernwood Av.
  SW16. . . . . 4F **117**
Ferranti Cl. SE18 . . . . . . 4F **83**
Ferrers Rd. SW16. . . . . 5F **117**
Ferrey M. SW9. . . . . 5C **90**
Ferriby Cl. N1. . . . . 4C **48**
Ferrier Ind. Est.
  SW18 . . . . *2D 101*
    (off Ferrier St.)
Ferrier Point *E16* *4C 68*
    (off Forty Acre La.)
Ferrier St. SW18 . . . . . 2D **101**
Ferrings SE21. . . . . 3A **120**
Ferris Rd. SE22 . . . . . . 2C **106**
Ferron Rd. E5. . . . . 5D **37**
Ferrybridge Ho.
  SE11. . . . . *4C 76*
    (off Lambeth Wlk.)
Ferry Ho. *E5*. *3D 37*
    (off Harrington Rd.)
Ferry La. SW13 . . . . 2B **84**
Ferry Rd. SW13 . . . . 3C **84**
Ferry St. E14 . . . . 1E **95**
Festing Rd. SW15 . . . . . 1F **99**
Festival Ct. E8 . . . . *4B 50*
    (off Holly St.)
Festoon Way E16 . . . . . 1F **83**
Fetter La.
  EC4 . . . . 3C **16** (5C **62**)
    (not continuous)
Fettes Ho. *NW8* *1F 59*
    (off Wellington Rd.)
Ffinch St. SE8 . . . . 3C **94**
Field Cl. NW2. . . . . 4C **28**
Field Ct. SW19. . . . . . . 3C **114**
  WC1. . . . . . . 1A **16** (4B **62**)
Fieldgate Mans. *E1* *4C 64*
    (off Fieldgate St.,
    not continuous)
Fieldgate St. E1 . . . . . . 4C **64**
Field Ho. *NW6* *2F 57*
    (off Harvist Rd.)
Fieldhouse Rd.
  SW12. . . . . 1E **117**
Fielding Ct. *WC2* *3D 15*
    (off Tower St.)
Fielding Ho. NW6 . . . . . 2C **58**
  W4 . . . . 2A *84*
    (off Devonshire St.)
Fielding M. *SW13* *2D 85*
    (off Jenner Pl.)

Fielding Rd. W4 . . . . . . 4A *70*
  W14. . . . . 4F *71*
Fieldings, The SE23. . . 1E **121**
Fielding St. SE17 . . . . . 2E **91**
Field Point E7. . . . . 1C **54**
Field Rd. E7 . . . . 1B **54**
  W6 . . . . 1A **86**
Fields Est. E8. . . . . 4C **50**
Fieldside Rd.
  BR1: Brom 5F **123**
Field St. WC1 . . . 1F **7** (2B **62**)
Fieldsway Ho. N5. . . . . 2C **48**
Fieldview SW18 . . . . . . 1F **115**
Fieldway Cres. N5 . . . . 2C **48**
Fife Rd. E16. . . . . 4C **68**
Fife Ter. N1 . . . . 1B **62**
Fifield Path SE23 . . . . . 3F **121**
Fifth Av. W10 . . . . 2A **58**
Fig Tree Cl. NW10 . . . . 5A **42**
Figure Ct. *SW3*. *1B 88*
    (off West Rd.)
Filey Av. N16. . . . . 3C **36**
Filigree Ct. SE16 . . . . . 2B **80**
Fillebrook Rd. E11 . . . . 3F **39**
Filmer Chambers
  SW6 . . . . *4A 86*
    (off Filmer Rd.)
Filmer Rd. SW6. . . . . . . 4A **86**
Filton Ct. *SE14* *3E 93*
    (off Farrow La.)
Finborough Ho.
  SW10 . . . . *2E 87*
    (off Finborough Rd.)
Finborough Rd.
  SW10 . . . . 1D **87**
Finborough Theatre, The
  . . . . *2D 87*
    (off Finborough Rd.)
Finch Av. SE27 . . . . . . 4F **119**
Finchdean Ho. SW15. . . 5B **98**
Finch Ho. *SE8* *3D 95*
    (off Bronze St.)
Finch La.
  EC3. . . . . . . 3C **18** (5F **63**)
Finchley Pl. NW8 . . . . . 1F **59**
Finchley Rd. NW2 . . . . . 1B **30**
  NW3 . . . . 1C **44**
  NW8 . . . . 5F **45**
  NW11 . . . . 1B **30**
Finch Lodge *W9*. *4C 58*
    (off Admiral Wlk.)
Finch M. SE15 . . . . 4B **92**
Finch's Ct. E14. . . . . . . 1D **81**
Finden Rd. E7. . . . . 2E **55**
Findhorn St. E14 . . . . . 5E **67**
Findon Cl. SW18 . . . . . 4C **100**
Findon Rd. W12. . . . . . . 3C **70**
Fingal St. SE10 . . . . . . 1B **96**
Fingest Ho. *NW8* *3A 60*
    (off Lilestone St.)
Finland Rd. SE4. . . . . . 1A **108**
Finland St. SE16 . . . . . 4A **80**
Finlay St. SW6. . . . . . . 4F **85**
Finmere Ho. N4 . . . . . . 2E **35**
Finnemore Ho. *N1* *5E 49*
    (off Britannia Row)
Finn Ho. *N1* *1C 10*
    (off Bevenden St.)
Finnis St. E2 . . . . 2D **65**

FINSBURY 3F 9 (2C 62)
Finsbury Av.
  EC2. . . . . . . 1C 18 (4F 63)
    (not continuous)
Finsbury Av. Sq. EC2. . . 5D 11
Finsbury Cir.
  EC2. . . . . . . 1C 18 (4F 63)
Finsbury Est.
  EC1. . . . . . . 2C 8 (2C 62)
Finsbury Leisure Cen.
  . . . . 3F 9 (2E 63)
Finsbury Mkt.
  EC2. . . . . . . 4D 11 (3A 64)
FINSBURY PARK. 3C 34
Finsbury Pk. Av. N4 . . . 1E 35
Finsbury Pk. Rd. N4. . . 4D 35
    (not continuous)
Finsbury Pavement
  EC2. . . . . . . 5C 10 (4F 63)
Finsbury Sq.
  EC2. . . . . . . 4C 10 (3F 63)
Finsbury St.
  EC2. . . . . . . 5B 10 (4F 63)
Finsen Rd. SE5. . . . . . 2E 105
Finstock Rd. W10 . . . . . 5F 57
Finwhale Ho. E14. . . . . 4D 81
    (off Glengall Gro.)
Fiona Ct. NW6 . . . . . . 1C 58
Firbank Cl. E16. . . . . . 4F 69
Firbank Rd. SE15. . . . . 5D 93
Fircroft Rd. SW17 . . . 2B 116
Firecrest Dr. NW3 . . . . 5D 31
Firefly Gdns. E6 . . . . . 3F 69
Fir Gro. Rd. SW9 . . . . . 5C 90
Firhill Rd. SE6 . . . . . . 4C 122
Fir Ho. W10 . . . . 3A 58
    (off Droop St.)
Firle Ho. W10 . . . . 4E 57
    (off Sutton Way)
Firs, The E6 . . . . 4F 55
  SE26. . . . . 5D 121
    (Border Rd.)
  SE26. . . . . 5E 121
    (Waverley Ct.)
Firsby Rd. N16 . . . . 3C 36
Firs Cl. SE23 . . . . 5A 108
First Av. E13 . . . . 2C 68
  SW14 . . . . 1A 98
  W3 . . . . 2B 70
  W10 . . . . 3B 58
First St. SW3 . . . . 5A 74
Firth Gdns. SW6 . . . . . . 4A 86
Firth Ho. E2 . . . . 2C 64
    (off Barnet Gro.)
Firtree Cl. SW16. . . . . . 5E 117
Fir Tree Ho. SE14. . . . . . 3E 93
    (off Avonley Rd.)
Fir Trees Cl. SE16 . . . . . 2A 80
Fisher Athletic FC 2F 79
Fisher Cl. E9 . . . . 2F 51
Fisher Ho. E1 . . . . 1E 79
    (off Cable St.)
  N1. . . . . 5C 48
    (off Barnsbury Est.)
Fishermans Dr. SE16 . . . 3F 79
Fisherman's Pl. W4 . . . . 2B 84
Fisherman's Wlk.
  E14. . . . . 2C 80

Fisher's Cl. SW16. . . . . 3F 117
Fishers Ct. SE14. . . . . . 4F 93
Fisher's La. W4 . . . . 5A 70
Fisher St. E16 . . . . 4C 68
  WC1 . . . . 1F 15 (4B 62)
Fisherton St. NW8 . . . . . 3F 59
Fishmongers Hall Wharf
  EC4 . . . . 5B 18
Fishponds Rd.
  SW17 . . . . 4A 116
Fish St. Hill
  EC3. . . . . . . 5C 18 (1F 77)
Fish Wharf
  EC3. . . . . . . 5C 18 (1F 77)
Fisons Rd. E16. . . . . . . 2C 82
Fitness First Health Club
  Islington 1D 9 (1D 63)
  Lewisham 1E 109
  Tooting Bec 3C 116
    (off Balham High Rd.)
Fitrooms 2B 86
Fitzalan St. SE11 . . . . . 5C 76
Fitzgeorge Av. W14 . . . . 5A 72
Fitzgerald Av. SW14. . . . 1A 98
Fitzgerald Ct. E10 . . . . . 3D 39
    (off Leyton Grange Est.)
Fitzgerald Ho. E14. . . . . 5D 67
    (off E. India Dock Rd.)
  SW9 . . . . 5C 90
Fitzgerald Rd. E11 . . . . 1C 40
  SW14 . . . . 1A 98
Fitzhardinge Ho. W1 . . 2B 12
    (off Portman Sq.)
Fitzhardinge St.
  W1. . . . . 2B 12 (5C 60)
Fitzhugh Gro. SW18 . . 4F 101
Fitzjames Av. W14. . . . . 5A 72
Fitzjohn's Av. NW3. . . . . 1E 45
Fitzmaurice Ho.
  SE16. . . . . 5D 79
    (off Rennie Est.)
Fitzmaurice Pl.
  W1. . . . . 1E 21 (2D 75)
Fitzneal St. W12 . . . . . . 5B 56
FITZROVIA 5E 5
Fitzroy Cl. N6 . . . . 3B 32
Fitzroy Ct. N6 . . . . 1E 33
  W1 . . . . 4A 6
Fitzroy Ho. E14. . . . . . . 4B 66
    (off Wallwood St.)
  SE1 . . . . 1B 92
    (off Coopers Rd.)
Fitzroy M. W1. . . . . 4F 5
Fitzroy Pk. N6. . . . . 3B 32
Fitzroy Rd. NW1. . . . . . 5C 46
Fitzroy Sq. W1. . . 4F 5 (3E 61)
Fitzroy St. W1 . . 4F 5 (3E 61)
    (not continuous)
Fitzroy Yd. NW1. . . . . . 5C 46
Fitzsimmons Ct.
  NW10 . . . . 5A 42
Fitzwarren Gdns. N19. . . 3E 33
Fitzwilliam Hgts.
  SE23. . . . . 2E 121
Fitzwilliam M. E16. . . . . 2C 82
Fitzwilliam Rd.
  SW4 . . . . 1E 103
Five Bell All. E14. . . . . . 5B 66
    (off Three Colt St.)

Five Oaks M.
  BR1: Brom 3C 124
Fives Ct. SE11 . . . . 4D 77
Fiveways Rd. SW9. . . . . 5C 90
Flack Ct. E10 . . . . 2D 39
Fladbury Rd. N15. . . . . . 1F 35
Fladgate Rd. E11. . . . . . 1A 40
Flamborough Ho.
  SE15. . . . . 4C 92
    (off Clayton Rd.)
Flamborough St. E14. . . 5A 66
Flamborough Wlk.
  E14. . . . . 5A 66
    (off Flamborough St.)
Flamingo Ct. SE8. . . . . . 3C 94
    (off Hamilton St.)
Flamstead Ho. SW3. . . . 1A 88
    (off Cale St.)
Flamsteed Rd. SE7 . . . . 1F 97
Flanchford Rd. W12. . . . 4B 70
Flanders Ct. E17 . . . . . . 2A 38
Flanders Mans. W4 . . . . 5B 70
Flanders Rd. W4 . . . . . . 5A 70
Flanders Way E9 . . . . . . 3F 51
    (not continuous)
Flank St. E1 . . . . 1C 78
Flansham Ho. E14. . . . . 5B 66
    (off Clemence St.)
Flask Wlk. NW3 . . . . 1E 45
Flatford Ho. SE6. . . . . . 4E 123
Flather Cl. SW16. . . . . . 5E 117
Flatiron Yd. SE1. . . . . . . 2A 26
    (off Union St.)
Flavell M. SE10 . . . . 1A 96
Flaxley Ho. SW1 . . . . . . 1D 89
    (off Abbots Mnr.)
Flaxman Ct. W1. . . . . . . 3B 14
  WC1 . . . . 2C 6
    (off Flaxman Ter.)
Flaxman Ho. SE1. . . . . . 5D 25
    (off London Rd.)
  W4 . . . . 1A 84
    (off Devonshire St.)
Flaxman Leisure Cen.
  . . . . 5E 91
Flaxman Rd. SE5. . . . . 1D 105
Flaxman Ter.
  WC1 . . . . 2C 6 (2F 61)
Flecker Ho. SE5. . . . . . . 3F 91
    (off Lomond Gro.)
Fleece Wlk. N7 . . . . 3A 48
Fleetbank Ho. EC4. . . . . 3C 16
    (off Whitefriars St.)
Fleet Bldg. EC4 . . . . . . 2D 17
Fleetfield WC1 . . . . 1E 7
    (off Birkenhead St.)
Fleet Ho. E14. . . . . 1A 80
    (off Victory Pl.)
Fleet Pl. EC4 . . 2D 17 (5D 63)
    (not continuous)
Fleet Rd. NW3 . . . . 2A 46
Fleet Sq. WC1. . 2A 8 (2B 62)
Fleet St. EC4 . . 3B 16 (5C 62)
Fleet St. Hill E1 . . . . 3C 64
Fleetway WC1 . . . . 1E 7
    (off Birkenhead Rd.)
Fleetwood Cl. E16 . . . . . 4F 69
Fleetwood Rd. NW10. . . 2C 42
Fleetwood St. N16 . . . . . 4A 36

Fleming Cl. W9 . . . . 3C **58**
Fleming Ct. W2. . . . . 4F **59**
  (off St Mary's Sq.)
Fleming Ho. N4 . . . . 3E **35**
SE16 . . . . 3C **78**
  (off George Row)
Fleming Lodge W9 . . . . 4C **58**
  (off Admiral Wlk.)
Fleming Rd. SE17 . . . . . 2D **91**
Flemming Cl. SW10 . . . . 2E **87**
  (off Park Wlk.)
Flempton Rd. E10 . . . . . 3A **38**
Fletcher Bldgs. WC2 . . . 3E **15**
  (off Martlett Ct.)
Fletcher Ho. SE15 . . . . . 3E **93**
  (off Clifton Way)
Fletcher La. E10 . . . . . . 2E **39**
Fletcher Path SE8 . . . . . 3C **94**
Fletcher St. E1 . . . . 1C **78**
Fletching Rd. E5 . . . . . . 5E **37**
SE7 . . . . 2E **97**
Fleur-de-Lis St.
E1. . . . . 4E **11** (3B **64**)
Fleur Gates SW19. . . . . 5F **99**
Flimwell Cl.
BR1: Brom 5A **124**
Flinders Ho. E1 . . . . 2D **79**
  (off Green Bank)
Flint Cl. E15 . . . . 4B **54**
Flintmill Cres. SE3 . . . . . 5F **97**
  (not continuous)
Flinton St. SE17 . . . . . . 1A **92**
Flint St. SE17 . . . . 5F **77**
Flitcroft St.
WC2 . . . . 3C **14** (5F **61**)
Flitton Ho. N1 . . . . 4D **49**
  (off The Sutton Est.)
Flock Mill Pl. SW18. . 1D **115**
Flockton St. SE16 . . . . . 3C **78**
Flodden Rd. SE5 . . . . . . 4E **91**
Flood St. SW3 . . . . 1A **88**
Flood Wlk. SW3 . . . . . . 2A **88**
Flora Cl. E14 . . . . 5D **67**
Flora Gdns. W6 . . . . . . 5D **71**
  (off Albion Gdns.)
Floral Pl. N1 . . . . 2F **49**
Floral St.
WC2 . . . . 4D **15** (1A **76**)
Florence Cantwell Wlk.
N19. . . . . 2A **34**
  (off Jessie Blythe La.)
Florence Ct. E5 . . . . . . 5C **36**
N1. . . . . 4D **49**
  (off Florence St.)
SW19 . . . . 5A **114**
W9 . . . . 2E **59**
  (off Maida Va.)
Florence Ho. SE16 . . . . 1D **93**
  (off Rotherhithe New Rd.)
W11. . . . . 1F **71**
  (off St Ann's Rd.)
Florence Mans. NW4 . . . 1D **29**
  (off Vivian Av.)
Florence Nightingale Mus.
. . . . 4F **23** (3B **76**)
Florence Rd. E6 . . . . . . 5E **55**
E13 . . . . 1C **68**
N4 . . . . 2B **34**
  (not continuous)

Florence Rd. SE14 . . . . 4B **94**
SW19 . . . . 5D **115**
N1. . . . . 4D **49**
Florence St. E16 . . . . . 3B **68**
Florence Ter. SE14. . . . 4B **94**
SW15 . . . . 3A **112**
Florence Way
SW12 . . . . 1B **116**
Flores Ho. E1 . . . . 4F **65**
  (off Shandy St.)
Florey Lodge W9 . . . . . 4C **58**
  (off Admiral Wlk.)
Floris Pl. SW4 . . . . 1E **103**
Florys Ct. SW19 . . . . . 1A **114**
Floss St. SW15 . . . . . . 5E **85**
Flower & Dean Wlk.
E1. . . . . 1F **19** (4B **64**)
Flower M. NW11 . . . . . 1A **30**
Flowerpot Cl. N15 . . . . 1B **36**
Flowers Cl. NW2 . . . . . 5C **28**
Flowersmead SW17. . . 2C **116**
Flowers M. N19 . . . . . . 4E **33**
Flower Wlk., The
SW7 . . . . 3E **73**
Floyd Rd. SE7. . . . . 1E **97**
Fludyer St. SE13 . . . . . 2A **110**
Flynn Ct. E14 . . . . 1C **80**
  (off Garford St.)
Foley Ho. E1. . . . . 5E **65**
  (off Tarling St.)
Foley St. W1 . . 1F **13** (4E **61**)
Folgate St.
E1. . . . . 5E **11** (4A **64**)
  (not continuous)
Foliot Ho. N1 . . . . 1B **62**
  (off Priory Grn. Est.)
Foliot St. W12 . . . . 5B **56**
Folkstone Ho. SE17 . . . 1A **92**
  (off Kinglake St.)
Follett Ho. SW10 . . . . . 3F **87**
  (off Worlds End Est.)
Follett St. E14 . . . . 5E **67**
Follingham Ct. N1 . . . . 1E **11**
  (off Drysdale Pl.)
Folly M. W11 . . . . 5B **58**
Folly Wall E14 . . . . 3E **81**
Fonda Ct. E14. . . . . . . 1C **80**
  (off Premiere Pl.)
Fontarabia Rd.
SW11 . . . . 2C **102**
Fontenelle Gdns.
SE5 . . . . 4A **92**
Fontenoy Ho. SE11 . . . 5D **77**
  (off Kennington La.)
Fontenoy Rd. SW12. . 2D **117**
Fonthill Ho. SW1 . . . . 1D **89**
  (off Sutherland St.)
W14 . . . . 4A **72**
  (off Russell Rd.)
Fonthill M. N4 . . . . 4B **34**

Fonthill Rd. N4. . . . . . . 3B **34**
Fontley Way SW15. . . . 5C **98**
Footpath, The SW15 . . 4C **98**
Forber Ho. E2 . . . . 2E **65**
  (off Cornwall Av.)
Forbes Cl. NW2 . . . . . . 5C **28**
Forbes St. E1 . . . . 5C **64**
Forburg Rd. N16 . . . . . 3C **36**
Ford Cl. E3 . . . . 1A **66**
Fordel Rd. SE6 . . . . . . 1E **123**
Fordham Ho. SE14. . . . 3A **94**
  (off Angus St.)
Fordham St. E1 . . . . . . 5C **64**
Fordie Ho. SW1 . . . . . . 4B **74**
  (off Sloane St.)
Fordingley Rd. W9. . . . 2B **58**
Fordington Ho.
SE26. . . . . 3C **120**
Fordmill Rd. SE6 . . . . 2C **122**
Ford Rd. E3 . . . . 1B **66**
Fords Pk. Rd. E16 . . . . 4C **68**
Ford Sq. E1 . . . . 4D **65**
Ford St. E3 . . . . 5A **52**
E16 . . . . 5B **68**
Fordwych Rd. NW2 . . . 1A **44**
Fordyce Rd. SE13. . . . 4E **109**
Foreign St. SE5 . . . . . . 5D **91**
Foreland Ho. W11 . . . . 1A **72**
  (off Walmer Rd.)
Foreshore SE8 . . . . 5B **80**
Forest Bus. Pk. E10 . . 2F **37**
Forest Cl. E11 . . . . 1C **40**
Forest Cft. SE23. . . . . 2D **121**
Forest Dr. E12. . . . . . . 5F **41**
Forest Dr. E. E11 . . . . 2F **39**
Forest Dr. W. E11. . . . 2E **39**
Forester Ho. E14 . . . . 1A **80**
  (off Victory Pl.)
Forester Rd. SE15 . . . 1D **107**
FOREST GATE 2C **54**
Forest Ga. Retreat
E7 . . . . 2C **54**
  (off Odessa Rd.)
Forest Glade E11 . . . . 1A **40**
Forest Gro. E8 . . . . . . 3B **50**
FOREST HILL 2E **121**
Forest Hill Bus. Cen.
SE23 . . . . 2E **121**
  (off Clyde Va.)
Forest Hill Ind. Est.
SE23 . . . . 2E **121**
Forest Hill Pool 2E **121**
Forest Hill Rd.
SE22 . . . . 3D **107**
SE23 . . . . 3D **107**
Forestholme Cl.
SE23 . . . . 2E **121**
Forest La. E7 . . . . 2A **54**
E15 . . . . 2A **54**
Forest Lodge SE23 . . 3E **121**
  (off Dartmouth Rd.)
Forest Point E7 . . . . . . 2D **55**
  (off Windsor Rd.)
Fore St. EC2 . . 1A **18** (4E **63**)
Fore St. Av.
EC2 . . . . 1B **18** (4F **63**)
Forest Rd. E7 . . . . 1C **54**
E8 . . . . 3B **50**
E11 . . . . 2F **39**

Forest Side E7 . . . . 1D 55
Forest St. E7 . . . . 2C 54
Forest Vw. Rd. E11 . . . . . . 2B 40
Forest Vw. Av. E10 . . . . . . 1F 39
Forest Vw. Rd. E12 . . . . . 1F 55
Forest Way N19 . . . . 4E 33
Forfar Rd. SW11 . . . . 4C 88
Forge Pl. NW1 . . . . 3C 46
Forges Rd. E12 . . . . 4F 41
Forman Pl. N16 . . . . 1B 50
Formby Ct. N7 . . . . 2C 48
(off Morgan Rd.)
Formosa Ho. E1 . . . . 3A 66
(off Ernest St.)
Formosa St. W9 . . . . 3D 59
Formunt Cl. E16 . . . . 4B 68
Forres Gdns. NW11 . . . 1C 30
Forrester Path SE26 . . 4E 121
Forset Ct. W1 . . . . 5A 60
(off Edgware Rd.)
Forset St. W1 . . . . 5A 60
Forster Ho.
BR1: Brom 4F 123
Forster Rd. E17 . . . . 1A 38
SW2 . . . . 5A 104
Forston St. N1 . . . . 1E 63
Forsyte Ho. SW3 . . . . 1A 88
(off Chelsea Mnr. St.)
Forsyth Gdns. SE17 . . . . 2D 91
Forsyth Ho. E9 . . . . 4E 51
(off Frampton Pk. Rd.)
SW1 . . . . 1E 89
(off Tachbrook St.)
Fortescue Av. E8 . . . . 4D 51
Fortess Gro. NW5 . . . . 2E 47
Fortess Rd. NW5 . . . . 2D 47
Fortess Wlk. NW5 . . . . 2D 47
Fortess Yd. NW5 . . . . 1D 47
Forthbridge Rd.
SW11 . . . . 2C 102
Fortis Cl. E16 . . . . 5E 69
Fortnam Rd. N19 . . . . 4F 33
Fort Rd. SE1 . . . . 5B 78
Fortrose Cl. E14 . . . . 5F 67
Fortrose Gdns. SW2 . . . 1A 118
Fort St. E1 . . . . 1E 19 (4A 64)
E16 . . . . 2D 83
Fortuna Cl. N7 . . . . 3B 48
Fortune Ct. E8 . . . . 4B 50
(off Queensbridge Rd.)
Fortunegate Rd.
NW10 . . . . 5A 42
FORTUNE GREEN 2C 44
Fortune Grn. Rd.
NW6 . . . . 1C 44
Fortune Ho. EC1 . . . . 4A 10
(off Fortune St.)
SE11 . . . . 5C 76
(off Marylee Way)
Fortune St.
EC1 . . . . 4A 10 (3E 63)
Fortune Theatre 3E 15
(off Russell St.)
Fortune Way NW10 . . . . 2C 56
Forty Acre La. E8 . . . . . . 4C 68
Forum Cl. E3 . . . . 5C 52
Forum Magnum Sq.
SE1 . . . . 3A 24
(off York Rd.)

Forward Bus. Cen., The
E16 . . . . 3F 67
Fosbrooke Ho. SW8 . . . . 3A 90
(off Davidson Gdns.)
Fosbury M. W2 . . . . 1D 73
Foscote Cl. W9 . . . . 3C 58
(off Foscote M.)
Foscote M. W9 . . . . 3C 58
Foscote Rd. NW4 . . . . . . 1D 29
Foskett Rd. SW6 . . . . . . 5B 86
Fossdene Rd. SE7 . . . . . 1D 97
Foss Ho. NW8 . . . . 1D 59
(off Carlton Hill)
Fossil Ct. SE1 . . . . 5D 27
(off Long La.)
Fossil Rd. SE13 . . . . . . 1C 108
Foss Rd. SW17 . . . . 4F 115
Foster Cl. E16 . . . . 1B 82
(off Tarling Rd.)
NW1 . . . . 4E 47
(off Royal College St.)
Foster Ho. SE14 . . . . 4B 94
Foster La.
EC2 . . . . 2F 17 (5E 63)
Foster Rd. E13 . . . . 3C 68
W3 . . . . 1A 70
W4 . . . . 1A 84
Foster's Way SW18 . . . 1D 115
Fothergill Cl. E13 . . . . . . 1C 68
Foubert's Pl.
W1 . . . . 3F 13 (5E 61)
Foulden Rd. N16 . . . . . . 1B 50
Foulden Ter. N16 . . . . . . 1B 50
Foulis Ter. SW7 . . . . 1F 87
Foulser Rd. SW17 . . . . . 3B 116
Founders Cl. EC2 . . . . . . 2B 18
Founders Ho. SW1 . . . . . 1F 89
(off Aylesford St.)
Foundling Ct. WC1 . . . . . 3D 7
(off Brunswick Cen.)
Foundling Mus., The
. . . . 3E 7 (3A 62)
Foundry Cl. SE16 . . . . . . 2A 80
Foundry Ho. E14 . . . . . . 4D 67
(off Morris Rd.)
Foundry M. NW1 . . . . 3A 6
Foundry Pl. E1 . . . . 4E 65
(off Redman's Rd.)
SW18 . . . . 5D 101
Fountain Ct.
EC4 . . . . 4B 16 (1C 76)
SE23 . . . . 2F 121
SW1 . . . . 5D 75
(off Buckingham Pal. Rd.)
Fountain Dr. SE19 . . . . . 4B 120
Fountain Grn. Sq.
SE16 . . . . 3C 78
Fountain Ho. NW6 . . . . . 4A 44
SE16 . . . . 3C 78
(off Bermondsey Wall E.)
W1 . . . . 1B 20
(off Park St.)
Fountain M. N5 . . . . 1E 49
(off Highbury Grange)
NW3 . . . . 3B 46
Fountain Pl. SW9 . . . . . . 4C 90
Fountain Rd. SW17 . . . . 5F 115
Fountain Sq. SW1 . . . . . 5D 75
Fountayne Rd. N16 . . . . 4C 36

Fount St. SW8 . . . . 3F 89
Fournier St.
E1 . . . . 5F 11 (4B 64)
Fourscore Mans. E8 . . . 4C 50
(off Shrubland Rd.)
Four Seasons Cl. E3 . . . 1C 66
Fourth Av. W10 . . . . 3A 58
Fovant Ct. SW8 . . . . 5E 89
Fowey Cl. E1 . . . . 2D 79
Fowey Ho. SE11 . . . . 1C 90
(off Kennings Way)
Fowler Cl. SW11 . . . . . . 1F 101
Fowler Ho. N15 . . . . 1F 35
(off South Gro.)
Fowler Rd. E7 . . . . 1C 54
N1 . . . . 5D 49
Fowlers M. N19 . . . . 4E 33
(off Holloway Rd.)
Fownes St. SW11 . . . . . 1A 102
Fox & Knot St. EC1 . . . . . 5E 9
Foxberry Rd. SE4 . . . . . 1A 108
Foxborough Gdns.
SE4 . . . . 3C 108
Foxbourne Rd.
SW17 . . . . 2C 116
Fox Cl. E1 . . . . 3E 65
E16 . . . . 4C 68
Foxcombe Cl. E6 . . . . . . 1F 69
Foxcombe Rd.
SW15 . . . . 1C 112
Foxcote SE5 . . . . 1A 92
Foxcroft WC1 . . . . 1A 8
(off Penton Ri.)
Foxes Dale SE3 . . . . . . 1C 110
Foxfield NW1 . . . . 5D 47
(off Arlington Rd.)
Foxglove St. W12 . . . . . . 1B 70
Foxham Rd. N19 . . . . 5F 33
Foxhole Rd. SE9 . . . . . . 3F 111
Foxley Cl. E8 . . . . 2C 50
Foxley Rd. SW9 . . . . 3C 90
Foxley Sq. SW9 . . . . 4D 91
Foxmore St. SW11 . . . . . 4B 88
Fox Rd. E16 . . . . 4B 68
Foxwell M. SE4 . . . . 1A 108
Foxwell St. SE4 . . . . 1A 108
Foxwood Rd. SE3 . . . . . 2B 110
Foyle Rd. SE3 . . . . 2B 96
Framfield Rd. N5 . . . . 2D 49
Framlingham Cl. E5 . . . . . 4E 37
Frampton NW1 . . . . 4F 47
(off Wrotham Rd.)
Frampton Ho. NW8 . . . . 3F 59
(off Frampton St.)
Frampton Pk. Est. E9 . . 4E 51
Frampton Pk. Rd. E9 . . 3E 51
Frampton St. NW8 . . . . 3F 59
Francemary Rd.
SE4 . . . . 3C 108
Frances Ct. E17 . . . . 1C 38
Franche Ct. Rd.
SW17 . . . . 3E 115
Francis Barber Cl.
SW16 . . . . 5B 118
Franciscan Rd.
SW17 . . . . 5B 116
Francis Chichester Way
SW11 . . . . 4C 88
Francis Cl. E14 . . . . 5F 81

Francis Ct. EC1 . . . . 5D 9
  SE14 . . . . 2F 93
   (off Myers La.)
Francis Ho. E17 . . . . 1B 38
  N1 . . . . 5A 50
   (off Colville Est.)
  SW10 . . . . 3D 87
   (off Coleridge Gdns.)
Francis M. SE12 . . . . 5C 110
Francis Rd. E10 . . . . 3E 39
Francis St. E15 . . . . 2A 54
  SW1 . . . . 5A 22 (5E 75)
Francis Ter. N19 . . . . 5E 33
Francis Wlk. N1 . . . . 5B 48
Franconia Rd. SW4 . . . . 3F 103
Frank Beswick Ho.
  SW6 . . . . 2B 86
   (off Clem Attlee Ct.)
Frank Burton Cl.
  SE7 . . . . 1D 97
Frank Dixon Cl.
  SE21 . . . . 5A 106
Frank Dixon Way
  SE21 . . . . 1A 120
Frankfurt Rd. SE24 . . . . 3E 105
Frankham Ho. *SE8* 3C 94
   (off Frankham St.)
Frankham St. SE8 . . . . . . 3C 94
Frank Ho. *SW8* 3A 90
   (off Wyvil Rd.)
Frankland Cl. SE16 . . . . 4D 79
Frankland Rd. SW7 . . . . 4F 73
Franklin Bldg. E14 . . . . . 3C 80
Franklin Cl. SE13 . . . . . 4D 95
  SE27 . . . . 3D 119
Franklin Ho. *E1* 2D 79
   (off Watts St.)
  E14 . . . . 5F 67
   (off E. India Dock Rd.)
Franklin Pl. SE13 . . . . . 4D 95
Franklin Sq. W14 . . . . . . 1B 86
Franklin's Row SW3 . . . 1B 88
Franklin St. E3 . . . . 2D 67
  N15 . . . . 1A 36
Franklyn Rd. NW10 . . . . 3B 42
Frank Soskice Ho.
  SW6 . . . . 2B 86
   (off Clem Attlee Ct.)
Frank St. E13 . . . . 3C 68
Frank Whymark Ho.
  SE16 . . . . 3E 79
   (off Rupack St.)
Fransfield Gro.
  SE26 . . . . 3D 121
Frans Hals Ct. E14 . . . . 4F 81
Franthorne Way
  SE6 . . . . 2D 123
Fraser Cl. E6 . . . . 5F 69
Fraser Ct. *E14* 1E 95
   (off Ferry St.)
  SW11 . . . . 4A 88
   (off Surrey La. Est.)
Fraser Rd. E17 . . . . 1D 39
Fraser St. W4 . . . . 1A 84
Frazier St.
  SE1 . . . . 4B 24 (3C 76)
Frean St. SE16 . . . . 4C 78
Frearson Ho. *WC1* 1A 8
   (off Penton Ri.)

Freda Corbet Cl.
  SE15 . . . . 3C 92
Frederica St. N7 . . . . 4B 48
Frederick Charrington Ho.
  E1 . . . . 3E 65
   (off Wickford St.)
Frederick Cl. W2 . . . . . . 1B 74
Frederick Ct. *SW3* 5B 74
   (off Duke of York Sq.)
Frederick Cres. SW9 . . 3D 91
Frederick Dobson Ho.
  W11 . . . . 1A 72
   (off Cowling Cl.)
Frederick Rd. SE17 . . . 2D 91
Frederick's Pl.
  EC2 . . . . 3B 18 (5F 63)
Frederick Sq. *SE16* . . . 1A 80
   (off Sovereign Cres.)
Frederick's Row
  EC1 . . . . 1D 9 (2D 63)
Frederick St.
  WC1 . . . . 2F 7 (2B 62)
Frederick Ter. E8 . . . . . 4B 50
Frederic M. *SW1* 4A 20
Frederic St. E17 . . . . . . 1A 38
Fred Styles Ho. SE7 . . 2E 97
Fred White Wlk. N7 . . . 3A 48
Freedom St. SW11 . . . 5B 88
Freegrove Rd. N7 . . . . . 2A 48
   (not continuous)
Freeling Ho. *NW8* 5F 45
   (off Dorman Way)
Freeling St. N1 . . . . 4B 48
   (Carnoustie Dr.)
  N1 . . . . 4A 48
   (Pembroke St.)
Freemantle St. SE17 . . 1A 92
Freemasons Rd. E16 . . 4D 69
Free Trade Wharf E1 . . 1F 79
Freke Rd. SW11 . . . . . . 1C 102
Fremantle Ho. *E1* 3D 65
   (off Somerford St.)
Fremont St. E9 . . . . 5D 51
   (not continuous)
French Ordinary Ct.
  EC3 . . . . 4E 19
French Pl. E1 . . . 2E 11 (2A 64)
Frendsbury Rd. SE4 . . 2A 108
Frensham Dr. SW15 . . 3B 112
   (not continuous)
Frensham St. SE15 . . . 2C 92
Frere St. SW11 . . . . 5A 88
Freshfield Av. E8 . . . . . 4B 50
Freshfield Cl. SE13 . . . 2F 109
Freshford St. SW18 . . 3E 115
Freshwater Cl.
  SW17 . . . . 5C 116
Freshwater Ct. *W1* 4A 60
   (off Crawford St.)
Freshwater Rd.
  SW17 . . . . 5C 116
Freston Rd. W10 . . . . . . 1F 71
  W11 . . . . 1F 71
Freswick Ho. *SE8* 5F 79
   (off Chilton Gro.)
Freud Mus., The 3F 45
Frewell Ho. *EC1* 5B 8
   (off Bourne Est.)
Frewin Rd. SW18 . . . . 1F 115

Friar M. SE27 . . . . 3D 119
Friars Av. SW15 . . . . . . 3B 112
Friars Cl. SE1 . . . . 2E 25
Friars Gdns. W3 . . . . . . 5A 56
Friars Mead E14 . . . . . 4E 81
Friars Pl. La. W3 . . . . . 1A 70
Friars Rd. E6 . . . . 5F 55
Friar St. EC4 . . . 3E 17 (5D 63)
Friars Way W3 . . . . 5A 56
Friary Ct. SW1 . . . . 2A 22
Friary Est. SE15 . . . . . . 2C 92
   (not continuous)
Friary Rd. SE15 . . . . . . 3C 92
  W3 . . . . 5A 56
Friday St.
  EC4 . . . . 4F 17 (1E 77)
Frideswide Pl. NW5 . . . 2E 47
Freightliners City Farm
  . . . . 3C 48
Friendly Pl. SE13 . . . . . 4D 95
Friendly St. SE8 . . . . . . 5C 94
Friendly St. M. SE8 . . . 5C 94
Friendship Ho. *SE1* . . . 4E 25
   (off Belvedere Pl.)
Friendship Way E15 . . 5E 53
Friends House 2B 6
Friend St. EC1 . . 1D 9 (2D 63)
Friern Rd. SE22 . . . . . . 5C 106
Frigate Ho. E14 . . . . 5E 81
   (off Stebondale St.)
Frigate M. SE8 . . . . 2C 94
Frimley Cl. SW19 . . . . 2A 114
Frimley St. E1 . . . . 3F 65
   (off Frimley Way)
Frimley Way E1 . . . . . . 3F 65
Frinstead Ho. *W10* . . . 1F 71
   (off Freston Rd.)
Frinton Ct. E6 . . . . 2F 69
  N15 . . . . 1A 36
Friston St. SW6 . . . . . . 5D 87
Frith Ho. *NW8* 3F 59
   (off Frampton St.)
Frith Rd. E11 . . . . 1E 53
Frith St. W1 . . 3B 14 (5F 61)
Frithville Ct. *W12* 2E 71
   (off Frithville Gdns.)
Frithville Gdns. W12 . . 2E 71
Frobisher Ct. *SE10* . . . 2F 95
   (off Old Woolwich Rd.)
  SE23 . . . . 2D 121
  W12 . . . . 3E 71
   (off Lime Gro.)
Frobisher Cres. EC2 . . 5A 10
   (off Beech St.)
Frobisher Gdns. E10 . . 2D 39
Frobisher Ho. *E1* 2D 79
   (off Watts St.)
  SW1 . . . . 2F 89
   (off Dolphin Sq.)
Frobisher Pas. E14 . . . 2C 80
Frobisher Pl. Pioneer Cen.
  SE15 . . . . 4E 93
Frobisher St. SE10 . . . 2A 96
Frogley Rd. SE22 . . . . . 2B 106
Frogmore SW18 . . . . . . 3C 100
Frogmore Ind. Est.
  N5 . . . . 2E 49
Frognal NW3 . . . . 1E 45
Frognal Cl. NW3 . . . . . . 2E 45

Frognal Ct. NW3 . . . . 3E **45**
Frognal Gdns. NW3 . . . . . 1E **45**
Frognal La. NW3 . . . . 2D **45**
Frognal Pde. NW3 . . . . . . 3E **45**
Frognal Ri. NW3 . . . . 5E **31**
Frognal Way NW3 . . . . . . 1E **45**
Froissart Rd. SE9 . . . . . 3F **111**
Frome Ho. SE15 . . . . . . 2D **107**
Frome St. N1 . . . . 1E **63**
Frontenac NW10 . . . . 4D **43**
Frostic Wlk. E1 . . . . 4C **64**
Froude St. SW8 . . . . 5D **89**
Fruiterers Pas. EC4 . . . . 5A **18**
. . . . (off Queen St. Pl.)
Fryday Gro. M.
  SW12 . . . . 5E **103**
. . . . (off Weir Rd.)
Fryent Cres. NW9 . . . . . . 1A **28**
Fryent Flds. NW9 . . . . . . 1A **28**
Fryent Gro. NW9 . . . . 1A **28**
Fry Ho. E6 . . . . 4E **55**
Frying Pan All. E1 . . . . . . 1F **19**
Fry Rd. E6 . . . . 4F **55**
  NW10 . . . . 5B **42**
Fulbeck Ho. N7 . . . . 3B **48**
. . . . (off Sutterton St.)
Fulbeck Rd. N19 . . . . 1E **47**
Fulbourne St. E1 . . . . . . 4D **65**
Fulbrook M. N19 . . . . 1E **47**
Fulcher Ho. N1 . . . . 5A **50**
. . . . (off Colville Est.)
  SE8 . . . . 1B **94**
Fulford St. SE16 . . . . 3D **79**
FULHAM 5A **86**
FULHAM BROADWAY
. . . . 3C **86**
Fulham B'way. SW6 . . . . . 3C **86**
Fulham B'way. Shop. Cen.
  SW6 . . . . 3C **86**
. . . . (off Fulham B'way.)
Fulham Ct. SW6 . . . . 4C **86**
Fulham FC 4F **85**
Fulham High St.
  SW6 . . . . 5A **86**
Fulham Palace 5A **86**
Fulham Pal. Rd.
  SW6 . . . . 1E **85**
  W6 . . . . 1E **85**
Fulham Pk. Gdns.
  SW6 . . . . 5B **86**
Fulham Pk. Rd. SW6 . . . . 5B **86**
Fulham Pools 2A **86**
Fulham Rd. SW3 . . . . 3D **87**
  SW6 . . . . 5A **86**
. . . . (Fulham High St.)
  SW6 . . . . 3D **87**
. . . . (King's Rd.)
  SW10 . . . . 3D **87**
Fuller Cl. E2 . . . . 3C **64**
. . . . (off Cheshire St.)
Fuller's Griffin Brewery &
  Vis. Cen. 2B **84**
Fullerton Rd.
  SW18 . . . . 3D **101**
Fullwood's M.
  N1 . . . . 1C **10** (2F **63**)
Fulmar Ho. SE16 . . . . . . 5F **79**
. . . . (off Tawny Way)
Fulmead St. SW6 . . . . . . 4D **87**

Fulmer Ho. NW8 . . . . 3A **60**
. . . . (off Mallory St.)
Fulmer Rd. E16 . . . . 4F **69**
Fulneck E1 . . . . 4E **65**
. . . . (off Mile End Rd.)
Fulready Rd. E10 . . . . . . 1F **39**
Fulthorp Rd. SE3 . . . . . . 5B **96**
Fulton M. W2 . . . . 1E **73**
Fulwood Pl.
  WC1 . . . . 1A **16** (4B **62**)
Fulwood Wlk.
  SW19 . . . . 1A **114**
Funland 5B **14**
. . . . (in Trocadero Cen.)
Furber St. W6 . . . . 4D **71**
Furley Ho. SE15 . . . . 3C **92**
. . . . (off Peckham Rd.)
Furley Rd. SE15 . . . . 3C **92**
Furlong Rd. N7 . . . . 3C **48**
Furmage St. SW18 . . . . 5D **101**
Furneaux Av.
  SE27 . . . . 5D **119**
Furness Ho. SW1 . . . . . . 1D **89**
. . . . (off Abbots Mnr.)
Furness Rd. NW10 . . . . . 1C **56**
  SW6 . . . . 5D **87**
Furnival Mans. W1 . . . . . 1F **13**
. . . . (off Wells St.)
Furnival St.
  EC4 . . . . 2B **16** (5C **62**)
Furrow La. E9 . . . . 2E **51**
Fursecroft W1 . . . . 5B **60**
. . . . (off George St.)
Further Grn. Rd.
  SE6 . . . . 5A **110**
FURZEDOWN 5D **117**
Furzedown Dr.
  SW17 . . . . 5D **117**
Furzedown Rd.
  SW17 . . . . 5D **117**
Furzefield Rd. SE3 . . . . . 2D **97**
Furze St. E3 . . . . 4C **66**
Fusion Health & Leisure Cen.
. . . . 5D **77**
Fye Foot La. EC4 . . . . . . 4F **17**
. . . . (off Queen Victoria St.)
Fyfield N4 . . . . 4C **34**
. . . . (off Six Acres Est.)
Fyfield Ct. E7 . . . . 3C **54**
Fyfield Rd. SW9 . . . . . . 1C **104**
Fynes St. SW1 . . . . 5F **75**

G

Gable Ct. SE26 . . . . 4D **121**
Gables Cl. SE5 . . . . 4A **92**
  SE12 . . . . 1C **124**
Gabriel Ho. N1 . . . . 5D **49**
. . . . (off Islington Grn.)
  SE11 . . . . 5B **76**
Gabrielle Ct. NW3 . . . . . 3F **45**
Gabriel M. NW2 . . . . 4B **30**
Gabriel St. SE23 . . . . . . 5F **107**
Gabriels Wharf
  SE1 . . . . 1B **24** (2C **76**)
Gad Cl. E13 . . . . 2D **69**
Gaddesden Ho. EC1 . . . . 2C **10**
. . . . (off Cranwood St.)

Gadebridge Ho. SW3 . . . 1A **88**
. . . . (off Cale St.)
Gadsbury Cl. NW9 . . . . . 1B **28**
Gadsden Ho. W10 . . . . . 3A **58**
. . . . (off Hazlewood Cres.)
Gadwall Cl. E16 . . . . 5D **69**
Gage Brown Ho. W10 . . 5F **57**
. . . . (off Bridge Cl.)
Gage Rd. E16 . . . . 4A **68**
Gage St. WC1 . . . . . . 5E **7** (4A **62**)
Gainford Ho. E2 . . . . 2D **65**
. . . . (off Ellsworth St.)
Gainford St. N1 . . . . 5C **48**
Gainsborough Ct.
  SE16 . . . . 1D **93**
. . . . (off Stubbs Dr.)
  SE21 . . . . 2A **120**
  W12 . . . . 3E **71**
Gainsborough Gdns.
  NW3 . . . . 5F **31**
  NW11 . . . . 2B **30**
Gainsborough Ho.
  E14 . . . . 3C **80**
. . . . (off Cassilis Rd.)
  E14 . . . . 1A **80**
. . . . (off Victory Pl.)
  SW1 . . . . 5F **75**
. . . . (off Erasmus St.)
Gainsborough Mans.
  W14 . . . . 2A **86**
. . . . (off Queen's Club Gdns.)
Gainsborough M.
  SE26 . . . . 3D **121**
Gainsborough Rd.
  E11 . . . . 2A **40**
  E15 . . . . 2A **68**
  W4 . . . . 5B **70**
Gainsborough St. E9 . . . . 3B **52**
Gainsborough Studios E.
  N1 . . . . 5F **49**
. . . . (off Poole St.)
Gainsborough Studios Nth.
  N1 . . . . 5F **49**
. . . . (off Poole St.)
Gainsborough Studios Sth.
  N1 . . . . 5F **49**
. . . . (off Poole St.)
Gainsborough Studios W.
  N1 . . . . 5F **49**
. . . . (off Poole St.)
Gainsfield Ct. E11 . . . . . 5A **40**
Gainsford St.
  SE1 . . . . 3F **27** (3B **78**)
Gairloch Ho. NW1 . . . . . 4F **47**
. . . . (off Stratford Vs.)
Gairloch Rd. SE5 . . . . . . 5A **92**
Gaisford St. NW5 . . . . . . 3E **47**
Gaitskell Ct. SW11 . . . . . 5A **88**
Gaitskell Ho. E6 . . . . 5F **55**
  SE17 . . . . 2A **92**
. . . . (off Villa St.)
Gala Bingo
  Camberwell 3E **91**
  Stratford 5F **53**
  Surrey Quays 4F **79**
Galahad Rd.
  BR1: Brom 4C **124**
Galata Rd. SW13 . . . . . . 3C **84**
Galatea Sq. SE15 . . . . . 1D **107**

Galaxy Bldg. E14 . . . . . . 5C 80
   (off Crews St.)
Galaxy Ho. EC2 . . . . 3C 10
   (off Leonard St.)
Galbraith St. E14 . . . . 4E 81
Galena Arches W6 . . . . . . 5D 71
   (off Galena Rd.)
Galena Ho. W6 . . . . 5D 71
   (off Galena Rd.)
Galena Rd. W6 . . . . 5D 71
Galen Pl.
  WC1 . . . . 1E 15 (4A 62)
Galesbury Rd.
  SW18 . . . . 4E 101
Gales Gdns. E2 . . . . 2D 65
Gale St. E3 . . . . 4C 66
Galgate Cl. SW19 . . . . . 1F 113
Galleon Cl. SE16 . . . . . . 3F 79
Galleon Ho. E14 . . . . 5E 81
   (off Glengarnock Av.)
Gallery Cl. SE1 . . . . 4B 26
   (off Pilgrimage St.)
SW10 . . . . 2E 87
Gallery Rd. SE21 . . . . . . 1F 119
Galleywall Rd. SE16 . . . 5D 79
Galleywall Rd. Trad. Est.
  SE16 . . . . 5D 79
   (off Galleywall Rd.)
Galleywood Ho. W10 . . . 4E 57
   (off Sutton Way)
Gallia Rd. N5 . . . . 2D 49
Gallions Rd. SE7 . . . . . . 5D 83
Galliver Pl. E5 . . . . 1D 51
Gallon Cl. SE7 . . . . 5E 83
Galloway Rd. W12 . . . . . 2C 70
Gallus Sq. SE3 . . . . 1D 111
Galsworthy Av. E14 . . . . 5A 66
Galsworthy Cl. NW2 . . . 1A 44
Galsworthy Cres.
  SE3 . . . . 4E 97
Galsworthy Ho. W11 . . . 5A 58
   (off Elgin Cres.)
Galsworthy Rd. NW2 . . . 1A 44
Galsworthy Ter. N16 . . . 5A 36
Galton St. W10 . . . . 2A 58
Galveston Ho. E1 . . . . . . 3A 66
   (off Harford St.)
Galveston Rd.
  SW15 . . . . 3B 100
Galway Cl. SE16 . . . . . . 1D 93
   (off Masters Dr.)
Galway Ho. E1 . . . . 4F 65
   (off White Horse La.)
EC1 . . . . 2A 10
Galway St.
  EC1 . . . . 2A 10 (2E 63)
Gambetta St. SW8 . . . . . 5D 89
Gambia St.
  SE1 . . . . 2E 25 (2D 77)
Gambier Ho. EC1 . . . . . . 2A 10
   (off Mora St.)
Gamboie Rd. SW17 . . . . 4A 116
Gamlen Rd. SW15 . . . . . 2F 99
Gamuel Cl. E17 . . . . 1C 38
Gandhi Cl. E17 . . . . 1C 38
Gandolfi St. SE15 . . . . . 2A 92
Ganton St.
  W1 . . . . 4F 13 (1E 75)

Gap Rd. SW19 . . . . 5C 114
Garbett Ho. SE17 . . . . . . 2D 91
   (off Doddington Gro.)
Garbutt Pl.
  W1 . . . . 5C 4 (4C 60)
Garden Cl. SE12 . . . . . . 3D 125
SW15 . . . . 5E 99
Garden Ct. EC4 . . . . 4B 16
NW8 . . . . 2F 59
   (off Garden Rd.)
W11 . . . . 1A 72
   (off Clarendon Rd.)
Garden Ho. SW7 . . . . . . 4D 73
   (off Cornwall Gdns.)
Garden Ho., The W6 . . . 2F 85
   (off Bothwell St.)
Garden La.
  BR1: Brom 5D 125
SW2 . . . . 1B 118
Garden M. W2 . . . . 1C 72
Garden Pl. E8 . . . . 5B 50
Garden Rd. NW8 . . . . . . 2F 59
Garden Row
  SE1 . . . . 5D 25 (4D 77)
Garden Royal SW15 . . . . 4F 99
Gardens, The SE22 . . . . 2C 106
Garden St. E1 . . . . 4F 65
Garden Ter. SW1 . . . . . . 1F 89
SW7 . . . . 3A 74
   (off Trevor Pl.)
Garden Vw. E7 . . . . 1E 55
Garden Wlk.
  EC2 . . . . 2D 11 (2A 64)
Gardiner Av. NW2 . . . . . 2E 43
Gardiner Ho. SW11 . . . . 4A 88
Gardner Cl. E11 . . . . 1D 41
Gardner Ct. EC1 . . . . . . 3D 9
   (off Brewery Sq.)
N5 . . . . 1E 49
Gardner Ind. Est.
  SE26 . . . . 5B 122
Gardner Rd. E13 . . . . . . 3D 69
Gardners La.
  EC4 . . . . 4F 17 (1E 77)
Gardnor Rd. NW3 . . . . . 1F 45
Gard St. EC1 . . . . . . 1E 9 (2D 63)
Gareth Ct. SW16 . . . . . . 3F 117
Gareth Gro.
  BR1: Brom 4C 124
Garfield Rd. NW6 . . . . . 4A 44
   (off Willesden La.)
Garfield M. SW11 . . . . . 1C 102
Garfield Rd. E13 . . . . . . 3B 68
SW11 . . . . 1C 102
SW19 . . . . 5E 115
Garford St. E14 . . . . 1C 80
Garganey Ct. NW10 . . . 3A 42
   (off Elgar Av.)
Garland Ct. E14 . . . . 1C 80
   (off Premiere Pl.)
SE17 . . . . 5E 77
   (off Wansey St.)
Garlands Ho. NW8 . . . . 1E 59
   (off Carlton Hill)
Garlick Hill
  EC4 . . . . 4A 18 (1E 77)
Garlies Rd. SE23 . . . . . 3A 122
Garlinge Rd. NW2 . . . . . 3B 44
Garnault M. EC1 . . . . . . 2C 8

Garnault Pl.
  EC1 . . . . 2C 8 (2C 62)
Garner St. E2 . . . . 1C 64
Garnet Ho. E1 . . . . 2E 79
   (off Garnet St.)
Garnet Rd. NW10 . . . . . 3A 42
Garnet St. E1 . . . . 1E 79
Garnett Rd. NW3 . . . . . . 2B 46
Garnham Cl. N16 . . . . . . 4B 36
Garnham St. N16 . . . . . . 4B 36
Garnies Cl. SE15 . . . . . . 3B 92
Garrad's Rd. SW16 . . . . 3F 117
Garrard Wlk. NW10 . . . . 3A 42
Garratt Cl. SW18 . . . . . . 5D 101
Garratt La. SW17 . . . . . . 3E 115
SW18 . . . . 4D 101
Garratt Ter. SW17 . . . . . 4A 116
Garraway Ct. SW13 . . . . 3E 85
   (off Wyatt Dr.)
Garrett Cl. W3 . . . . 4A 56
Garrett Ho. SE1 . . . . 3D 25
   (off Burrows M.)
W12 . . . . 5D 57
   (off Du Cane Rd.)
Garrett St.
  EC1 . . . . 3A 10 (3E 63)
Garrick Av. NW11 . . . . . 1A 30
Garrick Cl. SW18 . . . . . . 2E 101
Garrick Ct. E8 . . . . 4B 50
   (off Jacaranda Gro.)
Garrick Ho. W1 . . . . 2D 21
W4 . . . . 2A 84
Garrick Ind. Est.
  NW9 . . . . 1B 28
Garrick Rd. NW9 . . . . . . 1B 28
Garrick St.
  WC2 . . . . 4D 15 (1A 76)
Garrick Theatre 5D 15
   (off Charing Cross Rd.)
Garrick Yd. WC2 . . . . . . 4D 15
Garrison Rd. E3 . . . . 5C 52
Garsdale Ter. W14 . . . . . 1B 86
   (off Aisgill Av.)
Garsington M. SE4 . . . . 1B 108
Garson Ho. W2 . . . . 1F 73
   (off Gloucester Ter.)
Garston Ho. N1 . . . . 4D 49
   (off The Sutton Est.)
Garter Way SE16 . . . . . . 3F 79
Garth Ho. NW2 . . . . 4B 30
Garthorne Rd. SE23 . . . 5F 107
Garthorne Road
  Nature Reserve 5F 107
Garth Rd. NW2 . . . . 4B 30
Gartmoor Gdns.
  SW19 . . . . 1B 114
Garton Pl. SW18 . . . . . . 4E 101
Gartons Way SW11 . . . . 1E 101
Garvary Rd. E16 . . . . . . 5D 69
Garway Rd. W2 . . . . 5D 59
Gascoigne Pl.
  E2 . . . . 1F 11 (2B 64)
   (not continuous)
Gascony Av. NW6 . . . . . 4C 44
Gascoyne Ho. E9 . . . . . . 4A 52
Gascoyne Rd. E9 . . . . . . 4F 51
Gaselee St. E14 . . . . 2E 81
   (off Baffin Way)
Gaskarth Rd. SW12 . . . . 4D 103

Gaskell Rd. N6 . . . . 1B 32
Gaskell St. SW4 . . . . 5A 90
Gaskin St. N1 . . . . 5D 49
Gaspar Cl. SW5 . . . . 5D 73
   (off Courtfield Gdns.)
Gaspar M. SW5 . . . . 5D 73
Gassiot Rd. SW17 . . . . . 4B 116
Gasson Ho. SE14 . . . . . . 2F 93
   (off John Williams Cl.)
Gastein Rd. W6 . . . . 2F 85
Gastigny Ho. EC1 . . . . . . 2A 10
Gataker Ho. SE16 . . . . . . 4D 79
   (off Slippers Pl.)
Gataker St. SE16 . . . . . . 4D 79
Gatcombe Ho. SE22 . . . . 1A 106
Gatcombe Rd. E16 . . . . . 2C 82
  N19 . . . . 5F 33
Gate Cinema 2C 72
   (off Notting Hill Ga.)
Gateforth St. NW8 . . . . . 3A 60
Gate Hill Ct. W11 . . . . . . 2B 72
   (off Ladbroke Ter.)
Gate Ho. N1 . . . . 4F 49
   (off Ufton Rd.)
Gatehouse Sq. SE1 . . . . . 1A 26
Gatehouse Theatre . . . 3C 32
Gateley Ho. SE4 . . . . . . 2F 107
   (off Coston Wlk.)
Gateley Rd. SW9 . . . . . . 1B 104
Gate Lodge W9 . . . . 4C 58
   (off Admiral Wlk.)
Gate M. SW7 . . . . 3A 74
   (off Rutland Ga.)
Gatesborough St.
  EC2 . . . . 3D 11 (3A 64)
Gates Ct. SE17 . . . . 1E 91
Gatesden WC1 . . 2F 7 (2A 62)
Gateside Rd.
  SW17 . . . . 3B 116
Gate St. WC2 . . 2F 15 (5B 62)
Gate Theatre, The 2C 72
   (off Pembridge Rd.)
Gateway SE17 . . . . 2E 91
Gateway Arc. N1 . . . . . . 1D 63
   (off Upper St.)
Gateway Bus. Cen.
  BR3: Beck. 5A 122
Gateway Ind. Est.
  NW10 . . . . 2B 56
Gateway M. E8 . . . . 2B 50
Gateway Rd. E10 . . . . . . 5D 39
Gateways, The SW3 . . . . 5A 74
   (off Sprimont Pl.)
Gathorne St. E2 . . . . 1F 65
Gatliff Cl. SW1 . . . . 1D 89
   (off Ebury Bri. Rd.)
Gatliff Rd. SW1 . . . . 1D 89
   (not continuous)
Gatonby St. SE15 . . . . . . 4B 92
Gattis Wharf N1 . . . . 1A 62
   (off New Wharf Rd.)
Gatton Rd. SW17 . . . . . . 4A 116
Gatwick Ho. E14 . . . . . . 5B 66
   (off Clemence St.)
Gatwick Rd. SW18 . . . . . 5B 100
Gauden Cl. SW4 . . . . . . 1F 103
Gauden Rd. SW4 . . . . . . 5F 89
Gaugin Ct. SE16 . . . . . . 1D 93
   (off Stubbs Dr.)

Gaumont Ter.
  W12 . . . . 3E 71
   (off Lime Gro.)
Gaunt St.
  SE1 . . . . 5F 25 (4E 77)
Gautrey Rd. SE15 . . . . . . 5E 93
Gavel St. SE17 . . . . 5F 77
Gaverick M. E14 . . . . . . 5C 80
Gavestone Cres.
  SE12 . . . . 5D 111
Gavestone Rd.
  SE12 . . . . 5D 111
Gaviller Pl. E5 . . . . 1D 51
Gawber St. E2 . . . . 2E 65
Gawsworth Cl. E15 . . . . . 2B 54
Gawthorne Ct. E3 . . . . . . 1C 66
Gay Cl. NW2 . . . . 2D 43
Gaydon Ho. W2 . . . . 4D 59
   (off Bourne Ter.)
Gayfere St.
  SW1 . . . . 5D 23 (4A 76)
Gayford Rd. W12 . . . . . . 3B 70
Gay Ho. N16 . . . . 2A 50
Gayhurst SE17 . . . . 2F 91
   (off Hopwood Rd.)
Gayhurst Ho. NW8 . . . . . 3A 60
   (off Mallory St.)
Gayhurst Rd. E8 . . . . . . 4C 50
Gaymead NW8 . . . . 5D 45
   (off Abbey Rd.)
Gaynesford Rd.
  SE23 . . . . 2F 121
Gay Rd. E15 . . . . 1F 67
Gaysley Ho. SE11 . . . . . . 5C 76
   (off Hotspur St.)
Gay St. SW15 . . . . 1F 99
Gayton Cres. NW3 . . . . . 1F 45
Gayton Rd. NW3 . . . . . . 1F 45
Gayville Rd. SW11 . . . . . 4B 102
Gaywood Cl. SW2 . . . . . 1B 118
Gaywood St.
  SE1 . . . . 5E 25 (4D 77)
Gaza St. SE17 . . . . 1D 91
Gaze Ho. E14 . . . . 5F 67
   (off Blair St.)
Gazelle Ho. E15 . . . . 3A 54
Gean Ct. E11 . . . . 1F 53
Gearing Cl. SW17 . . . . . 4C 116
Geary Rd. NW10 . . . . . . 2C 42
Geary St. N7 . . . . 2B 48
Gedling Pl.
  SE1 . . . . 5F 27 (4B 78)
Geere Rd. E15 . . . . 5B 54
Gees Ct. W1 . . 3C 12 (5C 60)
Gee St. EC1 . . 3F 9 (3E 63)
Geffrye Ct. N1 . . . . 1A 64
Geffrye Est. N1 . . . . 1A 64
Geffrye Mus. 1F 11
Geffrye St.
  E2 . . . . 1F 11 (1B 64)
Geldart Rd. SE15 . . . . . . 3D 93
Geldeston Rd. E5 . . . . . . 4C 36
Gellatly Rd. SE14 . . . . . . 5E 93
Gemini Bus. Cen.
  E16 . . . . 3F 67
Gemini Bus. Est.
  SE14 . . . . 5A 80
Gemini Cl. E1 . . . . 1C 78
   (off Vaughan Way)

General Wolfe Rd.
  SE10 . . . . 4F 95
Geneva Ct. NW9 . . . . . . 1A 28
Geneva Dr. SW9 . . . . . . 2C 104
Genoa Av. SW15 . . . . . . 3E 99
Genoa Ho. E1 . . . . 3F 65
   (off Ernest St.)
Gentry Gdns. E13 . . . . . . 3C 68
Geoffrey Cl. SE5 . . . . . . 5E 91
Geoffrey Ct. SE4 . . . . . . 5B 94
Geoffrey Gdns. E6 . . . . . 1F 69
Geoffrey Ho. SE1 . . . . . . 5C 26
   (off Pardoner St.)
Geoffrey Jones Ct.
  NW10 . . . . 5C 42
Geoffrey Rd. SE4 . . . . . . 1B 108
George Beard Rd.
  SE8 . . . . 5B 80
George Belt Ho. E2 . . . . . 2F 65
   (off Smart St.)
George Ct. WC2 . . . . 5E 15
George Downing Est.
  N16 . . . . 4B 36
George Eliot Ho.
  SW1 . . . . 5E 75
   (off Vauxhall Bri. Rd.)
George Elliston Ho.
  SE1 . . . . 1C 92
   (off Old Kent Rd.)
George Eyre Ho.
  NW8 . . . . 1F 59
   (off Cochrane St.)
George Gillett Ct.
  EC1 . . . . 3A 10
George Inn Yd.
  SE1 . . . . 2B 26 (2F 77)
George La. SE13 . . . . . . 4D 109
George Lansbury Ho.
  NW10 . . . . 4A 42
George Lindgren Ho.
  SW6 . . . . 3B 86
   (off Clem Attlee Ct.)
George Loveless Ho.
  E2 . . . . 1F 11
   (off Diss St.)
George Lowe Ct. W2 . . . 4D 59
   (off Bourne Ter.)
George Mathers Rd.
  SE11 . . . . 5D 77
George M. NW1 . . . . 2A 6
  SW9 . . . . 5C 90
George Padmore Ho.
  E8 . . . . 5C 50
   (off Brougham Rd.)
George Peabody Ct.
  NW1 . . . . 4A 60
   (off Burne St.)
George Potter Ho.
  SW11 . . . . 5F 87
   (off George Potter Way)
George Potter Way
  SW11 . . . . 5F 87
George Row SE16 . . . . . . 3C 78
George's Rd. N7 . . . . . . 2B 48
George's Sq. SW6 . . . . . 2B 86
   (off North End Rd.)
George St. E16 . . . . 5B 68
   (not continuous)
  W1 . . . . 2A 12 (5B 60)

George Tingle Ho.
 SE1 . . . . 5F 27
Georgetown Cl.
 SE19. . . . . .5A 120
Georgette Pl. SE10. . . . . 3E 95
George Walter Ct.
 SE16. . . . . 5E 79
 (off Millender Wlk.)
George Wyver Cl.
 SW19 . . . . .5A 100
George Yd.
 EC3. . . . . 3C 18 (5F 63)
 W1 . . . . 4C 12 (1C 74)
Georgiana St. NW1 . . . . . 5E 47
Georgian Ct. SE9 . . . . . . 5E 51
 NW4 . . . . 1D 29
 SW16 . . . . .4A 118
Georgian Ho. E16. . . . . . .2C 82
 (off Capulet M.)
Georgina Gdns. E2 . . . . . 2B 64
Geraint Rd.
 BR1: Brom 4C 124
Geraldine Rd.
 SW18 . . . . .3E 101
Geraldine St.
 SE11 . . . . . . 5D 25 (4D 77)
Gerald M. SW1 . . . . 5C 74
 (off Gerald Rd.)
Gerald Rd. E16. . . . . 3B 68
 SW1 . . . . 5C 74
Gerard Pl. E9 . . . . 4F 51
Gerard Rd. SW13 . . . . . . 4B 84
Gerards Cl. SE16 . . . . . . 1E 93
Germander Way E15 . . . 2A 68
Gernigan Ho. SW18 . . . . 4F 101
Gernon Rd. E3 . . . . 1A 66
Geron Way NW2 . . . . 3D 29
Gerrard Ho. SE14 . . . . . . .3E 93
 (off Briant St.)
Gerrard Pl.
 W1 . . . . 4C 14 (1F 75)
Gerrard Rd. N1. . . . . 1D 63
Gerrard St.
 W1 . . . . 4C 14 (1F 75)
Gerridge Ct. SE1 . . . . 5C 24
 (off Gerridge St.)
Gerridge St.
 SE1 . . . . 5C 24 (4C 76)
Gerry Raffles Sq. E15. . . 4F 53
Gertrude St. SW10 . . . . . 2E 87
Gervase St. SE15. . . . . . . 3D 93
Ghent St. SE6. . . . . .2C 122
Ghent Way E8 . . . . 3B 50
Giant Arches Rd.
 SE24 . . . . .5E 105
Gibbings Ho. SE1 . . . . . . 4E 25
 (off King James St.)
Gibbins Rd. E15 . . . . 4E 53
Gibbon Ho. NW8. . . . . . . .3F 59
 (off Fisherton St.)
Gibbon Rd. SE15 . . . . 5E 93
 W3 . . . . 1A 70
Gibbon's Rents SE1 . . . . 2D 27
Gibbons Rd. NW10. . . . . . 3A 42
Gibbon Wlk. SW15. . . . . . 2C 98
Gibbs Av. SE19 . . . . .5F 119
Gibbs Cl. SE19 . . . . 5F 119
Gibbs Grn. W14 . . . . 1B 86
 (not continuous)

Gibbs Grn. Cl. W14 . . . . 1B 86
Gibbs Sq. SE19. . . . . . . .5F 119
Gibney Ter.
 BR1: Brom 4B 124
Gibraltar Wlk. E2 . . . . . . 2B 64
 (off Padbury Ct.)
Gibson Cl. E1 . . . . 3E 65
Gibson Gdns. N16 . . . . . . 4B 36
Gibson Rd. SE11 . . . . 5B 76
Gibsons Hill SW16. . . . . .5D 119
 (not continuous)
Gibson Sq. N1 . . . . 5C 48
Gibson St. SE10 . . . . 1A 96
Gideon Rd. SW11 . . . . . . 1C 102
Gielgud Theatre 4B 14
 (off Shaftesbury Av.)
Giesbach Rd. N19 . . . . . . 4F 33
Giffen Sq. Mkt. SE8 . . . . .3C 94
 (off Giffen St.)
Giffin St. SE8 . . . . 3C 94
Gifford Ho. SE10. . . . . . . .1F 95
 (off Eastney St.)
 SW1 . . . . .1E 89
 (off Churchill Gdns.)
Gifford St. N1. . . . . 4A 48
Gift La. E15 . . . . 5A 54
Gilbert Bri. EC2 . . . . .5A 10
 (off Gilbert Ho.)
Gilbert Collection 4A 16
 (off Strand)
Gilbert Ho. E2 . . . . 2F 65
 (off Usk St.)
 EC2 . . . . 5A 10
 SE8 . . . . 2C 94
 SW1 . . . . 1D 89
 (off Churchill Gdns.)
 SW8 . . . . 3A 90
 (off Wyvil Rd.)
 SW13 . . . . 3D 85
 (off Trinity Chu. Rd.)
Gilbert Pl.
 WC1 . . . . 1D 15 (4A 62)
Gilbert Rd. SE11 . . . . 5C 76
Gilbert Scott SW18 . . . . . 4A 100
Gilbert Sheldon Ho.
 W2 . . . . .4F 59
 (off Edgware Rd.)
Gilbertson Ho. E14 . . . . . .4C 80
 (off Mellish St.)
Gilbert St. E15 . . . . 1A 54
 W1 . . . . 3C 12 (5C 60)
Gilbey Rd. SW17 . . . . . . 4A 116
Gilbeys Yd. NW1 . . . . 4C 46
Gilby Ho. E9 . . . . 3F 51
Gilda Cres. N16 . . . . 3C 36
Gildea St.
 W1 . . . . 1E 13 (4D 61)
Gilden Cres. NW5 . . . . . . 2C 46
Giles Coppice
 SE19. . . . . 4B 120
Giles High St.
 WC2 . . . . 2C 14 (5F 61)
Giles Ho. SE16. . . . . .4C 78
 (off Old Jamaica Rd.)
 W11 . . . . .1C 58
 (off Westbourne Gro.)
Gilesmead SE5. . . . . 4F 91
Gilkes Cres. SE21 . . . . . 4A 106
Gilkes Pl. SE21 . . . . 4A 106

Gillam Ho. SE16. . . . . 5E 79
 (off Silwood St.)
Gillan Ct. SE12 . . . . 3D 125
Gill Av. E16 . . . . 5C 68
Gillender St. E3 . . . . 3E 67
 E14 . . . . 3E 67
Gillespie Rd. N5 . . . . 5C 34
Gillett Av. E6. . . . . 1F 69
Gillett Pl. N16 . . . . 2A 50
Gillett St. N16 . . . . 2A 50
Gillfoot NW1. . . . . .1F 5
 (off Hampstead Rd.)
Gillian St. SE13 . . . . 3D 109
Gillies Ho. NW6 . . . . .4F 45
 (off Hilgrove Rd.)
Gillies St. NW5 . . . . 2C 46
Gillingham M. SW1 . . . . . 5E 75
Gillingham Rd. NW2 . . . . 5A 30
Gillingham Row
 SW1 . . . . 5E 75
Gillingham St. SW1 . . . . . 5E 75
Gillison Wlk. SE16. . . . . . 4D 79
Gillman Dr. E15 . . . . 5B 54
Gillman Ho. E2. . . . . 1C 64
 (off Pritchard's Rd.)
Gillray Ho. SW10 . . . . 2F 87
 (off Ann La.)
Gill St. E14. . . . . 5B 66
Gilmore Rd. SE13. . . . . . 2F 109
Gilpin Av. SW14 . . . . 2A 98
Gilpin Cl. W2 . . . . 4E 59
 (off Porteus Rd.)
Gilpin Rd. E5 . . . . 1A 52
Gilray Ho. W2. . . . . .1F 73
 (off Gloucester Ter.)
Gilstead Rd. SW6 . . . . . . 5D 87
Gilston Rd. SW10. . . . . . . 1E 87
Gilton Rd. SE6 . . . . 3A 124
Giltspur St.
 EC1 . . . . 2E 17 (5D 63)
Ginger Apartments
 SE1 . . . . .3B 78
 (off Cayenne Ct.)
Ginsburg Yd. NW3 . . . . . . 1E 45
Gipsy Hill SE19 . . . . 4A 120
Gipsy La. SW15. . . . . 1D 99
Gipsy Moth IV 2E 95
Gipsy Rd. SE27 . . . . 4E 119
Gipsy Rd. Gdns.
 SE27 . . . . 4E 119
Giralda Cl. E16. . . . . 4F 69
Giraud St. E14 . . . . 5D 67
Girdler's Rd. W14. . . . . . . 5F 71
Girdlestone Wlk. N19. . . . 4E 33
Girdwood Rd. SW18. . . . 5A 100
Girling Ho. N1 . . . . .5A 50
 (off Colville Est.)
Gironde Rd. SW6 . . . . 3B 86
Girton Rd. SE26 . . . . 5F 121
Girton Vs. W10. . . . . 5F 57
Gisburn Ho. SE15. . . . . . . 2C 92
 (off Friary Est.)
Gissing Wlk. N1. . . . . 4C 48
Gittens Cl.
 BR1: Brom 4B 124
Given Wilson Wlk.
 E13 . . . . 1B 68
Gladding Rd. E12. . . . . . . 1F 55

Glade, The SE7 . . . . 3E 97
Gladesmore Community
School & Sports Cen.
. . . . 1C 36
Gladesmore Rd. N15 . . . 1B 36
Gladiator St. SE23 . . . 5A 108
Glading Ter. N16 . . . . . . 5B 36
Gladsmuir Rd. N19 . . . . 3E 33
Gladstone Ct. SW1 . . . . 5F 75
(off Regency St.)
Gladstone Ct. Bus. Cen.
SW8 . . . . 4D 89
(off Pagden St.)
Gladstone Ho. E14 . . . . 5C 66
(off E. India Dock Rd.)
Gladstone M. NW6 . . . . 4B 44
Gladstone Pde. NW2 . . . 4E 29
Gladstone Pk. Gdns.
NW2 . . . . 5D 29
Gladstone Pl. E3 . . . . . 1B 66
Gladstone St.
SE1 . . . . 5D 25 (4D 77)
Gladstone Ter. SE27 . . . 5E 119
(off Bentons La.)
SW8 . . . . 4D 89
Gladwell Rd.
BR1: Brom 5C 124
N8 . . . . 1B 34
Gladwin Ho. NW1 . . . . . 1A 6
(off Werrington St.)
Gladwyn Rd. SW15 . . . . 1F 99
Gladys Dimson Ho.
E7 . . . . 2B 54
Gladys Rd. NW6 . . . . . . 4C 44
Glaisher St. SE8 . . . . . 2C 94
Glamis Pl. E1 . . . . 1E 79
Glamis Rd. E1 . . . . 1E 79
Glanville Rd. SW2 . . . . 3A 104
Glasbrook Rd. SE9 . . . . 5F 111
Glaserton Rd. N16 . . . . 2A 36
Glasford St. SW17 . . . . 5B 116
Glasgow Ho. W9 . . . . . . 1D 59
(off Maida Va.)
Glasgow Rd. E13 . . . . . 1D 69
Glasgow Ter. SW1 . . . . 1E 89
Glasier Ct. E15 . . . . . . 4A 54
Glaskin M. E9 . . . . 3A 52
Glasshrook Rd. SE9 . . . . 5F 111
Glass Art Gallery, The
. . . . 4D 27 (3A 78)
Glasshill St.
SE1 . . . . . . 3E 25 (3D 77)
Glass Ho. WC2 . . . . 3D 15
(off New Compton St.)
Glass Ho., The SE1 . . . . 4D 27
(off Royal Oak Yd.)
Glasshouse Flds. E1 . . . 1F 79
Glasshouse St.
W1 . . . . 5A 14 (1E 75)
Glasshouse Wlk.
SE11 . . . . 1A 90
Glasshouse Yd.
EC1 . . . . 4F 9 (3E 63)
Glasslyn Rd. N8 . . . . . . 1F 33
Glass St. E2 . . . . 3D 65
Glassworks Studios
E2 . . . . 1E 11
(off Basing Pl.)
Glastonbury Ct. SE14 . . . 3E 93
(off Farrow La.)

Glastonbury Ho.
SE12 . . . . 3B 110
(off Wantage Rd.)
SW1 . . . . 1D 89
(off Abbots Mnr.)
Glastonbury Pl. E1 . . . . 5E 65
Glastonbury St. NW6 . . . 2B 44
Glaucus St. E3 . . . . 4D 67
Glazbury Rd. W14 . . . . . 5A 72
Glazebrook Cl. SE21 . . . 2F 119
Glebe, The SE3 . . . . . . 1A 110
SW16 . . . . 4F 117
Glebe Cl. W4 . . . . 1A 84
Glebe Ho. SE16 . . . . . . 4D 79
(off Slippers Pl.)
Glebe Hyrst SE19 . . . . . 4A 120
Glebelands E10 . . . . . . 4D 39
Glebelands Cl. SE5 . . . . 1A 106
Glebe Pl. SW3 . . . . 2A 88
Glebe Rd. E8 . . . . 4B 50
NW10 . . . . 3C 42
SW13 . . . . 5C 84
Glebe St. W4 . . . . 1A 84
Glebe Ter. E3 . . . . 2D 67
W4 . . . . 1A 84
Gledhow Gdns. SW5 . . . . 5E 73
Gledstanes Rd.
W14 . . . . 1A 86
Glegg Pl. SW15 . . . . . . 2F 99
Glenaffric Av. E14 . . . . . 5E 81
Glen Albyn Rd.
SW19 . . . . 2F 113
Glenallan Ho. W14 . . . . 5B 72
(off North End Cres.)
Glenalvon Way SE18 . . . 5F 83
Glenarm Rd. E5 . . . . . . 1E 51
Glenavon Rd. E15 . . . . . 4A 54
Glenbow Rd.
BR1: Brom 5A 124
Glenbrook Rd. NW6 . . . 2C 44
Glenburnie Rd.
SW17 . . . . 3B 116
Glencairne Cl. E16 . . . . 4F 69
Glencoe Mans. SW9 . . . . 3C 90
(off Mowll St.)
Glendall St. SW9 . . . . . 2B 104
Glendarvon St.
SW15 . . . . 1F 99
Glendower Gdns.
SW14 . . . . 1A 98
Glendower Pl. SW7 . . . . 5F 73
Glendower Rd.
SW14 . . . . 1A 98
Glendown Ho. E8 . . . . . 2C 50
Glendun Ct. W3 . . . . . . 1A 70
Glendun Rd. W3 . . . . . . 1A 70
Gleneagle M. SW16 . . . 5F 117
Gleneagle Rd.
SW16 . . . . 5F 117
Gleneagles Cl. SE16 . . . 1D 93
Gleneldon M.
SW16 . . . . 4A 118
Gleneldon Rd.
SW16 . . . . 4A 118
Glenelg Rd. SW2 . . . . . 3A 104
Glenfarg Rd. SE6 . . . . . 1E 123
Glenfield Rd. SW12 . . . . 1E 117

Glenfinlas Way SE5 . . . . 3D 91
Glenforth St. SE10 . . . . 1B 96
Glengall Gro. E14 . . . . . 4D 81
Glengall Pas. NW6 . . . . 5C 44
(off Priory Pk. Rd.)
Glengall Rd. NW6 . . . . . 5B 44
SE15 . . . . 1B 92
Glengall Ter. SE15 . . . . 2B 92
Glengarnock Av. E14 . . . 5E 81
Glengarry Rd. SE22 . . . 3A 106
Glenhurst Av. NW5 . . . . 1C 46
Glenhurst Ct. SE19 . . . . 5B 120
Glenilla Rd. NW3 . . . . . 3A 46
Glenister Rd. SE10 . . . . 1B 96
Glenkerry Ho. E14 . . . . 5E 67
(off Burcham St.)
Glenloch Rd. NW3 . . . . 3A 46
Glenluce Rd. SE3 . . . . . 2C 96
Glen M. E17 . . . . 1B 38
Glenmore Rd. NW3 . . . . 3A 46
Glennie Ct. SE22 . . . . . 1C 120
Glennie Ho. SE10 . . . . . 4E 95
(off Blackheath Hill)
Glennie Rd. SE27 . . . . 3C 118
Glenparke Rd. E7 . . . . . 3D 55
(not continuous)
Glenridding NW1 . . . . . . 1A 6
(off Ampthill Est.)
Glen Rd. E13 . . . . 3E 69
E17 . . . . 1B 38
Glenrosa St. SW6 . . . . . 5E 87
Glenrose Ct. SE1 . . . . . 5D 27
(off Long La.)
Glenroy St. W12 . . . . . . 5E 57
Glensdale Rd. SE4 . . . . 1B 108
Glenshaw Mans.
SW9 . . . . 3C 90
(off Brixton Rd.)
Glentanner Way
SW17 . . . . 3F 115
Glen Ter. E14 . . . . 3E 81
(off Manchester Rd.)
Glentham Gdns.
SW13 . . . . 2D 85
Glentham Rd. SW13 . . . 2C 84
Glenthorne M. W6 . . . . 5D 71
Glenthorne Rd. W6 . . . . 5D 71
Glenthorpe Av. SW15 . . . 2C 98
Glenton Rd. SE13 . . . . 2A 110
Glentworth St.
NW1 . . . . . . 4A 4 (3B 60)
Glenville Gro. SE8 . . . . 3B 94
Glenville M. SW18 . . . 5D 101
Glenville M. Ind. Est.
SW18 . . . . 5C 100
Glenwood Av. NW9 . . . . 3A 28
Glenwood Rd. N15 . . . . 1D 35
SE6 . . . . 1B 122
Glenworth Av. E14 . . . . 5F 81
Gliddon Dr. E5 . . . . . . 1C 50
Gliddon Rd. W14 . . . . . 5A 72
Global App. E3 . . . . 1D 67
Globe, The
SE1 . . . . 4B 26 (3E 77)
Globe Pond Rd.
SE16 . . . . 2A 80
Globe Rd. E1 . . . . 2E 65
E2 . . . . 2E 65
E15 . . . . 2B 54

Globe Rope Wlk.
E14 . . . . 5D 81
(off E. Ferry Rd.)
Globe St.
SE1 . . . . 5B 26 (4F 77)
Globe Ter. E2 . . . . . . 2E 65
GLOBE TOWN 2F 65
Globe Town Mkt. E2 . . 2F 65
Globe Wharf SE16 . . . 1F 79
Globe Yd. W1 . . . . . . 3D 13
Gloucester W14 . . . . 5B 72
(off Mornington Av.)
Gloucester Arc. SW7 . . 5E 73
Gloucester Av. NW1 . . 4C 46
Gloucester Cir. SE10 . . 3E 95
Gloucester Cl. NW10 . . 4A 42
Gloucester Ct.
EC3 . . . . 5E 19 (1A 78)
NW11 . . . . 2B 30
(off Golders Grn. Rd.)
SE22 . . . . 1C 120
Gloucester Cres.
NW1 . . . . 5D 47
Gloucester Dr. N4 . . . 4D 35
Gloucester Gdns.
NW11 . . . . 2B 30
W2 . . . . 5E 59
Gloucester Ga. NW1 . . 1D 61
(not continuous)
Gloucester Ga. M.
NW1 . . . . 1D 61
Gloucester Ho. E16 . . 2C 82
(off Gatcombe Rd.)
NW6 . . . . 1C 58
(off Cambridge Rd.)
SW9 . . . . 3C 90
Gloucester M. E10 . . . 2C 38
W2 . . . . 5E 59
Gloucester M. W. W2 . . 5E 59
Gloucester Pk. Apartments
SW7 . . . . 5E 73
Gloucester Pl.
NW1 . . . . . . 4A 4 (3B 60)
W1 . . . . 5A 4 (3B 60)
Gloucester Pl. M.
W1 . . . . . . 1A 12 (4B 60)
Gloucester Rd. E10 . . 2C 38
E11 . . . . 1D 41
SW7 . . . . 4E 73
Gloucester Sq. E2 . . . 5C 50
W2 . . . . 5F 59
Gloucester St. SW1 . . 1E 89
Gloucester Ter. W2 . . 5D 59
Gloucester Wlk. W8 . . 3C 72
Gloucester Way
EC1 . . . . . . 2C 8 (2C 62)
Glover Ho. NW6 . . . . 4E 45
(off Harben Rd.)
SE15 . . . . 2D 107
Glycena Rd. SW11 . . 1B 102
Glyn Ct. SW16 . . . . 3C 118
Glynde M. SW3 . . . . 4A 74
(off Walton St.)
Glynde Reach WC1 . . . 2E 7
Glynde St. SE4 . . . . 4B 108
Glynfield Rd. NW10 . . 4A 42
Glyn Rd. E5 . . . . 5F 37
Glyn St. SE11 . . . . . 1B 90
Glynwood Ct. SE23 . . 2E 121

Goater's All. SW6 . . . 3B 86
(off Dawes Rd.)
Godalming Rd. E14 . . 4D 67
Godbold Rd. E15 . . . . 3A 68
Goddard Pl. N19 . . . . 5E 33
Godfree Ct. SE1 . . . . 3B 26
(off Long La.)
Godfrey Ho. EC1 . . . . 2B 10
Godfrey St. E15 . . . . 1E 67
SW3 . . . . 1A 88
Goding St. SE11 . . . . 1A 90
Godley Cl. SE14 . . . . 4E 93
Godley Rd. SW18 . . . 1F 115
Godliman St.
EC4 . . . . 3E 17 (5D 63)
Godman Rd. SE15 . . . 5D 93
Godolphin Ho. NW3 . . 4A 46
(off Fellows Rd.)
Godolphin Pl. W3 . . . 1A 70
Godolphin Rd. W12 . . 2D 71
(not continuous)
Godstone Ho. SE1 . . . 5C 26
(off Pardoner St.)
Godwin Cl. N1 . . . . . 1E 63
Godwin Ct. NW1 . . . . 1E 61
(off Chalton St.)
Godwin Ho. E2 . . . . . 1B 64
(off Thurtle Rd.)
NW6 . . . . 1D 59
(off Tollgate Gdns.,
not continuous)
Godwin Rd. E7 . . . . . 1D 55
Goffers Rd. SE3 . . . . 4A 96
Golborne Gdns. W10 . . 3A 58
Golborne Ho. W10 . . . 3A 58
(off Adair Rd.)
Golborne M. W10 . . . 4A 58
Golborne Rd. W10 . . . 4A 58
Goldbeaters Ho. W1 . . 3C 14
(off Manette St.)
Goldcrest Cl. E16 . . . 4F 69
Golden Cross M.
W11 . . . . 5B 58
(off Portobello Rd.)
Golden Hinde . . 1B 26 (2F 77)
Golden Hind Pl. SE8 . . 5B 80
(off Grove St.)
Golden La.
EC1 . . . . 3F 9 (3E 63)
Golden La. Est.
EC1 . . . . 4F 9 (3E 63)
Golden Lane Leisure Cen.
. . . . 4F 9
Golden Plover Cl.
E16 . . . . 5C 68
Golden Sq.
W1 . . . . . . 4A 14 (1E 75)
Golden Yd. NW3 . . . . 1F 45
(off Holly Mt.)
Golders Ct. NW11 . . . 2B 30
Golders Gdns. NW11 . . 2A 30
GOLDERS GREEN . . . 1A 30
Golders Grn. Crematorium
NW11 . . . . 2C 30
Golders Grn. Cres.
NW11 . . . . 2B 30
Golders Grn. Rd.
NW11 . . . . 1A 30

Golderslea NW11 . . . 3C 30
Golders Mnr. Dr.
NW11 . . . . 1F 29
Golders Pk. Cl.
NW11 . . . . 3C 30
Golders Way NW11 . . 2B 30
Goldhawk Ind. Est.
W6 . . . . 4D 71
Goldhawk M. W12 . . . 3D 71
Goldhawk Rd. W6 . . . 5B 70
W12 . . . . 5B 70
Goldhurst Ter. NW6 . . 4D 45
Goldie Ho. N19 . . . . . 2F 33
Golding St. E1 . . . . . 5C 64
Golding Ter. E1 . . . . . 5C 64
SW11 . . . . 5C 88
Goldington Bldgs.
NW1 . . . . 5F 47
(off Royal College St.)
Goldington Cres.
NW1 . . . . 1F 61
Goldington St. NW1 . . 1F 61
Goldman Cl. E2 . . . . 3C 64
Goldney Rd. W9 . . . . 3C 58
Goldsboro' Rd. SW8 . . 4F 89
Goldsborough Ho.
E14 . . . . 1D 95
(off St Davids Sq.)
Goldsmith Av. E12 . . . 3F 55
NW9 . . . . 1A 28
Goldsmith Ct. WC2 . . 2E 15
(off Stukeley St.)
Goldsmith Rd. E10 . . 3C 38
SE15 . . . . 4C 92
Goldsmith's Bldgs.
W3 . . . . 2A 70
Goldsmiths Cl. W3 . . 2A 70
Goldsmiths College . . 4A 94
Goldsmith's Pl. NW6 . . 5D 45
(off Springfield La.)
Goldsmith's Row E2 . . 1C 64
Goldsmith's Sq. E2 . . 1C 64
Goldsmith St.
EC2 . . . . 2A 18 (5E 63)
Goldsworthy Gdns.
SE16 . . . . 1E 93
Goldthorpe NW1 . . . . 5E 47
(off Camden St.)
Goldwell Ho. SE22 . . 1A 106
Goldwin Cl. SE14 . . . 4E 93
Goldwing Cl. E16 . . . 5C 68
Gollogly Ter. SE7 . . . 1E 97
Gomm Rd. SE16 . . . . 4E 79
Gondar Gdns. NW6 . . 2B 44
Gonson St. SE8 . . . . 2D 95
Gonston Cl. SW19 . . 2A 114
Gonville St. SW6 . . . 1A 100
Gooch Ho. E5 . . . . . 5D 37
EC1 . . . . 5B 8
(off Portpool La.)
Goodall Ho. SE4 . . . . 2F 107
Goodall Rd. E11 . . . . 5E 39
Goodfaith Ho. E14 . . . 1D 81
(off Simpson's Rd.)
Goodge Pl.
W1 . . . . . . 1A 14 (4E 61)
Goodge St.
W1 . . . . . . 1A 14 (4E 61)

Goodhall St. NW10 . . . . 2B **56**
(not continuous)
Goodhart Pl. E14 . . . . . 1A **80**
Goodhope Ho. E14 . . . . 1D **81**
(off Poplar High St.)
Goodinge Cl. N7 . . . . . . 3A **48**
Gooding Ho. SE7 . . . . . 1E **97**
Goodman Cres.
SW2 . . . . 2A **118**
Goodman Rd. E10 . . . . . 2E **39**
Goodman's Ct. E1 . . . . . 4F **19**
Goodman's Stile E1 . . 5C **64**
Goodmans Yd.
E1 . . . . 4F **19** (1B **78**)
Goodrich Ct. W10 . . . . . 5F **57**
Goodrich Ho. E2 . . . . . . 1E **65**
(off Sewardstone Rd.)
Goodson Rd. SE22 . . 4B **106**
Goodson Rd. NW10 . . . . 4A **42**
Goodson St. N1 . . . . . . 1C **62**
Goodspeed Ho. E14 . . . . 1D **81**
(off Simpson's Rd.)
Goods Way NW1 . . . . . . 1A **62**
Goodway Gdns. E14 . . . 5F **67**
Goodwill Ho. E14 . . . . . 1D **81**
(off Simpson's Rd.)
Goodwin Cl. SE16 . . . . . 4B **78**
Goodwin Rd. W12 . . . . . 3C **70**
Goodwins Ct.
WC2 . . . . 4D **15** (1A **76**)
Goodwin St. N4 . . . . . . 4C **34**
Goodwood Cl. W1 . . . . . 5E **5**
(off Devonshire St.)
Goodwood Rd. SE14 . . 3A **94**
Goodyear Pl. SE5 . . . . . 2E **91**
Goodyer Ho. SW1 . . . . . 1F **89**
(off Tachbrook St.)
Goodyers Gdns. NW4 . . 1F **29**
Goose Grn. Trad. Est.
SE22 . . . . 2B **106**
Gophir La.
EC4 . . . . 4B **18** (1F **77**)
Gopsall St. N1 . . . . 5F **49**
Gordon Av. SW14 . . . . . 2A **98**
Gordonbrock Rd.
SE4 . . . . 3C **108**
Gordon Cl. E17 . . . . 1C **38**
N19 . . . . 3E **33**
Gordon Ct. W12 . . . . . . 5E **57**
Gordondale Rd.
SW19 . . . . 2C **114**
Gordon Gro. SE5 . . . . . 5D **91**
Gordon Ho. E1 . . . . 1E **79**
(off Glamis Rd.)
SE10 . . . . 3D **95**
(off Tarves Way)
SW1 . . . . 4E **75**
(off Greencoat Pl.)
Gordon Ho. Rd. NW5 . . 1C **46**
Gordon Mans. W14 . . . . 4F **71**
(off Addison Gdns.)
WC1 . . . . 4B **6**
(off Torrington Pl.)
Gordon Pl. W8 . . . . 3C **72**
Gordon Rd. E11 . . . . . . 1C **40**
E15 . . . . 1E **53**
SE15 . . . . 5D **93**
Gordon Sq.
WC1 . . . . 3B **6** (3F **61**)

Gordon St. E13 . . . . . . 2C **68**
WC1 . . . . 3B **6** (3F **61**)
Gorefield Ho. NW6 . . . . 1C **58**
(off Gorefield Pl.)
Gorefield Pl. NW6 . . . . 1C **58**
Gore Rd. E9 . . . . 5E **51**
Gore St. SW7 . . . . 4E **73**
Gorham Ho. SE16 . . . . . 3F **79**
(off Wolfe Cres.)
Gorham Pl. W11 . . . . . . 1A **72**
Goring St. EC3 . . . . 2E **19**
Gorleston St. W14 . . . . 5A **72**
(not continuous)
Gorse Cl. E16 . . . . 5C **68**
Gorsefield Ho. E14 . . . . 1C **80**
(off E. India Dock Rd.)
Gorse Ri. SW17 . . . . . . 5C **116**
Gorst Rd. NW10 . . . . . . 3A **56**
SW11 . . . . 4B **102**
Gorsuch Pl.
E2 . . . . 1F **11** (2B **64**)
Gorsuch St.
E2 . . . . 1F **11** (1B **64**)
Gosberton Rd.
SW12 . . . . 1B **116**
Gosfield St.
W1 . . . . 1F **13** (4E **61**)
Goslett Yd.
WC2 . . . . 3C **14** (5F **61**)
Gosling Ho. E1 . . . . 1E **79**
(off Sutton St.)
Gosling Way SW9 . . . . 4C **90**
GOSPEL OAK 1C **46**
Gosport Ho. E17 . . . . . . 1B **38**
Gosset St. E2 . . . . 2B **64**
Gosterwood St. SE8 . . 2A **94**
Goswell Pl. EC1 . . . . . . 2E **9**
Goswell Rd.
EC1 . . . . 1D **9** (1D **63**)
Gothic Ct. SE5 . . . . 3E **91**
(off Wyndham Rd.)
Gottfried M. NW5 . . . . . 1E **47**
Goudhurst Rd.
BR1: Brom 5A **124**
Gough Ho. N1 . . . . 5D **49**
(off Windsor St.)
Gough Rd. E15 . . . . 1B **54**
Gough Sq.
EC4 . . . . 3C **16** (5C **62**)
Gough St.
WC1 . . . . 3A **8** (3B **62**)
Gough Wlk. E14 . . . . . . 5C **66**
Goulden Ho. SW11 . . 5A **88**
Goulden Ho. App.
SW11 . . . . 5A **88**
Gouldman Ho. E1 . . . . . 3E **65**
(off Wyllen Cl.)
Gould Ter. E8 . . . . 2D **51**
Goulston St.
E1 . . . . 2F **19** (5B **64**)
Goulton Rd. E5 . . . . 1D **51**
Gourley Pl. N15 . . . . . . 1A **36**
Gourley St. N15 . . . . . . 1A **36**
Govan St. E2 . . . . 5C **50**
Gover Ct. SW4 . . . . 5A **90**
Govier Cl. E15 . . . . 4A **54**
Gowan Av. SW6 . . . . . . 4A **86**
Gowan Ho. E2 . . . . 2F **11**
(off Chambord St.)

Gowan Rd. NW10 . . . . . 3D **43**
Gowan Ct. SW4 . . . . . . 4E **103**
Gower Ct.
WC1 . . . . 3B **6** (3F **61**)
Gower Ho. SE17 . . . . . . 1E **91**
(off Morecambe St.)
Gower M.
WC1 . . . . 1C **14** (4F **61**)
Gower M. Mans. WC1 . . 5C **6**
(off Gower M.)
Gower Pl.
WC1 . . . . 3A **6** (3F **61**)
Gower Rd. E7 . . . . 3C **54**
Gower St.
WC1 . . . . 3A **6** (3E **61**)
Gower's Wlk. E1 . . . . . . 5C **64**
Gowlett Rd. SE15 . . . . 1C **106**
Gowrie Rd. SW11 . . . . 1C **102**
Gracechurch St.
EC3 . . . . 4C **18** (1F **77**)
Grace Cl. SE9 . . . . 3F **125**
Gracedale Rd.
SW16 . . . . 5D **117**
Gracefield Gdns.
SW16 . . . . 3A **118**
Gracehill E1 . . . . 4E **65**
(off Hannibal Rd.)
Grace Ho. SE11 . . . . . . 2B **90**
(off Vauxhall St.)
Grace Jones Cl. E8 . . . 3C **50**
Grace Path SE26 . . . . . 4E **121**
Grace Pl. E3 . . . . 2D **67**
Graces All. E1 . . . . 1C **78**
Graces M. NW8 . . . . . . 1E **59**
SE5 . . . . 5F **91**
Grace's Rd. SE5 . . . . . 5A **92**
Grace St. E3 . . . . 2D **67**
Gradient, The
SE26 . . . . 4C **120**
Graduate Pl. SE1 . . . . . 5D **27**
Grafton Cres. NW1 . . . . 3D **47**
Grafton Gdns. N4 . . . . . 1E **35**
Grafton Ho. SE8 . . . . . . 1B **94**
Grafton M. W1 . . 4F **5** (3E **61**)
Grafton Pl.
NW1 . . . . 2C **6** (2F **61**)
Grafton Rd. NW5 . . . . . 2C **46**
Graftons, The W2 . . . . 5C **30**
Grafton Sq. SW4 . . . . . 1E **103**
Grafton St.
W1 . . . . 5E **13** (1D **75**)
Grafton Ter. NW5 . . . . . 2B **46**
Grafton Way
W1 . . . . 4F **5** (3E **61**)
WC1 . . . . 4A **6** (3E **61**)
Grafton Yd. NW5 . . . . . 3D **47**
Graham Ct. SE14 . . . . . 2F **93**
(off Myers La.)
Graham Lodge NW4 . . 1D **29**
Graham Rd. E8 . . . . 3C **50**
E13 . . . . 3C **68**
NW4 . . . . 1D **29**
Graham St. N1 . . 1F **9** (1D **63**)
Graham Ter. SW1 . . . . 5C **74**
Grainger Ct. SE5 . . . . . 3E **91**
Grainstore, The E16 . . 1C **82**
Graphne Cl. E11 . . . . . . 4F **39**
Grampian Gdns.
NW2 . . . . 3A **30**

Grampians, The W6 . . . . . 3F 71
(off Shepherd's Bush Rd.)
Gramsci Way SE6 . . . . . 3D 123
Granada St. SW17 . . . . 5B 116
Granard Av. SW15 . . . . 3D 99
Granard Ho. E9 . . . . 3F 51
Granard Rd. SW12 . . . . 5B 102
Granary Rd. E1 . . . . 3D 65
Granary Sq. N1 . . . . 3C 48
Granary St. NW1 . . . . . 5F 47
Granby Pl. SE1 . . . . 4B 24
(off Station App. Rd.)
Granby St. E2 . . . . 3C 64
(not continuous)
Granby Ter.
NW1 . . . . 1F 5 (1E 61)
(not continuous)
Grand Av. EC1 . . 5E 9 (4D 63)
(not continuous)
Grandfield Ct. W4 . . . . . 2A 84
Grandison Rd.
SW11 . . . . 3B 102
Grand Junc. Wharf
N1 . . . . 1E 63
Grand Pde. N4 . . . . . . 1D 35
Grand Pde. M.
SW15 . . . . 3A 100
Grand Union W2 . . . . . . 4F 59
(off Harbet Rd.)
Grand Union Cen.
W10 . . . . 3F 57
(off West Row)
Grand Union Ct. W9 . . 4B 58
Grand Union Cres.
E8 . . . . 5C 50
Grand Union Wlk.
NW1 . . . . 4D 47
(off Kentish Town Rd.)
Grand Vitesse Ind. Cen.
SE1 . . . . 2E 25
(off Dolben St.)
Grand Wlk. E1 . . . . 3A 66
Granfield St. SW11 . . . . 4F 87
Grange, The E17 . . . . . . 1A 38
(off Grange Rd.)
SE1 . . . . 5F 27 (4B 78)
SW19 . . . . 5F 113
W14 . . . . 5B 72
Grange Ct. NW10 . . . . . 5A 28
(off Neasden La.)
WC2 . . . . 3A 16 (5B 62)
Grangecourt Rd.
N16 . . . . 3A 36
Grangefield NW1 . . . . . 4F 47
(off Marquis Rd.)
Grange Gdns. NW3 . . . 5D 31
Grange Gro. N1 . . . . . . 3E 49
Grange Ho. NW10 . . . . 4D 43
SE1 . . . . 5F 27 (4B 78)
Grange La. SE21 . . . . . 2B 120
Grange Lodge
SW19 . . . . 5F 113
Grangemill Rd. SE6 . . . 3C 122
Grangemill Way
SE6 . . . . 2C 122
Grange Mus. of
Community History
. . . . 1A 42
Grange Pk. Rd. E10 . . . 3D 39
Grange Pl. NW6 . . . . . . 4C 44

Grange Rd. E10 . . . . . . 3C 38
E13 . . . . 2B 68
E17 . . . . 1A 38
(not continuous)
N6 . . . . 1C 32
NW10 . . . . 3D 43
SE1 . . . . 5E 27 (4A 78)
SW13 . . . . 4C 84
Grange St. N1 . . . . 5F 49
Grange Wlk.
SE1 . . . . 5E 27 (4B 78)
Grange Wlk. M. SE1 . . . 5E 27
Grange Way NW6 . . . . . 4C 44
Grangewood St. E6 . . . 5F 55
Grange Yd.
SE1 . . . . 5F 27 (4B 78)
Granite Apartments
E15 . . . . 3F 53
Granleigh Rd. E11 . . . . . 4A 40
Gransden Av. E8 . . . . . 4D 51
Gransden Ho. SE8 . . . . 1B 94
Gransden Rd. W12 . . . . 3B 70
Grantbridge St. N1 . . . . 1D 63
Grantham Ct. SE16 . . . . 3F 79
(off Eleanor Cl.)
Grantham Ho. SE15 . . . 2C 92
(off Friary Est.)
Grantham Pl.
W1 . . . . 2D 21 (2D 75)
Grantham Rd. SW9 . . . 5A 90
W4 . . . . 3A 84
Grantley Ho. SE14 . . . . 2F 93
(off Myers La.)
Grantley St. E1 . . . . 2F 65
Grant Mus. of Zoology &
Comparative Anatomy
. . . . 4B 6
Grant Rd. SW11 . . . . . 2F 101
Grants Quay Wharf
EC3 . . . . 5C 18 (1F 77)
Grant St. E13 . . . . 2C 68
N1 . . . . 1C 62
Grant Ter. N16 . . . . 2C 36
(off Castlewood Rd.)
Grantully Rd. W9 . . . . . 2D 59
Granville Arc. SW9 . . . 2C 104
Granville Ct. N1 . . . . . . 5A 50
N4 . . . . 1B 34
SE14 . . . . 3A 94
(off Nynehead St.)
Granville Gro. SE13 . . . 1E 109
Granville Ho. E14 . . . . . 5C 66
(off E. India Dock Rd.)
Granville Pk. SE13 . . . . 1E 109
Granville Pl. SW6 . . . . . 3D 87
W1 . . . . 3B 12 (5C 60)
Granville Point NW2 . . . 4B 30
Granville Rd. E17 . . . . . 1D 39
N4 . . . . 1B 34
NW2 . . . . 4B 30
NW6 . . . . 1C 58
(not continuous)
SW18 . . . . 5B 100
Granville Sq. SE15 . . . . 3A 92
WC1 . . . . 2A 8 (2B 62)
Granville St.
WC1 . . . . 2A 8 (2B 62)

Grape St.
WC2 . . . . 2D 15 (5A 62)
Graphite Sq. SE11 . . . . 1B 90
Grasmere NW1 . . . . 2E 5
(off Osnaburgh St.)
Grasmere Av. SW15 . . . 4A 112
Grasmere Ct. SE26 . . . 5C 120
SW13 . . . . 2C 84
(off Verdun Rd.)
Grasmere Point SE15 . . 3E 93
(off Old Kent Rd.)
Grasmere Rd. E13 . . . . 1C 68
SW16 . . . . 5B 118
Grassmount SE23 . . . . 2D 121
Gratton Rd. W14 . . . . . 4A 72
Gratton Ter. NW2 . . . . . 5F 29
Gravel La. E1 . . 2F 19 (5B 64)
Gravely Ho. SE8 . . . . . 5A 80
(off Chilton Gro.)
Gravenel Gdns.
SW17 . . . . 5A 116
(off Nutwell St.)
Graveney Rd. SW17 . . . 4A 116
Gravesend Rd. W12 . . . 1C 70
Gray Ho. SE17 . . . . 1E 91
(off King & Queen St.)
Grayling Cl. E16 . . . . . . 3A 68
Grayling Rd. N16 . . . . . 4F 35
Grayling Sq. E2 . . . . . . 2C 64
(off Nelson Gdns.)
Grayshott Rd. SW11 . . . 5C 88
Gray's Inn N1 . . . 5A 8 (4B 62)
Gray's Inn Bldgs. EC1 . . 4B 8
(off Rosebery Av.)
Gray's Inn Pl.
WC1 . . . . 1A 16 (4B 62)
Gray's Inn Rd.
WC1 . . . . 1E 7 (2A 62)
Gray's Inn Sq.
WC1 . . . . 5B 8 (4B 62)
Grayson Ho. EC1 . . . . . 2A 10
Grays Ter. E7 . . . . 3E 55
Gray St. SE1 . . 4C 24 (3C 76)
Grayswood Point
SW15 . . . . 1C 112
Gray's Yd. W1 . . . . 3C 12
Grazebrook Rd. N16 . . . 4F 35
Grazeley Ct. SE19 . . . . 5A 120
Gt. Acre Ct. SW4 . . . . . 2F 103
Gt. Arthur Ho. EC1 . . . . 4F 9
(off Golden La. Est.)
Gt. Bell All.
EC2 . . . . 2B 18 (5F 63)
Great Brownings
SE21 . . . . 4B 120
Gt. Castle St.
W1 . . . . 2E 13 (5D 61)
Gt. Central St. NW1 . . . 4B 60
Gt. Central Way
NW10 . . . . 1A 42
Gt. Chapel St.
W1 . . . . 2B 14 (5F 61)
Gt. Chart St. SW11 . . . 2F 101
Gt. Chertsey Rd. W4 . . . 4A 84
Great Chu. La. W6 . . . . 5F 71
Great Coll. St.
SW1 . . . . 5D 23 (4A 76)
Great Cft. WC1 . . . . 2E 7
(off Cromer St.)

Gt. Cross Av. SE10 . . . . . 3F **95**
    (not continuous)
Gt. Cumberland M.
  W1 . . . . 3A **12** (5B **60**)
Gt. Cumberland Pl.
  W1 . . . . 2A **12** (5B **60**)
Gt. Dover St.
  SE1 . . . . 4A **26** (3E **77**)
Gt. Eastern Ent. Cen.
  E14 . . . . 3D **81**
Gt. Eastern Rd. E15 . . . . 4F **53**
Gt. Eastern St.
  EC2 . . . . 2D **11** (2A **64**)
Gt. Eastern Wlk. EC2 . . 1E **19**
Gt. Eastern Wharf
  SW11 . . . . 3A **88**
Greatfield NW5 . . . . 2E **47**
Greatfield Cl. N19 . . . 1E **47**
  SE4 . . . . 2C **108**
Gt. George St.
  SW1 . . . . 4C **22** (3F **75**)
Gt. Guildford Bus. Sq.
  SE1 . . . . 2F **25** (2C **77**)
Gt. Guildford St.
  SE1 . . . . 1F **25** (2C **77**)
Great Hall 1B **88**
Greatham Wlk.
  SW15 . . . . 1C **112**
Gt. James St.
  WC1 . . . . 5F **7** (4B **62**)
Gt. Marlborough St.
  W1 . . . . 3F **13** (5E **61**)
Gt. Maze Pond
  SE1 . . . . 3C **26** (3F **77**)
    (not continuous)
Gt. Newport St.
  WC2 . . . . 4D **15** (1A **76**)
Gt. New St.
  EC4 . . . . 2C **16** (5C **62**)
Great Nth. Rd. N6 . . . . 1B **32**
Greatorex Ho. E1 . . . . 4C **64**
    (off Spelman St.)
Greatorex St. E1 . . . . . 4C **64**
Gt. Ormond St.
  WC1 . . . . 5E **7** (4A **62**)
Gt. Percy St.
  WC1 . . . . 1A **8** (2B **62**)
Gt. Peter St.
  SW1 . . . . 5B **22** (4F **75**)
Gt. Portland St.
  W1 . . . . 4E **5** (3D **61**)
Gt. Pulteney St.
  W1 . . . . 4A **14** (1E **75**)
Gt. Queen St.
  WC2 . . . . 3E **15** (5A **62**)
Gt. Russell St.
  WC1 . . . . 2C **14** (5F **61**)
Gt. St Helen's
  EC3 . . . . 2D **19** (5A **64**)
Gt. St Thomas Apostle
  EC4 . . . . 4A **18** (1E **77**)
Gt. Scotland Yd.
  SW1 . . . . 2D **23** (2A **76**)
Gt. Smith St.
  SW1 . . . . 5C **22** (4F **75**)
Great Spilmans
  SE22 . . . . 3A **106**
Gt. Suffolk St.
  SE1 . . . . 2E **25** (2D **77**)

Gt. Sutton St.
  EC1 . . . . 4E **9** (3D **63**)
Gt. Swan All.
  EC2 . . . . 2B **18** (5F **63**)
    (not continuous)
Gt. Titchfield St.
  W1 . . . . 4E **5** (3D **61**)
Great Twr. St.
  EC3 . . . . 4D **19** (1A **78**)
Gt. Trinity La.
  EC4 . . . . 4A **18** (1E **77**)
Great Turnstile
  WC1 . . . . 1A **16** (4B **62**)
Gt. Turnstile Ho.
  WC1 . . . . 4B **62**
    (off Gt. Turnstile)
Gt. Western Rd. W9 . . . 4B **58**
  W11 . . . . 4B **58**
Great W. Rd. W4 . . . . . 1B **84**
  W6 . . . . 1B **84**
Gt. Winchester St.
  EC2 . . . . 2C **18** (5F **63**)
Gt. Windmill St.
  W1 . . . . 4B **14** (1F **75**)
Great Yd. SE1 . . . . 3E **27**
Greaves Cotts. E14 . . . 4A **66**
Greaves Pl. SW17 . . . 4A **116**
Greaves Twr. SW10 . . . 3E **87**
    (off Worlds End Est.)
Grebe Cl. E7 . . . . 2B **54**
Grebe Ct. E14 . . . . 3E **81**
    (off River Barge Cl.)
  SE8 . . . . 2B **94**
    (off Dorking Cl.)
Grecian Cres. SE19 . . . 5D **119**
Greek Cl. W1 . . . 3C **14** (5F **61**)
Greek St. W1 . . . 3C **14** (5F **61**)
Green, The
  BR1: Brom 3C **124**
    (not continuous)
  E11 . . . . 1D **41**
  E15 . . . . 3A **54**
  SW19 . . . . 5F **113**
  W3 . . . . 5A **56**
Greenacre Sq. SE16 . . . 3F **79**
Grn. Arbour Ct. EC1 . . 2D **17**
    (off Old Bailey)
Greenaway Gdns.
  NW3 . . . . 1D **45**
Greenaway Ho. NW8 . . . 5E **45**
    (off Boundary Rd.)
  WC1 . . . . 2B **8**
    (off Fernsbury St.)
Green Bank E1 . . . . 2D **79**
Greenbay Rd. SE7 . . . . 3F **97**
Greenberry St. NW8 . . . 1A **60**
Green Cl. NW11 . . . . . . 2E **31**
Greencoat Mans.
  SW1 . . . . 4E **75**
    (off Greencoat Row)
Greencoat Pl.
  SW1 . . . . 5A **22** (5E **75**)
Greencoat Row SW1 . . 4E **75**
Greencourt Ho. E1 . . . . 3F **65**
    (off Mile End Rd.)
Greencrest Pl. NW2 . . . 5C **28**
Greencroft Cl. E6 . . . . 4F **69**
Greencroft Gdns.
  NW6 . . . . 4D **45**

Green Dale SE5 . . . . . . 2F **105**
  SE22 . . . . 3A **106**
Grn. Dale Cl. SE22 . . . 3A **106**
Grn. Dragon Ct. SE1 . . 1B **26**
Grn. Dragon Ho.
  WC2 . . . . 2E **15**
    (off Dragon Yd.)
Grn. Dragon Yd. E1 . . . 4C **64**
Greene Ct. SE14 . . . . . 2F **93**
    (off Samuel Cl.)
Greene Ho. SE1 . . . . 5B **26**
    (off Burbage Cl.)
Greenend Rd. W4 . . . . . 3A **70**
Greenfell Ho. SW4 . . . . 1F **103**
Greenfell Mans. SE8 . . 2D **95**
Greenfield Gdns.
  NW2 . . . . 4A **30**
Greenfield Ho.
  SW19 . . . . 1F **113**
Greenfield Rd. E1 . . . . 4C **64**
  N15 . . . . 1A **36**
Greengate Lodge
  E13 . . . . 1D **69**
    (off Hollybush St.)
Greengate St. E13 . . . . 1D **69**
Greenham Cl.
  SE1 . . . . 4B **24** (3C **76**)
Greenham Ho. E9 . . . . . 5E **51**
    (off Templecombe Rd.)
Greenheath Bus. Cen.
  E2 . . . . 3D **65**
    (off Three Colts La.)
Greenhill NW3 . . . . 1F **45**
Greenhill Gro. E12 . . . 1F **55**
Greenhill Pk. NW10 . . . 5A **42**
Greenhill Rd. NW10 . . . 5A **42**
Greenhill's Rents
  EC1 . . . . 5D **9** (4D **63**)
Greenhills Ter. N1 . . . . 3F **49**
Grn. Hundred Rd.
  SE15 . . . . 2C **92**
Greenhurst Rd.
  SE27 . . . . 5C **118**
Greenland Ho. E1 . . . . 3A **66**
    (off Ernest St.)
Greenland M. SE8 . . . . 1F **93**
Greenland Pl. NW1 . . . 5D **47**
Greenland Quay SE16 . . 5F **79**
Greenland Rd. NW1 . . . 5E **47**
Greenland St. NW1 . . . 5D **47**
Green La. NW4 . . . . . . 1F **29**
Green Lanes N4 . . . . . . 3E **35**
  N16 . . . . 1D **35**
Greenleaf Cl. SW2 . . . . 5C **104**
Greenleaf Rd. E6 . . . . 5E **55**
GREEN MAN RDBT. . . . 2B **40**
Greenman St. N1 . . . . 4E **49**
Greenoak Way
  SW19 . . . . 4F **113**
Green Pk. 3E **21** (3D **75**)
Green Point E15 . . . . . 3A **54**
Greenroof Way
  SE10 . . . . 4B **82**
    (off School Bank Rd.)
Greenscape SE10 . . . . 4B **82**
    (not continuous)
Green's Ct. W1 . . . . . . 4B **14**
  W11 . . . . 2B **72**
    (off Lansdowne M.)

Greenshields Ind. Est.
E16 . . . . 3C **82**
Greenside Cl. SE6 . . . . 2F **123**
Greenside Rd. W12 . . . . 4C **70**
Greenstead Gdns.
SW15 . . . . 3D **99**
Greenstone M. E11 . . . . 1C **40**
Green St. E7 . . . . 3D **55**
E13 . . . . 3D **55**
W1 . . . . 4B **12** (1C **74**)
Greenstreet Hill SE14 . . 5F **93**
Green Ter.
EC1 . . . . 2C **8** (2C **62**)
Greenview Cl. W3 . . . . . 2A **70**
Green Wlk.
SE1 . . . . 5D **27** (4A **78**)
Green Way SE9 . . . . 3F **111**
Greenway Cl. N4 . . . . . . 4E **35**
Greenwell St.
W1 . . . . 4E **5** (3D **61**)
GREENWICH 3E **95**
Greenwich Bus. Pk.
SE10 . . . . 3D **95**
Greenwich Chu. St.
SE10 . . . . 2E **95**
Greenwich Cinema . . . 3E **95**
Greenwich Commercial Cen.
SE10 . . . . 3D **95**
Greenwich Ct. E1 . . . . . 5D **65**
(off Cavell St.)
Greenwich Cres. E6 . . . 4F **69**
Greenwich Gateway Vis. Cen.
. . . . 2E **95**
Greenwich High Rd.
SE10 . . . . 4D **95**
Greenwich Ind. Est.
SE7 . . . . 5D **83**
SE10 . . . . 3D **95**
Greenwich Mkt. SE10 . . 2E **95**
GREENWICH MILLENNIUM
VILLAGE 4B **82**
Greenwich Pk. 3F **95**
Greenwich Pk. St.
SE10 . . . . 2F **95**
Greenwich Quay SE8 . . 2D **95**
Greenwich Shop. Pk.
SE7 . . . . 5D **83**
Greenwich Sth. St.
SE10 . . . . 4D **95**
Greenwich Theatre . . . 3E **95**
Greenwich Vw. Pl.
E14 . . . . 4D **81**
Greenwich Yacht Club
. . . . 4C **82**
Greenwood Ho. SE4 . . . 2F **107**
Greenwood Pl. NW5 . . . 2D **47**
Greenwood Rd. E8 . . . . 3C **50**
E13 . . . . 1B **68**
Greenwood Ter.
NW10 . . . . 5A **42**
Greenwood Theatre . . . 3F **77**
Green Yd.
WC1 . . . . 3A **8** (3B **62**)
Green Yd., The EC3 . . . 3D **19**
Greet Ho. SE1 . . . . 4C **24**
Greet St. SE1 . . . 2C **24** (2C **76**)
Greg Cl. E10 . . . . 1E **39**
Gregor M. SE3 . . . . 3C **96**
Gregory Cres. SE9 . . . . 5F **111**

Gregory Pl. W8 . . . . 3D **73**
Greig Ter. SE17 . . . . 2D **91**
Grenada Ho. E14 . . . . . . 1B **80**
(off Limehouse C'way.)
Grenada Rd. SE7 . . . . . . 3E **97**
Grenade St. E14 . . . . . . 1B **80**
Grenard Cl. SE15 . . . . . . 3C **92**
Grendon Ho. E9 . . . . 4E **51**
(off Shore Pl.)
N1 . . . . 1B **62**
(off Calshot St.)
Grendon St. NW8 . . . . . 3A **60**
Grenfell Ho. SE5 . . . . . . 3E **91**
Grenfell Rd. W11 . . . . . . 1F **71**
Grenfell Twr. W11 . . . . . 1F **71**
Grenfell Wlk. W11 . . . . . 1F **71**
Grenier Apartments
SE15 . . . . 3D **93**
Grenville Ho. E3 . . . . . . 1A **66**
(off Arbery Rd.)
SE8 . . . . 2C **94**
(off New King St.)
SW1 . . . . 2F **89**
(off Dolphin Sq.)
Grenville M. N19 . . . . . . 3A **34**
SW7 . . . . 5E **73**
Grenville Pl. SW7 . . . . . 4E **73**
Grenville Rd. N19 . . . . . 3A **34**
Grenville St.
WC1 . . . . 4E **7** (3A **62**)
Gresham Gdns.
NW11 . . . . 3A **30**
Gresham Lodge E17 . . . 1D **39**
Gresham Pl. N19 . . . . . . 4F **33**
Gresham Rd. E16 . . . . . . 5D **69**
NW10 . . . . 2A **42**
SW9 . . . . 1C **104**
Gresham St.
EC2 . . . . 2F **17** (5E **63**)
Gresham Way
SW19 . . . . 3D **115**
Gresham Way Ind. Est.
SW19 . . . . 3D **115**
(off Gresham Way)
Gresley Cl. E17 . . . . 1A **38**
Gresley Rd. N19 . . . . . . 3E **33**
Gressenhall Rd.
SW18 . . . . 4B **100**
Gresse St.
W1 . . . . 1B **14** (5F **61**)
Greswell St. SW6 . . . . . 4F **85**
Gretton Ho. E2 . . . . 2E **65**
(off Globe Rd.)
Greville Ct. E5 . . . . 1D **51**
(off Napoleon Rd.)
Greville Hall NW6 . . . . . 1D **59**
Greville Ho. SW1 . . . . . . 5B **20**
(off Halkin Arc.)
Greville Lodge E13 . . . . 5D **55**
Greville M. NW6 . . . . . . 5D **45**
(off Greville Rd.)
Greville Pl. NW6 . . . . . . 1D **59**
Greville Rd. NW6 . . . . . . 1D **59**
Greville St.
EC1 . . . . 1B **16** (4C **62**)
(not continuous)
Grey Cl. NW11 . . . . 1E **31**
Greycoat Gdns. SW1 . . . 4F **75**
(off Greycoat St.)

Greycoat Pl.
SW1 . . . . 5B **22** (4F **75**)
Greycoat St. SW1 . . . . . 4F **75**
Greycot Rd.
BR3: Beck. 5C **122**
Grey Eagle St.
E1 . . . . 4F **11** (3B **64**)
Greyfriars SE26 . . . . 3C **120**
(off Wells Pk. Rd.)
Greyfriars Pas.
EC1 . . . . 2E **17** (5D **63**)
Greyhound Ct.
WC2 . . . . 4A **16** (1B **76**)
Greyhound La.
SW16 . . . . 5A **118**
Greyhound Mans.
W6 . . . . 2A **86**
(off Greyhound Rd.)
Greyhound Rd.
NW10 . . . . 2D **57**
W6 . . . . 2F **85**
W14 . . . . 2F **85**
(off White City Est.)
Greyladies Gdns.
SE10 . . . . 5E **95**
Greystead Rd. SE23 . . . 5E **107**
Greystoke Ho. SE15 . . . 2C **92**
(off Peckham Pk. Rd.)
Greystoke Pl.
EC4 . . . . 2B **16** (5C **62**)
Greystone Path E11 . . . 2B **40**
(off Mornington Rd.)
Greyswood St.
SW16 . . . . 5D **117**
Grey Turner Ho. W12 . . 5C **56**
Grierson Ho. SW16 . . . . 4E **117**
Grierson Rd. SE23 . . . . 5F **107**
Griffin Cl. NW10 . . . . . . 2D **43**
Griffin Ct. W4 . . . . 1B **84**
Griffin Ho. E14 . . . . 5D **67**
(off Ricardo St.)
N1 . . . . 5A **50**
(off New Era Est.)
W6 . . . . 5F **71**
(off Hammersmith Rd.)
Griggs Cl. SE1 . . . . 5E **27**
(off Grigg's Pl.)
Grigg's Pl. SE1 . . . . 5E **27**
Griggs Rd. E10 . . . . 1E **39**
Grimaldi Ho. N1 . . . . . . 1B **62**
(off Calshot St.)
Grimsby St. E2 . . . . 3B **64**
Grimsel Path SE5 . . . . . 3D **91**
Grimshaw Cl. N6 . . . . . . 2C **32**
Grimston Rd. SW6 . . . . 5B **86**
Grimthorpe Ho. EC1 . . . 3D **9**
Grimwade Cl. SE15 . . . . 1E **107**
Grindall Ho. E1 . . . . 3D **65**
(off Darling Row)
Grindal St.
SE1 . . . . 4B **24** (3C **76**)
Grindley Ho. E3 . . . . 4B **66**
(off Leopold St.)
Grinling Pl. SE8 . . . . . . 2C **94**
Grinstead Rd. SE8 . . . . 1A **94**
Grisedale NW1 . . . . 1F **5**
(off Cumberland Mkt.)
Grittleton Rd. W9 . . . . . 3C **58**

Grizedale Ter. SE23 . . . 2D **121**
Grocer's Hall Ct.
  EC2 . . . . 3B **18** (5F **63**)
Grocer's Hall Gdns.
  EC2 . . . . 3B **18**
Groombridge Ho.
  SE17 . . . . 1A **92**
    (off Kinglake St.)
Groombridge Rd. E9 . . . 4F **51**
Groome Cres. SW18 . . . 5F **101**
Groome Ho. SE11 . . . . . 5B **76**
Groomfield Cl.
  SW17 . . . . 4C **116**
Groom Pl.
  SW1 . . . . 5C 20 (4C **74**)
Grosse Way SW15 . . . . 4D **99**
Grosvenor Av. N5 . . . . . 2E **49**
  SW14 . . . . 1A **98**
Grosvenor Cotts.
  SW1 . . . . 5C **74**
Grosvenor Ct. E10 . . . . 3D **39**
  NW6 . . . . 5F **43**
  SE5 . . . . 2E **91**
Grosvenor Ct. Mans.
  W2 . . . . 5B **60**
    (off Edgware Rd.)
Grosvenor Cres.
  SW1 . . . . . . 4C 20 (3C **74**)
Grosvenor Cres. M.
  SW1 . . . . . . 4B 20 (3C **74**)
Grosvenor Est. SW1 . . . 5F **75**
Grosvenor Gdns. E6 . . . 2F **69**
  NW2 . . . . 3E **43**
  NW11 . . . . 1B **30**
  SW1 . . . . . . 5D 21 (4D **75**)
  SW14 . . . . 1A **98**
Grosvenor Gdns. M. E.
  SW1 . . . . 5E **21**
Grosvenor Gdns. M. Nth.
  SW1 . . . . 5D **21**
Grosvenor Gdns. M. Sth.
  SW1 . . . . 5E **21**
Grosvenor Ga.
  W1 . . . . 5B 12 (1C **74**)
Grosvenor Hill
  SW19 . . . . 5A **114**
  W1 . . . . 4D 13 (1D **75**)
Grosvenor Hill Ct.
  W1 . . . . 4D **13**
    (off Bourdon St.)
Grosvenor Pk. SE5 . . . . 3E **91**
Grosvenor Pk. Rd.
  E17 . . . . 1C **38**
Grosvenor Pl.
  SW1 . . . . . . 4C 20 (3C **74**)
Grosvenor Ri. E. E17 . . . 1D **39**
Grosvenor Rd. E6 . . . . . 5F **55**
  E7 . . . . 3D **55**
  E10 . . . . 3E **39**
  E11 . . . . 1D **41**
  SW1 . . . . 2D **89**
Grosvenor Sq.
  W1 . . . . 4C 12 (1C **74**)
Grosvenor St.
  W1 . . . . 4D 13 (1D **75**)
Grosvenor Studios
  SW1 . . . . 5C **74**
    (off Eaton Ter.)
Grosvenor Ter. SE5 . . . . 3E **91**

Grosvenor Way E5 . . . . 4E **37**
Grosvenor Wharf Rd.
  E14 . . . . 5F **81**
Grotes Bldgs. SE3 . . . . 5A **96**
Grote's Pl. SE3 . . . . . . 5A **96**
Groton Rd. SW18 . . . . 2D **115**
Grotto Ct.
  SE1 . . . . 3E 25 (3D **77**)
Grotto Pas.
  W1 . . . . 5C 4 (4C **60**)
GROVE, THE 1C **120**
Grove, The E15 . . . . . . 3A **54**
  N4 . . . . 2B **34**
  N6 . . . . 3C **32**
  N8 . . . . 1F **33**
  NW11 . . . . 2A **30**
Grove Cl. SE23 . . . . . . 1A **122**
Grove Cotts. SW3 . . . . . 2A **88**
    (off Chelsea Mnr. St.)
  W4 . . . . 2A **84**
Grove Ct. NW8 . . . . 2F **59**
    (off Grove End Rd.)
  SW10 . . . . 1E **87**
    (off Drayton Ggns.)
Grove Cres. Rd. E15 . . . 3F **53**
Grovedale Rd. N19 . . . . 4F **33**
Grove Dwellings E1 . . . 4E **65**
Grove End NW5 . . . . . . 1D **47**
Grove End Gdns.
  NW8 . . . . 1F **59**
    (off Grove End Rd.)
Grove End Ho. NW8 . . . 2F **59**
    (off Grove End Rd.)
Grove End Rd. NW8 . . . 1F **59**
Grove Gdns. NW8 . . . . 2A **60**
Grove Grn. Rd. E11 . . . . 5E **39**
Grove Hall Ct. NW8 . . . 2E **59**
Grovehill Ct.
  R1: Brom 5B **124**
Grove Hill Rd. SE5 . . . . 1A **106**
Grove Ho. SW3 . . . . . . 2A **88**
    (off Chelsea Mnr. St.)
Groveland Ct. EC4 . . . . 3A **18**
Grovelands Cl. SE5 . . . . 5A **92**
Grovelands Rd. N15 . . . 1C **36**
Grove La. SE5 . . . . 4F **91**
Grove La. Ter. SE5 . . . . 5F **91**
Grove Mans. W6 . . . . . 3E **71**
    (off Hammersmith Gro.)
Grove M. W6 . . . . 4E **71**
GROVE PARK 3D **125**
Grove Pk. E11 . . . . 1D **41**
  SE5 . . . . 5A **92**
Grove Pk. Rd. SE9 . . . . 3E **125**
Grove Pas. E2 . . . . 1D **65**
Grove Pl. NW3 . . . . 5F **31**
  SW12 . . . . 5D **103**
Grover Ct. SE13 . . . . . . 5D **95**
Grover Ho. SE11 . . . . . . 1B **90**
Grove Rd. E3 . . . . 5F **51**
  E11 . . . . 2B **40**
  E17 . . . . 1D **39**
  N15 . . . . 1A **36**
  NW2 . . . . 3E **43**
  SW13 . . . . 5B **84**
Groveside Ct. SW11 . . . 5F **87**
Grove St. SE8 . . . . 5B **80**
Grove Ter. NW5 . . . . . . 5D **33**
Grove Ter. M. NW5 . . . . 5D **33**
Grove Va. SE22 . . . . . . 2B **106**

Grove Vs. E14 . . . . 1D **81**
Groveway SW9 . . . . 4B **90**
Grummant Rd. SE15 . . . 4B **92**
Grundy St. E14 . . . . . . 5D **67**
Guardian Ct. SE12 . . . . 3A **110**
Guards Memorial
  . . . . 2C 22 (2F **75**)
Guards' Mus.
  . . . . 4A 22 (3E **75**)
Gubyon Av. SE24 . . . . . 3D **105**
Guerin Sq. E3 . . . . 2B **66**
Guernsey Gro. SE24 . . . 5E **105**
Guernsey Ho. N1 . . . . . 3E **49**
    (off Douglas Rd. Nth.)
Guernsey Rd. E11 . . . . 3F **39**
Guibal Rd. SE12 . . . . . 5D **111**
Guildford Ct. SW8 . . . . 3A **90**
    (off Guildford Rd.)
Guildford Gro. SE10 . . . 4D **95**
Guildford Rd. SW8 . . . . 4A **90**
Guildhall
  City 2A 18 (5E **63**)
  Westminster
  . . . . 4D 23 (3A **76**)
Guildhall Art Gallery
  . . . . 2B 18 (5F **63**)
Guildhall Bldgs. EC2 . . . 2B **18**
Guildhall Library
  . . . . 2A 18 (5E **63**)
Guildhall Offices EC2 . . 2A **18**
Guildhall Yd.
  EC2 . . . . . . 2A 18 (5E **63**)
Guildhouse St. SW1 . . . 5E **75**
Guild Rd. SE7 . . . . 2F **97**
Guilford Pl.
  WC1 . . . . 4F 7 (3B **62**)
Guilford St.
  WC1 . . . . 4D 7 (3A **62**)
Guillemot Ct. SE8 . . . . . 2B **94**
    (off Alexandra Cl.)
Guilsborough Cl.
  NW10 . . . . 4A **42**
Guinea Ct. E1 . . . . 1C **78**
    (off Royal Mint St.)
Guinness Cl. E9 . . . . . . 4A **52**
Guinness Ct. EC1 . . . . . 2A **10**
  EC3 . . . . 3F **19**
  NW8 . . . . 5A **46**
  SE1 . . . . 3D **27**
  SW3 . . . . 5B **74**
Guinness Sq. SE1 . . . . . 5A **78**
Guinness Trust SW3 . . . 5B **74**
Guinness Trust Bldgs.
  SE11 . . . . 1D **91**
  W6 . . . . 1F **85**
    (off Fulham Pal. Rd.)
Guinness Trust Est.
  E15 . . . . 5B **54**
    (off John St.)
  N16 . . . . 3A **36**
Guion Rd. SW6 . . . . . . 5B **86**
Gulland Wlk. N1 . . . . . . 3E **49**
    (off Church Rd.)
Gulliver's Ho. EC1 . . . . 4F **9**
Gulliver St. SE16 . . . . . 4A **80**
Gulston Wlk. SW3 . . . . . 5B **74**
    (off Blackland Ter.)
Gun Ho. E1 . . . . 2D **79**
    (off Wapping High St.)

Gunmaker's La. E3. . . . . 5A 52
E9. . . . . 5A 52
Gunnell Cl. SE26 . . . . . 4C 120
Gunners Rd. SW18. . . . . 2F 115
Gunpowder Sq. EC4 . . . 2C 16
(off Gough Sq.)
not continuous)
Gunstor Rd. N16. . . . . . . 1A 50
Gun St. E1 . . . 1F 19 (4B 64)
Gunter Gro. SW10 . . . . . 2E 87
Gunter Hall Studios
SW10 . . . . 2E 87
(off Gunter Gro.)
Gunterstone Rd. W14. . . . 5A 72
Gunthorpe St. E1 . . . . . 4B 64
Gunton Rd. E5. . . . . . . 5D 37
Gunwhale Cl. SE16. . . . . 2F 79
Gun Wharf E1 . . . . 2E 79
(off Wapping High St.)
Gun Wharf Bus. Cen.
E3. . . . . 5A 52
(off Old Ford Rd.)
Gurdon Ho. E14 . . . . . . 5C 66
(off Dod St.)
Gurdon Rd. SE7 . . . . . . 1C 96
Gurney Cl. E15. . . . . . . 2A 54
Gurney Ho. E2 . . . . 1C 64
(off Goldsmiths Row)
Gurney Rd. E15 . . . . . . 2A 54
SW6 . . . . 1E 101
Guthrie Ct. SE1. . . . . . . 4C 24
Guthrie St. SW3 . . . . . . 1F 87
Gutter La.
EC2. . . . . . . 2F 17 (5E 63)
Guy Barnett Gro.
SE3. . . . . 1C 110
Guyscliff Rd. SE13 . . . . 3E 109
Guy St. SE1 . . . 3C 26 (3F 77)
Gwalior Rd. SW15 . . . . . 2F 99
Gwendolen Av. SW15 . . . 2F 99
Gwendolen Cl. SW15 . . . 3F 99
Gwendoline Av. E13. . . . 5D 55
Gwendwr Rd. W14. . . . . 1A 86
Gwent Ct. SE16. . . . . . . 2F 79
(off Rotherhithe St.)
Gwilym Maries Ho.
E2. . . . . 2D 65
(off Blythe St.)
Gwyn Cl. SW6. . . . . 3E 87
Gwynne Cl. W4. . . . . . . 2B 84
Gwynne Ho. E1. . . . . . . 4D 65
(off Turner St.)
SW1 . . . . 1C 88
(off Lwr. Sloane St.)
WC1 . . . . 2B 8
(off Lloyd Baker St.)
Gwynne Pl.
WC1 . . . . 2A 8 (2B 62)
Gwynne Rd. SW11 . . . . . 5F 87
Gylcote Cl. SE5. . . . . . 2F 105

Haberdashers Ct.
SE14 . . . . 1F 107
Haberdasher St.
N1 . . . . 1C 10 (2F 63)
Habington Ho. SE5. . . . . 3F 91
(off Notley St.)
Habitat Cl. SE15 . . . . . 5D 93
Habitat Sq. SE10 . . . . . 4B 82
(off Teal St.)
Hackford Rd. SW9 . . . . . 4B 90
Hackford Wlk. SW9 . . . . 4B 90
Hackington Cres.
BR3: Beck. 5C 122
HACKNEY 3D 51
Hackney City Farm 1C 64
Hackney Empire Theatre
. . . . 3D 51
Hackney Gro. SE8 . . . . . 3D 51
Hackney Rd.
E2. . . . . . . 2F 11 (2B 64)
HACKNEY WICK 3B 52
HACKNEY WICK 3A 52
Haddington Ct.
SE10 . . . . 3D 95
(off Tarves Way)
Haddington Rd.
BR1: Brom 3F 123
Haddo Ho. SE10. . . . . . 2D 95
(off Haddo St.)
Haddon Ct. W3. . . . . . . 1B 70
Haddonfield SE8. . . . . . 5F 79
Haddon Hall St. SE1. . . 4F 77
(off Rephidim St.)
Haddo St. SE10 . . . . . . 2D 95
Haden Ct. N4. . . . . 4C 34
Hadfield Ho. E1 . . . . . . 5C 64
(off Ellen St.)
Hadleigh Cl. E1 . . . . . . 3E 65
Hadleigh Ho. E1 . . . . . . 3E 65
(off Hadleigh Cl.)
Hadleigh St. E2 . . . . . . 2E 65
Hadley Cl. N16. . . . . . . 3C 36
Hadley Gdns. W4 . . . . . 1A 84
Hadley St. NW1. . . . . . . 3D 47
(not continuous)
Hadlow Ho. SE17. . . . . . 1A 92
(off Kinglake St.)
Hadrian Cl. E3 . . . . 5C 52
(off Garrison Rd.)
Hadrian Est. E2 . . . . . . 1C 64
Hadrian St. SE10 . . . . . 1A 96
Hadstock Ho. NW1. . . . . 1C 6
(off Ossulston St.)
Hadyn Pk. Ct. W12. . . . . 3C 70
(off Curwen Rd.)
Hadyn Pk. Rd. W12 . . . 3C 70
Hafer Rd. SW11 . . . . . . 2B 102
Hafton Rd. SE6. . . . . . 1A 124
HAGGERSTON 4B 50
Haggerston Rd. E8. . . . . 4B 50
Haggerston Studios
E8. . . . . 5B 50
(off Kingsland Rd.)
Hague St. E2 . . . . 2C 64
Haig Ho. E2 . . . . 1C 64
(off Shipton St.)
Haig Rd. E. E13. . . . . . . 2E 69
Haig Rd. W. E13. . . . . . . 2E 69
Hailes Cl. SW19. . . . . . 5E 115

Hailsham Av. SW2 . . . . 2B 118
Haimo Rd. SE9. . . . . . . 3F 111
Hainault Rd. E11 . . . . . . 3E 39
Haines St. SW8 . . . . . . 3E 89
Hainford Cl. SE4. . . . . . 2F 107
Hainthorpe Rd.
SE27. . . . . 3D 119
Hainton Cl. E1 . . . . 5D 65
Halberd M. E5 . . . . 4D 37
Halcomb St. N1 . . . . . . 5A 50
Halcrow St. E1 . . . . 4D 65
Halcyon Wharf E1 . . . . . 2C 78
(off Hermitage Wall)
Haldane Pl. SW18. . . . . 1D 115
Haldane Rd. E6 . . . . . . 2F 69
SW6 . . . . 3B 86
Haldon Rd. SW18 . . . . . 4B 100
Hale Ho. SW1. . . . . 1F 89
(off Lindsay Sq.)
Hale Path SE27. . . . . . 4D 119
Hale Rd. E6 . . . . 3F 69
Hales Prior N1 . . . . 1F 7
(off Calshot St.)
Hales St. SE8. . . . . 3C 94
Hale St. E14. . . . . 1D 81
Halesworth Cl. E5 . . . . . 4E 37
Halesworth Rd.
SE13. . . . . 1D 109
Haley Rd. NW4. . . . . . . 1E 29
Half Moon Ct. EC1 . . . . 1F 17
Half Moon Cres. N1. . . . 1B 62
(not continuous)
Half Moon La. SE24. . . . 4E 105
Half Moon Pas.
E1. . . . . 3F 19 (5B 64)
(not continuous)
Half Moon St.
W1 . . . . 1E 21 (2D 75)
Halford Rd. E10 . . . . . . 1F 39
SW6 . . . . 2C 86
Haliday Ho. N1. . . . . 3F 49
(off Mildmay St.)
Haliday Wlk. N1. . . . . . . 3F 49
Halidon Cl. E9 . . . . 2E 51
Halifax St. SE26. . . . . . 3D 121
Haliwell Ho. NW6 . . . . . 5D 45
(off Mortimer Cres.)
Halkett Ho. E2 . . . . 5E 51
(off Waterloo Gdns.)
Halkin Arc.
SW1. . . . . 5A 20 (4B 74)
Halkin M.
SW1. . . . . 5B 20 (4C 74)
Halkin Pl.
SW1. . . . . 5B 20 (4C 74)
Halkin St.
SW1. . . . . 4C 20 (3C 74)
Hall, The St. W1 . . . . . 1C 110
Hallam Cl. W3. . . . . 5E 5
(off Hallam St.)
Hallam Ho. SW1 . . . . . . 1E 89
(off Churchill Gdns.)
Hallam M. W1. . . 5E 5 (4D 61)
Hallam Rd. SW13. . . . . 1D 99
Hallam St.
W1 . . . . 4E 5 (3D 61)
Hallane Ho. SE27. . . . . 5E 119
Hall Dr. SE26 . . . . 5E 121
Halley Gdns. SE13 . . . . 2F 109

Halley Ho. *E2* *1C 64*
(off Pritchards Rd.)
SE10 . . . . *1B 96*
(off Armitage Rd.)
Halley Rd. E7 . . . . 3E 55
E12 . . . . 3E 55
Halley St. E14 . . . . . . 4A 66
Hallfield Est. W2 . . . . 5E 59
(not continuous)
Hall Ga. NW8 . . . . 2F 59
Halliford St. N1 . . . . . . 4E 49
Halling Ho. *SE1* *4C 26*
(off Long La.)
Hallings Wharf Studios
E15 . . . . 5F 53
Halliwell Ct. SE22 . . . 3C 106
Halliwell Rd. SW2 . . . 4B 104

Hall Oak Wlk. NW6 . . . 3B 44
Hall Pl. W2 . . . . 3F 59
(not continuous)
Hall Rd. E15 . . . . 1F 53
NW8 . . . . 2E 59
Hall St. EC1 . . . . 1E 9 (2D 63)
Hallsville Rd. E16 . . . . 5B 68
Hallswelle Rd. NW11 . . 1B 30
Hall Twr. *W2* *4F 59*
(off Hall Pl.)
Hall Vw. SE9 . . . . 2F 125

Halpin Pl. SE17 . . . . . . 5F 77
Halsbrook Rd. SE3 . . . 1E 111
Halsbury Ho. *N7* *1B 48*
(off Biddestone Rd.)
Halsbury Rd. W12 . . . . 2D 71
Halsey M. SW3 . . . . . . 5B 74
Halsey St. SW3 . . . . . . 5B 74
Halsmere Rd. SE5 . . . . 4D 91
Halstead Ct. E17 . . . . 2B 38
N1 . . . . *1C 10*
(off Fairbank Est.)
Halstead Rd. E11 . . . . 1C 40
Halston Cl. SW11 . . . 4B 102
Halstow Rd. NW10 . . . 2F 57
SE10 . . . . 1C 96
Halton Cross St. N1 . . 5D 49
Halton Mans. N1 . . . . 4D 49
Halton Pl. N1 . . . . 5E 49
Halton Rd. N1 . . . . 4D 49
Halyard Ho. E14 . . . . . 4E 81
Hamara Ghar E13 . . . . 5E 55
Hambalt Rd. SW4 . . . 3E 103
Hambledon *SE17* *2F 91*
(off Villa St.)
Hambledon Ct.
SE22 . . . . 2A 106
Hambledon Pl.
SE21 . . . . 1A 120
Hambledon Rd.
SW18 . . . . 5B 100
Hamble St. SW6 . . . . 1D 101
Hambley Ho. *SE16* *5D 79*
(off Camilla Rd.)
Hambridge Way
SW2 . . . . 5C 104
Hambro Rd. SW16 . . . 5F 117
Hamfrith Rd. E15 . . . . 3B 54
Hamilton Bldgs.
EC2 . . . . 4E 11

Hamilton Cl. NW8 . . . . 2F 59
SE16 . . . . 3A 80
Hamilton Ct. SE6 . . . 1B 124
SW15 . . . . 1A 100
W9 . . . . *2E 59*
(off Maida Va.)
Hamilton Gdns. NW8 . . . 2E 59
Hamilton Hall *NW8* *1E 59*
(off Hamilton Ter.)
Hamilton Ho. E14 . . . . 1D 95
(off St Davids Sq.)
E14 . . . . 1B 80
(off Victory Pl.)
NW8 . . . . *2F 59*
(off Hall Rd.)
W4 . . . . 2A 84
W8 . . . . *3D 73*
(off Vicarage Ga.)
Hamilton La. N5 . . . . . 1D 49
Hamilton Lodge *E1* . . . *3E 65*
(off Cleveland Gro.)
Hamilton M. SW18 . . . 1C 114
W1 . . . . 3D 21 (3D 75)
Hamilton Pk. N5 . . . . . 1D 49
Hamilton Pk. W. N5 . . 1D 49
Hamilton Pl. N19 . . . . 5F 33
W1 . . . . . . 2C 20 (2C 74)
Hamilton Rd. E15 . . . . 2A 68
NW10 . . . . 2C 42
NW11 . . . . 2F 29
SE27 . . . . 4F 119
W4 . . . . 3A 70
Hamilton Rd. Ind. Est.
SE27 . . . . 4F 119
(off Hamilton Rd.)
Hamilton Sq.
SE1 . . . . . . 3C 26 (3F 77)
Hamilton St. SE8 . . . . 2C 94
Hamilton Ter. NW8 . . . 1D 59
Hamlea Cl. SE12 . . . . 3C 110
Hamlet, The SE5 . . . . 1F 105
Hamlet Cl. SE13 . . . . 2A 110
Hamlet Ct. *SE11* *1D 91*
(off Opal St.)
W6 . . . . 5C 70
Hamlet Gdns. W6 . . . . 5C 70
Hamlet Ind. Est. E9 . . 4C 52
Hamlet M. SE21 . . . . 1F 119
Hamlet Sq. NW2 . . . . 5A 30
Hamlets Way E3 . . . . . 3B 66
Hamlet Way
SE1 . . . . . . 3C 26 (3F 77)
Hammelton Grn.
SW9 . . . . 4D 91
Hammerfield Ho.
SW3 . . . . *1A 88*
(off Cale St.)
Hammersley Ho.
SE14 . . . . *3E 93*
(off Pomeroy St.)
HAMMERSMITH 5E 71
Hammersmith Bri.
W6 . . . . 1D 85
Hammersmith Bri. Rd.
W6 . . . . 1E 85
HAMMERSMITH BROADWAY
. . . . 5E 71
Hammersmith B'way.
W6 . . . . 5E 71

HAMMERSMITH FLYOVER
. . . . 1E 85
Hammersmith Flyover
W6 . . . . 1E 85
Hammersmith Gro.
W6 . . . . 3E 71
Hammersmith Ind. Est.
W6 . . . . 2E 85
Hammersmith Rd.
W6 . . . . 5F 71
W14 . . . . 5F 71
Hammersmith Ter.
W6 . . . . 1C 84
Hammett St.
EC3 . . . . . . 4F 19 (1B 78)
Hammond Ct. *E10* *4D 39*
(off Crescent Rd.)
Hammond Ho. E14 . . . 4C 80
(off Tiller Rd.)
SE14 . . . . *3E 93*
(off Lubbock St.)
Hammond Lodge *W9* . . *4C 58*
(off Admiral Wlk.)
Hammond St. NW5 . . . 3E 47
Hamond Sq. N1 . . . . . 1A 64
Ham Pk. Rd. E7 . . . . . 4B 54
E15 . . . . 4B 54
Hampden Cl. NW1 . . . 1F 61
Hampden Gurney St.
W1 . . . . 3A 12 (5B 60)
Hampden Ho. SW9 . . . 5C 90
Hampden Rd. N19 . . . 4F 33
Hampshire Hog La.
W6 . . . . 1D 85
Hampshire St. NW5 . . 3F 47
Hampson Way SW8 . . 4B 90
HAMPSTEAD 1F 45
Hampstead Gdns.
NW11 . . . . 1C 30
HAMPSTEAD GARDEN
SUBURB 1E 31
Hampstead Ga. NW3 . . 2E 45
Hampstead Grn.
NW3 . . . . 2A 46
Hampstead Gro.
NW3 . . . . 5E 31
Hampstead Heath 4F 31
Hampstead Heath Info. Cen.
. . . . 1C 46
(off Lissenden Gdns.)
Hampstead High St.
NW3 . . . . 1F 45
Hampstead Hill Gdns.
NW3 . . . . 1F 45
Hampstead La. N6 . . . 3F 31
NW3 . . . . 3F 31
Hampstead Lodge
NW1 . . . . *4A 60*
(off Bell St.)
Hampstead Mus. 1F 45
(in Burgh House)
Hampstead Rd.
NW1 . . . . . . 1F 5 (1E 61)
Hampstead Sq. NW3 . . 5E 31
Hampstead Theatre . . . 4F 45
Hampstead Wlk. E3 . . . 5B 52
Hampstead Way
NW11 . . . . 1B 30
Hampstead W. NW6 . . 3C 44

Hampton Cl. NW6 . . . . .2C 58
Hampton Ct. N1 . . . . . . .3D 49
  SE16 . . . . .1F 79
   (off King & Queen Wharf)
Hampton Rd. E7 . . . . . . .2D 55
  E11 . . . . .3F 39
Hampton St. SE17 . . . . .5D 77
Hamston Ho. W8 . . . . . .4D 73
   (off Kensington Ct. Pl.)
Ham Yd. W1 . . .4B 14 (1F 75)
Hanameel St. E16 . . . . . .2C 82
Hana M. E5 . . . . .1D 51
Hanbury Dr. E11 . . . . . . .2B 40
Hanbury Ho. E1 . . . . . . .4C 64
   (off Hanbury St.)
  SW8 . . . . .3A 90
   (off Regent's Bri. Gdns.)
Hanbury M. N1 . . . . .5E 49
Hanbury St.
  E1 . . . . .5F 11 (4B 64)
Hancock Nunn Ho.
  NW3 . . . . .3B 46
   (off Fellows Rd.)
Hancock Rd. E3 . . . . . . .2E 67
Handa Wlk. N1 . . . . .3F 49
Hand Ct.
  WC1 . . . . .1A 16 (4B 62)
Handel House Mus. 4D 13
   (off Brook St.)
Handel Mans.
  SW13 . . . . .3E 85
  WC1 . . . . .3E 7
   (off Handel St.)
Handel Pl. NW10 . . . . . .3A 42
Handels Bus. Cen.
  SW8 . . . . .2A 90
Handel St.
  WC1 . . . . . . .3D 7 (3A 62)
Handen Rd. SE12 . . . . . .3A 110
Handforth Rd. SW9 . . . . .3C 90
Handley Gro. NW2 . . . . .5F 29
Handley Rd. E9 . . . . .4E 51
Hands Wlk. E16 . . . . . . .5C 68
Hanford Cl. SW18 . . . . . .1C 114
Hanford Row SW19 . . . . .5E 113
Hanging Sword All.
  EC4 . . . . .3C 16
Hankey Ho. SE1 . . . . . . .4C 26
   (off Manciple St.)
Hankey Pl.
  SE1 . . . . .4C 26 (3F 77)
Hanley Gdns. N4 . . . . . .3B 34
Hanley Rd. N4 . . . . .3A 34
Hanmer Wlk. N7 . . . . . . .4B 34
Hannah Barlow Ho.
  SW8 . . . . .4B 90
Hannah Mary Way
  SE1 . . . . .5C 78
Hannay La. N8 . . . . .2F 33
Hannay Wlk. SW16 . . . . .2F 117
Hannell Rd. SW6 . . . . . .3A 86
Hannen Rd. SE27 . . . . . .3D 119
Hannibal Rd. E1 . . . . . . .4E 65
Hannington Rd.
  SW4 . . . . .1D 103
Hanover Av. E16 . . . . . . .2C 82
Hanover Ct. SW15 . . . . . .2B 98
  W12 . . . . .2C 70
   (off Uxbridge Rd.)

Hanover Flats W1 . . . . . .4C 12
   (off Binney St.,
     not continuous)
Hanover Gdns. SE11 . . . .2C 90
Hanover Ga. NW1 . . . . . .2A 60
Hanover Ga. Mans.
  NW1 . . . . .3A 60
   (off Park Rd.)
Hanover Ho. E14 . . . . . . .2B 80
   (off Westferry Cir.)
  NW8 . . . . .1A 60
   (off St John's Wood High St.)
  SW9 . . . . .1C 104
Hanover Mans. SW2 . . . .3C 104
   (off Barnwell Rd.)
Hanover Mead NW11 . . .1A 30
Hanover Pk. SE15 . . . . . .4C 92
Hanover Pl. E3 . . . . .2B 66
  WC2 . . . . .3E 15 (5A 62)
Hanover Rd. NW10 . . . . .4E 43
Hanover Sq.
  W1 . . . . .3E 13 (5D 61)
Hanover Steps W2 . . . . .5A 60
   (off St George's Flds.)
Hanover St.
  W1 . . . . .3E 13 (5D 61)
Hanover Ter. NW1 . . . . . .2A 60
Hanover Ter. M.
  NW1 . . . . .2A 60
Hanover Trad. Est.
  N7 . . . . .2A 48
Hanover Yd. N1 . . . . . . .1E 62
   (off Noel Rd.)
Hansard M. W14 . . . . . . .3F 71
Hanscomb M. SW4 . . . . .2E 103
Hans Ct. SW3 . . . . .4B 74
   (off Hans Rd.)
Hans Cres.
  SW1 . . . . .5A 20 (4B 74)
Hansler Rd. SE22 . . . . . .3B 106
Hanson Cl. SW12 . . . . . .5D 103
Hanson Ct. E17 . . . . .1D 39
Hanson St. W1 . . .5F 5 (4E 61)
Hans Pl.
  SW1 . . . . .5A 20 (4B 74)
Hans Rd.
  SW3 . . . . .5A 20 (4B 74)
Hans St.
  SW1 . . . . .5A 20 (4B 74)
Hanway Pl.
  W1 . . . . .2B 14 (5F 61)
Hanway St.
  W1 . . . . .2B 14 (5F 61)
Hanwell Ho. W2 . . . . . . .4C 58
   (off Brunel Rd.)
Hanworth Ho. SE5 . . . . . .3D 91
   (off Camberwell New Rd., not
     continuous)
Harad's Pl. E1 . . . . .1C 78
Harben Pde. NW3 . . . . . .4E 45
   (off Finchley Rd.)
Harben Rd. NW6 . . . . . . .4E 45
Harberson Rd. E15 . . . . .5B 54
  SW12 . . . . .1D 117
Harberton Rd. N19 . . . . .3E 33
Harbet Rd. W2 . . . . .4F 59
Harbinger Rd. E14 . . . . . .5D 81
Harbledown Ho. SE1 . . . .4B 26
   (off Manciple St.)

Harbledown Rd.
  SW6 . . . . .4C 86
Harbord Cl. SE5 . . . . . . .5F 91
Harbord Ho. SE16 . . . . . .5F 79
   (off Cope St.)
Harbord St. SW6 . . . . . . .4F 85
Harborough Rd.
  SW16 . . . . .4B 118
Harbour Av. SW10 . . . . . .4E 87
Harbour Club Leisure
  Cen., The. 5E 87
Harbour Exchange Sq.
  E14 . . . . .3D 81
Harbour Quay E14 . . . . . .2E 81
Harbour Reach SW6 . . . . .4E 87
Harbour Rd. SE5 . . . . . . .1E 105
Harbour Yd. SW10 . . . . . .4E 87
Harbridge Av. SW15 . . . . .5B 98
Harbut Rd. SW11 . . . . . . .2F 101
   (not continuous)
Harcombe Rd. N16 . . . . . .5A 36
Harcourt Bldgs. EC4. . . . .4B 16
Harcourt Ho. W1 . . . . . . .2D 13
   (off Cavendish Sq.)
Harcourt Rd. E15 . . . . . . .1B 68
  SE4 . . . . .1B 108
Harcourt St. W1 . . . . .4A 60
Harcourt Ter. SW10 . . . . .1D 87
Hardcastle Ho. SE14 . . . .4A 94
   (off Loring Rd.)
Hardel Ri. SW2 . . . . .1D 119
Hardel Wlk. SW2 . . . . . . .5C 104
Harden Ct. SE7 . . . . .5F 83
Harden Ho. SE5 . . . . .5A 92
Harden's Manorway
  SE7 . . . . .4F 83
   (not continuous)
Harders Rd. SE15 . . . . . .5D 93
Hardess St. SE24 . . . . . . .1E 105
Harding Cl. SE17 . . . . . . .2E 91
Hardinge La. E1 . . . . .5E 65
   (not continuous)
Hardinge Rd. NW10 . . . . .5D 43
Hardinge St. E1 . . . . .1E 79
   (not continuous)
Harding Ho. SW13 . . . . . .2D 85
   (off Wyatt Dr.)
Hardington NW1 . . . . . . .4C 46
   (off Belmont St.)
Hardman Rd. SE7 . . . . . .1D 97
Hardwicke M. WC1 . . . . . .2A 8
Hardwick Ho. NW8 . . . . . .3A 60
   (off Lilestone St.)
Hardwick St.
  EC1 . . . . .2C 8 (2C 62)
Hardwicks Way
  SW18 . . . . .3C 100
Hardwidge St.
  SE1 . . . . .3D 27 (3A 78)
Hardy Av. E16. . . . . .2C 82
Hardy Cl. SE16 . . . . .3F 79
Hardy Cotts. SE10 . . . . . .2F 95
Hardy Ho. SW4. . . . . .5E 103
Hardy Rd. SE3 . . . . .3B 96
Hare & Billet Rd. SE3. . . .4F 95
Hare Ct. EC4 . . .3B 16 (5C 62)
Harecourt Rd. N1 . . . . . . .3E 49
Haredale Rd. SE24. . . . . .2E 105
Haredon Cl. SE23. . . . . . .5F 107

Harefield M. SE4 . . . . . 1B 108
Harefield Rd. SE4 . . . . . 1B 108
Hare Pl. EC4 . . . . 3C 16
   (off Pleydell St.)
Hare Row E2 . . . . 1D 65
Hare Wlk. N1 . . . . 1A 64
   (not continuous)
Harewood Av. NW1 . . . . 3A 60
Harewood Pl.
  W1 . . . . 3E 13 (5D 61)
Harewood Row NW1 . . . 4A 60
Harfield Gdns. SE5 . . . . 1A 106
Harfleur Ct. SE11 . . . . . 5D 77
   (off Opal St.)
Harford Ho. SE5 . . . . . . 2E 91
   (off Bethwin Rd.)
  W11 . . . . 4B 58
Harford M. N19 . . . . . . 5F 33
Harford St. E1 . . . . 3A 66
Hargood Rd. SE3 . . . . . 4E 97
Hargrave Mans. N19 . . . 4F 33
Hargrave Pk. N19 . . . . . 4E 33
Hargrave Pl. N7 . . . . . . 2F 47
Hargrave Rd. N19 . . . . . 4E 33
Hargraves Ho. W12 . . . 1D 71
   (off White City Est.)
Hargwyne St. SW9 . . . 1B 104
Haringey Pk. N8 . . . . . . 1A 34
Harkness Ho. E1 . . . . . . 5C 64
   (off Christian St.)
Harland Rd. SE12 . . . . 1C 124
Harlequin Ct. E1 . . . . . . 1C 78
   (off Thomas More St.)
  NW10 . . . . 3A 42
   (off Mitchellbrook Way)
Harlescott Rd. SE15 . . . 2F 107
HARLESDEN 1B 56
Harlesden Gdns.
  NW10 . . . . 5B 42
Harlesden La. NW10 . . . 5C 42
Harlesden Plaza
  NW10 . . . . 1B 56
Harlesden Rd. NW10 . . . 5C 42
Harleston Cl. E5 . . . . . . 4E 37
Harley Ct. E11 . . . . 2C 40
Harleyford Ct. SE11 . . . 2B 90
   (off Harleyford Rd.)
Harleyford Rd. SE11 . . . 2B 90
Harleyford St. SE11 . . . 2C 90
Harley Gdns. SW10 . . . 1E 87
Harley Gro. E3 . . . . 2B 66
Harley Ho. E11 . . . . 2F 39
  NW1 . . . . 4C 4
Harley Pl.
  W1 . . . . 1D 13 (4D 61)
Harley Rd. NW3 . . . . . . 4F 45
  NW10 . . . . 1A 56
Harley St. W1 . . . 4D 5 (3D 61)
Harley Vs. NW10 . . . . . 1A 56
Harling Ct. SW11 . . . . . 5B 88
Harlinger St. SE18 . . . . 4F 83
Harlowe Cl. E8 . . . . 5C 50
Harlowe Ho. E8 . . . . . . 5B 50
   (off Clarissa St.)
Harlynwood SE5 . . . . . . 3E 91
   (off Wyndham Rd.)
Harman Cl. NW2 . . . . . 5A 30
  SE1 . . . . 1C 92

Harman Dr. NW2 . . . . . 5A 30
Harmon Ho. SE8 . . . . . 5B 80
Harmont Ho. W1 . . . . . 1D 13
   (off Harley St.)
Harmony Cl. NW11 . . . . 1A 30
Harmood Gro. NW1 . . . 4D 47
Harmood Ho. NW1 . . . . 4D 47
   (off Harmood St.)
Harmood Pl. NW1 . . . . 4D 47
Harmood St. NW1 . . . . 3D 47
Harmsworth M. SE1 . . . 4D 77
Harmsworth St.
  SE17 . . . . 1D 91
Harold Cl. SE16 . . . . . . 3F 79
   (off Christopher Cl.)
Harold Est. SE1 . . . . . . 4A 78
Harold Gibbons Ct.
  SE7 . . . . 2E 97
Harold Ho. E2 . . . . 1F 65
   (off Mace St.)
Harold Laski Ho. EC1 . . 2E 9
   (off Percival St.)
Harold Maddison Ho.
  SE17 . . . . 1D 91
   (off Penton Pl.)
Harold Pl. SE11 . . . . . . 1C 90
Harold Rd. E11 . . . . 3A 40
  E13 . . . . 5D 55
  NW10 . . . . 2A 56
Haroldstone Rd. E17 . . . 1F 37
Harold Wilson Ho.
  SW6 . . . . 2B 86
   (off Clem Attlee Ct.)
Harp All.
  EC4 . . . . 2D 17 (5D 63)
Harp Bus. Cen., The
  NW2 . . . . 4C 28
Harpenden Rd. E12 . . . . 4E 41
  SE27 . . . . 3D 119
Harpenmead Point
  NW2 . . . . 4B 30
Harper Ho. SW9 . . . . . 1D 105
Harper M. SW17 . . . . . 3E 115
Harper Rd.
  SE1 . . . . 5A 26 (4E 77)
Harp Island Cl.
  NW10 . . . . 4A 28
Harp La. EC3 . . . 5D 19 (1A 78)
Harpley Sq. E1 . . . . 3F 65
Harpsden St. SW11 . . . 4C 88
Harpur M.
  WC1 . . . . 5F 7 (4B 62)
Harpur St.
  WC1 . . . . 5F 7 (4B 62)
Harraden Rd. SE3 . . . . 4E 97
Harrier Av. E11 . . . . . . 1D 41
Harriet Cl. E8 . . . . 5C 50
Harriet Ho. SW6 . . . . . 3D 87
   (off Wandon Rd.)
Harriet St.
  SW1 . . . . 4A 20 (3B 74)
Harriet Tubman Cl.
  SW2 . . . . 5B 104
Harriet Wlk.
  SW1 . . . . 4A 20 (3B 74)
HARRINGAY 1D 35
Harrington Ct. SW7 . . . 5F 73
   (off Harrington Rd.)
  W10 . . . . 2B 58

Harrington Gdns.
  SW7 . . . . 5D 73
Harrington Hill E5 . . . . 3D 37
Harrington Ho. NW1 . . . 1F 5
   (off Harrington St.)
Harrington Rd. E11 . . . 3A 40
  SW7 . . . . 5F 73
Harrington Sq. NW1 . . . 1E 61
Harrington St.
  NW1 . . . . 1F 5 (1E 61)
   (not continuous)
Harrington Way
  SE18 . . . . 4F 83
Harriott Cl. SE10 . . . . . 5B 82
Harriott Ho. E1 . . . . . . 4E 65
   (off Jamaica St.)
Harris Bldgs. E1 . . . . . . 5C 64
   (off Burslem St.)
Harris Ho. SW9 . . . . . . 1C 104
   (off St James's Cres.)
Harris Lodge SE6 . . . . 1E 123
Harrison Ho. SE17 . . . . 1F 91
   (off Brandon St.)
Harrisons Ct. SE14 . . . . 2F 93
   (off Myers La.)
Harrison St.
  WC1 . . . . 2E 7 (2A 62)
Harris St. E17 . . . . 2B 38
  SE5 . . . . 3F 91
Harrods 5A 20 (4B 74)
Harrogate Ct. SE12 . . . 5C 110
  SE26 . . . . 3C 120
   (off Droitwich Cl.)
Harrold Ho. NW3 . . . . . 4F 45
Harroway Rd. SW11 . . . 5F 87
Harrowby St. W1 . . . . . 5A 60
Harrow Club Sports Cen.
  . . . . 1F 71
Harrowgate Ho. E9 . . . . 3F 51
Harrowgate Rd. E9 . . . . 3A 52
Harrow Grn. E11 . . . . . 5A 40
Harrow La. E14 . . . . . . 1D 81
Harrow Lodge NW8 . . . 3F 59
   (off Northwick Ter.)
Harrow Pl.
  E1 . . . . 2E 19 (5A 64)
Harrow Rd. E6 . . . . 5F 55
  E11 . . . . 5A 40
  NW10 . . . . 2D 57
  W2 . . . . 4E 59
   (not continuous)
  W9 . . . . 3A 58
  W10 . . . . 3A 58
Harrow Rd. Bri. W2 . . . 4E 59
Harrow St. NW1 . . . . . . 4A 60
   (off Daventry St.)
Harry Hinkins Ho.
  SE17 . . . . 1E 91
   (off Bronti Cl.)
Harry Lambourn Ho.
  SE15 . . . . 3D 93
   (off Gervase St.)
Hartfield Ter. E3 . . . . . 1C 66
Hartham Cl. N7 . . . . . . 2A 48
Hartham Rd. N7 . . . . . . 2A 48
Harting Rd. SE9 . . . . . . 3F 125
Hartington Ct. SW4 . . . 4A 90
Hartington Ho. SW1 . . . 1F 89
   (off Drummond Ga.)

Hartington Rd. E16 . . . . 5D **69**
  E17 . . . . 1A **38**
  SW8 . . . . 4A **90**
Hartismere Rd. SW6 . . . 3B **86**
Hartlake Rd. E9 . . . . 3F **51**
Hartland NW1 . . . . 5E **47**
  (off Royal College St.)
Hartland Rd. E15 . . . . . 4B **54**
  NW1 . . . . 4D **47**
  NW6 . . . . 1B **58**
Hartley Av. E6 . . . . 5F **55**
Hartley Ho. SE1 . . . . 5B **78**
  (off Longfield St.)
Hartley Rd. E11 . . . . 3B **40**
Hartley St. E2 . . . . 2E **65**
  (not continuous)
Hartmann Rd. E16 . . . . . 2F **83**
Hartnoll St. N7 . . . . 2B **48**
Harton St. SE8 . . . . 4C **94**
Hartop Point SW6 . . . . . 3A **86**
  (off Pellant Rd.)
Hartshorn All. EC3 . . . . 3E **19**
Hart's La. SE14 . . . . 4A **94**
Hart St. EC3 . . . . 4E **19** (1A **78**)
Hartswood Gdns.
  W12 . . . . 4B **70**
Hartswood Rd. W12 . . . . 3B **70**
Hartsworth Cl. E13 . . . . 1B **68**
Hartwell Ho. SE7 . . . . . . 1D **97**
  (off Troughton Rd.)
Hartwell St. E8 . . . . 3B **50**
Harvard Ct. NW6 . . . . . . 2D **45**
Harvard Ho. SE17 . . . . . 2D **91**
  (off Doddington Gro.)
Harvard Rd. SE13 . . . . . 3E **109**
Harvey Gdns. E11 . . . . . 3B **40**
  SE7 . . . . 1E **97**
Harvey Ho. E1 . . . . 3D **65**
  (off Brady St.)
  N1 . . . . 5F **49**
  (off Colville Est.)
  SW1 . . . . 1F **89**
  (off Aylesford St.)
Harvey Lodge W9 . . . . . 4C **58**
  (off Admiral Wlk.)
Harvey Point E16 . . . . . 4C **68**
  (off Fife Rd.)
Harvey Rd. E11 . . . . 3A **40**
  SE5 . . . . 4F **91**
  (not continuous)
Harvey's Bldgs.
  WC2 . . . . 5E **15** (1A **76**)
Harvey St. N1 . . . . 5F **49**
Harvington Wlk. E8 . . . . 4C **50**
Harvist Est. N7 . . . . 1C **48**
Harvist Rd. NW6 . . . . 1F **57**
Harwood Ct. N1 . . . . 5F **49**
  (off Colville Est.)
  SW15 . . . . 2E **99**
Harwood M. SW6 . . . . . . 3C **86**
Harwood Point SE16 . . . 3B **80**
Harwood Rd. SW6 . . . . . 3C **86**
Harwood Ter. SW6 . . . . . 4D **87**
Haseley End SE23 . . . . . 5E **107**
Haselrigge Rd. SW4 . . . 2F **103**
Haseltine Rd. SE26 . . . . 4B **122**
Hasker St. SW3 . . . . 5A **74**
Haslam Cl. N1 . . . . 4C **48**
Haslam St. SE15 . . . . . . 3B **92**

Haslemere Av. NW4 . . . . 1F **29**
  SW18 . . . . 2D **115**
Haslemere Ind. Est.
  SW18 . . . . 2D **115**
Haslemere Rd. N8 . . . . . 2F **33**
Haslers Wharf E3 . . . . . 5A **52**
  (off Old Ford Rd.)
Hassard St. E2 . . . . 1B **64**
Hassendean Rd. SE3 . . . 2D **97**
Hassett Rd. E9 . . . . 3F **51**
Hassocks Cl. SE26 . . . . . 3D **121**
Hassop Rd. NW2 . . . . 1F **43**
Hassop Wlk. SE9 . . . . . . 4F **125**
Hasted Rd. SE7 . . . . 1F **97**
Hastings Cl. SE15 . . . . . 3C **92**
Hastings Ho. W12 . . . . . 1D **71**
  (off White City Est.)
  WC1 . . . . 2D **7**
  (off Hastings St.)
Hastings St.
  WC1 . . . . 2D **7** (2A **62**)
Hat & Mitre Ct. EC1 . . . . 4E **9**
Hatcham M. Bus. Cen.
  SE14 . . . . 4F **93**
  (off Hatcham Pk. Rd.)
Hatcham Pk. M.
  SE14 . . . . 4F **93**
Hatcham Pk. Rd.
  SE14 . . . . 4F **93**
Hatcham Rd. SE15 . . . . . 2E **93**
Hatchard Rd. N19 . . . . . . 4F **33**
Hatchers M. SE1 . . . . . . 4E **27**
Hatchfield Ho. N15 . . . . . 1A **36**
  (off Albert Rd.)
Hatcliffe Almshouses
  SE10 . . . . 1A **96**
  (off Tuskar St.)
Hatcliffe Cl. SE3 . . . . . . 1B **110**
Hatcliffe St. SE10 . . . . . 1B **96**
Hatfield Cl. SE14 . . . . . . 3F **93**
Hatfield Ct. SE3 . . . . 3C **96**
Hatfield Ho. EC1 . . . . 4F **9**
Hatfield Rd. E15 . . . . 2A **54**
  W4 . . . . 3A **70**
Hatfields
  SE1 . . . . 1C **24** (2C **76**)
Hathaway Ho.
  N1 . . . . 1D **11** (1A **64**)
Hatherley Ct. W2 . . . . . . 5D **59**
  (off Hatherley Gro.)
Hatherley Gdns. E6 . . . . 2F **69**
  N8 . . . . 1A **34**
Hatherley Gro. W2 . . . . . 5D **59**
Hatherley St. SW1 . . . . . 5E **75**
Hathersage Ct. N1 . . . . . 2F **49**
Hathorne Cl. SE15 . . . . . 5D **93**
Hathway St. SE15 . . . . . 5F **93**
Hathway Ter. SE14 . . . . . 5F **93**
  (off Hathway St.)
Hatley Rd. N4 . . . . 4B **34**
Hatteraick St. SE16 . . . . 3E **79**
Hatton Gdn.
  EC1 . . . . 5C **8** (4C **62**)
Hatton Pl. EC1 . . . 5C **8** (4C **62**)
Hatton Row NW8 . . . . . . 3F **59**
  (off Hatton St.)
Hatton St. NW8 . . . . 3F **59**
Hatton Wall
  EC1 . . . . 5C **8** (4C **62**)

Haunch of Venison Yd.
  W1 . . . . 3D **13** (5D **61**)
Hauteville Ct. Gdns.
  W6 . . . . 4B **70**
  (off South Side)
Havana Rd. SW19 . . . . . 2C **114**
Havannah St. E14 . . . . . 3C **80**
Havelock Cl. W12 . . . . . . 1D **71**
Havelock Ho. SE23 . . . . 1E **121**
Havelock Rd. SW19 . . . . 5E **115**
Havelock St. N1 . . . . 5A **48**
Havelock Ter. SW8 . . . . . 4D **89**
Havelock Ter. Arches
  SW8 . . . . 4D **89**
  (off Havelock Ter.)
Havelock Wlk. SE23 . . . . 1E **121**
Haven Cl. SW19 . . . . 3F **113**
Haven M. E3 . . . . 4B **66**
  N1 . . . . 4C **48**
Havenpool NW8 . . . . 5D **45**
  (off Abbey Rd.)
Haven St. NW1 . . . . 4D **47**
Haverfield Rd. E3 . . . . . . 2A **66**
Haverhill Rd. SW12 . . . . 1E **117**
Havering NW1 . . . . 4D **47**
  (off Castlehaven Rd.)
Havering St. E1 . . . . 5F **65**
Haversham Pl. N6 . . . . . 4B **32**
Haverstock Hill NW3 . . . 2A **46**
Haverstock Pl. N1 . . . . . 1E **9**
  (off Haverstock St.)
Haverstock Rd. NW5 . . . 2C **46**
Haverstock St.
  N1 . . . . 1E **9** (1D **63**)
Havil St. SE5 . . . . 3A **92**
Havisham Ho. SE16 . . . . 3C **78**
Hawarden Gro.
  SE24 . . . . 5E **105**
Hawarden Hill NW2 . . . . 5C **28**
Hawbridge Rd. E11 . . . . 3F **39**
Hawes St. N1 . . . . 4D **49**
Hawgood St. E3 . . . . 4C **66**
Hawke Ho. E1 . . . . 3F **65**
  (off Ernest St.)
Hawke Pl. SE16 . . . . 3F **79**
Hawke Rd. SE19 . . . . 5F **119**
Hawkesbury Rd.
  SW15 . . . . 3D **99**
Hawkesfield Rd.
  SE23 . . . . 2A **122**
Hawke Twr. SE14 . . . . . . 2A **94**
Hawkins Ho. SE8 . . . . . . 2C **94**
  (off New King St.)
  SW1 . . . . 2E **89**
  (off Dolphin Sq.)
Hawkins Way SE6 . . . . . 5C **122**
Hawkley Gdns.
  SE27 . . . . 2D **119**
Hawkshaw Cl. SW2 . . . . 5A **104**
Hawkshead NW1 . . . . . . 1F **5**
Hawkshead Rd.
  NW10 . . . . 4B **42**
  W4 . . . . 3A **70**
Hawkslade Rd.
  SE15 . . . . 3F **107**
Hawksley Rd. N16 . . . . . 5A **36**
Hawks M. SE10 . . . . 3E **95**
Hawksmoor Cl. E6 . . . . . 5F **69**
Hawksmoor M. E1 . . . . . 1D **79**

Hawksmoor Pl. E2 . . . . . 3C 64
   (off Cheshire St.)
Hawksmoor St. W6 . . . . . 2F 85
Hawkstone Rd. SE16 . . . 5E 79
Hawkwell Wlk. N1 . . . . 5E 49
   (off Maldon Cl.)
Hawkwood Mt. E5 . . . . . 3D 37
Hawley Cres. NW1 . . . . 4D 47
Hawley M. NW1 . . . . . . 4D 47
Hawley Rd. NW1 . . . . . 4D 47
   (not continuous)
Hawley St. NW1 . . . . . . 4D 47
Hawstead Rd. SE6 . . . 4D 109
Hawthorn Av. E3 . . . . . . 5B 52
Hawthorn Cres.
SW17 . . . . 5C 116
Hawthorne Cl. N1 . . . . 3A 50
Hawthorne Ho. N15 . . . 1C 36
SW1 . . . . 1E 89
   (off Churchill Gdns.)
Hawthorn Rd. NW10 . . . 4C 42
Hawthorn Ter. N19 . . . . 3F 33
   (off Calverley Gro.)
Hawthorn Wlk. W10 . . 3A 58
Hawtrey Rd. NW3 . . . . 4A 46
Hay Cl. E15 . . . . 4A 54
Haycroft Gdns.
NW10 . . . . 5C 42
Haycroft Rd. SW2 . . . 3A 104
Hay Currie St. E14 . . . 5D 67
Hayday Rd. E16 . . . . . . 4C 68
   (not continuous)
Hayden Piper Ho.
SW3 . . . . 2B 88
   (off Caversham St.)
Hayden's Pl. W11 . . . . 5B 58
Haydon Pk. Rd.
SW19 . . . . 5C 114
Haydons Rd. SW19 . . 5D 115
Haydon St.
EC3 . . . . 4F 19 (1B 78)
Haydon Wlk.
E1 . . . . 3F 19 (5B 64)
Haydon Way SW11 . . . 2F 101
Hayes Ct. SE5 . . . . . . 3E 91
   (off Camberwell New Rd.)
SW2 . . . . 1A 118
Hayes Cres. NW11 . . . 1B 30
Hayesens Ho. SW17 . . 4E 115
Hayes Gro. SE22 . . . . 1B 106
Hayes Pl. NW1 . . . . . . 3A 60
Hayfield Pas. E1 . . . . . 3E 65
Hayfield Yd. E1 . . . . . 3E 65
Haygarth Pl. SW19 . . . 5F 113
Hay Hill W1 . . . . 5E 13 (1D 75)
Hayles Bldgs. SE11 . . . 5D 77
   (off Elliotts Row)
Hayles St. SE11 . . . . . 5D 77
Hayling Cl. N16 . . . . . 2A 50
Haymans Point SE11 . . 5B 76
Hayman St. N1 . . . . . . 4D 49
Haymarket
SW1 . . . . 5B 14 (1F 75)
Haymarket Arc. SW1 . . 5B 14
Haymarket Ct. E8 . . . . 4B 50
   (off Jacaranda Gro.)
Haymarket Theatre Royal
. . . . 5C 14
   (off Haymarket)

Haymerle Ho. SE15 . . . 2C 92
   (off Haymerle Rd.)
Haymerle Rd. SE15 . . . 2C 92
Hayne Ho. W11 . . . . . 2A 72
   (off Penzance Pl.)
Haynes Cl. SE3 . . . . . 1A 110
Haynes La. SE19 . . 5A 120
Hay's Galleria
SE1 . . . . 1D 27 (2A 78)
Hay's La.
SE1 . . . . 1D 27 (2A 78)
Hay's M. W1 . . 1D 21 (2D 75)
Hay St. E2 . . . . 5C 50
Hayter Ct. E11 . . . . . . 4D 41
Hayter Rd. SW2 . . . . 3A 104
Hayton Cl. E8 . . . . 3B 50
Hayward Ct. SW4 . . . 5A 90
   (off Clapham Rd.)
Hayward Gallery 2A 24
Hayward Gdns.
SW15 . . . . 4E 99
Hayward Ho. N1 . . . . 1C 62
   (off Penton St.)
Hayward's Pl.
EC1 . . . . 3D 9 (3D 63)
Haywards Yd. SE4 . . 3B 108
   (off Lindal Rd.)
Hazelbank Rd. SE6 . . 2F 123
Hazelbourne Rd.
SW12 . . . . 4D 103
Hazel Cl. N19 . . . . . . 4E 33
Hazeldean Rd. NW10 . . 4A 42
Hazeldon Rd. SE4 . . . 3A 108
Hazel Gro. SE26 . . . . 4F 121
Hazelhurst Ct. SE6 . . 5E 123
   (off Beckenham Hill Rd.)
Hazelhurst Rd.
SW17 . . . . 4E 115
Hazellville Rd. N19 . . 2F 33
Hazelmere Ct. SW2 . . 1B 118
Hazelmere Rd. NW6 . . 5B 44
Hazel Rd. E15 . . . . . . 2A 54
NW10 . . . . 2D 57
   (not continuous)
Hazel Way SE1 . . . . . 5B 78
Hazelwood Ct. NW10 . . 5A 28
Hazelwood Ho. SE8 . . 5A 80
Hazelwood Rd. E17 . . 1A 38
Hazlebury Rd. SW6 . . 5D 87
Hazlewell Rd. SW15 . . 3E 99
Hazlewood Cl. E5 . . . 5A 38
Hazlewood Cres.
W10 . . . . 3A 58
Hazlewood Twr. W10 . . 3A 58
   (off Golborne Gdns.)
Hazlitt M. W14 . . . . . 4A 72
Hazlitt Rd. W14 . . . . . 4A 72
Headbourne Ho.
SE1 . . . . 5C 26 (4F 77)
Headcorn Rd.
BR1: Brom 5B 124
Headfort Pl.
SW1 . . . . 4C 20 (3C 74)
Headington Rd.
SW18 . . . . 2E 115
Headlam Rd. SW4 . . . 4F 103
   (not continuous)
Headlam St. E1 . . . . . 3D 65
Headley Ct. SE26 . . . 5E 121

Head's M. W11 . . . . . 5C 58
Head St. E1 . . . . 5F 65
   (not continuous)
Heald St. SE14 . . . . . 4C 94
Healey Ho. SW9 . . . . 3C 90
Healey St. NW1 . . . . 3D 47
Hearn's Bldgs. SE17 . . 5F 77
Hearnshaw St. E14 . . 5A 66
Hearn M.
EC2 . . . . 4E 11 (3A 64)
Hearnville Rd.
SW12 . . . . 1C 116
Heath Brow NW3 . . . 5E 31
Heath Cl. NW11 . . . . 2D 31
Heathcock Ct. WC2 . . 5E 15
   (off Exchange Ct.)
Heathcote St.
WC1 . . . . 3F 7 (3B 62)
Heath Cft. NW11 . . . . 3D 31
Heath Dr. NW3 . . . . . 1D 45
Heathedge SE26 . . . . 2D 121
Heather Cl. N7 . . . . . 5B 34
SE13 . . . . 5F 109
SW8 . . . . 1D 103
Heather Gdns. NW11 . . 1A 30
Heather Ho. E14 . . . . 5E 67
   (off Dee St.)
Heatherley Ct. E5 . . . 5C 36
Heather Rd. NW2 . . . 4B 28
SE12 . . . . 2C 124
Heather Wlk. W10 . . 3A 58
Heatherwood Cl. E12 . . 4E 41
Heathfield Av.
SW18 . . . . 5F 101
Heathfield Cl. E16 . . . 4F 69
Heathfield Gdns.
NW11 . . . . 1F 29
SE3 . . . . 5A 96
   (off Baizdon Rd.)
SW18 . . . . 4F 101
Heathfield Ho. SE3 . . 5A 96
Heathfield Pk. NW2 . . 3E 43
Heathfield Rd.
SW18 . . . . 4E 101
Heathfield Sq.
SW18 . . . . 5F 101
Heathfield St. W11 . . 1A 72
   (off Portland Rd.)
Heathgate NW11 . . . . 1D 31
Heathgate Pl. NW3 . . 2B 46
Heath Hurst Rd.
NW3 . . . . 1A 46
Heathland Rd. N16 . . 3A 36
Heath La. SE3 . . . . . 5F 95
   (not continuous)
Heathlee Rd. SE3 . . . 2B 110
Heathmans Rd.
SW6 . . . . 4B 86
Heath Mead SW19 . . 3F 113
Heathpool Ct. E1 . . . 3D 65
Heath Ri. SW15 . . . . 4F 99
Heath Rd. SW8 . . . . . 5D 89
Heath Royal SW15 . . 4F 99
Heath Side NW3 . . . . 1F 45
Heathstan Rd. W12 . . 5C 56
Heath St. NW3 . . . . . 5E 31
Heathview NW5 . . . . 1C 46

Heathview Gdns.
 SW15 . . . . 5E **99**
Heath Vs. NW3 . . . . 5F **31**
Heathville Rd. N19. . . . . . 2A **34**
Heathwall St.
 SW11 . . . . 1B **102**
Heathway SE3 . . . . 3C **96**
Heathway Ct. NW3. . . . . . 4C **30**
Heathwood Gdns.
 SE7 . . . . 5F **83**
Heathwood Point
 SE23 . . . . 3F **121**
Heaton Ho. *SW10.* *2E 87*
 (off Seymour Wlk.)
Heaton Rd. SE15 . . . . 5D **93**
Heaven Tree Cl. N1 . . . . . 3E **49**
Heaver Rd. SW11. . . . . . . 1F **101**
Hebden Ct. E2 . . . . 5B **50**
Hebdon Rd. SW17 . . . . . . 3A **116**
Heber Mans. *W14* *2A 86*
 (off Queen's Club Gdns.)
Heber Rd. NW2. . . . . 2F **43**
 SE22 . . . . 4B **106**
Hebron Rd. W6. . . . . 4E **71**
Heckfield Pl. SW6 . . . . . . 3C **86**
Heckford Ho. *E14.* *5D 67*
 (off Grundy St.)
Heckford St. E1 . . . . 1F **79**
Heckford St. *SW9.* *3C 90*
 (off Caldwell St.)
Hector Ct. *SW9.* *3C 90*
Hector Ho. *E2.* *1D 65*
 (off Old Bethnal Grn. Rd.)
Heddington Gro. N7. . . . . 2B **48**
Heddon St.
 W1 . . . . 4F **13** (1E **75**)
 (not continuous)
Hedgegate Ct. *W11* *5B 58*
 (off Powis Ter.)
Hedgers Gro. E9. . . . . 3A **52**
Hedger St. SE11. . . . . 5D **77**
Hedge Wlk. SE6. . . . . 5D **123**
Hedgley M. SE12 . . . . 3B **110**
Hedgley St. SE12 . . . . 3B **110**
Hedingham Cl. N1 . . . . . . 4E **49**
Hedley Ho. *E14.* *4E 81*
 (off Stewart St.)
Hedley Row N5 . . . . 2F **49**
Hedsor Ho. *E2.* *3F 11*
 (off Ligonier St.)
Hega Ho. *E14.* *4E 67*
 (off Ullin St.)
Heidegger Cres.
 SW13 . . . . 3D **85**
Heigham Rd. E6 . . . . 4F **55**
Heights, The SE7 . . . . 1E **97**
Heiron St. SE17 . . . . 2D **91**
Helby Rd. SW4 . . . . 4F **103**
Heldar Ct.
 SE1. . . . . 4C **26** (3F **77**)
Helder Gro. SE12 . . . . 5B **110**
Helena Pl. E9. . . . . 5D **51**
Helena Rd. E13 . . . . 1B **68**
 E17. . . . . 1C **38**
 NW10. . . . . 2D **43**
Helena Sq. *SE16* *1A 80*
 (off Sovereign Cres.)
Helen Gladstone Ho.
 SE1. . . . . *3D 25*
 (off Surrey Row)

Helen Ho. *E2* *1D 65*
 (off Old Bethnal Grn. Rd.)
Helen Mackay Ho.
 E14. . . . . *5F 67*
 (off Blair St.)
Helen Peele Cotts.
 SE16 . . . . *4E 79*
 (off Lower Rd.)
Helenslea Av. NW11 . . . . 3C **30**
Helen's Pl. E2. . . . . 2E **65**
Helen Taylor Ho.
 SE16 . . . . *4C 78*
 (off Evelyn Lowe Est.)
Heliport Ind. Est.
 SW11 . . . . 5F **87**
Helix Cl. *W11.* *2F 71*
 (off Swanscombe Rd.)
Helix Gdns. SW2 . . . . 4B **104**
Helix Rd. SW2 . . . . 4B **104**
Hellings St. E1. . . . . 2C **78**
Helme Cl. SW19 . . . . 5B **114**
Helmet Row
 EC1 . . . . 2A **10** (3E **63**)
Helmsdale Ho. *NW6* *1D 59*
 (off Carlton Va.)
Helmsley Pl. E8 . . . . 4D **51**
Helmsley St. E8 . . . . 4D **51**
Helperby Rd. NW10 . . . . . 4A **42**
Helsby Ct. *NW8* *3F 59*
 (off Pollitt Dr.)
Helsinki Sq. SE16 . . . . . . 4A **80**
Helston *NW1* *5E 47*
 (off Camden St.)
Helston Ct. *N15* *1A 36*
 (off Culvert Rd.)
Helston Ho. *SE11.* *1C 90*
 (off Kennings Way)
Helvetia St. SE6 . . . . 2B **122**
Hemans St. SW8 . . . . 3F **89**
Hemans St. Est. SW8. . . 3F **89**
Hemberton Rd.
 SW9 . . . . 1A **104**
Hemingford Rd. N1 . . . . . 5B **48**
Hemingway Cl. NW5 . . . 1C **46**
Hemlock Rd. W12 . . . . . . 1B **70**
 (not continuous)
Hemming St. E1. . . . . 3C **64**
Hemp Wlk. SE17 . . . . 5F **77**
Hemstal Rd. NW6 . . . . . . 4C **44**
Hemsworth Ct. N1 . . . . . . 1A **64**
Hemsworth St. N1 . . . . . . 1A **64**
Hemus Pl. SW3 . . . . 1A **88**
Hen & Chicken Ct.
 EC4 . . . . *3B 16*
 (off Fleet St.)
Hen & Chickens Theatre
 . . . . *3D 49*
 (off St Paul's Rd.)
Henchman St. W12 . . . . . 5B **56**
Henderson Ct. *NW3* *2F 45*
 (off Fitzjohn's Av.)
 SE14 . . . . *2F 93*
 (off Myers La.)
Henderson Dr. NW8 . . . . 3F **59**
Henderson Rd. E7 . . . . . . 3E **55**
 SW18 . . . . 5A **102**
Hendham Rd.
 SW17 . . . . 2A **116**
HENDON 1D **29**

Hendon FC. 4F **29**
Hendon Ho. NW4 . . . . . . 1F **29**
Hendon Pk. Mans.
 NW4 . . . . 1E **29**
Hendon Pk. Row
 NW11 . . . . 1B **30**
Hendon Way NW2 . . . . . . 2F **29**
 NW4 . . . . 1D **29**
Hendon Youth Sports Cen.
 . . . . 2F **29**
Hendre *SE1* *5A 78*
 (off Old Kent Rd.)
Hendre Rd. SE1 . . . . 5A **78**
Hendrick Av. SW12 . . . . . 5B **102**
Heneage La.
 EC3 . . . . 3E **19** (5A **64**)
Heneage Pl.
 EC3 . . . . 3E **19** (5A **64**)
Heneage St. E1 . . . . 4B **64**
Henfield Cl. N19 . . . . 3E **33**
Hengist Rd. SE12. . . . . . . 5D **111**
Hengrave Rd. SE23 . . . . . 4E **107**
Henley Cl. *SE16* *3E 79*
 (off St Marychurch St.)
Henley Ct. NW2 . . . . 3F **43**
Henley Dr. SE1 . . . . 5B **78**
Henley Ho. *E2.* *3F 11*
 (off Swanfield St.)
Henley Prior N1 . . . . 1F **7**
 (off Affleck St.)
Henley Rd. NW10 . . . . . . 5E **43**
Henley St. SW11 . . . . 5C **88**
Hennel Cl. SE23 . . . . 3E **121**
Hennessy Ct. E10 . . . . . . 1E **39**
Henniker Gdns. E6 . . . . . 2F **69**
Henniker M. SW3 . . . . 2F **87**
Henniker Point E15 . . . . . 2A **54**
 (off Leytonstone Rd.)
Henniker Rd. E15 . . . . 2F **53**
Henning St. SW11 . . . . . 4A **88**
Henrietta Cl. SE8 . . . . . . 2C **94**
Henrietta Ho. *N15* *1A 36*
 (off St Ann's Rd.)
 W6 . . . . *1E 85*
 (off Queen Caroline St.)
Henrietta M.
 WC1 . . . . 3E **7** (3A **62**)
Henrietta Pl.
 W1. . . . . 3D **13** (5D **61**)
Henrietta St. E15 . . . . 2E **53**
 WC2 . . . . 4E **15** (1A **76**)
Henriques St. E1 . . . . 5C **64**
Henry Cooper Way
 SE9 . . . . 3F **125**
Henry Dickens Ct.
 W11 . . . . 1F **71**
Henry Doulton Dr.
 SW17 . . . . 4C **116**
Henry Ho.
 SE1 . . . . 2B **24** (2C **76**)
 SW8 . . . . *3A 90*
 (off Wyvil Rd.)
Henry Jackson Rd.
 SW15 . . . . 1F **99**
Henry Purcell Ho.
 E16. . . . . *2D 83*
 (off Evelyn Rd.)
Henry Rd. N4 . . . . 3E **35**
Henryson Rd. SE4 . . . . . . 3C **108**

Henry Tate M.
  SW16 . . . . 5C **118**
Henry Wise Ho. SW1 . . . 5E **75**
  (off Vauxhall Bri. Rd.)
Hensford Gdns.
  SE26 . . . . 4D **121**
Henshall St. N1 . . . . 3F **49**
Henshaw St. SE17 . . . . . 5F **77**
Henslowe Rd. SE22 . . 3C **106**
Henslow Ho. SE15 . . . . 3C **92**
  (off Peckham Pk. Rd.)
Henson Av. NW2 . . . . . . 2E **43**
Henstridge Pl. NW8 . . 5A **46**
Henty Cl. SW11 . . . . . . 3A **88**
Henty Wlk. SW15 . . . . . 3D **99**
Henwick Rd. SE9 . . . . . 1F **111**
Hepburn M. SW11 . . . 3B **102**
Hepplestone Cl.
  SW15 . . . . 4D **99**
Hepscott Rd. E9 . . . . . . 3C **52**
Hepworth Ct. N1 . . . . . . 5D **49**
  (off Gaskin St.)
  NW3 . . . . 2A **46**
Hera Ct. E14 . . . . 5C **80**
  (off Homer Dr.)
Herald's Pl. SE11 . . . . 5D **77**
  (off Gilbert Rd.)
Herald St. E2 . . . . 3D **65**
Herbal Hill
  EC1 . . . . 4C **8** (3C **62**)
Herbal Hill Gdns. EC1 . . 4C **8**
  (off Herbal Hill)
Herbal Pl. EC1 . . . . 4C **8**
Herbert Cres.
  SW1 . . . . . . 5A **20** (4B **74**)
Herbert Gdns.
  NW10 . . . . 1D **57**
Herbert Ho. E1 . . . . 2F **19**
  (off Old Castle St.)
Herbert M. SW2 . . . . . . 4C **104**
Herbert Morrison Ho.
  SW6 . . . . 2B **86**
  (off Clem Attlee Ct.)
Herbert Rd. E12 . . . . . . 1F **55**
  E17 . . . . 2B **38**
  NW9 . . . . 1C **28**
Herbert St. E13 . . . . . . 1C **68**
  NW5 . . . . 3C **46**
Herbrand Est.
  WC1 . . . . 3D **7** (3A **62**)
Herbrand St.
  WC1 . . . . 3D **7** (3A **62**)
Hercules Ct. SE14 . . . . 2A **94**
Hercules Pl. N7 . . . . . . 5A **34**
  (not continuous)
Hercules Rd.
  SE1 . . . . 5A **24** (4B **76**)
Hercules St. N7 . . . . . . 5A **34**
Hercules Wharf E14 . . 1A **82**
  (off Orchard Pl.)
Hercules Yd. N7 . . . . . . 5A **34**
  (off Old Church St.)
Hereford Bldgs. SW3 . . 2F **87**
Hereford Gdns.
  SE13 . . . . 3A **110**
Hereford Ho. NW6 . . . . 1C **58**
  (off Carlton Va.)
  SW3 . . . . 4A **74**
  (off Ovington Gdns.)

Hereford Ho. SW10 . . . 3D **87**
  (off Fulham Rd.)
Hereford M. W2 . . . . . . 5C **58**
Hereford Pl. SE14 . . . . 3B **94**
Hereford Retreat
  SE15 . . . . 3C **92**
Hereford Rd. E3 . . . . . . 1B **66**
  E11 . . . . 1D **41**
  W2 . . . . 5C **58**
Hereford Sq. SW7 . . . . 5E **73**
Hereford St. E2 . . . . . . 3C **64**
Hereward Rd.
  SW17 . . . . 4B **116**
Heritage Cl. SW9 . . . . 1D **105**
Heritage Ct. SE8 . . . . . 1F **93**
  (off Trundley's Rd.)
Heritage Pl. SW18 . . . 1E **115**
Herlwyn Gdns.
  SW17 . . . . 4B **116**
Her Majesty's Theatre
  . . . . 1B **22**
  (off Haymarket)
Hermes Cl. W9 . . . . 3C **58**
Hermes Ct. SW2 . . . . 4B **104**
  SW9 . . . . 4C **90**
  (off Southey Rd.)
Hermes St.
  N1 . . . . . . 1B **8** (1C **62**)
Herm Ho. N1 . . . . 3E **49**
Hermiston Av. N8 . . . . 1A **34**
Hermitage, The
  SE13 . . . . 5E **95**
  SE23 . . . . 1E **121**
  SW13 . . . . 4B **84**
Hermitage Ct. E1 . . . . 2C **78**
  (off Knighten St.)
  NW2 . . . . 5C **30**
Hermitage Gdns.
  NW2 . . . . 5C **30**
Hermitage La. NW2 . . . 5C **30**
Hermitage Rd. N4 . . . . 2D **35**
  N15 . . . . 1F **35**
  SE19 . . . . 5F **119**
Hermitage Rooms 4A **16**
  (off Strand)
Hermitage Row E8 . . . 2C **50**
Hermitage St. W2 . . . . 4F **59**
Hermitage Vs. SW6 . . 2C **86**
  (off Lillie Rd.)
Hermitage Wall E1 . . . 2C **78**
Hermitage Waterside
  E1 . . . . 2C **78**
  (off Thomas More St.)
Hermit Pl. NW6 . . . . . . 5D **45**
Hermit Rd. E16 . . . . . . 4B **68**
Hermit St.
  EC1 . . . . . . 1D **9** (2D **63**)
Hermon Hill E11 . . . . . 1C **40**
Herndon Rd. SW18 . . 3E **101**
Herne Cl. NW10 . . . . . 2A **42**
HERNE HILL 3E **105**
Herne Hill SE24 . . . . . 4E **105**
Herne Hill Ho.
  SE24 . . . . 4D **105**
  (off Railton Rd.)
Herne Hill Rd. SE24 . . 1E **105**
Herne Hill Stadium . . . 4F **105**
Herne Pl. SE24 . . . . . . 3D **105**
Heron Cl. NW10 . . . . . 3A **42**

Heron Ct. E14 . . . . 4E **81**
  (off New Union Cl.)
Herondale Av.
  SW18 . . . . 1F **115**
Heron Dr. N4 . . . . 4E **35**
Herongate Rd. E12 . . . 4E **41**
Heron Ho. E6 . . . . 4F **55**
  NW8 . . . . 1A **60**
  (off Newcourt St.)
  SW11 . . . . 3A **88**
  (off Searles Cl.)
Heron Ind. Est. E15 . . . 1D **67**
Heron Pl. SE16 . . . . . . 2A **80**
  W1 . . . . 2C **12**
  (off Thayer St.)
Heron Quay E14 . . . . . 2C **80**
Heron Rd. SE24 . . . . . 2E **105**
Herons, The E11 . . . . . 1B **40**
Heron's Lea N6 . . . . . . 1B **32**
Herrick Ho. N16 . . . . . 1F **49**
  (off Howard Rd.)
  SE5 . . . . 3F **91**
  (off Elmington Est.)
Herrick Rd. N5 . . . . . . 5E **35**
Herrick St. SW1 . . . . . 5F **75**
Herries St. W10 . . . . . 1A **58**
Herringham Rd. SE7 . . 4E **83**
Hersant Cl. NW10 . . . . 5C **42**
Herschell M. SE5 . . . . 1E **105**
Herschell Rd. SE23 . . 5A **108**
Hersham Cl. SW15 . . . 5C **98**
Hertford Av. SW14 . . . 3A **98**
Hertford Pl.
  W1 . . . . 4A **6** (3E **61**)
Hertford Rd. N1 . . . . . . 5A **50**
  (not continuous)
Hertford St.
  W1 . . . . 2D **21** (2D **75**)
Hertslet Rd. N7 . . . . . . 5B **34**
Hertsmere Ho. E14 . . . 1C **80**
  (off Hertsmere Rd.)
Hertsmere Rd. E14 . . . 2C **80**
Hervey Rd. SE3 . . . . . . 4D **97**
Hesewall Cl. SW4 . . . . 5E **89**
Hesketh Pl. W11 . . . . . 1A **72**
Hesketh Rd. E7 . . . . . . 5C **40**
Heslop Rd. SW12 . . . 1B **116**
Hesper M. SW5 . . . . . 5D **73**
Hesperus Ct. E14 . . . . 5D **81**
Hesperus Cres. E14 . . 5D **81**
Hessel St. E1 . . . . 5D **65**
Hestercombe Av.
  SW6 . . . . 5A **86**
Hester Rd. SW11 . . . . 3A **88**
Hestia Ho. SE1 . . . . . . 4D **27**
Heston Ho. SE8 . . . . . . 4C **94**
Heston St. SE14 . . . . . 4C **94**
Hetherington Rd.
  SW4 . . . . 2A **104**
Hethpool Ho. W2 . . . . 3F **59**
  (off Hall Pl.)
Hetley Rd. W12 . . . . . . 2D **71**
Hevelius Cl. SE10 . . . . 1B **96**
Hever Ho. SE15 . . . . . 2F **93**
  (off Lovelinch Cl.)
Heversham Ho. SE15 . . 2E **93**
Hewer St. W10 . . . . . . 4F **57**
Hewett St.
  EC2 . . . . 4E **11** (3A **64**)

Hewison St. E3........1B 66
Hewitt Rd. N8.........1C 34
Hewlett Ho. SW8.....3D 89
  (off Havelock Ter.)
Hewlett Rd. E3........1A 66
Hexagon, The N6.....3B 32
Hexal Rd. SE6........3A 124
Hexham Rd. SE27....2E 119
  (off Lewis St.)
Heybridge NW1........3D 47
  (off Lewis St.)
Heybridge Av.
  SW16..............5B 118
Heybridge Way E10..2A 38
Heydon Ho. SE14.....4E 93
  (off Kender St.)
Heyford Av. SW8......3A 90
Heyford Ter. SW8......3A 90
Heygate St. SE17......5E 77
Heylyn Sq. E3.........2B 66
Heysham La. NW3.....5D 31
Heysham Rd. N15.....1F 35
Heythorp St. SW18...1B 114
Heywood Ho. SE14....2F 93
  (off Myers La.)
Heyworth Rd. E5.......1D 51
  E15................2B 54
Hibbert Ho. E14.......4C 80
  (off Tiller Rd.)
Hibbert Rd. E17.......2B 38
Hibbert St. SW11......1F 101
Hichisson Rd. SE15...3E 107
Hickes Ho. NW6.......4F 45
Hickin Cl. SE7.........5F 83
Hickin St. E14.........4E 81
Hickleton NW1.........5E 47
  (off Camden St.)
Hickling Ho. SE16.....4D 79
  (off Slippers Pl.)
Hickman Cl. E16.......4F 69
Hickmore Wlk. SW4...1F 103
Hicks Cl. SW11........1A 102
Hicks St. SE8.........1A 94
Hide Pl. SW1..........5F 75
Hider Cl. SE3.........3E 97
Hides St. N7...........3B 48
Hide Twr. SW1.........5F 75
  (off Regency St.)
Higgins Ho. N1........5A 50
  (off Colville Est.)
Higginson Ho. NW3...4B 46
  (off Fellows Rd.)
Higgs Ind. Est.
  SE24..............1D 105
Highbank Way N8.....1C 34
High Bri. SE10........1F 95
Highbridge Ct. SE14..3E 93
  (off Farrow La.)
High Bri. Wharf SE10.1F 95
  (off High Bri.)
Highbrook Rd. SE3....1F 111
HIGHBURY...........1D 49
HIGHBURY CORNER...3D 49
Highbury Cres. N5....2D 49
Highbury Est. N5......2E 49
Highbury Grange N5..1E 49
Highbury Gro. N5.....2D 49
Highbury Gro. Ct. N5..3E 49
Highbury Hill N5......5C 34
Highbury New Pk. N5..2E 49

Highbury Pk. N5.......5D 35
Highbury Pk. M. N5...1E 49
Highbury Pl. N5.......3D 49
Highbury Pool........3D 49
Highbury Quad. N5...5E 35
Highbury Rd. SW19..5A 114
Highbury Sta. Rd. N1..3C 48
Highbury Ter. N5......2D 49
Highbury Ter. M. N5..2D 49
Highclere St. SE26...4A 122
Highcliffe Dr. SW15..4B 98
  (not continuous)
Highcliffe Gdns.
  IG4: Ilf..............1F 41
Highcombe SE7.......2D 97
Highcombe Cl. SE9...1F 125
Highcroft Est. N19....2A 34
Highcroft Gdns.
  NW11..............1B 30
Highcroft Rd. N19....2A 34
Highcross Way
  SW15..............1C 112
Highdown Rd. SW15..4D 99
Highfield Av. NW11...2F 29
Highfield Cl. SE13....4F 109
Highfield Ct. NW11...1A 30
Highfield Gdns.
  NW11..............1A 30
Highfield M. NW6.....4D 45
  (off Compayne Gdns.)
Highfield Rd. NW11...1A 30
Highfields Gro. N6....3B 32
HIGHGATE...........2C 32
Highgate Av. N6.......2D 33
Highgate Cemetery
  N6.................3C 32
Highgate Cl. N6.......2C 32
Highgate Edge N2....1A 32
Highgate Hgts. N6....1E 33
Highgate High St. N6..3C 32
  N19................3D 33
Highgate Rd. SE26...3C 120
Highgate Rd. NW5....5C 32
Highgate Spinney N8..1F 33
Highgate Wlk. SE23...2E 121
Highgate W. Hill N6...3C 32
Highgate Wood School
  Sports Cen.........1E 33
High Hill Est. E5......3D 37
High Hill Ferry E5....3D 37
High Holborn
  WC1........2D 15 (5A 62)
Highland Cft.
  BR3: Beck..........5D 123
Highland Rd. SE19...5A 120
Highlands Cl. N4.....2A 34
Highlands Heath
  SW15..............5E 99
Highland Ter. SE13...1D 109
  (off Algernon Rd.)
High Level Dr. SE26..4C 120
Highlever Rd. W10....4E 57
High Meads Rd. E16..5F 69
Highmore Rd. SE3....3A 96
High Mt. NW4.........1C 28
High Pde., The
  SW16..............3A 118

High Point N6.........2C 32
High Rd. N15.........1B 36
  NW10..............3A 42
High Rd. Leyton E10..1D 39
  E15................1E 53
High Rd. Leytonstone
  E11................1A 54
  E15................1A 54
High Sheldon N6......1B 32
Highshore Rd. SE15..5B 92
  (not continuous)
Highstone Av. E11....1C 40
Highstone Ct. E11....1B 40
  (off New Wanstead)
Highstone Mans.
  NW1...............4E 47
  (off Camden Rd.)
High St. E11.........1C 40
  E13................1C 68
  E15................1E 67
  SW19..............5F 113
High St. Colliers Wood
  SW19..............5A 116
High St. Harlesden
  NW10..............1B 56
High St. M. SW19.....5A 114
High St. Nth. E12.....2F 55
High Timber St.
  EC4........4F 17 (1E 77)
High Trees SW2......1C 118
Hightrees Ho.
  SW12..............4C 102
Highview N6..........1E 33
Highway, The E1......1C 78
Highway Bus. Pk., The
  E1.................1F 79
  (off Heckford St.)
Highway Trad. Cen., The
  E1.................1F 79
  (off Heckford St.)
Highwood Rd. N19...5A 34
Highworth St. NW1...4A 60
  (off Daventry St.)
Hi-Gloss Cen. SE8...1A 94
Hilary Cl. SW6........3D 87
Hilary Rd. W12........5B 56
  (not continuous)
Hilborough Ct. E8....4B 50
Hilda Rd. E6..........4F 55
  E16................3A 68
  (not continuous)
Hilda Ter. SW9........5C 90
Hildenborough Gdns.
  BR1: Brom.........5A 124
Hildreth St. SW12....1D 117
Hildreth St. M.
  SW12..............1D 117
Hildyard Rd. SW6....2C 86
Hiley Rd. NW10.......2E 57
Hilgrove Rd. NW6....4E 45
Hillary Ct. W12........3E 71
  (off Titmuss St.)
Hillbeck Cl. SE15.....3E 93
Hillbeck Cl. SE15.....2E 93
  (off Hillbeck Cl.)
Hillboro Ct. E11......2F 39
Hillbrook Rd.
  SW17..............3B 116
Hillbury Rd. SW17...3D 117

Hill Cl. NW2 . . . . 5D 29
   NW1 . . . . 1C 30
Hillcourt Est. N16 . . . . . . 3F 35
Hillcourt Rd. SE22 . . . 4D 107
Hillcrest N6 . . . . 2C 32
   SE24 . . . . 2F 105
   W11 . . . . 1B 72
    (off St John's Gdns.)
Hillcrest Cl. SE26 . . . . . 4C 120
Hill Crest Gdns. NW2 . . . 5C 28
Hillcrest Rd.
   BR1: Brom 5C 124
Hilldrop Cres. N7 . . . . . . 2F 47
Hilldrop Est. N7 . . . . 2F 47
    (not continuous)
Hilldrop La. N7 . . . . 2F 47
Hilldrop Rd. BR1: Brom 5D 125
   N7 . . . . 2F 47
Hillersden Ho. SW1 . . . . 1D 89
    (off Ebury Bri. Rd.)
Hillersdon Av. SW13 . . . 5C 84
Hillery Cl. SE17 . . . . 5F 77
Hill Farm Rd. W10 . . . . . 4E 57
Hillfield Ct. NW3 . . . . . . 2A 46
Hillfield Ho. N5 . . . . 2E 49
Hillfield Rd. NW6 . . . . . . 2B 44
Hillgate Pl. SW12 . . . . . 5D 103
   W8 . . . . 2C 72
Hillgate St. W8 . . . . 2C 72
Hillgate Wlk. N6 . . . . 1E 33
Hill Ho. E5 . . . . 3D 37
    (off Harrington Hill)
Hill Ho. Rd. SW16 . . . . . 5B 118
Hilliard Ho. E1 . . . . 2D 79
    (off Prusom St.)
Hilliards Ct. E1 . . . . 2E 79
Hillier Ho. NW1 . . . . 4F 47
    (off Camden Sq.)
Hillier Rd. SW11 . . . . . . 4B 102
Hillingdon St. SE17 . . . . 2D 91
Hillman Dr. W10 . . . . 3E 57
Hillman St. E8 . . . . 3D 51
Hillmarton Rd. N7 . . . . . 2A 48
Hillmarton Ter. N7 . . . . . 2A 48
    (off Hillmarton Rd.)
Hillmead Dr. SW9 . . . . . 2D 105
Hillmore Cl. SE13 . . . . . . 1F 109
    (off Belmont Hill)
Hillmore Gro. SE26 . . . . 5A 122
Hill Path NW16 . . . . 5B 118
Hill Ri. SE23 . . . . 1D 121
Hillrise Mans. N19 . . . . . 2A 34
    (off Warltersville Rd.)
Hillrise Rd. N19 . . . . 2A 34
Hill Rd. NW8 . . . . 2E 59
Hillsboro' Rd. SE22 . . . . 3A 106
Hillsborough Ct.
   NW6 . . . . 5D 45
    (off Mortimer Cres.)
Hillside N8 . . . . 1F 33
   NW5 . . . . 5C 32
   NW10 . . . . 5A 42
   SE10 . . . . 3F 95
    (off Crooms Hill)
Hillside Cl. NW8 . . . . . . 1D 59
Hillside Est. N15 . . . . . . 1B 36
Hillside Gdns. N6 . . . . . 1D 33
   SW2 . . . . 2C 118
Hillside Pas. SW16 . . . . 2B 118

Hillside Rd. N15 . . . . . . 2A 36
   SW2 . . . . 2B 118
Hillsleigh Rd. W8 . . . . . 2B 72
Hills Pl. W1 . . . 3F 13 (5E 61)
Hillstowe St. E5 . . . . . . 5E 37
Hill St. W1 . . . 1C 20 (2C 74)
Hilltop Ct. NW8 . . . . . . 4E 45
    (off Alexandra Rd.)
Hilltop Ho. N6 . . . . 2F 33
Hilltop Rd. NW6 . . . . . . 4C 44
Hill Vw. NW3 . . . . 5B 46
    (off Ainger Rd.)
Hill Vw. Gdns. NW9 . . . 1A 28
Hillway N6 . . . . 4C 32
   NW9 . . . . 3A 28
Hill-Wood Ho. NW1 . . . 1A 6
    (off Polygon Rd.)
Hillworth Rd. SW2 . . . . 5C 104
Hillyard Ho. SW9 . . . . . 4C 90
Hillyard St. SW9 . . . . . 4C 90
Hillyfield Cl. E9 . . . . . . 2A 52
Hilly Flds. Cres.
   SE4 . . . . 1C 108
   SE13 . . . . 1C 108
Hilsea Point SW15 . . . . 1D 113
Hilsea St. E5 . . . . 1E 51
Hilton Ho. SE4 . . . . . . 2F 107
Hilton's Wharf SE10 . . 2D 95
    (off Norman Rd.)
Hilversum Cres.
   SE22 . . . . 3A 106
Himley Rd. SW17 . . . . . 5A 116
Hinchinbrook Ho.
   NW6 . . . . 5D 45
    (off Mortimer Cres.)
Hinckley Rd. SE15 . . . . 2C 106
Hind Cl. EC4 . . . 3C 16 (5C 62)
Hinde Ho. W1 . . . . 2C 12
    (off Hinde St.)
Hinde M. W1 . . . . 2C 12
Hinde St. W1 . . . 2C 12 (5C 60)
Hind Gro. E14 . . . . 5C 66
Hindhead Cl. N16 . . . . . 3A 36
Hindhead Point
   SW15 . . . . 1D 113
Hind Ho. N7 . . . . 1C 48
   SE14 . . . . 2F 93
    (off Myers La.)
Hindlip Ho. SW8 . . . . . . 4F 89
Hindmans Rd. SE22 . . . 3C 106
Hindmarsh Cl. E1 . . . . . 1C 78
Hindon Ct. SW1 . . . . . . 5E 75
    (off Guildhouse St.)
Hindrey Rd. E5 . . . . 2D 51
Hindsley's Pl. SE23 . . . 2E 121
Hinstock NW6 . . . . 5D 45
    (off Belsize Rd.)
Hinton Ct. E10 . . . . 4D 39
    (off Leyton Grange Est.)
Hinton Rd. SE24 . . . . . 1D 105
Hippodrome M. W11 . . 1A 72
Hippodrome Pl. W11 . . 1A 72
Hiroshima Prom.
   SE7 . . . . 4E 83
Hitcham Rd. E17 . . . . . 2B 38
Hitchin Sq. E3 . . . . 1A 66
Hithe Gro. SE16 . . . . . 4E 79
Hither Farm Rd.
   SE3 . . . . 1E 111

Hitherfield Rd.
   SW16 . . . . 2B 118
HITHER GREEN 4A 110
Hither Grn. La.
   SE13 . . . . 3E 109
Hitherwood Dr.
   SE19 . . . . 4B 120
HMP Brixton SW2 . . . . 4A 104
HMP Pentonville N7 . . 3B 48
HMP Wandsworth
   SW18 . . . . 5F 101
HMP Wormwood Scrubs
   W12 . . . . 5C 56
HMS Belfast . . 1D 27 (2A 78)
Hoadly Ho. SE1 . . . . . . 2F 25
    (off Pepper St.)
Hoadly Rd. SW16 . . . . 3F 117
Hobart Pl.
   SW1 . . . . 5D 21 (4D 75)
Hobbes Wlk. SW15 . . . 3D 99
Hobbs Ct. SE1 . . . . . . 3B 78
    (off Mill St.)
Hobbs Pl. N1 . . . . 5A 50
Hobbs Pl. Est. N1 . . . . 1A 64
    (off Hobbs Pl.)
Hobbs Rd. SE27 . . . . . 4E 119
Hobday St. E14 . . . . . . 5D 67
Hobson's Pl. E1 . . . . . . 4C 64
Hobury St. SW10 . . . . . 2E 87
Hocker St. E2 . . 2F 11 (2B 64)
Hockett Cl. SE8 . . . . . . 5A 80
Hockley Av. E6 . . . . . . 1F 69
Hockliffe Ho. W10 . . . . 4E 57
    (off Sutton Way)
Hockney Ct. SE16 . . . . 1D 93
    (off Rossetti Rd.)
Hocroft Av. NW2 . . . . . 5B 30
Hocroft Ct. NW2 . . . . . 5B 30
Hocroft Rd. NW2 . . . . . 5B 30
Hocroft Wlk. NW2 . . . . 5B 30
Hodes Row NW3 . . . . . 1C 46
Hodford Rd. NW11 . . . . 3B 30
Hodister Cl. SE5 . . . . . 3E 91
Hodnet Gro. SE16 . . . . 5F 79
Hoe St. E17 . . . . 1C 38
Hoever Ho. SE6 . . . . . . 4E 123
Hofland Rd. W14 . . . . . 4A 72
Hogan M. W2 . . . . 4E 59
Hogan Way E5 . . . . . . 4C 36
Hogarth Bus. Pk. W4 . . 2A 84
Hogarth Cl. E16 . . . . . . 4F 69
Hogarth Ct. E1 . . . . . . 5C 64
    (off Batty St.)
   EC3 . . . . 4E 19 (5A 64)
   NW1 . . . . 4E 47
    (off St Pancras Way)
   SE19 . . . . 4B 120
Hogarth Ho. SW1 . . . . 5F 75
    (off Erasmus St.)
Hogarth Ind. Est.
   NW10 . . . . 3C 56
Hogarth La. W4 . . . . . . 2A 84
Hogarth Pl. SW5 . . . . . 5D 73
    (off Hogarth Rd.)
Hogarth Rd. SW5 . . . . 5D 73
HOGARTH RDBT. 2A 84
Hogarth's House 2A 84
    (off Hogarth La.)

Hogarth Ter. W4 . . . . . . 2A 84
Hogshead Pas. E1 . . . . 1D 79
    (off Reunion Row)
Holbeach M. SW12 . . . 1D 117
Holbeach Rd. SE6 . . . . 5C 108
Holbeck Row SE15 . . . . 3C 92
Holbein Ho. SW1 . . . . . . 1C 88
    (off Holbein M.)
Holbein M. SW1 . . . . . . 1C 88
Holbein Pl. SW1 . . . . . . 5C 74
Holberton Gdns.
  NW10 . . . . 2D 57
HOLBORN 1F 15 (4C 62)
Holborn EC1 . . 1B 16 (4C 62)
  WC1 . . . . 4B 62
Holborn Cir.
  EC1 . . . . . . 1C 16 (4C 62)
Holborn Pl. WC1 . . . . . . 1F 15
Holborn Rd. E13 . . . . . . 3D 69
Holborn Viaduct
  EC1 . . . . . . 1C 16 (4C 62)
Holbrook Cl. NW19 . . . . 3D 33
Holbrooke Ct. N7 . . . . . 5A 34
Holbrook Rd. E15 . . . . . 1B 68
Holburne Cl. SE3 . . . . . 4E 97
Holburne Gdns. SE3 . . . 4F 97
Holburne Rd. SE3 . . . . . 4E 97
Holcombe Ho. SW9 . . . 1A 104
    (off Landor Rd.)
Holcombe Pl. SE4 . . . . 1A 108
    (off St Asaph Rd.)
Holcombe St. W6 . . . . . 5D 71
Holcroft Ct. W1 . . . . 5F 5
Holcroft Rd. SW11 . . . 1F 101
Holcroft Rd. E9 . . . . . . 4E 51
Holdenby Rd. SE4 . . . 3A 108
Holden Ho. N1 . . . . 5E 49
    (off Prebend St.)
  SE8 . . . . 3C 94
Holden St. SW11 . . . . . 5C 88
Holdernesse Rd.
  SW17 . . . . 3B 116
Holderness Ho. SE5 . . . 1A 106
Holderness Way
  SE27 . . . . 5D 119
Holford Ho. SE16 . . . . . 5D 79
    (off Camilla Rd.)
  WC1 . . . . 1A 8
    (off Gt. Percy St.)
Holford M. WC1 . . . . 1B 8
Holford Pl.
  WC1 . . . . 1A 8 (2B 62)
Holford Rd. NW3 . . . . . 5E 31
Holford St.
  WC1 . . . . 1B 8 (2B 62)
    (off Cruikshank St.)
Holford Yd. WC1 . . . . . . 1B 8
Holgate Av. SW11 . . . . 1F 101
Holgate St. SE7 . . . . . . 4F 83
Holland Dr. SE23 . . . . . 3A 122
Holland Gdns.
  W14 . . . . 4A 72
Holland Gro. SW9 . . . . . 3C 90
Holland Ho. NW10 . . . . . 1D 57
    (off Holland Rd.)
HOLLAND PARK 2B 72
Holland Pk. 3B 72
Holland Pk. W11 . . . . . . 2A 72
Holland Pk. Av. W11 . . . 3A 72

Holland Pk. Ct. W14 . . . 3A 72
    (off Holland Pk. Gdns.)
Holland Pk. Gdns.
  W14 . . . . 3A 72
Holland Pk. Mans.
  W14 . . . . 2A 72
    (off Holland Pk. Av.)
Holland Pk. M. W11 . . . 2A 72
Holland Pk. Rd. W14 . . 4B 72
HOLLAND PARK
  ROUNDABOUT 3F 71
Holland Pk. Ter. W11 . . 2A 72
    (off Portland Rd.)
Holland Pk. Theatre
  (Open Air) 3B 72
    (in Holland Pk.)
Holland Pas. N1 . . . . . . 5E 49
    (off Basire St.)
Holland Pl. W8 . . . . 3D 73
    (off Kensington Chu. St.)
Holland Pl. Chambers
  W8 . . . . 3D 73
    (off Holland Pl.)
Holland Ri. Ho. SW9 . . 3B 90
    (off Clapham Rd.)
Holland Rd. E15 . . . . . . 2A 68
  NW10 . . . . 5C 42
  W14 . . . . 3F 71
Holland St.
  SE1 . . . . . . 1E 25 (2D 77)
  W8 . . . . 3D 73
Holland Vs. Rd. W14 . . 3A 72
Holland Wlk. N19 . . . . . 3F 33
  W8 . . . . 2B 72
Hollar Rd. N16 . . . . 5B 36
Hollen St. W1 . . 2B 14 (5F 61)
Holles Ho. SW9 . . . . . . 5C 90
Holles St.
  W1 . . . . 2E 13 (5D 61)
Holley Rd. W3 . . . . 3A 70
Holliday Sq. SW11 . . . 1F 101
    (off Fowler Cl.)
Hollies, The E11 . . . . . . 1C 40
    (off New Wanstead)
Hollies Way SW12 . . . 5C 102
Hollingbourne Rd.
  SE24 . . . . 3E 105
Hollins Ho. N7 . . . . 1A 48
Hollisfield WC1 . . . . 2E 7
    (off Cromer St.)
HOLLOWAY 5A 34
Holloway Ho. NW2 . . . . 5E 29
    (off Stoll Cl.)
Holloway Rd. E11 . . . . . 5F 39
  N7 . . . . 1B 48
  N19 . . . . 4F 33
Hollyberry La. NW3 . . . 1E 45
Hollybush Cl. E11 . . . . . 1C 40
Hollybush Gdns. E2 . . . 2D 65
Hollybush Hill E11 . . . . 1B 40
  NW3 . . . . 1E 45
Hollybush Ho. E2 . . . . . 2D 65
Hollybush Pl. E2 . . . . . . 2D 65
Hollybush Steps NW3 . . 1E 45
    (off Holly M.)
Hollybush St. E13 . . . . . 2D 69
Holly Bush Va. NW3 . . . 1E 45
Hollybush Wlk.
  SW9 . . . . 2D 105

Holly Cl. NW10 . . . . . . 4A 42
Hollycroft Av. NW3 . . . . 5C 30
Hollydale Rd. SE15 . . . . 4E 93
Hollydene SE13 . . . . . . 4F 109
  SE15 . . . . 4D 93
Hollydown Way E11 . . . 5F 39
Holly Gro. SE15 . . . . . . 5B 92
Holly Hedge Ter.
  SE13 . . . . 3F 109
Holly Hill NW3 . . . . 1E 45
Holly Ho. W10 . . . . 3A 58
    (off Hawthorn Wlk.)
Holly Lodge Gdns.
  N6 . . . . 4C 32
Holly Lodge Mans.
  N6 . . . . 4C 32
Holly M. SW10 . . . . 1E 87
Holly Mt. NW3 . . . . 1E 45
Hollymount Cl. SE10 . . . 4E 95
Holly Pk. N4 . . . . 2A 34
    (not continuous)
Holly Pk. Est. N4 . . . . . 2B 34
Holly Pl. NW3 . . . . 1E 45
    (off Holly Berry La.)
Holly Rd. E11 . . . . 2B 40
  W4 . . . . 5A 70
Holly St. E8 . . . . 4B 50
Holly Tree Cl. SW19 . . . 1F 113
Holly Tree Ho. SE4 . . . 1B 108
    (off Brockley Rd.)
Holly Vw. Cl. NW4 . . . . 1C 28
Holly Village N6 . . . . . . 4D 33
Holly Vs. W6 . . . . 4D 71
    (off Wellesley Av.)
Holly Wlk. NW3 . . . . . . 1E 45
Hollywood Bowl
  Surrey Quays 4F 79
Hollywood Ct. SW10 . . . 2E 87
    (off Hollywood Ct.)
Hollywood M. SW10 . . . 2E 87
Hollywood Rd. SW10 . . . 2E 87
Holman Ho. E2 . . . . 2F 65
    (off Roman Rd.)
Holman Hunt Ho. W6 . . 1A 86
    (off Field Rd.)
Holman Rd. SW11 . . . . 5F 87
Holmbrook NW1 . . . . . . 1E 61
    (off Eversholt St.)
Holmbury Ct. SW17 . . . 3B 116
Holmbury Ho. SE24 . . . 3D 105
Holmbury Vw. E5 . . . . . 3D 37
Holmbush Rd.
  SW15 . . . . 4A 100
Holmcote Gdns. N5 . . . 2E 49
Holm Ct. SE12 . . . . . . 3D 125
Holmdale Gdns. NW4 . . 1F 29
Holmdale Rd. NW6 . . . . 2C 44
Holmdale Ter. N15 . . . . 2A 36
Holmdene Av. SE24 . . . 3E 105
Holmead Rd. SW6 . . . . 3D 87
Holmefield Ho. W10 . . . 3A 58
    (off Hazlewood Cres.)
Holme Lacey Rd.
  SE12 . . . . 4B 110
Holmesdale Ho.
  NW6 . . . . 5C 44
    (off Kilburn Va.)
Holmesdale Rd. N6 . . . 2D 33

Holmesley Rd.
  SE23 . . . . 4A **108**
Holmes Pl. SW10 . . . . . 2E **87**
Holmes Place Health Club
  Barbican 5F **9**
    (off Aldersgate St.)
  Hammersmith. 5F **71**
    (off Hammersmith Rd.)
  Merton. 5E **115**
  St Luke's 4B **10**
Holmes Rd. NW5 . . . . . 2D **47**
Holmes Ter. SE1 . . . . . 3B **24**
Holmewood Gdns.
  SW2 . . . . 5B **104**
Holmewood Rd.
  SW2 . . . . 5A **104**
Holmfield Cl. NW3 . . . 2A **46**
Holmhurst SE13 . . . . . 4F **109**
Holmleigh Rd. N16 . . . 3A **36**
Holmleigh Rd. Est.
  N16 . . . . 3A **36**
Holmoak Cl. SW15 . . . 4B **100**
Holm Oak M. SW4 . . . 3A **104**
Holmsdale Ho. E14 . . . 1D **81**
    (off Poplar High St.)
Holmshaw Cl. SE26 . . 4A **122**
Holmside Rd. SW12 . . 4C **102**
Holmsley Ho. SW15 . . 5B **98**
    (off Tangley Gro.)
Holm Wlk. SE3 . . . . . . 5C **96**
Holmwood Vs. SE7 . . . 1C **96**
Holne Chase N2 . . . . . 1E **31**
Holness Rd. E15 . . . . . 3B **54**
Holocaust Memorial Garden
  . . . . 3A **20**
Holroyd Rd. SW15 . . . . 2E **99**
Holst Ct. SE1 . . . . 5B **24**
    (off Westminster Bri. Rd.)
Holst Mans. SW13 . . . 2E **85**
Holsworthy Sq. WC1 . . 4A **8**
Holt Ct. E15 . . . . 2E **53**
Holt Ho. SW2 . . . . 4C **104**
Holton St. E1 . . . . 3F **65**
Holwood Pl. SW4 . . . . 2F **103**
Holybourne Av.
  SW15 . . . . 5C **98**
Holyhead Cl. E3 . . . . . . 2C **66**
Holyoake Ct. SE16 . . . 3B **80**
Holyoak Rd. SE11 . . . . 5D **77**
Holyport Rd. SW6 . . . . 3F **85**
Holyrood M. E16 . . . . . 2C **82**
    (off Badminton M.)
Holyrood St.
  SE1 . . . . 2D **27** (2A **78**)
Holywell Cen. 3D **11**
    (off Phipp St.)
Holywell Cl. SE3 . . . . . 2C **96**
  SE16 . . . . 1D **93**
Holywell La.
  EC2 . . . . 3E **11** (3A **64**)
Holywell Row
  EC2 . . . . 4D **11** (3A **64**)
Homecroft Rd. SE26 . . 5E **121**
Homefield Ho. SE23 . . 3F **121**
Homefield Rd.
  SW19 . . . . 5F **113**
  W4 . . . . 1B **84**
Homefield St.
  N1 . . . . 1D **11** (1A **64**)

Homeleigh Ct.
  SW16 . . . . 3A **118**
Homeleigh Rd.
  SE15 . . . . 3F **107**
Home Pk. Rd.
  SW19 . . . . 4B **114**
Homer Dr. E14 . . . . 5C **80**
Home Rd. SW11 . . . . . 5A **88**
Homer Rd. E9 . . . . 3A **52**
Homer Row W1 . . . . . . 4A **60**
Homer St. W1 . . . . 4A **60**
HOMERTON 2F **51**
Homerton Gro. E9 . . . . 2F **51**
Homerton High St.
  E9 . . . . 2F **51**
Homerton Rd. E9 . . . . . 2A **52**
Homerton Row E9 . . . . 2E **51**
Homerton Ter. E9 . . . . . 3E **51**
    (not continuous)
Homesdale Cl. E11 . . . 1C **40**
Homestall Rd. SE22 . . 3E **107**
Homestead Pk. NW2 . . 5B **28**
Homestead Rd. SW6 . . 3B **86**
Homewalk Ho.
  SE26 . . . . 4D **121**
Homewoods SW12 . . . 5E **103**
Homildon Ho. SE26 . . 3C **120**
Honduras St.
  EC1 . . . . 3F **9** (3E **63**)
Honeybourne Rd.
  NW6 . . . . 2D **45**
Honeybrook Rd.
  SW12 . . . . 5E **103**
Honey La. EC2 . . . . 3A **18**
Honey La. Ho. SW10 . . 2D **87**
    (off Finborough Rd.)
Honeyman Cl. NW6 . . . 4F **43**
Honeywell Rd.
  SW11 . . . . 4B **102**
Honeywood Rd.
  NW10 . . . . 1B **56**
Honiton Gdns. SE15 . . 5E **93**
    (off Gibbon Rd.)
Honiton Rd. NW6 . . . . 1B **58**
Honley Rd. SE6 . . . . . . 5D **109**
HONOR OAK 4E **107**
Honor Oak Crematorium
  SE23 . . . . 3F **107**
HONOR OAK PARK . . . 5A **108**
Honor Oak Pk. SE23 . . 4E **107**
Honor Oak Ri. SE23 . . 4E **107**
Honor Oak Rd.
  SE23 . . . . 1E **121**
Hood Ct. EC4 . . . . 3C **16**
Hood Ho. SE5 . . . . 3F **91**
    (off Elmington Est.)
  SW1 . . . . 1F **89**
    (off Dolphin Sq.)
Hooke Ho. E3 . . . . 1A **66**
    (off Gernon Rd.)
Hookham Ct. SW8 . . . 4F **89**
Hooks Cl. SE15 . . . . . . 4D **93**
Hooper Rd. E16 . . . . . . 5C **68**
Hooper's Ct. SW3 . . . . 3B **74**
Hooper Sq. E1 . . . . 5C **64**
    (off Hooper St.)
Hooper St. E1 . . . . 5C **64**
Hoop La. NW11 . . . . . . 2B **30**
    (not continuous)

Hope Cl. N1 . . . . 3E **49**
  SE12 . . . . 3D **125**
Hope Ct. NW10 . . . . . . 2F **57**
    (off Chamberlayne Rd.)
Hopedale Rd. SE7 . . . . 2D **97**
Hopefield Av. NW6 . . . 1A **58**
Hope Sq. EC2 . . . . 1D **19**
Hope St. SW11 . . . . . . 1F **101**
Hopetown St. E1 . . . . . 4B **64**
Hopewell St. SE5 . . . . 3F **91**
Hopewell Yd. SE5 . . . . 3F **91**
    (off Hopewell St.)
Hope Wharf SE16 . . . . 3E **79**
Hop Gdns.
  WC2 . . . . 5D **15** (1A **76**)
Hopgood St. W12 . . . . 2E **71**
Hopkins Ho. E14 . . . . . 5C **66**
    (off Canton St.)
Hopkins M. E15 . . . . . . 5B **54**
Hopkinsons Pl. NW1 . . 5C **46**
Hopkins Rd. E10 . . . . . 2D **39**
Hopkins St.
  W1 . . . . 3A **14** (5E **61**)
Hopping La. N1 . . . . . . 3D **49**
Hop St. SE10 . . . . 5B **82**
    (off School Bank Rd.)
Hopton Rd. SW16 . . . . 5A **118**
Hopton's Gdns. SE1 . . 1E **25**
Hopton St.
  SE1 . . . . 5D **17** (1D **77**)
Hopwood Cl. SW17 . . . 3E **115**
Hopwood Rd. SE17 . . . 2F **91**
Hopwood Wlk. E8 . . . . 4C **50**
Horace Rd. E7 . . . . 1D **55**
Horatio Ct. SE16 . . . . . 2E **79**
    (off Rotherhithe St.)
Horatio Ho. E2 . . . . 1B **64**
    (off Horatio St.)
  W6 . . . . 1F **85**
    (off Fulham Pal. Rd.)
Horatio Pl. E14 . . . . . . 2E **81**
    (off Preston's Rd.)
Horatio St. E2 . . . . 1B **64**
Horbury Cres. W11 . . . 1C **72**
Horbury M. W11 . . . . . 1B **72**
Horder Rd. SW6 . . . . . 4A **86**
Hordle Prom. E.
  SE15 . . . . 3B **92**
Hordle Prom. Sth.
  SE15 . . . . 3B **92**
    (off Quarley Way)
Horizon Bldg. E14 . . . . 1C **80**
    (off Hertsmere Rd.)
Horizon Way SE7 . . . . 5D **83**
Horle Wlk. SE5 . . . . . . 5D **91**
Horley Rd. SE9 . . . . . . 4F **125**
Hormead Rd. W9 . . . . . 3B **58**
Hornbeam Cl. SE11 . . 5C **76**
Hornbeam Sq. E3 . . . . 5B **52**
Hornblower Cl. SE16 . . 4A **80**
Hornby Cl. NW3 . . . . . 4F **45**
Hornby Ho. SE11 . . . . . 2C **90**
    (off Clayton St.)
Horncastle Cl. SE12 . . 5C **110**
Horncastle Rd.
  SE12 . . . . 5C **110**
Horndean Cl. SW15 . . 1C **112**
Horner Ho. N1 . . . . 5A **50**
    (off Whitmore Est.)

Horne Way SW15 . . . . . . 5E **85**
Hornfair Rd. SE7 . . . . . . 2E **97**
Horniman Dr. SE23 . . 1D **121**
Horniman Mus. 1D **121**
Horn La. SE10 . . . . 1C **96**
   (not continuous)
Horn Link Way SE10 . . . . 5C **82**
HORN PARK 3D **111**
Horn Pk. Cl. SE12 . . . 3D **111**
Hornpark La. SE12 . . 3D **111**
Hornsey La. N6 . . . . 3D **33**
Hornsey La. Est. N19 . . 2F **33**
Hornsey La. Gdns.
  N6 . . . . 2E **33**
Hornsey Ri. N19 . . . . . . 2F **33**
Hornsey Ri. Gdns.
  N19 . . . . 2F **33**
Hornsey Rd. N7 . . . . . . 3A **34**
  N19 . . . . 3A **34**
Hornsey St. N7 . . . . . . 2B **48**
HORNSEY VALE 1B **34**
Hornshay St. SE15 . . 2E **93**
Hornton Ct. W8 . . . . . . 3C **72**
   (off Kensington High St.)
Hornton Pl. W8 . . . . . . 3D **73**
Hornton St. W8 . . . . . . 3C **72**
Horsa Rd. SE12 . . . . . 5E **111**
Horse & Dolphin Yd.
  W1 . . . . 4C **14**
Horseferry Pl. SE10 . . 2E **95**
Horseferry Rd. E14 . . 1A **80**
  SW1 . . . . 4F **75**
Horseferry Rd. Est.
  SW1 . . . . 5B **22**
Horseguards Av.
  SW1 . . . . . . 2D **23** (2A **76**)
Horse Guards Parade
  . . . . 2D **23** (2A **76**)
Horse Guards Rd.
  SW1 . . . . . . 2C **22** (2F **75**)
Horsell Rd. N5 . . . . . . 2C **48**
   (not continuous)
Horselydown La.
  SE1 . . . . 3F **27** (3B **78**)
Horselydown Mans.
  SE1 . . . . 3F **27**
   (off Lafone St.)
Horsemongers M.
  SE1 . . . . 4A **26**
Horse Ride
  SW1 . . . . . . 2B **22** (2E **75**)
Horseshoe Cl. E14 . . . 1E **95**
  NW2 . . . . 4D **29**
Horseshoe Ct. EC1 . . . . 3E **9**
   (off Brewhouse Yd.)
Horseshoe M. SW2 . . 2A **104**
Horseshoe Wharf
  SE1 . . . . 1B **26**
   (off Clink St.)
Horse Yd. N1 . . . . 5D **49**
   (off Essex Rd.)
Horsfeld Gdns.
  SE9 . . . . 3F **111**
Horsfeld Rd. SE9 . . . . 3F **111**
Horsfield Ho. N1 . . . . . . 4E **49**
   (off Northampton St.)
Horsford Rd. SW2 . . 3B **104**
Horsley St. SE17 . . . . . 2F **91**

Horsman Ho. SE5 . . . . . 2E **91**
   (off Bethwin Rd.)
Horsman St. SE5 . . . . . 2E **91**
Horsmonden Rd.
  SE4 . . . . 3B **108**
Hortensia Ho. SW10 . . 3E **87**
   (off Gunter Gro.)
Hortensia Rd. SW10 . . 3E **87**
Horton Av. NW2 . . . . . . 1A **44**
Horton Ho. SE15 . . . . . 2E **93**
  SW8 . . . . 3B **90**
  W6 . . . . 1A **86**
   (off Field Rd.)
Horton Rd. E8 . . . . 3D **51**
Horton St. SE13 . . . . . 1D **109**
Horwood Ho. E2 . . . . . . 2D **65**
   (off Pott St.)
  NW8 . . . . 3A **60**
   (off Paveley St.)
Hosack Rd. SW17 . . . 2C **116**
Hoser Av. SE12 . . . . . 2C **124**
Hosier La.
  EC1 . . . . . . 1D **17** (4D **63**)
Hoskins Cl. E16 . . . . . . 5E **69**
Hoskins St. SE10 . . . . . 1F **95**
Hospital Rd. E9 . . . . . . 2F **51**
Hospital Way SE13 . . . 5F **109**
Hotham Rd. SW15 . . . . 1E **99**
Hotham St. E15 . . . . . . 5A **54**
Hothfield Pl. SE16 . . . . 4E **79**
Hotspur St. SE11 . . . . . 5C **76**
Houghton Cl. E8 . . . . . . 3B **50**
Houghton St.
  WC2 . . . . . . 3A **16** (5B **62**)
   (not continuous)
Houndsditch
  EC3 . . . . 2E **19** (5A **64**)
Houseman Way SE5 . . . 3F **91**
Houses of Parliament
  . . . . 5E **23** (4A **76**)
Houston Rd. SE23 . . . 2A **122**
Hove Av. E17 . . . . 1B **38**
Hoveden Rd. NW2 . . . . 2A **44**
Hove St. SE15 . . . . 3E **93**
   (off Culmore Rd.)
Howard Bldg. SW8 . . 2D **89**
Howard Cl. NW2 . . . . . 1A **44**
Howard Ho. E16 . . . . . . 2D **83**
   (off Wesley Av.)
  SE8 . . . . 2B **94**
   (off Evelyn St.)
  SW1 . . . . 1E **89**
   (off Dolphin Sq.)
  SW9 . . . . 1D **105**
   (off Barrington Rd.)
  W1 . . . . 4E **5**
   (off Cleveland St.)
Howard M. N5 . . . . 1D **49**
Howard Rd. E11 . . . . . . 5A **40**
  N15 . . . . 1A **36**
  N16 . . . . 1F **49**
  NW2 . . . . 1F **43**
Howard's La. SW15 . . 2D **99**
Howards Rd. E13 . . . . . 2C **68**
Howarth Ct. E15 . . . . . 2D **53**
   (off Clays La.)
Howbury Rd. SE15 . . 1E **107**
Howden St. SE15 . . . . 1C **106**
Howell Ct. E10 . . . . 2D **39**

Howell Wlk. SE1 . . . . . 5D **77**
Howick Pl.
  SW1 . . . . . . 5A **22** (4E **75**)
Howie St. SW11 . . . . . 3A **88**
Howitt Cl. N16 . . . . 1A **50**
  NW3 . . . . 3A **46**
Howitt Rd. NW3 . . . . . . 3A **46**
Howland Est. SE16 . . . 4E **79**
Howland Ho. SW16 . . 3A **118**
Howland M. E.
  W1 . . . . 5A **6** (4E **61**)
Howland St.
  W1 . . . . 5F **5** (4E **61**)
Howland Way SE16 . . . 3A **80**
Howletts Rd. SE24 . . 4E **105**
Howley Pl. W2 . . . . 4E **59**
Howsman Rd. SW13 . . 2C **84**
Howson Rd. SE4 . . . . 2A **108**
How's St. E2 . . . . 1B **64**
HOXTON 1A **64**
Hoxton Hall Theatre . . 1A **64**
   (off Hoxton Rd.)
Hoxton Mkt. N1 . . . . . . 2D **11**
Hoxton Sq.
  N1 . . . . 2D **11** (2A **64**)
Hoxton St.
  N1 . . . . 2E **11** (5A **50**)
Hoylake Rd. W3 . . . . . . 5A **56**
Hoyland Cl. SE15 . . . . . 3D **93**
Hoyle Rd. SW17 . . . . . 5A **116**
Hoy St. E16 . . . . 5B **68**
Hubbard Rd. SE27 . . 4E **119**
Hubbard St. E15 . . . . . 5A **54**
Huberd Ho. SE1 . . . . . . 5C **26**
   (off Manciple St.)
Hubert Gro. SW9 . . . . 1A **104**
Hubert Ho. NW8 . . . . . . 3A **60**
   (off Ashbridge St.)
Hubert Rd. E6 . . . . 2F **69**
Hucknall Cl. NW8 . . . . . 3F **59**
   (off Cunningham Pl.)
Huddart St. E3 . . . . 4B **66**
   (not continuous)
Huddleston Cl. E2 . . . . 1E **65**
Huddlestone Rd. E7 . . . 1B **54**
  NW2 . . . . 3D **43**
Huddleston Rd. N7 . . . 5E **33**
Hudson Bldg. E1 . . . . . 4C **64**
   (off Chicksand St.)
Hudson Cl. E15 . . . . . . 5C **54**
  W12 . . . . 1D **71**
Hudson Ct. E14 . . . . . . 1C **94**
   (off Maritime Quay)
Hudson Ho. SW10 . . . . 3E **87**
   (off Hortensia Rd.)
  W11 . . . . 5A **58**
   (off Ladbroke Gro.)
Hudson's Pl. SW1 . . . . 5D **75**
Huggin Ct. EC4 . . . . . . 4A **18**
Huggin Hill
  EC4 . . . . . . 4F **17** (1E **77**)
Huggins Pl. SW2 . . . . 1B **118**
Hughan Rd. E15 . . . . . 2F **53**
Hugh Astor Ct. SE1 . . . 5E **25**
   (off Keyworth St.)
Hugh Cubitt Ho. N1 . . . 1B **62**
   (off Collier St.)

Hugh Dalton Av.
SW6 . . . . 2B 86
Hughenden Ho. NW8 . . . . 3A 60
(off Jerome Cres.)
Hughendon Ter. E15 . . . 1E 53
Hughes Ct. N7 . . . . 2F 47
Hughes Ho. E2 . . . . 2E 65
(off Sceptre Ho.)
SE8 . . . . 2C 94
(off Benbow St.)
SE17 . . . . 5D 77
(off Peacock St.)
Hughes Mans. E1 . . . . . 3C 64
Hughes M. SW11 . . . . . 3B 102
Hughes Ter. E16 . . . . . . 4B 68
(off Clarkson Rd.)
SW9 . . . . 1D 105
(off Styles Gdns.)
Hugh Gaitskell Cl.
SW6 . . . . 2B 86
Hugh Gaitskell Ho.
N16 . . . . 4B 36
Hugh M. SW1 . . . . 5D 75
Hugh Platt Ho. E2 . . . . . 1D 65
(off Patriot Sq.)
Hugh St. SW1 . . . . 5D 75
Hugo Ho. SW1 . . . . 5A 20
(off Sloane St.)
Hugon Rd. SW6 . . . . . . 1D 101
Hugo Rd. N19 . . . . 1E 47
Huguenot Pl. E1 . . . . . . 4B 64
SW18 . . . . 3E 101
Huguenot Sq. SE15 . . . 1D 107
Hullbridge M. N1 . . . . . 5F 49
Hull Cl. SE16 . . . . 3F 79
Hull St. EC1 . . . . 2F 9 (2E 63)
Hulme Pl.
SE1 . . . . 4A 26 (3E 77)
Humber Dr. W10 . . . . . . 3F 57
Humber Rd. NW2 . . . . . 4D 29
SE3 . . . . 2B 96
Humberstone Rd.
E13 . . . . 2E 69
Humberton Cl. E9 . . . . . 2A 52
Humber Trad. Est.
NW2 . . . . 4D 29
Humbolt Rd. W6 . . . . . . 2A 86
Hume Ct. N1 . . . . 4D 49
(off Hawes St.)
Hume Ho. W11 . . . . 2F 71
(off Queensdale Cres.)
Hume Ter. E16 . . . . 4D 69
Humphrey St. SE1 . . . . 1B 92
Hungerford Ho. SW1 . . . 2E 89
(off Churchill Gdns.)
Hungerford La. WC2 . . . 1E 23
(not continuous)
Hungerford Rd. N7 . . . . 3F 47
Hungerford St. E1 . . . . . 5D 65
Hunsdon Rd. SE14 . . . . 3F 93
Hunslett St. E2 . . . . . . 2E 65
Hunstanton Ho.
NW1 . . . . 4A 60
(off Cosway St.)
Hunt Cl. W11 . . . . 2F 71
Hunter Cl.
SE1 . . . . 5C 26 (4F 77)
Hunter Ho. SE1 . . . . . . 4E 25
(off Lancaster St.)

Hunter Ho. SW5 . . . . . . 1C 86
(off Old Brompton Rd.)
SW8 . . . . 3F 89
(off Fount St.)
WC1 . . . . 3E 7
(off Hunter St.)
Hunterian Mus., The . . . 2A 16
(off Portugal St.)
Hunter Lodge W9 . . . . . 4C 58
(off Admiral Wlk.)
Hunters Cl. SW12 . . . . 1C 116
Hunters Mdw. SE19 . . . 4A 120
Hunter St.
WC1 . . . . 3E 7 (3A 62)
Hunter Wlk. E13 . . . . . . 1C 68
Huntingdon St. E16 . . . 5B 68
N1 . . . . 4B 48
Huntingfield Rd.
SW15 . . . . 2C 98
Huntley St.
WC1 . . . . 4A 6 (3E 61)
Hunton St. E1 . . . . 4C 64
Hunt's Cl. SE3 . . . . 5C 96
Hunt's Ct.
WC2 . . . . 5C 14 (1F 75)
Hunts La. E15 . . . . 1E 67
Huntsman St. SE17 . . . . 5A 78
Huntspill St. SW17 . . . . 3E 115
Hunts Slip Rd.
SE21 . . . . 3A 120
Huntsworth M.
NW1 . . . . 3A 4 (3B 60)
Hurdwick Pl. NW1 . . . . . 1E 61
(off Hampstead Rd.)
Hurleston Ho. SE8 . . . . 1B 94
Hurley Cres. SE16 . . . . 3F 79
Hurley Ho. SE11 . . . . . . 5D 77
HURLINGHAM 1D 101
Hurlingham Bus. Pk.
SW6 . . . . 1C 100
Hurlingham Club, The
. . . . 1C 100
Hurlingham Ct.
SW6 . . . . 1B 100
Hurlingham Gdns.
SW6 . . . . 1B 100
Hurlingham Retail Pk.
SW6 . . . . 1D 101
Hurlingham Rd. SW6 . . . 5B 86
Hurlingham Sq.
SW6 . . . . 1C 100
Hurlingham Stadium
. . . . 1B 100
Hurlock St. N5 . . . . 5D 35
Huron Rd. SW17 . . . . . 2C 116
Huron University 4F 73
Hurren Cl. SE3 . . . . . . 1A 110
Hurry Cl. E15 . . . . 4A 54
Hurst Av. N6 . . . . 1E 33
Hurstbourne Ho.
SW15 . . . . 4B 98
(off Tangley Gro.)
Hurstbourne Rd.
SE23 . . . . 1A 122
Hurst Cl. NW11 . . . . . . 1D 31
Hurst Cl. E6 . . . . 4F 69
(off Tollgate Rd.)
Hurstdene Gdns.
N15 . . . . 2A 36

Hurst Ho. WC1 . . . . 1A 8
(off Penton Ri.)
Hurst St. SE24 . . . . 4D 105
Hurstway Rd. W11 . . . . . 1F 71
Hurstway Wlk. W11 . . . . 1F 71
Husborne Ho. SE8 . . . . 5A 80
(off Chilton Gro.)
Huson Cl. NW3 . . . . . . 4A 46
Hutchings St. E14 . . . . 3C 80
Hutchings Wharf E14 . . 3C 80
(off Hutchings St.)
Hutchins Cl. E15 . . . . . 4E 53
Hutchinson Ho. NW3 . . . 4B 46
SE14 . . . . 3E 93
Hutton Cl. N4 . . . . 3B 34
(off Victoria Rd.)
Hutton St.
EC4 . . . . 4C 16 (5D 63)
Huxbear St. SE4 . . . . . 3B 108
Huxley Ho. NW8 . . . . . . 3F 59
(off Fisherton St.)
Huxley Rd. E10 . . . . . . 4E 39
Huxley St. W10 . . . . . . 2A 58
Hyacinth Rd. SW15 . . . 1C 112
HYDE, THE 1B 28
Hyde, The NW9 . . . . . . 1B 28
Hyde Cl. E13 . . . . 1C 68
Hyde Cres. NW9 . . . . . 1A 28
Hyde Est. Rd. NW9 . . . . 1B 28
Hyde Farm M.
SW12 . . . . 1F 117
Hyde Ind. Est., The
NW9 . . . . 1B 28
Hyde La. SW11 . . . . . . 4A 88
Hyde Pk. 1A 20 (2A 74)
Hyde Pk. Barracks 3A 74
(off Knightsbridge)
HYDE PARK CORNER
. . . . 3D 75
Hyde Pk. Cnr.
W1 . . . . 3C 20 (3C 74)
Hyde Pk. Cres. W2 . . . . 5A 60
Hyde Pk. Gdns. W2 . . . 1F 73
Hyde Pk. Gdns. M.
W2 . . . . 1F 73
(not continuous)
Hyde Pk. Ga. SW7 . . . . 3E 73
(not continuous)
Hyde Pk. Ga. M.
SW7 . . . . 3E 73
Hyde Pk. Mans. NW1 . . 4A 60
(off Cabbell St., not continu-
ous)
Hyde Pk. Pl. W2 . . . . . . 1A 74
Hyde Pk. Sq. W2 . . . . . 5A 60
Hyde Pk. Sq. M. W2 . . . 5A 60
(off Southwick Pl.)
Hyde Pk. St. W2 . . . . . . 5A 60
Hyde Pk. Towers W2 . . 1E 73
Hyderabad Way E15 . . . 4A 54
Hyde Rd. N1 . . . . 5A 50
Hyde's Pl. N1 . . . . 4D 49
Hyde St. SE8 . . . . 2C 94
Hydethorpe Rd.
SW12 . . . . 1E 117
Hyde Va. SE10 . . . . . . 3E 95
Hydra Bldg., The EC1 . . 2C 8
Hyndewood SE23 . . . . 3F 121
Hyndman St. SE15 . . . . 2D 93

Hyperion Ho. E3 . . . . . 1A 66
   (off Arbery Rd.)
SW2 . . . . 4B 104
Hyson Ho. SE16 . . . . . 1D 93
Hythe Ho. SE16 . . . . . 3E 79
   (off Swan Rd.)
W6 . . . . 5E 71
   (off Shepherd's Bush Rd.)
Hythe Ho. NW10 . . . . . 2B 56
Hythe Ho. Ind. Est.
NW10 . . . . 2C 56

I

Ian Bowater Ct. N1 . . . . 1C 10
   (off East St.)
Ian Ct. SE23 . . . . 2E 121
Ibberton Ho. SW8 . . . . . 3B 90
   (off Meadow Rd.)
W14 . . . . 4A 72
   (off Russell Rd.)
Ibbotson Av. E16 . . . . . 5B 68
Ibbott St. E1 . . . . 3E 65
Iberia Ho. N19 . . . . 2F 33
Ibex Ho. E15 . . . . 2A 54
   (off Forest La.)
Ibis Ct. SE8 . . . . 2B 94
   (off Edward Pl.)
Ibsley Gdns. SW15 . . . . 1C 112
ICA Cinema 2C 22
   (off The Mall)
ICA Theatre 2B 78
   (off Lafone St.)
Iceland Rd. E3 . . . . 5C 52
Iceland Wharf SE8 . . . . . 5A 80
Ice Wharf Marina N1 . . . 1A 62
   (off New Wharf Rd.)
Ickburgh Est. E5 . . . . . . 4D 37
Ickburgh Rd. E5 . . . . . . 5D 37
Icknield Ho. SW3 . . . . . 1A 88
   (off Cale St.)
Icon Apartments SE1 . . . 5D 27
   (off Cluny Pl.)
Idaho Bldg. SE10 . . . . . 4D 95
   (off Deal's Gateway)
Ida St. E14 . . . . 5E 67
   (not continuous)
Idlecombe Rd.
SW17 . . . . 5C 116
Idmiston Rd. E15 . . . . . 1B 54
SE27 . . . . 3E 119
Idol La.
EC3 . . . . 5D 19 (1A 78)
Idonia St. SE8 . . . . 3C 94
Iffley Rd. W6 . . . . 4D 71
Ifield Rd. SW10 . . . . . . 2D 87
Ightham Ho. SE17 . . . . . 5A 78
   (off Beckway St.)
Ikon Ho. E1 . . . . 1E 79
   (off Devonport St.)
Ilbert St. W10 . . . . 2F 57
Ilchester Gdns. W2 . . . . 1D 73
Ilchester Mans. W8 . . . . 4C 72
   (off Abingdon Rd.)
Ilchester Pl. W14 . . . . . 4B 72
Ildersly Gro. SE21 . . . . 2F 119
Ilderton Rd. SE16 . . . . . 1E 93

Ilderton Wharf SE15 . . . 2E 93
   (off Rollins St.)
Ilex Rd. NW10 . . . . 3B 42
Ilex Way SW16 . . . . . . 5C 118
Ilford Ho. N1 . . . . 3F 49
   (off Dove Rd.)
Ilfracombe Flats SE1 . . . 3A 26
   (off Marshalsea Rd.)
Ilfracombe Rd.
BR1: Brom 3B 124
Iliffe St. SE17 . . . . 1D 91
Iliffe Yd. SE17 . . . . 1D 91
   (off Crampton St.)
Ilkeston Ct. E5 . . . . 1F 51
   (off Overbury St.)
Ilkley Rd. E16 . . . . 4E 69
Ilminster Gdns.
SW11 . . . . 2A 102
Ilsley Ct. SW8 . . . . 5E 89
Imani Mans. SW11 . . . . 5F 87
IMAX Cinema
. . . . 2B 24 (2C 76)
Imber St. N1 . . . . 5F 49
Imperial Av. N16 . . . . . 1A 50
Imperial College of Science,
Technology & Medicine
Imperial Coll. Rd. 4F 73
Wilson House 5A 60
   (off Star La.)
Imperial Coll. Rd.
SW7 . . . . 4F 73
Imperial Ct. N6 . . . . . . 1E 33
NW8 . . . . 1A 60
   (off Prince Albert Rd.)
SE11 . . . . 1C 90
Imperial Cres. SW6 . . . . 5E 87
Imperial Ho. E3 . . . . . . 2A 66
   (off Grove Rd.)
E14 . . . . 1B 80
   (off Victory Pl.)
Imperial M. E6 . . . . 1F 69
Imperial Pde. EC4 . . . . . 3D 17
   (off New Bri. St.)
Imperial Rd. SW6 . . . . . 4D 87
Imperial Sq. SW6 . . . . . 4D 87
Imperial St. E3 . . . . 2E 67
Imperial War Mus.
. . . . 5C 24 (4C 76)
Imperial Wharf SW6 . . . 5E 87
Imre Cl. W12 . . . . 2D 71
Inchmery Rd. SE6 . . . . . 2D 123
Independent Pl. E8 . . . . 2B 50
Independents Rd.
SE3 . . . . 1B 110
Inderwick Rd. N8 . . . . . 1B 34
Indescon Ct. E14 . . . . . 3D 81
Indiana Bldg. SE8 . . . . . 4C 94
   (off Deal's Gateway)
India Pl. WC2 . . . . 4F 15
India St. EC3 . . . 3F 19 (5B 64)
India Way W12 . . . . . . 1D 71
Indigo M. E14 . . . . 1E 81
N16 . . . . 5F 35
Indus Ct. SE15 . . . . 3B 92
   (off Amstel Ct.)
Indus Rd. SE7 . . . . 3E 97
Infirmary Ct. SW3 . . . . 2B 88
   (off West Rd.)
Ingal Rd. E13 . . . . 3C 68

Ingate Pl. SW8 . . . . 4D 89
Ingatestone Rd. E12 . . . 3E 41
Ingelow Ho. W8 . . . . . . 3D 73
   (off Holland St.)
Ingelow Rd. SW8 . . . . . 5D 89
Ingersoll Rd. W12 . . . . . 2D 71
Ingestre Pl.
W1 . . . . 3A 14 (5E 61)
Ingestre Rd. E7 . . . . . . 1C 54
NW5 . . . . 1D 47
Ingham Rd. NW6 . . . . . 1C 44
Inglebert St.
EC1 . . . . 1B 8 (2C 62)
Ingleborough St.
SW9 . . . . 5C 90
Ingleby Rd. N7 . . . . 5A 34
Inglefield Sq. E1 . . . . . . 2D 79
   (off Prusom St.)
Inglemere Rd.
SE23 . . . . 3F 121
Inglesham Wlk. E9 . . . . 3B 52
Ingleside Gro. SE3 . . . . 2B 96
Inglethorpe St. SW6 . . . 4F 85
Ingleton St. SW9 . . . . . 5C 90
Inglewood Cl. E14 . . . . . 5C 80
Inglewood Rd. NW6 . . . 2C 44
Inglis St. SE5 . . . . 4D 91
Ingoldisthorpe Gro.
SE15 . . . . 2B 92
Ingram Av. NW11 . . . . . 2E 31
Ingram Cl. SE11 . . . . . . 5B 76
Ingram Ho. E3 . . . . 5A 52
Ingrave St. SW11 . . . . . 1F 101
Ingrebourne Ho.
BR1: Brom 5F 123
   (off Brangbourne Rd.)
NW8 . . . . 4F 59
   (off Broadley St.)
Ingress St. W4 . . . . 1A 84
Inigo Jones Rd. SE7 . . . 3F 97
Inigo Pl. WC2 . . . . 4D 15
Inkerman Rd. NW5 . . . . 3D 47
Inkerman Ter. W8 . . . . . 4C 72
   (off Allen St.)
Inkster Ho. SW11 . . . . . 1A 102
Inman Rd. NW10 . . . . . 5A 42
SW18 . . . . 5E 101
Inner Circ.
NW1 . . . . 2B 4 (2C 60)
Inner Ct. SW3 . . . . 2A 88
Inner Pk. Rd. SW19 . . . 1F 113
Inner Temple La.
EC4 . . . . 3B 16
Innes Gdns. SW15 . . . . 4D 99
Innis Ho. SE17 . . . . . . 1A 92
   (off East St.)
Inniskilling Rd. E13 . . . 1E 69
Innis St. SE15 . . . . 3A 92
Innovation Cen., The
E14 . . . . 3E 81
   (off Marsh Wall)
Inns of Court & City
Yeomanry Mus. 1A 16
   (off Chancery La.)
Inskip Cl. E10 . . . . 4D 39
Institute of Archaeology
. . . . 3F 61
Institute of Classical Studies
. . . . 3F 61

Institute of Contemporary Arts
. . . . 1C 22
Institute Pl. E8 . . . . 2D 51
Integer Gdns. E11 . . . . 2F 39
International Bus. Pk.
E15 . . . . 5F 53
International Ho. E1 . . . . 5F 19
(off St Katharine's Way)
Inver Cl. E5 . . . . 4E 37
Inver Ct. W2 . . . . 5D 59
W6 . . . . 4C 70
Inverforth Cl. NW3 . . . . . 4E 31
Invergarry Ho. NW6 . . . 1D 59
(off Carlton Va.)
Inverine Rd. SE7 . . . . . . 1D 97
Invermead Cl. W6 . . . . . 4C 70
Inverness Ct. SE6 . . . . . 1B 124
Inverness Gdns. W8 . . . . 2D 73
Inverness M. W2 . . . . . . 1D 73
Inverness Pl. W2 . . . . . . 1D 73
Inverness St. NW1 . . . . . 5D 47
Inverness Ter. W2 . . . . . 5D 59
Inverton Rd. SE15 . . . . . 2F 107
Invicta Plaza
SE1 . . . . 1D 25 (2D 77)
Invicta Rd. SE3 . . . . 3C 96
Invicta Sq. E3 . . . . 4C 66
Inville Rd. SE17 . . . . 1F 91
Inville Wlk. SE17 . . . . . . 1F 91
Inwen Ct. SE8 . . . . 1A 94
Inwood Ct. NW1 . . . . . . 4E 47
(off Rochester Sq.)
Inworth St. SW11 . . . . . . 5A 88
Inworth Wlk. N1 . . . . . . 5E 49
(off Popham St.)
Iona Cl. SE6 . . . . 5C 108
Ion Ct. E2 . . . . 1C 64
Ionian Bldg. E14 . . . . . . 1A 80
Ionian Ho. E1 . . . . 3F 65
(off Duckett St.)
Ion Sq. E2 . . . . 1C 64
Ipsden Bldgs. SE1 . . . . . 2C 24
Ipswich Ho. SE4 . . . . . . 3F 107
Ireland Yd. EC4 . . . . . . 5D 63
Irene Rd. SW6 . . . . 4C 86
Ireton St. E3 . . . . 3C 66
Iris Ct. SE14 . . . . 4E 93
(off Briant St.)
Iron Bri. Cl. NW10 . . . . 2A 42
Iron Bri. Ho. NW1 . . . . 4B 46
Iron Mill Pl. SW18 . . . . 4D 101
Iron Mill Rd. SW18 . . . 4D 101
Ironmonger La.
EC2 . . . . . 3A 18 (5E 63)
Ironmonger Pas.
EC1 . . . . 2A 10
(off Ironmonger Row)
Ironmonger Row
EC1 . . . . . 2A 10 (2E 63)
Ironmonger Row Baths
. . . . 2A 10
Ironmongers Pl. E14 . . . 5C 80
Ironside Cl. SE16 . . . . . 3F 79
Ironside Ho. E9 . . . . . . 1A 52
Iron Works E3 . . . . 5C 52
Irvine Cl. E14 . . . . 4D 67
Irvine Ho. N7 . . . . 3B 48
(off Caledonian Rd.)
Irving Gro. SW9 . . . . . . 5B 90

Irving Ho. SE17 . . . . . . 1D 91
(off Doddington Gro.)
Irving Mans. W14 . . . . 2A 86
(off Queen's Club Gdns.)
Irving M. N1 . . . . 3E 49
Irving Rd. W14 . . . . . . 4F 71
Irving St.
WC2 . . . . . 5C 14 (1F 75)
Irving Way NW9 . . . . . 1C 28
Irwell Est. SE16 . . . . . . 4E 79
Irwin Gdns. NW10 . . . . 5D 43
Isaac Way SE1 . . . . . . 3A 26
(off Lant St.)
Isabella Ho. SE11 . . . . 1D 91
(off Othello Cl.)
W6 . . . . 1E 85
(off Queen Caroline St.)
Isabella Rd. E9 . . . . . . 2E 51
Isabella St.
SE1 . . . . . . 2D 25 (2D 77)
Isabel St. SW9 . . . . . . 4B 90
Isambard M. E14 . . . . . 4E 81
Isambard Pl. SE16 . . . . 2E 79
Isel Way SE22 . . . . . . 3A 106
Isis Cl. SW15 . . . . 2E 99
Isis Ho. NW8 . . . . 3F 59
(off Church St. Est.)
Isis St. SW18 . . . . 2E 115
Island Ho. E15 . . . . . . 2E 67
Island Row E14 . . . . . . 5B 66
Islay Wlk. N1 . . . . 3E 49
(off Douglas Rd. Sth.)
Isleden Ho. N1 . . . . . . 5E 49
(off Prebend St.)
Isledon Rd. N7 . . . . . . 5C 34
ISLEDON VILLAGE . . . 5C 34
Isley Ct. SW8 . . . . 5E 89
ISLINGTON 4D 49
Islington Grn. N1 . . . . 5D 49
Islington High St. N1 . . 1C 62
(not continuous)
Islington Mus. 4D 49
Islington Pk. M. N1 . . . 4D 49
Islington Pk. St. N1 . . . 4C 48
Islington Pl. N1 . . . . . 5C 48
Islington Tennis Cen.
. . . . 3A 48
Islip St. NW5 . . . . 2E 47
Ismailia Rd. E7 . . . . . . 4D 55
Isom Cl. E13 . . . . 2D 69
Ivanhoe Ho. E3 . . . . . 1A 66
(off Grove Rd.)
Ivanhoe Rd. SE5 . . . . . 1B 106
Ivatt Pl. W14 . . . . 1B 86
Iveagh Cl. E9 . . . . 5F 51
Iveagh Ct. E1 . . . . 3F 19
Iveagh Ho. SW9 . . . . . 5D 91
SW10 . . . . 3E 87
(off King's Rd.)
Ive Farm Cl. E10 . . . . . 4C 38
Ive Farm La. E10 . . . . . 4C 38
Iveley Rd. SW4 . . . . . . 5E 89
Iver Ho. N1 . . . . 5A 50
(off New Era Est.)
Iverna Ct. W8 . . . . 4C 72
Iverna Gdns. W8 . . . . . 4C 72
Iverson Rd. NW6 . . . . . 3B 44
Ives Rd. E16 . . . . 4A 68
Ives St. SW3 . . . . 5A 74

Ivestor Ter. SE23 . . . . . 5E 107
Ivimey St. E2 . . . . 2C 64
Ivinghoe Ho. N7 . . . . . 2F 47
Ivor Ct. N8 . . . . 1A 34
NW1 . . . . 3B 60
(off Gloucester Pl.)
Ivories, The N1 . . . . . . 4E 49
(off Northampton St.)
Ivor Pl. NW1 . . . . 4A 4 (3B 60)
Ivor St. NW1 . . . . 4E 47
Ivorydown
BR1: Brom 4C 124
Ivory Ho. E1 . . . . 2B 78
Ivory Sq. SW11 . . . . . 1E 101
Ivybridge Ct. NW1 . . . 4D 47
(off Lewis St.)
Ivybridge La.
WC2 . . . . . 5E 15 (1A 76)
Ivychurch La. SE17 . . . 1B 92
Ivy Ct. SE16 . . . . 1C 92
(off Argyle Way)
Ivydale Rd. SE15 . . . . 1F 107
Ivyday Gro. SW16 . . . 3B 118
Ivy Gdns. N8 . . . . 1A 34
Ivy Lodge W11 . . . . . . 2C 72
(off Notting Hill Ga.)
Ivymount Rd.
SE27 . . . . 3C 118
Ivy Rd. E16 . . . . 5C 68
E17 . . . . 1C 38
NW2 . . . . 1E 43
SE4 . . . . 2B 108
SW17 . . . . 5A 116
Ivy St. N1 . . . . 1A 64
Ixworth Pl. SW3 . . . . . 1A 88

J

Jacana Ct. E1 . . . . 1B 78
(off Star Pl.)
Jacaranda Gro. E8 . . . . 4B 50
Jack Clow Rd. E15 . . . . 1A 68
Jack Dash Ho. E14 . . . 3E 81
(off Lawn Ho. Cl.)
Jack Dash Way E6 . . . 3F 69
Jackman Ho. E1 . . . . . 2D 79
(off Watts St.)
Jackman St. NW10 . . . 5A 28
Jackman St. E8 . . . . . . 5D 51
Jackson Cl. E9 . . . . . . 4E 51
Jackson Ct. E7 . . . . . . 3D 55
Jackson Rd. N7 . . . . . 1B 48
Jacksons La. N6 . . . . . 2C 32
Jacksons Lane Theatre
. . . . 1D 33
(off Jacksons La.)
Jacks Pl. E1 . . . . 5F 11
(off Corbet Pl.)
Jack Walker Ct. N5 . . . 1D 49
Jacobin Lodge N7 . . . 2A 48
Jacob Mans. E1 . . . . . 5D 65
(off Commercial Rd.)
Jacobs Ho. E13 . . . . . 2E 69
(off New City Rd.)
Jacob St. SE1 . . . . . . 3C 78
Jacob's Well M.
W1 . . . . 1C 12 (4C 60)

Jacotts Ho. *W10* 3E **57**
James Stewart Ho.
  NW6 . . . . 4B **44**
Jacqueline Creft Ter.
  N6 . . . . 1C **32**
    (off Grange Rd.)
Jacqueline Ho. *NW1* . . . 5B **46**
    (off Regent's Pk. Rd.)
Jade Cl. E16 . . . . 5F **69**
  NW2 . . . . 2F **29**
Jade Ter. NW6 . . . . 4E **45**
Jaffray Pl. SE27 . . . . . 4D **119**
Jaggard Way SW12 . . . 5D **102**
Jagger Ho. *SW11* 4B **88**
    (off Rosenau Rd.)
Jago Wlk. SE5 . . . . 3F **91**
Jake Russell Wlk.
  E16 . . . . 1E **83**
Jamaica Rd.
  SE1 . . . . 4F **27** (3B **78**)
  SE16 . . . . 3B **78**
Jamaica St. E1 . . . . 5E **65**
James Allens School
  Swimming Pool . . . 3A **106**
James Anderson Ct.
  E2 . . . . 1A **64**
    (off Kingsland Rd.)
James Av. NW2 . . . . 2E **43**
James Boswell Ct.
  SW16 . . . . 4B **118**
James Brine Ho. *E2* . . . 1F **11**
    (off Ravenscroft St.)
James Campbell Ho.
  E2 . . . . 1E **65**
    (off Old Ford Rd.)
James Cl. E13 . . . . 1C **68**
  NW11 . . . . 1A **30**
James Collins Cl.
  W9 . . . . 3B **58**
James Ct. *N1* 5E **49**
    (off Raynor Pl.)
James Docherty Ho.
  E2 . . . . 1D **65**
    (off Patriot Sq.)
James Hammett Ho.
  E2 . . . . 1F **11**
    (off Ravenscroft St.)
James Hill Ho. *W10* . . . 3A **58**
    (off Kensal Rd.)
James Ho. *E1* 3A **66**
    (off Solebay St.)
  SE16 . . . . 3F **79**
    (off Wolfe Cres.)
  SW8 . . . . 3A **90**
    (off Wheatsheaf La.)
James Joyce Wlk.
  SE24 . . . . 2D **105**
James La. E10 . . . . 2E **39**
  E11 . . . . 2F **39**
James Lind Ho. *SE8* . . . 5B **80**
    (off Grove St.)
James Middleton Ho.
  E2 . . . . 2D **65**
    (off Middleton St.)
Jameson Ct. *E2* 1E **65**
    (off Russia La.)
Jameson Ho. *SE11* 1B **90**
    (off Glasshouse Wlk.)
Jameson Lodge N6 . . . . 1E **33**
Jameson St. W8 . . . . . . 2C **72**

James St.
  W1 . . . . 3C **12** (5C **60**)
  WC2 . . . . 3E **15** (1A **76**)
James Stroud Ho.
  SE17 . . . . 1E **91**
    (off Bronti Cl.)
James Ter. SW14 . . . . . . 1A **98**
    (off Church Path)
Jamestown Rd. NW1 . . 5D **47**
Jamestown Way E14 . . 1F **81**
Jamuna Cl. E14 . . . . 4A **66**
Jane Austen Hall
  E16 . . . . 2D **83**
    (off Wesley Av.)
Jane Austen Ho.
  SW1 . . . . 1E **89**
    (off Churchill Gdns.)
Jane St. E1 . . . . 5D **65**
Janet Adegoke Leisure Cen.
  . . . . 1C **70**
Janet St. E14 . . . . 4C **80**
Janeway Pl. SE16 . . . . . 3D **79**
Janeway St. SE16 . . . . . 3C **78**
Jansen Wlk. SW11 . . . . 1F **101**
Janson Cl. E15 . . . . 2A **54**
  NW10 . . . . 5A **28**
Janson Rd. E15 . . . . 2A **54**
Japan Cres. N4 . . . . 3B **34**
Jardine Rd. E1 . . . . 1F **79**
Jarman Ho. *E1* 4E **65**
    (off Jubilee St.)
  SE16 . . . . 5F **79**
    (off Hawkstone Rd.)
Jarrett Cl. SW2 . . . . . . 1D **119**
Jarrow Rd. SE16 . . . . . . 5E **79**
Jarrow Way E9 . . . . 1B **52**
Jarvis Rd. SE22 . . . . . . 2A **106**
Jasmin Cl. SE12 . . . . . . 4C **110**
Jasmine Ct. SW19 . . . . . 5C **114**
Jasmine Sq. E3 . . . . 5B **52**
    (off Hawthorn Av.)
Jasmin Lodge SE16 . . . 1D **93**
    (off Sherwood Gdns.)
Jason Ct. *SW9* 4C **90**
    (off Southey Rd.)
  W1 . . . . 2C **12**
Jasper Pas. SE19 . . . . . 5B **120**
Jasper Rd. E16 . . . . 5F **69**
  SE19 . . . . 5B **120**
Jasper Wlk. N1 . . . . 1B **10**
    (off Nile St.)
Java Wharf SE1 . . . . . . 3B **78**
    (off Shad Thames)
Jay M. SW7 . . . . 3E **73**
Jean Darling Ho.
  SW10 . . . . 2F **87**
    (off Milman's St.)
Jean Ho. SW17 . . . . . . 5A **116**
Jean Pardies Ho. *E1* . . 4E **65**
    (off Jubilee St.)
Jebb Av. SW2 . . . . 4A **104**
    (not continuous)
Jebb St. E3 . . . . 1C **66**
Jedburgh Rd. E13 . . . . . 2E **69**
Jedburgh St. SW11 . . . 2C **102**
Jeddo M. W12 . . . . 3B **70**
Jeddo Rd. W12 . . . . 3B **70**

Jefferson Bldg. E14 . . . . 3C **80**
Jeffrey Row SE12 . . . . . 3D **111**
Jeffrey's Pl. NW1 . . . . . 4E **47**
Jeffreys Rd. SW4 . . . . . 5A **90**
Jeffrey's St. NW1 . . . . . 4E **47**
Jeffreys Wlk. SW4 . . . . 5A **90**
Jeger Av. E2 . . . . 5B **50**
Jeken Rd. SE9 . . . . 2E **111**
Jelf Rd. SW2 . . . . 3C **104**
Jellicoe Ho. *E2* 1C **64**
    (off Ropley St.)
  NW1 . . . . 3D **61**
Jellicoe Rd. E13 . . . . . . 3C **68**
Jemotts Ct. SE14 . . . . . 2F **93**
    (off Myers La.)
Jenkinson Ho. *E2* 2F **65**
    (off Usk St.)
Jenkins Rd. E13 . . . . . . 3D **69**
Jenner Av. W3 . . . . 4A **56**
Jenner Ho. SE3 . . . . 2A **96**
    (off Restell Cl.)
  WC1 . . . . 3E **7**
    (off Hunter St.)
Jenner Pl. SW13 . . . . . . 2D **85**
Jenner Rd. N16 . . . . 5B **36**
Jennifer Ho. SE11 . . . . . 5C **76**
    (off Reedworth St.)
Jennifer Rd.
  BR1: Brom 3B **124**
Jenningsbury Ho.
  SW3 . . . . 1A **88**
    (off Cale St.)
Jennings Ho. SE10 . . . . 1F **95**
    (off Old Woolwich Rd.)
Jennings Rd. SE22 . . . . 4B **106**
Jenny Hammond Cl.
  E11 . . . . 5B **40**
Jephson Ct. SW4 . . . . . 5A **90**
Jephson Ho. SE17 . . . . . 2D **91**
    (off Doddington Gro.)
Jephson Rd. E7 . . . . 4E **55**
Jephson St. SE5 . . . . . . 4F **91**
Jephtha Rd. SW18 . . . . 4C **100**
Jepson Ho. SW6 . . . . . . 4D **87**
    (off Pearscroft Rd.)
Jerdan Pl. SW6 . . . . 3C **86**
Jeremiah St. E14 . . . . . . 5D **67**
Jeremy Bentham Ho.
  E2 . . . . 2C **64**
    (off Mansford St.)
Jermyn St.
  SW1 . . . . 1F **21** (2E **75**)
Jermyn Street Theatre
  . . . . 5B **14**
    (off Jermyn St.)
Jerningham Ct. SE14 . . . 4A **94**
Jerningham Rd.
  SE14 . . . . 5A **94**
Jerome Cres. NW8 . . . . 3A **60**
Jerome Ho. NW1 . . . . . . 4A **60**
    (off Lisson Gro.)
  SW7 . . . . 5F **73**
    (off Glendower Pl.)
Jerome St.
  E1 . . . . 5F **11** (3B **64**)
Jerrard St. SE13 . . . . . 1D **109**
Jerrold St.
  N1 . . . . 1E **11** (1A **64**)
Jersey Ho. N1 . . . . 3E **49**

Jersey Rd. E11 . . . . 3F **39**
  E16 . . . . 5E **69**
  N1 . . . . 3E **49**
Jersey St. E2 . . . . 2D **65**
Jerusalem Pas.
  EC1 . . . . 4D **9** (3D **63**)
Jervis Bay Ho. E14 . . . . . 5F **67**
  (off Blair St.)
Jervis Ct. SE10 . . . . 4E **95**
  (off Blissett St.)
  W1 . . . . 3E **13**
Jervis Rd. SW6 . . . . 2B **86**
Jerviston Gdns.
  SW16 . . . . 5C **118**
Jerwood Space Art Gallery
  . . . . 3F **25**
Jessam Av. E5 . . . . 3D **37**
Jessel Ho. SW1 . . . . 5F **75**
  (off Page St.)
  WC1 . . . . 2D **7**
  (off Judd St.)
Jessel Mans. W14 . . . . . 2A **86**
  (off Queen's Club Gdns.)
Jesse Rd. E10 . . . . 3E **39**
Jessica Rd. SW18 . . . . . 4E **101**
Jessie Blythe La.
  N19 . . . . 2A **34**
Jessie Duffett Ho.
  SE5 . . . . 3E **91**
  (off Pitman St.)
Jessie Wood Ct.
  SW9 . . . . 3C **90**
  (off Caldwell St.)
Jesson Ho. SE17 . . . . . . 5F **77**
  (off Orb St.)
Jessop Ct. N1 . . . . 1D **63**
Jessop Rd. SE24 . . . . . . 2D **105**
Jessop Sq. E14 . . . . 2C **80**
  (off Heron Quay)
Jevington Way
  SE12 . . . . 1D **125**
Jevons Ho. NW8 . . . . 4F **45**
  (off Hilgrove Rd.)
Jewel House 5F **19**
  (in The Tower of London)
Jewel Tower 5D **23**
  (off College M.)
Jewish Mus.
  Camden Town 5D **47**
Jewry St.
  EC3 . . . . . . 3F **19** (5B **64**)
Jew's Row SW18 . . . . . 2D **101**
Jews' Wlk. SE26 . . . . . . 4D **121**
Jeymer Av. NW2 . . . . . . 2D **43**
Jeypore Pas.
  SW18 . . . . 4E **101**
Jeypore Rd. SW18 . . . . . 5E **101**
Jim Griffiths Ho.
  SW6 . . . . 2B **86**
  (off Clem Attlee Ct.)
Joan Bicknell Cen., The
  . . . . 2F **115**
Joan Cres. SE9 . . . . 5F **111**
Joanna Ho. W6 . . . . 1E **85**
  (off Queen Caroline St.)
Joan St. SE1 . . 2D **25** (2D **77**)
Jocelin Ho. N1 . . . . 5B **48**
  (off Barnsbury Est.)
Jocelyn St. SE15 . . . . . . 4C **92**

Jockey's Flds.
  WC1 . . . . 5A **8** (4B **62**)
Jodane St. SE8 . . . . 5B **80**
Jodrell Rd. E3 . . . . 5B **52**
Joe Hunte Ct. SE27 . . . 5D **119**
Johanna St.
  SE1 . . . . 4B **24** (3C **76**)
John Adam St.
  WC2 . . . . 5E **15** (1A **76**)
John Aird Ct. W2 . . . . . . 4E **59**
  (off Howley Pl.,
  not continuous)
John Archer Way
  SW18 . . . . 4F **101**
John Ashby Cl. SW2 . . . 4A **104**
John Baird Ct. SE26 . . . 4E **121**
John Barker Ct. NW6 . . . 4A **44**
John Barnes Wlk.
  E15 . . . . 3B **54**
John Betts' Ho. W12 . . . 4B **70**
  (off Bush Rd.)
John Brent Ho. SE8 . . . . 5F **79**
  (off Bush Rd.)
John Buck Ho. NW10 . . . 5B **42**
John Campbell Rd.
  N16 . . . . 2A **50**
John Carpenter St.
  EC4 . . . . 4D **17** (1D **77**)
John Cartwright Ho.
  E2 . . . . 2D **65**
  (off Old Bethnal Grn. Rd.)
John Drinkwater Cl.
  E11 . . . . 2B **40**
John Fearon Wlk.
  W10 . . . . 2A **58**
  (off Dart St.)
John Felton Rd.
  SE16 . . . . 3C **78**
John Fielden Ho. E2 . . . 2D **65**
  (off Canrobert St.)
John Fisher St. E1 . . . . 1C **78**
John Harrison Way
  SE10 . . . . 4B **82**
John Horner M. N1 . . . . 1E **63**
John Islip St. SW1 . . . . 5F **75**
John Kennedy Ct. N1 . . . 3F **49**
  (off Newington Grn. Rd.)
John Kennedy Ho.
  SE16 . . . . 5F **79**
  (off Rotherhithe Old Rd.)
John Knight Lodge
  SW6 . . . . 3C **86**
John McDonald Ho.
  E14 . . . . 4E **81**
  (off Glengall Gro.)
John McKenna Wlk.
  SE16 . . . . 4C **78**
John Masefield Ho.
  N15 . . . . 1F **35**
  (off Fladbury Rd.)
John Maurice Cl.
  SE17 . . . . 5F **77**
John Orwell Sports Cen.
  . . . . 2D **79**
John Parker Sq.
  SW11 . . . . 1F **101**
John Parry Ct. N1 . . . . . 1A **64**
  (off Hare Wlk.)
John Penn Ho. SE14 . . . 3B **94**
  (off Amersham Va.)

John Penn St. SE13 . . . . 4D **95**
John Penry Ho. SE1 . . . . 1C **92**
  (off Marlborough Gro.)
John Prince's St.
  W1 . . . . 2E **13** (5D **61**)
John Pritchard Ho.
  E1 . . . . 3C **64**
  (off Buxton St.)
John Ratcliffe Ho.
  NW6 . . . . 2C **58**
  (off Chippenham Gdns.)
John Rennie Wlk.
  E1 . . . . 1D **79**
John Roll Way SE16 . . . 4C **78**
John Ruskin St. SE5 . . . 3D **91**
John Scurr Ho. E14 . . . . 5A **66**
  (off Ratcliffe La.)
John Silkin La. SE8 . . . . 1F **93**
John's M.
  WC1 . . . . 4A **8** (3B **62**)
John Smith Av. SW6 . . . 3B **86**
John Smith M. E14 . . . . 1F **81**
Johnson Cl. E8 . . . . 5C **50**
Johnson Ho. E2 . . . . 2C **64**
  (off Roberta St.)
  NW1 . . . . 1E **61**
  (off Cranleigh St.)
  NW3 . . . . 4B **46**
  (off Adelaide Rd.)
  SW1 . . . . 5C **74**
  (off Cundy St.)
  SW8 . . . . 3F **89**
  (off Wandsworth Rd.)
Johnson Lodge W9 . . . 4C **58**
  (off Admiral Wlk.)
Johnson Mans. W14 . . . 2A **86**
  (off Queen's Club Gdns.)
Johnson's Ct. EC4 . . . . 5C **62**
Johnson's Pl. SW1 . . . . 1E **89**
Johnson St. E1 . . . . 1F **79**
John Spencer Sq. N1 . . . 3D **49**
John's Pl. E1 . . . . 5D **65**
Johnston Cl. SW9 . . . . . 4B **90**
Johnston Ct. E10 . . . . . 5D **39**
Johnstone Ho. SE13 . . 1F **109**
  (off Belmont Hill)
Johnston Ter. NW2 . . . . 5F **29**
John Strachey Ho.
  SW6 . . . . 2B **86**
  (off Clem Attlee Ct.)
John St. E15 . . . . 5B **54**
  WC1 . . . . 4A **8** (3B **62**)
John Strype Ct. E10 . . . 3D **39**
John Trundle Ct. EC2 . . . 5F **9**
John Trundle Highwalk
  EC2 . . . . 5F **9**
  (off Beech St.)
John Tucker Ho. E14 . . 4C **80**
  (off Mellish St.)
John Wesley Highwalk
  EC2 . . . . 1F **17**
  (off Barbican)
John Wheatley Ho.
  SW6 . . . . 2B **86**
  (off Clem Attlee Ct.)
John Williams Cl.
  SE14 . . . . 2F **93**
John Woolley Cl.
  SE13 . . . . 2A **110**

Joiners Arms Yd.
SE5 . . . . 4F 91
Joiners Pl. N5 . . . . 1F 49
Joiner St.
SE1 . . . . 2C 26 (2F 77)
Joiners Yd. N1 . . . . 1E 7
(off Caledonia St.)
Jonathan St. SE11 . . . 1B 90
Jones Ho. E14 . . . . 5F 67
(off Blair St.)
Jones M. SW15 . . . . . . 2A 100
Jones Rd. E13 . . . . 3D 69
Jones St.
W1 . . . . 5D 13 (1D 75)
Jonson Ho. SE1 . . . . . . 5C 26
(off Burbage Cl.)
Jordan Ct. SW15 . . . . . . 2F 99
Jordan Ho. N1 . . . . 5F 49
(off Colville Est.)
SE4 . . . . 2F 107
(off St Norbert Rd.)
Jordans Ho. NW8 . . . . . 3F 59
(off Capland St.)
Joscoyne Ho. E1 . . . . . 5D 65
(off Philpot St.)
Joseph Conrad Ho.
SW1 . . . . 5E 75
(off Tachbrook St.)
Joseph Ct. N16 . . . . . . 1A 36
(off Amhurst Pk.)
SE14 . . . . 3F 93
Josephine Av. SW2 . . . 3B 104
Joseph Irwin Ho.
E14 . . . . 1B 80
(off Gill St.)
Joseph Lister Ct. E7 . . . 4C 54
Joseph Powell Cl.
SW12 . . . . 4E 103
Joseph Priestley Ho.
E2 . . . . 2D 65
(off Canrobert St.)
Joseph Ray Rd. E11 . . . 4A 40
Joseph St. E3 . . . . 3B 66
Joseph Trotter Cl. EC1 . . . 2C 8
Joshua St. E14 . . . . . . 5E 67
Joslings Cl. W12 . . . . . 1C 70
Josseline Ct. E3 . . . . . 1A 66
(off Ford St.)
Joubert Mans. SW3 . . . 1A 88
(off Jubilee Pl.)
Joubert St. SW11 . . . . . 5B 88
Jowett St. SE15 . . . . . . 3B 92
Jowitt Ho. E2 . . . . 2F 65
(off Morpeth St.)
Joyce Page Cl. SE7 . . . 2F 97
Joyce Wlk. SW2 . . . . . 4C 104
Jubb Powell Ho. N15 . . . 1A 36
Jubilee, The SE10 . . . . 3D 95
Jubilee Bldgs. NW8 . . . 5F 45
Jubilee Cl. NW9 . . . . . . 1A 28
NW10 . . . . 1A 56
Jubilee Cres. E14 . . . . . 4E 81
Jubilee Hall Sports Cen.
. . . . 4E 15
(off Tavistock St.)
Jubilee Ho. SE11 . . . . . 5C 76
(off Reedworth St.)
WC1 . . . . 3F 7

Jubilee Mans. E1 . . . . . 5E 65
(off Jubilee St.)
Jubilee Mkt. WC2 . . . . . 4E 15
Jubilee Pl. SW3 . . . . . 1A 88
Jubilee Pl. Shop. Mall
E14 . . . . 2D 81
(off Bank St.)
Jubilee Sports Cen. & Baths
. . . . 2B 58
Jubilee St. E1 . . . . 5E 65
Jubilee Walkway
SE1 . . . . . . 5E 17 (1D 77)
Jubilee Yd. SE1 . . . . . . 3F 27
Judd St.
WC1 . . . . 2D 7 (2A 62)
Jude St. E16 . . . . 5B 68
Judges Wlk. NW3 . . . . . 5E 31
Juer St. SW11 . . . . 3A 88
Julia Ct. E17 . . . . 1D 39
Julia Garfield M.
E16 . . . . 2D 83
(not continuous)
Julian Ho. SE21 . . . . . 4A 120
Julian Pl. E14 . . . . 1D 95
Julian Tayler Path
SE23 . . . . 2D 121
Julia St. NW5 . . . . 1C 46
Juliet Ho. N1 . . . . 1A 64
(off Arden Est.)
Juliette Rd. E13 . . . . . . 1C 68
Julius Ho. E14 . . . . 5F 67
(off E. India Dock Rd.)
Julius Nyerere Cl.
N1 . . . . 5B 48
(off Copenhagen St.)
Junction App.
SE13 . . . . 1E 109
SW11 . . . . 1A 102
Junction Av. NW10 . . . 3E 57
Junction M. W2 . . . . . . 5A 60
Junction Pl. W2 . . . . . . 5F 59
(off Praed St.)
Junction Rd. E13 . . . . . 1D 69
N19 . . . . 1E 47
Juniper Cl. W8 . . . . 4D 73
(off St Mary's Pl.)
Juniper Cres. NW1 . . . . 4C 46
Juniper Ho. SE14 . . . . . 3E 93
W10 . . . . 3A 58
(off Fourth Av.)
Juniper St. E1 . . . . 1E 79
Juno Ct. SW9 . . . . 3C 90
(off Caldwell St.)
Juno Way SE14 . . . . . . 2F 93
Juno Way Ind. Est.
SE14 . . . . 2F 93
Jupiter Ct. SW9 . . . . . . 3C 90
(off Caldwell St.)
Jupiter Ho. E14 . . . . . . 1D 95
(off St Davids Sq.)
Jupiter Way N7 . . . . . . 3B 48
Jupp Rd. E15 . . . . 4F 53
Jupp Rd. W. E15 . . . . . 5F 53
Jura Ho. SE16 . . . . 5F 79
(off Plough Way)
Jurston Ct. SE1 . . . . . . 4C 24
Justice Wlk. SW3 . . . . . 2A 88
Justines Pl. E2 . . . . 2F 65
Jutland Cl. N19 . . . . . . 3A 34

Jutland Ho. SE5 . . . . . . 5E 91
Jutland Rd. E13 . . . . . . 3C 68
SE6 . . . . 5E 109
Juxon Ho. EC4 . . . . 3E 17
(off St Paul's Chyd.)
Juxon St. SE11 . . . . . . 5B 76
JVC Bus. Pk. NW2 . . . . 3C 28

K

Kambala Rd. SW11 . . . 1F 101
Kangley Bri. Rd.
SE26 . . . . 5B 122
Kangley Bus. Cen.
SE26 . . . . 5B 122
Karanjia Ct. NW2 . . . . . 3E 43
Kara Way NW2 . . . . . . 1F 43
Karen Ter. E11 . . . . 4B 40
Kashmir Rd. SE7 . . . . . 3F 97
Kassala Rd. SW11 . . . . 4B 88
Katherine Cl. SE16 . . . . 2F 79
Katherine Ct. SE23 . . . 1D 121
Katherine Gdns.
SE9 . . . . 2F 111
Katherine Ho. W10 . . . 3A 58
(off Portobello Rd.)
Katherine Rd. E6 . . . . . 2E 55
E7 . . . . 2E 55
Katherine Sq. W11 . . . . 2A 72
Kathleen Godfree Ct.
SW19 . . . . 5C 114
Kathleen Rd.
SW11 . . . . 1B 102
Kay Rd. SW9 . . . . 5A 90
Kay St. E2 . . . . 1C 64
E15 . . . . 4F 53
Kean Ho. SE17 . . . . . . 2D 91
Kean St.
WC2 . . . . 3F 15 (5B 62)
Keats Av. E16 . . . . 2D 83
Keats Cl. E11 . . . . 1D 41
NW3 . . . . 1A 46
SE1 . . . . 5B 78
SW19 . . . . 5F 115
Keats Est. N16 . . . . 4B 36
(off Kyverdale Rd.)
Keats Gro. NW3 . . . . . . 1A 46
Keats House NW3 . . . . 1A 46
Keats Ho. E2 . . . . 2E 65
(off Roman Rd.)
SE5 . . . . 3E 91
(off Elmington Est.)
SW1 . . . . 1E 89
(off Churchill Gdns.)
Keats Pl. EC2 . . . . 1B 18
(off Moorfields)
Kebbell Ter. E7 . . . . . . 2D 55
(off Claremont Rd.)
Keble Pl. SW13 . . . . . . 2D 85
Keble St. SW17 . . . . . . 4E 115
Kedge Ho. E14 . . . . 4C 80
(off Tiller Rd.)
Kedleston Wlk. E2 . . . . 2D 65
Keedonward Rd.
BR1: Brom 5A 124
Keel Cl. SE16 . . . . 2F 79
Keel Ct. E14 . . . . 1F 81
(off Newport Av.)

Keeley St.
    WC2 . . . . 3F **15** (5B **62**)
Keeling Ho. E2 . . . . 1D **65**
    (off Claredale St.)
Keeling Rd. SE9 . . . . 3F **111**
Keelson Ho. E14 . . . . 4C **80**
    (off Mellish St.)
Keens Cl. SW16 . . . . 5F **117**
Keen's Yd. N1 . . . . 3D **49**
Keep, The SE3 . . . . 5C **96**
Keepier Wharf E14 . . . . . 1F **79**
    (off Narrow St.)
Keeton's Rd. SE16 . . . . . 4D **79**
    (not continuous)
Keevil Dr. SW19 . . . . 5F **99**
Keighley Cl. N7 . . . . 2A **48**
Keildon Rd. SW11 . . . . . . 2B **102**
Keir, The SW19. . . . . . . 5E **113**
Keir Hardie Ct.
    NW10 . . . . 4B **42**
Keir Hardie Est. E5 . . . . . 3D **37**
Keir Hardie Ho. N19 . . . . . 2F **33**
    W6 . . . . 2F **85**
    (off Fulham Pal. Rd.)
Keith Connor Cl.
    SW8 . . . . 1D **103**
Keith Gro. W12 . . . . 3C **70**
Keith Ho. NW6 . . . . 1D **59**
    (off Carlton Va.)
    SW8 . . . . 3A **90**
    (off Wheatsheaf La.)
Kelbrook Rd. SE3 . . . . . . 5F **97**
Kelby Ho. N7 . . . . 3B **48**
    (off Sutterton St.)
Kelceda Cl. NW2 . . . . 4C **28**
Kelfield Ct. W10 . . . . 5F **57**
Kelfield Gdns. W10 . . . . . 5F **57**
Kelfield M. W10 . . . . 5F **57**
Kelland Rd. E13 . . . . 3C **68**
Kellaway Rd. SE3 . . . . . . 5F **97**
Keller Cres. E12 . . . . 1F **55**
Kellerton Rd. SE13 . . . . . 3A **110**
Kellet Ho's. WC1 . . . . 2E **7**
    (off Tankerton St.)
Kellett Ho. N1 . . . . 5A **50**
    (off Colville Est.)
Kellett Rd. SW2 . . . . 2C **104**
Kellino St. SW17 . . . . . . 4B **116**
Kellow Ho. SE1 . . . . 3B **26**
    (off Tennis St.)
Kell St. SE1 . . . . 5E **25** (4D **77**)
Kelly Av. SE15 . . . . 3B **92**
Kelly Cl. NW10 . . . . 5A **28**
Kelly Ct. E14 . . . . 1C **80**
    (off Garford St.)
Kelly M. W9 . . . . 3B **58**
Kelly St. NW1 . . . . 3D **47**
Kelman Cl. SW4 . . . . 5F **89**
Kelmore Gro. SE22 . . . . . 2C **106**
Kelmscott Gdns.
    W12 . . . . 4C **70**
Kelmscott Leisure Cen.
    . . . . 1B **38**
Kelmscott Rd.
    SW11 . . . . 3A **102**
Kelross Pas. N5 . . . . 1E **49**
Kelross Rd. N5 . . . . 1E **49**
Kelsall Cl. SE3 . . . . 5D **97**
Kelsey St. E2 . . . . 3C **64**

Kelso Ho. E14 . . . . 4E **81**
Kelso Pl. W8 . . . . 4D **73**
Kelvedon Ho. SW8 . . . . . 4A **90**
Kelvedon Rd. SW6 . . . . . 3B **86**
Kelvin Ct. W11 . . . . 1C **72**
Kelvin Gro. SE26 . . . . . . 3D **121**
Kelvington Rd.
    SE15 . . . . 3F **107**
Kelvin Rd. N5 . . . . 1E **49**
Kember St. N1 . . . . 4B **48**
Kemble Ho. SW9 . . . . . . 1D **105**
    (off Barrington Rd.)
Kemble Rd. SE23 . . . . . . 1F **121**
Kemble St.
    WC2 . . . . 3F **15** (5B **62**)
Kemerton Rd. SE5 . . . . . 1E **105**
Kemeys St. E9 . . . . 2A **52**
Kemp Ct. SW8 . . . . 3A **90**
    (off Hartington Rd.)
Kempe Ho. SE1 . . . . 4F **77**
    (off Burge St.)
Kempe Rd. NW6 . . . . 1F **57**
Kemp Ho. E2 . . . . 1F **65**
    (off Sewardstone St.)
    W1 . . . . 4B **14**
    (off Berwick St.)
Kempis Way SE22 . . . . . 3A **106**
Kemplay Rd. NW3 . . . . . 1F **45**
Kemps Ct. W1 . . . . 3B **14**
    (off Hopkins St.)
Kemps Dr. E14 . . . . 1C **80**
Kempsford Gdns.
    SW5 . . . . 1C **86**
Kempsford Rd. SE11 . . . . 5C **76**
    (not continuous)
Kemps Gdns. SE13 . . . . . 3E **109**
Kempson Rd. SW6 . . . . . 4C **86**
Kempthorne Rd. SE8 . . . . 5B **80**
Kempton Ct. E1 . . . . 4D **65**
Kempton Ho. N1 . . . . 5A **50**
    (off Hoxton St.)
Kemsing Ho. SE1 . . . . . . 4C **26**
    (off Long La.)
Kemsing Rd. SE10 . . . . . 1C **96**
Kemsley SE13 . . . . 3D **109**
Kenbrook Ho. NW5 . . . . . 2E **47**
    W14 . . . . 4B **72**
Kenbury Gdns. SE5 . . . . 5E **91**
Kenbury Mans. SE5 . . . . 5E **91**
    (off Kenbury St.)
Kenbury St. SE5 . . . . 5E **91**
Kenchester Cl. SW8 . . . . 3A **90**
Kendal NW1 . . . . 1E **5**
    (off Augustus St.)
Kendal Cl. SW9 . . . . 3D **91**
Kendale Rd.
    BR1: Brom 5A **124**
Kendal Ho. E9 . . . . 5E **51**
    N1 . . . . 1B **62**
    (off Priory Grn. Est.)
Kendall Pl.
    W1 . . . . 1B **12** (4C **60**)
Kendal Pl. SW15 . . . . . . 3B **100**
Kendal Rd. NW10 . . . . . . 1C **42**
Kendal Steps W2 . . . . . . 5A **60**
    (off St George's Flds.)
Kendal St. W2 . . . . 5A **60**
Kender Est. SE14 . . . . . . 4E **93**
    (off Queen's Rd.)

Kender St. SE14 . . . . 3E **93**
Kendoa Rd. SW4 . . . . . . 2F **103**
Kendon Cl. E11 . . . . 1D **41**
Kendrick Ct. SE15 . . . . . 4D **93**
    (off Woods Rd.)
Kendrick M. SW7 . . . . . . 5F **73**
Kendrick Pl. SW7 . . . . . . 5F **73**
Kenilford Rd. SW12 . . . . 5D **103**
Kenilworth Av.
    SW19 . . . . 5C **114**
Kenilworth Rd. E3 . . . . . 1A **66**
    NW6 . . . . 5B **44**
Kenley Wlk. W11 . . . . . . 1A **72**
Kenlor Rd. SW17 . . . . . . 5F **115**
Kenmont Gdns.
    NW10 . . . . 2D **57**
Kenmure Rd. E8 . . . . 2D **51**
Kenmure Yd. E8 . . . . 2D **51**
Kennacraig Cl. E16 . . . . . 2C **82**
Kennard Ho. SW11 . . . . . 5C **88**
Kennard Rd. E15 . . . . . . 4F **53**
Kennard St. SW11 . . . . . 4C **88**
Kennedy Cl. E13 . . . . 1C **68**
Kennedy Cox Ho.
    E16 . . . . 4B **68**
    (off Burke St.)
Kennedy Ho. SE11 . . . . . 1B **90**
    (off Vauxhall Wlk.)
Kennedy Wlk. SE17 . . . . 5F **77**
    (off Elsted St.)
Kennet Cl. SW11 . . . . . . 2F **101**
Kennet Ct. W9 . . . . 4C **58**
    (off Elmfield Way)
Kenneth Campbell Ho.
    NW8 . . . . 3F **59**
    (off Orchardson St.)
Kenneth Ct. SE11 . . . . . . 5C **76**
Kenneth Cres. NW2 . . . . 2D **43**
Kennet Ho. NW8 . . . . . . 3F **59**
    (off Church St. Est.)
Kenneth Younger Ho.
    SW6 . . . . 2B **86**
    (off Clem Attlee Ct.)
Kennet Rd. W9 . . . . 3B **58**
Kennet St. E1 . . . . 2C **78**
Kennett Wharf La.
    EC4 . . . . 5A **18**
Kenninghall Rd. E5 . . . . . 5C **36**
Kenning Ho. N1 . . . . 5A **50**
    (off Colville Est.)
Kenning St. SE16 . . . . . . 3E **79**
Kennings Way SE11 . . . . 1C **90**
KENNINGTON 2C **90**
Kennington Grn.
    SE11 . . . . 1C **90**
Kennington Gro.
    SE11 . . . . 2B **90**
Kennington La. SE11 . . . . 1B **90**
KENNINGTON OVAL . . . 2C **90**
Kennington Oval
    SE11 . . . . 2B **90**
Kennington Pal. Ct.
    SE11 . . . . 1C **90**
    (off Sancroft St.)
Kennington Pk. Gdns.
    SE11 . . . . 2D **91**
Kennington Pk. Ho.
    SE11 . . . . 1C **90**
    (off Kennington Pk. Pl.)

Kennington Pk. Pl.
SE11 . . . . 2C 90
Kennington Pk. Rd.
SE11 . . . . 2C 90
Kennington Rd.
SE1 . . . . 5B 24 (4C 76)
SE11 . . . . 5B 24 (4C 76)
Kennistoun Ho. NW5 . . . . 2E 47
Kennoldes SE21 . . . . . . 2F 119
(off Croxted Rd.)
Kennyland Ct. NW4 . . . . 1D 29
(off Hendon Way)
Kenrick Pl.
W1 . . . . 1B 12 (4C 60)
KENSAL GREEN 2E 57
Kensal Ho. W10 . . . . . . 3F 57
(off Ladbroke Gro.)
KENSAL RISE 1F 57
Kensal Rd. W10 . . . . . . 3A 58
KENSAL TOWN 3A 58
Kensal Wharf W10 . . . . 3F 57
KENSINGTON 3D 73
Kensington Arc. W8 . . . . 3D 73
(off Kensington High St.)
Kensington Cen.
W14 . . . . 5A 72
(not continuous)
Kensington Chu. Ct.
W8 . . . . 3D 73
Kensington Chu. St.
W8 . . . . 2C 72
Kensington Chu. Wlk.
W8 . . . . 3D 73
(not continuous)
Kensington Ct. SE16 . . . . 2F 79
(off King & Queen Wharf)
W8 . . . . 3D 73
Kensington Ct. Gdns.
W8 . . . . 4D 73
(off Kensington Ct. Pl.)
Kensington Ct. M.
W8 . . . . 4D 73
(off Kensington Ct. Pl.)
Kensington Ct. Pl.
W8 . . . . 4D 73
Kensington Gdns. 2E 73
Kensington Gdns. Sq.
W2 . . . . 5D 59
(not continuous)
Kensington Ga. W8 . . . . 4E 73
Kensington Gore
SW7 . . . . 3E 73
Kensington Hall Gdns.
W14 . . . . 1B 86
Kensington Hgts. W8 . . . 2C 72
Kensington High St.
W8 . . . . 4B 72
W14 . . . . 4B 72
Kensington Ho. W8 . . . . 3D 73
(off Kensington Ct.)
W14 . . . . 3F 71
Kensington Mall W8 . . . . 2C 72
Kensington Mans.
SW5 . . . . 1C 86
(off Trebovir Rd.,
not continuous)
Kensington Palace 3D 73
Kensington Pal. Gdns.
W8 . . . . 2D 73

Kensington Pk. Gdns.
W11 . . . . 1B 72
Kensington Pk. M.
W11 . . . . 5B 58
Kensington Pk. Rd.
W11 . . . . 5B 58
Kensington Pl. W8 . . . . 2C 72
Kensington Rd. SW7 . . . 3D 73
W8 . . . . 3D 73
Kensington Sports Cen.
. . . . 1A 72
Kensington Sq. W8 . . . . 4D 73
Kensington Village
W14 . . . . 5B 72
Kensington W. W14 . . . . 5A 72
Kensworth Ho. EC1 . . . . 2C 10
(off Cranwood St.)
Kent Ct. E2 . . . . 1B 64
Kent Ho. SE1 . . . . 1B 92
SW1 . . . . 1F 89
(off Aylesford St.)
W4 . . . . 1A 84
(off Devonshire St.)
W8 . . . . 3D 73
(off Kensington Ct.)
W11 . . . . 2B 72
(off Boyne Ter. M.)
Kent Ho. Rd. SE26 . . . . 5A 122
Kentish Bldgs.
SE1 . . . . 2B 26 (3F 77)
KENTISH TOWN 2D 47
Kentish Town Forum . . . 2D 47
Kentish Town Ind. Est.
NW5 . . . . 2D 47
Kentish Town Rd.
NW1 . . . . 4D 47
NW5 . . . . 4D 47
Kentish Town Sports Cen.
. . . . 3D 47
Kentmere Ho. SE15 . . . . 2E 93
Kenton Ct. SE26 . . . . . 4A 122
(off Adamsrill Rd.)
W14 . . . . 4B 72
Kenton Ho. E1 . . . . . . 3E 65
(off Mantus Cl.)
Kenton Rd. E9 . . . . . . 3F 51
Kenton St.
WC1 . . . . 3D 7 (3A 62)
Kent Pk. Ind. Est.
SE15 . . . . 2D 93
Kent Pas. NW1 . . . . . . 3B 60
Kent St. E2 . . . . 1B 64
E13 . . . . 2E 69
Kent Ter. NW1 . . . . . . 2A 60
Kent Wlk. SW9 . . . . . . 2D 105
Kentwell Cl. SE4 . . . . . 2A 108
Kent Wharf SE8 . . . . . . 3D 95
(off Creekside)
Kentwode Grn. SW13 . . . 3C 84
Kent Yd. SW7 . . . . 3A 74
Kenward Rd. SE9 . . . . . 3E 111
Kenward Way SW11 . . . . 5C 88
Kenway Rd. SW5 . . . . . 5D 73
Ken Wilson Ho. E2 . . . . 1C 64
(off Pritchards Rd.)
Kenwood Cl. NW3 . . . . 3F 31
Kenwood House 3A 32
Kenwood Ho. SW9 . . . . 2D 105
Kenwood Rd. N6 . . . . . 1B 32

Kenworthy Rd. E9 . . . . 2A 52
Kenwrick Ho. N1 . . . . . 5B 48
(off Barnsbury Est.)
Kenwyn Dr. NW2 . . . . . 4A 28
Kenwyn Rd. SW4 . . . . . 2F 103
Kenya Rd. SE7 . . . . . . 3F 97
Kenyon Mans. W14 . . . . 2A 86
(off Queen's Club Gdns.)
Kenyon St. SW6 . . . . . 4F 85
Kepler Ho. SE10 . . . . . 1B 96
(off Armitage Rd.)
Kepler Rd. SW4 . . . . . . 2A 104
Keppel Ho. SE8 . . . . . . 1B 94
SW3 . . . . 5A 74
(off Elystan St.)
Keppel Row
SE1 . . . . 2F 25 (2E 77)
Keppel St.
WC1 . . . . 5C 6 (4F 61)
Kerbela St. E2 . . . . . . 3C 64
Kerbey St. E14 . . . . . . 5D 67
Kerfield Cres. SE5 . . . . 4F 91
Kerfield Pl. SE5 . . . . . . 4F 91
Kerridge Ct. N1 . . . . . . 3A 50
(off Balls Pond Rd.)
Kerrier Ho. SW10 . . . . . 3E 87
(off Stadium St.)
Kerrington Ct. W12 . . . . 3E 71
(off Uxbridge Rd.)
Kerrison Rd. E15 . . . . . 5F 53
SW11 . . . . 1A 102
Kerry N7 . . . . 3A 48
Kerry Cl. E16 . . . . 5D 69
Kerry Ho. E1 . . . . 5E 65
(off Sidney St.)
Kerry Path SE14 . . . . . 2B 94
Kerry Rd. SE14 . . . . . . 2B 94
Kersey Gdns. SE9 . . . . 4F 125
Kersfield Ho. SW15 . . . . 4F 99
Kersfield Rd. SW15 . . . . 4F 99
Kershaw Cl. SW18 . . . . 4F 101
Kersley M. SW11 . . . . . 4B 88
Kersley Rd. N16 . . . . . . 4A 36
Kersley St. SW11 . . . . . 5B 88
Kerswell Cl. N15 . . . . . 1A 36
Kerwick Cl. N7 . . . . . . 4A 48
Keslake Mans. NW10 . . . 1F 57
(off Station Ter.)
Keslake Rd. NW6 . . . . . 1F 57
Keston Ho. SE17 . . . . . 1A 92
(off Kinglake St.)
Keston Rd. SE15 . . . . . 1C 106
Kestrel Av. E6 . . . . . . 4F 69
SE24 . . . . 3D 105
Kestrel Cl. NW10 . . . . . 2A 42
Kestrel Ho. EC1 . . . . . . 1F 9
(off Pickard St.)
Kestrel Pl. SE14 . . . . . 2A 94
Keswick Av. SW15 . . . . 5A 112
Keswick Broadway
SW15 . . . . 3B 100
(off Up. Richmond Rd.)
Keswick Cl. SE6 . . . . . 1B 124
SE13 . . . . 3D 109
Keswick Ho. SE5 . . . . . 5E 91
Keswick Rd. SW15 . . . . 3A 100
Kett Gdns. SW2 . . . . . . 3B 104
Kettlebaston Rd. E10 . . . 3B 38

Kettleby Ho. *SW9*. 1D **105**
 (off Barrington Rd.)
Ketton Ho. *W10*. 3E **57**
 (off Sutton Way)
Kevan Ho. SE5. . . . . 3E **91**
Keybridge Ho. *SW8*. . . . 2A **90**
 (off Miles St.)
Key Cl. E1. . . . . 3E **65**
Keyes Ho. *SW1*. 1F **89**
 (off Dolphin Sq.)
Keyham Ho. *W2*. 2F **43**
Keyham Ho. *W2*. 4C **58**
 (off Park Rd.)
Key Ho. SE11. . . . . 2C **90**
Keymer Rd. SW2. . . . . . . 2B **118**
Keynsham Gdns.
 SE9. . . . . 3F **111**
Keynsham Rd. SE9. . . . . . 3F **111**
Keyse Rd. SE1. . . . . 4B **78**
Keystone Cres.
 N1. . . . . 1E **7** (1A **62**)
Keyworth Cl. E5. . . . . 1A **52**
Keyworth Pl. SE1. . . . . . . 5E **25**
Keyworth
 SE1. . . . . 5E **25** (4D **77**)
Kezia M. SE8. . . . . 1A **94**
Kezia St. SE8. . . . . 1A **94**
Khama Rd. SW17. . . . . . . 4A **116**
Khartoum Rd. E13. . . . . . 2D **69**
 SW17. . . . . 4F **115**
Khyber Rd. SW11. . . . . . . 5A **88**
Kibworth St. SW8. . . . . . . 3B **90**
KIDBROOKE. 5D **97**
Kidbrooke Est. SE3. . . . . 1E **111**
Kidbrooke Gdns. SE3. . . . 5C **96**
Kidbrooke Green
 Nature Reserve. 1E **111**
Kidbrooke Gro. SE3. . . . . 4C **96**
Kidbrooke La. SE9. . . . . . 2F **111**
Kidbrooke Pk. Cl.
 SE3. . . . . 4D **97**
Kidbrooke Pk. Rd.
 SE3. . . . . 4D **97**
Kidbrooke Way SE3. . . . . 5D **97**
Kidderpore Av. NW3. . . . . 1C **44**
Kidderpore Gdns.
 NW3. . . . . 1C **44**
Kierbeck Bus. Complex
 E16. . . . . 3D **83**
Kiffen St.
 EC2. . . . . 3C **10** (3F **63**)
Kilbrennan Ho. *E14*. . . . 5E **67**
 (off Findhorn St.)
KILBURN. 1B **58**
Kilburn Bri. NW6. . . . . . . 5C **44**
Kilburn Ga. NW6. . . . . . . 1D **59**
Kilburn High Rd.
 NW6. . . . . 4B **44**
Kilburn Ho. *NW6*. 1B **58**
 (off Malvern Pl.)
Kilburn La. W9. . . . . 2A **58**
 W10. . . . . 2F **57**
Kilburn Pk. Rd. NW6. . . . 2C **58**
Kilburn Pl. NW6. . . . . 5C **44**
Kilburn Priory NW6. . . . . 5D **45**
Kilburn Sq. NW6. . . . . . . 5C **44**
Kilburn Va. NW6. . . . . . . 5D **45**
Kilburn Va. Est. *NW6*. . . 5D **45**
 (off Kilburn Va.)

Kilby Ct. *SE10*. 4B **82**
 (off School Bank Rd.)
Kildare Ct. *W2*. 5C **58**
 (off Kildare Ter.)
Kildare Gdns. W2. . . . . . . 5C **58**
Kildare Rd. E16. . . . . 4C **68**
Kildare Ter. W2. . . . . 5C **58**
Kildare Wlk. E14. . . . . . . 5C **66**
Kildoran Rd. SW2. . . . . . 3A **104**
Kilgour Rd. SE23. . . . . . . 4A **108**
Kilkie St. SW6. . . . . 5E **87**
Killarney Rd.
 SW18. . . . . 4E **101**
Killearn Rd. SE6. . . . . . . 1F **123**
Killick St. N1. . . . 1F **7** (1B **62**)
Killieser Av. SW2. . . . . . 2A **118**
Killip Cl. E16. . . . . 5B **68**
Killoran Ho. *E14*. 4E **81**
 (off Galbraith St.)
Killowen Rd. E9. . . . . 3F **51**
Killyon Rd. SW8. . . . . 5E **89**
Killyon Ter. SW8. . . . . . . 5E **89**
Kilmaine Rd. SW6. . . . . . 3A **86**
Kilmarsh Rd. W6. . . . . . . 5E **71**
Kilmington Rd.
 SW13. . . . . 2C **84**
Kilmore Ho. *E14*. 5D **67**
 (off Vesey Path)
Kilmorie Rd. SE23. . . . . . 1A **122**
Kilmuir Ho. *SW1*. 5C **74**
 (off Bury St.)
Kiln Ct. E14. . . . . 1B **80**
 (off Newell St.)
Kilner Ho. *E16*. 4D **69**
 (off Freemasons Rd.)
 SE11. . . . . 2C **90**
 (off Clayton St.)
Kilner St. E14. . . . . 4C **66**
Kiln M. SW17. . . . . 5F **115**
Kiln Pl. NW5. . . . . 2C **46**
Kilravock St. W10. . . . . . 2A **58**
Kimbell Gdns. SW6. . . . . 4A **86**
Kimbell Pl. SE3. . . . . 2E **111**
Kimber Ct. *SE1*. 5D **27**
 (off Long La.)
Kimberley Av. E6. . . . . . . 1F **69**
 SE15. . . . . 5D **93**
Kimberley Gdns. N4. . . . 1D **35**
Kimberley Ho. *E14*. 4E **81**
 (off Galbraith St.)
Kimberley Rd. E11. . . . . . 4F **39**
 E16. . . . . 3B **68**
 NW6. . . . . 5A **44**
 SW9. . . . . 5A **90**
Kimber Rd. SW18. . . . . . 5C **100**
Kimble Ho. *NW8*. 3A **60**
 (off Lilestone St.)
Kimble Rd. SW19. . . . . . 5F **115**
Kimbolton Cl. SE12. . . . . 4B **110**
Kimbolton Ct. *SW3*. 5A **74**
 (off Fulham Rd.)
Kimbolton Row *SW3*. . . 5A **74**
 (off Fulham Rd.)
Kimmeridge Rd.
 SE9. . . . . 4F **125**
Kimpton Ho. SW15. . . . . 5C **98**
Kimpton Rd. SE5. . . . . . . 4F **91**
Kinburn St. SE16. . . . . . . 3F **79**
Kincaid Rd. SE15. . . . . . . 3D **93**

Kincardine Gdns. W9. . . . 3C **58**
 (off Harrow Rd.)
Kinder Ho. N1. . . . . 1F **63**
 (off Cranston Est.)
Kindersley Ho. *E1*. 5C **64**
 (off Pinchin St.)
Kinder St. E1. . . . . 5D **65**
Kinefold Ho. N7. . . . . 3A **48**
Kinfauns Rd. SW2. . . . . . 2C **118**
King Alfred Av. SE6. . . . . 4C **122**
 (not continuous)
King & Queen St.
 SE17. . . . . 1E **91**
King & Queen Wharf
 SE16. . . . . 1F **79**
King Arthur Cl. SE15. . . . 3E **93**
King Charles I Island
 WC2. . . . . 1D **23**
King Charles Ct.
 SE17. . . . . 2D **91**
 (off Royal Rd.)
King Charles Ho.
 SW6. . . . . 3D **87**
 (off Wandon Rd.)
King Charles's Ct.
 SE10. . . . . 2E **95**
 (off Park Row)
King Charles St.
 SW1. . . . . 3C **22** (3F **75**)
King Charles Ter. *E1*. . . 1D **79**
 (off Sovereign Cl.)
King Charles Wlk.
 SW19. . . . . 1A **114**
King Ct. E10. . . . . 2D **39**
King David La. E1. . . . . . 1E **79**
Kingdon Ho. *E14*. 4E **81**
 (off Galbraith St.)
Kingdon Rd. NW6. . . . . . 3C **44**
King Edward III M.
 SE16. . . . . 3D **79**
King Edward Bldg.
 EC1. . . . . 5D **63**
King Edward Mans.
 E8. . . . . 5D **51**
 (off Mare St.)
King Edward M.
 SW13. . . . . 4C **84**
King Edward Rd. E10. . . . 3E **39**
King Edwards Mans.
 SW6. . . . . 3C **86**
 (off Fulham Rd.)
King Edward's Rd.
 E9. . . . . 5D **51**
King Edward St.
 EC1. . . . . 2F **17** (5E **63**)
King Edward Wlk.
 SE1. . . . . 5C **24** (4C **76**)
Kingfield St. E14. . . . . . . 5E **81**
Kingfisher Av. E11. . . . . . 1D **41**
Kingfisher Ct. *E14*. 3E **81**
 (off River Barge Cl.)
 SE1. . . . . 4A **26**
 (off Swan St.)
 SW19. . . . . 2F **113**
Kingfisher Ho.
 SW18. . . . . 1E **101**
 W14. . . . . 4B **72**
 (off Melbury Rd.)
Kingfisher M. SE13. . . 2C **108**

Kingfisher Sq. *SE8* **2B 94**
    (off Clyde St.)
Kingfisher Way
NW10 . . . . .3A **42**
King Frederick IX Twr.
SE16 . . . . .4B **80**
King George IV Ct.
SE17 . . . .*1F 91*
    (off Dawes St.)
King George VI Memorial
. . . . .2B **22** (2F **75**)
King George Av. E16 . . .5E **69**
King George St.
SE10 . . . . .3E **95**
Kingham Cl. SW18 . . .5E **101**
W11 . . . . .3A **72**
King Henry's Reach
W6 . . . . .2E **85**
King Henry's Rd.
NW3 . . . . .4A **46**
King Henry's Stairs
E1 . . . . .2D **79**
King Henry St. N16 . . .2A **50**
King Henry's Wlk. N1 . .3A **50**
King Henry Ter. *E1* *1D 79*
    (off Sovereign Cl.)
Kinghorn St.
EC1 . . . . . . .1F **17** (4E **63**)
King Ho. W12 . . . . . . .5D **57**
King James Ct. SE1 . . .4E **25**
King James St.
SE1 . . . . . . .4E **25** (3D **77**)
King John Ct.
EC2 . . . . . . .3E **11** (3A **64**)
King John St. E1 . . . . .4F **65**
King John's Wlk.
SE9 . . . . .5F **111**
    (not continuous)
Kinglake Est. SE17 . . .1A **92**
Kinglake St. SE17 . . . .1A **92**
    (not continuous)
Kinglet Cl. E7 . . . . . . .3C **54**
Kingly Ct. W1 . . . . . . .4A **14**
Kingly St. W1 . . .3F **13** (5E **61**)
Kingsand Rd. SE12 . . .2C **124**
Kings Arms Ct. E1 . . . .4C **64**
Kings Arms Yd.
EC2 . . . . . . .2B **18** (5F **63**)
Kings Av.
BR1: Brom 5B **124**
SW4 . . . . .1F **117**
SW12 . . . . .1F **117**
King's Bench St.
SE1 . . . . . . .3E **25** (3D **77**)
King's Bench Wlk.
EC4 . . . . . . .3C **16** (5C **62**)
Kingsbridge Ct. *E14* . . .*4C 80*
    (off Dockers Tanner Rd.)
NW1 . . . .*4D 47*
    (off Castlehaven Rd.)
Kingsbridge Rd.
W10 . . . . .1F **15**
KINGSBURY GREEN . .1A **28**
Kingsbury Rd. N1 . . . .3A **50**
NW9 . . . . .1A **28**
Kingsbury Ter. N1 . . . .3A **50**
Kingsbury Trad. Est.
NW9 . . . . .1A **28**
Kingsclere Cl. SW15 . .5C **98**

Kingscliffe Gdns.
SW19 . . . . .1B **114**
Kings Cl. E10 . . . . .2D **39**
Kings Coll. Ct. NW3 . . .4A **46**
Kings College London
Chelsea Campus *1F 87*
    (off Chelsea Sq.)
Dental Institute 5F **91**
Hampstead Campus
. . . . .1C **44**
St Thomas' Campus
. . . .*4B 76*
    (off Lambeth Pal. Rd.)
Strand Campus
. . . . .4A **16** (1B **76**)
Waterloo Campus . . .2B **24**
King's College London
School of Medicine
St Thomas' Hospital
Campus 5E **23**
King's Coll. Rd. NW3 . .4A **46**
King's College School of
Medicine & Dentistry
. . . . .5E **91**
Kingscote St.
EC4 . . . . . . .4D **17** (1D **77**)
Kings Ct. E13 . . . . . . .5D **55**
N7 . . . .*4B 48*
    (off Caledonian Rd.)
NW8 . . . .*5B 46*
    (off Prince Albert Rd.)
SE1 . . . . . . .3E **25** (3D **77**)
W6 . . . . .5C **70**
Kings Ct. Nth. SW3 . . .1A **88**
Kingscourt Rd.
SW16 . . . . .3F **117**
Kings Ct. Sth. *SW3* *1A 88*
    (off Chelsea Mnr. Gdns.)
King's Cres. N4 . . . . . .5E **35**
Kings Cres. Est. N4 . . .4E **35**
Kingscroft SW4 . . . . .4A **104**
Kingscroft Rd. NW2 . . .3B **44**
King's Cross Bri. N1 . . .1E **7**
King's Cross Rd.
WC1 . . . . . . .1F **7** (2B **62**)
Kingsdale Gdns. W11 . .2F **71**
Kingsdown Av. W3 . . . .1A **70**
Kingsdown Cl. *SE16* . . .*1D 93*
    (off Masters Dr.)
W10 . . . . .5F **57**
Kingsdown Ho. E8 . . . .2C **50**
Kingsdown Rd. E11 . . .5A **40**
N19 . . . . .4F **33**
Kingsfield Ho. SE9 . . . .3F **125**
Kingsford St. NW5 . . . .2B **46**
King's Gdns. NW6 . . . .4C **44**
Kings Gth. M. SE23 . . .2E **121**
Kingsgate Est. N1 . . . .3A **50**
Kingsgate Ho. SW9 . . .4C **90**
Kingsgate Mans.
WC1 . . . .*1F 15*
    (off Red Lion Sq.)
Kingsgate Pde. SW1 . . .5A **22**
Kingsgate Pl. NW6 . . . .4C **44**
Kingsgate Rd. NW6 . . .4C **44**
Kingsground SE9 . . . . .5F **111**
King's Gro. SE15 . . . . .3D **93**
    (not continuous)

Kings Hall Leisure Cen.
. . . . .2E **51**
Kingshall M. SE13 . . .1E **109**
Kings Hall Rd.
BR3: Beck 5A **122**
Kings Head Pas.
SW4 . . . .*2F 103*
    (off Clapham Pk. Rd.)
Kings Head Theatre *5D 49*
    (off Upper St.)
King's Head Yd.
SE1 . . . . . . .2B **26** (2F **77**)
Kingshill *SE17* *5E 77*
    (off Brandon St.)
Kingshold Rd. E9 . . . . .4E **51**
Kingsholm Gdns.
SE9 . . . . .2F **111**
Kings Ho. SW8 . . . .*3A 90*
    (off Sth. Lambeth Rd.)
SW10 . . . .*2F 87*
    (off Park Wlk.)
King's Ho. Studios
SW10 . . . .*2F 87*
    (off Lamont Rd. Pas.)
Kingshurst Rd.
SE12 . . . . .5C **110**
Kings Keep SW15 . . . .3F **99**
KINGSLAND 3A **50**
Kingsland NW8 . . . . . .5A **46**
Kingsland Grn. E8 . . . .3A **50**
Kingsland High St.
E8 . . . . .3B **50**
Kingsland Pas. E8 . . . .3A **50**
Kingsland Rd.
E2 . . . . .2E **11** (2A **64**)
E8 . . . . .2A **64**
E13 . . . . .2E **69**
Kingsland Shop. Cen.
E8 . . . . .3B **50**
Kingslawn Cl. SW15 . . .3D **99**
Kingsley Ct. NW2 . . . . .3D **43**
Kingsley Flats *SE1* *5A 78*
    (off Old Kent Rd.)
Kingsley Ho. *SW3* *2F 87*
    (off Beaufort St.)
Kingsley Mans. *W14* . . .*2A 86*
    (off Greyhound Rd.)
Kingsley M. E1 . . . . . .1D **79**
W8 . . . . .4D **73**
Kingsley Pl. N6 . . . . . .2C **32**
Kingsley Rd. E7 . . . . . .4C **54**
NW6 . . . . .5B **44**
SW19 . . . . .5D **115**
Kingsley St. SW11 . . .1B **102**
Kingsley Way N2 . . . . .1E **31**
Kings Mall W6 . . . . . . .5E **71**
Kings Mans. *SW3* *2A 88*
    (off Lawrence St.)
Kingsmead Av. NW9 . . .2A **28**
Kingsmead Ct. N6 . . . .2F **33**
Kingsmead Ho. E9 . . . .1A **52**
Kingsmead Rd.
SW2 . . . . .2C **118**
King's Mead Way
E9 . . . . .1A **52**
Kingsmere Cl. SW15 . .1F **99**
Kingsmere Pl. N16 . . . .3F **35**
Kingsmere Rd.
SW19 . . . . .2F **113**

King's M. SW4 . . . . 3A **104**
WC1 . . . . . . 4A **8** (3B **62**)
Kingsmill *NW8* 1F **59**
(off Kingsmill Ter.)
Kingsmill Ho. *SW3* 1A **88**
(off Cale St.)
Kingsmill Ter. NW8 . . . . . . 1F **59**
Kingsnorth Ho. W10 . . . 5F **57**
Kings Pde. NW10 . . . . . . 5E **43**
W12 . . . . 4C **70**
Kings Pas. E11 . . . . 2A **40**
King's Pl.
SE1 . . . . 4F **25** (3E **77**)
King Sq. EC1 . . . . 2F **9** (2E **63**)
King's Quay *SW10* 4E **87**
(off Chelsea Harbour Dr.)
Kings Reach Twr.
SE1 . . . . 1C **24**
Kingsridge SW19 . . . . . . 2A **114**
Kings Rd. E6 . . . . 5E **55**
E11 . . . . 2A **40**
NW10 . . . . 4D **43**
SW3 . . . . 2F **87**
SW6 . . . . 3D **87**
SW10 . . . . 3D **87**
SW14 . . . . 1A **98**
SW19 . . . . 5C **114**
King's Scholars' Pas.
SW1 . . . . 4E **75**
(off Carlisle Pl.)
King's Ter. NW1 . . . . 5E **47**
Kingsthorpe Rd.
SE26 . . . . 4F **121**
Kingston By-Pass
SW15 . . . . 5A **112**
SW20 . . . . 5A **112**
Kingston Ho. NW6 . . . . . 4A **44**
Kingston Ho. E. *SW7* . . . 3A **74**
(off Prince's Ga.)
Kingston Ho. Nth.
SW7 . . . . 3A **74**
(off Prince's Ga.)
Kingston Ho. Sth.
SW7 . . . . 3A **74**
(off Ennismore Gdns.)
Kingston Rd. SW15 . . . 2C **112**
SW19 . . . . 2C **112**
Kingston Sq. SE19 . . . 5F **119**
Kingston University
Kingston Hill 5A **112**
Roehampton Vale Cen.
. . . . 3B **112**
KINGSTON VALE 4A **112**
Kingston Va. SW15 . . . 4A **112**
(not continuous)
Kingstown St. NW1 . . . . 5C **46**
King St. E13 . . . . 3C **68**
EC2 . . . . . . 3A **18** (5E **63**)
SW1 . . . . . . 2A **22** (2E **75**)
W6 . . . . 5C **70**
WC2 . . . . . . 4D **15** (1A **76**)
King St. Cloisters
W6 . . . . 5D **71**
(off Clifton Wlk.)
Kings Wlk. Shop. Cen.
SW3 . . . . 1B **88**
Kingswater Pl.
SW11 . . . . 3A **88**

Kingsway
WC2 . . . . 2F **15** (5B **62**)
Kingsway Mans. *WC1* . . . 5F **7**
(off Red Lion Sq.)
Kingsway Pde. N16 . . . . 5F **35**
(off Albion Rd.)
Kingsway Pl. EC1 . . . . . . 3C **8**
(off Sans Wlk.)
Kingswear Rd. NW5 . . . 5D **33**
Kings Wharf *E8* 5A **50**
(off Kingsland Rd.)
Kingswood E2 . . . . 1E **65**
(off Cyprus St.)
Kingswood Av. NW6 . . . 5A **44**
Kingswood Cl. SW8 . . . 3A **90**
Kingswood Ct. NW6 . . . 4C **44**
(off West End La.)
Kingswood Dr. SE19 . . 4A **120**
Kingswood Est.
SE21 . . . . 4A **120**
Kingswood Pl. SE13 . . . 2A **110**
Kingswood Rd. E11 . . . 2A **40**
SW2 . . . . 4A **104**
Kings Yd. E15 . . . . 3C **52**
SW15 . . . . 1E **99**
(off Lwr. Richmond Rd.)
Kingthorpe Ter.
NW10 . . . . 3A **42**
Kington Ho. NW6 . . . . . 5D **45**
(off Mortimer Cres.)
Kingward Ho. E1 . . . . . . 4C **64**
(off Hanbury St.)
Kingweston Cl. NW2 . . . 5A **30**
King William La.
SE10 . . . . 1A **96**
King William's Ct.
SE10 . . . . 2F **95**
(off Park Row)
King William St.
EC4 . . . . . . 3C **18** (5F **63**)
King William Wlk.
SE10 . . . . 2E **95**
(not continuous)
Kingwood Rd. SW6 . . . 4A **86**
Kinloch Dr. NW9 . . . . . . 2A **28**
Kinloch St. N7 . . . . 5B **34**
Kinnaird Av.
BR1: Brom 5B **124**
Kinnear Rd. W12 . . . . . 3B **70**
Kinnerton Pl. Nth.
SW1 . . . . 4A **20**
Kinnerton Pl. Sth.
SW1 . . . . 4A **20**
Kinnerton St.
SW1 . . . . 4B **20** (3C **74**)
Kinnerton Yd. SW1 . . . . 4B **20**
Kinnoul Rd. W6 . . . . 2A **86**
Kinross Ct. SE16 . . . . . 1B **124**
Kinsale Rd. SE15 . . . . . 1C **106**
Kinsella Gdns.
SW19 . . . . 5D **113**
Kinsham Ho. *E2* 3C **64**
(off Ramsey St.)
Kintore Way SE1 . . . . . . 5B **78**
Kintyre Ct. SW2 . . . . . . 5A **104**
Kintyre Ho. E14 . . . . 2E **81**
(off Coldharbour)
Kinveachy Gdns. SE7 . . 1F **97**
Kinver Rd. SE26 . . . . . . 4E **121**

Kipling Dr. SW19 . . . . . . 5F **115**
Kipling Est.
SE1 . . . . 4C **26** (3F **77**)
Kipling Ho. E16 . . . . 2D **83**
(off Southampton M.)
SE5 . . . . 3F **91**
(off Elmington Est.)
Kipling St.
SE1 . . . . 4C **26** (3F **77**)
Kippington Dr. SE9 . . . 1F **125**
Kirby Est. SE16 . . . . 4D **79**
Kirby Gro.
SE1 . . . . 3D **27** (3A **78**)
Kirby St. EC1 . . . . 5C **8** (4C **62**)
Kirkdale SE26 . . . . 2D **121**
Kirkdale Cnr. SE26 . . . . 4E **121**
Kirkdale Rd. E11 . . . . . . 3A **40**
Kirkeby Ho. *EC1* 5B **8**
(off Leather La.)
Kirkland Ho. *E14* 1D **95**
(off St Davids Sq.)
E14 . . . . 1D **95**
(off Westferry Rd.)
Kirkland Ter.
BR3: Beck 5C **122**
Kirkland Wlk. E8 . . . . . . 3B **50**
Kirkman Pl. W1 . . . . 1B **14**
Kirkmichael Rd. E14 . . . 5E **67**
Kirkside Rd. SE3 . . . . . . 2C **96**
Kirkstall Gdns. SW2 . . 1A **118**
Kirkstall Rd. SW2 . . . . . 1F **117**
Kirkstead Ct. E5 . . . . 1F **51**
Kirkstone *NW1* 1F **5**
(off Harrington St.)
Kirk St. WC1 . . . . 4F **7**
(off Lamb's Conduit St.)
Kirkwall Pl. E2 . . . . 2E **65**
Kirkwood Pl. NW1 . . . . . 4C **46**
Kirkwood Rd. SE15 . . . 5D **93**
Kirtley Ho. SW8 . . . . . . 4E **89**
Kirtley Rd. SE26 . . . . . . 4A **122**
Kirtling St. SW8 . . . . 3E **89**
Kirton Cl. W4 . . . . 5A **70**
Kirton Gdns.
E2 . . . . 2F **11** (2B **64**)
Kirton Lodge SW18 . . . 4D **101**
Kirton Rd. E13 . . . . 1E **69**
Kirwyn Way SE5 . . . . . . 3D **91**
Kitcat Ter. E3 . . . . 2C **66**
Kitchen Ct. E10 . . . . 4D **39**
Kitchener Rd. E7 . . . . . . 3D **55**
Kite Pl. *E2* 2C **64**
(off Lampern Sq.)
Kite Yd. *SW11* 4B **88**
(off Cambridge Rd.)
Kitson Rd. SE5 . . . . 3F **91**
SW13 . . . . 4C **84**
Kittiwake Ct. *SE1* 4A **26**
(off Swan St.)
SE8 . . . . 2B **94**
(off Abinger Gro.)
Kitto Rd. SE14 . . . . 5F **93**
Kiver Rd. N19 . . . . 4F **33**
Klea Av. SW4 . . . . 4E **103**
Kleine Wharf N1 . . . . 5A **50**
Klein's Wharf *E14* 4C **80**
(off Westferry Rd.)
Knapdale Cl. SE23 . . . . 2D **121**
Knapmill Rd. SE6 . . . . . 2C **122**

Knapmill Way SE6 . . . . . 2D **123**
Knapp Cl. NW10 . . . . 3A **42**
Knapp Rd. E3 . . . . 3C **66**
Knapton M. SW17 . . . . 5C **116**
Knaresborough Dr.
  SW18 . . . . 1D **115**
Knaresborough Pl.
  SW5 . . . . 5D **73**
Knatchbull Rd.
  NW10 . . . . 5A **42**
  SE5 . . . . 5D **91**
Knebworth Ho. SW8 . . . 5F **89**
Knebworth Rd. N16 . . . 1A **50**
Kneller Rd. SE4 . . . . . 2A **108**
Knighten St. E1 . . . . . . 2D **79**
Knighthead Point
  E14 . . . . 3C **80**
Knight Ho. SE17 . . . . . 5A **78**
  (off Tatum St.)
Knightland Rd. E5 . . . . 4D **37**
Knightleas Ct. NW2 . . . 3E **43**
Knightleys Ct. E10 . . . 3A **38**
  (off Wellington Rd.)
Knighton Pk. Rd.
  SE26 . . . . 5F **121**
Knighton Rd. E7 . . . . . 5C **40**
Knightrider Ct. EC4. . . . 4E **17**
Knightrider St.
  EC4 . . . . 4E **17** (5D **63**)
Knights Arc. SW1 . . . . . 4A **20**
KNIGHTSBRIDGE 3A **74**
Knightsbridge
  SW1 . . . . 4A **20** (3B **74**)
  SW7 . . . . 3B **74**
Knightsbridge Ct.
  SW1 . . . . 4A **20**
Knightsbridge Grn.
  SW1 . . . . 3B **74**
  (not continuous)
Knights Cl. E9 . . . . 2E **51**
Knights Ct.
  BR1: Brom 3B **124**
Knights Hill SE27 . . . . 5D **119**
Knight's Hill Sq.
  SE27 . . . . 4D **119**
Knights Ho. SW8 . . . . . 3A **90**
  (off Sth. Lambeth Rd.)
  SW10 . . . . 3E **87**
  (off Hortensia Rd.)
Knight's Rd. E16 . . . . . 3C **82**
Knight's Wlk. SE11 . . . 5D **77**
  (not continuous)
Knightswood Ct. N6 . . . 2F **33**
Knivet Rd. SW6 . . . . . . 2C **86**
Knobs Hill Rd. E15 . . . 5D **53**
Knockholt Rd. SE9 . . . 3F **111**
Knoll Ct. SE19 . . . . 5B **120**
  (off Farquhar Rd.)
Knoll Ho. NW8 . . . . 1E **59**
  (off Carlton Hill)
Knoll Rd. SW18 . . . . . . 3E **101**
Knollys Cl. SW16 . . . . 3C **118**
Knolly's Ho. WC1 . . . . . . 3D **7**
  (off Tavistock Pl.)
Knollys Rd. SW16 . . . 3B **118**
Knot Ho. SE1 . . . . 2B **78**
  (off Horselydown La.)
Knottisford St. E2 . . . . 2E **65**
Knotts Grn. M. E10 . . . 1D **39**

Knotts Grn. Rd. E10 . . . 1D **39**
Knowlden Ho. E1 . . . . . . 1E **79**
  (off Cable St.)
Knowle Cl. SW9 . . . . . 1C **104**
Knowles Hill Cres.
  SE13 . . . . 3F **109**
Knowles Ho. SW18 . . . 4D **101**
  (off Neville Gill Cl.)
Knowles Wlk. SW4 . . . . 1E **103**
Knowlton Ho. SW9 . . . . 4C **90**
  (off Cowley Rd.)
Knowsley Rd. SW11 . . . 5B **88**
Knox Ct. SW4 . . . . 5A **90**
Knox Rd. E7 . . . . 3B **54**
Knox St. W1 . . . . 5A **4** (4B **60**)
Knoyle Ho. W14 . . . . 4A **72**
  (off Russell Rd.)
Knoyle St. SE14 . . . . . . 2A **94**
Kohat Rd. SW19 . . . . . 5D **115**
Kossuth St. SE10 . . . . . 1A **96**
Kotree Way SE1 . . . . . . 5C **78**
Kramer M. SW1 . . . . . . 1C **86**
Kreedman Wlk. E8 . . . . 2C **50**
Krupnik Pl. EC2 . . . . . . 2E **11**
Kubrick Bus. Est. E7 . . 1D **55**
  (off Station App.)
Kuhn Way E7 . . . . 2C **54**
Kylemore Cl. E6 . . . . . . 1F **69**
Kylemore Rd. NW6 . . . . 4C **44**
Kylestrome Ho. SW1 . . . 5C **74**
  (off Cundy St.)
Kynance M. SW7 . . . . . 4D **73**
Kynance Pl. SW7 . . . . . 4E **73**
Kynaston Av. N16 . . . . . 5B **36**
Kynaston Rd.
  BR1: Brom 5C **124**
  N16 . . . . 5A **36**
Kyrle Rd. SW11 . . . . . . 4C **102**
Kyverdale Rd. N16 . . . . 2B **36**

L

Laburnum Cl. SE15 . . . . 3E **93**
Laburnum Ct. E2 . . . . . . 5B **50**
  SE16 . . . . 3E **79**
  (off Albion St.)
Laburnum St. E2 . . . . . . 5B **50**
La Caye Apartments
  E14 . . . . 5F **81**
  (off Glenaffric Av.)
Lacewing Cl. E13 . . . . . 2C **68**
Lacey M. E3 . . . . 1C **66**
Lacine Ct. SE16 . . . . . . 3F **79**
  (off Christopher Cl.)
Lackington St.
  EC2 . . . . 5C **10** (4F **63**)
Lackland Ho. SE1 . . . . . 1B **92**
  (off Rowcross St.)
Lacland Ho. SW10 . . . . 3F **87**
  (off Worlds End Est.)
Lacon Ho. WC1 . . . . 5F **7**
  (off Theobalds Rd.)
Lacon Rd. SE22 . . . . . 2C **106**
Lacy Rd. SW15 . . . . 2F **99**
  (not continuous)
Ladas Rd. SE27 . . . . . 4E **119**
Ladbroke Cres. W11 . . . 5A **58**
Ladbroke Gdns. W11 . . 1B **72**

Ladbroke Gro. W10 . . . . 3F **57**
  W11 . . . . 5A **58**
Ladbroke Gro. Ho.
  W11 . . . . 1B **72**
  (off Ladbroke Gro.)
Ladbroke M. W11 . . . . . 2A **72**
Ladbroke Rd. W11 . . . . 2B **72**
Ladbroke Sq. W11 . . . . 1B **72**
Ladbroke Ter. W11 . . . . 1B **72**
Ladbroke Wlk. W11 . . . 2B **72**
Ladlands SE22 . . . . . . 5C **106**
Ladycroft Rd. SE13 . . . 1D **109**
Lady Dock Path
  SE16 . . . . 3A **80**
Ladyfern Ho. E3 . . . . . . 4C **66**
  (off Gail St.)
Lady Margaret Ho.
  SE17 . . . . 2F **91**
  (off Westmoreland Rd.)
Lady Margaret Rd.
  N19 . . . . 2E **47**
  NW5 . . . . 2E **47**
Lady May Ho. SE5 . . . . 3E **91**
  (off Pitman St.)
Lady Micos Almshouses
  E1 . . . . 5E **65**
  (off Aylward St.)
Ladyship Ter. SE22 . . . 5C **106**
Ladysmith Av. E6 . . . . . 1F **69**
Ladysmith Rd. E16 . . . . 2B **68**
Lady Somerset Rd.
  NW5 . . . . 1D **47**
LADYWELL 3D **109**
Ladywell Arena
  Ladywell 4D **109**
Ladywell Cl. SE4 . . . . 3C **108**
Ladywell Hgts. SE4 . . 4B **108**
Ladywell Leisure Cen.
  . . . . 3E **109**
Ladywell Rd. SE4 . . . . 3C **108**
  SE13 . . . . 3C **108**
Ladywell St. E15 . . . . . 5B **54**
LA Fitness
  Aldgate 4F **19**
  (off Portsoken St.)
  Bayswater 1D **73**
  (off Queen's M.)
  Bloomsbury 5F **7**
  (off Conduit St.)
  Golders Green 2B **30**
  Gospel Oak 1D **47**
  Leadenhall 3E **19**
  (off Billiter St.)
  Marylebone
  . . . . 5A **4** (4B **60**)
  Novello 1B **76**
  (off Tavistock St.)
  Piccadilly 5B **14**
  (off Regent St.)
  St Pauls 1F **17**
  (off King Edward St.)
  South Kensington . . . 5A **74**
  Sydenham 4E **121**
  Victoria 5F **21**
  (off Bressenden Pl.)
  West India Quay 1C **80**
Lafone St.
  SE1 . . . . 3F **27** (3B **78**)
Lagado M. SE16 . . . . . . 2F **79**

Lagonier Ho. *EC1* *2A 10*
  (off Dingley Rd.)
Laing St. SE5 . . . . 3E **91**
Lainson St. SW18 . . . . . 5C **100**
Lairdale Cl. SE21 . . . . . 1E **119**
Laird Ho. *SE5* *3E 91*
  (off Redcar St.)
Lairs Cl. N7 . . . . 2A **48**
Laitwood Rd. SW12 . . . 1D **117**
Lakanal *SE5* *4A 92*
  (off Dalwood St.)
Lake Av. BR1: Brom . . 5C **124**
Lake Cl. SW19 . . . . 5B **114**
Lake Ho. *SE1* *4F 25*
  (off Southwark Bri. Rd.)
Lake Ho. Rd. E11 . . . . . 5C **40**
Laker Ct. SW4 . . . . 4A **90**
Laker Ind. Est. *BR3* . . *5A 122*
  (off Kent Ho. La.)
Lake Rd. E10 . . . . 2D **39**
  SW19 . . . . 5B **114**
Laker Pl. SW15 . . . . . . 4A **100**
Lakeside Ct. N4 . . . . 4E **35**
Lakeside Rd. W14 . . . . . 4F **71**
Lakeside Ter. EC2. . . . . . 5A **10**
Lake Vw. Ct. *SW1* *5E 21*
  (off Bressenden Pl.)
Lake Vw. Est. E3 . . . . . 1A **66**
Lakeview Rd. SE27 . . . 5C **118**
Lakis Cl. NW3 . . . . 1E **45**
Laleham Ho. *E2* *3F 11*
  (off Camlet St.)
Laleham Rd. SE6 . . . . . 5E **109**
Lalor St. SW6 . . . . 5A **86**
Lambard Ho. *SE10* *3E 95*
  (off Langdale Rd.)
Lamb Ct. *E14* *1A 80*
  (off Narrow St.)
Lamberhurst Ho.
  SE15 . . . . 2E **93**
Lamberhurst Rd.
  SE27 . . . . 4C **118**
Lambert Jones M.
  EC2 . . . . 5F **9**
Lambert Rd. E16 . . . . . . 5D **69**
  SW2 . . . . 3A **104**
Lambert St. N1 . . . . 4C **48**
LAMBETH 5F **23** (4B **76**)
Lambeth Bri. SE1 . . . . . . 5A **76**
  SW1 . . . . 5A **76**
Lambeth Crematorium
  SW17 . . . . 4E **115**
Lambeth High St.
  SE1 . . . . 5B **76**
Lambeth Hill
  EC4 . . . . . . 4F **17** (1E **77**)
Lambeth Palace
  . . . . 5F **23** (4B **76**)
Lambeth Pal. Rd.
  SE1 . . . . . . 5F **23** (4B **76**)
Lambeth Rd.
  SE1 . . . . . . 5B **24** (5B **76**)
Lambeth Towers
  SE11 . . . . 5B **24**
Lambeth Wlk. SE11 . . . 5B **76**
  (not continuous)
Lambfold Ho. N7 . . . . . 3A **48**
Lamb Ho. *SE5* *3E 91*
  (off Elmington Est.)

Lamb Ho. SE10 . . . . 2E **95**
  (off Haddo St.)
Lamb La. E8 . . . . 4D **51**
Lamble St. NW5 . . . . 2C **46**
Lambolle Pl. NW3 . . . . . 3A **46**
Lambolle Rd. NW3 . . . . 3A **46**
Lambourn Cl. NW5 . . . . 1E **47**
Lambourne Av.
  SW19 . . . . 4B **114**
Lambourne Gro.
  SE16 . . . . 1F **93**
Lambourne Ho. *NW8* . . . *4F 59*
  (off Broadley St.)
  SE16 . . . . 5F **79**
Lambourne Pl. SE3 . . . . 4D **97**
Lambourne Rd. E11 . . . 2E **39**
Lambourn Rd. SW4 . . . 1D **103**
Lambrook Ho. SE15 . . . 4C **92**
Lambrook Ter. SW6 . . . 4A **86**
Lamb's Bldgs.
  EC1 . . . . 4B **10** (3F **63**)
Lamb's Conduit Pas.
  WC1 . . . . 5F **7** (4B **62**)
Lamb's Conduit St.
  WC1 . . . . 4F **7** (3B **62**)
  (not continuous)
Lambscroft Av. SE9 . . . 3E **125**
Lambs Health & Fitness
  . . . . 4B **10**
Lamb's M. N1 . . . . 5D **49**
Lamb's Pas.
  EC1 . . . . 5B **10** (3F **63**)
Lamb St. E1 . . . 5F **11** (4B **64**)
Lambton M. *N19* *3A 34*
  (off Lambton Rd.)
Lambton Pl. W11 . . . . . 1B **72**
Lambton Rd. N19 . . . . . 3A **34**
Lamb Wlk.
  SE1 . . . . . . 4D **27** (3A **78**)
LAMDA Theatre *5C 72*
  (off Logan Pl.)
Lamerock Rd.
  BR1: Brom 4B **124**
Lamerton St. SE8 . . . . . 2C **94**
Lamington St. W6 . . . . . 5D **71**
Lamlash St. SE11 . . . . . 5D **77**
Lamley Ho. *SE10* *3D 95*
  (off Ashburnham Pl.)
Lammas Grn. SE26 . . . 3D **121**
Lammas Rd. E9 . . . . 4F **51**
  E10 . . . . 4A **38**
Lammermoor Rd.
  SW12 . . . . 5D **103**
Lamont Rd. SW10 . . . . . 2F **87**
Lamont Rd. Pas.
  SW10 . . . . *2F 87*
  (off Lamont Rd.)
Lampard Gro. N16 . . . . 3B **36**
Lampern Sq. E2 . . . . . . 2C **64**
Lampeter Cl. NW9 . . . . 1A **28**
Lampeter Sq. W6 . . . . . 2A **86**
Lamplighter Cl. E1 . . . . 3E **65**
Lampmead Rd.
  SE12 . . . . 3B **110**
Lamp Office St.
  WC1 . . . . 4F **7**
Lampton Ho. Cl.
  SW19 . . . . 4F **113**
Lanain Ct. SE12 . . . . . 5B **110**

Lanark Ho. *SE1* *1C 92*
  (off Old Kent Rd.)
Lanark Mans. *W9* *3E 59*
  (off Lanark Rd.)
  W12 . . . . *3E 71*
  (off Pennard Rd.)
Lanark M. W9 . . . . 2E **59**
Lanark Pl. W9 . . . . 3E **59**
Lanark Rd. W9 . . . . 1D **59**
Lanark Sq. E14 . . . . 4D **81**
Lanbury Rd. SE15 . . . . 2F **107**
Lancashire Ct. W1 . . . . 4E **13**
Lancaster Av.
  SE27 . . . . 2D **119**
  SW19 . . . . 5F **113**
Lancaster Cl. N1 . . . . . . 4A **50**
  W2 . . . . *1D 73*
  (off St Petersburgh Pl.)
Lancaster Ct. SE27 . . . 2D **119**
  SW6 . . . . 3B **86**
  W2 . . . . *1E 73*
  (off Lancaster Ga.)
Lancaster Dr. E14 . . . . . 2E **81**
  NW3 . . . . 3A **46**
Lancaster Gdns.
  SW19 . . . . 5A **114**
Lancaster Ga. W2 . . . . . 1E **73**
Lancaster Gro. NW3 . . . 3F **45**
Lancaster Hall *E16* *2C 82*
  (off Wesley Av.,
  not continuous)
Lancaster House *3F 21*
Lancaster Lodge
  11 . . . . *5A 58*
  (off Lancaster Rd.)
Lancaster M. SW18 . . . 3D **101**
  W2 . . . . *1E 73*
Lancaster Pl.
  SW19 . . . . 5F **113**
  WC2 . . . . . . 4F **15** (1B **76**)
Lancaster Rd. E7 . . . . . 4C **54**
  E11 . . . . 4A **40**
  N4 . . . . 2B **34**
  NW10 . . . . 2C **42**
  SW19 . . . . 5F **113**
  W11 . . . . 5A **58**
Lancaster Stables
  NW3 . . . . 3A **46**
Lancaster St.
  SE1 . . . . . . 4D **25** (3D **77**)
Lancaster Ter. W2 . . . . 1F **73**
Lancaster Wlk. W2 . . . . 2E **73**
Lancefield Ct. W10 . . . 1A **58**
Lancefield Ho.
  SE15 . . . . 2D **107**
Lancefield St. W10 . . . . 2B **58**
Lancell St. N16 . . . . 4B **36**
Lancelot Pl. SW7 . . . . . 3B **74**
Lancer Sq. W8 . . . . 3D **73**
Lancey Cl. SE7 . . . . 5F **83**
Lanchester Ct. *W2* *5B 60*
  (off Seymour St.)
Lanchester Rd. N6 . . . . 1B **32**
Lanchester Way
  SE14 . . . . 4E **93**
Lancing St.
  NW1 . . . . . . 2B **6** (2F **61**)
Lancresse Ct. *N1* *5A 50*
  (off De Beauvoir Est.)

Landale Ho. *SE16*. 4E **79**
  (off Lower Rd.)
Landcroft Rd. *SE22* . . 3B **106**
Landells Rd. *SE22* 4B **106**
Landford Rd. *SW15* 1E **99**
Landgrove Rd.
  SW19 . . . . 5C **114**
Landin Ho. *E14*. 5C **66**
  (off Thomas Rd.)
Landleys Fld. *N7* 2F **47**
  (off Long Mdw.)
Landmann Ho. *SE16* . . . 5D **79**
  (off Rennie Est.)
Landmann Way *SE14* . . . 1F **93**
Landmark Hgts. *E5*. 1A **52**
Landmark Ho. *W6* 1E **85**
  (off Hammersmith Bri. Rd.)
Landon Pl.
  SW1. . . . . 5A **20** (4B **74**)
Landon's Cl. *E14* 2E **81**
Landon Wlk. *E14* 1D **81**
Landor Ho. *SE5*. 3F **91**
  (off Elmington Est.)
  W2 . . . . 4C **58**
  (off Brunel Est.)
Landor Rd. *SW9*. 1A **104**
Landor Theatre 1A **104**
Landor Wlk. *W12* 3C **70**
Landrake *NW1* 5E **47**
  (off Plender St.)
Landridge Rd. *SW6* 5B **86**
Landrock Rd. *N8* 1A **34**
Landseer Ho. *NW8* 3F **59**
  (off Frampton St.)
  SW1 . . . . 5F **75**
  (off Herrick St.)
  SW11 . . . . 4C **88**
Landseer Rd. *N19* 5A **34**
  (not continuous)
Landulph Ho. *SE11* 1C **90**
  (off Kennings Way)
Landward Ct. *W1* 5A **60**
  (off Harrowby St.)
Lane, The *NW8* 1E **59**
  SE3. . . . . 1C **110**
Lane Cl. *NW2* 5D **29**
Lane End *SW15* 4F **99**
Lanercost Cl. *SW2* 2C **118**
Lanercost Rd. *SW2* . . . 2C **118**
Lanesborough Ct. *N1*. . . 1D **11**
  (off Fanshaw St.)
Lanesborough Pl.
  SW1 . . . . 3C **20**
Laneway *SW15* 3D **99**
Laney Ho. *EC1* 5B **8**
  (off Leather La.)
Lanfranc Rd. *E3* 1A **66**
Lanfrey Pl. *W14* 1B **86**
Langbourne Av. *N6*. . . . 4C **32**
Langbourne Ct. *E17* . . . 1A **38**
Langbourne Mans.
  N6. . . . . 4C **32**
Langbourne Pl. *E14* . . . 1D **95**
Langbrook Rd. *SE3* 1F **111**
Langdale *NW1* 1F **5**
  (off Stanhope Pl.)
Langdale Cl. *SE17* 2E **91**
Langdale Ho. *SW1* 1E **89**
  (off Churchill Gdns.)

Langdale Rd. *SE10* 3E **95**
Langdale St. *E1* 5D **65**
Langdon Ct. *EC1* 1E **9**
  (off City Rd.)
  NW10 . . . . 5A **42**
Langdon Ho. *E14* 5E **67**
Langdon Pk. Rd. *N6* . . . 2E **33**
Langdon Way *SE1* 5C **78**
Langford Cl. *E8* 2C **50**
  NW8 . . . . 1E **59**
Langford Ct. *NW8* 1E **59**
  (off Abbey Rd.)
Langford Grn. *SE5* 1A **106**
Langford Ho. *SE8* 2C **94**
Langford M. *N1* 4C **48**
Langford Pl. *NW8* 1E **59**
Langford Rd. *SW6* 5D **87**
Langham Mans.
  SW5. . . . . 1D **87**
  (off Earl's Ct. Sq.)
Langham Pl.
  W1. . . . . 1E **13** (4D **61**)
  W4 . . . . 2A **84**
Langham St.
  W1. . . . . 1E **13** (4D **61**)
Langholm Cl. *SW12* . . . 5F **103**
Langhorne Ct. *NW8* 4F **45**
  (off Dorman Way)
Lang Ho. *SW8* 3A **90**
  (off Hartington Rd.)
Langland Gdns. *NW3*. . . 2D **45**
Langland Ho. *SE5*. 3F **91**
  (off Edmund St.)
Langler Rd. *NW10* 1E **57**
Langley Cl.
  WC2. . . . . . . 4D **15** (1A **76**)
Langley Cres. *E11* 2E **41**
Langley Dr. *E11* 2D **41**
Langley Ho. *W2* 4C **58**
  (off Alfred Rd.)
Langley La. *SW8* 2B **90**
Langley Mans. *SW8*. . . . 2B **90**
  (off Langley La.)
Langley St.
  WC2 . . . . 3D **15** (5A **62**)
Langmead St. *SE27*. . . . 4D **119**
Langmore Ho. *E1*. 5C **64**
  (off Stutfield St.)
Langport Ho. *SW9* 5D **91**
Langroyd Rd. *SW17*. . . . 2B **116**
Langside Av. *SW15* 2C **98**
Langston Hughes Cl.
  SE24. . . . . 2D **105**
Lang St. *E1* 3E **65**
Langthorn Ct.
  EC2. . . . . 2B **18** (5F **63**)
Langthorne Ct.
  BR1: Brom 4E **123**
Langthorne Rd. *E11* . . . 5E **39**
Langthorne St. *SW6*. . . . 3F **85**
Langton Cl.
  WC1 . . . . 3A **8** (3B **62**)
Langton Ho. *SE11* 5B **76**
  (off Lambeth Wlk.)
Langton Pl. *SW18* 1C **114**
Langton Ri. *SE23* 5D **107**
Langton Rd. *NW2*. 5E **29**
  SW9 . . . . 3D **91**
Langton St. *SW10* 2E **87**

Langton Way *SE3*. 4B **96**
Langtry Pl. *SW6*. 2C **86**
Langtry Rd. *NW8* 5D **45**
Langtry Wlk. *NW8* 5D **45**
Lanhill Rd. *W9*. 3C **58**
Lanier Rd. *SE13* 4F **109**
Lannoy Point *SW6* 3A **86**
  (off Pellant Rd.)
Lanrick Ho. *E14* 5F **67**
  (off Lanrick Rd.)
Lanrick Rd. *E14* 5F **67**
Lansbury Est. *E14* 5D **67**
Lansbury Gdns. *E14*. . . . 5F **67**
Lanscombe Wlk.
  SW8 . . . . 4A **90**
Lansdell Ho. *SW2* 4C **104**
  (off Tulse Hill)
Lansdowne Ct. *W11*. . . . 1A **72**
  (off Lansdowne Ri.)
Lansdowne Cres.
  W11 . . . . 1A **72**
Lansdowne Dr. *E8* 3C **50**
Lansdowne Gdns.
  SW8 . . . . 4A **90**
Lansdowne Grn. Est.
  SW8 . . . . 4A **90**
Lansdowne Gro.
  NW10 . . . . 1A **42**
Lansdowne Hill
  SE27 . . . . 3D **119**
Lansdowne Ho. *W11*. . . . 2B **72**
  (off Ladbroke Rd.)
Lansdowne La. *SE7* 2F **97**
Lansdowne M. *SE7*. 1F **97**
  W11 . . . . 2B **72**
Lansdowne Pl.
  SE1. . . . . 5C **26** (4F **77**)
Lansdowne Ri. *W11*. . . . 1A **72**
Lansdowne Rd. *E11*. . . . 4B **40**
  E17 . . . . 1C **38**
  W11 . . . . 1A **72**
Lansdowne Row
  W1. . . . . 1E **21** (2D **75**)
Lansdowne Ter.
  WC1 . . . . 4E **7** (3A **62**)
Lansdowne Wlk.
  W11 . . . . 2B **72**
Lansdowne Way *SW8*. . . 4F **89**
Lansdowne Wood Cl.
  SE27 . . . . 3D **119**
Lansdowne Workshops
  SE7 . . . . 1E **97**
Lansdown Rd. *E7* 4E **55**
Lantern Cl. *SW15*. 2C **98**
Lanterns Ct. *E14* 3D **81**
Lant Ho. *SE1*. 4F **25**
  (off Toulmin St.)
Lant St. *SE1*. 3F **25** (3E **77**)
Lanvanor Rd. *SE15* 5E **93**
Lanyard Ho. *SE8* 5B **80**
Lapford Cl. *W9*. 3B **58**
Lapse Wood Wlk.
  SE23. . . . . 1D **121**
Lapwing Ct. *SE1*. 4A **26**
  (off Swan St.)
Lapwing Twr. *SE8* 2B **94**
  (off Taylor Cl.)
Lapworth Ct. *W2* 4D **59**
  (off Delamere Ter.)

Lara Cl. SE13 . . . . 4E 109
Larch Av. W3 . . . . 2A 70
Larch Cl. E13 . . . . 3D 69
N19 . . . . 4E 33
SE8 . . . . 2B 94
SW12 . . . . 2D 117
Larch Ct. SE1 . . . . 4D 27
    (off Royal Oak Yd.)
W9 . . . . 4C 58
    (off Admiral Wlk.)
Larch Ho. SE16 . . . . . . 3E 79
    (off Ainsty Est.)
W10 . . . . 3A 58
    (off Rowan Wlk.)
Larch Rd. E10 . . . . 4C 38
NW2 . . . . 1E 43
Larcom St. SE17 . . . . . 5E 77
Larden Rd. W3 . . . . 2A 70
Larissa St. SE17 . . . . . 1F 91
Larkbere Rd. SE26 . . . 4A 122
Larkhall La. SW4 . . . . . 5F 89
Larkhall Ri. SW4 . . . . . 1E 103
    (not continuous)
Lark Row E2 . . . . 5E 51
Larkspur Cl. E6 . . . . . . 4F 69
Larnach Rd. W6 . . . . . . 2F 85
Larpent Av. SW15 . . . . 3E 99
Lascelles Cl. E11 . . . . . 4F 39
Lascelles Ho. NW1 . . . . 3A 60
    (off Harewood Av.)
Lassell St. SE10 . . . . . . 1F 95
Lasseter Pl. SE3 . . . . . . 2A 96
Latchmere Leisure Cen.
    . . . . 5B 88
Latchmere Pas.
    SW11 . . . . 5A 88
Latchmere Rd. SW11 . . 5B 88
Latchmere St. SW11 . . 5B 88
Latham Ct. SW5 . . . . . . 5C 72
    (off W. Cromwell Rd.)
Latham Ho. E1 . . . . 5F 65
    (off Chudleigh St.)
Latimer Ho. E9 . . . . 3F 51
W11 . . . . 1B 72
    (off Kensington Pk. Rd.)
Latimer Ind. Est.
    W10 . . . . 5E 57
Latimer Pl. W10 . . . . . . 5E 57
Latimer Rd. E7 . . . . 1D 55
N15 . . . . 1A 36
W10 . . . . 4E 57
    (not continuous)
Latona Ct. SW9 . . . . . . 3C 90
    (off Caldwell St.)
Latona Rd. SE15 . . . . . 2C 92
Lattimer Pl. W4 . . . . . . 3A 84
Latvia St. SE17 . . . . . . 1E 91
    (off Sutherland Sq.)
Latymer Ct. W6 . . . . . . 5F 71
Latymer Upper School
    Sports Cen. 1C 84
Lauderdale House 3D 33
Lauderdale Ho. SW9 . . 4C 90
    (off Gosling Way)
Lauderdale Mans.
    W9 . . . . 2D 59
    (off Lauderdale Rd.,
        not continuous)
Lauderdale Pde. W9 . . 3D 59

Lauderdale Pl. EC2 . . . . 5F 9
    (off Beech St.)
Lauderdale Rd. W9 . . . 2D 59
Lauderdale Twr. EC2 . . . 5F 9
Laud St. SE11 . . . . 1B 90
Launcelot Rd.
    BR1: Brom 4C 124
Launcelot St.
    SE1 . . . . 4B 24 (3C 76)
Launceston Pl. W8 . . . . 4E 73
Launch St. E14 . . . . . . 4E 81
Laundress La. N16 . . . . 5C 36
Laundry La. N1 . . . . 5E 49
Laundry M. SE23 . . . . 5A 108
Laundry Rd. W6 . . . . . . 2A 86
Laura Pl. E5 . . . . 1E 51
Laura Ter. N4 . . . . 4D 35
Laurel Bank Gdns.
    SW6 . . . . 5B 86
Laurelbrook SE6 . . . . 3A 124
Laurel Cl. N19 . . . . 4E 33
SW17 . . . . 5A 116
Laurel Gro. SE26 . . . . 4F 121
Laurel Ho. SE8 . . . . . . 2B 94
Laurel Rd. SW13 . . . . . 5C 84
Laurels, The NW10 . . . 5D 43
Laurel St. E8 . . . . 3B 50
Laurence Cl. E10 . . . . . 2D 39
Laurence M. W12 . . . . . 3C 70
Laurence Pountney Hill
    EC4 . . . . 4B 18 (1F 77)
Laurence Pountney La.
    EC4 . . . . 4B 18 (1F 77)
Laurie Gro. SE14 . . . . . 4A 94
Laurie Ho. SE1 . . . . 5E 25
    (off St George's Rd.)
W8 . . . . 2C 72
    (off Airlie Gdns.)
Laurier Rd. NW5 . . . . . 5D 33
Lauriston Ho. E9 . . . . . . 4E 51
    (off Lauriston St.)
Lauriston Rd. E9 . . . . . . 4E 51
SW19 . . . . 5F 113
Lausanne Rd. SE15 . . . 4E 93
Lavell St. N16 . . . . 1F 49
Lavender Cl. SW3 . . . . . 2F 87
Lavender Gdns.
    SW11 . . . . 2B 102
Lavender Gro. E8 . . . . . 4C 50
Lavender Hill SW11 . . 2A 102
Lavender Ho. SE16 . . . . 2F 79
    (off Rotherhithe St.)
Lavender Pond Nature Res.
    . . . . 2A 80
Lavender Rd. SE16 . . . . 2A 80
SW11 . . . . 1F 101
Lavender Sq. E11 . . . . . 5F 39
Lavender St. E15 . . . . . 3A 54
Lavender Sweep
    SW11 . . . . 2B 102
Lavender Ter. SW11 . . 1A 102
Lavender Wlk.
    SW11 . . . . 2B 102
Lavendon Ho. NW8 . . . 3A 60
    (off Paveley St.)
Lavengro Rd. SE27 . . . 2E 119
Lavenham Rd.
    SW18 . . . . 2B 114
Lavers Rd. N16 . . . . . . 5A 36

Laverstoke Gdns.
    SW15 . . . . 5B 98
Laverton M. SW5 . . . . . 5D 73
Laverton Pl. SW5 . . . . . 5D 73
Lavina Gro. N1 . . . . 1B 62
Lavington Cl. E9 . . . . . . 3B 52
Lavington St.
    SE1 . . . . 2E 25 (2D 77)
Lavisham Ho.
    BR1: Brom 5D 125
Lawes Ho. W10 . . . . . . 2B 58
    (off Lancefield St.)
Lawford Rd. N1 . . . . . . 4A 50
NW5 . . . . 3E 47
Lawfords Wharf NW1 . . 4E 47
    (off Lyme St.)
Lawless Ho. E14 . . . . . . 1E 81
    (off Bazely St.)
Lawless St. E14 . . . . . . 1D 81
Lawley St. E5 . . . . 1E 51
Lawn Dr. E7 . . . . 1F 55
Lawn La. SW8 . . . . 2A 90
Lawn Rd. NW3 . . . . 2B 46
Lawns, The SE3 . . . . . 1B 110
SW19 . . . . 5B 114
Lawnside SE3 . . . . 2B 110
Lawn Ter. SE3 . . . . . . 1A 110
Lawrence Av. NW10 . . 5A 42
Lawrence Bldgs. N16 . . 5B 36
Lawrence Cl. E3 . . . . . . 2C 66
W12 . . . . 1D 71
Lawrence Ct. N16 . . . . 5B 36
    (off Smalley Rd. Est.)
Lawrence Ho. SW1 . . . . 5F 75
    (off Cureton St.)
Lawrence La.
    EC2 . . . . 2A 18 (5E 63)
Lawrence Mans.
    SW1 . . . . 1D 89
    (off Sutherland St.)
SW3 . . . . 2A 88
    (off Lawrence St.)
Lawrence Pl. N1 . . . . . . 5A 48
    (off Brydon Wlk.)
Lawrence Rd. E6 . . . . . 5F 55
E13 . . . . 5D 55
Lawrence St. E16 . . . . . 4B 68
SW3 . . . . 2A 88
Lawrence Trad. Est.
    SE10 . . . . 5A 82
Lawrie Pk. Av.
    SE26 . . . . 5D 121
Lawrie Pk. Cres.
    SE26 . . . . 5D 121
Lawrie Pk. Gdns.
    SE26 . . . . 4D 121
Lawrie Pk. Rd.
    SE26 . . . . 5D 121
Lawson Cl. E16 . . . . . . 4E 69
SW19 . . . . 3F 113
Lawson Ct. N4 . . . . 3B 34
    (off Lorne Rd.)
Lawson Ho. W12 . . . . . 1D 71
    (off White City Est.)
Law St. SE1 . . . . . 5C 26 (4F 77)
Lawton Rd. E3 . . . . 2A 66
    (not continuous)
E10 . . . . 3E 39

Laxfield Ct. E8 . . . . 5C 50
(off Pownall Rd.)
Laxford Ho. SW1 . . . . . . 5C 74
(off Cundy St.)
Laxley Cl. SE5 . . . . 3D 91
Laxton Pl.
NW1 . . . . 3E 5 (3D 61)
Layard Rd. SE16 . . . . . 5D 79
Layard Sq. SE16 . . . . . 5D 79
Laybourne Ho. E14 . . . . 3C 80
(off Admirals Way)
Laycock St. N1 . . . . 3C 48
Layfield Cl. NW4 . . . . . . 2D 29
Layfield Cres. NW4 . . . . 2D 29
Layfield Ho. SE10 . . . . . 1C 96
(off Kemsing Rd.)
Layfield Rd. NW4 . . . . . 2D 29
Laystall Ct. WC1 . . . . . . 4B 8
(off Mt. Pleasant)
Laystall St.
EC1 . . . . 4B 8 (3C 62)
Layton's Bldgs.
SE1 . . . . 3B 26 (3F 77)
Layzell Wlk. SE9 . . . . . . 1F 125
Lazenby Ct. WC2 . . . . . . 4D 15
Leabank Sq. E9 . . . . 3D 52
Leabank Vw. N15 . . . . . . 1C 36
Lea Bon Ct. E15 . . . . 5B 54
(off Plaistow Gro.)
Leabourne Rd. N16 . . . . 2C 36
LEA BRIDGE 5F 37
Lea Bri. Ind. Cen.
E10 . . . . 3A 38
Lea Bri. Rd. E5 . . . . 5E 37
E10 . . . . 5E 37
Lea Ct. E13 . . . . 2C 68
Leacroft Av. SW12 . . . . 5B 102
Leadale Rd. N15 . . . . . . 1C 36
N16 . . . . 1C 36
Leadenhall Mkt.
EC3 . . . . 3D 19 (5A 64)
Leadenhall Pl.
EC3 . . . . 3D 19 (5A 64)
Leadenhall St.
EC3 . . . . 3D 19 (5A 64)
Leadenham Ct. E3 . . . . . 3C 66
Leaf Gro. SE27 . . . . . . 5C 118
Leafy Oak Rd.
SE12 . . . . 4E 125
Leagrave St. E5 . . . . 5E 37
Lea Hall Gdns. E10 . . . . 3C 38
Lea Hall Rd. E10 . . . . . . 3C 38
Lea Ho. NW8 . . . . 3A 60
(off Salisbury St.)
Leahurst Rd. SE13 . . . . 3F 109
(not continuous)
LEA INTERCHANGE . . . 2C 52
Leake Ct.
SE1 . . . . 4A 24 (3B 76)
Leake St.
SE1 . . . . 3A 24 (3B 76)
(not continuous)
Lealand Rd. N15 . . . . . . 1B 36
Leamington Av.
BR1: Brom 5E 125
E17 . . . . 1C 38
Leamington Cl.
BR1: Brom 4E 125

Leamington Ho. W11 . . . 4B 58
(off Leamington Rd. Vs.)
Leamington Rd. Vs.
W11 . . . . 4B 58
Leamore St. W6 . . . . 5E 71
LEAMOUTH 1A 82
Leamouth Rd. E6 . . . . . . 4F 69
E14 . . . . 5F 67
Leander Ct. SE8 . . . . . . 4C 94
Leander Rd. SW2 . . . . . 4B 104
Lea Pk. Trad. Est.
E10 . . . . 2B 38
Leaside Rd. E5 . . . . 3E 37
Leasowes Rd. E10 . . . . . 3C 38
Lea Sq. E3 . . . . 5B 52
Leathardale St. E1 . . . . . 3E 65
(Harpley Sq.)
E1 . . . . 2F 65
(Portelet Rd.)
Leather Gdns. E15 . . . . . 5A 54
Leatherhead Cl. N16 . . . 3B 36
Leather La.
EC1 . . . . 5B 8 (4C 62)
(not continuous)
Leathermarket, The
SE1 . . . . 4D 27
Leathermarket Ct.
SE1 . . . . 4D 27 (3A 78)
Leathermarket St.
SE1 . . . . 4D 27 (3A 78)
Leather St. E1 . . . . 1F 79
Leathwaite Rd.
SW11 . . . . 2B 102
Leathwell Rd. SE8 . . . . . 5D 95
Lea Vw. Ho. E5 . . . . 3D 37
Leaway E10 . . . . 3F 37
Lebanon Gdns.
SW18 . . . . 4C 100
Lebanon Rd. SW18 . . . 3C 100
Lebrun Sq. SE3 . . . . . . 2D 111
Lebus Ho. NW8 . . . . 1A 60
(off Cochrane St.)
Lechmere Rd. NW2 . . . . 3D 43
Leckford Rd. SW18 . . . . 2E 115
Leckhampton Pl.
SW2 . . . . 5C 104
Lecky St. SW7 . . . . 1F 87
Leclair Ho. SE3 . . . . 1D 111
Leconfield Av. SW13 . . . 1B 98
Leconfield Ho. SE5 . . . . 2A 106
Leconfield Rd. N5 . . . . . 1F 49
Le Cordon Bleu London
Culinary Arts Institute
. . . . 1C 12
(off Marylebone La.)
Leda Ct. SW9 . . . . 3C 90
(off Caldwell St.)
Ledam Ho. EC1 . . . . 5B 8
(off Bourne Est.)
Ledbury Ho. SE22 . . . . . 1A 106
W11 . . . . 5B 58
(off Colville Rd.)
Ledbury M. Nth. W11 . . . 1C 72
Ledbury M. W. W11 . . . . 1C 72
Ledbury Rd. W11 . . . . . 5B 58
Ledbury St. SE15 . . . . . 3C 92
LEE 4C 110
Lee Bri. SE13 . . . . 1E 109

Lee Chu. St. SE13 . . . . . 2A 110
Lee Conservancy Rd.
E9 . . . . 2B 52
Lee Ct. SE13 . . . . 2F 109
(off Lee High Rd.)
Leeds Ct. EC1 . . . . 3D 9
(off St John St.)
Leefern Rd. W12 . . . . . . 3C 70
Leegate SE12 . . . . 3B 110
LEE GREEN 3B 110
Lee High Rd. SE12 . . . . 1E 109
SE13 . . . . 1E 109
Lee Ho. EC2 . . . . 1A 18
(off Monkwell Sq.)
Leeke St. WC1 . . . 1F 7 (2B 62)
Leeland Way NW10 . . . . 1B 42
Lee Pk. SE3 . . . . 2B 110
Leerdam Dr. E14 . . . . . . 4E 81
Lee Rd. SE3 . . . . 1B 110
Lees Ct. W1 . . . . 4B 12
(off Lees Pl.)
Lees Ho. SE17 . . . . 1F 91
(off Merrow St.)
Leeside Ct. SE16 . . . . . . 2F 79
(off Rotherhithe St.)
Leeside Cres. NW11 . . . 1A 30
Leeson Rd. SE24 . . . . . 2C 104
Lees Pl. W1 . . . 4B 12 (1C 74)
Lee St. E8 . . . . 5B 50
Lee Ter. SE3 . . . . 1A 110
SE13 . . . . 1A 110
Lee Valley Cycle Circuit
. . . . 2D 53
Lee Valley Ice Cen. 4F 37
Lee Valley Sports Cen.
. . . . 1D 53
Leeve Ho. W10 . . . . 2B 58
(off Lancefield St.)
Leeward Ct. E1 . . . . 1C 78
Leeward Gdns.
SW19 . . . . 5A 114
Leeward Ho. N1 . . . . 5A 50
(off New Era Est.)
Leeway SE8 . . . . 1B 94
Leewood Cl. SE12 . . . . . 4B 110
Lefevre Wlk. E3 . . . . 1C 66
Leff Ho. NW6 . . . . 5A 44
Lefroy Ho. SE1 . . . . 4F 25
(off Southwark Bri. Rd.)
Lefroy Rd. W12 . . . . 3B 70
Legard Rd. N5 . . . . 5D 35
Legatt Rd. SE9 . . . . 3F 111
Leggatt Rd. E15 . . . . . . 1E 67
Legge St. SE13 . . . . 3E 109
Leghorn Rd. NW10 . . . . 1B 56
Legion Cl. N1 . . . . 4C 48
Legion Ter. E3 . . . . 5B 52
Leicester Ct. W9 . . . . . . 4C 58
(off Elmfield Way)
WC2 . . . . 4C 14
Leicester Flds. WC2 . . . 5C 14
Leicester Ho. SW9 . . . . 1D 105
(off Loughborough Rd.)
Leicester Pl.
WC2 . . . . 4C 14 (1F 75)
Leicester Rd. E11 . . . . . 1D 41
NW10 . . . . 4A 42
Leicester Sq.
WC2 . . . . 5C 14 (1F 75)

Leicester St.
WC2 . . . . 4C **14** (1F **75**)
Leigham Av. SW16 . . . . 3A **118**
Leigham Cl. SW16 . . . . 3B **118**
Leigham Ct. Rd.
SW16 . . . . 2A **118**
Leigham Hall Pde.
SW16 . . . . *3A 118*
(off Streatham High Rd.)
Leigham Va. SW2 . . . . 3B **118**
SW16 . . . . 3B **118**
Leigh Gdns. NW10 . . . 1E **57**
Leigh Orchard Cl.
SW16 . . . . 3B **118**
Leigh Pl. EC1 . . 5B **8** (4C **62**)
Leigh Rd. E10 . . . . 2E **39**
N5 . . . . 1D **49**
Leigh St. WC1 . . 2D **7** (2A **62**)
Leighton Cres. NW5 . . . 2E **47**
Leighton Gdns.
NW10 . . . . 1D **57**
Leighton Gro. NW5 . . . 2E **47**
Leighton Ho. *SW1* . . . *5F 75*
(off Herrick St.)
Leighton House Art
Gallery & Mus. 4B **72**
Leighton Mans. *W14* . . *2A 86*
(off Greyhound Rd.)
Leighton Pl. NW5 . . . . 2E **47**
Leighton Rd. NW5 . . . . 2E **47**
Leila Parnell Pl. SE7 . . 2E **97**
Leinster Gdns. W2 . . . 5E **59**
Leinster M. W2 . . . . . . 1E **73**
Leinster Pl. W2 . . . . . . 5E **59**
Leinster Sq. W2 . . . . . . 5C **58**
(not continuous)
Leinster Ter. W2 . . . . . 1E **73**
Leitch Ho. *NW8* *4F 45*
(off Hilgrove Rd.)
Leithcote Gdns.
SW16 . . . . 4B **118**
Leithcote Path
SW16 . . . . 3B **118**
Leith Mans. *W9* *2D 59*
(off Grantully Rd.)
Leith Yd. *NW6* *5C 44*
(off Quex Rd.)
Lelitia Cl. E8 . . . . 5C **50**
Leman Pas. *E1* *5C 64*
(off Leman St.)
Leman St. E1 . . . . 5B **64**
Le May Av. SE12 . . . . . 3D **125**
Lemmon Rd. SE10 . . . . 2A **96**
Lemna Rd. E11 . . . . 2B **40**
Le Moal Ho. *E1* *4E 65*
(off Stepney Way)
Lemsford Ct. N15 . . . . 1C **36**
Lemsford Ct. N4 . . . . . 4E **35**
Lemuel St. SW18 . . . . . 4E **101**
Lena Gdns. W6 . . . . . . 4E **71**
Lenanton Steps *E14* . . *3C 80*
(off Manilla St.)
Lendal Ter. SW4 . . . . . 1F **103**
Len Freeman Pl.
SW6 . . . . 2B **86**
W6 . . . . *5B 70*
(off Goldhawk Rd.)
Lenham Ho. *SE1* *4C 26*
(off Long La.)

Lenham Rd. SE12 . . . . 2B **110**
Lennard Rd. SE20 . . . . 5F **121**
Lennon Rd. NW2 . . . . . 2E **43**
Lennox Gdns. NW10 . . 1B **42**
SW1 . . . . 4B **74**
Lennox Gdns. M.
SW1 . . . . 4B **74**
Lennox Lewis Cen.
E5 . . . . *4E 37*
(off Theydon Rd.)
Lennox Rd. E17 . . . . . . 1B **38**
N4 . . . . 4B **34**
Lens Rd. E7 . . . . 4E **55**
Lenthall Ho. *SW1* *1E 89*
(off Churchill Gdns.)
Lenthall Rd. E8 . . . . . . 4C **50**
Lenthorp Rd. SE10 . . . 5B **82**
Lentmead Rd.
BR1: Brom 3B **124**
Len Williams Ct.
NW6 . . . . 1C **58**
Leof Cres. SE6 . . . . . . 5D **123**
Leonard Ct. W8 . . . . . . 4C **72**
WC1 . . . . 3C **6** (3F **61**)
Leonard Pl. N16 . . . . . . 1A **50**
Leonard Rd. E7 . . . . . . 1C **54**
Leonard St.
EC2 . . . . 3C **10** (3F **63**)
Leonora Ho. *W9* *3E 59*
(off Lanark Rd.)
Leontine Cl. SE15 . . . . 3C **92**
Leopards Ct. EC1 . . . . . 5B **8**
Leopold Av. SW19 . . . . 5B **114**
Leopold Bldgs. *E2* . . . *1F 11*
(off Columbia Rd.)
Leopold M. E9 . . . . 5E **51**
Leopold Rd. E17 . . . . . 1C **38**
NW10 . . . . 4A **42**
SW19 . . . . 4B **114**
Leopold St. E3 . . . . 4B **66**
Leopold Ter. SW19 . . . 5B **114**
Leopold Wlk. *SE11* . . . *1B 90*
(off Tyers St.)
Leo St. SE15 . . . . 3D **93**
Leo Yd. EC1 . . . . 4E **9**
Leppoc Rd. SW4 . . . . . 3F **103**
Leroy St. SE1 . . . . 5A **78**
Lerry Cl. W14 . . . . 2B **86**
Lescombe Cl. SE23 . . . 3A **122**
Lescombe Rd. SE23 . . . 3A **122**
Lesley Ct. *SW1* *5B 22*
(off Strutton Ground)
Leslie Ho. *SW8* *3A 90*
(off Wheatsheaf La.)
Leslie Prince Ct. SE5 . . 3F **91**
Leslie Rd. E11 . . . . 1E **53**
E16 . . . . 5D **69**
Lessar Av. SW4 . . . . . . 4E **103**
Lessingham Av.
SW17 . . . . 4B **116**
Lessing St. SE23 . . . . . 5A **108**
Lester Av. E15 . . . . 3A **68**
Leswin Pl. N16 . . . . 5B **36**
Leswin Rd. N16 . . . . . . 5B **36**
Letchford Gdns.
NW10 . . . . 2C **56**
Letchford M. NW10 . . . 2C **56**
Letchmore Ho. *W10* . . *3E 57*
(off Sutton Way)

Letchworth St.
SW17 . . . . 4B **116**
Lethbridge Cl. SE13 . . . 4E **95**
Letterstone Rd. SW6 . . 3B **86**
Lettice St. SW6 . . . . . . 4B **86**
Lett Rd. E15 . . . . 4F **53**
Lettsom St. SE5 . . . . . . 5A **92**
Lettsom Wlk. E13 . . . . . 1C **68**
Leucha Rd. E17 . . . . . . 1A **38**
Levana Cl. SW19 . . . . . 1A **114**
Levant Ho. *E1* *3F 65*
(off Ernest St.)
Levehurst Ho. SE27 . . . 5E **119**
Levendale Rd.
SE23 . . . . 2A **122**
Levenhurst Way SW4 . . 5A **90**
Leven Rd. E14 . . . . 4E **67**
Leverett St. SW3 . . . . . 5A **74**
Leverington Pl.
N1 . . . . 2C **10** (2F **63**)
Leverson St. SW16 . . . 5E **117**
Leverstock Ho. *SW3* . . *1A 88*
(off Cale St.)
Lever St. EC1 . . 2E **9** (2D **63**)
Leverton Pl. NW5 . . . . . 2E **47**
Leverton St. NW5 . . . . . 2E **47**
Levison Way N19 . . . . . 3F **33**
Levita Ho. NW1 . . . . . . 1C **6**
(not continuous)
Lewesdon Cl. SW19 . . 1F **113**
Lewes Ho. *SE1* *3E 27*
(off Druid St.)
SE15 . . . . *2C 92*
(off Friary Est.)
Leweston Pl. N16 . . . . . 2B **36**
Lew Evans Ho.
SE22 . . . . 3C **106**
Lewey Ho. *E3* *3B 66*
(off Joseph St.)
Lewin Rd. SW14 . . . . . 1A **98**
SW16 . . . . 5F **117**
Lewis Ct. *SE16* *1D 93*
(off Stubbs Dr.)
Lewis Gro. SE13 . . . . . 2E **109**
LEWISHAM 1E **109**
Lewisham Bus. Cen.
SE14 . . . . 2F **93**
Lewisham Cen.
SE13 . . . . 2E **109**
Lewisham Crematorium
SE6 . . . . 2B **124**
Lewisham Hgts.
SE23 . . . . 1E **121**
Lewisham High St.
SE13 . . . . 4D **109**
Lewisham Hill SE13 . . . 5E **95**
Lewisham Lions Cen.
. . . . 1E **93**
Lewisham Model Mkt.
SE13 . . . . *2E 109*
(off Lewisham High St.)
Lewisham Pk. SE13 . . . 3E **109**
Lewisham Rd. SE13 . . . 4D **95**
Lewisham St.
SW1 . . . . 4C **22** (3F **75**)
Lewisham Way SE4 . . . 4B **94**
SE14 . . . . 4B **94**
Lewis Ho. *E14* *2E 81*
(off Coldharbour)

Lewis Pl. E8 . . . . 2C **50**
Lewis Silkin Ho.
  SE16 . . . . 2E **93**
  (off Lovelinch Cl.)
Lewis St. NW1 . . . . 3D **47**
  (not continuous)
Lexham Gdns. W8 . . . . . 5C **72**
Lexham Gdns. M.
  W8 . . . . 4D **73**
Lexham Ho. W8 . . . . . . 5D **73**
  (off Lexham Gdns.)
Lexham M. W8 . . . . 5C **72**
Lexham Wlk. W8 . . . . . . 4D **73**
Lexington Apartments
  EC1 . . . . 3C **10** (3F **63**)
Lexington St.
  W1 . . . . 4A **14** (1E **75**)
Lexton Gdns. SW12 . . . 1F **117**
Leybourne Ho. E14 . . . . 5B **66**
  (off Dod St.)
  SE15 . . . . 2E **93**
Leybourne Rd. E11 . . . . 3B **40**
  NW1 . . . . 4D **47**
Leybourne St. NW1 . . . 4D **47**
Leybridge Ct. SE12 . . . 3C **110**
Leyden Mans. N19 . . . . 2A **34**
Leyden St.
  E1 . . . . 1F **19** (4B **64**)
Leydon Cl. SE16 . . . . . . 2F **79**
Leyes Rd. E16 . . . . 5F **69**
Leyland Ho. E14 . . . . . . 1D **81**
  (off Hale St.)
Leyland Rd. SE12 . . . . . 3C **110**
Leylands SW18 . . . . . . 4B **100**
Leylang Rd. SE14 . . . . . 3F **93**
Leys Ct. SW9 . . . . 5C **90**
Leysdown Ho. SE17 . . . 1A **92**
  (off Madron St.)
Leysfield Rd. W12 . . . . 4C **70**
Leyspring Rd. E11 . . . . . 3B **40**
LEYTON 4E **39**
Leyton Bus. Cen.
  E10 . . . . 4C **38**
Leyton Ct. SE23 . . . . . 1E **121**
Leyton FC Ground 3B **38**
Leyton Grange Est.
  E10 . . . . 3C **38**
Leyton Grn. Rd. E10 . . . 1E **39**
Leyton Grn. Twr. E10 . . 1E **39**
  (off Leyton Grn. Rd.)
Leyton Grn. Towers
  E10 . . . . 1E **39**
  (off Leyton Grn. Rd.)
Leyton Ind. Village
  E10 . . . . 2F **37**
Leyton Leisure Lagoon
  . . . . 2D **39**
Leyton Orient FC 5D **39**
Leyton Pk. Rd. E10 . . . . 5E **39**
Leyton Rd. E15 . . . . 2E **53**
LEYTONSTONE 5A **40**
Leytonstone Ho.
  E11 . . . . 2B **40**
  (off Hanbury Dr.)
Leytonstone Rd. E15 . . . 2A **54**
Leyton Way E11 . . . . . . 2A **40**
Leywick St. E15 . . . . . . 1A **68**
Liardet St. SE14 . . . . . . 2A **94**
Liberia Rd. N5 . . . . 3D **49**

Liberty Ho. E1 . . . . 1C **78**
  (off Ensign St.)
Liberty M. SW12 . . . . . 4D **103**
Liberty St. SW9 . . . . . . 4B **90**
Libra Rd. E3 . . . . 1B **66**
  E13 . . . . 1C **68**
Library Mans. W12 . . . . 3E **71**
  (off Pennard Rd.)
Library Pde. NW10 . . . . 5A **42**
  (off Craven Pk. Rd.)
Library Pl. E1 . . . . 1D **79**
Library St.
  SE1 . . . . 5D **25** (3D **77**)
Lichfield Rd. E3 . . . . . . 2A **66**
  E6 . . . . 2F **69**
  NW2 . . . . 1A **44**
Lickey Ho. W14 . . . . . . 2B **86**
  (off North End Rd.)
Lidcote Gdns. SW9 . . . . 5B **90**
Liddell Gdns. NW10 . . . 1E **57**
Liddell Rd. NW6 . . . . . . 3C **44**
Liddington Rd. E15 . . . . 5B **54**
Liddon Rd. E13 . . . . 2D **69**
Liden Cl. E17 . . . . 2B **38**
Lidfield Rd. N16 . . . . . . 1F **49**
Lidgate Rd. SE15 . . . . . 3B **92**
Lidiard Rd. SW18 . . . . . 2E **115**
Lidlington Pl. NW1 . . . . 1E **61**
Lidyard Rd. N19 . . . . . . 3E **33**
Liffords Pl. SW13 . . . . . 5B **84**
Lifford St. SW15 . . . . . . 2F **99**
Lighter Cl. SE16 . . . . . . 5A **80**
Lighterman Ho. E14 . . . 1E **81**
Lighterman M. E1 . . . . . 5F **65**
Lightermans Rd.
  E14 . . . . 3C **80**
Lightermans Wlk.
  SW18 . . . . 2C **100**
Light Horse Ct. SW3 . . . 1C **88**
  (off Royal Hospital Rd.)
Ligonier St.
  E2 . . . . 3F **11** (3B **64**)
Lilac Ct. E13 . . . . 5E **55**
Lilac Ho. SE4 . . . . 1C **108**
Lilac Pl. SE11 . . . . 5B **76**
Lilac St. W12 . . . . 1C **70**
Lilburne Rd. SE9 . . . . . 3F **111**
Lilestone Ho. NW8 . . . . 3F **59**
  (off Frampton St.)
Lilestone St. NW8 . . . . . 3A **60**
Lilford Ho. SE5 . . . . 5E **91**
Lilford Rd. SE5 . . . . 5D **91**
Lilian Barker Cl.
  SE12 . . . . 3C **110**
Lilian Cl. N16 . . . . 5A **36**
Lilian Rd. SW13 . . . . . . 2C **84**
Lillian Ho. SW6 . . . . . . 2A **86**
  (off Lillie Rd.)
Lillie Mans. SW6 . . . . . 2A **86**
  (off Lillie Rd.)
Lillie Rd. SW6 . . . . 2A **86**
Lillie Road Fitness Cen.
  . . . . 3F **85**
Lillieshall Rd. SW4 . . . . 1D **103**
Lillie Yd. SW6 . . . . 2C **86**
Lillington St. N7 . . . . . . 1C **48**
Lillington Gdns. Est.
  SW1 . . . . 5E **75**
  (off Vauxhall Bri. Rd.)
Lilliput Ct. SE12 . . . . . . 3D **111**

Lily Cl. W14 . . . . 5F **71**
  (not continuous)
Lily Nichols Ho. E16 . . . 2F **83**
  (off Connaught Rd.)
Lily Pl. EC1 . . . . . . 5C **8** (4C **62**)
Lily Rd. E17 . . . . 1C **38**
Lilyville Rd. SW6 . . . . . 4B **86**
Limborough Ho. E14 . . . 4C **66**
  (off Thomas Rd.)
Limburg Rd. SW11 . . . . 2A **102**
Limeburner La.
  EC4 . . . . 3D **17** (5D **63**)
Lime Cl. E1 . . . . 2C **78**
Lime Ct. E11 . . . . 4A **40**
  (off Trinity Cl.)
  E17 . . . . 1E **39**
Lime Gro. W12 . . . . 3E **71**
Limeharbour E14 . . . . . 4D **81**
LIMEHOUSE 5B **66**
Limehouse C'way.
  E14 . . . . 1B **80**
Limehouse Ct. E14 . . . . 5C **66**
Limehouse Cut E14 . . . 4D **67**
  (off Morris Rd.)
Limehouse Flds. Est.
  E14 . . . . 4A **66**
Limehouse Link E14 . . . 5A **66**
Lime Kiln Dr. SE7 . . . . . 2D **97**
Limerick Cl. SW12 . . . . 5E **103**
Limerston St. SW10 . . . 2E **87**
Limes, The SW18 . . . . . 4C **100**
  W2 . . . . 1C **72**
Limes Av. NW11 . . . . . . 2A **30**
  SW13 . . . . 5B **84**
Limes Ct. NW6 . . . . . . 4A **44**
  (off Brondesbury Pk.)
Limes Fld. Rd.
  SW14 . . . . 1A **98**
Limesford Rd. SE15 . . . 2F **107**
Limes Gdns. SW18 . . . . 4C **100**
Limes Gro. SE13 . . . . . 2E **109**
Lime St. EC3 . . . . 4D **19** (1A **78**)
Lime St. Pas.
  EC3 . . . . 3D **19** (5A **64**)
Limes Wlk. SE15 . . . . . 2E **107**
Limetree Cl. SW2 . . . . . 1B **118**
Lime Tree Ct. E3 . . . . . 4C **66**
Limetree Ter. SE6 . . . . . 1B **122**
Limetree Wlk.
  SW17 . . . . 5C **116**
Lime Wlk. E15 . . . . 5A **54**
Limpsfield Av.
  SW19 . . . . 2F **113**
Linacre Cl. SE15 . . . . . 1D **107**
Linacre Ct. W6 . . . . 1F **85**
Linacre Rd. NW2 . . . . . 3D **43**
Linale Ho. N1 . . . . 1B **10**
Linberry Wlk. SE8 . . . . . 5B **80**
Linchmere Rd.
  SE12 . . . . 5B **110**
Lincoln Av. SW19 . . . . . 3F **113**
  SE12 . . . . 3E **125**
Lincoln Ho. SE5 . . . . . . 3C **90**
  SW3 . . . . 3B **74**
Lincoln M. NW6 . . . . . . 5B **44**
  SE21 . . . . 2F **119**
Lincoln Rd. E7 . . . . 3F **55**
  E13 . . . . 3D **69**

Lincolns Inn Flds.
WC2 . . . . 2F 15 (5B 62)
Lincoln's Inn Hall
. . . . 2A 16 (5B 62)
Lincoln St. E11 . . . . . . 4A 40
SW3 . . . . 5B 74
Lincombe Rd.
BR1: Brom 3B 124
Lindal Rd. SE4 . . . . . 3B 108
Linden Av. NW10 . . 1F 57
Linden Ct. W12. . . . . 2E 71
Linden Gdns. W2 . . . . 1C 72
W4 . . . . 1A 84
Linden Gro. SE15 . . 1D 107
Linden Lea. SE8 . . . . 2B 94
(off Abinger Gro.)
Linden Lea N2 . . . . . . 1E 31
Linden Mans. N6 . . . . 3D 33
(off Hornsey La.)
Linden M. N1 . . . . 2F 49
W2 . . . . 1C 72
Linden Wlk. N19. . . . . 4E 33
Lindfield Gdns. NW3 . . 2D 45
Lindfield St. E14 . . . . 5C 66
Lindisfarne Way E9 . . 1A 52
Lindley Est. SE15 . . . 3C 92
Lindley Ho. E1 . . . . . 4E 65
(off Lindley St.)
SE15. . . . . 3C 92
(off Peckham Pk. Rd.)
Lindley Rd. E10 . . . . . 4E 39
Lindley St. E1 . . . . . . 4E 65
Lindop Ho. E1 . . . . . . 3A 66
(off Mile End Rd.)
Lindore Rd. SW11 . . 2B 102
Lindo St. SE15 . . . . . 5E 93
Lindrop St. SW6 . . . . 5C 87
Lindsay Ct. SW11 . . . 4F 87
(off Battersea High St.)
Lindsay Ho. SW7 . . . 4E 73
(off Gloucester St.)
Lindsay Sq. SW1 . . . . 1F 89
Lindsell St. SE10 . . . . 4E 95
Lindsey M. N1 . . . . . . 4E 49
Lindsey St.
EC1 . . . . 5E 9 (4D 63)
Lind St. SE8 . . . . 5C 94
Lindway SE27 . . . . . 5D 119
Linfield WC1 . . . . 2F 7
(off Sidmouth St.)
Linford Christie Stadium
. . . . 4C 56
Linford Ho. E2 . . . . . . 5C 50
(off Whiston Rd.)
Linford St. SW8 . . . . . 4E 89
Lingard Ho. E14 . . . . 4E 81
(off Marshfield St.)
Lingards Rd. SE13 . . 2E 109
Lingfield Ho. SE1 . . . 4E 25
Lingfield Rd.
SW19 . . . . 5F 113
Lingham Ct. SW9 . . . . 5A 90
Lingham St. SW9 . . . . 5A 90
Ling Rd. E16 . . . . 4C 68
Lings Coppice SE21 . . 2F 119
Lingwell Rd. SW17 . . 3A 116
Lingwood Rd. E5 . . . . 2C 36
Linhope St. NW1 . . . . 3B 60
Link, The NW2 . . . . . . 3C 28

Linkenholt Mans.
W6 . . . . 5B 70
(off Stamford Brook Av.)
Link Ho. E3 . . . . 1D 67
W10. . . . . 5F 57
(off Kingsdown Cl.)
Link Rd. E1 . . . . 1C 78
E12 . . . . 4F 41
Links Rd. NW2 . . . . . 4B 28
Link St. E9 . . . . 3E 51
Linksview N2 . . . . . . 1B 32
(off Gt. North Rd.)
Links Yd. E1 . . . . 4B 64
(off Spelman St.)
Linkway N4 . . . . 2E 35
Linkwood Wlk. NW1 . . 4F 47
Linley Sambourne House
. . . . 4C 72
(off Stafford Ter.)
Linnell Cl. NW11 . . . . 1D 31
Linnell Dr. NW11 . . . . 1D 31
Linnell Ho. E1 . . . . . . 5F 11
(off Folgate St.)
Linnell Rd. SE5 . . . . . 5A 92
Linnet M. SW12 . . . . 5C 102
Linom Rd. SW4 . . . . 2A 104
Linscott Rd. E5 . . . . . 1E 51
Linsey Ct. E10 . . . . . 3C 38
(off Grange Rd.)
Linsey St. SE16 . . . . 5C 78
(not continuous)
Linslade Ho. E2 . . . . . 5C 50
NW8 . . . . 3A 60
(off Paveley St.)
Linstead Hall SW7 . . . 4F 73
(off Princes Gdns.)
Linstead St. NW6 . . . . 4C 44
Linstead Way SW18 . . 5A 100
Lintaine Cl. W6 . . . . . 2A 86
Linthorpe Rd. N16 . . . 2A 36
Linton Cl. SE7 . . . . . . 1E 97
Linton Ct. NW1 . . . . . 4E 47
(off Agar Gro.)
Linton Gdns. E6 . . . . . 5F 69
Linton Gro. SE27 . . . 5D 119
Linton Ho. E3 . . . . . . 4C 66
(off St Paul's Way)
Linton St. N1 . . . . . . 5E 49
(not continuous)
Linver Rd. SW6 . . . . . 5C 86
Lion Cl. SE4 . . . . . . 4C 108
Lion Ct. E1 . . . . 1F 79
(off The Highway)
N1. . . . . 5B 48
(off Copenhagen St.)
SE1. . . . . 2D 27
(off Magdalen St.)
Lionel Gdns. SE9 . . . 3F 111
Lionel Ho. W10 . . . . . 4A 58
(off Portobello Rd.)
Lionel Mans. W14 . . . 4F 71
(off Haarlem Rd.)
Lionel M. W10 . . . . . 4A 58
Lionel Rd. SE9 . . . . . 3F 111
Lion Gate M. SW18 . . 5C 100
Lion Mills E2 . . . . . . 1C 64
Lions Cl. SE9 . . . . . . 3E 125
Lion Yd. SW4 . . . . . 2F 103

Liphook Cres. SE23 . . 5E 107
Lipton Rd. E1 . . . . . . 5F 65
Lisburne Rd. NW3 . . . 1B 46
Lisford St. SE15 . . . . 4B 92
Lisgar Ter. W14 . . . . . 5B 72
Liskeard Gdns. SE3 . . 4C 96
Liskeard Ho. SE11 . . . 1C 90
(off Kennings Way)
Lisle Cl. SW17 . . . . . 4D 117
Lisle Ct. NW2 . . . . . . 5A 30
Lisle St.
WC2 . . . . 4C 14 (1F 75)
Lismore SW19 . . . . . 5B 114
(off Woodside)
Lismore Cir. NW5 . . . . 2C 46
Lismore Ho. SE15 . . . 1D 107
Lismore Wlk. N1 . . . . 3E 49
(off Clephane Rd. Nth.)
Lissenden Gdns.
NW5 . . . . 1C 46
(not continuous)
Lissenden Mans.
NW5 . . . . 1C 46
Lisson Grn. Est.
NW8 . . . . 3A 60
(off Tresham Cres.)
LISSON GROVE 4A 60
Lisson Gro. NW1 . . . . 3F 59
NW8 . . . . 3F 59
Lisson Ho. NW1 . . . . . 4A 60
(off Lisson St.)
Lisson St. NW1 . . . . . 4A 60
Lister Cl. W3 . . . . 4A 56
Lister Ct. N16 . . . . . . 4A 36
Listergate Ct. SW15 . . 2E 99
Lister Ho. E1 . . . . 4C 64
SE3 . . . . 2A 96
(off Restell Cl.)
Lister Lodge W9 . . . . 4C 58
(off Admiral Wlk.)
Lister Rd. E11 . . . . . . 3A 40
Liston Rd. SW4 . . . . . 1E 103
Listowel Cl. SW9 . . . . 3C 90
Listria Pk. N16 . . . . . 4A 36
Litcham Ho. E1 . . . . . 2F 65
(off Longnor Rd.)
Litchfield Av. E15. . . . 3A 54
Litchfield Ct. E17. . . . 1C 38
Litchfield Gdns.
NW10 . . . . 3C 42
Litchfield St.
WC2 . . . . 4C 14 (1F 75)
Litchfield Way
NW11 . . . . 1E 31
Lithos Rd. NW3 . . . . . 3D 45
Lit. Albany St.
NW1 . . . . 2E 5 (2D 61)
(Albany St.)
NW1 . . . . 3E 5
(Longford St.)
Little Angel Theatre . . 5D 49
(off Cross St.)
Lit. Argyll St.
W1 . . . . 3F 13 (5E 61)
Lit. Boltons, The
SW5 . . . . 1D 87
SW10 . . . . 1D 87
Little Bornes SE21 . . . 4A 120
Littlebourne SE13 . . . 5A 110

Littlebourne Ho.
  SE17 . . . . 1A *92*
  (off Kinglake St.)
Little Britain
  EC1 . . . . . . 1E **17** (4D *63*)
Little Brownings
  SE23 . . . . 2D *121*
Littlebury Rd. SW4 . . . 1F *103*
Lit. Chelsea Ho.
  SW10 . . . . 2E *87*
  (off Netherton Gro.)
Lit. Chester St.
  SW1 . . . . . 5D **21** (4D *75*)
Little Cloisters
  SW1 . . . . . 5D **23** (4A *76*)
Little Coll. La. EC4 . . . . **4B 18**
  (off College St.)
Little Coll. St.
  SW1 . . . . . 5D **23** (4A *76*)
Littlecombe SE7 . . . . 2D *97*
Littlecombe Cl.
  SW15 . . . . 4F *99*
Littlecote Cl. SW19 . . . 5A *100*
Lit. Dean's Yd. SW1 . . . 5D **23**
Little Dimocks
  SW12 . . . . 2D *117*
Lit. Dorrit Ct.
  SE1 . . . . . . 3A **26** (3E *77*)
Lit. Edward St.
  NW1 . . . . 1E **5** (2D *61*)
Lit. Essex St. WC2 . . . . 4B **16**
Littlefield Cl. N19 . . . . . 1E *47*
Lit. George St.
  SW1 . . . . . 4D **23** (3A *76*)
Little Grn. St. NW5 . . . 1D *47*
Little Heath SE7 . . . . . . 2F *97*
Little Holt E11 . . . . 1C *40*
Lit. London St. SE1 . . . 3B *78*
  (off Wolseley St.)
Lit. Marlborough St.
  W1 . . . . 3F **13**
Lit. Newport St.
  WC2 . . . . . . 4C **14** (1F *75*)
Lit. New St.
  EC4 . . . . . . 2C **16** (5C *62*)
Lit. Portland St.
  W1 . . . . . . 2E **13** (5E *61*)
Lit. Russell St.
  WC1 . . . . . . 1D **15** (4A *62*)
Lit. St James's St.
  SW1 . . . . . 2F **21** (2E *75*)
Little Sanctuary
  SW1 . . . . . 4C **22** (3F *75*)
Lit. Smith St.
  SW1 . . . . . 5C **22** (4F *75*)
Lit. Somerset St.
  E1 . . . . . . 3F **19** (5B *64*)
Lit. Titchfield St.
  W1 . . . . . . 1F **13** (4E *61*)
Littleton Ho. SW1 . . . . . 1E *89*
  (off Lupus St.)
Littleton St. SW18 . . . . 2E *115*
Lit. Trinity La.
  EC4 . . . . . . 4A **18** (1E *77*)
Little Turnstile
  WC1 . . . . . . 1F **15** (4B *62*)
Littlewood SE13 . . . . . . 4E *109*
Livermere Ct. E8 . . . . . . 5B *50*
  (off Queensbridge Rd.)

Livermere Rd. E8 . . . . . . 5B *50*
Liverpool Gro. SE17 . . . . 1E *91*
Liverpool Rd. E10 . . . . . 1E **39**
  E16 . . . . 4A *68*
  N1 . . . . 4C *48*
  N7 . . . . 2C *48*
Liverpool St.
  EC2 . . . . . . 1D **19** (4A *64*)
Livesey Mus. for Children
  . . . . 2D *93*
Livesey Pl. SE15 . . . . . . 2C *92*
Livingstone Ct. E10 . . . . 1E **39**
Livingstone Ho. SE5. . . . 3E *91*
  (off Wyndham Rd.)
Livingstone Lodge
  W9 . . . . 4C *58*
  (off Admiral Wlk.)
Livingstone Mans.
  W14 . . . . 2A *86*
  (off Queen's Club Gdns.)
Livingstone Pl. E14 . . . . 1E *95*
Livingstone Rd. E15. . . . 5E *53*
  E17 . . . . 1D *39*
  SW11 . . . . 1F *101*
Livingwell Health Club
  Greville Rd. 1D *59*
  (within Regents Plaza)
Livonia St.
  W1 . . . . . . 3A **14** (5E *61*)
Lizard St.
  EC1 . . . . . . 2A **10** (2E *63*)
Lizban St. SE3 . . . . 3D *97*
Lizmans Ter. W8 . . . . . . 4C *72*
  (off Earl's Ct. Rd.)
Llandovery Ho. E14 . . . . 3E *81*
  (off Chipka St.)
Llanelly Rd. NW2 . . . . . . 4B *30*
Llanvanor Rd. NW2 . . . . 4B *30*
Llewellyn St. SE16 . . . . . 3C *78*
Lloyd Baker St.
  WC1 . . . . . . 2A **8** (2B *62*)
  (not continuous)
Lloyd's Av.
  EC3 . . . . . . 3E **19** (5A *64*)
Lloyds' Building
  . . . . 3D **19** (5A *64*)
Lloyd's Pl. SE3 . . . . 5A *96*
Lloyd Sq.
  WC1 . . . . . . 1B **8** (2C *62*)
Lloyd's Row
  EC1 . . . . . . 2C **8** (2C *62*)
Lloyd St. WC1 . . . 1B **8** (2C *62*)
Lloyds Wharf SE1 . . . . . . 3B *78*
  (off Mill St.)
Lloyd Vs. SE4 . . . . 5C *94*
Loampit Hill SE13 . . . . . 5C *94*
LOAMPIT VALE 1E *109*
Loampit Va. SE13 . . . . . 1D *109*
Loanda Cl. E8 . . . . 5B *50*
Loats Rd. SW2 . . . . 4A *104*
Lobelia Cl. E6 . . . . 4F *69*
Locarno Rd. SW16 . . . . 5E *117*
Lochaber Rd. SE13 . . . . 2A *110*
Lochaline St. W6 . . . . . . 2E *85*
Lochinvar St.
  SW12 . . . . 5D *103*
Lochmore Ho. SW1 . . . . 5C *74*
  (off Cundy St.)
Lochnagar St. E14 . . . . . 4E *67*

Lockbridge Ct. W9 . . . . . 4C *58*
  (off Woodfield Rd.)
Lock Bldg., The E15 . . . 1E *67*
Lock Chase SE3 . . . . . . 1A *110*
Locke Ho. SW8 . . . . 4E *89*
  (off Wadhurst Rd.)
Lockesfield Pl. E14 . . . . 1D *95*
Lockgate Cl. E9 . . . . 2B *52*
Lockhart Cl. N7 . . . . 3B *48*
Lockhart Ho. SE10 . . . . . 3D *95*
  (off Tarves Way)
Lockhart St. E3 . . . . 3B *66*
Lockhurst St. E5 . . . . . . 1F *51*
Lockington Rd. SW8 . . . 4D *89*
Lock Keepers Quay
  SE16 . . . . 4F *79*
  (off Brunswick Quay)
Lockmead Rd. N15 . . . . 1C *36*
  SE13 . . . . 1E *109*
Lock M. NW5 . . . . 3F *47*
  (off Northpoint Sq.)
Locksfields SE17 . . . . . . 5F *77*
  (off Catesby St.)
Lockside E14 . . . . 1A *80*
  (off Narrow St.)
Locksley Est. E14 . . . . . 5B *66*
Locksley St. E14 . . . . . . 4B *66*
Locksons Cl. E14 . . . . . . 4D *67*
Lock Vw. Ct. E14 . . . . . . 1A *80*
  (off Narrow St.)
Lockwood Cl. SE26 . . . . 4F *121*
Lockwood Ho. SE11 . . . . 2C *90*
Lockwood Sq. SE16 . . . . 4D *79*
Lockyer Est. SE1 . . . . . . 4C *26*
  (not continuous)
Lockyer Ho. SE10 . . . . . 1B *96*
  (off Armitage Rd.)
  SW8 . . . . 3F *89*
  (off Wandsworth Rd.)
  SW15 . . . . 1F *99*
Lockyer St.
  SE1 . . . . . . 4C **26** (3F *77*)
Locton Grn. E3 . . . . 5B *52*
Loddiges Ho. E9 . . . . . . 4E *51*
Loddiges Rd. E9 . . . . . . 4E *51*
Loddon Ho. NW8 . . . . . . 3F *59*
  (off Church St. Est.)
Loder St. SE15 . . . . 3E *93*
Lodge Av. SW14 . . . . . . 1A *98*
Lodge Rd. NW8 . . . . 2F *59*
Lodore Gdns. NW9 . . . . 1A *28*
Lodore St. E14 . . . . 5E *67*
Loftie St. SE16 . . . . 3C *78*
Lofting Ho. N1 . . . . 4C *48*
  (off Liverpool Rd.)
Lofting Rd. N1 . . . . 4B *48*
Loftus Road 2D *71*
Loftus Rd. W12 . . . . 2D *71*
Loftus Vs. W12 . . . . 2D *71*
  (off Loftus Rd.)
Logan M. W8 . . . . 5C *72*
Logan Pl. W8 . . . . 5C *72*
Loggetts SE21 . . . . 2A *120*
Lohmann Ho. SE11 . . . . 2C *90*
  (off Kennington Oval)
Lolesworth Cl.
  E1 . . . . 1F **19** (4B *64*)
Lollard St. SE11 . . . . . . 5B *76*
  (not continuous)

Loman St.
SE1 . . . . 3E 25 (3D 77)
Lomas Dr. E8 . . . . 4B 50
(off Richmond Rd.)
Lomas St. E1 . . . . 4C 64
Lombard Bus. Cen., The
SW11 . . . . 5F 87
Lombard Ct.
EC4 . . . . 4C 18 (1F 77)
Lombard La.
EC4 . . . . 3C 16 (5C 62)
Lombard Rd. SW11 . . . 5F 87
Lombard St.
EC3 . . . . 3C 18 (5F 63)
Lombard Trad. Est.
SE7 . . . . 5D 83
Lombard Wall SE7 . . . 4D 83
(not continuous)
Lombardy Pl. W2 . . . . . 1D 73
Lomond Gro. SE5 . . . . . 3F 91
Lomond Ho. SE5 . . . . . 3F 91
Loncroft Rd. SE5 . . . . 2A 92
Londesborough Rd.
N16 . . . . 1A 50
Londinium Twr. E1 . . . . 4F 19
(off W. Tenter St.)
London Apollo 1E 85
London Aquarium
. . . . 3F 23 (3B 76)
London Arena 4D 81
London Bri.
EC4 . . . . 5C 18 (2F 77)
SE1 . . . . 1C 26 (2F 77)
London Bri. St.
SE1 . . . . 2C 26 (2F 77)
London Bri. Wlk.
SE1 . . . . 1C 26
(off Duke St. Hill)
London Business School
. . . . 3A 4 (3B 60)
London Canal Mus. . . . 1A 62
LONDON CITY AIRPORT
. . . . 2F 83
London City College . . 2B 24
London Coliseum . . . 5D 15
(off St Martin's La.)
London College of
Fashion, The
Hackney. 4E 51
(off Mare St.)
St Luke's . . . 4F 9 (3E 63)
London Dungeon 2C 26
London Eye. . . . 3F 23 (3B 76)
London Flds. E. Side
E8 . . . . 4D 51
London Flds. W. Side
E8 . . . . 4C 50
London Fire Brigade Mus.
. . . . 3E 77
London Fruit Exchange
E1 . . . . 1F 19
(off Brushfield St.)
London Group Bus. Pk.
NW2 . . . . 3B 28
London Guildhall University
Coke St. 5C 64
London Ho. NW8 . . . . 1A 60
(off Avenue Rd.)
WC1 . . . . 3F 7 (3B 62)

London La. E8 . . . . 4D 51
London Master Bakers
Almshouses E10 . . 1D 39
London Metropolitan University
Benwell Rd. 2C 48
City of London 3F 19
(off Jewry St.)
Hornsey St. 2B 48
Manningtree St.
. . . . 2F 19 (5C 64)
London M. W2 . . . . 5F 59
London Palladium . . . 3F 13
(off Argyll St.)
London Regatta Cen.
. . . . 1F 83
London Rd. E13 . . . . . 1C 68
SE1 . . . . . . 5D 25 (4D 77)
SE23 . . . . 1D 121
London School of Economics
& Politics, The
. . . . 3A 16 (5B 62)
London South Bank University
. . . . 5E 25 (4D 77)
London South Bank University
Sports Cen. 5E 25
(in London South
Bank University)
London Stock Exchange
. . . . 2E 17
(off Paternoster Sq.)
London St.
EC3 . . . . 4E 19 (1A 78)
W2 . . . . 5F 59
London Telecom Tower, The
. . . . 5F 5 (4E 61)
London Television Cen., The
. . . . 1B 24 (2C 76)
London Ter. E2 . . . . . . 1C 64
London Transport Mus.
. . . . 4E 15 (1A 76)
London Underwriting Cen.
EC3 . . . . 4E 19
London Wall
EC2 . . . . 1A 18 (4E 63)
London Wall Bldgs.
EC2 . . . . 1C 18
London Wetland Cen.
. . . . 4D 85
London Wharf E2 . . . . 5D 51
(off Wharf Pl.)
London Wildlife Trust
. . . . 5F 47
London Wildlife Trust Cen. for
Wildlife Gardening
. . . . 1B 106
London Zoo 1C 60
Long Acre
WC2 . . . . . . 4D 15 (1A 76)
Longbeach Rd.
SW11 . . . . 1B 102
Longberrys NW2 . . . . . 5B 30
Longbridge Way
SE13 . . . . 3E 109
Longdown Rd. SE6 . . 4C 122
Long Dr. W3 . . . . 5A 56
Longfellow Rd. E17 . . . 1B 38
Longfellow Way SE1 . . 5B 78
Longfield Cres.
SE26 . . . . 3E 121

Longfield Est. SE1 . . . 5B 78
Longfield St. SW18 . . . 5C 100
Longford Ct. E5 . . . . . 1F 51
(off Pedro St.)
Longford Ho.
BR1: Brom 5F 123
(off Brangbourne Rd.)
E1 . . . . 5E 65
(off Jubilee St.)
Longford St.
NW1 . . . . 3E 5 (3D 61)
Longford Wlk. SW2 . . 5C 104
Longhedge Ho.
SE26 . . . . 4C 120
(off High Level Dr.)
Longhedge St. SW11 . . 5C 88
Longhill Rd. SE6 . . . . 2A 124
Longhope Cl. SE15 . . . 2A 92
Longhurst Ho. W10 . . . 2B 58
(off Lancefield St.)
Longhurst Rd. SE13 . . 3F 109
Longland Ct. SE1 . . . . 1C 92
Longlands Ct. W11 . . . 1B 72
(off Westbourne Gro.)
Long La. EC1 . . 1E 17 (4D 63)
SE1 . . . . 4B 26 (3F 77)
Longleat Ho. SW1 . . . 1F 89
(off Rampayne St.)
Longleigh Ho. SE5 . . . 4A 92
(off Peckham Rd.)
Long Lents Ho.
NW10 . . . . 5A 42
(off Shrewsbury Cres.)
Longley Ct. SW8 . . . . 4A 90
Longley Ho. SW17 . . . 5A 116
Longley St. SE1 . . . . . 5C 78
Longley Way NW2 . . . 5E 29
Longman Ho. E2 . . . . . 1F 65
(off Mace St.)
E8 . . . . 5B 50
(off Haggerston Rd.)
Long Mark Rd. E16 . . . 4F 69
Longmead
SE27 . . . . 5E 119
Long Mdw. NW5 . . . . . 2F 47
Longmead Rd.
SW17 . . . . 5B 116
Long Mill SE10 . . . . . 4D 95
(off Greenwich High Rd.)
Longmoore St. SW1 . . 5E 75
Longmoor Point
SW15 . . . . 1D 113
(off Norley Vale)
Longmore Gdns. Est.
SW1 . . . . 5E 75
(off Vauxhall Bri. Rd.)
Longnor Est. E1 . . . . . 2F 65
Longnor Rd. E1 . . . . . 2F 65
Long Pond Rd. SE3 . . 4A 96
Longridge Ho.
SE1 . . . . 5A 26 (4E 77)
Longridge Rd. SW5 . . 5C 72
Long Rd. SW4 . . . . . . 2D 103
Long's Ct. WC2 . . . . . 5C 14
Longshore SE8 . . . . . 5B 80
Longshott Ct. SW5 . . . 5C 72
(off W. Cromwell Rd.)
Longstaff Cres.
SW18 . . . . 4C 100

Longstaff Rd. SW18. . . 4C 100
Longstone Av. NW10 . . 4B 42
Longstone Ct. SE1 . . . . 4B 26
　(off Gt. Dover St.)
Longstone Rd.
　SW17 . . . . 5D 117
Long St. E2 . . . 1F 11 (2B 64)
Longthorpe Ct. W6 . . . . 5C 70
　(off Invermead Cl.)
Longton Av. SE26 . . . . 4C 120
Longton Gro. SE26. . . 4D 121
Longville Rd. SE11 . . . 5D 77
Long Wlk. SE1 . . . . 5E 27
SW13 . . . . 5A 84
Long Wall E15. . . . . . . 2F 67
Long Yd. WC1 . . . 4F 7 (3B 62)
Longwood Dr. SW15. . . 4C 98
Lonsdale Av. E6 . . . . . . 2F 69
Lonsdale Cl. E6 . . . . . . 3F 69
SE9 . . . . 3F 125
Lonsdale Ho. W11 . . . . 5B 58
　(off Lonsdale Rd.)
Lonsdale M. W11. . . . . 5B 58
　(off Lonsdale Rd.)
Lonsdale Pl. N1 . . . . . . 4C 48
Lonsdale Rd. E11. . . . . 1B 40
NW6 . . . . 5B 44
SW13 . . . . 4B 84
W4 . . . . 5B 70
W11 . . . . 5B 58
Lonsdale Sq. N1. . . . . . 4C 48
Lonsdale Yd. W11 . . . . 1C 72
Lopez Ho. SW9. . . . . . 1A 104
Loraine Cotts. N7 . . . . . 1B 48
Loraine Rd. N7. . . . . . . 1B 48
Lord Amory Way
　E14 . . . . 3E 81
Lordell Pl. SW19 . . . . 5E 113
Lorden Wlk. E2. . . . . . . 2C 64
Lord Hills Bri. W2 . . . . 4D 59
Lord Hills Rd. W2 . . . . 4D 59
Lord Holland La.
　SW9 . . . . 5C 90
Lord Napier Pl. W6 . . . 1C 84
Lord North St.
　SW1. . . . . . 5D 23 (4A 76)
Lord Roberts M.
　SW6 . . . . 3D 87
Lords Cl. SE21 . . . . . . 2E 119
Lord's Cricket Ground
　. . . . . 2F 59
Lordship Gro. N16 . . . . 4F 35
Lordship La. SE22 . . . . 2B 106
Lordship La. Est.
　SE21 . . . . 5C 106
Lordship Pk. N16 . . . . . 4E 35
Lordship Pk. M. N16 . . 4E 35
Lordship Pl. SW3 . . . . . 2A 88
Lordship Rd. N16 . . . . . 3F 35
Lordship Ter. N16 . . . . . 4F 35
Lords Vw. NW8 . . . . . . 2F 59
Loreburn Ho. N7. . . . . . 1B 48
Lorenzo St.
　WC1. . . . . . 1F 7 (2B 62)
Loring Rd. SE14 . . . . . . 4A 94
Loris Rd. W6 . . . . 4E 71
Lorn Ct. SW9 . . . . 5C 90
Lorne Cl. NW8 . . . . 2A 60
Lorne Gdns. W11 . . . . . 3F 71

Lorne Ho. E1 . . . . 4A 66
　(off Ben Jonson Rd.)
Lorne Rd. E7 . . . . 1D 55
E17 . . . . 1C 38
N4 . . . . 3B 34
Lorn Rd. SW9 . . . . 5B 90
Lorraine Ct. NW1. . . . . 4D 47
Lorrimore Rd. SE17. . . 2D 91
Lorrimore Sq. SE17 . . 2D 91
Lorton Ho. NW6 . . . . . . 5C 44
　(off Kilburn Va.)
Lothair Rd. Nth. N4 . . . 1D 35
Lothair Rd. Sth. N4 . . . 2C 34
Lothbury EC2. . 2B 18 (5F 63)
Lothian Rd. SW9 . . . . . 4D 91
Lots Rd. SW10 . . . . 3E 87
Lotus Cl. SE21 . . . . . . 3F 119
Loubet St. SW17 . . . . . 5B 116
Loudoun Rd. NW8 . . . . 5E 45
Loughborough Est.
　SW9 . . . . 1D 105
Loughborough Pk.
　SW9 . . . . 2D 105
Loughborough Rd.
　SW9 . . . . 5C 90
Loughborough St.
　SE11 . . . . 1B 90
Lough Rd. N7 . . . . 2B 48
Louisa Cl. E9 . . . . 5F 51
Louisa Gdns. E1 . . . . . 3F 65
Louisa St. E1 . . . . 3F 65
Louise Aumonier Wlk.
　N19 . . . . 2A 34
　(off Jessie Blythe La.)
Louise Bennett Cl.
　SE24 . . . . 2D 105
Louise De Marillac Ho.
　E1 . . . . 4E 65
　(off Smithy St.)
Louise Rd. E15. . . . . . . 3A 54
Louise White Ho.
　N19 . . . . 3F 33
Louisville Rd.
　SW17 . . . . 3C 116
Louvaine Rd. SW11 . . . 2F 101
Lovat Cl. NW2 . . . . 5B 28
Lovat La.
　EC3 . . . . . . 4D 19 (1A 78)
　(not continuous)
Lovatt Ct. SW12. . . . . . 1D 117
Lovegrove St. SE1 . . . . 1C 92
Lovegrove Wlk. E14. . . 2E 81
Lovelace Rd. SE21 . . . 2E 119
Lovelace Rd. SE21. . . 2E 119
Lovelinch Cl. SE15. . . . 2E 93
Lovell Ho. E8 . . . . 5C 50
　(off Shrubland Rd.)
Lovell Pl. SE16 . . . . 4A 80
Loveridge M. NW6. . . . 3B 44
Loveridge Rd. NW6 . . . 3B 44
Lovers Wlk. SE10 . . . . . 2F 95
W1. . . . . 1B 20 (2C 74)
Low Cross Wood La.
　SE21 . . . . 3B 120
Lowden Rd. SE24 . . . . 2D 105

Lowder Ho. E1 . . . . 2D 79
　(off Wapping La.)
Lowe Av. E16 . . . . 4C 68
Lowell Ho. SE5 . . . . 3E 91
　(off Wyndham Est.)
Lowell St. E14 . . . . 5A 66
Lwr. Addison Gdns.
　W14 . . . . 3A 72
Lwr. Belgrave St.
　SW1 . . . . . . 5D 21 (4D 75)
LOWER CLAPTON 1D 51
Lwr. Clapton Rd. E5. . . 5D 37
Lwr. Clarendon Wlk.
　W11 . . . . 5A 58
　(off Clarendon Rd.)
Lower Comn. Sth.
　SW15 . . . . 1D 99
Lwr. Grosvenor Pl.
　SW1 . . . . . . 5E 21 (4D 75)
LOWER HOLLOWAY . . . 2B 48
Lwr. James St.
　W1 . . . . 4A 14 (1E 75)
Lwr. John St.
　W1 . . . . 4A 14 (1E 75)
Lwr. Lea Crossing
　E14 . . . . 1A 82
　E16 . . . . 1A 82
Lower Mall W6 . . . . . . 1D 85
Lower Marsh
　SE1 . . . . . . 4B 24 (3C 76)
Lwr. Merton Ri. NW3. . 4A 46
Lwr. Richmond Rd.
　SW15 . . . . 1D 99
Lower Rd.
　SE1 . . . . . . 3B 24 (3C 76)
　SE8 . . . . 5F 79
　SE16 . . . . 3E 79
　(not continuous)
Lwr. Robert St. WC2 . . 5E 15
　(off Robert St.)
Lwr. Sloane St. SW1 . . 5C 74
LOWER SYDENHAM
　. . . . . 4F 121
Lwr. Sydenham Ind. Est.
　SE26 . . . . 5B 122
Lower Ter. NW3 . . . . . . 5E 31
SE27 . . . . 5D 119
　(off Woodcote Pl.)
Lwr. Thames St.
　EC3 . . . . . . 5C 18 (1F 77)
Lowerwood Ct. W11 . . 5A 58
　(off Westbourne Pk. Rd.)
Lowestoft Cl. E5. . . . . . 4E 37
　(off Mundford Rd.)
Loweswater Ho. E3 . . . 3B 66
Lowfield Rd. NW6 . . . . 4C 44
Low Hall La. E17. . . . . . 1A 38
Low Hall Mnr. Bus. Cen.
　E17 . . . . 1A 38
Lowman Rd. N7 . . . . . . 1B 48
Lowndes Cl. SW1. . . . . 4C 74
Lowndes Ct.
　SW1. . . . . . 5A 20 (4B 74)
W1. . . . . 3F 13
Lowndes Lodge SW1. . 5A 20
　(off Lowndes St.)
Lowndes Pl. SW1. . . . . 4C 74
Lowndes Sq.
　SW1. . . . . . . 4A 20 (3B 74)

Lowndes St.
SW1 . . . . . 5A **20** (4C **74**)
Lowood Ct. SE19 . . . . . 5B **120**
(off Farquhar Rd.)
Lowood Ho. E1 . . . . 1E **79**
(off Bewley St.)
Lowood St. E1 . . . . . . 1D **79**
Lowry Ct. SE16 . . . . 1D **93**
(off Stubbs Dr.)
Lowry Ho. E14 . . . . 3C **80**
(off Cassilis Rd.)
Lowther Gdns. SW7 . . . 3F **73**
Lowther Hill SE23 . . . 5A **108**
Lowther Ho. E8 . . . . 5B **50**
(off Clarissa St.)
SW1 . . . . 1E **89**
(off Churchill Gdns.)
Lowther Rd. N7 . . . . . . 2C **48**
SW13 . . . . 4B **84**
Lowth Rd. SE5 . . . . 4E **91**
Loxford Av. E6 . . . . 1F **69**
Loxham St.
WC1 . . . . 2E **7** (2A **62**)
Loxley Cl. SE26 . . . . . 5F **121**
Loxley Rd. SW18 . . . . 1F **115**
Loxton Rd. SE23 . . . . 1F **121**
LSO St Lukes 3A **10**
(off St Lukes Cl.)
Lubbock Ho. E14 . . . . . 1D **81**
(off Poplar High St.)
Lubbock St. SE14 . . . . . 3E **93**
Lucan Ho. N1 . . . . 5F **49**
(off Colville Est.)
Lucan Pl. SW3 . . . . 5A **74**
Lucas Av. E13 . . . . 5D **55**
Lucas Cl. NW10 . . . . . . 4C **42**
Lucas Ct. SE26 . . . . . . 5A **122**
SW11 . . . . 4C **88**
Lucas Ho. SW10 . . . . . . 3D **87**
(off Coleridge Gdns.)
Lucas Sq. NW11 . . . . . . 1C **30**
Lucas St. SE8 . . . . 4C **94**
Lucerne M. W8 . . . . 2C **72**
Lucerne Rd. N5 . . . . 1D **49**
Lucey Rd. SE16 . . . . . . 4C **78**
Lucey Way SE16 . . . . . . 4C **78**
Lucien Ho. SW17 . . . . 4C **116**
SW19 . . . . 2D **115**
Lucorn Cl. SE12 . . . . . 4B **110**
Lucy Brown Ho. SE1 . . 2A **26**
Ludgate B'way.
EC4 . . . . 3D **17** (5D **63**)
Ludgate Cir.
EC4 . . . . 3D **17** (5D **63**)
Ludgate Hill
EC4 . . . . 3D **17** (5D **63**)
Ludgate Sq.
EC4 . . . . 3E **17** (5D **63**)
Ludham NW5 . . . . 2B **46**
Ludlow St. EC1 . . 3F **9** (3E **63**)
Ludovick Wlk. SW15 . . 2A **98**
Ludwell Ho. W14 . . . . . 4A **72**
(off Russell Rd.)
Ludwick M. SE14 . . . . . 3A **94**
Luffman Rd. SE12 . . . . 3D **125**
Lugard Ho. W12 . . . . . . 2D **71**
Lugard Rd. SE15 . . . . . . 5D **93**
Luke Ho. E1 . . . . 5D **65**
(off Tillman St.)

Luke St. EC2 . . . 3D **11** (3A **64**)
Lukin St. E1 . . . . 5E **65**
Lullingstone Ho.
SE15 . . . . 2E **93**
(off Lovelinch Cl.)
Lullingstone La.
SE13 . . . . 4F **109**
Lulot Gdns. N19 . . . . . . 4D **33**
Lulworth NW1 . . . . 4F **47**
(off Wrotham Rd.)
SE17 . . . . 1F **91**
(off Portland St.)
Lulworth Ct. N1 . . . . . . 4A **50**
(off St Peter's Way)
Lulworth Ho. SW8 . . . . 3B **90**
Lulworth Rd. SE9 . . . . 2F **125**
SE15 . . . . 5D **93**
Lumiere Bldg., The
E7 . . . . 2F **55**
(off Romford Rd.)
Lumiere Ct. SW17 . . . 2C **116**
Lumina Bldgs. E14 . . . . 2E **81**
(off Prestons Rd.)
Lumley Ct.
WC2 . . . . . 5E **15** (1A **76**)
Lumley Flats SW1 . . . 1C **88**
(off Holbein Pl.)
Lumley St.
W1 . . . . 3C **12** (5C **60**)
Lumsdon NW8 . . . . 5D **45**
(off Abbey Rd.)
Luna Ho. SE16 . . . . 3C **78**
Lund Point E15 . . . . 5E **53**
Lundy Wlk. N1 . . . . 3E **49**
Lunham Rd. SE19 . . . . 5A **120**
Luntley Pl. E1 . . . . 4C **64**
(off Chicksand St.)
Lupin Cl. SW2 . . . . 2D **119**
Lupin Ct. SE11 . . . . 5B **76**
Lupin Point SE1 . . . . . . 3B **78**
(off Abbey St.)
Lupton Cl. SE12 . . . . . 3D **125**
Lupton St. NW5 . . . . . . 1E **47**
(not continuous)
Lupus St. SW1 . . . . 1D **89**
Luralda Wharf E14 . . . . 1F **95**
Lurgan Av. W6 . . . . 2F **85**
Lurline Gdns. SW11 . . . 4C **88**
Luscombe Way SW8 . . . 3A **90**
Lushington Rd.
NW10 . . . . 1D **57**
SE6 . . . . 4D **123**
Lushington Ter. E8 . . . . 2C **50**
Luther King Cl. E17 . . . 1B **38**
Luton Ho. E13 . . . . 3C **68**
(off Luton Rd.)
Luton Pl. SE10 . . . . 3E **95**
Luton Rd. E13 . . . . 3C **68**
Luton St. NW8 . . . . 3F **59**
Lutton Ter. NW3 . . . . . . 1E **45**
(off Lakis Cl.)
Luttrell Av. SW15 . . . . . 3D **99**
Lutwyche Rd. SE6 . . . . 2B **122**
Lutyens Ho. SW1 . . . . . 1E **89**
(off Churchill Gdns.)
Luxborough Ho. W1 . . . 5B **4**
(off Luxborough St.)
Luxborough St.
W1 . . . . 5B **4** (4C **60**)

Luxborough Twr. W1 . . . 5B **4**
Lux Cinema 2D **11**
(off Hoxton Sq.)
Luxemburg M. E15 . . . . 2A **54**
Luxemburg Gdns. W6 . . 5F **71**
Luxfield Rd. SE9 . . . . . 1F **125**
Luxford St. SE16 . . . . . . 5F **79**
Luxmore St. SE4 . . . . . . 4B **94**
Luxor St. SE5 . . . . 1E **105**
Lyall Av. SE21 . . . . 4A **120**
Lyall M.
SW1 . . . . 5B **20** (4C **74**)
Lyall M. W. SW1 . . . . . 4C **74**
Lyall St.
SW1 . . . . 5B **20** (4C **74**)
Lyal Rd. E3 . . . . 1A **66**
Lycett Pl. W12 . . . . 3C **70**
Lyceum Theatre 4F **15**
Lydden Gro. SW18 . . . . 5D **101**
Lydden Rd. SW18 . . . . 5D **101**
Lyden Ho. E1 . . . . 2F **65**
(off Westfield Way)
Lydford NW1 . . . . 5E **47**
(off Royal College St.)
Lydford Cl. N16 . . . . . . 2A **50**
(off Pellerin Rd.)
Lydford Rd. N15 . . . . . . 1F **35**
NW2 . . . . 3E **43**
W9 . . . . 3B **58**
Lydhurst Av. SW2 . . . . 2B **118**
Lydney Cl. SW19 . . . . . 2A **114**
Lydon Rd. SW4 . . . . . . 1E **103**
Lyford Rd. SW18 . . . . . 5F **101**
Lygon Ho. E2 . . . . 2B **64**
(off Gosset St.)
SW6 . . . . 4A **86**
(off Fulham Pal. Rd.)
Lygon Pl.
SW1 . . . . 5D **21** (4D **75**)
Lyham Cl. SW2 . . . . . . 4A **104**
Lyham Rd. SW2 . . . . . 3A **104**
Lyly Ho. SE1 . . . . 5C **26**
(off Burbage Cl.)
Lyme Farm Rd.
SE12 . . . . 2C **110**
Lyme Gro. E9 . . . . 4E **51**
Lyme Gro. Ho. E9 . . . . . 4E **51**
(off Lyme Gro.)
Lymer Av. SE19 . . . . . . 5B **120**
Lyme St. NW1 . . . . 4E **47**
Lyme Ter. NW1 . . . . 4E **47**
Lyminge Gdns.
SW18 . . . . 1A **116**
Lymington Lodge E14 . . 4F **81**
(off Schooner Cl.)
Lymington Rd. NW6 . . . 3D **45**
Lympstone Gdns.
SE15 . . . . 3C **92**
Lynbrook Gro. SE15 . . . 3A **92**
Lynch Cl. SE3 . . . . 5B **96**
Lynch Wlk. SE8 . . . . . . 2B **94**
(off Prince St.)
Lyncott Cres. SW4 . . . . 2D **103**
Lyncourt SE3 . . . . 5F **95**
Lyncroft Gdns. NW6 . . . 2C **44**
Lyncroft Mans. NW6 . . . 2C **44**
Lyndale NW2 . . . . 1B **44**
Lyndale Av. NW2 . . . . . 5B **30**
Lyndale Cl. SE3 . . . . . . 2B **96**

Lynde Ho. SW4 . . . . . . 1F **103**
Lyndhurst Cl. NW10 . . . 5A **28**
Lyndhurst Cl. NW8 . . . . 5F **45**
   (off Finchley Rd.)
Lyndhurst Dr. E10 . . . . . 2E **39**
Lyndhurst Gdns.
  NW3 . . . . 2F **45**
Lyndhurst Gro. SE15 . . . 5A **92**
Lyndhurst Lodge E14 . . . 5F **81**
   (off Millennium Dr.)
Lyndhurst Rd. NW3 . . . . 2F **45**
Lyndhurst Sq. SE15 . . . . 4B **92**
Lyndhurst Ter. NW3 . . . . 2F **45**
Lyndhurst Way SE15 . . . 4B **92**
Lyndon Yd. SW17 . . . . . 4E **115**
Lyneham Wlk. E5 . . . . . 2A **52**
Lynette Av. SW4 . . . . . . 4D **103**
Lyn M. E3 . . . . 2B **66**
  N16 . . . . 1A **50**
Lynmouth Rd. E17 . . . . . 1A **38**
  N16 . . . . 3B **36**
Lynne Cl. SE23 . . . . 5B **108**
Lynne Ct. NW6 . . . . 4D **45**
   (off Priory Rd.)
Lynne Way NW10 . . . . . 4A **42**
Lynn Ho. SE15 . . . . 2D **93**
   (off Friary St.)
Lynn M. E11 . . . . 4A **40**
Lynn Rd. E11 . . . . 4A **40**
  SW12 . . . . 5D **103**
Lynsted Gdns. SE9 . . . . 1F **111**
Lynton Cl. NW10 . . . . . . 2A **42**
Lynton Est. SE1 . . . . . . 5C **78**
Lynton Ho. W2 . . . . 5E **59**
   (off Hallfield Est.)
Lynton Mans. SE1 . . . . . 5B **24**
   (off Kennington Rd.)
Lynton Rd. N8 . . . . 1F **33**
   (not continuous)
  NW6 . . . . 1B **58**
  SE1 . . . . 5B **78**
Lynwood Rd. SW17 . . . . 3B **116**
Lynx Way E16 . . . . 1F **83**
Lyon Ho. NW8 . . . . 3A **60**
   (off Broadley St.)
Lyon Ind. Est. NW2 . . . . 4D **29**
Lyons Pl. NW8 . . . . 3F **59**
Lyon St. N1 . . . . 4B **48**
Lyons Wlk. W14 . . . . . . 5A **72**
Lyric Ct. E8 . . . . 4B **50**
   (off Holly St.)
Lyric M. SE26 . . . . 4E **121**
Lyric Rd. SW13 . . . . . . 4B **84**
Lyric Theatre
  Hammersmith 5E **71**
  *Westminster 4B **14**
   (off Shaftesbury Av.)
Lysander Gro. N19 . . . . 3F **33**
Lysander Ho. E2 . . . . . . 1D **65**
   (off Temple St.)
Lysander M. N19 . . . . . 3E **33**
Lysia Ct. SW6 . . . . 3F **85**
   (off Lysia St.)
Lysias Rd. SW12 . . . . . 4D **103**
Lysia St. SW6 . . . . 3F **85**
Lysons Wlk. SW15 . . . . 2C **98**
Lytcott Gro. SE22 . . . . . 3A **106**
Lytham St. SE17 . . . . . 1F **91**
Lyttelton Cl. NW3 . . . . . 4A **46**

Lyttelton Ho. E9 . . . . . . 4E **51**
   (off Well St.)
Lyttelton Rd. E10 . . . . . 5D **39**
Lyttelton Theatre 1B **24**
  (in Royal National Theatre)
Lytton Cl. N2 . . . . 1F **31**
Lytton Gro. SW15 . . . . . 3F **99**
Lytton Rd. E11 . . . . 2A **40**
Lyveden Rd. SE3 . . . . . . 3D **97**

M

Mabledon Ct. WC1 . . . . . 2C **6**
   (off Mabledon Pl.)
Mabledon Pl.
  WC1 . . . . 2C **6** (2F **61**)
Mablethorpe Rd.
  SW6 . . . . 3A **86**
Mabley St. E9 . . . . 2A **52**
Macarthur Cl. E7 . . . . . . 3C **54**
Macarthur Ter. SE7 . . . . 2F **97**
Macartney Ho.
  SE10 . . . . 3F **95**
   (off Chesterfield Wlk.)
  SW9 . . . . 4C **90**
   (off Gosling Way)
Macaulay Cl. SW4 . . . . 1D **103**
Macaulay Rd. E6 . . . . . . 1F **69**
  SW4 . . . . 1D **103**
Macaulay Sq. SW4 . . . . 2D **103**
McAuley Cl. SE1 . . . . . . 5B **24**
Macaulay Ho. W10 . . . . 4A **58**
   (off Portobello Rd.)
Macaulay M. SE13 . . . . 4E **95**
Macbeth Ho. N1 . . . . . . 1A **64**
Macbeth St. W6 . . . . . . 1D **85**
McCall Cl. SW4 . . . . . . 5A **90**
McCall Cres. SE7 . . . . . 1F **97**
McCall Ho. N7 . . . . 1A **48**
MCC Cricket Mus. and Tours
   . . . . 2F **59**
Macclesfield Ho.
  EC1 . . . . 2F **9**
   (off Central St.)
Macclesfield Rd.
  EC1 . . . . 1F **9** (2E **63**)
Macclesfield St.
  W1 . . . . 4C **14** (1F **75**)
McCoid Way
  SE1 . . . . 4F **25** (3E **77**)
McCrone M. NW3 . . . . . 3F **45**
McCullum Rd. E3 . . . . . 5B **52**
McDermott Cl.
  SW11 . . . . 1A **102**
McDermott Rd.
  SE15 . . . . 1C **106**
Macdonald Ho.
  SW11 . . . . 5C **88**
   (off Dagnall St.)
Macdonald Rd. E7 . . . . 1C **54**
  N19 . . . . 4E **33**
McDowall Cl. E16 . . . . . 4B **68**
McDowall Rd. SE5 . . . . 4E **91**
Macduff Rd. SW11 . . . . 4C **88**
Mace Cl. E1 . . . . 2D **79**
Mace St. E2 . . . . 1F **65**
McEwen Way E15 . . . . . 5F **53**
Macey Ho. SW11 . . . . . 4A **88**

Macey St. SE10 . . . . . . 2E **95**
   (off Thames St.)
Macfarland Gro.
  SE15 . . . . 3A **92**
Macfarlane Rd. W12 . . . 2E **71**
Macfarren Pl.
  NW1 . . . . 4C **4** (3C **60**)
McGlashon Ho. E1 . . . . 3C **64**
   (off Hunton St.)
McGrath Rd. E15 . . . . . 2B **54**
McGregor Ct. N1 . . . . . 1E **11**
Macgregor Rd. E16 . . . . 4E **69**
McGregor Rd. W11 . . . . 5B **58**
Machell Rd. SE15 . . . . . 1E **107**
McIndoe Ct. N1 . . . . . . 5F **49**
   (off Sherborne St.)
Macintosh Ho. W1 . . . . 5C **4**
   (off Beaumont St.)
McIntosh Ho. SE16 . . . . 5E **79**
   (off Millender Wlk.)
Mackay Ho. W12 . . . . . 1D **71**
   (off White City Est.)
Mackay Rd. SW4 . . . . . 1D **103**
Mackennal St. NW8 . . . 1A **60**
Mackenzie Cl. W12 . . . . 1D **71**
Mackenzie Ho. NW2 . . . 5C **28**
Mackenzie Rd. N7 . . . . 3B **48**
Mackenzie Wlk. E14 . . . 2C **80**
McKerrell Rd. SE15 . . . . 4C **92**
Mackeson Rd. NW3 . . . 1B **46**
Mackie Rd. SW2 . . . . . 5C **104**
Mackintosh La. E9 . . . . 2F **51**
Macklin St.
  WC2 . . . . 2E **15** (5A **62**)
Mackonochie Ho. EC1 . . 5B **8**
   (off Baldwins Gdns.)
Mackrow Wlk. E14 . . . . 1E **81**
Mack's Rd. SE16 . . . . . 5C **78**
Mackworth Ho. NW1 . . . 1F **5**
   (off Augustus St.)
Mackworth St.
  NW1 . . . . 1F **5** (2E **61**)
McLaren Ho. SE1 . . . . . 4D **25**
   (off St Georges Cir.)
Maclaren M. SW15 . . . . 2E **99**
Maclean Rd. SE23 . . . . 4A **108**
McLeod Ct. SE22 . . . . . 1C **120**
McLeod's M. SW7 . . . . 5D **73**
Macleod St. SE17 . . . . . 1E **91**
Maclise Ho. SW1 . . . . . 5A **76**
   (off Marsham St.)
Maclise Rd. W14 . . . . . 4A **72**
Macmillan Ho. NW8 . . . 2A **60**
   (off Lorne Cl.)
McMillan Ho. SE4 . . . . 1A **108**
   (off Arica Rd.)
  SE14 . . . . 4A **94**
McMillan St. SE8 . . . . . 2C **94**
Macmillan Way
  SW17 . . . . 4D **117**
Macnamara Ho.
  SW10 . . . . 3F **87**
   (off Worlds End Est.)
McNeil Rd. SE5 . . . . . . 5A **92**
Maconochies Rd.
  E14 . . . . 1D **95**
Macquarie Way E14 . . . 5D **81**

Macready Ho. *W1* *4A 60*
(off Crawford St.)
Macready Pl. *N7* 1A 48
(not continuous)
Macroom Ho. *W9* *2B 58*
(off Macroom Rd.)
Macroom Rd. *W9* 2B 58
Mac's Pl. *EC4* 2B 16
Madame Tussaud's
. . . . . *4B 4* (3C 60)
Maddams St. *E3* 3D 67
Maddocks Ho. *E1* *1D 79*
(off Cornwall St.)
Maddock Way *SE17* 2D 91
Maddox St.
W1 . . . . . 4E 13 (1D 75)
Madeira Rd. *E11* 3F 39
SW16 . . . . . 5A 118
Madinah Rd. *E8* 3C 50
Madison, The *SE1* *3B 26*
(off Long La.)
Madison Ho. *E14* 1B 80
(off Victory Pl.)
Madras Pl. *N7* 3C 48
Madrid Rd. *SW13* 4C 84
Madrigal La. *SE5* 3D 91
Madron St. *SE17* 1A 92
Mafeking Av. *E6* 1F 69
Mafeking Rd. *E16* 3B 68
Magazine Ga. *W2* 2A 74
Magdala Av. *N19* 4E 33
Magdalene Cl. *SE15* 5D 93
Magdalen Ho. *E16* *2D 83*
(off Keats Av.)
Magdalen Pas. *E1* 1B 78
Magdalen Rd.
SW18 . . . . . 1E 115
Magdalen St.
SE1 . . . . . 2D 27 (2A 78)
Magee St. *SE11* 2C 90
Magellan Ct. *NW10* *4A 42*
(off Brentfield Rd.)
Magellan Ho. *E1* *3F 65*
(off Ernest St.)
Magellan Pl. *E14* 5C 80
Magnin Ct. *E8* 5C 50
Magnolia Cl. *E10* 4C 38
Magnolia Gdns. *E10* 4C 38
Magnolia Ho. *SE8* *2B 94*
(off Evelyn St.)
Magnolia Lodge *W8* *4D 73*
(off St Mary's Ga.)
Magnolia Pl. *SW4* 3A 104
Magpie All.
EC4 . . . . . 3C 16 (5C 62)
Magpie Cl. *E7* 2B 54
Magpie Pl. *SE14* 2A 94
Magri Wlk. *E1* 4E 65
Maguire St. *SE1* 3B 78
Mahatma Gandhi Ind. Est.
SE24 . . . . . 2D 105
Mahogany Cl. *SE16* 2A 80
Maida Av. *W2* 4E 59
MAIDA HILL 3B 58
MAIDA VALE 2D 59
Maida Va. *W9* 1D 59
Maiden La. *NW1* 4F 47
SE1 . . . . . 2A 26 (2E 77)
WC2 . . . . . 5E 15 (1A 76)

Maiden Pl. *NW5* 5E 33
Maiden Rd. *E15* 4A 54
Maidenstone Hill
SE10 . . . . . 4E 95
Maidstone Bldgs. M.
SE1 . . . . . 2A 26 (2E 77)
Maidstone Ho. *E14* *5D 67*
(off Carmen St.)
Mail Coach Yd. *E2* 1E 11
Main Mill *SE10* *3D 95*
(off Greenwich High St.)
Mais Ho. *SE26* 2D 121
Maismore St. *SE15* 2C 92
Maitland Cl. *SE10* 3D 95
Maitland Ct. *W2* *1F 73*
(off Lancaster Ter.)
Maitland Ho. *E2* *1E 65*
(off Waterloo Gdns.)
SW1 . . . . . *2E 89*
(off Churchill Gdns.)
Maitland Pk. Est.
NW3 . . . . . 3B 46
Maitland Pk. Rd.
NW3 . . . . . 3B 46
Maitland Pk. Vs.
NW3 . . . . . 3B 46
Maitland Pl. *E5* 1D 51
Maitland Rd. *E15* 3B 54
SE26 . . . . . 5F 121
Maize Row *E14* 1B 80
Major Cl. *SW9* 1D 105
Major Rd. *E15* 2F 53
SE16 . . . . . 4C 78
Makepeace Av. *N6* 4C 32
Makepeace Mans.
N6 . . . . . 4C 32
Makins St. *SW3* 5A 74
Malabar Ct. *W12* *1D 71*
(off India Way)
Malabar St. *E14* 3C 80
Malam Ct. *SE11* 5C 76
Malam Gdns. *E14* 1D 81
Malbrook Rd. *SW15* 2D 99
Malcolm Ct. *E7* 3B 54
NW4 . . . . . 1C 28
Malcolm Cres. *NW4* 1C 28
Malcolm Ho. *N1* *1A 64*
(off Arden Est.)
Malcolm Pl. *E2* 3E 65
Malcolm Rd. *E1* 3E 65
Malcolm Sargent Ho.
E16 . . . . . *2D 83*
(off Evelyn Rd.)
Malcolmson Ho.
SW1 . . . . . *1F 89*
(off Aylesford St.)
Malden Ct. *N4* 1E 35
Malden Cres. *NW1* 3C 46
Malden Pl. *NW5* 2C 46
Malden Rd. *NW5* 2B 46
Maldon Cl. *E15* 2A 54
N1 . . . . . 5E 49
SE5 . . . . . 1A 106
Malet Pl. *WC1* 4B 6 (3F 61)
Malet St.
WC1 . . . . . 4B 6 (3F 61)
Maley Av. *SE27* 2D 119
Malfort Rd. *SE5* 1A 106
Malham Rd. *SE23* 1F 121

Malham Rd. Ind. Est.
SE23 . . . . . 1F 121
Malibu Cl. *SE26* 3D 121
Mall, The *E15* 4F 53
SW1 . . . . . 2C 22 (3E 75)
Mallams M. *SW9* 1D 105
Mallard Cl. *E9* 3B 52
NW6 . . . . . 1C 58
Mallard Ho. *NW8* *1A 60*
(off Barrow Hill Est.)
Mallards *E11* *2C 40*
(off Blake Hall Rd.)
Mall Chambers *W8* *2C 72*
(off Kensington Mall)
Mall Galleries 1C 22
Mall Gallery *WC2* *3D 15*
(in Thomas Neals Shop. Mall)
Malling *SE13* 3D 109
Mallinson Rd.
SW11 . . . . . 3A 102
Mallinson Sports Cen.
. . . . . 2B 32
Mallon Gdns. *E1* *2F 19*
(off Commercial St.)
Mallord St. *SW3* 2F 87
Mallory Bldgs. *EC1* *4D 9*
(off St John St.)
Mallory Cl. *E14* 4D 67
SE4 . . . . . 2A 108
Mallory St. *NW8* 3A 60
Mallow St.
EC1 . . . . . 3B 10 (3F 63)
Mall Rd. *W6* 1D 85
Mall Vs. *W6* *1D 85*
(off Mall Rd.)
Malmesbury *E2* *1E 65*
(off Cyprus St.)
Malmesbury Rd. *E3* 2B 66
E16 . . . . . 4A 68
Malmesbury Ter. *E16* 4B 68
Malmsey Ho. *SE11* 1B 90
Malmsmead Ho. *E9* *2B 52*
(off King's Mead Way)
Malpas Rd. *E8* 2D 51
SE4 . . . . . 5B 94
Malta Rd. *E10* 3C 38
Malta St. *EC1* 3D 9 (3D 63)
Maltby St.
SE1 . . . . . 4F 27 (3B 78)
Malthouse Dr. *W4* 2B 84
Malthouse Pas.
SW13 . . . . . *5B 84*
(off Maltings Cl.)
Malting Ho. *E14* 1B 80
(off Oak La.)
Maltings Cl. *E3* 2E 67
SW13 . . . . . 5B 84
Maltings Lodge *W4* *2A 84*
(off Corney Reach Way)
Maltings Pl. *SE1* 4E 27
SW6 . . . . . 4D 87
Malton M. *W10* 5A 58
Malton Rd. *W10* 5A 58
Maltravers St.
WC2 . . . . . 4A 16 (1B 76)
Malva Cl. *SW18* 3D 101
Malvern Cl. *W10* 4B 58

Malvern Ct. SW7 . . . . . . 5F 73
(off Onslow Sq.)
W12 . . . . 3C 70
(off Hadyn Pk. Rd.)
Malvern Gdns. NW2. . . . . 4A 30
Malvern Ho. N16 . . . . 3B 36
Malvern M. NW6 . . . . 2C 58
Malvern Pl. NW6 . . . . 2B 58
Malvern Rd. E6. . . . . 5F 55
E8 . . . . 4C 50
E11 . . . . 4A 40
NW6 . . . . 1B 58
(not continuous)
Malvern Ter. N1 . . . . 5C 48
Malwood Rd. SW12. . . . . 4D 103
Malyons Rd. SE13 . . . . . 4D 109
Malyons Ter. SE13 . . . . . 3D 109
Managers St. E14 . . . . . . 2E 81
Manaton Cl. SE15 . . . . . 1D 107
Manbey Gro. E15 . . . . . . 3A 54
Manbey Pk. Rd. E15 . . . . 3A 54
Manbey Rd. E15 . . . . 3A 54
Manbey St. E15 . . . . 3A 54
Manbre Rd. W6 . . . . 2E 85
Manchester Ct. E16 . . . . . 5D 69
(off Garvary Rd.)
Manchester Dr. W10 . . . . 3A 58
Manchester Gro. E14 . . . 1E 95
Manchester Ho.
SE17 . . . . 1E 91
Manchester M. W1. . . . . 1B 12
Manchester Rd. E14. . . . 1E 95
N15 . . . . 1F 35
Manchester Sq.
W1. . . . . 2B 12 (5C 60)
Manchester St.
W1. . . . . 1B 12 (4C 60)
Manchuria Rd.
SW11 . . . . 4C 102
Manciple St.
SE1. . . . . 4B 26 (3F 77)
Mandalay Rd. SW4 . . . 3E 103
Mandarin Ct. NW10 . . . . 3A 42
(off Mitchellbrook Way)
SE8 . . . . 2B 94
Mandarin St. E14 . . . . . 1C 80
Mandela Cl. W12. . . . . . 1D 71
Mandela Ho. E2 . . . . 2F 11
(off Virginia Rd.)
SE5. . . . . 5D 91
Mandela Rd. E16 . . . . . . 5C 68
Mandela St. NW1 . . . . . 5E 47
SW9 . . . . 3C 90
(not continuous)
Mandela Way SE1 . . . . . 5A 78
Mandel Ho. SW18 . . . . . 2C 100
Manderley W14 . . . . 4B 72
(off Oakwood La.)
Mandeville Cl. SE3 . . . . 3B 96
Mandeville Ho. SE1. . . . . 1B 92
(off Rolls Rd.)
SW4 . . . . 3E 103
Mandeville M. SW4 . . . 2B 103
Mandeville Pl.
W1. . . . . 2C 12 (5C 60)
Mandeville St. E5. . . . . . 5A 38
Mandrake Rd.
SW17 . . . . 3B 116
Mandrake Way E15 . . . . 4A 54

Mandrell Rd. SW2. . . . . 3A 104
Manette St.
W1. . . . . 3C 14 (5F 61)
Manfred Rd. SW15 . . . . 3B 100
Manger Rd. N7. . . . . 3A 48
Manilla St. E14 . . . . 3C 80
Manitoba Ct. SE16. . . . . . 3E 79
(off Canada Est.)
Manley Ct. N16 . . . . 5B 36
Manley Ho. SE11. . . . . . 5C 76
Manley St. NW1. . . . . . . 5C 46
Mannebey Prior N1 . . . . 1A 8
(off Cumming St.)
Manningford Cl.
EC1. . . . . 1D 9 (2D 63)
Manning Ho. W11 . . . . . 5A 58
(off Westbourne Pk. Rd.)
Manningtree Cl.
SW19 . . . . 1A 114
Manningtree St. E1 . . . . 5C 64
Manny Shinwell Ho.
SW6 . . . . 2B 86
(off Clem Attlee Ct.)
Manor, The SE23 . . . . . 5E 107
Manor Av. E7 . . . . 1E 55
SE4. . . . . 5B 94
Manor Brook SE3 . . . . . 2C 110
Manor Ct. E10 . . . . 3D 39
N2. . . . . 1B 32
SW2 . . . . 3B 104
SW3 . . . . 1A 88
(off Hemus Pl.)
SW6 . . . . 4D 87
SW16 . . . . 3A 118
Manor Est. SE16 . . . . . . 5D 79
Manorfield Cl. N19. . . . . 1E 47
(off Fulbrook M.)
Manor Flds. SW15 . . . . . 4F 99
Manor Gdns. N7. . . . . . . 5A 34
SW4 . . . . 5E 89
(off Larkhall Ri.)
W4 . . . . 1A 84
Manor Gro. SE15 . . . . . . 2E 93
Manorhall Gdns. E10. . . 3C 38
MANOR HOUSE 2F 35
MANOR HOUSE 2E 35
Manor Ho. NW1. . . . . . . 4A 60
(off Marylebone Rd.)
Manor Ho. Ct. W9 . . . . . . 3E 59
(off Warrington Gdns.)
Manor Ho. Dr. NW6 . . . . 4F 43
Manor Ho. Gdn. E11 . . . 1D 41
Manor La. SE12 . . . . . . 3A 110
SE13. . . . . 3A 110
Manor La. Ter. SE13 . . . 2A 110
Manor M. NW6. . . . . 1C 58
(off Cambridge Av.)
SE4. . . . . 5B 94
Manor Mt. SE23. . . . . . . 1E 121
Manor Pde. N16. . . . . . . 4B 36
NW10 . . . . 1B 56
(off High St. Harlesden)
MANOR PARK 1F 55
Manor Pk. SE13 . . . . . . 2F 109
Manor Pk. Crematorium
E7 . . . . 1E 55
Manor Pk. Pde.
SE13 . . . . 2F 109
(off Lee High Rd.)

Manor Pk. Rd. E12. . . . . 1F 55
(not continuous)
NW10 . . . . 5B 42
Manor Pl. SE17 . . . . 1D 91
Manor Rd. E10. . . . . 2C 38
E15 . . . . 1A 68
N16 . . . . 4F 35
Manor Way SE3 . . . . 2B 110
Manorway SE7 . . . . 5F 83
Manresa Rd. SW3 . . . . . 1A 88
Mansard Beeches
SW17 . . . . 5C 116
Mansell St.
E1. . . . . 3F 19 (5B 64)
Mansel Rd. SW19 . . . . . 5A 114
Manse Rd. N16 . . . . 5B 36
Mansfield Ct. E2. . . . . 5B 50
(off Whiston Rd.)
Mansfield Hgts. N2 . . . . 1A 32
Mansfield Ho. N1. . . . . . . 5A 50
(off New Era Est.)
Mansfield M.
W1. . . . . 1D 13 (4D 61)
Mansfield Pl. NW3. . . . . 1E 45
Mansfield Rd. E11. . . . . 1D 41
NW3 . . . . 2B 46
Mansfield St.
W1. . . . . 1D 13 (4D 61)
Mansford St. E2 . . . . . . 1C 64
Mansion Cl. SW9 . . . . . . 4C 90
(not continuous)
Mansion Cottage Vis.
Info. Cen. 3A 32
Mansion Gdns. NW3 . . . 5D 31
Mansion House
. . . . 3B 18 (5F 63)
Mansion Ho. Pl.
EC4. . . . . 3B 18 (5F 63)
Mansions, The SW5 . . . 1D 87
Manson M. SW7. . . . . . . 5F 73
Manson Pl. SW7. . . . . . . 5F 73
Manston NW1. . . . . 4E 47
(off Agar Gro.)
Manstone Rd. NW2 . . . . 2A 44
Manston Ho. W14 . . . . . 4A 72
(off Russell Rd.)
Mantilla Rd. SW17 . . . . 4C 116
Mantle Ct. SW18 . . . . . . 4D 101
(off Mapleton Rd.)
Mantle Rd. SE4 . . . . 1A 108
Mantle Way E15. . . . . . . 4A 54
Mantua St. SW11 . . . . . 1F 101
Mantus Cl. E1. . . . . 3E 65
Mantus Rd. E1 . . . . 3E 65
Manville Gdns.
SW17 . . . . 3D 117
Manville Rd. SW17 . . . . 2C 116
Manwood Rd. SE4 . . . . . 3B 108
Manygates SW12. . . . . . 2D 117
Mapesbury Ct. NW2. . . . 2A 44
Mapesbury M. NW4 . . . . 1C 28
Mapesbury Rd. NW2 . . . 4A 44
Mapeshill Pl. NW2 . . . . . 3E 43
Mapes Ho. NW6. . . . . . . 4B 44
Mape St. E2. . . . . 3D 65
(not continuous)
Maple Av. W3. . . . . 2A 70

Maple Cl. N16 . . . . 1C 36
SW4 . . . . 4F 103
Maple Ct. SE6 . . . . 1D 123
Maplecroft Cl. E6 . . . . . 5F 69
Mapledene Est. E8 . . . . 4C 50
Mapledene Rd. E8 . . . . . 4B 50
Maple Ho. SE8 . . . . 3B 94
(off Idonia St.)
Maple Leaf Sq. SE16 . . . 3F 79
Maple Lodge W8 . . . . . 4D 73
(off Abbots Wlk.)
Maple M. NW6 . . . . 1D 59
SW16 . . . . 5B 118
Maple Pl. W1 . . . 5A 6 (3E 61)
Maple Rd. E11 . . . . 1A 40
Maples Pl. E1 . . . . 4D 65
Maplestead Rd.
SW2 . . . . 5B 104
Maple St. E2 . . . . 1D 65
W1 . . . . 5F 5 (4E 61)
Mapleton Cres.
SW18 . . . . 4D 101
Mapleton Rd. SW18 . . . . 4C 100
(not continuous)
Maple Tree M. SE3 . . . . 4F 97
Maple Wlk. W10 . . . . . . 2F 57
Maplin Ho. E16 . . . . 5C 68
Maplin St. E3 . . . . 2B 66
Mapperley Cl. E11 . . . . . 1B 40
Marabou Cl. E12 . . . . . 2F 55
Marathon Ho. NW1 . . . . 5A 4
(off Marylebone Rd.)
Marban Rd. W9 . . . . . . 2B 58
Marble Arch 4A 12
MARBLE ARCH 1B 74
Marble Arch
W1 . . . . 4A 12 (1B 74)
Marble Arch Apartments
W1 . . . . 5B 60
(off Harrowby St.)
Marble Dr. NW2 . . . . . . 3F 29
Marble Ho. W9 . . . . . . 3B 58
Marble Quay E1 . . . . . . 2C 78
Marbles Ho. SE5 . . . . . 2E 91
(off Grosvenor Ter.)
Marbrook Ct. SE12 . . . . 3E 125
Marcella Rd. SW9 . . . . . 5C 90
Marchant Ct. SE1 . . . . . 1B 92
Marchant Ho. N1 . . . . . 5A 50
(off New Era Est.)
Marchant Rd. E11 . . . . . 4F 39
Marchant St. SE14 . . . . 2A 94
Marchbank Rd. W14 . . . . 2B 86
March Ct. SW15 . . . . . . 2D 99
Marchmont St.
WC1 . . . . 3D 7 (3A 62)
Marchwood Cl. SE5 . . . . 3A 92
Marcia Rd. SE1 . . . . . . 5A 78
Marcilly Rd. SW18 . . . . 3F 101
Marcon Ct. E8 . . . . 2D 51
(off Amhurst Rd.)
Marconi Rd. E10 . . . . . . 3C 38
Marcon Pl. E8 . . . . 3D 51
Marco Polo Ho.
SW8 . . . . 3D 89
Marco Rd. W6 . . . . 4E 71
Marcus Ct. E15 . . . . . . 5A 54
Marcus Garvey M.
SE22 . . . . 4D 107

Marcus Garvey Way
SE24 . . . . 2C 104
Marcus St. E15 . . . . . . 5B 54
SW18 . . . . 4D 101
Marcus Ter. SW18 . . . . 4D 101
Marden Ho. E8 . . . . 2D 51
Marden Sq. SE16 . . . . . 4D 79
Mardyke Ho. SE17 . . . . 5F 77
(off Mason St.)
Maresfield Gdns.
NW3 . . . . 2E 45
Mare St. E2 . . . . 1D 65
E8 . . . . 2D 51
Margaret Bldgs. N16 . . . 3B 36
Margaret Ct. W1 . . . . . 2F 13
Margaret Herbison Ho.
SW6 . . . . 2B 86
(off Clem Attlee Ct.)
Margaret Ho. W6 . . . . . 1E 85
(off Queen Caroline St.)
Margaret Ingram Cl.
SW6 . . . . 2B 86
Margaret Rd. N16 . . . . . 3B 36
Margaret St.
W1 . . . . 2E 13 (5D 61)
Margaretta Ter. SW3 . . . 2A 88
Margaretting Rd. E12 . . . 3E 41
Margaret Way IG4: Ilf. . . 1F 41
Margaret White Ho.
NW1 . . . . 1C 6
(off Chalton St.)
Margate Rd. SW2 . . . . . 3A 104
Margery Fry Ct. N7 . . . . 5A 34
Margery Pk. Rd. E7 . . . . 3C 54
Margery St.
WC1 . . . . 2B 8 (2C 62)
Margery Ter. E7 . . . . . . 3C 54
(off Margery Pk. Rd.)
Margin Dr. SW19 . . . . . 5F 113
Margravine Gdns.
W6 . . . . 1F 85
Margravine Rd. W6 . . . . 1F 85
Marham Gdns.
SW18 . . . . 1A 116
Maria Cl. SE1 . . . . 5D 79
Marian Ct. E9 . . . . 2E 51
Marian Pl. E2 . . . . 1D 65
Marian St. E2 . . . . 1D 65
Maria Ter. E1 . . . . 4F 65
Maribor SE10 . . . . 3E 95
(off Burney St.)
Marie Curie SE5 . . . . . 4A 92
Marie Lloyd Gdns.
N19 . . . . 2A 34
Marie Lloyd Ho. N1 . . . . 1B 10
(off Murray Gro.)
Marie Lloyd Wlk.
E8 . . . . 3B 50
Marigold All. SE1 . . . . . 5D 17
Marigold St. SE16 . . . . 3D 79
Marine Ct. E11 . . . . . . 4A 40
Marinefield Rd.
SW6 . . . . 5D 87
Marinel Ho. SE5 . . . . . 3E 91
Mariners M. E14 . . . . . 5F 81
Marine St. SE16 . . . . . 4C 78
Marine Twr. SE8 . . . . . 2B 94
(off Abinger Gro.)

Marion Ho. NW1 . . . . . 5B 46
(off Regent's Pk. Rd.)
Marion M. SE21 . . . . . . 3F 119
Marischal Rd. SE13 . . . 1F 109
Maritime Ind. Est.
SE7 . . . . 5D 83
Maritime Quay E14 . . . . 1C 94
Maritime St. E3 . . . . . . 3B 66
Marius Mans.
SW17 . . . . 2C 116
Marius Rd. SW17 . . . . . 2C 116
Marjorie Gro. SW11 . . . 2B 102
Marjorie M. E1 . . . . . . 5F 65
Market Ct. W1 . . . . 2F 13
Market Dr. W4 . . . . 3A 84
Market Entrance
SW8 . . . . 3E 89
Market Est. N7 . . . . . . 3A 48
Market La. W12 . . . . . . 3E 71
Market M.
W1 . . . . 2D 21 (2D 75)
Market Pde. E10 . . . . . 1E 39
(off High Rd.)
N16 . . . . 3C 36
(off Oldhill St.)
Market Pav. E10 . . . . . 5C 38
Market Pl. SE16 . . . . . 5C 78
(not continuous)
W1 . . . . 2F 13 (5E 61)
Market Rd. N7 . . . . 3A 48
Market Row SW9 . . . . . 2C 104
Market Sq. E14 . . . . . . 5D 67
Market St. E1 . . . . 4B 64
Market Way E14 . . . . . 5D 67
Market Yd. M.
SE1 . . . . 5D 27 (3A 78)
Markham Pl. SW3 . . . . . 1B 88
Markham Sq. SW3 . . . . 1B 88
Markham St. SW3 . . . . 1A 88
Mark Ho. E2 . . . . 1F 65
(off Sewardstone Rd.)
Markhouse Av. E17 . . . . 1A 38
Markhouse Pas. E17 . . . 1B 38
(off Markhouse Rd.)
Markhouse Rd. E17 . . . 1B 38
Markland Ho. W10 . . . . 1F 71
(off Darfield Way)
Mark La. EC3 . . . . 4E 19 (1A 78)
Markmanor Av. E17 . . . . 2A 38
Mark Sq.
EC2 . . . . 3D 11 (3A 64)
Markstone Ho. SE1 . . . . 4D 25
(off Lancaster St.)
Mark St. E15 . . . . 4A 54
EC2 . . . . 3D 11 (3A 64)
Mark Wade Cl. E12 . . . . 3F 41
Markwell Cl. SE26 . . . . 4D 121
Markyate Ho. W10 . . . . 3E 57
(off Sutton Way)
Marland Ho. SW1 . . . . . 5A 20
(off Sloane St.)
Marlborough SW19 . . . . 1F 113
(off Inner Pk. Rd.)
W9 . . . . 2E 59
(off Maida Va.)
Marlborough Av. E8 . . . 5C 50
(not continuous)
Marlborough Cl.
SE17 . . . . 5E 77

Marlborough Ct. W1. . . . . .4F **13**
W8 . . . . .5C **72**
(off Pembroke Rd.)
Marlborough Cres.
W4 . . . . .4A **70**
Marlborough Flats
SW3 . . . . .5A **74**
(off Walton St.)
Marlborough Ga. Ho.
W2 . . . . .1F **73**
(off Elms M.)
Marlborough Gro.
SE1 . . . . .1C **92**
Marlborough Hill
NW8 . . . . .1E **59**
Marlborough House
. . . . .2A **22** (2E **75**)
Marlborough Ho. *E16*. . .2C **82**
(off Hardy Av.)
NW1 . . . . .3E **5**
(off Osnaburgh St.)
Marlborough La. SE7. . .2E **97**
Marlborough Lodge
NW8 . . . . .1E **59**
(off Marlborough Pl.)
Marlborough Mans.
NW6 . . . . .2D **45**
(off Canon Hill)
Marlborough M.
SW2 . . . . .2B **104**
Marlborough Pl.
NW8 . . . . .1E **59**
Marlborough Rd. E7. . . .4E **55**
E15 . . . . .1A **54**
N19 . . . . .4F **33**
(not continuous)
SW1 . . . . . . .2A **22** (2E **75**)
Marlborough St.
SW3 . . . . .5A **74**
Marlborough Yd. N19. . .4F **33**
Marlbury *NW8* 5D **45**
(off Abbey Rd.)
Marler Rd. SE23. . . . . .1A **122**
Marley Ho. *W11*. 1F **71**
(off St Ann's Rd.)
Marley Wlk. NW2. . . . . .2E **43**
Marloes Rd. W8. . . . . . .4D **73**
Marlow Ct. NW6. . . . . . .4F **43**
SE14. . . . . .3A **94**
(off Batavia Rd.)
Marlowe Ct. SE19. . . . .5B **120**
SW3 . . . . .5A **74**
(off Petyward)
Marlowe Ho. *SE8*. 1B **94**
(off Bowditch)
Marlowe Path SE8 . . . . .2C **94**
Marlowes, The NW8. . . .5F **45**
Marlow Ho. *E2* 2F **11**
(off Calvert Av.)
SE1 . . . . .5F **27**
(off Maltby St.)
W2 . . . . .5D **59**
(off Hallfield Est.)
Marlow Way NW6. . . . . .3F **79**
Marlow Workshops
E2 . . . . .2F **11**
(off Virginia Rd.)
Marl Rd. SW18. . . . . . .2E **101**

Marlton St. SE10 . . . . . .1B **96**
Marmara Apartments
E16. . . . . .1C **82**
(off Western Gateway)
Marmion M. SW11. . . . .1C **102**
Marmion Rd. SW11. . . . .2C **102**
Marmont Rd. SE15. . . . .4C **92**
Marmora Ho. *E1*. 4A **66**
(off Ben Jonson Rd.)
Marmora Rd. SE22. . . . .4E **107**
Marne St. W10. . . . . . . .2A **58**
Marney Rd. SW11. . . . . .2C **102**
Marnfield Cres.
SW2 . . . . .1C **118**
Marnham Av. NW2. . . . . .1A **44**
Marnock Ho. *SE17*. 1F **91**
(off Brandon St.)
Marnock Rd. SE4. . . . . .3B **108**
Maroon St. E14. . . . . . . .4A **66**
Maroons Way SE6 . . . . .5C **122**
Marqueen Ct. *W8*. 3D **73**
(off Kensington Chu. St.)
Marquess Rd. N1. . . . . . .3F **49**
Marquess Rd. Nth.
N1. . . . . .3F **49**
Marquess Rd. Sth.
N1. . . . . .3E **49**
Marquis Ct. *N4*. 3B **34**
(off Marquis Rd.)
Marquis Rd. N4 . . . . . . .3B **34**
NW1 . . . . .3F **47**
Marrick Cl. SW15. . . . . . .2C **98**
Marrick Ho. *NW6*. 5D **45**
(off Mortimer Cres.)
Marriett Ho. SE6 . . . . . .4E **123**
Marriott Rd. E15 . . . . . . .5A **54**
N4. . . . . .3B **34**
Marriotts Cl. NW9 . . . . . .1B **28**
Marryat Ho. *SW1* 1E **89**
(off Churchill Gdns.)
Marryat Pl. SW19 . . . . . .4A **114**
Marryat Rd. SW19 . . . . . .5F **113**
Marryat Sq. SW6 . . . . . . .4A **86**
Marsala Rd. SE13 . . . . . .2D **109**
Marsden Rd. SE15. . . . .1B **106**
Marsden St. NW5. . . . . . .3C **46**
(not continuous)
Marshall Cl. SW18. . . . . .4E **101**
Marshall Ho. *N1*. 1F **63**
(off Cranston Est.)
NW6 . . . . .1B **58**
(off Albert Rd.)
SE1 . . . . .5E **27**
SE17. . . . . .1F **91**
(off East St.)
Marshall Rd. E10. . . . . . .5D **39**
Marshall's Pl.
SE16. . . . . . .5F **27** (4B **78**)
Marshall St.
W1. . . . . .3A **14** (5E **61**)
Marshalsea Rd.
SE1 . . . . .3A **26** (3E **77**)
Marsham Ct.
SW1 . . . . .5F **75**
Marsham St.
SW1 . . . . .5C **22** (4F **75**)
Marshbrook Cl. SE3 . . . .1F **111**
Marsh Cen., The *E1*. 2F **19**
(off Whitechapel High St.)

Marsh Ct. E8 . . . . .3C **50**
Marsh Dr. NW9 . . . . .1B **28**
Marshfield St. E14. . . . . .4E **81**
Marsh Ga. Bus. Cen.
E15 . . . . .5E **53**
Marshgate Cen., The
E15 . . . . .5D **53**
Marshgate La. E15 . . . . .4D **53**
(not continuous)
Marshgate Sidings
(Bow Depot) E15 . . . . .5D **53**
Marshgate Trad. Est.
E15 . . . . .4D **53**
Marsh Hill E9 . . . . .2A **52**
Marsh Ho. SW1 . . . . .1F **89**
(off Aylesford St.)
SW8 . . . . .4E **89**
Marsh La. E10 . . . . .4B **38**
Marsh St. E14 . . . . .5D **81**
Marsh Wall E14 . . . . .2C **80**
Marshwood Ho.
NW6 . . . . .5C **44**
(off Kilburn Va.)
Marsland Cl. SE17. . . . . .1D **91**
Marsom Ho. *N1* 1B **10**
(off Fairbank Est.)
Marston Cl. NW6 . . . . . . .4E **45**
Marston Ho. SW9. . . . . . .5C **90**
Marsworth Ho. *E2* 5C **50**
(off Whiston Rd.)
Martaban Rd. N16. . . . . .4B **36**
Martara M. SE17 . . . . . . .1E **91**
Martello St. E8. . . . . .4D **51**
Martello Ter. E8. . . . . . . .4D **51**
Martell Rd. SE21 . . . . . .3F **119**
Martel Pl. E8 . . . . .3B **50**
Martha Ct. E2. . . . . .1D **65**
Martha Rd. E15 . . . . .3A **54**
Martha's Bldgs.
EC1. . . . . . . .3B **10** (3F **63**)
Martha St. E1 . . . . .5E **65**
Martin Ct. *E14*. 3E **81**
(off River Barge Cl.)
Martindale Av. E16 . . . . . .1C **82**
Martindale Ho. *E14* 1D **81**
(off Poplar High St.)
Martindale Rd.
SW12 . . . . .5D **103**
Martineau Est. E1. . . . . . .1E **79**
Martineau Ho. *SW1* 1E **89**
(off Churchill Gdns.)
Martineau M. N5 . . . . .1D **49**
Martineau Rd. N5 . . . . . . .1D **49**
Martin Ho.
SE1 . . . . .5A **26** (4E **77**)
SW8 . . . . .3A **90**
(off Wyvil Rd.)
Martin La.
EC4. . . . . . . .4C **18** (1F **77**)
(not continuous)
Martins, The SE26. . . . . .5D **121**
Martlett Ct.
WC2. . . . . . . .3E **15** (5A **62**)
Marton Cl. SE6. . . . . .3C **122**
Marton Rd. N16 . . . . .4A **36**
Martys Yd. NW3 . . . . .1F **45**
Marvell Ho. *SE5*. 3F **91**
(off Camberwell Rd.)
Marvels Cl. SE12. . . . . . .2D **125**

Marvels La. SE12...... 2D **125**
(not continuous)
Marville Rd. SW6....... 3B **86**
Marvin St. E8 .... 3D **51**
Mary Adelaide Cl.
SW15 .... 4A **112**
Mary Ann Gdns. SE8 ... 2C **94**
Mary Bayly Ho. W11 ... 2A **72**
(off Wilsham St.)
Mary Datchelor Cl.
SE5 .... 4F **91**
Mary Flux Ct. SW5..... 1D **87**
(off Bramham Gdns.)
Mary Grn. NW8 .... 5D **45**
Mary Holben Ho.
SW16 .... 5E **117**
Mary Ho. W6 .... 1E **85**
(off Queen Caroline St.)
Mary Jones Ho. E14... 1C **80**
(off Garford St.)
Maryland Ind. Est.
E15 .... 2A **54**
(off Maryland Rd.)
Maryland Pk. E15...... 2A **54**
(not continuous)
Maryland Point E15 ... 3A **54**
(off The Grove)
Maryland Rd. E15...... 2F **53**
Maryland Sq. E15...... 2A **54**
Marylands Rd. W9 ..... 3C **58**
Maryland St. E15 ...... 2F **53**
Maryland Wlk. N1 ..... 5E **49**
(off Popham St.)
Mary Lawrenson Pl.
SE3 .... 3C **96**
MARYLEBONE... 5C **4** (4C **60**)
Marylebone Cricket Club
.... 2F **59**
MARYLEBONE FLYOVER
.... 4F **59**
Marylebone Fly-Over
W2................... 4F **59**
Marylebone High St.
W1 .... 5C **4** (4C **60**)
Marylebone La.
W1 .... 1C **12** (4C **60**)
Marylebone M.
W1 .... 1D **13** (4D **61**)
Marylebone Pas.
W1 .... 2A **14** (5E **61**)
Marylebone Rd.
NW1 .... 5A **4** (4A **60**)
Marylebone St.
W1 .... 1C **12** (4C **60**)
Marylee Way SE11..... 5B **76**
Mary Macarthur Ho.
E2 .... 2F **65**
(off Warley St.)
W6 .... 2A **86**
Maryon Ho. NW6 ..... 4E **45**
(off Goldhurst Ter.)
Maryon M. NW3....... 1A **46**
Maryon Rd. SE7 ...... 5F **83**
SE18 .... 5F **83**
Mary Pl. W11......... 1A **72**
Marys Ct. NW1........ 3A **60**
(off Palgrave Gdns.)
Mary Seacole Cl.
E8 .... 5B **50**

Mary Smith Ct. SW5 ... 5C **72**
(off Trebovir Rd.)
Marysmith Ho. SW1.... 1F **89**
(off Cureton St.)
Mary St. E16 .... 4B **68**
N1 .... 5E **49**
Mary Ter. NW1........ 5D **47**
Mary Wharrie Ho.
NW3 .... 4B **46**
(off Fellows Rd.)
Marzell Ho. W14 ...... 1B **86**
(off North End Rd.)
Masbro' Rd. W14 ...... 4F **71**
Mascalls Ct. SE7 ...... 2E **97**
Mascalls Rd. SE7 ..... 2E **97**
Mascotte Rd. SW15 ... 2F **99**
Mascotts Cl. NW2 ..... 5D **29**
Masefield Ho. NW6 .... 2C **58**
(off Stafford Rd.)
Mashie Rd. W3 .... 5A **56**
Maskall Cl. SW2 ...... 1C **118**
Maskell Rd. SW17 .... 3E **115**
Maskelyne Cl. SW11 ... 4A **88**
Mason Cl. E16 .... 1C **82**
SE16 .... 1C **92**
Mason Ho. E9......... 4E **51**
(off Frampton Pk. Rd.)
SE1 .... 5C **78**
(off Simms Rd.)
Mason's Arms M.
W1 .... 3E **13** (5D **61**)
Mason's Av.
EC2 .... 2B **18** (5F **63**)
Masons Pl.
EC1 .... 1E **9** (2E **63**)
Mason St. SE17 .... 5F **77**
Masons Yd.
EC1 .... 1E **9** (2D **63**)
SW1 .... 1A **22** (2E **75**)
SW19 .... 5F **113**
Massey Ct. E6 .... 5E **55**
(off Florence Rd.)
Massie Rd. E8 .... 3C **50**
Massingberd Way
SW17 .... 4D **117**
Massinger St. SE17 ... 5A **78**
Massingham St. E1 ... 3F **65**
Mast Ct. SE16 .... 5A **80**
(off Boat Lifter Way)
Master Gunners Pl.
SE18 .... 3F **97**
Masterman Ho. SE5.... 3F **91**
(off Elmington Est.)
Masterman Rd. E6 .... 2F **69**
Masters Cl. SW16 .... 5E **117**
Masters Dr. SE16..... 1D **93**
Masters Lodge E1 .... 5E **65**
(off Johnson St.)
Masters St. E1 .... 4F **65**
Mast Ho. Ter. E14 .... 5C **80**
(not continuous)
Mastmaker Ct. E14 ... 3C **80**
Mastmaker Rd. E14 ... 3C **80**
Matcham Rd. E11 .... 5A **40**
Matham Gro. SE22.... 2B **106**

Mathews Yd.
WC2.......... 2D **15** (5A **62**)
Mathieson Ct. SE1 .... 4E **25**
(off King James St.)
Mathison Ho. SW10.... 3E **87**
(off Coleridge Gdns.)
Matilda Gdns. E3...... 1C **66**
Matilda Ho. E1........ 2C **78**
(off St Katherine's Way)
Matilda St. N1 .... 5B **48**
Matisse Ct.
EC1............. 3B **10** (3F **63**)
Matlock Cl. SE24 ..... 2E **105**
Matlock Ct. NW8 ..... 1E **59**
(off Abbey Rd.)
SE5 .... 2F **105**
W11 .... 1C **72**
(off Kensington Pk. Rd.)
Matlock Rd. E10....... 1E **39**
Matlock St. E14 ...... 5A **66**
Maton Ho. SW6....... 3B **86**
(off Estcourt Rd.)
Matrimony Pl. SW4 ... 5E **89**
Matson Ho. SE16...... 4D **79**
Matthew Cl. W10 ..... 3F **57**
Matthew Parker St.
SW1 .... 4C **22** (3F **75**)
Matthews Ho. E14 .... 4C **66**
(off Burgess St.)
Matthews St. SW11.... 5B **88**
Matthias Rd. N16...... 2A **50**
Mattison Rd. N4....... 1C **34**
Maude Ho. E2 .... 1C **64**
(off Ropley St.)
Maude Rd. SE5 .... 4A **92**
Maud Gdns. E13 ...... 5B **54**
Maudlins Grn. E1...... 2C **78**
Maud Rd. E10 .... 5E **39**
E13 .... 1B **68**
Maud St. E16......... 4B **68**
Maud Wilkes Cl.
NW5 .... 2E **47**
Mauleverer Rd.
SW2 .... 3A **104**
Maundeby Wlk.
NW10 .... 3A **42**
Maunsel St. SW1 ..... 5F **75**
Maurer Ct. SE10 ...... 4B **82**
Mauretania Bldg. E1 .. 1F **79**
(off Jardine Rd.)
Maurice Bishop Ter.
N6.................... 1C **32**
(off View Rd.)
Maurice Ct. E1 .... 2F **65**
Maurice Drummond Ho.
SE10................. 4D **95**
(off Catherine Gro.)
Maurice St. W12 ..... 5D **57**
Mauritius Rd. SE10 ... 5A **82**
Maury Rd. N16........ 4C **36**
Maverton Rd. E3 ..... 5C **52**
Mavis Wlk. E6 .... 4F **69**
(off Greenwich Cres.)
Mavor Ho. N1......... 5B **48**
(off Barnsbury Est.)
Mawbey Ho. SE1 ..... 1B **92**
Mawbey Pl. SE1...... 1B **92**
Mawbey Rd. SE1 ..... 1B **92**
Mawbey St. SW8...... 3A **90**

Mawdley Ho. SE1. . . . . . . 4D **25**
Mawson Ct. N1 . . . . 5F **49**
  (off Gopsall St.)
Mawson Ho. EC1 . . . . 5B **8**
  (off Baldwins Gdns.)
Mawson La. W4 . . . . 2B **84**
Maxden Ct. SE15. . . . . 1B **106**
Maxilla Wlk. W10. . . . . . 5F **57**
Maxted Rd. SE15. . . . . 1B **106**
Maxwell Ct. SE22. . . . 1C **120**
  SW4 . . . . 3F **103**
Maxwell Rd. SW6 . . . . . 3D **87**
Maya Cl. SE15. . . . . 5D **93**
Mayall Rd. SE24. . . . . 3D **105**
Maybourne Cl.
  SE26. . . . . 5D **121**
Maybury Ct. W1. . . . . . . 1C **12**
  (off Marylebone St.)
Maybury Gdns.
  NW10. . . . . 3D **43**
Maybury M. N6. . . . . 2E **33**
Maybury Rd. E13 . . . . . . 3E **69**
Maybury St. SW17. . . . . 5A **116**
Mayday Gdns. SE3 . . . . . 5F **97**
Maydew Ho. SE16 . . . . . 5E **79**
  (off Abbeyfield Est.)
Maydwell Ho. E14 . . . . . 4C **66**
  (off Thomas Rd.)
Mayerne Rd. SE9 . . . . . 3F **111**
Mayeswood Rd.
  SE12. . . . . 4E **125**
MAYFAIR 5D **13** (1D **75**)
Mayfair M. NW1 . . . . 4B **46**
  (off Regents Pk. Rd.)
Mayfair Pl.
  W1. . . . . 1E **21** (2D **75**)
Mayfield Av. W4. . . . . . . 5A **70**
Mayfield Cl. E8. . . . . . . 3B **50**
  SW4 . . . . 3F **103**
Mayfield Gdns. NW4 . . . . 1F **29**
Mayfield Ho. E2 . . . . 1D **65**
  (off Cambridge Heath Rd.)
Mayfield Mans.
  SW15. . . . . 3B **100**
Mayfield Rd. E8 . . . . . . 4B **50**
  E13 . . . . 3B **68**
  N8. . . . . 1B **34**
  W12 . . . . 3A **70**
Mayfield Rd. Flats
  N8. . . . . 1B **34**
Mayflower Cl. SE16 . . . . 5F **79**
Mayflower Rd. SW9. . . . 1A **104**
Mayflower St. SE16 . . . . 3E **79**
Mayford NW1 . . . . 1E **61**
  (not continuous)
Mayford Cl. SW12 . . . . 5B **102**
Mayford Rd. SW12 . . . . 5B **102**
Maygood St. N1. . . . . . . 1C **62**
Maygrove Rd. NW6 . . . . 3B **44**
Mayhew Ct. SE5. . . . . . 2F **105**
Mayhill Rd. SE7 . . . . . . 2D **97**
Maylands Ho. SW3 . . . . . 5A **74**
  (off Elystan St.)
Maylie Ho. SE16 . . . . . . 3D **79**
  (off Marigold St.)
Maynard Cl. SW6. . . . . . 3D **87**
Maynard Rd. E17 . . . . . . 1E **39**
Maynards Quay E1 . . . . . 1E **79**
Mayne Ct. SE26 . . . . . 5D **121**

Mayo Ho. E1 . . . . 4E **65**
  (off Lindley St.)
Mayola Rd. E5 . . . . 1E **51**
Mayo Rd. NW10 . . . . . . 3A **42**
Mayow Rd. SE23 . . . . . . 4F **121**
  SE26 . . . . 4F **121**
May Rd. E13. . . . . 1C **68**
May's Bldgs. M.
  SE10 . . . . 3E **95**
Mays Cl. SE10 . . . . 3F **95**
  WC2 . . . . . . 5D **15** (1A **76**)
Maysoule Rd.
  SW11 . . . . 2F **101**
Mayston M. SE10. . . . . . 1C **96**
  (off Ormiston Rd.)
May St. W14 . . . . 1B **86**
  (North End Rd.)
  W14 . . . . 1B **86**
  (Vereker Rd.)
Maythorne Cotts.
  SE13 . . . . 4F **109**
Mayton St. N7 . . . . 5B **34**
May Tree Ho. SE4 . . . . . 1B **108**
  (off Wickham Rd.)
Maytree Wlk. SW2. . . . . 2C **118**
Mayville Est. N16. . . . . . 2A **50**
Mayville Rd. E11. . . . . . 4A **40**
May Wlk. E13. . . . . 1D **69**
Mayward Ho. SE5 . . . . . 4A **92**
  (off Peckham Rd.)
May Wynne Ho. E16 . . . . 1D **83**
  (off Murray Sq.)
Maze Hill SE3 . . . . 3B **96**
  SE10 . . . . 2A **96**
Maze Hill Lodge
  SE10 . . . . 2F **95**
  (off Park Vista)
Mazenod Av. NW6 . . . . . 4C **44**
Meadbank Studios
  SW11 . . . . 3A **88**
  (off Parkgate Rd.)
Mead Cl. NW1 . . . . 3C **46**
Meadcroft Rd. SE11. . . . 2D **91**
  (not continuous)
Meader Ct. SE14 . . . . . . 3F **93**
Mead Ho. W11 . . . . 2B **72**
  (off Ladbroke Rd.)
Meadow Bank SE3 . . . . 1B **110**
Meadowbank NW3. . . . . 4B **46**
Meadowbank Cl.
  SW6 . . . . 3E **85**
Meadowbank Rd.
  NW9 . . . . 2A **28**
Meadow Cl. SE6. . . . . . 5C **122**
Meadow Ct. N1 . . . . 1A **64**
Meadowcourt Rd.
  SE3 . . . . 2B **110**
Meadow La. SE12 . . . . . 3D **125**
Meadow M. SW8 . . . . . 2B **90**
Meadow Pl. SW8 . . . . . 3A **90**
  W4 . . . . 3A **84**
Meadow Rd. SW8 . . . . . 3B **90**
Meadow Row SE1 . . . . . 4E **77**
Meadowside SE9 . . . . . 2E **111**
Meadowside Leisure Cen.
  . . . . 2E **111**
Meadowsweet Cl.
  E16 . . . . 4F **69**

Meadowview Rd.
  SE6. . . . . 5B **122**
Mead Path SW17 . . . . . 4E **115**
Mead Pl. E9. . . . . 3E **51**
Mead Row
  SE1 . . . . . . 5B **24** (4C **76**)
Meads Cl. E15 . . . . 3B **54**
Meadway NW11. . . . . . . 1C **30**
Meadway, The SE3. . . . . 5F **95**
Meadway Cl. NW11. . . . . 1D **31**
Meadway Ga. NW11 . . . . 1C **30**
Meakin Est.
  SE1 . . . . . . 5D **27** (4A **78**)
Meanley Rd. E12 . . . . . . 1F **55**
Meard St.
  W1 . . . . 3B **14** (5F **61**)
  (not continuous)
Meath Ho. SE24. . . . . . 4D **105**
  (off Dulwich Rd.)
Meath Rd. E15 . . . . 1B **68**
Meath St. SW11. . . . . . 4D **89**
Mecca Bingo
  Camden. 5D **47**
  (off Arlington Rd.)
  Earlsfield. 1D **115**
  Fulham Broadway. . . . 3C **86**
  (off Vanston Pl.)
  Haggerston 1B **64**
  (off Hackney Rd.)
  Islington 4E **49**
  Kilburn 5C **44**
Mecklenburgh Pl.
  WC1 . . . . 3F **7** (3B **62**)
Mecklenburgh Sq.
  WC1 . . . . 3F **7** (3B **62**)
Mecklenburgh St.
  WC1 . . . . 3F **7** (3B **62**)
Medburn St. NW1. . . . . . 1F **61**
Medebourne Cl.
  SE3 . . . . 1C **110**
Mede Ho.
  BR1: Brom 5D **125**
  (off Pike Cl.)
Medfield St. SW15. . . . . 5C **98**
Medhurst Cl. E3 . . . . . . 1A **66**
  (not continuous)
Median Rd. E5 . . . . 2E **51**
Medina Gro. N7 . . . . . . 5C **34**
Medina Rd. N7. . . . . . . 5C **34**
Medland Ho. E14. . . . . . 1A **80**
Medlar St. SE5. . . . . . . 4E **91**
Medley Rd. NW6 . . . . . . 3C **44**
Medora Rd. SW2 . . . . . 5B **104**
Medusa Rd. SE6 . . . . . 4D **109**
Medway Bldgs. E3. . . . . 1A **66**
  (off Medway Rd.)
Medway Ho. NW11 . . . . 1D **31**
  WC1 . . . . 2D **7**
  (off Judd St.)
Medway Ho. NW8 . . . . . 3A **60**
  (off Penfold St.)
  SE1 . . . . 4C **26**
  (off Hankey Pl.)
Medway M. E3. . . . . . . 1A **66**
Medway Rd. E3 . . . . . . 1A **66**
Medway St. SW1 . . . . . 4F **75**
Medwin St. SW4 . . . . . 2B **104**
Meerbrook Rd. SE3 . . . . 1E **111**
Meeson Rd. E15. . . . . . 4B **54**

Meeson St. *E5* 1A **52**
Meeson's Wharf *E15* 1E **67**
Meeting Fld. Path *E9* . . . 3E **51**
Meeting Ho. All. *E1* 2D **79**
Meeting Ho. La.
  SE15. . . . . 4D **93**
Megabowl
  Streatham Hill 2A **118**
Mehetabel Rd. *E9*. 2E **51**
Melba Way *SE13* 4D **95**
Melbourne Ct. *W9* 3E **59**
  (off Randolph Av.)
Melbourne Gro.
  SE22 . . . . 2A **106**
Melbourne Ho. *W8*. 2C **72**
  (off Kensington Pl.)
Melbourne Mans.
  W14 . . . . 2A **86**
  (off Musard Rd.)
Melbourne M. *SE6* 5E **109**
  SW9 . . . . 4C **90**
Melbourne Pl.
  WC2. . . . . 3A **16** (5B **62**)
Melbourne Rd. *E10* 2D **39**
Melbourne Sq. *SW9* 4C **90**
Melbourne Ter. *SW6* 3D **87**
  (off Moore Pk. Rd.)
Melbray M. *SW6* 5B **86**
Melbreak Ho. *SE22* 1A **106**
Melbury Ct. *W8* 4B **72**
Melbury Dr. *SE5*. 3A **92**
Melbury Ho. *SW8* 3B **90**
  (off Richborne Ter.)
Melbury Rd. *W14*. 4B **72**
Melbury Ter. *NW1* 3A **60**
Melchester *W11*. 5B **58**
  (off Ledbury Rd.)
Melchester Ho. *N19* 5F **33**
  (off Wedmore St.)
Melcombe Ct. *NW1* 5A **4**
  (off Melcombe Pl.)
Melcombe Ho. *SW8*. 3B **90**
  (off Dorset Rd.)
Melcombe Pl. *NW1* 4B **60**
Melcombe Regis Ct.
  W1 . . . . 1C **12**
  (off Weymouth St.)
Melcombe St.
  NW1. . . . . 4A **4** (3B **60**)
Meldon Cl. *SW6*. 4D **87**
Melfield Gdns. *SE6* 4E **123**
Melford Ct. *SE1* 5E **27**
  (off Fendall St.)
  SE22 . . . . 1C **120**
  (not continuous)
Melford Pas. *SE22* 5C **106**
Melford Rd. *E11* 4A **40**
  SE22 . . . . 5C **106**
Melgund Rd. *N5*. 2C **48**
Melina Ct. *SW15* 1C **98**
Melina Pl. *NW8* 2F **59**
Melina Rd. *W12* 3D **71**
Melior Ct. *N6* 1E **33**
Melior Pl.
  SE1 . . . . 3D **27** (3A **78**)
Melior St.
  SE1 . . . . 3D **27** (3A **78**)
Meliot Rd. *SE6* 2F **123**
Mellish Flats *E10* 2C **38**

Mellish Ho. *E1*. 5D **65**
  (off Varden St.)
Mellish Ind. Est.
  SE18 . . . . 4F **83**
Mellish St. *E14* 4C **80**
Mellison Rd. *SW17* 5A **116**
Mellitus St. *W12* 4B **56**
Mell St. *SE10* 1A **96**
Melody La. *N5* 2E **49**
Melody Rd. *SW18* 3E **101**
Melon Pl. *W8* 3C **72**
Melon Rd. *E11* 5A **40**
  SE15. . . . . 4C **92**
Melrose Av. *NW2* 2D **43**
  SW19 . . . . 2B **114**
Melrose Cl. *SE12* 1C **124**
Melrose Gdns. *W6* 4E **71**
Melrose Ho. *E14* 4D **81**
  (off Lanark Sq.)
  NW6 . . . . 2C **58**
  (off Carlton Va.)
  SW1 . . . . 1D **89**
  (off Sutherland St.)
Melrose Rd. *SW13*. 5B **84**
  SW18 . . . . 4B **100**
Melrose Ter. *W6* 4E **71**
Melthorpe Gdns. *SE3* . . 4F **97**
Melton Ct. *SW7* 5F **73**
Melton St.
  NW1. . . . . 2A **6** (2E **61**)
Melville Ct. *SE8* 5A **80**
  W12 . . . . 4D **71**
  (off Goldhawk Rd.)
Melville Ho. *SE10* 4E **95**
Melville Pl. *N1* 4E **49**
Melville Rd. *SW13*. 4C **84**
Melwood Ho. *E1* 5D **65**
  (off Watney Mkt.)
Melyn Cl. *N7* 1E **47**
Memel Ct. *EC1* 4F **9**
Memel St. *EC1*. . 4F **9** (3E **63**)
Memorial Av. *E12*. 4F **41**
  E15. . . . . 2A **68**
Menard Ct. *EC1* 2A **10**
  (off Galway St.)
Mendham Ho. *SE1*. 5D **27**
  (off Cluny Pl.)
Mendip Cl. *SE26* 4E **121**
Mendip Ct. *SE14* 2E **93**
  (off Avonley Rd.)
  SW11 . . . . 1E **101**
Mendip Dr. *NW2*. 4A **30**
Mendip Ho's. *E2* 2E **65**
  (off Welwyn St.)
Mendip Rd. *SW11* 1E **101**
Mendora Rd. *SW6* 3A **86**
Menelik Rd. *NW2* 1A **44**
Menier Chocolate Factory
  . . . . 2A **26**
  (off O'Meara St.)
Menotti St. *E2* 3C **64**
Menteath Ho. *E14* 5C **66**
  (off Dod St.)
Mentmore Ter. *E8* 4D **51**
Mentone Mans.
  SW10 . . . . 3D **87**
  (off Fulham Rd.)
Mepham St.
  SE1 . . . . 2B **24** (2C **76**)

Merbury Cl. *SE13*. 3E **109**
Mercator Pl. *E14* 1C **94**
Mercator Rd. *SE13* 2F **109**
Mercer Bldg. *EC2*. 3E **11**
  (off Bateman's Row)
Mercer Ho. *SW1* 1D **89**
  (off Ebury Bri. Rd.)
Merceron Ho's. *E2* 2E **65**
  (off Globe Rd.)
Merceron St. *E1*. 3D **65**
Mercers Cl. *SE10*. 5B **82**
Mercer's Cotts. *E1* 5A **66**
  (off White Horse Rd.)
Mercers M. *N19* 5F **33**
Mercers Pl. *W6* 5F **71**
Mercers Rd. *N19* 5F **33**
  (not continuous)
Mercer St.
  WC2. . . . . 3D **15** (5A **62**)
Merchant Ct. *E1* 2E **79**
  (off Wapping Wall)
Merchants Ho. *SE10* . . . 1F **95**
  (off Collington St.)
Merchants Row *SE10* . . . 1F **95**
  (off Hoskins St.)
Merchant St. *E3* 2B **66**
Merchiston Rd. *SE6* . . . 2F **123**
Mercia Gro. *SE13*. 2E **109**
Mercia Ho. *SE5* 5E **91**
  (off Denmark Rd.)
Mercier Rd. *SW15* 3A **100**
Mercury Ct. *E14*. 5C **80**
  (off Homer Dr.)
Mercury Way *SE14* 2F **93**
Mercy Ter. *SE13*. 3D **109**
Mere Cl. *SW15*. 5F **99**
Meredith Av. *NW2* 2E **43**
Meredith Ho. *N16* 2A **50**
Meredith M. *SE4* 2B **108**
Meredith St. *E13* 2C **68**
  EC1 . . . . 2D **9** (2D **63**)
Meredyth Rd. *SW13* . . . 5C **84**
Meretone Cl. *SE4*. 2A **108**
Mereton Mans. *SE8*. . . . 4C **94**
  (off Brookmill Rd.)
Mereworth Ho. *SE15* . . . 2E **93**
Merganser Ct. *SE8*. 2B **94**
  (off Edward St.)
Meriden Ct. *SW3* 1A **88**
  (off Chelsea Mnr. St.)
Meriden Ho. *N1* 5A **50**
  (off Wilmer Gdns.)
Meridian Ct. *SE16* 3C **78**
  (off Nth. Flock St.)
Meridian Ga. *E14* 3D **81**
Meridian Ho. *SE10* 5A **82**
  (off Azof St.)
  SE10 . . . . 3E **95**
  (off Royal Hill)
Meridian Pl. *E14*. 3D **81**
Meridian Point *SE8* 2D **95**
Meridian Rd. *SE7* 3F **97**
Meridian Sq. *E15*. 4F **53**
Meridian Trad. Est.
  SE7. . . . . 5D **83**
Merifield Rd. *SE9* 2E **111**
Merivale Rd. *SW15* . . . 2A **100**
Merlin Gdns.
  BR1: Brom 3C **124**

Merlin Ho. SW18 . . . . . . 2E **101**
Merlin Rd. E12 . . . . 4F **41**
Merlins Ct. WC1 . . . . 2B **8**
   (off Margery St.)
Merlin St.
  WC1 . . . . 2B **8** (2C **62**)
Mermaid Ct. E8 . . . . 4B **50**
  (off Celandine Dr.)
SE1 . . . . 3B **26** (3F **77**)
SE16 . . . . 2B **80**
Mermaid Ho. E14 . . . . 1E **81**
   (off Bazely St.)
Mermaid Twr. SE8 . . . . . . 2B **94**
  (off Abinger Gro.)
Meroe Ct. N16 . . . . 4A **36**
Merredene St. SW2 . . 4B **104**
Merriam Av. E9 . . . . 3B **52**
Merrick Sq.
  SE1 . . . . 5B **26** (4F **77**)
Merriman Rd. SE3 . . . . . 4E **97**
Merrington Rd. SW6 . . 2C **86**
Merritt Rd. SE4 . . . . 3B **108**
Merritt's Bldgs. EC2 . . . 4D **11**
Merrivale NW1 . . . . 5E **47**
  (off Camden St.)
Merrow St. SE17 . . . . . . 1F **91**
Merrow Wlk. SE17 . . . . . 1F **91**
Merryfield SE3 . . . . 5B **96**
Merryfield Ho. SE9 . . 3E **125**
  (off Grove Pk. Rd.)
Merryfields Way
  SE6 . . . . 5D **109**
Merryweather Ct.
  N19 . . . . 5E **33**
Merthyr Ter. SW13 . . . . . 2D **85**
Merton Av. W4 . . . . 5B **70**
Merton La. N6 . . . . 4B **32**
Merton Ri. NW3 . . . . 4A **46**
Merton Rd. E17 . . . . 1E **39**
  SW18 . . . . 4C **100**
Mertoun Ter. W1 . . . . . . 4B **60**
  (off Seymour Pl.)
Merttins Rd. SE4 . . . . . . 3F **107**
  SE15 . . . . 3F **107**
Meru Cl. NW5 . . . . 1C **46**
Mervan Rd. SW2 . . . . . 2C **104**
Messent Rd. SE9 . . . . . 3E **111**
Messina Av. NW6 . . . . . 4C **44**
Messiter Ho. N1 . . . . 5B **48**
  (off Barnsbury Est.)
Meteor St. SW11 . . . . . 2C **102**
Methley St. SE11 . . . . . 1C **90**
Methwold Rd. W10 . . . . 4F **57**
Metro Bus. Cen., The
  SE26 . . . . 5B **122**
Metro Central Hgts.
  SE1 . . . . 5F **25**
Metropolis SE11 . . . . . . 4D **77**
  (off Oswin St.)
Metropolitan Bus. Cen.
  N1 . . . . 4A **50**
  (off Enfield Rd.)
Metropolitan Cl.
  E14 . . . . 4C **66**
Metropolitan Sta. Bldgs.
  W6 . . . . 5E **71**
  (off Beadon Rd.)
Metropolitan Wharf
  E1 . . . . 2E **79**

Mews, The IG4: Ilf 1F **41**
N1 . . . . 5E **49**
SE22 . . . . 3C **106**
Mews St. E1 . . . . 2C **78**
Mexborough NW1 . . . . . 5E **47**
Mexfield Rd. SW15 . . 3B **100**
Meymott St.
  SE1 . . . . . . 2D **25** (2D **77**)
Meynell Cres. E9 . . . . . 4F **51**
Meynell Gdns. E9 . . . . . 4F **51**
Meynell Rd. E9 . . . . 4F **51**
Meyrick Ho. E14 . . . . . . 4C **66**
  (off Burgess St.)
Meyrick Rd. NW10 . . . 3C **42**
  SW11 . . . . 1F **101**
Miah Ter. E1 . . . . 2C **78**
Miall Wlk. SE26 . . . . . 4A **122**
Micawber Ct. N1 . . . . . . 1A **10**
  (off Windsor Ter.)
Micawber Ho.
  SE16 . . . . 3C **78**
  (off Llewellyn St.)
Micawber St.
  N1 . . . . 1A **10** (2E **63**)
Michael Cliffe Ho.
  EC1 . . . . 2D **9**
Michael Faraday Ho.
  SE17 . . . . 1A **92**
  (off Beaconsfield Rd.)
Michael Manley Ind. Est.
  SW8 . . . . 5E **89**
  (off Clyston St.)
Michael Rd. E11 . . . . . . 3B **40**
  SW6 . . . . 4D **87**
Michaels Cl. SE13 . . . 2A **110**
Michael Sobell Leisure Cen.
  . . . . 5B **34**
Michael Stewart Ho.
  SW6 . . . . 2B **86**
  (off Clem Attlee Ct.)
Michelangelo Ct.
  SE16 . . . . 1D **93**
  (off Stubbs Dr.)
Micheldever Rd.
  SE12 . . . . 4A **110**
Michelle Cl. W3 . . . . . . 1A **70**
Michelson Ho. SE11 . . 5B **76**
  (off Black Prince Rd.)
Michigan Ho. E14 . . . . 4C **80**
Mickledore NW1 . . . . . . 1A **6**
  (off Ampthill Est.)
Micklethwaite Rd.
  SW6 . . . . 2C **86**
Mickleton Ho. W2 . . . . . 4C **58**
  (off Brunel Est.)
Middle Dartrey Wlk.
  SW10 . . . . 3E **87**
  (off Dartrey Wlk.)
Middlefield NW8 . . . . . . 5F **45**
Middle La. N8 . . . . 1A **34**
Middle La. M. N8 . . . . . 1A **34**
Middle Pk. Av. SE9 . . 4F **111**
Middle Rd. E13 . . . . 1C **68**
Middlesex CC Club . . . 2F **59**
Middlesex Ct. W4 . . . . . 5B **70**
Middlesex Filter Beds
  Nature Reserve 5F **37**
Middlesex Pas. EC1 . . . 1E **17**

Middlesex Pl. E9 . . . . . . 3E **51**
  (off Elsdale St.)
Middlesex St.
  E1 . . . . 1E **19** (4A **64**)
Middlesex University
  The Archway Campus
  . . . . 3E **33**
Middlesex Wharf E5 . . . 4E **37**
Middle St. EC1 . . . 5F **9** (4E **63**)
Middle Temple La.
  EC4 . . . . 3B **16** (5C **62**)
Middleton Dr. SE16 . . . 3F **79**
Middleton Gro. N7 . . . . 2A **48**
Middleton Ho. E8 . . . . . 4C **50**
  SE1 . . . . 5B **26**
  (off Burbage Cl.)
  SW1 . . . . 5F **75**
  (off Causton St.)
Middleton M. N7 . . . . . . 2A **48**
Middleton Pl. W1 . . . . . 1F **13**
Middleton Rd. E8 . . . . . 4B **50**
  NW11 . . . . 2C **30**
Middleton St. E2 . . . . . 2D **65**
Middleton Way
  SE13 . . . . 2F **109**
Middleway NW11 . . . . . 1D **31**
Middle Yd.
  SE1 . . . . . . 1D **27** (2A **78**)
Midford Pl.
  W1 . . . . 4A **6** (3E **61**)
Midhope Ho. WC1 . . . . . 2E **7**
  (off Midhope St.)
Midhope St.
  WC1 . . . . 2E **7** (2A **62**)
Midhurst SE26 . . . . 5E **121**
Midhurst Ho. E14 . . . . . 5B **66**
  (off Salmon La.)
Midhurst Way E5 . . . . . 1C **50**
Midland Pde. NW6 . . . . 3D **45**
Midland Pl. E14 . . . . . . 1E **95**
Midland Rd. E10 . . . . . . 2E **39**
  NW1 . . . . 1C **6** (1F **61**)
Midland Ter. NW2 . . . . . 5F **29**
  NW10 . . . . 3A **56**
Midmoor Rd. SW12 . . 1E **117**
Midship Cl. SE16 . . . . . 2F **79**
Midship Point E14 . . . . 3C **80**
  (off The Quarterdeck)
Midstrath Rd. NW10 . . 1A **42**
Midway Ho. EC1 . . . . . . 1D **9**
Midwood Cl. NW2 . . . . 5D **29**
Mighell Av. IG4: Ilf 1F **41**
Milborne Gro. SW10 . . 1E **87**
Milborne St. E9 . . . . 3E **51**
Milborough Cres.
  SE12 . . . . 4A **110**
Milcote St.
  SE1 . . . . . . 4D **25** (3D **77**)
Mildenhall Rd. E5 . . . . . 1E **51**
Mildmay Av. N1 . . . . 3F **49**
Mildmay Gro. Nth.
  N1 . . . . 2F **49**
Mildmay Gro. Sth.
  N1 . . . . 2F **49**
Mildmay Pk. N1 . . . . 2F **49**
Mildmay Rd. N16 . . . . . 2A **50**
Mildmay Rd. N1 . . . . 2F **49**
Mildmay St. N1 . . . . 3F **49**
MILE END 3B **66**

Mile End Pk. 3A 66
Mile End Pk. Leisure Cen.
. . . . 4A 66
Mile End Pl. E1 . . . . 3F 65
Mile End Rd. E1 . . . . 4E 65
E3 . . . . 4E 65
Mile End Stadium 4B 66
Miles Bldgs. NW1 . . . . 4A 60
(off Penfold Pl.)
Miles Ct. E1 . . . . 5D 65
(off Tillman St.)
Miles Ho. SE10 . . . . 1A 96
(off Tuskar St.)
Miles Pl. NW1 . . . . 4F 59
(off Broadley St.)
Miles St. SW8 . . . . 2A 90
Miles St. Bus. Est.
SW8 . . . . 2A 90
(off Miles St.)
Milfoil St. W12 . . . . 1C 70
Milford La.
WC2 . . . . 4A 16 (1C 76)
Milford M. SW16 . . . . . . 3B 118
Milford Towers SE6 . . . 5D 109
Milk St. BR1: Brom . . 5D 125
EC2 . . . . 2A 18 (5E 63)
Milkwell Yd. SE5 . . . . . . 4E 91
Milkwood Rd. SE24 . . . 3D 105
Milk Yd. E1 . . . . 1E 79
Millais Ho. SW1 . . . . . . 5A 76
(off Marsham St.)
Millais Rd. E11 . . . . 1E 53
Millard Cl. N16 . . . . 2A 50
Millard Ho. SE8 . . . . . . 1B 94
(off Leeway)
Millbank
SW1 . . . . 5D 23 (4A 76)
Millbank Ct. SW1 . . . . . 5A 76
(off John Islip St.)
Millbank Twr. SW1 . . . . 5A 76
Millbank Way SE12 . . . 3C 110
Millbrook Ho. SE15 . . . . 2C 92
(off Peckham Pk. Rd.)
Millbrook Pas. SW9 . . . 1D 105
Millbrook Pl. NW1 . . . . 1E 61
(off Hampstead Rd.)
Millbrook Rd. SW9 . . . 1D 105
Mill Ct. E10 . . . . 5E 39
Millcroft Ho. SE6 . . . . . 4E 123
(off Melfield Gdns.)
Millender Wlk. SE16 . . . 5E 79
(off New Rotherhithe Rd.)
Millennium Bridge
. . . . 5E 17 (1D 77)
Millennium Bri. Ho.
EC4 . . . . 4F 17
(off Up. Thames St.)
Millennium Bus. Cen.
NW2 . . . . 4D 29
Millennium Cl. E16 . . . . 5D 69
Millennium Dome
The O2 . . . . 2A 82
Millennium Dr. E14 . . . . 5F 81
Millennium Pl. E2 . . . . 1D 65
Millennium Sq.
SE1 . . . . 3F 27 (3B 78)
Millennium Way
SE10 . . . . 3A 82

Miller Cl.
BR1: Brom 5D 125
Miller Rd. SW19 . . . . . . 5F 115
Miller's Av. E8 . . . . 2B 50
Millers Mdw. Cl.
SE3 . . . . 2B 110
Miller's Ter. E8 . . . . 2B 50
Miller St. NW1 . . . . 1E 61
(not continuous)
Millers Way W6 . . . . 3E 71
Millers Wharf Rd. E1 . . . 2C 78
(off St Katherine's Way)
Miller Wlk.
SE1 . . . . 2C 24 (2C 76)
Millfield N4 . . . . 4C 34
Millfield La. N6 . . . . 3A 32
(not continuous)
Millfield Pl. N6 . . . . 4C 32
Mill Gdns. SE26 . . . . . 3D 121
Millgrove St. SW11 . . . . 4C 88
Millharbour E14 . . . . . . 3D 81
Mill Hill SW13 . . . . 5C 84
Mill Hill Rd. SW13 . . . . . 5C 84
(off St Katherine's Way)
Milligan St. E14 . . . . 1B 80
Milliners Ho. SE1 . . . . . 4E 27
(off Bermondsey St.)
SW18 . . . . 2C 100
Millington Ho. N16 . . . . 5F 35
Mill La. NW6 . . . . 2B 44
Millman M. WC1 . . . . 4F 7
(off Millman Ct.)
Millman M.
WC1 . . . . 4F 7 (3B 62)
Millman Pl. WC1 . . . . 4A 8
(off Millman St.)
Millman St.
WC1 . . . . 4F 7 (3B 62)
Millmark Gro. SE14 . . . . 5A 94
MILL MEADS 1F 67
Mill Pl. E14 . . . . 5A 66
Mill Pond Cl. SW8 . . . . . 3F 89
Millpond Est. SE16 . . . . 3D 79
Mill Rd. E16 . . . . 2D 83
Mill Row N1 . . . . 5A 50
Mills Ct. EC2 . . . . 3D 11
(off Curtain Rd.)
Mills Gro. E14 . . . . 5E 67
Millshot Cl. SW6 . . . . . . 4E 85
Mills Ho. SW8 . . . . 4E 89
(off Thessaly Rd.)
Millstream Ho.
SE16 . . . . 3D 79
(off Jamaica Rd.)
Millstream Rd.
SE1 . . . . 4F 27 (3B 78)
Mill St. SE1 . . . . 3B 78
W1 . . . . 4F 13 (1D 75)
MILLWALL 5D 81
Millwall Dock Rd.
E14 . . . . 4C 80
Millwall FC 1E 93
Millwood St. W10 . . . . . 4A 58
Mill Yd. E1 . . . . 1C 78
Milman Rd. NW6 . . . . . . 1F 57
Milman's Ho. SW1 . . . . 1D 89
(off Warwick Way)

Milman's Ho. SW10 . . . . 2F 87
(off Milman's St.)
Milman's St. SW10 . . . . 2F 87
Milne Gdns. SE9 . . . . . . 3F 111
Milner Ct. SE15 . . . . 3B 92
(off Colegrove Rd.)
Milner Pl. N1 . . . . 5C 48
Milner Rd. E15 . . . . 2A 68
Milner Sq. N1 . . . . 4D 49
Milner St. SW3 . . . . 5B 74
Milo Gdns. SE22 . . . . . 4B 106
Milo Rd. SE22 . . . . 4B 106
Milrood Ho. E1 . . . . 4F 65
(off Stepney Grn.)
Milroy Wlk.
SE1 . . . . 1D 25 (2D 77)
Milson Rd. W14 . . . . 4F 71
Milstead Ho. E5 . . . . 2D 51
Milton Av. E6 . . . . 4F 55
N6 . . . . 2E 33
Milton Cl. N2 . . . . 1E 31
SE1 . . . . 5B 78
Milton Ct.
EC2 . . . . 5B 10 (4F 63)
SE14 . . . . 2B 94
(not continuous)
SW18 . . . . 3C 100
Milton Ct. Rd. SE14 . . . . 2A 94
Milton Ct. Wlk. EC2 . . . 5B 10
(off Silk St.)
Milton Gdn. Est.
N16 . . . . 1F 49
Milton Gro. N16 . . . . 1F 49
Milton Ho. E2 . . . . 2E 65
(off Roman Rd.)
SE5 . . . . 3F 91
(off Elmington Est.)
Milton Mans. W14 . . . . 2A 86
(off Queen's Club Gdns.)
Milton Pk. N6 . . . . 2E 33
Milton Pl. N7 . . . . 2C 48
(off Eastwood Cl.)
Milton Rd. N6 . . . . 2E 33
NW9 . . . . 2C 28
SE24 . . . . 3D 105
SW19 . . . . 5E 115
Milton St.
EC2 . . . . 5B 10 (4F 63)
Milverton Ho. SE6 . . . . 3A 122
Milverton Rd. NW6 . . . . 4E 43
Milverton St. SE11 . . . . 1C 90
Milward St. E1 . . . . 4D 65
Mimosa Lodge
NW10 . . . . 2B 42
Mimosa St. SW6 . . . . . . 4B 86
Minard Rd. SE6 . . . . . . 5A 110
Mina Rd. SE17 . . . . 1A 92
Minchin Ho. E14 . . . . . . 5C 66
(off Dod St.)
Mincing La.
EC3 . . . . 4D 19 (1A 78)
Minehead Rd.
SW16 . . . . 5B 118
Minera M. SW1 . . . . 5C 74
Minerva Cl. SW9 . . . . . . 3C 90
(not continuous)
Minerva Lodge N7 . . . . . 3B 48
Minerva Rd. NW10 . . . . 2A 56
Minerva St. E2 . . . . 1D 65

Minerva Wlk.
EC1 . . . . 2E **17** (5D **63**)
Minet Av. NW10 . . . . 1A **56**
Minet Gdns. NW10 . . . . . 1A **56**
Minet Rd. SW9 . . . . 5D **91**
Minford Gdns. W14 . . . . . 3F **71**
Minford Ho. W14 . . . . 3F **71**
(off Minford Gdns.)
Mingard Wlk. N7 . . . . 4B **34**
Ming St. E14 . . . . 1C **80**
Miniver Pl. EC4 . . . . 4A **18**
Minnow St. SE17 . . . . 5A **78**
Minnow Wlk. SE17 . . . . . . 5A **78**
Minories EC3 . . . 3F **19** (5B **64**)
Minshill St. SW8 . . . . 4F **89**
Minson Rd. E9 . . . . 5F **51**
Minstead Gdns.
SW15 . . . . 5B **98**
Minster Ct. EC3 . . . . 4E **19**
Minster Pavement
EC3 . . . . 4E **19**
(off Mincing La.)
Minster Rd. NW2 . . . . 2A **44**
Mint Bus. Pk. E16 . . . . . . 4D **69**
Mintern St. N1 . . . . 1F **63**
Minton Ho. SE11 . . . . 5C **76**
(off Walnut Tree Wlk.)
Minton M. NW6 . . . . 3D **45**
Mirabel Rd. SW6 . . . . 3B **86**
Miranda Cl. E1 . . . . 4E **65**
Miranda Ho. N1 . . . . 1D **11**
(off Crondall St.)
Miranda Rd. N19 . . . . 3E **33**
Mirfield St. SE7 . . . . 5F **83**
Mirror Path SE9 . . . . 3E **125**
Missenden SE17 . . . . 1F **91**
(off Roland Way)
Missenden Ho. NW8 . . 3A **60**
(off Jerome Cres.)
Missenden Villa Wlk.
SE17 . . . . 1F **91**
(off Inville Rd.)
Mission, The E14 . . . . . . 5B **66**
(off Commercial Rd.)
Mission Pl. SE15 . . . . 4C **92**
Mistral SE5 . . . . 4A **92**
Mitali Pas. E1 . . . . 5C **64**
(not continuous)
Mitcham Ho. SE5 . . . . 4E **91**
Mitcham La. SW16 . . . . . . 5E **117**
Mitcham Rd. SW17 . . . . . 5B **116**
Mitchellbrook Way
NW10 . . . . 3A **42**
Mitchell Ho. W12 . . . . . . 1D **71**
(off White City Est.)
Mitchell's Pl. SE21 . . . . . 4A **106**
(off Aysgarth Rd.)
Mitchell St.
EC1 . . . . 3F **9** (3E **63**)
(not continuous)
Mitchell Wlk. E6 . . . . 4F **69**
(off Allhallows Rd.)
Mitchison Rd. N1 . . . . . . 3F **49**
Mitford Bldgs. SW6 . . . 3C **86**
(off Dawes St.)
Mitford Rd. N19 . . . . 4A **34**
Mitre, The E14 . . . . 1B **80**
Mitre Ct. EC2 . . . . 2A **18**

Mitre Ho. SW3 . . . . 1B **88**
(off King's Rd.)
Mitre Rd. E15 . . . . 1A **68**
SE1 . . . . 3C **24** (3C **76**)
Mitre Sq.
EC3 . . . . 3E **19** (5A **64**)
Mitre St. EC3 . . . 3E **19** (5A **64**)
W10 . . . . 3D **57**
Mitre Yd. SW3 . . . . 5A **74**
Mizen Ct. E14 . . . . 3C **80**
(off Alpha Gro.)
Moat Dr. E13 . . . . 1E **69**
Moatfield NW6 . . . . 4A **44**
Moatlands Ho. WC1 . . . . . 2E **7**
(off Cromer St.)
Moat Pl. SW9 . . . . 1B **104**
Moberly Rd. SW4 . . . . . . 5F **103**
Moberly Sports &
Education Cen. 2F **57**
(off Chamberlayne Rd.)
Mobil Ct. WC2 . . . . 3A **16**
(off Clement's Inn)
Mocatta Ho. E1 . . . . 3D **65**
(off Brady St.)
Modbury Gdns. NW5 . . . . 3C **46**
Modder Pl. SW15 . . . . . . 2F **99**
Model Bldgs. WC1 . . . . . . 2A **8**
Model Farm Cl. SE9 . . . . 3F **125**
Modern Ct. EC4 . . . . 2D **17**
Modling Ho. E2 . . . . 1F **65**
(off Mace St.)
Moelwyn N7 . . . . 2F **47**
Moffat Ct. SW19 . . . . 5C **114**
Moffat Ho. SE5 . . . . 3E **91**
Moffat Rd. SW17 . . . . . . 4B **116**
Mohawk Ho. E3 . . . . 1A **66**
(off Gernon Rd.)
Mohmmad Khan Rd.
E11 . . . . 3B **40**
Moland Mead SE16 . . . . 1F **93**
(off Crane Mead)
Molasses Ho. SW11 . . . . 1E **101**
(off Clove Hitch Quay)
Molasses Row
SW11 . . . . 1E **101**
Mole Ho. NW8 . . . . 3F **59**
(off Church St. Est.)
Molesford Rd. SW6 . . . . 4C **86**
Molesworth Ho.
SE17 . . . . 2D **91**
(off Brandon Est.)
Molesworth St.
SE13 . . . . 2E **109**
Mollis Ho. E3 . . . . 4C **66**
(off Gale St.)
Molly Huggins Cl.
SW12 . . . . 5E **103**
Molton Ho. N1 . . . . 5B **48**
(off Barnsbury Est.)
Molyneux Dr. SW17 . . . . 4D **117**
Molyneux St. W1 . . . . . . 4A **60**
Monarch Dr. E16 . . . . 4F **69**
Monarch Ho. W8 . . . . . . 4C **72**
(off Earl's Ct. Rd.)
W8 . . . . 4C **72**
(off Kensington High St.)
Monarch M. E17 . . . . 1D **39**
SW16 . . . . 5C **118**

Mona Rd. SE15 . . . . 5E **93**
Mona St. E16 . . . . 4B **68**
Moncks Row
SW18 . . . . 4B **100**
Monck St.
SW1 . . . . 5C **22** (4F **75**)
Monckton Ct. W14 . . . . . 4B **72**
(off Strangways Ter.)
Monclar Rd. SE5 . . . . 2F **105**
Moncorvo Cl. SW7 . . . . . 3A **74**
Moncrieff Cl. E6 . . . . 5F **69**
Moncrieff Pl. SE15 . . . . . 5C **92**
Moncrieff St. SE15 . . . . . 5C **92**
Monday All. N16 . . . . 4A **36**
(off High St.)
Monega Rd. E7 . . . . 3E **55**
E12 . . . . 3E **55**
Monet Ct. SE16 . . . . 1D **93**
(off Stubbs Dr.)
Moneyer Ho. N1 . . . . . . 1B **10**
(off Fairbank Est.)
Mongers Almshouses
E9 . . . . 4F **51**
(off Church Cres.)
Monica Shaw Ct.
NW1 . . . . 1F **61**
(off Purchese St.,
not continuous)
Monier Rd. E3 . . . . 4C **52**
Monk Ct. W12 . . . . 2C **70**
Monk Dr. E16 . . . . 1C **82**
Monk Pas. E16 . . . . 1C **82**
(off Monk Dr.)
Monkton Ho. E5 . . . . 2D **51**
SE16 . . . . 3F **79**
(off Wolfe Cres.)
Monkton St. SE11 . . . . . . 5C **76**
Monkwell Sq.
EC2 . . . . 1A **18** (4E **63**)
Monmouth Pl. W2 . . . . . . 5D **59**
(off Monmouth Rd.)
Monmouth Rd. W2 . . . . . . 5C **58**
Monmouth St.
WC2 . . . . 3D **15** (5A **62**)
Monnery Rd. N19 . . . . . . 5E **33**
Monro Ho. SE1 . . . . 1C **92**
Monroe Ho. NW8 . . . . . . 2A **60**
(off Lorne Cl.)
Monro Way E5 . . . . 1C **50**
Monsell Ct. N4 . . . . 5D **35**
Monsell Rd. N4 . . . . 5C **34**
Monson Rd. NW10 . . . . . 1C **56**
SE14 . . . . 3F **93**
Montacute Rd. SE6 . . . . . 5B **108**
Montagu Ct. W1 . . . . 1A **12**
(off Montagu Sq.)
Montague Av. SE4 . . . . . 2B **108**
Montague Cl.
SE1 . . . . 1B **26** (2F **77**)
Montague Ho. E16 . . . . . 2D **83**
(off Wesley Av.)
N1 . . . . 5A **50**
(off New Era Est.)
Montague Pl.
WC1 . . . . 5C **6** (4F **61**)
Montague Rd. E8 . . . . 2C **50**
E11 . . . . 4B **40**
N8 . . . . 1B **34**
Montague Sq. SE15 . . . . 3E **93**

Montague St.
EC1. . . . . 1F **17** (4E **63**)
WC1. . . . . 5D **7** (4A **62**)
Montagu Mans.
W1. . . . . 5A **4** (4B **60**)
Montagu M. Nth.
W1. . . . . 1A **12** (4B **60**)
Montagu M. Sth.
W1. . . . . 2A **12** (5B **60**)
Montagu M. W.
W1. . . . . 2A **12** (5B **60**)
Montagu Pl.
W1. . . . . 1A **12** (4B **60**)
Montagu Rd. NW4 . . . 1C **28**
Montagu Row
W1. . . . . 1A **12** (4B **60**)
Montagu Sq.
W1. . . . . 1A **12** (4B **60**)
Montagu St.
W1. . . . . . . 2A **12** (5B **60**)
Montaigne Cl. SW1 . . . . 5F **75**
Montana Bldg. *SE10* . . 4D **95**
(off Deal's Gateway)
Montana Gdns.
SE26. . . . . 5B **122**
Montana Rd. SW17 . . 3C **116**
Montcalm Ho. E14 . . . . 5B **80**
Montcalm Rd. SE7 . . . . 3F **97**
Montclare St.
E2. . . . . 3F **11** (3B **64**)
Monteagle Ct. N1. . . . . 1A **64**
Monteagle Way E5 . . . . 5C **36**
SE15. . . . . 1D **107**
Montefiore Ct. N16. . . . 3B **36**
Montefiore St. SW8. . . . 5D **89**
Montego Cl. SE24 . . . 2C **104**
Montem Rd. SE23 . . . 5B **108**
Montem St. N4 . . . . . . 3B **34**
Montenotte Rd. N8. . . . 1E **33**
Montesquieu Ter.
E16 . . . . *5B 68*
(off Clarkson Rd.)
Montevetro SW11. . . . . 4F **87**
Montford Pl. SE11 . . . . 1C **90**
Montfort Ho. *E2* *2E 65*
(off Victoria Pk. Sq.)
E14 . . . . *4E 81*
(off Galbraith St.)
Montfort Pl. SW19 . . . . 1F **113**
Montgomerie M.
SE23 . . . . 5E **107**
Montgomery Lodge
E1 . . . . *3E 65*
(off Cleveland Gro.)
Montgomery St. E14 . . 2D **81**
Montholme Rd.
SW11 . . . . 4B **102**
Monthope Rd. E1 . . . . 4C **64**
Montolieu Gdns.
SW15 . . . . 3D **99**
Montpelier Gdns. E6. . . 2F **69**
Montpelier Gro. NW5 . . 2E **47**
Montpelier M. SW7 . . . 4A **74**
Montpelier Pl. E1 . . . . . 5E **65**
SW7 . . . . 4A **74**
Montpelier Ri. NW11. . . 2A **30**
Montpelier Sq. SE15 . . 4D **93**
Montpelier Row SE3 . . . 5B **96**
Montpelier Sq. SW7 . . . 3A **74**

Montpelier St. SW7 . . . 4A **74**
Montpelier Ter. SW7 . . . 3A **74**
Montpelier Va. SE3 . . . 5B **96**
Montpelier Wlk.
SW7 . . . . 4A **74**
Montpelier Way
NW11 . . . . 2A **30**
Montreal Pl.
WC2. . . . . . . 4F **15** (1B **76**)
Montrell Rd. SW2 . . . 1A **118**
Montrose Av. NW6 . . . 1A **58**
Montrose Ct. SE6 . . . 2B **124**
SW7 . . . . 3F **73**
Montrose Ho. E14 . . . . 4C **80**
SW1 . . . . *4C 20*
(off Montrose Pl.)
Montrose Pl.
SW1. . . . . . . 4C **20** (3C **74**)
Montrose Way SE23 . . 1F **121**
Montserrat Rd. SE19 . . 5F **119**
Montserrat Rd.
SW15 . . . . 2A **100**
Monument, The *4C 18*
(off Monument St.)
Monument Gdns.
SE13 . . . . 3E **109**
Monument St.
EC3. . . . . . . 4C **18** (1F **77**)
Monza St. E1 . . . . 1E **79**
Moodkee St. SE16 . . . . 4E **79**
Moody Rd. SE15 . . . . . 4B **92**
Moody St. E1 . . . . 2F **65**
Moon Ct. SE12 . . . . . 2C **110**
Moon St. N1 . . . . 5D **49**
Moorcroft Rd.
SW16 . . . . 3A **118**
Moore Cl. *N1* *5D 49*
(off Gaskin St.)
Moorehead Way
SE3 . . . . 1C **110**
Moore Ho. *E1* *1E 79*
(off Cable St.)
E2 . . . . *2E 65*
(off Roman Rd.)
E14 . . . . 3C **80**
SE10 . . . . *1B 96*
(off Armitage Rd.)
Moore Pk. Ct. *SW6* . . . *3D 87*
(off Fulham Rd.)
Moore Pk. Rd. SW6 . . . 3C **86**
Moore St. SW19 . . . . . 5E **119**
Moore St. SW3. . . . . . 5B **74**
Moore Wlk. E7 . . . . . . 1C **54**
Moorey Cl. E15 . . . . . . 5B **54**
Moorfields
EC2. . . . . . . 1B **18** (4F **63**)
Moorfields Highwalk
EC2 . . . . *1B 18*
(off Moorfields,
not continuous)
Moorgate
EC2. . . . . . . 2B **18** (5F **63**)
Moorgate Pl. EC2. . . . . 2B **18**
Moorgreen Ho. EC1 . . . 1D **9**
Moorhouse Rd. W2 . . . 5C **58**
Moorings, The. *E16* . . *4E 69*
(off Prince Regent La.)
Moorland Rd.
SW9 . . . . 2D **105**

Moor La. EC2. . . 1B **18** (4F **63**)
(not continuous)
Moor Pl. EC2. . . 1B **18** (4F **63**)
Moorside Rd.
BR1: Brom 3A **124**
Moor St. W1 . . . 3C **14** (5F **61**)
Moran Ho. *E1*. *2D 79*
(off Wapping La.)
Morant St. E14. . . . . . . 1C **80**
Mora Rd. NW2 . . . . . . 1E **43**
Mora St. EC1. . . 2A **10** (2E **63**)
Morat St. SW9 . . . . 4B **90**
Moravian Cl. SW3 . . . . 2F **87**
Moravian Pl. SW10 . . . 2F **87**
Moravian St. E2 . . . . . 1E **65**
Moray Ho. *E1*. *3A 66*
(off Harford St.)
Moray M. N7 . . . . 4B **34**
Moray Rd. N4 . . . . 4B **34**
Mordaunt Ho. *NW10* . . *5A 42*
(off Stracey Rd.)
Mordaunt Rd. NW10 . . 5A **42**
Mordaunt St. SW9 . . . 1B **104**
Morden Hill SE13 . . . . 5E **95**
Morden La. SE13 . . . . . 4E **95**
(not continuous)
Morden Rd. SE3. . . . . . 5C **96**
Morden Rd. M. SE3 . . . 5C **96**
Morden St. SE13 . . . . . 4D **95**
Morden Wharf SE10. . . *4A 82*
(off Morden Wharf Rd.)
Morden Wharf Rd.
SE10. . . . . 4A **82**
Mordern Ho. *NW1* . . . *3A 60*
(off Harewood Av.)
Mordred Rd. SE6 . . . 2A **124**
Morecambe Cl. E1 . . . . 4F **65**
Morecambe St. SE17 . . 5E **77**
More Cl. E16 . . . . 5B **68**
W14. . . . . 5F **71**
Moreland Cotts. *E3* . . . *1C 66*
(off Fairfield Rd.)
Moreland Ct. NW2 . . . . 5C **30**
Moreland St.
EC1 . . . . 1E **9** (2D **63**)
Morella Rd. SW12 . . . 5B **102**
More London Pl.
SE1 . . . . 2D **27** (2A **78**)
More London Riverside
SE1 . . . . 2A **78**
Moremead Rd. SE6 . . . 4B **122**
Morena St. SE6 . . . . . 5D **109**
Moresby Rd. E5. . . . . . 3D **37**
Moresby Wlk. SW8 . . . 5E **89**
More's Gdn. *SW3* *2F 87*
(off Cheyne Wlk.)
Moreton Cl. E5. . . . . . . 4D **37**
N15. . . . . 1F **35**
SW1 . . . . *1E 89*
(off Moreton Ter.)
Moreton Ho. SE16 . . . . 4D **79**
Moreton Pl. SW1 . . . . . 1E **89**
Moreton Rd. N15 . . . . . 1F **35**
Moreton St. SW1 . . . . . 1E **89**
Moreton Ter. SW1 . . . . 1E **89**
Moreton Ter. M. Nth.
SW1 . . . . 1E **89**
Moreton Ter. M. Sth.
SW1 . . . . 1E **89**

Morgan Ho. *SW1* 5E **75**
　(off Vauxhall Bri. Rd.)
SW8 . . . . 4E **89**
　(off Wadhurst Rd.)
Morgan Mans. *N7* 2C **48**
　(off Morgan Rd.)
Morgan Rd. N7 . . . . 2C **48**
W10 . . . . 4B **58**
Morgan St. E3 . . . . 2A **66**
E16 . . . . 4B **68**
Moriarty Cl. N7 . . . . 1A **48**
Morie St. SW18 . . . . 3D **101**
Morieux Rd. E10 . . . . . . 3B **38**
Moring Rd. SW17 . . . . . 4C **116**
Morkyns Wlk. SE21 . . . . 3A **120**
Morland Cl. NW11 . . . . . 3D **31**
Morland Ct. *W12* 3D **71**
　(off Coningham Rd.)
Morland Est. E8 . . . . . . 4C **50**
Morland Gdns. NW10 . . . 4A **42**
Morland Ho. *NW1* 1A **6**
　(off Werrington St.)
NW6 . . . . 5C **44**
SW1 . . . . 5A **76**
　(off Marsham St.)
W11 . . . . 5A **58**
　(off Lancaster Rd.)
Morland M. N1 . . . . 4C **48**
Morland Rd. E17 . . . . . . 1F **37**
Morley Rd. E10 . . . . 3E **39**
E15 . . . . 1B **68**
SE13 . . . . 2E **109**
Morley St.
SE1 . . . . . . 5C **24** (4C **76**)
Morna Rd. SE5 . . . . 5E **91**
Morning La. E9 . . . . 3E **51**
Mornington Av. W14 . . . . 5B **72**
Mornington Av. Mans.
W14 . . . . 5B **72**
　(off Mornington Av.)
Mornington Ct. *NW1* . . . 1E **61**
　(off Mornington Cres.)
Mornington Cres.
NW1 . . . . 1E **61**
Mornington Gro. E3 . . . . 2C **66**
Mornington M. SE5 . . . . 4E **91**
Mornington Pl. NW1 . . . . 1E **61**
SE8 . . . . 3B **94**
　(off Mornington Rd.)
Mornington Rd. E11 . . . . 2B **40**
　(not continuous)
SE8 . . . . 3B **94**
Mornington Sports &
　Leisure Cen. 5D **47**
　(off Stanmore Pl.)
Mornington St. NW1 . . . . 1D **61**
Mornington Ter. NW1 . . . 5D **47**
Morocco St.
SE1 . . . . . . 4D **27** (3A **78**)
Morocco Wharf *E1* 2D **79**
　(off Wapping High St.)
Morpeth Gro. E9 . . . . . . 5F **51**
Morpeth Mans. *SW1* . . . 5E **75**
　(off Morpeth Ter.)
Morpeth Rd. E9 . . . . 5F **51**
Morpeth St. E2 . . . . 2E **65**
Morpeth Ter. SW1 . . . . . 4E **75**
Morrel Ct. *E2* 1C **64**
　(off Goldsmiths Row)

Morrells Yd. SE11 . . . . . 1C **90**
　(off Cleaver St.)
Morris Blitz Ct. N16 . . . . 1B **50**
Morris Gdns. SW18 . . . . 5C **100**
Morris Ho. *E2* 2E **65**
　(off Roman Rd.)
NW8 . . . . 3A **60**
　(off Salisbury St.)
Morrish Rd. SW2 . . . . . 5A **104**
Morrison Bldgs. Nth.
E1 . . . . 5C **64**
　(off Commercial Rd.)
Morrison Ho. *SW2* 1C **118**
　(off High Trees)
Morrison Rd. SW9 . . . . . 5C **90**
Morrison St. SW11 . . . . 1C **102**
Morris Pl. N4 . . . . 4C **34**
Morris Rd. E14 . . . . 4D **67**
E15 . . . . 1A **54**
Morris Ho. SE16 . . . . . . 3D **79**
　(off Cherry Gdn. St.)
Morris St. E1 . . . . 5D **65**
Morse Cl. E13 . . . . 2C **68**
Morshead Mans. *W9* . . . 2C **58**
　(off Morshead Rd.)
Morshead Rd. W9 . . . . . 2C **58**
Mortain Ho. *SE16* 5D **79**
　(off Roseberry St.)
Morten Cl. SW4 . . . . . . 4F **103**
Mortham St. E15 . . . . . . 5A **54**
Mortimer Cl. NW2 . . . . . 4B **30**
SW16 . . . . 2F **117**
Mortimer Ct. *NW8* 1E **59**
　(off Abbey Rd.)
Mortimer Cres. NW6 . . . 5D **45**
Mortimer Est. *NW6* . . . 5D **45**
　(off Mortimer Pl.)
Mortimer Ho. W11 . . . . . 2F **71**
W14 . . . . 5A **72**
　(off North End Rd.)
Mortimer Mkt.
WC1 . . . . . . 4A **6** (3E **61**)
Mortimer Pl. NW6 . . . . . 5D **45**
Mortimer Rd. N1 . . . . . . 4A **50**
　(not continuous)
NW10 . . . . 2E **57**
Mortimer Sq. W11 . . . . . 1F **71**
Mortimer St.
W1 . . . . 2E **13** (5E **61**)
Mortimer Ter. NW5 . . . . 1D **47**
Mortlake High St.
SW14 . . . . 1A **98**
Mortlake Rd. E16 . . . . . . 5D **69**
Mortlock Cl. SE15 . . . . . 4D **93**
Mortlock Ct. E7 . . . . 1F **55**
Morton Ho. SE17 . . . . . . 2D **91**
Morton M. SW5 . . . . . . 5D **73**
Morton Pl. SE1 . . . . 4C **76**
Morton Rd. E15 . . . . 4B **54**
N1 . . . . 4E **49**
Morval Rd. SW2 . . . . . . 3C **104**
Morven Rd. SW17 . . . . . 3B **116**
Morville Ho. *SW18* 4F **101**
　(off Fitzhugh Gro.)
Morville St. E3 . . . . 1C **66**
Morwell St.
WC1 . . . . . . 1B **14** (4F **61**)
Moscow Mans. *W8* 5C **72**
　(off Cromwell Rd.)

Moscow Pl. W2 . . . . 1D **73**
Moscow Rd. W2 . . . . . . 1C **72**
Mosedale *NW1* 2E **5**
　(off Cumberland Mkt.)
Moseley Row *SE10* 5B **82**
　(off School Bank Rd.)
Mosque Ter. *E1* 4C **64**
　(off Fieldgate St.)
Mosque Twr. *E1* 4C **64**
　(off Fieldgate St.)
E3 . . . . 1A **66**
　(off Ford St.)
Mossbury Rd.
SW11 . . . . 1A **102**
Moss Cl. E1 . . . . 4C **64**
Mossford St. E3 . . . . . . 3B **66**
Mossington Gdns.
SE16 . . . . 5E **79**
Mossop St. SW3 . . . . . . 5A **74**
Mostyn Gdns. NW10 . . . 2F **57**
Mostyn Gro. E3 . . . . 1C **66**
Mostyn Rd. SW9 . . . . . . 4C **90**
Motcomb St.
SW1 . . . . . . 5B **20** (4C **74**)
Mothers Sq. *E5* 1D **51**
　(off Hana M.)
Motley Av. EC2. . . . . 4D **11**
Motley St. SW8 . . . . 5E **89**
MOTTINGHAM 2F **125**
Mottingham Gdns.
SE9 . . . . 1F **125**
Mottingham La.
SE9 . . . . 1E **125**
SE12 . . . . 1E **125**
Mottingham Rd.
SE9 . . . . 2F **125**
Moules Ct. SE5 . . . . 3E **91**
Moulins Rd. E9 . . . . 4E **51**
Moulsford Ho. N7 . . . . . . 2F **47**
W2 . . . . 4C **58**
　(off Brunel Est.)
Moundfield Rd. N16 . . . . 1C **36**
Mounsey Ho. *W10* 2A **58**
　(off Third Av.)
Mount, The E5 . . . . 4D **37**
　(not continuous)
NW3 . . . . 5E **31**
W8 . . . . 2C **72**
　(off Bedford Gdns.)
Mountacre Cl. SE26 . . . 4B **120**
Mt. Adon Pk. SE22 . . . . 5C **106**
Mountague Pl. E14 . . . . 1E **81**
Mountain Ho. SE11 . . . . 5B **76**
Mt. Angelus Rd.
SW15 . . . . 5B **98**
Mt. Ash Rd. SE26 . . . . . 3D **121**
Mountbatten Cl.
SE19 . . . . 5A **120**
Mountbatten Ct.
SE16 . . . . 2E **79**
　(off Rotherhithe St.)
Mountbatten Ho. *N6* . . . 2C **32**
　(off Hillcrest)
Mountbatten M.
SW18 . . . . 5E **101**
Mt. Carmel Chambers
W8 . . . . 3C **72**
　(off Dukes La.)
Mount Ct. SW15 . . . . . . 1A **100**

Mounteari Gdns.
SW16 . . . . 3B 118
Mt. Ephraim La.
SW16 . . . . 3F 117
Mt. Ephraim Rd.
SW16 . . . . 3F 117
Mountfield Cl. SE6 . . . 5F 109
Mountfield Ter. SE6 . . 5F 109
Mountford Rd. E8 . . . . 2C 50
Mountfort Cres. N1 . . . 4C 48
Mountfort Ter. N1 . . . . 4C 48
Mount Gdns. SE26 . . . 3D 121
Mountgrove Rd. N5 . . . 5D 35
Mountjoy Cl. EC2 . . . . 1A 18
(off Thomas More Highwalk)
Mountjoy Ho. EC2 . . . . 1F 17
Mount Lodge N6 . . . . . 1E 33
EC1 . . . . 2E 9 (2D 63)
Mt. Nod Rd. SW16 . . . . 3B 118
Mt. Pleasant SE27 . . . . 4E 119
WC1 . . . . 4B 8 (3C 62)
Mt. Pleasant Cres.
N4 . . . . 3B 34
Mt. Pleasant Hill E5 . . . 4D 37
Mt. Pleasant La. E5 . . . 3D 37
Mt. Pleasant Rd.
NW10 . . . . 4E 43
SE13 . . . . 4D 109
Mt. Pleasant Vs. N4 . . . 2B 34
Mount Rd. NW2 . . . . . . 5D 29
NW4 . . . . 1C 28
SW19 . . . . 2C 114
Mount Row
W1 . . . . 5D 13 (1D 75)
Mountsfield Ct.
SE13 . . . . 4F 109
Mounts Pond Rd. SE3 . . 5F 95
(not continuous)
Mount Sq., The NW3 . . 5E 31
Mount St.
W1 . . . . 5B 12 (1C 74)
Mount St. M.
W1 . . . . 5D 13 (1D 75)
Mount Ter. E1 . . . . 4D 65
Mount Vernon NW3 . . . 1E 45
Mountview Cl.
NW11 . . . . 3D 31
Mount Vw. Rd. N4 . . . . 2A 34
Mount Vs. SE27 . . . . . 3D 119
Mowatt Cl. N19 . . . . . . 3F 33
Mowbray Rd. NW6 . . . . 4A 44
Mowlem St. E2 . . . . . . 1D 65
Mowll St. SW9 . . . . . . 3C 90
Moxon Cl. E13 . . . . 1B 68
Moxon St.
W1 . . . . 1B 12 (4C 60)
Moye Cl. E2 . . . . 1C 64
Moyers Rd. E10 . . . . . . 2E 39
Moylan Rd. W6 . . . . . . 2A 86
Moyle Ho. SW1 . . . . . . 1E 89
(off Churchill Gdns.)
Moyne Ho. SW9 . . . . . . 3D 105
Moyser Rd. SW16 . . . . 5D 117
Mozart St. W10 . . . . . . 2B 58
Mozart Ter. SW1 . . . . . 5C 74
Mudlarks Blvd. SE10 . . 4B 82
Mudlarks Way SE10 . . . 4B 82
(not continuous)

Muir Dr. SW18 . . . . . . 4A 102
Muirfield W3 . . . . 5A 56
Muirfield Cl. SE16 . . . . 1D 93
Muirfield Cres. E14 . . . 4D 81
Muirkirk Rd. SE6 . . . . . 1E 123
Muir Rd. E5 . . . . 1C 50
Mulberry Bus. Cen.
SE16 . . . . 3F 79
Mulberry Cl. NW3 . . . . 1F 45
SE7 . . . . 2F 97
SE22 . . . . 3C 106
SW3 . . . . 2F 87
SW16 . . . . 4E 117
Mulberry Ct. E11 . . . . . 1F 53
(off Langthorne Rd.)
EC1 . . . . 2E 9
(off Tompion St.)
SW3 . . . . 2F 87
(off King's Rd.)
Mulberry Ho. E2 . . . . . 2E 65
(off Victoria Pk.)
SE8 . . . . 2B 94
Mulberry Housing
Co-operative SE1 . . 1C 24
Mulberry M. SE14 . . . . 4B 94
Mulberry Pl. E14 . . . . . 1E 81
(off Clove Cres.)
SE9 . . . . 2F 111
W6 . . . . 1C 84
Mulberry Rd. E8 . . . . . 4B 50
Mulberry St. E1 . . . . . . 5C 64
Mulberry Wlk. SW3 . . . 2F 87
SW6 . . . . 2B 86
Mulkern Rd. N19 . . . . . 3F 33
(not continuous)
Mullen Twr. WC1 . . . . . 4B 8
(off Mt. Pleasant)
Muller Rd. SW4 . . . . . . 4F 103
Mullet Gdns. E2 . . . . . 2C 64
Mulletsfield WC1 . . . . . 2E 7
(off Cromer St.)
Mull Wlk. N1 . . . . 3E 49
(off Clephane Rd.)
Mulready Ho. SW1 . . . . 5A 76
(off Marsham St.)
Mulready Rd. NW8 . . . . 3A 60
Multi Way W3 . . . . 3A 70
Multon Ho. E9 . . . . 4E 51
Multon Rd. SW18 . . . . . 5F 101
Mulvaney Way
SE1 . . . . 4C 26 (3F 77)
(not continuous)
Mumford Mills SE10 . . 4D 95
(off Greenwich High Rd.)
Mumford Rd. SE24 . . . 3D 105
Muncaster Rd.
SW11 . . . . 3B 102
Muncies M. SE6 . . . . . 2E 123
Mundania Ct. SE22 . . . 4D 107
Mundania Rd. SE22 . . . 4D 107
Munday Ho. SE1 . . . . . 5B 26
(off Deverell St.)
Munday Rd. E16 . . . . . 1C 82
Munden St. W14 . . . . . 5A 72
Mundford Rd. E5 . . . . . 4E 37
Mund St. W14 . . . . 1B 86
Mundy Ho. W10 . . . . . . 2A 58
(off Dart St.)

Mundy St.
N1 . . . . 1D 11 (2A 64)
Munnings Ho. E16 . . . . 2D 83
(off Portsmouth M.)
Munro Ho.
SE1 . . . . 4B 24 (3C 76)
Munro M. W10 . . . . . . 4A 58
(not continuous)
Munro Ter. SW10 . . . . . 3F 87
Munster Ct. SW6 . . . . . 5B 86
Munster M. SW6 . . . . . 3A 86
Munster Rd. SW6 . . . . . 3A 86
Munster Sq.
NW1 . . . . 2E 5 (2D 61)
Munton Rd. SE17 . . . . . 5E 77
Murchison Ho. W10 . . . 4A 58
(off Ladbroke Gro.)
Murchison Rd.
E10 . . . . 4E 39
Murdoch Ho. SE16 . . . . 4E 79
(off Moodkee St.)
Murdock Cl. E16 . . . . . 5B 68
Murdock St. SE15 . . . . 2D 93
Murfett Cl. SW19 . . . . . 2A 114
Muriel Ct. E10 . . . . 2D 39
Muriel St. N1 . . . . 1B 62
(not continuous)
Murillo Rd. SE13 . . . . . 2F 109
Murphy Ho. SE1 . . . . . 5E 25
(off Borough Rd.)
SE1 . . . . 3F 77
(Long La.)
Murphy St.
SE1 . . . . 4B 24 (3C 76)
Murray Gro.
N1 . . . . 1A 10 (1E 63)
Murray M. NW1 . . . . . . 4F 47
Murray Rd. SW19 . . . . 5F 113
Murray Sq. E16 . . . . . . 5C 68
Murray St. NW1 . . . . . 4E 47
Murray Ter. NW3 . . . . . 1E 45
Mursell Est. SW8 . . . . 4B 90
Musard Rd. W6 . . . . . . 2A 86
Musbury St. E1 . . . . . . 5E 65
Muscal W6 . . . . 2A 86
(off Field Rd.)
Muscatel Pl. SE5 . . . . . 4A 92
Muschamp Rd.
SE15 . . . . 1B 106
Muscott Ho. E2 . . . . . . 5C 50
(off Whiston Rd.)
Muscovy St.
EC3 . . . . 4E 19 (1A 78)
Museum Chambers
WC1 . . . . 1D 15
(off Bury Pl.)
Mus. in Docklands, The
. . . . 1C 80
Museum La. SW7 . . . . . 4F 73
Mus. of Brands, Packaging
and Advertising 5B 58
(off Colville M.)
Mus. of Classical Archaeology
. . . . 3B 6
(off Gower Pl.)
Mus. of Garden History
. . . . 4B 76
Mus. of London
. . . . 1F 17 (4E 63)

Mus. of the Order of St John
. . . . 4D 9
(off St John's La.)
Museum Pas. E2 . . . . . 2E 65
Museum St.
WC1. . . . . 1D 15 (4A 62)
Musgrave Ct. SW11 . . . . 4A 88
Musgrave Cres.
SW6 . . . . 3C 86
Musgrave Rd. SE14 . . . . 4F 93
Musjid Rd. SW11 . . . . . 5F 87
Muston Rd. E5 . . . . 4D 37
Mustow Pl. SW6 . . . . . . 5B 86
Muswell Hill Rd. N6 . . . . 1C 32
N10 . . . . 1D 33
Mutrix Rd. NW6 . . . . . . 5C 44
Mutton Pl. NW1 . . . . . . 3C 46
Myatt Rd. SW9 . . . . 4D 91
Myatts Flds. Sth.
SW9 . . . . 5C 90
(off St Lawrence Way)
Mycenae Rd. SE3 . . . . . 3C 96
Myddelton Pas.
EC1 . . . . 1C 8 (2C 62)
Myddelton Sq.
EC1 . . . . 1C 8 (2C 62)
Myddelton St.
EC1 . . . . 2C 8 (2C 62)
Myddleton Av. N4 . . . . . 4E 35
Myddleton Ho. N1 . . . . . 1B 8
Myers Ho. SE5 . . . . 3E 91
(off Bethwin Rd.)
Myers La. SE14 . . . . . . 2F 93
Myles Ct. SE16 . . . . 4E 79
(off Neptune St.)
Mylis Cl. SE26 . . . . 4D 121
Mylius Cl. SE14 . . . . . . 3E 93
Mylne Cl. W6 . . . . 1C 84
Mylne St. EC1 . . 1B 8 (2C 62)
Myrdle Ct. E1 . . . . 5C 64
(off Myrdle St.)
Myrdle St. E1 . . . . 4C 64
Myron Pl. SE13 . . . . 1E 109
Myrtleberry Cl. E8 . . . . . 3B 50
(off Beechwood Rd.)
Myrtle Rd. E17 . . . . 1A 38
Myrtle Wlk.
N1 . . . . 1D 11 (1A 64)
Mysore Rd. SW11 . . . . . 1B 102
Myton Rd. SE21 . . . . . . 3F 119
Mytton Ho. SW8 . . . . . . 3B 90
(off St Stephens Ter.)

M

N1 Shop. Cen. N1 . . . . . 1C 62
N16 Fitness Cen. 1F 49
Nadine St. SE7 . . . . 1E 97
Nagasaki Wlk. SE7 . . . . 4D 83
NAG'S HEAD 5A 34
Nags Head Ct. EC1 . . . . 4A 10
Nags Head Shop. Cen.
N7 . . . . 1B 48
Nainby Ho. SE11 . . . . . 5C 76
(off Hotspur St.)
Nairne Gro. SE24 . . . . . 3F 105
Nairn St. E14 . . . . 4E 67
Naldera Gdns. SE3 . . . . 2C 96

Nalton Ho. NW6 . . . . . . 4E 45
(off Belsize Rd.)
Namba Roy Cl.
SW16 . . . . 4B 118
Nankin St. E14 . . . . 5C 66
Nansen Rd. SW11 . . . . . 1C 102
Nant Ct. NW2 . . . . 4B 30
Nantes Cl. SW18 . . . . . 2E 101
Nantes Pas.
E1 . . . . 5F 11 (4B 64)
Nant Rd. NW2 . . . . 4B 30
Nant St. E2 . . . . 2D 65
Naoroji St.
WC1 . . . . 2B 8 (2C 62)
Napier Av. E14 . . . . 1C 94
SW6 . . . . 1B 100
Napier Cl. SE8 . . . . 3B 94
W14 . . . . 4A 72
Napier Ct. N1 . . . . 1F 63
(off Cropley St.)
SE12 . . . . 3D 125
SW6 . . . . 1B 100
(off Ranelagh Gdns.)
Napier Gro. N1 . . . . 1E 63
Napier Ho. SE17 . . . . . . 2D 91
(off Cook's Rd.)
Napier Pl. W14 . . . . 4B 72
Napier Rd. E11 . . . . 1A 54
E15 . . . . 1A 68
(not continuous)
NW10 . . . . 2D 57
W14 . . . . 4B 72
Napier St. SE8 . . . . 3B 94
(off Napier Cl.)
Napier Ter. N1 . . . . 4D 49
Napoleon Rd. E5 . . . . . . 5D 37
Narbonne Av. SW4 . . . . 3E 103
Narborough St. SW6 . . . 5D 87
Narcissus Rd. NW6 . . . . 2C 44
Narford Rd. E5 . . . . 5C 36
Narrow St. E14 . . . . 1A 80
Narvic Ho. SE5 . . . . 5E 91
Narwhal Inuit Art Gallery
. . . . 5A 70
Nascot St. W12 . . . . 5E 57
Naseby Cl. NW6 . . . . . . 4E 45
Naseby Rd. SE19 . . . . . 5F 119
Nashe Ho. SE1 . . . . 5B 26
(off Burbage Cl.)
Nash Ho. E14 . . . . 3C 80
(off Alpha Gro.)
NW1 . . . . 1D 61
(off Pk. Village E.)
SW1 . . . . 1D 89
(off Lupus St.)
Nash Pl. E14 . . . . 2D 81
Nash Rd. SE4 . . . . 2A 108
Nash St. NW1 . . 1E 5 (2D 61)
Nasmyth St. W6 . . . . . . 4D 71
Nassau Rd. SW13 . . . . . 4B 84
Nassau St.
W1 . . . . 1F 13 (4E 61)
Nassington Rd. NW3 . . . 1B 46
Natal Rd. SW16 . . . . . . 5F 117
Nathan Ho. SE11 . . . . . 5C 76
(off Reedworth St.)
Nathaniel Cl.
E1 . . . . 1F 19 (4B 64)
Nathaniel Ct. E17 . . . . . 2A 38

National Army Mus. 2B 88
National Film Theatre, The
. . . . 1A 24
National Gallery
. . . . 5C 14 (1F 75)
National Maritime Mus.
. . . . 2F 95
National Portrait Gallery
. . . . 5C 14
National Ter. SE16 . . . . . 3D 79
(off Bermondsey Wall E.)
National Theatre
. . . . 1A 24 (2B 76)
Natural History Mus.
. . . . 4F 73
Nautilus Bldg., The
EC1 . . . . 1C 8
(off Myddelton Pas.)
Naval Ho. E14 . . . . 1F 81
(off Quixley St.)
Naval Row E14 . . . . 1E 81
Navarino Gro. E8 . . . . . 3C 50
Navarino Mans. E8 . . . . 3C 50
Navarino Rd. E8 . . . . . . 3C 50
Navarre St.
E2 . . . . 3F 11 (3B 64)
Navenby Wlk. E3 . . . . . 3C 66
Navy St. SW4 . . . . 1F 103
Naxos Bldg. E14 . . . . . . 3B 80
Nayim Pl. E8 . . . . 2D 51
Nayland Ho. SE6 . . . . . . 4E 123
Naylor Ho. SE17 . . . . . . 5F 77
(off Flint St.)
W10 . . . . 2A 58
(off Dart St.)
Naylor Rd. SE15 . . . . . . 3D 93
Nazareth Gdns.
SE15 . . . . 5D 93
Nazrul St. E2 . . 1F 11 (2B 64)
Neagle Ho. NW2 . . . . . 5E 29
(off Stoll Cl.)
Nealden St.
SW9 . . . . 1B 104
Neal St.
WC2 . . . . 3D 15 (5A 62)
Neal's Yd.
WC2 . . . . 3D 15 (5A 62)
NEASDEN 5A 28
Neasden Cl. NW10 . . . . 2A 42
NEASDEN JUNC. 1A 42
Neasden La. NW10 . . . . 5A 28
Neasden La. Nth.
NW10 . . . . 5A 28
Neate Ho. SW1 . . . . 1E 89
(off Lupus St.)
Neate St. SE5 . . . . 2A 92
(not continuous)
Neathouse Pl. SW1 . . . . 5E 75
Neatscourt Rd. E6 . . . . . 4F 69
Nebraska Bldg. SE8 . . . . 4D 95
(off Deal's Gateway)
Nebraska St.
SE1 . . . . 4B 26 (3F 77)
Neckinger
SE16 . . . . 5F 27 (4B 78)
Neckinger Est.
SE16 . . . . 5F 27 (4B 78)
Neckinger St. SE1 . . . . . 3B 78
Nectarine Way SE13 . . . 5D 95

Needham Ho. *SE11* 1C **90**
(off Marylee Way)
Needham Ho. W11. . . . . 5C **58**
Needham Ter. NW2. . . . . 5F **29**
Needleman St. SE16 . . . . 3F **79**
Needwood Ho. N4 . . . . . 3E **35**
Neeld Cres. NW4 . . . . . 1D **29**
Neil Wates Cres.
SW2 . . . . 1C **118**
Nelgarde Rd. SE6. . . . . 5C **108**
Nella Rd. W6 . . . . 2F **85**
Nelldale Rd. SE16 . . . . . 5E **79**
Nell Gwynn Ho. SW3 . . . 5A **74**
Nello James Gdns.
SE27 . . . . 4F **119**
Nelson Cl. NW6 . . . . . . 2C **58**
Nelson Ct.
SE1 . . . . 3E **25** (3D **77**)
SE16 . . . . 2E **79**
(off Brunel Rd.)
Nelson Gdns. E2. . . . . . 2C **64**
Nelson Ho. *SW1* 2E **89**
(off Dolphin Sq.)
Nelson Mandela Ho.
N16. . . . . 4C **36**
Nelson Mandela Rd.
SE3 . . . . 1E **111**
Nelson Pas.
EC1 . . . . 1A **10** (2E **63**)
Nelson Pl. N1 . . . 1E **9** (1D **63**)
Nelson Rd. N8 . . . . 1B **34**
SE10 . . . . 2E **95**
Nelson's Column
. . . . 1C **22** (2A **76**)
Nelson Sq.
SE1 . . . . 3D **25** (3D **77**)
Nelson's Row SW4 . . . . 2F **103**
Nelson St. E1 . . . . 5D **65**
E16 . . . . 1B **82**
(not continuous)
Nelsons Yd. *NW1* 1E **61**
(off Mornington Cres.)
Nelson Ter. N1. . 1E **9** (1D **63**)
Nelson Wlk. SE16 . . . . . 2A **80**
Nepaul Rd. SW11. . . . . 5A **88**
Nepean St. SW15. . . . . 4C **98**
Neptune Ct. *E14* 5C **80**
(off Homer Dr.)
Neptune Ho. *SE16* 4E **79**
(off Moodkee St.)
Neptune St. SE16 . . . . . 4E **79**
Nesbit Rd. SE9 . . . . . . 2F **111**
Nesbitt Cl. SE3 . . . . . . 1A **110**
Nesham Ho. *N1* 5A **50**
(off Hoxton St.)
Nesham St. E1 . . . . 1C **78**
Ness St. SE16. . . . . . . 4C **78**
Nestor Ho. *E2* 1D **65**
(off Old Bethnal Grn. Rd.)
Netheravon Rd. W4 . . . 5B **70**
Netheravon Rd. Sth.
W4 . . . . 1B **84**
Netherby Rd. SE23 . . . 5E **107**
Netherfield Rd.
SW17 . . . . 3C **116**
Netherford Rd. SW4 . . . 5E **89**
Netherhall Gdns.
NW3 . . . . 3E **45**
Netherhall Way NW3 . . . 2E **45**

Netherleigh Cl. N6 . . . . 3D **33**
Netherton Gro. SW10 . . 2E **87**
Netherton Rd. N15 . . . . 1F **35**
Netherwood Pl. *W14* . . . 4F **71**
(off Netherwood Rd.)
Netherwood Rd. W14 . . . 4F **71**
Netherwood St. NW6 . . . 4B **44**
Netley *SE5* 4A **92**
(off Redbridge Gdns.)
Netley Rd. E17 . . . . 1B **38**
Netley St.
NW1 . . . . 2F **5** (2E **61**)
Nettlecombe *NW1* 4F **47**
(off Agar Gro.)
Nettleden Ho. SW3 . . . . 5A **74**
(off Marlborough St.)
Nettlefold Pl. SE27 . . . 3D **119**
Nettleton Ct. *EC2* 1F **17**
(off London Wall)
Nettleton Rd. SE14 . . . . 4F **93**
Neuchatel Rd. SE6. . . . 2B **122**
Nevada St. SE10 . . . . . 2E **95**
Nevern Mansions
SW5 . . . . 1C **86**
(off Nevern Sq.)
Nevern Pl. SW5 . . . . . . 5C **72**
Nevern Rd. SW5 . . . . . 5C **72**
Nevern Sq. SW5. . . . . . 5C **72**
Nevil Ho. *SW9* 5D **91**
(off Loughborough Est.)
Nevill Ct. EC4. . . . . 2C **16**
SW10 . . . . 3E **87**
(off Edith Ter.)
Neville Cl. E11. . . . . 5B **40**
NW1 . . . . 1F **61**
NW6 . . . . 1B **58**
SE15 . . . . 4C **92**
Neville Cl. *NW8* 1F **59**
(off Abbey Rd.)
Neville Dr. N2. . . . . 1E **31**
Neville Gill Cl.
SW18 . . . . 4C **100**
Neville Rd. E7 . . . . 4C **54**
NW6 . . . . 1B **58**
Nevilles Ct. NW2 . . . . . 5C **28**
Neville St. SW7 . . . . . . 1F **87**
Neville Ter. SW7 . . . . . . 1F **87**
Nevill Rd. N16 . . . . 1A **50**
Nevinson Cl. SW18 . . . . 4F **101**
Nevis Rd. SW17 . . . . . 2C **116**
Nevitt Ho. *N1* 1F **63**
(off Cranston Est.)
Newall Ho. SE1 . . . . . . 5A **26**
(off Bath Ter.)
Newarke Ho. SW9 . . . . 5D **91**
Newark St. E1 . . . . 4D **65**
(not continuous)
New Atlas Wharf *E14*. . . 4C **80**
(off Arnhem Pl.)
New Baltic Wharf
SE8 . . . . 1A **94**
(off Evelyn St.)
New Barn St. E13. . . . . 3C **68**
NEW BECKENHAM . . . 5B **122**
New Bentham Ct. *N1* . . 4E **49**
(off Ecclesbourne Rd.)
Newbery Ho. *N1* 4E **49**
(off Northampton St.)
Newbold Cotts. E1 . . . . 5E **65**

Newbolt Ho. *SE17* 1F **91**
(off Brandon St.)
New Bond St.
W1. . . . . 3D **13** (5D **61**)
Newbridge Point
SE23 . . . . 3F **121**
(off Windrush La.)
New Bri. St.
EC4 . . . . 3D **17** (5D **63**)
New Broad St.
EC2 . . . . 1D **19** (4A **64**)
Newburgh St.
W1. . . . . 3A **14** (5E **61**)
New Burlington M.
W1 . . . . 4F **13** (1E **75**)
New Burlington Pl.
W1 . . . . 4F **13** (1E **75**)
New Burlington St.
W1 . . . . 4F **13** (1E **75**)
Newburn Ho. *SE11*. 1B **90**
(off Newburn St.)
Newburn St. SE11 . . . . 1B **90**
Newbury Ho. SW9 . . . . 5D **91**
W2 . . . . 5D **59**
(off Hallfield Est.)
Newbury M. NW5. . . . . 3C **46**
Newbury St.
EC1 . . . . 1F **17** (4E **63**)
New Bus. Cen., The
NW10 . . . . 2B **56**
New Butt La. SE8. . . . . 3C **94**
New Butt La. Nth.
SE8 . . . . 3C **94**
(off Hales St.)
Newby *NW1* 2F **5**
(off Robert St.)
Newby Ho. *E14*. 1E **81**
(off Newby Pl.)
Newby Pl. E14 . . . . 1E **81**
Newby St. SW8 . . . . . 1D **103**
New Caledonian Mkt.
SE1 . . . . 5E **27**
New Caledonian Wharf
SE16 . . . . 4B **80**
Newcastle Cl.
EC4 . . . . 2D **17** (5D **63**)
Newcastle Ct.
EC4. . . . . 4A **18**
(off College Hill)
Newcastle Ho. *W1*. 5B **4**
(off Luxborough St.)
Newcastle Pl. W2. . . . . 4F **59**
Newcastle Row
EC1 . . . . 4C **8** (3C **62**)
New Cavendish St.
W1. . . . . 1C **12** (4C **60**)
New Change
EC4 . . . . 3F **17** (5E **63**)
New Charles St.
EC1 . . . . 1E **9** (2D **63**)
NEW CHARLTON 5E **83**
New Chiswick Pool 3A **84**
New Church Rd. SE5 . . 3E **91**
(not continuous)
New City Rd. E13 . . . . . 2E **69**
New College Ct.
NW3 . . . . 3E **45**
(off Finchley Rd.)
New College M. N1 . . . 4C **48**

New College Pde.
 NW3 . . . . 3F 45
 (off Finchley Rd.)
Newcombe Gdns.
 SW16 . . . . 4A 118
Newcombe St. W8 . . . . 2C 72
Newcomen Rd. E11 . . . 5B 40
 SW11 . . . . 1F 101
Newcomen St.
 SE1 . . . . 3B 26 (3F 77)
New Compton St.
 WC2 . . . . 3C 14 (5F 61)
New Concordia Wharf
 SE1 . . . . 3C 78
New Ct. EC4 . . . . 4B 16
Newcourt Ho. E2 . . . . . . 2D 65
 (off Pott St.)
Newcourt St. NW8 . . . . 1A 60
New Covent Garden Market
 . . . . 3F 89
New Coventry St.
 W1 . . . . 5C 14 (1F 75)
New Crane Pl. E1 . . . . . 2E 79
New Crane Wharf E1 . . . 2E 79
 (off New Crane Pl.)
New Cres. Yd. NW10 . . 1B 56
NEW CROSS 3B 94
NEW CROSS 4B 94
NEW CROSS GATE 4F 93
NEW CROSS GATE 4F 93
New Cross Rd. SE14 . . 3F 93
 SE15 . . . . 3E 93
Newdigate Ho. E14 . . . . 5B 66
 (off Norbiton Rd.)
Newell St. E14 . . . . 5B 66
New End NW3 . . . . 1E 45
New End Sq. NW3 . . . . 1F 45
New End Theatre
 Hampstead. 5E 31
Newent Cl. SE15 . . . . . 3A 92
New Era Est. N1 . . . . . . 5A 50
 (off Phillipp St.)
New Era Ho. N1 . . . . 5A 50
 (off New Era Est.)
New Fetter La.
 EC4 . . . . 2C 16 (5C 62)
Newfield Ri. NW2 . . . . . 5C 28
Newgate St.
 EC1 . . . . 2E 17 (5D 63)
New Globe Wlk.
 SE1 . . . . 1F 25 (2E 77)
New Goulston St.
 E1 . . . . 2F 19 (5B 64)
New Grn. Pl. SE19 . . . . 5A 120
Newham College of
 Further Education
 Stratford Campus . . . 4A 54
Newham Leisure Cen.
 . . . . 4E 69
Newham's Row
 SE1 . . . . 4E 27 (4A 78)
Newham Way E6 . . . . . 4B 68
 E16 . . . . 4B 68
Newhaven Gdns.
 SE9 . . . . 2F 111
Newhaven La. E16 . . . . 3B 68
New Hope Ct. NW10 . . 2D 57
 (off Harrow Rd.)
Newick Rd. E5 . . . . 1D 51

NEWINGTON 4E 77
Newington Barrow Way
 N7 . . . . 5B 34
Newington Butts SE1 . . 5D 77
 SE11 . . . . 5D 77
Newington C'way.
 SE1 . . . . 5E 25 (4D 77)
Newington Ct. Bus. Cen.
 SE1 . . . . 5F 25
Newington Grn. N1 . . . 2F 49
 N16 . . . . 2F 49
Newington Grn. Mans.
 N16 . . . . 2F 49
Newington Grn. Rd.
 SE17 . . . . 5E 77
Newington Ind. Est.
 SE17 . . . . 5E 77
New Inn B'way.
 EC2 . . . . 3E 11 (3A 64)
New Inn Pas. WC2 . . . . 3A 16
New Inn Sq. EC2 . . . . . 3E 11
New Inn St.
 EC2 . . . . 3E 11 (3A 64)
New Inn Yd.
 EC2 . . . . 3E 11 (3A 64)
New Jubilee Wharf
 E1 . . . . 2E 79
 (off Wapping Wall)
New Kent Rd. SE1 . . . . 4E 77
New Kings Rd.
 SW6 . . . . 5B 86
New King St. SE8 . . . . . 2C 94
Newland Ct. EC1 . . . . . 2B 10
Newland Ho. SE14 . . . . 2F 93
 (off John Williams Cl.)
NEWLANDS 3F 107
Newlands NW1 . . . . 1F 5
 (off Harrington St.)
Newlands Pk. SE26 . . . 5E 121
Newlands Quay E1 . . . . 1E 79
New London Ct. EC3 . . 4E 19
New London Theatre . . 2E 15
 (off Drury La.)
New Lydenburg
 Commercial Est.
 SE7 . . . . 4E 83
New Lydenburg St.
 SE7 . . . . 4E 83
Newlyn NW1 . . . . 5E 47
 (off Plender St.)
Newman Pas.
 W1 . . . . 1A 14 (4E 61)
Newman Rd. E13 . . . . . 2D 69
Newman's Ct. EC3 . . . . 3C 18
Newman's Row
 WC2 . . . . 1A 16 (4B 62)
Newman St.
 W1 . . . . 1A 14 (4E 61)
Newman Yd.
 W1 . . . . 2B 14 (5E 61)
Newmarket Grn.
 SE9 . . . . 5F 111
Newmill Ho. E3 . . . . . . 3E 67
New Mount St. E15 . . . 4F 53
Newnes Path SW15 . . . 2D 99
Newnham Ter.
 SE1 . . . . 5B 24 (4C 76)
New Nth. Pl.
 EC2 . . . . 3D 11 (3A 64)

New Nth. Rd.
 N1 . . . . 1C 10 (4E 49)
New Nth. St.
 WC1 . . . . 5F 7 (4B 62)
Newnton Cl. N4 . . . . . . 2F 35
 (not continuous)
New Orleans Wlk.
 N19 . . . . 2F 33
New Oxford St.
 WC1 . . . . 2C 14 (5F 61)
New Pk. Pde. SW2 . . . . 5A 104
 (off New Pk. Rd.)
New Pk. Rd. SW2 . . . . 1F 117
New Pl. Sq. SE16 . . . . 4D 79
New Plaistow Rd.
 E15 . . . . 5A 54
New Players Theatre
 . . . . 2A 76
 (off Craven St.)
Newport Av. E13 . . . . . 3D 69
 E14 . . . . 1F 81
Newport Ct.
 WC2 . . . . 4C 14 (1F 75)
Newport Ho. E3 . . . . . . 2A 66
 (off Strahan Rd.)
Newport Pl.
 W1 . . . . 4C 14 (1F 75)
Newport Rd. E10 . . . . . 4E 39
 SW13 . . . . 4C 84
Newport St. SE11 . . . . 5B 76
New Priory Ct. NW6 . . . 4C 44
 (off Mazenod Av.)
New Providence Wharf
 E14 . . . . 2F 81
Newquay Ho. SE11 . . . 1C 90
Newquay Rd. SE6 . . . . 2D 123
New Quebec St.
 W1 . . . . 3A 12 (5B 60)
New Ride SW1 . . . . 3B 74
 SW7 . . . . 3A 20 (3A 74)
New River Ct. N5 . . . . . 1E 49
New River Head
 EC1 . . . . 1C 8 (2C 62)
New River Wlk. N1 . . . . 3E 49
New River Way N4 . . . . 2F 35
New Rd. E1 . . . . 4D 65
 E12 . . . . 4F 41
 N8 . . . . 1A 34
New Rochford St.
 NW5 . . . . 2B 46
New Row
 WC2 . . . . 4D 15 (1A 76)
New Spitalfields Mkt.
 E10 . . . . 5D 39
New Spring Gdns. Wlk.
 SE11 . . . . 1A 90
New Sq.
 WC2 . . . . 2B 16 (5C 62)
New Sq. Pas. WC2 . . . . 2B 16
Newstead Ho. N1 . . . . . 1C 62
 (off Tolpuddle St.)
Newstead Rd. SE12 . . . 5B 110
Newstead Way
 SW19 . . . . 4F 113
New St. EC2 . . . 1E 19 (4A 64)
New St. Hill
 BR1: Brom 5D 125
New St. Sq.
 EC4 . . . . 2C 16 (5C 62)

Newton Cl. E17 . . . . 1A 38
Newton Ct. W8 . . . . 3C 72
(off Kensington Chu. St.)
Newton Gro. W4 . . . . 5A 70
Newton Ho. E1 . . . . 1D 79
(off Cornwall St.)
NW8 . . . . 5D 45
(off Abbey Rd.)
Newton Mans. W14 . . . 2A 86
(off Queen's Club Gdns.)
Newton Pl. E14 . . . . . . 5C 80
Newton Point E16 . . . . . . 5B 68
(off Clarkson Rd.)
Newton St. E15 . . . . 2F 53
NW2 . . . . 1E 43
W2 . . . . 5D 59
Newton St.
WC2 . . . . 2E 15 (5A 62)
Newton's Yd. SW18 . . . . 3C 100
New Twr. Bldgs. E1 . . . . 2D 79
Newtown St. SW11 . . . . 4D 89
New Turnstile WC1 . . . . 1F 15
New Union Cl. E14 . . . . . . 4E 81
New Union St.
EC2 . . . . 1B 18 (4F 63)
New Wanstead E11 . . . . 1B 40
New Wharf Rd. N1 . . . . . . 1A 62
New Zealand Way
W12 . . . . 1D 71
Next Generation Club
Carlton 4C 58
Nexus Ct. E11 . . . . 3A 40
Niagra Cl. N1 . . . . 1E 63
Niagra Ct. SE16 . . . . . . 4E 79
(off Canada Est.)
Nicholas Ct. SE12 . . . 1C 124
W4 . . . . 2A 84
(off Corney Reach Way)
Nicholas La.
EC4 . . . . 4C 18 (1F 77)
(not continuous)
Nicholas M. W4 . . . . 2A 84
Nicholas Pas. EC3 . . . . 3C 18
Nicholas Rd. E1 . . . . . . 3E 65
Nicholas Stacey Ho.
SE7 . . . . 1D 97
(off Frank Burton Cl.)
Nicholay Rd. N19 . . . . . . 3F 33
(not continuous)
Nicholl Ho. N4 . . . . 3E 35
Nichollsfield Wlk. N7 . . 2B 48
Nicholls Point E15 . . . . 5C 54
(off Park Gro.)
Nicholl St. E2 . . . . 5C 50
Nichols Cl. N4 . . . . 3C 34
(off Osborne Rd.)
Nichols Ct. E2 . . . . 1B 64
Nicholson Ho. SE17 . . . . 1F 91
Nicholson St.
SE1 . . . . 2D 25 (2D 77)
Nickleby Ho. SE16 . . . . 3C 78
(off Parkers Row)
W11 . . . . 2F 71
Nickols Wlk. SW18 . . . . 2D 101
Nicolas Ct. E13 . . . . . . 2D 69
Nicoll Ct. NW10 . . . . . . 5A 42
Nicoll Pl. NW4 . . . . 1D 29
Nicoll Rd. NW10 . . . . . . 5A 42

Nicosia Rd. SW18 . . . . 5A 102
Niederwald Rd.
SE26 . . . . 4A 122
Nigel Ho. EC1 . . . . 5B 8
(off Portpool La.)
Nigel Playfair Av.
W6 . . . . 5D 71
Nigel Rd. E7 . . . . 2E 55
SE15 . . . . 1C 106
Nigeria Rd. SE7 . . . . . . 3E 97
Nightingale Ct. E14 . . . . 3E 81
(off Ovex Cl.)
N4 . . . . 4B 34
(off Tollington Pk.)
SW6 . . . . 4D 87
(off Maltings Pl.)
Nightingale Gro.
SE13 . . . . 3F 109
Nightingale Ho. E1 . . . . 2C 78
(off Thomas More St.)
E2 . . . . 5A 50
(off Kingsland Rd.)
W12 . . . . 5E 57
(off Du Cane Rd.)
Nightingale La.
SW4 . . . . 5B 102
SW12 . . . . 5B 102
Nightingale Lodge
W9 . . . . 4C 58
(off Admiral Wlk.)
Nightingale M. E3 . . . . 1F 65
E11 . . . . 1C 40
SE11 . . . . 5D 77
Nightingale Pl.
SW10 . . . . 2E 87
(not continuous)
Nightingale Rd. E5 . . . . 5D 37
N1 . . . . 3E 49
NW10 . . . . 1B 56
Nightingale Sq.
SW12 . . . . 5C 102
Nightingale Wlk.
SW4 . . . . 4D 103
Nile Cl. N16 . . . . 5B 36
Nile Rd. E13 . . . . 1E 69
Nile St. N1 . . . . . . 1A 10 (2E 63)
Nile Ter. SE15 . . . . . . 1B 92
Nimegen Way SE22 . . 3A 106
Nimrod Ho. E16 . . . . . . 4D 69
(off Vanguard Cl.)
Nimrod Pas. N1 . . . . . . 3A 50
Nimrod Rd. SW16 . . . . 5D 117
Nina Mackay Cl.
E15 . . . . 5A 54
Nine Elms La. SW8 . . . . 3E 89
Nine Elms La. SW8 . . . . 3E 89
Nipponzan Myohoji
Peace Pagoda . . 2B 88
Nirvana Apartments
N1 . . . . 5D 49
(off Islington Grn.)
Nisbet Ho. E9 . . . . . . 2F 51
Nita Ct. SE12 . . . . . . 1C 124
Niton St. SW6 . . . . . . 3F 85
Nobel Ho. SE5 . . . . . . 5E 91
Noble Cl. E1 . . . . 1D 79
Noblefield Hgts. N2 . . 1A 32
Noble M. N16 . . . . . . 5F 35
(off Albion Rd.)

Noble St.
EC2 . . . . . . 2F 17 (5E 63)
Noel Coward Ho.
SW1 . . . . 5E 75
(off Vauxhall Bri. Rd.)
Noel Ho. NW6 . . . . . . 4F 45
(off Harben Rd.)
Noel Rd. E6 . . . . 3F 69
N1 . . . . 1D 63
Noel St. W1 . . . . 3A 14 (5E 61)
Noel Ter. SE23 . . . . 2E 121
Noko W10 . . . . 2F 57
Nolan Way E5 . . . . . . 1C 50
Noll Ho. N7 . . . . 4B 34
(off Tomlins Wlk.)
Norbiton Rd. E14 . . . . 5B 66
Norbroke St. W12 . . . . 1B 70
Norburn St. W10 . . . . 4A 58
Norcombe Ho. N19 . . . . 5F 33
(off Wedmore St.)
Norcott Rd. N16 . . . . 4C 36
Norcroft Gdns.
SE22 . . . . 5C 106
Norden Ho. E2 . . . . . . 2D 65
(off Pott St.)
Norfolk Av. N15 . . . . 1B 36
Norfolk Cres. W2 . . . . 5A 60
Norfolk Ho. EC4 . . . . 4F 17
SE3 . . . . 2A 96
(off Restell Cl.)
SE8 . . . . 4C 94
SW1 . . . . 5F 75
(off Page St.)
Norfolk Ho. Rd.
SW16 . . . . 3F 117
Norfolk Mans.
SW11 . . . . 4B 88
(off Prince of Wales Dr.)
Norfolk M. W10 . . . . 4A 58
(off Blagrove Rd.)
Norfolk Pl. W2 . . . . . . 5F 59
(not continuous)
Norfolk Rd. NW8 . . . . 5F 45
NW10 . . . . 4A 42
Norfolk Row SE1 . . . . 5B 76
(not continuous)
Norfolk Sq. W2 . . . . . . 5F 59
Norfolk Sq. M. W2 . . . . 5F 59
(off London St.)
Norfolk St. E7 . . . . . . 2C 54
Norfolk Ter. W6 . . . . 1A 86
Norgrove St. SW12 . . 5C 102
Norland Ho. W11 . . . . 2F 71
(off Queensdale Cres.)
Norland Pl. W11 . . . . 2A 72
Norland Rd. W11 . . . . 2F 71
Norland Sq. W11 . . . . 2A 72
Norland Sq. Mans.
W11 . . . . 2A 72
(off Norland Sq.)
Norley Va. SW15 . . . . 1C 112
Norlington Rd. E10 . . 3E 39
E11 . . . . 3E 39
Norman Butler Ho.
W10 . . . . 3A 58
(off Ladbroke Gro.)
Normanby Cl.
SW15 . . . . 3B 100
Normanby Rd. NW10 . . 1B 42

Norman Ct. N4 . . . . 2C 34
NW10 . . . . 4C 42
Normand Gdns. W14 . . . 2A 86
(off Greyhound Rd.)
Normand Mans. W14 . . . 2A 86
(off Normand M.)
Normand M. W14 . . . . . . 2A 86
Normand Rd. W14 . . . . . 2B 86
Normandy Cl. SE26 . . . 3A 122
Normandy Ho. E14 . . . . . 3E 81
(off Plevna St.)
Normandy Rd. SW9 . . . . 4C 90
Normandy Ter. E16. . . . . 5D 69
Norman Gro. E3 . . . . 1A 66
Norman Ho. SW8 . . . . . . 3A 90
(off Wyvil Rd.)
Normanhurst Rd.
SW2 . . . . 2B 118
Norman Rd. E11 . . . . 4F 39
SE10. . . . . 3D 95
Norman St.
EC1 . . . . 2A 10 (2E 63)
Normanton Av.
SW19 . . . . 2C 114
Normanton St. SE23 . . 2F 121
Normington Cl.
SW16 . . . . 5C 118
Norrice Lea N2 . . . . 1F 31
Norris Ho. E9 . . . . 5E 51
(off Handley Rd.)
N1. . . . . 5A 50
(off Colville Est.)
SE8 . . . . 1B 94
(off Grove St.)
Norris St.
SW1 . . . . 5B 14 (1F 75)
Norroy Rd. SW15 . . . . . . 2F 99
Norstead Pl. SW15. . . . 2C 112
Nth. Access Rd. E17. . . . 1F 37
NORTH ACTON 4A 56
Nth. Acton Rd. NW10. . . 1A 56
Northampton Gro. N1 . . 2F 49
Northampton Pk. N1. . . . 3E 49
Northampton Rd.
EC1 . . . . 3C 8 (3C 62)
Northampton Row
EC1 . . . . 3C 8
Northampton Sq.
EC1 . . . . 2D 9 (2D 63)
Northampton St. N1. . . . 4E 49
Nth. Audley St.
W1. . . . . 3B 12 (5C 60)
North Av. NW10 . . . . 2E 57
Northaw Ho. W10. . . . . . 3E 57
(off Sutton Way)
North Bank NW8 . . . . . . 2A 60
NORTH BECKTON 4F 69
Nth. Birkbeck Rd.
E11 . . . . 5F 39
North Block SE1 . . . . . . 3A 24
(off York Rd.)
Nth. Boundary Rd.
E12 . . . . 5F 41
Northbourne Rd.
SW4 . . . . 3F 103
Nth. Branch Av.
NW10 . . . . 2E 57
Northbrook Rd.
SE13 . . . . 3A 110

Northburgh St.
EC1 . . . . 4E 9 (3D 63)
Nth. Carriage Dr. W2 . . 1A 74
(off Bayswater Rd.)
Northchurch SE17. . . . . 1F 91
(not continuous)
Northchurch Ho. E2 . . . 5C 50
(off Whiston Rd.)
Northchurch Rd. N1 . . . 4F 49
(not continuous)
Northchurch Ter. N1. . . 4A 50
Nth. Circular Rd.
NW2 . . . . 5A 28
NW4 . . . . 2E 29
NW10 . . . . 2A 42
NW11 . . . . 2E 29
Nth. Colonnade, The
E14. . . . . 2C 80
Northcote M. SW11 . . . 2A 102
Northcote Rd. NW10 . . . 4A 42
SW11 . . . . 3A 102
North Ct. SE24 . . . . . . 1D 105
SW1 . . . . 5D 23
(off Gt. Peter St.)
W1 . . . . 5A 6 (4E 61)
North Cres. E16 . . . . 3F 67
WC1 . . . . 5B 6 (4F 61)
Northcroft Ct. W12. . . . . 3C 70
North Crofts SE23 . . . . 1D 121
Nth. Cross Rd.
SE22 . . . . 3B 106
Northdene Gdns.
N15. . . . . 1B 36
Northdown St.
N1 . . . . 1F 7 (1A 62)
North Dr. SW16 . . . . 4E 117
NORTH END 4E 31
North End NW3. . . . . 4E 31
North End Av. NW3. . . . . 4E 31
(not continuous)
North End Cres. W14. . . 5B 72
North End Ho. W14 . . . . 5A 72
North End Pde. W14 . . . 5A 72
(off North End Rd.)
North End Rd. NW11 . . . 3C 30
SW6 . . . . 2B 86
W14 . . . . 5A 72
North End Way NW3 . . . 4E 31
Northern Hgts. N8 . . . . . 2F 33
(off Crescent Rd.)
Northern Rd. E13. . . . . . 1D 69
Northesk Ho. E1 . . . . . . 3D 65
(off Tent St.)
Nth. Eyot Gdns. W6 . . . 1B 84
Northey St. E14 . . . . 1A 80
Northfield Ho. SE15. . . . 2C 92
Northfield Rd. N16. . . . . 2A 36
Northfields SW18. . . . . . 2C 100
Northfields Prospect
Bus. Cen. SW18. . . . 2C 100
Northfleet Ho. SE1. . . . . 3B 26
(off Tennis St.)
Nth. Flock St. SE16 . . . 3C 78
Nth. Flower Wlk. W2 . . . 1E 73
(off Lancaster Wlk.)
North Gdn. E14. . . . . 2C 80
North Ga. NW8 . . . . 1A 60
(off Prince Albert Rd.)
Northgate Ct. SW9 . . . . 1C 104

Northgate Dr. NW9. . . . . 1A 28
Northgate Ho. E14 . . . . . 1C 80
(off E. India Dock Rd.)
Nth. Gower St.
NW1 . . . . 2A 6 (2E 61)
North Gro. N6. . . . . 2C 32
N15. . . . . 1F 35
North Hill N6 . . . . 1B 32
Nth. Hill Av. N6 . . . . 1B 32
North Ho. SE8 . . . . 1B 94
Northiam WC1 . . . . 2E 7
(off Cromer St.)
Northiam St. E9 . . . . 5D 51
Northington St.
WC1. . . . . 4A 8 (3B 62)
NORTH KENSINGTON
. . . . 4F 57
Northlands St. SE5. . . . . 5E 91
North Lodge E16 . . . . . . 2D 83
(off Wesley Av.)
Nth. Lodge Cl. SW15. . . 3F 99
North Mall SW18 . . . . 3D 101
(off Buckhold Rd.)
North M. WC1 . . . 4A 8 (3B 62)
Northolme Rd. N5 . . . . . 1E 49
Northover
BR1: Brom 3B 124
North Pas. SW18 . . . . . . 3C 100
Northpoint Sq. NW1 . . . 3F 47
Nth. Pole Rd. W10. . . . . 4E 57
Northport St. N1 . . . . . . 5F 49
North Ride W2 . . . . 1A 74
North Ri. W2 . . . . 5A 60
North Rd. N6 . . . . 2C 32
N7 . . . . 3A 48
SW19 . . . . 5E 115
North Row
W1 . . . . 4A 12 (1B 74)
Nth. Row Bldgs. W1 . . . 4B 12
(off North Row)
North Several SE3 . . . . . 5F 95
Nth. Side Wandsworth Comn.
SW18 . . . . 3F 101
North Sq. NW11 . . . . 1C 30
Northstead Rd.
SW2 . . . . 2C 118
North St. E13. . . . . 1D 69
SW4 . . . . 1E 103
North St. Pas. E13. . . . . 1D 69
Nth. Tenter St. E1 . . . . . 5B 64
North Ter. SW3 . . . . 4A 74
Northumberland All.
EC3 . . . . 3E 19 (5A 64)
(not continuous)
Northumberland Av.
E12 . . . . 3E 41
WC2. . . . . 1D 23 (2A 76)
Northumberland Ho.
SW1 . . . . 1D 23
(off Northumberland Av.)
Northumberland Pl.
W2 . . . . 5C 58
Northumberland Rd.
E17. . . . . 2C 38
Northumberland St.
WC2. . . . . 1D 23 (2A 76)
Northumbria St. E14 . . . 5C 66
Nth. Verbena Gdns.
W6 . . . . 1C 84

North Vw. SW19 . . . . . . 5E 113
Northview N7 . . . . 5A 34
Northview Cres.
NW10 . . . . 1B 42
North Vs. NW1 . . . . 3F 47
North Wlk. W2 . . . . 1D 73
Northway NW11 . . . . . . 1D 31
Northway Rd. SE5 . . . . 1E 105
Northways Pde. NW3 . . . 4F 45
(off College Cres.,
not continuous)
Nth. Western
Commercial Cen.
NW1 . . . . 4A 48
Northwest Pl. N1 . . . . . . 1C 62
North Wharf Rd. W2 . . . 2E 81
(off Coldharbour)
Nth. Wharf Rd. W2 . . . . 4F 59
Northwick Cl. NW8 . . . . 3F 59
Northwick Ho. NW8 . . . . 3E 59
(off St John's Wood Rd.)
Northwick Ter. NW8 . . . . 3F 59
Northwold Rd. E5 . . . . . 4B 36
N16 . . . . 4B 36
Northwood Est. E5 . . . . . 4C 36
Northwood Hall N6 . . . . 2E 33
Northwood Ho.
SE27 . . . . 4F 119
Northwood Rd. N6 . . . . . 2D 33
SE23 . . . . 1B 122
Northwood Way
SE19 . . . . 5F 119
Nth. Woolwich Rd.
E16 . . . . 2B 82
Nth. Worple Way
SW14 . . . . 1A 98
Norton Folgate
E1 . . . . 5E 11 (4A 64)
Norton Folgate Ho.
E1 . . . . 5F 11
(off Puma Ct.)
Norton Ho. E1 . . . . 5D 65
(off Bigland St.)
E2 . . . . 1F 65
(off Mace St.)
SW1 . . . . 4F 75
(off Arneway St.)
SW9 . . . . 5B 90
(off Aytoun Rd.)
Norton Rd. E10 . . . . 3B 38
Norway Ga. SE16 . . . . . 4A 80
Norway Pl. E14 . . . . 5B 66
Norway St. SE10 . . . . . . 2D 95
Norway Wharf E14 . . . . . 5B 66
(off Norway Pl.)
Norwich Ho. E14 . . . . . . 5D 67
(off Cordelia St.)
Norwich Rd. E7 . . . . 2C 54
Norwich St.
EC4 . . . . 2B 16 (5C 62)
Norwood Cl. NW2 . . . . . 5A 30
Norwood High St.
SE27 . . . . 3D 119
Norwood Ho. E14 . . . . . 1D 81
(off Poplar High St.)
NORWOOD NEW TOWN
. . . . 5E 119
Norwood Pk. Rd.
SE27 . . . . 5E 119

Norwood Rd. SE24 . . . . 1D 119
SE27 . . . . 2D 119
Notley St. SE5 . . . . 3F 91
Notting Barn Rd.
W10 . . . . 3F 57
Nottingdale Sq. W11 . . . 2A 72
Nottingham Av. E16 . . . . 4E 69
Nottingham Ct.
WC2 . . . . 3D 15 (5A 62)
Nottingham Ho.
WC2 . . . . 3D 15
(off Shorts Gdns.)
Nottingham Pl.
W1 . . . . 4B 4 (4C 60)
Nottingham Rd. E10 . . . . 1E 39
SW17 . . . . 1B 116
Nottingham St.
W1 . . . . 5B 4 (4C 60)
Nottingham Ter. NW1 . . . 4B 4
NOTTING HILL 1B 72
Notting Hill Ga. W11 . . . 2C 72
Nottingwood Ho.
W11 . . . . 1A 72
(off Clarendon Rd.)
Nova Bldg. E14 . . . . . . 5C 80
Nova Ct. E. E14 . . . . . . 2E 81
(off Yabsley St.)
Nova Ct. W. E14 . . . . . . 2E 81
(off Yabsley St.)
Novello St. SW6 . . . . . . 4C 86
Novel Sq. SE10 . . . . . . 4B 82
(off Bank Rd.)
Nowell Rd. SW13 . . . . . 2C 84
Noyna Rd. SW17 . . . . . 3B 116
Nubia Way
BR1: Brom 3A 124
Nuding Cl. SE13 . . . . . . 1C 108
Nuffield Lodge N6 . . . . . 1E 33
W9 . . . . 4C 58
(off Admiral Wlk.)
Nugent Rd. N19 . . . . . . 3A 34
Nugent Ter. NW8 . . . . . 1E 59
NUNHEAD 1D 107
Nunhead Cres.
SE15 . . . . 1D 107
Nunhead Est. SE15 . . . . 2D 107
Nunhead Grn. SE15 . . . . 1D 107
Nunhead Gro. SE15 . . . . 1D 107
Nunhead La. SE15 . . . . 1D 107
Nunhead Pas. SE15 . . . . 1C 106
Nursery Cl. SE4 . . . . . . 5B 94
SW15 . . . . 2F 99
Nursery La. E2 . . . . 5B 50
E7 . . . . 3C 54
W10 . . . . 4E 57
Nursery Rd. E9 . . . . 3E 51
E12 . . . . 4F 41
SW9 . . . . 2B 104
Nursery Row SE17 . . . . 5F 77
Nutbourne St. W10 . . . . 2A 58
Nutbrook St. SE15 . . . . 1C 106
Nutcroft Rd. SE15 . . . . 3D 93
Nutfield Rd. E15 . . . . . . 1E 53
NW2 . . . . 5C 28
SE22 . . . . 2B 106
Nutford Pl. W1 . . . . 5B 60
Nuthurst Av. SW2 . . . . . 2B 118
Nutley Ter. NW3 . . . . . . 3E 45

Nutmeg Cl. E16 . . . . . . 3A 68
Nutmeg La. E14 . . . . . . 5F 67
Nuttall St. N1 . . . . 1A 64
Nutter La. E11 . . . . 1E 41
Nutt St. SE15 . . . . 3B 92
Nutwell St. SW17 . . . . . 5A 116
Nye Bevan Est. E5 . . . . 5F 37
Nye Bevan Ho. SW6 . . . 3B 86
(off St Thomas's Way)
Nynehead St. SE14 . . . . 3A 94
Nyon Gro. SE6 . . . . 2B 122
Nyssa Ct. E15 . . . . 2A 68
(off Teasel Way)
Nyton Cl. N19 . . . . 3A 34

O

O2, The
(Millennium Dome)
. . . . 2A 82
O2 Cen. NW3 . . . . 3E 45
Oak Apple Ct. SE12 . . . . 1C 124
Oakbank Gro. SE24 . . . . 2E 105
Oakbrook Cl.
BR1: Brom 4D 125
Oakbury Rd. SW6 . . . . . 5D 87
Oak Cott. Cl. SE6 . . . . . 1B 124
Oak Ct. SE15 . . . . 3B 92
(off Sumner Rd.)
Oak Cres. E16 . . . . 4A 68
Oakcroft Rd. SE13 . . . . 5F 95
Oakdale Rd. E7 . . . . 4D 55
E11 . . . . 4F 39
N4 . . . . 1E 35
SE4 . . . . 1E 107
SE15 . . . . 1E 107
SW16 . . . . 5A 118
Oakdene SE15 . . . . 4D 93
Oakden St. SE11 . . . . . . 5C 76
Oake Ct. SW15 . . . . 3A 100
Oakeford Ho. W14 . . . . . 4A 72
(off Russell Rd.)
Oakend Ho. N4 . . . . 2F 35
Oakeshott Av. N6 . . . . . 4C 32
Oakey La.
SE1 . . . . 5B 24 (4C 76)
Oakfield Ct. N8 . . . . 2A 34
NW2 . . . . 2F 29
Oakfield Gdns.
SE19 . . . . 5A 120
(not continuous)
Oakfield Ho. E3 . . . . 4C 66
(off Gale St.)
Oakfield Rd. E6 . . . . 5F 55
N4 . . . . 1C 34
SW19 . . . . 3F 113
Oakfields Rd. NW11 . . . . 1A 30
Oakfield St. SW10 . . . . . 2E 87
Oakford Rd. NW5 . . . . . 1E 47
Oak Gro. NW2 . . . . 1A 44
Oakhall Ct. E11 . . . . 1D 41
Oak Hall Rd. E11 . . . . . 1D 41
Oakham Cl. SE6 . . . . . . 2B 122
Oakham Ho. W10 . . . . . 3E 57
(off Sutton Way)
Oakhill Av. NW3 . . . . . . 1D 45
Oakhill Ct. SE23 . . . . . . 4E 107
Oak Hill Pk. NW3 . . . . . 1D 45

Oak Hill Pk. M. NW3 . . . . 1E **45**
Oakhill Pl. SW15 . . . . 3C **100**
Oakhill Rd. SW15 . . . . . 3B **100**
Oak Hill Way NW3 . . . . . 1D **45**
   (not continuous)
Oak Ho. W10 . . . . 3A **58**
   (off Sycamore Wlk.)
Oakhurst Gro. SE22 . . 2C **106**
Oakington Rd. W9 . . . . . 3C **58**
Oakington Way N8 . . . . 2A **34**
Oakland Rd. E15 . . . . . . 1F **53**
Oaklands Ct. NW10 . . . . 5A **42**
   (off Nicoll Rd.)
Oaklands Est. SW4 . . . 4E **103**
Oaklands Gro. W12 . . . . 2C **70**
Oaklands M. NW2 . . . . . 1F **43**
   (off Oaklands Rd.)
Oaklands Pas. NW2 . . . . 1F **43**
   (off Oaklands Rd.)
Oaklands Pl. SW4 . . . . 2E **103**
Oaklands Rd. NW2 . . . . 1F **43**
Oak La. E14 . . . . 1B **80**
Oakley Cres. EC1 . . . . . 1D **63**
Oakley Dr. SE13 . . . . . 4F **109**
Oakley Gdns. SW3 . . . . 2A **88**
Oakley Ho. SW1 . . . . . . 5B **74**
   (off Sloane St.)
Oakley Pl. SE1 . . . . 1B **92**
Oakley Rd. N1 . . . . 4F **49**
Oakley Sq. NW1 . . . . . . 1E **61**
Oakley St. SW3 . . . . . . 2A **88**
Oakley Studios SW3. . . 2A **88**
   (off Up. Cheyne Row)
Oakley Wlk. W6 . . . . . . 2F **85**
Oakley Yd. E2 . . . . 3B **64**
Oak Lodge E11 . . . . . . 1C **40**
   W8 . . . . 4D **73**
   (off Chantry Sq.)
Oakman Ho. SW19 . . . 1F **113**
Oakmead Rd. SW12 . . 1C **116**
Oak Pk. Gdns.
   SW19 . . . . 1F **113**
Oak Pk. M. N16 . . . . . . 5B **36**
Oak Pl. SW18 . . . . 3D **101**
Oakridge La.
   BR1: Brom 5F **123**
Oakridge Rd.
   BR1: Brom 4F **123**
Oaks, The NW6 . . . . . . 4F **43**
   (off Brondesbury Pk.)
   NW10 . . . . 4D **43**
Oaks Av. SE19 . . . . . . 5A **120**
Oaksford Av. SE26 . . 3D **121**
Oakshade Rd.
   BR1: Brom 4F **123**
Oakshaw Rd. SW18 . . 5D **101**
Oakshott Ct.
   NW1. . . . . 1B **6** (1F **61**)
   (not continuous)
Oak St. E14 . . . . 3E **81**
   (off Stewart St.)
Oak Tree Gdns.
   BR1: Brom 5D **125**
Oak Tree Ho. W9 . . . . . 3C **58**
   (off Shirland Rd.)
Oak Tree Rd. NW8 . . . . 2A **60**
Oakview Lodge
   NW11 . . . . 2B **30**
   (off Beechcroft Av.)

Oakview Rd. SE6 . . . . 5D **123**
Oak Village NW5 . . . . . 1C **46**
Oak Vs. NW11 . . . . 1B **30**
   (off Hendon Pk. Row)
Oak Way W3. . . . . 2A **70**
Oakwood Bus. Pk.
   NW10 . . . . 3A **56**
Oakwood Ct. E6 . . . . . . 5F **55**
   W14 . . . . 4B **72**
Oakwood Dr. SE19 . . . . 5F **119**
Oakwood Ho. E9. . . . . . 3E **51**
   (off Frampton Pk. Ct.)
Oakwood La. W14 . . . . 4B **72**
Oakwood Mans. W14. . . 4B **72**
   (off Oakwood Ct.)
Oakworth Rd. W10 . . . . 4E **57**
Oasis Sports Cen.
   . . . . 2D **15** (5A **62**)
Oast Ct. E14 . . . . 1B **80**
   (off Newell St.)
Oast Lodge W4. . . . . . . 3A **84**
   (off Corney Reach Way)
Oatfield Ho. N15 . . . . . 1A **36**
   (off Perry Ct.)
Oat La. EC2 . . . . 2A **18** (5E **63**)
Oatwell Ho. SW3 . . . . . 1A **88**
   (off Marlborough St.)
Oban Cl. E13 . . . . 3E **69**
Oban Ho. E14 . . . . 5F **67**
   (off Oban St.)
Oban Rd. E13 . . . . 2E **69**
Oban St. E14 . . . . 5F **67**
Oberon Ho. N1 . . . . . . 1A **64**
   (off Arden Est.)
Oberstein Rd. SW11. . 2F **101**
Oborne Cl. SE24 . . . . 3D **105**
O'Brien Ho. E2 . . . . . . 2F **65**
   (off Roman Rd.)
Observatory Gdns.
   W8 . . . . 3C **72**
Observatory M. E14 . . . 5F **81**
Observatory Rd.
   SW7 . . . . 4F **73**
Occupation Rd. SE17 . . 1E **91**
Ocean Est. E1. . . . . . . 4A **66**
   (Ben Jonson Rd.)
   E1 . . . . 3F **65**
   (Ernest St.)
Ocean Music Venue . . 3D **51**
   (off Mare St.)
Ocean St. E1. . . . . 4F **65**
Ocean Wharf E14 . . . . 3B **80**
Ockbrook E1 . . . . 4E **65**
   (off Hannibal Rd.)
Ockendon M. N1 . . . . . 3F **49**
Ockendon Rd. N1 . . . . 3F **49**
Ockley Rd. SW16 . . . . 4A **118**
Octagon, The SW10 . . 3D **87**
   (off Coleridge Gdns.)
Octagon Arc.
   EC2 . . . . . 1D **19** (4A **64**)
Octagon Ct. SE16 . . . . 2F **79**
   (off Rotherhithe St.)
Octavia Ho. SW1 . . . . . 4F **75**
   (off Medway St.)
   W10 . . . . 3A **58**
Octavia M. W10 . . . . . 3B **58**
Octavia St. SW11 . . . . 4A **88**
Octavius St. SE8 . . . . . 3C **94**

Odeon Cinema
   Camden Town 5D **47**
   (off Parkway)
   Charing Cross. 5C **14**
   (off Panton St.)
   Covent Garden 3C **14**
   (off Shaftesbury Av.)
   Greenwich 5B **82**
   Holloway 5A **34**
   Kensington 4C **72**
   (off Kensington High St.)
   Leicester Sq. 5C **14**
   (off Leicester Sq.)
   Marble March. 3A **12**
   (off Edgware Rd.)
   Putney 1A **100**
   Rotherhithe 4F **79**
   Streatham 3A **118**
   Swiss Cen. 4B **14**
   (off Wardour St.)
   Swiss Cottage. 4F **45**
   Tottenham Ct. Rd. . . 1B **14**
   (off Tottenham Ct. Rd.)
   West End 5C **14**
   (off Leicester Sq.)
   Whiteleys 5D **59**
   (off Queensway)
Odeon Cl. E16 . . . . 4C **68**
   NW10 . . . . 5A **42**
   (off St Albans Rd.)
Odessa Rd. E7 . . . . 5B **40**
   NW10 . . . . 1C **56**
Odessa St. SE16 . . . . . 3B **80**
Odette Duval Ho. E1. . . 4E **65**
   (off Stepney Way)
Odger St. SW11 . . . . . 5B **88**
Odhams Wlk.
   WC2 . . . . . . 3E **15** (5A **62**)
Odin Ho. SE5 . . . . 5E **91**
O'Donnell Ct.
   WC1 . . . . 3E **7** (3A **62**)
Odontological Mus., The
   . . . . 2A **16**
   (in The Royal College of
    Surgeons)
O'Driscoll Ho. W12 . . 5D **57**
Offa's Mead E9. . . . . . . 1B **52**
Offenbach Ho. E2 . . . . 1F **65**
   (off Mace St.)
Offerton Rd. SW4 . . . 1E **103**
Offham Ho. SE17 . . . . 5A **78**
   (off Beckway St.)
Offley Rd. SW9 . . . . . . 3C **90**
Offord Rd. N1 . . . . 4B **48**
Offord St. N1 . . . . 4B **48**
Ogilvie Ho. E1 . . . . 5F **65**
   (off Stepney C'way.)
Oglander Rd.
   SE15 . . . . 2B **106**
Ogle St. W1 . . . . . 5F **5** (4E **61**)
O'Gorman Ho. SW10 . . 3E **87**
   (off King's Rd.)
Ohio Bldg. SE8. . . . . . . 4D **95**
   (off Deal's Gateway)
Ohio Rd. E13 . . . . 3B **68**
Oil Mill La. W6 . . . . 1C **84**
Okeburn Rd. SW17 . . 5C **116**
Okehampton Rd.
   NW10 . . . . 5E **43**

Olaf Ct. *W8* *3C 72*
(off Kensington Chu. St.)
Olaf St. *W11* *1F 71*
Oldacre M. *SW12* *5C 102*
Old Bailey
EC4 . . . . *3E 17 (5D 63)*
Old Bailey
(Central Criminal Court)
. . . . *2E 17 (5D 63)*
Old Barge Ho. All.
SE1 . . . . *5C 16*
Old Barracks *W8* *3D 73*
Old Barrack Yd.
SW1 . . . . . . *4B 20 (3C 74)*
(not continuous)
Old Barrowfield *E15* . . . *5A 54*
Old Bellgate Pl. *E14* . . . *4C 80*
Old Bethnal Grn. Rd.
E2 . . . . *2C 64*
Old Billingsgate Mkt.
EC3 . . . . *5C 18*
(off Lwr. Thames St.)
Old Billingsgate Wlk.
EC3 . . . . . . *5D 19 (1A 78)*
Old Bond St.
W1 . . . . . . *5F 13 (1E 75)*
Old Brewer's Yd.
WC2 . . . . . . *3D 15 (5A 62)*
Old Brewery M. *NW3* . . *1F 45*
Old Broad St.
EC2 . . . . . . *2C 18 (5F 63)*
Old Bromley Rd.
BR1: Brom *5F 123*
Old Brompton Rd.
SW5 . . . . *1C 86*
SW7 . . . . *1C 86*
Old Bldgs. *WC2* *2B 16*
Old Burlington St.
W1 . . . . . . *4F 13 (1E 75)*
Oldbury Ho. *W2* *4D 59*
(off Harrow Rd.)
Oldbury Pl.
W1 . . . . . . *5C 4 (4C 60)*
Old Canal M. *SE15* *1B 92*
Old Castle St.
E1 . . . . *2F 19 (5B 64)*
Old Cavendish St.
W1 . . . . . . *2D 13 (5D 61)*
Old Change Ct. *EC4* . . . *3F 17*
Old Chapel Pl. *SW9* . . . *5C 90*
Old Chelsea M. *SW3* . . . *2A 88*
Old Chiswick Yd. *W4* . . *2A 84*
(off Pumping Sta. Rd.)
Old Church La. *NW9* . . . *4A 28*
Old Church Rd. *E1* *5F 65*
Old Church St. *SW3* . . . *1F 87*
Old Compton St.
W1 . . . . . . *4B 14 (1F 75)*
Old Ct. Ho. *W8* *3D 73*
(off Old Ct. Pl.)
Old Ct. Pl. *W8* *3D 73*
Old Curiosity Shop . . . *3A 16*
(off Portsmouth St.)
Old Dairy M. *NW5* *3D 47*
SW12 . . . . *1C 116*
Old Devonshire Rd.
SW12 . . . . *5D 103*
Old Dover Rd. *SE3* *3C 96*

Oldegate Ho. *E6* *4F 55*
Old Farm Cl. *SW17* . . . *2A 116*
Oldfield Gro. *SE16* *5F 79*
Oldfield Ho. *W4* *1A 84*
(off Devonshire Rd.)
Oldfield M. *N6* *2E 33*
Oldfield Rd. *N16* *5A 36*
NW10 . . . . *4B 42*
SW19 . . . . *5A 114*
W3 . . . . *3B 70*
Old Fish St. Hill *EC4* . . . *4F 17*
(off Victoria St.)
Old Fleet La.
EC4 . . . . . . *2D 17 (5D 63)*
Old Ford Rd. *E2* *1E 65*
E3 . . . . *1A 66*
Old Forge M. *W12* *3D 71*
Old Forge Rd. *N19* *4F 33*
Old Gloucester St.
WC1 . . . . *5E 7 (4A 62)*
Oldhill St. *N16* *3C 36*
Old Hospital Cl.
SW12 . . . . *1B 116*
Old Ho. Cl. *SW19* *5A 114*
Old Jamaica Rd.
SE16 . . . . *4C 78*
Old James St. *SE15* . . *1D 107*
Old Jewry
EC2 . . . . . . *3B 18 (5F 63)*
Old Kent Rd. *SE1* *5A 78*
SE15 . . . . *5A 78*
Old Mnr. Ct. *NW8* *1E 59*
Old Mnr. Yd. *SW5* *5D 73*
Old Mkt. Sq.
E2 . . . . . . *1F 11 (2B 64)*
Old Marylebone Rd.
NW1 . . . . *4A 60*
Old Mitre Ct.
EC4 . . . . . . *3C 16 (5C 62)*
Old Montague St. *E1* . . *4C 64*
Old Nichol St.
E2 . . . . *3F 11 (3B 64)*
Old Nth. St. *WC1* *5F 7*
Old Nursery Ct. *E2* *1B 64*
(off Dunloe St.)
OLD OAK COMMON . . . *4A 56*
Old Oak Comn. La.
NW10 . . . . *4A 56*
W3 . . . . *4A 56*
Old Oak La. *NW10* *2A 56*
Old Oak Rd. *W3* *1B 70*
Old Orchard, The
NW3 . . . . *1B 46*
Old Pal. Yd.
SW1 . . . . . *5D 23 (4A 76)*
Old Paradise St.
SE11 . . . . *5B 76*
Old Pk. Av. *SW12* *4C 102*
Old Pk. La.
W1 . . . . . . *2D 21 (2D 75)*
Old Post Office La.
SE3 . . . . *1D 111*
Old Pye St.
SW1 . . . . . *5B 22 (4F 75)*
Old Pye St. Est. *SW1* . . . *5B 22*
(off Old Pye St.)
Old Quebec St.
W1 . . . . . . *3A 12 (5B 60)*

Old Queen St.
SW1 . . . . . . *4C 22 (3F 75)*
Old Red Lion Theatre . . . *1C 8*
(off St John St.)
Oldridge Rd. *SW12* . . . *5C 102*
Old Rd. *SE13* *2A 110*
Old Royal Free Pl.
N1 . . . . *5C 48*
Old Royal Free Sq.
N1 . . . . *5C 48*
Old Royal Naval College
. . . . *1F 95*
Old School Cl. *SE10* . . . *4A 82*
Old School Cres. *E7* . . . *3C 54*
Old School Sq. *E14* . . . *5C 66*
(off Pelling St.)
Old Seacoal La.
EC4 . . . . . . *2D 17 (5D 63)*
Old Sth. Lambeth Rd.
SW8 . . . . *3A 90*
Old Spitalfields Market
. . . . *5F 11 (4B 64)*
Old Sq. *WC2* . . *2B 16 (5B 62)*
Old Stable M. *N5* *5E 35*
Oldstead Rd.
BR1: Brom *4E 123*
OLD STREET *3F 63*
Old St. *E13* *1D 69*
EC1 . . . . *3F 9 (3E 63)*
Old Sun Wharf *E14* . . . *1A 80*
(off Narrow St.)
Old Swan Wharf
SW11 . . . . *4F 87*
Old Thackeray School
SW8 . . . . *5D 89*
Old Theatre Ct. *SE1* . . . *1A 26*
(off Porter St.)
Old Town *SW4* *1E 103*
Old Vic Theatre, The. . . *3C 24*
Old Woolwich Rd.
SE10 . . . . *2F 95*
Old York Rd. *SW18* . . . *3D 101*
O'Leary Sq. *E1* *4E 65*
Olga St. *E3* *1A 66*
Olinda Rd. *N16* *1B 36*
Oliphant St. *W10* *2F 57*
Olive Blythe Ho.
W10 . . . . *3A 58*
(off Ladbroke Gro.)
Olive Ct. *N1* *5C 48*
(off Liverpool Rd.)
Oliver Goldsmith Est.
SE15 . . . . *4C 92*
Oliver Ho. *SE16* *3C 78*
(off George Row)
SW8 . . . . *3A 90*
(off Wyvil Rd.)
Oliver M. *SE15* *5C 92*
Olive Rd. *E13* *2E 69*
NW2 . . . . *1E 43*
Oliver Rd. *E10* *4D 39*
Olivers Wharf *E1* *2D 79*
(off Wapping High St.)
Olivers Yd.
EC1 . . . . *3C 10 (3F 63)*
Olive Tree Ho. *SE15* . . . *2E 93*
(off Sharratt St.)
Olivette St. *SW15* *1F 99*
Olive Waite Ho. *NW6* . . *4C 44*

Olivier Theatre 1B 24
  (in Royal National Theatre)
Ollerton Grn. E3 . . . . 5B 52
Ollgar Cl. W12 . . . . 2B 70
Olliffe St. E14 . . . . 4E 81
Olmar St. SE1 . . . . 2C 92
Olney Ho. NW8 . . . . 3A 60
  (off Tresham Cres.)
Olney Rd. SE17 . . . . 2D 91
  (not continuous)
Olympia 4A 72
Olympia M. W2 . . . . 1D 73
Olympian Ct. E14 . . . . . . 5C 80
  (off Homer Dr.)
Olympia Way W14 . . . . . 4A 72
Olympus Sq. E5 . . . . 5C 36
O'Mahoney Ho.
  SW17 . . . . 3E 115
Oman Av. NW2 . . . . 1E 43
O'Meara St.
  SE1 . . . . 2A 26 (2E 77)
Omega Cl. E14 . . . . 4D 81
Omega Ho. SW10 . . . . . 3E 87
  (off King's Rd.)
Omega Pl. N1 . . . . 1E 7
Omega St. SE14 . . . . . . 4C 94
Omega Works E3 . . . . . 4C 52
Ommaney Rd.
  SE14 . . . . 4F 93
Ondine Ho. SE15 . . . . . 2B 106
Onega Ga. SE16 . . . . . . 4A 80
O'Neill Ho. NW8 . . . . . . 1A 60
  (off Cochrane St.)
One Owen St. EC1 . . . . . 1D 9
  (off Goswell St.)
One Tree Cl. SE23 . . . . . 4E 107
Ongar Rd. SW6 . . . . 2C 86
Onra Rd. E17 . . . . 2C 38
Onslow Cl. W10 . . . . . . 2B 58
Onslow Ct. SW7 . . . . . . 1E 87
  (off Drayton Gdns.)
Onslow Cres. SW7 . . . . . 5F 73
Onslow Gdns. SW7 . . . . . 5F 73
Onslow M. E. SW7 . . . . . 5F 73
Onslow M. W. SW7 . . . . . 5F 73
Onslow Sq. SW7 . . . . . . 5F 73
Onslow St.
  EC1 . . . . 4C 8 (3C 62)
Ontario St.
  SE1 . . . . 5E 25 (4D 77)
Ontario Way E14 . . . . . . 1C 80
  (not continuous)
Onyx M. E15 . . . . 3B 54
Opal Cl. E16 . . . . 5F 69
Opal M. NW6 . . . . 5B 44
Opal St. SE11 . . . . 1D 91
Open Air Stage 3A 32
Open Air Theatre 4C 42
Openview SW18 . . . . . . 1E 115
  (Parsifal College) . . . 1C 44
Openview SW18 . . . . . . 1E 115
  (off Wedmore St.)
Operating Theatre Mus.
  . . . . 2C 26
Ophelia Gdns. NW2 . . . . 5A 30
Ophelia Ho. W6 . . . . . . 1F 85
  (off Fulham Pal. Rd.)
Ophir Ter. SE15 . . . . 4C 92

Opie Ho. NW8 . . . . 1A 60
  (off Townshend Est.)
Oppenheim Rd. SE13 . . . 5E 95
Oppidans Rd. NW3 . . . . 4B 46
Orange Gro. E11 . . . . . . 5A 40
  (not continuous)
Orange Pl. SE16 . . . . . . 4E 79
Orangery Gallery, The
  . . . . 3B 72
Orange St.
  WC2 . . . . . . 5C 14 (1F 75)
Orange Tree Ct. SE5 . . . 3A 92
  (off Havil St.)
Orange Yd. W1 . . . . 3C 14
Oratory La. SW3 . . . . . . 1F 87
Orbain Rd. SW6 . . . . . . 3A 86
Orbel St. SW11 . . . . 4A 88
Orb St. SE17 . . . . 5F 77
Orchard, The NW11 . . . . 1C 30
  SE3 . . . . 5A 96
  W4 . . . . 5A 70
Orchard Bus. Cen.
  SE26 . . . . 5B 122
Orchard Cl. N1 . . . . 4E 49
  NW2 . . . . 5C 28
  SE23 . . . . 4E 107
  W10 . . . . 4B 58
Orchard Ct. E10 . . . . . . 3D 39
Orchard Dr. SE3 . . . . . . 5F 95
Orchard Hill SE13 . . . . . 5D 95
Orchard Ho. SE5 . . . . . . 4E 91
  (off County Gro.)
  SE16 . . . . 4E 79
  SW6 . . . . 3B 86
  (off Varna St.)
  W1 . . . . 2B 12
  (off Fitzhardinge St.)
  W12 . . . . 2C 70
Orchard Mead Ho.
  NW2 . . . . 4C 30
Orchard M. N1 . . . . 4F 49
  N6 . . . . 2D 33
  SW17 . . . . 3E 115
Orchard Pl. E5 . . . . 2D 51
  E14 . . . . 1A 82
  (not continuous)
Orchard Rd. N6 . . . . 2D 33
  SE3 . . . . 5A 96
Orchardson Ho. NW8 . . . 3F 59
  (off Orchardson St.)
Orchardson St. NW8 . . . 3F 59
Orchard Sq. W14 . . . . . . 1B 86
Orchard St.
  W1 . . . . 3B 12 (5C 60)
Orchard Studios W6 . . . 5F 71
  (off Brook Grn.)
Orchard Ter. NW10 . . . . 1B 42
Orchard Wharf E14 . . . . 1A 82
  (off Orchard Pl.)
Orchid Cl. E6 . . . . 4F 69
Orchid St. W12 . . . . 1C 70
Orde Hall St.
  WC1 . . . . 4F 7 (3B 62)
Ordell Rd. E3 . . . . 1B 66
Ordnance Cres. SE10 . . . 3F 81
Ordnance Hill NW8 . . . . 5F 45
Ordnance M. NW8 . . . . . 1F 59
Ordnance Rd. E16 . . . . . 4B 68
Oregano Dr. E14 . . . . . . 5F 67

Oregon Bldg. SE10 . . . . 4D 95
  (off Deal's Gateway)
Orestes M. NW6 . . . . . . 2C 44
Orford Ct. SE27 . . . . . . 2D 119
Orford Rd. E17 . . . . 1C 38
  SE6 . . . . 3D 123
Oriana Ho. E14 . . . . 1B 80
  (off Victory Pl.)
Oriel Ct. NW3 . . . . 1E 45
Oriel Dr. SW13 . . . . 2E 85
Oriel Pl. NW3 . . . . 1E 45
  (off Heath St.)
Oriel Rd. E9 . . . . 3F 51
Oriental Ho. E14 . . . . . . 2F 83
Oriental St. E14 . . . . 1C 80
  (off Pennyfields)
Orient Ind. Pk. E10 . . . . 4C 38
Orient St. SE11 . . . . 5D 77
Orient Way E5 . . . . 5F 37
  E10 . . . . 3A 38
Orient Wharf E1 . . . . . . 2E 79
  (off Wapping High St.)
Orion E14 . . . . 5C 80
  (off Crews St.)
Orion Bus. Cen. SE14 . . 1F 93
Orion Ho. E1 . . . . 3D 65
  (off Coventry Rd.)
Orkney Ho. N1 . . . . 5B 48
  (off Bemerton Est.)
Orkney St. SW11 . . . . . 5C 88
Orlando Rd. SW4 . . . . . 1E 103
Orleston M. N7 . . . . 3C 48
Orleston Rd. N7 . . . . . . 3C 48
Orlop St. SE10 . . . . 1A 96
Ormanton Rd. SE26 . . . 4C 120
Orme Ct. W2 . . . . 1D 73
Orme Ct. M. W2 . . . . . . 1D 73
  (off Orme La.)
Orme Ho. E8 . . . . 5B 50
Orme La. W2 . . . . 1D 73
Ormeley Rd. SW12 . . . . 1D 117
Orme Sq. W2 . . . . 1D 73
Ormiston Gro. W12 . . . . 2D 71
Ormiston Rd. SE10 . . . . 1C 96
Ormond Cl.
  WC1 . . . . 5E 7 (4A 62)
Ormonde Ct. NW8 . . . . . 5B 46
  (off St Edmund's Cl.)
  SW15 . . . . 2E 99
Ormonde Ga. SW3 . . . . 1B 88
Ormonde Pl. SW1 . . . . . 5C 74
Ormonde Ter. NW8 . . . . 5B 46
Ormond Ho. N16 . . . . . . 4F 35
Ormond M.
  WC1 . . . . 4E 7 (3A 62)
Ormond Rd. N19 . . . . . . 3A 34
Ormond Yd.
  SW1 . . . . 1A 22 (2E 75)
Ormrod Ct. W11 . . . . . . 5A 58
  (off Westbourne Pk. Rd.)
Ormsby Lodge W4 . . . . 4A 70
Ormsby Pl. N16 . . . . 5B 36
Ormsby St. E2 . . . . 1B 64
Ormside St. SE15 . . . . . 2E 93
Ornan Rd. NW3 . . . . 2A 46
Orpen Ho. SW5 . . . . 5C 72
  (off Trebovir Rd.)
Orpen Wlk. N16 . . . . 5A 36
Orpheus St. SE5 . . . . . . 4F 91

Orsett M. W2 . . . . 5D **59**
(not continuous)
Orsett St. SE11 . . . . 1B **90**
Orsett Ter. W2 . . . . 5D **59**
Orsman Rd. N1. . . . . 5A **50**
Orton St. E1 . . . . 2C **78**
Orville Rd. SW11 . . . . . . 5F **87**
Orwell Ct. E8 . . . . 5C **50**
(off Pownall Rd.)
N5 . . . . 1E **49**
Orwell Rd. E13 . . . . 1E **69**
Osbaldeston Rd. N16 . . 4C **36**
Osberton Rd. SE12 . . . . 3C **110**
Osbert St. SW1 . . . . 5F **75**
Osborn Cl. E8 . . . . 5C **50**
Osborne Ct. E10 . . . . . . 2D **39**
Osborne Gro. N4 . . . . . . 3C **34**
Osborne Ho. E16 . . . . . . 2C **82**
(off Wesley Av.)
Osborne Rd. E7 . . . . 2D **55**
E9 . . . . 3B **52**
E10 . . . . 4D **39**
N4 . . . . 3C **34**
NW2 . . . . 3D **43**
Osborne Ter. SW17 . . . . 5B **116**
(off Church La.)
Osborn La. SE23 . . . . . . 5A **108**
Osborn St. E1 . . . . 4B **64**
Osborn Ter. SE3 . . . . . . 2B **110**
Oscar Faber Pl. N1. . . . 4A **50**
Oscar St. SE8 . . . . 5C **94**
(not continuous)
Oseney Cres. NW5 . . . . 2E **47**
Osier Ct. E1. . . . . 3F **65**
(off Osier St.)
Osier La. SE10 . . . . 4B **82**
(off School Bank Rd.)
Osier M. W4 . . . . 2A **84**
Osiers Est., The
SW18 . . . . 2C **100**
Osiers Rd. SW18 . . . . . 2C **100**
Osier St. E1 . . . . 3E **65**
Osier Way E10 . . . . 5D **39**
Oslac Rd. SE6 . . . . 5D **123**
Oslo Ct. NW8 . . . . 1A **60**
(off Prince Albert Rd.)
Oslo Ho. SE5 . . . . 5E **91**
(off Carew St.)
Oslo Sq. SE16 . . . . 4A **80**
Osman Cl. N15 . . . . 1F **35**
Osmani School Sports Cen.
. . . . 4C **64**
Osman Rd. W6 . . . . 4E **71**
Osmington Ho. SW8. . . 3B **90**
(off Dorset Rd.)
Osmund St. W12 . . . . . . 4B **56**
Osnaburgh St.
NW1 . . . . 4E **5** (3D **61**)
(Euston Rd.)
NW1 . . . . 2E **5**
(Robert St.)
Osnaburgh Ter.
NW1 . . . . 3E **5** (3D **61**)
Osprey Cl. E6 . . . . 4F **69**
Osprey Ct. E1 . . . . 1C **78**
(off Star Pl.)
Osprey Est. SE16 . . . . . 5A **80**
Osprey Ho. E14 . . . . 1A **80**
(off Victory Pl.)

Ospringe Ho. SE1 . . . . . 3C **24**
(off Wootton St.)
Ospringe Rd. NW5 . . . . 1E **47**
Osram Ct. W6 . . . . 4E **71**
Osric Path N1 . . . . 1A **64**
Ossian M. N4 . . . . 2B **34**
Ossian Rd. N4 . . . . 2B **34**
Ossington Bldgs.
W1 . . . . 5B **4** (4C **60**)
Ossington Cl. W2 . . . . . 1C **72**
Ossington St. W2 . . . . . 1C **72**
Ossory Rd. SE1 . . . . 2C **92**
Ossulston St.
NW1 . . . . 1C **6** (1F **61**)
Ostade Rd. SW2 . . . . . . 5B **104**
Ostend Pl. SE11 . . . . . . 5E **77**
Osten M. SW7 . . . . 4D **73**
Osterley Ho. E14 . . . . . . 5D **67**
(off Giraud St.)
Osterley Rd. N16 . . . . . . 1A **50**
Oswald Bldg. SW8 . . . . 2D **89**
Oswald's Mead E9 . . . . 1A **52**
Oswald St. E5 . . . . 5F **37**
Oswald Ter. NW2 . . . . . 5E **29**
Osward Rd. SW17 . . . . . 2B **116**
Oswell Ho. E1 . . . . 2D **79**
(off Farthing Flds.)
Oswin St. SE11 . . . . 5D **77**
Oswyth Rd. SE5 . . . . . . 5A **92**
Otford Cres. SE4 . . . . . . 4B **108**
Otford Ho. SE1 . . . . 5C **26**
(off Staple St.)
SE15 . . . . 2E **93**
(off Lovelinch Cl.)
Othello Cl. SE11 . . . . . . 1D **91**
Otis St. E3 . . . . 2E **67**
Otley Ho. N5. . . . . 5C **34**
Otley Rd. E16 . . . . 5E **69**
Otley Ter. E5 . . . . 5F **37**
Ottaway Ct. E5 . . . . 5C **36**
Ottaway St. E5 . . . . 5C **36**
Otterburn Ho. SE5 . . . . 3E **91**
(off Sultan St.)
Otterburn St. SW17 . . . 5B **116**
Otter Cl. E15 . . . . 5E **53**
Otterden St. SE6 . . . . . . 4C **122**
Otto Cl. SE26 . . . . 3D **121**
Otto St. SE17 . . . . 2D **91**
Oulton Cl. E5 . . . . 4E **37**
Oulton Rd. N15. . . . . 1F **35**
Ouseley Rd. SW12 . . . . 1B **116**
Outer Circ.
NW1 . . . . 1D **5** (1A **60**)
Outgate Rd. NW10 . . . . 4B **42**
Outram Pl. N1 . . . . 5A **48**
Outram Rd. E6 . . . . 5F **55**
Outwich St. EC3 . . . . . . 2E **19**
Outwood Ho. SW2 . . . . 5B **104**
(off Deepdene Gdns.)
Oval, The E2 . . . . 1D **65**
Oval Cricket Ground, The
. . . . 2B **90**
Oval House Theatre . . . 2C **90**
(off Kennington Oval)
Oval Mans. SE11 . . . . . 2B **90**
Oval Pl. SW8 . . . . 3B **90**
Oval Rd. NW1 . . . . 5D **47**
Oval Way SE11 . . . . 1B **90**
Overbrae BR3: Beck. . . 5C **122**

Overbury Rd. N15. . . . . 1F **35**
Overbury St. E5 . . . . . . 1F **51**
Overcliff Rd. SE13 . . . . 1C **108**
Overdown Rd. SE6 . . . . 4C **122**
Overhill Rd. SE22 . . . . . 5C **106**
Overlea Rd. E5. . . . . 2C **36**
Oversley Ho. W2 . . . . . . 4C **58**
(off Alfred Rd.)
Overstone Ho. E14. . . . . 5C **66**
(off E. India Dock Rd.)
Overstone Rd. W6 . . . . . 4E **71**
Overstrand Mans.
SW11 . . . . 4B **88**
Overton Ct. E11 . . . . 2C **40**
Overton Dr. E11 . . . . 2C **40**
Overton Ho. SW15 . . . . 5B **98**
(off Tangley Gro.)
Overton Rd. E10. . . . . . . 3A **38**
SW9 . . . . 5C **90**
Overy Ho.
SE1 . . . . 4D **25** (3D **77**)
Ovex Cl. E14. . . . . 3E **81**
Ovington Ct. SW3 . . . . . 4A **74**
(off Brompton Rd.)
Ovington Gdns. SW3 . . 4A **74**
Ovington M. SW3 . . . . . 4A **74**
(off Ovington Gdns.)
Ovington Sq. SW3 . . . . 4A **74**
Ovington St. SW3 . . . . . 5A **74**
Owen Mans. W14 . . . . . 2A **86**
(off Queen's Club Gdns.)
Owens M. E11 . . . . 4A **40**
Owen's Row
EC1 . . . . 1D **9** (2D **63**)
Owen St. EC1 . . . 1D **9** (1D **63**)
(not continuous)
Owens Way SE23 . . . . . 5A **108**
Owgan Cl. SE5 . . . . 3F **91**
Oxberry Av. SW6 . . . . . . 5A **86**
Oxendon St.
SW1 . . . . 5B **14** (1F **75**)
Oxenford St. SE15 . . . . 1B **106**
Oxenham Ho. SE8 . . . . . 2C **94**
(off Benbow St.)
Oxenholme NW1 . . . . . . 1F **5**
(off Hampstead Rd.)
Oxestall's Rd. SE8. . . . . 1A **94**
Oxford & Cambridge Mans.
NW1 . . . . 4A **60**
(off Old Marylebone Rd.)
Oxford Av. NW10 . . . . . . 2D **57**
Oxford Cir. W1 . . . . 3F **13**
Oxford Cir. Av.
W1 . . . . 3F **13** (5E **61**)
Oxford Ct. EC4 . . . . 4B **18**
W9 . . . . 4C **58**
(off Elmfield Way)
Oxford Dr.
SE1 . . . . 2D **27** (2A **78**)
Oxford Gdns. W10 . . . . . 5E **57**
Oxford Ga. W6 . . . . 5F **71**
Oxford Pl. NW10 . . . . . . 5A **28**
(off Press Rd.)
Oxford Rd. E15 . . . . 3F **53**
(not continuous)
N4 . . . . 3C **34**
NW6 . . . . 1C **58**
SE19 . . . . 5F **119**
SW15 . . . . 2A **100**

Oxford Sq. W2 . . . . 5A 60
Oxford St.
  W1 . . . . 3B 12 (5C 60)
Oxgate Cen. NW2 . . . . . . 4D 29
Oxgate Ct. NW2 . . . . 4C 28
Oxgate Ct. Pde. NW2 . . . . 4C 28
Oxgate Gdns. NW2 . . . . . . 5D 29
Oxgate La. NW2 . . . . 4D 29
Oxgate Pde. NW2 . . . . . . 4C 28
Oxley Cl. SE1 . . . . 1B 92
Oxleys Rd. NW2 . . . . 5D 29
Oxonian St. SE22 . . . . . . 2B 106
Oxo Tower Wharf
  SE1 . . . . 5C 16 (1C 76)
Oxzygeem Sports Cen.
  . . . . 4D 105
Oystercatcher Cl.
  E16 . . . . 5D 69
Oystergate Wlk. EC4 . . . . 5B 18
Oyster Row E1 . . . . 5E 65
Oyster Wharf SW11 . . . . 5F 87
Ozolins Way E16 . . . . . . 5C 68

P

Pablo Neruda Cl.
  SE24 . . . . 2D 105
Pace Pl. E1 . . . . 5D 65
Pacific Ho. E1 . . . . 3F 65
  (off Ernest St.)
Pacific Rd. E16 . . . . 5C 68
Pacific Wharf SE16 . . . . 2F 79
Packenham Ho. E2 . . . . . 2B 64
  (off Wellington Row)
Packington Sq. N1 . . . . . . 5E 49
  (not continuous)
Packington St. N1 . . . . . 5D 49
Padbury SE17 . . . . 1A 92
  (off Bagshot St.)
Padbury Ct. E2 . . . . 2B 64
Padbury Ho. NW8 . . . . . 3A 60
  (off Tresham Cres.)
Paddenswick Rd.
  W6 . . . . 4C 70
PADDINGTON 5F 59
Paddington Bowling &
  Sports Club 3D 59
Paddington Grn. W2 . . . . 4F 59
Paddington St.
  W1 . . . . 5B 4 (4C 60)
Paddington Wlk. W2 . . . . 4F 59
  (off Hermitage St.)
Paddock Cl. SE3 . . . . 5C 96
  SE26 . . . . 4F 121
Paddock Rd. NW2 . . . . . . 5C 28
Paddock Way SW15 . . . . 5E 99
Padfield Rd. SE5 . . . . . . 1E 105
Padstow Ho. E14 . . . . . . 1B 80
  (off Three Colt St.)
Pagden St. SW8 . . . . 4D 89
Pageant Cres. SE16 . . . . 2A 80
Pageantmaster Ct.
  EC4 . . . . 3D 17
Page Grn. Rd. N15 . . . . . 1C 36
Page Grn. Ter. N15 . . . . 1B 36
Page Ho. SE10 . . . . 2E 95
  (off Welland St.)
Page St. SW1 . . . . 5F 75

Page's Wlk.
  SE1 . . . . 5E 27 (5A 78)
Pages Yd. W4 . . . . 2B 84
Paget Ho. E2 . . . . 1E 65
  (off Bishop's Way)
Paget Rd. N16 . . . . 3F 35
Paget St.
  EC1 . . . . 1D 9 (2D 63)
Pagham Ho. W10 . . . . . . 3E 57
  (off Sutton Way)
Pagnell St. SE14 . . . . . . 3B 94
Pagoda Gdns. SE3 . . . . . 5F 95
Pagoda Gro. SE27 . . . . . 2E 119
Paignton Rd. N15 . . . . . . 1A 36
Painsthorpe Rd. N16 . . . . 5A 36
Painswick Ct. SE15 . . . . 3B 92
  (off Daniel Gdns.)
Painted Hall
  Greenwich 2E 95
Painters M. SE16 . . . . . . 5C 78
Pakeman Ho. SE1 . . . . . 3E 25
  (off Surrey Row)
Pakeman St. N7 . . . . 5B 34
Pakenham Cl.
  SW12 . . . . 1C 116
Pakenham St.
  WC1 . . . . 2A 8 (2B 62)
Pakington Ho. SW9 . . . . 5A 90
  (off Stockwell Gdns. Est.)
Palace Av. W8 . . . . 3D 73
Palace Bingo 5E 77
  (off Elephant & Castle)
Palace Ct. NW3 . . . . 2D 45
  W2 . . . . 1D 73
  (off Moscow Rd.,
    not continuous)
Palace Gdns. M. W8 . . . . 2D 73
Palace Gdns. Ter.
  W8 . . . . 2C 72
Palace Ga. W8 . . . . 3E 73
Palace Grn. W8 . . . . 2D 73
Palace Mans. W14 . . . . 5A 72
  (off Hammersmith Rd.)
Palace M. SW1 . . . . 5C 74
  (off Eaton Ter.)
  SW6 . . . . 3C 86
Palace Pl.
  SW1 . . . . 5F 21 (4E 75)
Palace Pl. Mans.
  W8 . . . . 3D 73
  (off Kensington Ct.)
Palace Rd. N8 . . . . 1F 33
  (not continuous)
  SW2 . . . . 1B 118
Palace St.
  SW1 . . . . 5F 21 (4E 75)
Palace Theatre
  Soho 3C 14
  (off Shaftesbury Av.)
Palace Vw. SE12 . . . . . . 2C 124
Palace Wharf W6 . . . . . . 3E 85
  (off Rainville Rd.)
Palamon Ct. SE1 . . . . . . 1B 92
  (off Cooper's Rd.)
Palamos Rd. E10 . . . . . . 3C 38
Palatine Av. N16 . . . . . . 1A 50
Palatine Rd. N16 . . . . . . 1A 50
Palemead Ct. SW6 . . . . . 4F 85
Palermo Rd. NW10 . . . . 1C 56

Palewell Comn. Dr.
  SW14 . . . . 3A 98
Palfrey Pl. SW8 . . . . . . 3B 90
Palgrave Gdns. NW1 . . . . 3A 60
Palgrave Ho. SE5 . . . . . 3E 91
  (off Wyndham Est.)
Palgrave Rd. W12 . . . . . 4B 70
Palissy St.
  E2 . . . . 2F 11 (2B 64)
  (not continuous)
Palladino Ho.
  SW17 . . . . 5A 116
  (off Laurel Cl.)
Palladium Ct. E8 . . . . . . 4B 50
  (off Queensbridge Rd.)
Pallant Ho. SE1 . . . . . . 5C 26
Pallett Way SE18 . . . . . 4F 97
Palliser Ct. W14 . . . . . . 1A 86
  (off Palliser Rd.)
Palliser Ho. E1 . . . . 3F 65
  (off Ernest St.)
  SE10 . . . . 2F 95
  (off Trafalgar Rd.)
Palliser Rd. W14 . . . . . . 1A 86
Pall Mall
  SW1 . . . . . . 2A 22 (2E 75)
Pall Mall E.
  SW1 . . . . 1C 22 (2F 75)
Pall Mall Pl. SW1 . . . . . 2A 22
Palm Cl. E10 . . . . 5D 39
Palm Ct. SE15 . . . . 3B 92
  (off Garnies Cl.)
Palmer Pl. N7 . . . . 2C 48
Palmer Rd. E13 . . . . 3D 69
Palmer's Rd. E2 . . . . . . 1F 65
Palmerston Ct. E3 . . . . . 1F 65
  (off Old Ford Rd.)
Palmerston Ho. SE1 . . . . 4B 24
  (off Westminster Bri. Rd.)
  W8 . . . . 2C 72
  (off Kensington Pl.)
Palmerston Mans.
  W14 . . . . 2A 86
  (off Queen's Club Gdns.)
Palmerston Rd. E7 . . . . . 3D 55
  NW6 . . . . 4B 44
  (not continuous)
Palmerston Way
  SW8 . . . . 3D 89
Palmer St.
  SW1 . . . . 5B 22 (4F 75)
  (not continuous)
Palm Tree Ho. SE14 . . . . 3F 93
  (off Barlborough St.)
Palyn Ho. EC1 . . . . 2A 10
  (off Ironmonger Row)
Pamela Ho. E8 . . . . 5B 50
  (off Haggerston Rd.)
Panama Ho. E1 . . . . 4F 65
  (off Beaumont Sq.)
Pancras La.
  EC4 . . . . 3B 18 (5E 63)
Pancras Rd.
  NW1 . . . . 1D 7 (1F 61)
Pandian Way NW5 . . . . . 3F 47
Pandora Rd. NW6 . . . . . 3C 44
Pangbourne NW1 . . . . . 2F 5
  (off Stanhope St.)

Pangbourne Av. W10 . . . . 4E 57
Pankhurst Av. E16 . . . . . . 2D 83
Pankhurst Cl. SE14 . . . . . . 3F 93
Panmure Cl. N5 . . . . 1D 49
Panmure Rd. SE26 . . . . . 3D 121
Panorama Ct. N6 . . . . 1E 33
Pansy Gdns. W12 . . . . . . 1C 70
Panton St.
    SW1 . . . . 5B 14 (1F 75)
Paper Bldgs. EC4 . . . . . . 4C 16
Papillons Wlk. SE3 . . . . . . 5C 96
Papworth Gdns. N7 . . . . . 2B 48
Papworth Way SW2 . . . . 5C 104
Parade, The N4 . . . . 3C 34
    SE4 . . . . 5B 94
        (off Up. Brockley Rd.)
    SE26 . . . . 3D 121
        (off Wells Pk. Rd.)
    SW11 . . . . 3B 88
Parade Mans. NW4 . . . . . 1D 29
Parade M. SE27 . . . . 2D 119
Paradise Pas. N7 . . . . 2C 48
Paradise Rd. SW4 . . . . . . 5A 90
Paradise Row E2 . . . . 2D 65
Paradise St. SE16 . . . . . . 3D 79
Paradise Wlk. SW3 . . . . . 2B 88
Paragon, The SE3 . . . . . . 5B 96
Paragon Cl. E16 . . . . 5C 68
Paragon M. SE1 . . . . 5F 77
Paragon Pl. SE3 . . . . 5B 96
Paragon Rd. E9 . . . . 3E 51
Paramount Bldg. EC1 . . . . 3D 9
        (off St John St.)
Paramount Ct. WC1 . . . . . 4A 6
Parbury Rd. SE23 . . . . . 4A 108
Pardoe Rd. E10 . . . . 2D 39
Pardoner Ho. SE1 . . . . . . 5C 26
        (off Pardoner St.)
Pardoner St.
    SE1 . . . . 5C 26 (4F 77)
        (not continuous)
Pardon St.
    EC1 . . . . 3E 9 (3D 63)
Parfett St. E1 . . . . 4C 64
        (not continuous)
Parfitt Cl. NW3 . . . . 3E 31
Parfrey St. W6 . . . . 2E 85
Paris Gdn.
    SE1 . . . . . . 1D 25 (2D 77)
Paris Ho. E2 . . . . 1D 65
        (off Old Bethnal Grn. Rd.)
Park, The N6 . . . . 1C 32
    NW11 . . . . 3D 31
    SE23 . . . . 1E 121
Park App. SE16 . . . . 4D 79
Park Av. E15 . . . . 3A 54
    NW2 . . . . 2D 43
    NW10 . . . . 2D 43
    NW11 . . . . 3D 31
    SW14 . . . . 2A 98
Park Av. Nth. NW10 . . . . . 2D 43
Park Bus. Cen.
    NW6 . . . . 2C 58
Park Cl. E9 . . . . 5E 51
    NW2 . . . . 5D 29
    SW1 . . . . 3B 74
    W4 . . . . 2A 84
    W14 . . . . 4B 72
Park Club, The 2A 70

Park Ct. E17 . . . . 1D 39
    SE21 . . . . 3E 119
    SE26 . . . . 5D 121
    SW11 . . . . 4D 89
    W6 . . . . 5C 70
Park Cres.
    W1 . . . . 4D 5 (3D 61)
Park Cres. M. E.
    W1 . . . . 4E 5 (3D 61)
Park Cres. M. W.
    W1 . . . . 4D 5 (3D 61)
Parkcroft Rd. SE12 . . . 5B 110
Park Dr. NW11 . . . . 3D 31
    SE7 . . . . 2F 97
    SW14 . . . . 3A 98
Park Dwellings
    NW3 . . . . 2B 46
Park End NW3 . . . . 1A 46
Parker Cl. E16 . . . . 2F 83
Parker Ho. E14 . . . . 3C 80
        (off Admirals Way)
Parker M.
    WC2 . . . . 2E 15 (5A 62)
Parke Rd. SW13 . . . . 4C 84
Parkers Row SE1 . . . . . . 3C 78
Parker St. E16 . . . . 2F 83
    WC2 . . . . 2E 15 (5A 62)
Parkfield Av. SW14 . . . . . 2A 98
Parkfield Ct. SE14 . . . . . . 4B 94
        (off Parkfield Rd.)
Parkfield Ind. Est.
    SW11 . . . . 5C 88
Parkfield Rd. NW10 . . . . . 4D 43
    SE14 . . . . 4B 94
Parkfields SW15 . . . . 2E 99
Parkfields Av. NW9 . . . . . 3A 28
Parkfield St. N1 . . . . 1C 62
Park Gdns. E10 . . . . 3C 38
Park Ga. SE3 . . . . 1B 110
Parkgate N1 . . . . 5F 49
        (off Southgate Rd.)
Parkgate M. N6 . . . . 2E 33
Parkgate Rd. SW11 . . . . . 3A 88
Park Gro. E15 . . . . 5C 54
Park Gro. Rd. E11 . . . . . . 4A 40
Park Hall SE10 . . . . 3F 95
        (off Crooms Hill)
Park Hall Rd. SE21 . . . . 3E 119
Park Hall Trad. Est.
    SE21 . . . . 3E 119
Parkham St. SW11 . . . . . 4A 88
Park Hill SE23 . . . . 2D 121
    SW4 . . . . 3F 103
Park Hill Ct. SW17 . . . . . 3B 116
Parkhill Rd. NW3 . . . . 2B 46
Parkhill Wlk. NW3 . . . . . . 2B 46
Parkholme Rd. E8 . . . . . . 3B 50
Park Ho. E9 . . . . 4E 51
        (off Shore Rd.)
Park Ho. Pas. N6 . . . . . . 2C 32
Parkhouse St. SE5 . . . . . 3F 91
Parkhurst Ct. N7 . . . . 1A 48
Parkhurst Rd. N7 . . . . . . 1A 48
Parkinson Ho. E9 . . . . . . 4E 51
        (off Frampton Pk. Rd.)
    SW1 . . . . 5E 75
        (off Tachbrook St.)
Parkland Ct. E15 . . . . . . 2A 54
        (off Maryland Pk.)

Parkland Ct. W14 . . . . . . 3A 72
        (off Holland Pk. Av.)
Parkland Gdns.
    SW19 . . . . 1F 113
Parklands N6 . . . . 2D 33
Parklands Rd.
    SW16 . . . . 5D 117
Park La. E15 . . . . 5F 53
    W1 . . . . 4A 12 (1B 74)
Park Lee Ct. N16 . . . . . . 2A 36
Park Lodge NW8 . . . . 4F 45
    W14 . . . . 4B 72
        (off Kensington High St.)
Park Lofts SW2 . . . . 3A 104
        (off Mandrell Rd.)
Park Lorne NW8 . . . . 2A 60
        (off Park Rd.)
Park Mans. NW4 . . . . 1D 29
    NW8 . . . . 1A 60
        (off Allitsen Rd.)
    SW1 . . . . 4A 20
        (off Knightsbridge)
    SW8 . . . . 2A 90
    SW11 . . . . 4B 88
        (off Prince of Wales Dr.)
Parkmead SW15 . . . . 4D 99
Park M. SE10 . . . . 1B 96
    SE24 . . . . 5E 105
    W10 . . . . 1A 58
Park Pde. NW10 . . . . 1B 56
    N1 . . . . 4F 49
        (off Downham Rd.)
    SW1 . . . . 2F 21 (2E 75)
Park Pl. Vs. W2 . . . . 4E 59
Park Ri. SE23 . . . . 1A 122
Park Ri. Rd. SE23 . . . . . 1A 122
Park Rd. E6 . . . . 5E 55
    E10 . . . . 3C 38
    E12 . . . . 3D 41
    E15 . . . . 5C 54
    E17 . . . . 1B 38
    N8 . . . . 1F 33
    NW1 . . . . 3A 4 (2A 60)
    NW4 . . . . 2C 28
    NW8 . . . . 2A 60
    NW10 . . . . 5A 42
    SW19 . . . . 5A 116
    W2 . . . . 4C 58
    W4 . . . . 2A 84
Park Rd. Nth. W4 . . . . . . 1A 84
Park Road Swimming Pool
        . . . . 1F 33
Park Row SE10 . . . . 1F 95
    SW2 . . . . 4C 104
Park Side NW2 . . . . 5C 28
Parkside SE3 . . . . 3B 96
    SW1 . . . . 3A 20
    SW19 . . . . 3F 113
    W3 . . . . 2A 70
Parkside Av. SW19 . . . . . 5F 113
Parkside Bus. Est.
    SE8 . . . . 2A 94
        (Blackhorse Rd.)
    SE8 . . . . 2A 94
        (Rolt St.)
Parkside Ct. E11 . . . . 1C 40
        (off Wanstead Pl.)
Parkside Cres. N7 . . . . . 5C 34

Parkside Est. E9 . . . . 5E **51**
Parkside Gdns.
  SW19 . . . . 4F **113**
Parkside Rd. SW11 . . . 4C **88**
Park Sq. E.
  NW1 . . . . 3D **5** (3D **61**)
Park Sq. M.
  NW1 . . . . 4D **5** (3C **60**)
Park Sq. W.
  NW1 . . . . 3D **5** (3D **61**)
Parkstead Rd. SW15 . . . 3C **98**
Park Steps W2 . . . . 1A **74**
  (off St George's Flds.)
Parkstone Rd. SE15 . . . 5C **92**
Park St. SE1 . . . 1F **25** (2E **77**)
  W1 . . . . . . 4B **12** (1C **74**)
Parkthorne Rd.
  SW12 . . . . 5F **103**
Park Towers W1 . . . . 2D **21**
  (off Brick St.)
Park Vw. N5 . . . . 1E **49**
  SE8 . . . . 1F **93**
  (off Trundleys Rd.)
Park Vw. Apartments
  SE16 . . . . 4D **79**
  (off Banyard Rd.)
Parkview Ct. SW6 . . . . . 5A **86**
  SW18 . . . . 4C **100**
Park Vw. Est. E2 . . . . . . 1F **65**
Park Vw. Gdns. NW4 . . 1E **29**
Park Vw. Ho. SE24 . . . 4D **105**
  (off Hurst St.)
Park Vw. Mans. N4 . . . 1D **35**
Park Vw. M. SW9 . . . . . 5B **90**
Park Vw. Rd. NW10 . . . 1B **42**
Park Village E.
  NW1 . . . . 1E **5** (1D **61**)
Park Village W. NW1 . . 1D **61**
Parkville Rd. SW6 . . . . 3B **86**
Park Vista SE10 . . . . . . 2F **95**
Park Wlk. N6 . . . . 2C **32**
  SE10 . . . . 3F **95**
  SW10 . . . . 2E **87**
Park Way NW11 . . . . . . 1A **30**
Parkway NW1 . . . . 5D **47**
Park W. W2 . . . . 5A **60**
  (off Edgware Rd.)
Park W. Pl. W2 . . . . 5A **60**
Park Wharf SE8 . . . . . . 1A **94**
  (off Evelyn St.)
Parkwood NW8 . . . . 5B **46**
  (off St Edmund's Ter.)
Parkwood M. N6 . . . . . 1D **33**
Parkwood Rd.
  SW19 . . . . 5B **114**
Parliament Ct. E1 . . . . . 1E **19**
Parliament Hill 5B **32**
Parliament Hill NW3 . . 1A **46**
Parliament Hill Fields
  . . . . 5C **32**
Parliament Hill Lido . . 1C **46**
Parliament Hill Mans.
  NW5 . . . . 1C **46**
Parliament Sq.
  SW1 . . . . 4D **23** (3A **76**)
Parliament St.
  SW1 . . . . 3D **23** (3A **76**)
Parliament Vw. SE1 . . . 5B **76**
Parma Cres. SW11 . . . . 2B **102**

Parmiter Ind. Est. E2 . . . 1D **65**
  (off Parmiter St.)
Parmiter St. E2 . . . . 1D **65**
Parmoor Ct. EC1 . . . . . . 3F **9**
Parnell Cl. W12 . . . . 4D **71**
Parnell Ho.
  WC1 . . . . 1C **14** (4F **61**)
Parnell Rd. E3 . . . . 5B **52**
  (not continuous)
Parnham St. E14 . . . . . . 5A **66**
  (not continuous)
Parolles Rd. N19 . . . . . . 3E **33**
Parr Ct. N1 . . . . 1F **63**
  (off Nth. Nth. Rd.)
Parr Ho. E16 . . . . 2D **83**
  (off Beaulieu Av.)
Parrington Ho. SW4 . . . 4F **103**
Parr Rd. E6 . . . . 5F **55**
Parr St. N1 . . . . 1F **63**
Parry Ho. E1 . . . . 2D **79**
  (off Green Bank)
Parry Rd. W10 . . . . 2A **58**
  (not continuous)
Parry St. SW8 . . . . 2A **90**
Parsifal Rd. NW6 . . . . . . 2C **44**
Parsonage St. E14 . . . . . 5E **81**
PARSONS GREEN 5B **86**
Parson's Grn. SW6 . . . . 4C **86**
Parson's Grn. La.
  SW6 . . . . 4C **86**
Parsons Ho. W2 . . . . 3F **59**
  (off Hall Pl.)
Parsons Lodge NW6 . . . 4D **45**
  (off Priory Rd.)
Parson's Rd. E13 . . . . . . 1E **69**
Parthenia Rd. SW6 . . . . 4C **86**
Partington Cl. N19 . . . . . 3F **33**
Partridge Cl. E16 . . . . . . 4F **69**
Partridge Ct. EC1 . . . . . . 3D **9**
Pascall Ho. SE17 . . . . . . 2E **91**
  (off Draco St.)
Pascal St. SW8 . . . . 3F **89**
Pascoe Rd. SE13 . . . . . . 3F **109**
Pasley Cl. SE17 . . . . 1D **91**
Passfield Dr. E14 . . . . . . 4D **67**
Passfield Hall WC1 . . . . 3F **61**
  (off Endsleigh Pl.)
Passfields SE6 . . . . 3D **123**
  W14 . . . . 1B **86**
  (off Star St.)
Passing All. EC1 . . . . . . 4E **9**
Passmore House E2 . . . 5B **50**
  (off Kingsland Rd.)
Passmore St. SW1 . . . . 1C **88**
Paston Cl. E5 . . . . 5F **37**
Paston Cres. SE12 . . . . 5D **111**
Pastor Ct. N6 . . . . 1E **33**
Pastor St. SE11 . . . . 5D **77**
  (not continuous)
Pasture Rd. SE6 . . . . 1B **124**
Patcham Ter. SW8 . . . . . 4D **89**
Patent Ho. E14 . . . . 4D **67**
  (off Morris Rd.)
Paternoster La.
  EC4 . . . . 3E **17** (5D **63**)
Paternoster Row
  EC4 . . . . 3F **17** (5E **63**)
Paternoster Sq.
  EC4 . . . . 3E **17** (5D **63**)

Paterson Ct. EC1 . . . . . . 2B **10**
Pater St. W8 . . . . 4C **72**
Pathfield Rd. SW16 . . . 5F **117**
Patience Rd. SW11 . . . 5A **88**
Patio Cl. SW4 . . . . 4F **103**
Patmore Est. SW8 . . . . 4E **89**
Patmore Ho. N16 . . . . . 2A **50**
Patmore St. SW8 . . . . . 4E **89**
Patmos Lodge
  SW9 . . . . 4D **91**
  (off Elliott Rd.)
Patmos Rd. SW9 . . . . . 3D **91**
Paton Cl. E3 . . . . 2C **66**
Paton Ho. SW9 . . . . . . 5B **90**
  (off Stockwell Rd.)
Paton St. EC1 . . . 2F **9** (2E **63**)
Patrick Coman Ho.
  EC1 . . . . 2D **9**
  (off St John St.)
Patrick Connolly Gdns.
  E3 . . . . 2D **67**
Patrick Pas. SW11 . . . . 5A **88**
Patrick Rd. E13 . . . . . . 2E **69**
Patriot Sq. E2 . . . . 1D **65**
Patrol Pl. SE6 . . . . 4D **109**
Pat Shaw Ho. E1 . . . . . 3F **65**
  (off Globe Rd.)
Patshull Pl. NW5 . . . . . 3E **47**
Patshull Rd. NW5 . . . . 3E **47**
Pattenden Rd. SE6 . . . 1B **122**
Patten Ho. N4 . . . . 3E **35**
Patten Rd. SW18 . . . . . 5A **102**
Patterdale NW1 . . . . . . 2E **5**
  (off Osnaburgh St.)
Patterdale Rd. SE15 . . . 3E **93**
Pattern Ho.
  EC1 . . . . 3D **9** (3D **63**)
Pattina Wlk. SE16 . . . . 2A **80**
  (off Capstan Way)
Pattinson Point E16 . . . 4C **68**
  (off Fife Rd.)
Pattison Ho. E1 . . . . . . 5F **65**
  (off Wellesley St.)
  SE1 . . . . 3A **26**
  (off Redcross Way)
Pattison Rd. NW2 . . . . 5C **30**
Paul Cl. E15 . . . . 4A **54**
Paulet Rd. SE5 . . . . . . 5D **91**
Paul Ho. W10 . . . . 3A **58**
  (off Ladbroke Gro.)
Pauline Ho. E1 . . . . 4C **64**
  (off Old Montague St.)
Paul Julius Cl. E14 . . . 1F **81**
Pauls Ho. E3 . . . . 4B **66**
  (off Timothy Rd.)
Paul St. E15 . . . . 5A **54**
  EC2 . . . . 4C **10** (3F **63**)
Paul's Wlk.
  EC4 . . . . 4E **17** (1E **77**)
Paultons Ho. SW3 . . . . 2F **87**
  (off King's Rd.)
Paultons Sq. SW3 . . . . 2F **87**
Paultons St. SW3 . . . . 2F **87**
Pauntley St. N19 . . . . . 3E **33**
Pavan Ct. E2 . . . . 2E **65**
  (off Sceptre Rd.)
Paveley Dr. SW11 . . . . 3A **88**
Paveley Ho. N1 . . . . . . 1B **62**
  (off Priory Grn. Est.)

Paveley St. NW8 . . . . . . 2A **60**
Pavement, The E11 . . . . 3E **39**
　　　(off Hainault Rd.)
SW4 . . . . 2E **103**
Pavilion NW8 . . . . 2F **59**
Pavilion, The
　SW8 . . . . 3F **89**
Pavilion Ct. NW6 . . . . . . 2C **58**
　　　(off Stafford Rd.)
Pavilion Pde. W12 . . . . . 5E **57**
　　　(off Wood La.)
Pavilion Rd.
　SW1 . . . . 4A 20 (4B **74**)
Pavilion Sq. SW17 . . . . 3B **116**
Pavilion St.
　SW1 . . . . 5A 20 (4B **74**)
Pavilion Ter. W12 . . . . . 5E **57**
　　　(off Wood La.)
Pawsey Cl. E13 . . . . 5D **55**
Paxton Ct. SE12 . . . . . . 3E **125**
　SE26 . . . . 4A **122**
　　　(off Adamsrill Rd.)
Paxton Pl. SE27 . . . . . . 4A **120**
Paxton Rd. SE23 . . . . . . 3A **122**
　W4 . . . . 2A **84**
Paxton Ter. SW1 . . . . . . 2D **89**
Paymal Ho. E1 . . . . 4E **65**
　　　(off Stepney Way)
Payne Ho. N1 . . . . 5B **48**
　　　(off Barnsbury Est.)
Paynell Ct. SE3 . . . . . . 1A **110**
Payne Rd. E3 . . . . 1D **67**
Paynesfield Av.
　SW14 . . . . 1A **98**
Payne St. SE8 . . . . 3B **94**
Paynes Wlk. W6 . . . . . . 2A **86**
Peabody Av. SW1 . . . . . 1D **89**
Peabody Bldgs. E1 . . . . 1C **78**
　　　(off John Fisher St.)
　EC1 . . . . 4A **10**
　　　(off Roscoe St.)
　SW3 . . . . 2A **88**
　　　(off Cheyne Row)
Peabody Cl. SE10 . . . . . 4D **95**
　SW1 . . . . 1D **89**
Peabody Ct. EC1 . . . . . . 4A **10**
　　　(off Roscoe St.)
　SE5 . . . . 4F **91**
　　　(off Kimpton Rd.)
Peabody Est. E1 . . . . . . 1F **79**
　　　(off Glamis Pl.)
　E2 . . . . 1D **65**
　　　(off Minerva St.)
　EC1 . . . . 4A **10**
　　　(off Dufferin St.,
　　　　not continuous)
　EC1 . . . . 4C **8**
　　　(off Farringdon La.)
　N1 . . . . 5E **49**
　SE1 . . . . 2C 24 (2C **76**)
　　　　　　(Duchy St.)
　SE1 . . . . 3A **26**
　　　　(Marshalsea Rd.)
　SE1 . . . . 2F 25 (2E **77**)
　　　　(Southwark St.)
　SE24 . . . . 5D **105**
　SW1 . . . . 5E **75**
　　　(off Vauxhall Bri. Rd.)
　SW3 . . . . 2A **88**

Peabody Est. SW6 . . . . . 2C **86**
　　　(off Lillie Rd.)
　SW11 . . . . 2A **102**
　W6 . . . . 1E **85**
　W10 . . . . 4E **57**
Peabody Hill SE21 . . . . 1D **119**
Peabody Sq.
　SE1 . . . . 4D 25 (3D **77**)
　　　(not continuous)
Peabody Ter. EC1 . . . . . 4C **8**
　　　(off Farringdon La.)
Peabody Twr. EC1 . . . . . 4A **10**
　　　(off Golden La.)
Peabody Trust SE17 . . . . 5F **77**
　　　(off Rodney Rd.)
Peabody Yd. N1 . . . . . . 5E **49**
Peach Gro. E11 . . . . 5F **39**
Peach Rd. W10 . . . . 2F **57**
Peachum Rd. SE3 . . . . . 2B **96**
Peachwalk M. E3 . . . . . 1F **65**
Peacock St. SE17 . . . . . 5D **77**
Peacock Theatre 3F **15**
　　　(off Portugal St.)
Peacock Wlk. E16 . . . . . 5D **69**
　　　(off Mortlake Rd.)
　N6 . . . . 2D **33**
Peacock Yd. SE17 . . . . . 1D **91**
　　　(off Iliffe St.)
Peak, The SE26 . . . . . . 3E **121**
Peak Fitness
　Crossharbour 3D **81**
Peak Hill SE26 . . . . . . 4E **121**
Peak Hill Av. SE26 . . . . 4E **121**
Peak Hill Gdns.
　SE26 . . . . 4E **121**
Peak Ho. N4 . . . . 3E **35**
　　　(off Woodberry Down Est.)
Pearcefield Av.
　SE23 . . . . 1E **121**
Pearce Ho. SW1 . . . . . . 5F **75**
　　　(off Causton St.)
Pear Cl. SE14 . . . . 3A **94**
Pear Ct. SE15 . . . . 3B **92**
　　　(off Thruxton Way)
Pearcroft Rd. E11 . . . . . 4F **39**
Peardon St. SW8 . . . . . 5D **89**
Pearfield Rd.
　SE23 . . . . 3A **122**
Pearl Cl. NW2 . . . . 2F **29**
Pearl St. E1 . . . . 2D **79**
Pearman St.
　SE1 . . . . 5C 24 (4C **76**)
Pear Pl. SE1 . . . . 3B 24 (3C **76**)
Pear Rd. E11 . . . . 5F **39**
Pearscroft Ct. SW6 . . . . 4D **87**
Pearscroft Rd.
　SW6 . . . . 4D **87**
Pearse St. SE15 . . . . . . 2A **92**
Pearson Cl. SE5 . . . . . . 4E **91**
　　　(off Camberwell New Rd.)
Pearson M. SW4 . . . . . . 1F **103**
　　　(off Slievemore Cl.)
Pearson's Av. SE14 . . . . 4C **94**
Pearson St. E2 . . . . 1B **64**
Peartree SE26 . . . . 5A **122**
Peartree Av. SW17 . . . . 3E **115**
Pear Tree Cl. E2 . . . . . . 5B **50**
Pear Tree Ct.
　EC1 . . . . 4C 8 (3C **62**)

Pear Tree Ho. SE4 . . . . 1B **108**
Peartree La. E1 . . . . 1E **79**
Pear Tree St.
　EC1 . . . . 3E 9 (3E **63**)
Peartree Way SE10 . . . . 5C **82**
Peary Ho. NW10 . . . . . . 4A **42**
Peary Pl. E2 . . . . 2E **65**
Peckarmans Wood
　SE26 . . . . 3C **120**
Peckett Sq. N5 . . . . 1E **49**
Peckford Pl. SW9 . . . . . 5C **90**
PECKHAM 4C **92**
Peckham Gro. SE15 . . . . 3A **92**
Peckham High St.
　SE15 . . . . 4C **92**
Peckham Hill St.
　SE15 . . . . 3C **92**
Peckham Pk. Rd.
　SE15 . . . . 3C **92**
Peckham Pulse Health &
　Leisure Cen. 4C **92**
Peckham Rd. SE5 . . . . . 4A **92**
　SE15 . . . . 4A **92**
Peckham Rye SE15 . . . . 1C **106**
　SE22 . . . . 2C **106**
Peckham Sq. SE15 . . . . 4C **92**
Pecks Yd. E1 . . . . 5F **11**
　　　(off Hanbury St.)
Peckwater St. NW5 . . . . 2E **47**
Pedlar's Wlk. N7 . . . . . . 2B **48**
Pedley St. E1 . . . . 3B **64**
Pedro St. E5 . . . . 5F **37**
Pedworth Gdns.
　SE16 . . . . 5E **79**
Peebles Ho. NW6 . . . . . 1D **59**
　　　(off Carlton Va.)
Peek Cres. SW19 . . . . . 5F **113**
Peel Gro. E2 . . . . 1E **65**
　　　(not continuous)
Peel Pas. W8 . . . . 2C **72**
Peel Pct. NW6 . . . . 1C **58**
Peel St. W8 . . . . 2C **72**
Peerless St.
　EC1 . . . . 2B 10 (2F **63**)
Pegasus Cl. N16 . . . . . . 1F **49**
Pegasus Ct. NW10 . . . . 2D **57**
　　　(off Trenmar Gdns.)
Pegasus Ho. E1 . . . . . . 3F **65**
　　　(off Beaumont Sq.)
Pegasus Pl. SE11 . . . . . 2C **90**
　SW6 . . . . 4C **86**
Pegley Gdns.
　SE12 . . . . 2C **124**
Pekin Cl. E14 . . . . 5C **66**
　　　(off Pekin St.)
Pekin St. E14 . . . . 5C **66**
Peldon Wlk. N1 . . . . 5D **49**
　　　(off Popham St.)
Pelham Cl. SE5 . . . . . . 1A **106**
Pelham Ct. SW3 . . . . . . 5A **74**
　　　(off Fulham Rd.)
Pelham Cres. SW7 . . . . 5A **74**
Pelham Ho. W14 . . . . . . 5B **72**
　　　(off Mornington Av.)
Pelham Pl. SW7 . . . . . . 5A **74**
Pelham St. SW7 . . . . . . 5F **73**
Pelican Est. SE15 . . . . . 4B **92**
Pelican Ho. SE5 . . . . . . 4B **92**
　SE8 . . . . 5B **80**

Pelican Pas. E1 . . . . . . 3E 65
Pelican Wlk. SW9 . . . . . 2D 105
Pelican Wharf E1 . . . . . . 2E 79
  (off Wapping Wall)
Pelier St. SE17 . . . . 2E 91
Pelinore Rd. SE6 . . . . . . 2A 124
Pella Ho. SE11 . . . . 1B 90
Pellant Rd. SW6 . . . . . . 3A 86
Pellatt Rd. SE22 . . . . . . 3B 106
Pellerin Rd. N16 . . . . . . 2A 50
Pellew Ho. E1 . . . . 3D 65
  (off Somerford St.)
Pelling St. E14 . . . . 5C 66
Pelly Rd. E13 . . . . 5C 54
  (not continuous)
Pelter St. E2 . . . 1F 11 (1B 64)
  (not continuous)
Pelton Rd. SE10 . . . . . . 1A 96
Pember Rd. NW10 . . . . . 2F 57
Pemberton Ct. E1 . . . . . 2F 65
  (off Portelet Rd.)
Pemberton Gdns.
  N19 . . . . 5E 33
Pemberton Ho.
  SE26 . . . . 4C 120
  (off High Level Dr.)
Pemberton Pl. E8 . . . . . 4D 51
Pemberton Rd. N4 . . . . 1C 34
Pemberton Row
  EC4 . . . . . . 2C 16 (5C 62)
Pemberton Ter. N19 . . . . 5E 33
Pembridge Cres.
  W11 . . . . 1C 72
Pembridge Gdns. W2 . . 1C 72
Pembridge M. W11 . . . . 1C 72
Pembridge Pl.
  SW15 . . . . 3C 100
  W2 . . . . 1C 72
Pembridge Rd. W11 . . . . 1C 72
Pembridge Sq. W2 . . . . 1C 72
Pembridge Studios
  W11 . . . . 1C 72
  (off Pembridge Vs.)
Pembridge Vs. W2 . . . . 1C 72
  W11 . . . . 1C 72
Pembroke W14 . . . . 5B 72
  (off Mornington Av.)
Pembroke Av. N1 . . . . . 5A 48
Pembroke Bldgs.
  NW10 . . . . 2C 56
Pembroke Cl.
  SW1 . . . . . 4C 20 (3C 74)
Pembroke Cotts. W8 . . . 4C 72
  (off Pembroke Sq.)
Pembroke Ct. W8 . . . . . 4C 72
  (off Sth. Edwardes Sq.)
Pembroke Gdns. W8 . . . 5B 72
Pembroke Gdns. Cl.
  W8 . . . . 4C 72
Pembroke Ho. SW1 . . . . 5B 20
  (off Chesham Ho.)
  W2 . . . . 5D 59
  (off Hallfield Est.)
Pembroke M. E3 . . . . . . 2A 66
  W8 . . . . 4C 72
Pembroke Pl. W8 . . . . . 4C 72
Pembroke Rd. E17 . . . . 1D 39
  N15 . . . . 1B 36
  W8 . . . . 5B 72

Pembroke Sq. W8 . . . . . 4C 72
Pembroke St. N1 . . . . . 4A 48
  (not continuous)
Pembroke Studios
  W8 . . . . 4B 72
Pembroke Ter. NW8 . . . . 5F 45
  (off Queen's Ter.)
Pembroke Vs. W8 . . . . . 5C 72
Pembroke Wlk. W8 . . . . 5C 72
Pembrook M. SW11 . . . 2F 101
Pembry Cl. SW9 . . . . . . 4C 90
Pembury Cl. E5 . . . . . . 2D 51
Pembury Ho. E5 . . . . . . 2D 51
Pembury Pl. E5 . . . . . . 2D 51
Pembury Rd. E5 . . . . . . 2D 51
Pemell Cl. E1 . . . . 3E 65
Pemell Ho. E1 . . . . 3E 65
  (off Pemell Cl.)
Penally Pl. N1 . . . . 5F 49
Penang Ho. E1 . . . . 2D 79
  (off Prusom St.)
Penang St. E1 . . . . 2D 79
Penarth Cen. SE15 . . . . 2E 93
Penarth St. SE15 . . . . . 2E 93
Penberth Rd. SE6 . . . . . 2E 123
Pencombe M. W11 . . . . 1B 72
Pencraig Way SE15 . . . . 2D 93
Penda's Mead E9 . . . . . 1A 52
Pendennis Ho. SE8 . . . . 5A 80
Pendennis Rd.
  SW16 . . . . 4A 118
Penderry Ri. SE6 . . . . . 2F 123
Penderyn Way N7 . . . . . 1F 47
Pendle Ho. SE26 . . . . . 3C 120
Pendle Rd. SW16 . . . . . 5D 117
Pendlestone Rd. E17 . . . 1D 39
Pendley Ho. E2 . . . . . . 5C 50
  (off Whiston Rd.)
Pendragon Rd.
  BR1: Brom 3B 124
Pendragon Wlk.
  NW9 . . . . 1A 28
Pendrell Ho. WC2 . . . . . 3C 14
  (off New Compton St.)
Pendrell Rd. SE4 . . . . . 5A 94
Pendulum M. E8 . . . . . . 2B 50
Penerley Rd. SE6 . . . . . 1D 123
Penfield Lodge W9 . . . . 4C 58
  (off Admiral Wlk.)
Penfields Ho. N7 . . . . . 3A 48
Penfold Pl. NW1 . . . . . 4A 60
Penfold St. NW1 . . . . . 4A 60
  NW8 . . . . 3F 59
Penford Gdns. SE9 . . . . 1F 111
Penford St. SE5 . . . . . . 5D 91
Penge Ho. SW11 . . . . . 1F 101
Penge Rd. E13 . . . . 5E 55
Penhall Rd. SE7 . . . . . . 5F 83
Penhurst Pl. SE1 . . . . . 5A 24
Peninsula Apartments
  W2 . . . . 4A 60
  (off Praed St.)
Peninsula Ct. E14 . . . . . 4D 81
  (off E. Ferry Rd.)
Peninsula Hgts. SE1 . . . 1A 90
Peninsular Pk. SE7 . . . . 5C 82
Peninsular Pk. Rd.
  SE7 . . . . 5C 82
Penley Ct.
  WC2 . . . . 4A 16 (1B 76)

Penmayne Ho. SE11 . . . 1C 90
  (off Kennings Way)
Pennack Rd. SE15 . . . . 2B 92
Penn Almshouses
  SE10 . . . . 4E 95
  (off Greenwich Sth. St.)
Pennant M. W8 . . . . . . 5D 73
Pennant Mans. W12 . . . 3E 71
  (off Goldhawk Rd.)
Pennard Rd. W12 . . . . . 3E 71
Penner Cl. SW19 . . . . . 2A 114
Pennethorne Cl. E9 . . . 5E 51
Pennethorne Ho.
  SW11 . . . . 1F 101
Pennethorne Rd.
  SE15 . . . . 3D 93
Penn Ho. NW8 . . . . 3A 60
  (off Mallory St.)
Pennine Dr. NW2 . . . . . 4F 29
Pennine La. NW2 . . . . . 4A 30
Pennine Pde. NW2 . . . . 4A 30
Pennington Cl.
  SE27 . . . . 4F 119
Pennington Ct. SE16 . . 2A 80
Pennington St. E1 . . . . 1D 79
Pennington Way
  SE12 . . . . 2D 125
Penn Rd. N7 . . . . 2A 48
Penn St. N1 . . . . 5F 49
Pennyfields E14 . . . . . . 1C 80
  (not continuous)
Pennyford Ct. NW8 . . . . 3F 59
  (off St John's Wood Rd.)
Penny M. SW12 . . . . . . 5D 103
Pennymoor Wlk. W9 . . . 3B 58
  (off Ashmore Rd.)
Penpoll Rd. E8 . . . . 3D 51
Penrith Cl. SW15 . . . . . 3A 100
Penrith Pl. SE27 . . . . . 2D 119
Penrith Rd. N15 . . . . . . 1F 35
Penrith St. SW16 . . . . . 5E 117
Penrose Gro. SE17 . . . . 1E 91
Penrose Ho. SE17 . . . . 1E 91
  (not continuous)
Penrose St. SE17 . . . . . 1E 91
Penryn Ho. SE11 . . . . . 1D 91
  (off Seaton Cl.)
Penryn St. NW1 . . . . . . 1F 61
Penry St. SE1 . . . . 5A 78
Pensbury Pl. SW8 . . . . 5E 89
Pensbury St. SW8 . . . . 5E 89
Penshurst NW5 . . . . . . 3C 46
Penshurst Ho. SE15 . . . 2E 93
  (off Lovelinch Cl.)
Penshurst Rd. E9 . . . . . 4F 51
Pentagram Yd. W11 . . . 5C 58
  (off Needham Rd.)
Pentland Cl. NW11 . . . . 4A 30
Pentland Gdns.
  SW18 . . . . 4E 101
Pentland St. SW18 . . . . 4E 101
Pentlow St. SW15 . . . . 1E 99
Pentney Rd. SW12 . . . . 1E 117
Penton Gro. N1 . . . . . . 1C 62
Penton Ho. N1 . . . . 1B 8
  (off Pentonville Rd.)
Penton Pl. SE17 . . . . . 1D 91
Penton Ri.
  WC1 . . . . 1A 8 (2B 62)

Penton St. N1 . . . . . . 1C 62
PENTONVILLE 1B 62
Pentonville Rd.
N1 . . . . 1F 7 (1B 62)
Pentridge St. SE15 . . . 3B 92
Penwith Rd.
SW18 . . . . 2C 114
Penwood Ho. SW15 . . 4B 98
Penwortham Rd.
SW16 . . . . 5D 117
Penywern Rd. SW5 . . 1C 86
Penzance Ho. SE11 . . . 1C 90
(off Seaton Cl.)
Penzance Pl. W11 . . . . 2A 72
Penzance St. W11 . . . . 2A 72
Peony Ct. SW3 . . . . . . 2E 87
Peony Gdns. W12 . . . . 1C 70
Peperfield WC1 . . . . . . 2F 7
(off Cromer St.)
Pepler Ho. W10 . . . . . 3A 58
(off Wornington Rd.)
Pepler M. SE5 . . . . . . 1B 92
Peploe Rd. NW6 . . . . . 1F 57
Peppermead Sq.
SE13 . . . . 3C 108
Peppermint Pl. E11 . . . 5A 40
Pepper St. E14 . . . . . . 4D 81
SE1 . . . . . 3F 25 (3E 77)
Peppie Cl. N16 . . . . . . 4A 36
Pepys Cres. E16 . . . . . 2C 82
Pepys Ho. E2 . . . . 2E 65
(off Kirkwall Pl.)
Pepys Rd. SE14 . . . . . 4F 93
Pepys St.
EC3 . . . . . . 4E 19 (1A 78)
Perceval Av. NW3 . . . . 2A 46
Perch St. E8 . . . . 1B 50
Percival David Foundation of
Chinese Art 3C 6
Percival St.
EC1 . . . . 3D 9 (3D 63)
Percy Cir.
WC1 . . . . 1A 8 (2B 62)
Percy Laurie Ho.
SW15 . . . . 2F 99
(off Nursery Cl.)
Percy M. W1 . . . . 1B 14
Percy Pas. W1 . . . . . . 1B 14
Percy Rd. E11 . . . . . . 2A 40
E16 . . . . 4A 68
W12 . . . . 3C 70
Percy St. W1 . . 1B 14 (4F 61)
Percy Yd.
WC1 . . . . 1A 8 (2B 62)
Peregrine Cl. NW10 . . 2A 42
Peregrine Ct. SE8 . . . . 2C 94
(off Edward St.)
SW16 . . . . 4B 118
Peregrine Ho. EC1 . . . . 1E 9
Perham Rd. W14 . . . . . 1A 86
Perifield SE21 . . . . . . 1E 119
Periton Rd. SE9 . . . . . 2F 111
Perkins Ho. E14 . . . . . 4B 66
(off Wallwood St.)
Perkin's Rents
SW1 . . . . . . 5B 22 (4F 75)
Perkins Sq.
SE1 . . . . . . 1A 26 (2E 77)
Perks Cl. SE3 . . . . . . 1A 110

Perley Ho. E3 . . . . . . 4B 66
(off Weatherley Cl.)
Perran Rd. SW2 . . . . . 1D 119
Perren St. NW5 . . . . . 3D 47
Perrers Rd. W6 . . . . . 5D 71
Perring Est. E3 . . . . . . 4C 66
(off Gale St.)
Perrin Ho. NW6 . . . . . 2C 58
Perrin's Ct. NW3 . . . . 1E 45
Perrin's La. NW3 . . . . 1E 45
Perrin's Wlk. NW3 . . . 1E 45
Perronet Ho. SE1 . . . . 5E 25
Perry Av. W3 . . . . 5A 56
Perry Ct. E14 . . . . 1C 94
(off Maritime Quay)
N15 . . . . 1A 36
Perryfield Way
NW9 . . . . 1B 28
Perry Hill SE6 . . . . . . 3B 122
Perrymead St. SW6 . . 4C 86
Perryn Ho. W3 . . . . . . 1A 70
Perryn Rd. SE16 . . . . . 4D 79
W3 . . . . 2A 70
Perry Ri. SE23 . . . . . . 3A 122
Perry's Pl.
W1 . . . . . . 2B 14 (5F 61)
Perry Va. SE23 . . . . . . 2E 121
Persant Rd. SE6 . . . . . 2A 124
Perseverance Pl.
SW9 . . . . 3C 90
Perseverance Works
E2 . . . . 1E 11
(off Kingsland Rd.)
Perth Av. NW9 . . . . . . 2A 28
Perth Cl. SE5 . . . . 2F 105
Perth Ho. N1 . . . . 4B 48
(off Bemerton Est.)
Perth Rd. E10 . . . . . . 3A 38
E13 . . . . 1D 69
N4 . . . . 3C 34
Perystreete SE23 . . . . 2E 121
Peter Av. NW10 . . . . . 4D 43
Peter Best Ho. E1 . . . . 5D 65
(off Nelson St.)
Peterboat Cl. SE10 . . 5A 82
Peterborough Ct.
EC4 . . . . . . 3C 16 (5C 62)
Peterborough M.
SW6 . . . . 5C 86
Peterborough Rd.
E10 . . . . 1E 39
SW6 . . . . 5C 86
Peterborough Vs.
SW6 . . . . 4D 87
Peter Butler Ho. SE1 . . 3C 78
(off Wolseley St.)
Peterchurch Ho.
SE15 . . . . 2D 93
(off Commercial Way)
Petergate SW11 . . . . . 2E 101
Peter Heathfield Ho.
E15 . . . . 5F 53
(off Wise Rd.)
Peter Ho. SW8 . . . . . . 3A 90
(off Luscombe Way)
Peterley Bus. Cen.
E2 . . . . 1D 65
Peter Pan Statue 2F 73

Peter Scott Vis. Cen., The
. . . . 4D 85
Peters Ct. W2 . . . . 5D 59
(off Porchester Rd.)
Petersfield Ri.
SW15 . . . . 1D 113
Petersham Ho. SW7 . . 5F 73
(off Kendrick M.)
Petersham La. SW7 . . 4E 73
Petersham M. SW7 . . . 4E 73
Petersham Pl. SW7 . . . 4E 73
Peter's Hill
EC4 . . . . . . 4F 17 (1E 77)
Peter Shore Ct. E1 . . . 4F 65
(off Beaumont Sq.)
Peter's La.
EC1 . . . . . . 5E 9 (4D 63)
(not continuous)
Peter's Path SE26 . . . . 4D 121
Peterstow Cl.
SW19 . . . . 2A 114
Peter St. W1 . . 4B 14 (1F 75)
Petherton Cl. NW10 . . 5F 43
(off Tiverton Rd.)
Petherton Ho. N4 . . . . 3E 35
(off Woodberry Down Est.)
Petherton Rd. N5 . . . . 2E 49
Petiver Cl. E9 . . . . 4E 51
Petley Rd. W6 . . . . . . 2F 85
Peto Pl. NW1 . . 3E 5 (3D 61)
Peto St. Nth. E16 . . . . 5B 68
Petrie Cl. NW2 . . . . . . 3A 44
Petrie Mus. of
Egyptian Archaeology
. . . . 4B 6
Petros Gdns. NW3 . . . 3E 45
Petticoat La.
E1 . . . . 1F 19 (4A 64)
Petticoat Lane Market
. . . . 2F 19
(off Middlesex St.)
Petticoat Sq.
E1 . . . . 2F 19 (5B 64)
Petticoat Twr. E1 . . . . 2F 19
Pettiward Cl. SW15 . . 2E 99
Pett St. SE18 . . . . 5F 83
Petty France
SW1 . . . . . . 5A 22 (4E 75)
Petty Wales
EC3 . . . . . . 5E 19 (1A 78)
Petworth St. SW11 . . . 4A 88
Petyt Pl. SW3 . . . . . . 2A 88
Petyward SW3 . . . . . . 5A 74
Pevensey Cl. E1 . . . . . 4F 65
(off Ben Jonson Rd.)
Pevensey Rd. E7 . . . . 1B 54
SW17 . . . . 4F 115
Peverill Ho. SE1 . . . . . 5C 26
Peyton Pl. SE10 . . . . . 3E 95
Pharamond Way2 . . . . 3F 43
Pheasant Cl. E16 . . . . 5D 69
Pheasantry Ho. SW3 . . 1A 88
(off Jubilee Pl.)
Phelp St. SE17 . . . . . . 2F 91
Phene St. SW3 . . . . . . 2A 88
Philadelphia Ct.
SW10 . . . . 3E 87
(off Uverdale Rd.)
Philbeach Gdns. SW5 . 1C 86

Phil Brown Pl. SW8 . . . 1D *103*
   (off Wandsworth Rd.)
Philchurch Pl. E1 . . . . . . 5C **64**
Philia Ho. NW1 . . . . 4E **47**
   (off Farrier St.)
Philip Ct. W2 . . . . 4F **59**
   (off Hall Pl.)
Philip Ho. NW6 . . . . 5D **45**
   (off Mortimer Pl.)
Philip Jones Ct. N4 . . . . 3B **34**
Philip Mole Ho. W9 . . . . 3C **58**
   (off Chippenham Rd.)
Philippa Gdns. SE9. . . 3F **111**
Philip Sq. SW8 . . . . 5D **89**
Philip St. E13 . . . . 3C **68**
Philip Wlk. SE15 . . . . . . 1C **106**
   (not continuous)
Phillimore Ct. W8 . . . . . . 3C **72**
   (off Kensington High St.)
Phillimore Gdns.
  NW10 . . . . 5E **43**
  W8 . . . . 3C **72**
Phillimore Gdns. Cl.
  W8 . . . . 4C **72**
Phillimore Pl. W8 . . . . . . 4C **72**
Phillimore Ter. W8 . . . . 4C **72**
   (off Allen St.)
Phillimore Wlk. W8 . . . 4C **72**
Phillipp St. N1 . . . . 5A **50**
Philpot La.
  EC3 . . . . 4D **19** (1A **78**)
Philpot Sq. SW6. . . . . 1D **101**
Philpot St. E1 . . . . 5D **65**
Phineas Pett Rd.
  SE9 . . . . 1F **111**
Phipps Ho. SE7 . . . . . . 1D **97**
   (off Woolwich Rd.)
  W12 . . . . 1D **71**
   (off White City Est.)
Phipp St.
  EC2 . . . . 3D **11** (3A **64**)
Phoebeth Rd. SE4 . . . . 3C **108**
Phoenix Bus. Cen.
  E3 . . . . 4C **66**
   (off Bow Comn. La.)
Phoenix Cl. E8 . . . . 5B **50**
Phoenix Ct. E1 . . . . 3D **65**
   (off Buckhurst St.)
  E14 . . . . 5C **80**
  NW1 . . . . 1C **6**
   (off Purchese St.)
  SE14 . . . . 2A **94**
   (off Chipley St.)
Phoenix Lodge Mans.
  W6. . . . . 5F **71**
   (off Brook Grn.)
Phoenix Pk. NW2 . . . . . 4C **28**
Phoenix Pl.
  WC1 . . . . 3A **8** (3B **62**)
Phoenix Rd.
  NW1 . . . . 1B **6** (2F **61**)
Phoenix Sports & Fitness Cen.
  . . . . 1C **70**
Phoenix St.
  WC2 . . . . 3C **14** (5F **61**)
Phoenix Theatre 3C **14**
   (off Charing Cross Rd.)
Phoenix Wharf E1 . . . . 2D **79**
   (off Wapping High St.)

Phoenix Wharf Rd.
  SE1 . . . . 4F **27**
Phoenix Yd. WC1 . . . . . . 2A **8**
Photographers' Gallery
  . . . . 4D **15**
   (off Gt. Newport St.)
Physic Pl. SW3 . . . . 2B **88**
Piazza, The WC2 . . . . . . 4E **15**
   (not continuous)
Piccadilly
  W1 . . . . 2E **21** (2D **75**)
Piccadilly Arc. SW1 . . . 1F **21**
Piccadilly Circus
  . . . . 5B **14** (1F **75**)
Piccadilly Cir.
  W1 . . . . 5B **14** (1F **75**)
Piccadilly Ct. N7 . . . . . . 3B **48**
   (off Caledonian Rd.)
Piccadilly Pl. W1 . . . . . . 5A **14**
Piccadilly Theatre 4A **14**
   (off Denman St.)
Pickard St.
  EC1 . . . . 1E **9** (2D **63**)
Pickering Cl. E9 . . . . 4F **51**
Pickering Ho. W2 . . . . . . 5E **59**
   (off Hallfield Est.)
Pickering M. W2 . . . . . . 5D **59**
Pickering Pl. SW1 . . . . . 2A **22**
Pickering St. N1 . . . . 5D **49**
Pickets St. SW12 . . . . . 5D **103**
Picketts Ter. SE22 . . . . 3C **106**
Pickfords Wharf N1 . . . . 1E **63**
  SE1 . . . . 1B **26** (2F **77**)
Pickwick Ho. SE16 . . . . 3C **78**
   (off George Row)
  W11 . . . . 2F **71**
   (off St Ann's Rd.)
Pickwick Rd. SE21 . . . 5F **105**
Pickwick St.
  SE1 . . . . 4F **25** (3E **77**)
Pickworth Cl. SW8 . . . . 3A **90**
Picton Pl.
  W1 . . . . 3C **12** (5C **60**)
Picton St. SE5 . . . . 3F **91**
Picture Ho. SW16 . . . . . 2A **118**
Pied Bull Yard N1 . . . . . 5D **49**
   (off Theberton St.)
  WC1 . . . . 1D **15**
   (not continuous)
Pier Head E1 . . . . 2D **79**
   (not continuous)
Pierhead Wharf E1 . . . 2D **79**
   (off Wapping High St.)
Pier Ho. SW3 . . . . 2A **88**
Piermont Grn. SE22 . . 3D **107**
Piermont Rd. SE22 . . . 3D **107**
Pierpoint Bldg. E14 . . . 3B **80**
Pierrepont Arc. N1 . . . . 1D **63**
   (off Islington High St.)
Pierrepont Row N1 . . . 1D **63**
   (off Camden Pas.)
Pier St. E14 . . . . 5E **81**
   (not continuous)
Pier Ter. SW18 . . . . 2D **101**
Pietra Lara Bldg. EC1. . 3F **9**
   (off Pear Tree St.)
Piggott Ho. E2 . . . . 1F **65**
   (off Sewardstone Rd.)
Pigott St. E14. . . . . 5C **66**
Pike Cl. BR1: Brom . . . 5D **125**

Pikemans Ct. SW5 . . . . . 5C **72**
   (off W. Cromwell Rd.)
Pikethorne SE23 . . . . . 2F **121**
Pilgrimage St.
  SE1 . . . . 4B **26** (3F **77**)
Pilgrim Hill SE27 . . . . . 4E **119**
Pilgrim Ho. SE1 . . . . . . 5C **26**
   (off Lansdowne Pl.)
Pilgrims Cloisters
  SE5 . . . . 3A **92**
   (off Sedgmoor Pl.)
Pilgrim's La. NW3 . . . . . 1F **45**
Pilgrims M. E14 . . . . 1A **82**
Pilgrim's Pl. NW3 . . . . . 1F **45**
Pilgrim St.
  EC4 . . . . 3D **17** (5D **63**)
Pilgrims Way N19 . . . . . 3F **33**
Pilkington Rd. SE15 . . . 5D **93**
Pilot Cl. SE8 . . . . 2B **94**
Pilot Ind. Cen. NW10 . . 3A **56**
Pilsden Cl. SW19 . . . . 1F **113**
Pilton Pl. SE17 . . . . 1E **91**
   (off King & Queen St.)
Pilton Pl. Est. SE17 . . . 1E **91**
PIMLICO 1E **89**
Pimlico Ho. SW1 . . . . . . 1D **89**
   (off Ebury Bri. Rd.)
Pimlico Rd. SW1 . . . . . 1C **88**
Pimlico Wlk. N1 . . . . . . 1D **11**
Pinchin & Johnsons Yd.
  E1 . . . . 1C **78**
   (off Pinchin St.)
Pinchin St. E1 . . . . 1C **78**
Pincombe Ho. SE17 . . . 1F **91**
   (off Orb St.)
Pincott Pl. SE4 . . . . . . 1F **107**
Pindar St.
  EC2 . . . . 5D **11** (4A **64**)
Pindock M. W9 . . . . 3D **59**
Pine Apple Ct. SW1 . . . 5A **22**
Pine Av. E15 . . . . 2F **53**
Pine Cl. E10 . . . . 4D **39**
  N19 . . . . 4E **33**
Pinedene SE15 . . . . 4D **93**
Pinefield Cl. E14 . . . . . . 1C **80**
Pine Gro. N4 . . . . 4A **34**
  SW19 . . . . 5B **114**
Pine Ho. SE16 . . . . 3E **79**
   (off Ainsty Est.)
  W10 . . . . 3A **58**
   (off Droop St.)
Pinehurst Ct. W11 . . . . 5B **58**
   (off Colville Gdns.)
Pinemartin Cl. NW2 . . . 5E **29**
Pine M. NW10 . . . . 1F **57**
Pine Rd. NW2 . . . . 1E **43**
Pine St. EC1 . . . 3C **8** (3C **62**)
Pine Tree Ho. SE14 . . . 3F **93**
   (off Reaston St.)
Pinewood Cl. SW4 . . . . 4F **103**
Pinfold Rd. SW16 . . . . 4A **118**
Pinkerton Pl. SW16 . . . 4F **117**
Pinnace Ho. E14 . . . . . . 4E **81**
   (off Manchester Rd.)
Pinnacle Way E14 . . . . 5A **66**
   (off Commercial Rd.)
Pinnell Rd. SE9 . . . . . . 2F **111**
Pinner Ct. NW8 . . . . 3F **59**
   (off St John's Wood Rd.)

Pinners Pas. *EC2* 2C **18**
  (off Austin Friars)
Pintail Cl. E6 . . . . 4F **69**
Pintail Ct. *SE8* 2B **94**
  (off Pilot Cl.)
Pinter Ho. *SW9* 5A **90**
  (off Grantham Rd.)
Pinto Way SE3 . . . . 2D **111**
Pioneer Cl. E14 . . . . 4D **67**
Pioneer Ho. *WC1* 1F **7**
  (off Britannia St.)
Pioneer St. SE15 . . . . 4C **92**
Pioneer Way W12 . . . . 5D **57**
Piper Cl. N7 . . . . 2B **48**
Pipers Ho. *SE10* 1F **95**
  (off Collington St.)
Pippin Cl. NW2 . . . . 5C **28**
Pippin Ho. *W10* 1F **71**
  (off Freston Rd.)
Pirbright Rd. SW18 . . . . 1B **114**
Pirie Cl. SE5 . . . . 1F **105**
Pirie St. E16 . . . . 2D **83**
Pitchford St. E15 . . . . 4F **53**
Pitfield Est.
  N1 . . . . 1D **11** (2A **64**)
Pitfield St.
  N1 . . . . 1D **11** (2A **64**)
Pitfold Cl. SE12 . . . . 4C **110**
Pitfold Rd. SE12 . . . . 4C **110**
Pitman Ho. SE8 . . . . 4C **94**
Pitman St. SE5 . . . . 3E **91**
  (not continuous)
Pitmaston Ho. *SE13* *5E* **95**
  (off Lewisham Rd.)
Pitsea Pl. E1 . . . . 5F **65**
Pitsea St. E1 . . . . 5F **65**
Pitt Cres. SW19 . . . . 4D **115**
Pitt's Head M.
  W1 . . . . 2C **20** (2C **74**)
Pitt St. W8 . . . . 3C **72**
Pixley St. E14 . . . . 5B **66**
Place, The. *2C 6*
  (off Duke's Rd.)
Plaisterers Highwalk
  EC2 . . . . 1F **17**
  (off Noble St.)
PLAISTOW. 1D **69**
Plaistow Gro. E15 . . . . 5B **54**
Plaistow Pk. Rd.
  E13 . . . . 1D **69**
Plaistow Rd. E15 . . . . 5B **54**
Plaistow Wharf E16 . . . . . 3C **82**
Plane St. SE26 . . . . 3D **121**
Planetree Ct. *W6* *5F 71*
  (off Brook Grn.)
Plane Tree Ho. *SE8* *2A 94*
  (off Etta St.)
Plane Tree Wlk.
  SE19 . . . . 5A **120**
Plantain Gdns. E11 . . . . . . *5F 39*
  (off Hollydown Way,
   not continuous)
Plantain Pl.
  SE1 . . . . 3B **26** (3F **77**)
Plantation, The SE3 . . . . . 5C **96**
Plantation Pl. EC3 . . . . 4D **19**
Plantation Wharf
  SW11 . . . . 1E **101**

Plasel Ct. *E13* *5D 55*
  (off Pawsey Cl.)
PLASHET. 3F **55**
Plashet Gro. E6 . . . . 5E **55**
Plashet Rd. E13 . . . . 5C **54**
Plassy Rd. SE6 . . . . 5D **109**
Plate Ho. *E14*. *1D 95*
  (off Burrells Wharf Sq.)
Platina St. EC2. . . . . 3C **10**
Plato Rd. SW2 . . . . 2A **104**
Platt, The SW15 . . . . 1F **99**
Platt's La. NW3 . . . . 1C **44**
Platt St. NW1 . . . . 1F **61**
Plaxton Ct. E11 . . . . 5B **40**
Playfair Ho. *E14*. *5C 66*
  (off Saracen St.)
Playfair Mans. *W14*. . . . *2A 86*
  (off Queen's Club Gdns.)
Playfair St. W6. . . . . 1E **85**
Playfield Cres.
  SE22 . . . . 3B **106**
Playford Rd. N4 . . . . 4B **34**
  (not continuous)
Playgreen Way SE6 . . . 3C **122**
Playhouse Ct. *SE1* *3F 25*
  (off Southwark Bri. Rd.)
Playhouse Theatre *1E 23*
  (off Northumberland Av.)
Playhouse Yd.
  EC4 . . . . 3D **17** (5D **63**)
Playscape Pro Racing
  Karting Track 5F **117**
Plaza Cinema *5B 14*
  (off Regent St.)
Plaza Hgts. E10 . . . . 5E **39**
Plaza Pde. NW6 . . . . 1D **59**
Plaza Shop. Cen., The
  W1 . . . . 2A **14** (5E **61**)
Pleasance, The
  SW15 . . . . 2D **99**
Pleasance Rd. SW15. . . . . 3D **99**
Pleasance Theatre *3A 48*
  (off Carpenters M.)
Pleasant Pl. N1 . . . . 4D **49**
Pleasant Row NW1 . . . . . . 5D **47**
Plender Pl. *NW1* *5E 47*
  (off Plender St.)
Plender St. NW1 . . . . 5E **47**
Pleshey Rd. N7. . . . . 1F **47**
Plessey Bldg. *E14* *5C 66*
  (off Dod St.)
Plevna Cres. N15. . . . . 1A **36**
Plevna St. E14 . . . . 4E **81**
Pleydell Av. W6 . . . . 5B **70**
Pleydell Ct. *EC4*. *3C 16*
  (off Lombard La.)
Pleydell Est. EC1 . . . . 2A **10**
Pleydell St. EC4. . . . . 3C **16**
Plimsoll Cl. E14. . . . . 5D **67**
Plimsoll Rd. N4 . . . . 5C **34**
Plough Ct.
  EC3. . . . . 4C **18** (1F **77**)
Plough La. SE22 . . . . 4B **106**
  SW17 . . . . 5D **115**
  SW19 . . . . 5D **115**
Ploughmans Cl. NW1 . . . 5F **47**
Plough M. SW11 . . . . 2F **101**
Plough Pl.
  EC4 . . . . 2C **16** (5C **62**)

Plough Rd. SW11 . . . . 1F **101**
Plough St. E1. . . . . 5B **64**
Plough Ter. SW11 . . . . 2F **101**
Plough Way SE16. . . . . 5F **79**
Plough Yd.
  EC2 . . . . 4E **11** (3A **64**)
Plover Ho. *SW9* *3C 90*
  (off Brixton Rd.)
Plover Way SE16 . . . . 4A **80**
Plowden Bldgs. EC4 . . . . . 4B **16**
Plumber's Row E1 . . . . 4C **64**
Plumbridge St. SE10 . . . . 4E **95**
Plume Ho. *SE10* *2D 95*
  (off Creek Rd.)
Plummer Rd. SW4 . . . . 5F **103**
Plumtree Ct.
  EC4. . . . . 2D **17** (5D **63**)
Plymouth Ho. *SE10* *4D 95*
  (off Devonshire Dr.)
Plymouth Rd. E16 . . . . 4C **68**
Plymouth Wharf E14 . . . 5F **81**
Plympton Av. NW6 . . . . 4B **44**
Plympton Pl. NW8 . . . . 3A **60**
Plympton Rd. NW6 . . . . . . 4B **44**
Plympton St. NW8 . . . . . . 3A **60**
Pocklington Cl. *W12* . . . *4C 70*
  (off Ashchurch Pk. Vs.)
Pocklington Ct.
  SW15 . . . . 1C **112**
Pocklington Lodge
  W12 . . . . 4C **70**
Pocock St.
  SE1 . . . . 3D **25** (3D **77**)
Podmore Rd. SW18 . . . . . 2E **101**
Poet's Rd. N5 . . . . 2F **49**
Point, The *W2* *5F 59*
  (off Nth. Wharf Rd.)
Point Cl. SE10 . . . . 4E **95**
Pointers Cl. E14. . . . . 1D **95**
Point Hill SE10. . . . . 3E **95**
Point Pleasant
  SW18 . . . . 2C **100**
Point Ter. *E7* *2D 55*
  (off Claremont Rd.)
Point West SW7. . . . . 5D **73**
Poland St.
  W1 . . . . 3A **14** (5E **61**)
Polebrook Rd. SE3 . . . . . 1E **111**
Polecroft La. SE6 . . . . 2B **122**
Polesworth Ho. *W2* *4C 58*
  (off Alfred Rd.)
Pollard Cl. E16. . . . . 1C **82**
  N7 . . . . 1B **48**
Pollard Ho. *N1* *1F 7*
  (off Northdown St.)
Pollard Row E2 . . . . 2C **64**
Pollard St. E2. . . . . 2C **64**
Pollen St.
  W1 . . . . 3F **13** (5E **61**)
Pollitt Dr. NW8 . . . . 3F **59**
Pollock Ho. *W10* *3A 58*
  (off Kensal Rd.)
Pollock's Toy Mus.
  . . . . 5A **6** (4E **61**)
Polperro Ho. *W2*. *4C 58*
  (off Brunel Est.)
Polperro M. SE11 . . . . 5D **77**
Polsted Rd. SE6. . . . . 5B **108**
Polworth Rd. SW16 . . . 5A **118**

Polychrome Ct. *SE1* *4D 25*
    (off Waterloo Rd.)
Polygon, The *NW8* *5F 45*
    (off Avenue Rd.)
SW4 . . . . 2E **103**
Polygon Rd.
NW1 . . . . 1B **6** (1F **61**)
Pomell Way
E1 . . . . 2F **19** (5B **64**)
Pomeroy Ho. *E2* *1F 65*
    (off St James's Av.)
W11 . . . . *5A 58*
    (off Lancaster Rd.)
Pomeroy St. *SE14* 3E **93**
Pomfret Rd. *SE5* 1D **105**
Pomoja La. *N19* 4A **34**
Pomona Ho. *SE8* *5A 80*
    (off Evelyn St.)
Pond Cl. *SE3* 5C **96**
Pond Cotts. *SE21* 1A **120**
Ponder St. *N7* 4B **48**
    (not continuous)
Pond Farm Est. *E5* 5E **37**
Pondfield Ho. *SE27* . . 5E **119**
Pond Ho. *SW3* 5A **74**
Pond Mead *SE21* 4F **105**
Pond Pl. *SW3* 5A **74**
Pond Rd. *E15* 1A **68**
SE3 . . . . 5B **96**
Pond Sq. *N6* 3C **32**
Pond St. *NW3* 2A **46**
Ponler St. *E1* 5D **65**
Ponsard Rd. *NW10* . . . 2D **57**
Ponsford St. *E9* 3E **51**
Ponsonby Ho. *E2* *1E 65*
    (off Bishop's Way)
Ponsonby Pl. *SW1* 1F **89**
Ponsonby Rd. *SW15* . . . 5D **99**
Ponsonby Ter. *SW1* . . . 1F **89**
Pontefract Rd.
BR1: Brom 5B **124**
Ponton Rd. *SW8* 3F **89**
Pont St. *SW1* . . . 5A **20** (4B **74**)
Pont St. M.
SW1 . . . . . . 5A **20** (4B **74**)
Pontypool Pl.
SE1 . . . . 3D **25** (3D **77**)
Pool Cl. *BR3*: Beck . . . 5C **122**
Pool Ct. *SE6* 2C **122**
Poole Ct. *N1* *4A 50*
    (off St Peter's Way)
Poole Ho. *SE11* *4C 76*
    (off Lambeth Wlk.)
Poole Rd. *E9* 3F **51**
Pooles Bldgs. *WC1* 4B **8**
Pooles La. *SW10* 3E **87**
Pooles Pk. *N4* 4C **34**
Poole St. *N1* 5F **49**
Pooley Ho. *E1* 2F **65**
Pool Ho. *NW8* *4F 59*
    (off Penfold St.)
Poolmans St. *SE16* 3F **79**
Poonah St. *E1* 5E **65**
Pope Ho. *SE5* *3F 91*
    (off Elmington Est.)
SE16 . . . . *5D 79*
    (off Manor Est.)
Pope's Head All.
EC3 . . . . . 3C **18** (5F **63**)

Pope's Rd. *SW9* 1C **104**
Pope St. *SE1* . . . 4E **27** (3A **78**)
Popham Rd. *N1* 5E **49**
Popham St. *N1* 5D **49**
    (not continuous)
POPLAR 1D **81**
Poplar Bath St. *E14* . . . 5D **67**
Poplar Bus. Pk. *E14* . . . 1E **81**
Poplar Cl. *E9* 2B **52**
Poplar Ct. *SW19* 5C **114**
Poplar Gro. *W6* 3E **71**
Poplar High St.
E14 . . . . 1D **81**
Poplar Ho. *SE4* *2B 108*
    (off Wickham Rd.)
SE16 . . . . *3F 79*
    (off Woodland Cres.)
Poplar M. *W12* 2E **71**
Poplar Pl. *W2* 1D **73**
Poplar Rd. *E12* 4F **41**
SE24 . . . . 2E **105**
Poplars Av. *NW2* 3E **43**
Poplars Rd. *E17* 1D **39**
Poplar Wlk. *SE24* 1E **105**
    (not continuous)
Poppins Ct.
EC4 . . . . 3D **17** (5D **63**)
Poppleton Rd. *E11* 1A **40**
Porchester Cl. *SE5* 2E **105**
Porchester Ct. *N1* *1D 73*
    (off Porchester Gdns.)
Porchester Gdns.
W2 . . . . 1D **73**
Porchester Gdns. M.
W2 . . . . 5D **59**
Porchester Ga. *W2* *1D 73*
    (off Bayswater Rd.,
    not continuous)
Porchester Ho. *E1* *5D 65*
    (off Philpot St.)
Porchester Leisure Cen.
. . . . 5D **59**
Porchester Mead
BR3: Beck 5B **122**
Porchester M. *W2* 5D **59**
Porchester Pl. *W2* 5A **60**
Porchester Rd. *W2* 5D **59**
Porchester Sq. *W2* 5D **59**
Porchester Ter. *W2* 1E **73**
Porchester Ter. Nth.
W2 . . . . 5D **59**
Porchester Wlk. *W2* . . . *5D 59*
    (off Porchester Ter. Nth.)
Porden Rd. *SW2* 2B **104**
Porlock Ho. *SE26* 3C **120**
Porlock St.
SE1 . . . . 3C **26** (3F **77**)
Porson St. *SE13* 1D **109**
Portal Cl. *SE27* 3C **118**
Portal Way *W3* 4A **56**
Portbury Cl. *SE15* 4C **92**
Port Cres. *E13* 3D **69**
Portcullis Ho. *SW1* 4D **23**
Portelet Ct. *N1* *5A 50*
    (off De Beauvoir Est.)
Portelet Rd. *E1* 2F **65**
Porten Ho's. *W14* *4A 72*
    (off Porten Rd.)
Porten Rd. *W14* 4A **72**

Porters Lodge, The
SW10 . . . . *3E 87*
    (off Coleridge Gdns.)
Porter Sq. *N19* 3A **34**
Porter St.
SE1 . . . . 1A **26** (2E **77**)
W1 . . . . 5A **4** (4B **60**)
Porters Wlk. *E1* *1D 79*
    (off Balkan Wlk.)
Porteus Rd. *W2* 4E **59**
Portgate Cl. *W9* 3B **58**
Porthcawe Rd.
SE26 . . . . 4A **122**
Port Ho. *E14* *1D 95*
    (off Burrells Wharf Sq.)
Portia Ct. *SE11* *1D 91*
    (off Opal St.)
Portia Way *E3* 3B **66**
Porticos, The *SW3* *2F 87*
    (off King's Rd.)
Portinscale Rd.
SW15 . . . . 3A **100**
Portishead Ho. *W2* *4C 58*
    (off Brunel Est.)
Portland Av. *N16* 2B **36**
Portland Ct. *N1* *4A 50*
    (off St Peter's Way)
SE1 . . . . *5B 26*
    (off Gt. Dover St.)
SE14 . . . . *2A 94*
    (off Whitcher Cl.)
Portland Cres. *SE9* . . . 2F **125**
Portland Gdns. *N4* 1D **35**
Portland Gro. *SW8* 4B **90**
Portland Ho. *SW1* 5F **21**
Portland M.
W1 . . . . 3A **14** (5E **61**)
Portland Pl.
W1 . . . . 4D **5** (3D **61**)
Portland Rd. *N4* 3D **35**
    (not continuous)
Portland Rd.
BR1: Brom 4E **125**
SE9 . . . . 2F **125**
W11 . . . . 1A **72**
Portland Sq. *E1* 2D **79**
Portland St. *SE17* 1F **91**
Portland Wlk. *SE17* 2F **91**
Portman Av. *SW14* 1A **98**
Portman Cl.
W1 . . . . 2A **12** (5B **60**)
Portman Ga. *NW1* 3A **60**
Portman Mans. *W1* *5A 4*
    (off Chiltern St.)
Portman M. Sth.
W1 . . . . 3B **12** (5C **60**)
Portman Pl. *E2* 2E **65**
Portman Sq.
W1 . . . . 2B **12** (5C **60**)
Portman St.
W1 . . . . 3B **12** (5C **60**)
Portman Towers
W1 . . . . 2A **12** (5B **60**)
Port Meers Cl. *E17* 1B **38**
Portnall Ho. *W9* *2B 58*
    (off Portnall Rd.)
Portnall Rd. *W9* 1B **58**
Portobello Ct. Est.
W11 . . . . 5B **58**

Portobello M. W11 . . . . . 1C 72
Portobello Rd. W10 . . . . 4A 58
W11 . . . . 5B 58
Portobello Road Market
. . . . 4A 58
Portpool La.
EC1 . . . . 5B 8 (4C 62)
Portree St. E14 . . . . . . 5F 67
Portsdown Av. NW11 . . 1B 30
Portsdown M. NW11 . . . 1B 30
Portsea Hall W2 . . . . . . 5B 60
(off Portsea Pl.)
Portsea M. W2 . . . . 5A 60
(off Portsea Pl.)
Portsea Pl. W2 . . . . 5A 60
Portslade Rd. SW8 . . . . 5E 89
Portsmouth M. E16 . . . . 2D 83
Portsmouth St.
SW15 . . . . 5D 99
Portsmouth St.
WC2 . . . . . . 3F 15 (5B 62)
Portsoken St.
E1 . . . . 4F 19 (1B 78)
Portswood Pl. SW15 . . 4B 98
Portugal St.
WC2 . . . . . . 3F 15 (5B 62)
Portway E15 . . . . 5B 54
Portway Gdns. SE18 . . . 3F 97
Pory Ho. SE11 . . . . 5B 76
(off Lambeth Wlk.)
Poseidon Ct. E14 . . . . . 5C 80
(off Homer Dr.)
Postern, The EC2 . . . . . 1A 18
Post Office App. E7 . . . 2D 55
Post Office Ct. EC3 . . . 3C 18
(off Barbican)
Post Office Way SW8 . . 3F 89
Potier St.
SE1 . . . . 5C 26 (4F 77)
Potter Cl. SE15 . . . . 3A 92
Potterne Cl. SW19 . . . . 5F 99
Potters Flds.
SE1 . . . . 2E 27 (2A 78)
Potter's La. SW16 . . . . 5F 117
Potters Lodge E14 . . . . 1E 95
(off Manchester Rd.)
Potters Rd. SW6 . . . . . . 5E 87
Pottery La. W11 . . . . . . 2A 72
Pottery St. SE16 . . . . . . 3D 79
Pott St. E2 . . . . 2D 65
Poulton Cl. E8 . . . . 3D 51
Poulton Ho. W3 . . . . . . 4A 56
(off Victoria Rd.)
Poultry EC2 . . . 3B 18 (5F 63)
Pound La. NW10 . . . . . . 3C 42
Pound Pk. Rd. SE7 . . . . 5F 83
Pountney Rd.
SW11 . . . . 1C 102
Povey Ho. SE17 . . . . . . 5A 78
(off Tatum St.)
Powell Ho. W2 . . . . 5D 59
(off Gloucester Ter.)
Powell Rd. E5 . . . . 5D 37
Powell's Wlk. W4 . . . . . 2A 84
Powergate Bus. Pk.
NW10 . . . . 2A 56
Powerleague Soccer Cen.
Catford 1C 122
Powerscroft Rd. E5 . . . . 1E 51

Powis Ct. W11 . . . . 5B 58
(off Powis Gdns.)
Powis Gdns. NW11 . . . . 2B 30
W11 . . . . 5B 58
Powis M. W11 . . . . 5B 58
Powis Pl.
WC1 . . . . 4E 7 (3A 62)
Powis Rd. E3 . . . . 2D 67
Powis Sq. W11 . . . . 5B 58
(not continuous)
Powis Ter. W11 . . . . 5B 58
Powlesland Ct. E1 . . . . . 5A 66
(off White Horse Rd.)
Powlett Ho. NW1 . . . . . 3D 47
(off Powlett Pl.)
Powlett Pl. NW1 . . . . . . 4C 46
(not continuous)
Pownall Rd. E8 . . . . 5B 50
Powster Rd.
BR1: Brom 5C 124
Poynders Ct. SW4 . . . . 4E 103
Poynders Gdns.
SW4 . . . . 5E 103
Poynders Rd. SW4 . . . . 4E 103
Poynings Rd. N19 . . . . . 5E 33
Poynter Ho. NW8 . . . . . 3F 59
(off Fisherton St.)
W11 . . . . 2F 71
(off Queensdale Cres.)
Poyntz Rd. SW11 . . . . . 5B 88
Poyser St. E2 . . . . 1D 65
Praed M. W2 . . . . 5F 59
Praed St. W2 . . . . 5F 59
Pragel St. E13 . . . . 1E 69
Pragnell Rd. SE12 . . . . 2D 125
Prague Pl. SW2 . . . . . . 3A 104
Prah Rd. N4 . . . . 4C 34
Prairie St. SW8 . . . . 5C 88
Pratt M. NW1 . . . . 5E 47
Pratt St. NW1 . . . . 5E 47
Pratt Wlk. SE11 . . . . . . 5B 76
Prayle Gro. NW2 . . . . . . 3F 29
Preachers Ct. EC1 . . . . . 5E 9
(off Charterhouse Sq.)
Prebend Gdns. W4 . . . . 5B 70
W6 . . . . 5B 70
(not continuous)
Prebend Mans. W4 . . . . 5B 70
(off Chiswick High Rd.)
Prebend St. N1 . . . . 5E 49
Precinct, The N1 . . . . . . 5E 49
Premier Cinema 5C 92
Premier Cnr. W9 . . . . . . 1B 58
Premiere Pl. E14 . . . . . . 1C 80
Premier Ho. N1 . . . . 4D 49
(off Waterloo Ter.)
Premier Pl. SW15 . . . . 2A 100
Prendergast Rd.
SE3 . . . . 1A 110
Prentice Ct. SW19 . . . . 5B 114
Prentis Rd. SW16 . . . . . 4F 117
Prentiss Ct. SE7 . . . . . . 5F 83
Presburg St. E5 . . . . . . 5F 37
Prescot St. E1 . . . . 1B 78
Prescott Ho. SE17 . . . . 2D 91
(off Hillingdon St.)
Prescott Pl. SW4 . . . . . 1F 103
Presentation M.
SW2 . . . . 2B 118

President Dr. E1 . . . . . . 2D 79
President Ho.
EC1 . . . . 2E 9 (2D 63)
President Quay E1 . . . . 2B 78
(off St Katherine's Way)
President St. EC1 . . . . . . 1F 9
Press Ct. SE1 . . . . 1C 92
Press Ho. NW10 . . . . . . 5A 28
Press M. NW10 . . . . 5A 28
Prestage Way E14 . . . . 1E 81
Prestbury Rd. E7 . . . . . 4E 55
Prested Rd. SW11 . . . . 2A 102
Preston Cl. SE1 . . . . . . 5A 78
Preston Dr. E11 . . . . . . 1E 41
Preston Gdns. NW10 . . 3B 42
Preston Ho. SE1 . . . . . . 5A 78
(off Preston Cl.)
SE1 . . . . 5F 27
(off Stanworth St.)
Preston Pl. NW2 . . . . . . 3C 42
Preston Rd. E11 . . . . . . 1A 40
SE19 . . . . 5D 119
Preston's Rd. E14 . . . . . 1E 81
Preston St. E2 . . . . 1F 65
Prestwich Ter. SW4 . . . 3E 103
Prestwood Ho.
SE16 . . . . 4D 79
(off Drummond Rd.)
Prestwood St.
N1 . . . . 1A 10 (1E 63)
Pretoria Rd. E11 . . . . . . 3F 39
E16 . . . . 3B 68
SW16 . . . . 5D 117
Priam Ho. E2 . . . . 1D 65
(off Old Bethnal Grn. Rd.)
Price Cl. SW17 . . . . . . 3B 116
Price Ho. N1 . . . . 5E 49
(off Britannia Row)
Price's Ct. SW11 . . . . . 1F 101
Price's St.
SE1 . . . . 2E 25 (2D 77)
Price's Yd. N1 . . . . 5B 48
Prichard Ct. N7 . . . . 3B 48
Prideaux Ho. WC1 . . . . 2B 62
(off Prideaux Pl.)
Prideaux Pl. W3 . . . . . . 1A 70
WC1 . . . . 1A 8 (2B 62)
Prideaux Rd. SW9 . . . . 1A 104
Priestfield Rd.
SE23 . . . . 3A 122
Priestley Cl. N16 . . . . . . 2B 36
Priestley Ho. EC1 . . . . 3A 10
(off Old St.)
Priestley Way NW2 . . . 3C 28
Priest's Bri. SW14 . . . . 1A 98
Priest's Ct. EC2 . . . . . . 2F 17
(off Foster La.)
Prima Rd. SW9 . . . . 3C 90
Prime Meridian Line . . . 3F 95
Primrose Cl. E3 . . . . . . 1C 66
SE6 . . . . 5E 123
Primrose Ct. SW12 . . . 5F 103
Primrose Gdns.
NW3 . . . . 3A 46
PRIMROSE HILL 5C 46
Primrose Hill
EC4 . . . . 3C 16 (5C 62)
Primrose Hill Ct.
NW3 . . . . 4B 46

Primrose Hill Rd.
NW3 . . . . 4B 46
Primrose Hill Studios
NW1 . . . . 5C 46
Primrose Mans.
SW11 . . . . 4C 88
Primrose M. NW1 . . . . 4B 46
(off Sharpleshall St.)
SE3 . . . . 3C 96
Primrose Rd. E10 . . . 3D 39
Primrose Sq. E9 . . . . 4E 51
Primrose St.
EC2 . . . . . . 5D 11 (4A 64)
Primrose Wlk. SE14 . . 3A 94
Primula St. W12 . . . 5C 56
Prince Albert Ct.
NW8 . . . . 5B 46
(off Prince Albert Rd.)
Prince Albert Rd.
NW1 . . . . 2A 60
NW8 . . . . 2A 60
Prince Arthur M.
NW3 . . . . 1E 45
Prince Arthur Rd.
NW3 . . . . 2E 45
Prince Charles Cinema
. . . . 4C 14
Prince Charles Dr.
NW4 . . . . 2E 29
Prince Charles Rd.
SE3 . . . . 5B 96
Prince Consort Rd.
SW7 . . . . 4E 73
Princedale Rd. W11 . . 2A 72
Prince Edward Mans.
W2 . . . . 1C 72
(off Moscow Rd.)
Prince Edward Rd.
E9 . . . . 3B 52
Prince Edward Theatre
. . . . 3C 14
(off Old Compton St.)
Prince George Rd.
N16 . . . . 1A 50
Prince Henry Rd.
SE7 . . . . 3F 97
Prince John Rd.
SE9 . . . . 3F 111
Princelet St.
E1 . . . . . . 5F 11 (4B 64)
Prince of Orange Ct.
SE16 . . . . 4E 79
(off Lower Rd.)
Prince of Orange La.
SE10 . . . . 3E 95
Prince of Wales Dr.
SW8 . . . . 3D 89
SW11 . . . . 4A 88
Prince of Wales Mans.
SW11 . . . . 4C 88
Prince of Wales Pas.
NW1 . . . . 2F 5
Prince of Wales Rd.
E16 . . . . 5E 69
NW5 . . . . 3C 46
SE3 . . . . 5B 96
Prince of Wales Ter.
W4 . . . . 1A 84
W8 . . . . 3D 73

Prince of Wales Theatre
. . . . 5B 14
(off Coventry St.)
Prince Regent Ct.
NW8 . . . . 1A 60
(off Avenue Rd.)
SE16 . . . . 1A 80
(off Edward Sq.)
Prince Regent La.
E13 . . . . 2D 69
E16 . . . . 2D 69
Prince Regent M.
NW1 . . . . 2F 5
Princes Arc. SW1 . . . 1A 22
Princes Cir.
WC2 . . . . . . 2D 15 (5A 62)
Princes Cl. N4 . . . . . 3D 35
SW4 . . . . 1E 103
Prince's Ct. SE16 . . . 4B 80
SW3 . . . . 4B 74
(off Brompton Rd.)
Princes Ct. Bus. Cen.
E1 . . . . 1D 79
Prince's Gdns. SW7 . . 4F 73
Prince's Ga. SW7 . . . 3F 73
(not continuous)
Prince's Ga. Ct.
SW7 . . . . 3F 73
Prince's Ga. M. SW7 . . 4F 73
Princes Ho. W11 . . . 1B 72
Princes M. W2 . . . . . 1D 73
W6 . . . . 1D 85
(off Down Pl.)
Princes Pde. NW11 . . 1A 30
(off Golders Grn. Rd.)
Princes Pk. Av.
NW11 . . . . 1A 30
Princes Pl. SW1 . . . . 1A 22
W11 . . . . 2A 72
Prince's Ri. SE13 . . . 5E 95
Princes Riverside Rd.
SE16 . . . . 2F 79
Princes Rd. SW14 . . . 1A 98
SW19 . . . . 5C 114
Princess Alice Ho.
W10 . . . . 3E 57
Princess Ct. N6 . . . . 2E 33
W1 . . . . 4B 60
(off Bryanston Pl.)
W2 . . . . 1D 73
(off Queensway)
Princess Cres. N4 . . . 4D 35
Princess Louise Cl.
W2 . . . . 4F 59
Princess Mary Ho.
SW1 . . . . 5F 75
(off Vincent St.)
Princess May Rd.
N16 . . . . 1A 50
Princess M. NW3 . . . 2F 45
Princess of Wales
Memorial Fountain
. . . . 3F 73
Princes Sq. W2 . . . . 1D 73
(not continuous)
Princess Rd. NW1 . . . 5C 46
NW6 . . . . 1C 58
Princess St.
SE1 . . . . . . 5E 25 (4D 77)

Princes St.
EC2 . . . . . . 3B 18 (5F 63)
W1 . . . . . . 3E 13 (5D 61)
Princes Ter. E13 . . . 5D 55
Prince's Twr. SE16 . . 3E 79
(off Elephant La.)
Prince St. SE8 . . . . . 2B 94
Princes Way SW19 . . 5F 99
Prince's Yd. W11 . . . 2A 72
Princethorpe Ho.
W2 . . . . 4D 59
(off Woodchester Sq.)
Princethorpe Rd.
SE26 . . . . 4F 121
Princeton Ct. SW15 . . 1F 99
Princeton St.
WC1 . . . . . . 1F 15 (4B 62)
Principal Sq. E9 . . . . 2F 51
Pringle Gdns. SW16 . . 4E 117
(not continuous)
Printers Inn Ct. EC4 . . 5C 62
Printers M. E3 . . . . . 5A 52
Printer St.
EC4 . . . . . . 2C 16 (5C 62)
Printing Ho. Yd.
E2 . . . . . . 1E 11 (2A 64)
Printon Ho. E14 . . . . 4B 66
(off Wallwood St.)
Print Village SE15 . . 5B 92
Printwork Apartments
SE1 . . . . 5D 27
(off Long La.)
Priolo Rd. SE7 . . . . . 1E 97
Prior Bolton St. N1 . . 3D 49
Prioress Rd. SE27 . . . 3D 119
Prioress St.
SE1 . . . . . . 5C 26 (4A 78)
Prior St. SE10 . . . . . 3E 95
Priory, The SE3 . . . . 2B 110
Priory Apartments, The
SE6 . . . . 1D 123
Priory Av. W4 . . . . . 5A 70
Priory Ct. E6 . . . . . . 5E 55
E9 . . . . 2F 51
EC4 . . . . 3E 17
(off Pilgrim St.)
SW8 . . . . 4F 89
Priory Gdns. N6 . . . . 1D 33
SW13 . . . . 1B 98
W4 . . . . 5A 70
Priory Grn. Est. N1 . . 1B 62
Priory Gro. SW8 . . . . 4A 90
Priory Ho. E1 . . . . . . 5F 11
(off Folgate St.)
EC1 . . . . 3D 9
(off Sans Wlk.)
SW1 . . . . 1F 89
(off Rampayne St.)
Priory La. SW15 . . . . 4A 98
Priory Mans. SW10 . . 1E 87
(off Drayton Gdns.)
Priory M. SW8 . . . . . 4A 90
Priory Pk. SE3 . . . . . 1B 110
Priory Pk. Rd. NW6 . . 5B 44
Priory Rd. E6 . . . . . . 5F 55
NW6 . . . . 5D 45
Priory St. E3 . . . . . . 2D 67
Priory Ter. NW6 . . . . 5D 45
Priory Wlk. SW10 . . . 1E 87

Pritchard Ho. *E2*. *1D* **65**
(off Ada Pl.)
Pritchard's Rd. *E2*. *5C* **50**
Priter Rd. SE16. . . . . *4C* **78**
Priter Way SE16. . . . . . . *4C* **78**
Probert Rd. SW2. . . . . . *3C* **104**
Probyn Ho. *SW1*. *5F* **75**
(off Page St.)
Probyn Rd. SW2. . . . . . . *2D* **119**
Procter Ho. *SE1*. *1C* **92**
(off Avondale Sq.)
SE5 . . . . *3F* **91**
(off Picton St.)
Procter St.
WC1. . . . . 1F **15** (4B **62**)
Project Ho. *E3*. *3F* **67**
Prologis Pk. E16. . . . . . . *3F* **67**
Promenade, The
W4 . . . . *5A* **84**
Promenade App. Rd.
W4 . . . . *3A* **84**
Prospect Cl. SE26. . . . *4D* **121**
Prospect Cotts.
SW18. . . . . *2C* **100**
Prospect Ho. *N1*. *1C* **62**
(off Donegal St.)
SE1. . . . . *5D* **25**
W10. . . . . *5F* **57**
(off Bridge Cl.)
Prospect Pl. *E1*. *2E* **79**
(not continuous)
N7. . . . . *1A* **48**
NW2. . . . . *5B* **30**
NW3. . . . . *1E* **45**
SE8 . . . . *2B* **94**
(off Evelyn St.)
W4 . . . . *1A* **84**
Prospect Quay
SW18 . . . . *2C* **100**
(off Lightermans Wlk.)
Prospect Rd. NW2. . . . . *5B* **30**
Prospect St. SE16. . . . . *4D* **79**
Prospect Va. SE18. . . . . *5F* **83**
Prospect Wharf E1 . . . . *1E* **79**
Prospero Rd. N19. . . . . . *3F* **33**
Protea Cl. E16 . . . . *3B* **68**
Prothero Rd. SW6 . . . . . *3A* **86**
Proud Ho. *E1* *5D* **65**
(off Amazon St.)
Prout Gro. NW10 . . . . . . *1A* **42**
Prout Rd. E5. . . . . *5D* **37**
Provence St. N1. . . . . . . *1E* **63**
Providence Cl. E9. . . . . . *5F* **51**
Providence Ct.
W1. . . . . 4C **12** (1C **74**)
Providence Pl. N1. . . . . . *5D* **49**
Providence Row N1 . . . . *1F* **7**
Providence Row Cl.
E2. . . . . *2D* **65**
Providence Sq. SE1 . . . . *3C* **78**
Providence Twr.
SE16. . . . . *3C* **78**
(off Bermondsey Wall W.)
Providence Yd. *E2*. *2C* **64**
(off Ezra St.)
Provost Ct. *NW3*. *3B* **46**
(off Eton Rd.)
Provost Est. N1. . . . . *1B* **10**
Provost Rd. NW3 . . . . . . *4B* **46**

Provost St.
N1. . . . . 1B **10** (1F **63**)
Prowse Pl. NW1. . . . . . . *4E* **47**
Prudent Pas. EC2. . . . . . *2A* **18**
Prusom's Island *E1* *2E* **79**
(off Cinnamon St.)
Prusom St. E1. . . . . *2D* **79**
Pryors, The NW3 . . . . . . *5F* **31**
Pudding La.
EC3. . . . . 5C **18** (1F **77**)
Pudding Mill La. E15. . . . *5D* **53**
Puddle Dock
EC4. . . . . 4E **17** (1D **77**)
(not continuous)
Pugin Ct. *N1*. *4C* **48**
(off Liverpool Rd.)
Pulborough Rd.
SW18. . . . . *5B* **100**
Pulford Rd. N15. . . . . . . *1F* **35**
Pulham Ho. SW8. . . . . . *3B* **90**
(off Dorset Rd.)
Pullen's Bldgs. *SE17*. . . *1F* **77**
(off Iliffe St.)
Pullman Ct. SW2. . . . . *1A* **118**
Pullman Gdns. SW15. . . *4E* **99**
Pullman M. SE12. . . . . *3D* **125**
Pulross Rd. SW9 . . . . . *1B* **104**
Pulteney Cl. E3 . . . . *5B* **52**
Pulteney Ter. N1. . . . . . . *5B* **48**
(not continuous)
Pulton Ho. *SE4*. *2A* **108**
(off Turnham Rd.)
Pulton Pl. SW6. . . . . *3C* **86**
Puma Ct. E1. . . 5F **11** (4B **64**)
Pump Ct.
EC4. . . . . 3B **16** (5C **62**)
Pump Ho. Cl. SE16. . . . . *3E* **79**
Pumphouse Educational
Mus., The *2A* **80**
(off Lavender Rd.)
Pump House Gallery, The
. . . . *3C* **88**
Pump Ho. M. *E1*. *1C* **78**
(off Hooper St.)
Pump House Steam &
Transport Mus. *1A* **38**
Pumping Ho. *E14*. *1F* **81**
(off Naval Row)
Pumping Sta. Rd.
W4. . . . . *3A* **84**
Pump La. SE14. . . . . *3E* **93**
Punderson's Gdns.
E2. . . . . *2D* **65**
Purbeck Dr. NW2 . . . . . . *4F* **29**
Purbeck Ho. SW8. . . . . . *3B* **90**
(off Bolney St.)
Purbrook Est.
SE1. . . . . 4E **27** (3A **78**)
Purbrook St.
SE1. . . . . 5E **27** (4A **78**)
Purcell Cres. SW6 . . . . . *3F* **85**
(not continuous)
Purcell Ho. *SW10*. *2F* **87**
(off Milman's St.)
Purcell Mans. W14 . . . . . *2A* **86**
(off Queen's Club Gdns.)
Purcell M. NW10 . . . . . . *4A* **42**
Purcell Room *1A* **24**
(in South Bank)

Purcell St. N1 . . . . *1A* **64**
Purchese St.
NW1. . . . . 1C **6** (1F **61**)
Purday Ho. *W10*. *2A* **58**
(off Bruckner St.)
Purdon Ho. SE15. . . . . . *4C* **92**
(off Peckham High St.)
Purdy St. E3. . . . . *3D* **67**
Purelake M. SE13 . . . . . *1F* **109**
(off Marischal Rd.)
Purley Av. NW2 . . . . *4A* **30**
Purley Pl. N1 . . . . *4D* **49**
Purneys Rd. SE9 . . . . . . *2F* **111**
Purser Ho. *SW2*. *4C* **104**
(off Tulse Hill)
Pursers Cross Rd.
SW6. . . . . *4B* **86**
(not continuous)
Purves Rd. NW10 . . . . . *2D* **57**
Pusey Ho. E14. . . . . *5C* **66**
(off Saracen St.)
Puteaux Ho. *E2*. *1F* **65**
(off Mace St.)
PUTNEY *2F* **99**
Putney Arts Theatre *2F* **99**
Putney Bri. SW6 . . . . . *1A* **100**
Putney Bri. App.
SW6. . . . . *1A* **100**
Putney Bri. Rd.
SW15. . . . . *2A* **100**
SW18. . . . . *2A* **100**
Putney Comn. SW15 . . . *1E* **99**
Putney Exchange Shop. Cen.
SW15. . . . . *2F* **99**
PUTNEY HEATH *4E* **99**
Putney Heath SW15. . . . *5D* **99**
Putney Heath La.
SW15. . . . . *4F* **99**
Putney High St.
SW15. . . . . *2F* **99**
Putney Hill SW15 . . . . . *5F* **99**
(not continuous)
Putney Leisure Cen. . . . *2E* **99**
Putney Pk. Av. SW15 . . . *2C* **98**
Putney Pk. La. SW15 . . . *2D* **99**
(not continuous)
PUTNEY VALE *3C* **112**
Putney Va. Crematorium
SW15. . . . . *2C* **112**
Putney Wharf SW15. . . *1A* **100**
Pylon Trad. Est. E16 . . . *3A* **68**
Pymers Mead SE21 . . . *1E* **119**
Pynfolds SE16. . . . . *3D* **79**
Pynnersmead SE24 . . . *3E* **105**
Pyrford Ho. SW9 . . . . . *2D* **105**
Pyrland Rd. N5. . . . . *2F* **49**
Pyrmont Gro. SE27. . . . *3D* **119**
Pytchley Rd. SE22 . . . . *1A* **106**

Q

Q Bldg., The E15. . . . . . . *3A* **54**
(off The Grove)
Quad Ct. SE1 . . . . *5E* **27**
(off Grigg's Pl.)
Quadrangle, The E15. . . . *3A* **54**
SE24. . . . . *3E* **105**

Quadrangle, The
SW6 . . . . 3A **86**
(Fulham)
SW6 . . . . 4E **87**
(Sands End)
W2 . . . . 5A **60**
W12 . . . . *5D 57*
(off Du Cane Rd.)
Quadrangle Cl. SE1 . . . 5A **78**
Quadrant, The W10 . . . 2F **57**
Quadrant Arc. W1 . . . . 5A **14**
Quadrant Bus. Cen.
NW6 . . . . 5A **44**
Quadrant Gro. NW5 . . . 2B **46**
Quadrant Ho. SE1 . . . . 1D **25**
Quaggy Wlk. SE3 . . . . 2C **110**
Quain Mans. *W14* 2A **86**
(off Queen's Club Gdns.)
Quainton St. NW10 . . . 5A **28**
Quaker Ct. *E1* *4F 11*
(off Quaker St.)
EC1 . . . . 3B **10**
Quakers Pl. E7 . . . . . . 2F **55**
Quaker St.
E1 . . . . 4F **11** (3B **64**)
Quality Ct. WC2 . . . . . 2B **16**
Quantock Gdns. NW2 . . 4F **29**
Quantock Ho. N16 . . . . 3B **36**
Quantock M. *SE15* *5C 92*
(off Alpha St.)
Quarrendon St. SW6 . . . 5C **86**
Quarry Rd. SW18 . . . . . 4E **101**
Quarterdeck, The
E14 . . . . 3C **80**
Quarter Mile La. E10 . . 1D **53**
Quastel Ho. *SE1* *4B 26*
(off Long La.)
Quay Ho. *E14* *3C 80*
(off Admirals Way)
Quayside Cotts. *E1* *2C 78*
(off Mews St.)
Quayside Ct. *SE16* *2F 79*
(off Abbotshade Rd.)
Quayside Ho. E14 . . . . 2B **80**
W10 . . . . 3A **58**
Quay Vw. Apartments
E14 . . . . *4C 80*
(off Arden Cres.)
Quebec M.
W1 . . . . 3A **12** (5B **60**)
Quebec Way SE16 . . . . 3F **79**
Quebec Way Ind. Est.
SE16 . . . . 3A **80**
Quebec Wharf *E8* *5A 50*
(off Kingsland Rd.)
E14 . . . . 5C **66**
Quedgeley Ct. *SE15* . . . *2B 92*
(off Ebley Cl.)
Queen Alexandra Mans.
WC1 . . . . *2D 7*
(off Bidborough St.)
Queen Alexandra's Ct.
SW19 . . . . 5B **114**
Queen Anne Ho.
E16 . . . . *2C 82*
(off Hardy Av.)
Queen Anne M.
W1 . . . . 1E **13** (4D **61**)
Queen Anne Rd. E9 . . . 3F **51**

Queen Anne's Ct.
SE10 . . . . *1F 95*
(off Park Row)
Queen Anne's Gdns.
W4 . . . . 4A **70**
Queen Anne's Ga.
SW1 . . . . 4B **22** (3F **75**)
Queen Anne's Gro.
W4 . . . . 4A **70**
Queen Anne St.
W1 . . . . 2D **13** (5D **61**)
Queen Anne's Wlk.
WC1 . . . . 4E **7**
Queen Anne Ter. *E1* . . . *1D 79*
(off Sovereign Cl.)
Queensbridge Sports &
Community Cen. . . . 4B **50**
Queen Caroline St.
W6 . . . . 1E **85**
(not continuous)
Queen Catherine Ho.
SW6 . . . . *3D 87*
(off Wandon Rd.)
Queen Elizabeth Bldgs.
WC2 . . . . 4B **16**
Queen Elizabeth Hall
. . . . 1A **24**
Queen Elizabeth Ho.
SW12 . . . . 5C **102**
Queen Elizabeth II
Conference Cen
. . . . 4C **22** (3F **75**)
Queen Elizabeth's Cl.
N16 . . . . 4F **35**
Queen Elizabeth's Coll.
SE10 . . . . 3E **95**
Queen Elizabeth St.
SE1 . . . . 3E **27** (3A **78**)
Queen Elizabeth's Wlk.
N16 . . . . 3F **35**
Queen Elizabeth Wlk.
SW13 . . . . 4C **84**
Queenhithe
EC4 . . . . 4A **18** (1E **77**)
Queen Isabella Way
EC1 . . . . *2E 17*
(off King Edward St.)
Queen Margaret Flats
E2 . . . . *2D 65*
(off St Jude's Rd.)
Queen Margaret's Gro.
N1 . . . . 2A **50**
Queen Mary Ho. *E16* . . *2D 83*
(off Wesley Av.)
Queen Mary Rd.
SE19 . . . . 5D **119**
Queen Marys Bldgs.
SW1 . . . . *5E 75*
(off Stillington St.)
Queen Mary's Ct.
SE10 . . . . *2F 95*
(off Park Row)
Queen Mother Sports
Cen., The *5E 75*
(off Vauxhall Bri. Rd.)
Queen of Denmark Ct.
SE16 . . . . 4B **80**
Queensberry M. W.
SW7 . . . . 5F **73**

Queensberry Pl. E12 . . 2F **55**
SW7 . . . . 5F **73**
Queensberry Way
SW7 . . . . 5F **73**
Queensborough M.
W2 . . . . 1E **73**
Queensborough Pas.
W2 . . . . *1E 73*
(off Queensborough M.)
Queensborough Studios
W2 . . . . *1E 73*
(off Queensborough M.)
Queensborough Ter.
W2 . . . . 1D **73**
Queensbridge Ct. *E2* . . *5B 50*
(off Queensbridge Rd.)
Queensbridge Rd. E2 . . 3B **50**
E8 . . . . 3B **50**
Queensbury St. N1 . . . . 4E **49**
Queen's Chapel of the
Savoy, The *5F 15*
(off Savoy St.)
Queen's Cir. SW8 . . . . 3D **89**
Queen's Club Gdns.
W14 . . . . 2A **86**
Queen's Club, The (Tennis)
. . . . 1A **86**
Queens Ct. E11 . . . . . 2A **40**
NW6 . . . . 2D **45**
NW8 . . . . *1F 59*
(off Queen's Ter.)
NW11 . . . . 1B **30**
SE23 . . . . 2D **121**
W2 . . . . *1D 73*
(off Queensway)
Queen's Cres. NW5 . . . 3C **46**
Queenscroft Rd.
SE9 . . . . 3F **111**
Queensdale Cres.
W11 . . . . 2F **71**
(not continuous)
Queensdale Pl. W11 . . . 2A **72**
Queensdale Rd.
W11 . . . . 2F **71**
Queensdale Wlk.
W11 . . . . 2A **72**
Queensdown Rd. E5 . . . 1D **51**
Queens Dr. E10 . . . . . 2C **38**
N4 . . . . 4D **35**
Queen's Elm Pde.
SW3 . . . . *1F 87*
(off Old Church St.)
Queen's Elm Sq.
SW3 . . . . 1F **87**
Queen's Gallery
. . . . 4E **21** (3D **75**)
Queen's Gdns. NW4 . . . 1E **29**
W2 . . . . 1E **73**
Queen's Ga. SW7 . . . . 3E **73**
Queens Ga. Gdns.
SW7 . . . . 4E **73**
SW15 . . . . 2D **99**
Queensgate Ho. *E3* . . . *1B 66*
(off Hereford Rd.)
Queen's Ga. M. SW7 . . 4E **73**
Queen's Ga. Pl. SW7 . . 4E **73**
Queensgate Pl. NW6 . . 4C **44**
Queen's Ga. Pl. M.
SW7 . . . . 4E **73**

Queen's Ga. Ter.
  SW7 . . . . 4E 73
Queens Ga. Vs. E9 . . . . 4A 52
Queen's Gro. NW8 . . . . 5F 45
Queen's Gro. Studios
  NW8 . . . . 5F 45
Queen's Head Pas.
  EC4 . . . . . 2F 17 (5E 63)
Queen's Head La.
  N1 . . . . 5D 49
Queen's Head Yd.
  SE1 . . . . 2B 26
Queens House, The . . 2F 95
Queens Ho. SE17 . . . . 2F 91
    (off Merrow St.)
  SW8 . . . . 3A 90
    (off Sth. Lambeth Rd.)
  W2 . . . . 1D 73
    (off Queensway)
Queens Ice Bowl . . 1D 73
    (off Queensway)
Queensland Pl. N7 . . 1C 48
Queensland Rd. N7 . . 1C 48
Queen's Mans. W6 . . . 5F 71
    (off Brook Grn.)
Queen's Mkt. E13 . . . . 5E 55
Queensmead NW8 . . . . 5F 45
Queensmere Cl.
  SW19 . . . . 2F 113
Queensmere Ct.
  SW13 . . . . 3B 84
Queensmere Rd.
  SW19 . . . . 2F 113
Queen's M. W2 . . . . . 1D 73
    (not continuous)
Queensmill Rd. SW6 . . 3F 85
Queens Pde. NW2 . . . 3E 43
    (off Willesden La.)
  NW4 . . . . 1E 29
    (off Queens Rd.)
Queens Pk. Ct. W10 . . 2F 57
Queen's Pk. Rangers FC
  . . . . 2D 71
Queens Pk. School
  Sports Cen. 5F 43
    (within school)
Queen Sq.
  WC1 . . . . . 4E 7 (3A 62)
Queen Sq. Pl. WC1 . . . 4E 7
    (off Up. Thames St.)
Queens Quay EC4 . . . . 4F 17
    (off Up. Thames St.)
Queens Ride SW13 . . 1C 98
  SW15 . . . . 1C 98
Queens Rd. E11 . . . . . 2F 39
  E13 . . . . 5D 55
  E17 . . . . 1B 38
  NW4 . . . . 1E 29
  SE14 . . . . 4E 93
  SE15 . . . . 4D 93
  SW14 . . . . 1A 98
  SW19 . . . . 5C 114
Queens Rd. W. E13 . . 1C 68
Queen's Row SE17 . . . 2F 91
Queens Ter. E1 . . . . . 3E 65
  E13 . . . . 5D 55
  NW8 . . . . 5F 45
Queen's Theatre
  Westminster 4B 14
    (off Shaftesbury Av.)

Queensthorpe Rd.
  SE26 . . . . 4F 121
Queenstown M. SW8 . . 5D 89
Queenstown Rd.
  SW8 . . . . 2D 89
Queen St.
  EC4 . . . . . 4A 18 (1E 77)
    (not continuous)
  W1 . . . . . . 1D 21 (2D 75)
Queen St. Pl.
  EC4 . . . . . 4A 18 (1E 77)
Queensville Rd.
  SW12 . . . . 5F 103
Queen's Wlk. N5 . . . . 2D 49
  SW1 . . . . . 2F 21 (2E 75)
Queen's Wlk., The
  SE1 . . . . . . 5C 16 (1C 76)
    (Oxo Tower Wharf)
  SE1 . . . . . . 1C 26 (2A 78)
    (Tooley St.)
  SE1 . . . . . . 1A 24 (2B 76)
    (Waterloo Rd.)
Queen's Way NW4 . . . 1E 29
Queensway W2 . . . . . 5D 59
Queens Wharf W6 . . . 1E 85
Queenswood Ct.
  SE27 . . . . 4F 119
  SW4 . . . . 3A 104
Queenswood Gdns.
  E11 . . . . 3D 41
Queens Wood Rd.
  N10 . . . . 1D 33
Queenswood Rd.
  SE23 . . . . 3F 121
Queen's Yd.
  WC1 . . . . . . 4A 6 (4E 61)
Queen Victoria Memorial
  SW1 . . . . . 2F 21 (3E 75)
Queen Victoria Seaman's Rest
  E14 . . . . 5D 67
    (off E. India Dock Rd.)
Queen Victoria St.
  EC4 . . . . . 4D 17 (1D 77)
Queen Victoria Ter.
  E1 . . . . 1D 79
    (off Sovereign Cl.)
Quemerford Rd. N7 . . 2B 48
Quendon Ho. W10 . . . 3E 57
    (off Sutton Way)
Quenington Ct. SE15 . . 2B 92
Quentin Ho. SE1 . . . . 4C 24
    (off Gray St., not continuous)
Quentin Pl. SE13 . . . . 1A 110
Quentin Rd. SE13 . . . . 1A 110
Quernmore Cl.
  BR1: Brom 5C 124
Quernmore Rd.
  BR1: Brom 5C 124
  N4 . . . . 1C 34
Querrin St. SW6 . . . . . 5E 87
Quest, The W11 . . . . . 1A 72
    (off Clarendon Rd.)
Quested Ct. E8 . . . . . . 2D 51
    (off Brett Rd.)
Quex M. NW6 . . . . . . 5C 44
Quex Rd. NW6 . . . . . . 5C 44
Quick Rd. W4 . . . . . . 1A 84
Quick St. N1 . . . . 1D 63
Quick St. M. N1 . . . . . 1D 63

Quickswood NW3 . . . . 4A 46
Quill La. SW15 . . . . . . 2F 99
Quill St. N4 . . . . 5C 34
Quilp St. SE1 . . 3F 25 (3E 77)
    (not continuous)
Quilter Ho. W10 . . . . . 2B 58
    (off Dart St.)
Quilter St. E2 . . . . . . 2C 64
Quilting Ct. SE16 . . . . 3F 79
    (off Garter Way)
Quince Ho. SE13 . . . . 5D 95
    (off Quince Rd.)
Quinton Ho. SW8 . . . . 3A 90
    (off Wyvil Rd.)
Quinton St. SW18 . . 2E 115
Quixley St. E14 . . . . . 1F 81
Quorn Rd. SE22 . . . . 2A 106

R

Rabbit Row W8 . . . . . 2C 72
Raby St. E14 . . . . 5A 66
Raceway, The (Go-Kart Track)
  . . . . 3A 48
Racine SE5. . . . . 4A 92
    (off Peckham Rd.)
Rackham M. SW16 . . 5E 117
Rackstraw Ho. NW3. . . 4B 46
Racton Rd. SW6 . . . . 2C 86
RADA 5B 6
    (off Chenies St.)
Radbourne Av. NW10 . . 1C 56
Radcliffe Ho. SE16 . . . 5D 79
    (off Anchor St.)
Radcliffe Path SW8 . . . 5D 89
Radcliffe Rd.
  SE1 . . . . . . 5E 27 (4A 78)
Radcliffe Sq. SW15 . . . 4F 99
Radcot Point SE23 . . . 3F 121
Radcot St. SE11 . . . . . 1C 90
Raddington Rd. W10 . . 4A 58
Radfield Est. NW10 . . 2A 56
Radford Ho. E14 . . . . 4D 67
    (off St Leonard's Rd.)
  N7 . . . . 2B 48
Radford Rd. SE13 . . . 4E 109
Radipole Rd. SW6 . . . 4B 86
Radisson Ct. SE1 . . . . 5D 27
    (off Long La.)
Radius Apartments N1 . . 1F 7
    (off Caledonian Rd.)
Radland Rd. E16 . . . . 5B 68
Radlet Av. SE26 . . . . 3D 121
Radlett Cl. E7. . . . . . . 3B 54
Radlett Pl. NW8 . . . . . 5A 46
Radley Ct. SE16 . . . . . 3F 79
Radley Ho. NW1 . . . . . 3A 4
    (off Gloucester Pl.)
Radley M. W8 . . . . . . 4C 72
Radley Sq. E5 . . . . . . 4E 37
Radley Ter. E16 . . . . . 4B 68
    (off Hermit Rd.)
Radlix Rd. E10. . . . . . 3C 38
Radnor Ho. EC1 . . . . . 2A 10
    (off Bath St.)

Radnor Lodge W2 . . . . . . 5F **59**
(off Radnor M.)
Radnor M. W2 . . . . 5F **59**
Radnor Pl. W2 . . . . 5A **60**
Radnor Rd. NW6 . . . . 5A **44**
SE15 . . . . 3C **92**
Radnor St.
EC1 . . . . 2A **10** (2E **63**)
Radnor Ter. W14 . . . . 5B **72**
Radnor Wlk. E14 . . . . . . 5C **80**
(off Barnsdale Av.)
SW3 . . . . 1A **88**
Radstock St. SW11 . . . . . 3A **88**
(not continuous)
Radway Ho. W2 . . . . 4C **58**
(off Alfred Rd.)
Raeburn Cl. NW11 . . . . . 1E **31**
Raeburn St. SW2 . . . . . 2A **104**
Ragged School Mus. 4A **66**
Raglan Cl. SE12 . . . . . . 3C **110**
Raglan Rd. E17 . . . . 1E **39**
Raglan St. NW5 . . . . 3D **47**
Ragwort Ct. SE26 . . . . . 5D **121**
Railey M. NW5 . . . . 2E **47**
Railton Rd. SE24 . . . . . . 2C **104**
Railway App. N4 . . . . 1C **34**
SE1 . . . . 2C **26** (2F **77**)
Railway Arches E2 . . . . . . 1F **11**
(off Geffrye St.)
E7 . . . . 1C **54**
(off Winchelsea Rd.)
E8 . . . . 4D **51**
(off Mentmore Ter.)
E10 . . . . 2D **39**
(off Capworth St.)
E11 . . . . 4A **40**
(off Leytonstone High Rd.)
E11 . . . . 3F **39**
(off The Sidings)
E17 . . . . 1C **38**
(off Yunus Khan Cl.)
W12 . . . . 3E **71**
(off Shepherd's Bush Mkt.)
Railway Av. SE16 . . . . . . 3E **79**
(not continuous)
Railway Children Wlk.
BR1: Brom 2C **124**
SE12 . . . . 2C **124**
Railway Cotts. E15 . . . . . 1A **68**
(off Baker's Row)
SW19 . . . . 4D **115**
W6 . . . . 3E **71**
(off Sulgrave Rd.)
Railway Gro. SE14 . . . . . 3B **94**
Railway M. E3 . . . . 2C **66**
(off Wellington Way)
W10 . . . . 5A **58**
Railway Ri. SE22 . . . . . 2A **106**
Railway Side SW13 . . . . 1A **98**
(not continuous)
Railway St. N1 . . . . 1A **62**
Railway Ter. SE13 . . . . . 3D **109**
Rainbow Av. E14 . . . . . . 1D **95**
Rainbow Ct. SE14 . . . . . . 2A **94**
(off Chipley St.)
Rainbow Quay SE16 . . . . 4A **80**
(not continuous)
Rainbow St. SE5 . . . . 3A **92**

Rainbow Theatre 4C **34**
Raines Est. Ct. N16 . . . . 4B **36**
Raine St. E1 . . . . 2D **79**
Rainham Cl. SW11 . . . . 4A **102**
Rainham Ho. NW1 . . . . . 5E **47**
(off Bayham Pl.)
Rainham Rd. NW10 . . . . 2E **57**
Rainhill Way E3 . . . . 2C **66**
(not continuous)
Rainsborough Av.
SE8 . . . . 5A **80**
Rainsford St. W2 . . . . . . 5A **60**
Rainton Rd. SE7 . . . . 1C **96**
Rainville Rd. W6 . . . . 2E **85**
Raleana Rd. E14 . . . . . . 2E **81**
Raleigh Ct. SE16 . . . . . . 2F **79**
(off Clarence M.)
W12 . . . . 3E **71**
(off Scott's Rd.)
Raleigh Gdns. SW2 . . . . 4B **104**
Raleigh Ho. E14 . . . . 3D **81**
(off Admirals Way)
SW1 . . . . 2F **89**
(off Dolphin Sq.)
Raleigh M. N1 . . . . 5D **49**
(off Packington St.)
Raleigh St. N1 . . . . 5D **49**
Ralph Brook Ct. N1 . . . . 1C **10**
(off Chart St.)
Ralph Ct. W2 . . . . 5D **59**
(off Queensway)
Ralston St. SW3 . . . . 1B **88**
Ramac Ind. Est. SE7 . . . . 5D **83**
Ramac Way SE7 . . . . 5D **83**
Ramar Ho. E1 . . . . 4C **64**
(off Hanbury St.)
Rambler Cl. SW16 . . . . . 4E **117**
Rame Cl. SW17 . . . . . . 5C **116**
Ramillies Cl. SW2 . . . . . 4A **104**
Ramillies Pl.
W1 . . . . 3F **13** (5E **61**)
Ramillies Rd. W4 . . . . . . 5A **70**
Ramillies St.
W1 . . . . 3F **13** (5E **61**)
Rampart St. E1 . . . . 5D **65**
Rampayne St. SW1 . . . . . 1F **89**
Ram Pl. E9 . . . . 3E **51**
Ramsay Ho. NW8 . . . . . . 1A **60**
(off Townshend Est.)
Ramsay M. SW3 . . . . . . 2A **88**
Ramsay Rd. E7 . . . . 1A **54**
Ramsdale Rd.
SW17 . . . . 5C **116**
Ramsden Rd.
SW12 . . . . 4C **102**
Ramsey Cl. NW9 . . . . . . 1B **28**
Ramsey Ho. SW9 . . . . . . 3C **90**
Ramsey St. E2 . . . . 3C **64**
Ramsey Wlk. N1 . . . . 3F **49**
(off Handa Wlk.)
Ramsfort Ho. SE16 . . . . . 5D **79**
(off Camilla Rd.)
Ramsgate Cl. E16 . . . . . . 2D **83**
Ramsgate St. E8 . . . . 3B **50**
Ram St. SW18 . . . . 3D **101**
Rancliffe Gdns. SE9 . . . . 2F **111**
Randall Av. NW2 . . . . . . 4A **28**
Randall Cl. SW11 . . . . . . 4A **88**
Randall Pl. SE10 . . . . 3E **95**

Randall Rd. SE11 . . . . . . 1B **90**
Randall Row SE11 . . . . . . 5B **76**
(off Gulliver St.)
Randalls Rents SE16 . . . . 4B **80**
(off Gulliver St.)
Randell's Rd. N1 . . . . 5A **48**
(not continuous)
Randisbourne Gdns.
SE6 . . . . 3D **123**
Randlesdown Rd.
SE6 . . . . 4C **122**
(not continuous)
Randolph App. E16 . . . . . 5E **69**
Randolph Av. W9 . . . . . . 1D **59**
Randolph Cres. W9 . . . . . 3E **59**
Randolph Gdns.
NW6 . . . . 1D **59**
Randolph M. W9 . . . . 3E **59**
Randolph Rd. E17 . . . . . . 1D **39**
W9 . . . . 3E **59**
Randolph St. NW1 . . . . . . 4E **47**
Ranelagh Av. SW6 . . . . . 1B **100**
SW13 . . . . 5C **84**
Ranelagh Bri. W2 . . . . . . 4D **59**
Ranelagh Cotts. SW1 . . 1C **88**
(off Ranelagh Gro.)
Ranelagh Gdns.
SW6 . . . . 1A **100**
(not continuous)
W6 . . . . 5B **70**
Ranelagh Gdns. Mans.
SW6 . . . . 1A **100**
(off Ranelagh Gdns.)
Ranelagh Gro. SW1 . . . . 1C **88**
Ranelagh Ho. SW3 . . . . 1B **88**
(off Elystan Pl.)
Ranelagh Rd. E11 . . . . . . 1A **54**
E15 . . . . 1A **68**
NW10 . . . . 1B **56**
SW1 . . . . 1E **89**
Rangbourne Ho. N7 . . . . 2A **48**
Rangefield Rd.
BR1: Brom 5A **124**
Rangemoor Rd. N15 . . . . 1B **36**
Rangers House 4F **95**
Rangers Sq. SE10 . . . . . . 4F **95**
Rangoon St. EC3 . . . . 3F **19**
Rankine Ho. SE1 . . . . 5F **25**
(off Bath Ter.)
Ranmere St. SW12 . . . . 1D **117**
Rannoch Rd. W6 . . . . 2E **85**
Rannock Av. NW9 . . . . . . 2A **28**
Ransome's Dock Bus. Cen.
SW11 . . . . 3A **88**
Ransom Rd. SE7 . . . . 5E **83**
Ranston St. NW1 . . . . . . 4A **60**
Ranulf Rd. NW2 . . . . 1B **44**
Ranwell Cl. E3 . . . . 5B **52**
Raphael Ct. SE16 . . . . . . 1D **93**
(off Stubbs Dr.)
Raphael St. SW7 . . . . . . 3B **74**
Rapley Ho. E2 . . . . 2C **64**
(off Turin St.)
Raquel Ct. SE1 . . . . 3D **27**
(off Snowfields)
Rashleigh Ct. SW8 . . . . . 5D **89**
Rashleigh Ho. WC1 . . . . 2D **7**
(off Thanet St.)
Rastell Av. SW2 . . . . . . 2F **117**
RATCLIFF 4A **66**

Ratcliffe Cl. SE12 . . . . . 5C 110
Ratcliffe Ct. SE1 . . . . . . 4A 26
   (off Gt. Dover St.)
Ratcliffe Cross St. E1 . . 5F 65
Ratcliffe Ho. E14 . . . . . . 5A 66
Ratcliffe La. E14 . . . . . . 5A 66
Ratcliffe Orchard E1 . . 1F 79
Ratcliff Rd. E7 . . . . 2E 55
Rathbone Ho. E16 . . . . . 5B 68
   (off Rathbone St.)
NW6 . . . . 5C 44
Rathbone Mkt. E16 . . . . 4B 68
Rathbone Pl.
  W1 . . . . 1B 14 (4F 61)
Rathbone St. E16 . . . . . . 4B 68
  W1 . . . . 1A 14 (4E 61)
Rathcoole Gdns. N8 . . . 1B 34
Rathfern Rd. SE6 . . . . . 1B 122
Rathgar Rd. SW9 . . . . . 1D 105
Rathmell Dr. SW4 . . . . . 4F 103
Rathmore Rd. SE7 . . . . . 1D 97
Rattray Ct. SE6 . . . . 2B 124
Rattray Rd. SW2 . . . . . 2C 104
Raul Rd. SE15 . . . . 5C 92
Raveley St. NW5 . . . . . . 1E 47
   (not continuous)
Ravenet St. SW11 . . . . . 4D 89
   (not continuous)
Ravenfield Rd.
  SW17 . . . . 3B 116
Ravenhill Rd. E13 . . . . . 1E 69
Raven Ho. SE16 . . . . . . 5F 79
   (off Tawny Way)
Ravenna Rd. SW15 . . . . 3F 99
Raven Row E1 . . . . 4D 65
   (not continuous)
Ravensbourne Ct.
  SE6 . . . . 5C 108
Ravensbourne Ho.
  BR1: Brom 5F 123
  NW8 . . . . 4A 60
   (off Broadley St.)
Ravensbourne Mans.
  SE8 . . . . 2C 94
   (off Berthon St.)
Ravensbourne Pk.
  SE6 . . . . 5C 108
Ravensbourne Pk. Cres.
  SE6 . . . . 5B 108
Ravensbourne Pl.
  SE13 . . . . 5D 95
Ravensbourne Rd.
  SE6 . . . . 5B 108
Ravensbury Rd.
  SW18 . . . . 2C 114
Ravensbury Ter.
  SW18 . . . . 2D 115
Ravenscar NW1 . . . . . . 5E 47
   (off Bayham St.)
Ravenscar Rd.
  BR1: Brom 4A 124
Ravenscourt Av. W6 . . . 5C 70
Ravenscourt Gdns.
  W6 . . . . 5C 70
Ravenscourt Pk. W6 . . . 4C 70
Ravenscourt Pk. Mans.
  W6 . . . . 4D 71
   (off Paddenswick Rd.)
Ravenscourt Pl. W6 . . . 5D 71

Ravenscourt Rd. W6 . . . 5D 71
   (not continuous)
Ravenscourt Sq. W6 . . . 4C 70
Ravenscroft Av.
  NW11 . . . . 2B 30
   (not continuous)
Ravenscroft Cl. E16 . . . 4C 68
Ravenscroft Rd. E16 . . . 4C 68
Ravenscroft St. E2 . . . . 1B 64
Ravensdale Mans.
  N8 . . . . 1A 34
   (off Haringey Pk.)
Ravensdale Rd. N16 . . . 2B 36
Ravensdon St. SE11 . . . 1C 90
Ravenshaw St. NW6 . . . 2B 44
Ravenslea Rd.
  SW12 . . . . 5B 102
Ravensleigh Gdns.
  BR1: Brom 5D 125
Ravensmede Way
  W4 . . . . 5B 70
Ravens M. SE12 . . . . . . 3C 110
Ravenstone SE17 . . . . . 1A 92
Ravenstone Rd. NW9 . . 1B 28
Ravenstone St.
  SW12 . . . . 1C 116
Ravens Way SE12 . . . . . 3C 110
Ravenswood Rd.
  SW12 . . . . 5D 103
Ravensworth Ct.
  SW6 . . . . 3C 86
   (off Fulham Rd.)
Ravensworth Rd.
  NW10 . . . . 2D 57
Ravent Rd. SE11 . . . . . . 5B 76
Raven Wharf SE1 . . . . . 3F 27
   (off Lafone St.)
Ravey St.
  EC2 . . . . 3D 11 (3A 64)
Rav Pinter Cl. N16 . . . . 2A 36
Rawalpindi Ho. E16 . . . 3B 68
Rawchester Cl.
  SW18 . . . . 1B 114
Rawlings St. SW3 . . . . . 5B 74
Rawlinson Ct. NW2 . . . 2E 29
Rawlinson Ho. SE13 . . . 2F 109
   (off Mercator Rd.)
Rawlinson Point E16 . . . 4B 68
   (off Fox Rd.)
Rawreth Wlk. N1 . . . . . 5E 49
   (off Basire St.)
Rawson St. SW11 . . . . . 4C 88
   (not continuous)
Rawstone Wlk. E13 . . . 1C 68
Rawstorne Pl.
  EC1 . . . . 1D 9 (2D 63)
Rawstorne St.
  EC1 . . . . 1D 9 (2D 63)
   (not continuous)
Rayburne Ct. W14 . . . . 4A 72
Raydon St. N19 . . . . . . 4D 33
Rayford Av. SE12 . . . . . 5B 110
Ray Gunter Ho. SE17 . . 1D 91
   (off Marsland Cl.)
Ray Ho. N1 . . . . 5A 50
   (off Colville Est.)
W10 . . . . 5F 57
   (off Cambridge Gdns.)
Rayleigh Rd. E16 . . . . . 2D 83

Raymede Towers
  W10 . . . . 4F 57
   (off Treverton St.)
Raymond Bldgs.
  WC1 . . . . 5A 8 (4B 62)
Raymond Cl. SE26 . . . . 5E 121
Raymond Rd. E13 . . . . . 5E 55
  SW19 . . . . 5A 114
Raymouth Rd. SE16 . . . 5D 79
Raynald Ho. SW2 . . . . . 3A 118
Rayne Ho. SW12 . . . . . 4C 102
  W9 . . . . 3D 59
   (off Delaware Rd.)
Rayner Ct. W12 . . . . . . 3E 71
   (off Bamborough Gdns.)
Rayners Rd.
  SW15 . . . . 3A 100
Rayner Towers E10 . . . 2C 38
   (off Albany Rd.)
Raynes Av. E11 . . . . . . 2E 41
Raynham W2 . . . . 5A 60
   (off Norfolk Cres.)
Raynham Ho. E1 . . . . . . 3F 65
   (off Harpley Sq.)
Raynham Rd. W6 . . . . . 5D 71
Raynor Pl. N1 . . . . 4E 49
Ray St. EC1 . . . . 4C 8 (3C 62)
Ray St. Bri. EC1 . . . . . . 4C 8
Ray Wlk. N7 . . . . 4B 34
Reachview Cl. NW1 . . . 4E 47
Read Ct. E17 . . . . 1C 38
Reade Ho. SE10 . . . . . . 2F 95
   (off Trafalgar Gro.)
Reade Wlk. NW10 . . . . 4A 42
Read Ho. SE11 . . . . 2C 90
   (off Clayton St.)
Reading Ho. SE15 . . . . 2C 92
   (off Friary Est.)
  W2 . . . . 5E 59
   (off Hallfield Est.)
Reading La. E8 . . . . 3D 51
Reapers Cl. NW1 . . . . . 5F 47
Reardon Ho. E1 . . . . . . 2D 79
   (off Reardon St.)
Reardon Path E1 . . . . . 2D 79
   (not continuous)
Reardon St. E1 . . . . 2D 79
Reaston St. SE14 . . . . . 3F 93
Reckitt Rd. W4 . . . . 1A 84
Record St. SE15 . . . . . . 2E 93
Recovery St. SW17 . . . 5A 116
Recreation Rd.
  SE26 . . . . 4F 121
Rector St. N1 . . . . 5E 49
Rectory Chambers
  SW3 . . . . 2A 88
   (off Old Church St.)
Rectory Cres. E11 . . . . 1E 41
   (not continuous)
Rectory Fld. Cres.
  SE7 . . . . 3E 97
Rectory Gdns. SW4 . . . 1E 103
Rectory Gro. SW4 . . . . 1E 103
Rectory La. SW17 . . . . 5C 116
Rectory Orchard
  SW19 . . . . 4A 114
Rectory Rd. N16 . . . . . . 4B 36
  SW13 . . . . 5C 84
Rectory Sq. E1 . . . . 4F 65

Reculver Ho. SE15 . . . . . 2E 93
  (off Lovelinch Cl.)
Reculver Rd. SE16 . . . . . 1F 93
Red Anchor Cl. SW3 . . . 2F 87
Redan Pl. W2 . . . . 5D 59
Redan St. W14 . . . . 4F 71
Redan Ter. SE5 . . . . 5D 91
Redberry Gro. SE26 . . . 3E 121
Redbourne Ho. E14 . . . . 5B 66
  (off Norbiton Rd.)
Redbourn Ho. W10 . . . . . 3E 57
  (off Sutton Way)
REDBRIDGE 1F 41
Redbridge Gdns. SE5 . . 3A 92
Redbridge La. E.
  IG4: Ilf 1F 41
Redbridge La. W.
  E11 . . . . 1D 41
REDBRIDGE RDBT. 1F 41
Redburn St. SW3 . . . . . . 2B 88
Redcar St. SE5 . . . . 3E 91
Redcastle Cl. E1 . . . . . . 1E 79
Redchurch St.
  E2 . . . . 3F 11 (3B 64)
Redcliffe Cl. SW5 . . . . . 1D 87
  (off Old Brompton Rd.)
Redcliffe Ct. E5 . . . . 5D 37
  (off Napoleon Rd.)
Redcliffe Gdns.
  SW10 . . . . 1D 87
Redcliffe M. SW10 . . . . . 1D 87
Redcliffe Pl. SW10 . . . . . 2E 87
Redcliffe Rd. SW10 . . . . 1E 87
Redcliffe Sq. SW10 . . . . 1D 87
Redcliffe St. SW10 . . . . . 2D 87
Redclyffe Rd. E6 . . . . . . 5E 55
Redclyf Ho. E1 . . . . 3E 65
  (off Cephas St.)
Red Cow La.
  EC1 . . . . 3F 9 (3E 63)
Redcross Way
  SE1 . . . . 3A 26 (3E 77)
Redding Ho. SE18 . . . . . 4F 83
Reddins Rd. SE15 . . . . . 2C 92
Redenham Ho.
  SW15 . . . . 5C 98
  (off Ellisfield Dr.)
Rede Pl. W2 . . . . 5C 58
Redesdale St. SW3 . . . . 2A 88
Redfern Ho. E13 . . . . 5B 54
  (off Redriffe Rd.)
Redfern Rd. NW10 . . . . . 4A 42
  SE6 . . . . 5E 109
Redfield La. SW5 . . . . . . 5C 72
Redfield M. SW5 . . . . . . 5D 73
Redford Ho. W10 . . . . . . 2B 58
  (off Dowland St.)
Redford Wlk. N1 . . . . 5E 49
  (off Popham St.)
Redgate Ter. SW15 . . . . 4F 99
Redgrave Rd. SW15 . . . . 1F 99
Redgrave Ter. E2 . . . . . . 2C 64
  (off Derbyshire St.)
Redhill Ct. SW2 . . . . . . 2C 118
Redhill St.
  NW1 . . . . 1E 5 (1D 61)
Red Ho. Sq. N1 . . . . 3E 49
Redington Gdns.
  NW3 . . . . 1D 45

Redington Ho. N1 . . . . . . 1B 62
  (off Priory Grn. Est.)
Redington Rd. NW3 . . . . 5D 31
Redlands Way SW2 . . . 5B 104
Red Lion Cl. SE17 . . . . . 2F 91
  (off Red Lion Row)
Red Lion Ct.
  EC4 . . . . 3C 16 (5C 62)
  SE1 . . . . 1A 26 (2E 77)
Red Lion Row SE17 . . . . 2E 91
Red Lion Sq.
  SW18 . . . . 3C 100
  WC1 . . . . 1F 15 (4B 62)
Red Lion St.
  WC1 . . . . 5F 7 (4B 62)
Red Lion Yd. W1 . . . . . . 1C 20
Redlynch Ct. W14 . . . . . 3A 72
  (off Addison Cres.)
Redman Ho. EC1 . . . . 5B 8
  (off Bourne Est.)
  SE1 . . . . 4A 26
  (off Borough High St.)
Redman's Rd. E1 . . . . . . 4E 65
Redmead La. E1 . . . . 2C 78
Redmill Ho. E1 . . . . 3D 65
  (off Headlam St.)
Redmond Ho. N1 . . . . . . 5B 48
  (off Barnsbury Est.)
Redmore Rd. W6 . . . . . . 5D 71
Red Path E9 . . . . 3A 52
Red Pl. W1 . . . . 4B 12 (1C 74)
Red Post Hill SE21 . . . . 2F 105
  SE24 . . . . 2F 105
Red Post Ho. E6 . . . . . . 4F 55
Redriff Est. SE16 . . . . . . 4B 80
Redriff Rd. SE16 . . . . . . 5F 79
RED ROVER 2C 98
Redrup Ho. SE14 . . . . . . 2F 93
  (off John Williams Cl.)
Redruth Rd. E9 . . . . 5E 51
Redshank Ho. SE1 . . . . . 1B 92
  (off Avocet Cl.)
Red Sq. N16 . . . . 5F 35
Redstart Cl. E6 . . . . 4F 69
  SE14 . . . . 3A 94
Redvers St. N1 . . . . 1E 11
Redwald Rd. E5 . . . . 1F 51
Redwing Ct. SE1 . . . . . . 4A 26
  (off Swan St.)
Redwing M. SE5 . . . . . . 5E 91
Redwood Cl. E3 . . . . 1C 66
  SE16 . . . . 2A 80
  NW6 . . . . 4A 44
Redwood Ct. N19 . . . . . 2F 33
Redwood Mans.
  W8 . . . . 4D 73
  (off Chantry Sq.)
Redwood M. SW4 . . . . 1D 103
Redwoods SW15 . . . . . 1C 112
Reece M. SW7 . . . . 5F 73
Reed Cl. E16 . . . . 4C 68
  SE12 . . . . 3C 110
Reedham St. SE15 . . . . 5C 92
Reedholm Vs. N16 . . . . . 1F 49
Reed's Pl. NW1 . . . . 4E 47
Reedworth St. SE11 . . . 5C 76
Reef Ho. E14 . . . . 4E 81
  (off Manchester St.)

Rees St. N1 . . . . 5E 49
Reets Farm Cl. NW9 . . . 1A 28
Reeves Av. NW9 . . . . . . 2A 28
Reeves Ho. SE1 . . . . 4B 24
  (off Baylis Rd.)
Reeves M.
  W1 . . . . 5B 12 (1C 74)
Reeves Rd. E3 . . . . 3D 67
Reflection Ho. E2 . . . . . . 3C 64
  (off Cheshire St.)
Reform St. SW11 . . . . . . 5B 88
Regal Cl. E1 . . . . 4C 64
Regal Ct. NW6 . . . . 1B 58
  (off Malvern Rd.)
Regal La. NW1 . . . . 5C 46
Regal Pl. E3 . . . . 2B 66
  SW6 . . . . 3D 87
Regal Row SE15 . . . . . . 4E 93
Regan Way
  N1 . . . . 1D 11 (1A 64)
Regatta Point E14 . . . . . 3C 80
  (off Westferry Rd.)
Regency Ho. E16 . . . . . . 2C 82
  (off Pepys Cres.)
  NW1 . . . . 3E 5
  (off Osnaburgh St.)
  SW1 . . . . 5F 75
  (off Regency St.)
Regency Lawn NW5 . . . 5D 33
Regency Lodge NW3 . . . 4F 45
  (off Adelaide Rd.)
Regency M. NW10 . . . . . 3C 42
  SW9 . . . . 3D 91
Regency Pde. NW3 . . . . 4F 45
  (off Finchley Rd.)
Regency Pl. SW1 . . . . . . 5F 75
Regency St. NW10 . . . . . 3A 56
  SW1 . . . . 5F 75
Regency Ter. SW7 . . . . . 1F 87
  (off Fulham Rd.)
Regent Ct. NW8 . . . . . . 2A 60
  (off North Bank)
  W8 . . . . 4D 73
  (off Wright's La.)
Regent Ho. W14 . . . . . . 5A 72
  (off Windsor Way)
  W1 . . . . 4A 14 (1E 75)
Regent Pl. SW19 . . . . . 5E 115
  W1 . . . . 4A 14 (1E 75)
Regent Rd. SE24 . . . . . 4D 105
Regent's Bri. Gdns.
  SW8 . . . . 3A 90
Regents Canal Ho.
  E14 . . . . 5A 66
  (off Commercial Rd.)
Regents College 3A 4
Regents Ct. E8 . . . . 5B 50
  (off Pownall Rd.)
Regents Ga. Ho.
  E14 . . . . 1A 80
  (off Horseferry Rd.)
Regents M. NW8 . . . . . . 1E 59
REGENT'S PARK
  . . . . 2E 5 (2D 61)
Regent's Pk. . . . 1A 4 (1B 60)
Regent's Pk. Barracks
  . . . . 1E 5
Regents Pk. Est. NW1 . . 1F 5
Regent's Pk. Gdns. M.
  NW1 . . . . 5B 46

Regents Pk. Golf &
Tennis School......1B 60
Regent's Pk. Ho.
NW8 ....2A 60
(off Park Rd.)
Regent's Pk. Open Air Theatre
..............2B 4 (2C 60)
Regent's Pk. Rd.
NW1 ....4B 46
(not continuous)
Regent's Pk. Ter.
NW1 ....5D 47
Regent's Pl. SE3 .....5C 96
Regents Plaza NW6 ...1D 59
(off Kilburn High Rd.)
Regent Sq. E3 ....2D 67
WC1 ....2E 7 (2A 62)
Regent's Row E8 ......5C 50
Regent St. NW10 .....2F 57
SW1 ....2E 13 (1F 75)
W1 ....2E 13 (5D 61)
Regents Wharf E2 .....5D 51
(off Wharf Pl.)
N1 ....1B 62
Reginald Pl. SE8 ......3C 94
(off Deptford High St.)
Reginald Rd. E7 ......4C 54
SE8 ....3C 94
Reginald Sorenson Ho.
E11 ....2F 39
Reginald Sq. SE8 .....3C 94
Regina Point SE16 ....4E 79
Regina Rd. N4 ....3B 34
Regis Ct. NW1 ....4B 60
(off Melcombe Pl.)
Regis Ho. W1 ....5C 4
(off Beaumont St.)
Regis Pl. SW2 ....2B 104
Regis Rd. NW5 ......2D 47
Regnart Bldgs. NW1 ...3A 6
Reigate Rd.
BR1: Brom 3B 124
Reighton Rd. E5 .....5C 36
Reizel Cl. N16 ......3B 36
Relay Rd. W12 ....2E 71
Relf Rd. SE15 ......1C 106
Reliance Arc. SW9 ...2C 104
Reliance Sq.
EC2 ....3E 11 (3A 64)
Relton M. SW7 ....4A 74
Rembold Ho. SE10 ....4E 95
(off Blissett St.)
Rembrandt Cl. E14 ....4F 81
SW1 ....1C 88
(off Graham Ter.)
Rembrandt Ct.
SE16 ....1D 93
(off Stubbs Dr.)
Rembrandt Rd.
SE13 ....2A 110
Remembrance Rd.
E7 ....1F 55
Remington Rd. E6 .....5F 69
N15 ....1F 35
Remington St. N1 .....1D 63
Remnant St.
WC2 ....2F 15 (5B 62)
Remsted Ho. NW6 .....5D 45
(off Mortimer Cres.)

Remus Bldg., The
EC1 ....2C 8
(off Hardwick St.)
Remus Rd. E3 ....4C 52
Renaissance Wlk.
SE10 ....4B 82
(off Teal St.)
Rendle Ho. W10 ......3A 58
(off Wornington Rd.)
Rendlesham Rd. E5 ....1C 50
Renforth St. SE16 ....4E 79
Renfrew Ho. NW6 .....1D 59
(off Carlton Va.)
Renfrew Rd. SE11 ....5D 77
Renmuir St. SW17 ....5B 116
Rennell St. SE13 ....1E 109
Rennie Cotts. E1 .....3E 65
(off Pernell Cl.)
Rennie Ct. SE1 ......1D 25
Rennie Est. SE16 ....5D 79
Rennie Ho. SE1 ......5F 25
(off Bath Ter.)
Rennie St.
SE1 ....1D 25 (2D 77)
(not continuous)
Renoir Cinema
..............3E 7 (3A 62)
Renoir Ct. SE16 .....1D 93
(off Stubbs Dr.)
Rensburg Rd. E17 ....1F 37
Renters Av. NW4 .....1E 29
Renton Cl. SW2 .....4B 104
Rephidim St.
SE1 ....5D 27 (4A 78)
Replingham Rd.
SW18 ....1B 114
Reporton Rd. SW6 ....3A 86
Repton Ho. SW1 .....5E 75
(off Charlwood St.)
Reservoir Ct. E14 ....5A 66
Reservoir Rd. SE4 ....5A 94
Reservoir Studios E1 ...5F 65
(off Cable St.)
Resolution Way SE8 ...3C 94
(off Deptford High St.)
Restell Cl. SE3 ......2A 96
Reston Pl. SW7 ......3E 73
Restoration Sq.
SW11 ....4F 87
Restormel Ho. SE11 ...5C 76
(off Chester Way)
Retcar Cl. N19 ......4D 33
Retcar Pl. N19 ......4D 33
(off Retcar Cl.)
Retford St.
N1 ....1E 11 (1A 64)
Retreat, The SW14 ....1A 98
Retreat Ho. E9 ......3E 51
Retreat Pl. E9 ......3E 51
Reunion Row E1 .....1D 79
Reuters Plaza E14 ....2D 81
(off The Sth. Colonnade)
Reveley Sq. SE16 .....3A 80
Revelon Rd. SE4 .....2A 108
Revelstoke Rd.
SW18 ....2B 114
Reverdy Rd. SE1 .....5C 78
Review Rd. NW2 .....4B 28
Rewell St. SW6 ......3E 87

Rex Pl. W1 .....5C 12 (1C 74)
Reydon Av. E11 ......1E 41
Reynard Cl. SE4 .....1A 108
Reynard Pl. SE14 ....2A 94
Reynolah Gdns. SE7 ...1D 97
Reynolds Cl. NW11 ...2D 31
Reynolds Ho. E2 .....1E 65
(off Approach Rd.)
NW8 ....1F 59
(off Wellington Rd.)
SW1 ....5F 75
(off Erasmus St.)
Reynolds Pl. SE3 .....3D 97
Reynolds Rd. SE15 ...2E 107
Rheidol M. N1 ....1E 63
Rheidol Ter. N1 .....5E 63
Rhoda St. E2 ....3F 11 (3B 64)
Rhodes Ho. N1 ......1B 10
(off Fairbank St.)
Rhodesia Rd. E11 ....4F 39
SW9 ....5A 90
Rhodes St. N7 ......2B 48
Rhodeswell Rd. E14 ...4A 66
(not continuous)
Rhondda Gro. E3 .....2A 66
Rhyl St. NW5 ....3C 46
Ribblesdale Ho. NW6 ...5C 44
(off Kilburn Va.)
Ribblesdale Rd.
SW16 ....5D 117
Ribbon Dance M.
SE5 ....4F 91
Ricardo St. E14 .....5D 67
Ricards Rd. SW19 ...5B 114
Riceyman Ho. WC1 ....2B 8
(off Lloyd Baker St.)
Richard Anderson Ct.
SE14 ....3F 93
(off Monson Rd.)
Richard Burbidge Mans.
SW13 ....2E 85
(off Brasenose Dr.)
Richard Ho. SE16 ....5E 79
(off Silwood St.)
Richard Ho. Dr. E16 ...5F 69
Richard Neale Ho.
E1 ....1D 79
(off Cornwall St.)
Richard Robert
Residence, The
E15 ....3F 53
(off Salway Rd.)
Richardson Cl. E8 ....5B 50
Richardson Ct. SW4 ...5A 90
(off Studley Rd.)
Richardson Rd. E15 ...1A 68
Richardson's M. W1 ...4F 5
Richard's Pl. SW3 ....5A 74
Richard St. E1 ......5D 65
Richbell WC1 ....5E 7
(off Boswell St.)
Richbell Pl.
WC1 ....5F 7 (4B 62)
Richborne Ter. SW8 ...3B 90
Richborough Ho.
SE15 ....2E 93
(off Sharratt St.)
Richborough Rd.
NW2 ....1A 44

Richbourne Ct. W1 . . . . . . 5A 60
(off Harrowby St.)
Richford Ga. W6 . . . . 4E 71
Richford Rd. E15 . . . . 5B 54
Richford St. W6 . . . . 3E 71
Rich Ind. Est.
SE1 . . . . 5E 27 (4A 78)
SE15 . . . . 2D 93
Rich La. SW5 . . . . 1D 87
Richman Ho. SE8 . . . . 1B 94
(off Grove Rd.)
Richmond American University
in London, The
. . . . 4D 73
(off Ansdell St.)
Richmond Av. N1 . . . . 5B 48
NW10 . . . . 3E 43
Richmond Bldgs.
W1 . . . . 3B 14 (5F 61)
Richmond Cl. E17 . . . . 1B 38
Richmond College
(The American Institute
University in London)
. . . . 3D 73
Richmond Cotts. W14 . . . 5A 72
(off Hammersmith Rd.)
Richmond Ct. E8 . . . . 4D 51
(off Mare St.)
NW6 . . . . 4F 43
(off Willesden La.)
SW1 . . . . 4A 20
(off Sloane St.)
W14 . . . . 5A 72
(off Hammersmith Rd.)
Richmond Cres. N1 . . . . . 5B 48
Richmond Gro. N1 . . . . . . 4D 49
(not continuous)
Richmond Ho. NW1 . . . . . . 1E 5
(off Pk. Village E.)
SE17 . . . . 1F 91
(off Portland St.)
Richmond Mans.
SW5 . . . . 1D 87
(off Old Brompton Rd.)
Richmond M.
W1 . . . . 3B 14 (5F 61)
Richmond Rd. E7 . . . . 2D 55
(not continuous)
E8 . . . . 4B 50
E11 . . . . 4F 39
N15 . . . . 1A 36
Richmond St. E13 . . . . 1C 68
Richmond Ter.
SW1 . . . . 3D 23 (3A 76)
Richmond Way E11 . . . . . 4C 40
W12 . . . . 3F 71
W14 . . . . 3F 71
Richmount Gdns.
SE3 . . . . 1C 110
Rich St. E14 . . . . 1B 80
Rickard Cl. SW2 . . . . 1C 118
Rickett St. SW6 . . . . 2C 86
Rickman Ho. E1 . . . . 3E 65
(off Rickman St.)
Rickman St. E1 . . . . 3E 65
Rick Roberts Way
E15 . . . . 1A 80
Rickthorne Rd. N19 . . . . . 4A 34
Rickyard Path SE9 . . . . . . 2F 111

Riddell Ct. SE5 . . . . 1B 92
(off Albany Rd.)
Riddons Rd. SE12 . . . . . . 3E 125
Ridgdale St. E3 . . . . 1D 67
Ridgebrook Rd. SE3 . . . . 1F 111
Ridge Ct. SE22 . . . . 5C 106
Ridge Hill NW11 . . . . 3A 30
Ridge Rd. N8 . . . . 1B 34
NW2 . . . . 5B 30
Ridge Way E19 . . . . 5A 120
Ridgeway, The
NW11 . . . . 2A 30
Ridgeway Dr.
BR1: Brom 4D 125
Ridgeway Gdns. N6 . . . . . 2E 33
Ridgewell Cl. N1 . . . . 5E 49
SE26 . . . . 4B 122
Ridgmont Gdns.
WC1 . . . . 5B 6 (4F 61)
Ridgmont Pl.
WC1 . . . . 5B 6 (4F 61)
Ridgmount Rd.
SW18 . . . . 3D 101
Ridgmount St.
WC1 . . . . 5B 6 (4F 61)
Ridgway SW19 . . . . 5A 114
Ridgway Pl. SW19 . . . . . 5A 114
Ridgway Rd. SW9 . . . . . . 1D 105
Ridgwell Rd. E16 . . . . 4E 69
Riding, The NW11 . . . . 2B 30
Riding Ho. St.
W1 . . . . 1E 13 (4D 61)
Ridings Cl. N6 . . . . 2E 33
Ridley Ct. SW16 . . . . 5A 118
Ridley Rd. E7 . . . . 1E 55
E8 . . . . 2B 50
NW10 . . . . 1C 56
Riffel Rd. NW2 . . . . 2E 43
Rifle Ct. SE11 . . . . 2C 90
Rifle St. E14 . . . . 4D 67
Riga Ho. E1 . . . . 4F 65
(off Shandy St.)
Riga M. E1 . . . . 5C 64
(off Commercial Rd.)
Rigault Rd. SW6 . . . . 5A 86
Rigden St. E14 . . . . 5D 67
Rigeley Rd. NW10 . . . . . . 2C 56
Rigg App. E10 . . . . 3F 37
Rigge Pl. SW4 . . . . 2F 103
Riggindale Rd.
SW16 . . . . 5F 117
Riley Ho. SW10 . . . . 3F 87
Riley Rd. SE1 . . . . 5E 27 (4B 78)
Riley St. SW10 . . . . 2F 87
Rill Ho. SE5 . . . . 3F 91
(off Harris St.)
Rima Ho. SW3 . . . . 2F 87
(off Callow St.)
Rinaldo Rd. SW12 . . . . . . 5D 103
Ring, The W2 . . . . 4A 12 (1F 73)
(not continuous)
Ringcroft St. N7 . . . . 2C 48
Ringford Rd. SW18 . . . . . 3B 100
Ring Ho. E1 . . . . 1E 79
(off Sage St.)
Ringlet Cl. E16 . . . . 4D 69
Ringmer Av. SW6 . . . . 4A 86
Ringmer Gdns. N19 . . . . . 4A 34
Ringmore Ri. SE23 . . . . . 5D 107

Ring Rd. W12 . . . . 2E 71
Ringsfield Ho. SE17 . . . . . . 1E 91
(off Bronti Cl.)
Ringstead Rd. SE6 . . . . . . 5D 109
Ringwood Gdns. E14 . . . . 5C 80
SW15 . . . . 1C 112
Ringwood Rd. E17 . . . . . . 1B 38
Rio Cinema 2A 50
(off Kingsland High St.)
Ripley Gdns. SW14 . . . . . 1A 98
Ripley Ho. SW1 . . . . 2E 89
(off Churchill Gdns.)
Ripley M. E11 . . . . 1A 40
Ripley Rd. E16 . . . . 5E 69
Ripon Gdns. IG1: Ilf 1F 41
Ripplevale Gro. N1 . . . . . . 4B 48
Risborough SE17 . . . . 5E 77
(off Deacon Way)
Risborough Ho. NW8 . . . . 3A 60
(off Mallory St.)
Risborough St.
SE1 . . . . 3E 25 (3D 77)
Risdon Ho. SE16 . . . . 3E 79
(off Risdon St.)
Risdon St. SE16 . . . . 4E 79
Rise, The E11 . . . . 1C 40
NW10 . . . . 1A 42
Riseholme Ct. E9 . . . . 3B 52
Riseldine Rd. SE23 . . . . . 4A 108
Risinghill St. N1 . . . . 1B 62
Rising Sun Ct. EC1 . . . . 5E 9
Rita Rd. SW8 . . . . 2A 90
Ritches Rd. N15 . . . . 1E 35
Ritchie Ho. E14 . . . . 5F 67
(off Blair St.)
N19 . . . . 3F 33
SE16 . . . . 4E 79
(off Howland St.)
Ritchie St. N1 . . . . 1C 62
Ritherdon Rd.
SW17 . . . . 2C 116
Ritson Ho. N1 . . . . 5B 48
(off Barnsbury Est.)
Ritson Rd. E8 . . . . 3C 50
Riva Bingo 1A 118
Rivaz Pl. E9 . . . . 3E 51
Riven Ct. W2 . . . . 5D 59
(off Inverness Ter.)
Riverbank Rd.
BR1: Brom 3C 124
River Barge Cl. E14 . . . . . 3E 81
River Cl. E11 . . . . 1E 41
River Ct.
SE1 . . . . 5D 17 (1D 77)
Rivercourt Rd. W6 . . . . 5D 71
Riverdale SE13 . . . . 2E 109
Riverdale Dr. SW18 . . . . 1D 115
Riverdale Shop. Cen.
SE13 . . . . 1E 109
Riverfleet WC1 . . . . 1E 7
(off Birkenhead St.)
Riverford Ho. W2 . . . . 4C 58
(off Brunel St.)
River Ho. SE26 . . . . 3D 121
River Lodge SW1 . . . . 2E 89
(off Grosvenor Rd.)
Rivermead Ct. SW6 . . . . . 1B 100
Rivermead Ho. E9 . . . . 2A 52
River Pl. N1 . . . . 4E 49

Riversdale Rd. N5 . . . . . 5D 35
Riverside NW4 . . . . 2D 29
  SE7 . . . . 4D 83
  SW11 . . . . 3A 88
  WC1 . . . . 1E 7
    (off Birkenhead St.)
Riverside Apartments
  SE1 . . . . 2F 27
    (off Shad Thames)
Riverside Bus. Cen.
  SW18 . . . . 1D 115
Riverside Cl. E5 . . . . . . 3E 37
Riverside Ct. SE3 . . . . 2B 110
  SW8 . . . . 2F 89
Riverside Dr. NW11 . . . 1A 30
  W4 . . . . 3A 84
Riverside Gdns. W6. . . 1D 85
Riverside Ho. N1 . . . . . . 4E 49
    (off Canbury St.)
Riverside Mans. E1 . . . 2E 79
    (off Milk Yd.)
Riverside Rd. E15 . . . . 1E 67
  N15 . . . . 1C 36
  SW17 . . . . 4D 115
Riverside Studios 1E 85
    (off River Ter.)
Riverside Twr. SW6 . . . 5E 87
    (off The Boulevard)
Riverside Wlk. SE10 . . 4A 82
    (Morden Wharf Rd.)
  SE10 . . . . 3F 81
    (Tunnel Av.)
  SW6 . . . . 1A 100
  W4 . . . . 2B 84
    (off Chiswick Wharf)
Riverside Workshops
  SE1 . . . . 1A 26
    (off Park St.)
Riverside Yd. SW17 . . . 4E 115
River St. EC1 . . . . 1B 8 (2C 62)
  WC2 . . . . 5F 15
River Ter. W6 . . . . 1E 85
  WC2 . . . . 5E 15
Riverton Cl. W9 . . . . . . 2B 58
Riverview Ct. E14. . . . . 4B 80
Riverview Gdns.
  SW13 . . . . 2D 85
River Vw. Hgts.
  SE16 . . . . 3C 78
    (off Bermondsey Wall W.)
Riverview Pk. SE6 . . . 2C 122
River Wlk. W6 . . . . 3E 85
River Way SE10 . . . . . . 4B 82
Riverview Wlk.
  SE6 . . . . 3B 122
Rivet Ho. SE1 . . . . 1B 92
    (off Coopers Rd.)
Rivington Ct.
  NW10 . . . . 5C 42
Rivington Pl.
  EC2 . . . . 2E 11 (2A 64)
Rivington St.
  EC2 . . . . 2D 11 (2A 64)
Rivington Wlk. E8 . . . . 5C 50
Rixon St. N7 . . . . 5C 34
Roach Rd. E3 . . . . 4C 52
Roads Pl. N19 . . . . 4A 34
Roan St. SE10 . . . . 2E 95
Robert Adam St.
  W1 . . . . 2B 12 (5C 60)

Roberta St. E2 . . . . 2C 64
Robert Bell Ho. SE16. . 5C 78
    (off Rouel Rd.)
Robert Burns M.
  SE24 . . . . 3D 105
Robert Cl. W9 . . . . 3E 59
Robert Dashwood Way
  SE17 . . . . 5E 77
Robert Gentry Ho.
  W14 . . . . 1A 86
    (off Gledstanes Rd.)
Robert Jones Ho.
  SE16 . . . . 5C 78
    (off Rouel Rd.)
Robert Keen Cl.
  SE15 . . . . 4C 92
Robert Lowe Cl.
  SE14 . . . . 3F 93
Robert Morton Ho.
  NW8 . . . . 4E 45
Robert Owen Ho.
  SW6 . . . . 4F 85
Robert Runcie Cl.
  SW2 . . . . 2B 104
Roberts Cl. SE16 . . . . . 3F 79
Roberts Ct. N1 . . . . 5D 49
    (off Essex Rd.)
  NW10 . . . . 3A 42
Roberts M.
  SW1 . . . . . . 5B 20 (4C 74)
Robertson Gro.
  SW17 . . . . 5A 116
Robertson Rd. E15. . . . 5E 53
Robertson St. SW8 . . 1D 103
Roberts Pl.
  EC1 . . . . 3C 8 (3C 62)
Robert St.
  NW1 . . . . 2E 5 (2D 61)
  WC2 . . . . 5E 15 (1A 76)
Robert Sutton Ho. E1 . . 5E 65
    (off Tarling St.)
Robeson St. E3 . . . . . . 4B 66
Robin Ct. E14 . . . . 3E 81
  SE16 . . . . 5C 78
Robin Cres. E6 . . . . . . 4F 69
Robin Gro. N6 . . . . 4C 32
ROBIN HOOD 3A 112
Robin Hood Ct. EC4 . . 2C 16
    (off Shoe La.)
Robin Hood Gdns.
  E14 . . . . 1E 81
    (off Woolmore St.,
    not continuous)
Robin Hood La. E14. . . 1E 81
  SW15 . . . . 3A 112
Robin Hood Rd.
  SW19 . . . . 5C 112
Robin Hood Way
  SW15 . . . . 3A 112
  SW20 . . . . 3A 112
Robin Ho. NW8 . . . . . . 1A 60
    (off Barrow Hill Est.)
Robin Howard Dance Theatre
  . . . . 2C 6
    (in The Place)
Robinia Cres. E10 . . . . 4D 39
Robins Ct. SE12 . . . . . 3E 125
Robinscroft M. SE10 . . 4E 95
Robinson Cl. E11 . . . . . 5A 40

Robinson Ct. N1 . . . . . . 5D 49
    (off St Mary's Path)
Robinson Ho. E14 . . . . 4C 66
    (off Selsey St.)
  W10. . . . . 5F 57
    (off Bramley Rd.)
Robinson Rd. E2 . . . . . 1E 65
  SW17 . . . . 5A 116
Robinson St. SW3 . . . . 2B 88
Robinwood Pl.
  SW15 . . . . 4A 112
Robsart St. SW9 . . . . . 5B 90
Robson Av. NW10 . . . . 4C 42
Robson Ct. E6. . . . . . . 5F 69
Robson Rd. SE27 . . . . 3D 119
Roby Ho. EC1 . . . . 3F 9
    (off Mitchell St.)
Rocastle Rd. SE4. . . . . 3A 108
Rochdale Rd. E17 . . . . 2C 38
Rochdale Way SE8. . . . 3C 94
    (not continuous)
Roche Ho. E14. . . . . . . 1B 80
    (off Beccles St.)
Rochelle Cl. SW11. . . . 2F 101
Rochelle St.
  E2. . . . . 2F 11 (2B 64)
    (not continuous)
Rochemont Wlk. E8 . . . 5C 50
    (off Pownell Rd.)
Rochester Av. E13 . . . . 5E 55
Rochester Ct. E2 . . . . . 3D 65
    (off Wilmot St.)
  NW1 . . . . 4E 47
    (off Rochester Sq.)
Rochester Ho. SE1. . . . 4C 26
    (off Manciple St.)
  SE15 . . . . 2E 93
    (off Sharratt St.)
Rochester M. NW1. . . . 4E 47
Rochester Pl. NW1 . . . 3E 47
Rochester Rd. NW1 . . . 3E 47
Rochester Row SW1 . . 5E 75
Rochester Sq. NW1 . . . 4E 47
Rochester St. NW1 . . . 4F 75
Rochester Ter. NW1 . . . 3E 47
Rochester Wlk.
  SE1. . . . . 1B 26 (2F 77)
Rochester Way SE3 . . . 4D 97
  SE9 . . . . 5E 97
Rochester Way Relief Rd.
  SE3. . . . . 4D 97
  SE9 . . . . 2E 111
Rochford Cl. E6 . . . . . . 1F 69
Rochford Wlk. E8. . . . . 4C 50
Rochfort Ho. SE8 . . . . 1B 94
Rock Av. SW14. . . . . . . 1A 98
Rockbourne M.
  SE23 . . . . 1F 121
Rockbourne Rd.
  SE23 . . . . 1F 121
Rockell's Pl. SE22. . . . 4D 107
Rockfield Ho. SE10 . . . 2E 95
    (off Welland St.)
Rock Gro. Way SE16 . . 5C 78
    (not continuous)
Rockhall Rd. NW2 . . . . 1F 43
Rockhall Way NW2. . . . 5F 29
Rockhampton Cl.
  SE27 . . . . 4C 118

Rockhampton Rd.
  SE27 . . . . 4C 118
Rock Hill SE26 . . . . . . 4B 120
  (not continuous)
Rockingham Cl.
  SW15 . . . . 2B 98
Rockingham St.
  SE1 . . . . 5F 25 (4E 77)
Rockland Rd. SW15 . . . 2A 100
Rockley Ct. W14 . . . . 3F 71
  (off Rockley Rd.)
Rockley Rd. W14 . . . . . . 3F 71
Rocks La. SW13 . . . . . . 4C 84
Rock St. N4 . . . . 4C 34
Rockwell Gdns.
  SE19 . . . . 5A 120
Rockwood Pl. W12 . . . . 3E 71
Rocliffe St. N1 . . . . 1D 63
Rocombe Cres.
  SE23 . . . . 5E 107
Rocque Ho. SW6 . . . . . 3B 86
  (off Estcourt Rd.)
Rocque La. SE3 . . . . . . 1B 110
Rodale Mans.
  SW18 . . . . 4D 101
Rodborough Ct. W9 . . . 3C 58
  (off Hermes Cl.)
Rodborough Rd.
  NW11 . . . . 3C 30
Roden Ct. N6 . . . . 2F 33
Rodenhurst Rd.
  SW4 . . . . 4E 103
Roden St. N7 . . . . 5B 34
Roderick Ho. SE16 . . . . 5E 79
  (off Raymouth Rd.)
Roderick Rd. NW3 . . . . 1B 46
Rodgers Ho. SW4 . . . . . 5F 103
  (off Clapham Pk. Est.)
Rodin Ct. N1. . . . . 5D 49
  (off Essex Rd.)
Roding Ho. N1 . . . . 5C 48
  (off Barnsbury Est.)
Roding La. Sth.
  IG4: Ilf 1F 41
Roding M. E1 . . . . 2C 78
Roding Rd. E5 . . . . 1F 51
Rodmarton St.
  W1 . . . . 1A 12 (4B 60)
Rodmell WC1 . . . . 2E 7
  (off Regent Sq.)
Rodmere St. SE10 . . . . 1A 96
Rodmill La. SW2 . . . . . 5A 104
Rodney Ct. W9 . . . . 3E 59
Rodney Ho. E14 . . . . . . 5D 81
  (off Cahir St.)
N1. . . . . 1B 62
  (off Donegal St.)
SW1 . . . . 1E 89
  (off Dolphin Sq.)
W11 . . . . 1C 72
  (off Pembridge Cres.)
Rodney Pl. SE17. . . . . . 5E 77
Rodney Rd. SE17. . . . . . 5E 77
  (not continuous)
Rodney St. N1 . . . 1A 8 (1B 62)
Rodway Rd. SW15 . . . . 5C 98
Rodwell Rd. SE22 . . . . 4B 106
Roedean Cres.
  SW15 . . . . 4A 98

ROEHAMPTON 5C 98
Roehampton Cl.
  SW15 . . . . 2C 98
Roehampton Ga.
  SW15 . . . . 4A 98
Roehampton High St.
  SW15 . . . . 5C 98
ROEHAMPTON LANE
  . . . . 1D 113
Roehampton La.
  SW15 . . . . 2C 98
Roehampton Recreation Cen.
  . . . . 5C 98
Roehampton University
  . . . . 4B 98
Roehampton Va.
  SW15 . . . . 3B 112
Roffey St. E14 . . . . 3E 81
Rogate Ho. E5 . . . . 5C 36
Roger Dowley Ct. E2 . . 1E 65
Roger Harriss Almshouses
  E15 . . . . 5B 54
  (off Gift La.)
Rogers Ct. E14 . . . . 1C 80
  (off Premiere Pl.)
Rogers Est. E2 . . . . 2E 65
Rogers Ho. SW1 . . . . . . 5F 75
  (off Page St.)
Rogers Rd. E16 . . . . . . 5B 68
Roger St.
  WC1 . . . . 4A 8 (3B 62)
Rohere Ho.
  EC1 . . . . 1F 9 (2E 63)
Rojack Rd. SE23. . . . . . 1F 121
Rokeby Ho. SW12 . . . . 5D 103
  (off Lochinvar St.)
WC1 . . . . 4F 7
  (off Millman M.)
Rokeby Rd. SE4 . . . . . . 5B 94
Rokeby St. E15. . . . . . . 5F 53
Rokell Ho.
  BR3: Beck 5D 123
  (off Beckenham Hill Rd.)
Roland Gdns. SW7 . . . . 1E 87
Roland Ho. SW7 . . . . . . 1E 87
  (off Old Brompton Rd.)
Roland Mans. SW5 . . . . 1E 87
  (off Old Brompton Rd.)
Roland M. E1 . . . . 4F 65
Roland Way SE17 . . . . . 1F 91
SW7 . . . . 1E 87
Rollins St. SE15. . . . . . 2E 93
Rollit St. N7 . . . . 2C 48
Rolls Bldgs.
  EC4 . . . . 2B 16 (5C 62)
Rollscourt Av. SE24 . . . 3E 105
Rolls Pas. EC4 . . . . 2B 16
Rolls Rd. SE1 . . . . 1B 92
Rolt St. SE8 . . . . 2A 94
  (not continuous)
Roman Ct. N7. . . . . 3B 48
Romanfield Rd.
  SW2 . . . . 5B 104
Roman Ho. EC2 . . . . . . 1A 18
Roman Ri. SE19. . . . . . 5F 119
Roman Rd. E2 . . . . 2E 65
E3 . . . . 5B 52
E6 . . . . 3F 69

Roman Rd. NW2 . . . . . . 5E 29
W4 . . . . 5A 70
Roman Rd. Mkt. E3 . . . 5B 52
  (off Roman Rd.)
Roman Way N7 . . . . 3B 48
SE15 . . . . 3E 93
Roman Way Ind. Est.
  N7 . . . . 4B 48
  (off Roman Way)
Roma Read Cl.
  SW15 . . . . 5D 99
Romayne Ho. SW4 . . . . 1F 103
Romberg Rd. SW17 . . . 3C 116
Romborough Gdns.
  SE13 . . . . 3E 109
Romborough Way
  SE13 . . . . 3E 109
Romer Ho. W10 . . . . . . 2B 58
  (off Dowland St.)
Romero Cl. SW9 . . . . . . 1B 104
Romero Sq. SE3 . . . . . . 2E 111
Romeyn Rd.
  SW16 . . . . 3B 118
Romford Rd. E7 . . . . . . 3A 54
E12 . . . . 2E 55
E15 . . . . 3A 54
Romford St. E1. . . . . . . 4C 64
Romilly Ho. W11 . . . . . 1A 72
  (off Wilsham St.)
Romilly Rd. N4 . . . . 4D 35
Romilly St.
  W1 . . . . 4C 14 (1F 75)
Romily Ct. SW6 . . . . . . 5B 86
Rommany Rd. SE27 . . . 4F 119
  (not continuous)
Romney Cl. NW11 . . . . 3E 31
SE14 . . . . 3E 93
Romney Ct. NW3 . . . . . 3A 46
W12. . . . . 3F 71
  (off Shepherd's Bush Grn.)
Romney M.
  W1 . . . . 5B 4 (4C 60)
Romney Rd. SE10 . . . . . 2F 95
Romney Row NW2 . . . . 4F 29
  (off Brent Ter.)
Romney St. SW1 . . . . . 4A 76
Romola Rd. SE24 . . . . . 1D 119
Ronald Av. E15. . . . . . . 2A 68
Ronald Buckingham Ct.
  SE16 . . . . 3E 79
  (off Kenning St.)
Ronald Ho. SE3 . . . . . . 2E 111
Ronaldshay N4. . . . . . . 2C 34
Ronalds Rd. N5 . . . . . . 2C 48
  (not continuous)
Ronald St. E1 . . . . 5E 65
Rona Rd. NW3 . . . . 1C 46
Rona Wlk. N1 . . . . 3F 49
  (off Ramsey Wlk.)
Rondu Rd. NW2 . . . . . . 2A 44
Ronver Rd. SE12 . . . . . 1B 124
Rood La.
  EC3 . . . . 4D 19 (1A 78)
Roof Ter. Apartments, The
  EC1 . . . . 4E 9
  (off Gt. Sutton St.)
Rookery Rd. SW4 . . . . . 2E 103
Rookery Way NW9 . . . . 1B 28
Rooke Way SE10 . . . . . 1B 96

Rookstone Rd.
SW17 . . . . .5B 116
Rook Wlk. E6 . . . . . .5F 69
Rookwood Rd. N16 . . 2B 36
Roosevelt Memorial
. . . . .4C 12 (1C 74)
Rootes Dr. W10. . . . .4F 57
Ropemaker Rd.
SE16 . . . . .3A 80
Ropemaker's Flds.
E14 . . . . .1B 80
Ropemaker St.
EC2. . . . . . .5B 10 (4F 63)
Roper La.
SE1 . . . . . .4E 27 (3A 78)
Ropers Orchard SW3 . .2A 88
(off Danvers St.)
Ropers Wlk. SW2. . . .5C 104
Ropery Bus. Pk.
SE7 . . . . .5E 83
Ropery St. E3 . . . . . .3B 66
Rope St. SE16 . . . . . .5A 80
Rope Wlk. Gdns. E1 . . .5C 64
Ropewalk M. E8. . . . .4C 50
(off Middleton Rd.)
Ropley St. E2. . . . . . .1C 64
Rosa Alba M. N5 . . . . 1E 49
Rosalind Ho. N1 . . . . .1A 64
(off Arden Ho.)
Rosaline Rd. SW6 . . . .3A 86
Rosaline Ter. SW6 . . . .3A 86
(off Rosaline Rd.)
Rosamond St. SE26 . . .3D 121
Rosary Gdns. SW7 . . . .5E 73
Rosaville Rd. SW6. . . .3B 86
Roscoe St.
EC1 . . . . . . .4A 10 (3E 63)
(not continuous)
Roscoe St. Est.
EC1 . . . . . . .4A 10 (3E 63)
Rose All. EC2. . . . . . .1E 19
(off Bishopsgate)
SE1 . . . . . .1A 26 (2E 77)
Rose & Crown Ct.
EC2. . . . . .2A 18
Rose & Crown Yd.
SW1. . . . . .1A 22 (2E 75)
Rosebank SW6 . . . . . .3E 85
Rosebank Gdns. E3 . . .1B 66
Rosebank Rd. E17 . . . .1D 39
Rosebank Wlk. NW1. . .4F 47
Rosebay Ho. E3 . . . . .4C 66
(off Hawgood St.)
Roseberry Gdns. N4. . .1D 35
Roseberry Pl. E8 . . . . .3B 50
Roseberry St. SE16 . . .5D 79
Rosebery Av. E12 . . . .3F 55
EC1 . . . . . .4B 8 (3C 62)
Rosebery Ct. EC1 . . . .4B 8
(off Rosebery Av.)
W1 . . . . .1D 21
(off Charles St.)
Rosebery Gdns. N8 . . .1A 34
Rosebery Ho. E2 . . . . .1E 65
(off Sewardstone Rd.)
Rosebery Rd. SW2. . . .4A 104
Rosebery Sq. EC1 . . . .4B 8
Rosebury Rd. SW6 . . . .5D 87
Rose Bush Ct. NW3 . . .2B 46

Rose Ct. E1 . . . . .1F 19
E8 . . . . .4B 50
(off Richmond Rd.)
N1 . . . . .5D 49
(off Collin's Yd.)
SE16 . . . . .5F 79
Rosecroft Av. NW3 . . .5C 30
Rosecroft Gdns.
NW2 . . . . .5C 28
Rosedale Ct. N5. . . . .1D 49
Rosedale Ho. N16 . . . .3F 35
Rosedale Rd. E7 . . . . .2E 55
Rosedale Ter. W6 . . . .4D 71
(off Dalling Rd.)
Rosedene NW6. . . . . .5F 43
Rosedene Av.
SW16 . . . . .3B 118
Rosedene Ter. E10. . . .4D 39
Rosedew Rd. W6 . . . . .2F 85
Rosefield Gdns. E14 . . .1C 80
Roseford Ct. W12. . . . .3F 71
(off Shepherd's Bush Grn.)
Rosegate Ho. E3 . . . . .1B 66
(off Hereford Rd.)
Rosehart M. W11. . . . .5C 58
Rosehill Rd. SW18. . . .4E 101
Roseleigh Av. N5 . . . . .1D 49
Rosemary Branch Theatre
. . . . .5F 49
(off Penally Pl.)
Rosemary Ct. SE8 . . . .2B 94
(off Dorking Cl.)
Rosemary Dr. E14. . . . .5F 67
IG4: Ilf 1F 41
Rosemary Ho. N1 . . . . .5F 49
(off Branch Pl.)
NW10 . . . . .5D 43
(off Uffington Rd.)
Rosemary La. SE15. . . .3B 92
SW17 . . . . .3E 115
Rosemary St. N1 . . . . .5F 49
Rosemead NW9 . . . . . .2B 28
Rosemont Rd. NW3 . . . .3E 45
Rosemoor St. SW3 . . . .5B 74
Rosemount Point
SE23 . . . . .3F 121
Rosenau Cres. SW11. . .4B 88
Rosenau Rd. SW11 . . . .4A 88
Rosendale Rd.
SE21 . . . . .3F 119
SE24 . . . . .5E 105
Roseneath Rd.
SW11 . . . . .4C 102
Rosenthal Rd. SE6. . . .4D 109
Rosenthorpe Rd.
SE15 . . . . .3F 107
Roserton St. E14 . . . . .3E 81
Rose Sq. SW3 . . . . . . .1F 87
Rose St. EC4 . . .2E 17 (5D 78)
WC2. . . . . .4D 15 (1A 76)
(not continuous)
Rosethorn Cl. SW12. . . .5F 103
Rosetta Cl. SW8. . . . . .3A 90
(off Kenchester Cl.)
Roseveare Rd.
SE12 . . . . .4E 125
Rose Way SE12 . . . . . .3C 110
Roseway SE21 . . . . . . .4F 105
Rosewood Ct. E11 . . . .1F 53

Rosewood Gdns.
SE13 . . . . .5E 95
Rosewood Ho. SW8 . . .2B 90
(off Sth. Lambeth Rd.)
Rosewood Sq. W12 . . .5C 56
Rosher Cl. E15. . . . . . .4F 53
Roshni Ho. SW17 . . . .5A 116
Rosina St. E9 . . . . . . .3F 51
Roskell Rd. SW15 . . . .1F 99
Roslin Ho. E1 . . . . . . .1F 79
(off Brodlove La.)
Roslin Way
BR1: Brom 5C 124
Rosmead Rd. W11. . . .1A 72
Rosoman Pl.
EC1 . . . . . . .3C 8 (3C 62)
Rosoman St.
EC1 . . . . . . .2C 8 (2C 62)
Ross Ct. E5 . . . . .1D 51
(off Napoleon Rd.)
SW15 . . . . .5F 99
Rosscourt Mans.
SW1 . . . . .5F 21
(off Buckingham Pal. Rd.)
Rossdale Rd. SW15. . . .2E 99
Rosse M. SE3 . . . . . . .4D 97
Rossendale St. E5. . . . .4D 37
Rossendale Way
NW1 . . . . .4E 47
Rossetti Cl. WC1 . . . . .5B 6
(off Ridgmount Pl.)
Rossetti Gdn. Mans.
SW3 . . . . .2B 88
(off Flood St.)
Rossetti Ho. SW1. . . . .5F 75
(off Erasmus St.)
Rossetti M. NW8 . . . . .5F 45
Rossetti Rd. SE16 . . . .1D 93
Rossetti Studios
SW3 . . . . .2A 88
(off Flood St.)
Ross Ho. E1 . . . . .2D 79
(off Prusom St.)
Rossington St. E5 . . . .4C 36
Rossiter Rd. SW12 . . . .1D 117
Rosslyn Av. SW13 . . . .1A 98
Rosslyn Hill NW3. . . . .1F 45
Rosslyn Mans. NW6 . . .4E 45
(off Goldhurst Ter.)
Rosslyn M. NW3 . . . . .1F 45
Rosslyn Pk. M. NW3 . . .2F 45
Rosslyn Pk. RUFC 2B 98
Rossmore Cl. NW1 . . . .3A 60
(off Rossmore Rd.)
Rossmore Ct. NW1 . . . .3B 60
Rossmore Rd. NW1 . . . .3A 60
Ross Way SE9 . . . . . . .1F 111
Rostella Rd. SW17. . . .4F 115
Rostrevor Av. N15 . . . .1B 36
Rostrevor M. SW6 . . . .4B 86
Rostrevor Rd. SW6 . . . .4B 86
SW19 . . . . .5C 114
Rotary St.
SE1 . . . . . .5D 25 (4D 77)
(off Albany St.)
Rothay NW1 . . . . .1E 5
(off Mauritius Rd.)
Rothbury Cotts. SE10. . .5A 82
Rothbury Hall 5A 82

Rothbury Rd. E9 . . . . . 4B 52
Rotheley Ho. E9 . . . . . . 4E 51
(off Balcorne St.)
Rotherfield Ct. N1 . . . . . 4F 49
*(off Rotherfield St.,
not continuous)*
Rotherfield St. N1 . . . . . 4E 49
Rotherham Wlk. SE1 . . . 2D 25
ROTHERHITHE 3E 79
Rotherhithe Bus. Est.
SE16 . . . . 5D 79
Rotherhithe New Rd.
SE16 . . . . 1D 93
Rotherhithe Old Rd.
SE16 . . . . 5F 79
Rotherhithe St. SE16 . . . 3E 79
Rotherhithe Tunnel
SE16 . . . . 2F 79
Rother Ho. SE15 . . . . . . 2D 107
Rotherwick Ho. E1 . . . . 1C 78
(off Thomas More St.)
Rotherwick Rd.
NW11 . . . . 2C 30
Rotherwood Rd.
SW15 . . . . 1F 99
Rothery St. N1 . . . . 5D 49
(off St Marys Path)
Rothesay Ct. SE6 . . . . . 2B 124
SE11 . . . . 2C 90
(off Harleyford St.)
SE12 . . . . 3D 125
Rothley Ct. NW8 . . . . . . 3F 59
(off St John's Wood Rd.)
Rothsay Rd. E7 . . . . 4E 55
Rothsay St.
SE1 . . . . 5D 27 (4A 78)
Rothsay Wlk. E14 . . . . . 5C 80
(off Charnwood Gdns.)
Rothschild St. SE27 . . . 4D 119
Roth Wlk. N7 . . . . 4B 34
Rothwell St. NW1 . . . . . 5B 46
Rotten Row NW3 . . . . . 3E 31
SW1 . . . . 3A 20 (3A 74)
SW7 . . . . 3A 74
Rotterdam Dr. E14 . . . . . 4E 81
Rouel Rd. SE16 . . . . 4C 78
(Dockley Rd.)
SE16 . . . . 5C 78
(Southwark Pk. Rd.)
Roundacre SW19 . . . . . 2F 113
Roundel Cl. SE4 . . . . . . 2B 108
Roundhay Cl. SE23 . . . . 2F 121
Round Hill SE26 . . . . . . 2E 121
(not continuous)
Roundhouse, The 4C 46
(off Chalk Farm Rd.)
Roundtable Rd.
BR1: Brom 3B 124
Roundwood Rd.
NW10 . . . . 3B 42
Rounton Rd. E3 . . . . 3C 66
Roupell Rd. SW2 . . . . . . 1B 118
Roupell St.
SE1 . . . . 2C 24 (2C 76)
Rousden St. NW1 . . . . . 4E 47
Rouse Gdns. SE21 . . . . . 4A 120
Routemaster Cl.
E13 . . . . 2D 69
Routh Rd. SW18 . . . . . . 5A 102

Rover Ho. N1 . . . . 5A 50
(off Mill Row)
Rowallan Rd. SW6 . . . . 3A 86
Rowan Ct. E13 . . . . 1D 69
(off High St.)
SE15 . . . . 3B 92
(off Garnies Cl.)
SW11 . . . . 4B 102
Rowan Ho. SE16 . . . . . . 3F 79
(off Woodland Cres.)
Rowan Lodge W8 . . . . . 4D 73
(off Chantry Sq.)
Rowan Rd. W6 . . . . 5F 71
Rowans Complex N4 . . . 4C 34
Rowan Ter. W6 . . . . 5F 71
Rowan Wlk. E1 . . . . 1E 31
N19 . . . . 4E 33
W10 . . . . 3A 58
Rowberry Cl. SW6 . . . . . 3E 85
Rowcross St. SE1 . . . . . 1B 92
Rowditch La. SW11 . . . . 5C 88
Rowdon Av. NW10 . . . . . 4D 43
Rowe Ho. E9 . . . . 3E 51
Rowe La. E9 . . . . 2E 51
Rowena Cres. SW11 . . . 5A 88
Rowfant Rd. SW17 . . . . 1C 116
Rowhill Rd. E5 . . . . 1D 51
Rowington Cl. W2 . . . . . 4D 59
Rowland Ct. E16 . . . . . . 3B 68
Rowland Gro. SE26 . . . . 3D 121
Rowland Hill Ho.
SE1 . . . . 3D 25 (3D 77)
Rowland Hill St.
NW3 . . . . 2A 46
Rowlands Cl. N6 . . . . . . 1C 32
Rowley Gdns. N4 . . . . . . 2E 35
Rowley Ho. SE8 . . . . 1C 94
(off Watergate St.)
Rowley Rd. N15 . . . . 1E 35
Rowley Way NW8 . . . . . 5D 45
Rowntree Clifford Cl.
E13 . . . . 3C 68
Rowntree Cl. NW6 . . . . . 3C 44
Rowse Cl. E15 . . . . 5E 53
Rowstock Gdns. N7 . . . . 2F 47
Roxburghe Mans.
W8 . . . . 3D 73
(off Kensington Ct.)
Roxburgh Rd. SE27 . . . . 5D 119
Roxby Pl. SW6 . . . . 2C 86
Roxley Rd. SE13 . . . . . . 4D 109
Roxwell NW1 . . . . 3D 47
(off Hartland Rd.)
Roxwell Rd. W12 . . . . . . 3C 70
Roxwell Trad. Pk.
E10 . . . . 2A 38
Royal Academy of Arts
(Burlington House)
. . . . 5F 13 (1E 75)
Royal Academy of Music Mus.
. . . . 4C 4
Royal Air Force Memorial
. . . . 2E 23 (2A 76)
Royal Albert Hall 3F 73
Royal Albert Rdbt.
E16 . . . . 1F 83
(off Royal Albert Way)
Royal Albert Way E16. . 1F 83
Royal Arc. W1 . . . . 5F 13

Royal Av. SW3 . . . . 1B 88
Royal Av. Ho. SW3 . . . . 1B 88
(off Royal Av.)
Royal Belgrave Ho.
SW1 . . . . 5D 75
(off Hugh St.)
Royal Ceremonial Dress
Collection, The 2D 73
(in Kensington Palace)
Royal Cir. SE27 . . . . 3C 118
Royal Cl. N16 . . . . 3A 36
SE8 . . . . 2B 94
SW19 . . . . 3F 113
Royal College of Art . . . 3F 73
Royal College of Music
. . . . 4F 73
Royal College of Obstetricians
& Gynaecologists . . . 3B 60
Royal College of Physicians
. . . . 3D 5 (3D 61)
Royal College of Surgeons
. . . . 2A 16 (5B 62)
Royal Coll. St. NW1 . . . . 4E 47
Royal Connaught Apartments
E16 . . . . 2F 83
(off Connaught Rd.)
Royal Ct. EC3 . . . . 3C 18
(off Finch La.)
SE16 . . . . 4B 80
Royal Courts of Justice
. . . . 3A 16 (5C 62)
Royal Court Theatre . . . 5C 74
(off Sloane Sq.)
Royal Cres. W11 . . . . . . 2F 71
Royal Cres. M. W11 . . . . 2F 71
Royal Duchess M.
SW12 . . . . 5D 103
Royal Exchange
. . . . 3C 18 (5F 63)
Royal Exchange Av.
EC3 . . . . 3C 18
Royal Exchange Bldgs.
EC3 . . . . 3C 18
Royal Festival Hall
. . . . 2A 24 (2B 76)
Royal Fusiliers Mus.
. . . . 5F 19
(in The Tower of London)
Royal Geographical Society
. . . . 3F 73
(off Kensington Gore)
Royal Hill SE10 . . . . 3E 95
Royal Hill Ct. SE10 . . . . 3E 95
(off Greenwich High St.)
Royal Hospital Chelsea Mus.
. . . . 1C 88
Royal Hospital Rd.
SW3 . . . . 2B 88
Royal London Ind. Est.
NW10 . . . . 1A 56
Royal Mews, The
. . . . 5E 21 (4D 75)
Royal M.
SW1 . . . . 5E 21 (4D 75)
Royal Mint Ct.
EC3 . . . . 5F 19 (1B 78)
Royal Mint Pl. E1 . . . . . . 1C 78
Royal Mint St. E1 . . . . . 1B 78
Royal Naval Pl. SE14 . . . 3B 94

Royal Oak Ct. *N1* 1D **11**
    (off Pitfield St.)
Royal Oak Pl. SE22 . . . . 4D **107**
Royal Oak Rd. E8 . . . . 3D **51**
Royal Oak Yd.
  SE1 . . . . 4D **27** (3A **78**)
Royal Observatory Greenwich
  . . . . 3A **96**
Royal Opera Arc.
  SW1 . . . . 1B **22** (2F **75**)
Royal Opera House
  . . . . 3E **15** (3A **62**)
Royal Orchard Cl.
  SW18 . . . . 5A **100**
  SW6 . . . . 3A **86**
Royal Pde. SE3 . . . . 5B **96**
Royal Pde. M. *SE3.* *5B* **96**
    (off Royal Pde.)
Royal Pl. SE10 . . . . 3E **95**
Royal Rd. E16. . . . . 5F **69**
  SE17 . . . . 2D **91**
Royal St.
  SE1 . . . . 5A **24** (4B **76**)
Royal Twr. Lodge *E1* . . . 1C **78**
    (off Cartwright St.)
Royalty Mans. *W1* *3B* **14**
    (off Richmond M.)
Royalty M.
  W1 . . . . 3B **14** (5F **61**)
Royalty Studios *W11* . . . *5A* **58**
    (off Lancaster Rd.)
Royal Veterinary College
  Camden Town. 5F **47**
Royal Victoria Docks
  Watersports Cen. . . 1C **82**
Royal Victoria Patriotic Bldg.
  SW18 . . . . 4F **101**
Royal Victoria Pl.
  E16. . . . . 2D **83**
Royal Victoria Sq.
  E16. . . . . 1D **83**
Royal Victor Pl. E3 . . . . 1F **65**
Royal Westminster Lodge
  SW1 . . . . *5F* **75**
    (off Elverton St.)
Roycroft Cl. SW2 . . . . 1C **118**
Roydon Cl. *SW11* *5B* **88**
    (off Battersea Pk. Rd.)
Royle Bldg. *N1* *1E* **63**
    (off Wenlock Rd.)
Roy Sq. E14 . . . . 1A **80**
Royston Ct. *E13* *5C* **54**
    (off Stopford Rd.)
  SE24 . . . . 4E **105**
  W8 . . . . *2C* **72**
    (off Kensington Chu. St.)
Royston Gdns.
  IG1: Ilf. 1F **41**
Royston Ho. *SE15* 2D **93**
    (off Friary Est.)
Royston Pde. IG1: Ilf. . . 1F **41**
Royston St. E2 . . . . 1E **65**
Rozel Ct. N1. . . . . 5A **50**
Rozel Rd. SW4 . . . . 1E **103**
Rq33 SW18. . . . . 2C **100**
Rubens Gdns. *SE22* . . . *5C* **106**
    (off Lordship La.)
Rubens Pl. SW4 . . . . . . 2A **104**
Rubens St. SE6 . . . . 2B **122**

Ruby St. SE15 . . . . 2D **93**
Ruby Triangle SE15 . . . . 2D **93**
Ruckholt Cl. E10 . . . . . . 5D **39**
Ruckholt Rd. E9 . . . . 1C **52**
  E10 . . . . 1C **52**
Rucklidge Av. NW10 . . 1B **56**
Rucklidge Pas.
  NW10 . . . . *1B* **56**
    (off Rucklidge Av.)
Rudall Cres. NW3 . . . . . . 1F **45**
Rudbeck Ho. *SE15* *3C* **92**
    (off Peckham Pk. Rd.)
Ruddington Cl. E5 . . . . . 1A **52**
Rudge Ho. *SE16* *4C* **78**
    (off Jamaica Rd.)
Rudgwick Ter. NW8 . . . . 5A **46**
Rudloe Rd. SW12 . . . . . 5E **103**
Rudolf Pl. SW8 . . . . 2A **90**
Rudolph Rd. E13 . . . . . . 1B **68**
  NW6 . . . . 1C **58**
Rufford St. N1 . . . . 5A **48**
Rufus Bus. Cen.
  SW18 . . . . 2D **115**
Rufus Ho. *SE1* *5F* **27**
    (off Abbey St.)
Rufus St. N1 . . 2D **11** (2A **64**)
    (off Bishop King's Rd.)
Rugby Rd. W4 . . . . 3A **70**
Rugby St.
  WC1 . . . . 4F **7** (3B **62**)
Rugg St. E14 . . . . 1C **80**
Rugless Ho. *E14.* *3E* **81**
    (off E. Ferry Rd.)
Rugmere *NW1* *4C* **46**
    (off Ferdinand St.)
Ruislip St. SW17 . . . . . 4B **116**
Rumball Ho. *SE5* *3A* **92**
    (off Harris St.)
Rumbold Rd. SW6 . . . . 3D **87**
Rum Cl. E1 . . . . 1E **79**
Rumford Ho. *SE1* *5F* **25**
    (off Tiverton St.)
Rumsey M. N4 . . . . 5D **35**
Rumsey Rd. SW9 . . . . . . 1B **104**
Runacres Ct. SE17 . . . . 1E **91**
Runbury Circ. NW9 . . . . 4A **28**
Runcorn Pl. W11 . . . . . . 1A **72**
Rundell Cres. NW4 . . . . 1D **29**
Rundell Twr. SW8 . . . . . 4B **90**
Runnymede Ct.
  SW15 . . . . 1C **112**
Runnymede Ho. E9 . . . . 1A **52**
Rupack St. SE16. . . . . . . 3E **79**
Rupert Ct.
  W1 . . . . 4B **14** (1F **75**)
Rupert Gdns. SW9 . . . . 5D **91**
Rupert Ho. SE11 . . . . . . 5C **76**
  SW5 . . . . 5C **72**
    (off Nevern Sq.)
Rupert Rd. N19. . . . . 5F **33**
    (not continuous)
  NW6 . . . . 1B **58**
  W4 . . . . 4A **70**
Rupert St.
  W1 . . . . 4B **14** (1F **75**)
Rushbridge Cl. E8 . . . . . 2C **50**
Ruscoe Rd. E16 . . . . 5B **68**
Rusham Rd. SW12 . . . . 4B **102**

Rush Comn. M.
  SW2 . . . . 5B **104**
    (Cotherstone Rd.)
  SW2 . . . . 5A **104**
    (New Pk. Rd.)
Rushcroft Rd. SW2 . . . . 2C **104**
Rushcutters Ct. *SE16.* . . *5A* **80**
    (off Boat Lifter Way)
Rushey Grn. SE6 . . . . . . 5D **109**
Rushey Mead SE4 . . . . . 3C **108**
Rushford Rd. SE4 . . . . . 4B **108**
Rushgrove Pde. NW9 . . 1A **28**
Rush Hill M. *SW11* 1C **102**
    (off Rush Hill Rd.)
Rush Hill Rd. SW11. . . . 1C **102**
Rushmead E2. . . . . 2D **65**
Rushmere Pl. SW19. . . . 5F **113**
Rushmore Cres. E5 . . . . 1F **51**
Rushmore Ho. SW15 . . . 5C **98**
  W14 . . . . *4A* **72**
    (off Russell Rd.)
Rushmore Rd. E5. . . . . . 1E **51**
    (not continuous)
Rusholme Gro.
  SE19 . . . . 5A **120**
Rusholme Rd. SW15 . . . 4F **99**
Rushton Ho. SW8 . . . . . 5F **89**
Rushton St. N1 . . . . 1F **63**
Rushworth St.
  SE1 . . . . 3E **25** (3D **77**)
Ruskin Av. E12 . . . . 3F **55**
Ruskin Cl. NW11 . . . . . . 1D **31**
Ruskin Ct. *SE5* *1F* **105**
    (off Champion Hill)
Ruskin Ho. *SW1* *5F* **75**
    (off Herrick St.)
Ruskin Mans. *W14* *2A* **86**
    (off Queen's Club Gdns.)
Ruskin Pk. Ho. SE5 . . . 1F **105**
Ruskin Wlk. SE24 . . . . 3E **105**
Rusper Cl. NW2 . . . . . . 5E **29**
Rusper Ct. *SW9* *5A* **90**
    (off Clapham Rd.)
Russell Cl. SE7 . . . . 3E **97**
  W4 . . . . 2B **84**
Russell Ct. E10 . . . . 2D **39**
  SE15 . . . . *5D* **93**
    (off Heaton Rd.)
  SW1 . . . . 2A **22**
  SW16 . . . . 5B **118**
  WC1 . . . . 4D **7**
Russell Flint Ho.
  E16 . . . . *2D* **83**
    (off Pankhurst Av.)
Russell Gdns. NW11 . . . 1A **30**
  W14 . . . . 4A **72**
Russell Gdns. M.
  W14 . . . . 3A **72**
Russell Gro. SW9 . . . . . 3C **90**
Russell Ho. E14 . . . . 5C **66**
    (off Saracen St.)
  SW1 . . . . *1E* **89**
    (off Cambridge St.)
Russell Lodge *SE1.* . . . *5B* **26**
    (off Spurgeon St.)
Russell Mans. *WC1* *5E* **7**
    (off Southampton Row)
Russell Pde. NW11 . . . . 1A **30**
    (off Golders Grn. Rd.)

Russell Pl. NW3 . . . . 2A 46
  SE16 . . . . 4A 80
Russell Rd. E10 . . . . 1D 39
  E16 . . . . 5C 68
  N8 . . . . 1F 33
  N15 . . . . 1A 36
  NW9 . . . . 1B 28
  W14 . . . . 4A 72
Russell's Footpath
  SW16 . . . . 5A 118
Russell Sq.
  WC1 . . . . 4D 7 (4A 62)
Russell St.
  WC2 . . . . 4E 15 (1A 76)
Russell's Wharf Flats
  W10 . . . . 3B 58
Russell Yd.
  SW15 . . . . 2A 100
Russel Sq. Mans.
  WC1 . . . . 5E 7
    (off Southampton Row)
Russet Cres. N7 . . . . 2B 48
Russett Way SE13 . . . . 5D 95
Russia Dock Rd.
  SE16 . . . . 2A 80
Russia La. E2 . . . . 1E 65
Russia Row
  EC2 . . . . 3A 18 (5E 63)
Russia Wlk. SE16 . . . . 3A 80
Rusthall Av. W4 . . . . 5A 70
Rustic Wlk. E16 . . . . 5D 69
    (off Lambert Rd.)
Ruston M. W11 . . . . 5A 58
Ruston Rd. SE18 . . . . 4F 83
Ruston St. E3 . . . . 5B 52
Rust Sq. SE5 . . . . 3F 91
Rutford Rd. SW16 . . . . 5A 118
Ruth Ct. E3 . . . . 1A 66
Rutherford Ho. E1 . . . . 3D 65
    (off Brady St.)
Rutherford St. SW1 . . . . . . 5F 75
Ruth Ho. W10 . . . . 3A 58
    (off Kensal Rd.)
Ruthin Cl. NW9 . . . . 1A 28
Ruthin Rd. SE3 . . . . 2C 96
Ruthven St. E9 . . . . 5F 51
Rutland Ct. SE5 . . . . 2F 105
  SW7 . . . . 3A 74
    (off Rutland Gdns.)
Rutland Gdns. N4 . . . . 1D 35
  SW7 . . . . 3A 74
Rutland Gdns. M.
  SW7 . . . . 3A 74
Rutland Ga. SW7 . . . . 3A 74
Rutland Ga. M.
  SW7 . . . . 3A 74
    (off Rutland Ga.)
Rutland Gro. W6 . . . . 1D 85
Rutland Ho. W8 . . . . 4D 73
    (off Marloes Rd.)
Rutland M. NW8 . . . . 5D 45
Rutland M. E. SW7 . . . . . . 4A 74
    (off Ennismore St.)
Rutland M. Sth. SW7 . . . . 4A 74
    (off Ennismore St.)
Rutland M. W. SW7 . . . . . . 4A 74
    (off Rutland Ga.)
Rutland Pk. NW2 . . . . 3E 43
  SE6 . . . . 2B 122

Rutland Pk. Gdns.
  NW2 . . . . 3E 43
    (off Rutland Pk.)
Rutland Pk. Mans.
  NW2 . . . . 3E 43
Rutland Pl.
  EC1 . . . . 5E 9 (3D 63)
Rutland Rd. E7 . . . . 4F 55
  E9 . . . . 5F 51
  E17 . . . . 1C 38
Rutland St. SW7 . . . . 4A 74
Rutland Wlk. SE6 . . . . 2B 122
Rutley Cl. SE17 . . . . 2D 91
Rutt's Ter. SE14 . . . . 4F 93
Ruvigny Gdns. SW15 . . . . . 1F 99
Ryan Cl. SE3 . . . . 2D 111
Rycott Path SE22 . . . . 5C 106
Rycroft Sq. SE3 . . . . 5B 96
Rydal Gdns. NW9 . . . . 1A 28
  SW15 . . . . 5A 112
Rydal Rd. SW16 . . . . 4F 117
Rydal Water
  NW1 . . . . 2F 5 (2E 61)
Rydens Ho. SE9 . . . . 3E 125
Ryder Cl.
  BR1: Brom 5D 125
Ryder Ct. E10 . . . . 4D 39
  SW1 . . . . 1A 22
Ryder Dr. SE16 . . . . 1D 93
Ryder Ho. E1 . . . . 3E 65
    (off Colebert Av.)
Ryder M. E9 . . . . 2E 51
Ryder's Ter. NW8 . . . . 1E 59
Ryder St.
  SW1 . . . . 1A 22 (2E 75)
Ryder Yd.
  SW1 . . . . 1A 22 (2E 75)
Ryde Va. Rd. SW12 . . . . . . 2E 117
Rydons Cl. SE9 . . . . 1F 111
Rydon St. N1 . . . . 5E 49
Rydston Cl. N7 . . . . 4A 48
Ryecotes Mead
  SE21 . . . . 1A 120
Ryecroft Rd. SE13 . . . . 3E 109
  SW16 . . . . 5C 118
Ryecroft St. SW6 . . . . 4D 87
Ryedale SE22 . . . . 4D 107
Ryefield Path SW15 . . . . . 1C 112
Ryefield Rd. SE19 . . . . 5E 119
Rye Hill Pk. SE15 . . . . 2E 107
Rye Ho. SE16 . . . . 3E 79
    (off Swan Rd.)
  SW1 . . . . 1D 89
    (off Ebury Bri. Rd.)
Ryelands Cres.
  SE12 . . . . 4E 111
Rye La. SE15 . . . . 4C 92
Rye Pas. SE15 . . . . 1C 106
Rye Rd. SE15 . . . . 2F 107
Rye Wlk. SW15 . . . . 3F 99
Ryfold Rd. SW19 . . . . 3C 114
Rylandes Rd. NW2 . . . . . . 5C 28
Ryland Rd. NW5 . . . . 3D 47
Rylett Cres. W12 . . . . 3B 70
Rylett Rd. W12 . . . . 3B 70
Rylston Rd. SW6 . . . . 2B 86
Rymer St. SE24 . . . . 4D 105
Rysbrack St.
  SW3 . . . . 5A 20 (4B 74)

S

Saatchi Gallery 1B 88
Sabbarton St. E16 . . . . 5B 68
Sabella Ct. E3 . . . . 1B 66
Sabine Rd. SW11 . . . . 1B 102
Sable St. N1 . . . . 4D 49
Sach Rd. E5 . . . . 4D 37
Sackville Ho. SW16 . . . . . . 3A 118
Sackville St.
  W1 . . . . 5A 14 (1E 75)
Saddlers M. SW8 . . . . 4A 90
Saddle Yd.
  W1 . . . . 1D 21 (2D 75)
Sadler Ho. EC1 . . . . 1C 8
    (off Spa Grn. Est.)
Sadler's Wells Theatre
. . . . 1C 8
Saffron Av. E14 . . . . 1F 81
Saffron Cl. NW11 . . . . 1B 30
Saffron Ct. E15 . . . . 2A 54
    (off Maryland Pk.)
Saffron Hill
  EC1 . . . . 5C 8 (4C 62)
Saffron St.
  EC1 . . . . 5C 8 (4C 62)
Saffron Wharf SE1 . . . . . . 3B 78
    (off Shad Thames)
Sage M. SE22 . . . . 3B 106
Sage St. E1. . . . . 1E 79
Sage Way WC1 . . . . 2F 7
Saigasso Cl. E16 . . . . 5F 69
Sailacre Ho. SE10 . . . . 1B 96
    (off Woolwich Rd.)
Sail Ct. E14 . . . . 1F 81
    (off Newport Av.)
Sailmakers Ct. SW6 . . . . . . 5E 87
Sail St. SE11 . . . . 5B 76
Sainfoin Rd. SW17 . . . . . . 2C 116
Sainsbury Rd. SE19 . . . . . 5A 120
Sainsbury Wing 5C 14
    (in National Gallery)
St Agnes Cl. E9 . . . . 5E 51
St Agnes Pl. SE11 . . . . 2C 90
St Agnes Well EC1 . . . . 3C 10
St Aidan's Rd. SE22 . . . . . 4D 107
St Alban's Av. W4 . . . . 4A 70
St Albans Cl. NW11 . . . . . . 3C 30
St Albans Ct. EC2 . . . . 1A 18
St Alban's Gro. W8 . . . . . . 4D 73
St Alban's La. NW11 . . . . . 3C 30
St Albans Mans. W8 . . . . . 4D 73
    (off Kensington Ct. Pl.)
St Alban's Pl. N1 . . . . 5D 49
St Albans Rd. NW5 . . . . . . 5C 32
  NW10 . . . . 5A 42
St Alban's St.
  SW1 . . . . 5B 14 (1F 75)
    (not continuous)
St Albans Studios
  W8 . . . . 4D 73
    (off St Albans Gro.)
St Albans Ter. W6 . . . . 2A 86
St Albans Vs. NW5 . . . . . . 5C 32
St Alfege Pas. SE10 . . . . . . 2E 95
St Alfege Rd. SE7 . . . . 2F 97
St Alphage Gdn.
  EC2 . . . . 1A 18 (4E 63)

St Alphage Highwalk
EC2 . . . . 1A **18**
St Alphage Ho. EC2 . . 1B **18**
St Alphonsus Rd.
SW4 . . . . 2E **103**
St Amunds Cl. SE6 . . . . 4C **122**
St Andrews Chambers
W1 . . . . *1A 14*
(off Wells St.)
St Andrews Cl. NW2 . . 5D **29**
SE16 . . . . 1D **93**
St Andrew's Ct.
SW18 . . . . 2E **115**
St Andrew's Gro. N16 . . 3F **35**
St Andrew's Hill
EC4 . . . . 4E **17** (1D **77**)
(not continuous)
St Andrews Mans.
W1 . . . . *1B 12*
(off Dorset St.)
W14 . . . . *2A 86*
(off St Andrews Rd.)
St Andrews M. N16 . . . 3A **36**
SE3 . . . . 3C **96**
SW12 . . . . 1F **117**
St Andrew's Pl.
NW1 . . . . 3E **5** (3D **61**)
St Andrews Rd. E11 . . 1A **40**
E12 . . . . 4F **41**
E13 . . . . 2D **69**
NW10 . . . . 3D **43**
NW11 . . . . 1B **30**
W3 . . . . 1A **70**
W14 . . . . 2A **86**
St Andrews Sq. W11 . . 5A **58**
St Andrew St.
EC1 . . . . 1C **16** (4C **62**)
EC4 . . . . 4C **62**
St Andrews Way E3 . . 3D **67**
St Andrew's Wharf
SE1 . . . . 3B **78**
St Anne's Cl. N6 . . . . . 5C **32**
St Anne's Ct. NW6 . . . 5A **44**
W1 . . . . 3B **14** (5F **61**)
St Anne's Flats *NW1* . . *1B 6*
(off Doric Way)
St Anne's Pas. E14 . . 5B **66**
St Anne's Rd. E11 . . . . 4F **39**
St Anne's Row E14 . . . 5B **66**
St Anne's Trad. Est.
E14 . . . . *5B 66*
(off St Anne's Row)
St Anne St. E14 . . . . . 5B **66**
St Ann's Cres.
SW18 . . . . 4D **101**
St Ann's Gdns. NW5 . . 3C **46**
St Ann's Hill SW18 . . 3D **101**
St Ann's Ho. *WC1* *2B 8*
(off Margery St.)
St Ann's La.
SW1 . . . . . . 5C **22** (4F **75**)
St Ann's Pk. Rd.
SW18 . . . . 4E **101**
St Ann's Pas. SW13 . . 1A **98**
St Ann's Rd. N15 . . . . 1D **35**
SW13 . . . . 5B **84**
W11 . . . . 1F **71**
St Ann's St.
SW1 . . . . . . 5C **22** (4F **75**)

St Ann's Ter. NW8 . . . . 1F **59**
St Ann's Vs. W11 . . . . 2F **71**
St Anselms Ct.
SW16 . . . . 5A **118**
St Anselm's Pl.
W1 . . . . 4D **13** (1D **75**)
St Anthony's Cl. E1 . . 2C **78**
SW17 . . . . 2A **116**
St Anthony's Ct.
SW17 . . . . 2C **116**
St Anthony's Flats
NW1 . . . . *1B 6*
(off Aldenham St.)
St Antony's Rd. E7 . . . 4D **55**
St Asaph Rd. SE4 . . . . 1F **107**
St Aubins Ct. N1 . . . . . 5F **49**
St Aubyn's Av.
SW19 . . . . 5B **114**
St Augustine's Ho.
NW1 . . . . *1B 6*
(off Werrington St.)
St Augustine's Mans.
SW1 . . . . *5E 75*
(off Bloomburg St.)
St Augustine's Path
N5 . . . . 1E **49**
St Augustine's Rd.
NW1 . . . . 4F **47**
St Austell Rd. SE13 . . 5E **95**
St Barnabas Cl.
SE22 . . . . 3A **106**
St Barnabas Rd. E17 . . 1C **38**
St Barnabas St. SW1 . . 1C **88**
St Barnabas Ter. E9 . . 2F **51**
St Barnabas Vs.
SW8 . . . . 4A **90**
St Bartholomew's Cl.
SE26 . . . . 4D **121**
**St Bartholomew's
Hospital Mus.** 1E **17**
St Benedict's Cl.
SW17 . . . . 5C **116**
St Benet's Cl.
SW17 . . . . 2A **116**
St Benet's Pl.
EC3 . . . . 4C **18** (1F **77**)
St Bernard's Cl.
SE27 . . . . 4F **119**
St Bernards Ho. *E14* . . *4E 81*
(off Galbraith St.)
St Bernard's Rd. E6 . . 5F **55**
St Botolph Row
EC3 . . . . 3F **19** (5B **64**)
St Botolph St.
EC3 . . . . 2F **19** (5B **64**)
St Brelades Ct. N1 . . . 5A **50**
St Bride's Av. EC4 . . . 3D **17**
St Bride's Crypt Mus.
. . . . 3D **17**
(in St Bride's)
St Bride's Pas. EC4 . . 3D **17**
St Bride St.
EC4 . . . . 2D **17** (5D **63**)
St Catherine's Cl.
SW17 . . . . 2A **116**
St Catherine's Ct.
W4 . . . . 4A **70**
St Catherine's Dr.
SE14 . . . . 5F **93**

St Catherines M.
SW3 . . . . 5B **74**
St Catherines Twr.
E10 . . . . 2D **39**
St Cecelia's Pl. SE3 . . . 1C **96**
St Chad's Pl.
WC1 . . . . 1E **7** (2A **62**)
St Chad's St.
WC1 . . . . 1E **7** (2A **62**)
(not continuous)
St Charles Pl. W10 . . . 4A **58**
St Charles Sq. W10 . . 4F **57**
St Christopher's Ho.
NW1 . . . . *1E 61*
(off Bridgeway St.)
St Christopher's Pl.
W1 . . . . 2C **12** (5C **60**)
St Clair Rd. E13 . . . . . 1D **69**
St Clare St.
EC3 . . . . 3F **19** (5B **64**)
N7 . . . . 3B **48**
SE14 . . . . 2F **93**
(off Myers La.)
W11 . . . . *1F 71*
(off Stoneleigh St.)
St Clement's Hgts.
SE26 . . . . 3C **120**
St Clements Ho. *E1* . . . *1F 19*
(off Leyden St.)
St Clement's La.
WC2 . . . . 3F **15** (5B **62**)
St Clements Mans.
SW6 . . . . *2F 85*
(off Lillie Rd.)
St Clements St. N7 . . . 3C **48**
St Clements Yd.
SE22 . . . . 2B **106**
St Cloud Rd. SE27 . . . 4E **119**
St Columb's Ho.
W10 . . . . *4A 58*
(off Blagrove Rd.)
St Crispin's Cl. NW3 . . 1A **46**
St Cross St.
EC1 . . . . 5C **8** (4C **62**)
St Cuthbert's Rd.
NW2 . . . . 3B **44**
St Cyprian's St.
SW17 . . . . 4B **116**
St Davids Cl. *SE16* . . . *1D 93*
(off Masters Dr.)
St Davids M. *E3* *2A 66*
(off Morgan St.)
St David's Pl. NW4 . . . 2D **29**
St Davids Sq. E14 . . . 1D **95**
St Denis Rd. SE27 . . . 4F **119**
St Dionis Rd. E12 . . . . 5F **41**
SW6 . . . . 5B **86**
St Donatt's Rd. SE14 . . 4B **94**
St Dunstan's All. EC3 . . 4D **19**
St Dunstan's Av. W3 . . 1A **70**
St Dunstans Ct.
EC4 . . . . 3C **16** (5C **62**)
St Dunstans Hill
EC3 . . . . 5D **19** (1A **78**)
St Dunstan's La.
EC3 . . . . 5D **19** (1A **78**)
St Dunstan's Rd. E7 . . 3D **55**
W6 . . . . 1F **85**

St Edmund's Cl.
NW8 . . . . 5B 46
SW17 . . . . 2A 116
St Edmund's Cl. NW8 . . . 5B 46
(off St Edmund's Ter.)
St Edmunds Sq.
SW13 . . . . 2E 85
St Edmund's Ter.
NW8 . . . . 5A 46
St Edward's Cl.
NW11 . . . . 1C 30
St Edwards Cl. E10 . . . . 2D 39
NW11 . . . . 1C 30
St Elizabeth Ct. E10 . . . 2D 39
St Elmo Rd. W12 . . . . . . 2B 70
(not continuous)
St Elmos Rd. SE16 . . . . . 3A 80
St Ermin's Hill SW1 . . . . 5B 22
St Ervan's Rd. W10 . . . . 4B 58
St Eugene Ct. NW6 . . . . 5A 44
(off Salusbury Rd.)
St Faith's Rd. SE21 . . . 1D 119
St Fillans Rd. SE6 . . . . 1E 123
St Francis' Ho.
NW1 . . . . 1F 61
(off Bridgeway St.)
St Francis Rd. SE22 . . . 2A 106
St Frideswide's M.
E14 . . . . 5E 67
St Gabriel's Cl. E11 . . . . 4D 41
E14 . . . . 4D 67
St Gabriels Mnr. SE5 . . . 4D 91
(off Cormont Rd.)
St Gabriels Rd. NW2 . . . 2F 43
St George's Av. E7 . . . . 4D 55
N7 . . . . 1F 47
St George's Bldgs.
SE1 . . . . 4D 77
(off St George's Rd.)
St George's Cathedral
. . . . 1E 5 (2D 61)
St George's Cir.
SE1 . . . . 5D 25 (4D 77)
St George's Cl.
NW11 . . . . 1B 30
SW8 . . . . 4E 89
St Georges Ct.
EC4 . . . . 2D 17 (5D 63)
SW1 . . . . 1E 89
(off St George's Dr.)
SW3 . . . . 5A 74
(off Brompton Rd.)
SW7 . . . . 5A 74
(off South Ter.)
SW15 . . . . 2B 100
W8 . . . . 4E 73
St George's Dr. SW1 . . . 5D 75
ST GEORGE'S FIELD . . . 1A 74
St George's Flds. W2 . . 5A 60
St George's Gro.
SW17 . . . . 3F 115
St Georges Ho. NW1 . . . 1F 61
(off Bridgeway Av.)
SW11 . . . . 4C 88
(off Charlotte Despard Av.)
St George's La. EC3 . . . 4C 18
St George's Mans.
SW1 . . . . 1F 89
(off Causton St.)

St George's M. NW1 . . . 4B 46
SE1 . . . . 5C 24
SE8 . . . . 5B 80
St Georges Pde.
SE6 . . . . 2B 122
St George's Path
SE4 . . . . 2C 108
(off Adelaide St.)
St George's RC Cathedral
. . . . 5C 24 (4C 76)
St George's Rd. E7 . . . . 4D 55
E10 . . . . 5E 39
NW11 . . . . 1B 30
SE1 . . . . 5C 24 (4C 76)
W4 . . . . 3A 70
St Georges Sq. E7 . . . . 4D 55
E14 . . . . 1A 80
SE8 . . . . 5B 80
(not continuous)
SW1 . . . . 1F 89
St George's Sq. M.
SW1 . . . . 1F 89
St George's Ter. E6 . . . . 2F 69
(off Masterman Rd.)
NW1 . . . . 4B 46
SE15 . . . . 3C 92
(off Peckham Hill St.)
St George's Theatre . . . 1F 47
St George St.
W1 . . . . 3E 13 (1D 75)
St George's Way
SE15 . . . . 2A 92
St George's Wharf
SE1 . . . . 3F 27
(off Shad Thames)
St George Wharf
SW8 . . . . 2A 90
St Gerards Cl. SW4 . . . 3E 103
St German's Pl.
SE3 . . . . 4C 96
St German's Rd.
SE23 . . . . 1A 122
St Giles Cir.
W1 . . . . 2C 14 (5F 61)
St Giles Ct. WC2 . . . . . 2D 15
St Giles High St.
WC2 . . . . 2C 14 (5F 61)
St Giles Pas. WC2 . . . . 3C 14
St Giles Rd. SE5 . . . . . 3A 92
St Giles Ter. EC2 . . . . . 1A 18
(off Beech St.)
St Giles Twr. SE5 . . . . . 4A 92
(off Gables Cl.)
St Gilles Ho. E2 . . . . . . 1F 65
(off Mace St.)
St Gothard Rd.
SE27 . . . . 4F 119
(not continuous)
St Helena Ho. WC1 . . . . 2B 8
(off Margery St.)
St Helena Rd. SE16 . . . 5F 79
St Helena St.
WC1 . . . . 2B 8 (2C 62)
St Helen's Gdns.
W10 . . . . 4F 57
St Helen's Pl.
EC3 . . . . 2D 19 (5A 64)
St Helier Ct. N1 . . . . . . 5A 50
(off De Beauvoir Est.)

St Helier Ct. SE16 . . . . . 3F 79
(off Poolmans St.)
St Helier's Rd. E10 . . . . 1E 39
St Hilda's NW6 . . . . 4F 43
SW17 . . . . 2A 116
St Hilda's Rd. SW13 . . . 2D 85
St Hilda's Wharf E1 . . . . 2E 79
(off Wapping High St.)
St Hubert's Ho. E14 . . . 4C 80
(off Janet St.)
St Hughes Cl.
SW17 . . . . 2A 116
St James SE14 . . . . 4A 94
St James App.
EC2 . . . . 4D 11 (3A 64)
St James Ct. E2 . . . . . . 2C 64
(off Bethnal Grn. Rd.)
E12 . . . . 4E 41
SE3 . . . . 4D 97
SW1 . . . . 5A 22 (4E 75)
St James Gro. SW11 . . . 5B 88
St James Ind. M.
SE1 . . . . 1C 92
St James Mans.
NW6 . . . . 4C 44
(off West End La.)
SE1 . . . . 5B 24
(off Kennington Rd.)
St James M. E14 . . . . . . 4E 81
E17 . . . . 1A 38
(off St James's St.)
St James Residences
W1 . . . . 4B 14
(off Brewer St.)
St James' Rd. E15 . . . . . 2B 54
ST JAMES'S . . . 1B 22 (2F 75)
St James's
SW1 . . . . 1A 22 (2E 75)
St James's Av. E2 . . . . . 1E 65
St James's Chambers
SW1 . . . . 1A 22
(off Jermyn St.)
St James's Cl. NW8 . . . . 5B 46
(off St James's Ter. M.)
SW17 . . . . 2B 116
St James's Cres.
SW9 . . . . 1C 104
St James's Dr.
SW17 . . . . 1B 116
St James's Gdns.
W11 . . . . 2A 72
(not continuous)
St James's Mkt.
SW1 . . . . 5B 14 (1F 75)
St James's Palace
. . . . 2A 22 (3E 75)
St James's Pk.
. . . . 3B 22 (3F 75)
St James's Pas. EC3 . . . 3E 19
St James's Pl.
SW1 . . . . 2F 21 (2E 75)
St James's Rd. SE1 . . . . 2C 92
SE16 . . . . 4C 78
St James's Sq.
SW1 . . . . 1A 22 (2E 75)
St James's St. E17 . . . . . 1A 38
SW1 . . . . 1F 21 (2E 75)
St James's Ter. NW8 . . . 5B 46
(off Prince Albert Rd.)

St James's Ter. M.
NW8 . . . . 5B 46
St James's St. W6 . . . . 1E 85
St James's Wlk.
EC1 . . . . 3D 9 (3D 63)
St James Ter.
SW12 . . . . 1C 116
ST JOHNS 5C 94
St John's Av. NW10 . . 5B 42
SW15 . . . . 3F 99
St Johns Chu. Rd. E9 . . 2E 51
St John's Cl. SW6 . . . . 3C 86
St John's Ct. E1 . . . 2D 79
(off Scandrett St.)
N4 . . . . 4D 35
N5 . . . . 1D 49
SE13 . . . . 5E 95
W6 . . . . 5D 71
(off Glenthorne Rd.)
St John's Cres.
SW9 . . . . 1C 104
St Johns Dr. SW18 . . 1D 115
St John's Est. N1 . . . . 1F 63
SE1 . . . . 3F 27
St John's Gdns. W11 . . 1A 72
St John's Gate 4D 9
St John's Gro. N19 . . . 4E 33
SW13 . . . . 5B 84
St John's Hill SW11 . . 3F 101
St John's Hill Gro.
SW11 . . . . 2F 101
St Johns Ho. E14 . . . 5E 81
(off Pier St.)
SE17 . . . . 2F 91
(off Lytham St.)
St John's La.
EC1 . . . . 4D 9 (3D 63)
St John's Lodge NW3 . . 4A 46
(off King Henry's Rd.)
St John's M. W11 . . . . 5C 58
St John's Pk. SE3 . . . . 3B 96
St John's Pk. Mans.
N19 . . . . 5E 33
St John's Path EC1 . . . 4D 9
St Johns Pathway
SE23 . . . . 1E 121
St John's Pl.
EC1 . . . . 4D 9 (3D 63)
St John's Rd. E16 . . . . 5C 68
N15 . . . . 1A 36
NW11 . . . . 1B 30
SW11 . . . . 2A 102
St John's Sq.
EC1 . . . . 4D 9 (3D 63)
St John's Ter. E7 . . . . 3D 55
SW15 . . . . 3A 112
(off Kingston Va.)
W10 . . . . 3F 57
St John St.
EC1 . . . . 1C 8 (1C 62)
St John's Va. SE8 . . . . 5C 94
St John's Vs. N19 . . . . 4F 33
W8 . . . . 4D 73
(off St Mary's Pl.)
St John's Way N19 . . . 4E 33
ST JOHN'S WOOD 1F 59
St John's Wood Cl.
NW8 . . . . 2F 59
(off St John's Wood Rd.)

St John's Wood High St.
NW8 . . . . 1F 59
St John's Wood Pk.
NW8 . . . . 5F 45
St John's Wood Rd.
NW8 . . . . 3F 59
St John's Wood Ter.
NW8 . . . . 1F 59
St Josephs Almshouses
W6 . . . . 5F 71
(off Brook Grn.)
St Joseph's Cl. W10 . . 4A 58
St Joseph's College
Sports Cen. 5D 119
St Joseph's Cotts.
SW3 . . . . 5B 74
(off Cadogan St.)
St Josephs Ct. SE7 . . 2D 97
St Joseph's Flats NW1 . . 1B 6
(off Drummond Cres.)
St Joseph's Ho. W6 . . . 5F 71
(off Brook Grn.)
St Joseph's St. SW8 . . 4D 89
St Joseph's Va. SE3 . . 1F 109
St Jude's Rd. E2 . . . . 1D 65
St Jude St. N16 . . . . . 2A 50
St Julian's Cl.
SW16 . . . . 4C 118
St Julian's Farm Rd.
SE27 . . . . 4C 118
St Julian's Rd. NW6 . . 5C 44
St Katharine Docks
. . . . 5F 19 (2C 78)
St Katharine's Pct.
NW1 . . . . 1D 61
St Katharine's Way
E1 . . . . 1F 27 (2B 78)
(not continuous)
St Katherine's Row
EC3 . . . . 4E 19
St Katherines Wlk.
W11 . . . . 2F 71
(off St Ann's Rd.)
St Kilda's Rd. N16 . . . 3F 35
St Kitts Ter. SE19 . . . 5A 120
St Laurence Cl. NW6 . . 5F 43
St Lawrence Cotts.
E14 . . . . 2E 81
(off St Lawrence St.)
St Lawrence Ct. N1 . . . 4F 49
St Lawrence Ho. SE1 . . 5E 27
(off Purbrook St.)
St Lawrence St. E14 . . 2E 81
St Lawrence Ter.
W10 . . . . 4A 58
St Lawrence Way
SW9 . . . . 4C 90
St Leonard M. N1 . . . 1A 64
(off Hoxton St.)
St Leonard's Ct. N1 . . 1C 10
St Leonard's Rd. E14 . . 4D 67
(not continuous)
NW10 . . . . 3A 56
St Leonards Sq.
NW5 . . . . 3C 46
St Leonard's St. E3 . . 2D 67
St Leonard's Ter.
SW3 . . . . 1B 88
St Loo Av. SW3 . . . . 2A 88

St Loo Ct. SW3 . . . . 2A 88
(off St Loo Av.)
St Louis Rd. SE27 . . . 4F 119
St Lucia Dr. E15 . . . . 5B 54
ST LUKE'S 3A 10 (3E 63)
St Luke's Av. SW4 . . . 2F 103
St Luke's Cl.
EC1 . . . . 3A 10 (3E 63)
St Lukes Ct. E10 . . . 2D 39
(off Capworth St.)
W11 . . . . 5B 58
(off St Luke's Rd.)
St Luke's Est.
EC1 . . . . 2B 10 (2F 63)
St Luke's M. W11 . . . 5B 58
St Luke's Rd. W11 . . . 4B 58
St Luke's Sq. E16 . . . 5B 68
St Luke's St. SW3 . . . 1A 88
St Luke's Yd. W9 . . . . 1B 58
(not continuous)
St Margarets Rd.
EC2 . . . . 5F 63
St Margarets Ct.
SE1 . . . . 2A 26 (2E 77)
SW15 . . . . 2D 99
St Margaret's Cres.
SW15 . . . . 3D 99
St Margaret's Gro.
E11 . . . . 5B 40
St Margaret's La.
W8 . . . . 4D 73
St Margaret's Pas.
SE13 . . . . 1A 110
(not continuous)
St Margarets Rd. E12 . . 4E 41
NW10 . . . . 2E 57
SE4 . . . . 2B 108
St Margaret St.
SW1 . . . . 4D 23 (3A 76)
St Marks Cl. SE10 . . . 3E 95
SW6 . . . . 4C 86
St Marks Ct. E10 . . . 2D 39
(off Capworth St.)
NW8 . . . . 1E 59
(off Abercorn Pl.)
St Mark's Cres. NW1 . . 5C 46
St Mark's Gro. SW10 . . 3D 87
St Marks Ho. SE17 . . 2F 91
(off Lytham St.)
St Marks Ind. Est.
E16 . . . . 2F 83
St Mark's Pl. SW19 . . 5B 114
W11 . . . . 5A 58
St Mark's Ri. E8 . . . . 2B 50
St Mark's Rd. W10 . . . 4F 57
St Mark's Sq. NW1 . . 5C 46
St Mark St. E1 . . . . . 5B 64
St Mark's Vs. N4 . . . 4B 34
(off Moray Rd.)
St Martin-in-the-Fields Church
. . . . 5D 15
(off St Martin's La.)
St Martin's Almshouses
NW1 . . . . 5E 47
St Martin's Av. E6 . . . 1F 69
St Martin's Cl. NW1 . . 5E 47
St Martins Ct. EC4 . . 2F 17
(off Paternoster Row)

St Martins Ct. *N1* 5A **50**
  (off De Beauvoir Est.)
WC2 . . . . 4D **15** (1A **76**)
St Martins Est. SW2 . . . 1C **118**
St Martin's La.
WC2 . . . . 4D **15** (1A **76**)
St Martin's le-Grand
EC1 . . . . 2F **17** (5E **63**)
St Martin's Pl.
WC2 . . . . 5D **15** (1A **76**)
St Martin's Rd.
SW9 . . . . 5B **90**
St Martin's St.
WC2 . . . . 5C **14** (1F **75**)
  (not continuous)
St Martin's Theatre 4D **15**
  (off West St.)
St Martins Way
SW17 . . . . 3E **115**
St Mary Abbot's Ct.
W14 . . . . 4B **72**
  (off Warwick Gdns.)
St Mary Abbot's Pl.
W8 . . . . 4B **72**
St Mary Abbot's Ter.
W14 . . . . 4B **72**
St Mary at Hill
EC3 . . . . 5D **19** (1A **78**)
St Mary Axe
EC3 . . . . 3D **19** (5A **64**)
St Marychurch St.
SE16 . . . . 3E **79**
St Mary Graces Ct.
E1 . . . . 1B **78**
St Marylebone Cl.
NW10 . . . . 5A **42**
St Mary le-Park Ct.
SW11 . . . . 3A **88**
  (off Parkgate Rd.)
St Mary Newington Cl.
SE17 . . . . 1A **92**
  (off Surrey Sq.)
St Mary's Av. E11 . . . . . 2D **41**
St Mary's Ct. SE7 . . . . . 3F **97**
W6 . . . . 4B **70**
St Mary's Est. SE16 . . . . 3E **79**
  (off St Marychurch St.)
St Mary's Flats NW1 . . . 1B **6**
  (off Drummond Cres.)
St Mary's Gdns.
SE11 . . . . 5C **76**
St Mary's Ga. W8 . . . . . 4D **73**
St Mary's Gro. N1 . . . . . 3D **49**
SW13 . . . . 1D **99**
St Mary's Ho. *N1* 5D **49**
  (off St Mary's Path)
St Mary's Mans. W2 . . . . 4F **59**
St Mary's M. NW6 . . . . . 4D **45**
St Mary's Path *E1* 5C **64**
  (off Adler St.)
N1 . . . . 5D **49**
St Mary's Pl. W8 . . . . . . 4D **73**
St Mary's Rd. E10 . . . . . 5E **39**
E13 . . . . 1D **69**
NW10 . . . . 5A **42**
NW11 . . . . 2A **30**
SE15 . . . . 4E **93**
SW19 . . . . 5A **114**
St Mary's Sq. W2 . . . . . 4F **59**

St Mary's Ter. W2 . . . . . 4F **59**
St Mary's Twr. EC1 . . . . 4A **10**
  (off Fortune St.)
St Mary's Wlk. SE11 . . . 5C **76**
St Matthews Ct. E10 . . . 2D **39**
SE1 . . . . 4E **77**
  (off Meadow Row)
St Matthews Ho.
SE17 . . . . 2F **91**
  (off Phelp St.)
St Matthew's Lodge
NW1 . . . . 1E **61**
  (off Oakley Sq.)
St Matthew's Rd.
SW2 . . . . 2B **104**
St Matthew's Row E2 . . . 2C **64**
St Matthew St.
SW1 . . . . 5B **22** (4F **75**)
St Maur Rd. SW6 . . . . . 4B **86**
St Michael's All.
EC3 . . . . 3C **18** (5F **63**)
St Michaels Cl. E16 . . . . 4F **69**
St Michaels Ct. *E14* . . . 4E **67**
  (off St Leonards Rd.)
SE1 . . . . 4A **26**
  (off Trinity St.)
St Michael's Flats
NW1 . . . . 1B **6**
  (off Aldenham St.)
St Michael's Gdns.
W10 . . . . 4A **58**
St Michaels M. SW1 . . . 5C **74**
St Michael's Rd.
NW2 . . . . 1E **43**
SW9 . . . . 5B **90**
St Michael's St. W2 . . . . 5F **59**
St Michaels Ter. *N6* . . . 3C **32**
  (off South Gro.)
St Mildred's Ct.
EC2 . . . . 3B **18** (5F **63**)
St Mildreds Rd.
SE6 . . . . 5A **110**
SE12 . . . . 5A **110**
St Nicholas' Flats
NW1 . . . . 1B **6**
  (off Werrington St.)
St Nicholas Glebe
SW17 . . . . 5C **116**
St Nicholas Ho. *SE8* . . . 2C **94**
  (off Deptford Grn.)
St Nicholas St. SE8 . . . . 4B **94**
St Norbert Grn. SE4 . . . 2A **108**
St Norbert Rd. SE4 . . . . 3F **107**
St Olaf Ho. SE1 . . . . . . 1C **26**
St Olaf's Rd. SW6 . . . . . 3A **86**
St Olaf Stairs SE1 . . . . . 1C **26**
St Olave's Ct.
EC2 . . . . 3B **18** (5F **63**)
St Olave's Est.
SE1 . . . . 3E **27** (3A **78**)
St Olave's Gdns.
SE11 . . . . 5C **76**
St Olaves Ho. *SE11* . . . 5C **76**
  (off Walnut Tree Wlk.)
St Olave's Mans.
SE11 . . . . 5C **76**
  (off Walnut Tree Wlk.)
St Olave's Ter. SE1 . . . . 3E **27**
St Olav's Sq. SE16 . . . . 3E **79**

St Oswald's Pl. SE11 . . . 1B **90**
St Oswalds Studios
SW6 . . . . 2C **86**
  (off Sedlescombe Rd.)
St Oswulf St. SW1 . . . . 5F **75**
St Owen Ho. *SE1* 5F **27**
  (off Fendall St.)
ST PANCRAS . . . 2E **7** (3B **62**)
St Pancras Commercial Cen.
NW1 . . . . 5E **47**
  (off Pratt St.)
St Pancras Way NW1 . . . 4E **47**
St Paul's All. EC4 . . . . . 3E **17**
  (off St Paul's Chyd.)
St Paul's Arts Cen. 5C **80**
  (off Westferry Rd.)
St Paul's Av. NW2 . . . . . 3D **43**
SE16 . . . . 2F **79**
St Paul's Bldgs. EC1 . . . 3E **9**
  (off Dallington St.)
St Paul's Cathedral
. . . . 3F **17** (5E **63**)
St Paul's Chyd.
EC4 . . . . 3E **17** (5D **63**)
  (not continuous)
St Pauls Cl. SE7 . . . . . . 1F **97**
St Pauls Ct. SW4 . . . . . 3F **103**
St Pauls Courtyard
SE8 . . . . 3C **94**
  (off Crossfield St.)
St Paul's Cres. NW1 . . . 4F **47**
  (not continuous)
St Paul's Dr. E15 . . . . . 2F **53**
St Paul's M. NW1 . . . . . 4F **47**
St Paul's Pl. N1 . . . . . . 3F **49**
St Paul's Rd. N1 . . . . . . 3D **49**
St Paul's Shrubbery
N1 . . . . 3F **49**
St Paul's Studios
W14 . . . . 1A **86**
  (off Talgarth Rd.)
St Pauls Ter. SE17 . . . . 2D **91**
St Pauls Twr. *E10* 2D **39**
  (off Beaumont Rd.)
St Paul St. N1 . . . . 5E **49**
  (not continuous)
St Pauls Vw. Apartments
EC1 . . . . 2B **8**
  (off Amwell St.)
St Pauls Way E3 . . . . . . 4B **66**
St Peter's All. EC3 . . . . 3C **18**
  (off Cornhill)
St Peter's Av. E2 . . . . . 1C **64**
St Petersburgh M.
W2 . . . . 1D **73**
St Petersburgh Pl.
W2 . . . . 1D **73**
St Peter's Cen. E1 . . . . 2D **79**
  (off Reardon St.)
St Peter's Chu. Ct.
N1 . . . . 5D **49**
  (off St Peter's St.)
St Peter's Cl. E2 . . . . . 1C **64**
SW17 . . . . 2A **116**
St Peters Cl. NW4 . . . . . 1E **29**
SE12 . . . . 3B **110**
St Peter's Gdns.
SE27 . . . . 3C **118**
St Peter's Gro. W6 . . . . 5C **70**

St Peters Ho. SE17 . . . . . 2F 91
   WC1 . . . . 2E 7
   (off Regent Sq.)
St Peters M. N8 . . . . 1C 34
St Peters Pl. W9 . . . . 3D 59
St Peter's Rd. W6 . . . . . . 1C 84
St Peter's Sq. E2 . . . . 1C 64
   W6 . . . . 5B 70
St Peter's St. N1 . . . . 5D 49
St Peter's St. M. N1 . . . . 1D 63
   (off St Peters St.)
St Peter's Ter. SW6 . . . . 3B 86
St Peter's Vs. W6 . . . . . . 5C 70
St Peter's Way N1 . . . . . . 4A 50
St Philip Ho. WC1 . . . . . . 2B 8
   (off Lloyd Baker St.)
St Philip Sq. SW8 . . . . . . 5D 89
St Philip St. E8 . . . . 3C 50
St Philip St. SW8 . . . . . . 5D 89
St Philip's Way N1 . . . . . 5E 49
St Quentin Ho.
   SW18 . . . . 4F 101
St Quintin Av. W10 . . . . . 4E 57
St Quintin Gdns.
   W10 . . . . 4E 57
St Quintin Rd. E13 . . . . . 2D 69
St Regis Hgts. NW3 . . . . 5D 31
St Richard's Ho. NW1 . . . 1B 6
   (off Eversholt St.)
St Rule St. SW8 . . . . 5E 89
St Saviour's Coll.
   SE27 . . . . 4F 119
St Saviour's Est.
   SE1 . . . . 5F 27 (3B 78)
St Saviour's Rd.
   SW2 . . . . 3B 104
St Saviour's Wharf
   SE1 . . . . 3B 78
   (off Shad Thames)
   SE1 . . . . 3F 27
   (off Mill St.)
Saints Cl. SE27 . . . . 4D 119
Saints Dr. E7 . . . . 2F 55
St Silas Pl. NW5 . . . . 3C 46
St Simon's Av.
   SW15 . . . . 3E 99
St Stephen's Av. E17 . . . 1E 39
   W12 . . . . 2D 71
   (not continuous)
St Stephen's Cl. E17 . . . 1D 39
   NW8 . . . . 5A 46
St Stephens Ct. N8 . . . . 1B 34
St Stephen's Cres.
   W2 . . . . 5C 58
St Stephen's Gdns.
   SW15 . . . . 3B 100
   W2 . . . . 5C 58
   (not continuous)
St Stephens Gro.
   SE13 . . . . 1E 109
St Stephens Ho.
   SE17 . . . . 2F 91
   (off Lytham St.)
St Stephen's M. W2 . . . . 4C 58
St Stephens Pde. E7 . . . 4E 55
St Stephen's Rd. E3 . . . . 5A 52
   E6 . . . . 4E 55
   E17 . . . . 1D 39

St Stephen's Row
   EC4 . . . . 3B 18
St Stephen's Ter.
   SW8 . . . . 3B 90
St Stephen's Wlk.
   SW7 . . . . 5E 73
   (off Southwell Gdns.)
St Swithins La.
   EC4 . . . . 4B 18 (1F 77)
St Swithun's Rd.
   SE13 . . . . 4F 109
St Thomas Ct. E10 . . . . 2D 39
   (off Beaumont Rd.)
   NW1 . . . . 4E 47
   (off Wrotham Rd.)
St Thomas Ho. E1 . . . . . 5F 65
   (off W. Arbour St.)
St Thomas Rd. E16 . . . . 5C 68
St Thomas's Gdns.
   NW5 . . . . 3C 46
St Thomas's Pl. E9 . . . . 4E 51
St Thomas's Rd. N4 . . . . 4C 34
   NW10 . . . . 5A 42
St Thomas's Sq. E9 . . . . 4E 51
St Thomas St.
   SE1 . . . . 2C 26 (2F 77)
St Thomas's Way
   SW6 . . . . 3B 86
St Vincent Cl. SE27 . . . 5D 119
St Vincent De Paul Ho.
   E1 . . . . 4E 65
   (off Jubilee St.)
St Vincent Ho. SE1 . . . . 5F 27
   (off Fendall St.)
St Vincent St.
   W1 . . . . 1C 12 (4C 60)
Sala Ho. SE3 . . . . 2D 111
Salamanca Pl. SE1 . . . . 5B 76
Salamanca Sq. SE1 . . . . 5B 76
   (off Salamanca Pl.)
Salamanca St. SE1 . . . . 5B 76
   SE11 . . . . 5B 76
Salcombe Rd. E17 . . . . . 2B 38
   N16 . . . . 2A 50
Salcott Rd. SW11 . . . . . 3A 102
Salehurst Rd. SE4 . . . . 4B 108
Salem Rd. W2 . . . . 1D 73
Sale Pl. W2 . . . . 4A 60
Sale St. E2 . . . . 3C 64
Salford Ho. E14 . . . . 5E 81
   (off Seyssel St.)
Salford Rd. SW2 . . . . . . 1F 117
Salisbury Cl. SE17 . . . . 5F 77
Salisbury Ct.
   EC4 . . . . 3D 17 (5D 63)
   SE16 . . . . 4C 78
   (off Stork's Rd.)
Salisbury Ho. E14 . . . . . 5D 67
   (off Hobday St.)
   EC2 . . . . 1C 18
   (off London Wall)
   N1 . . . . 5D 49
   (off St Mary's Path)
   SW1 . . . . 1F 89
   (off Drummond Ga.)
   SW9 . . . . 3C 90
   (off Cranmer Rd.)
Salisbury Mans. N15 . . . 1D 35
Salisbury M. SW6 . . . . . 3B 86

Salisbury Pas. SW6 . . . . 3B 86
   (off Dawes Rd.)
Salisbury Pavement
   SW6 . . . . 3B 86
   (off Dawes Rd.)
Salisbury Pl. SW9 . . . . . 3D 91
   W1 . . . . 5A 4 (4B 60)
Salisbury Rd. E7 . . . . . . 3C 54
   E10 . . . . 4E 39
   E12 . . . . 2F 55
   E17 . . . . 1E 39
   N4 . . . . 1D 35
Salisbury Sq.
   EC4 . . . . 3C 16 (5C 62)
Salisbury St. NW8 . . . . . 3A 60
Salisbury Ter. SE15 . . . 1E 107
Salisbury Wlk. N19 . . . . 4E 33
Salmen Rd. E13 . . . . . . 1B 68
Salmon La. E14 . . . . . . 5A 66
Salmon M. NW6 . . . . . . 2C 44
Salmon St. E14 . . . . 5B 66
Salomons Rd. E13 . . . . 4E 69
Salop Rd. E17 . . . . 1F 37
Saltcoats Rd. W4 . . . . . 3A 70
Saltdene N4 . . . . 3B 34
Salterford Rd.
   SW17 . . . . 5C 116
Salter Rd. SE16 . . . . . . 2F 79
Salters Ct. EC4 . . . . 3A 18
Salter's Hall Ct. EC4 . . . 4B 18
Salter's Hill SE19 . . . . . 5F 119
Salters Rd. W10 . . . . . . 3F 57
Salters Row N1 . . . . 3F 49
   (off Tilney Gdns.)
Salter St. E14 . . . . 1B 80
   NW10 . . . . 2C 56
Salterton Rd. N7 . . . . . . 5B 34
Saltoun Rd. SW2 . . . . . 2C 104
Saltram Cres. W9 . . . . . 2B 58
Saltwell St. E14 . . . . 1C 80
Salvin Rd. SW15 . . . . . . 1F 99
Salway Pl. E15 . . . . 3F 53
Salway Rd. E15 . . . . 3F 53
Samantha Cl. E17 . . . . . 2B 38
Sam Bartram Cl. SE7 . . . 1E 97
Sambrook Ho. E1 . . . . . 4E 65
   (off Jubilee St.)
   SE11 . . . . 5C 76
   (off Hotspur St.)
Sambruck M. SE6 . . . . 1D 123
Samels Ct. W6 . . . . 1C 84
Samford Ho. N1 . . . . . . 5C 48
   (off Barnsbury Est.)
Samford St. NW8 . . . . . 3F 59
Samira Cl. E17 . . . . 1C 38
Sam Manners Ho.
   SE10 . . . . 1A 96
   (off Tuskar St.)
Sam March Ho. E14 . . . 5F 67
   (off Blair St.)
Sampson Ho.
   SE1 . . . . 1D 25 (2D 77)
Sampson St. E1 . . . . . . 2C 78

Samson St. E13 . . . . 1E 69
Samuda Est. E14 . . . . . . 4E 81
Samuel Cl. E8 . . . . 5B 50
SE14 . . . . 2F 93
Samuel Ct. N1 . . . . 2A 64
(off Pitfield St.)
Samuel Ho. E8 . . . . 5B 50
(off Clarissa St.)
Samuel Johnson Cl.
SW16 . . . . 4B 118
Samuel Jones Ind. Est.
SE15 . . . . 3A 92
Samuel Lewis Bldgs.
N1 . . . . 3C 48
Samuel Lewis Trust Dwellings
N16 . . . . 1A 36
SE5 . . . . 4E 91
(off Warner Rd.)
SW3 . . . . 5A 74
SW6 . . . . 3C 86
(off Vanston Pl.)
W14 . . . . 5B 72
(off Lisgar Ter.)
Samuel Richardson Ho.
W14 . . . . 5B 72
(off North End Cres.)
Samuel's Cl. W6 . . . . . . 5E 71
Samuel St. SE15 . . . . . . 3B 92
Sancroft Cl. NW2 . . . . . 5D 29
Sancroft Ho. SE11 . . . . . 1B 90
(off Sancroft St.)
Sancroft St. SE11 . . . . . 1B 90
Sanctuary, The SW1 . . . . 5C 22
Sanctuary M. E8 . . . . . . 3B 50
Sanctuary St.
SE1 . . . . 3A 26 (3E 77)
Sandale Cl. N16 . . . . . . 5F 35
Sandall Ho. E3 . . . . 1A 66
Sandall Rd. NW5 . . . . . . 3E 47
Sandal St. E15 . . . . 5A 54
Sandalwood Cl. E1 . . . . . 3A 66
Sandalwood Mans.
W8 . . . . 4D 73
(off Stone Hall Gdns.)
Sandbourne NW8 . . . . . . 5D 45
(off Abbey Rd.)
W11 . . . . 5C 58
(off Dartmouth Cl.)
Sandbourne Rd. SE4 . . . . 5A 94
Sandbrook Rd. N16 . . . . . 5A 36
Sandby Ho. NW6 . . . . . . 5C 44
Sandell St.
SE1 . . . . 3B 24 (3C 76)
Sanderling Ct. SE8 . . . . . 2B 94
(off Abinger Gro.)
Sanderling Lodge E1 . . . . 1B 78
(off Star Pl.)
Sanders Ho. WC1 . . . . . . 1B 8
(off Gt. Percy St.)
Sanderson Cl. NW5 . . . . . 1D 47
Sanderson Ho. SE8 . . . . . 1B 94
(off Grove St.)
Sanderstead Av.
NW2 . . . . 4A 30
Sanderstead Cl.
SW12 . . . . 5E 103
Sanderstead Rd.
E10 . . . . 3A 38
Sanders Way N19 . . . . . . 3F 33

Sandfield WC1 . . . . 2E 7
(off Cromer St.)
Sandford Ct. N16 . . . . . . 3A 36
Sandford Row SE17 . . . . . 1F 91
Sandford St. SW6 . . . . . . 3D 87
Sandgate Ho. E5 . . . . . . 2D 51
Sandgate La. SW18 . . . . . 1A 116
Sandgate St. SE15 . . . . . 2D 93
Sandgate Trad. Est.
SE15 . . . . 2D 93
(off Sandgate St.)
Sandham Ct. SW4 . . . . . 4A 90
Sandhills, The SW10 . . . . 2E 87
(off Limerston St.)
Sandhurst Ct. SW2 . . . . . 2A 104
Sandhurst Ho. E1 . . . . . . 4E 65
(off Wolsy St.)
Sandhurst Mkt. SE6 . . . . 1E 123
(off Sandhurst Rd.)
Sandhurst Rd. SE6 . . . . . 1F 123
Sandifer Dr. NW2 . . . . . . 5F 29
Sandilands Rd. SW6 . . . . 4D 87
Sandison St. SE15 . . . . . 1C 106
Sandland St.
WC1 . . . . 1A 16 (4B 62)
Sandlings, The SE15 . . . . 5D 93
Sandmere Rd. SW4 . . . . . 2A 104
Sandown Ct. SE26 . . . . . 3D 121
Sandpiper Cl. SE16 . . . . . 3B 80
Sandpiper Ct. E1 . . . . . . 1C 78
(off Thomas More St.)
E14 . . . . 4E 81
(off New Union Cl.)
SE8 . . . . 2C 94
(off Edward Pl.)
Sandpiper Ho.
SW18 . . . . 1E 101
Sandpit Rd.
BR1: Brom 5A 124
Sandridge St. N19 . . . . . 4E 33
Sandringham Cl.
SW19 . . . . 1F 113
Sandringham Ct.
SE16 . . . . 2F 79
(off King & Queen Wharf)
W1 . . . . 3A 14
(off Dufour's Pl.)
W9 . . . . 2F 59
(off Maida Va.)
Sandringham Flats
WC2 . . . . 4C 14
(off Charing Cross Rd.)
Sandringham Gdns.
N8 . . . . 1A 34
Sandringham Ho.
W14 . . . . 5A 72
(off Windsor Way)
Sandringham Rd.
BR1: Brom 5C 124
E7 . . . . 2E 55
E8 . . . . 2B 50
E10 . . . . 1F 39
NW2 . . . . 3D 43
NW11 . . . . 2A 30
Sandrock Rd. SE13 . . . . . 1C 108
SANDS END 4E 87
Sand's End La. SW6 . . . . 4D 87
Sandstone La. E16 . . . . . 1D 83
Sandstone Pl. N19 . . . . . 4D 33

Sandstone Rd.
SE12 . . . . 2D 125
Sandtoft Rd. SE7 . . . . . . 2D 97
Sandwell Cres. NW6 . . . . 3C 44
Sandwich Ho. SE16 . . . . . 3E 79
(off Swan Rd.)
WC1 . . . . 2D 7
(off Sandwich St.)
Sandwich St.
WC1 . . . . 2D 7 (2A 62)
Sandy Rd. NW3 . . . . 4D 31
(not continuous)
Sandys Row
E1 . . . . 1E 19 (4A 64)
Sanford La. N16 . . . . 5B 36
Sanford St. SE14 . . . . . . 2A 94
Sanford Ter. N16 . . . . . . 5B 36
Sanford Wlk. N16 . . . . . . 4B 36
SE14 . . . . 2A 94
Sangley Rd. SE6 . . . . . . 5D 109
Sangora Rd. SW11 . . . . . 2F 101
Sankey Ho. E2 . . . . 1E 65
(off St James's Av.)
Sansom Rd. E11 . . . . . . 4B 40
Sansom St. SE5 . . . . 4F 91
Sans Wlk.
EC1 . . . . 3C 8 (3C 62)
Santley Ho.
SE1 . . . . 4C 24 (3C 76)
Santley St. SW4 . . . . . . 2B 104
Santos Rd. SW18 . . . . . . 3C 100
Sapcote Trad. Cen.
NW10 . . . . 3B 42
Saperton Wlk. SE11 . . . . 5B 76
(off Juxon St.)
Sapperton Ct. EC1 . . . . . 3F 9
Sapperton Ho. W2 . . . . . 4C 58
(off Brunel Est.)
Sapphire Ct. E1 . . . . 1C 78
(off Cable St.)
Sapphire Rd. SE8 . . . . . . 5A 80
Saracens Head Yd.
EC3 . . . . 3F 19
Saracen St. E14 . . . . 5C 66
Sarah Ho. E1 . . . . 5D 65
(off Commercial Rd.)
Sarah St. N1 . . . . 1E 11 (2A 64)
Sarah Swift Ho. SE1 . . . . 3C 26
(off Kipling St.)
Sara La. Ct. N1 . . . . 1A 64
(off Stanway St.)
Saratoga Rd. E5 . . . . . . 1E 51
Sardinia St.
WC2 . . . . 3F 15 (5B 62)
Sarjant Path SW19 . . . . . 2F 113
(off Blincoe Cl.)
Sark Wlk. E16 . . . . 5D 69
Sarnesfield Ho.
SE15 . . . . 2D 93
(off Pencraig Way)
Sarratt Ho. W10 . . . . 4E 57
(off Sutton Way)
Sarre Rd. NW2 . . . . 2B 44
Sarsfeld Rd. SW12 . . . . . 1B 116
Sartor Rd. SE15 . . . . . . 2F 107
Sarum Ter. E3 . . . . 3B 66
Satanita Cl. E16 . . . . 5F 69
Satchwell Rd. E2 . . . . . . 2C 64
Satchwell St. E2 . . . . . . 2C 64

Sattar M. N16 . . . . 5F 35
        (off Clissold Rd.)
Saul Ct. SE15 . . . . 2B 92
Sauls Grn. E11 . . . . 5A 40
Saunders Cl. E14 . . . . . 1B 80
        (off Limehouse C'way.)
Saunders Ho. SE11 . . . . 3F 79
        (off Quebec Way)
Saunders Ness Rd.
E14 . . . . 1E 95
Saunders St. SE11 . . . . . 5C 76
Savage Gdns.
EC3 . . . . 4E 19 (1A 78)
        (not continuous)
Savannah Cl. SE15 . . . . . 3B 92
Savernake Ho. N4 . . . . . 2E 35
Savernake Rd. NW3 . . . . 1B 46
Savile Row
W1 . . . . 4F 13 (1E 75)
Saville Rd. E16 . . . . 2F 83
Savill Ho. SW4 . . . . . . 4F 103
Savona Ho. SW8 . . . . . 3E 89
        (off Savona St.)
Savona St. SW8 . . . . . . 3E 89
SAVOY CIRCUS 1B 70
Savoy Cl. E15 . . . . 5A 54
Savoy Cl. NW3 . . . . 5E 31
        SW5 . . . . 5C 72
        (off Cromwell Rd.)
        WC2 . . . . 5E 15 (1B 76)
Savoy Hill
WC2 . . . . 5F 15 (1B 76)
Savoy M. SW9 . . . . . . 1A 104
Savoy Pl.
WC2 . . . . 5E 15 (1A 76)
Savoy Row WC2 . . . . . . 4F 15
Savoy Steps WC2 . . . . . 5F 15
Savoy St.
WC2 . . . . 5F 15 (1B 76)
Savoy Theatre 5E 15
        (off Strand)
Savoy Way WC2 . . . . . . 5F 15
Sawkins Cl. SW19 . . . . . 2A 114
Sawley Rd. W12 . . . . . . 2C 70
Sawmill Yd. E3 . . . . 5A 52
Sawyer Ct. NW10 . . . . . 4A 42
Sawyer St.
SE1 . . . . 3F 25 (3E 77)
Saxby Rd. SW2 . . . . . . 5A 104
Saxonbury Ct. N7 . . . . . 2A 48
Saxon Cl. E17 . . . . 2C 38
Saxonfield Cl. SW2 . . . . 1B 118
Saxon Hall W2 . . . . 1D 73
        (off Palace Ct.)
Saxon Ho. E1 . . . . 1F 19
        (off Thrawl St.)
Saxon Rd. E3 . . . . 1B 66
Saxon Ter. SE6 . . . . 2B 122
Saxton Cl. SE13 . . . . . . 1F 109
Sayes Ct. SE8 . . . . 2B 94
Sayes Ct. St. SE8 . . . . . 2B 94
Scafell NW1 . . . . 1F 5
        (off Stanhope St.)
Scala St. W1 . . . . 5A 6 (4E 61)
Scampston M. W10 . . . . 5F 57
Scandrett St. E1 . . . . . . 2D 79
Scarba Wlk. N1 . . . . 3F 49
        (off Marquess Rd.)

Scarborough Rd. E11 . . . 3F 39
        N4 . . . . 3C 34
Scarborough St. E1 . . . . 5B 64
Scarlet Rd. SE6 . . . . . . 3A 124
Scarlette Mnr. Way
        SW2 . . . . 5C 104
Scarsbrook Rd. SE3 . . . . 1F 111
Scarsdale Pl. W8 . . . . . . 4D 73
Scarsdale Studios
        W8 . . . . 4C 72
        (off Stratford Rd.)
Scarsdale Vs. W8 . . . . . 4C 72
Scarth Rd. SW13 . . . . . 1B 98
Scawen Rd. SE8 . . . . . . 1A 94
Scawfell St. E2 . . . . 1B 64
Sceaux Gdns. SE5 . . . . . 4A 92
Sceptre Ct. EC3 . . . . . . 5F 19
        (off Tower Hill)
Sceptre Ho. E1 . . . . 3E 65
        (off Malcolm Rd.)
Sceptre Rd. E2 . . . . 2E 65
Schafer Ho.
        NW1 . . . . 2F 5 (2E 61)
Schiller International
University 2B 24
Schofield Wlk. SE3 . . . . 3C 96
Scholars Pl. N16 . . . . . . 5A 36
Scholars Rd. SW12 . . . . 1E 117
Scholefield Rd. N19 . . . . 4F 33
Scholey Ho. SW11 . . . . 1A 102
Schomberg Ho.
        SW1 . . . . 5F 75
        (off Page St.)
Schonfeld Sq. N16 . . . . 4F 35
School App.
        E2 . . . . 1E 11 (2A 64)
Schoolbank Rd.
        SE10 . . . . 4B 82
Schoolbell M. E3 . . . . . 1A 66
School Ho. SE1 . . . . 5A 78
        (off Page's Wlk.)
School Ho. La. E1 . . . . . 1F 79
School of Hygiene &
        Tropical Medicine 5C 6
School of Oriental &
        African Studies 4C 6
School Rd. NW10 . . . . . 3A 56
School Sq. SE10 . . . . . . 4B 82
Schooner Cl. E14 . . . . . 4F 81
        SE16 . . . . 3F 79
Schubert Rd. SW15 . . . . 3B 100
Science Mus. 4F 73
Sclater St.
        E1 . . . . 3F 11 (3B 64)
Scoble Pl. N16 . . . . 1B 50
Scoles Cres. SW2 . . . . . 1D 119
Scoop, The 2A 78
Scoresby St.
        SE1 . . . . 2D 25 (2D 77)
Scorton Ho. N1 . . . . 1A 64
        (off Whitmore Est.)
SCOTCH HOUSE 4B 74
Scoter Ct. SE8 . . . . 2B 94
        (off Abinger Gro.)
Scotia Bldg. E1 . . . . 1F 79
        (off Jardine Rd.)
Scotia Ct. SE16 . . . . 3E 79
        (off Canada Est.)
Scotia Rd. SW2 . . . . . . 5C 104

Scotland Pl.
        SW1 . . . . 2D 23 (2A 76)
Scotney Ho. E9 . . . . 3E 51
Scotsdale Rd.
        SE12 . . . . 3D 111
Scotson Ho. SE11 . . . . . 5C 76
        (off Marylee Way)
Scotswood St.
        EC1 . . . . 3C 8 (3C 62)
Scott Ellis Gdns.
        NW8 . . . . 2F 59
Scott Ho. E13 . . . . 1C 68
        (off Queens Rd. W.)
        E14 . . . . 3C 80
        (off Admirals Way)
        N1 . . . . 5F 49
        (off Sherborne St.)
        N7 . . . . 3B 48
        (off Caledonian Rd.)
        NW8 . . . . 3A 60
        (off Broadley St.)
        NW10 . . . . 4A 42
        (off Stonebridge Pk.)
        SE8 . . . . 1B 94
        (off Grove St.)
Scott Lidgett Cres.
        SE16 . . . . 3C 78
Scott Russell Pl. E14 . . . 1D 95
Scotts Ct. W12 . . . . 3E 71
        (off Scott's Rd.)
Scott's Rd. E10 . . . . 3E 39
        W12 . . . . 3D 71
Scott's Sufferance Wharf
        SE1 . . . . 4F 27
Scotts Ter. SE9 . . . . 2F 125
Scott St. E1 . . . . 3D 65
Scott's Yd.
        EC4 . . . . 4B 18 (1F 77)
Scoulding Ho. E14 . . . . . 4C 80
        (off Mellish St.)
Scoulding Rd. E16 . . . . . 5C 68
Scouler St. E14 . . . . 1E 81
Scout App. NW10 . . . . . 1A 42
Scout La. SW4 . . . . 1E 103
Scovell Cres. SE1 . . . . . 4F 25
Scovell Rd.
        SE1 . . . . 4F 25 (3E 77)
Screen on Baker Street
        (Cinema) 5A 4
        (off Baker St.)
Screen on the Green Cinema
        . . . . 5D 49
        (off Upper St.)
Screen on the Hill (Cinema)
        Belsize Pk. 2A 46
Scriven Ct. E8 . . . . 5B 50
Scriven St. E8 . . . . 5B 50
Scrooby St. SE6 . . . . . . 4D 109
Scrope Ho. EC1 . . . . 5B 8
        (off Bourne Est.)
Scrubs La. NW10 . . . . . 2C 56
Scrutton Cl. SW12 . . . . . 5F 103
Scrutton St.
        EC2 . . . . 4D 11 (3A 64)
Scutari Rd. SE22 . . . . . . 3E 107
Scylla Rd. SE15 . . . . . . 1C 106
        (not continuous)
Seabright St. E2 . . . . . . 2D 65
Seacole Cl. W3 . . . . 5A 56

Seacon Twr. E14 . . . . . . 3B **80**
Seaford Ho. *SE16* *3E* **79**
    (off Swan Rd.)
Seaford St.
  WC1 . . . . 2E **7** (2B **62**)
Seaforth Cres. N5 . . . . . . 2E **49**
Seaforth Pl. SW1 . . . . . . 5A **22**
Seager Bldgs. SE8 . . . . . 4C **94**
Seagrave Cl. E1 . . . . 4F **65**
Seagrave Lodge *SW6* . . . *2C* **86**
    (off Seagrave Rd.)
Seagrave Rd. SW6 . . . . . . 2C **86**
Seagry Rd. E11 . . . . 2C **40**
Seagull La. E16 . . . . 1C **82**
Seal Ho. *SE1* *5C* **26**
    (off Pardoner St.)
Seal St. E8 . . . . 1B **50**
Searles Cl. SW11 . . . . . . 3A **88**
Searles Rd. SE1 . . . . 5F **77**
Searson Ho. *SE17* *5D* **77**
    (off Canterbury Pl.)
Sears St. SE5 . . . . 3F **91**
Seaton Cl. E13 . . . . 3C **68**
  SE11 . . . . 1C **90**
  SW15 . . . . 1D **113**
Seaton Point *E5* *1C* **50**
    (off Nolan Way)
Sebastian Ho. *N1* *1D* **11**
    (off Hoxton St.)
Sebastian St.
  EC1 . . . . 2E **9** (2D **63**)
Sebbon St. N1 . . . . 4D **49**
Sebert Rd. E7 . . . . 2D **55**
Sebright Ho. *E2* *1C* **64**
    (off Coate St.)
Sebright Pas. E2 . . . . . . 1C **64**
Secker Ho. *SW9* *5D* **91**
    (off Loughborough Est.)
Secker St.
  SE1 . . . . . . 2B **24** (2C **76**)
Second Av. E13 . . . . 2C **68**
  SW14 . . . . 1A **98**
  W3 . . . . 2B **70**
  W10 . . . . 3A **58**
Sedan Way SE17 . . . . . . 1A **92**
Sedding St. SW1 . . . . . . 5C **74**
Sedding Studios
  SW1 . . . . *5C* **74**
    (off Sedding St.)
Seddon Highwalk *EC2* . . *5F* **9**
    (off Seddon Ho.)
Seddon Ho. EC2 . . . . 5F **9**
Seddon St.
  WC1 . . . . 2A **8** (2B **62**)
Sedgebrook Rd. SE3 . . . . 5F **97**
Sedgeford Rd. W12 . . . . . 2B **70**
Sedgehill Rd. SE6 . . . . . . 4C **122**
Sedgeway SE6 . . . . 1B **124**
Sedgmoor Pl. SE5 . . . . . . 3A **92**
Sedgwick Ho. *E3* *4C* **66**
    (off Gale St.)
Sedgwick Rd. E10 . . . . . . 4E **39**
Sedgwick St. E9 . . . . 2F **51**
Sedleigh Rd. SW18 . . . . . 4B **100**
Sedlescombe Rd.
  SW6 . . . . 2C **86**
Sedley Ct. SE26 . . . . 2D **121**
Sedley Ho. *SE11* *1B* **90**
    (off Newburn St.)

Sedley Pl.
  W1 . . . . 3D **13** (5D **61**)
Seeley Dr. SE21 . . . . 4A **120**
Seelig Av. NW9 . . . . 2C **28**
Seely Rd. SW17 . . . . 5C **116**
Seething La.
  EC3 . . . . 4E **19** (1A **78**)
Sefton St. SW15 . . . . 1E **99**
Segal Cl. SE23 . . . . 5A **108**
Sekforde St.
  EC1 . . . . 4D **9** (3D **63**)
Selbie Av. NW10 . . . . 2B **42**
Selborne Rd. SE5 . . . . . . 5F **91**
Selbourne Ho.
  SE1 . . . . 5B **26**
Selby Cl. E6 . . . . 4F **69**
Selby Ho. *W10* *2A* **58**
    (off Beethoven St.)
Selby Rd. E11 . . . . 5A **40**
  E13 . . . . 4D **69**
Selby Sq. *W10* *2A* **58**
    (off Dowland St.)
Selby St. E1 . . . . 3C **64**
Selcroft Ho. *SE10* *1B* **96**
    (off Glenister Rd.)
Selden Ho. *SE15* *5E* **93**
    (off Selden Rd.)
Selden Rd. SE15 . . . . 5E **93**
Selden Wlk. N7 . . . . 4B **34**
Seldon Ho. *SW1* *1E* **89**
    (off Churchill Gdns.)
  SW8 . . . . *3E* **89**
    (off Stewart's Rd.)
Selfridges 3B **12**
Selhurst Cl. SW19 . . . . . . 1F **113**
Selina Ho. *NW8* *3F* **59**
    (off Frampton St.)
Selkirk Rd. SW17 . . . . . . 4A **116**
Sellincourt Rd.
  SW17 . . . . 5A **116**
Sellons Av. NW10 . . . . . . 5B **42**
Selma Ho. *W12* *5D* **57**
    (off Du Cane Rd.)
Selman Ho. E9 . . . . 3A **52**
Selsdon Rd. E11 . . . . 2C **40**
  E13 . . . . 5E **55**
  NW2 . . . . 4B **28**
  SE27 . . . . 3C **118**
Selsdon Way E14 . . . . . . 4D **81**
Selsea Pl. N16 . . . . 2A **50**
Selsey St. E14 . . . . 4C **66**
Selway Ho. *SW8* *4A* **90**
    (off Sth. Lambeth Rd.)
Selwood Pl. SW7 . . . . . . 1F **87**
Selwoods SW2 . . . . 5C **104**
Selwood Ter. SW7 . . . . . . 1F **87**
Selworthy Cl. E11 . . . . . . 1C **40**
Selworthy Rd. SE6 . . . . . 3B **122**
Selwyn Ct. *E17* *1C* **38**
    (off Yunus Khan Cl.)
  SE3 . . . . 1B **110**
Selwyn Rd. E3 . . . . 1B **66**
  E13 . . . . 5D **55**
  NW10 . . . . 4A **42**
Semley Ga. E9 . . . . 3B **52**
Semley Ho. *SW1* *5D* **75**
    (off Semley Pl.)
Semley Pl. SW1 . . . . 5C **74**
Senate St. SE15 . . . . 5E **93**

Senators Lodge *E3* *1A* **66**
    (off Roman Rd.)
Senior St. W2 . . . . 4D **59**
Senlac Rd. SE12 . . . . 1D **125**
Senrab St. E1 . . . . 5F **65**
Sentamu Cl. SW2 . . . . . . 1D **119**
Seraph Ct. *EC1* *1F* **9**
    (off Moreland St.)
Serbin Cl. E10 . . . . 2E **39**
Serenaders Rd. SW9 . . . . 5C **90**
Sergeant Ind. Est.
  SW18 . . . . 4D **101**
Serica Ct. SE10 . . . . 3E **95**
Serjeants Inn
  EC4 . . . . 3C **16** (5C **62**)
Serlby Ct. *W14* *4B* **72**
    (off Somerset Sq.)
Serle St.
  WC2 . . . . 2A **16** (5B **62**)
Sermon La. EC4 . . . . 3F **17**
Serpentine, The 2A **74**
Serpentine Gallery 3F **73**
Serpentine Rd.
  W2 . . . . 2A **20** (2A **74**)
Setchell Rd. SE1 . . . . 5B **78**
Setchell Way SE1 . . . . . . 5B **78**
Seth St. SE16 . . . . 3E **79**
Settle Point *E13* *1C* **68**
    (off London Rd.)
Settle Rd. E13 . . . . 1C **68**
Settlers Ct. E14 . . . . 1F **81**
Settles St. E1 . . . . 4C **64**
Settrington Rd. SW6 . . . . 5D **87**
Seven Dials
  WC2 . . . . 3D **15** (5A **62**)
Seven Dials Ct. *WC2* . . . *3D* **15**
    (off Shorts Gdns.)
Seven Islands Leisure Cen.
  . . . . 4E **79**
Sevenoaks Rd. SE4 . . . . . 4A **108**
Seven Sisters Rd.
  N4 . . . . 5B **34**
  N7 . . . . 5B **34**
  N15 . . . . 4C **34**
Seven Stars Cnr. W6 . . . . 4C **70**
Seven Stars Yd. E1 . . . . . 5F **11**
Severnake Cl. E14 . . . . . . 5C **80**
Severn Av. W10 . . . . 2A **58**
Severn Way NW10 . . . . . . 2B **42**
Severus Rd. SW11 . . . . . 2A **102**
Seville Ho. *E1* *2C* **78**
    (off Hellings St.)
Seville M. N1 . . . . 4A **50**
Seville St.
  SW1 . . . . 4A **20** (3B **74**)
Sevington Rd. NW4 . . . . . 1D **29**
Sevington St. W9 . . . . 3D **59**
Sewardstone Rd. E2 . . . . 1E **65**
Seward St.
  EC1 . . . . 3E **9** (2D **63**)
Sewdley St. E5 . . . . 5F **37**
Sewell St. E13 . . . . 2C **68**
Sextant Av. E14 . . . . 5F **81**
Sexton Ct. *E14* *1F* **81**
    (off Newport Av.)
Sextons Ho. *SE10* *2E* **95**
    (off Bardsley La.)
Seymour Ct. NW2 . . . . . . 4D **29**
Seymour Gdns. SE4 . . . . 1A **108**

Seymour Ho. E16 . . . . . 2C 82
(off De Quincey M.)
NW1 . . . . 1C 6
(off Churchway)
WC1 . . . . 3D 7
(off Tavistock Pl.)
Seymour Leisure Cen.
. . . . 4B 60
Seymour M.
W1 . . . . . . 2B 12 (5C 60)
Seymour Pl.
W1 . . . . . 2A 12 (4B 60)
Seymour Rd. E6 . . . . . 1F 69
E10 . . . . 3B 38
N8 . . . . 1C 34
SW18 . . . . 5B 100
SW19 . . . . 3F 113
Seymour St.
W1 . . . . . . 3A 12 (5B 60)
W2 . . . . 5B 60
Seymour Wlk. SW10 . . . 2E 87
Seyssel St. E14 . . . . . 5E 81
Shaa Rd. W3 . . . . 1A 70
Shabana Rd. W12 . . . . 2D 71
Shackleton Cl.
SE23 . . . . 2D 121
Shackleton Ct. E14 . . . . 1C 94
(off Maritime Quay)
W12 . . . . 3D 71
Shackleton Ho. E1 . . . . 2E 79
(off Prusom St.)
NW10 . . . . 4A 42
SHACKLEWELL 1B 50
Shacklewell Grn. E8 . . . 1B 50
Shacklewell Ho. E8 . . . 1B 50
Shacklewell La. E8 . . . 2B 50
Shacklewell Rd. N16 . . 1B 50
Shacklewell Row
E8 . . . . 1B 50
Shacklewell St. E2 . . . . 2B 64
Shad Thames
SE1 . . . . . . 2F 27 (2B 78)
SHADWELL 1D 79
Shadwell Gdns. E1 . . . . 1E 79
Shadwell Pierhead
E1 . . . . 1E 79
Shadwell Pl. E1 . . . . . . 1E 79
(off Shadwell Gdns.)
Shaftesbury Av.
W1 . . . . 5B 14 (1F 75)
WC1 . . . . . 2D 15 (5A 62)
WC2 . . . . . 2D 15 (5A 62)
Shaftesbury Cen.
W10 . . . . 3F 57
(off Barlby Rd.)
Shaftesbury Ct. N1 . . . . 1F 63
(off Shaftesbury St.)
SW6 . . . . 4D 87
(off Maltings Pl.)
SW16 . . . . 3F 117
Shaftesbury Gdns.
NW10 . . . . 3A 56
Shaftesbury Lodge
E14 . . . . 5D 67
(off Upper Nth. St.)
Shaftesbury M. SE1 . . . . 3E 103
SW4 . . . . 3E 103
W8 . . . . 4C 72
(off Stratford Rd.)

Shaftesbury Pl. EC2 . . . . 1F 17
(off London Wall)
W14 . . . . 5B 72
(off Warwick Rd.)
Shaftesbury Point
E13 . . . . 1C 68
(off High St.)
Shaftesbury Rd. E7 . . . 4E 55
E10 . . . . 3C 38
E17 . . . . 1D 39
N19 . . . . 3A 34
Shaftesbury St. N1 . . . . 1E 63
(not continuous)
Shaftesbury Theatre . . . 2D 15
(off Shaftesbury Av.)
Shaftesbury Vs. W8 . . . 4C 72
(off Allen St.)
Shafto M. SW1 . . . . . . 4B 74
Shafton M. E9 . . . . . . 5F 51
Shafton Rd. E9 . . . . . . 5F 51
Shaftsbury Ct. SE5 . . . 2F 105
Shafts Ct.
EC3 . . . . . . 3D 19 (5A 64)
Shahjalal Ho. E2 . . . . . 1C 64
(off Pritchards Rd.)
Shakespeare Ho. E9 . . . 4E 51
(off Lyme Gro.)
Shakespeare Rd.
SE24 . . . . 3D 105
Shakespeare's Globe Theatre
& Exhibition
. . . . 1F 25 (2E 77)
Shakespeare Twr.
EC2 . . . . 5A 10
Shakspeare M. N16 . . . 1A 50
Shakspeare Wlk.
N16 . . . . 1A 50
Shalbourne Sq. E9 . . . . 3B 52
Shalcomb St. SW10 . . . 2E 87
Shalden Ho. SW15 . . . 4B 98
Shalfleet Dr. W10 . . . . 1F 71
Shalford Ct. N1 . . . . . . 1D 63
(off Charlton Pl.)
Shalford Ho.
SE1 . . . . . . 5C 26 (4F 77)
Shamrock St. SW4 . . . 1F 103
Shandon Rd. SW4 . . . . 4E 103
Shand St.
SE1 . . . . . . 3E 27 (3A 78)
Shandy St. E1 . . . . 4F 65
Shan Ho. WC1 . . . . . . 4F 7
Shanklin Rd. N8 . . . . . 1F 33
Shannon Cl. NW2 . . . . 5F 29
Shannon Ct. N16 . . . . . 5A 36
SE15 . . . . 3B 92
(off Garnies Cl.)
Shannon Gro. SW9 . . . 2B 104
Shannon Pl. NW8 . . . . 1A 60
Shanti Ct. SW18 . . . . . 1C 114
Shap St. E2 . . . . 1B 64
Shardcroft Av. SE24 . . 3D 105
Shardeloes Rd.
SE14 . . . . 5B 94
Shard's Sq. SE15 . . . . 2C 92
Sharnbrook Ho. W14 . . 2C 86
Sharon Gdns. E9 . . . . . 5E 51
Sharp Ho. SW8 . . . . . . 1D 103
Sharpleshall St.
NW1 . . . . 4B 46

Sharpness Ct. SE15 . . . . 3B 92
(off Daniel Gdns.)
Sharratt St. SE15 . . . . 2E 93
Sharsted St. SE17 . . . . 1D 91
Sharwood WC1 . . . . 1A 8
(off Penton Ri.)
Shaver's Pl. SW1 . . . . . 5B 14
Shawbrooke Rd.
SE9 . . . . 3E 111
Shawbury Rd.
SE22 . . . . 3B 106
Shaw Cres. E14 . . . . . 5A 66
Shawfield St. SW3 . . . . 1A 88
Shawford Ct. SW15 . . . 5C 98
Shaw Path
BR1: Brom 3B 124
Shaw Rd.
BR1: Brom 3B 124
SE22 . . . . 2A 106
Shaws Cotts. SE23 . . . 3A 122
Shaw Theatre . . . 2C 6 (2F 61)
Shearling Way N7 . . . . 3A 48
Shearman Rd. SE3 . . . 2B 110
Shearwater Ct. E1 . . . . 1C 78
(off Star Pl.)
SE8 . . . . 2B 94
(off Abinger Gro.)
Sheba Pl. E1 . . 4F 11 (3B 64)
Sheenewood SE26 . . . . 4D 121
Sheengate Mans.
SW14 . . . . 2A 98
Sheen Rd. SW 5C 48
Sheen Sports & Fitness Cen.
. . . . 2A 98
Sheepcote La. SW11 . . 5B 88
Sheep La. E8 . . . . 5D 51
Sheep Wlk. M.
SW19 . . . . 5F 113
Sheerwater Rd. E16 . . . 4F 69
Sheffield Sq. E3 . . . . . 2B 66
Sheffield St.
WC2 . . . . . . 3F 15 (5B 62)
Shelburne Rd. N7 . . . . 1B 48
Shelbury Rd. SE22 . . . 3D 107
Sheldon Av. N6 . . . . . 2A 32
Sheldon Cl. SE12 . . . . 3D 111
Sheldon Ct. SW8 . . . . . 3A 90
(off Lansdowne Grn.)
Sheldon Ho. N1 . . . . . . 5A 50
(off Kingsland Rd.)
Sheldon Rd. E2 . . . . . . 1C 64
(not continuous)
Sheldon Rd. NW2 . . . . 1F 43
Sheldon Sq. W2 . . . . . 4E 59
Sheldrake Ho. SE16 . . . 5F 79
(off Tawny Way)
Sheldrake Pl. W8 . . . . 3C 72
Shelduck Cl. E15 . . . . 2B 54
Shelduck Ct. SE8 . . . . 2B 94
(off Pilot Cl.)
Shelford Pl. N16 . . . . . 5F 35
Shelgate Rd.
SW11 . . . . 3A 102
Shelley Av. E12 . . . . . 3F 55
Shelley Cl. SE15 . . . . 5D 93
Shelley Ct. E10 . . . . . 2D 39
(off Skelton's La.)
N19 . . . . 3B 34

Shelley Ct. *SW3* 2B 88
    (off Tite St.)
Shelley Ho. *E2* 2E 65
    (off Cornwall Av.)
  N16 . . . . 1A 50
  SE17 . . . . 1E 91
    (off Browning St.)
  SW1 . . . . 2E 89
    (off Churchill Gdns.)
Shelley Rd. NW10 . . . . . . 5A 42
Shelley Way SW19 . . . . . 5F 115
Shellness Rd. E5 . . . . . . 2D 51
Shell Rd. SE13 . . . . 1D 109
Shellwood Rd. SW11 . . . . 5B 88
Shelmerdine Cl. E3 . . . . . 4C 66
Shelton St.
  WC2 . . . . 3D 15 (5A 62)
    (not continuous)
Shene Ho. *EC1* 5B 8
    (off Bourne Est.)
Shenfield Ho. *SE18* 4F 97
    (off Portway Gdns.)
Shenfield St.
  N1 . . . . 1E 11 (1A 64)
    (not continuous)
Shenley Rd. SE5 . . . . . . 4A 92
Shenstone Ho.
  SW16 . . . . 5E 117
Shepherdess Pl.
  N1 . . . . 1A 10 (2E 63)
Shepherdess Wlk.
  N1 . . . . 1A 10 (1E 63)
Shepherd Ho. *E14* 5D 67
    (off Annabel Cl.)
Shepherd Mkt.
  W1 . . . . 1D 21 (2D 75)
SHEPHERD'S BUSH 3E 71
Shepherds Bush
  Empire Theatre 3E 71
Shepherd's Bush Grn.
  W12 . . . . 3E 71
Shepherd's Bush Mkt.
  W12 . . . . 3E 71
    (not continuous)
Shepherd's Bush Pl.
  W12 . . . . 3F 71
Shepherd's Bush Rd.
  W6 . . . . 5E 71
Shepherds Cl. N6 . . . . . . 1D 33
  W1 . . . . 4B 12
    (off Lees Pl.)
Shepherds Cl. *W12* 3F 71
    (off Shepherd's Bush Grn.)
Shepherd's Hill N6 . . . . . 1D 33
Shepherds La. E9 . . . . . . 3F 51
Shepherd's Path
  NW3 . . . . 2F 45
    (off Lyndhurst Rd.)
Shepherds Pl.
  W1 . . . . 4B 12 (1C 74)
Shepherd St.
  W1 . . . . 2D 21 (2D 75)
Shepherds Wlk. NW2 . . . . 4C 28
  NW3 . . . . 2F 45
    (not continuous)
Sheppard Dr. SE16 . . . . . 1D 93
Sheppard Ho. *E2* 1C 64
    (off Warner Pl.)
  SW2 . . . . 1C 118

Sheppard St. E16 . . . . . . 3B 68
Shepperton Rd. N1 . . . . . 5E 49
Shepton Ho's. *E2* 2E 65
    (off Welwyn St.)
Sherard Ct. N7 . . . . 5A 34
Sherard Ho. *E9* 4E 51
    (off Frampton Pk. Rd.)
Sheraton Ho. SW1 . . . . . 2D 89
    (off Churchill Gdns.)
Sheraton St.
  W1 . . . . 3B 14 (5F 61)
Sherborne Ho. *SW1* 1D 89
    (off Winchester St.)
  SW8 . . . . 3B 90
    (off Bolney St.)
Sherborne La.
  EC4 . . . . 4B 18 (1F 77)
Sherborne St. N1 . . . . . . 5F 49
Sherboro Rd. N15 . . . . . . 1B 36
Sherbourne Cl. SW5 . . . . 5D 73
    (off Cromwell Rd.)
Sherbrooke Ho. *E2* 1E 65
    (off Bonner Rd.)
Sherbrooke Rd. SW6 . . . . 3A 86
Sherbrooke Ter. SW6 . . . . 3A 86
    (off Sherbrook Rd.)
Shere Ho. SE1 . . . . 5B 26
Sherfield Gdns.
  SW15 . . . . 4B 98
Sheridan Bldgs. *WC2* . . . 3E 15
    (off Martlett Ct.)
Sheridan Ct. NW6 . . . . . . 4E 45
    (off Belsize Rd.)
  SW5 . . . . 5D 73
    (off Barkston Gdns.)
Sheridan Ho. *E1* 5E 65
    (off Tarling St.)
  SE11 . . . . 5C 76
    (off Wincott St.)
Sheridan M. E11 . . . . 1D 41
Sheridan Pl. SW13 . . . . . 1B 98
Sheridan Rd. E7 . . . . 5B 40
Sheridan St. E1 . . . . 5D 65
Sheridan Wlk. NW11 . . . . 1C 30
Sheringham NW8 . . . . . . 5F 45
Sheringham Ho.
  NW1 . . . . 4A 60
    (off Lisson St.)
Sheringham Rd. N7 . . . . . 3B 48
Sherington Rd. SE7 . . . . . 2D 97
Sherlock Ct. *NW8* 5F 45
    (off Dorman Way)
Sherlock Holmes Mus.
  . . . . 4A 4
Sherlock M.
  W1 . . . . 5B 4 (4C 60)
Sherman Ho. *E14* 5E 67
    (off Dee St.)
Shernhall St. E17 . . . . . . 1E 39
Sherrard Rd. E7 . . . . 3E 55
  E12 . . . . 3E 55
Sherren Ho. E1 . . . . 3E 65
  NW10 . . . . 2D 43
Sherrick Grn. Rd.
  NW10 . . . . 2D 43
Sherriff Rd. NW6 . . . . . . 3C 44
Sherrin Rd. E10 . . . . 1D 53
Sherston Ct. *SE1* 5D 77
    (off Newington Butts)
  WC1 . . . . 2B 8

Sherwin Ho. *SE11* 2C 90
    (off Kennington Rd.)
Sherwin Rd. SE14 . . . . . 4F 93
Sherwood NW6 . . . . 4A 44
Sherwood Cl. SW13 . . . . 1D 99
Sherwood Ct. SW11 . . . . 1E 101
  W1 . . . . 4B 60
    (off Bryanston Pl.)
Sherwood Gdns. E14 . . . 5C 80
  SE16 . . . . 1C 92
Sherwood St.
  W1 . . . . 4A 14 (1E 75)
Shetland Rd. E3 . . . . 1B 66
Shifford Path SE23 . . . . . 3F 121
Shillaker Ct. W3 . . . . 2B 70
Shillibeer Pl. *W1* 4A 60
    (off Harcourt St.)
Shillingford St. N1 . . . . . 4D 49
Shillingstone Ho.
  W14 . . . . 4A 72
    (off Russell Rd.)
Shinfield St. W12 . . . . . . 5E 57
Ship & Mermaid Row
  SE1 . . . . 3C 26 (3F 77)
Shipka Rd. SW12 . . . . . 1D 117
Shiplake Ho. *E2* 2F 11
    (off Arnold Cir.)
Shipman Rd. E16 . . . . . . 5D 69
  SE23 . . . . 2F 121
Ship St. SE8 . . . . 4C 94
Ship Tavern Pas.
  EC3 . . . . 4D 19 (1A 78)
Shipton Ho. *E2* 1B 64
    (off Shipton St.)
Shipton St. E2 . . . . 1B 64
Shipway Ter. N16 . . . . . . 5B 36
Shipwright Rd.
  SE16 . . . . 3A 80
Shipwright Yd.
  SE1 . . . . 2D 27 (2A 78)
Ship Yd. E14 . . . . 1D 95
Shirburn Cl. SE23 . . . . . 5E 107
Shirebrook Rd. SE3 . . . . 1F 111
Shirehall Cl. NW4 . . . . . . 1F 29
Shirehall Gdns. NW4 . . . . 1F 29
Shirehall La. NW4 . . . . . . 1F 29
Shirehall Pk. NW4 . . . . . . 1F 29
Shire La. SW18 . . . . 5E 101
Shirland M. W9 . . . . 2B 58
Shirland Rd. W9 . . . . 2B 58
Shirlbutt St. E14 . . . . 1D 81
Shirley Gro. SW11 . . . . . 1C 102
Shirley Ho. SE5 . . . . 3F 91
    (off Picton St.)
Shirley Ho. Dr. SE7 . . . . . 3E 97
Shirley Rd. E15 . . . . 4A 54
  W4 . . . . 3A 70
Shirley St. E16 . . . . 5B 68
Shirlock Rd. NW3 . . . . . . 1B 46
Shobroke Cl. NW2 . . . . . 5E 29
Shoe La.
  EC4 . . . . 2C 16 (5C 62)
Shona Ho. E13 . . . . 4E 69
Shooters Hill Rd.
  SE3 . . . . 4F 95
  SE10 . . . . 4F 95
  SE18 . . . . 3E 97
Shoot Up Hill NW2 . . . . . 2A 44
Shore Bus. Cen. E9 . . . . 4E 51

SHOREDITCH
.............1D 11 (2A 64)
Shoreditch Ct. E8.......4B 50
(off Queensbridge Rd.)
Shoreditch High St.
E1...............1A 11 (3A 64)
Shoreditch Ho. N1....2C 10
Shoreham Cl.
SW18............3D 101
Shore Ho. SW8....1D 103
Shore M. E9.........4E 51
(off Shore Rd.)
Shore Pl. E9.........4E 51
Shore Rd. E9........4E 51
Shore Way SW9......5C 90
(off Crowhurst Cl.)
Shorncliffe Rd. SE1..1B 92
Shorndean St. SE6...1E 123
Shorrold's Rd. SW6...3B 86
Shorter St. E1........1B 78
Shortlands W6.......5F 71
Shortlands Rd. E10...2D 39
Short Rd. E11........4A 40
W4.................2A 84
Shorts Gdns.
WC2.........3D 15 (5A 62)
Short St. SE1...3C 24 (3C 76)
Short Wall E15........2E 67
Short Way SE9........1F 111
Shottendale Rd.
SW6...............4C 86
Shottery Cl. SE9.....3F 125
Shottfield Av. SW14..2A 98
Shottsford W2........5C 58
(off Talbot Rd.)
Shoulder of Mutton All.
E14...............1A 80
Shouldham St. W1...4A 60
Shrewsbury Ct. EC1...4A 10
Shrewsbury Cres.
NW10.............5A 42
Shrewsbury Ho. SW3..2A 88
(off Cheyne Wlk.)
SW8...............2B 90
(off Kennington Oval)
Shrewsbury M. W2....4C 58
(off Chepstow Rd.)
Shrewsbury Rd. E7...2F 55
W2................5C 58
Shrewsbury St. W10..3E 57
Shroffold Rd.
BR1: Brom.......4A 124
Shropshire Pl.
WC1.........4B 6 (3E 61)
Shroton St. NW1......4A 60
Shrubbery, The E11...1D 41
Shrubbery Cl. N1.....5E 49
Shrubbery Rd.
SW16............4A 118
Shrubland Rd. E8.....5B 50
E10...............2C 38
E17...............1C 38
Shrublands Cl.
SE26.............3E 121
Shuna Wlk. N1.......3F 49
Shurland Gdns.
SE15.............3B 92
Shuters Sq. W14.....1B 86
Shuttle St. E1........3C 64

Shuttleworth Rd.
SW11.............5A 88
Sibella Rd. SW4......5F 89
Sibthorpe Rd. SE12...4D 111
Sicilian Av. WC1......1E 15
Sidbury St. SW6.....4A 86
Sidcup Rd. SE9......4E 111
SE12.............4E 111
Siddons La.
NW1.........4A 4 (3B 60)
Siddons Rd. SE23....2A 122
Side Rd. E17.........1B 38
Sidford Ho. SE1......5A 24
Sidford Pl.
SE1..........5A 24 (4C 76)
Sidgwick Ho. SW9....5B 90
(off Lingham St.)
Sidings, The E11......3E 39
Sidings M. N7.......5C 34
Sidlaw Ho. N16......3B 36
Sidmouth Ho. SE15...3C 92
(off Lympstone Gdns.)
W1...............5A 60
(off Cato St.)
Sidmouth Pde. NW2...4E 43
Sidmouth Rd. E10....5E 39
NW2..............4E 43
Sidmouth St.
WC1..........2E 7 (2B 62)
Sidney Boyd Ct. NW6..4C 44
Sidney Est. E1.......5E 65
(Bromhead St.)
E1................4E 65
(Lindley St.)
Sidney Godley (VC) Ho.
E2................2E 65
(off Digby St.)
Sidney Gro.
EC1..........1D 9 (1D 63)
Sidney Ho. E2........1F 65
(off Old Ford Rd.)
Sidney Rd. E7.......5C 40
SW9..............5B 90
Sidney Sq. E1........4E 65
Sidney St. E1........4D 65
Sidworth St. E8......4D 51
Siebert Rd. SE3......2C 96
Siege Ho. E1........5D 65
(off Sidney St.)
Siemens Rd. SE18....4F 83
Sienna Ter. NW2.....4C 28
Sigdon Pas. E8......2C 50
Sigdon Rd. E8.......2C 50
Sigmund Freud Statue
...............3F 45
Signal Ho. E8........4D 51
(off Martello Ter.)
Signmakers Yd.
NW1..............5D 47
(off Delancey St.)
Silbury Ho. SE26....3C 120
Silbury St.
N1............1B 10 (2F 63)
Silchester Rd. W10...5F 57
Silesia Bldgs. E8.....4D 51
Silex St. SE1....4E 25 (3D 77)
Silk Cl. SE12........3C 110
Silk Ct. E2...........2C 64
(off Squirries St.)

Silk Mills Pas. SE13...5D 95
Silk Mills Path SE13...5D 95
(not continuous)
Silk Mills Sq. E9.....3B 52
Silks Ct. E11........3B 40
Silk St. EC2....5A 10 (4E 63)
Sillitoe Ho. N1.......5F 49
(off Colville Est.)
Silsoe Ho. NW1......1D 61
Silver Birch Cl. SE6...3B 122
Silverbirch Wlk.
NW5..............3C 46
Silverburn Ho. SW9...4D 91
(off Lothian Rd.)
Silver Cl. SE14......3A 94
Silverdale NW1......1F 5
(off Hampstead Rd.)
SE26.............4E 121
Silverdale Ct. EC1....3E 9
Silverdale Dr. SE9...2F 125
Silvermere Rd. SE6...5D 109
Silver Pl.
W1...........4A 14 (5E 61)
Silver Rd. SE13.....1D 109
(not continuous)
W12..............1F 71
Silverthorn NW8.....5D 45
(off Abbey Rd.)
Silverthorne Loft
SE17.............2F 91
(off Albany Rd.)
Silverthorne Rd.
SW8..............5D 89
Silverton Rd. W6....2F 85
SILVERTOWN........2E 83
Silvertown Viaduct
E16..............5B 68
Silvertown Way E16...5A 68
(not continuous)
Silver Wlk. SE16.....2A 80
Silvester Ho. E1......5D 65
(off Varden St.)
E2................2E 65
(off Sceptre Rd.)
W11..............5B 58
(off Basing St.)
Silvester Rd. SE22...3B 106
Silvester St.
SE1..........4B 26 (3F 77)
Silvocea Way E14....5F 67
Silwood Est. SE16....5E 79
Silwood St. SE16.....5E 79
(off Rotherhithe New Rd.)
Simla Ct. N7.........4A 48
(off Brewery Rd.)
Simla Ho. SE1.......4C 26
(off Kipling St.)
Simmonds Ct. SW5...5D 73
(off Earl's Ct. Gdns.)
Simms Rd. SE1......5C 78
Simnel Rd. SE12....5D 111
Simon Cl. W11.......1B 72
Simon Ct. W9........2C 58
(off Saltram Cres.)
Simonds Rd. E10....4C 38
Simone Ct. SE26.....3E 121
Simons Ct. N16......4B 36
Simons Wlk. E15.....2F 53
Simpson Dr. W3......5A 56

Simpson Ho. NW8 . . . . . . 3A 60
SE11 . . . . 1B 90
Simpson's Rd. E14 . . . . . . 1D 81
Simpson St. SW11 . . . . 5A 88
Simrose Ct. SW18 . . . . 3C 100
Sims Wlk. SE3 . . . . . . 2B 110
Sinclair Gdns. W14 . . . . 3F 71
Sinclair Gro. NW11 . . . . 1F 29
Sinclair Ho. WC1 . . . . . . 2D 7
    (off Sandwich St.)
Sinclair Mans. W12 . . . . 3F 71
    (off Richmond Way)
Sinclair Pl. SE4 . . . . . . 4C 108
Sinclair Rd. W14 . . . . . . 3F 71
Singer St.
    EC2. . . . . 2C 10 (2F 63)
Sir Abraham Dawes Cotts.
    SW15 . . . . 2B 100
Sir Alexander Cl. W3 . . . 2B 70
Sir Alexander Rd.
    W3 . . . . 2B 70
Sir Christopher France Ho.
    E1 . . . . 2A 66
Sirdar Rd. W11 . . . . 1F 71
Sirinham Point SW8. . . . 2B 90
    (off Meadow Rd.)
Sirius Bldg. E1 . . . . 1F 79
    (off Jardine Rd.)
Sir John Cass Hall E9. . . 4E 51
    (off Well St.)
Sir John Kirk Cl. SE5 . . . 3E 91
Sir John Soane's Mus.
    . . . . 2F 15 (5B 62)
Sir Nicholas Garrow Ho.
    W10 . . . . 3A 58
    (off Kensal Rd.)
Sir Oswald Stoll
    Foundation, The
    SW6 . . . . 3D 87
    (off Fulham Rd.)
Sir Oswald Stoll Mans.
    SW6 . . . . 3D 87
    (off Fulham Rd.)
Sir William Powell's
    Almshouses SW6. . . . 5A 86
Sise La. EC4 . . . 3B 18 (5F 63)
Siskin Ho. SE16 . . . . . . 5F 79
    (off Tawny Way)
Sispara Gdns.
    SW18 . . . . 4B 100
Sissinghurst Cl.
    BR1: Brom 5A 124
Sissinghurst Ho.
    SE15 . . . . 2E 93
    (off Sharratt St.)
Sissulu Ct. E6 . . . . 5E 55
Sister Mabel's Way
    SE15 . . . . 3C 92
Sisters Av. SW11 . . . . 1B 102
Sistova Rd. SW12 . . . . 1D 117
Sisulu Pl. SW9. . . . . . 1C 104
Sitarey Ct. W12 . . . . . . 2D 71
Sivill Ho. E2 . . . . 1F 11
    (off Columbia Rd.)
Siward Rd. SW17 . . . . 3E 115
Six Acres Est. N4 . . . . . 4B 34
Six Bridges Ind. Est.
    SE1 . . . . 1C 92
Sixth Av. W10 . . . . 2A 58

Skardu Rd. NW2 . . . . . . 2A 44
Skeena Hill SW18 . . . . 5A 100
Skeggs Ho. E14 . . . . . . 4E 81
    (off Glengall St.)
Skegness Ho. N7 . . . . . . 4B 48
    (off Sutterton St.)
Skelbrook St. SW18 . . . 2E 115
Skelgill Rd. SW15 . . . . 2B 100
Skelley Rd. E15 . . . . . . 4B 54
Skelton Cl. E8 . . . . 3B 50
Skelton Rd. E7 . . . . 3C 54
Skelton's La. E10 . . . . . 2D 39
Skelwith Rd. W6 . . . . . . 2E 85
Skenfrith Ho. SE15 . . . . 2D 93
    (off Commercial Way)
Sketchley Gdns.
    SE16 . . . . 1F 93
Skiers St. E15 . . . . 5A 54
Skiffington Cl. SW2 . . . 1C 118
Skinner Pl. SW1. . . . . . . 5C 74
    (off Bourne St.)
Skinners La.
    EC4 . . . . . . 4A 18 (1E 77)
Skinner's Row SE10. . . . 4D 95
Skinner St.
    EC1 . . . . 2D 9 (2C 62)
Skipsea Ho. SW18 . . . . 4A 102
Skipton Ho. SE4 . . . . . . 2A 108
Skipwith Ho. EC1 . . . . . . 5B 8
    (off Bourne Est.)
Skipworth Rd. E9 . . . . . . 5E 51
Skua Ct. SE8 . . . . 2B 94
    (off Dorking Cl.)
Skylark Ct. SE1 . . . . . . 4A 26
    (off Swan St.)
Skyline Ct. SE1 . . . . . . 4B 78
Skyline Plaza Bldg.
    E1 . . . . 5C 64
    (off Commercial Rd.)
Skylines E14. . . . . 3E 81
Skylines Village
    E14 . . . . 3E 81
Sladebrook Rd. SE3 . . . 1F 111
Sladen Pl. E5 . . . . 1D 51
Slade Twr. E10 . . . . 4C 38
    (off Leyton Grange Est.)
Slade Wlk. SE17 . . . . . . 2D 91
Slagrove Pl. SE13 . . . . 3C 108
Slaidburn St. SW10 . . . . 2E 87
Slaithwaite Rd.
    SE13 . . . . 2E 109
Slaney Cl. NW10 . . . . . . 4E 43
Slaney Pl. N7 . . . . 2C 48
Sleaford Ind. Est.
    SW8 . . . . 3E 89
Sleaford St. SW8 . . . . . . 3E 89
Sleigh Ho. E2 . . . . 2E 65
    (off Bacton St.)
Slievemore Cl.
    SW4 . . . . 1F 103
Sligo Ho. E1 . . . . 3F 65
    (off Beaumont Gro.)
Slindon Ct. N16 . . . . 5B 36
Slingsby Pl.
    WC2. . . . . . 4D 15 (1A 76)
Slippers Pl. SE16. . . . . . 4D 79
Slipway Ho. E14 . . . . . . 1D 95
    (off Burrells Wharf Sq.)
Sloane Av. SW3 . . . . . . 5A 74

Sloane Av. Mans.
    SW3 . . . . 5B 74
    (off Sloane Av.)
Sloane Ct. E. SW3 . . . . 1C 88
Sloane Ct. W. SW3 . . . . 1C 88
Sloane Gdns. SW1 . . . . 5C 74
Sloane Ga. Mans.
    SW1 . . . . 5C 74
    (off D'Oyley St.)
Sloane Ho. E9 . . . . 4E 51
    (off Loddiges Rd.)
Sloane Sq. SW1. . . . . . . 5C 74
Sloane St.
    SW1. . . . . . 4A 20 (3B 74)
Sloane Ter. SW1 . . . . . . 5C 74
Sloane Ter. Mans.
    SW1 . . . . 5C 74
    (off Sloane Ter.)
Sloman Ho. W10 . . . . . . 2A 58
    (off Beethoven St.)
Sly St. E1 . . . . 5D 65
Smallbrook M. W2 . . . . . 5F 59
Smalley Cl. N16. . . . . . . 5B 36
Smalley Rd. Est.
    N16. . . . . 5B 36
    (off Smalley Cl.)
Smallwood Rd.
    SW17 . . . . 4F 115
Smart's Pl.
    WC2 . . . . . . 2E 15 (5A 62)
Smart St. E2 . . . . 2F 65
Smeaton Ct.
    SE1 . . . . 5F 25 (4E 77)
Smeaton Rd.
    SW18 . . . . 5C 100
Smeaton St. E1 . . . . 2D 79
Smedley St. SW4 . . . . . . 5F 89
Smeed Rd. E3 . . . . 4C 52
Smiles Pl. SE13 . . . . . . 5E 95
Smith Cl. SE16 . . . . 2F 79
Smithfield (Central Markets)
    . . . . 1D 17
Smithfield St.
    EC1 . . . . . . 1D 17 (4D 63)
Smithies Ct. E15 . . . . . . 2E 53
Smith's Ct. W1. . . . . . . 4A 14
Smiths Point E13 . . . . . . 5C 54
    (off Brooks Rd.)
Smith Sq.
    SW1. . . . . . 5D 23 (4A 76)
Smith St. SW3 . . . . 1B 88
Smith's Yd. SW18 . . . . 2E 115
Smith Ter. SW3 . . . . . . 1B 88
Smithwood Cl.
    SW19 . . . . 1A 114
Smithy St. E1 . . . . 4E 65
Smokehouse Yd. EC1 . . . 5E 9
    (off St John St.)
Smugglers Way
    SW18 . . . . 2D 101
Smyrk's Rd. SE17 . . . . . 1A 92
Smyrna Rd. NW6. . . . . . 4C 44
Smythe St. E14 . . . . 1D 81
SNARESBROOK 1C 40
Snarsgate St. W10. . . . . 4E 57
Sneath Av. NW11. . . . . . 2B 30
Sneyd Rd. NW2 . . . . 1E 43
Snowberry Cl. E15. . . . . 1F 53
Snowbury Rd. SW6 . . . . 5D 87

Snowden St.
  EC2 . . . . 4D **11** (3A **64**)
Snowdon Aviary *5B 46*
  (in London Zoo)
Snowdon Dr. NW9 . . . . 1A **28**
Snow Hill
  EC1 . . . . 1D **17** (4D **63**)
Snow Hill Ct.
  EC1 . . . . 2E **17** (5D **63**)
  (not continuous)
Snowman Ho. NW6 . . . 5D **45**
Snowsfields
  SE1 . . . . 3C **26** (3F **77**)
Snowshill Rd. E12 . . . . 2F **55**
Soames St. SE15 . . . . 1B **106**
Soane Ct. NW1 . . . . . . *4E 47*
  (off St Pancras Way)
SOHO 3B **14** (5E **61**)
Soho Sq. W1 . . 2B **14** (5F **61**)
Soho St. W1 . . . 2B **14** (5F **61**)
Soho Theatre & Writers Cen.
  . . . . *3B 14*
  (off Dean St.)
Sojourner Truth Cl.
  E8 . . . . 3D **51**
Solander Gdns. *E1* . . . *1D 79*
  (off Cable St.)
  E1 . . . . 1E **79**
  (Highway, The)
Solarium Ct. *SE1* *5B 78*
  (off Alscot Rd.)
Soldene Ct. *N7* *2B 48*
  (off George's Rd.)
Solebay St. E1 . . . . . . 3A **66**
Solent Ho. *E1* *4A 66*
  (off Ben Jonson Rd.)
Solent Ri. E13 . . . . . . 2C **68**
Solent Rd. NW6 . . . . . 2C **44**
Soley M. WC1 . . 1B **8** (2C **62**)
Solna Av. SW15 . . . . . 3E **99**
Solomon's Pas.
  SE15 . . . . 2D **107**
Solon New Rd.
  SW4 . . . . 2A **104**
Solon New Rd. Est.
  SW4 . . . . 2A **104**
Solon Rd. SW2 . . . . . 2A **104**
Solway Cl. *E8* *3B 50*
  (off Queensbridge Rd.)
Solway Ho. *E1* *3F 65*
  (off Ernest St.)
Solway Rd. SE22 . . . . 2C **106**
Somali Rd. NW2 . . . . . 2B **44**
Sombourne Ho.
  SW15 . . . . *5C 98*
  (off Fontley Way)
Somer Ct. *SW6* *2C 86*
  (off Anselm Rd.)
Somerfield Ho. SE16 . . 1F **93**
Somerfield Rd. N4 . . . 4D **35**
  (not continuous)
Somerfield St. SE16 . . . 1F **93**
Somerford Gro. N16 . . . 1B **50**
Somerford Gro. Est.
  N16 . . . . 1B **50**
Somerford St. E1 . . . . 3D **65**
Somerford Way SE16 . . 3A **80**
Somerleyton Pas.
  SW9 . . . . 2D **105**

Somerleyton Rd.
  SW9 . . . . 2C **104**
Somers Cl. NW1 . . . . . 1F **61**
Somers Cres. W2 . . . . 5A **60**
Somerset Ct. NW1 . . . . 1F **61**
Somerset Est. SW11 . . 4F **87**
Somerset Gdns. N6 . . . 2C **32**
SE13 . . . . 5D **95**
Somerset House
  . . . . 4F **15** (1B **76**)
Somerset Ho. SW19 . . . 3F **113**
Somerset Rd. E17 . . . . 1C **38**
  SW19 . . . . 3F **113**
Somerset Sq. W14 . . . . 3A **72**
Somers Pl. SW2 . . . . . 5B **104**
Somers Rd. SW2 . . . . 4B **104**
SOMERS TOWN
  . . . . 1B **6** (2F **61**)
Somers Town Community
  Sports Cen. 1F **61**
Somerton Ho. WC1 . . . . 2C **6**
Somerton Rd. NW2 . . . 5A **30**
  SE15 . . . . 2D **107**
Somertrees Av.
  SE12 . . . . 2D **125**
Somerville Av. SW13 . . 2D **85**
Somerville Cl. SW9 . . . 4B **90**
Somerville Point
  SE16 . . . . 3B **80**
Sonderburg Rd. N7 . . . 4B **34**
Sondes St. SE17 . . . . . 2F **91**
Sonia Gdns. NW10 . . . 1B **42**
Sonning Ho. *E2* *2F 11*
  (off Swanfield St.)
Soper Cl. SE23 . . . . . . 1F **121**
Sophia Cl. N7 . . . . 3B **48**
Sophia Ho. *W6* *1E 85*
  (off Queen Caroline St.)
Sophia Rd. E10 . . . . . . 3D **39**
  E16 . . . . 5D **69**
Sophia Sq. *SE16* *1A 80*
  (off Sovereign Cres.)
Sopwith Way SW8 . . . . 3D **89**
Sorensen Ct. *E10* *4D 39*
  (off Leyton Grange Est.)
Sorrel Gdns. E6 . . . . . 4F **69**
Sorrel La. E14 . . . . . . 5F **67**
Sorrell Cl. SE14 . . . . . 3A **94**
  SW9 . . . . 5C **90**
Sotheby Rd. N5 . . . . . 5D **35**
Sotheran Cl. E8 . . . . . 5C **50**
Sotherby Lodge *E2* . . . *1E 65*
  (off Sewardstone Rd.)
Sotheron Rd. SW6 . . . 3D **87**
Soudan Rd. SW11 . . . . 4B **88**
Souldern Rd. W14 . . . . 4F **71**
Sth. Access Rd. E17 . . 2A **38**
Southacre *W2* *5A 60*
  (off Hyde Pk. Cres.)
Sth. Africa Rd. W12 . . . 2D **71**
Southall Pl.
  SE1 . . . . 4B **26** (3F **77**)
Southam Ho. *W10* . . . *3A 58*
  (off Southam St.)
Southampton Bldgs.
  WC2 . . . . 1B **16** (4C **62**)
Southampton M. E16 . . 2D **83**
Southampton Pl.
  WC1 . . . . 1E **15** (4A **62**)

Southampton Rd.
  NW5 . . . . 2B **46**
Southampton Row
  WC1 . . . . 5E **7** (4A **62**)
Southampton St.
  WC2 . . . . 4E **15** (1A **76**)
Southampton Way
  SE5 . . . . 3F **91**
Southam St. W10 . . . . 3A **58**
Sth. Audley St.
  W1 . . . . 5C **12** (1C **74**)
South Av. NW10 . . . . . 3E **57**
South Bank . . 1A **24** (3B **76**)
Sth. Bank Bus. Cen.
  SW8 . . . . 2F **89**
Sth. Birkbeck Rd.
  E11 . . . . 5F **39**
Sth. Black Lion La.
  W6 . . . . 1C **84**
South Block *SE1* *4F 23*
  (off Westminster Bri. Rd.)
Sth. Bolton Gdns.
  SW5 . . . . 1E **87**
Southborough Ho.
  SE17 . . . . *1A 92*
  (off Surrey Gro.)
Southborough Rd. E9 . . 5F **51**
Southbourne Gdns.
  SE12 . . . . 3D **111**
Sth. Branch Av.
  NW10 . . . . 3E **57**
SOUTH BROMLEY 1E **81**
Southbrook M.
  SE12 . . . . 4B **110**
Southbrook Rd.
  SE12 . . . . 4B **110**
Southbury NW8 . . . . . *5E 45*
  (off Loudoun Rd.)
Sth. Carriage Dr.
  SW1 . . . . 3A **20** (3B **74**)
  SW7 . . . . 3F **73**
Sth. Circular Rd.
  SW15 . . . . 2C **98**
Sth. City Ct. SE15 . . . . 3A **92**
South Cl. N6 . . . . 1D **33**
Sth. Colonnade, The
  E14 . . . . 2C **80**
Southcombe St. W14 . . 5A **72**
Southcote Rd. N19 . . . 1E **47**
Southcott Ho. *W9* . . . *3E 59*
  (off Clarendon Gdns.)
Southcott M. NW8 . . . . 1A **60**
South Cres. E16 . . . . . 3F **67**
  WC1 . . . . 1B **14** (4F **61**)
Southcroft Rd.
  SW16 . . . . 5D **117**
  SW17 . . . . 5C **116**
Sth. Croxted Rd.
  SE21 . . . . 3F **119**
Southdean Gdns.
  SW19 . . . . 2B **114**
Southdown N7 . . . . . . 3A **48**
South Eastern University
  . . . . 5B **34**
Sth. Eaton Pl. SW1 . . . 5C **74**
Sth. Edwardes Sq.
  W8 . . . . 4B **72**
SOUTHEND 4F **123**
South End W8 . . . . . . 4D **73**

South End Cl. NW3. . . . 1A 46
South End Grn. NW3 . . . 1A 46
Southend La. SE6. . . . . 4B 122
SE26. . . . . 4B 122
South End Rd.
NW3 . . . . 1A 46
Southend Rd.
BR3: Beck. 5D 123
South End Row W8 . . . 4D 73
Southerngate Way
SE14. . . . . 3A 94
Southern Gro. E3 . . . . 2B 66
Southern Rd. E13. . . . . 1D 69
Southern Row W10 . . . 3A 58
Southern St. N1. . . . . . 1B 62
Southern Way SE10 . . 5B 82
(off School Bank Rd.)
Southernwood Retail Pk.
SE1. . . . . 1B 92
Southerton Rd. W6. . . 5E 71
Sth. Esk Rd. E7. . . . . . 3E 55
Southey Ho. SE17. . . . 1E 91
(off Browning St.)
Southey M. E16 . . . . . . 2C 82
Southey Rd. N15 . . . . . 1A 36
SW9 . . . . 4C 90
Southfield Ct. E11 . . . . 5B 40
Southfield Rd. W4 . . . 3A 70
SOUTHFIELDS 1B 114
Southfields M.
SW18 . . . . 4C 100
Southfields Pas.
SW18 . . . . 4C 100
Southfields Rd.
SW18 . . . . 4C 100
Southfleet NW5 . . . . . 3C 46
Southgate Ct. N1 . . . . 4F 49
(off Downham Rd.)
Southgate Gro. N1 . . . 4F 49
South Ga. Rd. E12 . . . 5F 41
Southgate Rd. N1 . . . . 5F 49
South Gro. E17 . . . . . . 1B 38
N6. . . . . 3C 32
N15 . . . . 1F 35
South Gro. Ho. N6 . . . 3C 32
SOUTH HACKNEY . . . 4F 51
SOUTH HAMPSTEAD . . 4E 45
Sth. Hill Pk. NW3. . . . . 1A 46
Sth. Hill Pk. Gdns.
NW3 . . . . 5A 32
Southill St. E14 . . . . . 5D 67
Sth. Island Pl. SW9 . . 3B 90
SOUTH KENSINGTON
. . . . 5F 73
Sth. Kensington Sta. Arc.
SW7 . . . . 5F 73
(off Pelham St.)
SOUTH LAMBETH 3A 90
Sth. Lambeth Pl.
SW8 . . . . 2A 90
Sth. Lambeth Rd.
SW8 . . . . 2A 90
Southlands Dr.
SW19 . . . . 2F 113
South Lodge E16 . . . . 2D 83
(off Audley Dr.)
NW8 . . . . 1F 59
SW7 . . . . 3A 74
(off Knightsbridge)

South London Gallery
. . . . 4A 92
(off Peckham Rd.)
South London Theatre
. . . . 3D 119
(off Norwood High St.)
South Mall SW18. . . . . 4D 101
Southmead Rd.
SW19 . . . . 1A 114
Sth. Molton La.
W1. . . . . 3D 13 (5D 61)
Sth. Molton Rd. E16 . . 5C 68
Sth. Molton St.
W1. . . . . 3D 13 (5D 61)
Southmoor Way E9 . . 3B 52
Sth. Oak Rd. SW16 . . . 4B 118
Southolm St. SW11. . . 4D 89
Southover
BR1: Brom 5C 124
South Pde. SW3 . . . . . 1F 87
W4 . . . . 5A 70
South Pk. Cres. SE6. . . 1A 124
South Pk. Rd.
SW19 . . . . 5E 115
South Pl.
EC2. . . . . 5C 10 (4F 63)
South Pl. M.
EC2. . . . . 1C 18 (4F 63)
Sth. Quay Plaza E14 . . 3D 81
South Ri. W2 . . . . 1A 74
(off St George's Flds.)
South Rd. SE23. . . . . . 2F 121
Southrow SE3 . . . . 5B 96
Sth. Sea St. SE16 . . . . 4B 80
South Side W6. . . . . . . 4B 70
Southside N7 . . . . 1F 47
Southside Comn.
SW19 . . . . 5E 113
Southside Ind. Est.
SW8 . . . . 4E 89
(off Havelock Ter.)
Southside Shop. Cen.
SW18 . . . . 4D 101
South Sq. NW11. . . . . . 1D 31
WC1. . . . . 1B 16 (4C 62)
South St. W1. . . 1C 20 (2C 74)
Sth. Tenter St. E1 . . . . 1B 78
South Ter. SW7 . . . . . . 5A 74
SOUTH TOTTENHAM . . 1B 36
Southvale Rd. SE3 . . . 5A 96
Southview Av. NW10 . . 2B 42
Southview Cl.
SW17 . . . . 5C 116
Southview Rd.
BR1: Brom 4F 123
South Vs. NW1 . . . . . . 3F 47
Southville SW8. . . . . . 4F 89
SOUTHWARK
. . . . 3E 25 (2E 77)
Southwark Bri.
EC4. . . . . 5A 18 (1E 77)
SE1. . . . . 2A 26
(off Southwark Bri. Rd.)
Southwark Bri. Bus. Cen.
SE1. . . . . 2A 26
(off Southwark Bri. Rd.)
Southwark Bri. Office Village
SE1. . . . . 1A 26
Southwark Bri. Rd.
SE1 . . . . 5E 25 (4D 77)

Southwark Cathedral
. . . . 1B 26 (2F 77)
Southwark Pk. Est.
SE16. . . . . 4D 79
Southwark Pk. Rd.
SE16 . . . . 5B 78
Southwark Pk.
Sports Cen. Track . . 5E 79
Southwark Pk. Sports Complex
. . . . 5E 79
Southwark Playhouse
. . . . 2F 25
(off Gt. Guildford St.)
Southwark St.
SE1. . . . . 1D 25 (2D 77)
Southwater Cl. E14 . . . 5B 66
Southway NW11. . . . . . 1D 31
Southway Cl. W12. . . . 3D 71
(off Scott's Rd.)
Southwell Gdns.
SW7 . . . . 5E 73
Southwell Gro. Rd.
E11. . . . . 4A 40
Southwell Ho. SE16. . . 5D 79
(off Anchor St.)
Southwell Rd. SE5 . . . 1E 105
South W. India Dock Entrance
E14. . . . . 3E 81
Southwest Rd. E11. . . . 3F 39
Sth. Wharf Rd. W2 . . . 5F 59
Southwick M. W2. . . . . 5F 59
Southwick Pl. W2. . . . . 5A 60
Southwick St. W2. . . . . 5A 60
Southwick Yd. W2 . . . 5A 60
(off Titchborne Row)
SOUTH WIMBLEDON
. . . . 5D 115
Southwold Mans. W9. . 2C 58
(off Widley Rd.)
Southwold Rd. E5 . . . . 4D 37
Southwood Av. N6 . . . 2D 33
Southwood Ct. EC1 . . . 2D 9
(off Wynyatt St.)
NW11. . . . . 1D 31
Southwood Hall N6 . . . 1D 33
Barking Relief Rd.
E11. . . . . 1F 41
IG1: Ilf. 1F 41
IG4: Ilf. 1F 41
Southwood Hgts. N6. . 2D 33
Southwood Ho. W11 . . 1A 72
(off Avondale Pk. Rd.)
Southwood La. N6. . . . 3C 32
Southwood Lawn Rd.
N6. . . . . 2C 32
Southwood Mans. N6. . 1C 32
(off Southwood La.)
Southwood Pk. N6 . . . 2C 32
Southwood Smith Ho.
E2. . . . . 2D 65
(off Florida St.)
Southwood Smith St.
N1. . . . . 5D 49
Sth. Worple Av.
SW14 . . . . 1A 98
Sth. Worple Way
SW14 . . . . 1A 98
Southwyck Ho. SW9 . . 2D 105

Sovereign Cl. E1 . . . . . . 1D 79
Sovereign Ct. W8. . . . . . . 4D 73
   (off Wright's La.)
Sovereign Cres. SE16. . 1A 80
Sovereign Ho. E1. . . . . . . 3D 65
   (off Cambridge Heath Rd.)
Sovereign M. E2. . . . . . . 1B 64
Spa Ct. SW16 . . . . 4B 118
Spafield St.
  EC1 . . . . 3B 8 (3C 62)
Spa Grn. Est.
  EC1 . . . . 1C 8 (2D 63)
Spalding Ho. SE4. . . . . . 2A 108
Spalding Rd. NW4 . . . . . 2E 29
  SW17 . . . . 5D 117
Spanby Rd. E3 . . . . 3C 66
Spaniards Cl. NW11. . . . . 3F 31
Spaniards End NW3 . . . . 3E 31
Spaniards Rd. NW3 . . . . 4E 31
Spanish Pl.
  W1 . . . . 2C 12 (5C 60)
Spanish Rd. SW18. . . . . 3E 101
Sparkes Cotts. SW1 . . . . 5C 74
  (off Graham Ter.)
Sparke Ter. E16 . . . . 5B 68
  (off Clarkson Rd.)
Spa Rd.
  SE16 . . . . . . 5F 27 (4B 78)
Sparrick's Row
  SE1 . . . . 3C 26 (3F 77)
Sparrow Ho. E1 . . . . 3E 65
  (off Cephas Av.)
Sparsholt Rd. N19 . . . . . 3B 34
Sparta St. SE10 . . . . 4E 95
Speakers' Corner
  . . . . 4A 12 (1B 74)
Speakman Ho. SE4 . . . . 1A 108
  (off Arica Rd.)
Spearman Ho. E14 . . . . . 5C 66
  (off Up. North St.)
Spear M. SW5 . . . . 5C 72
Spears Rd. N19 . . . . 3A 34
Spectacle Works E13 . . . 2E 69
Spectrum Pl. SE17 . . . . . 2F 91
  (off Lytham St.)
Spedan Cl. NW3 . . . . . . 5E 31
Speechly M. E8 . . . . 2B 50
Speed Highwalk EC2 . . 5A 10
  (off Silk St.)
Speed Ho. EC2 . . . . 5A 10
Speedwell St. SE8 . . . . . 3C 94
Speedy Pl. WC1 . . . . 2D 7
Speke Ho. SE16 . . . . 3E 79
Speldhurst Rd. E9 . . . . . 4F 51
  W4 . . . . 4A 70
Spellbrook Wlk. N1 . . . . 5E 49
Spelman Ho. E1 . . . . 4C 64
  (off Spelman St.)
Spelman St. E1 . . . . 4C 64
  (not continuous)
Spence Cl. SE16 . . . . . . 3B 80
Spencer Cl. NW8 . . . . . . 1E 59
  (off Marlborough Pl.)
Spencer Dr. N2 . . . . 1E 31
Spencer House 2F 21
Spencer Ho. NW4 . . . . . 1D 29
Spencer Mans.
  W14 . . . . 2A 86
  (off Queen's Club Gdns.)

Spencer M. SW8 . . . . . . 4B 90
  (off Sth. Lambeth Rd.)
  W6 . . . . 2A 86
SPENCER PARK 3F 101
Spencer Pk. SW18 . . . . 3F 101
Spencer Pl. N1 . . . . 4D 49
Spencer Ri. NW5 . . . . . . 1D 47
Spencer Rd. E6 . . . . 5F 55
  N8 . . . . 1B 34
  (not continuous)
  SW18 . . . . 2F 101
Spencer St.
  EC1 . . . . 2D 9 (2D 63)
Spencer Wlk. NW3 . . . . . 1E 45
  (off Perrin's Ct.)
  NW3 . . . . 1F 45
  (Hampstead High St.)
  SW15 . . . . 2F 99
Spenlow Ho. SE16 . . . . . 4C 78
  (off Jamaica Rd.)
Spenser Gro. N16 . . . . . 2A 50
Spenser M. SE21 . . . . . 2F 119
Spenser Rd. SE24 . . . . . 3D 105
Spenser St.
  SW1 . . . . 5A 22 (4E 75)
Spens Ho. WC1 . . . . 4F 7
  (off Long Yd.)
Spensley Wlk. N16 . . . . . 5F 35
Spert St. E14 . . . . 1A 80
Spey St. E14 . . . . 4E 67
Spezia Rd. NW10 . . . . . 1C 56
Sphere, The E16 . . . . . . 5B 68
  (off Hallsville Rd.)
Spice Ct. E1 . . . . 1C 78
Spice Quay Hgts.
  SE1 . . . . 2B 78
Spicer Cl. SW9 . . . . 5D 91
Spindrift Av. E14 . . . . . . 5C 80
Spinnaker Ho. E14 . . . . . 3C 80
  (off Byng St.)
Spinney, The SW13 . . . . 3D 85
  SW16 . . . . 3E 117
Spinney Gdns.
  SE19 . . . . 5B 120
Spire Ho. W2 . . . . 1E 73
  (off Lancaster Ga.)
Spirit Quay E1 . . . . 2C 78
SPITALFIELDS
  . . . . 5F 11 (4B 64)
Spital Sq. E1 . . 5E 11 (4A 64)
Spital St. E1 . . . . 4C 64
Spital Yd. E1 . . 5E 11 (4A 64)
Splendour Wlk.
  SE16 . . . . 1E 93
  (off Verney Rd.)
Spode Ho. SE11 . . . . . . 5B 24
Spode Wlk. NW6 . . . . . . 2D 45
Sportsbank St. SE6 . . . . 5E 109
Sportsman Pl. E2 . . . . . . 5C 50
Spratt Hall Rd. E11 . . . . 1C 40
Spriggs Ho. N1 . . . . 4D 49
  (off Canonbury Rd.)
Sprimont Pl. SW3 . . . . . 1B 88
Springall St. SE15 . . . . . 3D 93
Springalls Wharf
  SE16 . . . . 3C 78
  (off Bermondsey Wall W.)
Springbank Rd.
  SE13 . . . . 4F 109

Springbank Wlk.
  NW1 . . . . 4F 47
Spring Ct. NW6 . . . . 3B 44
Springdale M. N16 . . . . . 1F 49
Springdale Rd. N16 . . . . 1F 49
Springett Ho. SW2 . . . . 3C 104
  (off St Matthews Rd.)
Springfield E5 . . . . 3D 37
Springfield Ct. NW3 . . . . 4A 46
  (off Eton Av.)
Springfield Gdns. E5 . . . 3D 37
  NW9 . . . . 1A 28
Springfield Gro. SE7 . . . 2E 97
Springfield La. NW6 . . . . 5D 45
Springfield Ri.
  SE26 . . . . 3D 121
Springfield Rd. E15 . . . . 2A 68
  E17 . . . . 1B 38
  NW8 . . . . 5E 45
  SE26 . . . . 5D 121
  SW19 . . . . 5B 114
Springfield Wlk.
  NW6 . . . . 5D 45
Spring Gdns. N5 . . . . . . 2E 49
  SW1 . . . . 1C 22 (2F 75)
  (not continuous)
Spring Hill E5 . . . . 2C 36
  SE26 . . . . 4E 121
Springhill Cl. SE5 . . . . . 1F 105
Spring Ho. WC1 . . . . 2B 8
Spring La. E5 . . . . 2D 37
Spring M. W1 . . 5A 4 (4B 60)
Spring Pk. Dr. N4 . . . . . . 3E 35
Spring Pas. SW15 . . . . . 1F 99
Spring Path NW3 . . . . . . 2F 45
Spring Pl. NW5 . . . . 2D 47
Springrice Rd. SE13 . . . 4F 109
Spring St. W2 . . . . 5F 59
Spring Tide Cl. SE15 . . . 4C 92
Spring Va. Ter. W14 . . . . 4F 71
Springwater WC1 . . . . . . 5F 7
Springwell Av. NW10 . . . 5B 42
Springwell Cl.
  SW16 . . . . 4B 118
Springwell Rd.
  SW16 . . . . 4C 118
Springwood Cl. E3 . . . . 1C 66
Sprowston M. E7 . . . . . . 3C 54
Sprowston Rd. E7 . . . . . 2C 54
Spruce Ho. SE16 . . . . . . 3F 79
  (off Woodland Cres.)
Sprules Rd. SE4 . . . . . . 5A 94
Spurgeon St. SE1 . . . . . 5B 26
Spurling Rd. SE22 . . . . . 2B 106
Spur Rd. SE1 . . 3B 24 (3C 76)
  SW1 . . . . 4F 21 (3E 75)
Spurstowe Rd. E8 . . . . . 3D 51
Spurstowe Ter. E8 . . . . . 2C 50
Square, The E10 . . . . . . 5E 39
  W6 . . . . 1E 85
Square Rigger Row
  SW11 . . . . 1E 101
Squarey St. SW17 . . . . . 3E 115
Squire Gdns. NW8 . . . . . 2F 59
  (off Grove End Rd.)
Squires Ct. SW4 . . . . . . 4A 90
  SW19 . . . . 4C 114
Squires Mt. NW3 . . . . . . 5F 31

Squirrels, The SE13 . . . 1F 109
Squirries St. E2 . . . . 2C 64
Stable M. NW5 . . . . 3D 47
SE6 . . . . 1A 124
Stables Gallery & Arts Cen.
. . . . 5C 28
Stables Lodge E8 . . . . . 4D 51
(off Mare St.)
Stables Mkt., The
NW1 . . . . 4D 47
Stables M. SE27 . . . . . 5E 119
Stables Way SE11 . . 1C 90
Stables Yd. SW18 . . . 4C 100
Stable Wlk. N1 . . . . . 1A 62
(off Wharfdale Rd.)
Stable Way W10 . . . . . 5E 57
Stable Yd. SW1 . . . . . . 3F 21
SW15 . . . . 1E 99
Stableyard, The SW9 . . 5B 90
Stable Yd. Rd.
SW1 . . . . 3A 22 (3E 75)
(not continuous)
Stacey Cl. E10 . . . . 1F 39
Stacey St. N7 . . . . 5C 34
WC2 . . . . . 3C 14 (5F 61)
Stack Ho. SW1 . . . . 5C 74
(off Cundy St.)
Stackhouse St. SW3 . . 5A 20
Stacy Path SE5 . . . . 3A 92
Stadium Rd. E. NW4 . . 2D 29
Stadium St. SW10 . . . . 3E 87
Staffa Rd. E10 . . . . . . 3A 38
Stafford Cl. E17 . . . . . . 1B 38
(not continuous)
NW6 . . . . 2C 58
Stafford Ct. SW8 . . . . 3A 90
W8 . . . . 4C 72
Stafford Cripps Ho.
E2 . . . . 2E 65
(off Globe Rd.)
SW6 . . . . 2B 86
(off Clem Attlee Ct.)
Stafford Ho. SE1 . . . . 1B 92
(off Cooper's Rd.)
Stafford Mans. SW1 . . 5F 21
(off Stafford Pl.)
SW4 . . . . 2A 104
SW11 . . . . 3B 88
(off Albert Bri. Rd.)
W14 . . . . 4F 71
(off Haarlem Rd.)
Stafford Pl.
SW1 . . . . . . 5F 21 (4E 75)
Stafford Rd. E3 . . . . . 1B 66
E7 . . . . 4E 55
NW6 . . . . 2C 58
Staffordshire St.
SE15 . . . . 4C 92
Stafford St.
W1 . . . . 1F 21 (2E 75)
Stafford Ter. W8 . . . . . 4C 72
Staff St. EC1 . . . 2C 10 (2F 63)
STAG LANE 2B 112
Stag La. SW15 . . . . . . 3B 112
Stainer Ho. SE3 . . . . 2E 111
Stainer St.
SE1 . . . . 2C 26 (2F 77)
Staining La.
EC2 . . . . . . 2A 18 (5E 63)

Stainsbury St. E2 . . . . . 1E 65
Stainsby Rd. E14 . . . . . 5C 66
Stainton Rd. SE6 . . . . . 4F 109
Stalbridge Flats W1 . . . . 3C 12
(off Lumley St.)
Stalbridge Ho. NW1 . . . . 1F 5
(off Harrington St.)
Stalbridge St. NW1 . . . 4A 60
Stalham St. SE16 . . . . . 4D 79
Stamford Bridge 3D 87
Stamford Brook Arches
W6 . . . . 5C 70
Stamford Brook Av.
W6 . . . . 4B 70
Stamford Brook Gdns.
W6 . . . . 4B 70
Stamford Brook Mans.
W6 . . . . 5B 70
(off Goldhawk Rd.)
Stamford Brook Rd.
W6 . . . . 4B 70
Stamford Bldgs.
SW8 . . . . 3A 90
(off Meadow Pl.)
Stamford Cl. NW3 . . . . . 5E 31
(off Heath St.)
Stamford Cotts.
SW10 . . . . 3D 87
(off Billing St.)
Stamford Ct. W6 . . . . . 5C 70
Stamford Ga. SW6 . . . . 3D 87
Stamford Gro. E.
N16 . . . . 3C 36
Stamford Gro. W.
N16 . . . . 3C 36
STAMFORD HILL 3B 36
Stamford Hill N16 . . . . 4B 36
Stamford Lodge N16 . . 2B 36
Stamford Rd. E6 . . . . . 5F 55
N1 . . . . 4A 50
Stamford St.
SE1 . . . . . . 2B 24 (2C 76)
Stamp Pl. E2 . . 1F 11 (1B 64)
Stanard Cl. N16 . . . . . 2A 36
Stanborough Pas. E8 . . 3B 50
Stanbridge Rd.
SW15 . . . . 1E 99
Stanbury Ct. NW3 . . . . 3B 46
Stanbury Rd. SE15 . . . 5D 93
(not continuous)
Standard St. SE6 . . . . 1D 123
Standard Pl. EC2 . . . . . 2E 11
Standard Rd. NW10 . . 3A 56
Standen Rd. SW18 . . . 5B 100
Standish Ho. SE3 . . . . 2D 111
(off Elford Cl.)
W6 . . . . 5C 70
(off St Peter's Gro.)
Standish Rd. W6 . . . . . 5C 70
Standlake Point
SE23 . . . . 3F 121
Stane Gro. SW4 . . . . . 5A 90
Stane Pas. SW16 . . . . 5A 118
Stanesgate Ho. SE15 . . 3C 92
(off Friary Est.)
Stane Way SE18 . . . . . 3F 97
Stanfield Ho. NW8 . . . . 3F 59
(off Frampton St.)
Stanfield Rd. E3 . . . . . 1A 66

Stanford Ct. SW6 . . . . . 4D 87
W8 . . . . 4D 73
(off Kingsley M.)
Stanford Pl. SE17 . . . . 5A 78
Stanford Rd. W8 . . . . . 4D 73
Stanford St. SW1 . . . . 5F 75
Stangate SE1 . . . . 5A 24
Stanhope Cl. SE16 . . . 3F 79
Stanhope Gdns. N4 . . . 1D 35
N6 . . . . 1D 33
SW7 . . . . 5E 73
Stanhope Ga.
W1 . . . . 2C 20 (2B 74)
Stanhope Ho. SE8 . . . . 3B 94
(off Adolphus St.)
Stanhope M. E. SW7 . . 5E 73
Stanhope M. Sth.
SW7 . . . . 5E 73
Stanhope M. W. SW7 . . 5E 73
Stanhope Pde.
NW1 . . . . 1F 5 (2E 61)
Stanhope Pl. W2 . . . . . 1B 74
Stanhope Rd. E17 . . . . 1D 39
N6 . . . . 1E 33
Stanhope Row
W1 . . . . 2D 21 (2D 75)
Stanhope St.
NW1 . . . . 1F 5 (1E 61)
Stanhope Ter. W2 . . . . 1F 73
Stanier Cl. W14 . . . . . . 1B 86
Stanlake M. W12 . . . . . 2E 71
Stanlake Rd. W12 . . . . 2E 71
Stanlake Vs. W12 . . . . 2E 71
Stanley Bri. Studios
SW6 . . . . 3D 87
(off King's Rd.)
Stanley Cl. SW8 . . . . . 2B 90
Stanley Cohen Ho.
EC1 . . . . 4F 9
(off Golden La. Est.)
Stanley Cres. W11 . . . . 1B 72
Stanley Gdns. NW2 . . . 2E 43
W3 . . . . 3A 70
W11 . . . . 1B 72
Stanley Gdns. M.
W11 . . . . 1B 72
(off Kensington Pk. Rd.)
Stanley Gro. SW8 . . . . 5C 88
Stanley Holloway Ct.
E16 . . . . 5C 68
(off Coolfin Rd.)
Stanley Ho. E14 . . . . . 5C 66
(off Saracen St.)
SW10 . . . . 3E 87
(off Coleridge Gdns.)
Stanley Mans. SW10 . . 2E 87
(off Park Wlk.)
Stanley M. SW10 . . . . 3E 87
(off Coleridge Gdns.)
Stanley Rd. E10 . . . . . 1D 39
E12 . . . . 2F 55
E15 . . . . 5F 53
NW9 . . . . 2C 28
Stanley St. SE8 . . . . . 3B 94
Stanley Studios
SW10 . . . . 2E 87
(off Fulham Rd.)
Stanley Ter. N19 . . . . . 4A 34
Stanliffe Ho. E14 . . . . 4C 80

Stanmer St. SW11 . . . . . 4A **88**
Stanmore Pl. NW1 . . . . . 5D **47**
Stanmore Rd. E11 . . . . . 3B **40**
Stanmore St. N1 . . . . . . 5B **48**
Stannard Cotts. E1 . . . . . 3E **65**
  (off Fox Cl.)
Stannard M. E8 . . . . 3C **50**
  (off Stannard Rd.)
Stannard Rd. E8 . . . . 3C **50**
Stannary Pl. SE11 . . . . . 1C **90**
Stannary St. SE11 . . . . . 2C **90**
Stansbury Ho. W10 . . . . 2A **58**
  (off Beethoven St.)
Stansbury Sq. W10 . . . . 2A **58**
Stansfeld Rd. E6 . . . . . . 4F **69**
  E16 . . . . 1F **83**
Stansfield Ho. SE1 . . . . . 5B **78**
  (off Balaclava Rd.)
Stansfield Rd. SW9 . . . . 1B **104**
Stanstead Gro. SE6 . . . . 1B **122**
Stanstead Rd. E11 . . . . . 1D **41**
  SE6 . . . . 1A **122**
  SE23 . . . . 1F **121**
Stanswood Gdns.
  SE5 . . . . 3A **92**
Stanthorpe Cl.
  SW16 . . . . 5A **118**
Stanthorpe Rd.
  SW16 . . . . 5A **118**
Stanton Ho. SE10 . . . . . 2E **95**
  (off Thames St.)
  SE16 . . . . 3B **80**
  (off Rotherhithe St.)
Stanton Rd. SE26 . . . . . 4B **122**
  SW13 . . . . 5B **84**
Stanton Sq. SE26 . . . . . 4B **122**
Stanton Way SE26 . . . . 4B **122**
Stanway Ct. N1 . . . . 1A **64**
  (not continuous)
Stanway St. N1 . . . . 1A **64**
Stanwick Rd. W14 . . . . . 5B **72**
Stanworth St.
  SE1 . . . . 4F **27** (4B **78**)
Stanyhurst SE23 . . . . . . 1A **122**
Staplefield Cl. SW2 . . . . 1A **118**
Stapleford Cl.
  SW19 . . . . 5A **100**
Staplehurst Rd.
  SE13 . . . . 3F **109**
Staple Inn WC1 . . . . 1B **16**
Staple Inn Bldgs.
  WC1 . . . . 1B **16** (4C **62**)
Staples Cl. SE16 . . . . . . 2A **80**
STAPLES CORNER 3D **29**
Staples Cnr. Bus. Pk.
  NW2 . . . . 3D **29**
Staple St.
  SE1 . . . . 4C **26** (3F **77**)
Stapleton Hall Rd.
  N4 . . . . 3B **34**
Stapleton Ho. E2 . . . . . . 2D **65**
  (off Ellsworth St.)
Stapleton Rd.
  SW17 . . . . 3C **116**
Stapleton Vs. N16 . . . . . 1A **50**
  (off Wordsworth St.)
Star All. EC3 . . . . 4E **19**
  (off Fenchurch St.)
Starboard Way E14 . . . . 4C **80**

Starcross St.
  NW1 . . . . 2A **6** (2E **61**)
Starfield Rd. W12 . . . . . 3C **70**
Star La. E16 . . . . 3A **68**
Starling Ho. NW8 . . . . . . 1A **60**
  (off Barrow Hill Est.)
Star Pl. E1 . . . . 1C **78**
Star Rd. W14 . . . . 2B **86**
Star St. W2 . . . . 5A **60**
Star Yd.
  WC2 . . . . 2B **16** (5C **62**)
Statham Gro. N16 . . . . . 1F **49**
Statham Ho. SW8 . . . . . 4E **89**
  (off Wadhurst Rd.)
Station App. E7 . . . . 1D **55**
  NW1 . . . . 4A **4** (3B **60**)
  NW10 . . . . 2B **56**
  SE3 . . . . 1D **111**
  SE12 . . . . 4C **110**
  (off Burnt Ash Hill)
  SE26 . . . . 4E **121**
  SW6 . . . . 1A **100**
  SW16 . . . . 5F **117**
Station App. Rd.
  SE1 . . . . 4A **24** (3C **76**)
Station Arc. W1 . . . . 4E **5**
  (off Gt. Portland St.)
Station Av. SW9 . . . . . . 1D **105**
Station Cres. SE3 . . . . . 1C **96**
Stationer's Hall Ct.
  EC4 . . . . 3E **17** (5D **63**)
Station Pde. E13 . . . . . . 5E **55**
  (off Green St.)
  NW2 . . . . 3E **43**
  SW12 . . . . 1C **116**
Station Pas. SE15 . . . . . 4E **93**
Station Path E8 . . . . 3D **51**
  (off Graham Rd.)
  SW6 . . . . 1B **100**
Station Pl. N4 . . . . 4C **34**
Station Ri. SE27 . . . . . . 2D **119**
Station Rd. E7 . . . . 1C **54**
  E12 . . . . 1F **55**
  E17 . . . . 1A **38**
  N19 . . . . 5E **33**
  NW4 . . . . 1C **28**
  NW10 . . . . 1B **56**
  SE13 . . . . 1E **109**
  SE20 . . . . 5E **121**
  SW13 . . . . 5B **84**
Station St. E15 . . . . 4F **53**
Station Ter. NW10 . . . . . 1F **57**
  SE5 . . . . 4E **91**
Station Ter. M. SE3 . . . . 1C **96**
Station Way SE15 . . . . . 5C **92**
Staton Ct. E10 . . . . 2D **39**
  (off Kings Cl.)
Staunton Ho. SE17 . . . . 5A **78**
  (off Tatum St.)
Staunton St. SE8 . . . . . . 2B **94**
Staveley NW1 . . . . 1F **5**
  (off Varndell St.)
Staveley Cl. E9 . . . . 2E **51**
  N7 . . . . 1A **48**
  SE15 . . . . 4D **93**
Staveley Gdns. W4 . . . . 4A **84**
Staveley Rd. W4 . . . . . . 3A **84**
Staverton Rd. NW2 . . . . 4E **43**
Stave Yd. Rd. SE16 . . . . 2A **80**

Stavordale Lodge
  W14 . . . . 4B **72**
  (off Melbury Rd.)
Stavordale Rd. N5 . . . . . 1D **49**
Stayner's Rd. E1 . . . . . . 3F **65**
Steadman St. EC1 . . . . . 3A **10**
  (off Old St.)
Stead St. SE17 . . . . 5F **77**
Stean St. E8 . . . . 5B **50**
Stebbing Ho. W11 . . . . . 2F **71**
  (off Queensdale Cres.)
Stebondale St. E14 . . . . 5E **81**
Stedham Pl. WC1 . . . . . 2D **15**
Steedman St. SE17 . . . . 5E **77**
Steele Ho. E15 . . . . 1A **68**
  (off Eve Rd.)
Steele Rd. E11 . . . . 1A **54**
Steele's M. Nth.
  NW3 . . . . 3B **46**
Steele's M. Sth.
  NW3 . . . . 3B **46**
Steele's Rd. NW3 . . . . . 3B **46**
Steele's Studios
  NW3 . . . . 3B **46**
Steel's La. E1 . . . . 5E **65**
Steelyard Pas. EC4 . . . . 5B **18**
Steen Way SE22 . . . . . . 3A **106**
Steep Hill SW16 . . . . . . 3F **117**
Steeple Cl. SW6 . . . . . . 5A **86**
  SW19 . . . . 5A **114**
Steeple Ct. E1 . . . . 3D **65**
Steeple Wlk. N1 . . . . 5E **49**
  (off New Nth. Rd.)
Steerforth St. SW18 . . . 2E **115**
Steers Way SE16 . . . . . 3A **80**
Stelfox Ho. WC1 . . . . . . 1A **8**
  (off Penton Ri.)
Stella Rd. SW17 . . . . . . 5B **116**
Stellman Cl. E5 . . . . 5C **36**
Stephan Cl. E8 . . . . 5C **50**
Stephendale Rd.
  SW6 . . . . 1D **101**
Stephen Fox Ho. W4 . . . 1A **84**
  (off Chiswick La.)
Stephen M.
  W1 . . . . 1B **14** (4F **61**)
Stephen Pl. SW4 . . . . . . 1E **103**
Stephens Ct. E16 . . . . . . 3B **68**
  SE4 . . . . 1A **108**
Stephenson Ho.
  SE1 . . . . 5F **25** (4E **77**)
Stephenson Rd. E17 . . . 1A **38**
Stephenson St. E16 . . . . 3A **68**
  NW10 . . . . 2A **56**
Stephenson Way
  NW1 . . . . 3A **6** (3E **61**)
Stephen's Rd. E15 . . . . . 5A **54**
Stephen St.
  W1 . . . . 1B **14** (4F **61**)
STEPNEY 4F **65**
Stepney C'way. E1 . . . . . 5F **65**
Stepney City Apartments
  E1 . . . . 4E **65**
Stepney Grn. E1 . . . . . . 4E **65**
Stepney Grn. Ct. E1 . . . . 4F **65**
  (off Stepney Grn.)
Stepney High St. E1 . . . . 4F **65**
Stepney Way E1 . . . . . . 4D **65**
Sterling Cl. NW10 . . . . . 4C **42**

Sterling Gdns. SE14 . . . . 2A 94
Sterling Ho. SE3 . . . . 2D 111
Sterling St. SW7 . . . . 4A 74
Sterndale Rd. W14 . . . . . . 4F 71
Sterne St. W12 . . . . 3F 71
Sternhall La. SE15 . . . 1C 106
Sternhold Av. SW2 . . . 2F 117
Sterry St.
  SE1 . . . . 4B 26 (3F 77)
Steucers La. SE23 . . . . 1A 122
Steve Biko La. SE6 . . . 4C 122
Steve Biko Lodge
  E13 . . . . 1C 68
    (off London Rd.)
Steve Biko Rd. N7 . . . . . 5C 34
Stevedore St. E1 . . . . 2D 79
Stevenage Rd. SW6 . . . . . 3F 85
Stevens Av. E9 . . . . 3E 51
Stevens Cl.
  BR3: Beck. 5C 122
Stevenson Cres.
  SE16 . . . . 1C 92
Stevenson Ho. NW8 . . . 5E 45
    (off Boundary Rd.)
Stevens St.
  SE1 . . . . 5E 27 (4A 78)
Steventon Rd. W12 . . . . . 1B 70
Steward St. E1 . . . . 4A 64
Stewart Rd. E15 . . . . 1F 53
Stewart's Gro. SW3 . . . . . 1F 87
Stewart's Rd. SW8 . . . . . 3E 89
Stewart St. E14 . . . . 3E 81
Stew La. EC4 . . . . 4F 17 (1E 77)
Stifford Ho. E1 . . . . 4E 65
    (off Stepney Way)
Stileman Ho. E3 . . . . 4B 66
    (off Ackroyd Dr.)
Stillingfleet Rd.
  SW13 . . . . 2C 84
Stillington St. SW1 . . . . . 5E 75
Stillness Rd. SE23 . . . . 4A 108
Stirling Ct. EC1 . . . . 3D 9
    (off St John St.)
Stirling Rd. E13 . . . . 1D 69
  SW9 . . . . 5A 90
Stockbeck NW1 . . . . 1A 6
    (off Ampthill Est.)
Stockfield Rd.
  SW16 . . . . 3B 118
Stockholm Ho. E1 . . . . . . 1C 78
    (off Swedenborg Gdns.)
Stockholm Rd. SE16 . . . 1E 93
Stockholm Way E1 . . . . . 2C 78
Stockhurst Cl. SW15 . . . 5E 85
Stockleigh Hall NW8 . . . 1A 60
    (off Prince Albert Rd.)
Stock Orchard Cres.
  N7 . . . . 2B 48
Stock Orchard St.
  N7 . . . . 2B 48
Stocks Pl. E14 . . . . 1B 80
Stock St. E13 . . . . 1C 68
Stockton Ct. SW1 . . . . . . 4F 75
    (off Rochester Row)
Stockton Ho. E2 . . . . 2D 65
    (off Ellsworth St.)
STOCKWELL 5B 90
Stockwell Av. SW9 . . . . 1B 104
Stockwell Gdns. SW9 . . 4B 90

Stockwell Gdns. Est.
  SW9 . . . . 5A 90
Stockwell Grn. SW9 . . . . 5B 90
Stockwell Grn. Ct.
  SW9 . . . . 5B 90
Stockwell La. SW9 . . . . . 5B 90
Stockwell M. SW9 . . . . . 5B 90
Stockwell Pk. Cres.
  SW9 . . . . 5B 90
Stockwell Pk. Est.
  SW9 . . . . 5B 90
Stockwell Pk. Rd.
  SW9 . . . . 4B 90
Stockwell Pk. Wlk.
  SW9 . . . . 1C 104
Stockwell Rd. SW9 . . . . . 5B 90
Stockwell St. SE10 . . . . 2E 95
Stockwell Ter. SW8 . . . . . 4B 90
Stoddart Ho. SW8 . . . . . 2B 90
Stofield Gdns. SE9 . . . . 3F 125
Stoford Cl. SW19 . . . . . 5A 100
Stokenchurch St.
  SW6 . . . . 4D 87
STOKE NEWINGTON . . 5B 36
Stoke Newington Chu. St.
  N16 . . . . 5F 35
Stoke Newington Comn.
  N16 . . . . 4B 36
Stoke Newington High St.
  N16 . . . . 5B 36
Stoke Newington Rd.
  N16 . . . . 2B 50
Stoke Pl. NW10 . . . . 2B 56
Stokesley St. W12 . . . . . 5B 56
Stokes Rd. E6 . . . . 3F 69
Stoll Cl. NW2 . . . . 5E 29
Stoms Path SE6 . . . . . . 5C 122
    (off Maroons Way)
Stondon Ho. E15 . . . . . . 5B 54
    (off John St.)
Stondon Pk. SE23 . . . . 4A 108
Stondon Wlk. E6 . . . . 1F 69
Stonebridge Cen.
  N15 . . . . 1B 36
Stonebridge Rd. N15 . . 1B 36
Stone Bldgs. WC2 . . . . . 1A 16
Stone Cl. SW4 . . . . 5E 89
Stonecutter St.
  EC4 . . . . 2D 17 (5D 63)
Stonefield N4 . . . . 4B 34
Stonefield St. N1 . . . . . . 5C 48
Stonefield Way SE7 . . . . 3F 97
Stone Hall W8 . . . . 4D 73
    (off Stone Hall Gdns.)
Stonehall Av. IG1: Ilf . . . 1F 41
Stone Hall Gdns. W8 . . . 4D 73
Stone Hall Rd. W8 . . . . . 4D 73
Stonehills Ct. SE21 . . . 3A 120
Stonehouse NW1 . . . . . . 5E 47
    (off Plender St.)
Stone Ho. Ct. EC2 . . . . . 1E 19
Stonehouse Ho. W2 . . . . 4C 58
    (off Brunel Est.)
Stone Lake Ind. Pk.
  SE7 . . . . 5E 83
Stone Lake Retail Pk.
  SE7 . . . . 5E 83
Stoneleigh M. E3 . . . . . . 1A 66
Stoneleigh Pl. W11 . . . . . 1F 71

Stoneleigh St. W11 . . . . . 1F 71
Stoneleigh Ter. N19 . . . . 4D 33
Stonell's Rd. SW11 . . . . 4B 102
Stonemason Ct. SE1 . . . . 4F 25
    (off Borough Rd.)
Stonenest St. N4 . . . . . . 3B 34
Stones End St.
  SE1 . . . . 4F 25 (3E 77)
Stoneyard La. E14 . . . . . 1D 81
Stoneycroft Cl.
  SE12 . . . . 5B 110
Stoney La.
  E1 . . . . 2E 19 (5B 64)
Stoney St.
  SE1 . . . . 1B 26 (2F 77)
Stonhouse St. SW4 . . . . 2F 103
Stonor Rd. W14 . . . . 5B 72
Stopes St. SE15 . . . . 3B 92
Stopford Rd. E13 . . . . . . 5C 54
  SE17 . . . . 1D 91
Stopher Ho. SE1 . . . . . . 4E 25
    (off Webber St.)
Storers Quay E14 . . . . . . 5F 81
Store St. E15 . . . . 2F 53
  WC1 . . . . 1B 14 (4F 61)
Storey Ct. NW8 . . . . 2F 59
    (off St John's Wood Rd.)
Storey Ho. E14 . . . . 1D 81
    (off Cottage St.)
Storey Rd. N6 . . . . 1B 32
Storey's Ga.
  SW1 . . . . 4C 22 (3F 75)
Stories M. SE5 . . . . 5A 92
Stories Rd. SE5 . . . . . . 1A 106
Stork Rd. E7 . . . . 3B 54
Stork's Rd. SE16 . . . . . . 4C 78
Stormont Lawn Tennis &
  Squash Club 1B 32
Stormont Rd. N6 . . . . . . 2B 32
  SW11 . . . . 1C 102
Storrington WC1 . . . . 2E 7
    (off Regent Sq.)
Story St. N1 . . . . 4B 48
Stothard Ho. E1 . . . . 3E 65
    (off Amiel St.)
Stothard St. E1 . . . . 3E 65
Stott Cl. SW18 . . . . 4F 101
Stoughton Cl. SE11 . . . . 5B 76
    (off Gibson Rd.)
  SW15 . . . . 1C 112
Stourcliffe Cl. W1 . . . . . . 5B 60
Stourcliffe St. W1 . . . . . . 5B 60
Stourhead Cl. SW19 . . . 5F 99
Stourhead Ho. SW1 . . . . 1F 89
    (off Tachbrook St.)
Stour Rd. E3 . . . . 4C 52
Stowage SE8 . . . . 2C 94
Stowe Ho. NW11 . . . . . . 1E 31
Stowe Rd. W12 . . . . 3D 71
Stracey Rd. E7 . . . . 1C 54
  NW10 . . . . 5A 42
Stradbroke Rd. N5 . . . . . 1E 49
Stradella Rd. SE24 . . . . 4E 105
Strafford Ho. SE8 . . . . . . 1B 94
    (off Grove St.)
Strafford St. E14 . . . . . . 3C 80
Strahan Rd. E3 . . . . 2A 66
Straightsmouth SE10 . . 3E 95
Strait Rd. E6 . . . . 1F 83

Strakers Rd. SE15 . . . . 2D **107**
Strale Ho. N1 . . . . 5A **50**
   (off Whitmore Est.)
Strand WC2 . . . 5E **15** (1A **76**)
Strand La.
  WC2 . . . . 4A **16** (1B **76**)
Strand Theatre 4F **15**
   (off Aldwych)
Strang Ho. N1 . . . . 5E **49**
Strang Print Room 3B **6**
Strangways Ter. W14 . . . 4B **72**
Stranraer Way N1 . . . . . 4A **48**
Strasburg Rd. SW11 . . . 4C **88**
STRATFORD 4F **53**
Stratford Cen., The
  E15 . . . . 4F **53**
Stratford Circus
(Performing Arts Cen.)
  . . . . 3F **53**
Stratford Gro. SW15 . . . 2F **99**
STRATFORD MARSH . . . 4D **53**
STRATFORD NEW TOWN
  . . . . 2E **53**
Stratford Office Village, The
  E15 . . . . 4A **54**
   (off Romford Rd.)
Stratford Picture House
  . . . . 3F **53**
Stratford Pl.
  W1 . . . . 3D **13** (5D **61**)
Stratford Rd. E13 . . . . . 5B **54**
   (not continuous)
  W8 . . . . 4C **72**
Stratford Shop. Cen.
  E15 . . . . 4F **53**
   (off The Stratford Cen.)
Stratford Studios W8 . . 4C **72**
Stratford Vs. NW1 . . . . 4E **47**
Stratham Ct. N19 . . . . . 5A **34**
   (off Alexander Rd.)
Strathan Cl. SW18 . . . . 4A **100**
Strathaven Rd.
  SE12 . . . . 4D **111**
Strathblaine Rd.
  SW11 . . . . 3F **101**
Strathdale SW16 . . . . . 5B **118**
Strathdon Dr. SW17 . . . 3F **115**
Strathearn Ho. W2 . . . . 1A **74**
   (off Strathearn Pl.)
Strathearn Pl. W2 . . . . 5A **60**
Strathearn Rd.
  SW19 . . . . 5C **114**
Stratheden Pde. SE3 . . . 3C **96**
Stratheden Rd. SE3 . . . 4C **96**
Strathleven Rd.
  SW2 . . . . 3A **104**
Strathmore Ct. NW8 . . . 2A **60**
   (off Park Rd.)
Strathmore Gdns.
  W8 . . . . 2C **72**
Strathmore Rd.
  SW19 . . . . 3C **114**
Strathnairn St. SE1 . . . 5C **78**
Strathray Gdns.
  NW3 . . . . 3A **46**
Strath Ter. SW11 . . . . . 2A **102**
Strathville Rd.
  SW18 . . . . 2C **114**
   (not continuous)

Stratton Ct. N1 . . . . 4A **50**
   (off Hertford Rd.)
Strattondale St. E14 . . . 4E **81**
Stratton St.
  W1 . . . . 1E **21** (2D **75**)
Strauss Rd. W4 . . . . 3A **70**
Streakes Fld. Rd.
  NW2 . . . . 4C **28**
Streamline Ct. SE22 . . . 1C **120**
   (off Streamline M.)
Streamline M. SE22 . . . 1C **120**
STREATHAM 5A **118**
Streatham Cl.
  SW16 . . . . 2A **118**
STREATHAM COMMON
  . . . . 5A **118**
Streatham Comn. Nth.
  SW16 . . . . 5A **118**
Streatham Comn. Sth.
  SW16 . . . . 5A **118**
Streatham Ct.
  SW16 . . . . 3A **118**
Streatham High Rd.
  SW16 . . . . 4A **118**
STREATHAM HILL 2A **118**
Streatham Hill SW2 . . . 2A **118**
Streatham Ice Arena
  . . . . 5F **117**
Streatham Leisure Cen.
  . . . . 5A **118**
STREATHAM PARK . . . 5E **117**
Streatham Pl. SW2 . . . 5A **104**
Streatham St.
  WC1 . . . . 2D **15** (5A **62**)
Streathbourne Rd.
  SW17 . . . . 2C **116**
Streatley Pl. NW3 . . . . 1E **45**
Streatley Rd. NW6 . . . . 4B **44**
Streetfield M. SE3 . . . . 1C **110**
Streimer Rd. E15 . . . . . 1E **67**
Strelley Way W3 . . . . . 1A **70**
Stretton Mans. SE8 . . . 1C **94**
Strickland Ct. SE15 . . . 1C **106**
Strickland Ho. E2 . . . . . 2F **11**
   (off Chambord St.)
Strickland Row
  SW18 . . . . 5F **101**
Strickland St. SE8 . . . . 5C **94**
Stride Rd. E13 . . . . 1B **68**
Stringer Ho. N1 . . . . 5A **50**
   (off Whitmore Est.)
Strode Rd. E7 . . . . 1C **54**
  NW10 . . . . 3C **42**
  SW6 . . . . 3A **86**
Strome Ho. NW6 . . . . . 1D **59**
   (off Carlton Va.)
Strone Rd. E7 . . . . 3E **55**
  E12 . . . . 3E **55**
Stronsa Rd. W12 . . . . . 3B **70**
Strood Ho. SE1 . . . . 4C **26**
   (off Staple St.)
Stroud Cres. SW15 . . . 3C **112**
STROUD GREEN 2B **34**
Stroud Grn. Rd. N4 . . . 3B **34**
Stroudley Ho. SW8 . . . 4E **89**
Stroudley Wlk. E3 . . . . 2D **67**
Stroud Rd. SW19 . . . . . 3C **114**
Strouts Pl.
  E2 . . . . 1F **11** (2B **64**)

Strudwick Ct. SW4 . . . . 4A **90**
   (off Binfield Rd.)
Strutton Ct. SW1 . . . . . 5B **22**
   (off Strutton Ground)
Strutton Ground
  SW1 . . . . 5B **22** (4F **75**)
Strype St. E1 . . 1F **19** (4B **64**)
Stuart Av. NW9 . . . . 2C **28**
Stuart Ho. E16 . . . . 2D **83**
   (off Beaulieu Av.)
  W14 . . . . 5A **72**
   (off Windsor Way)
Stuart Mill Ho. N1 . . . . . 1F **7**
   (off Killick St.)
Stuart Rd. NW6 . . . . . . 2C **58**
  SE15 . . . . 2E **107**
  SW19 . . . . 3C **114**
Stuart Twr. W9 . . . . 2E **59**
   (off Maida Va.)
Stubbs Dr. SE16 . . . . . 1D **93**
Stubbs Ho. E2 . . . . 2F **65**
   (off Bonner St.)
  SW1 . . . . 5F **75**
   (off Erasmus St.)
Stubbs Point E13 . . . . . 3C **68**
Stucley Pl. NW1 . . . . . . 4D **47**
Studdridge St. SW6 . . . 5C **86**
   (not continuous)
Studd St. N1 . . . . 5D **49**
Studholme Ct. NW3 . . . 1C **44**
Studholme St. SE15 . . . 3D **93**
Studio Pl. SW1 . . . . 4A **20**
Studios, The W8 . . . . . . 2C **72**
   (off Edge St.)
Studland SE17 . . . . 1F **91**
   (off Portland St.)
Studland Ho. E14 . . . . . 5A **66**
   (off Aston St.)
Studland Rd. SE26 . . . 5F **121**
Studland St. W6 . . . . . . 5D **71**
Studley Cl. E5 . . . . 2A **52**
Studley Ct. E14 . . . . . . 1F **81**
   (off Jamestown Way)
Studley Dr. IG4: Ilf 1F **41**
Studley Est. SW4 . . . . . 4A **90**
Studley Rd. E7 . . . . 3D **55**
  SW4 . . . . 4A **90**
Stukeley Rd. E7 . . . . . . 4D **55**
Stukeley St.
  WC2 . . . . 2E **15** (5A **62**)
Stumps Hill La.
  BR3: Beck 5C **122**
Stuneli Ho. SE14 . . . . . 2F **93**
   (off John Williams Cl.)
Sturdee Ho. E2 . . . . . . 1C **64**
   (off Horatio St.)
Sturdy Ho. E3 . . . . 1A **66**
   (off Gernon Rd.)
Sturdy Rd. SE15 . . . . . 5D **93**
Sturgeon Rd. SE17 . . . 1E **91**
Sturgess Av. NW4 . . . . 2D **29**
Sturge St.
  SE1 . . . . 3F **25** (3E **77**)
Sturmer Way N7 . . . . . 2B **48**
Sturminster Ho. SW8 . . 3B **90**
   (off Dorset Rd.)
Sturry St. E14 . . . . 5D **67**
Sturt St. N1 . . . 1A **10** (1E **63**)
Stutfield St. E1 . . . . . . 5C **64**

Styles Gdns. SW9 . . . . 1D **105**
Styles Ho. SE1 . . . . 3D **25**
Stylus Ho. E1 . . . . 5E **65**
Sudbourne Rd.
  SW2 . . . . 3A **104**
Sudbrooke Rd.
  SW12 . . . . 4B **102**
Sudbury Ct. *SW8* *4F* ***89***
  (off Allen Edwards Dr.)
Sudbury Cres.
  BR1: Brom 5C **124**
Sudbury Ho. SW18 . . . . 3D **101**
Sudeley St. N1 . . . . 1D **63**
Sudlow Rd. SW18 . . . . 3C **100**
Sudrey St.
  SE1 . . . . 4F **25** (3E **77**)
Suffield Ho. *SE17* *1D* ***91***
  (off Berryfield Rd.)
Suffolk Ct. E10 . . . . 2C **38**
Suffolk La.
  EC4 . . . . 4B **18** (1F **77**)
Suffolk Pl.
  SW1 . . . . 1C **22** (2F **75**)
Suffolk Rd. E13 . . . . 2C **68**
  N15 . . . . 1F **35**
  NW10 . . . . 4A **42**
  SW13 . . . . 3B **84**
Suffolk St. E7 . . . . 1C **54**
  SW1 . . . . 5C **14** (1F **75**)
Sugar Bakers Ct. EC3 . . 3E **19**
Sugar Ho. La. E15 . . . . 1E **67**
Sugar Loaf Wlk. E2 . . . 2E **65**
Sugar Quay EC3 . . . . . . 5E **19**
Sugar Quay Wlk.
  EC3 . . . . 5E **19** (1A **78**)
Sugden Rd. SW11 . . . . 1C **102**
Sugden St. SE5 . . . . 2F **91**
Sulby Ho. *SE4* 2A ***108***
  (off Turnham Rd.)
Sulgrave Gdns. W6 . . . . 3E **71**
Sulgrave Rd. W6 . . . . . . 4E **71**
Sulina Rd. SW2 . . . . . . 5A **104**
Sulivan Ct. SW6 . . . . . . 5C **86**
Sulivan Ent. Cen.
  SW6 . . . . 1D **101**
Sulivan Rd. SW6 . . . . . 1C **100**
Sulkin Ho. *E2* *2F* ***65***
  (off Knottisford St.)
Sullivan Av. E16 . . . . . . 4F **69**
Sullivan Cl. SW11 . . . . 1A **102**
Sullivan Ct. N16 . . . . . . 2B **36**
  SW5 . . . . *5C* ***72***
  (off Earls Ct. Rd.)
Sullivan Ho. *SE11* *5B* ***76***
  (off Vauxhall St.)
  SW1 . . . . *2D* ***89***
  (off Churchill Gdns.)
Sullivan Rd. SE11 . . . . 5C **76**
Sultan St. SE5 . . . . 3E **91**
Sumatra Rd. NW6 . . . . 2C **44**
Sumburgh Rd.
  SW12 . . . . 4C **102**
Summercourt Rd. E1 . . 5E **65**
Summerfield Av.
  NW6 . . . . 1A **58**
Summerfield St.
  SE12 . . . . 5B **110**
Summerhouse Rd.
  N16 . . . . 4A **36**

Summerley St.
  SW18 . . . . 2D **115**
Summersby Rd. N6 . . . 1D **33**
Summerskill Cl.
  SE15 . . . . 1D **107**
Summers St.
  EC1 . . . . 4B **8** (3C **62**)
SUMMERSTOWN . . . 3E **115**
Summerstown
  SW17 . . . . 3E **115**
Summit Av. NW9 . . . . . 1A **28**
Summit Cl. NW2 . . . . . 2A **44**
Summit Est. N16 . . . . . 2C **36**
Sumner Av. SE15 . . . . . 4B **92**
Sumner Bldgs. SE1 . . . 1F **25**
Sumner Ct. SW8 . . . . . 3A **90**
Sumner Est. SE15 . . . . 3B **92**
Sumner Ho. *E3* *4D* ***67***
  (off Watts Gro.)
Sumner Pl. M. SW7 . . . 5F **73**
Sumner Pl. M. SW7 . . . 5F **73**
Sumner Rd. SE15 . . . . . 2B **92**
Sumner St.
  SE1 . . . . 1E **25** (2D **77**)
Sumpter Cl. NW3 . . . . . 3E **45**
Sunbeam Cres. W10 . . 3E **57**
Sunbeam Rd. NW10 . . 3A **56**
Sunbury Av. SW14 . . . . 2A **98**
Sunbury Av. Pas.
  SW14 . . . . 2A **98**
Sunbury Ho. *E2* *2F* ***11***
  (off Swanfield St.)
  SE14 . . . . *2F* ***93***
  (off Myers La.)
Sunbury La. SW11 . . . . 4F **87**
  (not continuous)
Sunbury Workshops
  E2 . . . . *2F* ***11***
  (off Swanfield St.)
Sun Ct. EC3 . . . . 3C **18**
Suncroft Pl. SE26 . . . . 3E **121**
Sunderland Ct.
  SE22 . . . . 5C **106**
Sunderland Ho. *W2* . . . *4C* ***58***
  (off Brunel Est.)
Sunderland Mt.
  SE23 . . . . 2F **121**
Sunderland Rd.
  SE23 . . . . 1F **121**
Sunderland Ter. W2 . . . 5D **59**
Sunderland Way E12 . . 4F **41**
Sundew Av. W12 . . . . . 1C **70**
Sundew Cl. W12 . . . . . 1C **70**
Sundorne Rd. SE7 . . . . 1E **97**
Sundra Wlk. E1 . . . . 3F **65**
SUNDRIDGE 5D **125**
Sundridge Ho. *E9* *4F* ***51***
  (off Church Cres.)
Sunfields Pl. SE3 . . . . . 3D **97**
SUN-IN-THE-SANDS . . 3D **97**
Sun La. SE3 . . . . 3D **97**
Sunlight Cl. SW19 . . . . 5E **115**
Sunlight Sq. E2 . . . . . . 2D **65**
Sunningdale Av. W3 . . 1A **70**
Sunningdale Cl.
  SE16 . . . . 1D **93**
Sunningdale Gdns.
  W8 . . . . *4C* ***72***
  (off Stratford Rd.)

Sunninghill Rd.
  SE13 . . . . 5D **95**
Sunnydale Rd.
  SE12 . . . . 3D **111**
Sunnydene St.
  SE26 . . . . 4A **122**
Sunnyhill Cl. E5 . . . . . . 1A **52**
Sunnyhill Rd. SW16 . . 4A **118**
Sunnymead Rd.
  NW9 . . . . 2A **28**
  SW15 . . . . 3D **99**
Sunnyside NW2 . . . . . 5B **30**
  SW19 . . . . 5A **114**
Sunnyside Ho's.
  NW2 . . . . *5B* ***30***
  (off Sunnyside)
Sunnyside Pl.
  SW19 . . . . 5A **114**
Sunnyside Rd. E10 . . . 3C **38**
  N19 . . . . 2F **33**
Sun Pas. *SE16* *4C* ***78***
  (off Old Jamaica Rd.)
Sunray Av. SE24 . . . . . 2F **105**
Sun Rd. W14 . . . . 1B **86**
Sunset Rd. SE5 . . . . . . 2E **105**
  SW19 . . . . 5D **113**
Sun St. EC2 . . . . 5C **10** (4F **63**)
  (not continuous)
Sun St. Pas.
  EC2 . . . . 1D **19** (4A **64**)
Sun Wlk. E1 . . . . 1B **78**
Sunwell Cl. SE15 . . . . . 4D **93**
Sun Wharf *SE8* *3D* ***95***
  (off Creekside)
Surma Cl. E1 . . . . 3D **65**
Surrendale Pl. W9 . . . . 3C **58**
Surrey Canal Rd.
  SE14 . . . . 2E **93**
  SE15 . . . . 2E **93**

Surrey County Cricket Club
  . . . . 2B **90**

Surrey Docks Stadium
  . . . . 2F **79**

Surrey Docks
  Watersports Cen. 4A **80**
Surrey Gdns. N4 . . . . . 1E **35**
Surrey Gro. SE17 . . . . . 1A **92**
Surrey Ho. *SE16* *2F* ***79***
  (off Rotherhithe St.)
Surrey La. SW11 . . . . . 4A **88**
Surrey La. Est.
  SW11 . . . . 4A **88**
Surrey M. SE27 . . . . . . 4A **120**
Surrey Mt. SE23 . . . . . 1D **121**
Surrey Quays Rd.
  SE16 . . . . 4E **79**
Surrey Quays Shop. Cen.
  SE16 . . . . 4F **79**
Surrey Rd. SE15 . . . . . 3F **107**
Surrey Row
  SE1 . . . . 3D **25** (3D **77**)
Surrey Sq. SE17 . . . . . 1A **92**
Surrey Steps *WC2* *4A* ***16***
  (off Surrey St.)
Surrey St. E13 . . . . 2D **69**
  WC2 . . . . 4A **16** (1B **76**)
Surrey Ter. SE17 . . . . . 1A **92**
Surrey Water Rd.
  SE16 . . . . 2F **79**

Surridge Ct. SW9 . . . . . . 5A 90
(off Clapham Rd.)
Surr St. N7 . . . . 2A 48
Susan Constant Ct.
E14 . . . . 1F 81
(off Newport Av.)
Susannah St. E14 . . . . . . 5D 67
Susan Rd. SE3 . . . . 5D 97
Sussex Cl. N19 . . . . 4A 34
Sussex Cl. SE10 . . . . 2E 95
(off Roan St.)
W2 . . . . 5F 59
(off Spring St.)
Sussex Gdns. N4 . . . . . . 1E 35
N6 . . . . 1B 32
W2 . . . . 1F 73
Sussex Ga. N6 . . . . 1B 32
Sussex Lodge W2 . . . . . . 5F 59
(off Sussex Pl.)
Sussex Mans. SW7 . . . . . 5F 73
(off Old Brompton Rd.)
WC2 . . . . 4E 15
(off Maiden La.)
Sussex M. SE6 . . . . 5C 108
Sussex M. E. W2 . . . . 5F 59
(off Clifton Pl.)
Sussex M. W. W2 . . . . . . 1F 73
Sussex Pl.
NW1 . . . . 3A 4 (3B 60)
W2 . . . . 5F 59
W6 . . . . 1E 85
Sussex Sq. W2 . . . . 1F 73
Sussex St. E13 . . . . 2D 69
SW1 . . . . 1D 89
Sussex Way N7 . . . . 4A 34
N19 . . . . 3F 33
(not continuous)
Sutcliffe Cl. NW11 . . . . . 1D 31
Sutcliffe Pk. Athletics Track
. . . . 3E 111
Sutherland Av. W9 . . . . . 3C 58
Sutherland Ct. N16 . . . . . 5F 35
W9 . . . . 3C 58
(off Marylands Rd.)
Sutherland Gdns.
SW14 . . . . 1A 98
Sutherland Gro.
SW18 . . . . 4A 100
Sutherland Ho. W8 . . . . . 4D 73
Sutherland Pl. W2 . . . . . . 5C 58
Sutherland Point E5 . . . . 5D 37
(off Brackenfield Cl.)
Sutherland Rd. E3 . . . . . . 1B 66
W4 . . . . 2A 84
Sutherland Row SW1 . . . 1D 89
Sutherland Sq. SE17 . . . . 1E 91
Sutherland St. SW1 . . . . 1D 89
Sutherland Wlk.
SE17 . . . . 1E 91
Sutlej Rd. SE7 . . . . 3E 97
Sutterton St. N7 . . . . 3B 48
Sutton Ct. Rd. E13 . . . . . 2E 69
Sutton Est. EC1 . . . . 2C 10
W10 . . . . 4E 57
Sutton Est., The N1 . . . . 4D 49
SW3 . . . . 1A 88
Sutton La. EC1 . . . . 4E 9
(off Gt. Sutton St.)
Sutton Pl. E9 . . . . 2E 51

Sutton Rd. E13 . . . . 3B 68
Sutton Row
W1 . . . . 2C 14 (5F 61)
Sutton Sq. E9 . . . . 2E 51
Sutton St. E1 . . . . 1E 79
Sutton's Way
EC1 . . . . 4A 10 (3E 63)
Sutton Wlk.
SE1 . . . . 2A 24 (2B 76)
Sutton Way W10 . . . . 3E 57
Swaby Rd. SW18 . . . . . . 1E 115
Swaffield Rd.
SW18 . . . . 5D 101
Swains La. N6 . . . . 3C 32
Swainson Rd. W3 . . . . . . 3B 70
Swain St. NW8 . . . . 3A 60
(off Tresham Cres.)
Swallands Rd. SE6 . . . . . 3C 122
(not continuous)
Swallow Cl. SE14 . . . . . . 4F 93
Swallow Ct. SE1 . . . . 4A 26
(off Swan St.)
SE12 . . . . 5C 110
W9 . . . . 4C 58
(off Admiral Wlk.)
Swallow Dr. NW10 . . . . . 3A 42
Swallowfield NW1 . . . . . 2E 5
(off Munster Sq.)
Swallowfield Rd.
SE7 . . . . 1D 97
Swallow Gdns.
SW16 . . . . 5F 117
Swallow Ho. NW8 . . . . . . 1A 60
(off Barrow Hill Est.)
Swallow Pas. W1 . . . . . . 3E 13
(off Swallow Pl.)
Swallow Pl.
W1 . . . . 3E 13 (5D 61)
Swallow St.
W1 . . . . 5A 14 (1E 75)
Swanage Ct. N1 . . . . 4A 50
(off Hertford Rd.)
Swanage Ho. SW8 . . . . . 3B 90
(off Dorset Rd.)
Swanage Rd.
SW18 . . . . 4E 101
Swan App. E6 . . . . 4F 69
Swanbourne SE17 . . . . . 5E 77
(off Wansey St.)
Swanbourne Ho.
NW8 . . . . 3A 60
(off Capland St.)
Swan Cen., The
SW17 . . . . 3D 115
Swan Ct. E1 . . . . 1C 78
(off Star Pl.)
E14 . . . . 5B 66
(off Agnes St.)
SW3 . . . . 1A 88
SW6 . . . . 3C 86
(off Fulham Rd.)
Swandon Way
SW18 . . . . 3D 101
Swanfield St.
E2 . . . . 2F 11 (2B 64)
Swan Ho. N1 . . . . 4F 49
(off Oakley Rd.)
Swan La.
EC4 . . . . 5C 18 (1F 77)

Swanley Ho. SE17 . . . . . 1A 92
(off Kinglake Est.)
Swan Mead
SE1 . . . . 5D 27 (4A 78)
Swan M. SW6 . . . . 4B 86
SW9 . . . . 5B 90
Swanne Ho. SE10 . . . . . . 3E 95
(off Gloucester Cir.)
Swan Pas. E1 . . . . 1B 78
(off Royal Mint Pl.)
Swan Pl. SW13 . . . . 5B 84
Swan Rd. SE16 . . . . 3E 79
SE18 . . . . 4F 83
Swanscombe Ho.
W11 . . . . 2F 71
(off St Ann's Rd.)
Swanscombe Point
E16 . . . . 4B 68
(off Clarkson Rd.)
Swanscombe Rd. W4 . . . 1A 84
W11 . . . . 2F 71
Swan St. SE1 . . 5A 26 (4E 77)
Swanton Gdns.
SW19 . . . . 1F 113
Swan Wlk. SW3 . . . . 2B 88
Swanwick Cl. SW15 . . . . 5B 98
Swan Yd. N1 . . . . 3D 49
Swathling Ho. SW15 . . . . 4B 98
(off Tunworth Cres.)
Swaton Rd. E3 . . . . 3C 66
Swedeland Ct. E1 . . . . . . 1E 19
Swedenborg Gdns.
E1 . . . . 1D 79
Swedenborg Pl. E1 . . . . . 1D 79
(off Swedenborg Gdns.)
Sweden Ga. SE16 . . . . . . 4A 80
Swedish Quays SE16 . . . 4A 80
(not continuous)
Sweeney Cres.
SE1 . . . . 4F 27 (3B 78)
Swell Ct. E17 . . . . 1C 38
Swete St. E13 . . . . 1C 68
Sweyn Pl. SE3 . . . . 5C 96
Swift Lodge W9 . . . . 3C 58
(off Admiral Wlk.)
Swiftsden Way
BR1: Brom 5A 124
Swift St. SW6 . . . . 4B 86
Swinbrook Rd. W10 . . . . 4A 58
Swinburne Ct. SE5 . . . . . 2F 105
(off Basingdon Way)
Swinburne Ho. E2 . . . . . . 2E 65
(off Roman Rd.)
Swinburne Rd.
SW15 . . . . 2C 98
Swindon St. W12 . . . . . . 2D 71
Swinford Gdns.
SW9 . . . . 1D 105
Swingfield Ho. E9 . . . . . . 5E 51
(off Templecombe Rd.)
Swinley Ho. NW1 . . . . . . 1E 5
(off Redhill St.)
Swinnerton St. E9 . . . . . 2A 52
Swinton Pl.
WC1 . . . . 1F 7 (2B 62)
Swinton St.
WC1 . . . . 1F 7 (2B 62)
Swiss Cen. W1 . . . . 5B 14
SWISS COTTAGE 4F 45

Swiss Cottage Sports Cen.
. . . . 4F 45
Swiss Ct. WC2 . . . . 5C 14
Swiss Re Tower 2E 19
Swiss Ter. NW6. . . . . . . 4F 45
Switch Ho. E14 . . . . 1F 81
Sybil M. N4 . . . . 1D 35
Sybil Phoenix Cl.
SE8 . . . . 1F 93
Sybil Thorndike Casson Ho.
SW5 . . . . 1C 86
(off Kramer M.)
Sybourn St. E17 . . . . 2B 38
Sycamore Av. E3 . . . . . . 5B 52
Sycamore Cl. E16. . . . . . 3A 68
W3 . . . . 2A 70
Sycamore Ct. E7. . . . . . . 3C 54
NW6 . . . . 5C 44
(off Bransdale Cl.)
Sycamore Gdns. W6 . . . 3D 71
Sycamore Gro. SE6 . . . 4E 109
Sycamore Ho. SE1 . . . . 3F 79
(off Woodland Cres.)
W6 . . . . 3D 71
Sycamore Lodge W8 . . 4D 73
(off Stone Hall Pl.)
Sycamore M. SW4 . . . . 1E 103
Sycamore Rd.
SW19 . . . . 5E 113
Sycamore St.
EC1. . . . . 4F 9 (3E 63)
Sycamore Wlk. W10 . . 3A 58
Sydcote SE21 . . . . 1E 119
SYDENHAM 4E 121
Sydenham Av. SE26. . . 5D 121
Sydenham Cotts.
SE12 . . . . 2E 125
Sydenham Hill
SE23. . . . . 1D 121
SE26 . . . . 4B 120
Sydenham Pk. SE26. . . 3E 121
Sydenham Pk. Mans.
SE26. . . . . 3E 121
(off Sydenham Pk.)
Sydenham Pk. Rd.
SE26 . . . . 3E 121
Sydenham Pl. SE27. . . 3D 119
Sydenham Ri. SE23. . . 2D 121
Sydenham Rd. SE26. . . 4E 121
Sydmons Ct. SE23 . . . 5E 107
Sydner M. N16 . . . . 1B 50
Sydner Rd. N16. . . . . . . 1B 50
Sydney Cl. SW3 . . . . . . 5F 73
Sydney Gro. NW4 . . . . . 1E 29
Sydney M. SW3 . . . . . . 5F 73
Sydney Pl. SW7 . . . . . . 5F 73
Sydney Rd. E11 . . . . . . 1D 41
Sydney St. SW3 . . . . . 1A 88
Sylvan Gro. NW2 . . . . . 1F 43
SE15. . . . . 2D 93
Sylvan Rd. E7. . . . . 3D 55
E17. . . . . 1C 38
Sylvan Ter. SE15 . . . . . 2D 93
(off Sylvan Gro.)
Sylvester Path E8. . . . . 3D 51
Sylvester Rd. E8 . . . . . 3D 51
E17. . . . . 2B 38
Sylvia Ct. N1. . . . . 1F 63
(off Wenlock St.)

Symes M. NW1 . . . . 1E 61
Symington Ho. SE1 . . . 5B 26
(off Deverell St.)
Symington M. E9 . . . . . . 2F 51
Symister M. N1 . . . . 2D 11
Symons Cl. SE15 . . . . . 5E 93
Symons St. SW3 . . . . . . 5B 74
Symphony M. W10. . . . . 2A 58
Syon Lodge SE12. . . . . 5C 110
Syringa Ho. SE4 . . . . . . 1B 108

T

Tabard Ct. E14 . . . . 5E 67
(off Lodore St.)
Tabard Gdn. Est.
SE1 . . . . 4B 26 (4F 77)
Tabard Ho. SE1 . . . . . . 5C 26
(off Manciple St.)
Tabard St.
SE1 . . . . 3A 26 (3E 77)
Tabernacle Av. E13 . . . 3C 68
Tabernacle St.
EC2. . . . . 4C 10 (3F 63)
Tableer Av. SW4. . . . . . 3E 103
Tabley Rd. N7 . . . . 1A 48
Tabor Rd. W6. . . . . 4D 71
Tachbrook Est. SW1 . . 1F 89
Tachbrook M. SW1. . . . 5E 75
Tachbrook St. SW1. . . . 5E 75
(not continuous)
Tack M. SE4 . . . . 1C 108
Tadema Ho. NW8 . . . . . 3F 59
(off Penfold St.)
Tadema Rd. SW10 . . . . 3E 87
Tadmor St. W12 . . . . . . 2F 71
Tadworth Ho. SE1 . . . . 4D 25
Tadworth Rd. NW2 . . . . 4C 28
Taeping St. E14 . . . . . . 5D 81
Taffrail Ho. E14 . . . . . . 1D 95
(off Burrells Wharf Sq.)
Taft Way E3 . . . . 2D 67
Tailor Ho. WC1 . . . . 4E 7
(off Colonnade)
Tailworth St. E1 . . . . . . 4C 64
(off Chicksand St.)
Tait Ct. E3. . . . . 5B 52
(off St Stephen's Rd.)
SW8 . . . . 4A 90
(off Lansdowne Grn.)
Tait Ho. SE1 . . . . 2C 24
(off Greet St.)
Takhar M. SW11 . . . . . . 5A 88
Talacre Community
Sports Cen.
Kentish Town 3C 46
Talacre Rd. NW5 . . . . . 3C 46
Talbot Cl. EC3 . . . . 4C 18
Talbot Cres. NW4 . . . . . 1C 28
Talbot Gro. Ho. W11 . . 5A 58
(off Lancaster Rd.)
Talbot Ho. E14 . . . . 5D 67
(off Girauld St.)
N7 . . . . 5C 34
Talbot Pl. SE3 . . . . 5A 96
Talbot Rd. E7 . . . . 1C 54
N6 . . . . 1C 32
SE22 . . . . 2A 106

Talbot Rd. W2 . . . . 5B 58
W11 . . . . 5B 58
(not continuous)
Talbot Sq. W2 . . . . 5F 59
Talbot Wlk. NW10 . . . . 3A 42
W11 . . . . 5A 58
Talbot Yd.
SE1 . . . . 2B 26 (2F 77)
Talcott Path SW2 . . . . 1C 118
Talfourd Pl. SE15 . . . . 4B 92
Talfourd Rd. SE15 . . . . 4B 92
Talgarth Mans. W14 . . 1A 86
(off Talgarth Rd.)
Talgarth Rd. W6 . . . . . . 1F 85
W14. . . . . 1F 85
Talia Ho. E14 . . . . 4E 81
(off Manchester Rd.)
Talina Cen. SW6 . . . . . 4E 87
Talisman Sq. SE26. . . 4C 120
Tallack Rd. E10 . . . . . . 3B 38
Talleyrand Ho. SE5 . . . 5E 91
(off Lilford Rd.)
Tallis Cl. E16 . . . . 5D 69
Tallis Gro. SE7 . . . . 2D 97
Tallis St. EC4. . . 4C 16 (1C 76)
Tallis Vw. NW10 . . . . . 3A 42
Talma Gdns. Twic 4E 89
Talma Rd. SW2 . . . . . . 2C 104
Talwin St. E3 . . . . 2D 67
Tamar Cl. E3 . . . . 5B 52
Tamar Ho. E14 . . . . 3E 81
(off Plevna St.)
SE11 . . . . 1C 90
(off Kennington La.)
Tamarind Ct. SE1 . . . . . 3F 27
W8 . . . . 4D 73
(off Stone Hall Gdns.)
Tamarind Yd. E1 . . . . . 2C 78
(off Kennet St.)
Tamarisk Sq. W12 . . . . 1B 70
Tamar St. SE7 . . . . 4F 83
Tamplin Ho. W10 . . . . . 2B 58
(off Dowland St.)
Tamworth N7 . . . . 3A 48
Tamworth St. SW6 . . . . 2C 86
Tancred Rd. N4 . . . . . . 1D 35
Tanfield Av. NW2 . . . . . 1B 42
Tangley Gro. SW15 . . . 4B 98
Tangmere WC1 . . . . 2F 7
(off Sidmouth St.)
Tanhouse Fld. NW5 . . . 2F 47
(off Torriano Av.)
Tanhurst Ho. SW2 . . . . 5B 104
(off Redlands Way)
Tankerton Ho's. WC1 . . 2E 7
(off Tankerton St.)
Tankerton St.
WC1 . . . . 2E 7 (2A 62)
Tankridge Rd. NW2 . . . 4D 29
Tanner Ho. SE1 . . . . . . 4E 27
(off Tanner St.)
Tanneries, The E1 . . . . 3E 65
(off Cephas Av.)
Tanner Point E13 . . . . . 5C 54
(off Pelly Rd.)
Tanner's Hill SE8 . . . . . 4B 94
Tanner St.
SE1 . . . . 4E 27 (3A 78)
(not continuous)

Tannington Ter. N5. . . . . 5D 35
Tannsfeld Rd. SE26 . . . . 5F 121
Tansley Cl. N7. . . . . 2F 47
Tanswell St.
 SE1 . . . . 4B 24 (3C 76)
Tantallon Rd. SW12 . . . 1C 116
Tant Av. E16 . . . . 5B 68
Tanza Rd. NW3 . . . . . . 1B 46
Tapley Ho. SE1 . . . . 3C 78
 (off Wolseley St.)
Taplow SE17 . . . . 1F 91
 (off Thurlow St.)
Taplow Ho. E2 . . . . 2F 11
 (off Palissy St.)
Taplow St.
 N1 . . . . 1A 10 (1E 63)
Tappesfield Rd.
 SE15 . . . . 1E 107
Tapp St. E1 . . . . 3D 65
Tara Arts Cen. 1D 115
 (off Garratt La.)
Tara M. N8 . . . . 1A 34
Taransay Wlk. N1 . . . . . 3F 49
Taranto Ho. E1 . . . . 4F 65
 (off Master's St.)
Tarbert Rd. SE22 . . . . 3A 106
Tarbert Wlk. E1 . . . . 1E 79
Tariff Cres. SE8 . . . . . . 5B 80
Tarleton Gdns.
 SE23 . . . . 2D 121
Tarling Ho. E1 . . . . 5D 65
 (off Tarling St.)
Tarling Rd. E16 . . . . . . 5B 68
Tarling St. E1 . . . . 5D 65
Tarling St. Est. E1 . . . . . 5E 65
Tarnbrook Ct. SW1 . . . . 5C 74
 (off Whittaker St.)
Tarns, The NW1 . . . . . . 1F 5
 (off Varndell St.)
Tarn St. SE1 . . . . 4E 77
Tarplett Ho. SE14 . . . . . 2F 93
 (off John Williams Cl.)
Tarquin Ho. SE26 . . . . 4C 120
 (off High Level Dr.)
Tarragon Cl. SE14 . . . . 3A 94
Tarragon Gro. SE26 . . . 5F 121
Tarranbrae NW6 . . . . . 4A 44
Tarrant Ho. E2 . . . . 2E 65
 (off Roman Rd.)
 W14 . . . . 4A 72
 (off Russell Rd.)
Tarrant Pl. W1 . . . . 4B 60
Tarrington Cl. SW16 . . . 3F 117
Tartan Ho. E14 . . . . 5E 67
 (off Dee St.)
Tarver Rd. SE17 . . . . . . 1D 91
Tarves Way SE10 . . . . . 3D 95
Tasker Ho. E14 . . . . 4B 66
 (off Wallwood St.)
Tasker Rd. NW3 . . . . . . 2B 46
Tasman Ct. E14 . . . . . . 5D 81
 (off Westferry Rd.)
Tasman Ho. E1 . . . . 2D 79
 (off Clegg St.)
Tasman Rd. SW9 . . . . . 1A 104
Tasman Wlk. E16 . . . . . 5F 69
Tasso Rd. W6 . . . . 2A 86
Tasso Yd. W6 . . . . 2A 86
 (off Tasso Rd.)

Tatchbury Ho. SW15 . . . 4B 98
 (off Tunworth Cres.)
Tate Britain 5A 76
Tate Ho. E2 . . . . 1F 65
 (off Mace St.)
Tate Modern . . . 1E 25 (2D 77)
Tatham Pl. NW8 . . . . . . 1F 59
Tatnell Rd. SE23 . . . . . 4A 108
Tatsfield Ho. SE1 . . . . . 5C 26
 (off Pardoner St.)
Tatton Cres. N16 . . . . . 2B 36
Tatum St. SE17 . . . . 5F 77
Tauheed Cl. N4 . . . . 4E 35
Taunton Ho. W2 . . . . . . 5E 59
 (off Hallfield Est.)
Taunton M. NW1 . . . . . . 3B 60
Taunton Pl. NW1 . . . . . . 3B 60
Taunton Rd. SE12 . . . . 3A 110
Tavern Ct. SE1 . . . . 4E 77
 (off Falmouth Rd.)
Taverners Cl. W11 . . . . . 2A 72
Taverners Ct. E3 . . . . . . 2A 66
 (off Grove Rd.)
Taverner Sq. N5 . . . . . . 1E 49
Tavern La. SW9 . . . . . . 5C 90
Tavern Quay SE16 . . . . 5A 80
Tavistock Cl. N16 . . . . . 2A 50
Tavistock Ct. WC1 . . . . . 3C 6
 (off Tavistock Sq.)
 WC2 . . . . 4E 15
 (off Tavistock St.)
Tavistock Cres. W11 . . . 4B 58
 (not continuous)
Tavistock Ho.
 WC1 . . . . 3C 6 (3F 61)
Tavistock M. W11 . . . . . 5B 58
Tavistock Pl.
 WC1 . . . . 3D 7 (3A 62)
Tavistock Rd. E7 . . . . . . 1B 54
 E15 . . . . 3B 54
 N4 . . . . 1F 35
 NW10 . . . . 1B 56
 W11 . . . . 5B 58
 (not continuous)
Tavistock Sq.
 WC1 . . . . 3C 6 (3F 61)
Tavistock St.
 WC2 . . . . . . 4E 15 (1A 76)
Tavistock Ter. N19 . . . . 5F 33
Tavistock Twr. SE16 . . . 4A 80
Taviton St.
 WC1 . . . . 3B 6 (3F 61)
Tavy Cl. SE11 . . . . 1C 90
 (off White Hart St.,
 not continuous)
Tawny Way SE16 . . . . . 5F 79
Taybridge Rd.
 SW11 . . . . 1C 102
Tay Bldgs. SE1 . . . . 5D 27
Tayburn Cl. E14 . . . . . . 5E 67
Tayler Ct. NW8 . . . . 5F 45
Taylor Cl. SE8 . . . . 2B 94
Taylor Ct. E15 . . . . 2E 53
Taylors Grn. W3 . . . . . . 5A 56
Taylors La. NW10 . . . . . 3A 42
 SE26 . . . . 4D 121
Taymount Grange
 SE23 . . . . 2E 121

Taymount Ri. SE23. . . . 2E 121
Tayport Cl. N1 . . . . 4A 48
Tayside Ct. SE5 . . . . . . 2F 105
Teak Cl. SE16. . . . . 2A 80
Tealby Ct. N7 . . . . 2B 48
 (off George's Rd.)
Teal Cl. E16 . . . . 4F 69
Teal Ct. E1 . . . . 1C 78
 (off Star Pl.)
 SE8 . . . . 2B 94
 (off Abinger Gro.)
Teale St. E2 . . . . 1C 64
Tealing Dr. SE10 . . . . . . 4B 82
Teasel Way E15 . . . . . . 2A 68
Tea Trade Wharf
 SE1 . . . . 3B 78
 (off Shad Thames)
Ted Roberts Ho. E2 . . . . 1D 65
 (off Parmiter St.)
Tedworth Gdns. SW3 . . . 1B 88
Tedworth Sq. SW3 . . . . 1B 88
Tee, The W3. . . . . 5A 56
Teesdale Cl. E2 . . . . 1C 64
Teesdale Rd. E11 . . . . . 1B 40
Teesdale St. E2 . . . . . . 1D 65
Teesdale Yd. E2 . . . . . . 1D 65
 (off Teesdale St.)
Teignmouth Cl.
 SW4 . . . . 2F 103
Teignmouth Rd.
 NW2 . . . . 2F 43
Telegraph Hill NW3 . . . 5D 31
Telegraph Pas.
 SW2 . . . . 5A 104
 (off New Pk. Rd.)
Telegraph Pl. E14 . . . . . 5D 81
Telegraph Quarters
 SE10 . . . . 1F 95
 (off Park Row)
Telegraph Rd. SW15 . . . 5D 99
Telegraph St.
 EC2. . . . . 2B 18 (5F 63)
Telemann Sq. SE3 . . . . 2D 111
Telephone Pl. W14 . . . . 2B 86
Telfer Ho. EC1 . . . . 2E 9
Telferscot Rd.
 SW12 . . . . 1F 117
Telford Av. SW2 . . . . . . 1F 117
Telford Cl. E17 . . . . 2A 38
Telford Ho. SE1 . . . . . . 5F 25
 (off Tiverton St.)
 W10 . . . . 4A 58
 (off Portobello Rd.)
Telford Rd. NW9 . . . . . . 1C 28
 W10 . . . . 4A 58
Telfords Yd. E1. . . . . . . 1C 78
Telford Ter. SW1 . . . . . . 2E 89
Telford Way W3 . . . . . . 4A 56
Tell Gro. SE22 . . . . 2B 106
Tellson Av. SE18. . . . . . 4F 97
Temair Ho. SE10 . . . . . . 3D 95
 (off Tarves Way)
Temeraire St. SE16 . . . . 3E 79
Tempelhof Av. NW2 . . . . 3E 29
 NW4 . . . . 2E 29
Temperley Rd.
 SW12 . . . . 5C 102
Templar Ct. NW8 . . . . . 2F 59
 (off St John's Wood Rd.)

Templar Ho. NW2 . . . . . . 3B **44**
Templars Av. NW11 . . . . 1B **30**
Templars Ho. E15 . . . . 2D **53**
Templar St. SE5 . . . . . 5D **91**
Temple Av.
  EC4 . . . . 4C **16** (1C **76**)
Temple Bar 3B **16**
Temple Bar Gate 3E **17**
  (off Paternoster Sq.)
Temple Chambers
  EC4 . . . . 4C **16**
Temple Cl. E11 . . . . 2A **40**
Templecombe Rd. E9 . . 5E **51**
Temple Ct. E1 . . . . 4F **65**
  (off Rectory Sq.)
  SW8 . . . . 3A **90**
  (off Thorncroft St.)
Temple Dwellings E2 . . 1D **65**
  (off Temple St.)
TEMPLE FORTUNE . . . 1B **30**
Temple Fortune Hill
  NW11 . . . . 1C **30**
Temple Fortune La.
  NW11 . . . . 1B **30**
Temple Fortune Pde.
  NW11 . . . . 1B **30**
Temple Gdns. EC4 . . . . 4B **16**
  (off Middle Temple La.)
  NW11 . . . . 1B **30**
Temple Gro. NW11 . . . . 1C **30**
Temple La.
  EC4 . . . . 3C **16** (5C **62**)
Templemead Cl. W3 . . 5A **56**
Templemead Ho. E9 . . 1A **52**
Temple Mill La. E10 . . 1D **53**
  (not continuous)
  E15 . . . . 1E **53**
TEMPLE MILLS 1D **53**
Temple Mills E10 . . . . 5E **39**
Temple of Mithras (remains)
  . . . . 3B **18**
  (off Queen Victoria St.)
Temple Pl.
  WC2 . . . . 4A **16** (1B **76**)
Temple Rd. E6 . . . . 5F **55**
  NW2 . . . . 1E **43**
Temple St. E2 . . . . 1D **65**
Templeton Cl. N15 . . . . 1F **35**
  N16 . . . . 2A **50**
Templeton Pl. SW5 . . . 5C **72**
Templeton Rd. N15 . . . 1F **35**
Temple W. M.
  SE11 . . . . . . 5D **25** (4D **77**)
Templewood Av.
  NW3 . . . . 5D **31**
Templewood Gdns.
  NW3 . . . . 5D **31**
Templewood Point
  NW2 . . . . 4B **30**
  (off Granville Rd.)
Temple Yd. E2 . . . . 1D **65**
  (off Temple St.)
Tempus Wharf SE16 . . 3C **78**
  (off Bermondsey Wall W.)

Tenbury Cl. E7 . . . . 2F **55**
Tenbury Ct. SW2 . . . . . 1F **117**
Tenby Ho. W2 . . . . 5E **59**
  (off Hallfield Est.)
Tenby Mans. W1 . . . . . . 5C **4**
  (off Nottingham St.)
Tench St. E1 . . . . 2D **79**
Tenda Rd. SE16 . . . . . . 5D **79**
Tenham Av. SW2 . . . . . 1F **117**
Tenison Ct.
  W1 . . . . 4F **13** (1E **75**)
Tenison Way
  SE1 . . . . 2A **24** (2B **76**)
Tenniel Cl. W2 . . . . 1E **73**
Tennis St.
  SE1 . . . . 3B **26** (3F **77**)
Tennyson Av. E11 . . . . . 2C **40**
  E12 . . . . 4F **55**
Tennyson Ct. SW6 . . . . 4E **87**
  (off Imperial Rd.)
Tennyson Ho. SE17 . . . 1E **91**
  (off Browning St.)
Tennyson Mans.
  SW1 . . . . 1D **89**
  (off Sutherland St.)
  SW3 . . . . 2A **88**
  (off Lordship Pl.)
  W14 . . . . 2B **86**
  (off Queen's Club Gdns.)
Tennyson Rd. E10 . . . . 3D **39**
  E15 . . . . 4A **54**
  E17 . . . . 1B **38**
  NW6 . . . . 5B **44**
  SW19 . . . . 5E **115**
Tennyson St. SW8 . . . . 5D **89**
Tenterden Ho. SE17 . . . 1A **92**
  (off Surrey Gro.)
Tenterden St.
  W1 . . . . 3E **13** (5D **61**)
Tenter Ground
  E1 . . . . 1F **19** (4B **64**)
Tenter Pas. E1 . . . . 5B **64**
  (off Nth. Tenter St.)
Tent St. E1 . . . . 3D **65**
Tequila Wharf E14 . . . . 5A **66**
Terborch Way SE22 . . . 3A **106**
Teredo St. SE16 . . . . . . 4F **79**
Terence McMillan Stadium
  . . . . 3E **69**
Terence Messenger Twr.
  E10 . . . . 4D **39**
  (off Alpine Rd.)
Terling Cl. E11 . . . . 5B **40**
Terling Ho. W10 . . . . . . 4E **57**
  (off Sutton Way)
Terling Wlk. N1 . . . . 5E **49**
  (off Popham St.)
Terminus Pl. SW1 . . . . 4D **75**
Terrace, The E2 . . . . . . 2E **65**
  (off Old Ford Rd.)
  EC4 . . . . 3C **16**
  NW6 . . . . 5C **44**
  SE8 . . . . 5B **80**
  (off Longshore)

Terrace, The SE23 . . . . 5A **108**
  SW13 . . . . 5A **84**
Terrace Av. NW10 . . . . 3E **57**
Terrace Gdns. SW13 . . 5B **84**
Terrace Rd. E9 . . . . 4E **51**
  E13 . . . . 1C **68**
Terraces, The NW8 . . . . 1F **59**
  (off Queen's Ter.)
Terrace Wlk. SW11 . . . 3B **88**
  (off Albert Bri. Rd.)
Terrapin Rd.
  SW17 . . . . 3D **117**
Terretts Pl. N1 . . . . 4D **49**
  (off Upper St.)
Terrick St. W12 . . . . . . 5D **57**
Territorial Ho. SE11 . . . 5C **76**
  (off Reedworth St.)
Tessa Sanderson Pl.
  SW8 . . . . 1D **103**
  (off Daley Thompson Way)
Testerton Rd. W11 . . . . 1F **71**
  (off Hurstway Rd.)
Testerton Wlk. W11 . . . 1F **71**
Tetbury Pl. N1 . . . . 5D **49**
Tetcott Rd. SW10 . . . . 3E **87**
  (not continuous)
Teversham La. SW8 . . 4A **90**
Teviot Est. E14 . . . . 4D **67**
Teviot St. E14 . . . . 3E **67**
Tewkesbury Av.
  SE23 . . . . 1D **121**
Tewkesbury Cl. N15 . . 1F **35**
Tewkesbury Rd. N15 . . 1F **35**
Thackeray Ct. SW3 . . . 1B **88**
  (off Elystan Pl.)
  W14 . . . . 4A **72**
  (off Blythe Rd.)
Thackeray Ho. WC1 . . . 3D **7**
Thackeray M. E8 . . . . . 3C **50**
Thackeray Rd. E6 . . . . . 1F **69**
  SW8 . . . . 5D **89**
Thackeray St. W8 . . . . 4D **73**
Thakeham Cl. SE26 . . . 4D **121**
Thalia Cl. SE10 . . . . . . 2F **95**
Thame Rd. SE16 . . . . . 3F **79**
Thames Av. SW10 . . . . 4E **87**
Thames Barrier Ind. Area
  SE18 . . . . 4F **83**
  (off Faraday Way)
Thames Barrier Pk. . . . 3E **83**
Thames Barrier Vis. Cen.
  . . . . 4F **83**
Thamesbrook SW3 . . . 1A **88**
  (off Dovehouse St.)
Thames Circ. E14 . . . . 5C **80**
Thames Ct. SE15 . . . . 3B **92**
  (off Daniel Gdns.)
Thames Cres. W4 . . . . 3A **84**
Thames Exchange Bldg.
  EC4 . . . . 5A **18**
Thames Hgts. SE1 . . . . 3F **27**
  (off Gainsford St.)
Thames Ho. EC4 . . . . . 4A **18**
  (off Up. Thames St.)

Thames Ho. SW1 . . . 5A **76**
(off Millbank)
Thameside Ind. Est.
E16 . . . . 3F **83**
Thames Pl. SW15 . . . . . 1F **99**
(not continuous)
Thames Point SW6 . . . . 5E **87**
Thames Quay E14 . . . . 3D **81**
SW10 . . . . 4E **87**
(off Chelsea Harbour)
Thames Reach W6 . . . . . 2E **85**
(off Rainville Rd.)
Thames Rd. E16 . . . . . . 2F **83**
Thames Rd. Ind. Est.
E16 . . . . 3F **83**
Thames St. SE10 . . . . . 2D **95**
Thames Wlk. SW11 . . . 3A **88**
Thames Wharf Studios
W6 . . . . 2E **85**
(off Rainville Rd.)
Thanet Ho. WC1 . . . . . . 2D **7**
(off Thanet St.)
Thanet Lodge NW2 . . . . 3A **44**
(off Mapesbury Rd.)
Thanet St.
WC1 . . . . 2D **7** (2A **62**)
Thanet Wharf SE8 . . . . 2D **95**
(off Copperas St.)
Thane Vs. N7 . . . . 5B **34**
Thane Works N7 . . . . . . 5B **34**
Thant Cl. E10 . . . . 5D **39**
Thavie's Inn
EC4 . . . . 2C **16** (5C **62**)
Thaxted Ct. N1 . . . . 1C **10**
(off Fairbank Est.)
Thaxted Ho. SE16 . . . . . 5E **79**
(off Abbeyfield Est.)
Thaxton Rd. W14 . . . . . 2B **86**
Thayer St.
W1 . . . . 1C **12** (5C **60**)
The . . . . . .
Names prefixed with 'The'
for example 'The Alders' are
indexed under the main
name such as 'Alders, The'
Theatre Mus. 4E **15**
Theatrerites 2D **115**
Theatre Royal
Stratford 4F **53**
Theatre Sq. E15 . . . . . . 3F **53**
Theatre St. SW11 . . . . 1B **102**
Theatro Technis 5E **47**
(off Crowndale Rd.)
Theberton St. N1 . . . . . 5C **48**
Theed St.
SE1 . . . . 2C **24** (2C **76**)
Thelma Gdns. SE3 . . . . 4F **97**
Theobald Rd. E17 . . . . . 2B **38**
Theobalds St. N4 . . . . . 5E **35**
Theobald's Rd.
WC1 . . . . 5F **7** (4B **62**)
Theobald St. SE1 . . . . . 4F **77**
Theodore Ct.
SE13 . . . . 4F **109**

Theodore Rd. SE13 . . . 4F **109**
Therapia Rd. SE22 . . . . 4E **107**
Theresa Rd. W6 . . . . . . 5C **70**
Therfield Ct. N4 . . . . . . 4E **35**
Thermopylae Ga.
E14 . . . . 5D **81**
Theseus Wlk.
N1 . . . . 1E **9** (1D **63**)
Thessaly Ho. SW8 . . . . 3E **89**
(off Thessaly Rd.)
Thessaly Rd. SW8 . . . . 3E **89**
(not continuous)
Thesus Ho. E14 . . . . . . 5E **67**
(off Blair St.)
Thetford Ho. SE1 . . . . . 5F **27**
(off Maltby St.)
Theydon Rd. E5 . . . . . . 4E **37**
Theydon St. E17 . . . . . . 2B **38**
Third Av. E13 . . . . 2C **68**
E17 . . . . 1C **38**
W3 . . . . 2B **70**
W10 . . . . 2A **58**
Thirleby Rd.
SW1 . . . . 5A **22** (4E **75**)
Thirlmere NW1 . . . . 1E **5**
(off Cumberland Mkt.)
Thirlmere Ho. N16 . . . . 1F **49**
(off Howard Rd.)
Thirlmere Rd.
SW16 . . . . 4F **117**
Thirsk Rd. SW11 . . . . . 1C **102**
Thirza Ho. E1 . . . . 5E **65**
(off Devonport St.)
Thistle Gro. SW10 . . . . . 1E **87**
Thistle Ho. E14 . . . . 5E **67**
(off Dee St.)
Thistlewaite Rd. E5 . . . 5D **37**
Thistlewood Cl. N7 . . . . 4B **34**
Thistley Ct. SE8 . . . . . . 2D **95**
Thomas Baines Rd.
SW11 . . . . 1F **101**
Thomas Burt Ho. E2 . . . 2D **65**
(off Canrobert St.)
Thomas Darby Ct.
W11 . . . . 5A **58**
(off Lancaster Rd.)
Thomas Dean Rd.
SE26 . . . . 4B **122**
Thomas Dinwiddy Rd.
SE12 . . . . 2D **125**
Thomas Doyle St.
SE1 . . . . 5D **25** (4D **77**)
Thomas Hollywood Ho.
E2 . . . . 1E **65**
(off Approach Rd.)
Thomas La. SE6 . . . . . . 5C **108**
Thomas More Highwalk
EC2 . . . . 1F **17**
(off Beech St.)
Thomas More Ho.
EC2 . . . . 1F **17**
Thomas More Sq.
E1 . . . . 1C **78**
(off Thomas More St.)

Thomas More St. E1 . . . 1C **78**
Thomas Neal's Shop. Mall
WC2 . . . . 3D **15** (5A **62**)
Thomas Nth. Ter.
E16 . . . . 4B **68**
(off Barking Rd.)
Thomas Pl. W8 . . . . 4D **73**
Thomas Rd. E14 . . . . . . 5B **66**
Thomas Rd. Ind. Est.
E14 . . . . 4C **66**
Thompson Ho. SE14 . . . 2F **93**
(off John Williams Cl.)
W10 . . . . 3A **58**
(off Wornington Rd.)
Thompson Rd.
SE22 . . . . 4B **106**
Thompson's Av. SE5 . . . 3E **91**
Thomson Ho. E14 . . . . . 5C **66**
(off Saracen St.)
SE17 . . . . 5A **78**
(off Tatum St.)
SW1 . . . . 1F **89**
(off Bessborough Pl.)
Thorburn Ho. SW1 . . . . 4A **20**
(off Kinnerton St.)
Thorburn Sq. SE1 . . . . 5C **78**
Thoresby St.
N1 . . . . 1A **10** (2E **63**)
Thornaby Ho. E2 . . . . . . 2D **65**
(off Canrobert St.)
Thornbill Ho. SE15 . . . . 3C **92**
(off Bird in Bush Rd.)
Thornbury Cl. N16 . . . . 2A **50**
Thornbury Ct. W11 . . . . 1C **72**
(off Chepstow Vs.)
Thornbury Rd.
SW2 . . . . 4A **104**
Thornbury Sq. N6 . . . . . 3E **33**
Thornby Rd. E5 . . . . 5E **37**
Thorncliffe Rd.
SW2 . . . . 4A **104**
Thorncombe Rd.
SE22 . . . . 3A **106**
Thorncroft St. SW8 . . . 3A **90**
Thorndean St.
SW18 . . . . 2E **115**
Thorndike Cl. SW10 . . . 3E **87**
Thorndike Ho.
SW1 . . . . 1F **89**
(off Vauxhall Bri. Rd.)
Thorndike St. SW1 . . . . 5F **75**
Thorne Cl. E11 . . . . 1F **53**
E16 . . . . 5C **68**
Thorne Ho. E2 . . . . 2E **65**
(off Roman Rd.)
E14 . . . . 4E **81**
(off Launch St.)
Thorne Pas. SW13 . . . . 5A **84**
Thorne Rd. SW8 . . . . . . 3A **90**
Thorne St. SW13 . . . . . 1A **98**
Thornewill Ho. E1 . . . . 1E **79**
(off Cable St.)
Thorney Ct. W8 . . . . . . 3E **73**
(off Palace Ga.)

Thorney Cres.
  SW11 . . . . 3F **87**
Thorney St. SW1 . . . . . . 5A **76**
Thornfield Ho. *E14* *1C* **80**
  (off Rosefield Gdns.)
Thornfield Rd. W12 . . . . 3D **71**
  (not continuous)
Thornford Rd. SE13 . . 3E **109**
Thorngate Rd. W9 . . . . 3C **58**
Thorngrove Rd. E13 . . 5D **55**
Thornham Gro. E15 . . 2F **53**
Thornham Ind. Est.
  E15 . . . . 3F **53**
Thornham St. SE10 . . 2D **95**
Thornhaugh M.
  WC1 . . . . 4C **6** (3F **61**)
Thornhaugh St.
  WC1 . . . . 4C **6** (3F **61**)
Thornhill Bri. Wharf
  N1 . . . . 5B **48**
Thornhill Cres. N1 . . . 4B **48**
Thornhill Gdns. E10 . . 4D **39**
Thornhill Gro. N1 . . . . 4B **48**
Thornhill Ho. *W4* . . . *1A* **84**
  (off Wood St.)
Thornhill Ho's. N1 . . . 4C **48**
Thornhill M. SW15 . . 2B **100**
Thornhill Rd. E10 . . . . 4D **39**
  N1 . . . . 4C **48**
Thornhill Sq. N1 . . . . . 4B **48**
Thornicroft Ho. *SW9* . . *5B* **90**
  (off Stockwell Rd.)
Thornlaw Rd. SE27 . . 4C **118**
Thornley Pl. SE10 . . . 1A **96**
Thornsbeach Rd.
  SE6 . . . . 1E **123**
Thornsett Rd. SW18 . . 1D **115**
Thorn Ter. SE15 . . . . 1E **107**
Thornton Av. SW2 . . . 1F **117**
  W4 . . . . 5A **70**
Thornton Gdns.
  SW12 . . . . 1F **117**
Thornton Ho. *SE17* . . . *5A* **78**
  (off Townsend St.)
Thornton Pl.
  W1 . . . . 5A **4** (4B **60**)
Thornton Rd.
  BR1: Brom 5C **124**
  E11 . . . . 4F **39**
  SW12 . . . . 5F **103**
Thornton St. SW9 . . . 5C **90**
Thornton Way NW11 . . 1D **31**
Thorntree Rd. SE7 . . . 1F **97**
Thornville St. SE8 . . . 4C **94**
Thornwood Rd.
  SE13 . . . . 3A **110**
Thornycroft Ho. *W4* . . *1A* **84**
  (off Fraser St.)
Thorogood Gdns. E15 . . 2A **54**
Thorold Ho. *SE1* *3F* **25**
  (off Pepper St.)
Thorparch Rd. SW8 . . 4F **89**
Thorpebank Rd.
  W12 . . . . 2C **70**

Thorpe Cl. SE26 . . . . . 4F **121**
  W10 . . . . 5A **58**
Thorpedale Rd. N4 . . . 4A **34**
Thorpe Ho. *N1* *5B* **48**
  (off Barnsbury Est.)
Thorpe Rd. E7 . . . . . . 1B **54**
  N15 . . . . 1A **36**
Thorpewood Av.
  SE26 . . . . 2D **121**
Thorsden Way SE19 . . 5A **120**
Thorverton Rd. NW2 . . 5A **30**
Thoydon Rd. E3 . . . . . 1A **66**
Thrale Rd. SW16 . . . . 4E **117**
Thrale St.
  SE1 . . . . 2A **26** (2E **77**)
Thrasher Cl. E8 . . . . . . 5B **50**
Thrawl St. E1 . . 1F **19** (4B **64**)
Thrayle Ho. *SW9* *1B* **104**
  (off Benedict Rd.)
Threadgold Ho. *N1* . . . *3F* **49**
  (off Dovercourt Est.)
Threadneedle St.
  EC2 . . . . 2B **18** (5F **63**)
Three Barrels Wlk.
  EC4 . . . . *5A* **18**
  (off Queen St. Pl.)
Three Colt Cnr. *E2* . . . *3C* **64**
Three Colts La. E2 . . . 3D **65**
Three Colt St. E14 . . . 5B **66**
Three Cranes Wlk.
  EC4 . . . . *5A* **18**
Three Cups Yd. WC1 . . 1A **16**
Three Kings Yd.
  W1 . . . . 4D **13** (1D **75**)
Three Mill La. E3 . . . . 2E **67**
  (not continuous)
Three Mills 2E **67**
Three Oak La. SE1 . . . 3F **27**
Three Quays EC3 . . . . 5E **19**
Three Quays Wlk.
  EC3 . . . . 5E **19** (1A **78**)
Threshers Pl. W11 . . . 1A **72**
Thriftwood SE26 . . . . 3E **121**
Thring Ho. *SW9* *5B* **90**
  (off Stockwell Rd.)
Throckmorten Rd.
  E16 . . . . 5D **69**
Throgmorton Av.
  EC2 . . . . 2C **18** (5F **63**)
  (not continuous)
Throgmorton St.
  EC2 . . . . 2C **18** (5F **63**)
Thrush St. SE17 . . . . . 1E **91**
Thurbarn Rd. SE6 . . . 5D **123**
Thurland Ho. *SE16* . . . *5D* **79**
  (off Camilla Rd.)
Thurland Rd. SE16 . . . 4C **78**
Thurlby Rd. SE27 . . . 4C **118**
Thurleigh Av. SW12 . . 4C **102**
Thurleigh Ct. SW12 . . 4C **102**
Thurleigh Rd. SW12 . . 5B **102**
Thurlestone Rd.
  SE27 . . . . 3C **118**

Thurloe Cl. SW7 . . . . . 5A **74**
Thurloe Ct. *SW3* *5A* **74**
  (off Fulham Rd.)
Thurloe Pl. SW7 . . . . . 5F **73**
Thurloe Pl. M. *SW7* . . . *5F* **73**
  (off Thurloe Pl.)
Thurloe Sq. SW7 . . . . 5A **74**
Thurloe St. SW7 . . . . . 5F **73**
Thurlow Hill SE21 . . . 1E **119**
Thurlow Ho. SW16 . . . 3A **118**
Thurlow Pk. Rd.
  SE21 . . . . 2D **119**
Thurlow Rd. NW3 . . . . 2F **45**
Thurlow St. SE17 . . . . 1F **91**
  (not continuous)
Thurlow Ter. NW5 . . . 2C **46**
Thurlow Wlk. SE17 . . . 1A **92**
  (not continuous)
Thurnscoe NW1 . . . . . 5E **47**
  (off Pratt St.)
Thursley Gdns.
  SW19 . . . . 2F **113**
Thursley Ho. *SW2* . . . *5B* **104**
  (off Holmewood Gdns.)
Thurso Ho. NW6 . . . . 1D **59**
Thurso St. SW17 . . . . 4F **115**
Thurstan Dwellings
  WC2 . . . . *2E* **15**
  (off Newton St.)
Thurston Ind. Est.
  SE13 . . . . 1D **109**
Thurston Rd. SE13 . . . 5D **95**
Thurtle Rd. E2 . . . . . . 1B **64**
Thyme Cl. SE3 . . . . . 1E **111**
Tibbat's Rd. E3 . . . . . 3D **67**
Tibbenham Pl. SE6 . . 2C **122**
Tibberton Wlk. E13 . . 1B **68**
Tibberton Sq. N1 . . . . 5E **49**
Tibbet's Cl. SW19 . . . 1F **113**
TIBBET'S CORNER 5F **99**
Tibbet's Ride SW15 . . 5F **99**
Tiber Gdns. N1 . . . . . 5A **48**
Ticehurst Rd. SE23 . . 2A **122**
Tickford Ho. NW8 . . . . 2A **60**
Tidal Basin Rd. E16 . . 1B **82**
  (not continuous)
Tidbury Ct. *SW8* *3E* **89**
  (off Stewart's Rd.)
Tideswell Rd.
  SW15 . . . . 2E **99**
Tideway Ct. SE16 . . . 2F **79**
Tideway Ho. *E14* *3C* **80**
  (off Strafford St.)
Tideway Ind. Est.
  SW8 . . . . 2E **89**
Tideway Wlk. SW8 . . . 2E **89**
Tidey St. E3 . . . . 4C **66**
Tidworth Rd. E3 . . . . . 3C **66**
Tierney Rd. SW2 . . . . 1A **118**
Tiffany Hgts. SW18 . . 5C **100**
Tiger Ho. *WC1* *2C* **6**
  (off Burton St.)
Tiger Way E5 . . . . . . 1D **51**
Tilbrook Rd. SE3 . . . . 1E **111**

Tilbury Cl. SE15 . . . . 3B 92
Tilbury Ho. SE14 . . . . 2F 93
   (off Myers La.)
Tilbury Rd. E10 . . . . 2E 39
Tildesley Rd. SW15 . . . . . 4E 99
Tilehurst NW1 . . . . 2E 5
Tilehurst Rd. SW18 . . . . . 1F 115
Tile Kiln La. N6 . . . . 3D 33
Tile Kiln Studios N6 . . . . 2E 33
Tile Yd. E14 . . . . 5B 66
Tileyard Rd. N7 . . . . 4A 48
Tilford Gdns. SW19 . . . . . 1F 113
Tilford Ho. SW2 . . . . 5B 104
   (off Holmewood Gdns.)
Tilia Rd. E5 . . . . 1D 51
Tilia Wlk. SW9 . . . . 2D 105
Tilleard Ho. W10 . . . . 2A 58
   (off Herries St.)
Tiller Leisure Cen., The
. . . . 4C 80
Tiller Rd. E14 . . . . 4C 80
Tillett Sq. SE16 . . . . 3A 80
Tillet Way E2 . . . . 2C 64
Tilling Rd. NW2 . . . . 3E 29
Tillings Cl. SE5 . . . . 4E 91
Tillman St. E1 . . . . 5D 65
Tilloch St. N1 . . . . 4B 48
Tillotson Ct. SW8 . . . . 3F 89
   (off Wandsworth Rd.)
Tilney Ct.
  EC1 . . . . 3A 10 (3E 63)
Tilney Gdns. N1 . . . . 3F 49
Tilney St. W1 . . . 1C 20 (2C 74)
Tilson Cl. SE5 . . . . 3A 92
Tilson Gdns. SW2 . . . . . . 5A 104
Tilson Ho. SW2 . . . . 5A 104
Tilston Cl. E11 . . . . 5B 40
Tilton St. SW6 . . . . 2A 86
Timberland Cl. SE15 . . . . 3C 92
Timberland Rd. E1 . . . . . . 5D 65
Timber Mill Way
  SW4 . . . . 1F 103
Timber Pond Rd.
  SE16 . . . . 2F 79
Timber St. EC1 . . 3F 9 (3E 63)
Timberwharf Rd.
  N16 . . . . 1C 36
Timber Wharves Est.
  E14 . . . . 5C 80
   (off Charnwood Gdns.)
  E14 . . . . 5C 80
   (off Copeland Dr.)
Timbrell Pl. SE16 . . . . 2B 80
Time Sq. E8 . . . . 2B 50
Timor Ho. E1 . . . . 3A 66
   (off Duckett St.)
Timothy Cl. SW4 . . . . 3E 103
Timothy Rd. E3 . . . . 4B 66
Timperley Ct. SW19 . . . . . 1A 114
Timsbury Wlk.
  SW15 . . . . 1C 112
Tina Ct. SE6 . . . . 5B 108
Tindal St. SW9 . . . . 4D 91
Tinderbox All. SW14 . . . . 1A 98

Tinniswood Cl. N5 . . . . . . 2C 48
Tinsley Rd. E1 . . . . 4E 65
Tintagel Cres. SE22 . . . . 2B 106
Tintagel Gdns.
  SE22 . . . . 2B 106
Tintagel Ct. EC1 . . . . 3D 9
   (off St John St.)
Tintern Cl. SW15 . . . . 3A 100
Tintern Ho. NW1 . . . . 1E 5
   (off Augustus St.)
  SW1 . . . . 5D 75
   (off Abbots Mnr.)
Tintern Path NW9 . . . . . . 1A 28
   (off Fryent Gro.)
Tintern St. SW4 . . . . 2A 104
Tinto Rd. E16 . . . . 3C 68
Tinworth St. SE11 . . . . . . 1A 90
Tipthorpe Rd.
  SW11 . . . . 1C 102
Tiptree NW1 . . . . 4D 47
   (off Castlehaven Rd.)
Tisbury Ct. W1 . . . . 4B 14
Tisdall Ho. SE17 . . . . 5F 77
   (off Catesby St.)
Tisdall Pl. SE17 . . . . 5F 77
Tissington Ct. SE16 . . . . . 5E 79
Titan Bus. Est. SE8 . . . . . 3C 94
   (off Ffinch St.)
Titchborne Row W2 . . . . 5A 60
Titchfield Rd. NW8 . . . . . 5A 46
Titchwell Rd. SW18 . . . . . 1F 115
Tite St. SW3 . . . . 1B 88
Titmuss St. W12 . . . . 3E 71
Tiverton Rd. N15 . . . . 1F 35
  NW10 . . . . 5F 43
Tiverton St.
  SE1 . . . . 5F 25 (4E 77)
Tivoli Ct. SE16 . . . . 2B 80
Tivoli Gdns. SE18 . . . . . . 5F 83
   (not continuous)
Tivoli Rd. N8 . . . . 1F 33
  SE27 . . . . 5E 119
Tobacco Dock E1 . . . . . . 1D 79
Tobacco Quay E1 . . . . . . 1D 79
Tobago St. E14 . . . . 3C 80
Tobin Cl. NW3 . . . . 4A 46
Toby La. E1 . . . . 3A 66
Todber Ho. W14 . . . . 4A 72
   (off Russell Rd.)
Todds Wlk. N7 . . . . 4B 34
Tokenhouse Yd.
  EC2 . . . . 2B 18 (5F 63)
Token Yd. SW15 . . . . 2A 100
Toland Sq. SW15 . . . . . . 3C 98
Tolchurch W11 . . . . 5B 58
   (off Dartmouth Cl.)
Tolhurst Dr. W10 . . . . 2A 58
Tollard Ho. W14 . . . . 4B 72
Tollbridge Cl. W10 . . . . . 3A 58
Tollet St. E1 . . . . 3F 65
Tollgate Dr. SE21 . . . . . . 2A 120
Tollgate Gdns. NW6 . . . . 1D 59
Tollgate Ho. NW6 . . . . . . 1D 59
   (off Tollgate Gdns.)

Tollgate Rd. E6 . . . . 4E 69
  E16 . . . . 4E 69
Tollhouse Way N19 . . . . . 4E 33
Tollington Pk. N4 . . . . 4B 34
Tollington Pl. N4 . . . . 4B 34
Tollington Rd. N7 . . . . . . 1B 48
Tollington Way N7 . . . . . . 5A 34
Tolmers Sq.
  NW1 . . . . 3A 6 (3E 61)
   (not continuous)
Tolpaide Ho. SE11 . . . . . 5C 76
   (off Marylee Way)
Tolpuddle Av. E13 . . . . . . 5E 55
   (off Queens Rd.)
Tolpuddle St. N1 . . . . 1C 62
Tolsford Rd. E5 . . . . 2D 51
Tom Allen Arts Cen. 3F 53
Tom Blau Gallery 3F 27
   (off Queen Elizabeth St.)
Tom Groves Cl. E15 . . . . 2F 53
Tom Hood Cl. E15 . . . . . . 2F 53
Tom Jenkinson Rd.
  E16 . . . . 2C 82
Tomkyns Ho. SE11 . . . . . 5C 76
   (off Distin St.)
Tomline Ho. SE1 . . . . 2F 25
   (off Pepper St.)
Tomlin's Gro. E3 . . . . 2C 66
Tomlinson Cl. E2 . . . . 2B 64
Tomlins Ter. E14 . . . . 5A 66
Tomlins Wlk. N7 . . . . 4B 34
Tom Nolan Cl. E15 . . . . . 1A 68
Tompion Ho. EC1 . . . . . . 3E 9
   (off Percival St.)
Tompion St.
  EC1 . . . . 2D 9 (2D 63)
   (not continuous)
Tom Smith Cl. SE10 . . . . 2A 96
Tomson Ho. SE1 . . . . 5F 27
   (off Riley Rd.)
Tom Williams Ho.
  SW6 . . . . 2B 86
   (off Clem Attlee Ct.)
Tonbridge Ho's.
  WC1 . . . . 2D 7
   (off Tonbridge St.)
Tonbridge St.
  WC1 . . . . 1D 7 (2A 62)
Tonbridge Wlk. WC1 . . . . 1D 7
Toneborough NW8 . . . . . 5D 45
   (off Abbey Rd.)
Tonsley Hill SW18 . . . . . 3D 101
Tonsley Pl. SW18 . . . . . . 3D 101
Tonsley Rd. SW18 . . . . . 3D 101
Tonsley St. SW18 . . . . . . 3D 101
Tony Cannell M. E3 . . . . 2B 66
Took's Ct.
  EC4 . . . . 2B 16 (5C 62)
Tooley St.
  SE1 . . . . 1C 26 (2F 77)
Toomy Cen. E16 . . . . 2D 83
   (off Evelyn Rd.)
TOOTING 5A 116
TOOTING BEC 3B 116

Tooting Bec Gdns.
SW16 . . . . 4F **117**
(not continuous)
Tooting Bec Lido 4E **117**
Tooting Bec Rd.
SW16 . . . . 3C **116**
SW17 . . . . 3C **116**
Tooting B'way.
SW17 . . . . 5A **116**
TOOTING GRAVENEY
. . . . 5B **116**
Tooting Gro. SW17 . . 5A **116**
Tooting High St.
SW17 . . . . 5A **116**
Tooting Leisure Cen.
. . . . 4F **115**
Tooting Mkt. SW17 . . 4B **116**
Topaz Ct. E11 . . . . . . 3A **40**
Topaz Wlk. NW2 . . . . 2F **29**
Topham St. SE10 . . . . 3E **95**
(off Prior St.)
Topham St.
EC1 . . . . 3B **8** (3C **62**)
Topley St. SE9 . . . . . 2E **111**
Topmast Point E14 . . 3C **80**
Topp Wlk. NW2 . . . . . 4E **29**
Topsfield Cl. N8 . . . . 1F **33**
Topsfield Pde. N8 . . . 1A **34**
(off Tottenham La.)
Topsfield Rd. N8 . . . . 1A **34**
Topsham Rd. SW17 . . 3B **116**
Torbay Ct. NW1 . . . . . 4D **47**
Torbay Mans. NW6 . . . 5B **44**
(off Willesden La.)
Torbay Rd. NW6 . . . . 4B **44**
Torbay St. NW1 . . . . . 4D **47**
Tor Ct. W8 . . . . 3C **72**
Torcross Dr. SE23 . . 2E **121**
Tor Gdns. W8 . . . . . . 3C **72**
Tor Ho. N6 . . . . 1D **33**
Tornay Ho. E9 . . . . . . 4E **51**
N1 . . . . 1B **62**
(off Priory Grn. Est.)
Torquay St. W2 . . . . . 4D **59**
Torrance Cl. SE7 . . . . 2F **97**
Torrens Ct. SE5 . . . . 1F **105**
Torrens Rd. E15 . . . . 3B **54**
SW2 . . . . 3B **104**
Torrens Sq. E15 . . . . 3B **54**
Torrens St. EC1 . . . . 1C **62**
Torres Sq. E14 . . . . . 1C **94**
Torrey Dr. SW9 . . . . . 5C **90**
Torriano Av. NW5 . . . 2F **47**
Torriano Cotts. NW5 . 2E **47**
Torriano M. NW5 . . . . 2E **47**
Torridge Gdns. SE15 . 2E **107**
Torridon Ho. NW6 . . . 1D **59**
(off Randolph Gdns.)
Torridon Rd. SE6 . . . 5F **109**
SE13 . . . . 5A **110**
Torrington Ct. SE26 . 5C **120**
(off Crystal Pal. Pk. Rd.)
Torrington Pl. E1 . . . 2C **78**
WC1 . . . . 5B **6** (4F **61**)

Torrington Sq.
WC1 . . . . 4C **6** (3F **61**)
Tortington Ho. SE15 . . 3C **92**
(off Friary Est.)
Torwood Rd. SW15 . . 3C **98**
Tothill Ho. SW1 . . . . . 5F **75**
(off Page St.)
Tothill St.
SW1 . . . . 4C **22** (3F **75**)
Tottan Ter. E1 . . . . . . 5F **65**
Tottenhall NW1 . . . . . 4C **46**
(off Ferdinand St.)
Tottenham Ct. Rd.
W1 . . . . 4A **6** (3E **61**)
Tottenham La. N8 . . . 1A **34**
Tottenham M.
W1 . . . . 5A **6** (4E **61**)
Tottenham Rd. N1 . . . 3A **50**
Tottenham St.
W1 . . . . 1A **14** (4E **61**)
Totterdown St.
SW17 . . . . 4B **116**
Totteridge Ho. SW11 . 5F **87**
(off Yelverton Rd.)
Toulmin St.
SE1 . . . . 4F **25** (3E **77**)
Toulon St. SE5 . . . . . 3E **91**
Toulouse Ct. SE16 . . . 1D **93**
(off Rossetti Rd.)
Tounson Ct. SW1 . . . . 5F **75**
(off Montaigne Cl.)
Tourist Info. Cen.
City of London
. . . . 3F **17** (5E **63**)
Greenwich 2E **95**
Hackney 3D **51**
King's Cross 1D **7**
Leicester Sq.
. . . . 5C **14** (1F **75**)
Lewisham 2E **109**
Somers Town 2A **62**
Southwark
. . . . 1A **26** (2E **77**)
Waterloo International
Terminal . . . 3A **24** (3C **76**)
Tournay Rd. SW6 . . . . 3B **86**
Tours Pas. SW11 . . . . 2E **101**
Toussaint Wlk. SE16 . . 4C **78**
Tovy Ho. SE1 . . . . . . 1C **92**
(off Avondale Sq.)
Towcester Rd. E3 . . . 3D **67**
Tower 42 . . . . 2D **19** (5A **64**)
Tower Bri. E1 . . . . . . 2F **27**
SE1 . . . . 2F **27** (2B **78**)
Tower Bri. App.
E1 . . . . 1F **27** (2B **78**)
Tower Bri. Bus. Complex
SE16 . . . . 4C **78**
Tower Bri. Bus. Sq.
SE16 . . . . 5D **79**
Tower Bridge Experience
. . . . 1F **27**
Tower Bri. Plaza
SE1 . . . . 2F **27** (2B **78**)

Tower Bri. Rd.
SE1 . . . . 5D **27** (4A **78**)
Tower Bri. Sq. SE1 . . . 3F **27**
Tower Bri. Wharf E1 . . 2C **78**
Tower Bldgs. E1 . . . . 2D **79**
(off Brewhouse La.)
Tower Cl. NW3 . . . . . 2F **45**
Tower Ct. E5 . . . . 2B **36**
N1 . . . . 4E **49**
(off Canonbury St.)
NW8 . . . . 1A **60**
(off Mackennal St.)
WC2 . . . . 3D **15**
Towergate SE1 . . . . . 5A **78**
(off Page's Wlk.)
Tower Hamlets Rd.
E7 . . . . 1B **54**
TOWER HILL 1B **78**
Tower Hill
EC3 . . . . 5E **19** (1A **78**)
Tower Hill Ter. EC3 . . 5E **19**
Tower Ho. E1 . . . . . . 4C **64**
(off Fieldgate St.)
Tower Mill Rd. SE15 . 3A **92**
Tower of London, The
. . . . 5F **19** (1B **78**)
Tower of London
Vis. Cen., The
. . . . 5E **19** (1A **78**)
Tower Pl.
EC3 . . . . 5E **19** (1A **78**)
Tower Pl. E. EC3 . . . . 5E **19**
(off Lwr. Thames St.)
Tower Pl. W. EC3 . . . . 5E **19**
(off Lwr. Thames St.)
Tower Rd. NW10 . . . . 4C **42**
Tower Royal
EC4 . . . . 4B **18** (1F **77**)
Tower St.
WC2 . . . . 3D **15** (5A **62**)
Tower Wlk. SE1 . . . . . 5A **78**
(off Aberdour St.)
Towncourt Path N4 . . . 3E **35**
Town Hall Rd.
SW11 . . . . 1B **102**
Town Hall Wlk. N16 . . 1F **49**
(off Albion Rd.)
Townley Ct. E15 . . . . 3B **54**
Townley Rd. SE22 . . . 3A **106**
Townley St. SE17 . . . 1F **91**
(not continuous)
Townmead Bus. Cen.
SW6 . . . . 1E **101**
Townmead Rd. SW6 . . 1D **101**
Townsend Ho. SE1 . . . 5C **78**
(off Strathnairn St.)
Townsend La. NW9 . . 2A **28**
Townsend Rd. N15 . . . 1B **36**
Townsend St. SE17 . . 5A **78**
Townsend Yd. N6 . . . 3D **33**
Townshend Ct.
NW8 . . . . 1A **60**
(off Townshend Rd.)
Townshend Est. NW8 . 1A **60**

Townshend Rd. NW8 . . . 5A 46
(not continuous)
Towns Ho. SW4. . . . . 1F 103
Towpath, The SW10 . . . . . 4F 87
Towpath Wlk. E9. . . . . . . 2B 52
Towton Rd. SE27 . . . . . 2E 119
Toynbee St.
E1. . . . . 1F 19 (4B 64)
Toyne Way N6. . . . . 1B 32
Tracey Av. NW2 . . . . 2E 43
Tradescant Ho. E9 . . . . . 4E 51
(off Frampton Pk. Rd.)
Tradescant Rd. SW8. . . . . 3A 90
Tradewinds Ct. E1 . . . . . 1C 78
Trafalgar Av. SE15 . . . . . 1B 92
Trafalgar Chambers
SW3. . . . . 1F 87
(off South Pde.)
Trafalgar Cl. SE16 . . . . . 4A 80
Trafalgar Cl. E1. . . . . . . 2E 79
(off Wapping Wall)
Trafalgar Gdns. E1 . . . . . 4F 65
W8. . . . . 4D 73
(off South End Row)
Trafalgar Gro. SE10 . . . . 2F 95
Trafalgar Ho. SE17. . . . . 1E 91
(off Bronti Cl.)
Trafalgar M. E3. . . . . 3B 52
Trafalgar Point N1. . . . . . 4F 49
(off Downham Rd.)
Trafalgar Rd. SE10 . . . . . 2F 95
Trafalgar Square
. . . . 1D 23 (2A 76)
Trafalgar Sq.
WC2 . . . . 1C 22 (2F 75)
Trafalgar St. SE17. . . . . . 1F 91
Trafalgar Studios 1D 23
(off Whitehall)
Trafalgar Way E14 . . . . . 2E 81
Trafford Cl. E15 . . . . 2D 53
Trafford Ho. N1 . . . . 1F 63
(off Cranston Est.)
Trahorn Cl. E1 . . . . 3D 65
Traitors' Gate 1F 27
Tralee Ct. SE16 . . . . 1D 93
(off Masters Dr.)
Tramway Av. E15 . . . . . . 4A 54
Tranley M. NW3 . . . . 1A 46
(off Fleet Rd.)
Tranmere Rd.
SW18 . . . . 2E 115
Tranquil Pas. SE3. . . . . . 5B 96
(off Montpelier Va.)
Tranquil Va. SE3. . . . . . . 5A 96
Transept St. NW1. . . . . . 4A 60
Transom Sq. E14 . . . . . . 1D 95
Tranton Rd. SE16 . . . . . . 4C 78
Trappes Ho. SE16. . . . . . 5D 79
(off Camilla Rd.)
Travers Ho. SE10 . . . . . . 2F 95
(off Trafalgar Gro.)
Travers Rd. N7 . . . . 5C 34
Travis Ho. SE10 . . . . 4E 95

Treadgold Ho. W11. . . . . . 1F 71
(off Bomore Rd.)
Treadgold St. W11 . . . . . . 1F 71
Treadway St. E2. . . . . . . 1D 65
Treasury Pas. SW1 . . . . . 3D 23
Treaty St. N1 . . . . 5B 48
Trebeck St.
W1. . . . . 1D 21 (2D 75)
Trebovir Rd. SW5. . . . . . . 1C 86
Treby St. E3 . . . . 3B 66
Trecastle Way N7 . . . . . . 1F 47
Tredegar M. E3. . . . . 2B 66
Tredegar Rd. E3 . . . . 1B 66
Tredegar Sq. E3 . . . . 2B 66
Tredegar Ter. E3 . . . . 2B 66
Trederwen Rd. E8 . . . . . . 5C 50
Tredown Rd. SE26 . . . . . 5E 121
Tredwell Cl. SW2. . . . . . 2B 118
Tredwell Rd. SE27 . . . . . 4D 119
Treen Av. SW13 . . . . 1B 98
Tree Rd. E16. . . . . 5E 69
Treewall Gdns.
BR1: Brom. 4D 125
Trefil Wlk. N7. . . . . 1A 48
Trefoil Rd. SW18 . . . . . . 3E 101
Tregaron Av. N8 . . . . 1A 34
Tregarvon Rd.
SW11 . . . . 2C 102
Trego Rd. E9. . . . . 4C 52
Tregothnan Rd.
SW9 . . . . 1A 104
Tregunter Rd. SW10 . . . . 2D 87
Treherne Ct. SW9. . . . . . . 4D 91
SW17 . . . . 4C 116
Trehern Rd. SW14 . . . . . 1A 98
Trehurst St. E5 . . . . 2A 52
Trelawney Est. E9. . . . . . 3E 51
Trelawney Ho. SE1. . . . . . 2F 25
(off Pepper St.)
Trelawn Rd. E10. . . . . . . 5E 39
SW2 . . . . 3C 104
Trellick Twr. W10 . . . . . . 3B 58
(off Golborne Rd.)
Trellis Sq. E3 . . . . 2B 66
Tremadoc Rd. SW4. . . . . 2F 103
Tremaine Cl. SE4 . . . . . . 5C 94
Trematon Ho. SE11 . . . . . 1C 90
(off Kennings Way)
Tremlett Gro. N19. . . . . . 5E 33
Trenchard Ct. NW4. . . . . 1C 28
Trenchard St. SE10. . . . . 1F 95
Trenchold St. SW8 . . . . . 2A 90
Trendell Ho. E14 . . . . . . 5C 66
(off Dod St.)
Trenmar Gdns.
NW10 . . . . 2D 57
Trentham St. SW18 . . . . 1C 114
Trent Ho. SE15 . . . . 2E 107
Trent Rd. SW2 . . . . 3B 104
Treport St. SW18 . . . . . . 5D 101
Tresco Ho. SE11 . . . . 1C 90
(off Sancroft St.)
Tresco Rd. SE15. . . . . . . 2D 107
Tresham Cres. NW8 . . . . 3A 60

Tresham Wlk. E9 . . . . 2E 51
Tresidder Ho. SW4. . . . . 5F 103
Tressell Cl. N1. . . . . 4D 49
Tressillian Cres.
SE4. . . . . 1C 108
Tressillian Rd. SE4 . . . . 2B 108
Tress Pl. SE1. . . . . 1D 25
Trevanion Rd. W14 . . . . . 5A 72
Trevelyan Gdns.
NW10 . . . . 5E 43
Trevelyan Rd. E2 . . . . . . 2F 65
(off Morpeth St.)
Trevelyan Ho. SE5 . . . . . 3D 91
(off John Ruskin St.)
Trevelyan Rd. E15 . . . . . 1B 54
SW17 . . . . 5A 116
Trevenna Ho. SE23. . . . . 3F 121
(off Dacres Rd.)
Treveris St.
SE1 . . . . 2E 25 (2D 77)
Treverton St. W10 . . . . . 3F 57
Treverton Towers
W10. . . . . 4F 57
(off Treverton St.)
Treves Ho. E1. . . . . 3C 64
(off Vallance Rd.)
Treville St. SW15. . . . . . 5D 99
Treviso Rd. SE23 . . . . . . 2F 121
Trevithick Ho. SE16. . . . . 5D 79
(off Rennie Est.)
Trevithick St. SE8. . . . . . 2C 94
Trevone Ct. SW2 . . . . . . 5A 104
(off Doverfield Rd.)
Trevor Pl. SW7 . . . . 3A 74
Trevor Sq. SW7 . . . . 3B 74
Trevor St. SW7 . . . . 3A 74
Trevor Wlk. SW7 . . . . 3A 74
(off Trevor Pl., not continuous)
Trevose Ho. SE11. . . . . . 1B 90
(off Orsett St.)
Trewint St. SW18 . . . . . . 2E 115
Trewsbury Rd. SE26. . . . 5F 121
Triangle, The E8 . . . . 5D 51
EC1 . . . . 3E 9
Triangle Bus. Cen., The
NW10 . . . . 2B 56
Triangle Ct. E16. . . . . . . 4F 69
Triangle Est. SE11 . . . . . 1C 90
(off Kennington Rd.)
Triangle Pl. SW4 . . . . . . 2F 103
Triangle Rd. E8 . . . . 5D 51
Tricycle Cinema 4B 44
Tricycle Theatre 4B 44
Trident Bus. Cen.
SW17 . . . . 5B 116
Trident Ho. E14 . . . . 5E 67
(off Blair St.)
Trident Pl. SW3 . . . . 2F 87
(off Old Church St.)
Trident St. SE16 . . . . 5F 79
Trig La. EC4. . . . . . 4F 17 (1E 77)
Trigon Rd. SW8 . . . . 3B 90
Trilby Rd. SE23 . . . . 2F 121
Trimdon NW1 . . . . 5E 47

Trim St. SE14 . . . . 2B 94
Trinder Gdns. N19 . . . . 3A 34
Trinder Rd. N19 . . . . . . 3A 34
Trinidad Ho. E14. . . . . . 1B 80
　　　　(off Gill St.)
Trinidad St. E14 . . . . . . 1B 80
Trinity Buoy Wharf
　E14 . . . . 1A 82
　　　　(off Orchard Pl.)
Trinity Chu. Pas.
　SW13 . . . . 2D 85
Trinity Chu. Rd.
　SW13 . . . . 2D 85
Trinity Chu. Sq.
　SE1 . . . . . . 5A 26 (4E 77)
Trinity Cl. E8. . . . . 3B 50
　E11 . . . . 4A 40
Trinity Cl. NW3 . . . . . . 1F 45
　SE13 . . . . 2F 109
　SW4 . . . . 2E 103
Trinity College of Music
　. . . . . 2E 95
Trinity Ct. N1 . . . . 5A 50
　　　　(off Downham Rd.)
　NW2 . . . . 2E 43
　SE1 . . . . 5A 26
　　　　(off Brockham St.)
　SE7 . . . . 5F 83
　SE26 . . . . 3E 121
　SW9 . . . . 1B 104
　W2 . . . . 5E 59
　　　　(off Gloucester Ter.)
　WC1 . . . . 3F 7
Trinity Cres. SW17 . . . 2B 116
Trinity Gdns. E16 . . . . . 4B 68
　　　　(not continuous)
　SW9 . . . . 2B 104
Trinity Grn. E1. . . . . . . 3E 65
Trinity Gro. SE10 . . . . . 4E 95
Trinity Hospital (Almshouses)
　SE10 . . . . 1F 95
Trinity Ho. EC3 . . . . . . 4F 19
　SE1 . . . . 5A 26
　　　　(off Bath Ter.)
Trinity M. E1 . . . . 4E 65
　　　　(off Redman's Rd.)
　W10. . . . . 5F 57
Trinity Path SE23 . . . . 3E 121
Trinity Pl.
　EC3. . . . . . . 4F 19 (1B 78)
Trinity Ri. SW2. . . . . . . 1C 118
Trinity Rd. SW17 . . . . . 1A 116
　SW18 . . . . 2E 101
　SW19 . . . . 5C 114
Trinity Sq.
　EC3. . . . . . . 5E 19 (1A 78)
Trinity St. E16. . . . . 4B 68
　SE1 . . . . 4A 26 (3E 77)
　　　　(not continuous)
Trinity Twr. E1. . . . . 1C 78
　　　　(off Vaughan Way)
Trinity Wlk. NW3 . . . . . 3E 45
Trinity Way W3 . . . . . . 1A 70
Trio Pl. SE1 . . . . 4A 26 (3E 77)

Tristan Ct. SE8 . . . . 2B 94
　　　　(off Dorking Cl.)
Tristan Sq. SE3 . . . . . . 1A 110
Tristram Rd.
　BR1: Brom 4B 124
Triton Ho. E14 . . . . 5D 81
　　　　(off Cahir St.)
Triton Sq.
　NW1 . . . . 3F 5 (3E 61)
Tritton Rd. SE21 . . . . . . 3F 119
Trocadero Cen.
　. . . . . 5B 14 (1F 75)
Trocette Mans. SE1 . . . 5D 27
　　　　(off Bermondsey St.)
Trojan Ct. NW6. . . . . . . 4A 44
Trojan Ind. Est.
　NW10 . . . . 3B 42
Troon Cl. SE16 . . . . 1D 93
Troon Ho. E1 . . . . 5A 66
　　　　(off White Horse La.)
Tropical St. E1 . . . . 5A 66
Tropical Ct. W10. . . . . . 2F 57
　　　　(off Kilburn La.)
Trossachs Rd. SE22 . . . 3A 106
Trothy Rd. SE1 . . . . 5C 78
Trotman Ho. SE14 . . . . 4E 93
　　　　(off Pomeroy St.)
Trott St. SW11 . . . . 4A 88
Trotwood Ho. SE16 . . . . 3D 79
　　　　(off Wilson Gro.)
Troughton Rd. SE7. . . . 1D 97
Troutbeck NW1 . . . . 2E 5
Troutbeck Rd. SE14 . . . 4A 94
Trouville Rd. SW4 . . . . 4E 103
Trowbridge Rd. E9 . . . . 3B 52
Troy Ct. W8 . . . . 4C 72
　　　　(off Kensington High St.)
Troy Town SE15 . . . . . . 1C 106
Trumans Rd. N16 . . . . . 2B 50
Trumpington Rd. E7 . . . 1B 54
Trump St.
　EC2 . . . . 3A 18 (5E 63)
Trundle St.
　SE1 . . . . 3F 25 (3E 77)
Trundleys Rd. SE8 . . . . 1F 93
Trundley's Ter. SE8 . . . 5F 79
Truro Ho. W2 . . . . 4C 58
　　　　(off Brunel Est.)
Truro St. NW5. . . . . 3C 46
Truslove Rd. SE27 . . . . 5C 118
Trussley Rd. W6 . . . . . . 4E 71
Trust Wlk. SE21 . . . . . . 1D 119
Tryfan Cl. IG4: Ilf 1F 41
Tryon Cres. E9 . . . . 5E 51
Tryon St. SW3 . . . . 1B 88
Tubbs Rd. NW10 . . . . . 1B 56
Tucklow Wlk. SW15. . . . 5B 98
Tudor Cl. N6 . . . . 2E 33
　NW3 . . . . 2A 46
　SW2 . . . . 4B 104
Tudor Ct. E17 . . . . 2B 38
　N1. . . . . 3A 50
　SE16 . . . . 2F 79
　　　　(off Princes Riverside Rd.)

Tudor Gdns. SW13 . . . . 1A 98
Tudor Gro. E9 . . . . 4E 51
Tudor Ho. E9. . . . . 4E 51
　E16. . . . . 2D 83
　　　　(off Wesley Av.)
　W14. . . . . 5F 71
　　　　(off Windsor Way)
Tudor Rd. E6. . . . . 5E 55
　E9. . . . . 5D 51
Tudor Stacks SE24 . . . . 2E 105
Tudor St.
　EC4 . . . . 4C 16 (1C 76)
Tudway Rd. SE3. . . . . . 1D 111
TUFNELL PARK 1E 47
Tufnell Pk. Rd. N7 . . . . 1E 47
　N19 . . . . 1E 47
Tufton Ct. SW1. . . . . . . 5D 23
　　　　(off Tufton St.)
Tufton St.
　SW1. . . . . . . 5D 23 (4A 76)
Tugela St. SE6 . . . . 2B 122
Tullis Ho. E9. . . . . 4E 51
　　　　(off Frampton Pk. Rd.)
TULSE HILL 1D 119
Tulse Hill SW2 . . . . 4C 104
Tulse Hill Est. SW2 . . . 4C 104
Tulse Ho. SW2 . . . . 4C 104
Tulsemere Rd.
　SE27 . . . . 2E 119
Tunbridge Ho. EC1 . . . . 1C 8
Tunis Rd. W12 . . . . 2E 71
Tunley Grn. E14 . . . . . . 4B 66
Tunley Rd. NW10 . . . . . 5A 42
　SW17 . . . . 1C 116
Tunmarsh La. E13 . . . . 2D 69
Tunnel App. E14. . . . . . 1A 80
　SE10 . . . . 3A 82
　SE16 . . . . 3E 79
Tunnel Av. SE10 . . . . . . 3F 81
　　　　(not continuous)
Tunnel Av. Trad. Est.
　SE10 . . . . 3F 81
Tunnel Rd. SE16 . . . . . 3E 79
Tunstall Rd. SW9 . . . . . 2B 104
Tunworth Cres.
　SW15 . . . . 4B 98
Tun Yd. SW8 . . . . 5D 89
　　　　(off Silverthorne Rd.)
Tupelo Rd. E10 . . . . 4D 39
Tupman Ho. SE16 . . . . 3C 78
　　　　(off Scott Lidgett Cres.)
Turenne Cl. SW18 . . . . 2E 101
Turin St. E2 . . . . 2C 64
Turk's Head Yd.
　EC1 . . . . 5D 9 (4D 63)
Turk's Row SW3 . . . . . . 1B 88
Turle Rd. N4. . . . . 4B 34
Turlewray Cl. N4 . . . . . 3B 34
Turley Cl. E15. . . . . 5A 54
Turnagain La. EC4 . . . . 2D 17
Turnberry Cl. SE16. . . . 1D 93
Turnberry Quay E14 . . . 4D 81
Turnbull Ho. N1. . . . . . . 5D 49
Turnchapel M. SW4 . . . 1D 103

Turner Cl. NW11. . . . . . . 1D **31**
  SW9 . . . . 3D **91**
Turner Ct. SE16. . . . . 3E **79**
  (off Albion St.)
Turner Dr. NW11 . . . . 1D **31**
Turner Ho. E14 . . . . 3C **80**
  (off Cassilis Rd.)
  NW6 . . . . 2E **45**
  (off Dresden Cl.)
  NW8 . . . . 1A **60**
  (off Townshend Est.)
  SW1 . . . . 5F **75**
  (off Herrick St.)
Turner Pl. SW11 . . . . 3A **102**
Turner's All.
  EC3 . . . . 4D **19** (1A **78**)
Turners Ct. N15. . . . . 1F **35**
Turners Rd. E3 . . . . 4B **66**
Turner St. E1 . . . . 4D **65**
  E16 . . . . 5B **68**
Turners Wood
  NW11 . . . . 2E **31**
Turneville Rd. W14 . . . . . 2B **86**
Turney Rd. SE21. . . . . . . 5E **105**
TURNHAM GREEN. 5A **70**
Turnham Grn. Ter.
  W4 . . . . 5A **70**
Turnham Grn. Ter. M.
  W4 . . . . 5A **70**
Turnham Rd. SE4 . . . . . . 3A **108**
Turnmill St.
  EC1 . . . . 4D **9** (3D **63**)
Turnour Ho. E1. . . . . 5D **65**
  (off Walburgh St.)
Turnpike Cl. SE8 . . . . 3B **94**
Turnpike Ho.
  EC1 . . . . 2E **9** (2D **63**)
Turnpin La. SE10 . . . . . . 2E **95**
Turnstone Cl. E13 . . . . . . 2C **68**
Turnstone Ho. E1 . . . . . . 1C **78**
  (off Star Pl.)
Turpentine La. SW1 . . . . 1D **89**
Turpin Cl. E1 . . . . 1F **79**
Turpin Ho. SW11 . . . . . . 4D **89**
Turpins Yd. SE10 . . . . . . 3E **95**
Turpin Way N19 . . . . 4F **33**
  (not continuous)
Turquand St. SE17 . . . . . 5E **77**
Turret Gro. SW4 . . . . 1E **103**
Turville Ho. NW8 . . . . . . 3A **60**
  (off Grendon St.)
Turville St. E2 . . . . 3F **11**
Tuscan Ho. E2. . . . . 2E **65**
  (off Knottisford St.)
Tuskar St. SE10 . . . . 2A **96**
Tustin Est. SE15 . . . . 2E **93**
Tuttle Ho. SW1 . . . . 1F **89**
  (off Aylesford St.)
Tweedale Ct. E15 . . . . . . 2E **53**
Tweed Ho. E14 . . . . 1E **67**
  (off Teviot St.)
Tweedmouth Rd.
  E13 . . . . 1D **69**
Tweezer's All. WC2 . . . . . 4B **16**

Twelvetrees Cres. E3 . . . 3E **67**
  (not continuous)
  E16 . . . . 3F **67**
Twickenham Rd. E11 . . . 4E **39**
Twig Folly Cl. E2. . . . . . . 1F **65**
Twilley St. SW18 . . . . . . 5D **101**
Twine Ct. E1 . . . . 1E **79**
Twine Ter. E3 . . . . 3B **66**
  (off Ropery St.)
Twisden Rd. NW5 . . . . . . 1D **47**
Twycross M. SE10 . . . . . 1A **96**
Twyford Av. N2 . . . . 1A **36**
  (off Chisley Rd.)
Twyford Pl.
  WC2 . . . . 2F **15** (5B **62**)
Twyford St. N1 . . . . 5B **48**
Twynholm Mans.
  SW6 . . . . 3A **86**
  (off Lillie Rd.)
Tyas Rd. E16 . . . . 3B **68**
Tyburn Tree (site of) . . . 4A **12**
Tyburn Way
  W1. . . . . . . 4A **12** (1B **74**)
Tyers Est. SE1 . . . . 3D **27**
Tyers Ga.
  SE1 . . . . 4D **27** (3A **78**)
Tyers St. SE11 . . . . 1B **90**
Tyers Ter. SE11 . . . . 1B **90**
Tyler Cl. E2. . . . . 1B **64**
Tyler's Ct. W1. . . . . 3B **14**
Tyler St. SE10 . . . . 1A **96**
  (not continuous)
Tylney Av. SE19 . . . . 5B **120**
  (not continuous)
Tylney Ho. E1 . . . . 5D **65**
  (off Nelson St.)
Tylney Rd. E7 . . . . 1E **55**
Tyndale Ct. E14 . . . . 1D **95**
  (off Transom Sq.)
Tyndale La. N1. . . . . 4D **49**
Tyndale Mans. N1 . . . . . 4D **49**
  (off Upper St.)
Tyndale Ter. N1 . . . . 4D **49**
Tyndall Gdns. E10 . . . . . 4E **39**
Tyndall Rd. E10 . . . . 4E **39**
Tyneham Cl. SW11 . . . . . 1C **102**
Tyneham Rd. SW11. . . . . 5C **88**
Tynemouth St. SW6 . . . . 5E **87**
Tyne St. E1 . . . . 5B **64**
Tynsdale Rd. NW10 . . . . . 3A **42**
Tynwald Ho. SE26 . . . . . 3C **120**
Type St. E2 . . . . 1F **65**
Tyrawley Rd. SW6 . . . . . . 4D **87**
Tyrell Ho.
  BR3: Beck. 5D **123**
  (off Beckenham Hill Rd.)
Tyrols Rd. SE23 . . . . 1F **121**
Tyrrell Ho. SW1 . . . . 2E **89**
  (off Churchill Gdns.)
Tyrrell Rd. SE22 . . . . 2C **106**
Tyrrel Way NW9 . . . . 2B **28**
Tyrwhitt Rd. SE4 . . . . . . 1C **108**
Tysoe St. EC1 . . . . 2C **8** (2C **62**)

Tyson Gdns. SE23 . . . . . 5E **107**
Tyson Rd. SE23 . . . . 5E **107**
Tyssen Pas. E8. . . . . 3B **50**
Tyssen Rd. N16 . . . . 5B **36**
Tyssen St. E8 . . . . 3B **50**
  N1. . . . . 1A **64**
Tytherton E2 . . . . 1E **65**
  (off Cyprus St.)
Tytherton Rd. N19 . . . . . 5F **33**

U

Uamvar St. E14 . . . . 4D **67**
Udall St. SW1 . . . . 5E **75**
Udimore Ho. W10 . . . . . . 4E **57**
  (off Sutton Way)
Uffington Rd. NW10. . . . . 5C **42**
  SE27 . . . . 4C **118**
Ufford St.
  SE1 . . . . 3C **24** (3C **76**)
Ufton Gro. N1 . . . . 4F **49**
Ufton Rd. N1 . . . . 4F **49**
  (not continuous)
UGC Cinema
  St James's 5B **14**
  (off Haymarket)
Uhura Sq. N16 . . . . 5A **36**
Ujima Ct. SW16 . . . . 4A **118**
Ullathorne Rd.
  SW16 . . . . 4E **117**
Ullin St. E14 . . . . 4E **67**
Ullswater Cl. SW15 . . . . . 4A **112**
Ullswater Cres.
  SW15 . . . . 4A **112**
Ullswater Ho. SE15 . . . . . 2E **93**
  (off Hillbeck Cl.)
Ullswater Rd. SE27 . . . . . 2D **119**
  SW13 . . . . 3C **84**
Ulster Pl.
  NW1 . . . . 4D **5** (3D **61**)
Ulster Ter.
  NW1. . . . . . . 3C **4** (3C **60**)
Ulundi Rd. SE3 . . . . 2A **96**
Ulva Rd. SW15. . . . . 3F **99**
Ulverscroft Rd.
  SE22 . . . . 3B **106**
Ulverstone Rd.
  SE27 . . . . 2D **119**
Ulysses Rd. NW6 . . . . . . 2B **44**
Umberston St. E1 . . . . . . 5C **64**
Umbria St. SW15. . . . . . . 4C **98**
Umfreville Rd. N4 . . . . . . 1D **35**
Undercliff Rd. SE13 . . . . 1C **108**
Underhill Ho. E14 . . . . . . 4C **66**
  (off Burgess St.)
Underhill Pas. NW1. . . . . 5D **47**
  (off Camden High St.)
Underhill Rd. SE22 . . . . . 3C **106**
Underhill St. NW1 . . . . . . 5D **47**
Undershaft
  EC3 . . . . 3D **19** (5A **64**)
Undershaw Rd.
  BR1: Brom 3B **124**

Underwood Ct. E10 .... 3D 39
    (off Leyton Grange Est.)
Underwood Ho.
  W6 .... 4D 71
    (off Sycamore Gdns.)
Underwood Rd. E1... 3C 64
Underwood Row
  N1 ...... 1A 10 (2E 63)
Underwood St.
  N1 ...... 1A 10 (2E 63)
Undine Rd. E14 .... 5D 81
Undine St. SW17 ... 5B 116
Unicorn Bldg. E1.... 1F 79
    (off Jardine Rd.)
Unicorn Theatre 2A 78
Union Canal Wlk.
  W10 .... 3E 57
    (off Canal Way)
Union Cl. E11 ...... 1F 53
Union Cotts. E15 .... 4A 54
Union Ct. EC2... 2D 19
  SW4 .... 5A 90
  W9 .... 4C 58
    (off Elmfield Way)
Union Dr. E1........ 3A 66
Union Gro. SW8 .... 5F 89
Union M. SW4 ...... 5A 90
Union Pk. SE10 .... 1B 96
    (off Calvert Rd.)
Union Rd. SW4 ..... 5F 89
  SW8 .... 5F 89
Union Sq. N1 .... 5E 49
Union St. E15 ...... 5F 53
  SE1 .... 2D 25 (2D 77)
Union Theatre 2E 25
Union Wlk.
  E2........ 1E 11 (2A 64)
Union Wharf N1 .... 1E 63
    (off Wenlock Rd.)
  N1 .... 5E 49
    (Arlington Av.)
Union Yd.
  W1........ 3E 13 (5D 61)
Unit Workshops E1.... 5C 64
    (off Adler St.)
Unity Cl. NW10...... 3C 42
  SE19 .... 5E 119
Unity M. NW1 ...... 1F 61
Unity Way SE18 .... 4F 83
Unity Wharf SE1..... 3B 78
    (off Mill St.)
University College
  Department of Geological
  Sciences Collection
  .... 4B 6
University College London
  Campbell House..... 3B 6
    (off Taviton St.)
  Chemistry Building ... 3B 6
    (off Gordon St.)
  Gower St..... 4B 6 (3F 61)
University of East London
  Maryland House 3A 54
  Stratford Campus ... 3A 54

University of Greenwich
  Maritime Greenwich
  Campus.......... 2E 95
University of London
  College Hall........ 4B 6
    (off Malet St.)
  Institute of Education
  .... 3F 61
  Institute of
  Latin American Studies
  .... 3F 61
  Senate House
  .... 5C 6 (4F 61)
University of London Union
  .... 4C 6
University of North London
  Highbury Cres..... 3C 48
  Highbury Gro....... 2E 49
  Hornsey Rd. 1C 48
University of Westminster
  Marylebone Campus
  .... 5B 4 (4C 60)
University of Westminster
  (Cavendish Campus)
  Bolsover St.
  .... 5E 5 (4D 61)
  Hanson St. ... 5F 5 (4E 61)
University of Westminster
  (Regent Campus)
  Lit. Titchfield St. ... 1F 13
  Regent St.
  .... 2E 13 (5D 61)
  Wells St. 1A 14
University St.
  WC1........ 4A 6 (3E 61)
Unwin Cl. SE15 ...... 2C 92
Unwin Mans. W14 .... 2B 86
    (off Queen's Club Gdns.)
Unwin Rd. SW7 ...... 4F 73
Upbrook M. W2 ...... 5E 59
Upcerne Rd. SW10... 3E 87
Upcott Ho. E9........ 4E 51
    (off Frampton Pk. Rd.)
Upgrove Mnr. Way
  SW2 .... 5C 104
Upham Pk. Rd. W4 ... 5A 70
Upland M. SE22..... 3C 106
Upland Rd. E13 ..... 3C 68
  SE22 .... 3C 106
Uplands Rd. N8 ..... 1B 34
Upnall Ho. SE15..... 2E 93
Upnor Way SE17 .... 1A 92
Up. Addison Gdns.
  W14 .... 3A 72
Upper Bank St. E14 ... 2D 81
Up. Bardsey Wlk. N1.. 3E 49
    (off Douglas Rd. Nth.)
Up. Belgrave St.
  SW1........ 5C 20 (4C 74)
Up. Berenger Wlk.
  SW10 .... 3F 87
    (off Berenger Wlk.)
Up. Berkeley St.
  W1........ 3A 12 (5B 60)

Up. Blantyre Wlk.
  SW10 .... 3F 87
    (off Blantyre Wlk.)
Up. Brockley Rd.
  SE4............ 1B 108
    (not continuous)
Up. Brook St.
  W1........ 4B 12 (1C 74)
Up. Caldy Wlk.
  N1 .... 3E 49
    (off Arran Wlk.)
Up. Camelford Wlk.
  W11 .... 5A 58
    (off Cambourne M.)
  W11 .... 5A 58
    (off St Mark's Rd.)
Up. Cheyne Row
  SW3 .... 2A 88
    (off Old Chu. St.)
UPPER CLAPTON 4D 37
Up. Clapton Rd. E5 ... 3D 37
Up. Clarendon Wlk.
  W11 .... 5A 58
    (off Clarendon Rd.)
Up. Dartrey Wlk.
  SW10 .... 3E 87
    (off Whistler Wlk.)
Up. Dengie Wlk. N1... 5E 49
    (off Baddow Wlk.)
Upper Feilde W1 ...... 4B 12
    (off Park St.)
Up. Grosvenor St.
  W1........ 5B 12 (1C 74)
Upper Ground
  SE1 .... 1B 24 (2C 76)
Up. Gulland Wlk.
  N1 .... 4E 49
    (off Church Rd.)
Up. Hampstead Wlk.
  NW3 .... 1E 45
Up. Handa Wlk. N1 ... 3F 49
    (off Handa Wlk.)
Up. Hawkwell Wlk.
  N1 .... 5E 49
    (off Maldon Cl.)
UPPER HOLLOWAY 4E 33
Up. James St.
  W1........ 4A 14 (1E 75)
Up. John St.
  W1........ 4A 14 (1E 75)
Up. Lismore Wlk. N1... 3E 49
    (off Clephane Rd.)
Upper Lodge W8 ..... 2D 73
    (off Palace Grn.)
Upper Mall W6...... 1C 84
    (not continuous)
Upper Marsh
  SE1 .... 5A 24 (4B 76)
Up. Montagu St.
  W1........ 5A 4 (4B 60)
Upper Nth. St. E14... 4C 66
Upper Pk. Rd. NW3 ... 2B 46
Up. Phillimore Gdns.
  W8 .... 3C 72

Up. Ramsey Wlk. N1 . . . 3F **49**
(off Ramsey Wlk.)
Up. Rawreth Wlk. N1 . . . 5E **49**
(off Basire St.)
Up. Richmond Rd.
SW15 . . . . 2B **98**
Up. Richmond Rd. W.
SW14 . . . . 2A **98**
Upper Rd. E13 . . . . . . 2C **68**
Up. St Martin's La.
WC2 . . . . 4D **15** (1A **76**)
Upper St. N1 . . . . 1C **62**
UPPER SYDENHAM . . . 3D **121**
Up. Tachbrook St.
SW1 . . . . 5E **75**
Up. Talbot Wlk. W11 . . . 5A **58**
(off Talbot Wlk.)
Upper Ter. NW3 . . . . . 5E **31**
Up. Thames St.
EC4 . . . . 4E **17** (1D **77**)
Up. Tollington Pk. N4 . . 3C **34**
(not continuous)
Upperton Rd. E. E13 . . . 2E **69**
Upperton Rd. W.
E13 . . . . 2E **69**
UPPER TOOTING 4B **116**
Up. Tooting Pk.
SW17 . . . . 2B **116**
Up. Tooting Rd.
SW17 . . . . 4B **116**
Up. Tulse Hill SW2 . . . 5B **104**
Up. Whistler Wlk.
SW10 . . . . 3E **87**
(off Worlds End Est.)
Up. Wimpole St.
W1 . . . . 5C **4** (4C **60**)
Up. Woburn Pl.
WC1 . . . . . . 2C **6** (2F **61**)
Upstall St. SE5 . . . . . 4D **91**
UPTON 4C **54**
Upton Av. E7 . . . . 4C **54**
Upton Cl. NW2 . . . . . . 5A **30**
Upton Hgts. E7 . . . . . 4C **54**
Upton La. E7 . . . . 4C **54**
Upton Lodge E7 . . . . . 3C **54**
UPTON PARK 5F **55**
Upton Pk. 1E **69**
Upton Pk. Boleyn Cinema
. . . . 1F **69**
Upton Pk. Rd. E7 . . . . 4D **55**
Upwey Ho. N1 . . . . . . 5A **50**
Upwood Rd. SE12 . . . 4C **110**
Urban M. N4 . . . . 1D **35**
Urlwin St. SE5 . . . . . . 2E **91**
Urlwin Wlk. SW9 . . . . 4C **90**
Urmston Dr. SW19 . . . 1A **114**
Urmston Ho. E14 . . . . 5E **81**
(off Seyssel St.)
Ursula M. N4 . . . . 3E **35**
Ursula St. SW11 . . . . . 4A **88**
Urswick Rd. E9 . . . . . 2E **51**
Usborne M. SW8 . . . . 3B **90**
Usher Rd. E3 . . . . 5B **52**
Usk Rd. SW11 . . . . . 2E **101**

Usk St. E2 . . . . 2F **65**
Utah Bldg. SE10 . . . . 4D **95**
(off Deal's Gateway)
Utopia Village NW1 . . . 4C **46**
Uverdale Rd. SW10 . . . 3E **87**
Uxbridge Rd. W12 . . . 2C **70**
Uxbridge St. W8 . . . . . 2C **72**

V

Vaine Ho. E9 . . . . 3A **52**
Vaizeys Wharf SE7 . . . 4D **83**
Vale, The NW11 . . . . . 5F **29**
SW3 . . . . 2F **87**
W3 . . . . 2A **70**
Vale Cl. W9 . . . . 2E **59**
Vale Cotts. SW15 . . . 3A **112**
Vale Ct. W3 . . . . 2B **70**
W9 . . . . 2E **59**
Vale Cres. SW15 . . . . 4A **112**
Vale End SE22 . . . . . 2B **106**
Vale Est., The W3 . . . . 2A **70**
Vale Gro. N4 . . . . 2E **35**
W3 . . . . 3A **70**
Vale Lodge SE23 . . . . 2E **121**
Valentia Pl. SW9 . . . . 2C **104**
Valentine Ct. SE23 . . . 2F **121**
(not continuous)
Valentine Pl.
SE1 . . . . 3D **25** (3D **77**)
Valentine Rd. E9 . . . . . 3F **51**
Valentine Row
SE1 . . . . 4D **25** (3D **77**)
VALE OF HEALTH 5E **31**
Vale of Health
NW3 . . . . 5F **31**
Vale Pde. SW15 . . . . 3A **112**
Valerian Way E15 . . . . 2A **68**
Vale Ri. NW11 . . . . . . 3B **30**
Vale Rd. E7 . . . . 3D **55**
N4 . . . . 2E **35**
Vale Row N5 . . . . 5D **35**
Vale Royal N7 . . . . . . 4A **48**
Vale Royal Ho.
WC2 . . . . 4C **14**
(off Charing Cross Rd.)
Vale St. SE27 . . . . . . 3F **119**
Valeswood Rd.
BR1: Brom 5B **124**
Vale Ter. N4 . . . . 1E **35**
Valetta Gro. E13 . . . . . 1C **68**
Valetta Rd. W3 . . . . . 3A **70**
Valette Ho. E9 . . . . . . 3E **51**
Valette St. E9 . . . . . . 3E **51**
Valiant Ho. E14 . . . . . 3E **81**
(off Plevna St.)
SE7 . . . . 1E **97**
Vallance Rd. E1 . . . . . 2C **64**
E2 . . . . 2C **64**
Valley, The E1 . . . . . . 1E **97**
Valley Gro. SE7 . . . . . 1E **97**

Valley Leisure Cen., The
. . . . 1E **97**
(off The Valley)
Valley Rd. SW16 . . . . 5B **118**
Valley Side SE7 . . . . . 1F **97**
Valliere Rd. NW10 . . . 2C **56**
Val McKenzie Av. N7 . . 5C **34**
Valmar Rd. SE5 . . . . . 4E **91**
Valmar Trad. Est.
SE5 . . . . 4E **91**
Valnay St. SW17 . . . . 5B **116**
Valois Ho. SE1 . . . . . 5F **27**
(off The Grange)
Valonia Gdns.
SW18 . . . . 4B **100**
Vanbrugh Castle
SE10 . . . . 2A **96**
(off Maze Hill)
Vanbrugh Cl. E16 . . . . 4F **69**
Vanbrugh Ct. SE11 . . . 5C **76**
(off Wincott St.)
Vanbrugh Flds. SE3 . . . 2B **96**
Vanbrugh Hill SE3 . . . 2B **96**
SE10 . . . . 1B **96**
Vanbrugh Ho. E9 . . . . 4E **51**
(off Loddiges Rd.)
Vanbrugh Pk. SE3 . . . 3B **96**
Vanbrugh Pk. Rd.
SE3 . . . . 3B **96**
Vanbrugh Pk. Rd. W.
SE3 . . . . 3B **96**
Vanbrugh Rd. W4 . . . . 4A **70**
Vanbrugh Ter. SE3 . . . 4B **96**
Vanburgh Ho. E1 . . . . 5F **11**
(off Folgate St.)
Vancouver Ho. E1 . . . . 2D **79**
(off Reardon Path)
Vancouver Rd.
SE23 . . . . 2A **122**
Vanderbilt Rd.
SW18 . . . . 1D **115**
Vanderbilt Vs. W12 . . . 3F **71**
(off Sterne St.)
Vandome Cl. E16 . . . . 5D **69**
Vandon Ct. SW1 . . . . 5A **22**
(off Petty France)
Vandon Pas.
SW1 . . . . 5A **22** (4E **75**)
Vandon St.
SW1 . . . . 5A **22** (4E **75**)
Vandyke Cl. SW15 . . . 5F **99**
Vandyke Cross SE9 . . . 3F **111**
Vandy St.
EC2 . . . . 4D **11** (3A **64**)
Vane Cl. NW3 . . . . . . 2F **45**
Vane St. SW1 . . . . . . 5E **75**
Vange Ho. W10 . . . . . 4E **57**
(off Sutton Way)
Van Gogh Ct. E14 . . . . 4F **81**
Vanguard Bldg.
E14 . . . . 3B **80**
Vanguard Cl. E16 . . . . 4C **68**
Vanguard Ct. SE5 . . . . 4A **92**
Vanguard St. SE8 . . . . 4C **94**

Vanguard Trad. Est.
  E15 . . . . 5E 53
Vanneck Sq. SW15. . . . 3C 98
Vanoc Gdns.
  BR1: Brom 4C 124
Vansittart Rd. E7 . . . . 1B 54
Vansittart St. E14. . . . 3A 94
Vanston Pl. SW6 . . . . 3C 86
Vantage M. E14 . . . . . 2E 81
  (off Preston's Rd.)
Vantage Pl. W8 . . . . . 4C 72
Vantrey Ho. SE11 . . . . 5C 76
  (off Marylee Way)
Vant Rd. SW17 . . . . . 5B 116
Varcoe Rd. SE16 . . . . 1D 93
Vardens Rd. SW11 . . . 2F 101
Varden St. E1 . . . . . . 5D 65
Vardon Cl. W3 . . . . . 5A 56
Vardon Ho. SE10 . . . . 4E 95
Varley Ho. NW6 . . . . . 5C 44
Varley Rd. E16 . . . . . 5D 69
Varna Rd. SW6 . . . . . 3A 86
Varndell St.
  NW1 . . . . . 1F 5 (2E 61)
Varnishers Yd. N1 . . . . 1E 7
  (off York Rd.)
Vartry Rd. N15 . . . . . 1F 35
Vassall Ho. E3 . . . . . 2A 66
  (off Antill Rd.)
Vassall Rd. SW9 . . . . 3C 90
Vat Ho. SW8 . . . . . . 3A 90
  (off Rita Rd.)
Vauban Est. SE16 . . . . 4B 78
Vauban St. SE16 . . . . 4B 78
Vaudeville St. N4 . . . . 4C 34
Vaudeville Theatre . . . 5E 15
  (off Strand)
Vaughan Av. NW4 . . . . 1C 28
  W6 . . . . 5B 70
Vaughan Est. E2 . . . . 1F 11
Vaughan Ho. SE1 . . . . 3D 25
  (off Blackfriars Rd.)
  SW4 . . . . 5E 103
Vaughan Rd. E15 . . . . 3B 54
  SE5 . . . . 5E 91
Vaughan St. SE16 . . . . 3B 80
Vaughan Way E1 . . . . 1C 78
Vaughan Williams Cl.
  SE8 . . . . 3C 94
VAUXHALL 2A 90
Vauxhall Bri. SE1 . . . . 1A 90
  SW1 . . . . 1A 90
Vauxhall Bri. Rd.
  SW1 . . . . 4E 75
VAUXHALL CROSS . . . 1A 90
Vauxhall Distribution Pk.
  SW8 . . . . 2F 89
  (off Post Office Way)
Vauxhall Gro. SW8. . . . 2B 90
Vauxhall St. SE11 . . . . 1B 90
Vauxhall Wlk. SE11 . . . 1B 90
Vawdrey Cl. E1 . . . . . 3E 65
Veda Rd. SE13 . . . . . 2C 108
Velde Way SE22 . . . . 3A 106

Velletri Ho. E2 . . . . . 1F 65
  (off Mace St.)
Venables St. NW8 . . . . 3F 59
Vencourt Pl. W6 . . . . 5C 70
Venetian Rd. SE5 . . . . 5E 91
Venetia Rd. N4 . . . . . 1D 35
Venice Ct. NW8 . . . . . 3F 59
  (off Fisherton St.)
  SE5 . . . . 3E 91
  (off Bowyer St.)
Venner Rd. SE26 . . . . 5E 121
  (not continuous)
Venn Ho. N1 . . . . . . 5B 48
  (off Barnsbury Est.)
Venn St. SW4 . . . . . 2E 103
Ventnor Rd. SE14 . . . . 3F 93
Venture Ct. SE12 . . . . 5C 110
Venture Ho. W10 . . . . 5F 57
  (off Bridge Cl.)
Venue St. E14. . . . . . 4E 67
Venus Ho. E14 . . . . . 5C 80
  (off Westferry Rd.)
Vera Lynn Cl. E7 . . . . 1C 54
Vera Rd. SW6 . . . . . 4A 86
Verbena Cl. E16 . . . . 3B 68
Verbena Gdns. W6 . . . 1C 84
Verdant Ct. SE6 . . . . 5A 110
  (off Verdant La.)
Verdant La. SE6 . . . . 5A 110
Verdi Ho. W10 . . . . . 1A 58
  (off Herries St.)
Verdun Rd. SW13 . . . . 2C 84
Vere Ct. W2 . . . . . . 5D 59
  (off Westbourne Gdns.)
Vereker Rd. W14 . . . . 1A 86
Vere St. W1 . . 3D 13 (5D 61)
Verity Cl. W11 . . . . . 1A 72
Vermeer Ct. E14 . . . . 4F 81
Vermeer Gdns.
  SE15 . . . . 2E 107
Vermont Rd. SW18 . . . 4D 101
Verney Ho. NW8 . . . . 3A 60
  (off Jerome Cres.)
Verney Rd. SE16 . . . . 2C 92
Verney St. NW10 . . . . 5A 28
Verney Way SE16. . . . 1D 93
Vernon Cl. NW2 . . . . 5B 30
Vernon Ho. SE11 . . . . 1B 90
  (off Vauxhall St.)
  WC1 . . . . 1E 15
  (off Vernon Pl.)
Vernon Mans. W14 . . . 2B 86
  (off Queen's Club Mans.)
Vernon M. W14 . . . . . 5A 72
Vernon Pl.
  WC1 . . . . . 1E 15 (4A 62)
Vernon Ri.
  WC1 . . . . . . 1A 8 (2B 62)
Vernon Rd. E3 . . . . . 1B 66
  E11 . . . . 3A 40
  E15 . . . . 4A 54
  SW14 . . . . 1A 98
Vernon Sq.
  WC1 . . . . . 1A 8 (2B 62)

Vernon St. W14 . . . . . 5A 72
Vernon Yd. W11 . . . . . 1B 72
Verona Ct. SE14 . . . . 2F 93
  (off Myers La.)
  W4 . . . . 1A 84
Verona Rd. E7 . . . . . 4C 54
Veronica Ho. SE4 . . . . 1B 108
Veronica Rd. SW17 . . . 2D 117
Verran Rd. SW12 . . . . 5D 103
Verulam Av. E17 . . . . 1B 38
Verulam Bldgs. WC1 . . 5A 8
Verulam Ct. NW9 . . . . 2C 28
Verulam Ho. W6 . . . . 3E 71
  (off Hammersmith Gro.)
Verulam St.
  WC1 . . . . . . 5B 8 (4C 62)
Verwood Ho. SW8 . . . 3B 90
  (off Cobbett St.)
Verwood Lodge E14 . . 4F 81
  (off Manchester Rd.)
Veryan Ct. N8 . . . . . 1F 33
Vesage Ct. EC1 . . . . . 1C 16
  (off Leather La.)
Vesey Path E14 . . . . 5D 67
Vespan Rd. W12 . . . . 3C 70
Vesta Ct. SE1 . . . . . 4D 27
Vesta Rd. SE4 . . . . . 5A 94
Vestris Rd. SE23 . . . . 2F 121
Vestry Ct. SW1 . . . . . 4F 75
  (off Monck St.)
Vestry M. SE5 . . . . . 4A 92
Vestry Rd. SE5 . . . . . 4A 92
Vestry St. N1 . . 1B 10 (2F 63)
Vevey St. SE6 . . . . . 2B 122
Viaduct Bldgs.
  EC1 . . . . . . 1C 16 (4C 62)
Viaduct Pl. E2 . . . . . 2D 65
Viaduct St. E2 . . . . . 2D 65
Vian St. SE13 . . . . . 1D 109
Vibart Gdns. SW2 . . . 5B 104
Vibart Wlk. N1 . . . . . 5A 48
  (off Outram Pl.)
Vicarage Av. SE3 . . . . 3C 96
Vicarage Ct. W8 . . . . 3D 73
Vicarage Cres. SW11 . . 4F 87
Vicarage Gdns. W8 . . . 2C 72
Vicarage Ga. W8 . . . . 2D 73
Vicarage Gro. SE5 . . . 4F 91
Vicarage La. E15 . . . . 4A 54
Vicarage Path N8 . . . . 2A 34
Vicarage Rd. E10 . . . . 2C 38
  E15 . . . . 4B 54
  NW4 . . . . 1C 28
  SW14 . . . . 3A 98
Vicarage Wlk. SW11 . . 4F 87
Vicarage Way NW10 . . 5A 28
Vicars Cl. E9 . . . . . . 5E 51
  E15 . . . . 5C 54
Vicar's Hill SE13 . . . . 2D 109
Vicars Oak Rd.
  SE19 . . . . 5A 120
Vicar's Rd. NW5 . . . . 2C 46
Viceroy Ct. NW8 . . . . 1A 60
  (off Prince Albert Rd.)

Viceroy Rd. SW8 . . . . . . 4A 90
Vickery Ct. EC1 . . . . 3A 10
(off Mitchell St.)
Vickery's Wharf E14 . . . . 5C 66
Victor Cazalet Ho.
N1 . . . . 5D 49
(off Gaskin St.)
Victoria & Albert Mus.
. . . . 4F 73
Victoria Arc. SW1 . . . . . . 5E 21
(off Victoria St.)
Victoria Av. E6 . . . . 5F 55
EC2 . . . . 1E 19 (4A 64)
Victoria Bldgs. E8 . . . . . . 5D 51
(off Mare St.)
Victoria Chambers
EC2 . . . . 3D 11
(off Luke St.)
Victoria Colonnade
WC1 . . . . 1E 15
(off Southampton Row)
Victoria Cotts. E1 . . . . . . 4C 64
(off Deal St.)
Victoria Ct. SE1 . . . . 5A 78
(off Hendre Rd.)
SE26 . . . . 5E 121
Victoria Cres. N15 . . . . . 1A 36
SE19 . . . . 3A 120
Victoria Dock Rd.
E16 . . . . 5B 68
Victoria Dr. SW19 . . . . . . 5F 99
Victoria Emb.
EC4 . . . . 5A 16 (3A 76)
SW1 . . . . 3E 23 (3A 76)
WC2 . . . . 3E 23 (3A 76)
Victoria Gdns. W11 . . . . . 2C 72
Victoria Gro. W8 . . . . 4E 73
Victoria Gro. M.
W2 . . . . 1C 72
Victoria Hall E16 . . . . 2C 82
(off Wesley Av.,
not continuous)
Victoria Ho. SW1 . . . . . . 1D 89
(off Ebury Bri. Rd.)
SW1 . . . . 5F 75
(off Francis St.)
SW8 . . . . 3A 90
(off Sth. Lambeth Rd.)
Victoria Ind. Est.
W3 . . . . 4A 56
Victoria Mans.
NW10 . . . . 4D 43
SW8 . . . . 3A 90
(off Sth. Lambeth Rd.)
W14 . . . . 2B 86
(off Queen's Club Mans.)
Victoria M. E8 . . . . 3C 50
NW6 . . . . 5C 44
SW4 . . . . 2D 103
SW18 . . . . 1E 115
Victoria Mills Studios
E15 . . . . 5F 53
Victorian Gro. N16 . . . . . 1A 50
Victorian Rd. N16 . . . . . . 5A 36

Victoria Palace Theatre
. . . . 5F 21
(off Victoria St.)
Victoria Pk. Ct. E9 . . . . . 4E 51
(off Well St.)
Victoria Pk. Ind. Cen.
E9 . . . . 4C 52
(off Rothbury Rd.)
Victoria Pk. Rd. E9 . . . . . 5E 51
Victoria Pk. Sq. E2 . . . . . 2E 65
(off Fisherton St.)
Victoria Pas. NW8 . . . . . 3F 59
Victoria Pl. Shop. Cen.
SW1 . . . . 5D 75
(off Buckingham Pal. Rd.)
Victoria Point E13 . . . . . 1C 68
(off Victoria Rd.)
Victoria Ri. NW6 . . . . 4E 45
(off Hilgrove Rd.)
SW4 . . . . 1D 103
Victoria Rd. E11 . . . . 1A 54
E13 . . . . 1C 68
N4 . . . . 2B 34
NW6 . . . . 1B 58
NW10 . . . . 4A 56
W3 . . . . 4A 56
W8 . . . . 4E 73
Victoria Sq. SW1 . . . . . . 5E 21
Victoria St. E15 . . . . 4A 54
SW1 . . . . 5E 21 (4E 75)
Victoria Ter. N4 . . . . 3C 34
NW10 . . . . 3B 56
SW8 . . . . 5D 89
Victoria Way SE7 . . . . . . 1D 97
Victoria Wharf E2 . . . . . . 1F 65
(off Palmers Rd.)
E14 . . . . 1A 80
SE8 . . . . 1B 94
Victoria Works NW2 . . . . 4D 29
Victoria Yd. E1 . . . . 5C 64
Victor Rd. NW10 . . . . 2D 57
Victor Wharf SE1 . . . . . . 1B 26
(off Clink St.)
Victory Ct. W9 . . . . 3C 58
(off Hermes Cl.)
Victory Pl. E14 . . . . 1A 80
SE17 . . . . 5F 77
Victory Wlk. SE8 . . . . . . 4C 94
Victory Way SE16 . . . . . . 3A 80
Video Ct. N4 . . . . 2B 34
View Cl. N6 . . . . 2B 32
View Ct. SE12 . . . . 3E 125
View Cres. N8 . . . . 1F 33
Viewfield Rd. SW18 . . . . 4B 100
View Rd. N6 . . . . 2B 32
Vigilant Cl. SE26 . . . . . . 4C 120
Vigo St. W1 . . . . 5F 13 (1E 75)
Viking Cl. E3 . . . . 1A 66
Viking Ct. SW6 . . . . 2C 86
Viking Gdns. E6 . . . . 3F 69
Viking Ho. SE5 . . . . 5E 91
(off Denmark Rd.)
Viking Pl. E10 . . . . 3B 38

Village, The NW3 . . . . . . 4E 31
SE7 . . . . 2E 97
Village Cl. NW3 . . . . 2F 45
(off Belsize La.)
Village Ct. SE3 . . . . 1A 110
(off Hurren Cl.)
Village Mt. NW3 . . . . 1E 45
(off Perrins Ct.)
Village Way NW10 . . . . . 1A 42
SE21 . . . . 4F 105
Villa Rd. SW9 . . . . 1C 104
Villas on the Heath
NW3 . . . . 5E 31
Villa St. SE17 . . . . 1F 91
Villiers Cl. E10 . . . . 4C 38
Villiers M. NW2 . . . . 3C 42
Villiers Rd. NW2 . . . . 3C 42
Villiers St.
WC2 . . . . 5D 15 (2A 76)
Vince Ct. N1 . . . . 2F 63
Vincennes Est.
SE27 . . . . 4F 119
Vincent Cl. SE16 . . . . . . 3A 80
Vincent Ct. N4 . . . . 3A 34
SW9 . . . . 4B 90
W1 . . . . 2A 12
(off Seymour Pl.)
Vincent Gdns. NW2 . . . . 5B 28
Vincent Ho. SW1 . . . . . . 5F 75
(off Regency St.)
SW1 . . . . 5F 75
(off Vincent Sq.)
Vincent M. E3 . . . . 1C 66
Vincent Sq. SW1 . . . . . . 5F 75
Vincent Sq. Mans.
SW1 . . . . 5E 75
(off Walcott St.)
Vincent St. E16 . . . . 4B 68
SW1 . . . . 5F 75
Vincent Ter. N1 . . . . 1D 63
Vince St. EC1 . . 2C 10 (2F 63)
Vine Cotts. E1 . . . . 5E 65
(off Sidney Sq.)
Vine Ct. E1 . . . . 4C 64
Vinegar St. E1 . . . . 2D 79
Vinegar Yd.
SE1 . . . . 3D 27 (3A 78)
Vine Hill EC1 . . . 4B 8 (3C 62)
Vine La. SE1 . . 2E 27 (2A 78)
Vineries, The SE6 . . . . . 1C 122
Vine Rd. E15 . . . . 4B 54
SW13 . . . . 1B 98
Vinery Row W6 . . . . 4D 71
Vine Sq. W14 . . . . 1B 86
(off Star Rd.)
Vine St. EC3 . . . 3F 19 (5B 64)
W1 . . . . 5A 14 (1E 75)
Vine St. Bri.
EC1 . . . . 4C 8 (3C 62)
Vine Yd. SE1 . . . . 3A 26
Vineyard Cl. SE6 . . . . . . 1C 122
Vineyard Hill Rd.
SW19 . . . . 4B 114
Vineyard M. EC1 . . . . . . 3C 8

Vineyard Path SW14 . . . 1A *98*
(off Church Path)
Vineyard Wlk.
EC1 . . . . 3B 8 (3C *62*)
Viney Rd. SE13 . . . . . . 1D *109*
Vining St. SW9. . . . . . . 2C *104*
Vinopolis . . . 1A *26* (2E *77*)
Vinson Ho. *N1*. 1F *63*
(off Cranston Est.)
Vintners Ct.
EC4 . . . . 5A *18* (1E *77*)
Vintner's Pl. EC4. . . . . . 1E *77*
Viola Sq. W12 . . . . 1B *70*
Violet Cl. E16. . . . . 3A *68*
SE8 . . . . 2B *94*
Violet Hill NW8. . . . . . . 1E *59*
Violet Hill Ho. *NW8* . . . 1E *59*
(off Violet Hill,
not continuous)
Violet Rd. E3 . . . . 3D *67*
E17 . . . . 1C *38*
Violet St. E2. . . . . 3D *65*
VIP Trading Est. SE7. . . 5E *83*
Virgil Pl. W1. . . . . 4B *60*
Virgil St.
SE1 . . . . 5A *24* (4B *76*)
Virginia Ct. *SE16* 3F *79*
(off Eleanor Cl.)
WC1 . . . . 3C *6*
(off Burton St.)
Virginia Ho. *E14*. 1E *81*
(off Newby Pl.)
Virginia Rd.
E2. . . . . 2F *11* (2B *64*)
Virginia St. E1 . . . . 1C *78*
Virginia Wlk. SW2 . . . . 4B *104*
Visage *NW3* 4F *45*
(off Winchester Rd.)
Viscount Ct. *W2* 5C *58*
(off Pembridge Vs.)
Viscount St.
EC1. . . . . 4F 9 (3E *63*)
Vista, The SE9 . . . . 4F *111*
Vista Dr. IG4: Ilf 1F *41*
Vitae Apartments W6. . . 4C *70*
Vittoria St. *N1*. 5B *48*
(off High Rd.)
Vivian Av. NW4 . . . . 1D *29*
Vivian Comma Cl.
N4. . . . . 5D *35*
Vivian Mans. *NW4*. 1D *29*
(off Vivian Av.)
Vivian Rd. E3 . . . . 1A *66*
Vivian Sq. SE15 . . . . . . 1D *107*
Vixen M. *E8* 4B *50*
(off Haggerston Rd.)
Vogans Mill SE1. . . . . . 3B *78*
Vogler Ho. *E1* 1E *79*
(off Cable St.)
Vollasky Ho. *E1* 4C *64*
(off Daplyn St.)
Voltaire Rd. SW4 . . . . . 1F *103*
Volt Av. NW10 . . . . 2A *56*
Voluntary Pl. E11. . . . . . 1C *40*

Vorley Rd. N19. . . . . 4E *33*
Voss St. E2. . . . . 2C *64*
Voyager Bus. Est.
SE16. . . . . 4C *78*
(off Spa Rd.)
Vue Cinema
Finchley Rd. 3E *45*
(in O2 Cen.)
Fulham Broadway . . 3C *86*
Islington 1C *62*
Leicester Sq. 4C *14*
(off Cranbourn St.)
Shepherds Bush . . . 3F *71*
Vulcan Rd. SE4 . . . . 5B *94*
Vulcan Sq. E14. . . . . . . 5D *81*
Vulcan Ter. SE4. . . . . . . 5B *94*
Vulcan Way W3. . . . . . . 3B *48*
Vyner Rd. W3. . . . . 1A *70*
Vyner St. E2. . . . . 5D *51*

W

W12 W12 . . . . 3F *71*
Wadding St. SE17 . . . . . 5F *77*
Waddington Rd. E15 . . . 2F *53*
Waddington St. E15. . . . 3F *53*
Wade Ho. *SE1* 3C *78*
(off Parkers Row)
Wadeson St. E2 . . . . . . 1D *65*
Wade's Pl. E14 . . . . 1D *81*
Wadham Gdns.
NW3 . . . . 5A *46*
Wadham Rd. SW15 . . . 2A *100*
Wadhurst Rd. SW8. . . . . 4E *89*
W4 . . . . 4A *70*
Wadley Rd. E11. . . . . . . 2A *40*
Wager St. E3 . . . . 3B *66*
Waghorn Rd. E13. . . . . . 5E *55*
Waghorn St. SE15 . . . . 1C *106*
Wagner St. SE15 . . . . . . 3E *93*
Wainford Cl. SW19. . . . 1F *113*
Wainwright Ho. *E1* 2E *79*
(off Garnet St.)
Waite Davies Rd.
SE12. . . . . 5B *110*
Waite St. SE15. . . . . . . 2B *92*
Waithman St. *EC4* 3D *17*
(off Apothecary St.)
Wakefield Ct. SE26. . . . 5E *121*
Wakefield Gdns.
IG1: Ilf 1F *41*
Wakefield Ho. SE15. . . . 4C *92*
Wakefield M.
WC1. . . . . 2E 7 (2A *62*)
Wakefield Rd.
N15. . . . . 1B *36*
Wakefield St. E6. . . . . . 5F *55*
WC1. . . . . 2E 7 (3A *62*)
Wakeford Cl. SW4 . . . . 3E *103*
Wakeham St. N1 . . . . . . 3F *49*
Wakehurst Rd.
SW11 . . . . 3A *102*
Wakeling St. E14 . . . . . 5A *66*

Wakelin Ho. N1 . . . . 4D *49*
(off Sebbon St.)
SE23 . . . . 5A *108*
(off Brockley Pk.)
Wakelin Ho. E15 . . . . . . 1A *68*
Wakeman Ho.
NW10 . . . . 2F *57*
(off Wakeman Rd.)
Wakeman Rd. NW10 . . . 2E *57*
Wakley St.
EC1 . . . . 1D 9 (2D *63*)
Walberswick St.
SW8 . . . . 3A *90*
Walbrook
EC4. . . . . 4B *18* (1F *77*)
(not continuous)
Walbrook Ct. *N1*. 1A *64*
(off Hemsworth St.)
Walbrook Wharf EC4 . . 5A *18*
(off Bell Wharf La.)
Walburgh St. E1. . . . . . . 5D *65*
Walcorde Av. SE17. . . . . 5E *77*
Walcot Gdns. *SE11* 5C *76*
(off Kennington Rd.)
Walcot Sq. SE11 . . . . . . 5C *76*
Walcott St. SW1. . . . . . . 5E *75*
Waldeck Gro. SE27 . . . . 3D *119*
Waldemar Av. SW6 . . . . 4A *86*
Waldemar Rd.
SW19 . . . . 5C *114*
Walden Ct. SW8. . . . . . . 4F *89*
Walden Ho. SW1 . . . . . . 5C *74*
(off Pimlico Rd.)
SW11 . . . . 4C *88*
(off Dagnall St.)
Waldenshaw Rd.
SE23 . . . . 1E *121*
Walden St. E1 . . . . 5D *65*
(not continuous)
Waldo Cl. SW4. . . . . . . 3E *103*
Waldo Ho. *NW10*. 2D *57*
(off Waldo Rd.)
Waldo Rd. NW10 . . . . . 2C *56*
(not continuous)
Waldram Cres.
SE23 . . . . 1E *121*
Waldram Pk. Rd.
SE23 . . . . 1F *121*
Waldram Pl. SE23 . . . . 1E *121*
Waldron M. SW3 . . . . . . 2F *87*
Waldron Rd. SW18 . . . . 3E *115*
Walerand Rd. SE13 . . . . 5E *95*
Waleran Flats SE1 . . . . 5A *78*
Wales Cl. SE15 . . . . 3D *93*
Wales Farm Rd. W3 . . . 4A *56*
Waley St. E1. . . . . 4A *66*
Walford Ho. E1 . . . . 5C *64*
Walford Rd. N16 . . . . . . 1A *50*
WALHAM GREEN 4C *86*
Walham Grn. Ct.
SW6 . . . . 3D *87*
(off Waterford Rd.)
Walham Gro. SW6. . . . . 3C *86*
Walham Yd. SW6. . . . . . 3C *86*

Walker Ho.
NW1 . . . . 1B **6** (1F **61**)
Walker M. SW2 . . . . . . 3C **104**
Walker's Ct. W1 . . . . . 4B **14**
Walkerscroft Mead
SE21 . . . . 1E **119**
Walkers Lodge E14. . . . 3E **81**
(off Manchester Rd.)
Walkers Pl. SW15 . . . . 2A **100**
Walkinshaw Ct. N1. . . . 4E **49**
(off Rotherfield St.)
Wallace Collection
. . . . 2C **12** (5C **60**)
Wallace Ct. NW1 . . . . . 4A **60**
(off Old Marylebone Rd.)
Wallace Ho. N7 . . . . . . 3B **48**
(off Caledonian Rd.)
Wallace Rd. N1 . . . . . . 3E **49**
Wallace Way N19. . . . . 4F **33**
(off St John's Way)
Wallbutton Rd. SE4 . . . 5A **94**
Wallcote Av. NW2. . . . . 3F **29**
Wall Ct. N4 . . . . 3B **34**
(off Stroud Grn. Rd.)
Waller Rd. SE14 . . . . . . 4F **93**
Waller Way SE10 . . . . . 3D **95**
Wallflower St. W12 . . . . 1B **70**
Wallgrave Rd. SW5 . . . 5D **73**
Wallingford Av. W10. . . 4F **57**
Wallis All. SE1 . . . . 3A **26**
Wallis Cl. SW11 . . . . . . 1F **101**
Wallis Ho. SE14 . . . . . . 4A **94**
Wallis Rd. E9 . . . . 3B **52**
Wallis's Cotts. SW2 . . . 5A **104**
Wallorton Gdns.
SW14 . . . . 2A **98**
Wallside EC2 . . . . 1A **18**
Wall St. N1 . . . . 3F **49**
Wallwood Rd. E11 . . . . 2F **39**
Wallwood St. E14. . . . . 4B **66**
Walmer Ho. W10 . . . . . 5F **57**
(off Bramley Rd.)
Walmer Pl. W1 . . . . 4B **60**
(off Walmer St.)
Walmer Rd. W10 . . . . . 5E **57**
W11 . . . . 1A **72**
Walmer St. W1. . . . . . . 4B **60**
Walm La. NW2 . . . . 3E **43**
Walney Wlk. N1 . . . . . . 3E **49**
Walnut Cl. SE8 . . . . 2B **94**
Walnut Ct. W8 . . . . 4D **73**
(off St Mary's Ga.)
Walnut Gdns. E15. . . . . 2A **54**
Walnut Rd. E10 . . . . . . 4C **38**
Walnut Tree Cl.
SW13 . . . . 4B **84**
Walnut Tree Cotts.
SW19 . . . . 5A **114**
Walnut Tree Ho.
SW10 . . . . 2D **87**
(off Tregunter Rd.)
Walnut Tree Rd.
SE10 . . . . 1A **96**
(not continuous)

Walnut Tree Wlk.
SE11 . . . . 5C **76**
Walpole Ct. W14 . . . . . 4F **71**
(off Blythe Rd.)
Walpole Ho. SE1 . . . . . 4B **24**
(off Westminster Bri. Rd.)
Walpole M. NW8 . . . . . 5F **45**
Walpole Rd. E6 . . . . . . 4E **55**
SW19 . . . . 5F **115**
Walpole St. SW3 . . . . . 1B **88**
Walsham Cl. N16. . . . . . 3C **36**
Walsham Ho. SE14. . . . 5F **93**
SE17 . . . . 1F **91**
(off Blackwood St.)
Walsham Rd. SE14. . . . 5F **93**
Walsingham NW8. . . . . 5F **45**
Walsingham Lodge
SW13 . . . . 4C **84**
Walsingham Mans.
SW6 . . . . 3D **87**
(off Fulham Rd.)
Walsingham Pl.
SW4 . . . . 4C **102**
Walsingham Rd. E5 . . . 5C **36**
Walston Ho. SW1 . . . . . 1F **89**
(off Aylesford St.)
Walter Besant Ho. E1. . 2F **65**
(off Bancroft Rd.)
Walter Grn. Ho. SE15. . 4E **93**
(off Lausanne Rd.)
Walter Ho. SW10 . . . . . 3F **87**
(off Riley St.)
Walter Langley Ct.
SE16 . . . . 3E **79**
(off Brunel Rd.)
Walter Savil Twr. E17. . 1C **38**
(off Colchester Rd.)
Walters Cl. SE17 . . . . . 5F **77**
(off Brandon St.)
Walters Ho. SE17. . . . . 2D **91**
(off Otto St.)
Walter St. E2 . . . . 2F **65**
Walters Way SE23 . . . . 4F **107**
Walter Ter. E1 . . . . 5F **65**
Walterton Rd. W9 . . . . 3B **58**
Waltham Ho. NW8 . . . . 5E **45**
Walton Cl. E5 . . . . 5F **37**
NW2 . . . . 4D **29**
SW8 . . . . 3A **90**
Walton Dr. NW10 . . . . . 3A **42**
Walton Ho. E2. . . . . 3F **11**
(off Montclare St.)
SW1 . . . . 4B **74**
(off Lennox Gdns. M.)
Walton Pl.
SW3. . . . . . . 5A **20** (4B **74**)
Walton Rd. E13 . . . . . . 1E **69**
Walton St. SW3 . . . . . . 5A **74**
Walton Vs. N1 . . . . 4A **50**
(off Downham Rd.)
Walt Whitman Cl.
SE24 . . . . 2D **105**
WALWORTH 1E **91**
Walworth Pl. SE17 . . . . 1E **91**

Walworth Rd. SE17 . . . . 5E **77**
Wanborough Dr.
SW15 . . . . 1D **113**
Wandle Ho.
BR1: Brom 5F **123**
NW8 . . . . 4A **60**
(off Penfold St.)
Wandle Meadow Nature Pk.
. . . . 5E **115**
Wandle Recreation Cen.
. . . . 4D **101**
Wandle Rd. SW17 . . . . 2A **116**
Wandle Way SW18 . . . 1D **115**
Wandon Rd. SW6 . . . . . 3D **87**
(not continuous)
Wandsdown Pl. SW6. . . 3D **87**
WANDSWORTH 3D **101**
Wandsworth Bri.
SW6 . . . . 1D **101**
Wandsworth Bri. Rd.
SW6 . . . . 4D **87**
WANDSWORTH COMMON
. . . . 1B **116**
Wandsworth Comn. W. Side
SW18 . . . . 3E **101**
WANDSWORTH GYRATORY
. . . . 3D **101**
Wandsworth High St.
SW18 . . . . 3C **100**
Wandsworth Mus. . . . 3D **101**
Wandsworth Plain
SW18 . . . . 3D **101**
Wandsworth Rd.
SW8 . . . . 1D **103**
Wangford Ho. SW9 . . . 2D **105**
(off Loughborough Pk.)
Wanless Rd. SE24 . . . . 1E **105**
Wanley Rd. SE5 . . . . . . 2F **105**
Wanlip Rd. E13 . . . . . . 3D **69**
Wansbeck Rd. E9. . . . . 4B **52**
Wansey St. SE17 . . . . . 5E **77**
WANSTEAD 1D **41**
Wanstead Gdns.
IG4: Ilf 1F **41**
Wanstead La. IG1: Ilf . . 1F **41**
Wanstead Leisure Cen.
. . . . 1E **41**
Wanstead Pk. Av.
E12 . . . . 3F **41**
Wanstead Pk. Rd.
IG1: Ilf 1F **41**
Wanstead Pl. E11 . . . . 1C **40**
Wantage Rd. SE12. . . . 3B **110**
WAPPING 2D **79**
Wapping Dock St. E1. . 2D **79**
Wapping High St. E1 . . 2C **78**
Wapping La. E1 . . . . . . 1D **79**
Wapping Wall E1 . . . . . 2E **79**
Warbeck Rd. W12 . . . . 3D **71**
Warburton Cl. N1. . . . . 3A **50**
(off Culford St.)
Warburton Ho. E8 . . . . 5D **51**
(off Warburton St.)
Warburton Rd. E8 . . . . 5D **51**

Warburton St. E8 . . . . . 5D 51
Wardalls Gro. SE14 . . . . 3E 93
Wardalls Ho. SE8 . . . . . 2B 94
(off Staunton St.)
Wardell Ho. SE10 . . . . . 2E 95
(off Welland St.)
Warden Rd. NW5 . . . . . 3C 46
Wardens Gro.
SE1 . . . . 2F 25 (2E 77)
Wardle St. E9 . . . . 2F 51
Wardley St. SW18 . . . . 5D 101
Wardour M. W1 . . . . . . 3A 14
Wardour St.
W1 . . . . 2A 14 (5E 61)
Ward Point SE11 . . . . . 5C 76
Ward Rd. E15 . . . . 5F 53
N19 . . . . 5E 33
Wardrobe Pl. EC4 . . . . . 3E 17
Wardrobe Ter. EC4 . . . . 4E 17
Wards Wharf App.
E16 . . . . 2F 83
Wareham Ct. N1 . . . . . . 4A 50
(off Hertford Rd.)
Wareham Ho. SW8 . . . . 3B 90
Warehouse Way E16 . . 1D 83
Warfield Rd. NW10 . . . . 2F 57
Warfield Yd. NW10 . . . . 2F 57
(off Warfield Rd.)
Wargrave Av. N15 . . . . 1B 36
Wargrave Ho. E2 . . . . . 2F 11
(off Navarre St.)
Warham Rd. N4 . . . . . . 1C 34
Warham St. SE5 . . . . . . 3D 91
Waring St. SE27 . . . . . 4E 119
Warley Cl. E10 . . . . 3B 38
Warley St. E2 . . . . 2F 65
Warlingham Ct.
SE13 . . . . 4E 109
Warlock Rd. W9 . . . . . . 3B 58
Warlters Cl. N7 . . . . . . 1A 48
Warlters Rd. N7 . . . . . . 1A 48
Warltersville Mans.
N19 . . . . 2A 34
Warltersville Rd.
N19 . . . . 2A 34
Warmington Cl. E5 . . . . 5F 37
Warmington Rd.
SE24 . . . . 4E 105
Warmington St. E13 . . . 3C 68
Warmington Twr.
SE14 . . . . 4A 94
Warmsworth NW1 . . . . 5E 47
(off Pratt St.)
Warndon St. SE16 . . . . 5F 79
Warneford St. E9 . . . . . 5D 51
Warner Ct. E15 . . . . . . 2A 54
NW9 . . . . 2B 28
Warner Ho.
BR3: Beck 5D 123
NW8 . . . . 2E 59
SE13 . . . . 5D 95
(off Russett Way)
Warner Pl. E2 . . . . 1C 64

Warner Rd. SE5 . . . . . . 4E 91
Warner St.
EC1 . . . . 4B 8 (3C 62)
Warner Ter. EC1 . . . . . 4D 67
(off Broomfield St.)
Warner Yd. EC1 . . . . . . 4B 8
Warnford Ct. EC2 . . . . 2C 18
Warnford Ho.
SW15 . . . . 4A 98
(off Tunworth Cres.)
Warnham WC1 . . . . 2F 7
(off Sidmouth St.)
Warnham Ho. SW2 . . . 5B 104
(off Up. Tulse Hill)
Warple M. W3 . . . . 3A 70
Warple Way W3 . . . . . . 3A 70
(not continuous)
Warren, The SE7 . . . . . 2E 97
Warren Av. E10 . . . . . . 5E 39
Warren Cl. SE21 . . . . . 5E 105
Warren Ct. W1 . . . . 3A 6
(off Warren St.)
Warrender Rd. N19 . . . . 5E 33
Warren Dr., The E11 . . . 2E 41
Warren Gdns. E15 . . . . 2F 53
Warren Ho. W14 . . . . . 5B 72
(off Beckford Cl.)
Warren M. W1 . . . 4F 5 (3E 61)
Warren Pl. E1 . . . . 5F 65
(off Caroline St.)
Warren Rd. E10 . . . . . . 5E 39
E11 . . . . 1E 41
(not continuous)
NW2 . . . . 4B 28
Warren St. W1 . . . 4F 5 (3E 61)
Warren Wlk. SE7 . . . . . 2E 97
Warriner Gdns.
SW11 . . . . 4B 88
Warrington Cres. W9 . . 3E 59
Warrington Gdns.
W9 . . . . 3E 59
Warspite Ho. E14 . . . . . 5D 81
(off Cahir St.)
Warspite Rd. SE18 . . . . 4F 83
Warton Rd. E15 . . . . . . 4E 53
Warwick W14 . . . . 5B 72
(off Kensington Village)
Warwick Av. W2 . . . . . 3E 59
W9 . . . . 3D 59
Warwick Bldg. SW8 . . . 2D 89
Warwick Chambers
W8 . . . . 4C 72
(off Pater St.)
Warwick Cl. W8 . . . . . . 4B 72
(off Kensington High St.)
Warwick Ct. EC4 . . . . . 3E 17
(off Warwick La.)
WC1 . . . . 1A 16 (4B 62)
Warwick Cres. W2 . . . . 4E 59
Warwick Dr. SW15 . . . . 1D 99
Warwick Est. W2 . . . . . 4D 59
Warwick Gdns. N4 . . . . 1E 35
W14 . . . . 4B 72
Warwick Gro. E5 . . . . . 3D 37

Warwick Ho. E16 . . . . . 2C 82
(off Wesley Av.)
SW9 . . . . 5C 90
Warwick Ho. St.
SW1 . . . . 1C 22 (2F 75)
Warwick La.
EC4 . . . . 2E 17 (5D 63)
Warwick Mans SW5 . . . 5C 72
(off Cromwell Cres.)
Warwick Pas. EC4 . . . . 2E 17
(off Old Bailey)
Warwick Pl. W9 . . . . . . 4E 59
Warwick Pl. Nth.
SW1 . . . . 5E 75
Warwick Rd. E12 . . . . . 2F 55
E15 . . . . 3B 54
SW5 . . . . 5C 72
W14 . . . . 5B 72
Warwick Row
SW1 . . . . 5E 21 (4D 75)
Warwickshire Path
SE8 . . . . 3B 94
Warwickshire Rd.
N16 . . . . 1A 50
Warwick Sq.
EC4 . . . . 2E 17 (5D 63)
SW1 . . . . 1E 89
(not continuous)
Warwick Sq. M. SW1 . . 5E 75
Warwick St.
W1 . . . . 4A 14 (1E 75)
Warwick Ter. E17 . . . . . 1F 39
(off Lea Bri. Rd.)
Warwick Way SW1 . . . . 1D 89
Warwick Yd.
EC1 . . . . 4A 10 (3E 63)
Washington Bldg.
SE10 . . . . 4D 95
(off Deal's Gateway)
Washington Cl. E3 . . . . 2D 67
Washington Ho. SW3 . . 4A 20
(off Basil St.)
Washington Rd. E6 . . . . 4E 55
SW13 . . . . 3C 84
Wastdale Rd. SE23 . . . 1F 121
Waterbank Rd. SE6 . . . 3D 123
Water Brook La.
NW4 . . . . 1E 29
Watercress Pl. N1 . . . . 4A 50
Waterden Ct. W11 . . . . 2A 72
Waterden Cres. E15 . . . 2C 52
Waterden Rd. E15 . . . . 2C 52
Waterer Ho. SE6 . . . . . 4E 123
Waterfall Cotts.
SW19 . . . . 5F 115
Waterfall Rd.
SW19 . . . . 5F 115
Waterfall Ter. SW17 . . . 5A 116
Waterford Ho. W11 . . . 1B 72
(off Kensington Pk. Rd.)
Waterford Rd. SW6 . . . 3D 87
(not continuous)
Waterford Way
NW10 . . . . 2D 43

Waterfront Studios Bus. Cen.
  E16 . . . . 2C *82*
        (off Dock Rd.)
Water Gdns., The
  W2 . . . . 5A *60*
Watergate
  EC4 . . . . . . 4D **17** (1D *77*)
Watergate St.
  SE8 . . . . 2C *94*
Watergate Wlk.
  WC2 . . . . 1E **23** (2A *76*)
Waterhead NW1 . . . . 1F *5*
        (off Varndell St.)
Waterhouse Cl. E16 . . . 4F *69*
  NW3 . . . . 2F *45*
  W6 . . . . 5F *71*
Waterhouse Sq.
  EC1 . . . . . . 1B **16** (4C *62*)
Wateridge Cl. E14 . . . . 4C *80*
Water La. E15 . . . . 3A *54*
  EC3 . . . . . . 5E **19** (1A *78*)
  NW1 . . . . 4D *47*
  SE14 . . . . 3E *93*
Waterloo Bri. SE1 . . . . . 5A *16*
  WC2 . . . . 5F **15** (1B *76*)
Waterloo Cl. E9 . . . . . . 2E *51*
Waterloo Gdns. E2 . . . . 1E *65*
  N1 . . . . 4D *49*
Waterloo Pas. NW6 . . . 4B *44*
Waterloo Pl.
  SW1 . . . . . . 1B **22** (2F *75*)
Waterloo Rd. E6 . . . . . . 4E *55*
  E7 . . . . 2B *54*
  E10 . . . . 2C *38*
  NW2 . . . . 3C *28*
  SE1 . . . . . . 1A **24** (2B *76*)
Waterloo Ter. N1 . . . . . 4D *49*
Waterlow Ct. NW11 . . . 2D *31*
Waterlow Rd. N19 . . . . 3E *33*
Waterman Bldg. E14 . . . 3B *80*
Waterman St. SW15 . . . 1F *99*
Watermans Wlk.
  EC4 . . . . 5B *18*
  SE16 . . . . 3A *80*
Waterman Way E1 . . . . 2D *79*
Watermead Ho. E9 . . . . 2A *52*
Watermeadow La.
  SW6 . . . . 5E *87*
Watermead Rd. SE6 . . . 4E *123*
Water M. SE15 . . . . . . 2E *107*
Watermint Quay N16 . . 2C *36*
Water's Edge SW6 . . . . 4E *85*
      (off Palemead Cl.)
Waterside E17 . . . . 1E *37*
  N1 . . . . 1E *63*
  W2 . . . . 4F *59*
     (off Nth. Wharf Rd.)
Waterside Cl. E3 . . . . . 5B *52*
  SE16 . . . . 3C *78*
Waterside Ho. E14 . . . . 3D *81*
      (off Admirals Way)
Waterside Pl. NW1 . . . 5C *46*
Waterside Point
  SW11 . . . . 3A *88*

Waterside Twr. SW6 . . . 5E *87*
     (off The Boulevard)
Waterside Way
  SW17 . . . . 4E *115*
Waterson St.
  E2 . . . . 1E **11** (2A *64*)
Waters Pl. SW15 . . . . . 5E *85*
Waters Rd. SE6 . . . . . . 3A *124*
Water St. WC2 . . . . 4B *16*
Water Twr. Pl. N1 . . . . . 5C *48*
Waterview Ho. E14 . . . . 4A *66*
        (off Carr St.)
Waterworks La. E5 . . . . 4F *37*
Waterworks Rd.
  SW2 . . . . 4B *104*
Watford Cl. SW11 . . . . 4A *88*
Watford Rd. E16 . . . . . 4C *68*
Watford Way NW4 . . . 1D *29*
Watkins Ho. E14 . . . . . 3E *81*
      (off Manchester Rd.)
Watkinson Rd. N7 . . . . 3B *48*
Watling Ct. EC4 . . . . . . 3A *18*
Watling Gdns. NW2 . . . 3A *44*
Watling St.
  EC4 . . . . . . 3A **18** (5E *63*)
  SE15 . . . . 2A *92*
Watlington Gro.
  SE26 . . . . 5A *122*
Watney Mkt. E1 . . . . . . 5D *65*
Watney St. E1 . . . . 5D *65*
Watson Cl. N16 . . . . . . 2F *49*
Watson's M. W1 . . . . . . 4A *60*
Watsons St. SE8 . . . . . 3C *94*
Watson St. E13 . . . . . . 1D *69*
Wattisfield Rd. E5 . . . . 5E *37*
Wattsdown Cl. E13 . . . 5C *54*
Watts Gro. E3 . . . . 4C *66*
Watts Ho. W10 . . . . . . 4A *58*
     (off Wornington Rd.)
Watts Point E13 . . . . . . 5C *54*
      (off Brooks Rd.)
Watts St. E1 . . . . 2D *79*
  SE15 . . . . 4B *92*
Wat Tyler Rd. SE3 . . . . 5E *95*
  SE10 . . . . 5E *95*
Wavel Ct. E1 . . . . 2E *79*
       (off Garnet St.)
Wavelengths Leisure Pool
  . . . . 3C *94*
Wavel M. NW6 . . . . . . 4D *45*
Wavel Pl. SE26 . . . . . . 4B *120*
Wavendon Av. W4 . . . 1A *84*
Waveney Av. SE15 . . . 2D *107*
Waveney Cl. E1 . . . . . . 2C *78*
Waveney Ho. SE15 . . . 2D *107*
Waverley Ct. NW3 . . . . 3B *46*
  NW6 . . . . 4A *44*
  SE26 . . . . 5E *121*
Waverley Pl. N4 . . . . . . 4D *35*
Waverley Rd. N8 . . . . . 1A *34*
Waverton Ho. E3 . . . . . 5B *52*
Waverton Rd.
  SW18 . . . . 5E *101*

Waverton St.
  W1 . . . . 1D **21** (2C *74*)
Wavertree Ct. SW2 . . . 1A *118*
Wavertree Rd. SW2 . . . 1B *118*
Waxham NW3 . . . . 2B *46*
Waxlow Rd. NW10 . . . . 1A *56*
Wayford St. SW11 . . . . 5A *88*
Wayland Av. E8 . . . . . . 2C *50*
Wayland Ho. SW9 . . . . 5C *90*
      (off Robsart St.)
Waylett Ho. SE11 . . . . . 1B *90*
    (off Loughborough St.)
Waylett Pl. SE27 . . . . . 3D *119*
Wayman Ct. E8 . . . . . . 3D *51*
Wayne Kirkum Way
  NW6 . . . . 2B *44*
Waynflete Ho. SE1 . . . . 2F *25*
       (off Pepper St.)
Waynflete Sq. W10 . . . 1F *71*
Waynflete St. SW18 . . . 2E *115*
Wayside NW11 . . . . . . 3A *30*
Weald Cl. SE16 . . . . . . 1D *93*
Weald Sq. E5 . . . . 4C *36*
Weardale Rd. SE13 . . . 2F *109*
Wearmouth Ho. E3 . . . . 4B *66*
       (off Joseph St.)
Wear Pl. E2 . . . . 2D *65*
      (not continuous)
Wearside Rd. SE13 . . . 2D *109*
Weatherbury W2 . . . . . 5C *58*
      (off Talbot Rd.)
Weatherbury Ho.
  N19 . . . . 5F *33*
      (off Wedmore St.)
Weatherley Cl. E3 . . . . 4B *66*
Weavers Almshouses
  E11 . . . . 1B *40*
      (off Cambridge Rd.)
Weavers Ho. E11 . . . . . 1C *40*
     (off New Wanstead)
Weavers La.
  SE1 . . . . . . 2E **27** (2A *78*)
Weavers Ter. SW6 . . . . 2C *86*
    (off Micklethwaite Rd.)
Weaver St. E1 . . . . 3C *64*
Weavers Way NW1 . . . 5F *47*
Weaver Wlk. SE27 . . . . 4E *119*
Webb Cl. W10 . . . . 3E *57*
Webber Row
  SE1 . . . . 5C **24** (4C *76*)
Webber St.
  SE1 . . . . 3C **24** (3C *76*)
Webb Est. E5 . . . . 2C *36*
Webb Gdns. E13 . . . . . 3C *68*
Webb Ho. SW8 . . . . . . 3F *89*
Webb Pl. NW10 . . . . . . 2B *56*
Webb Rd. SE3 . . . . 2B *96*
Webb's Rd. SW11 . . . . 2B *102*
Webb St.
  SE1 . . . . 5D **27** (4A *78*)
Webheath NW6 . . . . . . 4B *44*
      (not continuous)
Webster Rd. E11 . . . . . 5E *39*
  SE16 . . . . 4C *78*

Weddell Ho. E1. . . . . 3F **65**
(off Duckett St.)
Wedderburn Ho.
SW1 . . . . 1C **88**
(off Lwr. Sloane St.)
Wedderburn Rd.
NW3 . . . . 2F **45**
Wedgewood Ho.
SW1 . . . . 1D **89**
(off Churchill Gdns.)
Wedgewood M.
W1 . . . . 3C **14** (5F **61**)
Wedgwood Ho. E2 . . . . 2F **65**
(off Warley St.)
SE11 . . . . 4C **76**
(off Lambeth Wlk.)
Wedgwood Wlk.
NW6 . . . . 2D **45**
(off Dresden Cl.)
Wedlake St. W10 . . . . . 3A **58**
Wedmore Gdns. N19 . . 4F **33**
Wedmore M. N19 . . . . . 5F **33**
Wedmore St. N19 . . . . . 5F **33**
Weech Rd. NW6 . . . . . . 1C **44**
Weedington Rd.
NW5 . . . . 2C **46**
Weedon Ho. W12 . . . . . 5C **56**
Weekley Sq. SW11 . . . 1F **101**
Weigall Rd. SE12 . . . . 3C **110**
Weighhouse St.
W1 . . . . 3C **12** (5C **60**)
Weimar St. SW15 . . . . 1A **100**
Weir Rd. SW12 . . . . . . 5E **103**
SW19 . . . . 3D **115**
Weir's Pas.
NW1 . . . . 1C **6** (2F **61**)
Weiss Rd. SW15 . . . . . 1F **99**
Welbeck Av.
BR1: Brom 4C **124**
Welbeck Ct. W14 . . . . . 5B **72**
(off Addison Bri. Pl.)
Welbeck Ho. W1 . . . . . 2D **13**
(off Welbeck St.)
Welbeck Rd. E6 . . . . . . 2F **69**
Welbeck St.
W1 . . . . 1C **12** (4C **60**)
Welbeck Way
W1 . . . . 2D **13** (5D **61**)
Welbury Ct. E8 . . . . . . 4A **50**
(off Kingsland Rd.)
Welby Ho. N19 . . . . . . 2F **33**
Welby St. SE5 . . . . 4D **91**
Welcome Ct. E17 . . . . . 2C **38**
(off Boundary Rd.)
Welfare Rd. E15 . . . . . 4A **54**
Welford Cl. E5 . . . . 5F **37**
Welford Ct. NW1 . . . . . 4D **47**
(off Castlehaven Rd.)
SW8 . . . . 5E **89**
W9 . . . . 4C **58**
(off Elmfield Way)
Welford Pl. SW19 . . . . 4A **114**
Welham Rd. SW16 . . . 5D **117**
SW17 . . . . 5C **116**

Welland Ct. SE6 . . . . . 2B **122**
(off Oakham Cl.)
Welland Ho. SE15 . . . . 2E **107**
Welland M. E1 . . . . 2C **78**
Welland St. SE10 . . . . . 2E **95**
Wellby Ct. E13 . . . . 5E **55**
Well Cl. SW16 . . . . 4B **118**
Wellclose Sq. E1 . . . . . 1C **78**
Wellclose St. E1 . . . . . 1C **78**
E3 . . . . 1A **66**
(off Driffield Rd)
Wellcome Cen. for
Medical Science 3B **6**
Wellcome Mus., The
. . . . 2A **16**
(in The Royal College of
Surgeons)
Well Cott. Cl. E11. . . . . 1E **41**
Well Ct. EC4 . . . 3A **18** (5E **63**)
(not continuous)
Weller Ct. W11 . . . . . . 2B **72**
(off Ladbroke Rd.)
Weller Ho. SE16 . . . . . 3C **78**
(off George Row)
Weller St.
SE1 . . . . 3F **25** (3E **77**)
Welles Ct. E14 . . . . 1C **80**
(off Premiere Pl.)
Wellesley Av. W6 . . . . . 4D **71**
Wellesley Cl. SE7 . . . . . 1E **97**
Wellesley Ct. NW2 . . . . 4C **28**
W9 . . . . 2E **59**
Wellesley Ho. NW1 . . . . 2C **6**
(off Wellesley Pl.)
SW1 . . . . 1D **89**
(off Ebury Bri. Rd.)
Wellesley Mans.
W14 . . . . 1B **86**
(off Edith Vs.)
Wellesley Pl.
NW1 . . . . . . 2B **6** (2F **61**)
NW5 . . . . 2C **46**
Wellesley Rd. E11 . . . . 1C **40**
E17 . . . . 1C **38**
NW5 . . . . 2C **46**
Wellesley St. E1 . . . . . 4F **65**
Wellesley Ter.
N1 . . . . 1A **10** (2E **63**)
Wellfield Rd.
SW16 . . . . 4A **118**
Wellfield Wlk.
SW16 . . . . 5B **118**
(not continuous)
Wellfit St. SE24 . . . . . 1D **105**
Wellgarth Rd.
NW11 . . . . 3D **31**
Welling Sq. N1 . . . . . . 5A **48**
Wellington Arch
. . . . 3C **20** (3C **74**)
Wellington Av. N15 . . . 1B **36**
Wellington Bldgs.
SW1 . . . . 1C **88**
Wellington Cl. SE14 . . . 4F **93**
W11 . . . . 5C **58**

Wellington Ct. NW8 . . . 1F **59**
(off Wellington Rd.)
SW1 . . . . 3B **74**
(off Knightsbridge)
SW6 . . . . 4D **87**
(off Maltings Pl.)
Wellington Gdns.
SE7 . . . . 2E **97**
Wellington Gro. SE10. . . 3F **95**
Wellington Ho. E16 . . . 2C **82**
(off Pepys Cres.)
NW3 . . . . 3B **46**
(off Eton Rd.)
SE17 . . . . 2E **91**
(off Merrow St.)
Wellington Mans.
E10 . . . . 3C **38**
W14 . . . . 2B **86**
(off Queen's Club Mans.)
Wellington M. N7 . . . . . 3B **48**
(off Roman Way)
SE7 . . . . 2E **97**
SE22 . . . . 2C **106**
SW16 . . . . 3F **117**
Wellington Monument
. . . . 3C **20**
Wellington Mus.
. . . . 3C **20** (3C **74**)
Wellington Pk. Est.
NW2 . . . . 4C **28**
Wellington Pas. E11 . . . 1C **40**
(off Wellington Rd.)
Wellington Pl. NW8 . . . 2F **59**
Wellington Rd. E7 . . . . 1B **54**
E10 . . . . 3A **38**
E11 . . . . 1C **40**
NW8 . . . . 1F **59**
NW10 . . . . 2F **57**
SW19 . . . . 2C **114**
Wellington Row E2 . . . . 2B **64**
Wellington Sq. SW3 . . . 1B **88**
Wellington St.
WC2 . . . . 4F **15** (1B **76**)
Wellington Ter. E1 . . . . 2D **79**
W2 . . . . 1C **72**
Wellington Way E3 . . . . 2C **66**
Wellmeadow Rd.
SE13 . . . . 4A **110**
(not continuous)
Well Pl. NW3 . . . . 5F **31**
Well Rd. NW3 . . . . 5F **31**
Wells Ct. NW6 . . . . 1C **58**
(off Cambridge Av.)
Wells Gdns. IG1: Ilf . . . 2F **41**
Wells Ho.
BR1: Brom 5D **125**
(off Pike Cl.)
EC1 . . . . 1C **8**
(off Spa Grn. Est.)
SE16 . . . . 4E **79**
(off Howland Est.)
W10 . . . . 3A **58**
(off Wornington Rd.)
Wells Ho. Rd. NW10 . . . 4A **56**

Wells M. W1 . . . 1A **14** (4E **61**)
Wells Pk. Rd. SE26 . . . 3C **120**
Wells Pl. SW18 . . . . . . 5E **101**
Wells Ri. NW8 . . . . 5B **46**
Wells Rd. W12 . . . . 3E **71**
Wells Sq. WC1. . . 2F **7** (2B **62**)
Wells Ter. N4 . . . . 4C **34**
Well St. E9 . . . . 4E **51**
E15 . . . . 3A **54**
Wells Way SE5 . . . . 2F **91**
SW7 . . . . 4F **73**
Wells Yd. N7 . . . . 2C **48**
Welmar M. SW4 . . . . . 3F **103**
 (off Northbourne Rd.)
Welsford St. SE1 . . . . . 5C **78**
 (not continuous)
Welsh Cl. E13. . . . . 2C **68**
Welsh Harp Nature Reserve
 . . . . 3A **28**
Welsh Ho. E1. . . . . 2D **79**
 (off Wapping La.)
Welshpool Ho. E8. . . . . 5C **50**
 (off Welshpool St.)
Welshpool St. E8 . . . . . 5C **50**
 (not continuous)
Welshside NW9 . . . . . . 1A **28**
 (off Ruthin Cl.)
Welshside Wlk. NW9 . . 1A **28**
Welstead Ho. E1 . . . . . 5D **65**
 (off Cannon St. Rd.)
Welstead Way W4 . . . . 5B **70**
Weltje Rd. W6 . . . . 5C **70**
Welton Cl. SE5 . . . . 4A **92**
Welton Ho. E1. . . . . . . 4F **65**
 (off Stepney Way)
Welwyn St. E2 . . . . 2E **65**
Wembury M. N6. . . . . . 2E **33**
Wembury Rd. N6 . . . . . 2D **33**
Wemyss Rd. SE3 . . . . . 5B **96**
Wendell Rd. W12. . . . . 4B **70**
Wendle Ct. SW8 . . . . . . 2A **90**
Wendling NW5 . . . . . . 2B **46**
Wendon St. E3 . . . . 5B **52**
Wendover SE17 . . . . . . 1A **92**
 (not continuous)
Wendover Ct. NW2 . . . 5C **30**
W1 . . . . 1B **12**
 (off Chiltern St.)
Wendover Ho. W1 . . . . 1B **12**
 (off Chiltern St.)
Wendover Rd. NW10 . . 1B **56**
SE9 . . . . 1F **111**
Wenham Ho. SW8 . . . . 3E **89**
Wenlake Ho. EC1 . . . . . 3F **9**
 (off Old St.)
Wenlock Barn Est.
 N1 . . . . 1F **63**
 (off Wenlock St.)
Wenlock Ct.
 N1 . . . . 1C **10** (1F **63**)
Wenlock Rd.
 N1 . . . . 1A **10** (1E **63**)

Wenlock St.
 N1 . . . . 1A **10** (1E **63**)
Wennington Rd. E3. . . . 1F **65**
Wensdale Ho. E5 . . . . . 4C **36**
Wentland Cl. SE6 . . . . . 2F **123**
Wentland Rd. SE6 . . . . 2F **123**
Wentworth Ct.
 SW18 . . . . 4D **101**
 (off Garratt La.)
 W6 . . . . 2A **86**
 (off Paynes Wlk.)
Wentworth Cres.
 SE15 . . . . 3C **92**
Wentworth Dwellings
 E1 . . . . 2F **19**
 (off Wentworth St.)
Wentworth M. E3 . . . . 3A **66**
 W3 . . . . 5A **56**
Wentworth Rd. E12. . . 1F **55**
 NW11 . . . . 1B **30**
Wentworth St.
 E1. . . . . 2F **19** (5B **64**)
Werrington St.
 NW1. . . . . . . 1B **6** (1E **61**)
Werter Rd. SW15. . . . . 2A **100**
Wesleyan Pl. NW5. . . . 1D **47**
Wesley Av. E16 . . . . . . 2C **82**
 NW10 . . . . 2A **56**
Wesley Cl. N7 . . . . 4B **34**
 SE17. . . . . 5D **77**
Wesley Ct. SE16 . . . . . 4D **79**
Wesley Rd. E10 . . . . . . 2E **39**
Wesley's House, Chapel &
 Mus. of Methodism
 . . . . 3C **10** (3F **63**)
Wesley Sq. W11. . . . . . 5A **58**
Wesley St.
 W1. . . . . 1C **12** (4C **60**)
Wessex Gdns.
 NW11 . . . . 3A **30**
Wessex Ho. SE1. . . . . . 1B **92**
Wessex St. E2 . . . . 2E **65**
Wessex Way NW11 . . . 3A **30**
Wesson Mead SE5 . . . . 3E **91**
 (off Camberwell Rd.)
Westacott Cl. N19. . . . 3F **33**
W. Arbour St. E1. . . . . 5F **65**
West Av. NW4. . . . . . . 1F **29**
West Bank N16. . . . . . . 2A **36**
WEST BECKTON 5F **69**
Westbere Rd. NW2 . . . 1A **44**
West Block SE1 . . . . . . 4A **24**
 (off Addington St.)
Westbourne Bri. W2 . . 4E **59**
Westbourne Ct. W2 . . . 4E **59**
Westbourne Cres.
 W2. . . . . 1F **73**
Westbourne Cres. M.
 W2. . . . . 1F **73**
 (off Westbourne Cres.)
Westbourne Dr.
 SE23 . . . . 2F **121**
Westbourne Gdns.
 W2 . . . . 5D **59**

WESTBOURNE GREEN
 . . . . 5B **58**
Westbourne Gro. W2. . 5C **58**
 W11 . . . . 1B **72**
Westbourne Gro. M.
 W11 . . . . 5C **58**
Westbourne Gro. Ter.
 W2 . . . . 5D **59**
Westbourne Ho.
 SW1 . . . . 1D **89**
 (off Ebury Bri. Rd.)
Westbourne Pk. Pas.
 W2 . . . . 4C **58**
 (not continuous)
Westbourne Pk. Rd.
 W2 . . . . 4C **58**
 W11 . . . . 5A **58**
Westbourne Pk. Vs.
 W2 . . . . 4C **58**
Westbourne Rd. N7 . . . 3B **48**
 SE26 . . . . 5F **121**
Westbourne St. W2 . . . 1F **73**
Westbourne Ter.
 SE23 . . . . 2F **121**
 (off Westbourne Dr.)
 W2 . . . . 5E **59**
Westbourne Ter. M.
 W2 . . . . 5E **59**
Westbourne Ter. Rd.
 W2 . . . . 4D **59**
Westbourne Ter. Rd. Bri.
 W2 . . . . 4E **59**
 (off Westbourne Ter. Rd.)
Westbridge Cl. W12. . . 3C **70**
Westbridge Rd.
 SW11 . . . . 4F **87**
WEST BROMPTON 2E **87**
Westbrook Ho. E2 . . . . 2E **65**
 (off Victoria Pk. Sq.)
Westbrook Rd. SE3 . . . 4D **97**
Westbury Ho. W11. . . . 4C **58**
 (off Aldridge Rd. Vs.)
Westbury Rd. E7 . . . . . 3D **55**
Westbury St. SW8 . . . . 5E **89**
 (off Portslade Rd.)
Westbury Ter. E7 . . . . . 3D **55**
W. Carriage Dr. W2 . . . 1A **74**
 (not continuous)
W. Central St.
 WC1. . . . . . . 2D **15** (5A **62**)
West Cen. Av. NW10 . . 3D **57**
Westcliffe Apartments
 W2. . . . . 4F **59**
Westcombe Ct. SE3 . . . 3B **96**
Westcombe Hill SE3 . . 3C **96**
 SE10. . . . . 3C **96**
Westcombe Pk. Rd.
 SE3 . . . . 2A **96**
Westcote Rd. SW16. . . 5E **117**
West Cotts. NW6 . . . . . 2C **44**
Westcott Cl. N15 . . . . . 1B **36**
Westcott Ho. E14. . . . . 1C **80**
Westcott Rd. SE17. . . . 2D **91**
Westcroft NW2. . . . . . . 1A **44**

Westcroft Est. NW2 . . . . . 1A 44
Westcroft Sq. W6 . . . . . . 5C 70
Westcroft Way NW2 . . . . . 1A 44
W. Cromwell Rd.
  SW5 . . . . 1B 86
  W14 . . . . 1B 86
W. Cross Route W10 . . . . 1F 71
  W11 . . . . 1F 71
  W12 . . . . 1F 71
Westdean Av. SE12 . . 1D 125
Westdean Cl. SW18 . . . 4D 101
Westdown Rd. E15 . . . . 1E 53
  SE6 . . . . 5C 108
West Dr. SW16 . . . . . . 4E 117
WEST DULWICH 2F 119
W. Eaton Pl. SW1 . . . . . 5C 74
W. Eaton Pl. M. SW1 . . . 5C 74
    (off W. Eaton Pl.)
W. Ella Rd. NW10 . . . . . 4A 42
West End Av. E10 . . . . . 1F 39
West End Cl. NW6 . . . . . 4D 45
West End La. NW6 . . . . . 2C 44
    (not continuous)
West End Quay W2 . . . . 4F 59
    (off Harbet Rd.)
Westerdale Rd. SE10 . . 1C 96
Westerham Rd. E10 . . . . 5E 47
    (off Bayham St.)
Westerham Ho. SE1 . . . 5C 26
Westerham Rd. E10 . . . 2D 39
Westerley Cres.
  SE26 . . . . 5B 122
Western Av. NW11 . . . 1F 29
  W5 . . . . 5A 56
Western Beach Apartments
  E16 . . . . 1C 82
Western Ct. NW6 . . . . . 1B 58
Western Gateway
  E16 . . . . 1C 82
Western La. SW12 . . . 5C 102
Western M. W9 . . . . . . 3B 58
Western Pl. SE16 . . . . . 3E 79
Western Rd. E13 . . . . . . 1E 69
  E17 . . . . 1E 39
  SW9 . . . . 1C 104
Western Ter. W6 . . . . . 1C 84
    (off Chiswick Mall)
Westferry Cir. E14 . . . . 2B 80
Westferry Rd. E14 . . . . 1B 80
Westfield Cl. SW10 . . . 3E 87
Westfield Ct. NW10 . . . 2F 57
    (off Chamberlayne Rd.)
Westfield Ho. SE16 . . . 5F 79
    (off Rotherhithe New Rd.)
  SW10 . . . . 3F 87
    (off Cremorne Est.)
  SW18 . . . . 1D 115
Westfields SW13 . . . . . 1B 98
Westfields Av. SW13 . . 1A 98
Westfield St. SE18 . . . . 4F 83
Westfield Way E1 . . . . . 2A 66
West Gdn. Pl. W2 . . . . . 5A 60
West Gdns. E1 . . . . 1D 79
  SW17 . . . . 5A 116

Westgate Cen., The
  E8 . . . . 5D 51
    (off Bocking St.)
Westgate Ct. SE12 . . . 1C 124
    (off Burnt Ash Hill)
  SW9 . . . . 1C 104
    (off Canterbury Cres.)
Westgate M. W10 . . . . 3A 58
    (off West Row)
Westgate St. E8 . . . . . . 5D 51
Westgate Ter. SW10 . . 2D 87
West Gro. SE10 . . . . . . 4E 95
Westgrove La. SE10 . . 4E 95
W. Halkin St.
  SW1 . . . . . 5B 20 (4C 74)
West Hallowes SE9 . . . 1F 125
WEST HAM 5B 54
W. Ham La. E15 . . . . . . 4F 53
    (not continuous)
WEST HAMPSTEAD . . . 3D 45
W. Hampstead M.
  NW6 . . . . 3D 45
West Ham United FC . . 1E 69
W. Harding St.
  EC4 . . . . . 2C 16 (5C 62)
W. Heath Av. NW11 . . . 3C 30
W. Heath Cl. NW3 . . . . 3C 30
W. Heath Ct. NW11 . . . 3C 30
W. Heath Dr. NW11 . . . 3C 30
W. Heath Gdns.
  NW3 . . . . 4C 30
W. Heath Rd. NW3 . . . . 4C 30
WEST HENDON 2C 28
WEST HILL 4B 100
West Hill SW15 . . . . . . 5F 99
  SW18 . . . . 5F 99
W. Hill Ct. N6 . . . . 5C 32
Westhill Ct. W11 . . . . . 1B 72
    (off Denbigh Rd.)
W. Hill Pk. N6 . . . . 4B 32
    (not continuous)
W. Hill Rd. SW18 . . . . 4B 100
Westhope Ho. E2 . . . . . 3C 64
    (off Derbyshire St.)
Westhorne Av. SE9 . . . 5C 110
  SE12 . . . . 5C 110
Westhorpe Rd. SW15 . . 1E 99
West Ho. Cl. SW19 . . 1A 114
W. India Av. E14 . . . . . 2C 80
W. India Dock Rd.
  E14 . . . . 1B 80
    (not continuous)
W. India Ho. E14 . . . . . 1C 80
    (off W. India Dock Rd.)
WEST KENSINGTON . . 5B 72
W. Kensington Ct.
  W14 . . . . 5B 72
    (off Edith Vs.)
W. Kensington Mans.
  W14 . . . . 1B 86
    (off Beaumont Cres.)
WEST KILBURN 2B 58
Westlake SE16 . . . . 5E 79
    (off Rotherhithe New Rd.)

Westland Pl.
  N1 . . . . 1B 10 (2F 63)
Westlands Ter.
  SW12 . . . . 4E 103
Westleigh Av. SW15 . . 3D 99
Westleigh Ct. E11 . . . . 1C 40
West Lodge E16 . . . . . . 2C 82
    (off Britannia Ga.)
W. London Crematorium &
  Chapel NW10 . . . . . . 3D 57
Westmacott Ho. NW8 . . 3F 59
    (off Hatton St.)
West Mall W8 . . . . 2C 72
    (off Palace Gdns. Ter.)
Westmark Point
  SW15 . . . . 1D 113
    (off Norley Vale)
Westmead SW15 . . . . . 4D 99
W. Mersea Cl. E16 . . . . 2D 83
West M. SW1 . . . . 5D 75
    (off W. Warwick Pl.)
Westmill Ct. N4 . . . . . . 4E 35
WESTMINSTER
  . . . . 4D 23 (3A 76)
Westminster Abbey
  . . . . 5D 23 (4F 75)
Westminster Abbey
  Chapter House 5D 23
    (in Westminster Abbey)
Westminster Abbey Mus.
  . . . . 5D 23
    (in Westminster Abbey)
Westminster Abbey
  Pyx Chamber 5D 23
    (in Westminster Abbey)
Westminster Bri.
  SE1 . . . . 3B 76
  SW1 . . . . 4E 23 (3A 76)
Westminster Bri. Rd.
  SE1 . . . . 4F 23 (3B 76)
Westminster Bus. Sq.
  SE11 . . . . 2B 90
Westminster Children's
  Sports Cen., The . . . 3F 59
Westminster Ct. E11 . . 1C 40
    (off Cambridge Pk.)
  NW8 . . . . 3F 59
    (off Lyons Pl.)
  SE16 . . . . 2F 79
    (off King & Queen Wharf)
Westminster Gdns.
  SW1 . . . . 5A 76
    (off Marsham St.)
Westminster Hall 4D 23
Westminster Ind. Est.
  SE18 . . . . 4F 83
Westminster Mans.
  SW1 . . . . 5C 22
    (off Gt. Smith St.)
Westminster Pal. Gdns.
  SW1 . . . . 5B 22
Westminster RC Cathedral
  . . . . 4E 75

Westmoor St. SE7 . . . . . 4E 83
Westmore St. SW15. . . 3A 100
Westmoreland Ho.
E16 . . . . 2C 82
(off Gatcombe Rd.)
Westmoreland Pl.
SW1 . . . . 1D 89
Westmoreland Rd.
SE17 . . . . 2F 91
(not continuous)
SW13 . . . . 4B 84
Westmoreland St.
W1 . . . . 1C 12 (4C 60)
Westmoreland Ter.
SW1 . . . . 1D 89
Westmoreland Wlk.
SE17 . . . . 2F 91
(not continuous)
Westmorland Cl. E12 . . . 4F 41
Westmorland Rd. E17. . . 1C 38
WEST NORWOOD 4E 119
W. Norwood Crematorium
SE27 . . . . 3E 119
Westonbirt St. SE15. . . 2B 92
(off Ebley Cl.)
Weston Ct. N4. . . . . . . 5E 35
W. One Ho. W1. . . . . . . 1F 13
(off Wells St.)
W. One Shop. Cen.
W1 . . . . 3C 12
Weston Ho. E9 . . . . 5E 51
(off King Edward's Rd.)
NW6 . . . . 4A 44
Weston London Heliport
. . . . 5F 87
Weston Pk. N8 . . . . 1A 34
Weston Ri.
WC1. . . . . . . 1A 8 (2B 62)
Weston St.
SE1 . . . . . . 4C 26 (3A 78)
(not continuous)
Weston Wlk. E8 . . . . . . 4D 51
Westover Hill NW3. . . . 4C 30
Westover Rd. SW18 . . . 5E 101
Westow Hill SE19. . . . 5A 120
West Pk. SE9 . . . . 2F 125
W. Parkside SE10. . . . . 3A 82
West Pl. SW19 . . . . . . 5E 113
West Point E14. . . . . . 1B 80
(off Grenade St.)
SE1 . . . . 1C 92
Westport Rd. E13. . . . . 3D 69
Westport St. E1. . . . . . 5F 65
W. Poultry Av.
EC1. . . . . . . 1D 17 (4D 63)
West Quarters W12 . . . 5C 56
West Quay SW10 . . . . . 4E 87
West Reservoir Cen. . . . 3E 35
West Ri. W2. . . . . 1A 74
(off St George's Flds.)
West Rd. E15 . . . . 5B 54
SE1 . . . . . . 3A 24 (3B 76)
SW3 . . . . 1B 88
SW4 . . . . 3F 103

West Row W10. . . . . . . 3A 58
Westrow SW15. . . . . . . 4E 99
W. Side Comn.
SW19 . . . . 5E 113
Westside Ct. W9 . . . . . . 3C 58
(off Elgin Av.)
West Smithfield
EC1. . . . . . . 1D 17 (4D 63)
West Sq.
SE11 . . . . . . 5D 25 (4D 77)
West St. E2 . . . . 1D 65
E11 . . . . 5A 40
E17. . . . . 1D 39
WC2 . . . . . . 3C 14 (5F 61)
W. Tenter St.
E1. . . . . 3F 19 (5B 64)
Westvale M. W3. . . . . . 3A 70
West Vw. Cl. NW10. . . . 2B 42
Westview Cl. W10 . . . . . 5E 57
Westville Rd. W12. . . . . 3C 70
W. Warwick Pl. SW1 . . . 5E 75
West Way NW10 . . . . . . 5A 28
Westway W2. . . . . 4B 58
W9 . . . . 4B 58
W10 . . . . 4B 58
W12 . . . . 1B 70
Westway Lodge W9 . . . . 4C 58
(off Amberley Rd.)
Westway Sports Cen.
. . . . 5F 57
Westwell M. SW16 . . . 5A 118
Westwell Rd. SW16. . . 5A 118
Westwell Rd. App.
SW16 . . . . 5A 118
Westwick Gdns. W14 . . . 3F 71
Westwood Bus. Cen.
NW10 . . . . 3A 56
Westwood Gdns.
SW13 . . . . 1B 98
Westwood Hill
SE26 . . . . 5C 120
Westwood Ho. W12. . . . 2E 71
(off Wood La.)
Westwood Pk.
SE23 . . . . 5D 107
Westwood Pl. SE26 . . . 4C 120
Westwood Rd. E16. . . . 2D 83
SW13 . . . . 1B 98
Wetherby Gdns. SW5. . . 5E 73
Wetherby Mans.
SW5 . . . . 1D 87
(off Earls Ct. Sq.)
Wetherby M. SW5 . . . . . 1D 87
Wetherby Pl. SW7 . . . . . 5E 73
Wetherden St. E17. . . . 2B 38
Wetherell Rd. E9 . . . . . 5F 51
Wevco Wharf SE15 . . . . 2D 93
Wevell Ho. N6 . . . . 2C 32
(off Hillcrest)
Wexford Ho. E1 . . . . . . 4E 65
(off Sidney St.)
Wexford Rd. SW12. . . . 5B 102
Weybourne St.
SW18 . . . . 2E 115

Weybridge Ct. SE16. . . . 1D 93
(off Argyle Way)
Weybridge Point
SW11 . . . . 5B 88
Weydown Cl. SW19 . . . 1A 114
Weyhill Rd. E1. . . . . . . 5C 64
Wey Ho. NW8. . . . . 3F 59
(off Salisbury St.)
Weyman Rd. SE3 . . . . . 4E 97
Weymouth Ct. E2. . . . . . 1B 64
(off Weymouth Ter.)
Weymouth Ho. SW8. . . . 3B 90
(off Bolney St.)
Weymouth M.
W1 . . . . 5D 5 (4D 61)
Weymouth St.
W1 . . . . 1C 12 (4C 60)
Weymouth Ter.
E2. . . . . 1F 11 (1B 64)
Weymouth Vs. N4 . . . . . 4B 34
(off Moray Rd.)
Whadcoat St. N4 . . . . . 4C 34
Whalebone Ct. EC2 . . . . 2B 18
Whalebone La. E15. . . . 4A 54
Whales Yd. E15. . . . . . . 4A 54
(off W. Ham La.)
Wharf, The
EC3 . . . . 1E 27 (2B 78)
Wharfdale Rd. N1 . . . . . 1A 62
Wharfdale Ct. E5 . . . . . 1F 51
Wharfedale Ho.
NW6 . . . . 5D 45
(off Kilburn Va.)
Wharfedale St.
SW10 . . . . 1D 87
Wharfedale Yard N1 . . . 1A 62
(off Wharfedale Rd.)
Wharf Pl. E2 . . . . 5D 51
Wharf Rd. N1. . . . 1F 9 (1E 63)
(Baldwin Ter.)
N1 . . . . 5F 47
(Camley St.)
Wharfside Rd. E16. . . . . 4A 68
Wharf St. E16. . . . . 4A 68
Wharf Vw. Ct. E14 . . . . . 5E 67
(off Athol Sq.)
Wharton Cl. NW10. . . . . 3A 42
Wharton Cotts.
WC1. . . . . . . 2B 8 (2C 62)
Wharton Ho. SE1 . . . . . 5F 27
(off Maltby St.)
Wharton St.
WC1. . . . . . . 2A 8 (2B 62)
Whatcott's Yd. N16 . . . 1A 50
Whateley Rd. SE22 . . . 3B 106
Whatman Ho. E14 . . . . 5B 66
(off Wallwood St.)
Whatman Rd. SE23 . . . 5F 107
Wheatfield Ho. W9 . . . . 2C 58
(off Kilburn Pk. Rd.)
Wheatland Ho.
SE22 . . . . 1A 106
Wheatlands Rd.
SW17 . . . . 3C 116

Wheatley Ho. SW15.... 5C 98
(off Ellisfield Dr)
Wheatley St.
W1........ 1C 12 (4C 60)
Wheat Sheaf Cl. E14.... 5D 81
Wheatsheaf La. SW6 ... 3E 85
SW8 .... 3A 90
(not continuous)
Wheatsheaf Ter.
SW6 .... 3B 86
Wheatstone Ho. W10... 4A 58
(off Telford Rd.)
Wheatstone Rd. W10... 4A 58
Wheeler Gdns. N1..... 5A 48
(off Outram Pl.)
Wheel Ho. E14........ 1D 95
(off Burrells Wharf Sq.)
Wheelwright St. N7..... 4B 48
Wheler Ho. E1 .... 4F 11
(off Quaker St.)
Wheler St.
E1......... 4F 11 (3B 64)
Whellock Rd. W4...... 4A 70
Whetstone Pk.
WC2........ 2F 15 (5B 62)
Whetstone Rd. SE3 ... 5E 97
Whewell Rd. N19...... 4A 34
Whidborne Bldgs.
WC1 .... 2E 7
(off Whidborne St.)
Whidborne Cl. SE8..... 5C 94
Whidborne St.
WC1........ 2E 7 (2A 62)
(not continuous)
Whinfell Cl. SW16 .... 5F 117
Whinyates Rd. SE9..... 1F 111
Whipps Cross E17..... 1F 39
Whipps Cross Rd.
E11 .... 1F 39
(not continuous)
Whiskin St.
EC1........ 2D 9 (2D 63)
Whistler M. SE15...... 3B 92
Whistlers Av. SW11 .... 3F 87
Whistler St. N5....... 2D 49
Whistler Twr. SW10 .... 3E 87
(off Worlds End Est.)
Whistler Wlk. SW10.... 3F 87
Whiston Ho. N1........ 4D 49
(off Richmond Gro.)
Whiston Rd. E2 .... 1B 64
Whitacre M. SE11 ..... 1C 90
Whitbread Rd. SE4.... 2A 108
Whitburn Rd. SE13 ... 2D 109
Whitby Ct. N7........ 1A 48
Whitby Ho. NW8....... 5E 45
(off Boundary Rd.)
Whitby St. E1... 3F 11 (3B 64)
(not continuous)
Whitcher Cl. SE14 .... 2A 94
Whitcher Pl. NW1...... 3E 47
Whitchurch Ho. W10 ... 5F 57
(off Kingsdown Cl.)
Whitchurch Rd. W11 ... 1F 71

Whitcomb Ct. WC2..... 5C 14
Whitcomb St.
WC2........ 5C 14 (1F 75)
Whiteadder Way E14... 5D 81
Whitear Wlk. E15...... 3F 53
Whitebeam Cl. SW9 ... 3B 90
White Bear Pl. NW3.... 1F 45
White Bear Yd. EC1.... 4B 8
(off Clerkenwell Rd.)
WHITECHAPEL 4C 64
Whitechapel Art Gallery
.... 5B 64
(off Whitechapel High St.)
Whitechapel High St.
E1....... 2F 19 (5B 64)
Whitechapel Rd. E1.... 5C 64
Whitechapel Sports Cen.
.... 4D 65
White Church La. E1 ... 5C 64
White Church Pas.
E1................ 5C 64
(off White Church La.)
WHITE CITY 1D 71
WHITE CITY 5E 57
White City Cl. W12..... 1E 71
White City Est. W12.... 1D 71
White City Rd. W12.... 1E 71
White Conduit St. N1... 1C 62
Whitecross Pl.
EC2........ 5C 10 (4F 63)
Whitecross St.
EC1........ 3A 10 (3E 63)
Whitefield Av. NW2 ... 3E 29
Whitefield Cl.
SW15 .... 4A 100
Whitefoot La.
BR1: Brom 4E 123
(not continuous)
Whitefoot Ter.
BR1: Brom 3B 124
Whitefriars St.
EC4........ 3C 16 (5C 62)
Whitehall
SW1........ 2D 23 (2A 76)
Whitehall Ct.
SW1........ 2D 23 (2A 76)
(not continuous)
Whitehall Gdns.
SW1 .... 2D 23
Whitehall Pk. N19 ..... 3E 33
Whitehall Pl. E7....... 2C 54
SW1........ 2D 23 (2A 76)
White Hart Ct. EC2.... 1D 19
White Hart La.
NW10 .... 3B 42
SW13 .... 1A 98
White Hart St.
EC4........ 2E 17 (5D 63)
SE11 .... 1C 90
White Hart Yd.
SE1........ 2B 26 (2F 77)
Whitehaven St. NW8 ... 3A 60
Whitehead Cl.
SW18 .... 5E 101

Whiteheads Gro.
SW3 .... 5A 74
White Heather Ho.
WC1 .... 2E 7
(off Cromer St.)
White Horse All. EC1... 5D 9
White Horse La. E1 .... 3F 65
Whitehorse M.
SE1........ 5C 24 (4C 76)
White Horse Rd. E1.... 4A 66
(not continuous)
White Horse St.
W1........ 2E 21 (2D 75)
White Horse Yd.
EC2........ 2B 18 (5F 63)
White Ho. SW4....... 5F 103
(off Clapham Pk. Est.)
SW11 .... 4F 87
White Ho., The NW1 ... 3E 5
Whitehouse Est. E10 ... 1E 39
White Kennett St.
E1........ 2E 19 (5A 64)
Whitelands Ho. SW3 ... 1B 88
(off Cheltenham Ter.)
Whitelegg Rd. E13..... 1B 68
Whiteley Rd. SE19 .... 5F 119
White Lion Ct. EC3 .... 3D 19
SE15 .... 2E 93
White Lion Hill
EC4 .... 4E 17 (1D 77)
White Lion St. N1..... 1C 62
White Lodge Cl. N2 ... 1F 31
White Lyon Ct. EC2.... 5F 9
White Post La. E9 ..... 4B 52
White Post St. SE15... 3E 93
White Rd. E15........ 4A 54
White's Grounds
SE1........ 4E 27 (3A 78)
White's Grounds Est.
SE1 .... 3E 27
White's Row
E1........ 1F 19 (4B 64)
Whites Sq. SW4...... 2F 103
Whitestone La. NW3 ... 5E 31
Whitestone Wlk.
NW3 .... 5E 31
Whiteswan M. W4 ..... 1A 84
Whitethorn Ho. E1..... 2E 79
(off Prusom St.)
Whitethorn Pas. E3 ... 3C 66
(off Whitethorn St.)
Whitethorn St. E3..... 4C 66
White Tower 5F 19
(in The Tower of London)
Whitfield Ho. NW8 .... 3A 60
(off Salisbury St.)
Whitfield Pl. W1...... 4F 5
Whitfield Rd. E6...... 4E 55
SE3 .... 4F 95
Whitfield St.
W1 .... 4F 5 (3E 61)
Whitgift Ho. SE11 .... 5B 76
SW11 .... 4A 88

Whitgift St. SE11 . . . . 5B 76
Whitley Ho. N1 . . . . 2E 89
   (off Churchill Gdns.)
Whitlock Dr. SW19 . . . . 5A 100
Whitman Ho. E2 . . . . 2E 65
   (off Cornwall Av.)
Whitman Rd. E3 . . . . 3A 66
Whitmore Est. N1 . . . . 5A 50
Whitmore Gdns.
  NW10 . . . . 1E 57
Whitmore Ho. N1 . . . . 5A 50
   (off Whitmore Est.)
Whitmore Rd. N1 . . . . 5A 50
Whitnell Way SW15 . . . . . 3E 99
Whitney Rd. E10 . . . . 2D 39
Whitstable Ho. W10 . . . . . 5F 57
   (off Silchester Rd.)
Whittaker Rd. E6 . . . . 4E 55
Whittaker St. SW1 . . . . . . 5C 74
Whittaker Way SE1 . . . . . 5C 78
Whitta Rd. E12 . . . . 1F 55
Whittell Gdns. SE26 . . . . 3E 121
Whittingham Ct. W4 . . . . 3A 84
Whittingstall Rd.
  SW6 . . . . 4B 86
Whittington Av.
  EC3 . . . . 3D 19 (5A 64)
Whittington Ct. N2 . . . . . 1B 32
Whittle Cl. E17 . . . . 1A 38
Whittlesey St.
  SE1 . . . . 2B 24 (2C 76)
Whitton NW3 . . . . 4B 46
Whitton Wlk. E3 . . . . 2C 66
Whitwell Rd. E13 . . . . 2C 68
Whitworth Ho.
  SE1 . . . . 5A 26 (4E 77)
Whitworth St. SE10 . . . . . 1A 96
Whorlton Rd. SE15 . . . . 1D 107
Whychcote Point
  NW2 . . . . 3E 29
   (off Whitefield Av.)
Whyteville Rd. E7 . . . . . . 3D 55
Whytlaw Ho. E3 . . . . 4B 66
   (off Baythorne St.)
Wickersley Rd.
  SW11 . . . . 5C 88
Wickers Oake SE19 . . . . 4B 120
Wicker St. E1 . . . . 5D 65
Wickfield Ho. SE16 . . . . . 3D 79
   (off Wilson Gro.)
Wickford Ho. E1 . . . . 3E 65
   (off Wickford St.)
Wickford St. E1 . . . . 3E 65
Wickham Cl. E1 . . . . 4E 65
Wickham Gdns. SE4 . . . . 1B 108
Wickham Ho. N1 . . . . 5A 50
   (off New Era Est.)
Wickham M. SE4 . . . . 5B 94
Wickham Rd. SE4 . . . . . . 2B 108
Wickham St. SE11 . . . . . . 1B 90
Wick La. E3 . . . . 5C 52
Wicklow Ho. N16 . . . . . . 3B 36
Wicklow St.
  WC1 . . . . 1F 7 (2B 62)

Wick M. E9 . . . . 3A 52
Wick Rd. E9 . . . . 3F 51
Wicks Cl. SE9 . . . . 4F 125
Wick Sq. E9 . . . . 3B 52
Wicksteed Ho. SE1 . . . . . 4E 77
Wickway Ct. SE15 . . . . . . 2B 92
   (off Cator St.)
Wickwood St. SE5 . . . . . 5D 91
Widdenham Rd. N7 . . . . . 1B 48
Widdin St. E15 . . . . 4A 54
Widegate St.
  E1 . . . . 1E 19 (4A 64)
Widford NW1 . . . . 3D 47
   (off Lewis St.)
Widford Ho. N1 . . . . 1D 63
   (off Colebrooke Rd.)
Widgeon Cl. E16 . . . . 5D 69
Widley Rd. W9 . . . . 2C 58
Wigan Ho. E5 . . . . 3D 37
Wightman Rd. N4 . . . . . . 1C 34
  N8 . . . . 1C 34
Wigmore Hall 2D 13
Wigmore Pl.
  W1 . . . . 2D 13 (5D 61)
Wigmore St.
  W1 . . . . 2C 12 (5C 60)
Wigram Ho. E14 . . . . 1D 81
   (off Wade's Pl.)
Wigram Rd. E11 . . . . 1E 41
Wigston Rd. E13 . . . . 3D 69
Wigton Pl. SE11 . . . . 1C 90
Wilberforce M. SW4 . . . . 2F 103
Wilberforce Rd. N4 . . . . . 4D 35
   (not continuous)
  NW9 . . . . 1C 28
Wilberforce Way
  SW19 . . . . 5F 113
Wilbraham Ho. SW8 . . . . 3A 90
   (off Wandsworth Rd.)
Wilbraham Mans.
  SW1 . . . . 5C 74
   (off Wilbraham Pl.)
Wilbraham Pl. SW1 . . . . 5B 74
Wilby M. W11 . . . . 2B 72
Wilcox Cl. SW8 . . . . 3A 90
   (not continuous)
Wilcox Ho. E3 . . . . 4B 66
   (off Ackroyd Dr.)
Wilcox Pl.
  SW1 . . . . 5A 22 (4E 75)
Wilcox Rd. SW8 . . . . 3A 90
Wild Ct. WC2 . . 3F 15 (5B 62)
   (not continuous)
Wildcroft Mnr. SW15 . . . 5E 99
Wildcroft Rd. SW15 . . . . 5E 99
Wilde Cl. E8 . . . . 5C 50
Wilde Ho. W2 . . . . 5D 59
   (off Gloucester Ter.)
  W2 . . . . 1F 73
   (off Gloucester Ter.)
Wilde Pl. SW18 . . . . 5F 101
Wilderness M. SW4 . . . . 2D 103
Wilderton Rd. N16 . . . . . 2A 36
Wildfell Rd. SE6 . . . . 5D 109

Wild Goose Dr. SE14 . . . . 4E 93
Wild Hatch NW11 . . . . . . 1C 30
Wild's Rents
  SE1 . . . . 5D 27 (4A 78)
Wild St. WC2 . . 3E 15 (5A 62)
Wildwood Cl. SE12 . . . . 5B 110
Wildwood Gro. NW3 . . . . 3E 31
Wildwood Ri. NW11 . . . . 3E 31
Wildwood Rd. NW11 . . . 1D 31
Wilfred Ct. N15 . . . . 1F 35
   (off South Gro.)
Wilfred Owen Cl.
  SW19 . . . . 5E 115
Wilfred St.
  SW1 . . . . 5F 21 (4E 75)
Wilkes St. E1 . . 5F 11 (4B 64)
Wilkie Ho. SW1 . . . . 1F 89
   (off Cureton St.)
Wilkins Ho. SW1 . . . . 2D 89
   (off Churchill Gdns.)
Wilkinson Ct. SW17 . . . . 4F 115
Wilkinson Ho. N1 . . . . 1F 63
   (off Cranston Est.)
Wilkinson Rd. E16 . . . . . . 5E 69
Wilkinson St. SW8 . . . . . 3B 90
Wilkin St. NW5 . . . . 3C 46
Wilkin St. M. NW5 . . . . . 3D 47
Wilks Pl. N1 . . . . 1A 64
Willan Wall E16 . . . . 1B 82
Willard St. SW8 . . . . 1D 103
Will Crooks Gdns.
  SE9 . . . . 2E 111
WILLESDEN 3C 42
Willesden Belle Vue Cinema
  . . . . 3D 43
   (within Library)
WILLESDEN GREEN . . . 3E 43
Willesden La. NW2 . . . . . 3E 43
  NW6 . . . . 3F 43
Willesden Section Ho.
  NW6 . . . . 3F 43
   (off Willesden La.)
Willesden Sports Cen.
  . . . . 5D 43
Willesden Sports Stadium
  . . . . 5D 43
Willes Rd. NW5 . . . . 3D 47
Willett Ho. E13 . . . . 1D 69
   (off Queens Rd. W.)
William IV St.
  WC2 . . . . 5D 15 (1A 76)
William Banfield Ho.
  SW6 . . . . 5B 86
   (off Munster Rd.)
William Blake Ho.
  SW11 . . . . 4A 88
William Bonney Est.
  SW4 . . . . 2F 103
William Caslon Ho.
  E2 . . . . 1D 65
   (off Patriot Sq.)
William Channing Ho.
  E2 . . . . 2D 65
   (off Canrobert St.)

William Cl. SE13 . . . . . . 1E 109
William Cobbett Ho.
  W8 . . . . 4D 73
  (off Scarsdale Pl.)
William Dromey Ct.
  NW6 . . . . 4B 44
William Dunbar Ho.
  NW6 . . . . 1B 58
  (off Albert Rd.)
William Dyce M.
  SW16 . . . . 4F 117
William Ellis Way
  SE16 . . . . 4C 78
  (off St James's Rd.)
William Evans Ho.
  SE8 . . . . 5F 79
  (off Bush Rd.)
William Farm La.
  SW15 . . . . 1D 99
William Fenn Ho. E2 . . 2C 64
  (off Shipton Rd.)
William Gdns.
  SW15 . . . . 3D 99
William Gibbs Ct.
  SW1 . . . . 5B 22
  (off Old Pye St.)
William Gunn Ho.
  NW3 . . . . 2A 46
William Guy Gdns.
  E3 . . . . 2D 67
William Harvey Ho.
  SW19 . . . . 1A 114
  (off Whitlock Dr.)
William Henry Wlk.
  SW8 . . . . 2F 89
William Hunt Mans.
  SW13 . . . . 2E 85
William Margrie Cl.
  SE15 . . . . 5C 92
William M.
  SW1 . . . . 4A 20 (3B 74)
William Morley Cl.
  E6 . . . . 5F 55
William Morris Ho.
  W6 . . . . 2F 85
William Morris Way
  SW6 . . . . 1E 101
William Paton Ho.
  E16 . . . . 5D 69
William Pl. E3 . . . . 1B 66
William Rathbone Ho.
  E2 . . . . 2D 65
  (off Florida St.)
William Rd.
  NW1 . . . . 2F 5 (2E 61)
William Rushbrooke Ho.
  SE16 . . . . 5C 78
  (off Rouel Rd.)
William Saville Ho.
  NW6 . . . . 1B 58
  (off Denmark Rd.)
William's Bldgs. E2 . . 3E 65
Williams Cl. N8 . . . . . . 1F 33
  SW6 . . . . 3A 86

Williams Ho. E9 . . . . . . 5D 51
  (off King Edward's Rd.)
  NW2 . . . . 5E 29
  (off Stoll Cl.)
  SW1 . . . . 5F 75
  (off Regency St.)
Williamson Cl. SE10 . . 1B 96
Williamson Ct. SE17 . . 1E 91
Williamson Rd. N4 . . . 1D 35
Williamson St. N7 . . . . 1A 48
William Sq. SE16 . . . . 1A 80
  (off Sovereign Cres.)
William St. E10 . . . . . . 1D 39
  SW1 . . . . 4A 20 (3B 74)
William White Ct.
  E13 . . . . 5E 55
  (off Green St.)
William Wood Ho.
  SE26 . . . . 3E 121
  (off Shrublands Cl.)
Willifield Way NW11 . . 1C 30
Willingham Cl. NW5 . . 2E 47
Willingham Ter. NW5 . . 2E 47
Willington Ct. E5 . . . . 5A 38
Willington Rd. SW9 . . 1A 104
Willis Ho. E14 . . . . 1D 81
  (off Hale St.)
Willis Rd. E15 . . . . 1B 68
Willis St. E14 . . . . 5D 67
Willoughby Highwalk
  EC2 . . . . 1B 18
  (off Moor La.)
Willoughby Ho. E1 . . . 2D 79
  (off Reardon Path)
  EC2 . . . . 5B 10
Willoughby M.
  SW4 . . . . 2D 103
  (off Wix's La.)
Willoughby Pas. E14 . . 2C 80
  (off W. India Av.)
Willoughby Rd. NW3 . . 1F 45
Willoughbys, The
  SW14 . . . . 1A 98
Willoughby Way SE7 . . 5D 83
Willow Av. SW13 . . . . 5B 84
Willow Bank SW6 . . . 1A 100
Willow Bri. Rd. N1 . . . 3E 49
  (not continuous)
Willowbrook Est.
  SE15 . . . . 3C 92
Willow Brook Rd.
  SE15 . . . . 3B 92
Willow Bus. Pk.
  SE26 . . . . 3E 121
Willow Cl. SE6 . . . . . . 1B 124
Willow Ct. E11 . . . . . . 4A 40
  (off Trinity Cl.)
  EC2 . . . . 3D 11
  NW6 . . . . 4A 44
  W4 . . . . 3A 84
  (off Corney Reach Way)
  W9 . . . . 4C 58
  (off Admiral Wlk.)

Willowdene N6 . . . . . . 2B 32
  SE15 . . . . 3D 93
Willow Gro. E13 . . . . . 1C 68
Willow Ho. W10 . . . . . 3F 57
  (off Maple Wlk.)
Willow Lodge SW6 . . . 4F 85
Willow Pl. SW1 . . . . . . 5E 75
Willow Rd. NW3 . . . . . 1F 45
Willows Ter. NW10 . . . 1B 56
  (off Rucklidge Av.)
Willow St.
  EC2 . . . . 3D 11 (3A 64)
Willow Tree Cl. E3 . . . 5B 52
  SW18 . . . . 1D 115
Willow Va. W12 . . . . . . 2C 70
Willow Wlk. SE1 . . . . . 4A 78
Willow Way SE26 . . . . 3E 121
  W11 . . . . 1F 71
Willsbridge Cl.
  SE15 . . . . 2A 92
Wilman Gro. E8 . . . . . 4C 50
Wilmcote Ho. W2 . . . . 4D 59
  (off Woodchester Sq.)
Wilment Ct. NW2 . . . . 5E 29
Wilmer Gdns. N1 . . . . 5A 50
  (not continuous)
Wilmer Lea Cl. E15 . . . 4E 53
Wilmer Pl. N16 . . . . . . 4B 36
Wilmers Ct. NW10 . . . 5A 42
  (off Lawrence Av.)
Wilmington Sq.
  WC1 . . . . 2B 8 (2C 62)
  (not continuous)
Wilmington St.
  WC1 . . . . 2B 8 (2C 62)
Wilmot Cl. SE15 . . . . . 3C 92
Wilmot Pl. NW1 . . . . . 4E 47
  (off St Pancras Way)
  NW1 . . . . 4E 47
  (Rochester Rd.)
Wilmot Rd. E10 . . . . . . 4D 39
  N17 . . . . 3D 65
Wilna Rd. SW18 . . . . . 5E 101
Wilsham St. W11 . . . . 2F 71
Wilshaw Ho. SE8 . . . . 3C 94
Wilshaw St. SE14 . . . . 4C 94
Wilson Gro. SE16 . . . . 3D 79
Wilson Rd. E6 . . . . 2F 69
  SE5 . . . . 4A 92
Wilson's Pl. E14 . . . . . 5B 66
Wilson's Rd. W6 . . . . . 1F 85
Wilson St.
  EC2 . . . . 5C 10 (4F 63)
Wilson Wlk. W6 . . . . . 5B 70
  (off Prebend Gdns.)
Wiltern Ct. NW2 . . . . . 3A 44
Wilton Av. W4 . . . . 1A 84
Wilton Ct. E1 . . . . 5D 65
  (off Cavell St.)
Wilton Cres.
  SW1 . . . . 4B 20 (3C 74)
Wilton St. E8 . . . . 3C 50
Wilton M. E8 . . . . 3D 51
  SW1 . . . . 5C 20 (4C 74)

Wilton Pl.
SW1 . . . . 4B **20** (3C **74**)
Wilton Rd. SW1 . . . . 4D **75**
Wilton Row
SW1 . . . . 4B **20** (3C **74**)
Wilton Sq. N1 . . . . 5F **49**
Wilton St.
SW1 . . . . . . 5D **21** (4D **75**)
Wilton Ter.
SW1 . . . . 5B **20** (4C **74**)
Wilton Vs. N1 . . . . 5F **49**
(off Wilton Sq.)
Wilton Way E8 . . . . 3C **50**
Wiltshire Cl. SW3 . . . . 5B **74**
Wiltshire Ct. N4 . . . . 3B **34**
(off Marquis Rd.)
Wiltshire Gdns. N4 . . . . . 1E **35**
Wiltshire Rd. SW9 . . . . 1C **104**
Wiltshire Row N1 . . . . . . 5F **49**
Wimbart Rd. SW2 . . . . . 5B **104**
WIMBLEDON 5F **113**
Wimbledon
All England Lawn Tennis &
Croquet Club 4A **114**
Wimbledon Common
. . . . 4B **112**
Wimbledon Greyhound &
Stadium 4E **115**
Wimbledon Hill Rd.
SW19 . . . . 5A **114**
Wimbledon Lawn Tennis Mus.
. . . . 3A **114**
Wimbledon Mus. of
Local History 5A **114**
WIMBLEDON PARK . 3C **114**
Wimbledon Pk. Ct.
SW19 . . . . 1B **114**
Wimbledon Pk. Rd.
SW18 . . . . 2A **114**
SW19 . . . . 2A **114**
Wimbledon Pk. Side
SW19 . . . . 3F **113**
Wimbledon Rd.
SW17 . . . . 4E **115**
Wimbledon Stadium Bus. Cen.
SW17 . . . . 3D **115**
Wimbledon Windmill Mus.
. . . . 2D **113**
Wimbolt St. E2 . . . . 2C **64**
Wimborne Cl. SE12 . . 3B **110**
Wimborne Ct.
SW12 . . . . 3E **117**
Wimborne Ho. E16 . . . . 1B **82**
(off Victoria Dock Rd.)
NW1 . . . . 3A **60**
(off Harewood Av.)
SW8 . . . . 3B **90**
(off Dorset Rd.)
SW12 . . . . 3E **117**
Wimbourne Ct. N1 . . . . 1F **63**
(off Wimbourne St.)
Wimbourne St. N1 . . . . 1F **63**
Wimpole M.
W1 . . . . 5D **5** (4D **61**)

Wimpole St.
W1 . . . . 1D **13** (4D **61**)
Winans Wlk. SW9 . . . . . 5C **90**
Winant Ho. E14 . . . . . . 1D **81**
(off Simpson's Rd.)
Wincanton Rd.
SW18 . . . . 5B **100**
Winchcomb Gdns.
SE9 . . . . 1F **111**
Winchelsea Cl. SW15 . . 3F **99**
Winchelsea Ho. SE16 . . 3E **79**
(off Swan Rd.)
Winchelsea Rd. E7 . . . . 5C **40**
NW10 . . . . 5A **42**
Winchendon Rd.
SW6 . . . . 4B **86**
Winchester Av. NW6 . . 5A **44**
Winchester Cl. SE17 . . 5D **77**
Winchester Ct. W8 . . . . 3C **72**
(off Vicarage Ga.)
Winchester Ho. SE18 . . 3F **97**
(off Portway Gdns.)
SW3 . . . . 2F **87**
(off Beaufort St.)
SW9 . . . . 3C **90**
W2 . . . . 5E **59**
(off Hallfield Est.)
Winchester Pl. E8 . . . . 2B **50**
N6 . . . . 3D **33**
Winchester Rd. N6 . . . . 2D **33**
NW3 . . . . 4F **45**
Winchester Sq. SE1 . . . 1B **26**
Winchester St. SW1 . . . 1D **89**
Winchester Wlk.
SE1 . . . . . . 1B **26** (2F **77**)
Winchester Wharf
SE1 . . . . 1B **26**
(off Clink St.)
Winchfield Ho. SW15 . . 4B **98**
Winchfield Rd.
SE26 . . . . 5A **122**
Winch Ho. E14 . . . . 4D **81**
(off Tiller Rd.)
SW10 . . . . 3E **87**
(off King's Rd.)
Winchilsea Ho. NW8 . . 2F **59**
(off St John's Wood Rd.)
Winckworth St. N1 . . . . 2C **10**
(off Brunswick Pl.)
Wincott St. SE11 . . . . . 5C **76**
Windermere NW1 . . . . . 2E **5**
(off Albany St.)
Windermere Av. NW6 . . 5A **44**
Windermere Ct.
SW13 . . . . 2B **84**
Windermere Ho. E3 . . . 3B **66**
Windermere Point
SE15 . . . . 3E **93**
(off Old Kent Rd.)
Windermere Rd. N19 . . 4E **33**
SW15 . . . . 4A **112**
Winders Rd. SW11 . . . . 5A **88**
(not continuous)
Windfield Cl. SE26 . . . . 4F **121**

Winding, The W2 . . . . . 4F **59**
(off Nth. Wharf Rd.)
Windlass Pl. SE8 . . . . . 5A **80**
Windlesham Gro.
SW19 . . . . 1F **113**
Windley Cl. SE23 . . . . . 2E **121**
Windmill WC1 . . . . 5F **7**
(off New Nth. St.)
Windmill Cl. SE1 . . . . . 5C **78**
(off Beatrice Rd.)
SE13 . . . . 5E **95**
Windmill Ct. NW2 . . . . . 3A **44**
Windmill Dr. NW2 . . . . . 5A **30**
SW4 . . . . 3D **103**
Windmill Hill NW3 . . . . 5E **31**
Windmill Ho. E14 . . . . . 5C **80**
Windmill La. E15 . . . . . 3F **53**
Windmill M. W4 . . . . . . 5A **70**
Windmill Pas. W4 . . . . . 5A **70**
Windmill Rd. SW18 . . 4F **101**
SW19 . . . . 2D **113**
W4 . . . . 5A **70**
Windmill Row SE11 . . . 1C **90**
Windmill St.
W1 . . . . 1B **14** (4F **61**)
(not continuous)
Windmill Wlk.
SE1 . . . . . . 2C **24** (2C **76**)
Windrose Cl. SE16 . . . . 3F **79**
Windrush Cl. SW11 . . . 2F **101**
Windrush Ho. NW8 . . . 3F **59**
(off Venables St.)
Windrush La. SE23 . . . 3F **121**
Windsock Cl. SE16 . . . . 5B **80**
Windsor Cen., The
N1 . . . . 5D **49**
(off Windsor St.)
Windsor Cl. SE27 . . . . . 4E **119**
Windsor Cotts. SE14 . . 3B **94**
(off Amersham Va.)
Windsor Ct. NW2 . . . . . 3A **44**
(off Chatsworth Rd.)
NW3 . . . . 1C **44**
NW11 . . . . 1A **30**
(off Golders Grn. Rd.)
SE16 . . . . 1F **79**
(off King & Queen Wharf)
SW3 . . . . 1A **88**
(off Jubilee Pl.)
SW11 . . . . 5F **87**
W2 . . . . 1D **73**
(off Moscow Rd.)
W10 . . . . 5F **57**
(off Bramley Rd.)
Windsor Gdns. W9 . . . . 4C **58**
Windsor Gro. SE27 . . . 4E **119**
Windsor Hall E16 . . . . 2D **83**
(off Wesley Av.)
Windsor Ho. E2 . . . . . . 2F **65**
(off Knottisford St.)
N1 . . . . 1E **63**
NW1 . . . . 1E **5**
Windsor M. SE6 . . . . . 1E **123**
SE23 . . . . 1A **122**

Windsor M. *SW18* 5E **101**
(off Wilna Rd.)
Windsor Pl. SW1 . . . . . . 4E **75**
Windsor Rd. E7 . . . . 2D **55**
 E10 . . . . 4D **39**
 E11 . . . . 3C **40**
 N7 . . . . 5A **34**
 NW2 . . . . 3D **43**
Windsor St. N1. . . . . 5D **49**
Windsor Ter.
 N1 . . . . 1A **10** (2E **63**)
Windsor Wlk. SE5. . . . . . 5F **91**
Windsor Way W14 . . . . . 5F **71**
Windsor Wharf E9 . . . . . 3C **52**
Windspoint Dr. SE15 . . . 2D **93**
Windus Rd. N16. . . . . . . 3B **36**
Windus Wlk. N16. . . . . . 3B **36**
Windy Ridge Cl.
 SW19 . . . . 5F **113**
Wine Cl. E1. . . . . 1E **79**
(not continuous)
Wine Office Ct.
 EC4 . . . . 2C **16** (5C **62**)
Winford St. SE15 . . . . . . 4D **93**
Winford Ho. E3. . . . . 4B **52**
Winforton St. SE10 . . . . 4E **95**
Winfrith Rd. SW18 . . . . . 5E **101**
Wingate Rd. W6 . . . . 4D **71**
Wingfield Ct. E14 . . . . . . 1F **81**
(off John Smith M.)
Wingfield Ho. E2 . . . . . . 2F **11**
(off Virginia Rd.)
 NW6 . . . . 1D **59**
(off Tollgate Gdns.)
Wingfield M. SE15 . . . . . 1C **106**
Wingfield Rd. E15 . . . . . 1A **54**
 E17 . . . . 1D **39**
Wingfield St. SE15 . . . . . 1C **106**
Wingford Rd. SW2 . . . . . 4A **104**
Wingmore Rd.
 SE24 . . . . 1E **105**
Wingrad Ho. E1 . . . . 4E **65**
(off Jubilee St.)
Wingrave SE17 . . . . 5F **77**
(not continuous)
Wingrave Rd. W6. . . . . . 2E **85**
Wingreen *NW8*. 5D **45**
(off Abbey Rd.)
Wingrove Rd. SE6 . . . . . 2A **124**
Winicotte Ho. *W2* 4F **59**
(off Paddington Grn.)
Winifred Ter. *E13* 1C **68**
(off Upper Rd.)
Winkfield Rd. E13 . . . . . 1D **69**
Winkley St. E2 . . . . 1D **65**
Winkworth Cotts. E1. . . . 3E **65**
(off Cephas St.)
Winlaton Rd.
 BR1: Brom 4F **123**
Winnett St.
 W1 . . . . 4B **14** (1F **75**)
Winnington Cl. N2 . . . . . 1F **31**
Winnington Ho. SE5. . . . 3E **91**
(off Wyndham Est.)

Winnington Ho. W10 . . . 3A **58**
(off Southern Row)
Winnington Rd. N2. . . . . 1F **31**
Winn Rd. SE12. . . . . 1C **124**
Winscombe St. N19. . . . . 4D **33**
Winsford Rd. SE6. . . . . . 3B **122**
Winsham Gro.
 SW11 . . . . 3C **102**
Winsham Ho. *NW1* 1C **6**
(off Churchway)
Winslade Rd. SW2. . . . . 3A **104**
Winslade Way SE6 . . . . 5D **109**
Winsland M. W2. . . . . . . 5F **59**
Winsland St. W2 . . . . . . 5F **59**
Winsley St.
 W1 . . . . 2A **14** (5E **61**)
Winslow SE17 . . . . 1A **92**
Winslow Cl. NW10. . . . . 5A **28**
Winslow Rd. W6 . . . . . . 2E **85**
Winstanley Est.
 SW11 . . . . 1F **101**
Winstanley Rd.
 SW11 . . . . 1F **101**
(not continuous)
Winston Av. NW9 . . . . . . 2A **28**
Winston Ho. WC1. . . . . . 3C **6**
Winston Rd. N16 . . . . . . 1F **49**
Winter Av. E6 . . . . 5F **55**
Winterbourne Ho.
 W11 . . . . 1A **72**
(off Portland Rd.)
Winterbourne Rd.
 SE6 . . . . 1B **122**
Winterbrook Rd.
 SE24 . . . . 4E **105**
Winterfold Cl.
 SW19 . . . . 2A **114**
Wintergreen Cl. E6. . . . . 4F **69**
Winterleys *NW6*. 1B **58**
(off Denmark Rd.)
Winter Lodge SE16 . . . . 1C **92**
(off Fern Wlk.)
Winterslow Ho. SE5. . . . 5E **91**
(off Flaxman Rd.)
Winterstoke Rd.
 SE6 . . . . 1B **122**
Winterton Ho. E1 . . . . . . 5E **65**
(off Deancross St.)
Winterton Pl. SW10 . . . . 2E **87**
Winterwell Rd.
 SW2 . . . . 3A **104**
Winthorpe Rd.
 SW15 . . . . 2A **100**
Winthrop Ho. W12. . . . . 1D **71**
(off White City Est.)
Winthrop St. E1. . . . . . . 4D **65**
Winton Way SW16. . . . . 5C **118**
Wireworks Ct. *SE1*. . . . 4F **25**
(off Gt. Sufolk St.)
Wirrall Ho. SE26 . . . . . . 3C **120**
Wisbech *N4* 3B **34**
(off Lorne Rd.)
Wisden Ho. SW8 . . . . . . 2B **90**
Wiseman Rd. E10 . . . . . 4C **38**

Wise Rd. E15 . . . . 5F **53**
Wiseton Rd. SW17. . . . . 1A **116**
Wishart Rd. SE3. . . . . . . 5F **97**
Wisley Ho. *SW1* 1F **89**
(off Rampayne St.)
Wisley Rd. SW11. . . . . . 3C **102**
Wisteria Rd. SE13 . . . . . 2F **109**
Wistow Ho. *E2* 5C **50**
(off Whiston Rd.)
Witanhurst La. N6 . . . . . 3C **32**
Witan St. E2. . . . . 2D **65**
Witchwood Ho.
 SW9 . . . . 1C **104**
(off Gresham Rd.)
Witham Ct. E10 . . . . 5D **39**
 SW17 . . . . 3B **116**
Witheringdon Rd. N5 . . . 2C **48**
Withers Pl.
 EC1 . . . . 3A **10** (3E **63**)
Withycombe Rd.
 SW19 . . . . 5F **99**
Withy Ho. *E1*. 3F **65**
(off Globe Rd.)
Witley Ct. WC1 . . . . 4D **7**
Witley Ho. SW2 . . . . 5A **104**
Witley Point *SW15*. . . . 1D **113**
(off Wanborough Dr.)
Witley Rd. N19. . . . . 4E **33**
Witney Path SE23. . . . . . 3F **121**
Wittersham Rd.
 BR1: Brom 5B **124**
Wivenhoe Cl. SE15 . . . . 1D **107**
Wiverton Rd. SE26. . . . . 5E **121**
Wixom Ho. SE3 . . . . 2E **111**
Wix's La. SW4 . . . . 1D **103**
Woburn Ct. *SE16*. 1D **93**
(off Masters Dr.)
Woburn Mans. *WC1*. . . . 5B **6**
(off Torrington Pl.)
Woburn M.
 WC1. . . . . 4C **6** (3F **61**)
Woburn Pl.
 WC1. . . . . 4D **7** (3A **62**)
Woburn Sq.
 WC1. . . . . 4C **6** (3F **61**)
Woburn Wlk.
 WC1. . . . . 2C **6** (2F **61**)
Wodeham Gdns. E1. . . . 4C **64**
Wodehouse Av.
 SE5 . . . . 4B **92**
Woking Cl. SW15. . . . . . 2B **98**
Wolcot Ho. *NW1* 1A **6**
(off Aldenham St.)
Wolfe Cres. SE7 . . . . . . 1F **97**
 SE16 . . . . 3F **79**
Wolfe Ho. *W12* 1D **71**
(off White City Est.)
Wolffe Gdns. E15. . . . . . 3B **54**
Wolfington Rd.
 SE27 . . . . 4D **119**
Wolfram Cl. SE13 . . . . . 3A **110**
Wolftencroft Cl.
 SW11 . . . . 1A **102**
Wollaston Cl. SE1 . . . . . 5E **77**

Wollaton Ho. *N1*. 1C **62**
(off Batchelor St.)
Wollett Ct. *NW1*. 4E **47**
(off St Pancras Way)
Wolseley Av. SW19. . . 2C **114**
Wolseley Rd. E7. . . . . . . 4D **55**
N8. . . . . 1F **33**
Wolseley St. SE1. . . . . . 3C **78**
Wolsey Cl. NW6. . . . . . . 4E **45**
SW11. . . . . *4A **88***
(off Westbridge Rd.)
Wolsey M. NW5. . . . . . . 3E **47**
Wolsey Rd. N1. . . . . 2F **49**
Wolsey St. E1. . . . . 4E **65**
Wolverley St. E2. . . . . . . 2D **65**
Wolverton SE17. . . . . . . 1A **92**
Wolverton Gdns. W6. . . 5F **71**
Womersley Rd. N8. . . . . 1B **34**
Wontner Cl. N1. . . . . 4E **49**
Wontner Rd. SW17. . . 2B **116**
Woodall Cl. E14. . . . . . . 1D **81**
Woodbank Rd.
BR1: Brom 3B **124**
Woodbastwick Rd.
SE26. . . . . 5F **121**
Woodberry Down N4 . . 2E **35**
Woodberry Down Est.
N4. . . . . 3E **35**
(Spring Pk. Dr.)
N4. . . . . 2E **35**
(Woodberry Gro.)
Woodberry Gro. N4 . . 2E **35**
Woodbine Pl. E11. . . . . . 1C **40**
Woodbine Ter. E9. . . . . . 3E **51**
Woodborough Rd.
SW15. . . . . 2D **99**
Woodbourne Av.
SW16. . . . . 3F **117**
Woodbourne Cl.
SW16. . . . . 3A **118**
Woodbridge Cl. N7. . . . 4B **34**
NW2. . . . . 5C **28**
Woodbridge Ho. E11 . . 3B **40**
Woodbridge St.
EC1 . . . . 3D **9** (3D **63**)
(not continuous)
Woodburn Cl. NW4. . . . 1F **29**
Woodbury Ho. SE26. . . 3C **120**
Woodbury St.
SW17. . . . . 5A **116**
Woodchester Sq. W2. . . 4D **59**
Woodchurch Rd.
NW6. . . . . 4C **44**
Wood Cl. E2. . . . . 3C **64**
NW9 . . . . 2A **28**
Woodcock Ho. E14. . . . . *4C **66***
(off Burgess St.)
Woodcocks E16. . . . . . . 4E **69**
Woodcombe Cres.
SE23. . . . . 1E **121**
Woodcote Ho. *SE8*. . . . *2B **94***
(off Prince St.)
Woodcote Pl. SE27. . . . 5D **119**
Woodcote Rd. E11 . . . . . 2C **40**

Woodcote Vs. *SE27* . . . 5E **119**
(off Woodcote Pl.)
Woodcroft M. SE8. . . . . 5A **80**
Wood Dene *SE15*. *4D **93***
(off Queen's Rd.)
Wood Dr. BR7: Chst . . . 5F **125**
Woodend SE17. . . . . . . 5E **119**
Wooder Gdns. E7. . . . . . 1C **54**
Woodfall Rd. N4. . . . . . . 4C **34**
Woodfall St. SW3. . . . . . 1B **88**
Woodfarrs SE5 . . . . 2F **105**
Wood Fld. NW3 . . . . 2B **46**
Woodfield Av.
SW16. . . . . 3F **117**
Woodfield Gro.
SW16. . . . . 3F **117**
Woodfield Ho. *SE23*. . . *3F **121***
(off Dacres Rd.)
Woodfield La.
SW16. . . . . 3F **117**
Woodfield Pl. W9. . . . . . 3B **58**
Woodfield Rd. W9 . . . . . 4B **58**
Woodford Ct. *W12*. *3F **71***
(off Shepherd's Bush Grn.)
Woodford Rd. E7. . . . . . 5D **41**
Woodger Rd. W12 . . . . . 3E **71**
Woodget Cl. E6. . . . . . . 5F **69**
Woodgrange Rd. E7. . . . 2D **55**
Woodhall *NW1* *2F **5***
(off Robert St.)
Woodhall Av. SE21. . . . 3B **120**
Woodhall Dr. SE21. . . . 3B **120**
Woodhall Ho.
SW18. . . . . 4F **101**
Woodham Rd. SE6. . . . 3E **123**
Woodhatch Cl. E6. . . . . 4F **69**
Woodheyes Rd.
NW10. . . . . 2A **42**
Woodhouse Gro. E12. . 3F **55**
Woodhouse Rd. E11. . . 5B **40**
Woodland Cl. SE19. . . 5A **120**
Woodland Ct. *E11* *1C **40***
(off New Wanstead)
Woodland Cres.
SE10. . . . . 2A **96**
SE16. . . . . 3F **79**
Woodland Gro. SE10. . 1A **96**
Woodland Hill SE19. . . 5A **120**
Woodland M. SW16. . . 3A **118**
Woodland Rd. SE19. . . 5A **120**
Woodlands NW11. . . . . 1A **30**
Woodlands, The N5 . . . 1E **49**
SE13. . . . . 5F **109**
Woodlands Art Gallery
. . . . 2C **96**
Woodlands Av. E11 . . . . 3D **41**
Woodlands Cl. NW11. . 1A **30**
Woodlands Ct.
NW10 . . . . *5F **43***
(off Wrentham Av.)
SE23. . . . . 5D **107**
Woodlands Ga.
SW15 . . . . *3B **100***
(off Woodlands Way)

Woodlands Hgts.
SE3. . . . . *2B **96***
(off Vanburgh Hill)
Woodlands Ho. NW6 . . 4A **44**
Woodlands Pk. Rd.
N15. . . . . 1D **35**
SE10. . . . . 2A **96**
(not continuous)
Woodlands Rd. E11. . . . 4A **40**
SW13. . . . . 1B **98**
Woodlands St. SE13. . . 5F **109**
Woodland St. E8. . . . . . 3B **50**
Woodlands Way
SW15 . . . . 3B **100**
Woodland Ter. SE7. . . . 5F **83**
Woodland Wlk.
BR1: Brom 4F **123**
(not continuous)
NW3. . . . . 2A **46**
SE10. . . . . 1A **96**
Wood La. N6 . . . . 1D **33**
NW9 . . . . 2A **28**
W12. . . . . 5E **57**
Woodlawn Cl.
SW15 . . . . 3B **100**
Woodlawn Rd. SW6 . . 3F **85**
Woodlea Rd. N16. . . . . 5A **36**
Woodleigh Gdns.
SW16 . . . . 3A **118**
Woodmans Gro.
NW10 . . . . 2B **42**
Woodman's M. W12 . . 4D **57**
Woodmere Cl.
SW11 . . . . 1C **102**
Woodnook Rd.
SW16 . . . . 5D **117**
Woodpecker M.
SE13. . . . . *2F **109***
(off Freshfield Cl.)
Woodpecker Rd.
SE14. . . . . 2A **94**
Wood Point *E16*. *4C **68***
(off Fife Rd.)
Woodquest Av.
SE24 . . . . 3E **105**
Woodriffe Rd. E11 . . . . 2F **39**
Woodrush Cl. SE14 . . . 3A **94**
Wood's Bldgs. *E1*. *4D **65***
(off Winthrop St.)
Woodseer St. E1. . . . . . 4B **64**
Woodsford *SE17*. *1F **91***
(off Portland St.)
Woodsford Sq. W14. . . 3A **72**
Woodside SW19. . . . . . 5B **114**
Woodside Av. N6 . . . . . 1B **32**
Woodside Ct. E12. . . . . 3E **41**
Woodside Ho.
SW19 . . . . 5B **114**
Woodside M. SE22 . . . 3B **106**
Woodside Rd. E13 . . . . 3E **69**
Woods M.
W1. . . . . 4B **12** (1C **74**)
Woodsome Rd.
NW5 . . . . 5C **32**

Woods Pl.
SE1 . . . . 5E **27** (4A **78**)
Woodspring Rd.
SW19 . . . . 2A **114**
Woods Rd. SE15 . . . . . . 2D **93**
Woodstock Av. NW11 . . 2A **30**
Woodstock Ct. SE11 . . 1B **90**
SE12 . . . . 4C **110**
Woodstock Gro. W12 . . 3F **71**
Woodstock M. W1 . . . . 1C **12**
Woodstock Rd. E7 . . . . 4E **55**
N4 . . . . 3C **34**
NW11 . . . . 2B **30**
W4 . . . . 5A **70**
Woodstock St.
W1. . . . . 3D **13** (5D **61**)
Woodstock Ter. E14 . . 1D **81**
Wood St.
EC2 . . . . 2A **18** (5E **63**)
W4 . . . . 1A **84**
Woodsyre SE26 . . . . . . 4B **120**
Wood Ter. NW2 . . . . . . 5D **29**
Woodthorpe Rd.
SW15 . . . . 2D **99**
Wood Va. N10 . . . . 1E **33**
SE23 . . . . 1D **121**
Wood Va. Est. SE23 . . 5E **107**
Woodvale Wlk.
SE27 . . . . 5E **119**
Woodvale Way NW11 . . 5F **29**
Woodview Cl. N4 . . . . . 2D **35**
SW15 . . . . 4A **112**
Woodville SE3 . . . . 3D **97**
Woodville Cl. SE12 . . 3C **110**
Woodville Gdns.
NW11 . . . . 2F **29**
Woodville Ho. SE1 . . . . 5F **27**
(off Grange Wlk.)
Woodville Rd. E11 . . . . 3B **40**
N16 . . . . 2A **50**
NW6 . . . . 1B **58**
NW11 . . . . 2F **29**
Woodward Av. NW4 . . 1C **28**
Woodwarde Rd.
SE22 . . . . 4A **106**
Woodwell St. SW18 . . 3E **101**
Wood Wharf SE10 . . . . 2E **95**
Wood Wharf Bus. Pk.
E14 . . . . 2D **81**
(not continuous)
Woodyard Cl. NW5 . . . . 2C **46**
Woodyard La. SE21 . . 3A **106**
Woodyates Rd.
SE12 . . . . 4C **110**
Woolacombe Rd.
SE3 . . . . 4E **97**
Woolcombes Ct.
SE16 . . . . 2F **79**
(off Princes Riverside Rd.)
Wooler St. SE17 . . . . . 1F **91**
Woolf M. WC1 . . . . 3C **6**
(off Burton Pl.)
Woolgar M. N16 . . . . . . 2A **50**
(off Gillett St.)

Woollaston Rd. N4 . . . . 1D **35**
Woolley Ho. SW9 . . . . 1D **105**
(off Loughborough Rd.)
Woollon Ho. E1 . . . . . . 5E **65**
(off Clark St.)
Woolmead Av. NW9 . . 2C **28**
Woolmore St. E14 . . . . 1E **81**
Woolneigh St. SW6 . . 1D **101**
Woolridge Way E9 . . . . 4E **51**
Woolstaplers Way
SE16 . . . . 4C **78**
Woolstone Ho. E2 . . . . 5C **50**
(off Whiston Rd.)
Woolstone Rd.
SE23 . . . . 2A **122**
Woolwich Chu. St.
SE18 . . . . 4F **83**
Woolwich Dockyard Ind. Est.
SE18 . . . . 4F **83**
Woolwich Rd. SE7 . . . . 1C **96**
SE10 . . . . 1B **96**
Wooster Gdns. E14 . . 5F **67**
Wooster Pl. SE1 . . . . . 5F **77**
(off Searles Rd.)
Wootton St.
SE1 . . . . 2C **24** (2C **76**)
Worcester Cl. NW2 . . 5D **29**
Worcester Ct. W9 . . . . 4C **58**
(off Elmfield Way)
Worcester Dr. W4 . . . . 3A **70**
Worcester Gdns.
SW11 . . . . 3B **102**
(off Grandison Rd.)
Worcester Ho. SE11 . . 5B **24**
(off Kennington Rd.)
. . . . 3C **90**
SW9 . . . .
(off Cranmer Rd.)
W2 . . . . 5E **59**
(off Hallfield Est.)
Worcester M. NW6 . . . 3D **45**
Worcester Rd.
SW19 . . . . 5B **114**
Wordsworth Av. E12 . . 4F **55**
Wordsworth Ho.
NW6 . . . . 2C **58**
(off Stafford Rd.)
Wordsworth Mans.
W14 . . . . 2B **86**
(off Queens Club Gdns.)
Wordsworth Pl. NW3 . . 2B **46**
Wordsworth Rd. N16 . . 1A **50**
SE1 . . . . 5B **78**
Worfield St. SW11 . . . . 3A **88**
Worgan St. SE11 . . . . 1B **90**
SE16 . . . . 5F **79**
Worland Rd. E15 . . . . 4A **54**
Worlds End Est.
SW10 . . . . 3F **87**
World's End Pas.
SW10 . . . . 3F **87**
(off Worlds End Est.)
World's End Pl.
SW10 . . . . 3F **87**
(off Worlds End Est.)

Worlidge St. W6 . . . . . 1E **85**
Worlingham Rd.
SE22 . . . . 2B **106**
Wormholt Rd. W12 . . . 1C **70**
Wormwood St.
EC2 . . . . 2D **19** (5A **64**)
Wornington Rd. W10 . . 3A **58**
(not continuous)
Wornum Ho. W10 . . . . 1A **58**
(off Kilburn La.)
Woronzow Rd. NW8 . . 5F **45**
Worple Rd. SW19 . . . . 5B **114**
Worple Rd. M.
SW19 . . . . 5B **114**
Worple St. SW14 . . . . 1A **98**
Worship St.
EC2 . . . . 4C **10** (3F **63**)
Worslade St. SW17 . . 4F **115**
Worsley Bri. Rd.
BR3: Beck. 5C **122**
SE26 . . . . 4B **122**
Worsley Gro. E5 . . . . . 1C **50**
Worsley Ho. SE23 . . . 2E **121**
Worsley Rd. E11 . . . . . 1A **54**
Worsopp Dr. SW4 . . . 3E **103**
Worth Gro. SE17 . . . . . 1F **91**
Worthing Cl. E15 . . . . . 5A **54**
Worthington Ho. EC1 . . 1C **8**
(off Myddelton Pas.)
Wortley Rd. E6 . . . . . . 4F **55**
Wotton Ct. E14 . . . . . . 1F **81**
(off Jamestown Way)
Wotton Rd. NW2 . . . . . 5E **29**
SE8 . . . . 2B **94**
Wouldham Rd. E16 . . . 5B **68**
Wragby Rd. E11 . . . . . 5A **40**
Wrayburn Ho. SE16 . . . 3C **78**
(off Llewellyn St.)
Wray Cres. N4 . . . . . . 4A **34**
Wren Av. NW2 . . . . 1E **43**
Wren Cl. E16 . . . . 5B **68**
Wren Ho. E3. . . . . 1A **66**
(off Gernon Rd.)
SW1 . . . . 1F **89**
(off Aylesford St.)
Wren Landing E14 . . . 2C **80**
Wrenn Ho. SW13 . . . . 2E **85**
Wren Rd. SE5 . . . . 4F **91**
Wren's Pk. Ho. E5 . . . 4D **37**
Wren St. WC1 . . 3A **8** (3B **62**)
Wrentham Av.
NW10 . . . . 1F **57**
Wrenthorpe Rd.
BR1: Brom 4A **124**
Wren Vw. N6 . . . . 2E **33**
Wrestlers Ct. EC2 . . . 2D **19**
Wrexham Rd. E3 . . . . 1C **66**
Wricklemarsh Rd.
SE3 . . . . 5D **97**
(not continuous)
Wrigglesworth St.
SE14 . . . . 3F **93**
Wright Cl. SE13 . . . . . 2F **109**
Wright Rd. N1 . . . . 3A **50**

Wrights Grn. SW4 . . . . . 2F **103**
Wright's La. W8 . . . . 4D **73**
Wright's Rd. E3 . . . . 1B **66**
   (not continuous)
Wrotham Ho. SE1 . . . . . . 5C **26**
   (off Law St.)
Wrotham Rd. NW1 . . . . . 4E **47**
Wrottesley Rd.
  NW10 . . . . 1C **56**
Wroughton Rd.
  SW11 . . . . 3B **102**
Wroxton Rd. SE15 . . . . . 5E **93**
Wulfstan St. W12 . . . . . 4B **56**
Wyatt Cl. SE16 . . . . 3B **80**
Wyatt Dr. SW13 . . . . . . 2D **85**
Wyatt Ho. NW8 . . . . 3F **59**
   (off Frampton St.)
  SE3 . . . . 5B **96**
Wyatt Pk. Rd. SW2 . . . 2A **118**
Wyatt Rd. E7 . . . . 3C **54**
  N5 . . . . 5E **35**
Wybert St.
  NW1 . . . . 3F **5** (3E **61**)
Wychcombe Studios
  NW3 . . . . 3B **46**
Wycherley Cl. SE3 . . . . . 3B **96**
Wychwood End N6 . . . . . 2E **33**
Wychwood Way
  SE19 . . . . 5F **119**
Wyclif Ct. EC1 . . . . 2D **9**
   (off Wyclif St.)
Wycliffe Rd. SW11 . . . . . 5C **88**
Wyclif St. EC1 . . . 2D **9** (2D **63**)
Wycombe Gdns.
  NW11 . . . . 4C **30**
Wycombe Ho. NW8 . . . . . 3A **60**
   (off Grendon St.)
Wycombe Pl. SW18 . . . . 4E **101**
Wycombe Sq. W8 . . . . . 2B **72**
Wydeville Mnr. Rd.
  SE12 . . . . 4D **125**
Wye St. SW11 . . . . 5F **87**
Wyfold Rd. SW6 . . . . . . 3A **86**
Wykeham Ct. NW4 . . . . . 1E **29**
   (off Wykeham Rd.)
Wykeham Ho. SE1 . . . . . 2F **25**
   (off Pepper St.)
Wykeham Rd. NW4 . . . . 1E **29**
Wyke Rd. E3 . . . . 4C **52**
Wyldes Cl. NW11 . . . . . 3E **31**
Wyleu St. SE23 . . . . . . 5A **108**
Wyllen Cl. E1 . . . . 3E **65**
Wymans Way E7 . . . . . . 1E **55**
Wymering Mans. W9 . . . 2C **58**
   (off Wymering Rd.,
   not continuous)
Wymering Rd. W9 . . . . . 2C **58**
Wymondham Ct.
  NW8 . . . . 5F **45**
   (off Queensmead)
Wymond St. SW15 . . . . . 1E **99**
Wynan Rd. E14 . . . . 1D **95**
Wyndcliff Rd. SE7 . . . . . 2D **97**
Wyndham Cres. N19 . . . 5E **33**

Wyndham Deedes Ho.
  E2 . . . . 1C **64**
   (off Hackney Rd.)
Wyndham Est. SE5 . . . . . 3E **91**
Wyndham Ho. E14 . . . . . 3D **81**
   (off Marsh Wall)
  SW1 . . . . 5C **74**
   (off Sloane Sq.)
Wyndham M. W1 . . . . . . 4B **60**
Wyndham Pl.
  W1 . . . . 1A **12** (4B **60**)
Wyndham Rd. E6 . . . . . . 4F **55**
  SE5 . . . . 3E **91**
Wyndhams Ct. E8 . . . . . 4B **50**
   (off Celandine Dr.)
Wyndham St. W1 . . . . . 4B **60**
Wyndham Yd. W1 . . . . . 4B **60**
Wyneham Rd. SE24 . . . 3F **105**
Wynell Rd. SE23 . . . . . 3F **121**
Wynford Ho. N1 . . . . . . 1B **62**
   (off Wynford Rd.)
Wynford Rd. N1 . . . . . . 1B **62**
Wynne Ho. SE14 . . . . . . 4F **93**
Wynne Rd. SW9 . . . . . . 5C **90**
Wynnstay Gdns. W8 . . . 4C **72**
Wynter St. SW11 . . . . . 2E **101**
Wynyard Ho. SE11 . . . . . 1B **90**
   (off Newburn St.)
Wynyard Ter. SE11 . . . . . 1B **90**
Wynyatt St.
  EC1 . . . . 2D **9** (2D **63**)
Wytham Ho. NW8 . . . . . 3F **59**
   (off Penfold St.)
Wythburn Ct. W1 . . . . . 2A **12**
   (off Wythburn Pl.)
Wythburn Pl.
  W1 . . . . 3A **12** (5B **60**)
Wythes Rd. E16 . . . . . . 2F **83**
Wyvil Rd. SW8 . . . . 3A **90**
Wyvis St. E14 . . . . 4D **67**

Y

Yabsley St. E14 . . . . . . 2E **81**
Yalding Ho. SE16 . . . . . 4C **78**
Yale Ct. NW6 . . . . 2D **45**
Yard, The N1 . . . . 1E **7**
   (off Caledonian Rd.)
Yardley St.
  WC1 . . . . 2B **8** (2C **62**)
   (not continuous)
Yarmouth Pl.
  W1 . . . . 2D **21** (2D **75**)
Yarnfield Sq. SE15 . . . . 4C **92**
Yarrell Mans. W14 . . . . 2B **86**
   (off Queen's Club Mans.)
Yarrow Cres. E6 . . . . . . 4F **69**
Yarrow Ho. E14 . . . . . . 4E **81**
   (off Stewart St.)
  W10 . . . . 4E **57**
   (off Sutton Way)

Yateley St. SE18 . . . . . . 4F **83**
Yates Ct. NW2 . . . . 3F **43**
   (off Willesden La.)
Yates Ho. E2 . . . . 2C **64**
   (off Roberta St.)
Yatton Ho. W10 . . . . . . 4E **57**
   (off Sutton Way)
Yeadon Ho. W10 . . . . . 4E **57**
   (off Sutton Way)
Yearby Ho. W10 . . . . . . 3E **57**
   (off Sutton Way)
Yeate St. N1 . . . . 4F **49**
Yeatman Rd. N6 . . . . . . 1B **32**
Yeats Cl. NW10 . . . . . . 2A **42**
  SE13 . . . . 5F **95**
Yeldham Ho. W6 . . . . . . 1F **85**
   (off Yeldham Rd.)
Yeldham Rd. W6 . . . . . . 1F **85**
Yeldham Vs. W6 . . . . . . 1F **85**
   (off Yeldham Rd.)
Yelverton Rd.
  SW11 . . . . 5F **87**
Yeoman Cl. SE27 . . . . . 3D **119**
Yeoman Ct. SE1 . . . . . . 1B **92**
   (off Cooper's Rd.)
Yeoman's Row SW3 . . . 4A **74**
Yeoman St. SE8 . . . . . . 5A **80**
Yeoman's Yd. E1 . . . . . 1B **78**
   (off Chamber St.)
Yeo St. E3 . . . . 4D **67**
Yeovil Ho. W10 . . . . . . 3E **57**
   (off Sutton Way)
Yerbury Rd. N19 . . . . . . 5F **33**
   (not continuous)
Yetev Lev Ct. E5 . . . . . . 3C **36**
Yewfield Rd. NW10 . . . . 3B **42**
Yew Gro. NW2 . . . . 1F **43**
Yew Ho. SE16 . . . . 3F **79**
   (off Woodland Cres.)
Yew Tree Cl. NW11 . . . . 1B **30**
   (off Bridge La.)
Yew Tree Lodge
  SW16 . . . . 4E **117**
Yew Tree Rd. W12 . . . . . 1B **70**
Yoakley Rd. N16 . . . . . . 4A **36**
Yoke Cl. N7 . . . . 3A **48**
Yolande Gdns. SE9 . . . . 3F **111**
Yonge Pk. N4 . . . . 5C **34**
York Av. SE17 . . . . 1E **91**
York Bri. NW1 . . . 3B **4** (3C **60**)
York Bldgs.
  WC2 . . . . 5E **15** (1A **76**)
York Cl. SE5 . . . . 5E **91**
   (off Lilford Rd.)
York Ga. NW1 . . . 4B **4** (3C **60**)
York Gro. SE15 . . . . . . 4E **93**
York Hill SE27 . . . . . . 3D **119**
York Ho. E16 . . . . 2C **82**
   (off De Quincey M.)
  SE1 . . . . 5A **24** (4B **76**)
  SW3 . . . . 1B **88**
   (off Turks Row)
  W1 . . . . 5A **4**
   (off York St.)

York Ho. W8 . . . . 3D 73
(off York Ho. Pl.)
York Ho. Pl. W8 . . . . 3D 73
Yorkley Ho. W10 . . . . 3E 57
(off Sutton Way)
York Mans. SW5 . . . . 1D 87
(off Earls Ct. Rd.)
SW11 . . . . 4C 88
(off Prince of Wales Dr.)
W1 . . . . 5B 4
(off Chiltern St.)
York M. NW5 . . . . 2D 47
York Pde. NW9 . . . . 1C 28
(off The Broadway)
York Pas. W8 . . . . 3D 73
(off York Ho. Pl.)
York Pl. SW11 . . . . 1F 101
WC2 . . . . 5E 15
York Pl. Mans.
W1 . . . . 5A 4
(off Baker St.)
York Ri. NW5 . . . . 5D 33
York Rd. E7 . . . . 3C 54
E10 . . . . 5E 39
E17 . . . . 1F 37
SE1 . . . . . . 3A 24 (3B 76)
SW11 . . . . 2E 101
SW18 . . . . 2E 101
SW19 . . . . 5E 115

York Rd. Bus. Cen.
SW11 . . . . 5F 87
Yorkshire Cl. N16 . . . . . . 5A 36
YORKSHIRE GREY. . . . 3F 111
Yorkshire Grey Pl.
NW3 . . . . 1E 45
Yorkshire Grey Yd.
WC1 . . . . 1F 15
Yorkshire Rd. E14 . . . . . . 5A 66
York Sq. E14 . . . . 5A 66
York St.
W1 . . . . 1A 12 (4B 60)
York St. Chambers
W1 . . . . 4B 60
(off York St.)
York Ter. E.
NW1 . . . . 4C 4 (3C 60)
York Ter. W.
NW1 . . . . 4B 4 (3C 60)
Yorkton St. E2 . . . . 1C 64
York Way N1 . . . 1E 7 (3A 48)
N7 . . . . 3F 47
York Way Ct. N1 . . . . 5A 48
York Way Est. N7 . . . . . . 3A 48
Young Ct. NW6 . . . . 4A 44
Young Rd. E16 . . . . 5E 69
Youngs Bldgs. EC1 . . . . . 3A 10
Youngs Ct. SW11 . . . . . . 4C 88
Young St. W8 . . . . 3D 73

Young Vic Theatre, The
. . . . 3C 24
Yoxall Ho. W10 . . . . 3E 57
(off Sutton Way)
Yukon Rd. SW12 . . . . . 5D 103
Yunus Khan Cl. E17 . . . . 1C 38

Z

Zampa Rd. SE16 . . . . . . 1E 93
Zander Ct. E2 . . . . 2C 64
Zangwill Rd. SE3 . . . . . . 4F 97
Zealand Ho. SE5 . . . . . . 5E 91
(off Denmark Rd.)
Zealand Rd. E3 . . . . 1A 66
Zennor Rd. SW12 . . . . . 1E 117
Zennor Rd. Ind. Est.
SW12 . . . . 1E 117
Zenobia Mans. W14 . . . . 2B 86
(off Queen's Club Mans.)
Zenoria St. SE22 . . . . . 2B 106
Zetland Ho. W8 . . . . 4D 73
(off Marloes Rd.)
Zetland St. E14 . . . . 4D 67
Zion Ho. E1 . . . . 5E 65
(off Jubilee St.)
Zoar St. SE1 . . . 1F 25 (2E 77)
Zoffany St. N19 . . . . 4F 33

HOSPITALS and HOSPICES
covered by this atlas.

N.B. Where Hospitals and Hospices are not named on the map,
the reference given is for the road in which they are situated.

ABBEY CHURCHILL LONDON, THE
...................................5C **24** (4C **76**)
22 Barkham Terrace
LONDON
SE1 7PW
Tel: 020 7928 5633

BARNES HOSPITAL 1A **98**
South Worple Way
LONDON
SW14 8SU
Tel: 020 8878 4981

BELVEDERE DAY HOSPITAL 5C **42**
341 Harlesden Road
LONDON
NW10 3RX
Tel: 020 8459 3562

BLACKHEATH BMI HOSPITAL, THE 1B **110**
40-42 Lee Terrace
LONDON
SE3 9UD
Tel: 020 8318 7722

BOLINGBROKE HOSPITAL 3A **102**
Bolingbroke Grove
LONDON
SW11 6HN
Tel: 020 7223 7411

BRITISH HOME, THE 5D **119**
Crown Lane
Streatham
LONDON
SW16 3JB
Tel: 020 8670 8261

CAMDEN MEWS DAY HOSPITAL 4E **47**
1-5 Camden Mews
LONDON
NW1 9DB
Tel: 020 7530 4780

CHARING CROSS HOSPITAL 2F **85**
Fulham Palace Road
LONDON
W6 8RF
Tel: 020 8846 1234

CHELSEA & WESTMINSTER HOSPITAL
...................................2E **87**
369 Fulham Road
LONDON
SW10 9NH
Tel: 020 8746 8000

CHILDREN'S HOSPITAL, THE (LEWISHAM)
...................................3D **109**
Lewisham University Hospital
Lewisham High Street
LONDON
SE13 6LH
Tel: 020 8333 3000

CROMWELL HOSPITAL, THE 5D **73**
162-174 Cromwell Road
LONDON
SW5 0TU
Tel: 020 7460 2000

DULWICH COMMUNITY HOSPITAL ...2A **106**
East Dulwich Grove
LONDON
SE22 8PT
Tel: 020 7346 6444

EASTMAN DENTAL HOSPITAL &
     DENTAL INSTITUTE, THE
...................................3F **7** (3B **62**)
256 Gray's Inn Road
LONDON
WC1X 8LD
Tel: 020 7915 1000

ELIZABETH GARRETT ANDERSON &
     OBSTETRIC HOSPITAL, THE
...................................4A **6** (3E **61**)
Huntley Street
LONDON
WC1E 6DH
Tel: 0845 1555 000

EVELINA CHILDREN'S HOSPITAL
...................................5F **23** (4B **76**)
St Thomas' Hospital
Lambeth Palace Road
LONDON
SE1 7EH
Tel: 020 7188 7188

FORDWYCH ROAD DAY HOSPITAL 2B **44**
85-87 Fordwych Road
LONDON
NW2 3TL
Tel: 020 8208 1612

GORDON HOSPITAL 5F **75**
Bloomburg Street
LONDON
SW1V 2RH
Tel: 020 8746 8733

GREAT ORMOND STREET HOSPITAL FOR
    CHILDREN 4E **7** (3A **62**)
Great Ormond Street
LONDON
WC1N 3JH
Tel: 020 7405 9200

GUY'S HOSPITAL 2C **26** (2F **77**)
St Thomas Street
LONDON
SE1 9RT
Tel: 020 7188 7188

GUY'S NUFFIELD HOUSE 3B **26** (3F **77**)
Newcomen Street
LONDON
SE1 1YR
Tel: 020 7188 5292

HAMMERSMITH HOSPITAL 5C **56**
Du Cane Road
LONDON
W12 0HS
Tel: 020 8383 1000

HARLEY STREET CLINIC 5D **5** (4D **61**)
35 Weymouth Street
LONDON
W1G 8BJ
Tel: 020 7935 7700

HEART HOSPITAL, THE 1C **12** (4C **60**)
16-18 Westmoreland Street
LONDON
W1G 8PH
Tel: 020 7573 8888

HIGHGATE HOSPITAL 1B **32**
17 View Road
LONDON
N6 4DJ
Tel: 020 8341 4182

HIGHGATE MENTAL HEALTH CENTRE
    . . . . .4D **33**
Dartmouth Park Hill
LONDON
N19 5NX
Tel: 020 7561 4000

HOMERTON UNIVERSITY HOSPITAL
    . . . . .2F **51**
Homerton Row
LONDON
E9 6SR
Tel: 020 8510 5555

HOSPITAL FOR TROPICAL DISEASES
    .4A **6** (3E **61**)
Mortimer Market,
Capper Street
LONDON
WC1E 6AU
Tel: 020 7387 9300

HOSPITAL OF ST JOHN & ST ELIZABETH
    . . . . .1F **59**
60 Grove End Road
LONDON
NW8 9NH
Tel: 020 7806 4000

KING EDWARD VII'S HOSPITAL
    SISTER AGNES 5C **4** (4C **60**)
5-10 Beaumont Street
LONDON
W1G 6AA
Tel: 020 7486 4411

KING'S COLLEGE HOSPITAL 5F **91**
Denmark Hill
LONDON
SE5 9RS
Tel: 020 7737 4000

LAMBETH HOSPITAL 1B **104**
108 Landor Road
LONDON
SW9 9NT
Tel: 020 7411 6100

LATIMER DAY HOSPITAL 5F **5** (4E **61**)
40 Hanson Street
LONDON
W1W 6UL
Tel: 020 7612 1645

LEWISHAM UNIVERSITY HOSPITAL
    . . . . .3D **109**
Lewisham High Street
LONDON
SE13 6LH
Tel: 020 8333 3000

LISTER HOSPITAL, THE 1D **89**
Chelsea Bridge Road
LONDON
SW1W 8RH
Tel: 020 7730 3417

LONDON BRIDGE HOSPITAL
    .1C **26** (2F **77**)
27 Tooley Street
LONDON
SE1 2PR
Tel: 020 7407 3100

LONDON CHEST HOSPITAL 1E **65**
Bonner Road
LONDON
E2 9JX
Tel: 020 7377 7000

LONDON CLINIC, THE 4C **4** (3C **60**)
20 Devonshire Place
LONDON
W1G 6BW
Tel: 020 7935 4444

LONDON INDEPENDENT BMI HOSPITAL, THE
............................4F **65**
1 Beaumont Square
LONDON
E1 4NL
Tel: 020 7780 2400

LONDON WELBECK HOSPITAL
............................1C **12** (4D **61**)
27 Welbeck Street
LONDON
W1G 8EN
Tel: 020 7224 2242

MARGARET CENTRE (HOSPICE) 1A **40**
Whipps Cross University Hospital
Whipps Cross Road
LONDON
E11 1NR
Tel: 020 8535 6605

MARIE CURIE HOSPICE, HAMPSTEAD, THE
............................2F **45**
11 Lyndhurst Gardens
LONDON
NW3 5NS
Tel: 020 7853 3400

MAUDSLEY HOSPITAL, THE 5F **91**
Denmark Hill
LONDON
SE5 8AZ
Tel: 020 7703 6333

MIDDLESEX HOSPITAL, THE ...1A **14** (4E **61**)
Mortimer Street
LONDON
W1T 3AA
Tel: 020 7636 8333

MILDMAY MISSION HOSPITAL (HOSPICE)
............................2F **11** (2B **64**)
Hackney Road
LONDON
E2 7NA
Tel: 020 7613 6300

MILE END HOSPITAL 3F **65**
Bancroft Road
LONDON
E1 4DG
Tel: 020 7377 7000

MOORFIELDS EYE HOSPITAL ...2B **10** (2F **63**)
162 City Road
LONDON
EC1V 2PD
Tel: 020 7253 3411

NHS WALK-IN CENTRE (CHARING CROSS)
............................1F **85**
Charing Cross Hospital
Fulham Palace Road
LONDON
W6 8RF
Tel: 020 8846 1234

NHS WALK-IN CENTRE (HACKNEY)
............................2F **51**
Homerton University Hospital
Homerton Row
LONDON
E9 6SR
Tel: 020 8510 5342

NHS WALK-IN CENTRE (LEYTONSTONE)
............................1F **39**
Whipps Cross University Hospital
Whipps Cross Road
LONDON
E11 1NR
Tel: 020 8539 5522

NHS WALK-IN CENTRE (LIVERPOOL STREET)
............................5E **11** (4A **64**)
Exchange Arcade
LONDON
EC2M 3WA
Tel: 0845 880 1242

NHS WALK-IN CENTRE (NEW CROSS)
............................3A **94**
40 Goodwood Road
LONDON
SE14 6BL
Tel: 020 7206 3100

NHS WALK-IN CENTRE (NEWHAM)
............................3E **69**
Glen Road
LONDON
E13 8SH
Tel: 020 7363 9200

NHS WALK-IN CENTRE (PARSONS GREEN)
............................4C **86**
5-7 Parsons Green
LONDON
SW6 4UL
Tel: 020 8846 6758

NHS WALK-IN CENTRE (SOHO)
............................3B **14** (5F **61**)
1 Frith Street
LONDON
W1D 3HZ
Tel: 020 7534 6500

NHS WALK-IN CENTRE (TOOTING) ...5A **116**
St George's Hospital
Blackshaw Road
LONDON
SW17 0QT
Tel: 020 8700 0505

NHS WALK-IN CENTRE (WHITECHAPEL)
............................4D **65**
The Royal London Hospital
174 Whitechapel Road
LONDON
E1 1BZ
Tel: 020 7943 1333

NHS WALK-IN CENTRE (WHITTINGTON)
.................................4E **33**
Whittington Hospital
Highgate Hill
LONDON
N19 5NF
Tel: 020 7272 3070

NATIONAL HOSPITAL FOR NEUROLOGY &
NEUROSURGERY, THE
.................................4E **7** (3A **62**)
Queen Square
LONDON
WC1N 3BG
Tel: 020 7837 3611

NEWHAM GENERAL HOSPITAL
.................................3E **69**
Glen Road
LONDON
E13 8SL
Tel: 020 7476 4000

NIGHTINGALE CAPIO DAY HOSPITAL
.................................4A **60**
1b Harewood Row
LONDON
NW1 6SE
Tel: 020 7725 9940

NIGHTINGALE CAPIO HOSPITAL
(ENFORD STREET) 4B **60**
23-24 Enford Street
LONDON
W1H 1DG
Tel: 020 7723 3635

NIGHTINGALE CAPIO HOSPITAL
(LISSON GROVE) 4A **60**
11-19 Lisson Grove
LONDON
NW1 6SH
Tel: 020 7535 7700

NIGHTINGALE CAPIO HOSPITAL
(RADNOR WALK) 1A **88**
1-5 Radnor Walk
LONDON
SW3 4BP
Tel: 020 7349 3900

PARKSIDE HOSPITAL 3F **113**
53 Parkside
LONDON
SW19 5NX
Tel: 020 8971 8000

PEMBRIDGE PALLIATIVE CARE CENTRE, THE
.................................4F **57**
St Charles Hospital
Exmoor Street
LONDON
W10 6DZ
Tel: 020 8962 4410 / 4411

PLAISTOW HOSPITAL 1E **69**
Samson Street
LONDON
E13 9EH
Tel: 020 8586 6200

PORTLAND HOSPITAL FOR WOMEN &
CHILDREN, THE 4E **5** (3D **61**)
205-209 Great Portland Street
LONDON
W1W 5AH
Tel: 020 7580 4400

PRINCESS GRACE HOSPITAL
(OUTPATIENTS), THE 4B **4** (3C **60**)
30 Devonshire Street
LONDON
W1G 6PU
Tel: 020 7908 3602

PRINCESS GRACE HOSPITAL, THE
.................................4B **4** (3C **60**)
42-52 Nottingham Place
LONDON
W1U 5NY
Tel: 020 7486 1234

PRINCESS LOUISE DAY HOSPITAL 4F **57**
St. Quintin Avenue
LONDON
W10 6DL
Tel: 020 8969 0133

QUEEN CHARLOTTE'S & CHELSEA HOSPITAL
.................................5C **56**
Du Cane Road
LONDON
W12 0HS
Tel: 020 8383 1111

QUEEN MARY'S HOSPITAL, ROEHAMPTON
.................................4C **98**
Roehampton Lane
LONDON
SW15 5PN
Tel: 020 8487 6000

QUEEN MARY'S HOUSE 5E **31**
23 East Heath Road
LONDON
NW3 1DU
Tel: 020 7431 4111

RAVENSCOURT PARK HOSPITAL 5C **70**
Ravenscourt Park
LONDON
W6 0NT
Tel: 020 8846 7777

RICHARD HOUSE CHILDREN'S HOSPICE
.................................1F **83**
Richard House Drive
LONDON
E16 3RG
Tel: 020 7511 0222

ROEHAMPTON HUNTERCOMBE HOSPITAL
.................................5C **98**
Holybourne Avenue
LONDON
SW15 4JL
Tel: 020 8780 6155

ROEHAMPTON PRIORY HOSPITAL 2B **98**
Priory Lane
LONDON
SW15 5JJ
Tel: 020 8876 8261

ROYAL BROMPTON HOSPITAL 1A **88**
Sydney Street
LONDON
SW3 6NP
Tel: 020 7352 8121

ROYAL BROMPTON HOSPITAL
(FULHAM WING) 1F **87**
Fulham Road
LONDON
SW3 6HP
Tel: 020 7352 8121

ROYAL FREE HOSPITAL, THE 2A **46**
Pond Street
LONDON
NW3 2QG
Tel: 020 7794 0500

ROYAL HOSPITAL FOR NEURO-DISABILITY
.................................4A **100**
West Hill
LONDON
SW15 3SW
Tel: 020 8780 4500

ROYAL LONDON HOMOEOPATHIC
HOSPITAL, THE 5E **7** (4A **62**)
Great Ormond Street
LONDON
WC1N 3HR
Tel: 0845 1555 000

ROYAL LONDON HOSPITAL, THE 4D **65**
Whitechapel Road
LONDON
E1 1BB
Tel: 020 7377 7000

ROYAL MARSDEN HOSPITAL (FULHAM), THE
.................................1F **87**
Fulham Road
LONDON
SW3 6JJ
Tel: 020 7352 8171

ROYAL NATIONAL ORTHOPAEDIC HOSPITAL
(CENTRAL LONDON OUTPATIENT DEPT.)
.....................4E **5** (3D **61**)
45-51 Bolsover Street
LONDON
W1W 5AQ
Tel: 020 7387 5070

ROYAL NATIONAL THROAT, NOSE &
EAR HOSPITAL 1F **7** (2B **62**)
330 Gray's Inn Road
LONDON
WC1X 8DA
Tel: 020 7915 1300

ST ANDREW'S HOSPITAL 3D **67**
Devas Street
LONDON
E3 3NT
Tel: 020 7476 4000

ST ANN'S HOSPITAL 1E **35**
St Ann's Road
LONDON
N15 3TH
Tel: 020 8442 6000

ST BARTHOLOMEW'S HOSPITAL
.................................1E **17** (4D **63**)
West Smithfield
LONDON
EC1A 7BE
Tel: 020 7377 7000

ST CHARLES HOSPITAL 4F **57**
Exmoor Street
LONDON
W10 6DZ
Tel: 020 8969 2488

ST CHRISTOPHER'S HOSPICE
.................................5E **121**
51-59 Lawrie Park Road
LONDON
SE26 6DZ
Tel: 020 8768 4500

ST CLEMENT'S HOSPITAL 2B **66**
2A Bow Road
LONDON
E3 4LL
Tel: 020 7377 7000

ST GEORGE'S HOSPITAL (TOOTING)
.................................5A **116**
Blackshaw Road
LONDON
SW17 0QT
Tel: 020 8672 1255

ST JOHN'S HOSPICE 1F **59**
Hospital of St John & St Elizabeth
60 Grove End Road
LONDON
NW8 9NH
Tel: 020 7806 4040

ST JOSEPH'S HOSPICE 5D **51**
Mare Street
LONDON
E8 4SA
Tel: 020 8525 6000

ST LUKE'S HOSPITAL FOR THE CLERGY
. . . . .4F **5** (3E **61**)
14 Fitzroy Square
LONDON
W1T 6AH
Tel: 020 7388 4954

ST MARY'S HOSPITAL 5F **59**
Praed Street
LONDON
W2 1NY
Tel: 020 7725 6666

ST PANCRAS HOSPITAL 5F **47**
4 St Pancras Way
LONDON
NW1 0PE
Tel: 020 7530 3500

ST THOMAS' HOSPITAL 5F **23** (4B **76**)
Lambeth Palace Road
LONDON
SE1 7EH
Tel: 020 7188 7188

SPRINGFIELD UNIVERSITY HOSPITAL
. . . . .3A **116**
61 Glenburnie Road
LONDON
SW17 7DJ
Tel: 020 8682 6000

TRINITY HOSPICE 2D **103**
30 Clapham Common North Side
LONDON
SW4 0RN
Tel: 020 7787 1000

UNIVERSITY COLLEGE HOSPITAL
. . . . .3A **6** (3E **61**)
235 Euston Road
LONDON
NW1 2BU
Tel: 0845 1555000

WELLINGTON HOSPITAL, THE 2F **59**
8a Wellington Place
LONDON
NW8 9LE
Tel: 020 7586 5959

WESTERN EYE HOSPITAL 4B **60**
171 Marylebone Road
LONDON
NW1 5QH
Tel: 020 7886 6666

WHIPPS CROSS UNIVERSITY HOSPITAL
. . . . .1F **39**
Whipps Cross Road
LONDON
E11 1NR
Tel: 020 8539 5522

WHITTINGTON HOSPITAL 4E **33**
Highgate Hill
LONDON
N19 5NF
Tel: 020 7272 3070

WILLESDEN CENTRE FOR HEALTH & CARE
. . . . .4C **42**
Robson Avenue
LONDON
NW10 3RY
Tel: 020 8438 7000

WOODBURY UNIT 1A **40**
178 James Lane
LONDON
E11 1NU
Tel: 020 85356478

RAIL, CROYDON TRAMLINK, DOCKLANDS LIGHT RAILWAY, RIVERBUS AND LONDON UNDERGROUND STATIONS

with their map square reference

A

Acton Central (Rail) 2A 70
Aldgate (Tube) 3F 19 (5B 64)
Aldgate East (Tube) 2F 19 (5B 64)
All Saints (DLR) 1D 81
Angel (Tube) 1C 62
Archway (Tube) 4E 33
Arsenal (Tube) 5C 34

B

Baker Street (Tube) 4A 4 (3B 60)
Balham (Rail & Tube) 1D 117
Bank (Tube & DLR) 3B 18 (5F 63)
Bankside Pier (Riverbus) 5F 17 (1E 77)
Barbican (Rail & Tube) 5F 9 (4E 63)
Barnes (Rail) 1C 98
Barnes Bridge (Rail) 5B 84
Barons Court (Tube) 1A 86
Battersea Park (Rail) 3D 89
Bayswater (Tube) 1D 73
Beckenham Hill (Rail) 5E 123
Bellingham (Rail) 3D 123
Belsize Park (Tube) 2A 46
Bermondsey (Tube) 4C 78
Bethnal Green (Rail) 3D 65
Bethnal Green (Tube) 2E 65
Blackfriars (Rail & Tube) 4D 17 (1D 77)
Blackfriars Millennium Pier (Riverbus)
. . . . .4C 16 (1C 76)
Blackheath (Rail) 1B 110
Blackwall (DLR) 1E 81
Bond Street (Tube) 3D 13 (5D 61)
Borough (Tube) 4A 26 (3E 77)
Bow Church (DLR) 2C 66
Bow Road (Tube) 2C 66
Brent Cross (Tube) 2F 29
Brixton (Rail & Tube) 2C 104
Brockley (Rail) 1A 108
Bromley-by-Bow (Tube) 2D 67
Brondesbury (Tube) 4B 44
Brondesbury Park (Rail) 5A 44

C

Cadogan Pier (Riverbus) 2A 88
Caledonian Road (Tube) 3B 48
Caledonian Road & Barnsbury (Rail)
. . . . .4B 48
Cambridge Heath (Rail) 1D 65
Camden Road (Rail) 4E 47
Camden Town (Tube) 5D 47
Canada Water (Tube) 3E 79
Canary Wharf (DLR & Tube) 2C 80
Canary Wharf Pier (Riverbus) 2B 80

Canning Town (Rail, Tube & DLR) 5A 68
Cannon Street (Rail & Tube)
. . . . .4B 18 (1F 77)
Canonbury (Rail) 2E 49
Catford (Rail) 5C 108
Catford Bridge (Rail) 5C 108
Chalk Farm (Tube) 4C 46
Chancery Lane (Tube) 1B 16 (4C 62)
Charing Cross (Rail & Tube) . .1D 23 (2A 76)
Charlton (Rail) 1E 97
Chelsea Harbour Pier (Riverbus) 4F 87
City Thameslink (Rail) 2D 17 (5D 63)
Clapham Common (Tube) 2E 103
Clapham High Street (Rail) 1F 103
Clapham Junction (Rail) 1A 102
Clapham North (Tube) 1A 104
Clapham South (Tube) 4D 103
Clapton (Rail) 4D 37
Covent Garden (Tube) 4E 15 (1A 76)
Cricklewood (Rail) 1F 43
Crofton Park (Rail) 3B 108
Crossharbour & London Arena (DLR & Tube)
. . . . .4D 81
Crouch Hill (Rail) 2B 34
Custom House for ExCeL (Rail & DLR)
. . . . .1D 83
Cutty Sark for Maritime Greenwich (DLR)
. . . . .2E 95

D

Dalston Kingsland (Rail) 2A 50
Denmark Hill (Rail) 5F 91
Deptford (Rail) 3C 94
Deptford Bridge (DLR) 4C 94
Devons Road (DLR) 3D 67
Dollis Hill (Tube) 2C 42
Drayton Park (Rail) 1C 48

E

Earl's Court (Tube) 5D 73
Earlsfield (Rail) 1E 115
East Acton (Tube) 5B 56
East Dulwich (Rail) 2A 106
East India (DLR) 1F 81
East Putney (Tube) 3A 100
Edgware Road (Tube) 4A 60
Elephant & Castle (Rail & Tube) 5E 77
Elmstead Woods (Rail) 5F 125
Elverson Road (DLR) 5D 95
Embankment (Tube) 1E 23 (2A 76)
Embankment Pier (Riverbus)
. . . . .1E 23 (2A 76)
Essex Road (Rail) 4E 49
Euston (Rail & Tube) 2B 6 (2F 61)
Euston Square (Tube) 3A 6 (3E 61)

Index to Stations

F

Farringdon (Rail & Tube) 5D 9 (4D 63)
Fenchurch Street (Rail) 4F 19 (1B 78)
Festival Pier (Riverbus) 1F 23 (2B 76)
Finchley Road (Tube) 3E 45
Finchley Road & Frognal (Rail) 2E 45
Finsbury Park (Rail & Tube) 4C 34
Forest Gate (Rail) 2C 54
Forest Hill (Rail) 2E 121
Fulham Broadway (Tube) 3C 86

G

Gipsy Hill (Rail) 5A 120
Gloucester Road (Tube) 5E 73
Golders Green (Tube) 3C 30
Goldhawk Road (Tube) 3E 71
Goodge Street (Tube) 5B 6 (4F 61)
Gospel Oak (Rail) 1C 46
Great Portland Street (Tube) . . .4E 5 (3D 61)
Greenland Pier (Riverbus) 4B 80
Green Park (Tube) 1E 21 (2E 75)
Greenwich (Rail & DLR) 3D 95
Greenwich Pier (Riverbus) 1E 95
Grove Park (Rail) 3D 125

H

Hackney Central (Rail) 3D 51
Hackney Downs (Rail) 2D 51
Hackney Wick (Rail) 3C 52
Hammersmith (Tube) 5E 71
Hampstead (Tube) 1E 45
Hampstead Heath (Rail) 1A 46
Harlesden (Rail & Tube) 1A 56
Harringay (Rail) 1C 34
Harringay Green Lanes (Rail) 1D 35
Haydons Road (Rail) 5E 115
Hendon (Rail) .1C 28
Hendon Central (Tube) 1D 29
Herne Hill (Rail) 4D 105
Heron Quays (DLR) 2C 80
Highbury & Islington (Rail & Tube) 3D 49
Highgate (Tube) 1D 33
High Street Kensington (Tube) 3D 73
Hilton Docklands Pier (Riverbus) 2B 80
Hither Green (Rail) 4A 110
Holborn (Tube) 1F 15 (5B 62)
Holland Park (Tube) 2B 72
Holloway Road (Tube) 2B 48
Homerton (Rail) 3F 51
Honor Oak Park (Rail) 4F 107
Hyde Park Corner (Tube) . . .3C 20 (3C 74)

I

Imperial Wharf (Rail) 4E 87
Island Gardens (DLR) 5E 81

K

Kennington (Tube) 1D 91

Kensal Green (Rail & Tube) 2E 57
Kensal Rise (Rail) 1F 57
Kensington Olympia (Rail & Tube) 4A 72
Kentish Town (Rail) 2E 47
Kentish Town West (Rail) 3D 47
Kidbrooke (Rail) 1D 111
Kilburn (Tube) .3B 44
Kilburn High Road (Rail) 5D 45
Kilburn Park (Tube) 1C 58
King's Cross (Rail) 1E 7 (1A 62)
King's Cross St Pancras (Tube)
. . . . .1D 7 (2A 62)
King's Cross Thameslink (Rail)
. . . . .1E 7 (2A 62)
Knightsbridge (Tube) 4A 20 (3B 74)

L

Ladbroke Grove (Tube) 5A 58
Ladywell (Rail) 3D 109
Lambeth North (Tube) 5B 24 (4C 76)
Lancaster Gate (Tube) 1F 73
Latimer Road (Tube) 1F 71
Lee (Rail) 4C 110
Leicester Square (Tube) 4C 14 (1A 76)
Lewisham (Rail & DLR) 1E 109
Leyton (Tube) .5E 39
Leyton Midland Road (Rail) 3E 39
Leytonstone (Tube) 3A 40
Leytonstone High Road (Rail) 4A 40
Limehouse (Rail & DLR) 5A 66
Liverpool Street (Rail & Tube)
. . . . .1D 19 (4A 64)
London Bridge (Rail & Tube)
. . . . .2C 26 (2F 77)
London Bridge City Pier (Riverbus)
. . . . .1D 27 (2A 78)
London Fields (Rail) 4D 51
Loughborough Junction (Rail) 1D 105
Lower Sydenham (Rail) 5B 122

M

Maida Vale (Tube) 2D 59
Manor House (Tube) 2E 35
Manor Park (Rail) 1F 55
Mansion House (Tube) 4A 18 (1E 77)
Marble Arch (Tube) 3A 12 (5B 60)
Maryland (Rail) 3A 54
Marylebone (Rail & Tube) 3B 60
Masthouse Terrace Pier (Riverbus) 1C 94
Maze Hill (Rail) 2A 96
Mile End (Tube) 3B 66
Millbank Millennium Pier (Riverbus)
. . . . .5A 76
Monument (Tube) 4C 18 (1F 77)
Moorgate (Rail & Tube) 1B 18 (4F 63)
Mornington Crescent (Tube) 1E 61
Mudchute (DLR) 5D 81

N

Neasden (Tube) 2A 42
New Cross (Rail & Tube) 3B 94
New Cross Gate (Rail & Tube) 4A 94

North Acton (Tube) 4A 56
North Dulwich (Rail) 3F 105
North Greenwich (Tube) 3A 82
Notting Hill Gate (Tube) 2C 72
Nunhead (Rail) 5E 93

O

Old Street (Rail & Tube) 2C 10 (3F 63)
Oval (Tube) 2C 90
Oxford Circus (Tube) 3F 13 (5E 61)

P

Paddington (Rail & Tube) 5F 59
Parsons Green (Tube) 4C 86
Peckham Rye (Rail) 5C 92
Penge East (Rail) 5E 121
Piccadilly Circus (Tube) 5B 14 (1F 75)
Pimlico (Tube) 1F 89
Plaistow (Tube) 1B 68
Pontoon Dock (DLR) 2E 83
Poplar (DLR) 1D 81
Prince Regent (DLR) 1E 83
Pudding Mill Lane (DLR) 5D 53
Putney (Rail) 2A 100
Putney Bridge (Tube) 1B 100
Putney Pier (Riverbus) 1A 100

Q

Queen's Park (Rail & Tube) 1B 58
Queens Road (Peckham) (Rail) 4E 93
Queenstown Road (Battersea) (Rail) . . .4D 89
Queensway (Tube) 1D 73

R

Ravenscourt Park (Tube) 5D 71
Rectory Road (Rail) 5B 36
Redbridge (Tube) 1F 41
Regent's Park (Tube) 4D 5 (3D 61)
Rotherhithe (Tube) 3E 79
Royal Albert (DLR) 1F 83
Royal Oak (Tube) 4D 59
Royal Victoria (DLR) 1C 82
Russell Square (Tube) 4D 7 (3A 62)

S

St James's Park (Tube) 5B 22 (3F 75)
St James Street (Rail) 1A 38
St Johns (Rail) 5C 94
St John's Wood (Tube) 1F 59
St Katharine's Pier (Riverbus)
. . . . .1F 27 (2B 78)
St Pancras (Rail) 1D 7 (1A 62)
St Paul's (Tube) 2F 17 (5E 63)
Savoy Pier (Riverbus) 5F 15 (1B 76)
Seven Sisters (Rail & Tube) 1B 36
Shadwell (Tube & DLR) 1D 79
Shepherd's Bush (Rail & Tube)
    Central Line 3F 71

Shepherd's Bush (Tube)
    Hammersmith & City Line 2E 71
Shoreditch (Tube) 3B 64
Silvertown (Rail) 2F 83
Sloane Square (Tube) 5C 74
Snaresbrook (Rail) 1C 40
South Bermondsey (Rail) 1E 93
Southfields (Tube) 1B 114
South Hampstead (Rail) 4E 45
South Kensington (Tube) 5F 73
South Quay (DLR) 3D 81
South Tottenham (Rail) 1B 36
Southwark (Tube) 2D 25 (2D 77)
Stamford Brook (Tube) 5B 70
Stamford Hill (Rail) 2A 36
Stepney Green (Tube) 3F 65
Stockwell (Tube) 4A 90
Stoke Newington (Rail) 4B 36
Stratford (Rail) 3F 53
Stratford International (Rail) 3E 53
Stratford Low Level (Rail, Tube & DLR)
. . . . .4F 53
Streatham (Rail) 5F 117
Streatham Hill (Rail) 2A 118
Surrey Quays (Tube) 5F 79
Swiss Cottage (Tube) 4F 45
Sydenham (Rail) 4E 121
Sydenham Hill (Rail) 3B 120

T

Temple (Tube) 4B 16 (1B 76)
Tooting Bec (Tube) 3C 116
Tooting Broadway (Tube) 5A 116
Tottenham Court Road (Tube)
. . . . .2C 14 (5F 61)
Tower Gateway (DLR) 4F 19 (1B 78)
Tower Hill (Tube) 4F 19 (1B 78)
Tower Millennium Pier (Riverbus)
. . . . .1E 27 (2A 78)
Tufnell Park (Tube) 1E 47
Tulse Hill (Rail) 2D 119
Turnham Green (Tube) 5A 70

U

Upper Holloway (Rail) 4F 33
Upton Park (Tube) 5E 55

V

Vauxhall (Rail & Tube) 1A 90
Victoria (Rail & Tube) 5D 75
Victoria Coach (Bus) 5D 75

W

Walthamstow Queens Road (Rail) 1C 38
Wandsworth Common (Rail) 1B 116
Wandsworth Road (Rail) 5E 89
Wandsworth Town (Rail) 2D 101
Wanstead (Tube) 1D 41
Wanstead Park (Rail) 1D 55
Wapping (Tube) 2E 79

Index to Stations

Warren Street (Tube) 3F 5 (3E 61)
Warwick Avenue (Tube) 3E 59
Waterloo (Rail & Tube) 3B 24 (3C 76)
Waterloo East (Rail) 2C 24 (2C 76)
Waterloo International (Rail) . .3B 24 (3C 76)
Waterloo Millennium Pier (Riverbus)
. . . . .3F 23 (3B 76)
Westbourne Park (Tube) 4B 58
West Brompton (Rail & Tube) 2C 86
Westcombe Park (Rail) . . . . . . : 1C 96
West Dulwich (Rail) 2F 119
Westferry (DLR) 1C 80
West Ham (Rail & Tube) 2A 68
West Hampstead (Rail) 3C 44
West Hampstead (Tube) 3D 45

West Hampstead Thameslink (Rail) . . .3C 44
West India Quay (DLR) 1C 80
West Kensington (Tube) 1B 86
Westminster (Tube) 4D 23 (3A 76)
Westminster Millennium Pier (Riverbus)
. . . . .3E 23 (3A 76)
West Norwood (Rail) 4D 119
West Silvertown (DLR) 2C 82
Whitechapel (Tube) 4D 65
White City (Tube) 1E 71
Willesden Green (Tube) 3E 43
Willesden Junction (Rail & Tube) 2B 56
Wimbledon (Rail, Tube & CT) 5B 114
Wimbledon Park (Tube) 3C 114
Woodgrange Park (Rail) 2F 55

Printed and bound in the United Kingdom by Polestar Wheatons Ltd., Exeter.